NAPOLEON BONAPARTE

Europe in 1789, Before Napoleon; and in 1814, Before His Defeat at Waterloo

Conquered "vassal" states

Conquered "allied" states

Conquered "rebellious" states

European "sovereign" states

NAPOLEON
BONAPARTE

ALAN SCHOM

HarperCollins*Publishers*

Frontispiece: *Emperor Napoleon, December 2, 1804.* Portrait by Maurin, lithograph by Delpech. *(Dawson Collection, Morrab Library of Penzance)*

HarperCollins books may be purchased for educational, business, or sales promotional use. For information please write: Special Markets Department, HarperCollins Publishers, Inc., 10 East 53rd Street, New York, NY 10022.

FIRST EDITION

Designed by Alma Hochhauser Orenstein
Maps by Paul J. Pugliese

Library of Congress Cataloging-in-Publication Data

Schom, Alan.
    Napoleon Bonaparte / by Alan Schom.
        p.   cm.
    Includes bibliographical references and index.
    ISBN 0-06-017214-2
    1. Napoleon I, Emperor of the French, 1769–1821. 2. France—Kings and rulers—Biography. 3. Corsica (France)—History—1789–1794. 4. France—History—Revolution, 1789–1799. 5. Napoleonic Wars, 1800–1815. I. Title.
    DC203.S36   1997
    944.05'092—dc21   97-5805

97 98 99 00 01 ❖/RRD 10 9 8 7 6 5 4 3 2 1

To the memory of Stefan Zweig (1881–1942),
who cherished and worked for a vision of Europe
far different from that of Napoleon.

And to Emile Zola (1840–1902),
who gave his life to the struggle for historical truth.

Why, man, he doth bestride the narrow world
Like a Colossus, and we petty men
Walk under his huge legs, and peep about
To find ourselves dishonourable graves.
Men at some time were masters of their fates.
—SHAKESPEARE, *JULIUS CAESAR*

. . . I may truly say, my soul hath been a stranger in the
course of my [life's] pilgrimage.
—FRANCIS BACON

Napoleon's empire, with all its faults, and all its glories, fell
and flushed away like snow at Easter till nothing remained
but His Majesty's ship Bellerophon *which awaited its suppli-*
ant refugees.
—SIR WINSTON CHURCHILL

C O N T E N T S

Illustrations follow pages 296 and 616.

MAPS

few weeks before our arrival [at Borodino in September, 1991], a peasant with a horse-drawn plow snagged two corpses just under the surface. One of them was a general, the other an infantryman," Baron de Méneval wrote me on February 26, 1996. The corpses were facing the former Russian position. The general was either Compère or Marion, both of whom were killed during that battle. The infantryman's skeletal hands were still grasping the rusting remains of his musket and bayonet. The guide at the Borodino Museum informed the baron that over the past few decades they had uncovered several dozen such human remains dating back to September 7, 1812. When visiting Eylau in September 1993, my friend the baron came across another newly discovered corpse—all of which reminds us just how close we are to the historical events of the past. We may sometimes try to forget history, but it does not forget us.

History has always fascinated me, but not the lifeless presentation of events of former times reduced to the dates of the reigns of kings and of battles and treaties—all but devoid of human association, of the men and women who actually created those events, and of the entire circumstances surrounding them. To correct such a myopic view and presentation one must introduce a sense of reality and understanding—in this case, the *full life* of Napoleon Bonaparte, whom the reader must see as a human being set in his own times. One must include his personal values, family, friends, associates, problems, character, and goals.

When I began my research a decade ago, I was astonished to find there was no one-volume biography covering all aspects of his life. I also found that most existing books tended to concentrate on "pieces" of his life—his military campaigns, or his foreign policy, or his administrative and political reforms—thereby revealing only part of the man. Over the last 150 years there have been thousands of these studies, most of them now out of print.

There have also been thousands of articles about Napoleon and his empire. Needless to say, deciding to set aside several years of my life to undertake such an enormous task as a one-volume biography of an individual about whom there was such a massive amount of primary and secondary research and source material was a decision I did not take lightly.

I began working on Napoleon in the summer of 1987, coming at him at first indirectly, so to speak, with research for my book on his attempt to invade England, concluding with Trafalgar, the great naval defeat of the French and Spanish fleets by Nelson's powerful squadron, which Napoleon only heard about, to his dismay, during the Austerlitz campaign. This was followed by my book on Napoleon's Hundred Days, which covers the period of his escape from exile on the island of Elba in the Mediterranean, his arrival on the south coast of France for a triumphal return to Paris, his raising of a new army to fight the large allied forces congregating against him, and his final battle and defeat at Waterloo.

It was after the completion of *One Hundred Days* that I decided, somewhat reluctantly, to commit myself to covering all of Napoleon's life from beginning to end, not just parts of it. I felt—and still do—that Napoleon badly needed to be dealt with fully and properly in one volume covering every aspect of his life and character, employing all the new research and archival documents.

This undertaking required visits to libraries and other archival sources on the Continent, in England, and in the United States, including the Bibliothèque Nationale, the Quai d'Orsay, and the Naval Museum in the Trocadero in Paris; the French Army and Navy Archives in Vincennes; the Musée Masséna in Nice; dozens of châteaux, including Talleyrand's Valencay, Malmaison, Fontainebleau, Pont de Briques in Boulogne, and Hougemont; public buildings, including in Paris the Conciergerie, the Naval Ministry, the Invalides, the Ecole Militaire, the National Assembly, and the Senate. In Britain I visited Oxford's Bodleian Library, the British Library, and various naval museums. In the United States I worked in the Main Library of the University of California, Berkeley, Yale's Sterling Memorial Library, and Dartmouth's Baker Library.

I also attempted to retrace Napoleon's steps through Egypt, Italy, Spain, throughout the whole of France, including its major ports on both coasts, through the Rhineland and up to Copenhagen, east by train to Berlin and Potsdam, across Bohemia to Vienna and Salzburg, along the Danube to Regensburg and Ulm, thence to Switzerland, and finally to Waterloo in Belgium. It has been a long, arduous, but fascinating odyssey requiring almost every minute of every day.

Being neutral about Napoleon has never been easy for Europeans. To the French he is almost universally a national hero, his excesses overlooked and unmentioned. By most other Europeans, whose ancestors suffered terribly under his conquests, he is, understandably, hated. My view of him is based upon what I found in the course of my research. I have attempted to suppress nothing, and have tried to be as impartial as humanly possible. As an American, whose young country at the time, apart from some minor naval clashes, was neither an enemy nor an ally of Napoleon, I have been able to avoid, I hope, emotional or nationalistic commitment to any one side. Using all I could glean from the French documents and memoirs available, I have endeavored to deal with every aspect of his character and life, whether regarding his private family life; or in the State Council; before diplomatic receptions; or on the field of battle. I have reexamined his many military campaigns, his treatment of those countries and peoples he conquered, his relations with colleagues and subordinates, and his ideas, motives, and performance.

My goal is to provide a balanced insight into Napoleon and his actions. And I hope that my biography will inspire my younger colleagues to undertake the multivolume study this subject so richly deserves and requires.

ACKNOWLEDGMENTS

I am indebted to many people and institutions for their help or advice over the years, although I should like to emphasize that I alone am responsible for the views expressed, and conclusions reached, in this book. I thank:

Librarians and archivists at the Bodleian Library, Oxford; the British Library, the Public Record Office, and Dr. Thomas Arkell, chairman of the Morrab Library, Penzance, for the use of many rare illustrations, and, in particular, Mrs. Gillian Green, who spent many hours selecting them; not to mention photographer W. J. Watton, the Hulton Deutsch Collection, for permission for some illustrations; Mr. Ian Robertson, director of the National Army Museum, London, and Miss Lucinda Brown, for permission to use this art gallery as the setting for the author photo; Dr. Lynn Orr and the associate curator of the San Francisco Fine Arts Museum, Dr. Marion C. Stewart; the curators of the National Maritime Museum, Greenwich, and the Royal Naval Museum, Portsmouth, as well as the faculty and staff of the Britannia Royal Naval College, Dartmouth, for their unstinting contributions.

In the United States the main library of the University of California, Berkeley, and the Baker Library at Dartmouth, aided me most generously in making available numerous rare first editions. Most of the research and writing, however, were carried out in France, of course, where, in addition to dozens of small museums and châteaux, the scene of events or the property of individuals discussed in this biography, I am much obliged to M. Jacques Perot, conservateur en chef of the Musée de l'Armée, at the Invalides, and to M. Gérard-Jean Chaduc, conservator of the "1789–1871 Department" also at the Invalides, and to the conservateur des Estampes, Musée Carnavalet, Mr. Bernard Chevallier, director of the museum at Malmaison, who patiently answered many questions about that property, while his colleague at Fontainebleau further aided me. I am also grateful to the curators of the Musée Bonnat of Bayonne; the Musée Masséna in Nice; the Musée de la Marine, Paris; and of the Services Historiques of the Army and Navy at Vincennes. Once again the Bibliothèque Nationale and the splendid new Archives Nationales of Paris proved a godsend. M. Philippe Martial, directeur de la Bibliothèque et des Archives du Sénat was of invaluable help, as were Général de Division Bruno Chaix, French Army (Ret.); Col. J-L. Reynaud (Ret.), and Col. Lawrence S. Burr, OBE, RAOC, at SHAPE. In the fields of science and medicine I was aided by Prof. Roger Hahn, University of California, Berkeley; and Drs. William Jago, F. Barham, and Bruce McCully. I am also indebted to my good friend, a former gunner and regimental commander, John Greenwood, for explanations of the technicalities of his art, not to mention the many books he made available to me from his personal library. Nor can I possibly omit Jeffery Burr, undoubtedly Britain's premier lawyer, for his advice and for making private library facilities available to me. David Chandler, the finest Napoleonic military authority of this century, helped me time and again, as only a very good friend could possibly do. Dr. Piers Branden, director of the Churchill College archives, Cambridge, expedited valuable research in my behalf; and I am grateful to Dr. Thomas Anfält of the University Library, University of Uppsala, Sweden, for his research into the Germaine de Staël papers. I should like to thank Count Alexandre Walewski and M. Jacques Jourquin for their help, and in particular Baron de Méneval, to whom I owe so much. I am grateful to the Prince and Princess Napoléon Murat for a delightful luncheon, Proctor Jones for his inimitable wit and many personal kindnesses, and Dr. Ben Weider for sharing with me the scientific evidence he has gathered concerning the poisoning of Napoleon. Special thanks are due to Byron Farwell for his encouragement. It would be most remiss on my part not to thank Françoise Coménie for her help and many kindnesses over the past several years, and without whose yeoman service, indeed, this book would never have been completed. Finally, I should like to express my special appreciation to my editor at HarperCollins, Buz Wyeth, for his wise counsel and inordinate understanding as the manuscript of this biography expanded far beyond the scope of the original project until it literally towered over his busy desk.

ALAN MORRIS SCHOM
Le Bois St.-Laumer
France

THE BONAPARTE FAMILY TREE

Carlo Maria Buonaparte m. 1764 Letizia Ramolino
1746–85   1750–1836

Joseph
1767–1844
King of Naples and of Spain

m. 1794
Julie Clary
1777–1845
––
two daughters

Napoleon
1769–1821
Emperor of the French

m. 1796
Joséphine de Beauharnais, divorced 1810
––

m. 1810
Marie Louise of Austria
––
one son
Napoléon-François-Joseph-Charles
1811–32
King of Rome, Duke of Reichstadt

Napoleon's stepson, Eugène de Beauharnais
1781–1824

m. 1806
Princess Auguste-Amélie of Bavaria
––
seven children

Lucien
1775–1840
Prince of Canino, French prince

m. 1795
1) Christine Boyer
1773–1800
––
four children

2) Alexandrine Jouberton
––
six sons, four daughters

Elisa
(Maria Anna)
1777–1820
Princess of Lucca and Piombino, Grand Duchess of Tuscany

m. 1797
Felix Bacciochi
1762–1841
––
five children

Louis
1778–1846
King of Holland (1806–10)

m. 1802 Hortense de Beauharnais
1783–1837
––
Children:
Napoléon-Louis-Charles (1802–7);
Napoléon-Louis (1804–31)
Charles-Louis-Napoléon (Napoléon III) (1808–73)

Pauline
(Paola Maria)
1780–1825
Duchess of Guastalla

m. 1797
1) Gen. Charles Leclerc
1772–1802
––
Louis-Napoléon
1798–1804

2) 1803, Prince Borghese (1775–1832)
no children

Caroline
(Maria Annunziata)
1782–1839
Grand Duchess of Berg (1806–8), Queen of Naples (1808–15)

m. 1800
Joachim Murat
(1767–1815)
––
four children

Jérôme
1784–1860
King of Westphalia

m. 1803
Elizabeth Patterson
(1785–1879)
divorced 1811
(United States)
––
one son

Bigamous "marriage" 1807
Princess Catherine of Württemberg
(1783–1835)
––
Jérôme-Napoléon
(1814–47)
Princesse Mathilde
(1820–1904)
Prince Napoléon
(1822–91)

CHAPTER 1

"A Dangerous Islander"

I was born even as my country was perishing.

n December 17, 1778, thirty-two-year-old Carlo Maria (or Charles, as he now called himself) Buonaparte boarded a coastal vessel in the Corsican port of Ajaccio. At his side, Joseph, ten, his eldest son; Napoleone, or "Nabulio," nine, the second surviving son; and Charles's brother-in-law, Joseph Fesch, waved to their brothers, sisters, and friends. They had just left their weatherbeaten four-story stone house in the Strada Malerba (Weedy Street), where Joseph and Nabulio had kissed their mother good-bye. They were bound for France, where Joseph would enter the Collège d'Autun, preparatory to a career in the church. Nabulio would continue on to the Royal Military School of Brienne-le-Château, where he would learn what to many Corsicans was still an elusive language, French, along with history, geography, mathematics, and the other courses required prior to entering the Ecole Militaire of Paris. The boys' amiable and mild young Uncle Fesch, their mother's half-brother, was off to the seminary at Aix-en-Provence to prepare for the priesthood. Such was the end of Napoleon's brief childhood.

Rushed home from high mass in the cathedral of Ajaccio on August 15, 1769, Letizia Buonaparte had barely reached the house when she gave birth to Napoleon, in the sparsely furnished drawing room. She had timed it too closely, as she did everything. Letizia Ramolino, the daughter of a state inspector of roads and bridges, and the stepdaughter of her mother's second husband, a banker named Fesch, was fourteen on June 2, 1764, when she married eighteen-year-old Carlo Maria di Buonaparte.

Originally from Lombardy, her family had gradually moved across much of Italy, including Florence and Naples, before setting out from Genoa for Corsica in the fifteenth century. Letizia was a slender, dark, not very tall girl who rarely smiled. Life was a serious, if not grim, affair for a female with no formal education, intended only to marry and bear children—as indeed she would—of whom eight ultimately survived. Her Corsican dialect of Italian was not flawless, and her grammar and writing were adequate at best; French was to remain a great mystery to her. As for books, she never read them in any language. But because France had purchased Corsica from the Genoese Republic on May 15, 1767—though conquering the defiant Corsicans, led by Pasquale Paoli, only the following year—she was destined to hear a lot of French spoken, in spite of her own antipathy to it and its people. She had brought a dowry of approximately seven thousand livres (considered quite respectable at the time) and a little land. She was a hard woman, a survivor of the rigors of tumultuous Corsican history, and was to prove a severe mother, reflected by her house with few furnishings, not even a single rug in the two lower stories the family occupied. The Buonaparte residence was hardly a welcoming place, and her brood found little kindness there. Although she attended mass when required—her husband's uncle, Lucien, was the archdeacon of Ajaccio—she was not "religious" by nature. She limited her world to her husband, who was rarely there; her children, who were always there; and the responsibilities involved in managing the family's income and affairs.

Charles Buonaparte's family had originally come from Florence to Ajaccio in 1520, where they were members of the small ruling "noble" (though titleless) class. Charles's first, and last, eminent ancestor, one Guglielmo di Buonaparte, had, as a nobleman, been a member of the municipal council of Florence in the thirteenth century, then under the control of the Ghibellines. But with the return of the Guelphs, he and his entire family were forced to flee the Tuscan capital and retire to Sarzana in Liguria and San Miniato, where they grew more and more impoverished, finally forcing Francesco di Buonaparte to sail to Corsica in the sixteenthth century for a fresh start.

Alas, the Buonaparti were not the best of businessmen, and although always educated, frequently serving in the law in one capacity or other, they left no fortunes behind. Indeed, when Charles had married Letizia in 1764, he was almost penniless. His law degree from Pisa enabled him to become "royal assessor" for the judicial region around Ajaccio. Though granted the title of equerry, his salary was only nine hundred francs a year.[1] But he had "expectations—the ailing Uncle Lucien, a priest with no family, promised to leave the good-natured if rather chaotic Charles his entire estate. And thus they now had the large house in Ajaccio, where the portrait of the island's French governor, Monsieur de Marbeuf, proudly hung in the otherwise dingy and unused drawing room.

Although a good Corsican patriot, Charles Buonaparte (the family never used the aristocratic particle, for which there was no title in any event), following Paoli's defeat by the French, had adapted quickly to the new political scene. He was one of those individuals who, although lazy by nature, are constantly devising new projects and schemes for the government to develop, in the hope of improving their own positions. But apart from getting himself elected one of the twelve members of the ruling municipal council of Ajaccio, most of Charles's schemes went awry. Nevertheless, at least his position in society was grounded in four generations of noble birth, and that opened many a door for him. Because of his ever growing number of progeny—now including Maria Anna (Elisa), Lucien, Louis, Maria Annunziata (Caroline), Paoletta (Pauline), and Jérôme—Charles Buonaparte needed all the help he could get, and thus, after dropping off the boys at Autun, he hastened on to Versailles, where he managed to secure a full scholarship for Napoleon at Brienne in January 1779.

Joseph and Napoleon went their separate ways for the first time on April 21, 1779. "I have never forgotten the day of our separation," Joseph later recalled. "I could not stop crying, while Napoleon spilled only one tear, and even that he tried in vain to hide."[2] If Joseph was very much his father's son, Napoleon was his mother's.

On May 15, 1779, the scrawny, undersize Napoleon passed by the concierge and into the dusty, lime-tree-lined courtyard of the establishment that was to be his home for the next six years. Run by a second-rate order of priests known as the Minimes, the Royal Military School included behind its massive walls the few remaining stone buildings, with moss-covered tiles, left of a former monastery. Donning his new uniform, including a light blue jacket with red cuffs, and dark blue breeches, Napoleon entered a new world. It was to change his life.

That he was there at the "king's expense" as a full scholarship student did not in itself distinguish him from the other 109 students, half of whom were in the same position. But his diminutive stature, his very limited French, distorted by a strong Corsican accent, his arrogance and continual chip-on-the-shoulder attitude, and his anger against France as the occupier of his beloved country set him off from the others. Proud, irascible, sometimes violent, ever self-conscious of being the outsider, he made no really close friends and only a few with whom he could even talk at all on a fairly regular basis, Louis de Bourrienne being one of them. By nature a loner, young Napoleon became doubly so now, and therefore was an ideal target for the bullies inevitably found in all boarding schools. That he was in an occasional rough scuffle was hardly surprising, for once getting the worst of what he had been dishing out for years to his good-natured brother Joseph. It was life in the barracks, nothing more, nothing less.

But despite the many drawbacks, Brienne did indeed open a whole new world to him, one unobtainable in Corsica. In addition to mathematics, ancient history, geography, some Latin literature (mostly in French translation), and German, and a smattering of science, he was introduced to the bewildering social graces of dance and music lessons, in which, if anything, he felt even more ill at ease. But unlike most of the other boys there, he was serious well beyond his years, knowing that apart from his own efforts, he could expect nothing from the world. His negligent if cheerful father, although now a Corsican delegate at Versailles, had no money to speak of.

Fortunately Napoleon had no special interest in personal wealth. Rather, he was determined to return to liberate occupied Corsica from the arrogant French who were holding his people in "slavery," as he put it. "I had even then the belief that my willpower was destined to make me triumph over the others,"[3] he asserted, and by the age of nine he was already a dedicated patriot boasting of his people, and especially of his hero, Paoli. To succeed—and he had no doubt that he would—required that he take advantage of everything the school, however humble, had to offer.

He needed special tutoring in French, which he was destined always to speak with a jarring Corsican accent, and was fascinated by classical history, reading eagerly (if only in translation) Cicero, Virgil, Tacitus, Suetonius, Horace, and Plutarch's *Lives*. "Napoleon shared his reading with me," his brother Joseph remarked. "It was always on ancient or modern historical subjects. And I would write to him about my own books, though they were less serious," Joseph preferring the epic poets to Caesar's *Commentaries* on the Gallic and civil wars.[4]

Napoleon had other passions that he did not share with his brother: geography and mathematics, in both of which he excelled. One of Napoleon's mathematics instructors was a strict, humorless man by the name of Jean-

Charles Pichegru, who within a few years would exchange a teaching career for one in the military. (During the Revolution he ultimately commanded the army that conquered Holland, which Napoleon in turn would later hand over to one of his brothers.) Apart from an annual invitation on the king's birthday to the château of the Comte Loménie de Brienne, Napoleon rarely escaped the high, forbidding stone walls enclosing his school. Nor did he much wish to do so, in hostile France. Instead he studied and studied and studied.

The French boys laughed at him, at everything about him, including his droll first name, Napoleone, which sounded like "*la paille-au-nez*," straw in the nose, and that is what they called him for months thereafter. But, grinning and bearing it, he studied even harder. Nor did he play games with the others, who took every occasion to taunt him. "I'll make you French pay, one day!" he would retaliate, shaking his small fist, which only increased their teasing. He was often disrespectful and outspoken in class. On one occasion he was disciplined by a master for disobedience and ordered to replace his uniform with rough clothing and then to eat dinner kneeling on the floor of the refectory with 109 smirking schoolboys looking on. Napoleon rebelled. "I'll eat standing up, Monsieur, and not on my knees!" he protested. "In *my family* we kneel only before God!" He stood there adamantly, then suddenly turned livid, seized by a violent attack that left him trembling, out of control, and vomiting. The school's superior rescinded the punishment, and a feverish Napoleon was taken back to his dormitory. He was to have other, much more serious attacks in the future, especially when exhausted or very tense.

Once a year the royal school inspectors examined each student individually in his subjects, the results of which determined the boy's future. The reports on Napoleon varied considerably. One described him as "distinguished . . . in mathematics" but "very poor in social accomplishments" and recommended him for a career as a naval officer. Another report found him "domineering, imperious, and stubborn." The final, determining one, issued in September 1784, recommended instead an army career for the boy.

The years passed in complete isolation from his family, as he never had money to return to Corsica for any of the school holidays, not even in summer. It was pretty grim, but the long spell was broken in June 1784, when his otherwise inattentive father stopped to visit him, with his sister Maria Anna (or Elisa, as she was now called) and brother Lucien in tow. Elisa was destined for a finishing school at St.-Cyr, while young Lucien was left at Brienne for a couple of years. It was the first time Napoleon had been called "Nabulio" since separating from the family at Autun, and it was the last time he would ever see his father.[5]

Charles Buonaparte stopped at the ancient Faculté de Médecine at

Montpellier, where he learned that he only had a few months to live. There he spent his last days with the Permon family, friends from Corsica. He died of cancer on February 24, 1785, at the age of thirty-nine.

On October 19, 1784, the fifteen-year-old "Napoleone de Buonaparte Esq." entered the gates of the Ecole Militaire in Paris, where he exchanged his old uniform for a light blue one with silver stripes on the sleeves and a red collar. He was now a "gentleman cadet" and beginning his first real military training, which after two years would lead to a king's commission in the royal army.

Founded by Louis XVI, the Ecole Militaire had been completed only in 1751. The cadets were assigned to various divisions. The wealthy were groomed to be cavalry officers. Napoleon, because of his strong background in mathematics, was one of the fourteen selected for the unaristocratic and unpopular artillery.

With War Minister Ségur at the helm, life at the Ecole Militaire was very strict indeed, especially compared to the rather lax existence at Brienne. Each *cadet gentilhomme* left his tiny individual monk's cell—barely large enough for an iron bed, a wooden chair, and a wardrobe—at the crack of dawn and was in chapel by 6:00 A.M. for prayers and mass, with more prayers at every meal. The day officially ended at 8:30 P.M., with each cadet back in his room. And what a day it was! The four instructing officers and eight drill sergeants kept the young men going, without a moment to themselves, all day long. Napoleon found daily drill in the large stone courtyard the most annoying and difficult of all the activities, with both sergeants and officers bellowing at him time and again for his slackness and unconcern, his mind forever elsewhere. As for the manual of arms, it was a positive bore, and week after week Napoleon was singled out for discipline. When the other cadets in his company were at "Present Arms," Napoleon would be at "Order Arms," and vice versa. "Civilize this dangerous islander," the drill instructor ordered Alexandre des Mazis, one of Napoleon's few friends. It was a tall order.

Except for German, which Napoleon loathed and nearly failed, his course work proved much more interesting. In addition to history, geography, literature, and German, there were higher courses on mathematics, physics, the construction of fortifications, and drawing, as well as talks on public law and philosophy. Of these, mathematics, fortifications, and, later, artillery, were Napoleon's favorites. His instructors' judgments of him were mixed. One referred to him as "a real Corsican by nationality and character" but acknowledged that he "would go far if circumstances permitted." His despairing German master simply gave up altogether, classifying him as "a wretch." But it was the report of artillery examiner Louis Monge—brother of Gaspard Monge, the mathematician and future founder of the Ecole Polytechnique—that saw the real Napoleon behind the face of a young boy:

> Reserved and studious, he prefers studying to any kind of amusement. He enjoys reading good authors and applies himself very well to the abstract sciences only, with a solid knowledge of mathematics and geography. He is quiet and solitary, capricious, haughty, and frightfully egotistical. He replies energetically to questions in class and is swift and sharp in his repartee at other times. He is most proud, ambitious, aspiring to everything. This young man merits our consideration and help.[6]

As if life had not been hard enough on Napoleon, the news of his father's death at the end of February 1785 struck him a very severe blow. This was one tragedy he could not conceal from Alexandre des Mazis. He disagreed with his father's having turned his back on the Corsican rebels holding out for independence from France and instead recognizing France and collaborating fully with its officials. And he had been hurt by his father's shameful neglect, even in Ajaccio. Nevertheless, Napoleon loved him deeply, much more so than he ever would his mother, despite his unflagging respect for her.

In Paris, unlike Brienne, he could escape now and then, for instance by spending an occasional day or two with the Permons, when they moved back to the capital from Montpellier. Madame Permon, as an old friend of his mother from her childhood in Ajaccio, always had a room waiting for him at their rather splendid Paris mansion. Both Monsieur and Madame Permon had always been kind to Napoleon, and they provided a real home and hearth for the homesick boy over the next several years, as he got to know their son and especially their daughter, Laure. Despite "his captivating smile," she admitted, "the disdainful twist of his mouth made you tremble." And when he was angry, "I could never look at that adorable face of his . . . without feeling a chill up my spine." But when he was in a good mood, he changed completely, becoming truly "charming" and "gentle."[7]

As the French navy had no academy, the Ecole Militaire provided its gunnery officers, and Napoleon was due to prepare to take the navy exams when it was announced that there would be none in 1785. Thus Napoleon, just turned sixteen, received his commission in the army artillery in the courtyard of the Ecole Militaire on September 28, 1785, ranked forty-second out of fifty-six students, among them his friend des Mazis and one

Louis de Phélippeaux. None of his family was present to celebrate the great moment, and, on trying on his new uniform with the silver clasp at the throat, 2nd Lt. Napoleon Buonaparte rushed over to the Permons for their approval. By November 6 he and des Mazis had reached their first posting, with the La Fère artillery regiment, at Valence. Napoleon Buonaparte's military career was about to begin.

"I know of nothing more handsome than the uniform of an artilleryman of La Fère," he proudly proclaimed after successfully completing an initial three-month training period with his new regiment. "Soldier I am, and that because it is a special gift I was endowed with at birth," he remarked.[8] Indeed, he had never looked handsomer, in his blue jacket with embroidered red cuffs, beneath that a muslin shirt with lace collar and cuffs, and the inevitable blue army breeches. He was now awarded the much-coveted epaulet with a gold fringe and a bright red silk cordon. This regiment was in fact *the* artillery school for the entire French army, and Napoleon had every right to be proud. He was already earning 920 livres per year, more than his father in his last position, but expenses in France were much greater, as were extra but obligatory regimental expenses.

"Even when I had finished my work and had nothing to do, I always vaguely felt that time was fleeting and I had not a moment to lose,"[9] he later recalled. Indeed, after his arrival at Valence, Second Lieutenant Buonaparte was scarcely seen outside his official regimental hours. He began an intensive five years during which almost every minute of his day and many hours of every night were occupied with four major preoccupations, if not obsessions: development of his career as a gunner; the financial problems encountered by his mother and family since the death of his father; his continuing private studies; and the liberation of Corsica from the French yoke. And although on rare occasions he did spare a few hours in society for the first time in his life, with introductions to the salons of women interested in finding suitable spouses for their daughters, they were few and far between. Still, he did request the hand of one young lady, though in vain. Then, simply dismissing this failure, he informed her mother, "My mother already has too many expenses to cope with, and I cannot permit myself to increase my own here, not to mention those resulting from the foolish entertainments of my comrades."[10] In other words, he had no suitable "prospects," and they should not consider him a possible son-in-law. Thus it was *his* decision to end this daydream of marriage to a wealthy young lady, without the personal means to support it. Napoleon would always have the last word.

Apart from artillery exercises, then, most of Napoleon's time at

Valence, from November 1785 to September 1786, was spent in the noisy room in which he was quartered, above a café. At times, given all he already had experienced, his thoughts naturally took a morbid turn. "Always alone, in the depths of my melancholy my thoughts dwell on death," he wrote, thinking not of his father's death but of his own. "What great rage brings me now to wish for my own destruction?" he asked himself. "No doubt because I see no place for myself in this world?" a question asked—and similarly answered—by many youths of his age. But in his case it was the overwhelming lack of prospects for any sort of future that got him down. Being not only of the lowest level of the nobility but also a foreigner, he saw no realistic future in a career in the Royal French Army. "As I must die sooner or later, why not kill myself?" he concluded, as he reflected on his impotence in the face of the French subjugation of his own country. "What would I see upon returning there? My fellow countrymen bound in chains. . . . When one's fatherland no longer exists, there is only one thing left for a true patriot to do: die."[11]

But instead of surrendering to death, Napoleon was saved by his innate drive, superior intelligence, and curiosity as he searched for answers to his questions. Not only would he continue to read voraciously over the next few years, filling a few dozen notebooks with his synopses and analyses, but he would later try to put them into action.

In the meantime he read and studied, read and studied. Given his home background and lack of solid formal education, the many volumes he pored over and the densely packed notebooks he filled soon covered an extraordinary range of subjects, probably unparalleled by any other French career officer. He read and wrote on the eighteenth-century English prime minister Sir Robert Walpole, a project for the total reorganization of the Régiment de La Fère; four different essays on the technical aspects of modern artillery and its development, including advice to one of his commanding officers; an analysis of Plato's *Republic*; a detailed study of the government of the ancient Persians; and much more on the geography, history, and government of ancient Greece, including warfare and mores. He then restlessly turned to ancient Egypt, Carthage, and even Assyria, while not forgetting a "philosophical and political history of the European commercial developments in the East and West Indies." He was always fascinated by England, studying it at considerable length and displaying a surprising knowledge and understanding of its historical and constitutional development. (How very different "the English" were from the rest of Europe, he noted.) Always impassioned about Friedrich II of Prussia, and making an analysis of such eighteenth-century works as the Abbé Marigny's *History of the*

Arabs Under the Caliphs and Amelot de la Houssaie's work *The Government of Venice*, he studied Machiavelli in detail, including his *History of Florence.* He went on to study the histories of the nobility and even of the Sorbonne. Inspired, he wrote an essay, "My Reflections on the State of Nature," and included an analysis of "happiness" and what it signified. His seemingly limitless curiosity still not quenched, he turned to a history of the Incas and of Cortés's conquest of Montezuma, filling page after page, returning always to the Greeks, including special studies of the general-politician, Alcibiades, and of course, Aristotle.[12]

"Formerly I was in love," and now realising its utter folly, indeed worse, he added, "I deny love's very existence." "Indeed, I go so far as to declare it harmful to society, to the individual happiness of man," the jaded lieutenant wrote. "Hence in brief I believe that love does more harm than good." To be sure, "Love offers incomparable pleasure," but, he added, it "perhaps results in even greater pain." Then, extrapolating, he came to the use of "love" as incorporated in the historical perspective of religion: "Religion was developed, and found a role by consoling the unfortunate peoples of the world," thereby permitting it "to enslave them forever," leading to what Napoleon referred to as "the empire of the priests," one which, he added, "probably will never end."[13]

Many a page he wrote, painfully, impatiently, in his all-but-illegible hand, which often even he was unable to decipher in the morning. He filled hundreds of folio pages between 1786 and 1791, including detailed advice to various commanding generals, such as Baron du Teil, suggesting an improved placement and trajectory of artillery, supported by mathematical proof.[14]

Napoleon then turned his attention to the reduction of transport costs from one arsenal to another.[15] Teil was much impressed by this unusual junior officer, whom he would not forget.

And thus on and on he went, night after night, while down below in the café, or in the officers' regimental mess, his fellow gunners were drinking, gambling, and whoring. The light never seemed to be out in his room, and yet somehow he seemed to muster enough strength to carry out his work at the battery the next day. He studied the geography of Switzerland and the history of Turkey, the government of India and the religion of the Aztecs.[16] His thirst for knowledge was unquenchable.

Of all the notebooks, letters, and memoirs he prepared during this period, the longest and most interesting were on tyrannical government, in particular that of unjust France over the beleaguered Corsicans. Napoleon was an indignant idealist, protesting the outrageous acts against the down-trodden of the world and the arrogance of power in general.

"The use of brute force is the law of the jungle; the power of reasoning, that of man," he began.[17] "How many vicissitudes are inflicted upon nations! ... Tyranny, oppression, and injustice are devastating the earth ... ," and the plight of Corsica provided a good example of "a small country that desires to be free but her neighbors wish to oppress."

The task of a nation's leader, however, is "to render the people over whom he rules happy, and to make society prosper. In order to do that, he, guided by the flame of reason, must balance with justice the rights of the men to whom he is responsible. To do that, one must be prepared to undertake whatever service the state requires. ... We are born to enjoy life," he went on, but that is quite unknown to the Corsican now "in French chains" as a result of the Bourbon monarchy and the administrators sent to that island. "I have read all the speeches by monarchist orators in which a poor effort is attempted to support a bad cause"—but which in reality was merely an excuse for the abuse of power, as in his homeland.

"Half the people of the world are ambitious and seek their happiness in attaining honors. The love of glory makes them desire positions of power, and take perilous risks [as leaders and administrators of a country], finding themselves enticed by this power of command." But, he argued, "the most alert ... among us oppose and reject this." The base of power of any tyrant or tyrannical government is "force"—the bayonet. "Are we going to have to continue watching the [French] military being given a free rein in their despotic rule [of Corsica]? Shall we continue to bow our heads beneath the triple yoke of the [French] army, governors, and financial officers" in their fiscal spoliation of our country? "How is it possible that an enlightened nation like France is not touched by our plight, a direct result of their actions? ... In the eyes of God, the worst crime is to tyrannize over men, but the next worse is to suffer such tyranny! ... Mankind! Mankind! How wretched you are in the state of bondage, but how great when you are impassioned by the flame of liberty!" Put an "end to the unjust French domination of Corsica." His homeland needed a savior, "but shall a William Tell appear?"[18]

Having by now worked himself into a furor over the rape of his homeland by the very French under whom he was serving, Second Lieutenant Buonaparte requested, and received, a five-and-a-half-month furlough.

Sailing from Toulon in the autumn of 1786, his ship reached his beloved Corsica on September 15, his first visit in six years. He was now seventeen, and after a further extension of his leave would not return to France until September of the following year.[19] Corsica's William Tell had arrived—or almost. In reality Napoleon's principal purpose at this time was not to save

Corsica but to help his poverty-stricken mother with some of the official paperwork for a final project prepared by his father just before his death and subsequently authorized by the royal government. This would result in the Buonapartes' receiving a few thousand francs for the draining of marshland and converting it into a fruit tree nursery. In addition his mother, Uncle Fesch, and Joseph would soon be acquiring one or two small vessels they were to employ in acts of piracy against ships of foreign powers, leading to criminal charges being brought against them. To what extent Napoleon knew about this is not clear, though when the scandal broke a few years later, he would be obliged to use all his influence to have the case quashed.

After a year's sojourn in Corsica, Napoleon rejoined his regiment in France only to apply for further leave because of the continuing family crisis, thereby resulting in a second stay in Ajaccio from January to June 1788.

These were chaotic times in France as well, with much political indecision and confusion as the Estates-General were summoned by Louis XVI in 1789, accompanied by the brutal attack on the Bastille and the slaughter of its small garrison by a mob on July 14. The newly created National Assembly abolished the feudal rights and privileges of the aristocracy, preparing the way for the downfall of the monarchy. On August 23 that same summer, Napoleon took the required new loyalty oath to "the Nation, the King, and the Law of the Land." Three days later the Declaration of the Rights of Man was decreed, followed in October by the introduction of martial law and then the seizure of church lands by the state in November.

Traveling to Versailles and Paris, where a new constitution was being drafted, the young officer was finally becoming aware of the terrible political convulsions taking place in France. But far from being dismayed by this turmoil, he applauded it: "Revolutions are ideal times for soldiers with a bit of wit and the courage to act,"[20] he boasted to a fellow gunner, even as he set out for Corsica for the third time in September 1789, inspired by all that he had just seen and heard. Unlike his previous sojourns, however, for the first time he was coming to participate "politically," even as the monarchical administration that he had so sharply criticized was being completely reorganized, permitting, he hoped, a new sense of justice to free the Corsicans from "their chains." Paoli, long in exile, would also be returning to the homeland the following year to urge his compatriots to take advantage of the Revolution, to replace a "bad cause" with democracy, revolutionary clubs, and their own National Guard.

But when the island's royalist governor closed the new club, Napoleon sent a petition of protest to the National Assembly in Paris. In the Corsican capital Napoleon supported the populace in a clash with the official French garrison there, and on November 5, 1789, the authorities requested his immediate expulsion to Ajaccio, where they hoped he would be out of harm's way. He could instead have been court-martialed for treason or mutiny and shot. In the meantime, the National Assembly had restored Corsican citizenship to the people. The cry for full independence was in the air, but the man required to lead this movement, Paoli, now sixty-four years old, was cautious.

Joseph Bonaparte, who had earlier changed his plans for a clerical career in favor of law studies at Pisa (which he never completed), was back in Corsica as well, working hand in hand with Napoleon. But there was great division among the islanders now, with the Catholic church supporting the king and opposing the revolution and the Civil Constitution of the Clergy (requiring priests to take the revolutionary loyalty oath), while others wanted ties with revolutionary France, and still others full independence. Napoleon and Joseph, though favoring independence, praised much of the work done by the Revolution, and in so doing narrowly escaped an irate pro-Catholic mob. Corsica was becoming a dangerous place.

A meeting between Napoleon and the by-now-dictatorial Paoli proved fruitless, and before sailing to France in January 1790, Napoleon convinced the Jacobin Club of Ajaccio to send a stinging letter of complaints to the city's ineffectual representative in the National Assembly. "Paoli was angry," Napoleon recalled. "We did not speak to each other again for a long time."[21]

Since his arrival at Valence after leaving the Ecole Militaire, Napoleon had been living under a most frugal regimen. He was supporting his thirteen-year-old brother Louis, who was now living with him, and sending money to his mother. What little remained was spent on books and stationery. As for food, a bit of bread and cheese sufficed. It was hardly surprising that he looked more sallow, more emaciated than ever, as Laure Permon noted with some anxiety. But this did not prevent Napoleon from entering an essay competition with the Académie de Lyon, entitled "What are the basic truths and feelings required to instill happiness in man?"[22] This was the last time he would waste his precious time on such philosophical ventures. No more theories for him. He had now fully graduated from "youth."

By September 10, 1791, First Lieutenant Buonaparte (he had been promoted in June) was back in Corsica for the fourth time in five years, now to support Joseph's candidacy for the Legislative Assembly. Failing to gain Paoli's backing, however, Joseph was soundly defeated by Charles-André Pozzo di Borgo (whose family had for years leased the third floor of the

Buonaparte house in Ajaccio). Napoleon would never forgive or forget this "betrayal."

The Buonapartes were still living in Ajaccio, although sides were being drawn up in the usual black-and-white, for-and-against Corsican manner. There remained the prorevolutionary French party, the growing pro-English faction supported more and more by Paoli, those who simply wanted independence, as well as a priesthood discontented with just about everyone except the Bourbon royalists. Nor had recent events in France helped matters: King Louis XVI's abortive attempt to flee the country in June and his subsequent arrest, the dissolution of the Constituent Assembly (renamed the Legislative Assembly) in September, the declaration of war by Austria in August, and the immediate national mobilization in order to meet that threat.

Events in Corsica itself clearly required a William Tell, Napoleon felt. He successfully rigged his own election as lieutenant colonel of the 2nd Battalion of Corsican Volunteers, although he was meeting strong resistance everywhere because of the anticlerical measures taken by the revolutionary government in Paris, including the closure of the island's monasteries, infuriating many of his fellow countrymen and further alienating them from Napoleon's volunteers and the revolutionary party. The result was scuffles and clashes, culminating in a vain attempt by Napoleon and his National Guardsmen to seize the Ajaccio citadel from the French garrison on April 8, 1792.

Napoleon had completely misjudged the situation, and it now backfired on him. Just about everyone was openly against him: Paoli (newly appointed lieutenant general and governor of Corsica by Paris), the French garrison, and most of the prochurch population of Ajaccio, who by now wanted a little calm. "Napoleon is the cause of all our woes," was heard in every quarter. Meanwhile, just to complicate matters, Napoleon had neglected to request an extension of his leave, which had expired in December, and on January 1, 1792, he had been marked AWOL, with the War Ministry then striking his name off the list of serving officers. Given all the chaos brother Napoleon had caused in Ajaccio these past few months, Joseph was only too grateful to see his ship disappearing over the horizon for France in May 1792.

Reaching Paris on May 28, Napoleon immediately set out to undo all the damage he had managed to inflict on his own career. At the same time he was developing political ties, frequently attending sessions of the newly renamed Legislative Assembly. After intensive weeks of politicking, Napoleon not only finally got all charges against him dropped but remarkably, also found himself fully reintegrated in his artillery regiment, with promotion to captain.[23]

Throughout the summer of 1792 Napoleon, along with Louis de Bourrienne, his old classmate from Brienne, observed the bizarre events taking place in Paris, including the storming of the Tuileries Palace by the masses on June 20 and then again on August 10, resulting in the public humiliation of Louis XVI and the slaughter of the Swiss Guards. Napoleon, witnessing the events from across the Carrousel and the Tuileries Palace at Bourrienne's brother's shop, felt as furious as he was hopeless to prevent the thousands of Parisians running amok, tearing through the palace. The experience further instilled in him an absolute loathing and fear of the masses, which he carried with him to his death.

These traumatic events also made Napoleon more impatient than ever to gain higher rank and command. Thus off he trudged to the Place de la Révolution (Concorde) to see the new naval minister, Gaspard Monge, requesting an appointment as lieutenant colonel of artillery in the French navy. Events were to intervene, however, preventing the otherwise well-disposed Monge from following through. On finally returning to the 1st Artillery Regiment at Valence after a long absence, Captain Buonaparte immediately applied for leave—again—using as his excuse the necessity of escorting his younger sister, Elisa, home to Corsica after her boarding school at St.-Cyr had been closed by the revolution.

Although Buonaparte had been absent more frequently than present throughout the past few years, his request was granted. On October 15, 1792, he set sail for Corsica with Elisa, never imagining that this would be the last time he would do so as a dedicated patriot. Despite his past disagreements with Paoli, he resumed his duties as lieutenant colonel and, under Paoli's orders as lieutenant general, took part in an attempted invasion of Sardinia, at Maddalena, following the successful French conquest of Savoy and Nice.

Setting sail on February 23, 1793, the small Corsican flotilla easily overwhelmed the tiny island of San Stefano, only to find the expedition's commander suddenly getting cold feet and ordering his men to reembark and return to Corsica.[24] For once Napoleon was speechless.

Meanwhile at Toulon eighteen-year-old Lucien Buonaparte was preparing the way for an even greater fiasco. Speaking before the Jacobin Club in that French port, he denounced Pasquale Paoli as "a traitor" who was preparing to hand over Corsica to the English. The club, endorsing this virulent attack, sent a copy to the Convention in Paris, where the deputy from the Department of the Var then repeated the warning of this teenage

Corsican hothead. Pandemonium filled the august building, followed by a vote calling for the immediate arrest of Governor Paoli, his delegate at the Convention, and Pozzo di Borgo. Even as troops were dispatched in Corsica to execute the orders from Paris, the entire island rose up against the treacherous Buonapartes, and menacing crowds surrounded the house in Ajaccio.

As for Napoleon, on returning from the Sardinian farce and learning what had happened in his absence, he wrote immediately to the Convention asking that body to revoke the arrest warrants. But it was already too late; by now even the Jacobin Club of Ajaccio was denouncing the Buonapartes. It was the excuse Paoli had long been looking for, and he demanded a complete break with France. Napoleon wrote to him in vain. "What scum!" Paoli had called Lucien on learning of his outrageous action. What he called Napoleon was no doubt worse.

Ajaccio was no longer safe even for Napoleon. He had to keep on the move, hiding first in a cave, then with a cousin, and later with friends. The Corsican police were looking for him everywhere. When in May, Commissaires Lacombe and Salicetti, the representatives of the Convention, reached Ajaccio with French troops to restore order and enforce the decrees of Paris, they met stiff resistance. Pozzo di Borgo for his part denounced *les frères Buonaparte,* while the governing council of Corsica in turn denounced Paris and condemned the Buonaparte family "to eternal execration and infamy."

A terrified Letizia fled with her children in the middle of the night, and by June 3, 1792, Napoleon, his mother, and siblings were all at Calvi, hiding with friends. As for Commissaires Salicetti and Lacombe, they too had to flee Ajaccio for their lives, while in Paris the Convention was drafting a further decree declaring "the traitor Paoli an outlaw," along with Pozzo di Borgo and others.

As for the Buonapartes, in the dark of night on June 10, 1793, the entire family secretly sailed for Toulon. Napoleon's new house and fields, which he had bought with Uncle Fesch, along with his mother's houses, properties, and vineyards, were seized and their living quarters ransacked by their neighbors. They had left Corsica with literally only the shirts on their backs. They had lost their entire source of revenue and now had only Napoleon's captain's pay to sustain their mother and six children. And all this because of the feckless, hotheaded Lucien, who still thought himself a great hero![25] The family never wanted to see Corsica again. Meanwhile, France was moving closer to an even more diabolical state of chaos and terror under the influence of Maximilien Robespierre and his Committee of Public Safety.

CHAPTER 2

"To Destiny"

Nature made me strong and determined . . . and you of gossamer and lace.

—To Josephine, 1796

he warm welcome the family received on landing at Toulon in June came as a pleasant shock, the members of the local Jacobin Club helping out the refugees by renting a house for them first in the suburb of La Valette and then in Marseilles. Lucien, the youngest Jacobin, responsible for this unexpected house moving, was given the sobering job of night watchman of a warehouse at nearby St.-Maximin. But for once it was Joseph who took expeditious action, going to Paris to lobby influential friends, returning in September as a newly appointed *commissaire de guerre* (a title unique to France at the time, something like a quartermaster or commissary officer) in charge of provisioning the army—a lucrative post with a salary of 6,000 francs a year, plus substantial bribes and the usual black-market deals, to which another 2,400 livres were added on his further appointment as commissioner of the Executive Committee of the Department of Corsica.[1] Hereafter the Buonapartes would not starve.

But it was in Paris that important things were happening that were to shape the lives of this family as well as much of Europe. Louis XVI had been executed on January 21, 1793, in the Place de la Révolution. France

had declared war on Austria back in April of the previous year, against
Great Britain and Holland in February 1793, and against Spain in March.
The country had been convulsed by riots ever since: food riots in hungry
Paris; royalist revolts in Brittany, the Vendée, and the West; the revolt of
royalist Lyons, soon to be suppressed in a bloody slaughter of civilians on
the orders of a former headmaster of a church school, one Joseph Fouché.
The Buonapartes had not yet made the acquaintance of that particular individual, but all eventually would—to their regret. A more ominous uprising
took place in Paris at the end of May, and politician Jean-Paul Marat was
then stabbed in his bathtub by Charlotte Corday. A new constitution was
voted on June 24, which soon would bring about a new and somewhat
more terrifying political order, as Robespierre became the tenth member of
the Committee of Public Safety in July. This was followed by a series of
stringent new laws regulating prices while also permitting neighbors to
denounce neighbors "as suspects"—which they often did just out of envy
or animosity, or even stemming from some long-standing feud. With an
English fleet and marines seizing Toulon in August, there would be more
than enough work for a very bright twenty-four-year-old officer by the
name of Napoleon Buonaparte, whose real military career was just about to
begin.

On November 30, 1793, Major Buonaparte (he had been promoted again)
studied the damp, cold, panoramic cluster of thirteen French batteries overlooking the inner and outer harbors of the principal French Mediterranean
naval base of Toulon. He was tired, having spent every day here without
respite since his arrival and appointment in September 17 as commander of
the two then-existing batteries of perhaps eight to ten guns, half of them
with no ammunition or else provided with the wrong caliber. His long
cloak and black knee-high boots were muddy, his uniform dank and wrin-
kled, but he had worked miracles in a mere two and a half months.

On his return to his artillery regiment—now attached to the so-called
Army of Italy at Nice—in June, after an absence of twenty-two months,
Napoleon had been reluctantly accepted back by Gen. Jean du Teil, whose
brother had commanded the artillery regiment back at Valence and Auxonne. Teil therefore already knew something about this young officer and
his checkered, intermittent career. The general also knew that his brother
held a very high opinion of Napoleon's abilities as a gunner. Therefore he
had accepted him back, but with caution, assigning him to organize convoys of munitions from Avignon to Nice, through sometimes hostile royalist territory.

Indeed, the revolts that had rocked the rest of France most of the year were still active in Provence, with proroyalist columns moving southward to attack such cities as Avignon and Marseilles, the latter being finally retaken by revolutionary forces on August 25. Then Toulon had revolted on August 27–28, throwing its superb anchorages open to an Anglo-Spanish war flotilla comprising a few dozen vessels, which had immediately landed nearly seventeen thousand Spaniards, French royalists, Neapolitans, Piedmontese, and a few British marines. The British fleet was under the command of the formidable Adm. Sir Samuel Hood, famous throughout the Royal Navy for his dramatic clashes with the French during the American Revolution. Hood was already approaching his fiftieth birthday and, with more than three decades of that spent at sea, would soon be retiring.

With only two thousand British troops, it was evident that Hood had not been sent here to conquer France, or even Toulon. The Admiralty no doubt expected the French to rise up against the harsh new laws and brutal acts of the Robespierre-dominated Committee of Public Safety. Nevertheless, Hood had done the best he could with the guns and troops at hand, protecting the narrow strait separating the large and small harbors with powerful batteries on the west side of the harbor at Fort Mulgrave (which they had just built), at Tour de la Balquier, and at L'Eguillette. Across the way on the eastern shore was placed another series of British batteries, beginning with Grosse Tour, Malbousquet, ringing the city of Toulon itself, reaching right up to Fort Croix, high atop the dominating Mt. Faron.

Initially the French, unable to cope, had watched helplessly as the British dug in, and the terrifying news reached Paris. There were just a few thousand French troops available, and their commander, General Carteaux, an artist by training and only an amateur soldier, was supported by a mere half dozen functioning cannon. Then, to compound matters, his artillery commander had been seriously wounded, just as Captain Buonaparte was approaching Marseilles en route to rejoin his regiment at Nice. Stopping at Marseilles, Napoleon had visited two "representatives" sent by the Committee of Public Safety to clean up all royalist pockets in the city, none other than Cristoforo Salicetti, whose Corsican assignment had ended in disaster and Napoleon's ultimate flight from that island, and another, named Gaspari. Salicetti and Napoleon at least had that in common. It was thanks to Salicetti that Napoleon had obtained Joseph's most lucrative position, as an army commissary officer. In fact, Napoleon had now stopped to see Salicetti to ask another favor, to place his younger brother Louis as a cadet officer. Delighted to see Napoleon at this critical moment, Salicetti instead asked a favor of him, that Napoleon transfer temporarily from his

regiment to replace the wounded artillery commander at Toulon. Most soldiers would simply have shrugged their shoulders on learning that they
would have only half a dozen or so cannon available with which to face
well over one hundred British guns. But to Napoleon it sounded like the
chance of a lifetime.

It was at this time that Napoleon met Louis Fréron and Paul François
de Barras, who had also been dispatched by the committee to cleanse
Provence of the royalist scourge. Barras, a former career officer himself,
seconded Salicetti's request, and Napoleon was duly appointed to a post
with many fascinating challenges from a gunner's viewpoint. Barras, the
renegade "Red Viscount" who had voted for the death of his king in January 1793, was busy now killing fellow aristocrats with Fréron, but spending more of his time pilfering vast amounts of silver, gold, jewelery, and
paintings from the châteaux and mansions of Marseilles's wealthy bourgeois
families. A debauched man from the time he entered the army, he had
received a dishonorable discharge after personally insulting the war minister. Barras was as ruthless as he was cunning, all of which was concealed
beneath the gracious manners of yesteryear and an obliging smile. He was
the antithesis of the crude, ruthless Fréron, who would one day attempt—
and fail—to become Napoleon's brother-in-law.

Napoleon thus avoided Fréron while he encouraged the interest Barras
showed in him. This was to pay unimaginable dividends, for Barras was a
man on the rise, soon to become a member of the five-man Directory,
which would replace the Committee of Public Safety. Indeed, it was thanks
to this much tainted voluptuary that Napoleon's career was to skyrocket,
and thanks to this same Barras that he was later to meet Barras's presiding
mistress, one Josephine de Beauharnais.

Thus it was that General du Teil was informed in September 1793 that
Captain Buonaparte had been temporarily seconded to the French army
units besieging loyalist-held Toulon. After carefully studying the irregular
topography of the Toulon region, which he already knew pretty well from
previous visits, he spent the next several weeks scavenging for cannon and
mortars from Avignon, Antibes, Nice, and Marseilles. Barras and Salicetti
watched in startled admiration as the twenty-four-year-old gunner went
out daily in every direction, inevitably returning with munitions, guns,
junior artillery officers, heavy beams for new batteries, and three hundred
horses, mules, and oxen to haul the new artillery pieces to their new sites. It
took weeks, but by the end of November the newly promoted major had
acquired more than ninety artillery pieces, including a goodly number of
the mighty twenty-four-pounders needed to reach the English forts and

vessels. "Before the week is out, Toulon will be yours,"[2] he told the commanding general.

Retaking the city was to prove a little more complicated than that, for not only were several hundred new gunners needed to man the thirteen new French batteries, but a new commanding general as well. First Carteaux was transferred for incompetence. His successor, "General" Doppet, a physician by profession and amateur soldier by preference, proved as disastrous a choice as his predecessor. Doppet in turn was dropped and replaced by a good professional officer, Gen. Jean François Dugommier, who finally took command on November 16.

Dugommier was the first of the commanders to appreciate Napoleon's full value, including his objectives; and, of course, this being a siege, cannon was king, infantry playing only a secondary role. Napoleon's ultimate aim was to isolate Toulon by land and sea. Thus he carefully sited his batteries to knock out those of his opponents, while peppering the Anglo-Spanish fleet to make life so hot for them that they would be forced to withdraw.

With the dramatic change brought about since Napoleon's arrival—and realizing that he was not going to receive sufficient support from the French on the mainland, thereby permitting more and more batteries to be brought to bear on him and his ships—Admiral Hood acknowledged that it was simply a matter of time before he would have to withdraw, and he issued those plans to his captains weeks in advance.

To force the British to do just that, Napoleon first wanted to knock out their powerful battery at L'Eguillette, situated at the top of the promontory at the entrance of the inner harbor. Once that was achieved, he would simply turn those English guns around and attack the hostile fleet. Next he wanted to seize Fort Mulgrave, and then Fort Malbousquet.

By the beginning of December he was at last ready with all his new batteries, including thirty-eight cannon just to neutralize Fort Mulgrave with a lethal crossfire. On November 25 General Dugommier had held a key war council formally adopting Napoleon's plan, which now went into effect, waiting only for Brig. Gen. André Masséna to arrive with his fresh troops to bring them up to full force. Meanwhile Napoleon never left his thundering guns, standing by them all day long, sleeping in or near the batteries every night, despite the heavy rain.

With all in readiness, Dugommier gave the signal for the all-out assault, which was launched on December 17 with the most devastating cannonading to date, followed by General Muiron's troops storming the powerful Fort Mulgrave, Masséna capturing Fort d'Artigues, and Napoleon himself taking Point L'Eguillette and another fort (under such heavy defensive fire by the British that he had one horse shot from beneath him, also receiving a minor bayonet wound in the thigh). Hood, his ships clustered in Toulon's smaller inner harbor, gave the evacuation orders, placing Capt. Sir William Sidney Smith—a man Napoleon would come into contact with time and again in his career—in charge of destroying the enormous French arsenal, stores, and ships. Although the arsenal was duly destroyed, along with ten French ships, the rest escaped when the Spanish in charge of that aspect of the operation failed to execute their orders.

At 9:00 A.M. on December 19, General Dugommier's revolutionary army finally occupied Toulon, and Major Buonaparte (promoted on October 18), the hero of the day, turned his cannon on the hundreds of "collaborators" (royalists) rounded up in the main square of Toulon, slaughtering them.[3] The main public buildings of the port were then leveled, to further discourage royalists throughout the country. This is how the revolutionary government dealt with such opposition, soon surpassed by the destruction of Lyons and the massacre of its civilian leaders, not to mention the horrifying mass drowning of citizens in the Loire at Nantes.

As for Citizen Buonaparte, who had arrived in Toulon a mere captain in charge of a wagon train en route for Nice back in mid-September, three months later, on December 22, 1793, he received a further promotion to brigadier general. For the first time in his military career, his name was briefly mentioned in every city and village of the land. "I cannot find praiseworthy enough words to describe Buonaparte's full worth," General du Teil wrote the war minister following the taking of Toulon. "He has a solid scientific knowledge of his profession and as much intelligence, if too much courage, *voilà*—there you have but a scant sketch of the virtues of this rare officer. It now only remains for you, Minister, to consecrate his talents to the glory of the Republic!"[4] At the age of twenty-five Napoleon Buonaparte had arrived—or nearly.

Praise attracts praise, and Napoleon's critical role in defeating the British at Toulon was now echoed everywhere, even by the tyrannically powerful "representatives." These political commissaires of the Committee of Public Safety sent to subdue and administer Provence, from the Rhône River to the Var, had enormous powers to appoint and replace even the highest officials and officers. Two such representatives, Fréron and Salicetti, wrote to Paris of their "satisfaction with the zeal and intelligence displayed by Citizen Buonaparte." Even more important to Napoleon, now at his new headquarters at Nice, were the reports sent by the more powerful and influential representatives of Paris in that city, Ricord and Maximilien Robespierre's twenty-nine-year-old brother, Augustin, who took up the cause of the hero of the day. Writing to his brother, the dreaded head of the Committee of Public Safety, after praising Napoleon to the hilt, Augustin declared him "to be worthy of rising merit."[5]

Following the capture of Toulon, and after being confirmed in his new rank, Napoleon was ordered to survey French defenses along the entire Mediterranean coast from Marseilles to Nice. In particular he found the Army of Italy, under the command of Gen. P. J. Dumerbion, to be in a most unmilitary state of apathy and preparedness. This would have to be corrected, he informed Representatives Ricord and Robespierre. But more important was the military policy for this region as laid down by Paris.

In addition to the Army of Italy, there was, just to the north, the Army of the Alps, with headquarters in the narrow mountain valley at Barcelonnette, both armies disputing military objectives on the other side of the Maritime Alps. The original targets—the Comté of Nice and the Duchy of Savoy—had been largely secured, with the exception of Piedmont. As the king of Sardinia was an ally of Austria, he was automatically a foe of France. And then there was the question of the Republic of Genoa, which had to be neutralized. But to complicate matters, not only were the Armies of the Alps and of Italy at odds with each other in the Parisian corridors of power, but the swaggering representatives of each region were equally jealous of one another.

Salicetti and Fréron, for instance, were a dangerous pair. Having rounded up the royalists of Marseilles and being responsible for the beheading of most of the 409 among them, they had added to their personal triumph by their support of Napoleon, resulting in his great victory at Toulon. But with Napoleon now literally out of their bailiwick, in Nice, where the rival commissars Ricord and Robespierre ruled, there was fresh anxiety and tension in the air. Napoleon was "their man," Fréron and Salicetti insisted, and they resented being shunted aside as their new brigadier general moved on. "Buonaparte has hardly deigned to look at me, he [is] now so high and mighty," Salicetti privately complained to Paris.[6] Little did Napoleon realize that he had a new, unscrupulous enemy who was only awaiting his moment to avenge this slight.

Champing at the bit, Napoleon was looking ahead to fresh action as he encouraged young Robespierre to put the Army of Italy in fighting shape. "It is up to you to make the Committee [of Public Safety] aware of our shameful inaction," he advised, explaining his willingness to "develop my plan that will permit me to conquer the whole of Italy with just 12 to 15,000 men."[7] (Meanwhile, of course, the Army of the Alps—to which Salicetti was now attached—had its own plans for Italian conquest, which left no room for the Army of Italy.)

Finally convinced by July 1794, Augustin Robespierre ordered Napoleon to carry out a one-man mission to the Republic of Genoa to sound out how its government stood vis-à-vis France. Accordingly, on July 11 Buonaparte set out for that Italian port, quite unaware of the rebellion taking place in Paris at that very moment, a strong counterreaction to the Jacobins and their horrifying massacres, destruction, and infamous new decrees—all authorized by Maximilien Robespierre and his Committee of Public Safety. The leaders of this new party were three Jacobins themselves taking refuge in the guise of the outraged: none other than Jean-Lambert Tallien, Fréron, and Barras (two of whom had been responsible for more than one massacre in Provence).

But shortly after Napoleon left Nice, Robespierre sent an urgent message to Augustin to return immediately to the capital, where Maximilien needed all the support he could muster. But it was already too late. Even as Napoleon sat negotiating with the Genoese and assessing the state of their military defenses, on July 27, 1794 (9 Thermidor), the "Thermidorians"* acted and overthrew Robespierre, his closest associates, and Augustin, who were dispatched to the Place de la Révolution and beheaded.[8] As for the 650 delegates to the National Convention, they were assigned to one of the thirteen ruling committees, their loyalties and political jealousies nicely divided, even as the Jacobin clubs throughout France were closed down by the newly reconstituted Committee of Public Safety, which included Fréron, Tallien, and Barras. *Plus ça change . . .*

In the meantime the unsuspecting Napoleon returned to Nice on July 29 only to find himself placed under arrest and incarcerated in the Fort Carré, facing the calm harbor of Antibes. He had in fact been denounced by his fellow countryman, a vengeful Salicetti, the same Salicetti who had just proclaimed "that my heart is filled with joy" on learning of the death of Robespierre, the same Robespierre with whom he had been working so closely for many months. His denunciation of Napoleon had been equally warm: "What was this general doing in a foreign country?" he asked the French authorities in outraged innocence, because of course, among other things, Napoleon's campaign plans had superseded his own. "There are strong suspicions of treason and fraud against him," Salicetti concluded.[9]

Much more relevant in the eyes of Paris, however, were Napoleon's friendly relations with the late terrorist Augustin Robespierre. And of course Napoleon's younger brother Lucien was a known Jacobin hothead. Men had

---

*So called because of their coup d'état on 9 Thermidor of the revolutionary calendar, which had been decreed in October 1793.

been executed for far less in revolutionary France. Fearing for his own life, Napoleon's commanding general, who had been fully aware of his subordinate's mission to Genoa, had immediately removed Buonaparte from his command.

Napoleon's fiercely loyal aide-de-camp, Andoche Junot, warmly advised his general to flee: "My conscience is clear," Napoleon informed Junot, "therefore do not do anything rash, or you will simply compromise me." Given a fair hearing, he felt confident he would have no problem explaining himself, and although he knew he had a real enemy in Fréron, he also had a friend and ally in the more influential Barras. Writing to another friend, Napoleon admitted to having been "affected by Robespierre's catastrophe, a man I liked and felt was completely honest. But," he added, "if he had been my own father I would have stabbed him myself if he had attempted to become a real tyrant."[10]

And then, just as unexpectedly as it had begun, his imprisonment ended. General Dumerbion, no doubt having second thoughts, released Napoleon on his own authority, merely requesting him not to leave the vicinity. He did refuse for the time being to reintegrate him into the Army of Italy, however, until he could demonstrate his ability "to regain our confidence, through his devotion to the public weal, and by his private actions." For, said his former commanding officer, "we are quite convinced of the services his military talents can still provide . . . at a time when men of his high caliber are extraordinarly rare."

In fact Buonaparte had been one of seventy-four general officers arrested after the fall of Robespierre. Then, for some inexplicable reason, the same Salicetti who had demanded Napoleon's arrest in the first place—perhaps after the intervention of his good friend Joseph Buonaparte—not only withdrew all allegations against Napoleon but even recommended his heading an expedition to liberate Corsica! In any event, with the British in command of the Mediterranean, no such French naval rescue would have been possible, and Napoleon for his part just wanted to get away from this infernal region, if not from France itself. In May 1795 he suddenly found himself ordered to join the Army of the West in his former rank of brigadier general, to command that army's artillery![11]

Despite the great relief he felt at being reinstated in the army and receiving a new posting, he hardly cared for the idea of being involved in a French civil war, for the Army of the West was in Brittany and the western departments with orders to put down French royalists and anyone else rebelling against the French government.

Thus he set out for Paris with Junot, his military school classmate Capt. Auguste Frédéric Louis Viesse de Marmont, and his own younger brother Louis. He delayed as much as possible en route, not arriving until the end of the month, by which time another revolution had taken place (on the twentieth), when a reaction to the return of the last of the Jacobins had been transformed into fear and force, resulting in flight of the remainder of Napoleon's influential friends from the capital. Although Napoleon managed to escape imprisonment again, the new government did its best to irritate him, by removing him from his artillery command, replacing it with an infantry brigade. *Quelle insulte . . .*

At first he pouted, then he requested a furlough, in order "to reestablish my health," holing up in an obscure hotel in the Latin Quarter of Paris with Junot and Marmont. He even considered applying for a post in the Ottoman Army. After a while, however, he was able to wangle a transfer to the general staff in Paris, as head of the Topographical Office. In the meantime he had submitted a plan to the government for the invasion of Italy. It interested them.[12]

As for his private life, it was in a shambles, as usual. Brother Joseph had married Julie Clary on August 1, 1794, in the village of Cuges, just outside Marseilles, but none of the Buonapartes had bothered to attend the ceremony—not even Letizia and Napoleon, who were then in nearby Nice. The bride's mother and two sisters, however, Eugénie Désirée and Honorine Blait, were present.

Through Joseph, Napoleon had earlier met the family, and an understanding of sorts was arrived at that he and Désirée would marry. But despite a brief discreet premarital tryst, the Clarys were none too happy at the prospect of yet another penniless Buonaparte in the family, especially the less-than-totally sociable brigadier. Thus Napoleon and Désirée parted on a wait-and-see basis. By the summer of 1795, however, no decision had been reached.

In mid-September Napoleon's alarmingly uncertain status was aggravated when he received orders to prepare to lead a special eight-man military mission to Turkey to organize and modernize the sultan's imperial artillery.[13] Napoleon had been hoping for something better. He remained optimistic at the announcement that General Barras was now heading the nation's defenses, and that most of the officers dismissed earlier for their lack of "republicanism" would now be reinstated. Seizing this opportunity, Napoleon went to see Barras at the Tuileries Palace on 12 Vendémiaire (October 3).

At midnight that same day, thousands of mostly working-class Parisians and royalists, marching under the banner of the self-proclaimed General

Danican, arrived at the Tuileries. At dawn the next day the rebels, several thousand strong, were in position, while Barras was impatiently awaiting several regiments from the suburbs. Summoning Napoleon during the early morning hours, he had ordered him to send for cannon and to defend the Tuileries. Time was clearly of the essence.

Napoleon had immediately dispatched a strapping twenty-seven-year-old cavalry officer with an incredible mop of dark curly hair, one Maj. Joachim Murat, to execute Barras's order. By 6:00 A.M. Murat appeared almost magically with a long convoy including forty powerful cannon, caissons, and gun crews, which Napoleon began placing where they would be most effective, before the Tuileries, while the nearby side streets were barred by regular army troops. But due to the congested medieval streets, he moved most of the heavy artillery pieces across the road before the Eglise St.-Roch, where he had a wider field of fire.

The first attack by Danican's rebel columns caught the troops at the Tuileries before they were fully deployed, but the regular regiments held their ground under heavy small-arms fire, and the attack was stalemated by two o'clock that afternoon. But at three o'clock Danican launched a more successful one, breaking through the defending troops and bursting into the Rue St.-Honoré, while other rebels threatened the National Assembly, across the Seine. Gaining control again, the defending regiments then succeeded in forcing the invading armed columns of rebels toward the Eglise St.-Roch. There Napoleon was waiting impatiently. He finally gave the order to open fire, and dozens of powerful cannon tearing huge red swaths through the mob of rebels, against which mere muskets were useless. Screaming, shouting, confused, the insurgents broke and fled. It took hours to clear the streets of the fourteen hundred corpses, as Napoleon summed up the day's events to Joseph: "The enemy attacked us at the Tuileries. We killed a great many of them. They killed thirty of our men and wounded another sixty. . . . Now all is quiet. As usual I did not receive a scratch. I could not be happier."[14]

The battle was over; the Tuileries, the seat of government, was safe, Barras was more secure than ever, and the last of the rebel positions were cleared by the following day, October 5.

A few days later Barras appeared in uniform before a grateful National Assembly with his generals, including Napoleon, but without naming any of them. Napoleon, whose face was still unknown to most people, no doubt was peeved, especially when suddenly none other than the former representative of Marseilles, Fréron, who had earlier endorsed Salicetti's insistence on Napoleon's arrest at Nice, suddenly scrambled up to the dais to address the hundreds of people present, including Barras. He pointed not to a smiling Barras but to Napoleon. "Do not forget, citizens," he boomed out, "that General Buona-Parte, . . . who had only that morning in which to station his cannon so cleverly, the fortunate results of which you have clearly seen yourselves," was the real hero of the day! An astonished Napoleon stood there speechless, not knowing that the same Fréron who had demanded his head the year before now needed him very much alive, for Fréron was madly in love with, of all people, Napoleon's lovely young sister Pauline. The names of "Buonaparte" and "Barras" rang through the jubilant crowd.

A fortnight later Napoleon was gazetted major general, and on October 25 Barras resigned as commander of the Army of the Interior. Divisional General Buonaparte was named to succeed him. Everywhere Napoleon's name was proclaimed throughout the former realm, this First Republic. He could no longer attend a performance of the Théâtre Français without receiving a rousing ovation. He would never again be forgotten, and it was now that he dropped the *u* in his name: Bonaparte had arrived.[15]

Throughout this period, despite the astonishing ups and downs in his career, Napoleon did enjoy some social life, especially at the Permon residence. There he would arrive, pale and thin, with his muddy boots and funny round hat and shapeless gray overcoat to visit young Laure, her brother, and her sister, but in particular their mother, Panoria. It was literally still the only foyer in Paris where he felt at home, except chez Bourrienne. But the Permons were special: They were family, and in Corsica that said everything.

The Permons, who had been out of Paris during the final illness of Monsieur Permon, returned just after the October events and Napoleon's elevation to commander of the Army of the Interior. When the Permons had left Paris, Napoleon's future was still in doubt. He was sharing a room with Junot and Marmont in a cheap Left Bank hotel. He had not a sou to spare for cabs or a horse, and his boots were always muddy from his long walks through the largely unpaved streets of the French capital. But according to Laure Permon:

> Muddy boots were out of the question. Bonaparte never appeared anywhere now but in a handsome carriage, and he lived in a very respectable house, in the Rue des Capucines. In brief, he had become a necessary and important personage, and all as if by magic. He came every day to see us, with the same kindness and familiarity. Sometimes, but very rarely, he brought along with him one of his aides-de-camp, either Junot or Muiron, or Uncle Fesch, a man of the mildest manners and most even temperament.

At this time the situation in Paris was desperate. Workers had no jobs, and people were starving. Napoleon would arrive in his carriage almost daily with dozens of loaves of bread for the Permons to distribute, but on strict orders not to say that this bounty had come from him.

Madame Permon was still in deep mourning. But Napoleon, as usual, was oblivious to anyone else's feelings. After pestering Madame Permon in vain to arrange for a marriage between Laure's brother and his sister Pauline, he then attempted a second alliance between Laure and Louis or Jérôme. Laure's mother rejected this suggestion as well, on the grounds of youth and both families' lack of fortune (the once wealthy Permons having lost almost everything during the Revolution).

"Indeed, my dear Napoleon," she had replied, "you are acting the high priest today. You are marrying everybody, even the youngsters," she laughed.

Bonaparte was embarrassed. He admitted that when he woke up that morning a "marriage-breeze" had swept over him. To prove it, he kissed Madame Permon's hand and now proposed the union of the two families by a marriage between *him* and *herself* "as soon as a regard to decency would allow." Madame Permon "stared at Bonaparte for some seconds with an astonishment bordering upon stupefaction, and then burst into so hearty a laugh" that the family heard her in the next room.

Napoleon continued to visit the Permons, and conversation in the drawing room was a little awkward for some time. Then one day a real storm developed out of the blue that eclipsed their misunderstanding and permanently destroyed the close ties he had maintained for so many years with this family.

It had all begun innocently enough, when Madame Permon asked Napoleon, now the great man, to obtain a commission in the élite special guards assigned to protect the National Assembly for the son of a Corsican cousin, a young man named Dimo Stephanopoli. Napoleon assured her that he would take care of it. A week later Madame Permon asked Napoleon if he had considered her recommendation. He replied that he had the war minister's promise. There was one more detail to take care of, and he would bring her the commission tomorrow.

When he arrived the next day, it turned out that with all his professional preoccupations he had completely forgotten his promise. "You owe this to me!" Madame Permon snapped at him. Napoleon explained that all the offices were closed for the weekend.

On Monday morning General Bonaparte called as usual on Madame Permon. On horseback and surrounded by numerous aides, he was in a convivial mood, but Madame Permon was quite beside herself. She had just received a message from Dimo saying that nothing had been done about his commission.

When Napoleon tried to kiss her hand, she snatched it violently from his and demanded to know whether he had the commission at last. Napoleon replied that he had been busy and again promised "tomorrow." Madame Permon flew into a rage. She accused him of lying to her and— worse—of dishonor. "You deserve a good thrashing!" she announced. "Could an enemy have served me worse?"

He tried to placate her, but to no avail. "What is done is done. With me words are nothing, actions are everything."

As Napoleon prepared to leave, he offered his hand. Madame Permon refused, silently folding her arms in front of her.

Napoleon had been severely humiliated before his subordinates, and that ended all normal relations with the one family he was truly fond of, in which he had been treated like a son. "We went several days without seeing him," said Laure. "He then called one evening when he knew we were at the theater, and at last stayed away altogether."[16]

In the future Napoleon would frequently make promises and simply forget about them. When reminded, he would merely shrug off his failure, never admitting he had wronged anyone. He developed a reputation as a notorious liar. He promised general officers, such as Baron Paul-Charles Henri Thiébault, promotion to higher rank, even before witnesses, and then did nothing about it for years. Napoleon would make enemy after enemy throughout his career, without a thought, for he had neither shame nor a sense of guilt. His word meant nothing, *tant pis!* Nor did he realize that this attitude lost him the respect of most of those around him—even those who otherwise genuinely admired his real military achievements—to the point that one day they would feel no compunction in abandoning him altogether.

Just as relations were ending between Napoleon and the Permons, they were beginning in another direction. Shortly after his sudden rise to power, following the October 4 cannonading, Major General Bonaparte, commander in chief of the Army of the Interior, met a woman he had no doubt heard mentioned frequently, along with some of her famous (some would say infamous) friends, such as Thérésia Tallien, Fortunée Hamelin, and Juliette Récamier, collectively known as the Merveilleuses because of the extraordinary costumes they wore. Their bacchanalia—"filthy orgies," one member of the Directory called them—held at the Chaumière, their cottage in the Champs-Elysées, were the talk and scandal of the town. Perhaps Napoleon had already met her there, but undoubtedly he had at least seen her fleetingly chez Barras, whose official mistress she now was. This was in the autumn of 1795, when her affair with Gen. Lazare Hoche was drawing to a close—or almost, with the announcement of Mme. Hoche's pregnancy and his refusal to divorce her, though he was still besotted by his mistress. The lady in question was of course Josephine, or Rose, as she was still called at this time.

To be sure, Hoche had not been her first lover since the execution of her estranged husband, Vicomte Alexandre de Beauharnais, a year and half earlier. There had been a chevalier, a count, and a duke, not to mention a few transient officers. The affair with the celebrated hero, Hoche, would linger to the end of 1795, when, with the dispersal of the Army of the West, he was named to head the newly forming Army of the West Coast, preparing for the invasion of Ireland.

Barras would prove to be the key to both Josephine's and Napoleon's lives and careers. Every woman in Paris found Barras eminently attractive: "Tall, dark, having a proud bearing, lively, and yet with a distinguished and most imposing air," the hard-to-please Victorine de Chastenay described him, the even-harder-to please Germaine de Staël fully concurring.

Josephine was not yet "Josephine." Born Marie Josèphe Rose Tascher de La Pagerie, on June 23, 1763, on the family sugar plantation at Les Trois Ilets in Martinique, she had been called Yvette by her family and then Rose after leaving school. At the age of eighteen, her father, Joseph Tascher de La Pagerie, a descendant of an old aristocratic family from the Loire, had left the court of Louis XVI, where he had been serving as a royal page, to seek his fortune in the fabled tropical Windward Islands of the Caribbean. Joseph was neither very bright nor a good businessman, and his plantation steadily declined, aided by one or two unusually destructive hurricanes and by his predilection for gambling, drink, and women. His great dream was to escape his tropical prison for the delights of Paris.

Rose's mother, née Rose Claire des Vergers de Sannois, was left with the management of the plantation and the raising of their three children, all girls: Catherine Désirée following one year after Rose, and Marie Françoise two years later, in 1766.[17]

Both parents were disappointed; they needed sons to manage the plantation and daughters-in-law with substantial dowries to restore it and pay their debts. Having three daughters had inflicted only further despair on a family hopelessly in debt, with the misfortune of having to provide three dowries instead of receive them. Thus Rose's father drank himself into a premature old age.

Education was not a priority for girls in colonial families, however prestigious their name, and at ten the almost illiterate Yvette was sent to a convent school at nearby Fort Royal, where dancing and music classes were the focus of the curriculum, with all scholarly subjects carefully omitted At the age of fourteen she returned home. She had grown prematurely almost into a woman, but she was little enhanced so far as knowledge was concerned, knowing nothing of mathematics, history, geography, or literature. The girl was a burden on the family and had to be married off.

And thus father and daughter (now called Rose) set sail for France in October 1777, where Joseph Tascher's sister, Désirée, agreed to look after the girl and find a suitable spouse for her. A marriage contract had been arranged with the son of Martinique's worthless former governor and lieutenant-general of all the French Windward Island possessions (then including Guadeloupe, Dominique, St. Lucia, Grenada, and Tobago)—the marquis de Beauharnais. Although the marquis's first choice had been Catherine Désirée, she had just died of tuberculosis and Rose was accepted in her stead. In September 1779 Joseph Tascher de La Pagerie and his daughter duly landed at Brest, where a carriage was waiting to fetch them to the imposing Beauharnais mansion in Paris. For Rose a new world had opened, and she was terribly excited.

After months of haggling the final marriage contract was signed, Rose's father agreeing to pay a dowry of one hundred thousand livres—the franc did not replace the livre until 1795—and the cost of her trousseau. He did not have a sou to his name but signed anyway—as he had his many gambling debts. In December 1779 the plump sixteen-year-old Rose married the self-styled Vicomte Alexandre de Beauharnais.

It did not prove a good match. After counseling his wife on what to study and read in order to repair her shocking—indeed embarrassing—illiteracy in every field and on every subject, he gave her long reading lists and thence repaired to his regiment in Brittany, where one of his many aristocratic mistresses was impatiently awaiting his return. Remaining at home with her in-laws during his long absences, Rose, ever a lazy child, proved an equally lazy student, doing little to improve herself. Nor did her husband mend his ways, one of his mistresses giving birth to a son, while Rose provided him with two children, a son, Eugène Rose, born in 1781, followed by a daughter, Hortense Eugénie, two years later.

Relations deteriorated quickly, the two rarely meeting. The dashing young husband finally sent her some acrimonious, even menacing letters, calling her "in my eyes, the vilest of creatures" and accusing her of having an affair and of providing him with a "bastard" daughter, Hortense, all of which was utter nonsense. Still not content, the soldier then kidnapped his son and sold all their furniture as well as all the jewelry he had given Rose, leaving her both bewildered and broke. A lawsuit was brought against Alexandre de Beauharnais, and he agreed to a separation. He would pay his wife five thousand livres per annum and retract all his unfounded accusations. That grotesque misalliance was effectively at an end.

Suddenly on her own, with two children to care for, Rose now applied herself to the reading and social education that she so badly needed in the French aristocratic circles of the day. She also acquired several agreeable gentlemen, much older than herself, to provide her with a little companionship—and financial help.

Finally reduced to a state of absolute poverty, however, in 1787 she borrowed enough money to sail back to Martinique, where she remained for the next two years, enjoying what social opportunities the local garrison officers and fellow planters could provide. But even there, with little to spend, she accumulated considerable debts to local merchants. It was a weakness she was never to overcome. If she saw a pretty pair of boots, or just some fetching lace, she had to buy them.

In the meantime, of course, the French Revolution had broken out, quickly making itself felt in the colonies as well. In the first week of September 1790 the white population of Martinique was warned that French mutineers and rebelling blacks were about to attack their settlements, which gave Rose the impetus she needed to leave. With the launching of the attack against Fort Royal and the French naval fleet, she was given emergency permission to sail to France.

The Paris she found in 1790 was emotionally a very different place from the city she had left. Most of the aristocrats who had not emigrated, such as Mirabeau, Lafayette, and Talleyrand, supported the initial revolutionary reforms. Her estranged husband, Alexandre, had been elected to the Constituent Assembly, while Rose remained politically undecided. But events moved quickly, including King Louis XVI's attempted flight from the country and return to Paris as a state prisoner in June 1791. The Constituent Assembly was replaced by the Legislative Assembly, and all sorts of traditional aristocratic rights and privileges were abolished. Then on April 20, 1792, France declared war on Austria.

Wartime France was very different indeed. By 1793 Rose's husband, now commanding the powerful Army of the Rhine, was defeated and fled from Mainz, for which he was arrested. Rose attempted to intervene on his behalf only to find herself arrested as well, in April 1794, perhaps because of her attempt to save her husband, or perhaps because she was an aristocrat and the prejudices of the masses ruled the day.

No sooner did she find herself imprisoned, in the former Carmelite monastery in Paris known as Les Carmes, than she discovered Beauharnais there. He was beheaded on July 22, and Josephine was informed she would inevitably follow. So the days passed in the crowded, fetid conditions of the dank stone prison. But after the active intervention of Citizen Jean-Lambert Tallien on her behalf, and the fall of Robespierre on July 27, 1794, much to her astonishment Rose suddenly found herself free.

By now she had acquired definite political views, which she shared with another liberated inmate of Les Carmes, Lazare Hoche, as they began their long liaison. It was months after her release that she became closely involved with the Chaumière crowd, which included Barras.

In mid-October 1795 Napoleon was invited for the first time to Rose's little house on the Rue Chantereine. Thereafter, at her request, they saw each other frequently. By now Napoleon had become quite the *grand homme* of the capital. Not only were his boots shining, but he kept an immaculate new coach drawn by four splendid horses, which took him regularly to the Opéra, where he maintained a private box. These were just the sort of things to appeal to the feckless Rose, who still continued to sleep with both Barras and Hoche, while—perhaps not yet realizing it—beginning a new romance with the Corsican general.

Napoleon for his part was now working hand-in-glove with Barras, seeing him almost daily after the Directory moved, on November 5, from the Tuileries into the Luxembourg Palace, where Barras headed both the Ministries of the Interior and of the Police, with Lazare Carnot temporarily at the War Office and Jean-François Reubell directing the Ministry of Foreign Affairs in the Hôtel Gallifet. Despite his debauched nightlife, somehow Barras managed to maintain a dignified air, in his long, old-fashioned military coat and glistening black boots, all enhanced by "a martial air." He was also very clever, a political survivor. He alone of the five ruling directors, however, rejected the absurd costume devised by the "art dictator of France," Jacques-Louis David, which included a scarlet toga, knee breeches, and an azure sash. It was a comedy, and he said so. That Rose was at the Luxembourg almost nightly, along with her inseparable friend, Thérésia Tallien, could hardly have been lost on the eagle-eyed Napoleon, nor could the continuing echoes of Rose's close ties with the mighty revolutionary hero, General Hoche.

But it was she who had encouraged Napoleon in the first place, writing on October 20: "You no longer come to see a friend who is fond of you. . . .

Come to lunch with me tomorrow.... Goodnight, *mon ami, je vous embrasse."* Signed "the Widow Beauharnais."

"No one desires your friendship more than I," he replied the same day. But within a matter of weeks the tone had changed, passion ringing through his replies—if not hers. "I awake every day with thoughts only of you.... Sweet and incomparable Josephine, what a strange effect you have on me!"[18] Napoleon did not like the name Rose—or the old reputation attached to it. He changed her name for her. And by the next letter he also had dropped the formal *vous* for *tu.* Indeed, despite the lady's reputation, Napoleon was soon pressing her to marry him, a suit she teasingly refused to take seriously. When it got down to basics, he was startled to learn that though her family did own a large property in Martinique, it was still deeply in debt, providing her with less than two thousand francs a year in income. By the end of the year Napoleon was sharing her nights alternately with Barras and Hoche. It was becoming a bit complicated, even by French standards.

Meanwhile, Napoleon's days had suddenly become extremely busy, as his revised campaign plan for the invasion of Italy was approved by War Minister Carnot in January 1796. In the last week of February, Napoleon was formally nominated as commander of the Army of Italy—Barras's dowry, the humorists quipped. A long-vacillating Josephine, over the protests of her friends and her own children, now finally agreed to a civil wedding with "Bonaparte," as she always called him. It was still pretty much of a joke, she told her friends.

A little before 7:00 P.M. on March 6, in the office of one of the arrondissement mayors of Paris, Josephine arrived in a white (Napoleon's favourite color for women) muslin dress and a tricolor sash, with a necklace of chains of her hair around her slender neck, bearing a medallion on which was engraved: "To Destiny." Jean-Lambert Tallien and his wife, Thérésia, Paul Barras, and her notary,* Calmelet, served as the bride's witnesses. Napoleon had sent only the eighteen-year-old Captain Le Marois. By 10:00 P.M., with no sign of the groom, the mayor gave up and stalked out. When Napoleon finally did arrive from his office, quite distrait, the various certificates and documents were hastily—and fraudulently—completed, Josephine giving her birth date as 1767 (instead of 1763), and Napoleon his as 1768 (instead of 1769), adding to his misdemeanor by naming Paris as the place of

---

*A French notary, one step below a lawyer, was an important and respected figure. He was responsible for handling one's investments, contracts, and so on, much as a solicitor does in England today.

his birth (not Ajaccio). These irregularities were compounded by two more, Napoleon's witness being underage (still technically a minor), and the mayor's replacement, one Collin, in fact not even legally authorized to per-form wedding ceremonies!

The bells of the Eglise St.-Roch were still ringing out the last seconds of the day as General and Madame Bonaparte passed on their way to number 6 Rue Chantereine. Two days later the bridegroom's carriage left the capital for the Comté de Nice and the invasion of Italy.

CHAPTER 3

"A New Alexander the Great"

For the first time, I no longer considered myself a mere general, but a man called upon to decide the fate of peoples.

he military situation in Europe was somewhat confused. France faced the remaining members of the First Coalition: the emperor of Austria; the king of Sardinia, Victor Amadeus III; and Great Britain. Habsburg-dominated northern Italy included the Duchy of Milan, Mantua, Modena, and Lucca, while a scion of the Austrian royal house reigned over the Duchy of Tuscany at Florence. A Spanish Bourbon, Ferdinand IV, ruled the southern part of the peninsula, including Naples and Sicily, while also controlling the Duchy of Parma in the north. There was considerable dissatisfaction in the Papal States, including Rome and Bologna, where signs of revolt had already appeared. To the north, the king of Sardinia had already lost Savoy and Nice to the French and was bent on revenge, leaving Piedmont as well as Lombardy in a tense state.

French strategy was to launch two northern armies across the Rhine, their objective to crush the Austrians and seize Vienna, where (it was hoped) Napoleon's Army of Italy would join them after sweeping across

northern Italy. The French government was concentrating its major effort
in the north, considering Napoleon's ragtag Army of Italy a mere sideshow.

The latter was indeed in a poor state on Napoleon's arrival at Nice in
late March 1796. He found its subcommanders—Gens. André Masséna,
Charles Pierre François Augereau, Jean Mathieu Philibert Sérurier, A. E. F.
Laharpe, and H. O. M. Stengel, not to mention his chief of staff, Brig. Gen.
Louis Alexandre Berthier—demoralized. Their spirits were hardly lifted on
seeing this stunted, grim-looking twenty-six-year-old foreigner, who was
their junior both in age and seniority of rank. Just another political general,
most of them had described him, this darling of the Directory whose new
wife, "that Beauharnais woman," was the talk of Paris. In fact, Napoleon
only had four friends with him, his aides-de-camp Col. Joachim Murat,
Major Junot, the twenty-two-year-old Captain Marmont, and his own
seventeen-year-old brother, Louis. Little did Bonaparte or any of these men
realize that over the next few years six of them were destined to become
legendary military figures as the marshals of an empire that was to seize,
shake, and throttle Europe and the world.

The background of these future marshals—most of them from working-
class families—was as varied as it was frequently startling. Masséna was
born in Nizza (Nice) in 1758. The small, dark, slender boy came from a
long line of grocers. If until the age of six life appeared to offer this young
subject of the king of Sardinia some stability and modest prospects, all was
much changed with his father's premature death.

His mother remarried quickly and soon abandoned André, leaving him
with one of his uncles. For the next few years the boy worked in the uncle's
pasta shop, preparing and cutting spaghetti. As for school, for the working
classes there was none. Approaching his tenth birthday, André fled over the
Var and into France, where a relative found him a position for the next several years as a cabin boy and then a sailor on long sea voyages. By the age of
seventeen, however, he never wanted to see another ship as long as he lived.
Unusually small and wiry, he was as fully grown as he ever would be. The
future did not seem bright; still illiterate, he had little to offer the world.

The Royal Italian Regiment of the French Army did accept him, however, and in its ranks he spent the next fourteen years. Quite intelligent, he
finally learned how to read and write and ultimately reached the rank of
sergeant-major in 1789, when he was automatically required to retire. The
coming of the Revolution was to prove his salvation: He was elected an officer of the National Guard and then advanced to a battalion of volunteers in
1791. By 1794 Masséna found himself a major general in the French army.

He may not have had "either education or good manners," as Captain Thiébault, just assigned to his regiment in Nice in 1796, remarked, "but his face reflected much wisdom and energy, while he had the penetrating eyes of an eagle." He was respected by his officers and men alike, who had real confidence in him. He bore himself "in a most dignified manner and proved to be provokingly audacious. His gestures were imperative ... and his speech brief and to the point."[1] His relations with an equally dapper Italian-speaking Bonaparte would not always be easy, given both men's proud, strong, independent nature.

If Masséna's youth seemed uninspiring, it had been a veritable bed of roses compared with that of Augereau. Born in Paris in 1757, the son of a household servant, the boy spent his childhood in the streets of the capital without any parental interest or supervision, and with the inevitable results. Recruited into the army at the age of seventeen, the tall, scarcely literate, gruff Augereau did not survive even in the barracks, being dishonorably discharged for a serious but hushed-up offense. Undiscouraged, the cold Augereau—"the brigand," his own troops would later call him—joined a private regiment of *carabiniers*. Instead of being grateful for a fresh start, however, Augereau deserted in Switzerland.

By now no one wanted the roughneck except the aging King Frederick of Prussia, on condition that he remain a private. After a few more years Augereau deserted again—or was he cashiered? Ever the optimist, the swashbuckling rogue decided to exchange dreary gray Prussian skies for the azure waters of Italy, serving for a while as a sergeant in the army of the king of the Two Sicilies, at Naples. For once ending his career honorably, he next established himself as a fencing master, at which he did well enough to marry the daughter of a Greek merchant. But when the French Revolution broke out in 1789, Augereau, regrettably a member of the barbarous French who had arrested the French royal family, was ordered to quit the kingdom forthwith. Returning eventually to France, he joined the Paris National Guard, transferring to a volunteer regiment two years later, and by the end of the next year the ex-sergeant suddenly found himself elected a major general! Only in France. . . . After campaigning in the western Pyrenees for two years, he now found himself in Nice facing a little Corsican general a full head shorter than himself and equally arrogant. They disliked each other on sight.

As for Sérurier, in him Bonaparte had a very different man indeed. Born in Laon fifty-four years earlier, the son of a "royal mole-catcher" for the breeding stables of Louis XV, the young man was surprisingly granted a commission in a militia battalion in 1755, then integrated into the regular army, serving in the Seven Years' War, but thereafter limited in advancement because he was not of noble birth. Thanks to the Revolution, however, he was a colonel by 1792 and was promoted to major general a year before joining Napoleon at Nice. He was one of the few general officers during the Empire to have served in a regular capacity as a career officer before the Revolution.

Born at Versailles in 1753, Alexandre Berthier also served as a regular army officer under Louis XV. His father had been commanding officer of the Royal Army Engineers, leading to his ennoblement in 1763. Unlike Augereau and Masséna, Berthier was well educated and welcome in drawing rooms, despite his emotional, high-strung nature. He took a commission as an engineering officer in 1770, serving under Lafayette in the American War of Independence. He continued his career under the revolutionary government, as a major general of the Versailles National Guard, and was now acting as Major General Bonaparte's chief of staff at Nice. He would remain at Napoleon's side, ever obedient, despite a constant flow of abuse from his chief, until the spring of 1814. But from the beginning the aloof Berthier disliked most of the French army commanders, a feeling they fully reciprocated.[2]

Lower on the totem pole was Napoleon's old friend and current aide-de-camp Captain Marmont. Born at Châtillon-sur-Seine in 1774, of an old aristocratic Burgundian family, he emerged from his royal military school in 1790 a second lieutenant and then went on to the artillery school at Châlons. He had met Bonaparte during the siege of Toulon, and they remained close thereafter.[3]

Joachim Murat's background also differed from that of his fellow commanding officers. Born in 1767 at La Bastide-Fortunière, in the Department of the Lot, the son of an estate steward with enough money to ensure his getting a reasonably good education at religious schools and seminaries, he then ran off at the age of twenty to enlist as a private in the cavalry. Thanks to the Revolution, he was promoted to second lieutenant in 1792, then major the following year. After serving in the north and Champagne, he worked under Napoleon's orders during the Paris rebellion of 13 Vendémiaire (October 4, 1795) and was promoted to colonel and senior aide-de-camp in 1796. Tall, broad-shouldered, relatively good-looking, and a boastful womanizer with an extraordinary taste for the bizarre in clothes, within a few weeks he was to grate on Bonaparte's nerves, a situation later aggravated by his seduction of Josephine. Murat's and Napoleon's relationship would be tenuous thereafter, in part because of the former's marriage to Napoleon's sister Caroline in 1800.[4]

There remained a few more officers with whom Bonaparte would soon be coming into contact who would also be rewarded with a marshal's baton. Capt. Jean Baptiste Bessières, the son of a barber, was born at Prayssac, in the Lot, in 1768. Like Murat he attended the Collège Saint-Michel of Cahors, where he did well, in preparation for the School of Medicine at Montpellier. But when he was only nineteen, his father's bankruptcy forced him to withdraw from his studies to take up the less inspiring trade of barber-surgeon. Soon—when he was elected second-in-command of a small local National Guard unit, where he was a close friend of Murat—he became yet another individual saved by the Revolution, whose blessings he fully supported. Joining the Army of the Western Pyrenees as a private, he was later elected an officer, when he first met General Augereau, who in turn brought him along to Nice for the expedition into Italy.

Jean Lannes quickly became a favorite of Napoleon.[5] Born in Lectoure in 1769, the son of a peasant who had neither the money nor the interest to educate the boy, he did not seem to have a promising future. Fortunately one of his brothers, a priest, taught him to read, write, add, and subtract, so that unlike Augereau and Masséna in their youth, he at least was literate, if at the most elementary level. He was apprenticed early, like many working-class boys of his generation, as a dyer, work he found so humiliating that he privately pressed on with his studies. Like most of Bonaparte's future generals, the young, handsome Lannes—before his numerous battle wounds disfigured him—too was saved from an anonymous, humdrum existence by the fruits of revolution. He joined the revolutionary army only to return to civilian life, working in a cloth shop until 1792. Then, at the age of twenty-three, he was elected second lieutenant in a volunteer battalion fighting with the Army of the Western Pyrenees, rising to the rank of major by the spring of 1796, although still personally unknown to his new commander in chief at Nice.

Such was the situation when Napoleon assumed command of his new army at the recently conquered capital of the former Comté de Nice. He immediately called for a full-dress review, which proved a long and painful ordeal, as he inspected every officer, every soldier, every cannon, and every caisson, his aides scribbling madly the mounting record of demerits. Nor was it entirely the fault of his subcommanders, for the Army of Italy—considered the least important of the French Republic's five armies—had been given the lowest priority. The men lacked anything like a regular uniform, some wearing only an old blue army coat over a strange assembly of civilian apparel, many hundreds of them even lacking a musket and bayonet. And their pay as usual was months in arrears. There was little artillery, all of it in

poor condition, and the horses, having been kept on half rations for the better part of a year, were thin and weak, seemingly incapable of any undertaking.

After summoning his commanders and informing them of his conclusions, Napoleon questioned them about the strength of their divisions—the
number and caliber of guns, munitions, wagons and vehicles, horses and
mules, and food and clothing supplies—all with a precision and in such
great detail as to leave them with the realization that their Gallic scorn of
Bonaparte had perhaps been rather premature. This Napoleon immediately
further confirmed by brutally putting down and disbanding some mutinous
battalions, leaving him with an effective field force of only thirty-seven
thousand men. His commanders learned another very disconcerting lesson
at this first meeting: When Napoleon Bonaparte gave an order, he expected
it to be executed then and there, if not the day before. All smug or disparaging smiles quickly disappeared as he cracked the whip.

Accordingly, after ordering what improvements he could effect in less
than one week, an impatient Major General Bonaparte set out from Nice at
the head of the Army of Italy on April 2, 1796, for the plains of Piedmont.[6]

"Soldiers! You are hungry and naked," he addressed them before setting out. "The government owes us much but can give us nothing. . . . I will
lead you into the most fertile plains on earth. Rich provinces, wealthy
towns, all will be yours for the taking. There you will find honor, and glory
and riches." With morale at rock bottom, Napoleon was promising them
full rations (for once), loot, and of course the inevitable *gloire*.[7] French
army pay, even for junior officers, was hardly sufficient to keep one alive,
and loot was the standard substitute of the day. They would return to
France laden with riches and covered in fame, or so he said.

As for Napoleon, he was preoccupied with two subjects only: the
bewitching Josephine, whom he had left on the third day of their marriage,
and this campaign. His invasion plans for Italy would make or break him,
but he considered this the opportunity of a lifetime. To be sure, just about
everyone had been against naming him to this command over senior divisional generals with experience in the field—no one more so than Carnot,
the rabid revolutionary and irate war minister, who argued constantly with
Bonaparte on every subject, including one of Carnot's own pet specialties,
fortifications. Nevertheless, he had been overruled by Barras, and
Napoleon was here. And thus, as he wrote Josephine, he was marching
along the hilly coastal corniche filled "with memories of the one woman in
my life, and my determination to triumph over destiny."[8]

He reached Savona on April 9 and decided to concentrate his force near

Carcare, where the two enemy armies joined. It was his hope to achieve a lightning victory—which would become a trademark of his military career.

With little help from Paris, Napoleon literally had to finance his own campaign as he proceeded. Accordingly, he had sent troops to invite the Senate and the wealthier merchants of the Republic of Genoa to provide war "loans" to the French, while demanding permission to continue on his way across their territory in order to attack their neighbors in Lombardy (with whom the Genoese were at peace).

Facing Napoleon were the combined forces of the Austrian and Piedmontese armies, about fifty-two thousand men. His aim was first to sever all communications between the two allied forces, then defeat them one at a time, beginning with the smaller, less formidable Sardinian army, led by the fifty-eight-year-old general Baron di Colli-Marchi. The septuagenarian Belgian general, J. P. de Beaulieu, commanded the Austrian army, including General Colli.

When Beaulieu received word of Napoleon's impending invasion, he was much alarmed and quickly set out from his GHQ at Milan down to Novi, ordering two divisions to move north and west to link up with him. The Austrian army was divided into three columns: a right wing, under General di Colli, was ordered to defend Stura and Tanaro; a center force, under Count d'Argenteau, was to cut off the left flank of the French army along the corniche at Savona; while Beaulieu himself headed the left wing en route for Voltri. From the outset, however, Beaulieu had problems with greatly dispersed troops, rarely in communication with one another or even with their own headquarters. Nor did the mountainous terrain help matters.

Acting quickly while Napoleon and his main force were still along the corniche, Argenteau reached Montenotte on April 9, 1796, catching the French off guard the next day and attacking them—unsuccessfully—at Monte Legino. Meanwhile, the same day, Beaulieu reached Genoa and set off for Voltri, where he attacked a surprised Laharpe, who was forced to retreat to Savona.

At first thrown off balance by this Austrian attack, which had anticipated his own offensive, Bonaparte ordered Masséna and Augereau to set out at once to Montenotte, which they did during the night of April 10–11. Argenteau's two thousand men suddenly found themselves in a disagreeable situation as dawn broke over the hills on the 11th. Greatly outnumbering their foe, the French launched a large-scale attack from both the front and the rear. With his position no longer tenable, Argenteau had no choice but

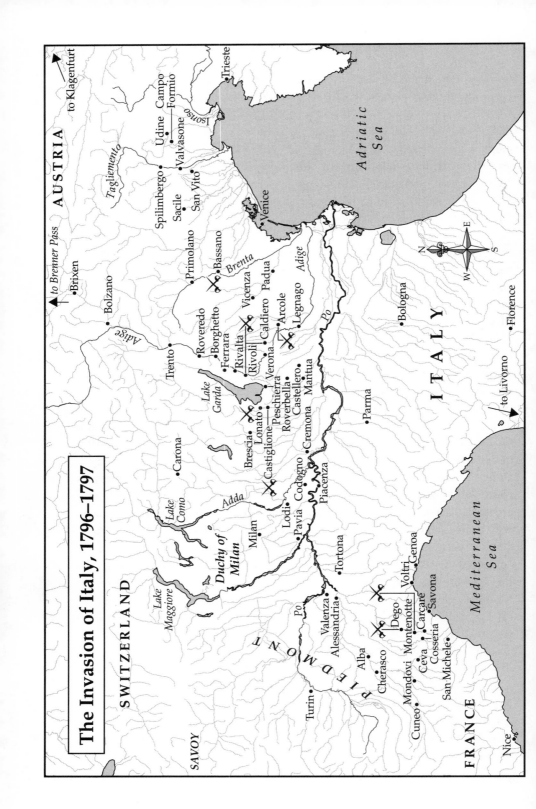

The Invasion of Italy, 1796–1797

to break out, which he did, fleeing northward up the Bormida di Spigno.

Montenotte thus marked Bonaparte's first battle and victory of the new campaign, and given the overall inordinate weaknesses of his army—no transport, guns, munitions, money, or even shoes or boots—he had to win rapidly and decisively at the outset or face defeat and expulsion from Italy. Speed was essential, and he was determined to maintain the momentum.

Meanwhile Beaulieu, having scattered the French along the coast at Voltri and learning of the minor defeat at Montenotte, set out for Dego on the twelfth. Napoleon was reassembling his troops around Carcare, assessing the changes—in particular concentrating on Colli's Piedmontese, now deployed at Millesimo, and the Austrians gathering at Dego. Both these towns were of critical importance to the French, controlling as they did the two vital main routes through the hills leading to the open plains of Piedmont to the north, which in turn joined the plains of Lombardy. Beaulieu therefore had to stop the French then and there, while they could still be easily contained. Bonaparte, on the other hand, was equally determined to defeat the Austrians and march north. Ordering Augereau to head the French left wing and march on Millesimo, he gave Masséna the French center, with Dego as his objective; while Laharpe, forming the right wing, was directed to the heights overlooking Cairo, just south of Dego.

They got off to a good start, Laharpe and Masséna taking Dego from the Austrians on the fourteenth, only to lose their advantage by celebrating their victory prematurely, their troops getting drunk and sacking the town. And that is how an Austrian commander found them on reaching Dego at three o'clock on the morning of the fifteenth, after a forced march from Voltri. Masséna, like many of his staff, was literally caught in bed with a village girl, barely having time to grab his sword and boots before leaping through the window and bounding over the rear wall. He had left no pickets or outposts of any kind, and now he paid for it. Indeed, Dego was retaken on the seventeenth only with the arrival of a furious Napoleon Bonaparte. Thanks to Masséna's ineptitude, the entire French schedule had been thrown out of kilter. Napoleon's plans for launching twenty-four thousand men against Colli's thirteen thousand Piedmontese was delayed by at least two days, long enough for Colli to get wind of these events and retreat from Ceva. A campaign that might have been concluded within a matter of weeks was now to extend many months. Nevertheless, with Ceva secured, the plains of Piedmont now lay open before the French, who had thus escaped Beaulieu's trap. Looking beyond to the snow-covered Alps, Napoleon commented, "Hannibal had to climb over them; we merely walked around them."[9]

Moving his camp to the castle of Lezegno, Napoleon watched as
Sérurier pushed Colli back from San Michele to Mondovi. There Colli
stopped just long enough to be defeated in a brief battle resulting in heavy
casualties. But during the French pursuit that followed, Napoleon's cavalry
commander was killed, Murat taking his place. The French then advanced
on Alba, Fossano, and Cherasco. The seizure of Cherasco—a major
stronghold with large quantities of badly needed supplies and munitions,
not to mention a few dozen cannon and fresh transport—on April 25 was
another important coup. For the first time in many weeks the men could eat
properly and even be paid.

Completely demoralized, undefended, and frankly terrified by the
reports of pillaging and rapine that preceded the approaching French army,
the representatives of King Victor Amadeus of Sardinia requested an
armistice at Turin with this awesome Bonaparte, to which he agreed on
April 28. The French were to be allowed to occupy Ceva, Cuneo, and
Tortona (or else Alessandria) and at the same time were granted the right of
free passage both to France and across Piedmontese territory to the Po and
beyond. The Sardinian king was forced to break with his Austrian allies,
while keeping his own troops in garrison with strict orders not to interfere
with the French. Thus, with the Armistice of Cherasco, Bonaparte had a
tentative legal foothold in Piedmont—but, until the Austrians could be neutralized permanently, far from a secure one. And they, for the moment at
least, were as astonished as the Piedmontese at the amazing French
advance.[10]

A proud Bonaparte now sent this armistice agreement back to Paris
with his aide-de-camp Colonel Murat, accompanied by none other than
Salicetti, the senior political commissar attached to his army, the very same
Salicetti who had earlier demanded his arrest. (How this transformation
occurred remains a mystery.) In any event, in less than two weeks
Napoleon had captured a series of towns, broken the Piedmontese army,
inflicted six thousand battle casualties, and taken thousands of prisoners.
But all this was due chiefly to the enemy's inferior numbers, poor leadership, and even poorer state of morale, determination, and confidence. Bonaparte therefore had yet to prove himself.

The victorious French army was still in pretty sad shape itself, forcing
its commander to call for strong reinforcements from France, which did
not, however, prevent him from preparing to launch the next stage of the
campaign. As he now informed Carnot, "I intend to catch up with the Austrians and defeat them before you have time to reply to this letter."

"Soldiers!" he addressed his troops:

In two weeks' time you have won six victories, taken twenty-one flags, fifty-five pieces of artillery, several forts, and conquered the richest part of Piedmont. You have taken fifteen thousand prisoners and killed or wounded another ten thousand men [sic]..... You have won battles without cannon, crossed rivers without bridges, made forced marches without shoes, drink or bread.... But soldiers! do not deceive yourselves, you have still achieved nothing, because you still have everything to do, for neither Turin nor Milan are yet in our hands! Soldiers, your country has the right to expect great things of you! There remain battles to fight, cities to take, rivers to cross.... And friends, I promise you will achieve it all!

And then, turning to the Piedmontese:

People of Italy! The French Army has just broken your chains of bondage. The French people are the friends of all peoples. Have confidence and work with us. Your property, your religion, and your customs will be respected."

After occupying Alessandria, French troops continued their pursuit of the Austrians, and by April 30, 1796, had crossed the Po. With fresh reinforcements Napoleon now had almost forty thousand men at his disposal, as he feinted a major crossing of the Po at Valenza with Sérurier's force, opposite Beaulieu's army concentrated on the north shore there. Instead, Napoleon would head the main force to strike at their rear farther downriver. And behind the Austrians lay Milan, the capital of Lombardy, his next objective.

By May 6 the army had moved up to its new positions, and before dawn the next morning, a special unit—including Colonel Lannes, 3,600 grenadiers, and 2,500 cavalry—set out for Piacenza, reaching it after a brisk five-hour march. If the troops were not fresh, they were willing, as Lannes led the first four battalions across the Po there. A few miles northwest, about halfway to Milan, lay the town of Lodi. Augereau was crossing the Po at Varetto, bringing news that Sérurier and Masséna were following.

That night, during violent, confused fighting between Napoleon's and Beaulieu's forces at Codogno, General Laharpe was mistakenly shot by his own men. Bonaparte hurriedly ordered his chief of staff, General Berthier, to replace him. Although his forces outnumbered the French, the indecisive seventy-three-year-old Beaulieu retreated to Lodi, on the River Adda. By the ninth, the last of Masséna's and Sérurier's divisions had crossed the Po after a forced march of sixty miles. Napoleon was bent on preventing Beaulieu from escaping once again, as he prepared for a final battle with the Austrian commander at Lodi. Alas, Beaulieu had already made good his retreat, crossing the Adda and falling back toward Cremona, leaving only one tough, largely Croatian division of ten thousand men to guard the vital bridgehead at Lodi as the French approached on May 10.

As usual, in the ensuing battle Bonaparte was in the heaviest part of the fighting, and after clearing Lodi he brought up twenty-four guns and concentrated on the Austrian troops on the far side of the Adda. A brief Austrian charge quickly collapsed as Masséna and Berthier headed a powerful French column against them, ultimately breaking the center of the Austrian position. Overwhelmed by vastly superior forces, the brave Austrians retreated to Brescia, having achieved their objective of delaying the French.

In the brief battle at Lodi, the Austrians had lost 153 dead and many hundreds of wounded and prisoners, compared with a much higher French casualty list. But with Lodi now theirs, and the Austrians gone, the road to Milan lay open. "They [the Directory] have seen nothing yet," an exhilarated Napoleon exclaimed to Captain Marmont. "That evening, for the first time, I no longer considered myself a mere general, but a man called upon to decide the fate of peoples," Bonaparte later remarked.[12]

But no sooner had he spoken than he received fresh orders from the five members of the Directory in Paris, informing him that Gen. François Etienne Christophe Kellermann would be transferred from Germany to take command of the principal part of the Army of Italy. Furious that a mere sideshow was to be allotted to him, Napoleon wrote back that same day: "I believe that to unite Kellermann and myself under joint command in Italy will prove fatal to us. I cannot serve with a man who believes himself to be Europe's finest general. . . . [Moreover,] unity of command is the most important thing in war."[13] To the flamboyant Corsican a competitor here was quite unacceptable. Instead he would leave the army, he informed the Directory. Off went the special courier to the French capital that same night, as Napoleon hurriedly marched on Milan before Kellermann could come to replace him. The Directory gave in: "Immortal glory to the conqueror of Lodi. Your plan is after all the only one to follow!" Kellermann would not be superseding him.[14]

On May 15 the magistrates of Milan duly threw open their gates to their liberator, treating him as a real hero who had released them from their long Austrian bondage. But instead of taking advantage of the goodwill of this large, prosperous capital, Napoleon, at the urging of the French commissars, including Salicetti, unleashed thousands of hungry, tired, victorious, womanless troops on the unsuspecting people of Milan, who became victims of an orgy of destroying, rapine, and killing. He had promised his men riches back at Nice, and now they were taking him at his word.

After veritable fortunes were stolen from the private citizens of this city in "war contributions," another ten million livres were taken from the dukes of Parma and Modena.[15] And the trains of war booty—gold, silver, jewels, and works of art—soon to be synonymous with the name of Bonaparte were making their long journey over the Alps to Paris. The French treasury, literally bankrupt at this point, welcomed Napoleon Bonaparte as its savior. To be sure, Napoleon paid a high price for the looting when large-scale revolts broke out at Milan and Pavia following his departure with the army on May 22. He ordered them to be put down brutally, followed by threats, imprisonment, executions, rape, and more days of looting. He even ordered Colonel Lannes to burn the nearby village of Biansco to the ground and round up all the boys and men and murder them. (Lannes, as usual, could be relied on to carry out his instructions with enthusiastic dedication.) Thereafter Bonaparte's name, along with that of the French, was dreaded and despised throughout the land. "The whole of Italy has been shaken," Commissar Salicetti glowed in a letter to Barras. "Our success everywhere, the bravery of the troops, along with Bonaparte's audacity and military operations frighten it. I think you should be well pleased with this army that everyone formerly dismissed as good for nothing and that instead has in such a short time accomplished everything."[16]

But Napoleon did not rest on his laurels. On May 28, at the head of an army of thirty thousand men, he set out from Brescia, determined to bring the Austrians to bay once and for all. It was not that easy, of course. After narrowly escaping capture by a detachment of Austrian cavalry on June 1— he was literally saved by his own aides-de-camp's swordsmanship— Napoleon decided to form his Guides (which later would be known as the famous Consular, then Imperial, Guard, commanded by Captain Bessières) to escort the commander-in-chief wherever he went thereafter.

Onward the French marched, seizing Peschiera, Castelnuovo, and Verona as they proceeded to their next major objective, the stout fortress of Mantua. Continuing to inform his superiors of his inability to face the French, the elusive Baron de Beaulieu remained on the run. After leaving a twelve-thousand-man garrison at Mantua, he marched north past Rovereto to Trent. Meanwhile Napoleon prepared to lay siege to Mantua, the last important city in Lombardy not yet in French hands. This impregnable citadel was surrounded and protected by two large lakes and malarial swamps, which would prove deadly to both sides. As for Genoa, it was now occupied and its senate threatened by the swaggering Murat and his troopers.

Major General Bonaparte also received orders from Paris to attack the pope and his domains, the Papal States, with the purpose of sending more loot to the thirsty French treasury. Napoleon's advance into the Papal States and Tuscany that June did indeed prove successful, thanks to Generals Augereau and Vaubois, and on the twenty-third Pope Pius VI requested, and was granted, an armistice. The terms were steep—an enormous indemnity in the form of gold and paintings from the Vatican and the occupation of Ancona. Terrified and utterly undefended, Florence, Ferrara, and Leghorn opened their gates to French military occupation as well. Among the categories of indemnity demanded of these latter cities were cannon, which were then hauled by mule and horse up to Mantua.

Throughout this period, literally from the moment he had left Nice, Napoleon had been imploring Josephine to join him as quickly as possible. With the capture of Milan, he had become more insistent and she more evasive. "I beseech you, do leave today with Murat [whom he had dispatched to Paris]," he had written following the Armistice of Cherasco.[17] "My happiness is knowing that you are happy, my joy that you are gay, my only pleasure in knowing that you are enjoying some as well." And then more passionately, "Never has a woman been loved with more devotion, fire, and tenderness." But he added, if she ever left him, "I would feel, that in losing your love, your heart, your adorable person, that I will have lost everything that makes life dear and worthwhile."

Napoleon wrote to her at least once a day for 127 days straight! Sometimes she did not even bother to read his letters immediately. And when she did, she often read aloud some of his more passionate, intimate passages to her friends, male and female alike. "Bonaparte," as she always referred to him, was "*si drôle!*" She grudgingly wrote a brief note usually once or twice a week, but sometimes not for two weeks. "Josephine, no letter from you," he chided her again from Milan on May 24. "No news from my good friend! Has she forgotten me already?" "All couriers arrive without a single letter from you . . . *mi dolce amore.* . . . Clearly your professed love for me was but a caprice. . . . It seems that you have made your choice, and you know with whom you want to replace me." He was dejected, and very jealous, thinking she was resuming her affair with Barras. "Drowning in my sorrow, perhaps I have written too harshly," he wrote again on June 14, now from Tortona, still without a sign of his wife, who had used for her excuse this time her alleged pregnancy. She could not possibly travel. (She was not pregnant.)

He was eating his heart out over her. "I went to Tortona to await your arrival. I waited every day, in vain." He literally rode up the highway several miles looking for her coach:

> I have just received your brief letter informing me that you are not coming here after all. . . . Ah, I had not realized that it was possible to suffer so deeply, so much pain, such frightful torment. . . . I send you a million kisses, and just remember that there is nothing as powerful as my love for you, which will last forever. . . . I feel from your lips, your heart, a flame that consumes me. . . . I kiss your heart, and then a little lower, and then much lower still.[18]

For the first—and only—time in his life, Napoleon Bonaparte was madly in love, while tormented by jealousy and uncertainty.

It was not just the opera, the theater, and the social gatherings of Paris that Josephine was so reluctant to forgo. Milan was an important, civilized capital as well, and the palace that the duke of Strebello put at Bonaparte's disposition was large and comfortable, with dozens of servants. At the same time, serving as the very nerve center of the French occupation, there was much activity there, with interesting people coming and going all the time. But it was only when Barras finally forced Josephine to join her husband that she did so. "She left as though she were going to a torture chamber instead of to Italy to reign as a sovereign," one friend recalled.[19]

She finally arrived at Milan at the end of June, in the company of one Lt. Hippolyte Charles, about to spend the third day of her almost-four-month-old marriage with her husband. If his initial joy in seeing her again was sumptuous, nevertheless duty beckoned and he was off again in a few days. "I am dying of boredom here," she wrote Thérésia Tallien. ". . . My husband does not merely love me, he absolutely worships me. I think he will go mad!"[20]

Napoleon's paranoia and mistrust of Josephine had in fact not been far off the mark, but instead of returning to Barras, she had begun a new passionate affair with Lieutenant Charles, nine years her junior. She had been seeing him daily, and no one had dared to say a word to Napoleon (nor would they for another two years). Indeed, Napoleon's need of, and hunger for, her presence was more ardent than ever. "My happiness," he wrote her, "is being near you. What nights together, *ma bonne amie!* . . . Oh, but surely you must have some faults in your character. Tell me!" Little did he realize what he was asking for.[21]

✳   ✳   ✳

Josephine or no Josephine, the war continued, as the dithering General Beaulieu was replaced as Austrian commander-in-chief by the younger, more dynamic Graf Würmser, who arrived at the end of June along with twenty-five-thousand fresh troops from the Rhine. With a total of fifty thousand men, Würmser had orders to destroy the French army and clear Italy of the invaders once and for all. A man of action, Würmser swept down from the north on both sides of Lake Garda. Taken unawares for a second time, Masséna was routed from the critically important stronghold of Verona on July 29,[22] while eighteen thousand Austrians descending along the western shore of the lake took the town of Salò, though they were finally stopped at Brescia on August 1 by Augereau. Meanwhile Napoleon rushed up all his reserves, including Sérurier's entire force besieging Mantua.

"I must take serious measures in the event of our defeat," Bonaparte confided to Berthier at the end of July. "The enemy have broken through our [French] lines in three places, cutting our communications with Milan and Verona." Then came the disastrous news of the fall of Verona, along with Salò, Rivoli, and Corona.[23] To prevent a complete collapse of the overextended French position, Bonaparte had to stop Würmser's separate troops from joining each other.

By August 5 Napoleon had brought up Sérurier's division to the heights overlooking Castiglione, giving him twenty-five thousand men (although Sérurier, ill with malaria, had been evacuated to France). In a little surprise of his own, Napoleon struck. In a night march Masséna and Augereau, attacked, forcing a startled Würmser to retreat over the Mincio. Bonaparte's rapid forced marches had once again paid off. Maintaining his momentum, he reached Verona on the night of August 7. Immediately Würmser—who had just arrived himself—and his men beat a panicky retreat.[24] Verona, Lonato, and Castiglione were now secured by Napoleon.

Both sides had paid a high price in the retaking of the plain, the French suffering some ten thousand casualties to the Austrians' seventeen thousand. The number of civilians dead, wounded, and displaced is not known, nor are the numbers of houses and buildings destroyed and women raped. Napoleon, realizing that not only his campaign but also his career were at stake, drove himself furiously, not to mention his horses, five of them dropping dead under him in just three days. Meanwhile, an exhausted and defeated Würmser fell back to Bassano, as Napoleon reassembled his troops at Verona. There, to bolster French morale and display his might and determination before the hostile Italian population, he gave his first full military review since entering Italy.[25] Another Austrian column also retreated north,

Masséna and Vaubois catching up with and defeating twenty-five thousand men at Rovereto on September 4. Two days later Napoleon force-marched his men to Bassano, where Lannes and Murat led French forces to another complete victory on September 8.

Now Würmser marched on Mantua. Napoleon responded by cutting the Austrians' line of communications with their most powerful fortress at Trieste. Nevertheless, Bonaparte was unable to prevent Würmser's larger force from defeating Masséna at Castellero and reaching Mantua safely on September 12. Würmser with his garrison of twenty-three thousand men at Mantua remained a force to be reckoned with. They had been partially successful in drawing Napoleon southward and preventing him from joining the French Army of the Rhine and Moselle, then on its way up the Danube to Vienna. Meanwhile that force was hurled back by a strong attack by Archduke Karl on September 19, however, ending the French threat to the Habsburg capital at least for the moment.

By now malaria and typhus were epidemic in the camps of both Würmser and Bonaparte. Fourteen thousand of Napoleon's men were incapacitated, leaving only nine thousand French troops permanently besieging Mantua again and another eighteen thousand available as a field force.

Nevertheless, after seizing Modena, Napoleon pulled off an important coup. By signing a treaty with Naples on October 10, he forestalled Neapolitan troops from coming to the aid of the pope. Taking advantage of the moment, Napoleon created three temporary artificial republics: the Cisalpine (around Milan), the Cispadena (combining Reggio and Modena), and the Transpadena (linking Bologna and Ferrara). He was gradually consolidating his hold over northern Italy.

Unknown to the French, however, Würmser's replacement, the fifty-year-old Hungarian-born Austrian commander, Baron Nicolas von Alvinzi, was descending from the north with another forty-six thousand men, with orders to advance on Verona in a pincer movement with the eighteen thousand Austrian soldiers already there. If they attacked in the north, and Würmser held down a large French force around Mantua, Napoleon's smaller divided army could be destroyed in isolated sections.

The fresh Austrian offensive began on November 4, attacking Trent and sending a small French force fleeing southward. Although inflicting serious casualties on Alvinzi's army, Masséna was unable to prevent the more powerful twenty-nine-thousand-man Austrian force from continuing toward Vicenza. All Napoleon's plans were a complete shambles.[26] At this point he prepared a fourth plan of operations. He would divide and attack the Austrian forces around Lake Garda (coincidentally Alvinzi had pre-

cisely the same objective against the French). Setting out in the rain from
Verona on November 11 with fifteen thousand men, Napoleon arrived at
Caldiero only to find it already securely in Alvinzi's hands. Attacking in the
continuing rain the next day, Masséna was defeated and the principal battery of French artillery captured. Although Alvinzi's army was suffering
heavy casualties, they nevertheless succeeded in throwing Bonaparte back,
thereby remaining masters of not only the Tyrol but also of all the territory
between Trent and the Adige. Napoleon himself, now down to an effective
force of just thirteen thousand men, was obliged to return in defeat to
Verona. "We were no longer in a position to take the offensive anywhere,"
he later admitted. "That Caldiero business, and that of the Tyrol had
strongly lowered the Army's morale.... [Moreover,] a large number of
men had been wounded two or three times at various battles. Morale thus
plummeted."[27]

"Perhaps the hour ... of my own death is at hand," an unusually discouraged Napoleon warned the Directory, even ordering Josephine to evacuate imperiled Milan for Genoa. But, when he finally dried off after several
days in the rain, Bonaparte's spirits rebounded. "We have to make just one
more effort and Italy is ours. To be sure Alvinzi outnumbers us, but half his
troops are green recruits.... Some reinforcements have reached us and the
rest will soon be on their way.... You beat Alvinzi," Napoleon urged his
men, "and I shall answer for the rest!"[28]

And with that General Bonaparte, at the head of twelve thousand men,
marched silently out of the "Camp of Verona" on the night of November
14, across the Adige River, following its open right bank in the direction of
Arcola to the east, one column advancing via Albaredo to Alpone, while the
main column reached Arcola itself at dawn. Between Arcola and Villanuova
just a few miles to the north lay a vast swampy area largely devoid of roads,
intersected instead by a mesh of dikes wide enough to serve as paths. Alvinzi, with his twenty-two thousand men at nearby Caldiero, apparently
felt quite secure for the moment.

Bonaparte's aim was to bypass Arcola and strike hard at Villanuova,
locking Alvinzi between the troops at Verona and Villanuova and cutting
off both his advance and retreat. "We are perhaps on the eve of losing
Italy," Napoleon had written the Directory before setting out now, because
despite all his brave words, few reinforcements had arrived. Given the
extremely weak position in which he found himself, Napoleon felt he had
only two choices: to face inevitable defeat or to attack.

He had made his choice and now watched as General Andréossy completed a temporary wooden bridge over the Adige at the village of Ronco,

Augereau's column crossing and marching northward. But they never reached Villanuova; they were stopped by heavy Austrian fire from Arcola on the opposite shore of the Ronco River. If this could not be overcome immediately, Napoleon's surprise plan for cutting off the Austrian rear would fail. Desperate, Bonaparte himself seized the French tricolor and prepared to lead Augereau's troops to the approaches of the well-defended bridgehead at Arcola. Augereau and others grabbed their impetuous commander-in-chief, roughly pulling him back, arguing with him to use a little common sense. The continuing hail of musket balls and cannon fire won the argument for them. In the chaos Napoleon lost his footing and fell off the crowded narrow dike into the surrounding swamp. Two officers immediately leapt in after him to haul out their weed- and mud-covered commander-in-chief, water gushing out of his high black boots. More or less simultaneously, Masséna marched out of the swamp to attack Arcola from another dike. Again and again Bonaparte urged Augereau to take the bridge at Arcola, but the Austrian defenders continued to beat back his attacks. Colonel Lannes, who had just arrived from Milan where he had been convalescing from a battle wound, personally intervened during one heavy fusillade, leaping before Napoleon and receiving three more musket balls intended for the French commander. Napoleon's aide-de-camp Muiron was killed trying to protect him, as was Gen. Jean Robert, while two other officers, Belliard and Vignelles, were badly wounded. Meanwhile, warned off, Alvinzi abandoned Caldiero with most of his army, escaping over the Alpone River. Arcola was still firmly in Austrian hands, and the French had been completely repulsed on all sides. But at least Verona was no longer threatened, and the Austrians were prevented from joining forces.[29]

By dawn of November 17, the third day of the battle, both sides were exhausted as the French recrossed the Adige in separate columns converging along dikes against Arcola, now held principally by a determined Croatian force. Unable to take the Arcola bridge the previous days, Andréossy had built another one over the Alpone, permitting Augereau to push back the Austrians with his nine thousand men, and after noon, Napoleon launched the final offensive against the village of Arcola. Masséna again emerged from the marsh, in conjunction with Augereau's attack against Arcola from the eastern shore of the Alpone, permitting the dapper Masséna finally to raise his hat on his sword to signal the final—and successful, as it turned out—assault. Despite later paintings showing Napoleon doing so, only Masséna was to cross that famous bridge, as Arcola fell to the French and Alvinzi withdrew to the northeast in the direction of Vicenza. The French had won again, if narrowly.[30]

Although Napoleon later boasted that the Austrians had suffered some 20,000 killed, wounded, or taken prisoner, in fact the figure came closer to 7,000 men, as opposed to 4,500 French casualties. "He entered Verona in triumph by the Venice Gate three days after his mysterious departure through the Milan Gate. It would be difficult to describe the astonishment and enthusiasm of the people," as the news spread of his victory at Arcola and the Austrians' retreat from Rivoli. "At long last, my adorable Josephine, I am among the living again," her triumphant husband wrote from Verona on November 19, "and I still retain my glory and honor. The enemy have been defeated at Arcola ... [though] I confess, I am a little weary."[31] And yet, if the third Austrian offensive had failed, so had Napoleon's objective of decisively defeating General Alvinzi.

November and December found both Napoleon and the Austrians licking their wounds and calling up reinforcements, still equally determined to continue the struggle. Field Marshal Alvinzi was gradually able to bring his strength up to 45,000 men around Bassano, preparatory to moving on Mantua, while Bonaparte got his effective strength up to 34,500, not counting 10,000 men still laying siege to Mantua with nearly eighty pieces of artillery.

On January 8, 1797, the great calm was broken as Augereau reported an Austrian attack before Legnago on the Adige, while another enemy force was reported back at Caldiero the next day. Masséna, meanwhile, was under attack at Verona. But it wasn't until the afternoon of the thirteenth that Bonaparte learned of Alvinzi's intentions and his troop strength. A fresh report informed him of a major Austrian attack at La Corona. Clearly Alvinzi was making his bid to link up with Würmser at Mantua, as he now advanced on Rivoli, just east of Lake Garda.

Napoleon immediately gave orders to march north. The transport of artillery and supplies was slow and difficult over the mountainous terrain, and just as arduous for foot-slogging troops under full kits. Riding ahead of his army, Bonaparte reached Joubert at Rivoli at two o'clock in the morning of January 14. Setting out on a reconnaissance mission, he saw for himself the three columns of the Austrian army below, and to their right, the unbridged Adige.

The battle began at first light, Joubert advancing alone at first with his ten thousand men and eighteen cannon toward the twelve thousand Austrians. By noon, the French force had increased to twenty-three thousand. Nevertheless, the Austrians were not easily intimidated by these superior forces, General Lusignan pulling a leaf out of Napoleon's own manual of maneuvers by falling on the French rear, taking them completely off guard and temporarily cutting their line of communications with the south. Sending in a half brigade to hold off the enterprising Austrians for the moment, Napoleon continued to focus on the main struggle in the Osteria Gorge before Rivoli.[32]

Joubert's troops were utterly exhausted by now, but Napoleon, sensing that the Austrians were equally so, realigned Joubert while pouring in a lethal stream of case shot* from a powerful battery, decimating the Austrian columns at point-blank range and blowing up two large Austrian ammunition wagons in the process. The intensity of the French attack, combined with the enormous explosions and overwhelming French numbers, including a cavalry charge through the Austrian line, shattered frayed Austrian nerves. At about the same time, General Lusignan's division found itself entrapped by Masséna's men before Rivoli, as well as advancing units from the south, with Napoleon as usual in the thick of battle directing everything—and losing two more horses in the process.

By late afternoon, feeling assured of the inevitable outcome, Napoleon left at the head of Masséna's division and drove south frantically to prevent the remaining Austrian column from reaching Mantua. Napoleon and Masséna's thoroughly exhausted men arrived too late to intervene as hoped, but the Austrians found a little surprise on reaching the marshy outskirts of Mantua. General Sérurier's division already held La Favorita and Fort St.-George before Mantua, thereby barring the route and cutting them off from the north and south. General Würmser's last attempted sortie from Mantua failed as well. Napoleon's arrival then forced the outmaneuvered Austrians to surrender at La Favorita. As a delighted young Lannes related to a friend: "The enemy's army is destroyed again. There was never such a bloody battle. We fought for three days and nights under a pelting rain and snow. . . . I decided to attack and fully succeeded."[33] And so had Napoleon with his big gamble.

Meanwhile, back at Rivoli, General Joubert, aided by Murat's cavalry, sent Alvinzi himself fleeing northward up the Adige and into the mountains.

On February 2, 1797, the great victory at Rivoli was followed by the dramatic surrender of Mantua and Würmser's entire garrison, another thirty thousand men, driven out by famine and illness ravaging their ranks. The gallant Würmser was allowed to leave with a few officers and the dignity he deserved. As for Alvinzi, he doubled back and sought refuge in the Papal States. To forestall that, an exhausted Napoleon drove into the Romagna with a small number of troops and forced Pius VI to surrender. Signing the Treaty of Tolentino on February 19, the pope agreed to deny further support to the Austrians and to pay an additional war indemnity

---

*A special kind of shell containing cartridges or shrapnel.

totaling thirty million francs, most of it reaching Paris after local deductions by Napoleon and company. Bonaparte had accomplished virtual miracles over the past few months, defeating three different Austrian commanders-in-chief, despite his inferior troop numbers and artillery and nonexistent logistical support.

Notwithstanding the catastrophic disasters in Italy, Vienna still refused to concede defeat and instead prepared for yet another campaign. But the triumphant French simply lacked the numbers and means with which to March on the Habsburg capital itself. The Directory, with gold and fresh success pouring in from only this one theater of war, at long last recognized the miracles wrought by the determined Bonaparte and agreed to dispatch an additional thirty thousand men to bring the Army of Italy up to a theoretical effective strength of eighty thousand.

Before all those reinforcements could arrive, however, and with only forty thousand men available, Napoleon left twenty thousand to guard against Archduke Karl's fifty thousand troops, well scattered throughout the Tyrol. With the remainder Napoleon and Joubert would head a two-pronged French drive on Vienna after all.

This was the first, but not the last, time Bonaparte would come up against the Archduke Karl, brother of Franz II (Holy Roman Emperor and, as Franz I, the Habsburg ruler of the Austrian Empire). A refined gentleman and in many respects a talented soldier and tactitian, Karl was nevertheless indecisive at critical moments and, like all Austrian commanders, now was plagued by very low morale in the ranks of an army conscripted from the empire's diverse provinces (including, among others, Hungarians, Czechs, Slovaks, Serbs, Croats, Silesians, Austrians, and Rhinelanders). Nor for the most part did he have the tough, resolute officer corps required in the circumstances.

Setting out separately in the last week of February, Napoleon's four divisions crossed the Brenta River, on March 1 overwhelmingly defeating an Austrian force at Primolano. The Austrians fell back to an area in the northeast, bent on retreat up one of the snow-covered mountain passes leading into Austria proper.

Delayed by heavy winter storms, for which the French were ill equipped, Napoleon and his forty-three thousand men took the most direct route to Vienna. They encountered heavy skirmishing with Archduke Karl's advance guard; nevertheless, despite this warning, the Austrians were taken by surprise when Napoleon heavily cannonaded positions along the Tagliamento River and crossed to the far shore, the Austrians giving way before them and withdrawing eastward to Udine.

Napoleon relentlessly pursued the fleeing enemy toward the Isonzo River, while Masséna pushed northward toward Tarvis in the Carnic Alps, which guarded the canyon and one of the mountain passes into Austria. The Austrians mounted stiff resistance, but at a price, Napoleon taking five thousand prisoners, four hundred wagons of supplies, thirty-two cannon, a large supply of munitions, and the entire baggage train. The recently arrived Gen. Jean-Baptiste Bernadotte then pursued the Austrians toward Laybach, Gen. C. F. J. Dugua's cavalry later securing the important arsenal and port of Trieste. Joubert reported similar success in the Tyrol near Bolzano (Bozen), Napoleon ordering him to straddle the main road at Brixen against any possible Austrian reinforcements descending from the Brenner Pass.

The by-now-splintered Austrian army continued to give way before the advancing French units, Napoleon entering Klagenfurt with three divisions on March 29, 1797. But with his own dwindling force equally dispersed over a large area, Bonaparte finally, reluctantly, conceded the impossibility of continuing his march on Vienna for the moment. Then the impetuous side of his nature took command, overriding reason. With his objective less than two hundred miles away, he decided to take a phenomenal chance by ordering Joubert from Brixen and Victor from the Romagna to join him at his new field headquarters at Klagenfurt to reinforce the several divisions already there. Even so, Napoleon lacked the numbers required to take Vienna single-handed.

Playing for time, Napoleon sent a courier to Archduke Karl on March 31, calling for a truce while pushing on to seize Leoben on April 7, with his advance guard reaching the Semmering Pass—only seventy-five miles from the Schönbrunn Palace. But Napoleon now paid the price for his impulsive decision of withdrawing most of his stronger units from the rear. Rebellions broke out in Venezia and the Tyrol, as well as Verona. Praying for a miracle, Bonaparte requested a five-day extension of the truce: "With a mere 50,000 men, surely you do not expect me to hold Italy *and* clobber the House of Austria as well!" an angry Bonaparte wrote the Directory.

On April 16 the French commander finally proposed his formal terms to the Austrians. After receiving instructions from the Schönbrunn, Archduke Karl reluctantly agreed to peace talks at Leoben on the 18th. Napoleon had won his gamble.

The Austrians agreed to pay a very high price indeed, ceding Belgium and Holland to France, along with the west bank of the Rhine, and the Ionian Islands. In addition they officially recognized Napoleon's new creation, the Cisalpine Republic (comprising Milan, Bologna, and Modena).

Napoleon for his part left Istria, Dalmatia, and the Friuli region (next to the Tyrol) in Austrian hands, while giving them the Republic of Venice.

Thus this long, painful, and most destructive Italian campaign came to an end, awaiting only the final peace treaty that would be signed that autumn at Campo Formio. Behind him, between Klagenfurt and Milan, Napoleon had left a wake of burned-out villages; uncounted civilian dead, maimed, and wounded; tens of thousands of homeless refugees; and major potentially friendly cities brutally sacked and occupied. Milan, Turin, Verona, Genoa, Pavia, Bologna, Mantua, and even Rome were forced to pay enormous war reparations and watch helplessly the endless trains of booty destined for Paris and the pockets of the conquering generals and the entire Bonaparte clan, which now became rich almost overnight.

"The little corporal," as the troops now affectionately dubbed Napoleon, had accomplished even more for himself. An international reputation as a formidable warlord, and a hero of France, he was easily the nation's most powerful man, apart from the five-member Directory itself. Starting a campaign with the misfits and leftovers of the principal armies of the north, he had led men—quite literally in rags and often barefoot—hundreds of miles over hills and mountains and dismal swamps to victory against the well-outfitted but demoralized, heterogeneous, and poorly officered regular armies of the Austrian emperor. Moreover, without the consent of Paris he had unilaterally dictated peace terms that would affect several European countries. At a single stroke he had become a negotiator to be reckoned with. The general who had commanded a few cannon before the Tuileries on 13 Vendémiaire had come a long way.

"I need a rest," Napoleon informed an anxious Directory. "I assure you that my only desire at this time is to return to private life."[34] While to Josephine the returning hero warned, "Take care, one of these fine nights I am going to come bursting through your bedroom door!"[35]

Napoleon's meteoric rise also caused the usual, inevitable professional rivalry, one Gen. C. F. de Malet denouncing "that stunted little man with the uncombed hair, that bastard of a Mandarin . . . will pay for . . . all his boastful glory!" while Gen. Henri J. G. Clarke proclaimed him "a new Alexander the Great!" to the Directory, a sentiment soon to be echoed across the whole of Europe.[36]

And when the Venetians attempted to rise up against this new Alexander, he simply had another region and city to sack, lengthening the already seemingly limitless booty trains, while ensuring confirmation of his territorial claims elsewhere, as news of this latest spine-tingling horror story reached a terrified Vienna.[37]

*   *   *

There was another side, however, to this extraordinary saga and conquest of northern Italy, as the twenty-eight-year-old Napoleon discovered on August 17, 1797, on receiving a letter addressed to "Citizen General Bonaparte, Commander in Chief of the Army of Italy," sent from a French field hospital by a young surgeon he had never heard of. It was the first of seventeen such letters over the next eighteen years, following one of his long list of subsequent victories and ultimate defeats.

"I hesitated a long time before letting my quill have its way," it began. "How could I, Jean-Baptiste Turiot, just another faceless citizen of our Nation under arms, a humble junior surgeon, have dared write personally to you, the conqueror of Italy?" Having been with Napoleon's Army of Italy since the Battle of Montenotte, on April 12, 1796, Turiot had followed in the wake of every battle thereafter, in the tracks of this "hero of triumphant *Liberty*," who had "come to the plains of Italy for the sole purpose of spreading the benefits of our revolution and its Equality among these still enslaved people here." There had to be bloodshed to achieve this noble, fraternal task, he insisted.

But the price paid had been high, and the army surgeons had seen the result: "My soul was baptized in the fire of these incessant bloody battles where I first learned of the abnegation and grandeur of our army surgeons." In fact everyone had suffered—far more grievously than apparently General Bonaparte had been informed, Turiot pointed out. They had lost most of their wounded because of the almost nonexistent ambulances and medical supplies of every category, including beds and basic field dressings. "Two thousand wounded lay in the streets of Brescia alone!" But Dr. Dominique-Jean Larrey in particular had done wonders, "and henceforth in battle if the name of General Bonaparte arouses ardent enthusiasm of our troops, that aroused by Dr. Larrey can be seen in the pale faces of our bullet-ridden soldiers, in the tears of their gratitude and hope." And yet much more was needed: a permanent, properly organized, well-equipped field medical corps, with a large staff of well-trained medical personnel. Attempts had been made, but "the Health Service will not be saved from the arbitrary acts of an incompetent government army administration until the lies and depredations of the army supply administrators are stopped from inflicting their evils on us." Only General Bonaparte had the power to intervene and stop these fraudulent operations, Turiot insisted, to prevent this large-scale incompetence and theft of medical supplies and funds.

> This month, even as the preliminary treaties are being signed at Leoben, our hospitals are still filled chock-a-block with 25,000 ill and wounded

men.... And yet most of the sick are the result of poor hygiene, con-
taminated or insufficient food, unhealthful camps, and the miasmas of
surrounding swamps.... [The present situation would not exist] if the
wounded were not herded into wretched hovels and then forced to lie
on damp stone or earth floors without mattresses, without covers, without even the most elementary care and attention that common decency
requires. [Because of the lack of food in our hospitals] the men are literally dying of hunger before our very eyes. At Bazzola a poor hospital
porter gave three francs of his own money to buy a little food in order
to save the lives of men dying of starvation.

Like an enormous fire, typhus is sweeping our hospitals and barracks.... Typhus, that mortal plague afflicting all campaigning armies,
is caused by the filth of these quarters, the lack of fresh air, the negligence of the troops [in their personal hygiene], and the total lack of concern by our own general staffs.... Indeed, even in our hospitals in
Milan ... the wounded and sick are relegated to disgusting places and
denied any sort of help *because the war commissars* [including Joseph
Bonaparte, earlier on] have stolen and sold army medical supplies, down
to the very hospital mattresses.

Whether Napoleon replied to Turiot is not known, but his reaction to
the letter's contents is. The corrupt *commissaires de guerre* responsible for
providing medical supplies to his various armies over the years—forming a
powerful lobby, with kickbacks to the War Ministry, commanding generals, and influential Parisian politicians—continued to thrive to the end of
Napoleon's career. Despite a few occasional promises by him, and even special legislation introduced years later, conditions in fact deteriorated. Little
did Turiot realize that these were still the good days. Worse, much worse,
was yet to come.[38]

CHAPTER 4

Crossroads

I have tasted command, I cannot give it up.

 was received by Buonaparte at the magnificent residence of Montebello, on [June 1, 1797], in the midst of a brilliant court, rather than the usual army headquarters I had expected," recalled diplomat Count Miot de Melito. "Strict etiquette already reigned round him. Even his aides-de-camp and officers were no longer received at his table, for he had become fastidious in the choice of guests whom he admitted to it. An invitation was an honour eagerly sought, and obtained only with great difficulty. . . . He was in no wise embarrassed or confused by these excessive honours, but received them as though he had been accustomed to them all his life. His reception rooms and an immense tent pitched before the palace were constantly filled with a crowd of generals, administrators, and the most distinguished noblemen of Italy, who came to solicit the favour of a momentary glance or the briefest interview. In a word, all bowed before the glory of his victories and the haughtiness of his demeanour. He was no longer the general of a triumphant Republic, but a conqueror on his own account, imposing his own laws on the vanquished."¹ At the seasoned age of twenty-seven, Divisional General Bonaparte had already achieved much of the success he had dreamed of as a youth. As commander in chief of the Army of Italy his forces had brought badly needed victories to the First

French Republic. The Austrian emperor had been ignominiously defeated, and praise of General Bonaparte rose from every village, town, and city of France, as hundreds of wagonloads of objets d'art, gems, gold, and silver emptied from the ancient palaces and churches of Venice and the fortified Renaissance cities of Lombardy streamed back to Paris to fill the empty treasury (and pockets) of the French Directory. Nor had General Bonaparte's troops forgone their share of the booty, generals, junior officers, and even NCOs becoming rich instantly (André Masséna surpassing them all). Generous shares of this loot were reserved for Napoleon's mother, Letizia, and brother Lucien, while Joseph and Louis, in Italy now, simply helped themselves. On a table in Bonaparte's study, Louis de Bourrienne safeguarded a large coffer filled with gold and silver coins with which to meet any immediate expenses. Napoleon had literally produced his own version of the Arabian Nights here on the plains of Lombardy, and Paris appreciated the results. The republicans in particular praised his achievements, and Bourbon sympathizers accepted the conquests for the fatherland, while secretly planning the return of Louis XVIII to his rightful throne. Nevertheless, the Directory found its new sword to be double-edged, for behind the riches and conquest remained the conqueror himself, a man of undisguised ambition.

Bonaparte clearly loved the glory, acclaim, and power he now wielded for the first time. It fitted him like a glove. The entire administration of northern Italy—quite exclusive of his army command—lay in his hands alone. At a word from him, ministers were dismissed or nobles stripped of titles and wealth, then imprisoned or even executed. *That* was power. An astonished Bourrienne, with his more modest goals, serving as Bonaparte's private secretary, simply took in the scene, the bad with the good. He was on the winning side, thanks to his formerly impecunious classmate at Brienne, who had later—when he was unemployed and awaiting a fresh army appointment, any appointment—hungrily partaken of numerous dinners provided by Bourrienne's young wife in their small Paris apartment. But now all had changed, and with it the rules of the game. Brothers Joseph and Lucien would never again be reduced to earning a living as warehouse guards, as they had been in Provence. Nor would Napoleon ever again go without a meal. Bourrienne and his wife, for their part, were no longer permitted to address the great man with the informal *tu* or even to dine with him, unless specifically invited. Now there were only senior generals, ambassadors, dukes, marquis, and counts.

Napoleon found it all exhilarating and did not want it to end. Therein lay the problem. The Directory was pressing him to conclude peace with the vanquished Austrians. But once this was done, large portions of the occupying forces would be withdrawn and the conquering hero ordered home. This was his first taste of the awe and power of an independent military command, where he alone could dictate all the rules, and he was still hungry. Once back in France, he would return to the boredom and restrictions of any other garrison commander, stripped of all political clout and any say in the dictation of French foreign policy, the glory and independence of Montebello but a fading memory.

During a long conversation with André Miot and Francesco Melzi d'Eril, Napoleon made no attempt to conceal his dread of returning to such a humdrum existence in France. "What I have done up to this point is nothing," the general told them during a two-hour interview in the gardens of Montebello:

> This is but the beginning of my career. Do you really think that I triumphed in Italy in order to aggrandise that pack of lawyers who form the Directory, men like Carnot and Barras? What an absurd idea! A republic of thirty million people, that is what the French want today! But that fad will pass, just like all the others. What they really want is Glory to gratify their Vanity, but as for Liberty, they do not know the meaning of the word.

The key to all was the army, he insisted, and the army would follow *his* wishes. "Let the Directory try to take this command from me, and they will see who is master. The nation," he continued, "must have a chief, a chief rendered illustrious by glory, and not by theories of government, by phrases, by speeches which the people do not understand. Give them baubles, that suffices for them; they will be amused and let themselves be led, so long as the end towards which they are heading is skilfully concealed from them." Then, turning to Melzi, he said: "We shall do what we like with Italy . . . we are going to create one or two republics of our own design here. . . ." As far as Austria was concerned, Napoleon would hold on to Lombardy and Mantua and give Austria Venice, while he remained in command with almost sovereign powers,

> unless by some blunder in Paris I am compelled to make peace; for it is not my intention to finish so promptly with Austria. Peace is not in my best interests. You can see for yourselves what my position is here, what I can do in Italy. If on the other hand peace is made, and I am no longer left at the head of the army . . . and must renounce power and the high position I have made for myself here . . . *I do not want to leave unless it*

is to play a rôle in France similar to the one I have here, and for that the
time has not yet come, the pear is not yet ripe.

But if the political situation in Paris were settled (this was before the coup
of 18 Fructidor, September 4, 1797), and "if peace becomes necessary to satisfy those boobies in Paris, then it is I who shall make it. For if I left it to
someone else [to dictate the terms and sign the treaty] then he would be
everyone's darling, and I quite forgotten."[2]

Of course Bonaparte couldn't achieve these goals single-handedly.
Conquering armies need successful generals, but such generals should know
their place and not steal the limelight. When the popular General
Bernadotte arrived with a division of the Army of the Rhine to Italy to
reinforce him, Napoleon quickly banished him to Paris, ostensibly to present the Directory with the twenty-one regimental flags taken by the
French at the Battle of Rivoli. And when in August 1797 the Directory then
wanted Napoleon to report back to Paris, purportedly to take command of
the troops of the capital to assure their planned September 4 coup,
Napoleon instead sent General Augereau, who was beginning to become
too assertive—and popular. Augereau duly quelled the extreme Jacobin
republicans and royalists, but when he was subsequently rewarded with
command of the Army of the Rhine, Napoleon was upset, jealous of any
laurels and glory that had escaped *him.*

In mid-July 1797, for the first time as supreme warlord, General Bonaparte summoned the five full army divisions under his command to Milan
to give an unprecedented review of French military might. In theory this
was a belated part of the Bastille Day celebrations, but in reality it was an
overt notice to Paris that he was the most powerful man in France. This he
reinforced by ordering each division to publish an address to the French
government—using the most arrogant language—threatening the monarchist faction in France, but which was clearly meant for the Directory.[3] As
the tens of thousands of victorious infantry-, cavalry-, and artillerymen
passed in review before their commander in chief, it was a staggering display not only of French power but of Napoleon's as well. "I have tasted
command, I cannot give it up," he was to repeat time and again thereafter.[4]
And Paris did indeed take heed.

In the third week of August, after quietly celebrating his twenty-eighth
birthday in Milan, Napoleon and Josephine, accompanied by Berthier and
Miot, set out for a brief trip to Lake Maggiore and a lovely villa on Isola
Bella. Because of the sweltering heat they left at night, and in the semidark-

ened carriage Napoleon grew unusually cheerful and "extremely attentive to his wife," as Miot delicately put it, "frequently taking little conjugal liberties that rather embarrassed Berthier and me." Later on a "gay and animated" Napoleon related "several anecdotes of his youth." They found Isola Bella, "the most beautiful of the lake's islands," a delight, Bonaparte momentarily removed from the pressures of work as commandant of an occupied country.[5] But this was only a two-day respite, and soon their carriage descended the mountain back into the intense heat of the valley below and the simmering politics of Milan.

Bernadotte, whose outspoken Jacobin sympathies had so annoyed Napoleon, was now out of the way, and Augereau was en route to Paris, while Miot traveled back to Turin to negotiate a new treaty with Piedmont and the king of Sardinia.[6]

It was in Paris, however, and not in Lombardy where the main event affecting Napoleon and his fresh Italian conquests was now taking place. With the backing of the newly arrived General Augereau, the coup d'état of September 4 was successfully executed. The republicans ousted monarchists and moderates and replaced them with hitherto minor, local Jacobin politicians: Gen. Jean Moulin, Louis Gohier, and Pierre Roger-Ducos. This reinforced a stronger Jacobin influence in the Luxembourg Palace and the former Bourbon Palace (where the Assembly of Five Hundred had earlier attempted to name Gaspard Monge, who would soon become a valued friend and ally of Napoleon's, to the Directory, an action precluded, however, by his absence in Italy). Meanwhile, ironically thanks to the successful coup, greater pressure was in turn brought to bear on Bonaparte, by Gen. H. J. G. Clarke, the Directory's negotiator with the Austrians at Udine.

Although the preliminaries to an Italian peace settlement had been concluded at Leoben back on April 15, Napoleon had managed to extend the negotiations at Udine for months, while he continued to expand his conquests. The behind-the-scenes activity was complex and intense. Napoleon's aide-de-camp Antoine Chamans Lavalette, who had been sent to Paris as his "negotiator" with the Directory, had in fact just dashed back to Udine to warn Bonaparte of the volatile situation in the capital: The new Directory had suddenly dismissed General Clarke both as negotiator and soldier but was also most upset about Bonaparte's intention of returning Venice to the Austrians. More important, Lavalette disclosed, the newly reconstructed Directory had dispatched a special courier to Udine—due any hour now—with instructions not only forbidding Bonaparte to sign the draft treaty but also ordering him back to France!

Napoleon conceded defeat. If he wanted to be the one who concluded the peace treaty, he would have to do so immediately. Reluctantly convoking all negotiators, at 10:00 P.M. on October 17, 1797, he and they signed the final draft Treaty of Campo Formio. Two hours later he dispatched Berthier and Monge with this binding international document to Paris. Shortly after their departure, the Directory's special courier arrived with the expected orders, informing Napoleon that they were "looking forward with the greatest pleasure to seeing the hero of 13 Vendémiaire once again."[7] Napoleon had outfoxed them, at least in part. Nevertheless, his own future seemed in doubt.

As a result of this important new treaty, among other things Austria now legally recognized the cession of Belgium and Holland as well as the left bank of the Rhine, not to mention the French conquest of Lombardy and acquisition of three Venetian islands: Corfu (Kérkira), Zante (Zákinthos), and Cephalonia (Kafillinía). In return Bonaparte had given Austria much of the Venetian Republic, including Venice—after first looting it, including some of the splendors of Venice's eleventh-century Byzantine Basilica of San Marco. (In fact it was at the insistence of Gaspard Monge that the French were able to include among the war booty from the Venetian capital several major paintings and the marvelous four bronze horses from San Marco, originally taken by the Venetians from Nero's triumphal arch in Rome.)

In addition to the Treaty of Campo Formio, Monge and Berthier left with the "Army flag."[8] This was an enormous tricolor flag, one side of which read, "To the Army of Italy, A Grateful Fatherland," while the reverse listed battles fought by Napoleon, and places taken, followed by the results of those campaigns, including the seizure of 150,000 prisoners, 170 regimental flags, 550 cannon, 600 pieces of light field artillery, five pontoon-bridge teams, nine sixty-four-gun ships of the line, twelve thirty-two-gun frigates, twelve corvettes, and eighteen galley vessels—outrageous lies, for the most part. This list was followed by the diplomatic results as well, including successful negotiations with the king of Sardinia, Genoa, the duke of Parma, the king of Naples, the pope, and of course with the Austrian emperor. The flag went on to mention all the places and peoples "liberated" by the French, including those of Bologna, Ferrara, Modena, Massa-Carrara, Romagna, Lombardy, Brescia, Bergamo, Mantua, Cremona, Chiavena, Bormio, the Valtellina, Genoa, Corfu, Ithaca, as well as various imperial fiefdoms. Then followed the names of some of the great works of art stolen and now en route to Paris.[9] The paintings of the great Italian masters would be safe from marauders at last!

The 150,000 Austrian prisoners allegedly taken were more soldiers than the Austrians ever sent into Italy. And the number of ships purportedly seized exceeded all the ships the entire French navy captured during the whole of the Consulate and Empire, 1799–1814. Thus the flag should be considered an early example of public relations rather than historical fact.

Reaching Paris on October 25, Monge and Berthier presented the Executive Directory with the new treaty and the flag. Meeting in special session the following day, the outmaneuvered directors begrudgingly ratified Campo Formio in unprecedented haste, for despite their pique, public enthusiasm for this peace treaty (and the man responsible for it) was unanimous, indeed hysterical. At the same time the directors issued fresh orders to Divisional General Bonaparte. After prefatory thanks for services rendered the French Republic—without the flow of that booty it (and they) could not have survived—the directors confirmed his transfer from his dangerously powerful and prestigious post as commander in chief of the Army of Italy and peremptorily ordered him home to take up his new command over the embryonic army forming on the Channel coast, intended for the invasion of England.

With these orders—including his own appointment as Napoleon's successor—in hand, Berthier was sent directly back to Italy. Upon his arrival at the Montebello Palace, it was his disagreeable task personally to inform his dour chief that he was relieving him of his command. A furious Napoleon, presented with a fait accompli, sent Josephine, Bourrienne, and Captain Charles on ahead to prepare the house in Paris, even as he handed over command. "I can no longer obey them," a seething Bonaparte confided to Miot during a brief stopover in Turin the next day. "I have made up my mind, if I cannot be master, then I shall simply leave France."[10] Continuing on to Basel and the German states, he spent the last week of November 1797 at the Congress of Rastadt, convened to implement the new treaty, to study the diplomatic situation there, before finally crossing the Rhine and the French frontier, to reach Paris on December 5.

The French capital, well prepared by Bonaparte's emissaries and successful publicity campaign, was ecstatic. A reluctant Directory, still under enormous public pressure, offered a sumptuous champagne reception for the conquering hero of the hour.[11] Greeted by a standing ovation of hundreds of the elect, Bonaparte entered the courtyard of the Luxembourg Palace, which had been hurriedly transformed into a colorfully festooned amphitheater of sorts, with rows of special temporary seating, as the choir of the Conservatoire sang patriotic hymns against a red-white-and-blue backdrop.

Foreign Minister Talleyrand addressed the distinguished assemblage, welcoming the father of the Treaty of Campo Formio, which gave France two new provinces, the Low Countries, and Lombardy. This was followed by a brief speech by Bonaparte himself into which he slipped—almost unperceived by anyone—his warning: "When the happiness of the French people is [one day] firmly seated on the best organic laws, the whole of Europe will become free."[12] The implications were great, and if his words did raise one or two eyebrows, they were quickly followed by Director Barras's own extravagant encomium, laced in irony. "The sublime revolution of the French people produced a new genius amid the history of famous men. The first among them all, Citizen General, you have cast aside all previous examples, and with the same arm with which you shattered the enemies of the republic, you have swept aside all heroic rivals cast up by antiquity."

An even more elegant fete was given in his honor a few days later by the combined councils (Ancients and Five Hundred) in the gallery of the Louvre, set against the hundreds of looted Michelangelos, Titians, Veroneses, Correggios, Carraccis, Raphaels, and Leonardos. Bonaparte made little attempt to conceal his boredom with these apparent signs of praise. The general did not find a palatial dinner with nearly eight hundred persons particularly convivial. Although he enjoyed the theater and attended it with Josephine, he was also upset when the limelight always shone on him as he entered his loge, accompanied by enormous peals of applause. While he quickly stepped back, attempting to hide, Josephine in her sparkling diamonds loved every minute of it, smiling and bowing. Never trusting such public demonstrations, he afterward confided to Bourrienne, "In Paris they never remember anything. . . . In this great Babylon, he whom they praise today, is forgotten on the morrow, replaced with the next, most recent hero of the day."[13]

In his case the clamor lasted well beyond "today," as the municipality of Paris ordered the changing of the name of the little street in which he lived, the Rue Chantereine ("Street of the Singing Frog"), to the Rue de la Victoire.[14] Great and lesser men came to pay their respects, and Bonaparte, now playing a new modest role, generally returned them. And despite an alleged abortive attempt to poison him, the festivities continued, one after another, although only one really interested him. Thanks to Monge's initiative and support, on December 28, 1797, Napoleon was welcomed as the newest member—in Sciences and Arts—of the prestigious Institut de France (which had recently replaced the Académie Française), where, as he put it, he received the only ovation "that really touched me."[15]

*   *   *

General Bonaparte's immediate responsibility was the command of the invasion army forming along the Channel, from Brest all the way up to the Batavian Republic on the North Sea. It could prove an extraordinary challenge, the kind Napoleon liked best—everything was at stake. If it succeeded, he, Napoleon Bonaparte, would be the first military commander to invade England since William the Conqueror in 1066. After his brilliant military and diplomatic successes in Italy, if all went well he could return to France with the English crown jewels, sweep away the Executive Directory, and seize the reins of power, to the unanimous acclaim of the whole of France. As Director Barras saw it, even if Napoleon failed, at least he would be sidetracked on an otherwise minor command along the Channel for months or even years. And afterward the ambitious troublemaker would end up just another army commander.

Bonaparte set out from Paris on February 10, 1798, on a whirlwind tour of the Channel ports, depots, and camps of the army gathering for the projected invasion. Interviewing officers, sailors, fishermen, coastal traders, and smugglers, he listened "with that patience, that presence of mind, that comprehensive tact and perspicacity that he possessed to such a high degree."[16] This invasion was, of course, just one of the ploys Bonaparte was considering as a means of bringing off the great coup to seize power. French troops on English soil could force their government to the negotiating table. But Napoleon cut short this coastal tour, apparently as a result of a special dispatch he received from Talleyrand, advising him to return posthaste to Paris in order to proceed to the Congress of Rastadt, where "our plenipotentiaries are urgently insisting on your presence."[17]

But on reaching the French capital on February 24 he learned that the mercurial diplomatic situation at Rastadt had altered yet again. He would *not* be going there after all. At the same time he submitted a negative report on the proposed invasion of England,[18] pointing out that everything was against such an attempt at this time. To begin with, if the element of surprise was to be achieved, the season was wrong—long, dark wintry nights being preferable for a successful Channel crossing. What is more, "without our being complete masters of the sea, our descent upon England will be rendered most risky and difficult.... Regardless of the efforts we might make now," he pointed out, "we will not achieve superiority of the seas *for several years to come*. A successful attempt on England now therefore seems too doubtful,"[19] he informed the Directory, while privately telling Bourrienne that Europe was "just a molehill. The truly great empires and revolutions have taken place only in the Orient."[20] To the directors he explained that there were now only ten French warships at Brest, and they without crews. Under such circumstances he had no intention of challenging the entire English navy in the Channel.[21] Nevertheless, the idea and strategy were sound for the future. France must begin to prepare in order to be ready to deliver that blow in several years' time.

Like Bonaparte, the Directory too was at a crossroads—indeed, in a state of considerable confusion. They had signed a decree favorable to the invasion, naming a three-man commission "to prepare, and execute the measures that General Bonaparte will prescribe to you relative to the expedition against England."[22] But at a special strategy conference, the Directory then reversed itself, shelving the Channel operation for the time being.[23]

Napoleon suggested instead two more viable alternatives, an invasion of (British—owned by the king) Hannover, or an expedition to "the Orient."[24] Of the two Bonaparte (with Talleyrand's full support) pressed for the latter. As early as July 3, 1797, Talleyrand had addressed the institute in Paris "on the advantages to be drawn from establishing new colonies" in the eastern Mediterranean.[25] In fact, on February 14, 1798—even before Bonaparte had returned from the Channel with his negative report on the English expedition—Talleyrand had submitted a lengthy formal proposal for the conquest of Egypt to the Directory.[26]

Reminding the five-man board that although Egypt had not always belonged to the Turks—they conquered it in the early sixteenth century—it was France's responsibility now to step in and save that unruly province, administering it in Turkey's name. The ostensible rationale for such an extraordinary act was twofold: the prejudicial acts carried out against French businessmen throughout Egypt, including forced "loans" extorted by the Mamelukes; and two humiliating public beatings of the French consul general, Charles Magallon. It was simply outrageous, the foreign minister insisted. In return for military intervention, France would receive adequate compensation, Egypt offering "the advantages of one of the most fortunate climates in the world," not to mention the land's rich agricultural production—"the cereals and vegetables are most abundant"—including rice, saffron, sugar, coffee, indigo, and cotton. As for the Ottoman sultan retaliating by declaring war on France, Talleyrand hastened to assure the wary Directory "that he would never do so" because of the cataclysm currently racking much of the tottering Ottoman Empire, particularly in Albania, the Peloponnesus, and Macedonia. The Turks had quite enough on their plate already. Nor "can England intimidate us," he continued, "for our war with her provides the perfect opportunity for a French invasion of Egypt. Threatened by a possible French descent upon the British Isles themselves at this time, she will hardly strip her coasts of naval protection in order to send those same ships to attack us in Egypt." What was more, once established in Egypt, France would be in a position to send a corps of fifteen thousand men from Suez "to chase the English out of India."[27] What sort of resistance would the French encounter in Egypt? he asked: "*A maximum of 8,000 Mameluke cavalry,* and moreover, they totally ignorant of modern tactics." With a mere twenty-five thousand men, France could hold the country, while "five ships of the line and six frigates [would] suffice to escort the troop vessels." As for the ruling Mamelukes, they would be abandoned by the enslaved Egyptian people, who would "look upon us with transports of joy [as we] free them from their oppressors." As for the invasion itself, it "will be easy. . . . [France] will be incurring only moderate expenses, for which the Republic will soon receive full compensation," from loot and the like. Summing up, the foreign minister remarked "that the conquest of Egypt would be but the just compensation for the wrongs and affronts inflicted on us by the Sublime Porte*. . . . Egypt was once a province of the Roman Empire and must now become one of ours."[28]

And so the Executive Directory decided to shelve the plans for England and instead concentrate on an expedition to Egypt.[29] To attain glory, wealth, power, and the possibility of peace with England, while ridding themselves of that hectoring and intimidating General Bonaparte, seemed to be the only possible answer. After all, fewer troops were needed in Europe now, thanks to the conclusion of peace with Austria, and once England was truly intimidated, peace would be universal.

*The sultan of the Ottoman empire and his government.

CHAPTER 5

The Decision

In order to truly destroy England, we must [also] seize Egypt. . . . How easy it will be, and even fool-proof.

he idea of the French colonizing Egypt was neither as new nor as palpably absurd as it might at first appear. After all, the Dutch were in the Far East, the Spaniards were in South America and even the South Pacific, and of course Great Britain—the only country with which France remained at war since the signing of the Treaty of Campo Formio—had a lucrative empire spanning several continents. What is more, French republicans felt they had the right and duty to bring the hard-earned fruits of their revolution to the rest of the world!

In 1769 the French foreign minister, the duc de Choiseul, had proposed to King Louis XV making a French colony of Egypt "to replace those in America, in the event they are lost to us"—but the idea was rejected. A few years later Foreign Minister Baron de Tott had reintroduced the project to Louis XVI, only to see it too rejected.

The Ottoman Empire, in a gradual state of decline, was already losing its grip on some of its more distant provinces. Algeria and Tunisia had long been merely nominal members of the sultan's realm, and Egypt was not much better, controlled as it was by the Mamelukes—formerly brought to Egypt as slaves, from the Caucasus and Circassia and later from the

Balkans, to form the country's élite military. On seizing Egypt for the new Ottoman Empire in 1517, Sultan Selim II had simply incorporated the Mamelukes in their traditional role, though by the 1790s Egypt was ruled de facto by twenty-four Mameluke beys, or princes, under a titular pasha appointed by the Sublime Porte.

The possibility of invading Egypt may have been brought to General Bonaparte's notice as early as April 1796 by French minister Raymond Verninae, when, on his return from his post with the Sublime Porte, he pointed out the interior disintegration of the Ottoman Empire, even as the pressure of foreign encroachment by both Russia and Austria grew. But the most persistent recent supporter for such an invasion had been a wealthy French businessman, long based in Cairo, Charles Magallon, who in his capacity as French honorary consul had direct access to Paris and the Foreign Ministry (and thus the Directory).

In August 1797 Magallon sent a memorandum to Paris pointing out the necessity and advantages of seizing Egypt. He proposed a French landing in the month of May (before the beginning of the great summer heat and the annual flooding of the Nile), claiming that "the conquest of the whole of Egypt may and must be executed within nine months [of arrival]. The three months of inundation [would] then give time in which to fortify Alexandria, Damietta, and Rosetta," which in turn would permit the French "to land an army in India and chase out the English," or else simply result in putting the French in a position "from which to annihilate English commerce with India"—all as a consequence of their new strategic position in Egypt, which in turn would enable the establishing of entrepôts in Cairo, Alexandria, and Marseilles, making those cities the greatest commercial centers in the world.[1] While Magallon's latest proposal was receiving a favorable hearing by Foreign Minister Talleyrand (with whom Bonaparte had remained in touch) during the summer of 1797, Gaspard Monge was independently encouraging the Corsican general to give serious thought to such an Egyptian venture. Monge's perspective was altogether different, however. He saw the seizure of Egypt as the triumph of French revolutionary ideals over the forces of ignorance and tyranny.[2] It was France's civic right to conquer.

In addition, throughout the spring and summer of 1797, a victorious Napoleon had been sending the Executive Directory in Paris a series of unsolicited international political analyses. On May 26, for instance, he encouraged the capture of Malta, an "island simply beyond all price to us, which sooner or later will fall to the English if we are so foolhardy as to permit it."[3] He added that along with the recently acquired Ionic islands of

Corfu, Zante, and Cephalonia—these were "of greater value than the whole of Italy." Not only were these islands "a source of riches and prosperity for our commerce," they were also strategic locations from which France could support its Turkish allies. But it was only after talking with Monge at Passeriano, near Udine, in September and October that he expanded this concept, arguing that "in order to truly destroy England, we must [also] seize Egypt."[4] (He was to take the same rather contradictory line throughout the venture, emphasizing the necessity of supporting the Turkish Empire while simultaneously advancing a project to strip that very empire of its choicest province.) Following the discussions with Monge, Bonaparte decided to send Treasury Comptroller Emile Poussielgue on a secret mission to Malta.

With the renewed possibility of a diplomatic role at Rastadt having faded yet again, Napoleon concentrated on the Egyptian operation, organizing it from beginning to end. On March 5 he submitted a long, formal analysis of the proposed expedition, including his estimate of the troops required—twenty-five thousand infantry, three thousand cavalry—"with which to seize Egypt and Malta."[5]

Napoleon's report was only a formality; the Directory had already consulted with him and decided on this course. That same day it issued a series of decrees launching the new operation. One included Napoleon's idea for an "Armaments Commission of the Mediterranean Coast" to oversee the entire process. Another decree authorized the provisioning of troops at Marseilles, Toulon, and other ports, and the assembling of a battle fleet to escort the expedition. Simultaneously the war minister was authorized to transfer the first million francs to the new Armaments Commission, to be followed by five hundred thousand francs every ten days thereafter to be allocated to the army and navy respectively until the preparations were completed. A separate decree ordered the naval minister to arm the warships at Toulon and victual them for a three-month voyage.[6] A spate of other orders and decrees by the Directory of that same date instructed army commanders in the Ligurian and Cisalpine Republics "to seize all ships" required by the Armaments Commission for the embarkation of troops at Genoa, while General Masséna was ordered to proceed to Civitavecchia to help prepare for the embarkation of troops and artillery there, and General Vaubois was ordered to do the same in Ajaccio.[7]

Although the actual destination was classified top secret and was revealed to only a handful of Bonaparte's most senior officers, the actual plan was set in motion in maddening haste, as government couriers set out from the War Ministry, the Naval Ministry, and the Luxembourg Palace—

for the Channel, Lyons, the Midi, Italy, Switzerland, and a dozen major French garrisons elsewhere. This was the beginning of an intensive flurry of activity, attended by an incessant flow of decrees and orders issued for the preparation of the invasion fleet, for its accompanying convoy of transport vessels, and of course for the gathering of the expeditionary army itself.

Two days later, on March 7, Rear Adm. François Paul Brueys d'Aigailliers was named commander-in-chief of the combined invasion fleet and convoy, accompanied by instructions for supplying the manpower, munitions, and artillery for this burgeoning force.[8] The following day Berthier was relieved of his command in Italy, with orders to proceed to Paris to take up his new posting as chief of staff of the "Armée d'Angleterre," as it was still officially called (to conceal its real purpose).[9] A week later Gen. Louis Desaix was sent to take over at Civitavecchia.[10]

In mid-March, War Minister Schérer notified the army commissaires of the eastern and southeastern departments of the country that large-scale troop movements were going to be taking place in their jurisdictions.[11] He also issued a series of orders to army commanders all over France and French-occupied territories, transferring units to Lyons, where General Bon was reorganizing and equipping most of them prior to sending them down the Rhône to the Mediterranean in hundreds of barges and other shallow craft.[12]

So thoroughly enforced—at least at certain levels—was the Directory's insistence on secrecy that one general who had never served with Bonaparte, Jean-Baptiste Kléber, and still ignorant of the expedition's ultimate destination, asked to be attached to the general staff of the "Armée de l'Angleterre."[13] Even more surprising, the acting naval minister himself was not apprised of the expedition's real objective until March 15![14]

Two weeks later, on March 30, General Bonaparte informed Chief Army Ordonnateur Sucy—who held a position equivalent in rank, pay, and importance to that of a quartermaster general—that the expeditionary force would be comprised of five army divisions requiring two months' food and munitions (for their use on reaching their destination), each division to stage at one of five principal embarkation ports: Marseilles, Toulon, Genoa, Ajaccio, and Civitavecchia. Gen. E. A. C. de Dommartin was to take command of the army's artillery, while its medical corps was to be headed by Dr. René Nicolas Desgenettes, seconded by Chief Army Surgeon Dominique Larrey, commanding eighteen medical doctors and surgeons as well as some three hundred nurses and pharmacists.[15] And although Bonaparte informed the "Armaments Commission for the Mediterranean Coast" on March 21 that "everything must be ready to sail" on April 9, so far none of the ports had a sufficient number of transport vessels ready, not to mention the escorting vessels, most of which were either being constructed or repaired, or were with Rear Admiral Brueys, returning from Corfu.[16]

This new expedition (and its controversial leader) had enemies, resulting in a potentially disastrous news leak to the semiofficial *Moniteur*. An item in that paper on April 1 announced that an expedition "of both a scientific and military nature" was forming, "having for its destination Egypt. By thus getting closer to the Indies [British India], its purpose will be to attack the English there."[17] Meanwhile, of course, most of Bonaparte's commanders and even most of the government's high officials had remained in complete ignorance. In a subsequent attempt at damage control, and further to confuse the British, on April 4 the *Moniteur* carried an official government announcement that "General Bonaparte will be leaving for Brest within the next ten days to take command of the Army of England."[18]

As for the naval arm of the enterprise, clearly the fleet and convoy would never sail on April 9 as ordered. Brueys's fleet, which had already been at sea off and on for well over a year, had left Corfu weeks earlier but had not yet arrived.[19] What is more, most of the warships would be in a poor state of repair after so many months at sea, while requiring largely new crews as a result of massive desertions. For all that, his tattered fleet of six French ships of the line and five commandeered Venetian battleships, attended by nine frigates (six of them French), were a welcome sight as they finally dropped anchor at Toulon on April 2.[20]

The welcome received by Admiral Brueys, his officers, and crews was short-lived, however. Scarcely had he stepped ashore after his long absence from home than a dismayed Brueys was informed, on behalf of the Armaments Commission and Napoleon Bonaparte, that all the warships under his command were "to set sail again without delay," with a respite only to revictual and take on troops for a new, undisclosed destination.[21] Rubbing salt into the wound, the commission also informed Brueys that the naval treasury was empty and could not pay his men and officers their nine months' back salaries![22]

Regardless of decisions made by men sitting at desks back in Paris, refitting and repairing an entire fleet required time, the admiral insisted. There was the further disagreeable task of unleashing press-gangs all along the coast to bring the ships' complements up to minimal strength. This of course meant that when they did eventually sail it would be with largely untrained crews, and even then with the strict proviso "with as few foreigners as possible," if the perennial problems of mass desertions and rampant misbehavior were to be checked.[23] To this was added the unusual decision

Brueys now took to dismiss a large number of incompetent or insubordinate officers, including five ships' captains.[24] What is more, he refused to put to sea again with less than six months' provisions rather than the three designated. The actual task of pressing thousands of new sailors would be an onerous one at best. Once accomplished, discipline had to be maintained, he argued, and present regulations against and punishments for insubordination by officers and seamen—a debilitating problem throughout the entire fleet—were far too lax. The juries created during the Revolution to hear more serious cases at courts-martial should be eliminated and greater authority assigned to the captain, "including the right to apply the death penalty for cowardice in combat." As for sailors who deserted in the face of the enemy, they "must be shot on the spot," and desertion while still in port, "which has paralyzed our naval forces," dealt with severely. "We now have to fight a powerful, well-trained enemy, with three times the number of vessels we have." He concluded in very tough language to his naval chief in Paris: "The campaign we are about to undertake will be decisive for us. Either we will see the annhilation of our own navy, or else we will become the preponderant naval force in the whole of Europe. In the final analysis, then, the outcome of the entire expedition depends on our own success at sea over our rivals."[25] It was blunt talk but badly needed, laced with a few home truths that had to be taken seriously by the politicians in Paris if the French navy was to be rebuilt from the ruins wrought by the French Revolution.

In addition to the chaotic rush to launch this armada, there were some very odd ingredients. Commander-in-Chief Bonaparte, for instance, had announced his immediate need for French, Greek, and Arabic printing presses, and the seconding to the expedition of numerous celebrated *savants* and scholars, including astronomers, geometricians, naturalists, a geologist, a chemist, archaeologists, various Orientalist-interpreters, a bevy of engineers on loan from the department of roads and bridges, even a balloon specialist, and a brilliant, talented artist who would one day reorganize the entire Louvre while laying the basis for new Egyptological studies—Vivant Denon.[26]

Thousands of troops soon converged on the Marseilles-Toulon area, most of them arriving by boat via the Rhône. And while the army paymaster was seeing to the disbursement of the first several million francs from Paris, the financially strapped Bonaparte was instructing General Schauenburg, then commanding the Armée d'Helvétie,* to seize three million

*The French army occupying Switzerland.

francs from the Swiss treasury in Bern and ship this sum under guard to Lyons.[27] Indeed, on top of the usual lack of the most elementary army supplies—shoes, muskets (of the twelve thousand additional ones just received, ten thousand were broken), artillery, gunpowder, not to mention transport vessels—the one commodity ever in short supply, crippling and delaying army and naval preparations alike, was ready cash (despite the earlier facile assurances of both Bonaparte and Talleyrand). The naval ordonnateur of Marseilles alone requested a staggering 5,837,377 francs for his port.[28] Meanwhile Gaspard Monge, who had just arrived at Civitavecchia to spur the embarkation preparations, found to his utter consternation that work was at a virtual standstill. He asked Bonaparte for 2,500,000 francs immediately.[29] In Corsica it was the same story, local suppliers refusing to cooperate until they were paid for past services.[30] Nor was the position of the French fleet any better: They were still owed 1,800,000 francs for the past nine months, leading Brueys to plead with Napoleon for funds. Nevertheless Brueys remained 100 percent behind Bonaparte, indeed almost pathetically so, praising him to the skies while assuring him of his unswerving personal devotion as well as of his "purest intentions . . . for a successful expedition . . . and my attachment to our republican government."[31]

Despite the authorized expenditure of millions of francs, the purchase of vast quantities of arms and muntions, an extraordinarily complex array of army transfers of thousands of troops to the Mediterranean ports, and the rushed repairs and construction of ships, not to mention the seizure of more than two hundred vessels for the proposed expedition, it was only on April 12, 1798, that the Executive Directory finally issued the two long-awaited critical decrees concerning all this activity. At the Luxembourg Palace, the Directory announced the creation of a military force to be called the "Army of the Orient," naming "Citizen Bonaparte, at present Commander in Chief of the Army of England," as its chief.[32] An accompanying decree confirmed that Bonaparte was to "direct the armed land and sea forces under his command against Egypt and seize that country." At the same time he was ordered "to chase the English from all their possessions in the East, or wherever he finds them . . . destroying their commercial houses in the Red Sea." He was to "cut off [and secure] the Isthmus of Suez and take all necessary measures required to assure the unimpeded and exclusive use of the Red Sea for the benefit of the French Republic," while maintaining "good relations with the Grand Seigneur [Ottoman sultan] and his immediate subjects, insofar as it is in his ability to do so."

In an introductory apologia for this unprovoked invasion and seizure of Ottoman territory, the Directory complained that the Mameluke beys "who have seized the government of Egypt"—making it appear as if this had just been done, instead of almost three hundred years earlier—"formed the closest ties with the English," becoming totally dependent on them. In consequence the Mamelukes had "carried out the most blatant hostilities and the most horribly cruel acts against the French people, whom they now daily harass, pillage, and murder," thereby leaving the French Republic with no recourse but to exercise "its duty of pursuing the enemies of the Republic in every quarter." The decree concluded that as England had gained complete control of the Cape of Good Hope, the French Republic had no alternative but to open . . . another route to reach "the Indies."[33] A third decree instructed Bonaparte also to "seize" Malta, because of "hostile acts" carried out against France by the Order of Malta and because of the declaration by its grand master five years earlier "insolently" refusing to recognize the newly formed first French Republic, resulting in "the paralysis of French navigation in the Mediterranean."[34] With these three decrees officially—if secretly—"promulgated," from the viewpoint of the French government, henceforth the entire operation was now perfectly legal, permitting them to proceed with a clear conscience.

In the midst of all this mayhem, the very next day Commander-in-Chief Bonaparte—as if not preoccupied enough with the innumerable problems encumbering the launching of this expedition—again reminded the world of his brilliance and the wide sweep of his outlook, as he presented the Directory with a "Note on the War with England."[35] In this lengthy analysis he informed the Directory that although the invasion plan for England had been postponed, it must not be discarded. In fact, he considered it an important element of the overall geopolitical strategy—one phase of a worldwide military operation, of which the invasion of Egypt was another—to bring haughty England to the negotiating table to conclude a lasting peace with France.

In this astonishing piece of Napoleona the commander in chief of the Army of the Orient presented one of the most illogical, indeed, preposterous pipe dreams of his career, calling for combined military operations to include twin landings in November 1798, one of forty thousand troops in England, launched from Boulogne in four hundred gunboats, and another of ten thousand men from Texel, in occupied Holland, destined for Scottish shores, while separate armies were conquering Egypt and India. He supported this proposal with an astonishingly lavish shipbuilding proposal for the French navy to counter the British fleet, including the expenditure of "forty to fifty million francs."[36]

As mad as the scheme appeared, so totally unrealistic in its expectations, given the very limited means available to France and its much smaller navy, nevertheless its triple objective of striking hard at England by simultaneous attacks on British India, Egypt, and British home shores was breathtaking. Bonaparte contended that only such a global operation could defeat England. But Bonaparte's ignorance of British naval strategy and the inferior quality of French naval training, officers, and crews was considerable too. This was one of his principal weaknesses throughout his military career: He would make plans for a sweeping campaign against a powerful enemy based on his own wishes, without attempting to understand or take into account the opposing military forces, dispositions, or strategy—or his own failings.

It is hard to say how Bonaparte had the temerity to present this fantastic scheme, at the risk of being considered an utterly irresponsible young man—he was, after all, only twenty-eight—or simply a madman. Given the temper of Europe, with an unsettled new peace treaty with Austria just signed, and England still fomenting unrest on the Continent in an attempt to form a new anti-French coalition, France could hardly afford to strip its own frontiers and shores of army and naval forces. Indeed, Bonaparte was having enough difficulty scraping together the thirty-eight thousand or so troops he needed for his immediate Egyptian expedition—as late as April 15 it was still nine thousand men short, excluding the navy's separate recruitment problems.[37]

Then there was the question of finding enough powerful ships of the line to escort the slow-sailing and vulnerable convoy of transport vessels for the invasion of England (Bonaparte apparently having forgotten to include such an escort for them), with his fifty ships at Brest held down by the British fleet off Ushant. Nor did Napoleon take into consideration the matter of the hundreds of transport vessels needed in the Channel and North Sea, Brueys encountering sufficient problems finding the three hundred or so envisaged for the Egyptian convoy. And where were the naval and transport vessels for the proposed landing in India to come from? The discrepancies continued to pile up, as in the case of Talleyrand's original proposal, which involved only five ships of the line as a naval escort for the Egyptian convoy, whereas Brueys estimated that he could not sail with fewer than thirteen battleships, exclusive of frigates and small naval escort vessels. Indeed, so short was Brueys of even unarmed transports that he was ordering additional vessels to be hastily built at Toulon and in Italy, while purchasing, borrowing, or simply confiscating foreign-owned neutral ships in Genoa, Marseilles, Civitavecchia, and Ajaccio.

The most elementary items required for an army, including muskets and shoes, were never found in sufficient quantities for the projected force for Egypt (Napoleon's official proposal had been only twenty-eight-thousand men). Even something so simple as an adequate flour supply was proving difficult, and then in Corsica they suddenly discovered that—because of unexpected drought, immobilizing the waterless mills—sufficient wheat could not be milled for the smaller convoy forming there. Even the lack of wood—for ships' ovens and later for the army in a barren Egypt—was to prove a trial.

In the final analysis, however, one fundamental weak link—on which ultimate success or failure depended—was, as Brueys rightly acknowledged, the French navy, in particular its lack of trained manpower. Desertions, poor pay and conditions, the risk of death, and unqualified and undisciplined landsmen and officers all took their toll. With officers little more reliable than their deserting crews, naval morale was the scandal of the armed forces, causing the newly promoted Vice Admiral Brueys no end of heartache—and he needed no fewer than 3,600 officers just for the fifty-six warships comprising his armada.[38] If he could not find adequate crews and officers for his thirteen ships of the line, how were they to be provided with the additional sixty-two proposed by Bonaparte for his fantastic simultaneous invasion plan for India, Egypt, and Great Britain? Amassing even the ten to fifteen million francs (the ultimate figure was never revealed) for only the Egyptian expedition was a nightmare. But for Napoleon's comprehensive project, it was a matter of fifty million francs—at a time when the French treasury was already on the verge of bankruptcy again, despite the vast booty channeled to France from occupied Holland, Belgium, Switzerland, and Italy. And, with the new peace treaty in place, there would be no more trains of booty and war contributions: Peace would prove the ruination of the treasury. Finally Napoleon had failed to take one more factor into consideration for his plan—time.

Back in March, when he had first submitted the Egyptian proposal, it was after declaring the impossibility of invading England "for several years" because it would take that long to find the ships and men to build a new navy. But a month later he was talking about launching a much larger army by November 1798—that very year. Ships had to be built and armaments ordered. It took weeks just to send out the orders for the timber, hemp, canvas, and other products needed for the construction of new vessels, which could then take up to two years to build. Additional cannon would have to be manufactured as well. In the best of circumstances, given unlimited funding, Bonaparte's great new plan would take at least two and a half years to implement, but he was proposing to launch this pipe dream in seven months.

Napoleon was never able to adapt his dreams to reality. Unfortunately Gaspard Monge was not available to study his latest proposal, nor was the practical Berthier. Nonetheless, what this great fantasy project did prove to the Directory was that General Bonaparte had a frighteningly brilliant brain, capable of coping with a vast, complicated—indeed global—strategy. If his plans were not feasible, they nevertheless were the product of a most extraordinary man, from whom much and anything might be expected— and perhaps feared—in the future. It was worth the price, and a relief to know, that he would soon be far away, at the other end of the Mediterranean.

To the spring of 1798, already so fraught with obstacles, decisions, and tension for Napoleon, was now added an element that first amazed and then stunned him. In March, Louise Compoint, a maid recently fired by Josephine under disagreeable circumstances, met with him to accuse his wife of carrying on an affair with a handsome young officer by the name of Louis-Hippolyle Quentin Charles, the very same Lieutenant Charles who had arrived in Milan with Josephine during the Italian campaign. What is more, the maid insisted, they were involved in illegal investments and speculations.[39] Napoleon, who knew only too well how vindictive and dishonest servants could be, questioned Josephine's archenemy in the Bonaparte clan (all of whom had in fact rejected her), his brother Joseph. After making several enquiries, Joseph met with Napoleon on March 19 to give his report, confirming everything . . . and more.

Josephine had met Charles in April 1796 and had been carrying on a passionate affair with him ever since. Throughout 1796 and 1797, during the Italian campaign, Napoleon's presence and that of his staff presented the lovers with some obstacles, but they managed to conclude in grand style with an orgy in Venice following the signing of the Treaty of Campo Formio, just prior to their return to France. Then, while Napoleon was en route to Rastadt, Josephine and Charles had again traveled together in her carriage (at Napoleon's expense), taking several weeks to cross the Alps, Charles leaving before the carriage crossed the frontier. On his wife's arrival in Paris on January 2, 1798—weeks late—Napoleon had been furious but totally unaware of the lieutenant sharing her favors and affections. Moreover Joseph, himself deeply involved in all sorts of business dealings and investments, including shady ones, informed his brother that Josephine and Charles were involved with Barras and others as investors in the Bodin

Company, which specialized first in war contracts—many of them fraudulent, and all enormously lucrative—with the Army of Italy, and later in the purchase and sale of hundreds of national properties, particularly in northern occupied lands, including estates, abbeys, and convents.

Napoleon summoned Josephine, and he and Joseph jointly presented the facts to her. She broke down in tears, calling it all lies. "Yes, my Hippolyte," she immediately wrote her lover afterward, informing him of the confrontation, "I hate them all. You, alone, have my love and tender thoughts. They must see how I loathe them . . . see the regrets and despair I feel in not being able to see you as often as I wish. . . . Oh! What have I done to those monsters to deserve this?" She even suggested divorcing Bonaparte, which Charles quickly discouraged.[40] Although they read her the riot act, Napoleon and Joseph lacked any written evidence or correspondence, and informed her that if she ever saw Charles alone again in his apartment (also the headquarters of the Bodin Company) or was involved in the Bodin Company's speculations, she would suffer the consequences.

Josephine defied everyone, not only continuing her not-so-secret rendezvous with the elegant Hippolyte Charles (who now resigned from the army in order to dedicate himself full-time to his prosperous business career) but also increasing her interests in the Bodin Company. Meanwhile Napoleon, apparently partially assuaged and taken in by Josephine's denials, instructed her to be more circumspect and a week later even bought her the house in the Rue de la Victoire. Involved night and day now with his various political and military plans, he had neither the time nor the emotion to spare for Josephine's transgressions. But as he was to learn later that summer, when he was far from French shores, Josephine's extramarital activities were even worse than he had imagined.[41]

Meanwhile the expedition was beginning to take shape, thanks to the energetic work of the hard-pressed Armaments Commission[42] directing all operations, aided by Treasury Comptroller Poussielgue. Although Bonaparte's initial sailing date of April 9 had come and gone, at least his senior team was more or less complete, including most of the army commanders—Kléber at Toulon, Reynier at Marseille, Desaix at Civitavecchia, Vaubois at Ajaccio, and Menard at Genoa, with Dommartin heading the Army's artillery, Dumas the cavalry, and Caffarelli the engineers.[43]

On April 17 Bonaparte ordered Brueys to prepare for a revised sailing date of April 27.[44] Yet it was not until the twenty-second that Napoleon officially confirmed the appointment of the admiral's senior fleet officers.[45] In reality it was sloppy, slapdash planning that only a miracle worker—a

Napoleon Bonaparte—could have thrown together at the last minute and then succeeded in pulling off, though leaving a nightmare of jangled nerves for lesser human beings in the lower echelons of command.

By April 22 the countdown for launching his fabled Egyptian expedition had just a few days to go. Bonaparte, who had done everything he could at this point—and barring the unforeseen—this time expected everything to go according to schedule. Accordingly he notified Brueys from Paris: "I am leaving [for Toulon] tomorrow night. Upon my arrival I hope to find the fleet all organized."[46] It was a brusque, impatient missive; he would tolerate no further excuses. Ready or not the fleet would sail in five days' time. But as so often during Bonaparte's life, the unexpected could—and now did—occur.

News brought from Vienna on April 23 by an exhausted French dispatch rider stopped Napoleon in his tracks and stunned the French capital. It transpired that on April 13 the recently defeated Austrians had hauled down the French national flag from over the entrance of the French Embassy and torn it to shreds—the very flag that Ambassador Bernadotte had hoisted at the request of the Directory to protest an Austrian military review celebrating the raising of the army to defend the capital against General Bonaparte's army in Styria in 1796. Since then, of course, the Austrians had been thoroughly defeated and the Peace of Campo Formio signed and ratified. It was a foolish act carried out by the emotional, patriotic Viennese, but it left Bernadotte no choice but to close the embassy in protest and leave the Habsburg capital.

The reaction in Paris was sharp and bitter. The Directory immediately ordered the transfer of army units from the Channel—already depleted by earlier transfers to the Egyptian expedition—to reinforce the French Armée de Mayence and the Armée d'Helvétie. Fear and rumors of war circulated in both the Council of Ancients and in the Bourbon Palace, where outspoken Jacobins were ready to take on the world to avenge the outrageous Austrian insult, while in the large stone courtyard of the Luxembourg Palace, special couriers came and went. In the Rue de la Victoire, General Bonaparte ordered his secretary, Bourrienne, to postpone his departure, as he contacted Foreign Minister Talleyrand, who always seemed to know more than anyone else, the Directory included. The general himself was in turn summoned urgently to the Luxembourg for consultations with the Directory, then ordered to remain ready, at its disposal.

By the following day, a special imperial Austrian diplomatic courier arrived from Vienna with a formal apology from the Austrian foreign secretary. As for the Directory, there was only relief to be seen on the faces of all, for the last thing they wanted—despite the outward fervent patriotic indignation filling the air and Jacobin hearts—was a fresh war, at least at this time. Accordingly that same day the Directory again summoned General Bonaparte, informing him that he—"Commanding General of the Army of England"—was to prepare to leave "immediately for [the Congress of] Rastadt where he is to confer with [the Austrian] minister . . . in order to put an end to all the difficulties existing between the House of Austria and the French Republic," including such matters as French intervention in Rome (where the French had arrested the pope and set up a Roman Republic), Naples, Tuscany, and Switzerland. Bonaparte was then "invested with the full powers to negotiate, conclude, and sign such agreement [as] he reaches."[47]

For Napoleon Bonaparte, it was an extraordinary, most unexpected piece of good fortune, coming out of the blue as it did, and he was quick to accept the challenge, anticipating the great prestige that would accrue to him in the event of his successfully negotiating a new, all-encompassing international accord. If there was one soldier in the whole of France the Austrians dreaded above all others, it was the tough little Corsican who had just stolen their precious holdings all across northern Italy, and the Directory—with the nudging of Talleyrand and Barras—was determined to make the most of that fear. Suddenly, one of the other balls Bonaparte had been juggling, the Egyptian expedition, was forgotten, replaced with prospects of a diplomatic coup at Rastadt. Nevertheless, Bonaparte did not discard his Egyptian expedition, instead explaining to Kléber in Toulon that he was delayed for several days. In the meantime he was handing over temporary overall command to Kléber, who was to carry on as usual and be ready to proceed as soon as he was notified.[48] After dispatching a shorter note to Brueys, he concentrated on his new objective.[49]

With Talleyrand's full support at the Foreign Ministry, and as the old protégé of Barras, who had launched his military career and was still the key man in the Directory, Napoleon was naturally buoyed up, bursting with fresh enthusiasm and plans, as he rushed back and forth between the Foreign Ministry and the Luxembourg, while writing to the senior Austrian diplomat of his arrival shortly at Rastadt where, thanks to Vienna's full apology, he anticipated a peaceful solution to their problems.[50] All the while, however, War Minister Schérer's orders to transfer thousands of troops to Mainz and northern Switzerland went into effect, reducing the Channel forces to a mere 47,500 men, while giving the Army of Mainz just over 50,000 men, and the Army of Helvetia 20,000.[51] Altogether France now had an effective standing army of 208,000 ready for European service (excluding the 29,000 men thus far transferred to the Egyptian expedition, and the 86,500 troops of the Army of the Interior, dispersed and garrisoned permanently throughout France). The country was prepared for anything, and the Austrian emperor had to take heed.[32]

Unfortunately for Bonaparte, however, he had no one to counsel caution. Gaspard Monge was not present or yet the full confidant he would become before the year was out, and apparently Foreign Minister Talleyrand could not restrain the swaggering claims of the Corsican general. The result was that in a private meeting with Barras, whom for the first time he now addressed as an equal, he confidentially boasted that he would probably abandon the Egyptian expedition. Alas, he did not confine his thoughts about his private aims and aspirations to Barras and Talleyrand.

Early in May he revealed all to the Directory, haranguing them in a blatantly cocky, offensive manner as to how they—he—could take full advantage of Austria's weakness at the bargaining table to wring sweeping new territorial concessions from their other European holdings. What is more, there should be an appropriate reward for him in the form of membership in the Directory itself. (A stunned Barras had earlier pointed out that at twenty-eight, Bonaparte was not eligible for that position, forty being the minimum age.) The directors were naturally shocked by Bonaparte's unilateral disregard of their official instructions to him, and by his ill-disguised thirst for personal glory, not to mention his irreverent manner. They wanted peace, and no part of Napoleon Bonaparte.

Barras, as a member of the Directory and hence witness to the whole incident, related, "Bonaparte was then quite mortified to see such a splendid opportunity escape them"—that is, at Rastadt, where a strong France could impose its will on a helpless victim—and "not having been able to achieve what he wanted by ruses and devious approach, to make himself—through the Directory—dictator of the affairs of all Europe, he no longer made any attempt to conceal his scorn of them." Foiled in this attempt, Napoleon acted like "the master dictating his wishes . . . [and finally] in the heat of the ensuing discussion went so far as to threaten us with his resignation from the Army altogether." Director Rewbell, who loathed the bumptious general, immediately thrust out a pen and paper—"Citizen General, sign here!" Having clearly overstepped himself this time, a humiliated Bonaparte withdrew "in the complete silence imposed by this stinging rebuff."[33] Following his departure, the five-man Directory reconvened, rescinding Bonaparte's diplomatic appointment and credentials and canceling his triumphant journey to Rastadt, and then ordered Barras personally to notify the general of these decisions.

Upon reaching the Rue de la Victoire that evening, an astonished Barras found the servants carrying out trunks to a waiting coach, and inside, Bonaparte still intent on leaving for Rastadt! Their meeting lasted barely a quarter of an hour, according to Bourrienne, as the two men ensconced themselves in Bonaparte's small study and Barras demanded the return of Bonaparte's now invalid diplomatic passport. "Barras left first, crossing the salon, scarcely exchanging a word with Madame Bonaparte. The general reappeared after him, seeing Barras to the door. Then, without saying a word to anyone, returned to his study, slamming the door behind him."[54]

Bonaparte dictated a quick note for Brueys, ordering him to embark the troops on May 9, while telling his old friend Gen. Maximilien Caffarelli that the Egyptian expedition was to proceed and he was leaving the next night for Toulon.[55]

This bitterly humiliating defeat, before the five most powerful men in France, was one that Bonaparte would neither forget nor forgive. He was determined to make them pay dearly. "They don't want any part of me," he confided to Bourrienne, just as he had done during his schooldays at Brienne. "They must be overthrown . . . but the time is not yet ripe . . . I've taken certain soundings . . . I would be standing all alone. Very well then, we will go to Egypt after all, that is where all the great opportunities for glory lie. . . . I am going to dazzle that lot yet."[56]

Divisional General Bonaparte set out from Paris with Josephine and Bourrienne in his heavily encumbered carriage on the night of May 3, heading for Lyons and the highway skirting the Rhône. Preoccupied with his immediate problems, he failed to notice a minor article in the *Moniteur* regarding the escape from prison of a troublesome POW, a young English naval captain by the name of Sir William Sidney Smith, aided by a former Ecole Militaire classmate of Napoleon, Louis de Phélippeaux, both of whom he was to encounter one day at the distant port of Acre.

Bonaparte spent the five days en route to Toulon silently brooding. But when he stepped down from the carriage at 6:00 A.M. on May 9, he was a different man. The decision had been made at last and now hardened to its reality. He was determined to succeed, ready to dazzle that lot!

The Armada

I shall now lead you into a country where by your future deeds you will surpass even your past achievements that have already so astonished the world.
—To the Army of the Orient, Toulon, May 1798

f General Bonaparte was exhausted after traveling for nearly six days and many hundreds of miles in a jolting carriage, he did not show it, and rather than resting or accompanying Josephine and Bourrienne to the imposing stone residence overlooking the large, bustling port of Toulon that had been reserved for him and his staff, he immediately ordered an unscheduled review of three half brigades just as they were about to embark. With the vigor reflecting his renewed determination, he would drive himself as relentlessly as he did his staff, and he took military reviews, like every other aspect of his life, seriously, as he now personally inspected men, muskets, bayonets, kits, artillery pieces, limbers,* and caissons.

He found harbors bursting with naval and merchant shipping and activity all along the French Mediterranean coast, with troops assigned to every port between Marseilles and Villefranche, including Hyères, St.-Tropez, and

---

*Limbers were two-wheeled gun carriages pulled by six to twelve horses, depending on the guns' caliber; caissons carried munitions.

Antibes.[1] Such enormous activity, in a region that was usually relatively calm, could not be concealed from the alert British and their royalist spies, and it was therefore essential to get the expedition under way as quickly as possible. The divisions at Ajaccio, Genoa, Civitavecchia, and Marseilles were attempting to get ready to sail and join the main force, and a frustrated Bonaparte had found it necessary yet again to postpone the sailing date from Toulon, rescheduled now for May 13–14.

Not even Bonaparte's unbounded energy and determination could dispel the stack of negative—and sometimes devastating—messages and reports awaiting him at Toulon, reports even from the ruthlessly efficient Ordonnateur Najac, who informed him that he still lacked the 1,800,000 francs in back pay for the naval crews, without which they refused to sail. Where was he to get this sum? What is more, the navy alone was already short 2,049 men (excluding crews for the convoy). But if push came to shove, the enterprising Najac argued, they could always force the passengers and troops to help crew the mighty warships![2] To make matters worse, the logistics for the expedition had been so badly handled that there was not enough food for the troops and seamen—chiefly because of the usual lack of funds—resulting in army officers breaking into the sealed provisions, intended for use in Egypt, already stored aboard the transports. There was not even fodder for the expedition's horses, Najac instead having to send seven hundred head over to Genoa, where others could worry about them.[3]

The report from General Reynier at Marseilles was no more encouraging. He declared that thirteen of the vessels assigned to transport his men and goods were plagued with a variety of problems, which in the long run meant delaying the sailing time. These vessels lacked not only sufficient crews but everything from mess kits to brooms, and at least ten days' pay to permit each soldier to buy the small personal items, such as tobacco, he would need for a long sea journey and many months of campaigning. Troops were missing basic parts of their uniforms, and some officers lacked mattresses. As for the hundreds of kegs of water just stored aboard, "they are already beginning to go bad."[4] What is more, Reynier's artillery officers and cart drivers had somehow "disappeared" from the port altogether.[5] It was a fiasco. To this was added Naval Ordonnateur Le Roy's report at Marseilles that an additional nine vessels there (including the convoy's two hospital ships) were in no condition to sail, all for the usual reason, "money being the thermometer of all activity," as he put it.[6] Meanwhile, an important senior officer upon whom Bonaparte had been counting, General Dugua, suddenly requested permission to be relieved of his command in Marseilles in order to return to Paris to serve a fresh term in the Council of

Five Hundred, as deputy for Calvados, which Napoleon refused out of hand.[7] Politics more important than the army?! Instead Dugua was ordered "to seize" five of the largest neutral ships he could find in port and get them over to Toulon.[8] It was not just transport vessels, crews, food, and supplies but thousands of troops who were now found to be "missing" as well. One of the first things General Bonaparte did on the very afternoon of his arrival at Toulon was personally to order all officers and soldiers of twelve different regiments and half brigades, who for whatever reason were absent from their units, to return to the port as quickly as possible.[9]

If the news was not exactly cheering, at least Napoleon—whose every word had to be heeded, with no Directory about to interfere—was in full charge here. He would succeed, and then he would deal with Paris. And yet in this dark hour, he did receive a most astonishing form of consolation from an unexpected quarter. The gruff General Kléber cryptically informed him that he "understood" Bonaparte's private political ambitions and appreciated the general's "vast genius," which Kléber's personal "devotion would do everything to second and see reach fruition."[10]

Meanwhile the French government attempted to put the British off the scent. To help explain the sudden disappearance of the much-talked-about "Minister Plenipotentiary Bonaparte" from Paris *and* Rastadt, as well as the obvious military preparations along the Mediterranean, they inserted in the *Moniteur* of May 8 the following item:

> It is said that General Bonaparte has left for Toulon, and that the fleet in that port, combined with the former squadron of the Venetian Navy, are to try to break the [British] blockade of Cadiz to free the Spanish fleet there, and then, together, proceed to Brest where, with that squadron, they will participate in the landings in England.[11]

By May 10 Najac, in charge of the embarkation at Toulon, had been able to board only twelve thousand troops and five hundred horses, whereas Reynier's entire division had already embarked, ready to sail from Marseilles.[12] Although the Armaments Commission in charge of the entire enterprise was attempting to create a semblance of organization, the inevitable constant tongue-lashing by a highly finicky Bonaparte at this stage caused more panic than order. Then a fresh last-minute setback occurred at Marseilles, when contrary gale-force winds not only delayed their already revised sailing date of May 10 but also caused considerable damage to ships in the otherwise protected harbor.[13] Somehow a much-harried Reynier nevertheless put to sea on the eleventh, reaching Toulon that same evening.[14] Bonaparte was one man who never accepted excuses.

The port of Toulon was still dark at five o'clock the next morning as a grim Napoleon was piped aboard the *Alceste* to receive General Reynier's personal report that the ships still under repair at Marseilles would be joining them shortly. Meanwhile Berthier ordered the last of the cavalry to be aboard four more ships by four o'clock the next morning.

But as usual the beleaguered Ordonnateur Najac brought the commander in chief more bad news. "Although it is my desire to fulfill your orders and needs as completely as it is in my power to do so," he began, nevertheless "my good will alone cannot suffice to provide the immense resources constantly necessitated by the presence of some 30,000 men." It boiled down to money problems, of course. He needed an additional 530,000 francs for various port expenses, 1,200,000 francs for the remainder of the unpaid naval salaries, and 1,451,450 francs for victualing, naval armament, and repairs—a grand total of 3,181,450 francs—*by midnight,* if they were to sail on schedule.[15] Bonaparte was staggered.

When he was not worrying about money, he was trying to cope with the manpower problem, aggravated by the daily desertion of hundreds of ratings (enlisted sailors) and merchant seamen.[16] And the situation with the army was even worse, as Berthier reported to Bonaparte now: Almost every half brigade was down to just fifteen hundred men, each having suffered desertions numbering from five to six hundred[17] even before reaching that port. This meant a loss of 25 percent of his army even before setting sail.

Just to keep the stunned Bonaparte in a perfectly foul mood, Brueys informed him that because of stormy seas and strong winds out of the south, the sailing date of May 13–14 would have to be postponed once again, probably for another five or six days.[18] This cacophony of problems hardly boded well.

On the other hand, it did give the love-smitten Bonaparte a few extra days in port with Josephine, and Bourrienne—who as usual worked seven days a week, from dawn to at least 11:00 P.M.—the opportunity at last to ask Napoleon how long he expected to be in Egypt. The reply was hardly reassuring for his secretary, who would be separated from his young wife and family. "A few months, or six years. It all depends on developments there. First I intend to colonize that country." And even if it took that long, "I am twenty-eight [*sic*] now and in six years would be only thirty-five. That is hardly old, and those six years—if all goes well—should give me the opportunity to reach India as well."[19]

Despite the astonishing panoply of mishaps, preparations for the Egyptian expedition were completed and most of the money somehow found.

The departure now depended only on the weather—until a series of disturbing naval intelligence reports reached GHQ at Toulon. An English squadron of twenty-seven warships had been sighted at Mahón, on Minorca, whereas all previous intelligence had indicated no major British presence in the Mediterranean for several months. Another source stated that Admiral Lord St. Vincent continued to remain off Cadiz with his entire fleet. A third report mentioned the sighting of fourteen vessels and frigates, along with a cutter, between the Tunisian and Sardinian Coasts. And when on the seventeenth Brueys sent out a ship to reconnoiter his proposed course to Malta, it was pursued by three British ships of the line and three frigates.[20] It was puzzling. What was Bonaparte to make of these conflicting figures and sightings? Additional sightings, notoriously inaccurate and often completely unfounded, were now coming in from Italy, yet the French had to be prepared. But for what? Where? Although still another report now informed Brueys of Rear Adm. Sir Horatio Nelson's return to the Mediterranean on May 9, nevertheless he had only three ships of the line and four escort frigates with him. Brueys did not know, of course, that the Admiralty was dispatching a sizable number of the largest British warships with which to reinforce this new squadron.[21] Whatever the precise number of enemy ships, the one thing the commander in chief did know for certain was that the sooner they got away the better, which the veering of the contrary easterly winds on May 17 finally made possible. Bonaparte authorized Brueys to set sail.[22]

At 5:00 P.M. on May 18 Brueys ordered the firing of six cannon, the final signal to all personnel on shore to return to their ships immediately. Bonaparte informed General Desaix at Civitavecchia that he hoped to put to sea the following morning.[23] Monge, who on Bonaparte's special instructions was helping Desaix, replied, "Here I am, transformed into an argonaut! This is another one of those miracles produced by our new Jason . . . who is going to carry the torch of enlightenment to a country which, for such a long time has remained in darkness, and where he is going to spread [republican] philosophical thought while carrying our national glory even farther afield."[24] As usual the exuberant Monge, despite his fifty-three years, was bubbling over with excitement and optimism—the perfect tonic for a grim Bonaparte, especially as it came from the one man in France the commander in chief admired perhaps above all others.

After a week of storms, with a beautiful day dawning on May 19, at 6:00 A.M. Brueys hoisted the signal from his flagship, the 118-gun *Orient*, for the fleet to weigh anchor and put to sea.[25] At General Bonaparte's personal orders, he also instructed the captains of all vessels to have the "March on England," a revolutionary hymn, "sung every evening."[26]

Then Bonaparte addressed the fleet: "Well, let me tell you, you have not yet done enough for the fatherland, nor the fatherland for you," he repeated from the Italian campaign. He was, he told his troops, about to lead them into a country where, by the services they were to render their country, they would surpass all past exploits. For this he promised each soldier on his return to France five acres of land (a promise he did not keep). "You are going to run fresh risks and share them with your brothers, the sailors. . . . Become the terror of your enemies on land and sea. Imitate the Roman soldiers of yore who fought Carthage on the plains and the Carthaginians on the sea." As he stepped back from the edge of the quarterdeck and the troops assembled below him on board the *Orient,* voices roared: "Vive la République immortelle! Vive Bonaparte!"[27] and broke into traditional revolutionary songs.

Despite the confusion and incredible obstacles the French had to hurdle in the slapdash mobilization effort, the armada was launched from all five ports, the ships of the line forming into three separate squadrons, a total of fifty-six naval vessels of all classes, manned by more than thirteen thousand officers and men.[28]

"Maintain strict discipline" throughout the fleet, Bonaparte had enjoined Brueys long before setting foot aboard the flagship, and "have a good bed prepared for me, as if you were expecting an invalid."[29] The commander in chief, who had once applied for a naval commission as a gunner, in fact disliked the sea and sailing and was inevitably seasick most of the time he was aboard any vessel, whatever the size and however calm the waters.

Both Bonaparte and Brueys were only too aware of the necessity of enforcing strict discipline, especially with every vessel practically bursting at the gunwales with supplies and humanity. The queen of the French navy, the splendid triple-deck *Orient* was perhaps worse off than the others in this respect, because it also carried many of the commanders of the expedition as well as the fleet commander, Vice Admiral Brueys. The inordinate number of officers aboard this ship proved a real test of endurance and ingenuity. Their number included Bonaparte's bevy of aides-de-camp and most of his senior staff with their own staff officers. Naturally Brueys had his own separate naval staff, headed by Rear Adm. Honoré Ganteaume, while the *Orient* remained under the immediate command of Flag Capt. Louis Casabianca (who had brought his nine-year-old son along in preparation for his early entry as a midshipman in four years' time). To these were added the high civilian and medical officials.[30] Altogether, a ship that ordinarily carried a complement of perhaps just over one thousand men maximum was now hosting nearly twice that number, every nook and cranny crammed with humanity and matériel—including Bonaparte's personal store of 4,800 bottles of wine—overflowing from the spacious holds to the main deck itself.

In all, the expedition was to comprise thirty-one generals. Sixteen of them had served prior to 1789 and were trained in the traditional Royal Army, but eleven had been NCOs only, with no formal officer's training, while five generals had been in the army fewer than nine years.[31]

In addition to the thousands of officers and men, the expedition included the variety of specialists required to keep the army self-sufficient in a hostile land, including blacksmiths, harness makers, carters (for the great variety of vehicles), and hundreds of horse handlers, bakers, cooks, tailors, and gunsmiths.

Dispersed among the 365 naval and transport vessels—exclusive of tons upon tons of food, wine, eaux-de-vie, water, clothing, and small arms—were 171 pieces of artillery, carriages, wagons, 757 other vehicles, scaling ladders, shovels, more than ten thousand picks and axes, not to mention forty-five thousand tons of gunpowder and twelve thousand tons of lead. In addition, some 1,330 horses were aboard makeshift stable ships.[32]

As part of a theoretically semiacademic mission, polymath Monge, chemist Claude-Louis Berthollet, and their colleagues had ordered dozens of crates of astronomical, chemical, physical, survey, surgical, and pharmaceutical instruments, accompanied by a reference library of several hundred tomes on science, philosophy, history, and geography, not to mention an array of what proved to be antiquated and all-but-useless maps of Egypt.[33]

The armada was spearheaded by thirteen battleships, sailing in three separate, parallel divisions or formations, preceding a convoy of 309 vessels. Spread out over several square miles of sea, and proceeding awkwardly at half the battleships' usual speed, it fell to the dynamic and resourceful thirty-seven-year-old Rear Adm. Denis Decrès and his three frigates to circle this ungainly herd of sail, snapping at their heels like well-trained sheepdogs, while keeping an eye out for an approaching enemy. These transport vessels flew many flags—French, Spanish, Ligurian, Tuscan, Ragusan, Maltese, Turkish, Venetian, Danish, and Swedish—the 309 captains and crew themselves representative of the colorful if captive diversity. Altogether, including seamen, troops, and civilians, the armada was ferrying more than 54,000 men, all theoretically self-sufficient in food and drink, not to mention hay and oats for the horses. Of the total number of men aboard, 36,826 were members of the expeditionary force.[34]

*   *   *

Brueys had charted the safest and most direct course for this unwieldy herd, and with the Toulon and Marseilles convoys having already combined, they sailed easterly now parallel to the French Mediterranean coast, past Nice and the spacious anchorage of Villefranche, and then Monaco, to the entrance of the Gulf of Genoa, where on May 21 they were joined by seventy-two vessels of Gen. Baraguey d'Hilliers's division out of Genoa.[35]

With that important maneuver completed, Brueys swung sharply south-southeast and headed to the Cape of Corsica, leaving behind the only world and security those troops—still ignorant of their ultimate destination—knew. Clearing the northern tip of Corsica and continuing almost due south along the east coast of the island, they were joined on May 27 by the fourth and smallest convoy of the expedition, comprising just twenty-two vessels, with supplies and Vaubois's Corsican division.

A by-now-very-tense Vice Admiral Brueys, with his first truly great command, the like of which would probably not be seen again by anyone in the Mediterranean for decades to come, and his career at stake, would soon be able to breathe a little more easily. There remained only one more rendezvous to complete the already sprawling armada: Desaix's overdue convoy out of Civitavecchia the following day.[36] With those additional fifty-six sail spotted by a lookout vessel, Bonaparte finally could inform the Directory: "Here we are, all united for the first time, sailing now toward our destination."[37]

Life on the flagship, with some two thousand men crammed aboard "a floating city," as Bourrienne called it—though one "without women"—was intensive, with constant comings and goings from Brueys's cabin and the commander in chief's much more spacious one with its large stern windows overlooking an azure sea. Naturally it was Bonaparte's cabin that became the center of their naval universe, where he appeared about ten each morning instead of his usual crack-of-dawn schedule on terra firma. Bonaparte was attended by Bourrienne from the moment he rose, and his quarters were inevitably filled with aides-de-camp, senior army officers, and some select members of the team of savants. Apart from occasional brief promenades on the quarterdeck with Admiral Brueys and Captain Casabianca—usually to discuss specifically naval questions—the general rarely left his quarters. Rare wines in endless number flowed, complimenting the delicacies that both Brueys and Bonaparte had provided on the generous scale one expected at sea, but all served as background for the long, frequently intensive conversations on all sorts of philosophical or scientific questions, lasting well into the early morning and rarely interrupted by music, which Bonaparte disliked.

*   *   *

Monge was in constant attendance, at Bonaparte's insistence and to Monge's delight. To this warm, outgoing, excitable scientist-mathematician, the doting father of two daughters, young Bonaparte became the adopted son he had never had.

On the face of it, no individual could have appeared a more unlikely candidate for Napoleon Bonaparte's combination general counselor, chief moral support, and confidant than Monge, the eldest son of a working-class family of Swiss origin, born in Beaune, just south of Dijon, in 1746.[38] All three Monge sons were well educated by the standards of their class. Gaspard was trained in the sciences and mathematics at the small Oratorian school at Beaune, then went on to the more important Oratorian College at Lyons, followed by the Collège de la Trinité in Lyons in 1764. Returning briefly to Beaune, he soon got a teaching position at the prestigious army engineering school, the Ecole de Génie de Mézières.

He worked his way up the ranks as soon as his unusual mathematical abilities were recognized. It was here that he encountered a talented pupil, Lazare Carnot, with whom he would be involved later during the French Revolution.[39] Over the next several years he taught mathematics, physics, and chemistry, writing famous treatises on various subjects. It was while teaching there that he married Marie-Catherine Huart Horbon, a thirty-one-year-old widow.[40] Thanks to a small fortune brought to him by his wife, the hitherto impecunious Monge was able to rise socially and politically; he also had more time for his own experiments.

Turning more to physics, Monge came into contact or corresponded with some of the more prominent scientists and philosophers of his day, and was made a member of the Académie Royale des Sciences.[41] Then he was named external examiner for naval officers and ultimately became a member of the prestigious Institut de France.

With the onset of the Revolution in 1789, Monge became a founder of the Jacobins, espousing extremist republican ideas, including the total destruction of the aristocracy and the execution of the king.[42]

In August 1792 he was duly rewarded with the Ministry of the Marine and, briefly, the premiership. As naval minister he had to face renewed warfare with England and the great mutinies ravaging the French navy, while on land French armies were gaining victories and conquering Belgium and Savoy.[43] Monge was responsible for sending out two unsuccessful expeditions—one to Sardinia, and another to help reconquer the island of Santo Domingo from the Haitian slave uprising led by Toussaint-Louverture.[44] By April 1793 Monge had made many political enemies, however, including

Georges-Jacques Danton, who forced him to resign that same month.[45]

Thereafter for the most part Monge focused on scientific matters, although he did serve on various government committees dealing with technical questions—preparations for large-scale manufacture of steel, muskets, and gunpowder, and on the famous committee charged with introducing the metric system.[46]

Thanks to Monge and his colleagues, Paris alone was soon producing up to 140,000 muskets a year, French bronze cannon factories increased from two to fifteen, and the number of steel mills rose from four to thirty.[47] Ever the zealous patriot, when Monge discovered workers and labor leaders hindering the manufacturing of armaments needed for hard-pressed French armies, he denounced them to the authorities.[48]

But with the fall of Robespierre in July 1794, Monge, who had been working under the direct orders of the Committee of Public Safety, was himself denounced and forced to go into hiding for several months until a writ for his arrest was withdrawn.

If Monge was renowned as a scientist, his name was later more closely associated with the work he did as one of the founders of the elite Ecole Polytechnique (created November 3, 1794).[49]

In May 1796 he was named to the newly created Commission on Arts and Science and ordered "to visit that part of Italy conquered by the victorious armies of the Republic, to gather all the artistic and scientific 'monuments' that you believe worthy of a place in our museums and libraries."[50] In other words he was given carte blanche to loot in any manner he saw fit.

It was during this seventeen-month mission that Monge met the victorious commander in chief of the Army of Italy, General Bonaparte, for the second time. (The first time had been back in August 1792 when a newly promoted Captain Bonaparte, temporarily finding his career blocked, had sought an interview with Naval Minister Monge, requesting a place as an artillery officer with the French avy. Although favorably impressed by the young man, nothing had come of it by the time Monge resigned in April 1793.)[51] Meeting in Milan on June 7, 1796, Monge and Bonaparte took an immediate liking to each other and quickly became fast friends. Monge, who was with the victorious General Bonaparte when he signed an armistice with the pope on June 23 of that same year, received an open invitation to Montebello, and became a frequent visitor there. When his government mission in Venice was completed in August 1797 he stopped at Passeriano to take his leave of Bonaparte. The general would not hear of his abandoning him prior to the signing of the peace treaty with the Austrians, eventually persuading him to postpone his departure for several weeks.

It was during those leisurely weeks at Passeriano that Napoleon privately aired his various possible projects for the future. One in particular appealed to him: an expedition to Egypt. The general returned to it, giving it much more weight and consideration, and Monge promised to gather further documentation himself.[52]

Their friendship now bound securely, the two men became virtually inseparable until the signing of the Treaty of Campo Formio, and on October 18 Napoleon entrusted him and Berthier with the original copy of that treaty to deliver personally to the Directory. Back in Paris as a senior influential member of the Institut de France, Monge—still enthralled by this extraordinary new relationship with Bonaparte—arranged for General Bonaparte's election to that distinguished body of savants that December.[53]

From Malta onward, where Monge transferred to the *Orient,* he spent more time with the commander in chief than anyone else aboard ship with the exception of Bourrienne. "Monge was invariably at his table," Bourrienne recalled. "This scholar, who had such a lively spirit, shared many of the same views as the commanding general, and with his stimulating mind roused Bonaparte's own lively imagination all the more."[54] But what Bourrienne—or indeed anyone else for that matter—did not yet quite grasp was the extent to which Monge had influenced Bonaparte's decisions, in particular at this stage regarding the Egyptian enterprise, although of course he had seen the numerous charts, statistics, learned articles, and maps on Egypt that Monge had earlier passed on to him.

Thus was cemented the unlikely friendship of the professional soldier and the civilian scientist that had developed during the peace negotiations a year earlier. Monge was to remain Napoleon's friend and confidant in all the years to follow—a man Bonaparte always trusted and relied on and who offered that unusual combination he sought—personal disinterestedness, integrity, and a sense of adventure in challenging the unknown. Monge was a rare hybrid of the practical mathematician (who based everything on balanced equations and mathematical proofs) and the dreamer. His lively imagination permitted fancy and theory to lead him to fresh, uncharted horizons, and like Napoleon, with a total disregard of the individuals around him. Curiously, it was Bourrienne who quite unconsciously put his finger on a real clue to one aspect of their relationship, when he remarked during the sea journey to Egypt on Bonaparte's "preference for those who cleverly defended an absurd proposition, as opposed to those who simply applied reason and sheer logic to do so."[55]

Naturally only such an individual could possibly have come up with, and justified, a major military expedition to the far end of the Mediterranean—to a country about which, in the final analysis, Bonaparte knew almost nothing.

Life aboard ship involved long hours drawing up orders and plans for the army, Malta, and Egypt, but there also was much free time for conversation. If there was one thing Bonaparte could not abide, it was boredom and inactivity. As Bourrienne related, "French foreign policy and politics were frequent subjects of discussion, but he especially liked to talk about the acclaim his latest campaign was receiving"—that is, when he was not incapacitated by seasickness.[56]

Among those nightly at table when these discussions took place, in addition to Monge, were Berthollet, Brueys, Ganteaume, Caffarelli, and other senior officers, and Bonaparte never seemed to rest, his brain teeming with new questions and proposals. He continually coaxed information out of his shipmates with practical, mundane questions, whether on politics or army campaigns. Then, sated, he would turn to religious ideas, or "whether the planets were inhabited," or the age of the world, or the probability or inevitability of the destruction of the planet Earth by water or fire. He was also fascinated by the interpretation of dreams.[57]

But with all divisions of the convoy at sea and events apparently dead on course, General Bonaparte now had some serious realities and anxieties to face alone, regarding the fate of his massive flotilla and the success or failure it could bring to his magical scheme of things. In particular the haunting possibility of a full-scale naval attack by the English was never far from Napoleon's mind, nor perhaps had he forgotten Admiral Brueys's prognostication back in April about the French naval fleet's fate in the event of such a confrontation, when he had declared that the campaign they were about to undertake "would prove decisive" for them.

To be sure, neither Brueys nor Bonaparte yet knew that Admiral Nelson's embryonic new fleet, which had swept through the Gut of Gibraltar on May 9 to oppose the French presence at Toulon, in fact involved only a few ships.[58] Although Nelson had been dispatched to the Mediterranean for the purpose of destroying the French fleet, the English rear admiral learned only while off the coast of Cartagena on May 28 that the French had already put to sea for an unknown destination, leaving the two navies already more than eight hundred miles apart.[59]

On June 2 Admiral Brueys's worst fears seemed realized, when the French sighted a distant "English vessel" that they believed to be the vanguard of the entire English Mediterranean fleet. Brueys quickly ordered four seventy-four-gun vessels and three frigates to reconnoiter the sea lanes before them.[60]

Fearful lest any part of the convoy fall prey to the seemingly ubiquitous English, Brueys urged Rear Admiral Blanquet to reach Malta as quickly as possible, and he signaled the three divisions of warships to form a single line of battle. At the same time Brueys ordered Rear Admiral Decrès to leave the convoy with his three frigates and proceed to Malta to blockade the port of Valletta, in preparation for his arrival.[61]

Bonaparte's other immediate preoccupation as the armada left the waters of Sicily behind was the seizure of Malta itself. It had to be accomplished within a few days of arrival, otherwise he risked tying up his entire force in a long siege—thereby permitting the Maltese to call on the British fleet for help—which in turn would postpone, perhaps permanently, the expedition toward its primary objective, the Ottoman province of Egypt.

The Order of the Knights Hospitalers of Saint John of Jerusalem, or, in more popular parlance, the Knights of Malta, had been recognized as a religious order of Crusaders by Pope Paschal II in 1113. When they lost Jerusalem to the Mameluke sultan Saladin in 1187, they found a new home on the strategically situated island of Rhodes, that is, until the arrival of the Ottoman Turks in the Middle East, when their powerful sultan, Suleiman the Magnificent, captured that island in 1522. By 1530, however, Habsburg Emperor Karl IV had found a new refuge for the knights, on the island of Malta, where they built an immense bastion of sprawling stone walls, protected by hundreds of cannon. When in 1565 Suleiman had attacked the knights there as well, he soon discovered the error of his ways. Although the Turks surrounded the fortress at Valletta and the entire island with hundreds of vessels and many tens of thousands of troops, after a continuous 233-day attack they had been forced to lift this fruitless siege, leaving behind some thirty thousand dead Turkish troops.

More recently Czar Paul I, hoping to play an active role in the Mediterranean for the first time, took the knights under Russia's protection, sponsoring a German general, Baron Hompesch, as their new grand master in July 1797.

In December 1797 Napoleon in turn had sent a couple of his own emissaries (with a coffer of gold) to Malta, well in advance of any authorization by the Directory of an expedition. The envoy, Treasury Comptroller Emile Poussielgue, and the Maltese spy accompanying him, gathered military intelligence on the layout of the fort and the number of troops, artillery, munitions, supplies, including information on the financial position of the knights. In addition a successful Poussielgue managed to win over—no doubt through substantial bribes—two Frenchmen, the treasurer of the order and the commissioner for fortification. Leaving Malta on March 3, Poussielgue had brought a most complete and favorable report to Bonaparte in Paris.

Despite the several miles of impressive battlements, whose detailed plans he had obtained, the very walls that had defied Suleiman's massive siege cannon for eight months were now, two centuries later, manned by a mere ten thousand Maltese militia (called up in emergencies only), mostly untrained civilians long unaccustomed to any military activity. In reality it turned out there was only a permanent fifteen-hundred-man native garrison to man both the walls and the nine hundred or so ancient cannon (most of which had not been fired in living memory), while the whole of this garrison was officered by 332 knights—fifty of them elderly—leaving only 272 on the active list, of whom 200 were in fact French. Given this background and the hefty bribes accepted, now in June 1798 Napoleon naturally expected little difficulty in the capture of the island fortress.[62]

On June 8, Admiral Brueys's armada finally caught sight of Malta, where they found Desaix's flotilla from Civitavecchia awaiting them, along with Decrès's frigate escort. The next day the combined force, now totaling 365 sail, dropped anchor off Valletta, after twenty-one days at sea.[63]

Needless to say, fear gripped the Maltese when they awoke on June 9 to find the Mediterranean before their ancient port covered as far as the eye could see with French ships, "a floating forest" of masts and sail. But senior French naval officers were, for their part, just as anxious, as their telescopes focused on the seemingly impregnable coast that Admiral Blanquet described as "bristling with fortifications ... defending both the port and the city from all sides."[64]

Bonaparte, with orders to seize the island but wishing to avoid the appearance of "the conqueror," signaled the port officer at Valletta, requesting permission to enter with the entire fleet to obtain fresh water. By ten o'clock that same morning he had his reply that only four ships would be allowed in at a time. That was fine. "A real pretext, no matter what, was needed" in order to attack them. General Desaix was immediately ordered aboard the *Orient* to consult with the commander in chief. "The dispositions have been taken to attack the island by military force," General Belliard recorded, and "the little man"—as he scathingly referred to Bonaparte—explained the role each was to play.[65] Desaix's division was to occupy the southeastern end of the island, General Vaubois's Corsican troops to land to the north, near the city of Valletta, Gen. Baraguey d'Hillier's Genoese division to land at the extreme southern end of the island, while Reynier's Marseilles division was to secure the smaller island of Gozo, just to the northwest.[66]

But first Bonaparte—ever with an eye to public opinion, and history—had one final legality to dispose of. On June 10 he duly ordered the French consul at Malta to deliver an official note of protest to the grand master of the Order of Knights, that the fleet had the right to enter a neutral port for water and that "Commander in Chief Bonaparte is most indignant" as a result of the negative reply he had just received. What is more, he was familiar with "the marked preference accorded English vessels, and with the proclamation made by the predecessor of Your Eminence [back in 1793, in which he had declined to recognize the new French Republic]." Bonaparte was therefore "resolved to take by force what ought to have been accorded by right . . . and I foresee the impossibility on your part of being able to prevent it."[67]

In fact the arrival of the fleet had not come as a surprise to the grand master, who had been informed of the situation in mid-May by a special dispatch from an Austrian diplomat at Rastadt. "I am writing to warn you, Monseigneur," the message began, "that the considerable expedition being prepared at Toulon is intended against Malta and Egypt. . . . You will surely be attacked, [but] if you surrender without defending yourselves, you will be dishonored in the eyes of all Europe," and therefore receive no outside support.[68]

To be sure, the French faced, among others, three principal forts controlling the entrance to the Valletta harbor, but with thousands of yards of battlements to defend and only the reduced actual force of 1,772 with which to man both them and the more than nine hundred cannon, mortars, and howitzers on the ramparts, Bonaparte was not seriously worried. He gave the signal for the attack to commence.[69]

Once again he was proved correct. Less than twenty-four hours after the opening of hostilities a Maltese spokesman appeared, at 9:00 A.M. on June 11 "requesting a suspension of arms." Quickly accepted by the French, by ten o'clock that evening a delegation of six Maltese plenipotentiaries arrived aboard the Orient, and after a minimal few hours of face-saving haggling, at three o'clock in the morning they duly signed the surrender, ceding Malta to the French Republic. The cost of the invasion to the French included three killed and half a dozen wounded, the Maltese losing "several men" as well as seven hundred prisoners.[70]

In the "convention" signed on board the Orient, the "Knights of the Order of St. John of Jerusalem . . . renounced all rights of sovereignty and property to the islands of Malta, Gozo, and Comino in favor of the French Republic."[71] In return France promised to "use its influence" at the

Congress of Rastadt to obtain for the grand master "an appropriate princi-pality" somewhere in the German states (which was never done) and a three-hundred-thousand-franc pension,[72] while the other knights were promised annual pensions of seven hundred francs apiece, though the two hundred French knights were also permitted to return to France. The promises were made, but the pensions were never delivered.

Barely waiting for the document of capitulation to be signed, Napoleon Bonaparte immediately released his triumphant Order of the Day to the French Army on June 13: "The Army is hereby notified that the enemy has surrendered! The standard of liberty floats over the forts of Malta."[73] The twenty-eight-year-old general, who the year before had returned to France with the Treaty of Campo Formio and the capitulation of the Habsburg emperor, had carried out his second phenomenal coup within eight months. He had every reason to be pleased with himself: All was going just as planned.

The swift and more or less bloodless occupation of the land now began, involving a thorough French reorganization of the country's administra-tion, including the judicial and religious institutions (priests were thereafter to be paid by the state, not the church). And simultaneously with the bestowal of French freedom began the inevitable looting, including confis-cation of all the public and private property belonging to the Knights of Malta and their order, not to mention numerous churches.

With the ink barely dry on the new treaty, on June 13 Bonaparte named "Citizen Berthollet" acting comptroller of the army, ordering him "to seize the gold, silver, and precious stones"—the vast celebrated treasure of the Knights of Malta accumulated since the twelfth century—located in the vaults of the Church of Saint John.[74] Before dusk had fallen, the first cartloads of strongboxes were on their way to the harbor of Valletta and the hold of the *Orient*. The French Republic had struck another blow for democracy.

Ultimately, and officially, Bonaparte notified the Directory that the loot taken from that church totaled 1,019,051 francs in gold and silver, with another 127,144 francs' worth of the same taken from the grand master's palace, while lesser amounts were taken from the Church of Saint Anthony, among others. Bonaparte claimed he was leaving nearly a million francs' worth of treasure behind "to cover garrison costs."[75] In fact, however, the sums seized in gold, silver, precious gems, statuary, and art objects—taken from private estates as well as from public buildings—totaled some seven million francs, five million of it in gold and another million in silver plate. This was suppressed in the official accounts rendered to Paris; Bonaparte and his generals had simply helped themselves.[76] As for the exact amount Napoleon got, Bourrienne remained loyally silent, merely noting that the

Maltese treasure was taken abroad the *Orient* and stored next to the three million francs seized earlier from the Swiss treasury in Bern.[77]

Under normal circumstances the conquest of Malta might have been enough to have returned General Bonaparte to Paris covered in glory once more. With Egypt as his main objective, however, he treated Malta as so incidental in the larger scheme of things that he longed to get away, rushing almost nonstop through the decrees, orders, decisions, and appointments he was drawing up over the next few days. As if to emphasize this, he remained aboard the *Orient* at night, going ashore only as required by immediate affairs. Included in the business of the day was the general's orders to the Knights of Malta to prepare a new treaty with Russia, which—like the Knights themselves—would now also lose any and all claim to the island. "The Russian Emperor," Napoleon informed the Directory on June 17, "ought to thank us now, since our occupation of Malta is saving his treasury 400,000 rubles [a year] in subsidies."[78]

General Bonaparte was rushing at this mad pace largely through fear of being caught there or else at sea en route to Egypt by Nelson's Mediterranean fleet. The French expeditionary force was told "to hold themselves ready to be able to sail at a moment's notice." And while they were being issued new, lighter cotton uniforms, the fleet and convoy were taking on fresh water, vegetables, food, and firewood, as well as more hay for the horses, while making room for some four hundred Maltese sheep.[79] By the evening of June 18, then, the Knights of Malta had left the island—except those few electing to join the French expedition, and some 350 Maltese as well.

After declaring the islands under effective French revolutionary rule, Bonaparte concluded by promising respect for private religious beliefs, including Islam, symbolizing this by the unheard-of gesture of freeing some two thousand North African and Turkish slaves chained to Maltese galleys.[80] Then, after appointing General Vaubois the new commander in Malta, at the head of a garrison of nearly four thousand French troops,[81] Napoleon finally found time to write to his brother Joseph, informing him of his latest coup and assuring him that, as usual, he was in excellent health. Napoleon also asked Joseph to send Josephine to join him in Egypt.[82] With the last courier now on his way to Paris, he instructed Brueys to prepare to put to sea early on the morrow. So far, so good.

The *Orient* now transformed into a veritable treasure ship worthy of the Spanish Main. Ten days after their arrival, on the morning of June 19, 1798, Admiral Brueys signaled the fleet to weigh anchor and chart a southeasterly course. If all went well, within two weeks' time they would be in sight of their secret destination at last.[83]

CHAPTER 7

Land of the Pharaohs

*You are about to undertake a conquest that will have an
incalculable effect upon world civilizations. . . . We will
succeed in all our enterprises, because Fate is on our side.*
— TO THE FRENCH ARMY, JUNE 22, 1798

 cannot . . . help feeling how . . . much depends upon its suc-
cess [that of Nelson's fleet], and how absolutely necessary it
is at this time to run some risk, in order, if possible, to bring
about a new system of affairs in Europe, which shall save us
all from being overrun by the exorbitant power of France,"
Earl Spencer, First Lord of the Admiralty, wrote to Vice
Admiral St. Vincent off Cádiz in April 1798.[1]

On entering the Mediterranean in the second week of May, Nelson's
three ships of the line and four frigates headed for the Gulf of Lyons. While
they were some seventy-five miles off the Hyères Islands, on the night of
May 20–21, the unexpected occurred: Nelson's embryonic squadron was
suddenly hit by a fierce gale, his own flagship, the seventy-four-gun *Vanguard*, on her beam and nearly capsizing as her foremast and main- and
mizzen topmasts were snapped, leaving her in near ruins.[2] By the time Nelson rendezvoused on June 7 with the reinforcements sent by St. Vincent, it
was of course too late. The French were long gone.

Despite his relative youth and the loss of an arm in the Canaries the year before, not to mention the vigorous protests of more senior admirals, the thirty-nine-year-old Nelson was considered by both the notoriously difficult Admiralty Board and the even more pernickety Admiral St. Vincent to be the right man—the only man—to tackle the French in the Mediterranean Sea.

It was on the junction on June 7 that Nelson received revised orders from Commander in Chief St. Vincent, instructing him specifically "to proceed in quest of the armament preparing by the enemy at Toulon and Genoa," though St. Vincent still had no idea of Bonaparte's objective (he suggested Naples, Sicily, Portugal, Spain, and Ireland as possible destinations).[3] Closer to the mark, the Right Hon. Henry Dundas, secretary of war, had other ideas on the matter, as he informed First Lord Spencer on June 2: "Did the instructions to Lord St. Vincent mention that Egypt might be the contemplation of Buonaparte's expedition? I may be whimsical, but I cannot help having a fancy of my own on that subject."[4]

Having learned only on May 28 of the escape of the French fleet from Toulon, and realizing that he had already missed a golden opportunity, Nelson now began a wide sea search for an opponent with a full ten-day head start, and with the additional disadvantage of having no hard evidence of either the French objective or even the direction in which they were sailing. Nevertheless St. Vincent's latest orders had given Nelson full scope to pursue the enemy "to any part of the Mediterranean, Adriatic, Morea Archipelago, or even into the Black Sea," and once finding them to "take, sink, burn or destroy" them, which is exactly what Nelson now had his heart set on doing.[5]

Thus began one of the most remarkable—and frequently frustrating—pursuits in naval history, as the British fleet headed "instinctively" to the southeast, stopping at Naples on June 17, then entering the Strait of Messina, where on June 22 Nelson was informed (incorrectly) that Bonaparte had taken, and already left, Malta. "If they pass Sicily," Nelson wrote Dundas, "I shall believe they are going on their scheme of possessing Alexandria,"[6] and hence he continued in that direction himself. Unknown to either Napoleon or Nelson, however, on June 23 the two fleets were in fact only seventy-eight miles apart![7] Ironically, so determined was Nelson to get Bonaparte that he now crowded all sail for Egypt, overtaking the unseen French on a parallel course, arriving in Alexandria on June 28. Finding no sign of the French warships or flotilla in the harbor, however, or even any news of them, within hours of his arrival the impatient rear admiral put to sea again, sailing on a northeasterly heading toward the coast of Anatolia, between the islands of Cyprus and Rhodes, before zigzagging on a more indecisive course to the southern coast of Crete and ultimately back to the Sicilian port of Syracuse. What again neither Bonaparte nor Nelson knew was that on June 29, even as the British were sailing from Alexandria, the French were approaching it. At one point the two opposing fleets, even closer than six days earlier, were only seventy-four miles apart, just a few hours' sailing time.[8]

Nelson was to learn of his astonishing near miss only three weeks later, when, cursing his own phenomenal bad luck and Napoleon's seemingly miraculous escape, he declared, "The devil's children have the devil's luck!" But, now determined to follow them even "to the Antipodes" if need be, after hastily revictualing at Syracuse, on July 24–25 he set out yet again for Alexandria.[9]

Late on the evening of June 27, slowed by weak winds and still some 180 miles northwest of the Egyptian coast, Vice Admiral Brueys ordered the frigate *Junon* to precede the armada to Alexandria to get a detailed report of the situation from the French consul there. Two days later, just hours after the British fleet had disappeared over the horizon, the *Junon* reached Alexandria to collect Consul Magallon (the nephew of Consul General Charles Magallon) and bring him back to an anxiously awaiting Bonaparte.

Vivant Denon, a passenger aboard the *Orient,* reported that the young consul informed the commander in chief "that a fleet of fourteen English warships" had left Alexandria before the arrival of the *Junon.* "This knowledge of the presence of the English darkened our horizon," Denon continued, "for they could now reappear at any moment." What is more, the favorable weather conditions had already begun to deteriorate, the wind becoming "very strong, swinging transports out of control, mixing the convoy with the fleet, rendering such a state of confusion that would have inevitably resulted in the greatest of disasters for us had the enemy then appeared." Although the dismay caused by this latest fiasco could be seen on everyone else's face, "I could not discern the slightest change in the general's expression," concluded the artist.[10] By now the French fleet was approaching Abukir Bay, "but it was this unexpected news of the English that decided him suddenly on the landing here at Marabut Beach," General Kléber related, "for the General's original plan had been to enter the delta by the two mouths of the Nile [at Rosetta and Damietta] simultaneously, while at the same time we were seizing Alexandria."[11]

As a result of the consul's report and Bonaparte's fresh instructions, at 6:45 A.M. on July 1 Admiral Brueys ordered the crews of his fleet to be piped to their action stations, while Rear Admiral Blanquet apprised the other ships of the new landing instructions.[12] At 8:00 A.M., with the armada still several miles north of Abukir, Brueys ordered the warships to leave the convoy and to form a separate battle line closer to shore. With that maneuver executed, they dropped anchor and prepared to land the troops. At 11:00 came the long-awaited order from the flagship to lower away the gunboats, sloops, and other boats serving as landing craft from the larger vessels. Napoleon's spur-of-the-moment revised debarkation orders had envisaged Kléber's division securing the far right of Marabut Beach, General Reynier's to the left of them, then Desaix's in the middle, with Menou's to its left, and—anchoring the extreme left flank—General Bon's division. That orderly plan was soon washed away by a raging storm.

As thousands of soldiers scrambled over the sides of dozens of ships, the real mayhem was just beginning. The high winds combined with nearly universal military incompetence to produce utter confusion throughout the vast armada. Fortunately the British were not in sight. In order to negotiate the shallows of the reef-strewn bay, Napoleon himself, bent on landing as quickly as possible, was unexpectedly forced to shift, when still four and half miles out, from one of the larger landing vessels to a smaller surfboat, delaying his arrival by at least another hour. The conditions that Admiral Blanquet had earlier described as "fair, fresh, the weather and sea beautiful," had by now been transformed into a "very rough night."[13] Even Berthier, who rarely referred to the sea if he could possibly avoid doing so, complained about "the violent wind that was churning up the sea, rendering it very difficult for the navigation of our boats, creating the greatest obstacles to the execution of our landing instructions."[14] In fact the gale-force winds were now heaving one boat on top of another, smashing some, overturning others, and hurling men and debris alike into the foaming surf, sometimes while they were still hundreds of yards from shore. Admiral Brueys, who was held responsible for this operation, had frantically attempted to dissuade Bonaparte from carrying out amphibious landings in raging seas, over uncharted reefs, destined for dark unknown beaches, beneath storm-laden skies—only to be overruled.[15] The chaos and disorder were complete. "The landing was rough," General Belliard conceded, as hundreds of craft bobbed out of control in the furious surf before being hurled ashore amid dozens of bodies of the dead and injured. Nevertheless, from the initial wave of boats about 2,500 men landed safely and assembled along the black expanse of Marabut Beach. But despite Bonaparte's orders, it proved utterly impossible to winch artillery and horses over the sides of the larger ships and transports into the landing craft below.

However, Bonaparte was not to be deterred from his objective, the seizure of Alexandria. At 2.30 A.M. three ragged columns now totaling perhaps 5,000 men formed in the howling wind. Bonaparte, with Generals Dumas (commander of the still-nonexistent cavalry), Dommartin (commanding the equally nonexistent artillery), and Caffarelli (the peg-legged commander of the army's engineers) at his side, moved out on foot to Fort Abukir and then west along the tempest-tossed shoreline. Despite the inability to land either food or water, they proceeded and a few hours later had come within one and a half miles of Alexandria, when hostile bedouin cavalry appeared out of the night, darting in and around the confused troops. This was the beginning of harassing tactics that would continue until the day the French left the country three years later.

Reaching the towering stone walls of the port, Napoleon moved the three partially formed "divisions" into position. Gen. Jacques F. Menou, who had advanced along the far right flank hugging the beach, had brought his men up between the triangular fort and the seawalls. Kléber's more powerful division drew up in the center, between the triangular fort and Pompey's Gate, facing the long southern walls of the city. Separated from them by several hundred yards, General Bon's division secured the left flank, attacking the Rosetta Gate at the extreme eastern end of the walls.[16] Although there were some brisk exchanges of small-arms fire—the defenders of walls having little powder for their artillery and even less desire to fight—the French (without artillery of their own) advanced, the commanding generals leading their troops into battle. By 11:00 A.M. the French had scaled walls and broken down city gates to take possession of this once-great seat of learning—but at a price. According to Berthier's report—his figures were always dictated by Napoleon and thus suspect—twenty-one French were killed and sixty wounded during the brief siege, with another twenty soldiers drowning during the night landings. Total casualty figures, including drowned, in fact amounted to a few hundred; among the wounded were General Menou, who was hurled down a wall and struck by large rocks, and General Kléber, who survived though shot in the head.[17] Shortly before noon a delegation from the besieged city emerged from Pompey's Gate, approached Bonaparte's headquarters, and surrendered then and there.

"I have come to restore your rights and to punish the usurpers," Bonaparte assured the people of Alexandria on July 2. "I respect God, his prophet, Muhammad, and the Koran far more than the Mamelukes do."[18] Determined to relieve the anxiety of the Egyptians and to assure them of his friendship, and hence to avoid the appearance of the traditional marauding conqueror, he announced severe restrictions on his troops' actions and harsh penalties for infractions thereof, including the firing squad for "any member of the army found to be guilty of pillaging or rape." On the other hand, all Mamelukes were to be arrested and their property and wealth confiscated. The Egyptians for their part were ordered to lay down their arms "within twenty-four hours" and to send official delegations from every community offering their formal submission to the French, in exchange for a promise of friendship and protection. Any village refusing to comply and caught "bearing arms against the French army, [was] to be burned." The one property the immobilized French did universally seize wherever they went, however, was transport in any form—horses, donkeys, oxen, and camels. With that one exception, the Egyptian people (as opposed to the ruling Mameluke class) were theoretically inviolable, at least so far as Napoleon was concerned. This included their religion, religious leaders, and institutions, all to be respected by the French. "Every Egyptian must thank God for the destruction of the Mameluke and cry out: 'Glory to the Sultan! Glory to the French army, his friend! Curses upon the Mamelukes, and happiness to the people of Egypt!'" Napoleon proclaimed.[19]

It was a new kind of warfare for the French, forbidden to lay hands on the conquered enemy, although in fact Napoleon was frequently to find it impossible to enforce his oft-repeated strictures and penalties against French violators, whose actions later kept undermining his policy. One of the problems was that among the guilty were to be found numerous senior army officers, sometimes flagrantly opposing their commander in chief, eroding his authority more and more. Nevertheless his policy was clear—to win the Egyptian people (not the Mamelukes) over and prepare the land for a reorganized government à la française and a peaceful conquest whenever possible, preparatory to establishing a French colony.

Some of the new regulations were hardly surprising—demanding that all inhabitants turn over their arms to the French, for example—but others were simply absurd, such as the demand that "every inhabitant [of Alexandria] wear the tricolor cocarde." Even more difficult, if not impossible, to execute was Napoleon's order requiring all French troops "to salute all high Muslim officials when bedecked in the French tricolor sash of office," this from an undisciplined army in which French soldiers frequently refused to salute even their own officers.[20] Regardless, the new orders were read before the troops. All Muslim institutions were to be respected; Bonaparte expressly forbade "every Frenchman, soldier or civilian alike, from entering a mosque or congregating before them . . . [and] those who contravene these orders will be shot." Nor would the troops be permitted to take the usual small liberties in the marketplace, Napoleon reminding them of the great importance he placed on "our soldiers paying for everything they take . . . and that the Turks [Egyptians] be neither robbed nor insulted. We must make friends of them, and restrict ourselves to making war only on the Mamelukes."²¹ Given these prescriptions, guarantees, and lofty sentiments, on July 4 the principal muftis and sheikhs of Alexandria signed a solemn declaration to support the new French regime.²² The conquest of Egypt could now begin in earnest.

With the city secured and the gates manned by French troops, what did the French themselves find as they stopped to look around them? "Awful sand, nothing alive to be seen in any direction, burning heat during the day, then cold at night," Col. Jean-Marie-René Savary succinctly summed it up. For the troops still camping along Marabut Beach after landing, it was grimmer still. "We lack simply everything. We have neither food [except the hard biscuit prebaked in France] nor the pots with which to cook it, even if we could find water."²³ In fact, whether seen from within or beyond the elongated walls of the port, the situation was hardly inspiring for the unprepared European suddenly dropped into a scene straight out of the *Arabian Nights.* The food problem likely could be solved within a matter of weeks, once French logistics were in place, but the land itself was quite another matter.

To begin with, Alexandria was built on one of the most peculiar sites ever conceived as a country's sole major port. Located on a long, slender spit of land—little more than a series of sand dunes—rarely more than a mile and a half wide and several miles long, the city itself faced the Mediterranean, with its back to the usually dried-up bed of Lake Mareotis and the briny waters of Lakes Abukir and Idku. They in turn cut the port off entirely from the mainland, apart from the narrow causeway separating Lakes Abukir and Mareotis, and the large canal linking Alexandria with Rahmaniya on the Nile—this panhandle the only direct land access from the port to the Nile and Cairo.

Nor did the immediate hinterland offer searching French eyes much relief: The lakes were surrounded by sand and, in the case of Lake Idku, by extensive marsh. But a couple of miles inland, along the canal from Alexandria (generally dried up for more than half the year), there were occasional patches of palm trees and small fields, large enough somehow to sustain more than a dozen villages and hamlets between Alexandria and Rahmaniya, including Birket and Damanhur. More than forty miles to the east, along the Egyptian coast from Alexandria, lay the mouth of the Rosetta branch of the Nile. To the west there was nothing but desert. Thus, Alexandria was so badly situated that if by some means a powerful foreign navy could reach and blockade it, and then land troops to either side of the port while securing the canal and causeway behind it, the chief link with the mainland—Egypt's only principal outlet on the Mediterranean—could be lost. (And this is precisely what the British were to do in 1801, when they took Alexandria from the French.)

Nor did the French find much to compensate for this dreary isolation when they entered the walls of this once-resplendent capital of Alexander the Great, the very memory of its fabled gardens and monumental library, the largest in the world, by now lost in the haze of dissipated centuries. Colonel Laugier's view, as he passed through Pompey's Gate, though clearly reflecting a total lack of imagination, was typical. "It is difficult to imagine an uglier city," he remarked. "There is not a single trace of its former splendor and the remains of the genius left by its founder. . . . Every door of every shabby dwelling bears the imprint of a despotism which knows how to destroy but never how to preserve. No repairs have been carried out on the inhabited houses, and the other half are mere ruins."[24]

General Bonaparte's original landing instructions had of course been altered unexpectedly because of the British naval threat. And the subsequent landings in Abukir Bay were hampered by the storm, rending temporarily impossible the landing of almost half the men and most of the horses, artillery, equipment, and food. Those units that did reach shore during the first twenty-four hours were in a state of utter confusion, one that in fact lasted for days and even weeks, leaving men to die of famine and thirst as a result of incompetent commissary operations and slack army organization.

At 5:00 A.M. on July 3, Bonaparte met with his artillery and engineering officers. They set out from French army headquarters in Alexandria for an inspection tour, though the last two divisions aboard the transports had not yet been landed. Going through the city, they checked on its water and food supplies, fortifications, and sites for barracks for the new French garrison.[25] Despite all the setbacks, Napoleon was determined to complete his work quickly, in order to push on to Cairo, for time was more than ever of the essence if he was to catch the Mameluke armies before they could rally sufficient force against him. The city first had to be organized, of course, which he was now doing with Berthier's able help, and yet one of his initial acts after feeding and housing his troops, set in motion by his sixth day in Egypt, was to arrange for the collection of taxes by Poussielgue and Magallon.[26] The former Muslim leaders were to be reinstated in their traditional posts, while the city came under martial law. Yet even as the troops continued to disembark and reassemble in their proper battalions and brigades, and garrisons were assigned to man Fort Abukir, the beachheads, and the city walls and to police the city, Napoleon's failure to put into effect previous reconnaissance, intelligence reports, and logistical planning was now felt with so cruel a vengeance as almost to destroy the expeditionary force from within, even before it confronted any major hostile military force.

The fact of the matter is that not just the landing but the entire campaign was a colossal foul-up from the very beginning, in consequence of Bonaparte's haste and oversights. It was a move at once as arrogant as it was irresponsible, and every member of his expedition was to suffer accordingly. In reality Napoleon knew little more than where the main cities of Egypt were located. For the most part, he did not know the location of the main food storage depots, wells, and cisterns along his proposed invasion route—and this during the hottest month of the year. And yet on the actual march inland, Napoleon brought almost no supplies of food or water, intending instead for the troops "to live off the land." Such a plan would have been difficult even in Europe. This, however, was not bountiful Europe, but a vast desert. The same criticism applies to transport; he brought just a few hundred horses with him, expecting somehow to find the horses, donkeys, oxen (and later camels) required for cavalry, artillery, and regular transport vehicles. Not only were large numbers of such transport animals not available in or near Alexandria, much to his chagrin, but he had no idea where to find them. As a result, even after reaching Cairo weeks later—and for months thereafter—his cavalry was still largely unmounted and useless; his wagons, carts, caissons, commissary, engineers, and baggage train all but immobilized.

The same lack of prior intelligence preparations led to a near debacle. Napoleon failed to establish where the principal granaries were maintained (actually they were at Rosetta and Damietta, but the weather had prevented landings there). Nor did it occur to him to determine the availability of grist mills to prepare the many tons of flour required, and then the existence of enough ovens, strategically located, in which to bake the bread. A simple item, bread, but one that almost undid all his plans.

Under normal circumstances, Berthier, as chief of staff, should have been held responsible for establishing this most elementary information months before the government had even authorized the invasion. Nor, as has been seen, had army and naval intelligence officers been dispatched to Egypt well in advance to ascertain the information required for all aspects of the logistics involved. Given the unique circumstances of this invasion, the entire responsibility for its failure then lay with Divisional General

Bonaparte alone. In fact the only "intelligence reports" he did possess were those provided by the merchant Charles Magallon and the treasurer, Poussielgue. He had not requested, dispatched, or received a single military intelligence report by a professional officer of any branch or service.

Thus it was that Bonaparte's isolated army found itself (as it would for months to come) without, among other basics, bread and even canteens for water. Hundreds of French troops died of thirst, hunger, malaria, sunstroke, and exhaustion.

Another major oversight on the commander in chief's part was the lack of any up-to-date maps. Napoleon did not know the main proposed routes for his army, and in what condition they would be found, in a country where roads for wheeled vehicles simply did not yet exist. He was especially ignorant of the extensive, complex canal system—with the exception of one or two major ones—that riddled the entire delta region and important areas of Upper Egypt as well, around al-Fayyum. Much to his surprise, in a country practically devoid of bridges, these canals proved to be an almost insurmountable barrier, whether dry or wet. His battalions and supply units had to cross and recross time and again wherever they went, and some of the larger canals were 120 feet wide. Transport wagons, artillery limbers, caissons, forges, baggage trains, and footslogging men in the ranks had to cope with these arduous, unfamiliar obstructions throughout their stay in Egypt.

Another result of relying on ancient maps was the failure to take into proper consideration the problem of sand dunes—and once encountering them, the best means of negotiating them—which played havoc with troops and transport from the moment they stepped ashore till they reached the very outskirts of Cairo.

Nor had resistance from local tribesmen and bedouins even occurred to Napoleon. He had believed his own propaganda that he was the friend of Islam and of the Egyptian *fellahs,* or peasants, and like them the enemy of the Turkish government under Mameluke rule. Expecting never to meet more than eight to ten thousand armed Mamelukes, and then in only one or two major battles, Napoleon instead encountered often-fierce armed resistance, even after areas had theoretically been secured. This included the canal route from Alexandria to Rahmaniya and later the river routes linking Cairo with Rosetta and Damietta, which were never made safe.

Any other military commander, under any other circumstances, within easy call of Paris, would not only have been removed immediately from his command but also court-martialed, if not shot, for such gross professional incompetence. But Napoleon was not at the beck and call of his superiors in

Paris (where the government remained largely ignorant of his acts) and as Admiral Nelson had already put it, "the devil's children have the devil's luck."

Meanwhile, despite his grievous head wound, General Kléber could still somehow command, at least for a few hours each day, before returning to his darkened room and bed. (His severe concussion and skull fracture would partially incapacitate him off and on for months to come.) With an acute shortage of seasoned senior officers, even badly wounded men had to remain on active duty. Nevertheless, appointed governor of Alexandria and of the surrounding province until he was fully recuperated, and left in charge with some 6,500 troops, Kléber coped surprisingly well.[27]

Napoleon had given his orders and was now ready to depart. Gen. Roger de Damas was to seize and fortify Abukir Bay and its small fort overlooking the French fleet and flotilla as they lay at anchor, while General Dugua was ordered to march to Rosetta, which Murat's cavalry were to seize in an advance attack. With that objective achieved, another convalescing divisional general, Menou, would then take over as governor of both the province and port of Rosetta, releasing Dugua to rejoin Napoleon and the main force. As for Admiral Brueys, he was to dispatch several dozen gunboats and smaller craft with troops, supplies, and munitions, first to Rosetta and then up the Nile to accompany Napoleon, although the admiral's battle fleet was to remain in Abukir Bay and "in such a manner as to be protected by the batteries that we establish there."[28]

Finally completing their landing on July 3–4 and reaching Alexandria, General Desaix's and Reynier's divisions were ordered by Bonaparte to serve as the advance units of the main body of the army on its march to Cairo. Preceding the rest of the army, they set out for Damanhur and Rahmaniya on the Nile, a position thirty-seven miles from Alexandria.[29] Although a few pieces of artillery and some ammunition were being landed at last, the rest would not be available for many weeks to come, Bonaparte enjoining Desaix before setting out not to use his light artillery: "You must conserve it for the big day when we come up against four or five thousand enemy cavalry."[30]

Gen. Louis Desaix, an unusually good-humored and self-confident if slapdash commander, and his troop, had set out as ordered, but the unrelenting summer sun, reaching well above one hundred degrees daily, and the great humidity along the swamps and canals, ringed by salt marsh, briny lakes, sand dunes, and occasional clumps of date palms, proved physically and mentally enervating, sapping his men from the very start. To this were

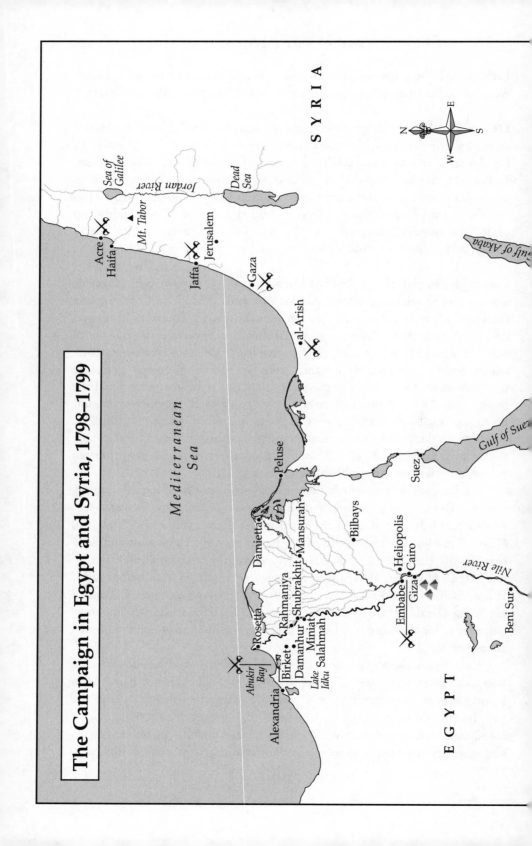

The Campaign in Egypt and Syria, 1798–1799

added sudden sporadic small bedouin attacks by screaming horsemen galloping out of nowhere, lunging and slashing at them with their scimitars or simply firing at them unseen from sand dunes and oases. Desaix's men, without canteens and each carrying just a small amount of rations of food and ammunition, soon found even the initial stage of their march to Damanhur taxing, then downright depressing, troops soon falling out and even dying of thirst by the time they reached Birket, a distance of only about twenty miles.

There this advance guard, greatly on edge, had made camp that night amid clouds of mosquitoes and had fallen asleep when, as Brigadier General Belliard related in his eyewitness account, "a bizarre incident" occurred. In the middle of the night something or someone spooked the horses, all tethered in a line. An artillery horse broke loose and suddenly started galloping right through the darkened camp, amid the dying embers of the fires maintained by the sleeping pickets. The exhausted troops, waking suddenly, and without orders, grabbed their muskets and started firing wildly in all directions, the sudden uproar and chaos then causing the other horses to panic and break loose, stampeding through the camp, trampling men, then fleeing into the night. By the time that lamps were lit and the men reassembled in their bivouac areas by their equally groggy and bewildered officers, and calm restored, it was discovered that they had shot three or four of their own men and had lost more than one hundred badly needed horses. "I do not know what to attribute their fear and panic to," Belliard confessed. "There must be someone here interested in stirring things up and spreading rumors. The troops are now so wrought up that if, during the night 25 or 30 Arabs attacked, I believe they would cause the entire division to stampede, so afraid of them are the men at this point."[31]

With General Reynier already marching to join Desaix on July 5, navy captain Perrée proceeded with several dozen boats to Rosetta, where on the following day General Dugua's division (Kléber's old division) was ordered to follow. That same day General Vial, temporarily heading Menou's division, set out on foot for Cairo, followed late the next afternoon by General Bonaparte, his staff, and Bon's division, over the by-now-well-trampled and dusty trail along the dried-up canal for Rahmaniya.[32]

Many of the complaints registered by Belliard concerning the problems encountered by Desaix's division as it marched painfully forward were echoed in the other four divisions, including Dugua's, in which

within three hours of leaving Alexandria [for Rosetta], any semblance of marching order had disappeared. Scarcely one and a half miles from

Alexandria one entered the desert, and by 10 A.M. the heat became so oppressive, and our thirst so great there amid the sand dunes, without water, that men were collapsing every step of the way . . . and later we were told that three had already died of thirst.[33]

This continued all the way to Rosetta. The lack of water crippled every French column, the situation aggravated by the poisoned or destroyed wells and cisterns they encountered in the course of their march.

Meanwhile Murat's and Damas's dragoons, sent as an advance column to take Rosetta, had fared better, and Colonel Laugier's spirits, like everyone else's, eventually picked up on reaching that point. "We made our entry there at noon," he recorded. "The city seemed pretty enough. All the inhabitants were standing before their houses, all the shops were open . . . [and] the sight of the Nile, as well as the large number of vessels there, excited us all. This spectacle was our first truly happy moment since arriving in Egypt."[34] And it was to prove one of the last. Rosetta was one of the few cities where tranquil gardens and fields lay undisturbed, the houses and shops of the people open, welcoming to the French.

With the arrival of the convalescing General Menou, who was to take command as military governor there, General Dugua then continued south with most of his division, up the Nile toward Cairo—some by land, some by boat—to rendezvous with General Bonaparte and the rest of the army, some thirty-three miles away at Rahmaniya.

Bonaparte and his staff, setting out just ahead of Bon's division on July 7, reached Damanhur by 8:00 A.M. on the eighth, only to be greeted with one of the many tragic stories attending the invasion, this one regarding the mysterious death of Brigadier General Mireur. Though he had little training and less than nine years' military experience, Mireur had risen quickly to the rank of brigadier. He had recently argued with Desaix about the folly of the whole expedition, insisting that they turn around. That evening he had wandered from camp at Damanhur, and his body was later found alone in the sand. Colonel Savary claimed that he had been killed by Arabs. But he had been found with his weapons, money, and uniform all intact, and Arabs always stripped and mutilated their victims. In fact, the despondent Mireur had ridden out into the desert, where he had shot himself in the head with his own pistol.[35] It had to be hushed up, and in any event, showing neither compassion nor understanding, Napoleon was furious with this treacherous act of betrayal—an abandonment of himself and the army.

In the eyes of many, Damanhur, the army's first major encampment after leaving Alexandria, seemed jinxed, boding ill for things to come—first stampeding horses, next Mireur's tragic suicide, and then the case of one of Napoleon's own aides-de-camp. While they were all settling in, some Arab horsemen somehow got through the pickets and approached Bonaparte himself, who immediately ordered his aide, Captain Croisier, to get some men together to chase them off. Leaping onto a horse, young Croisier quickly got fifteen guides together and attacked. During an exchange of gunfire, leaving Croisier in a weak position, Napoleon shouted out, "Get them, dammit! Charge!" but apparently Croisier was too cautious, and the Arabs escaped unharmed. "The General was beside himself with rage," Bourrienne recalled, "and when Croisier returned, he abused him royally, giving him a real dressing-down," all but accusing him of cowardice before the other officers and aides-de-camp. Reduced to tears, Croisier fled, later confiding to Bourrienne, "I shall not live this down. I am going to get myself killed. I cannot live dishonored in his eyes."[36] Although Croisier was involved in every wild skirmish thereafter, death defied his daring for months to come, until he finally fell beneath the walls of Acre the following year.

The fear of Arab attacks was real, their snipers and horsemen taking a heavy toll on the lengthening lines of French stragglers in particular, cutting their throats and stealing their few possessions. But apparently even more frightening for the French was the story now told by a few of the rare survivors of gang rape by Arabs, who sodomized the French before killing them. For the French—accustomed to raping the women and girls of conquered towns in Europe—this was shocking. When one soldier actually gave a firsthand report, Napoleon just brushed it off, laughing: He was alive, was he not, so what? But the raping and beheading of French stragglers continued all the way to Cairo; if nothing else it sometimes helped close up loose marching formations.

Meanwhile, on July 10, the first units of Desaix's and Reynier's divisions reached Rahmaniya, thereby completing the fifty-seven-mile trek from Alexandria to the Nile and the first leg of their march to Cairo.[37]

While Egyptian boats were sent down the Nile to Rosetta to help bring up troops and especially badly needed munitions and food, the French now encountered the first organized resistance by the Mamelukes. Some three hundred mounted "bedouin" (the French so misidentified them) followed and harassed them around Rahmaniya.[38] But even vicious saber attacks by enemy cavalry could not stifle the troops' reaction to the first sight of water and the Nile. Brigadier Belliard described the men's "cries of joy . . . everyone leaping with excitement" as, disregarding the orders of their officers, they broke rank, threw down their muskets and heavy packs, and leaped into the muddy water. "The soldiers simply threw themselves in, gulping water down like wild animals. In an instant the entire division was in the river, and a field of melon along the banks was soon devoured.... I do believe that the most dangerous enemy we shall have to fight in Egypt is thirst," he acknowledged.[39]

At Rahmaniya the leading four divisions were given a badly needed forty-eight hours' rest, though the grumbling resumed when it was discovered that despite wheat supplies there were no ovens, and hence still no bread. Then at 4:00 P.M. on July 12, General Desaix at the head of the column was ordered to resume the march and clear the still-uncharted route for the remainder of the army, while General Andréossy received orders to begin boarding several hundred artillerymen and their equipment on the Nile flotilla that was to accompany the army as it proceeded upriver. As they set out, the first reports reached Bonaparte's mobile headquarters of a large army under Egypt's most powerful Mameluke military commander, Murad Bey, blocking their path well to the south, just outside Cairo, and moving slowly in their direction, supported by a large and powerful river flotilla of their own.[40]

Delighted at the prospect of confronting the enemy on the battlefield, Bonaparte in turn ordered Desaix to advance quickly along the Nile as far as Shubrakhit and be ready to attack at dawn.[41]

Twelve days after the first units of the French expeditionary force had set foot on Egyptian territory, the two sides were jockeying for position preparatory to the clash that both hoped would be decisive.

At 2:00 A.M. Bonaparte ordered the army to break camp and advance on Shubrakhit, where intelligence reports informed him that an initial force of about four thousand Mameluke cavalry was already awaiting him, extending from that village to the banks of the river, where they were reinforced by several entrenched artillery batteries and eight to ten gunboats.[42] Occupying two hamlets before Shubrakhit, the five French divisions formed into five large, time-tested battle squares to meet the formidable Egyptian cavalry. No sooner had the French fixed their bayonets, however, than the enemy charged.

The French opened fire with howitzers and cannon. Foiled by this unexpectedly lethal barrage across the mass of their cavalry, the Mamelukes wheeled sharply to the left to sweep around the French rear instead.

Meanwhile, parallel to the army along the Nile, Captain Perrée was finding his boats outgunned by the stronger Mameluke gunboat division.

Sinking one French boat, the Mamelukes succeeded in boarding a French galley and a gunboat before being repulsed by an intensive firefight. But Arab artillery along the banks from the direction of Shubrakhit took the French by complete surprise. For a while Perrée's flotilla found "it becoming almost impossible to hold their own," forcing them to land General Zayoncheck's twelve hundred troops on the opposite (right) bank of the river, where they too came under withering Mameluke fire.[43] But despite enemy artillery and a wound in the arm, Perrée finally succeeded not only in repulsing the Mameluke onslaught but also in blowing up a large Egyptian gunboat, though all his men, including the scientists and civilians, had to take up muskets in order to save their necks. As Berthier later put it, "When it was a case of fighting the enemies of the fatherland, every Frenchman was a soldier."

Meanwhile the Mameluke cavalry, unimpeded by any countering French cavalry, continued to sweep northward well behind French lines as far as Miniat Salahmah, before being repelled by the "vigorous fusillade" of Reynier's, Vial's, and Dugua's infantry, then falling back to their own lines as suddenly as they had appeared. Quick to size up the situation, Bonaparte unleashed his small cavalry, backed by the infantry, ordering a full-scale pursuit and seizing their entire artillery at Shubrakhit in the process.

It turned out that the French had actually been facing twelve thousand enemy troops, peasants and slaves joining the three thousand or so Mameluke cavalry. But despite the original terror, the Battle of Shubrakhit had been easily won by the French in their first real, if brief, test of strength with their Egyptian opponents.[44] Berthier's battle report summed up French casualties as minimum and Egyptian figures at about three hundred. But the invaders still faced an entire, powerful army before them.

After pillaging Shubrakhit and then resting briefly, late on July 13 Bonaparte ordered the army to resume its march. Artillery and other wheeled vehicles in particular were soon sinking into seemingly bottomless sand dunes or getting stuck while crossing the innumerable small dry canals. For men lacking food and sleep ever since landing in Egypt, "this march [was] one of the hardest yet," according to one company commander, with large numbers of soldiers continuing to die of hunger, exposure, and exhaustion daily. But Bonaparte was unrelenting, pushing his weary men to the point that the entire army of bitter, undisciplined malcontents collapsed, disintegrated, or simply mutinied. "The army in general is grumbling," Belliard confessed, "and the officers by now equally discontent, let their famished soldiers break rank and wreak havoc on the villages along our route and steal whatever they wanted."[45] Even the threat of marauding bedouin no longer affected these men, as the number of stragglers increased. And due to Napoleon's slapdash "planning," there were still no food stores to be brought to exhausted troops at the end of the day, the commissary officers providing no logistical support whatsoever. The result was furious and half-demented French soldiers running amok through impoverished, undefended villages and hamlets as they passed, despite Napoleon's strict injunction to the contrary (including an immediate death penalty for the guilty). Until the army could provide food and drink for the troops, and a reasonable degree of relief from the sweltering heat, there was no way to maintain order and discipline.

The worst pillaging was committed by General Vial's battalions, who caused fear and panic wherever they went. "It is hard to imagine a more thoroughly ill-disciplined army," Colonel Laugier lamented more than once. "The tears of village men and the cries of their women create a terrible din," the women climbing up to the flat roofs of their mud houses, wailing, waving their shawls frantically back and forth, and "all that under the very eyes of the Commander in Chief himself. As he passed the scene, he angrily ordered General Dugua to remain behind with his men to restore order and find rations for the troops." Frustrated and exhausted after carrying heavy packs over seemingly endless sandy wastes, day after day, their throats parched and raw from the clouds of red dust kicked up by the preceding battalions, their feet bleeding and blistered from the sand rubbing in their shoes, (when they even *had* shoes), beset by infernal July temperatures hovering between 110 and 120 degrees—all this combined to leave men and officers alike near the end of their tether. "Instead of aiding the men, their commanders, the brigadier generals, increased it by their own insubordinate acts [before the divisional generals and even Napoleon] in front of the troops themselves," Laugier sadly remarked. When Dugua finally found a large store of beans, enough in fact for several brigades, the civilian quartermaster "simply refused to distribute them among the troops," an astonished Laugier noted. When then confronted by angry brigadiers, the quartermaster "protested that he was not their personal galley slave!"[46] although of course that is what he was being paid to be.

Hunger was now so rife as they passed through the last several miles of sand dunes that the French were reduced to killing the transport animals on which their very existence depended, including the donkeys carrying their baggage and munitions, even eating some of the dogs the officers had brought with them. Four more artillerymen in Desaix's advance division died anyway, their names added to the list of hundreds already recorded. Meanwhile bedouin cavalry continued to snipe along their flanks. And then when at last they did reach some more crops, those troops who followed found that Desaix's angry men had set fire to ripe grain still in the fields because they had no means of milling it, leaving nothing for the desperate and unruly divisions of Vial and Dugua, or for the peasants who had planted it. "By the time we arrived, we did not even know where to find hay and barley for our horses."[47] Bonaparte as usual omitted any mention of this catastrophic foul-up in his reports to Paris.

Instead he pushed on as fast as possible, now approaching Wardan, while ahead of them Murad Bey, who had escaped practically unscathed in his lightning attack, regrouped. If Bonaparte did not strike within the next few days, he would no longer have an army with which to face the foe. Finding himself virtually unheeded in his attempts to keep his own troops in hand, he did the only thing left for him to do: He pushed them on remorselessly to confront the enemy. One really good battle and a victorious entry into the Egyptian capital would solve all his problems, he felt. In any event, that was the only solution, apart from retreating to the sea and admitting defeat.

But even nearing Cairo did not cheer the troops as, to their dismay, they again encountered stretches of sand dunes. The nights were still very damp and cold, with river fog spreading inland. "This march is the worst yet," Belliard glumly reported.

On July 18, just three miles from Wardan, the situation changed drastically—as usual, in that land of stark contrasts. "There we suddenly came upon a rich valley, filled with splendid copses of sycamores and palm trees," which should have cheered up the disconsolate troops. But after days of sand-covered waste without any source of water whatsoever, upon reaching Wardan and the Nile again, the commissary officers still refused to gather and distribute food for the men. The famished troops mutinied. "Although the troops were clearly weary after their long march, that did not prevent them from pillaging and leaving a souvenir behind of our passage here," as Belliard put it.[48] By this time, at Wardan, Bonaparte—who had witnessed so many villages devastated by his swarm of men despite his threats—was at the end of his tether. "He went into a terrible rage about the pillaging," Colonel Savary confided to his personal journal. The situation was bad, Belliard agreed, and "if the Mamelukes had attacked us at this time, they would have done a lot of harm. The troops, worn out by the broiling heat, were just barely able to stagger along," while their artillery had proved unmaneuverable, often stuck in the sand dunes.[49]

Finally a desperate Bonaparte disobeyed his own instructions and ordered the seizure of local sheep and crops. He had no choice. It was also from there at Wardan that the first flicker of hope appeared for the army, hinting that the end—or at least their immediate goal—was in sight when "from above the sand dunes, at long last we saw the famous pyramids of Giza . . . and the high minarets of the city of Cairo, our promised land. This hope gave fresh courage to the weak among us," Colonel Savary acknowledged.[50] But for all that the discouragement of the army was still running deep, from outspoken brigadier generals to the lowest recruit, one angry trooper confronting the great man himself as he passed, snarling, "Well, general, you are going to lead us to India next, are you?" Bonaparte snapped back, "Certainly not with the likes of you!"[51]

What saved Bonaparte and his army at this point was Wardan itself— the vast fields, the rich coolness offered by the shade of its welcoming oases, and the abundance of food found there and along the Nile. The troops finally were fed and their anger momentarily appeased. But even before they had rested, Napoleon was ordering his sometimes disobedient and even outspokenly rude brigade commanders to have the men clean their sandy muskets and artillery in preparation for the forthcoming battle. Scouts were even now confirming the formation and extension of Murad Bey's large army standing between them and Cairo, supported by Ibrahim Bey's separate army on the east side of the Nile. The choice was no longer theirs. There would be a colossal confrontation, a head-on clash between Napoleon's twenty-four thousand men versus Murad's eighteen thousand, as well as Ibrahim's reputed one hundred thousand (mainly unarmed and untrained peasants).[52] If Napoleon wanted to reach Cairo, or even survive, he would first have to destroy the Mameluke hosts with their backs to the wall, protecting their homes, families, and all they owned.

Later, after a day's badly needed rest, the five divisions round Wardan formed by brigade once again and set out at 3:00 A.M. At 9:00 A.M. on July 20, Bonaparte and his staff mounted their horses, finally "leaving the sand dunes and the mountains behind," Savary happily noted. They had reached the point, known by the Arabs as the "Cow's Belly," where the Rosetta and Damietta branches joined, forming a larger single Nile River, further broadened by the formation of a series of long, largely treeless islands. "The plain we are crossing is lovely and rich and covered with several villages," the colonel continued, the French reaching al-Qaratayn by five that afternoon.[53]

The next day Captain Perrée's river flotilla joined them there, while General Zayoncheck continued to keep pace on the opposite side of the Nile.

Major Detroye had found the same disheartening marching conditions on the right bank of the river as well. "Nothing has been more difficult than our march to Cairo," he recorded in his journal. "The sky is burning, the earth hotter still from the sun. We arrive late and leave before sunrise. Our bivouacs are often made in constantly shifting sand, and the nights are soaking with river dampness." And although there was plenty of drinking water, from the Nile, and some meat from freshly slaughtered water buffalo, chickens, and pigeons, as well as watermelons and beans, there was "almost never any bread and no wine, no eau-de-vie." The only things he forgot to complain about were the vipers and the ubiquitous Egyptian scorpions. If food and drink were not the principal problem in this particular brigade, however, leadership was.

General Zayoncheck was hardly the ideal commanding officer on such a campaign, at least according to Major Detroye. "The general . . . appears to have all the qualities of an honest man, but none of those of a good general officer. Lacking character, energy, and basic forethought, he manages to let his troops go hungry here where food is so abundant." They were surrounded by food, but it was in fact rarely collected and distributed. "Failure to punish wrongs, combined with real need, results in pillaging, and every village we [in Zayoncheck's brigade] camp near is ravaged by us, while during the day's march the column is in utter disorder." But Napoleon and his chief of staff liked Zayoncheck, and Berthier's reports to the Directory as usual suppressed disagreeable truths, instead praising Zayoncheck as "an extremely good leader."[54]

With the confluence of the Damietta and Rosetta branches of the river behind them, the undulating horizon of furnacelike waves of heat, desert haze, and sand dunes of the left bank were giving way to immense flat fields of beans, watermelons, sugarcane, and black currants. These were interrupted by occasional yellow stretches of thistle gladiolas and blue indigo, amid numerous farming villages situated on raised mounds, surrounded by small orange and lemon groves. If a third of each village lay in ruins, and the habitable mud huts were "really filthy and stinking," the French at least found "the men to be quite tall and well built," though their women appeared "small, skinny, and hideous," with the children running around completely naked until the age of seven or eight. Nevertheless, given the swath of destruction they had left behind, surprisingly they found these villagers "very hospitable." As for their music, however, played by tambourines, cymbals, and flageolets, producing "most unpleasant sounds," they could have done without it.[55]

Meanwhile Captain Perrée's flotilla, with Monge, Berthollet, Bourrienne, and the other civilians aboard, along with hundreds of troops, was gradually being reduced in number, as several of the larger vessels ran aground in the low waters. By the time they reached the main channel of the Nile, Perrée found himself with only eight very crowded lateen-rigged feluccas (the workboats of the Nile) and a mere four gunboats.[56]

General Bonaparte's desire to close with Murad Bey's army on the plains now less than eighteen miles ahead of them was accompanied by considerable anxiety. The French cavalry, down to a few hundred mounted men, suffered from tactical inferiority and disintegrating morale, with almost no loyalty left to its commander in chief. The French had little hard evidence about Mameluke strategy; it was enough to know that the Mamelukes had resolved to fight them before Cairo, at a village called Imbabah.[57] Thus Bonaparte pushed relentlessly on. Finally at 4:00 P.M. his dust-covered column, several miles long, came to a halt near the villages of Waraq al-Hadar and Bashtil, just one and a half miles from Murad's imposing army.[58]

Murad Bey's army, combined with Ibrahim Bey's force across the river, looked impressive, if not intimidating. What the French did not know, however, was the fear that their earlier routing of Murad's forces at Shubrakhit was at this very moment causing in Cairo. This news, historian Abd al-Rahman wrote, "intensified the terror of the people.... The east and west banks were full of our artillery and troops ... despite all these preparations the [Mameluke] princes were frightened," and the wealthier families of Cairo arranging "to have transport laid on in the event of our military reverses, requiring them to flee, while government officers prevent the lesser inhabitants from attempting to leave the city." In the meantime Sayid Umar Effendi, leader of the sharifs [Muslim nobility], bearing the large green flag of the Prophet taken from the Citadel, was "escorted by several thousand men armed with sticks, loudly reciting prayers as they marched to reinforce the position at Bulaq. The whole of Egypt was in a state of turmoil and panic," al-Rahman continued, "everyone imploring Allah to give them a victory over the French." Left in the capital were the women, children, and elderly, hidden behind the faceless mud walls of their homes, the streets of Cairo abandoned to the bands of "murderers and brigands now controlling the city." Angry mobs seized most of the Europeans, Christian Arabs, Copts, Greeks, and Jews, along with everything of value from their churches, monasteries, synagogues, and homes. "They wanted to kill all the Jews and Christians," noted al-Rahman, and only strong intervention by the remaining Mameluke authorities prevented full-scale massacres. "Every day they learned that the French were getting closer and closer to Cairo, and no one in authority could agree as to what dispositions to take. The [Egyptian] troops had no confidence in their own armies, and nothing [efficacious] was done to meet the French."⁵⁹

Having reached Waraq and Bashtil, in the middle of the broad plain divided by a dry canal running from Imbabah almost straight to Bashil and several hundred yards beyond, Desaix's division, now in square formation, advanced slowly, anchoring the French right flank. Immediately to the left and connected only by a few pieces of light field artillery, was General Reynier's division and just beyond, Dugua—where Bonaparte directed operations—while far to their left, Bon's and Vial's troops hugged the banks of the Nile, with orders to cut off the Egyptians' retreat, silence their artillery, seize the village of Imbabah, and prevent Ibrahim's and Murad's forces from joining. Together the five French divisions formed "an impenetrable rampart of bayonets" totaling perhaps twenty-four thousand men.

Shrill, spine-chilling Muslim war cries and the sound of thundering hoofs announced the sudden unleashing of several thousand Mameluke cavalry, about half their force. They came, hurling themselves at Reynier's and Desaix's squares to the right, while to the extreme left Vial and Bon advanced in the same protective square formations toward Imbabah, even as a deadly artillery duel and small-arms fire broke out between the French flotilla and the much more powerful Arab gunboats and their land artillery emplacements.

As the full brunt of Mameluke cavalry charged Reynier's wall of steel and fire, it met with a well-ordered lethal blast of musketry and artillery, decimating the Arab ranks—but not stopping them—and "despite the liveliness of the [French] fusillade, they passed between our two divisions [Reynier's and Dugua's]"⁶⁰ and then swung off sharply to the right of the entire French position before turning back to Imbabah. At the same time the remainder of the Mameluke cavalry advanced far to Desaix's right, striking him unexpectedly hard from the rear. The French "square" was designed to repel an attack from any direction, and the Mameluke cavalry was also soon forced to continue back to Imbabah, leaving behind some three hundred or so dead and wounded. Meanwhile Vial and Bon successfully overran the Arab entrenchments around Imbabah, seizing sixty pieces of artillery and the village itself, causing part of Murad's force to panic and flee for the safety of the river, losing perhaps another fifteen hundred men in the process, chiefly by drowning. It was, said Berthier, "a frightful slaughter."⁶¹

Although Ibrahim Bey and many hundreds of his separate army on the opposite shore had boarded boats to cross over to Murad Bey's aid, they were too late and sent fleeing by Perrée's naval artillery. At the same time a strong wind churned up the muddy waters of the river, sweeping it in turn with curtains of reddish sand, blinding Ibrahim's troops and forcing them back to their side of the river, both sides' artillery firing nonstop all the while. "We were deafened by the noise," al-Rahman reported. "The very earth trembled, and the sky seemed to be falling upon us," as the blinding sand "brought night to the world."[62]

Within less than an hour the worst of the fighting was over, Murad Bey at the head of his now thoroughly broken cavalry galloping away to the south toward Giza and the Pyramids, and Ibrahim Bey fleeing east into the desert, disappearing almost magically from sight. The small number of French cavalry actually mounted, a few hundred at best, pursued Murad as far as Giza until about nine o'clock that evening before stopping.

Meanwhile, in nearby Cairo, tens of thousands of panic-stricken refugees, fleeing with whatever belongings they could carry, converged on the eastern gates of the city. But once beyond and in the countryside, they found themselves facing the poor Egyptians living in the outlying villages: "The unfortunate refugees were attacked by these Arabs, stripped of all their possessions ... and their women dishonored," lamented Abd al-Rahman. While on the other side of the city and the Nile the victorious French were scavenging the battlefield for loot. Many of the Egyptians remaining in Cairo pillaged the palaces of Ibrahim and Murad Bey as well as those of other princes, later setting several on fire. Whipped up by the strong desert winds, dozens of fires soon raged out of control across the city, spreading to Bulaq and to a large number of boats. "Never has there been such a night as this in the entire history of Cairo," a stunned al-Rahman commented, "no one can remember having seen anything like it."[63]

So ended the Battle of the Pyramids, on July 21, 1798. General Belliard put Egyptian losses at about 1,000 men killed or wounded, and the French at a mere 30. General Bon's more realistic numbers, however, put Egyptian casualties at 2,500 men killed or drowned, and the French total at well above one hundred.[64]

During the night Bonaparte ordered the building of a pontoon bridge over the remaining boats, linking Giza with Cairo. At about three o'clock in the morning, as flames licked the sky above the capital, Muslim religious officials arrived at Bonaparte's headquarters at Giza, accompanied by some of the more prominent European businessmen who had survived the slaughter, and a daunted Turkish ambassador.[65]

After accepting the surrender of Cairo in the early hours of the morning, a triumphant if weary Napoleon issued a "Proclamation to the People of Cairo," informing them that he had come as their "savior, to destroy the Mameluke race" and to protect the rest of the Egyptians and their commerce from them. "There is nothing to fear for your families, your houses, your property, and especially for the religion of the Prophet, which I esteem." The French had come to save the Egyptians, he insisted, not to destroy them.[66] At the same time he ordered General Bon's division to enter Cairo and seize the Citadel. By nightfall Cairo was securely in French hands.[67] Despite every possible obstacle, and their own logistical incompetence, the French had reached their objective, much to the amazement of just about everyone—except Napoleon Bonaparte.

Deep Water

*In this world one must appear friendly and make many
promises, but keep none.*

ugust 1, 1798: "Really beautiful weather," Lieutenant
Charrier aboard the eighty-gun *Franklin* off Alexandria
noted in his journal. "The wind out of the north-northwest;
a nice breeze, some swells. The second division sent on a
work detail ashore to dig wells."[1] Nothing to distinguish
this from the preceding days, that is, until that afternoon.
"At 2:00 P.M. the *Heureux* signaled the sighting of 12 sail to the west-
northwest. . . . They can be easily seen." It did not take long to confirm that
they were warships. The flagship immediately hoisted the signal to recall all
boats and men. The artillery captain in charge of the two mortars on the tiny
island opposite Fort Abukir, at the entrance of the bay, was ordered there
immediately. At three o'clock Admiral Brueys ordered his men to their action
stations to prepare for combat, while dispatching two brigs to reconnoiter.

The enemy force continued to come straight at the French. At four
o'clock two more vessels joined them: It was indeed the English navy. The
brig *Alerte* approached them at maximum cannon range in an attempt to
draw them into the unseen reefs of the bay, an old trick, but the English
paid no heed: "At 5 o'clock they [the English] continued on a direct star-
board tack," Lt. Charrier recorded:

The maneuver left little doubt in my mind that they intended to attack this very evening. Our Admiral Brueys ordered the men up into the main yard to break out the sail, but shortly thereafter, apparently convinced that we were too shorthanded to put to sea, he belayed that order. In fact we were at least two hundred men short of our best sailors aboard each vessel. He instead signaled his intention to fight at anchor.[2]

The fact that Brueys and the entire French battle fleet were still there in Egypt, in this most vulnerable position, was a bizarre tale in its own right. Bourrienne and Berthier succeeded in working with Bonaparte because they could to a certain degree anticipate and interpret his constant juggling of possibilities. Brueys, on the other hand, scarcely knew his commander in chief, and in any event his was not the kind of mind that coped easily with complex, fluid situations such as he now found in Abukir Bay. Both unimaginative and a worrier, as a career officer, he liked precise orders with a specific objective. He was an honest, diligent, thorough man who had seen his aristocratic class first removed from the nation's leadership and then decimated by the Reign of Terror throughout 1793 and 1794, leaving the once splendid Royal Navy, built up so painstakingly by Louis XVI, now an undisciplined, officerless shambles, with just a few minor younger officers along with one or two older men left to deal with the resultant chaos. Those few senior officers who had survived the republican bloodletting—compromisers and for the most part hardly brilliant—were willing to work with republican France, despite having seen their families and friends executed because of their aristocratic lineage. These survivors of their national shame were now in command of the navy. All of them—even the fleet's commander in chief, Brueys—were nervous, fearful of the constant threats and denunciations. Brueys could hardly forget the day in 1793 when he had been stripped of his rank because he was a "suspect," a noble. He had not been reintegrated until 1795, and then promoted to the rank of rear admiral only in November of the following year, when he was appointed commander of the squadron that captured the Ionian Isles and Corfu. It was all so bewildering, this topsy-turvy world created by the nation's revolutionary classes. And now to confuse matters all the more, he was in Egypt, of all places, and under the orders of a young man whom he genuinely respected as a military commander but hardly knew and never understood. Napoleon had a knack for quickly sizing up those about him, and he had cast Brueys as a lackey, a sycophant, a man broken by the Revolution, whom he could manipulate as he wished, unlike the difficult naval minister, Adm. Eustache de Bruix, whose fiery tongue and sense of personal honor kowtowed to no man's.

From the moment they had reached Egyptian waters and the fleet had dropped anchor in Abukir Bay, nothing had gone right for the unfortunate Brueys, first the disorganized landing in the wrong place, followed on July 3 by Berthier informing him that Bonaparte had been "very upset that during his attack on Alexandria you did not block the new port, to have prevented four large merchant vessels from having escaped and put to sea." Brueys had never received orders to leave Abukir Bay to do that, and in any case he had had his hands full keeping his fleet together during the raging storm while overseeing the landing of men and equipment. Then, Napoleon personally had ordered Brueys to bring his fleet into the old port of Alexandria the following day, July 4, "if the winds slacken and the channel is deep enough."[3]

Only at that point did it occur to Napoleon that there was another item he had failed to consider due to his lack of precampaign intelligence reports: whether or not his warships could even pass into this key port. But "if the water is not deep enough to permit the warships to enter, the following day they will take the appropriate measures" to otherwise land the artillery and other material, as well as the rest of the army." In any event, he would "notify the commander in chief . . . if the fleet [could] enter the port after all, or if instead he can at least defend it against a superior enemy fleet while at anchor in Abukir Bay. . . . Under those circumstances, he went on, "if the enemy appears with *a very superior force*, . . . the fleet will then withdraw to Corfu."[4] (As Nelson's fleet reportedly was about the same strength as his own, the Corfu contingency would not appear to apply here, Brueys's 1,287 guns far superior in number and fire-power to the British 1,012.)

As usual Napoleon issued his orders without considering how they would be carried out, or even if they *could* be. Surveying harbors by taking soundings by hand, even by well-qualified teams, to establish whether a deep-enough channel existed to accommodate the large, heavy warships, was a laborious, time-consuming task. It would actually take several weeks, not one or two days, as Napoleon now insisted. But essentially his expectations of Brueys were reduced to his remaining in Egypt for the time being, unless greatly outnumbered and outgunned by "a very superior force," as Bourrienne privately confirmed later.[5]

In any event, Brueys, though badly shaken by the chaotic landings that had begun on July 1, sent a dispatch to Cairo later on July 3: "Kindly accept my congratulations, my General, on your arrival in Egypt and its conquest, announced by the taking of Alexandria, which is the happiest omen for your continued success." He informed him that the soundings of the harbor channels would be undertaken immediately, although preliminary indications "are not satisfactory" (nor indeed were those to follow). But, he added, his position off Abukir could not be maintained, acknowledging that if any enemy navy "*of equal strength*" arrived at this time, they "*would destroy our entire fleet . . . if I had the misfortune to receive them while still at anchor there.*" Then, contradicting himself, he informed Bonaparte that "at the present time [however] I can find nowhere else, no alternative anchorage, . . . I would feel truly uneasy if failure to find the proper anchorage here forced me to leave you, I having no other desire than to be able to support you in some manner at least."[6] Napoleon did not correct, modify, or alter the admiral's conclusions.

Brueys had made his position reasonably clear: As no suitable channel had yet been found to permit the battle fleet to enter the safety of Alexandria harbor, he would remain in the partially protected anchorage of Abukir Bay until the ships were unloaded. Although fearful of meeting an English attack there, he did not want to leave Bonaparte and the entire army unprotected by sea and stranded in the event they met with military reverses ashore. Loyalty to Bonaparte and the army was paramount.

Other factors came into play as well, of course, determining the length of Brueys's sojourn—the time required to land and unload men, munitions, horses, artillery, and hundreds of vehicles, as well as the additional time necessary to obtain fresh naval supplies—rope, canvas, timber, and an entirely fresh food and water supply, enough at least to see the fleet through a two-month voyage, the bare minimum required for any major fleet putting to sea under any circumstances.

In a disturbing secret report of July 9, Naval Ordonnateur Jaubert informed Naval Minister Bruix that the port of Alexandria held "no naval provisions whatsoever, not even the basic facilities" such as drydocks, warehouses, and workshops. Moreover, it would take "at least a year" before these resources would be available. To further dash Bruix's hopes, he confided that in his opinion it was still uncertain whether smaller vessels would be able to enter the port and therefore certain that the larger ones could never do so.[7] Under the circumstances it was "generally felt that we must leave for Corfu immediately upon completing our landings," because the English were nearby and expected to arrive at any moment. He added that "Brueys had decided otherwise. . . . In consequence, there is a certain fatalism in the air, which is even beginning to undermine my own principles a little."[8]

As early as July 6 the first official report from Admiral Brueys's survey team stated that entry into Alexandria was "impracticable, or at best, dangerous." Brueys in turn broke the news to Bonaparte, adding, "Believe me, General, my greatest wish is to support your operations." Napoleon personally related to the Directory that same day: "This news completely upsets all my plans."[9] But in his report to the Directory the following month, he stated that he had categorically ordered Brueys "to enter Alexandria harbor within twenty-four hours" (a complete fabrication, of course, to cover his tracks).

After spending some days in Alexandria with Ordonnateur Jaubert, on July 7 Brueys returned to Abukir Bay. Because of shallow waters and reefs, he continued to anchor his fleet in a battle line nearly four miles offshore, and therefore beyond the range of protective land batteries, including the eight cannon at Fort Abukir at the tip of the peninsula and the mortars on Abukir Island. Brueys's principal preoccupation throughout the month of July was simply attempting to obtain fresh stores of food and water, both of which proved nearly impossible. The local wells along Abukir Bay were constantly under attack by marauding Arabs, and the principal source of food was still out of reach in the warehouses of Rosetta and Damietta. Even Jaubert, who strongly disliked Brueys and wanted to see the fleet sail immediately for Corfu before the English arrived, agreed that the situation was desperate and that Brueys could not possibly put to sea.[10]

By mid-July so grave was the dwindling food situation aboard the fleet that naval captains, ignoring the prescribed chain of command, were secretly writing to General Menou (no friend of Bonaparte), begging him for provisions. Even the usually recalcitrant Capt. Henri Alexandre Thévenard was angry: "Hunger is truly beginning to set in. How unhappy I am ever to have come to such a wretched country."[11] Poussielgue, the expedition's usually phlegmatic treasurer, implored Napoleon: "The fleet needs food most urgently." He had been left with no money despite the great Maltese treasure, which Napoleon refused to release, and therefore could not send the fleet food; the Egyptians would not sell to him without cash payment. Poussielgue estimated that Brueys needed an emergency shipment of 275 *tons* of rice, 330 tons of wood (for the ships' ovens), 80 head of cattle, and 150 sheep—to begin with.[12] When word finally reached Brueys late on July 24 that Menou was beginning to load five or six small vessels with emergency food relief, a grateful admiral thanked him warmly because the fleet was "truly on the verge of dying of hunger and thirst."[13] In fact the navy had provided Brueys with substantial provisions before sailing, but Napoleon had seized them and brought them ashore for the use of his army instead.

In a final letter of appeal, dated July 26, Brueys reminded Bonaparte that "we are floating between hope and despair." They were out of bread and almost out of water. What is more, his ships were still unprotected in the event of an attack. And if things were not bad enough, at least three thousand of his men were in the hospital, ashore in some capacity, or simply AWOL, including many rebellious officers. "Without food, or naval repairs," he told Bonaparte, "the fleet is now paralyzed."[14] Nevertheless, two days later, on receiving news of the spectacular French victory at the Battle of the Pyramids, the overjoyed Brueys rose from his sickbed to issue a victory proclamation to the fleet concluding: "*Vive la République, mes camarades!* Our brave brothers-in-arms have taken the city of Cairo, the capital of Egypt," and ordered a twenty-one-gun salute to be fired from every ship and frigate, and doubled their usual reduced rations of food and drink.[15]

On July 30 Napoleon finally replied, informing Brueys that he had already ordered "fifty boatloads of wheat and rice, which he would now find awaiting him in Alexandria, which he must enter most quickly." In fact Napoleon dispatched orders for those provisions to Damietta and Rosetta only that same day. Furthermore, Napoleon added, the English danger was now over. "The entire conduct of the English leads me to believe that they are limiting themselves to the blockade of Malta" and therefore would not be expected in Egyptian waters for the time being.[16]

This letter never reached the unfortunate Brueys nor, indeed, did these fabled fifty boatloads of supplies. It was a cruel hoax, leading the admiral to believe he would receive this food, and soon. But as Napoleon himself openly quipped time and again: "In this world one must appear friendly and make many promises, but keep none."[17] Meanwhile, apart from half a dozen small feluccas of rice, enough to feed the fleet for just another day or so, Brueys had received no provisions whatsoever—no meat, no vegetables, no wheat or flour, and precious little water. Weakened by a diet of half rations for the past few weeks, and with dysentery racking a large part of the crews remaining on board—Brueys himself was still convalescing from a near-fatal attack—the French fleet remained an anchored target that August 1, when Lieutenant Charrier reported the sighting of the British fleet on a direct course for Abukir Bay.

At the first sighting of the enemy, without waiting for orders, Rear Adms. Blanquet du Chayla and Pierre de Villeneuve had rushed aboard the *Orient,* where Brueys called an immediate war council that included chief of staff Rear Admiral Ganteaume and Commodore Casabianca. Voices and tempers rose as they discussed how best to cope with this unexpected situation. Blanquet was the only senior officer to vote to put to sea, the more cautious Villeneuve and Ganteaume supporting the equally prudent flag commander's view to fight at anchor. If the French were at a critical disadvantage now as a result of their failure to have posted frigates several miles offshore to warn them of any intruders, not to mention having been caught with a quarter of their battle crews ashore, they nevertheless held a distinct advantage in firepower over the British. In a sea fight their superiority in power and range could have made a great difference, but not here in close quarters. And with the British coming at them at a front angle, it was impossible for the French to bring their big guns around even to bear on them. To counterbalance the traditional British tactic of breaking through the battle line of their opponents and isolating each vessel, Brueys now ordered stream cables to be secured between ships, from bowsprits to sterns, in effect making one immense chain through which the British could not pass. But, as Lieutenant Charrier noted, like so many others "that order was not generally executed by the ships' captains," though most did drop a second main anchor, locking their formation in place.[18]

"I will bring the French Fleet to Action the moment I can lay hands upon them," a determined Admiral Nelson had promised time and again, and on July 25, with fresh word of the French in Egypt, he had set sail from Syracuse with his thirteen warships and one gunship on a direct course for Alexandria for a second time. Almost seven hundred miles later, off the coast of Egypt at dawn on August 1, Nelson dispatched two seventy-four-gun ships, ahead of the fleet to reconnoiter the situation. Taking a bearing on the Pharos and Pompey's Column, they duly reached Alexandria by noon. But finding only a few French ships in the old port—and not the war fleet itself—they continued eastward, making their discovery shortly afterward, immediately signaling the fleet and Admiral Nelson, "The Enemy is in Abukir Bay."[19] It was the moment Nelson had been waiting for since his arrival in the Mediterranean in May. It was now 3:00 P.M., which meant that they would not have many hours of daylight ahead of them if action began today, and Nelson had neither accurate charts of the bay nor local pilots. But he was determined not to let the French escape him once more after having traversed the entire length of the Mediterranean—some 2,600 miles—and halfway back again, to find them.

To the surprise of none of his captains, Nelson therefore immediately hoisted the general signal high above his double-deck flagship, the *Vanguard*: "Prepare for Battle and for Anchoring by the Stern. . . . I mean to attack the enemy's van and centre," he informed his captains at five o'clock, as they closed in on Abukir Bay, planning to attack the French ships in pairs, one on either side or at the bow and stern. If they lacked enough ships with which to attack the entire French battle line, at least they had a better chance of destroying or capturing those they could attack by applying this time-tested tactic. And then thirty minutes later, he hoisted the signal they were all eagerly, if nervously, waiting to receive: "Form Line of Battle as Convenient." At 6:20 P.M. the French ships in their turn finally hoisted their colors, opening fire as the first two British ships entered the bay.[20]

Nelson's plan was as dangerous as it was bold. Attacking in waters that he neither knew personally nor had a chart or pilot for. He was literally going in blind, and with the sun already nearing the horizon. Admiral Brueys for his part was taken completely by surprise, expecting the English to attack the following day, by which time he hoped to have the rest of his crews back onboard. But with a northerly breeze behind him and under a full press of sail, Nelson plowed through, in the process losing the seventy-four-gun ship *Culloden* when it ran aground (before the fight had even begun). With the sun quickly sinking, the British selected their opponents and dropped anchor alongside them. Nelson, despite a raging tooth and headache, and Brueys, still weakened by weeks of dysentery and raging fever, were both determined to fight to the end.

Cannonfire soon flashed generally across the western side of the bay as the thirteen French and fourteen British ships commenced a free-for-all.

That the French did as well as they did, given the weeks of very low rations, attrition by illness and greatly reduced crews (and most of them now under fire for the first time), was surprising, but the results not so. At 9:00 P.M. Captain Hood's *Zealous* captured the *Guerrier*, although another British ship, the *Bellerophon*, pierced by French thirty-six-pounders and left a floating ruin, was already out of action. The high point of the fierce onslaught came at approximately 10:15 P.M., when Brueys's *Orient*, the pride of the navy, blew up with most of its crew and officers, causing a deafening explosion and the ground to tremble at General Kléber's headquarters at Alexandria, more than fifteen miles away, where "a bright flash of flame as big as a warship rising rapidly in the air" was seen against the night sky, "the flame growing larger and larger, until it changed into a cloud of black smoke, mixed with showers of luminous sparks." Lieutenant Maissin, a survivor of the tragedy, recalled: "The explosion of the flagship was followed by a mournful silence, as both navies, struck with horror, ceased fire."[21] Later that night Kléber began receiving the first eyewitness reports from a boat he had dispatched to the scene, which, he acknowledged, "give the most painful details of the [French] squadron and of their battle."[22] In fact the preliminary results, which would take several more days to assemble, were indeed disastrous.

At 4:00 A.M., with the moon still high over the horizon, the French, having gathered some of their dead and wounded, opened fire again, much to the surprise of Nelson, as the *Tonnant*, totally dismasted but unvanquished, joined by the *Guillaume-Tell*, *Généreux* and *Timoléon* blazed away, however sporadically, from the end of the French battle line at several British ships. Just how much could human beings take? It seemed impossible, but the battle continued off and on the rest of the morning as the remaining ships were finally silenced and two almost untouched ships of the line, the seventy-four-Gun *Généreux* and the eighty-gun *Guillaume-Tell*, with Admiral Villeneuve aboard, escorted by two forty-gun frigates, the *Justice* and Admiral Decrès's *Diane*, slipped their cables around eleven o'clock and successfully escaped northward, the British too weary and battered to give serious chase.

The toll on ships and men was one of the most appalling in naval history. Of the thirteen French ships of the line, one had exploded, one had been destroyed by her own crew after running ashore, and nine had surrendered to the British. Regardless of one's perspective, French bravery and sheer perseverance under the most horrifying circumstances was in most cases nothing less than heroic. The once-mighty triple-deck *Tonnant*, though reduced to a hulk, kept her blackened colors flying from the splintered stump of her mainmast until the morning of July 3, when British sailors managed to board her, finding the decks littered with 200 of her crew and officers dead or wounded, out of a complement of 608. In addition five French ships of the line were entirely dismasted, while two others had lost two masts each. Of these the British were later able to sail six back, jury-rigged, as prizes to Gibraltar for repairs, and recommissioning into the Royal Navy. (The most famous of these, the *Spartiate*, was manned by the British against the French seven years later at Trafalgar.) The British captured and burned what was left of them.[23]

Nor were the British spared the inevitable rigors of battle. The *Bellerophon* was entirely dismasted by French guns—though she had never surrendered, nor indeed had any of the other British ships. Several others had lost some of their masts.[24] The British lost 218 men killed and 678 wounded. Admiral Nelson, with a head wound, later received a peerage for his gallant role.

Given the state of the French fleet, it was hardly surprising that its

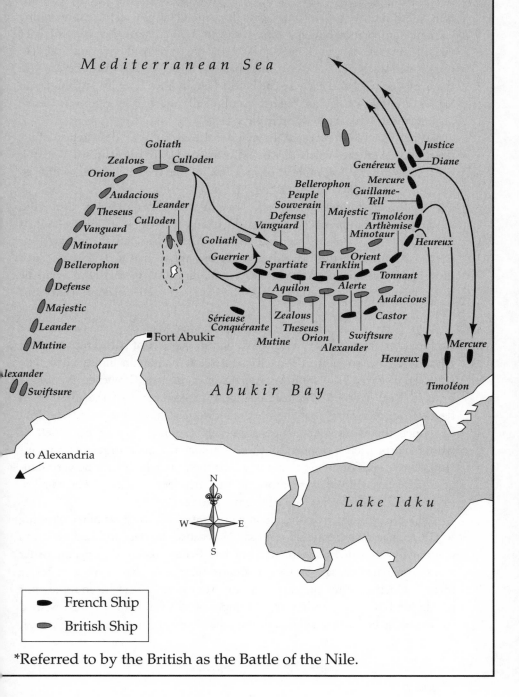

The Battle of Abukir Bay,* August 1, 1798

Mediterranean Sea

Abukir Bay

Lake Idku

Fort Abukir

to Alexandria

Goliath
Zealous   Culloden
Orion
Audacious
Theseus   Leander
Vanguard   Culloden
Minotaur
Bellerophon
Defense
Majestic
Leander
Mutine

Alexander
Swiftsure

Goliath
Guerrier
Sérieuse
Conquérante
Spartiate
Aquilon
Zealous
Theseus
Mutine   Orion
Alexander

Bellerophon
Peuple
Souverain
Defense
Vanguard
Majestic
Franklin
Orient
Alerte
Audacious
Castor
Swiftsure

Justice
Généreux   Diane
Mercure
Guillame-
Tell
Timoléon
Arthèmise
Minotaur
Heureux
Tonnant

Heureux   Mercure
Timoléon

N
W   E
S

British Ship

French Ship

British Ship

*Referred to by the British as the Battle of the Nile.

casualty figures were shocking. The French put their own dead at seventeen hundred killed or drowned, fifteen hundred wounded, and another three thousand taken prisoner. Of the eight thousand men manning the French fleet during the battle, only eighteen hundred escaped unscathed.[25] In addition to Admiral Brueys, French casualties included nine captains, including Captain Casabianca and his nine-year-old son. Despite Napoleon's later vicious remarks about Brueys, the forty-five-year-old vice admiral had fought courageously once hostilities had commenced. Wounded severely in the head and the hand early in the battle, half an hour later his left thigh and leg were blown off by an English cannonball, and still he refused to leave his quarterdeck where he soon expired.[26]

When Napoleon received the news of the almost total destruction of his fleet, he was, in the words of Louis Bourrienne, "simply stunned," it took some time for the full implications to sink in. Never in his career willing to accept responsibility for anything that went wrong—whether on land or sea—and instead quick to shift all blame to others, Napoleon naturally did so again now. In his reports to Paris he claimed it was all Brueys's fault. If he had only "obeyed orders" and entered Alexandria "within twenty-four hours" as directed, this would never have happened. Of course, no such orders had ever been given to the vice admiral. "If in this fatal event he made mistakes," Napoleon closed, "he expiated them through a glorious death."[27]

On Napoleon's orders Brueys had in fact had the harbor entrance explored for channels deep enough to permit his fleet of battleships to enter Alexandria. All soundings proved negative, as Napoleon himself had then reported to Paris. Four months after the naval disaster, however, Napoleon ordered Rear Admiral Ganteaume—now in command of the diminished fleet—to inform Paris that the fleet could indeed have entered Alexandria! For once the weak Ganteaume stood his ground, defying his chief. "I would accept such a responsibility only under the most urgent of circumstances, my opinion being that entry into the port will always be very dangerous for any ship drawing more than twenty feet of water." The smallest of the French fleet drew close to twenty-two feet.[28]

The other alternative Napoleon had mentioned, the possibility of going to Corfu, had been rendered impossible because the fleet still had not been completely unloaded or victualed, nor had Brueys received a specific order from Bonaparte to sail to Corfu, unless threatened by "a very superior force," which was not the case at all on August 1. Instead he could anchor in Abukir Bay if Alexandria proved impossible. Even if Brueys had wished to set sail, as he had considered doing when the British were first sighted, it had proved impossible because 3,000 men were on shore. With nearly empty water casks and food supplies sufficient for a few days at sea, no responsible fleet commander would have ordered his ships to put to sea for Corfu.

Nevertheless, when later reporting to the Directory, Napoleon persisted in accusing Brueys of having disobeyed orders by not entering the old port of Alexandria, which he could have done—nonsense, of course— and of remaining at anchor in Abukir without taking sufficient defensive precautions, which was partially true. Abukir had not been properly fortified, nor had the beach, and frigates had not been assigned to coastal waters to maintain a lookout for a powerful English fleet known to be in the vicinity (although Napoleon himself thought Nelson was blockading Malta). Finally Bonaparte again repeated the blatant lie to the Directory that, "Upon leaving Alexandria on [July 5] I ordered the admiral to enter the port of that city within twenty-four hours, or if he found that he could not do so, to promptly discharge the artillery and matériel, and sail for Corfu."[29] Napoleon continued, asserting that he left Alexandria believing that his (nonexistent) orders had been followed. As Bourrienne reminds us:

> The full truth was never to be found in Bonaparte's dispatches when that truth was even slightly unfavorable and when he was in a position to dissimulate. He was adept at disguising, altering, or suppressing it whenever possible. Frequently he even changed the dispatches of others and then had them printed, whenever their view differed from his own or might cast some aspersion on his reputation and actions. . . . He never hesitated to disguise the truth when he could make it embellish his own glory. He considered it sheer stupidity not to do so.[30]

So of course Napoleon failed to inform Paris that he had ignored Brueys's numerous pleas—and those of other officials—to revictual the fleet, just as he did not mention the fact that the navy had been weakened physically by living on reduced rations for some time before the battle took place. Nor did he mention that Admiral Brueys had nearly died of dysentery and was still very weak on the day of the battle. And naturally Napoleon could not reveal to Paris that he had failed to obtain the basic naval intelligence required for the commanding admiral under his orders, and that he had subsequently dispatched an entire battle fleet to a country without even knowing whether the ships could pass into the safety of that country's only harbor.

The full implications of the naval defeat soon began to make themselves felt. Without a navy, and with the loss of his important superior officers (Brueys was dead, and Villeneuve and Decrès had managed to escape to sea), Napoleon and his entire army now found themselves literally marooned. All around them lay vast stretches of remote, barren desert. The only other way out of Egypt was to the northeast, up the coast through the Turkish province of Syria, but large garrisons of Turkish troops blocked the way at Acre, Damascus, and Aleppo. Napoleon had informed his brother Joseph back in July that once in Cairo he hoped to return to France "within a couple of months." That now seemed impossible with the destruction of France's Mediterranean fleet. The entire sea lay open to the unchallenged supremacy of the British Royal Navy, which could do as it pleased, while the only other squadrons in the eastern Mediterranean, those of Russia and Turkey, were now against the French as well. This in turn meant British warships successfully sealing the Egyptian coast, preventing Napoleon not only from escaping from Egypt as he had been envisaging but also from receiving badly needed reinforcements, munitions, and supplies from France. One month after their arrival, Napoleon and his army were—to all intents and purposes—virtual prisoners in Egypt.

In the absence of Admiral Brueys it fell to Divisional General Bonaparte to notify the next of kin of the death of his commanding officers, and on September 4 he duly wrote to the father—himself a vice admiral of the French navy—of Henri-Alexandre Thévenard, captain of the *Aquilon*:

> Your son was killed by a cannonball while commanding on the quarter-deck. I now fulfill a very sad duty in informing you of this, Citizen General. But he died without suffering and with honor. That is the only consolation that can lessen a father's pain. All of us here are subject to the same fate. . . . Fortunate are those who die on the field of battle. They live eternally in the memory of posterity.[31]

It was a rare thoughtful moment for Napoleon. But it soon passed, for there were other, more pressing matters to cope with, such as extricating himself from his self-inflicted Egyptian debacle.

CHAPTER 9

In the Shadow of Defeat

*They [the Directors] have a grudge against me and hate me;
they will let me perish here.*

he real impact of the French invasion army's total isolation was apparent to one and all. English cruisers flagrantly patrolling Egyptian waters and blockading Alexandria were a constant reminder of just how drastically the French situation had changed, including the diminished likelihood of their being rescued by another French fleet. For no individual was their new, painful position more dramatically clear than for General Kléber, governor of Alexandria.

"We must renounce any further communication by sea, mon cher Général," he informed Menou at Rosetta on August 15, "until the English fleet disappears. . . . Therefore, keep your port closed until more favorable circumstances permit. . . . Here we are expecting to be bombarded any time."[1] Rosetta was one of the two outlets of the Nile and principal victualling point for both the navy and army. There was no longer a French navy to protect it, and with its garrison of only six hundred men and "neither artillery, munitions, nor money," it obviously couldn't protect itself. It was almost too much for General Menou, now at his wits' end, who requested that he be returned "to the head of my division rather than being left to go crazy in this place."[2] But for all his anxieties, Jacques (later Abdullah, when he converted to Islam) Menou still had enough consideration to think about the much more seriously ailing Kléber and his even more unenviable situation at Alexandria directly facing the English. "You must keep your spirits up and not let the problems depress you," he wrote on August 4.

But the epidemic of insubordination in the navy before and during the Battle of Abukir was prevalent in the army as well, and when on August 18 Berthier ordered Menou to hand over the gunboats and armed vessels under his command to newly promoted Rear Admiral Perrée (to be dispatched up the Nile), he blasted the chief of staff: "I have . . . nothing at all here and now you want to take away my gunboats and vessels, my sole means of defense. . . . I formally refuse."[3]

From his headquarters in Cairo, Napoleon did his best to conceal the gravity of the situation and the extent of the catastrophe. Writing to the French governor of Corfu, General Chabot, shortly after receiving news of Brueys's defeat and ordering him to assist Rear Admiral Villeneuve (who he erroneously thought had sailed to Corfu) "to begin to reorganize a new fleet" with which to relieve Egypt, he nevertheless assured him that "all goes perfectly well here."[4]

Following his victorious entry into Cairo on July 22, Napoleon had immediately begun setting up an entirely new government and administration for the country, including the naming of military governors as each new province was conquered. All operations were run from his luxurious new GHQ in the former palace of one Elfi Bey, which included Bonaparte's own residential wing, a sprawling structure built around a large courtyard, in reality a vast park of mosaic-lined fountains and tropical gardens complete with nightingales, surrounded and enclosed by elaborate Turkish galleries. Its massive walls were as strong as a fortress, with open spaces and gardens on either side of the main complex, while behind the palace long gardens extended down to the Nile. The palace faced the enormous, vaguely triangular Esbekiya Square, which, as events soon proved, provided an ideal field of fire in the event of an emergency, as well as an excellent area for reviewing and staging troops and mounting artillery batteries. Given the confines of the capital, it was probably the best strategically situated mansion in the Cairo area, with the added attraction of having larger buildings nearby that could be taken over by Berthier's large staff and Napoleon's elite personal guard, his Guides.

As head of the army of occupation, Napoleon decided to run the country on three different levels: the military, to "pacify" unconquered areas, followed by their consolidation by a military governor; through Muslim institutions and their officials (primarily over local, municipal, or provincial, and religious affairs); and ultimately by means of a purely French civil administration that reported, and was directly responsible to, Napoleon alone.

The military phase of operations was more or less self-explanatory, but the Muslim-Egyptian level required some consideration. Napoleon created a new puppet nine-man Egyptian divan, or municipal council, to cope with the daily administration of the capital and its population of three hundred thousand. This council was responsible for assuring the city's food supplies, policing, local tax collection, and public sanitation, while at the same time giving the Cairene residents the appearance of maintaining their own traditional institutions independent of the French.

First convened at five o'clock on the afternoon of July 25, only three days after the victorious French had swept into Cairo, the new divan was ordered to take the "Oath of Allegiance" to the French, promising "to do nothing to harm the army's interests." Time and again Napoleon insisted on the necessity of respecting local institutions and of establishing good public relations. The divan was to begin functioning at once, meeting daily at noon thereafter.[5] The new commandant of Cairo, General Dupuy, in addition to thousands of French troops, was given five Turkish companies with which to police the city's streets and markets. Similar divans and Egyptian police companies were gradually established in each newly secured province of the country, but with the difference that an intendant— in fact an Egyptian Copt*—was named to second the military governor in Egyptian administration and the collection of taxes, he in turn seconded by a French understudy who would one day replace him.[6] Ultimately there would be sixteen such provincial intendants under the orders of an intendant-general in Cairo, who was directly under French orders.

In addition to the military administration of the country, Napoleon created a powerful three-man Administrative Commission to sit in Cairo, composed of Monge, Berthollet, and Charles Magallon.[7] They were in charge of sequestering all Mameluke property and funds in the country, of collecting the nation's taxes, "direct and indirect," and of all national property and warehouses in general. At the same time Napoleon gave them the authority to appoint the various officials and subcommissions required to execute this vast undertaking, which included the naming of the intendants. These three men were to receive a special, separate civil salary for this time-consuming work (although Monge would soon also be appointed to a separate scientific task—as director of the Egyptian Institute). The commission carried out its tasks efficiently, seizing, organizing, and administering vast

*Christian.

amounts of property, while appointing the new intendant-general and the first six intendants (chiefly tax collectors) in August.

While ordering the seizure of all Mameluke property, including tens of thousands of their slaves, as "national property," Napoleon tried to assure the Egyptian population that as a part of his national policy, he would respect and maintain their historical institutions, including the traditional *shar'ia* civil courts. He also assured them that their title to personal real estate would be respected; however, innovations would be introduced.

What the French needed most desperately at this stage was hard cash. Thus the pressing work given Monge's Administrative Commission to seize all the government warehouses, whose contents would be sold and converted to cash or else—if in the form of useful commodities, such as food and clothing—distributed among the French army.[8] Taxes and customs duties would have to be collected, of course, and new money minted.

But as both Ibrahim and Murad Bey had managed to escape with most of the city's treasury holdings, beginning July 31 Napoleon issued a series of orders demanding immediate payment of more than three million French francs, chiefly from the wealthiest merchants of the country. All this was exclusive of large amounts seized from Mamelukes or extorted from important merchants of Cairo (those who monopolized the soap, sugar, and cloth markets), and of course exclusive of the regular tax collections, which were to follow.[9]

Nor could the army, with its own special needs, be forgotten. Napoleon ordered the creation of new barracks and more important, four new military hospitals for the Cairo area, totaling six hundred beds, to be operational within one week.[10] The construction of more large ovens by the engineers, to help feed the hungry troops, was also given top priority. What is more, Napoleon insisted on bread of "the highest quality." If the troops were well fed, he argued, they would not complain. And the men thus were not to be shortchanged by thieving civilian commissioners. The problem of theft in and by the army was rampant, but of particular immediate concern were Egyptian horses stolen or seized by French troops in or after battle, which were badly needed by the still largely unmounted French cavalry. Once in a while the Order of the Day contained lighter elements, though certainly not intended as such by the humorless Berthier: "Brigadier General Belliard has lost his greyhound. He asks anyone knowing anything of its whereabouts to notify him."[11]

Initial troop dispositions included Desaix's division camped upriver, south of Giza (preparatory to launching the attack against Murad Bey and his army); while General Bon's division occupied Cairo proper, supported by Menou's old division in nearby "Old Cairo" and Dugua's Division at the capital's river port of Bulaq; while on the eastern side of Cairo, Reynier's division straddled the desert route to Suez. Many units of these divisions would soon be dispersed in all directions in the expanding pacification effort. Meanwhile, in addition to everything else, Chief of Staff Berthier was given the complex and time-consuming task of organizing a mammoth central army camp at Giza, on the other side of the Nile, where hospitals, artillery and transport parks, and engineering and munitions depots were being built and fortified.

A constant flow of complaints about unruly French troops and even officers continued to reach Berthier, including confidential reports about seditious acts and materials encouraged and distributed by officers—all critical of Napoleon's Egyptian campaign. Even the daily routine of administering the army proved difficult; Dugua, Reynier, and Desaix regularly sending in sloppy reports or none at all, leaving Berthier frustrated and ignorant of troop levels and movements.[12]

Furthermore, the hitherto-much-praised Ordonnateur en Chef Sucy was in charge of supplying an army spread over thousands of square miles. Soon complaints started reaching GHQ that matériel and food shipments frequently were not reaching their destinations, particularly along the coast between Damietta and Alexandria. It would take several months before the full extent of Sucy's illegal seizure and sale of army property to the black market was fully disclosed and documented.

Meanwhile, with the regrouping of the army at the Egyptian capital, Napoleon now had to arrange for the complete subjugation of the country, for despite his letters to the Directory not even Rosetta and Damietta were secured. In fact the route the army had just taken, from Alexandria to Cairo, was under daily attack, involving French convoys. Even several army couriers dispatched to and from headquarters were killed—including one of Napoleon's favorite aides-de-camp, Julien—requiring beefed-up military escorts. While General Menou was still trying to cope with Egyptian dissidence around Rosetta, including the Nile passage up to Rahmaniya, General Vial was being dispatched to Damietta to secure that port and its valuable food depots. Zayoncheck was ordered to Menouf and the Delta to establish a French presence there, preparatory to securing the entire Damietta branch of the river and the interior, and expanding eastward.

In other words, despite his great victory at the Battle of the Pyramids, apart from a few strategic positions, including Alexandria and Cairo, the country was openly at war with the French army. No area was safe from uncoordinated small attacks. In addition there remained the two organized Mameluke armies still at large, those of Ibrahim Bey to the northeast of Cairo and of Murad Bey, following the Nile and network of canals south to al-Fayyum, Asyut, and even Aswan.

As for troops, of the thirty-three thousand or so men with whom Napoleon had set out fom Abukir Bay at the beginning of July, only about twenty thousand were actually available (with perhaps another six thousand in hospitals, on garrison duty, or otherwise detached). Berthier presented these shocking figures to Bonaparte on August 18. The results and implications were inescapable: He had lost seven thousand men in less than two months. Needless to say, the report was not passed on to Paris.

Despite the crude reality of having invaded and seized a foreign country, or perhaps *because* of this blatant aggression, Napoleon in later years emphasized what another generation would refer to as the French *"mission civilisatrice"* in the backward land of the pharaohs. He brought modern medicine, he boasted, not to mention a focus of attention on Egyptological studies, through the French discovery of the Rosetta stone in 1799, by Captain Bouchard, and artist Vivant Denon's discoveries at numerous splendid temple ruins at Thebes, Luxor, and Karnak (including the famous obelisks brought back to France and placed in the Tuileries Gardens and the Place de la Concorde). But perhaps Napoleon's greatest and most persistent personal claim concerned the founding of the Institut d'Egypte, in his eyes his finest civilizing accomplishment.[13]

Outwardly the creation of the Egyptian Institute on August 22, 1798, appeared a public relations contrivance, something to look good in the eyes of the Directory, the French people, and history, as well as to impress the Egyptians. It was in fact much more, directly and indirectly, thanks to the participation and work of Monge, Berthollet, and their colleagues. Monge in particular, who now saw Bonaparte almost daily in Cairo, had gradually influenced him as to the practical importance of having intellectuals (as opposed to politicians) serving as a guiding force in the formulation of a government and its direction and implementation. Bonaparte, who always preferred to think of himself as a *savant,* if somewhat *manqué* (he even signed most of his military orders with his title as member of the French Institute), likewise chose to associate with these intellectuals and scientists in his spare hours, rather than with rough soldiers. After witnessing all the work done by the scientific committee on behalf of war matériel production during the Revolution, both Bonaparte and Monge felt that these same scientists could be of similar use in this campaign.

Officially the institute had three general purposes: to propagate modern knowledge and technology throughout Egypt; to carry out research on natural history, industry, and the history of Egypt; and "to advise the government on the various problems put to it."[14] The last was in fact its principal task, serving as Egypt's first fully organized think tank on scientific matters.

The institute included four general divisions: mathematics (which included Bonaparte and Monge), physics, political economy (including former Executive Director Tallien, who had saved Josephine's life), and literature and the arts (including Vivant Denon, the future director of the Louvre). Short of qualified members, Bonaparte enlisted members of his staff and of the army.

The full-time civilian members were given quarters in the sequestered Mameluke palaces of Qassim Bey and Hassan Kashaf, a couple of miles south of the Elfi palace.[15] These two palaces served as living quarters for Berthollet and Monge, among others. They also housed botanical, physical, and chemistry laboratories, all the scientific collections made in the field, not to mention halls for the study and collection of Egyptian antiquities, as well as an already impressive research library in Latin, Greek, and Arabic.

The institute convened on August 23, with Monge, its first president, introducing the opening ceremonies, though it was clearly dominated by Bonaparte. He immediately set about assigning his advisory board its initial prosaic tasks—to improve army bread ovens for greater efficiency and productivity, study possible substitutes for hops in the preparation of beer for the troops, find the best means of purifying drinking water taken from the Nile, study the most practical choice of mills to be used in Egypt (water- or wind-powered), prepare for the production of gunpowder using Egyptian saltpeter deposits, along with the nonscientific but much more important question of what sort of judicial (civil and criminal) and educational systems to adopt in Egypt.[16] Bonaparte himself appeared at the institute several times a week, a pleasant diversion and civilized break from GHQ.

The institute proved of considerable practical help to Napoleon in coping with the technical problems facing him and the army, at the same time confirming the irrefutable establishment of Gaspard Monge as his second-in-command, on the civilian scene at least. As already noted, Monge, as a senior member of the separate political Administrative Commission, controlled most of the "native" administrative apparatus of Egypt. He now coordinated all scientific research in the country as well.

To go back a bit, after the Abukir naval disaster, the celebrations of Napoleon's twenty-ninth birthday on August 15 were hardly festive: Not even his nine aides-de-camp, including his stepson, Eugène de Beauharnais, or his ever-ailing and morose younger brother Louis Bonaparte, were able to offer more than perfunctory best wishes. The shadow of the naval defeat seemed to hang over everything. The drastically altered situation of Napoleon's army and position in the Middle East, with Egypt now literally isolated by a powerful British naval presence on the loose and unchallenged in the Mediterranean, forced Napoleon to scrap all his plans, including those for a campaign against India.

Napoleon had hoped to return to France with the conquest of Malta and the seizure of Egypt to his credit—and, as the conquering hero of the hour, seize the government. That was now impossible, the destruction of his fleet offsetting all previous victories. He needed fresh conquests, something really startling, before returning to Paris. What could be more dramatic than the seizure of the Holy Land, Damascus, and Constantinople itself?

The fact of the matter is that the publicly victorious Bonaparte had entered his newly captured capital of Cairo privately an unhappy, indeed disgruntled man, as no conquering hero should have been. Bourrienne and Monge were among the few who knew the reason for Napoleon's funk. To be sure, he found an Egypt with far greater and more complex problems than he had anticipated, including the total miscalculation of the resistance of the Egyptian people. But just as the lovesick Berthier was officially asking permission to return to Europe and the arms of his lovely Italian mistress, Countess Visconti, so too Napoleon now wanted to return to France because of—but not to—Josephine.

It all stemmed from a remark by one of his young aides-de-camp, Junot, regarding Josephine and the flagrant affair she was still having with Hippolyte Charles. To Napoleon, who had thought that nightmare was over, it came as a severe blow. A much-embarrassed Julien and General Berthier, when confronted by an irate Napoleon, had admitted that everyone was talking about it and that they had personally seen Josephine and Charles together often during the Italian campaign.[17] "All has been revealed," Napoleon wrote to his brother. "It's a sad situation to have so many conflicting sentiments about a single person in one's heart."[18] The situation was eating away at Napoleon, giving him no moment of rest, and—combined with the disastrous naval news from Alexandria—proved a double shock with which he found it hard to come to grips. He had to revise his thinking yet again.

He had of course burned his political bridges in Paris and had no real friends in the Directory. In any event, they would be in no particular hurry to come to his rescue, he believed, sighing aloud that they had "a grudge against me and hate me; they will let me perish here."[19] Even if they wanted to prepare a fresh fleet to relieve him, he had stripped the Mediterranean of most of its better warships; others would take time to build, repair, or somehow replace. And would events in Europe even permit the Directory to dispatch the fresh troops and vessels to Egypt, leaving French shores exposed and unprotected? In fact, Napoleon had to admit to himself what he never would publicly—that he had made a hash of his great Egyptian campaign, the greatest strategic and military gaffe of his life, because he had been cocky, headstrong, and thought he had all the answers, just like the preening Parisian political peacocks he so detested. He had not acted, weighed, and planned this campaign like a mature, professional soldier.

Then there was the problem here with the Mameluke armies, which he had hoped literally to annihilate on the battlefield but which had largely escaped, Ibrahim to the northeast and Murad to the south. Bonaparte found himself coping with an army of perhaps 20,000 deployable men dispersed into various smaller units all over the country. Desaix was already dispatched up the Nile, while Napoleon held two divisions in and around Cairo. Meanwhile, Kléber was in the coastal area. Far to the eastern side of the delta, General Dugua with Zayoncheck and a mere 4,274 men, was given the onerous task of trying to clear and pacify a wild region hitherto unknown to Napoleon, around Menouf.[20] Farther to the northeast, around Salheyeh, Reynier was trying to coordinate his actions with Dugua to clear that region of strong bedouin forces, at the same time securing the Damietta branch of the Nile for flotillas via canal to Damietta and Lake Manzalah. All this was to be anchored by new French forts and depots at Salheyeh and Peluse, to be used as a base from which to launch a possible drive up the Mediterranean to Syria. Then, of course, the large area of the delta between Damietta and Rosetta would also have to be quelled. As for General Dumas's cavalry, at this stage limited to 1,677 mounted men (with a small dromedary, or camel, corps being added), it was needed everywhere at once in this vast desert, where cavalry mobility was of far greater importance than in Europe—yet another major miscalculation by Napoleon.

The result was recalcitrance, intransigence, frustration, anger, and despair among a majority of the brigadiers and colonels in the field, rebelling against their impossible tasks, dispersed hither and thither and incapable of stanching resistance permanently, with little firepower and practically nonexistent logistical support: Supplies and reinforcements still were not reaching the army, hampered by the lack of accurate maps.

"Who could dare deny that a general sense of disgust pervaded the entire army and that the sole desire of its leaders, like everyone else, was to return to France: The number of requests to leave was truly heartbreaking," eyewitness Bourrienne lamented.[21] Discontent continued to swell, and the presence of Berthier's name at the top of that list did not help matters. When the valuable if fiery cavalry commander Gen. Alexandre Dumas* openly rebelled and quarreled with Napoleon before fellow officers, it was too much. The number of brigadiers opposing this campaign is not clear, but Bourrienne acknowledged that the feeling was "general," and it appears to have involved a large number. This of course trickled down to the junior officers and the men in the ranks, and the result was wanton bad discipline, refusal to execute orders, and at times chaos; open rebellion was averted only because the troops and their officers had no superior authority above Bonaparte to appeal to. In any event, there was certainly no place to flee to but the desert. The hours were long, the tasks unending, and the conditions appalling.

The men in the ranks balked at the introduction of rice, unfamiliar to them, as a main staple substitute. Bread would finally be available within the next few weeks, but not wine and eau-de-vie. There were coffee and sugar, however, but almost no cheese, another French staple. The principal source of drinking water, frequently the Nile, was hardly a healthy substitute for French wines (as the increasing number of dysentery cases resulting from its consumption dramatically attested). Just as bad, there was not enough European entertainment, and of course very few unmarried European women for these thousands of frustrated soldiers. Thus when officers and men were not working round the clock, there was little for them to do but sit around coffeehouses, gambling and grumbling. And since the men knew that reinforcements would not be in sight for months—perhaps years—to come, the grumbling soon turned ominous, focusing on the men's generals, and ultimately on the one general who had thought up this crackpot expedition in the first place. "Anxiety, unhappiness, nostalgia [for France] afflicted nearly everyone. . . . The positive illusion of the expedition had disappeared from the very beginning. Only the reality of the situation now remained: it was sad," bemoaned Bourrienne. How many "bitter complaints" there were from all units, and "these continuous complaints, without measure or moderation . . . greatly upset Bonaparte. . . . And that, I can say without the slightest exaggeration, is the truth of the matter."[22]

The full significance of this debacle was just beginning to make its impact on Napoleon. The military aspects he could not discuss with his

---

*Father of the future novelist of the same name.

otherwise sympathetic friend Monge, who was busy trying to solve the institute's problems, including the necessity of manufacturing replacements for their own dwindling supply of munitions. The French would in fact have to provide everything here themselves, something Napoleon had not anticipated when the sea channels were still open. And thus Napoleon found himself entirely isolated, apart from some quiet moments with the ever optimistic Monge. He remained the harried, hard-driven, frustrated, at times anguished young military commander who had gotten himself into very deep water from which he could rely on no one else to extricate him. The magnificent Elfi palace had become a torture chamber.

Outwardly, however, his show of confidence continued, as troops were reviewed and festivities celebrated in the grand manner. One of the principal planks of Napoleon's program was of course the observation of Egyptian and Muslim traditions and holy days, which included the age-old annual celebration marking the flooding of the Nile, dating back to pharaonic times. And although—with casualty and damage reports still arriving from Alexandria—he was hardly in a festive mood, at 6:00 A.M. on August 18, just four days after his return to Cairo, General Bonaparte, attended by three divisional generals, the general staff, and a bevy of brigadiers, Col. Louis Bonaparte and Eugène de Beauharnais, along with the highest Muslim dignitaries of the capital, reached Madkias. There the swelling river waters were about to break the main dike leading to the irrigation canals, officially opening the Feast of the Inundation of the Nile, as salvos from French gunboats and Citadel cannon announced the arrival of Bonaparte and his colorful retinue, attended by traditional Egyptian music and Muslim prayers, as workers dug away at the earth dike to release the first floodwaters of the year. Bonaparte—in full-dress uniform, covered by the mullah's traditional black robes—stood by, throwing handfuls of coins to the crowd of thousands; then he distributed caftans to the thirty-eight senior Muslim officials present.

Two days later fresh celebrations, known as the Feast of the Prophet Muhammad, began at the Elfi palace, continuing with illuminations at night and a great torchlit procession from the different quarters of the city, religious prayers being chanted throughout the night and for the next few days, "making an infernal racket," according to the none-too-tolerant Major Detroye. The festivities concluded on August 24 with a series of spectacles, as trainers of monkeys and bears entertained the public before Napoleon's reviewing stand, while snake charmers lured their friends out of baskets, women and children singing all the while, and the French garrison firing thundering celebratory salvos as the army's dashing cavalry and infantry units, accompanied by French army bands, executed military drills in Esbekiya Square. Following a sumptuous state feast in the palace, all gathered in the square, filled with tens of thousands of spectators, to watch the concluding fireworks display prepared by the army engineers—which regrettably fizzled due to the poor quality of powder.[23] Although the distraction offered by these twin feasts was brief, Bonaparte, determined to the very end to win over the Egyptian peasantry and Muslims in general, continued to do all in his power to show his respect for their religious beliefs.

Even before the celebrations concluded, on the eighteenth Napoleon had ordered Rear Admiral Perrée to convoy Brigadier General Marmont down the Nile to take charge of all fluvial communications between Rahmaniya and Alexandria in particular, where the more-than-one-hundred-foot-wide canal was beginning to fill and would now be of critical importance for the shipment of supplies and men between Alexandria and Rosetta and ultimately Cairo. Constant Bedouin attacks along the canal, by land and boat, still rendered it perilous even for strong French military escorts. What is more, the Arabs, intent on foiling the French invaders, kept destroying the banks of the canal in numerous places, requiring emergency work details directed by General Caffarelli's hard-pressed engineers. It was a demanding job, but Marmont was a capable and energetic young officer, who had been personally instructed by Napoleon (to whom he remained completely loyal throughout), that "you will write me in the greatest detail . . . to inform me on the situation regarding the English and how our fleet behaved during the battle [of Abukir]."[24]

Meanwhile Napoleon was sending his personal report to the Executive Directory in Paris (in duplicate form by a variety of messengers and small vessels) regarding the great naval clash with Nelson, somehow never actually mentioning the disaster itself, instead just suddenly informing them that the French had suffered some "800 wounded" (seventeen hundred had already been officially listed in Alexandria; other estimates suggested a much higher figure) and claimed he did not yet know the number of French killed in action, "but I am assured it is not very high" (although twelve hundred corpses had already been recovered). He praised Rear Admiral Villeneuve for escaping with two ships and two frigates, and also "the brave" Capt. Dupetit Thouars and Captain Casabianca, "who died calmly and courageously in the midst of the fire [that swept his ship]," but implied strong criticism of Brueys through praise of Ganteaume, who he said (quite incorrectly) had "opposed Brueys's tactics." Even Napoleon could not ignore the reality of the battle's consequences, however, as he instructed the Directory "to gather all our warships at Toulon, Malta, Ancona, and Corfu in order to prepare a fresh fleet" to be dispatched at once to Egypt with supplies and thousands of reinforcements.[25] That said it all.

In a similar attempt to put up a good front, he wrote to General Kléber two days later, assuring him that "my health has never been better. All goes very well indeed here, and the country is beginning to submit to our rule. . . . Every month [they had been in Egypt less than two months], every day, our position improves as a result of the proper measures we are taking to feed the Army and because of the fortifications we are raising." Then he closed: "I salute and embrace you with all my heart."[26]

That was in fact the last fond embrace Kléber, as governor of Alexandria, was to receive from Bonaparte. A series of acrimonious communications between the two began immediately. "The English do not permit our vessels either to enter or leave the port; commerce is stagnating, and customs therefore produce nothing whatsoever," Kléber informed Napoleon, and therein lay the crux of the problem: money, or rather, the lack thereof.[27] According to Bonaparte's principles, all maintenance costs for occupying a conquered people, in this case those of Alexandria, should invariably be borne by the conquered. But with the enforced closure of that port, most income naturally dried up. And now unexpectedly Kléber was required to find barracks for several thousand additional men (seventeen hundred wounded, plus three thousand prisoners shortly to be repatriated by the English, not to mention another eighteen hundred unharmed survivors), who would otherwise have been housed, clothed, and fed by the navy (at sea). What is more, the naval personnel—including officers—now under Rear Admiral Ganteaume's command, refused to comply with Kléber's orders. Kléber described them as rowdy, undisciplined, and arrogant, "men accustomed to living in a state of disorder, men familiar with every sort of vice," and he summed up the navy as "an infected cadaver."[28] In addition, Kléber informed Bonaparte that not only were his own army troops owed some three hundred thousand francs in back pay, but that normal monthly expenses required another two hundred thousand—all of which was nonexistent—and thus "we find ourselves at this time in a state of the most dire penury." Yet he had to meet these financial obligations, as well as those of the navy, and the building of fortifications against the British and the repairs of the Alexandria-Rahmaniya Canal. "It would be most unjust on your part, Citizen General, if you were to take as a sign of weakness or discouragement the vehemence with which I point out our needs and situation here," the otherwise tough but now bedridden Kléber protested. "As for myself, . . . you can count on my full support in any situation, and my obedience to every order you give me."[29] Napoleon instantly took him at his word and demanded a "loan" of five hundred thousand francs from local merchants. Kléber was astonished. At this very moment his reduced circumstances were forcing him to attempt to transfer a thousand wounded sailors to General Menou in Rosetta, because of the lack of food, medicines, money, and facilities in Alexandria, only to have them refused in turn by Menou, who was in equally dire financial straits.[30] To this addtional bad news, a daunted Kléber replied, "Only a bit of fabulous luck and our own national genius can extricate us now from this state of misery."[31]

So great were the immediate medical needs of the hospitals there, not to mention the increasing demands on food and clothing for the troops and sailors and the bills from hard-put local merchants, that a desperate Kléber unilaterally seized 100,000 francs Napoleon had just sent to Ordonnateur LeRoy for ship repairs and outfitting of the navy. Writing a week later, Kléber informed him, "Citizen General, if you really cannot appreciate what I have been trying to explain to you about how very critical our situation is here, then my contravention of your orders will no doubt displease you."[32] What is more, he pointed out, Ganteaume's unruly grounded sailors were now completely out of hand, ravaging Alexandria and terrifying the Egyptians, though fortunately several hundred had been reorganized into an infantry unit known as the "Nautical Legion" and seconded to the army. On top of everything, the troops still were not receiving their daily bread requirements and engineering commander Caffarelli's new defense plans for Alexandria were wholly unsatisfactory. Kléber, who did not have a second-in-command capable of relieving him of numerous anxieties, and in constant pain from his head wound, was at his wit's end. Finally, on September 3 he wrote to Bonaparte: "I see that my conduct does not comply with your orders. I therefore request permission to return to the command of my division."[33]

All this was too much for Bonaparte, who had the whole of Egypt's problems to contend with. In his reply to Kléber, he complained that the administration of Alexandria had cost twice as much as the rest of the army combined, which of course was utter nonsense, and implied sharply that Kléber was the most incompetent general in the French army. He ordered him to "return the [diverted] hundred thousand francs to the Navy immediately and not to contradict the dispositions I take hereafter."[34] On receipt of this stinging rebuke, Kléber fired back: "I desire, for my own satisfaction, that you have the Army Paymaster give you the receipts and expenses of this place to study. I do not think you will be able to disapprove of a single item." He closed with, "I must insist that you allow me to rejoin my division immediately."[35] Then, after receiving yet another sharp accusation of gross financial incompetence, the proud Kléber snapped: "When you wrote that letter, Citizen General, *you forgot that you were holding a historical record in your hands and also that you were addressing Kléber. . . . Accordingly, I hereby await by return courier, the order not only to relieve me of my functions here but also as a member of your army, until such time as you make yourself better acquainted with the real facts."*[36] After an unrepentant reply from Bonaparte, without permission Kléber simply handed over command of Alexandria to General Manscourt, his incompetent second-in-command, followed by a request that shook Napoleon, who now knew that he had indeed gone too far. "Today the state of my health and the consequences of my wound no longer permit me to associate myself with your brilliant career and campaign here, and I am thus asking General Caffarelli to obtain permission from you for me to return to France."[37] Kléber's resignation finally brought repentance and soothing words from the commander in chief of the Army of the Orient, with as close to an apology as Napoleon Bonaparte ever made to anyone: "I sincerely hope you will have a speedy recovery and that you appreciate the price I attach to your friendship. I am afraid we both got a little hot under the collar. . . . My respect for you is at least equal to that which you on occasion have shown for me." In closing, he said he hoped to see Kléber in Cairo in a few days.[38] As usual, Napoleon's language was easily open to interpretation.

Although the differences between the two proud men were partially resolved, at least superficially, and the faithful Kléber ultimately did withdraw his resignation from the army, their personal and professional relationships were never again the same, with nothing capable of dispelling "the deep aversion they continued to have for each other," as Bourrienne acknowledged.[39] Kléber's hitherto unwavering trust in Napoleon Bonaparte had been shattered forever, which Napoleon was to reciprocate with a vengeance when he abandoned the country the following year, naming Kléber his successor without even informing him in advance of the appointment or of his own departure. Napoleon may have respected the very few men who dared stand up to him, but as a true Corsican he neither forgave nor forgot. As for the unrepentant Kléber, he was ultimately to pay the supreme penalty.

Tivoli and Beyond

Calm has been completely restored in Cairo. . . . Every night
we have another thirty or so heads lopped off.
—To General Reynier, October 27, 1798

ews of General Bonaparte's activities aroused alarm throughout the Muslim community. He wished to convene the first assembly of all the notables of the sixteen Egyptian provinces, with the aim of reorganizing the land's civil and criminal judicial systems, as well as the land and property registration of the country to facilitate systematized fresh real estate taxation.[1] Alarm quickly gave way to open discontent in every quarter of the Egyptian capital, as it was learned that for the first time since the introduction of Islam into Egypt in the seventh century, all lands belonging to mosques, religious foundations, and Islamic brotherhoods would be taxed (although not the actual *masjid*, or mosque buildings).[2]

The Egyptians made no effort to conceal their anger and hostility. Rumors grew nastier and more persistent after the news on October 16 of the inclusion of the hitherto traditionally exempt sacrosanct religious properties. Further inflaming the population, the French, on Bonaparte's personal orders, had razed dozens of houses around the old Citadel, including at least two mosques,[3] to provide a better field of fire over the Arab quarter for the new French cannon and mortars being installed in the fortress. Napoleon had made the near-fatal blunder of treating the Muslims of Egypt as he had treated the Catholics of Italy, thinking nothing of destroying or desecrating their houses of worship and expecting the Arabs to acquiesce.

The sheikhs and *ulama* (doctors of Koranic law) responded by reading various Ottoman *firmans* (decrees) from Constantinople, proclaiming a *jihad,* or holy war, against the infidels. Religious leaders called for the "assembling of the troops of all the provinces of the [Ottoman] Empire" who under the "powerful protection of the Prophet" would "exterminate" these heathens, "and if it please God, reserve for Him to preside over their total destruction."[4] Napoleon, the master formulator of French public opinion, apparently paid little heed to these warnings. He controlled the only army in the capital. What could the unarmed, untrained masses possibly do? Clearly he had already forgotten the bloody days of the French Revolution, which he himself had helped quash more than once.

At dawn on October 21 crowds began circulating in the various Arab quarters of Cairo, crying out, "It's tyranny! Let God give victory to the true believers!" and attacking the homes of Muslim judicial officers who had been cooperating with the French.[5] At 8:00 A.M. Brigadier General Dupuy, commandant of the Cairo garrison, went with a small cavalry detachment to investigate. Almost immediately run through with a spear, he died on the spot, and his escort was cut down. Through the narrow, twisting streets, a firm nucleus of at least a thousand "Turks, armed with sticks and muskets," started rampaging, looting, and attacking anything French. The great insurrection had begun.

Meanwhile Bonaparte, attended by Generals Caffarelli and Dommartin, was making a routine inspection of new artillery installations and arsenals in the Old City and on the island of Rudah, when he was finally informed at 10:00 A.M. that the disturbances in the city were not mere isolated incidents and that General Dupuy had been murdered. Dropping everything and returning to Cairo, "we were greeted by a hail of stones," Major Detroye reported, as they passed through the Bulaq Gate. "Musketry could be heard in every part of the city and we began to come across more and more corpses as we advanced," finally reaching Esbekiya Square and the safety of a battery of fifteen pieces of artillery before Bonaparte's GHQ.

Not far away Caffarelli's headquarters, also serving as a warehouse for his sappers as well as the expedition's scientific instruments, was broken into, pillaged, and men and officers murdered. Although the Egyptian Institute and the Elfi palace were also coming under fire, the center of fighting was around al-Azhar Mosque, which some five thousand armed Muslims were using as a fortress. Additional artillery was being rushed up to the Citadel, situated on the high ground overlooking that mosque—the largest in Cairo—its enormous courtyard protected by high massive walls, but due to previous French indiscipline and slackness, it took many hours to get everything into a state of readiness. It was a grave decision, of course, for once Napoleon gave the order to begin the bombardment of al-Azhar, it would end any goodwill remaining between Muslims and the French.

The following day intense fighting resumed, in the midst of which one of Napoleon's favorite aides-de-camp, Colonel Sulkowski, at the head of a column of thirty-three soldiers he was escorting from a hospital in Belbeis, was attacked and killed, and the entire column massacred. By now the maze of passageways and streets round al-Azhar Mosque was completely barricaded, and the French found it impossible to enter "with cavalry or even infantry." But for some reason that is not clear, the full bombardment of al-Azhar did not begin until noon of that day, the pounding of heavy artillery then continuing until nightfall. According to Arab historian Abd al-Rahman, this roaring cannonade put the fear of hell into the Egyptians living in the vicinity of the mosque, while thousands more manning the barricades round the mosque were caught up in an intensive fire. "Cannonballs rained down on them from the heights," he noted, "shaking the very foundations of the houses, the sound deafening their ears."[6] After hours of bombardment, the French succeded in hacking their way through the massive doors of the mosque, followed by the furious saber-wielding cavalry and then the infantry, who destroyed everyone and everything in sight, including books, lamps, Korans, and religious artifacts, all thrown to the ground and trampled underfoot along with the dead defenders. Throughout that night and the following day, French troops "ran through the streets like devils," as al-Rahman put it, while a still-irate Bonaparte ordered General Bon—who had succeeded the unfortunate Dupuy as commandant of Cairo—"to have the great mosque razed to the ground."[7]

Then came the mopping-up operations and the question of public relations. The guilty had to be severely punished, but as General Bon put it, Napoleon "wanted to show himself to be as clement as he was terrible." Berthier instructed Dugua: "I wish to impress upon you, Citizen General, that some ringleaders who have worked up the riffraff of the country are responsible for this uprising," and "we carried out a real massacre of those scum" while "restoring order" to Cairo.[8] In fact Bonaparte deliberately let his troops go completely amok, slaughtering men, women, and children, even terrorizing women giving birth in the streets as they attempted to flee. And at 4:00 P.M. troops arrived in Esbekia Square with a donkey laden with bulging sacks. When they were opened, bleeding Arab heads rolled across the ground.[9] This was just the beginning.

Bonaparte did indeed set a terrible example while smoke was still rising from the ruins of al-Azhar Mosque. He ordered Berthier "to behead all prisoners taken with arms in their hands" and to throw "their headless corpses . . . into the river."[10] By October 27 Bonaparte could assure General Reynier that "calm has been completely restored in Cairo . . . every night we have another thirty or so heads lopped off," including fifteen of the most influential religious leaders of the city and members of the divan, who had urged this uprising.[11]

But hundreds of executions alone did not suffice. Napoleon beefed up the Citadel's garrisons and fortifications, laying in large stores of munitions and food. He also created three new smaller forts in Cairo to overlook the trouble spots, all three named after recently slain French officers: Fort Camin, Fort Dupuy, and Fort Sulkowski (the last built in a large mosque, complete with artillery placed in its minarets and a garrison of several hundred men and stabling for their horses within the mosque walls).[12] If the Egyptians had mistaken Napoleon's initial goodwill in attempting to win over the Muslim population for weakness, he was savagely disabusing them now.

As for the casualties resulting from the fighting alone, in a report to the Directory, Napoleon put French figures at 57 dead, and only 8 when writing to Reynier, whereas Major Detroye, attached to the Elfi palace, estimated at least 250 French dead and many hundreds wounded. Napoleon never submitted a corrected or revised report. As for Egyptian losses, Bonaparte thought initially about 2,500, although Belliard and Berthier suggested between 4,000 and 5,000 dead and many thousands more wounded.[13] "I cannot find the words to express [the horror] I felt," Bourrienne wrote, "but I must admit that this butchery at least assured public tranquillity for a long time thereafter."[14]

The fighting in some places throughout the country was heavy. Anxieties about the British blockade and their enforced geographical isolation were a grim reality, and the bitter aftermath of the bloody Cairene uprising of October 21–23 was still vividly in everyone's mind as they witnessed the new fortifications going up throughout the capital. But even so—nay, *especially* so, given such tumultuous uncertainties and unrelenting daily pressure—French troops and officers needed relaxation and amusement. (So far Napoleon's only personal attempt at diversion appears to have been a day's outing at the Pyramids, where, from the base of one massive structure, he watched Monge happily clamber to the top, despite the great heat.)

Although the European population of Cairo was not very large, a few enterprising souls were quick to see the need to fill this void in their daily lives with cafés, regimental concerts, French baths, tobacconists, and even a theatrical group. Women of course had to be found, and although for the most part the French disliked Arab women, they had to do for the rank and file. But what really enthralled just about everyone, bringing even the usually grim and unsociable Bonaparte himself to its long-deferred opening at the end of November 1798, was the inauguration of the Tivoli Gardens.

The mastermind of this enterprise, a former French bodyguard by the name of Dargeval, had wanted to create "the greatest and most beautiful" public gardens and house of amusement in Cairo. Located close to Esbekia Square, this sprawling oasis of several acres was "covered with orange, lemon, and other fragrant trees," amid fountains, tables and chairs, music and women, the focal point being an old mansion where one could find "all forms of entertainment, everything the heart could desire and that the limitations of Cairo could provide," not to mention "a reading room filled with reasonably current periodicals and books" to which were added "all that could contribute to the pleasure of the society frequenting this place." For a mere thirty-franc monthly subscription, one had full use of the entire facilities, this sum naturally exclusive of amounts spent *sur place,* during the daily hours of 4:00 to 10:00 P.M., after which, for security reasons, all officers were required to return to their quarters.

One evening, as General Bon's division went on parade in nearby Esbekia Square and a thirty-six-foot paper "montgolfière" (hot-air balloon) was successfully launched to a height of 250 feet above the city, Bonaparte himself made a grand appearance at the Tivoli Gardens, with his aides-de-camp, Berthier, and some staff officers in dress uniform. The few European women who greeted them were soon in great demand for dancing and quiet promenades among the orange blossoms, while in the mansion, gambling—assisted by more ladies—was the chief attraction, not to mention a restaurant with a few discreet private rooms and a separate café.[15] But the main attraction for Frenchmen deprived of female society for six months were the fifteen to twenty women decked out in their finery. Also popular was a fireworks display, including two Turks dressed up as devils and covered with sparklers.[16]

It was apparently on this occasion that Bonaparte met the ravishing Pauline Fourès, the twenty-year-old wife of a lieutenant of the Twenty-second Chasseurs. Although he was offered several young Arab women, Napoleon had found them unsympathetic, rejecting all but one young girl for a while, until encountering *la belle* Pauline, with whom he became quite taken during the ensuing weeks. And angry as he was, because of Josephine's outrageous and embarrassing infidelity with her own young lieutenant in France, he deliberately took Pauline Fourès as his mistress, quartering her in a little house next to the Elfi palace.

"Scandal has it that the young and pretty wife of a French officer has pleased the commander in chief," the staid Detroye recorded in his diary, "and that the husband was removed by sending him on a mission to France while arrangements have been taken most advantageously to please all parties. Details of his taking possession of her are openly talked about by everyone. It is said that the young woman rides in the general's carriage daily now."[17] Soon "the entire army" came to know about her, dubbing her the commander in chief's "Cleopatra." "This liaison was soon the talk of GHQ and the subject of nearly every conversation," Bourrienne relates, and it finally resulted in rendering Bonaparte a little less formidable, an occasional smile on his lips after weeks of bearing down on his staff and commanders. He added that Bonaparte badly wanted to have a child by Pauline. "But what could I do," Bonaparte remarked. "The silly little thing could not have any." Pauline later told Bourrienne, "Heavens! It isn't *my* fault!"[18] When Pauline's husband unexpectedly reappeared in Egypt—having been captured at sea and returned by the English—Bonaparte was furious. Pauline resolved the problem by asking for a quick divorce, which Napoleon gladly expedited, although it was later queried in France.[19]

For just about everyone else in the Army of the Orient, however, this campaign was proving unbearable: men without women, without hope, without either a present or a future. Tivoli or no, morale naturally continued to plummet. Senior officers openly cursed Napoleon, even before the troops, leading to a nasty but fortunately not fatal duel between one of Napoleon's most devoted young aides, Junot, and an embittered detractor, Brig. Gen. Pierre Lanusse.

The lovesick Berthier continued to pine after his Italian mistress, going into a schoolboy decline that at first amused Bonaparte but soon got on his nerves. Meanwhile General Manscourt proved to be as utterly incompetent a governor of Alexandria as everyone had predicted. Napoleon finally was forced to fire him and replace him with Menou.[20] (Manscourt proved to be not quite so hapless as he appeared, however, for then, pleading illness and with a disability certificate in hand from his doctor, he was ordered back to France, the envy of his critics.) General Dumas, too, criticized the folly of the Egyptian campaign and the incompetence of its direction, only to be rebuked angrily by Napoleon himself. "You have been talking sedition," he said to the cavalry general towering over him. "But your five feet ten inches

could not save you from being shot by a firing squad now if I ordered it!"
Dumas had then been allowed to return to France, never again to serve in
the French army.[21] Napoleon never forgot nor forgave what he considered
to be "a deserter." Napoleon's own aide-de-camp, his brother Louis, a
most promising career soldier, was now morose, chronically depressed, and
useless to everyone. To the relief of all those around him, he too was
granted permission to leave when a boat could safely get through the
British blockade.

The number of officers requesting permission to be repatriated soon
became staggering, as Bourrienne points out:

> All the letters that fell into the hands of the commander in chief [who
> had no compunction about intercepting his officers' private correspon-
> dence with their families] were unanimous in their complaints and their
> regrets. . . . No one who was in Egypt could deny the sad state of affairs
> . . . the awful misery there . . . and that is the undeniable truth of the
> matter.[22]

There had probably never been a situation like it in the entire history of the
French army—just about every officer lamented his role there and wished
for or actually did request a transfer to the homeland. This proved another
turning point in Napoleon's military career, causing him to put less and less
trust in his own men (and they in him), subtly shaping future relationships,
decisions, and actions in France even years later. Realizing he had to put a
halt to this panic and defection, he denied the vast majority of requests of
his officers to return home. Had he permitted the popular Kléber to resign
and return, for instance, it would have been the end: His entire army no
doubt would have mutinied or simply disintegrated.

To get around Napoleon's objections to any transfer whatsoever, most
officers flocked to the sympathetic head of the medical corps, Dr. Desgenettes, who by now despised Napoleon as much as they did themselves,
and who no doubt would have left Egypt himself had not duty required his
presence. The chief surgeon, Dr. Larrey, fully concurred, and after a noisy
row with Napoleon over hospital conditions and the continued to-do about
the issuing of medical certificates for men to be invalided home, relations
between GHQ and the medical corps swiftly declined.[23] (Napoleon retaliated by leaving Desgenettes and Larrey behind when he abandoned the
army the following year.)

When, despite his orders, Colonel Grobert, a valuable artillery officer,
did finally succeed in obtaining permission to return to France based on

medical grounds, Bonaparte denounced the "cowards, disloyal men, and those with little sense of duty" who were thus escaping his clutches. He made it harder to be granted a health certificate to return home. On the other hand he did not want an officer corps riddled with malcontents and deadbeats or, as he put it, men "who were not appreciative of the honor of being our companions-in-arms. Let them leave. I shall even facilitate their departure, but I do not want them to conceal their real motives of not wishing to share our exhausting work and dangers, by trumped-up illnesses."[24] It was in this mood that Napoleon had also authorized the departure of Quartermaster General Sucy, after having found him guilty of embezzlement and fraud, when Sucy obligingly complained of "my wound and problems with morale."[25] Had Napoleon publicized Sucy's grand theft, he felt it would have been one shock too many for an already demoralized army. As for Colonel Grobert, who was already dispatching his trunks to Alexandria, he was in for a jolt when he learned that Napoleon had personally torn up his disability certificate and had instead reassigned him to General Dommartin's bleak outpost at Salheyeh.

On learning that Bonaparte had canceled a certificate that he himself had prepared, Dr. Desgenettes insisted on an immediate interview at headquarters, resulting in a bitter exchange—something to which Napoleon was unaccustomed. As in the case of Kléber and General Dumas, relations between the medical corps director and Bonaparte were never again the same.[26] Every day the commander in chief was burning more bridges.

Although Napoleon continued to confide in Monge, he played some cards very close to his chest, in particular the possibility of his leaving Egypt with just a few of his collaborators to return to France. To what extent Napoleon mentioned this is not clear. To be sure, Monge knew that Josephine's blatant affair with Charles had left her husband the butt of many a ribald joke throughout the Army of the Orient. He also knew that the general's decision to flaunt his affair with Pauline Fourès was a form of retaliation (unlike the greater discretion he was to demonstrate with other mistresses later). Following the defeat of his fleet, Bonaparte had notified Admiral Ganteaume on September 1 that he wanted three or four of the remaining warships that had escaped destruction in Alexandria harbor to be rearmed and prepared to put to sea at a moment's notice.[27] He then sent funds to Alexandria that this work might be given top priority, for despite everything Napoleon was still intent on getting back to France to deal with both Josephine and the Directory. But apparently the more he reflected on the impact of the fleet's destruction, the more he realized the necessity of another resounding victory over "the Turks" to ensure the support he would require to overthrow the French government.

Following the naval debacle, Napoleon also conducted a highly discreet correspondence with the British fleet off the coast of Alexandria, attempting to arrange for some sort of signed truce, or even a peace treaty with the English.[28] Capt. Samuel Hood, the senior naval officer in charge of those cruisers, declined to play this game. Monge also encouraged Bonaparte to maintain—or attempt to maintain—negotiations with the Sublime Porte, while Napoleon for his part sent messages by land and sea to the sultan of the Ottoman Empire, purporting that the French were in Egypt to aid and work with the Turks, against the Austrians, the Russians, and the English. It was all rot, and both sides knew it; besides, there was not a single Russian or English soldier in Egypt.

On August 22 Napoleon had personally instructed Maj. Joseph Eugène Calmet-Beauvoisins to open negotiations with the Turks in Syria via Ahmet Pasha, known popularly as Djezzar, or "the Butcher." But upon reaching Jaffa, Djezzar's bluff son had treated the major arrogantly and rudely, not even permitting him to land.[29] After the officer returned to Cairo on September 11 with this bad news, the next day Napoleon ordered Capt. Mailly de Châteaubriand to set out immediately on another one-man mission to attempt to open contact with the Turkish army. Alas, this young man found himself in Turkish chains in a dank dungeon in Acre, where he was later decapitated by Djezzar.[30]

By December, then, when Napoleon dispatched a third emissary, by the name of Beauchamp, on the diplomatic errand of establishing direct relations with Constantinople, he was in a pretty foul temper, and his letter of instructions reflected this less conciliatory mood. In Constantinople, in conjunction with "our minister . . . you will demand that the Frenchmen arrested in Syria be released." At the same time, "you will inform the Sublime Porte that we want to be his friends, that the purpose of our expedition to Egypt is to punish the Mamelukes and the English, and to prevent the partitioning of the Ottoman Empire" by the Austrian and Russian emperors. He was "proudly and imperiously [to] demand" that the Sultan release all French citizens in Constantinople, "for failure to do so will be regarded as a declaration of war."[31] But what Napoleon really wanted was compromise. If the Porte had already declared war on France (which he had done back in September) and had had France's ministers arrested (which in fact was the case), Beauchamp was to say that Napoleon was returning a Turkish ship held in Alexandria as proof of the French government's desire for friendly relations. Unfortunately, not only was Beauchamp's sailing date delayed until February 13, 1799—when the very purpose had been canceled by subsequent events—but the caravelle was intercepted off Rhodes and Beauchamp imprisoned, while the ship and Beauchamp's written orders reached Constantinople only on April 14. It was a total fiasco.[32]

The fact of the matter is that the Ottoman sultan, upon learning of the French seizure of Egypt in the first week of September 1798, had had the French chargé d'affaires arrested, and with him most of the French colony in Constantinople. Napoleon first received word of the Porte's not-so-sublime actions and his declaration of war on France on October 9 from a Greek ship putting into Damietta. Even Talleyrand realized that France's invasion of Egypt would be the most difficult point to negotiate with the Porte.[33]

The news of Napoleon's initial successful landing in Egypt in the first week of July reached Paris only on September 10, accompanied by cheering crowds and the usual celebratory cannonfire from the Ecole Militaire. Later that same day, with the thunder of artillery still reverberating through the French capital, a special courier from Toulon, galloping across the Place de la Révolution, reined in sharply at the Rue Royale and dashed into the Naval Ministry to hand Admiral Bruix a dispatch announcing the news of Brueys's defeat by Nelson at Abukir.[34]

The full implications of the Abukir Bay naval disaster were already being felt all across the Mediterranean, as Britain's Royal Navy that same month attacked the French garrisons at Corfu (which surrendered on March 3, 1799), while General Vaubois, who was personally ordered to surrender Malta, managed to hold out against the British until September 4, 1800. Thus the two strategically situated new French naval bases were cut off completely and of no further use to France. To be sure, Napoleon knew nothing of this yet, nor of the later capture of Villeneuve and Decrès after attempting to escape Malta, where they had ultimately fled from the Battle of Abukir. With the destruction of its principal battle fleet, France had lost all significant clout, military and diplomatic, throughout the Mediterranean. Hence the futility of Bonaparte's desperate efforts to negotiate with the Turks in Syria or Constantinople.

Talleyrand, who had deceived Bonaparte about his private, personal support of him and his Egyptian expedition, and about his own intention to serve as ambassador to the Sublime Porte, drafted a letter for Jean-Baptiste Treilhard, the president of the Executive Directory, who dispatched it over his own signature to Bonaparte on November 4, 1798: "You can imagine the Directory's regrets and the difficulty they have in understanding the details of your expedition to date." Because of the naval defeat, Treilhard continued. France now found itself in a great dilemma vis-à-vis the other European powers and throughout the Mediterranean. "It is to this terrible event, which you so greatly feared and anticipated when you found the fleet could not leave the Egyptian coast, that we must attribute all our international problems." This "fleet disaster" had undermined French foreign policy in every sphere.[35] Because of it Malta was blockaded, there were fresh troubles in Italy, and the British and Austrians were closer than ever to forming a new anti-French coalition including Russia and Prussia. What is more, the government was now forced to decree the emergency conscription of another two hundred thousand young men, while General Joubert had been sent to head the Army of Italy, and Gen. Jean-Baptiste Jourdan was preparing the Army of the Rhine. If war broke out, Treilhard contended, Italy would no doubt be the place. Nevertheless "the external enemy will be conquered . . . and the imperishable republic . . . strong through the union of all members of its government, will emerge victorious from all attacks. . . . You must therefore arrange to rely entirely on yourself, at least for some time to come." In the final analysis, Director Treilhard closed, Bonaparte was left with three choices: he could remain in Egypt and simply bide his time; he could march to India; or he could march to Constantinople. Then he closed with a scathing dig at the mighty man who just months before had personally challenged and bullied this same Directory: "No matter how you resolve to act, we expect from the genius and luck of Bonaparte nothing less than sweeping operations and illustrious results."[36] Treilhard (and Talleyrand, whose hand was evident throughout this draft) had the last bitter laugh after all—or so it would seem for the moment. As for the recipient of this attack, Bonaparte would not receive it until March 25, 1799, in Acre, during yet another military setback.[37]

From a military viewpoint Napoleon, as commander in chief of the Army of the Orient, had several objectives on reaching Cairo, all of which he hoped to achieve more or less simultaneously: He had to secure Alexandria and the entire coastline between there and Damietta; to occupy and secure the two lower branches of the Nile between Cairo and Rosetta and the capital and Damietta; and to pacify the upper courses of the Nile from Cairo southward to Aswan and up to Wadi Halfa. In addition he had to pursue and destroy the armies of the two Mameluke princes, Murad Bey, who had fled along the Nile south of Cairo, and Ibrahim Bey, who had disappeared with the remnants of his army to the northeast toward al-Arish.

Despite this sweeping program of pacification in Egypt and the reduced size of his army (to twenty thousand men), Napoleon made the decision to march on Syria, which required securing not only the Delta but also the desert stretches to the east of the Damietta branch of the Nile, linking Cairo with the trade routes to Syria. This meant hastening the occupation of the Damietta branch, including the important canal leading from Mansûra to Lake Manzalah, and the route from Cairo passing Heliopolis, Balbais, Qaram, Salheyeh, and Peluse. Much to his surprise, he was to find the area round Damietta, Mansura, and the Shakiyah Provinces, to the east of the Damietta branch of the Nile, untamed and openly hostile, requiring reinforcements with fresh troops and the building of barracks, depots, and fortifications in the more inaccessible but strategically important areas around Salheyeh and Peluse (modern Port Said). Only when they had been secured could he launch his invasion of Syria and drive toward Acre, Damascus, and the Bosporus.

On August 25 General Desaix had finally sailed upriver from Giza with four battalions totaling 3,200 men to seek and destroy Murad Bey and his army and to pacify the entire southern region of the Nile between Cairo and the Sudan. Desaix first confronted Murad Bey's 9,000 Mamelukes at the Battle of Sediman on October 7, defeating and routing them. It proved a hollow victory, however: Murad lost only 400 men (to Desaix's 110) as he escaped practically unscathed into the desert.[38] By the end of October, Desaix's ranks were thinning due to ophthalmia* and dysentery. Stalwart and unrelenting, however, he ultimately passed Bani Sur, Abu Jirja, Mania, Manfalut, and Asyut, clashing with the Mamelukes at Sawqui (January 2), Samhud (January 22), Banut (March 8–10), Bir al-Bar (April 2), and Kassai (May 30, 1799).[39] Brig. Gen. Louis Davout ultimately inflicted the greatest casualties on Murad at Bani Adin on April 16, leaving behind two thousand Egyptian dead, a tally that did not, however, prevent the ever elusive Murad Bey from slipping through his fingers once again.[40]

Meanwhile, to the north the campaign continued much as before. Gen. Jacques Menou finally succeeded Manscourt at Alexandria on November 28, joining the command of that province with his own at Rosetta.[41] In mid-October General Dugua, with 4,274 men, was sent as governor to Damietta, with orders from Bonaparte "to pursue the Arabs and punish them vigorously."[42] General Andréossy was sent to Lake Manzalah on a special mission to help prepare the invasion route to Syria, while Damas, Murat, and the infamous Lanusse conquered the northeast.[43]

---

*Severe inflammation of the eye, frequently leading to temporary blindness; common across North Africa even today.

Napoleon had been seriously considering the invasion of Syria at least as early as September, when he asked General Reynier to prepare a study of the route[44] and ordered the ruthless cavalry commander Murat to do "all the harm possible" to the Arabs of that region. "My intention," he said, "is to destroy them."[45] Napoleon ordered Dugua to take his entire division and to make himself "sovereign master" by "beheading the opposition and taking hostages. . . . Burn their villages, make a terrible example of them."[46]

On December 3 Bonaparte ordered General Bon to march on Suez, to secure that port and gain control of all commerce on the Red Sea, while establishing friendly contact with the Arabs on the other side of that sea, at Yanbu and Jidda (to prevent them from further aiding Murad). Reaching Suez on December 7, Bon quickly accomplished his mission.[47]

Meanwhile, in the far northeastern corner of Egypt, Napoleon was gathering only extremely patchy intelligence reports from Reynier on Ibrahim Bey's forces at al-Arish (where he had been halted by Djezzar, who would not permit him to advance to Damascus), estimating Ibrahim's total forces at about 2,300 men. At the same time some of Bon's and Caffarelli's men were continuing to build forts at Peluse and Katiyah, to secure the invasion route northward, and Ganteaume was ordered by Bonaparte to prepare naval transport ships, with cannon, siege artillery, and supplies, to accompany the proposed expedition into Syria.[48]

With all finally in order, and Cairo now calm once again, Napoleon issued a parting message to the Cairenes, informing them that he had forgiven their bloody uprising and trespasses: "God has ordered me to be lenient and merciful. The day will come when everyone will have proof that I am following higher orders now and that in consequence no man can touch me." Then he added one of his many equivocal messages to the Muslims—messages that he would later try to delete from French history. He announced that after the enemies of Islam had been defeated, and Islam "defeats the cross, I will come from the far West to fulfill the task He has imposed upon me"; that is, to become their leader.[49]

Having delivered this proclamation, Napoleon, escorted by some three hundred crack troops and accompanied by Berthier, Dommartin, Caffarelli, Ganteaume, Monge, Berthollet, and others, set out from Cairo, crossing the Eastern Desert and arriving at Suez on December 27. After a quick tour of inspection, he left again three days later, adding a side trip to study the ruins of the ancient Suez Canal, which he hoped to restore. Then, returning via Balbais, he reached Cairo on January 6, 1799, now firmly determined to strike into Syria as quickly as possible.[50]

Road to Damascus

I will create a great new empire in the Orient that will truly establish my place in posterity.

he Syrian campaign was to be Napoleon's final full-scale military expedition in the Middle East, and it seemed doomed almost from the beginning. Berthier, who had finally received permission to return to Europe and his Italian mistress, had changed his mind, deciding to throw in his lot with Bonaparte once again.[1] Otherwise there was little in the way of good news. Morale continued to decline; thousands of troops were blinded and hospitalized by a seemingly incurable eye virus; while Desgenettes's December reports now confirmed that bubonic plague was sweeping the country from Alexandria to Cairo (it alone would ultimately kill another two thousand Frenchmen). Fear, lassitude, and general apathy were everywhere prevalent. The Ottoman sultan's declaration of war against the French Republic on September 9, 1798, had been the final blow, effectively sealing the fate of the French. But if Napoleon had no navy with which to counter the British squadron off the Egyptian coast, his troops could still march, and that is just what he was set on having them do. With a total effective force by now down to fewer than twenty thousand men, however, the thirteen thousand he was preparing to launch against Djezzar Pasha's force—in excess of forty thousand, awaiting them to the north, pro-

tected by mighty fortresses and large cavalry units—appeared daring if not utterly foolhardy.

On January 31, 1799, the first of the four partial divisions set out from Cairo overland via Balbais, Salheyeh, and Katia, Kléber in command of his own and Reynier's divisions. With the basic stores of food and munitions now in place, Reynier departed through sand dunes and under the unrelenting Egyptian sun, reaching Katia on February 4, and on the sixteenth left for the sprawling oasis of al-Arish. Even as Kléber's division was setting out from Katia on February 11, Bonaparte was heading north from Cairo with Bon's and Lannes's divisions (Lannes having replaced Vial).

Leaving in his berlin (a light traveling carriage) on the eleventh, and attended by these final two divisions, a grim Bonaparte—with the latest report in his pocket of the British bombardment of Alexandria on February 3—set out on the road to Damascus and war that would either make or break him. The enemy was closing in on all sides, and this was his last chance. By marching up to Acre Napoleon hoped to win over Djezzar from the Ottoman sultan, and with his aid smash the two Ottoman armies advancing by land and sea transport to recapture Egypt, aided by the British navy.

But as General Reynier discovered on reaching the coastal town of al-Arish, French army intelligence had proved faulty once again. Ordered to build a small fort there to hold off Ibrahim's followers, an astonished Reynier instead found a large stone fortress already in place, manned by some 2,300 well-armed and -supplied Mameluke and Albanian troops. The siege of this fort bogged down until Bonaparte's arrival there on February 16, its nine hundred survivors surrendering three days later. On the twenty-second they proceeded up the strip of desert coast to Gaza, which fell to them two days later, and after seizing al-Ramleh on March 1, reached Jaffa on the third.

At dawn on March 7 General Berthier sent an officer to Abd Allah Aga, the commanding officer of Jaffa: "God is good and merciful," his message began in the traditional Islamic manner, explaining that Bonaparte, who now surrounded the port city, "was touched by the woes that would befall [Jaffa] if it had to be taken by assault" and offered "the safety of its garrison and protection to the city" should it surrender under his terms now.[2] The defiant Turkish commander, however, instead seized and beheaded the unfortunate French truce officer, his only return message his bleeding head delivered on a pike. The French opened fire immediately and as Napoleon later reported to the Directory, by five o'clock that same afternoon: "We were masters of the city, which for the next twenty-four hours was pillaged by us and subject to all the horrors of war in their most hideous forms."[3]

On surrendering, the entire garrison of four thousand men was disarmed and marched out before two of Bonaparte's aides-de-camp, Eugène de Beauharnais and Captain Croisier, who promised them that their lives would be spared and then had them bound and paraded before Napoleon's tent. Coming out and looking at the mass of men filling the field before him, he turned to Bourrienne and said: "What the devil have they [Beauharnais and Croisier] involved me in now? What am I supposed to do with them?" Complaining that there was neither enough food nor water nor even the troops with which to escort them all the way back to Egypt as POWs, Napoleon called a war council to consider the possibilities, which ended in stalemate. This state continuing, an angry Bonaparte appeared on March 10 announcing his decision through Berthier: "The order was given and executed to shoot them."[4] Half the men were taken away to the beach, lined up and shot or bayoneted (to save ammunition). "As they stepped forward they found death and perished in the surf. . . . I shall limit myself to these few details of this horrible necessity of which I was an eyewitness. . . . That atrocious scene still makes me shiver whenever I think about it . . . the day of that blood-bath,"[5] Bourrienne recalled years afterward. The final death toll was thought to be about two thousand Arab troops. But simultaneously the French were struck down by another affliction over which they had no control; bubonic plague began rapidly to thin French ranks.

Leaving Jaffa, they marched on Haifa, Kléber easily taking it on March 16. But Haifa was just one of two fortified emplacements controlling the small bay separating it from Acre.

Once again as a result of faulty army intelligence, on reaching the walls of Acre the next day, the French found themselves before another immense fortress with massive stone battlements many feet thick and nearly two miles in circumference, well defended by some 250 cannon strategically situated on the harbor against attack either by land or sea. Although the garrison numbered only five thousand men, as the French were without a navy or heavy siege guns, these men could concentrate on fewer than fifteen hundred feet of ramparts facing the land on either side of the ancient citadel Djezzar used as his headquarters and residence. This small area in turn was buttressed by four formidable stone towers. Djezzar, a former Bosnian slave, may have been in his seventies but for all that he was a tough old character, fearful of no one. What is more, Sir Sidney Smith's small squadron had arrived in the nick of time two days earlier, adding more mobile guns to cover the shoreline and seize the flotilla bringing up half of Napoleon's siege guns and supplies from Alexandria as they arrived off the port of Haifa. In fact, Smith provided hundreds of trained British gunners and dozens of cannon.[6] In addition, an émigré, Louis de Phélippeaux (Napoleon's old classmate from the Ecole Militaire and now an official member of Smith's squadron), also helped advise the Turks on their artillery against the French. Although the rest of the French siege guns were being brought up by Admiral Pérrée from Damietta, they would take another month and a half to do so, too little and too late. To make matters worse, Smith escorted transport vessels bearing the Ottoman Army of Rhodes, destined to bolster Djezzar's garrison by many thousands. Had Napoleon arrived just ten days earlier, as originally planned (instead of being held up at al-Arish), before Smith appeared, the odds of his seizing Acre might perhaps have been greater. But now of course the situation looked bleak. Nevertheless, bringing up his four divisions, he began the one military operation he had always dreaded, the traditional medieval siege of enemy ramparts by trench, mine, and tunnel.

Meanwhile, fearful of being caught outside the walls of Acre in a pincer formed by another Turkish army approaching from Damascus, on March 30 Napoleon sent his trusted aide-de-camp Junot with five hundred men to reconnoiter the interior. Near Nazareth on April 10 they found themselves hopelessly outnumbered and -maneuvered by an enemy force of thousands. Fortunately Kléber arrived in the nick of time with a contingent of fifteen hundred, and with these two thousand men briefly succeeded in routing some six thousand Arabs near Cana on the eleventh. On April 15 a cavalry column led by Murat drove inland north of the Sea of Galilee, taking a critical crossing of the Jordan River, to cut off any further flow of troop reinforcements from Damascus. But once again French intelligence and timing proved faulty. A substantial army out of Damascus, comprising twenty-five thousand cavalry and ten thousand infantry, now came unexpectedly face to face with Kléber's force near the foot of snow-covered Mt. Tabor. Outnumbered, outmaneuvered, with munitions running low and his retreat cut off, even Kléber, it seemed, could not get out of this situation. Then suddenly Napoleon himself appeared over the rock-strewn hills at the head of Bon's infantry division. Kléber's astonishment was exceeded only by that of the Turkish force, still outnumbering them nearly 9 to 1. Caught completely unawares by Napoleon's opening cannonfire, the overwhelmingly superior but ill-disciplined Arab cavalry panicked, scattering before the French, and were last seen dashing for the road to Damascus. Napoleon's phenomenal luck had once again intervened to give him the surprise victory on April 16, 1799, known as the Battle of Mt. Tabor, permitting the French to extricate themselves and rejoin the rest of the troops before the siege of Acre. In a single blow Napoleon had saved thousand of French troops, and diverted the lethal pincer movement that would have entrapped him at Acre.

The brief triumph at Mt. Tabor was to be the last good military news to come Napoleon's way, for back at Acre the stalemate continued, and then the situation declined. Moreover, General Caffarelli, who had had an arm shattered by a cannonball and then amputated under primitive conditions, died on April 18, deeply upsetting Bonaparte, who had lost not only an irreplaceable chief of engineers but also one of the very few soldiers in the entire army he genuinely liked, admired, and counted on. Worse, Monge, who had come down with dysentery shortly after his arrival at Acre, was fighting for his life. He had nearly expired twice and was not expected to live, and on his return Napoleon spent hours at his bedside as Monge lay in a coma, occasionally covering his friend with an extra blanket. Thanks to a rugged constitution, however, the indomitable geometrician passed through the crisis by the end of April.[7]

Beyond that welcome news there was little to cheer up the French commander in chief. To be sure the second, smaller shipment of siege cannon that had reached Jaffa on April 15 was finally dragged overland, reaching Acre at the end of the month, permitting Bonaparte to launch his much-vaunted "major assault" on Djezzar's fortress. Between May 1 and 10 five such assaults were made, and although one of the towers was partially destroyed, and a temporary breach made, it was to no avail, as the daily toll of plague and battle casualties rose. To make matters worse during these final assaults, General Lannes was again severely wounded and put out of action, and on May 10 General Bon was killed, as was Napoleon's aide-de-camp Croisier.

With three senior generals—Caffarelli, Bon, and Lannes—dead or in the hospital all within the span of a few weeks, Desgenettes handing him a roster of 2,300 sick and wounded, ammunition and food supplies running low, and the Acre defenses stronger than before he arrived, thanks to reinforcements from Rhodes and Sir Sidney Smith's naval guns, on May 17 Bonaparte announced his decision to lift this siege and to return to Cairo. He had had enough. But as usual he had to save face, which in this case he did with such a bald-faced lie as to make even his weary troops laugh. Issuing his Proclamation of Mt. Tabor, he proclaimed his great victory over the Turks, declaring: "After having maintained our army in the heat of Syria for these past three months with only a handful of men, after capturing 40 guns and 6,000 prisoners, after having razed to the ground the fortifications of Gaza, Jaffa, Haifa, and Acre, we will now return to Egypt." Bourrienne, to whom Napoleon dictated this absurd fabrication (before the still-standing walls of Acre), described all this as "wounding the truth." The reason for now abandoning the siege of Acre and the entire Syrian campaign, Napoleon announced, was the necessity of fending off a large-scale Turkish landing expected at Alexandria.[8]

Spiking his enormous siege guns after less than three weeks' use, and leaving General Reynier's haggard division to form the rear guard of his column, Napoleon set out from Acre on May 20, with the convalescing Monge at his side in his berlin, as Kléber's much battered division led the way back. The road from Mt. Carmel to Jaffa over the next four days was depressing for the flagging stream of French troops. "A devouring thirst rising from the complete lack of water and excessive heat, an exhausting march through burning sand dunes, combined to demoralize the men," Bourrienne attested. "I saw officers with amputated limbs thrown from the stretchers by their bearers. . . . I saw amputees, the wounded, those suffering from plague, left by the roadside, . . . while our march was lit up by the villages, hamlets, and towns, and their fields of rich crops, all torched by our angry men. The entire countryside was on fire." The officers in charge

> everywhere themselves spread desolation in their wake, wanting to avenge their military reverses and relieve their sufferings through some form of action. We were entirely surrounded by the dying, pillagers, and arsonists. . . . The brilliant sun in a beautiful sky was hidden by the pall of smoke from our constant conflagrations. We had the sea to our right, and to our left and behind us, the desert we ourselves were laying waste as we advanced.[9]

Reaching Jaffa on May 24, Bonaparte found no boats waiting to evacuate the wounded. In fact Rear Admiral Perrée had abandoned the army and returned to Egypt after delivering the cannon. Knowing he could not carry them himself, but not wishing to leave them to be mutilated by the Turks and Arabs, Napoleon ordered Desgenettes to poison his hospital patients instead. The appalled head of the medical corps adamantly refused and flew into a rage. Nevertheless, Napoleon did make some well-publicized visits to the hospital containing amputees, wounded, plague victims, and ophthalmic cases. Then, instructing that the worst cases be left behind, he ordered the mining of the city's walls, blowing up the battlements as they departed.

By May 30, having already begun to jettison its stretcher cases,

Napoleon's straggling army reached Gaza, followed by four more grueling days trekking through the Sinai, reaching the newly fortified French garrison at Kadia on June 3. On June 14, 9,760 tattered troops (out of the nearly 13,000 men who had set out with them) reached the gates of Cairo.[10]

Bonaparte's return to Cairo was preceded by his latest *Army Bulletin.* He was returning with "many prisoners and flags. I razed Djezzar's Palace to the ground, along with the ramparts of Acre. There is not a stone left standing, and all the city's inhabitants have left by sea. Djezzar is seriously wounded." Lies, every one of his claims, from beginning to end. "I must confess I had found it painful recording these official words at his dictation," Bourrienne acknowledged, but when he protested, Napoleon replied with a smile: "*Mon cher*, you are a simpleton. You really don't understand a thing."[11] Bourrienne had to agree; he did not understand this man.

Even before reaching Cairo with his defeated remnants, and the bad news he received there of various revolts in the country during his absence, Napoleon had made up his mind to execute his long-prepared plans to abandon the army and return to France. The excuse he would use was that France was again at war with Austria and Russia—that French armies were faltering and needed his presence to recoup their recent losses. To be sure, the newspapers he had been shown at Acre, courtesy of the ever gallant Sir Sidney Smith, and others later in Egypt that month, had confirmed the deteriorating military position of the French Republic as well as the political situation in Paris. But all that was mere pretext. He had played all his cards here and failed completely. He had lost approximately three thousand men in the Syrian campaign, in addition to the seven thousand or so lost earlier in Egypt. Three of his aides-de-camp had been killed, several generals as well, and numerous others badly wounded more than once. Much of his officer corps had openly protested his command and their very presence in Egypt. Even his own brother Louis had abandoned him. The chief quartermaster of the entire army had been proved a colossal crook and dishonorably dismissed. Despite all the loot taken, there was not enough left in the treasury to pay even what remained of the dwindling army, reduced thus far by nearly one-third since its arrival. The country had revolted against his rule, Cairo leading the way in its destructive torment, and the plague was still taking its daily toll on Egyptians and French alike. And of course his navy had been sunk or captured. His splendid, ill-conceived expedition was a total failure.

Thus Napoleon Bonaparte returned to his palace in Esbekia Square on June 14 a greatly disillusioned man. If he had hoped for some unexpected good news now in Cairo, he found none, not even a glimmer. What is more, the Ottoman squadron escorted by the Royal Navy's cruisers under Commodore Sir Sidney Smith were now at sea, reportedly heading for Alexandria. He would have to rally his army and sea defenses once more, and then he would sail for France. He had notified Ordonnateur LeRoy well before the old year was out to arm and victual several frigates for a secret destination, and on June 21 reiterated that same order to Rear Admiral Ganteaume.[12] He would leave behind in Egypt an utter shambles, a much reduced army, weakened and in disarray and low morale, with opposition growing daily, even in the usually mute medical corps, chiefly as a result of a final row during the first reconvening of the Egyptian Institute in June.

It all began when Napoleon requested the formation of a committee to report on the effects of the plague during the Syrian campaign, making it perfectly clear that these statistics would be used to explain away his extraordinarily heavy casualties there. General headquarters would be absolved of its own sin and the medical corps held responsible for the high mortality rate. This was simply too much of a lie for Dr. Desgenettes. He leaped to his feet and accused Napoleon personally of having ordered him to poison hundreds of their own wounded and plague victims, in order not to have to bring them back to Egypt, and of making the medical corps responsible for his own military mistakes and for the blunders of his "oriental despotism. . . . I know, gentlemen, I know full well, General, that you want to lord it over everyone. I also know that I have been quite carried away and have said things that will have repercussions far from here. But I shall not retract a single word!" He then and there tendered his resignation from the army and requested permission to return to France. An equally livid Bonaparte categorically refused, though Desgenettes was the last person he wanted to meet in Egypt thereafter.[13]

One of his first tasks on returning to the capital was the most difficult, notifying Paris of the current situation. Napoleon announced that "the campaign in Syria had one great result: we are now the masters of the entire desert, and in consequence we have disconcerted all the projects of our enemies for invading us this year. . . . Our situation here is most reassuring."[14] The fact is, his last outpost at al-Arish was barely holding on, while most of Egypt, including the entire southern two-thirds of the country, was not yet under firm French control, Desaix's victories there proving fleeting, for want of supplies and sufficient troops to to garrison pacified areas. Although admitting that the plague had struck hard at Alexandria and Jaffa, Napoleon informed the Directory that it had bypassed Cairo and the rest of Egypt. (The hospitals of Cairo had been crowded with thousands of plague victims for months.) He did admit that the army had lost 5,344 men, and therefore he requested a minimum of 6,000 reinforcements quickly. He added that if he were given 15,000 more, "we [could] go anywhere, even to Constantinople." And while asking for an additional one hundred surgeons and physicians, and admitting that in fact "by next season we will be reduced to 15,000 men," which after deducting the hospitalized, laborers, and so on, "will leave us with 12,000," including every branch of service. If he rounded off casualties to 6,000, this added to 15,000 would have accounted for a total of 21,000, which did not explain what had happened to the remaining 12,000 required to bring the figure back to the original 33,000 or so with whom he had landed on July 1, 1798. Clearly he thought the Directors did not know how to add and subtract. Nonetheless, with his remaining 12,000 men, he conceded, "we will not be in a position to meet a combined land and sea attack." That being the case, "if it is impossible to send us the help I have requested, then it will be necessary for us to make peace here."[15]

Less than a fortnight after proclaiming that Egypt was perfectly safe from foreign invasion "this year," he received a special courier from General Marmont, now acting commander of Alexandria, with a most urgent top-secret dispatch. On that very day, July 11, 1799, the Turkish Army of Rhodes, aboard some sixty troop transports, escorted by British and Russian warships, had anchored in Abukir Bay. What is more, Gen. Mustapha Pasha was landing some fifteen thousand troops, who were quickly overrunning the new French batteries there, and Fort Abukir had fallen while Alexandria was under heavy bombardment. With the added news that Ibrahim Bey's troops were now re-forming in Gaza, and that Murad Bey was threatening Cairo itself from the south as well, Bonaparte had to act quickly and redeploy his remaining twelve to thirteen thousand men.

"If the landing indeed proves serious, it will be necessary to evacuate the whole of Upper Egypt while leaving a few of your men to garrison the forts there," Napoleon instructed Desaix on July 15. "Inform General Reynier about the news I have just received [from Alexandria] and of the necessity to concentrate his troops," Bonaparte ordered General Berthier, sending similar instructions by special courier to Kléber (now at Damietta) and others, as Napoleon called in the few remaining French troops at al-Arish and Katia to return to Rosetta and Alexandria.[16] Panic swept army headquarters as every spare company was brought in, practically evacuating the entire northeastern desert contiguous to the Sinai, in addition to the southern portion of the country. For good measure, a desperate Bonaparte ordered General Dugua to have the hundreds of prisoners in Cairo shot while attracting the least amount of public attention possible. Napoleon instructed General Marmont to take up a defensive position between Abukir and Rosetta and "to fall upon the flanks of the enemy" as the army asembled around Birket.[17]

Setting out for Giza with his general staff at 4:00 A.M. on July 16, Napoleon managed to rally and dazzle his men. Even the by now highly critical Bourrienne confessed his admiration. "I must render all justice to his imperturbable presence of mind, to his promptness of decision, to his rapidity of execution, which at this period of his life never abandoned him on all the great occasions.[18] Reaching al-Rahmaniyah three days later, he ordered Marmont to hold at Alexandria and Kléber to secure Rosetta, while Bonaparte himself held the middle of the French position at Birket, supported by Murat's cavalry between there and Abukir. He told Kléber that he did not expect the enemy to have as many troops as the French.[19]

Perhaps even Napoleon's spirits flagged a bit between July 20 and 22, when reports of the continued arrival of more enemy ships doubled the original estimate of 60.[20] Lannes's and Rampon's divisions (formerly Bon's) were nearing al-Rahmaniyah, while General Dugua was preparing to strip Cairo of most of its remaining garrison, with some twelve hundred men already en route. The hospitals in Cairo were ransacked for any men capable of standing and holding a musket, Berthier hoping to "give the Turks a lesson that will finally assure the possession of Egypt for France."[21] "Maintain the greatest vigilance," Bonaparte reminded Marmont. "No officer, especially no senior officer, is to undress at night; call the men to quarters frequently at night to ensure that every man knows the position to which he is assigned," and for good measure watchdogs were to be posted just outside the walls.[22] Only an obviously grave threat could have forced Bonaparte literally to strip the entire country of all French forces to confront the Turkish landings. Ibrahim Bey's anticipated army sweeping out of the Sinai only aggravated matters, as Bonaparte alerted Dugua to this fresh danger.[23] He further summoned General Desaix to collect what remained of Reynier's division up there and to march on Ibrahim. As for the position at Abukir, Napoleon assured Desaix that he would "attack and throw them back into the sea."[24] He made these plans and pronouncements with little artillery to field and no realistic idea of the number of troops he would face.

On July 22 Napoleon ordered General Lannes's division and General Lanusse (now temporarily heading Rampon's division) to take up their position at Birket, while General Menou secured Lake Madiah (he was to be joined there by General Kléber).[25] At 9:00 P.M. on July 24, on reaching his field headquarters near Birket, Napoleon ordered Murat, with the avant-garde of the army's cavalry and supported by four infantry battalions, to attack the Turkish landing force in five hours' time, with Lannes to Murat's right, and Lanusse to his left.[26] Marmont was to attack to the far west, between Alexandria and Abukir Bay, while Kléber was to push toward Abukir from Rosetta.

At 2:00 A.M. on July 25, what little artillery the French could muster suddenly thundered all along the line as ten thousand troops attacked Mustapha Pasha's roughly equal force.[27] Slashing his way straight through the Turkish line, Murat pushed past their entrenchments along the neck of land separating them from the sea and the lakes, with no Turkish cavalry to oppose him. The French next attacked the Turks' second line of defense, which was supported by thirty or so gunboats. "The cavalry then decided the victory for us," Napoleon related (truthfully, for a change) to the Directory, "swinging through the Turkish right, making a terrible slaughter . . . [as] the enemy threw themselves into the water to try to reach their boats a couple of miles out, all drowning in the process. It was the most horrible thing I have ever seen."[28]

It took only eleven hours for Napoleon to win a decisive victory over the Turks. Some 2,000 of them had been killed in battle, and up to 4,000 more died fleeing to the beach or drowning in the surf. A further 2,500 or so who had taken refuge in Fort Abukir at the top of the peninsula surrendered to Menou a week later. Napoleon reported French casualties at fewer than 500 (Berthier's more realistic count gave a figure of just under 1,000). But no matter how it was reckoned, it was Napoleon's first real victory—so far as disabling an enemy force was concerned—since arriving in Egypt.

Two days after the battle, Napoleon dispatched his key commanders back to their old posts—Desaix to Upper Egypt, Lanusse to Menouf, and Kléber back to Damietta.[29] But Napoleon's countenance no doubt fell when questioning their principal prisoner taken in the field, no less than the Turkish commander in chief, Mustapha Pasha, from whom he discovered that a fresh army was already en route from Damascus to Cairo. Thus Napoleon now sent Reynier back to Salheyeh to strengthen fortifications in that quarter. In a rare display of praise for someone other than himself, in the special Order of the Day, of July 27, 1799, Napoleon singled out Gen. Joachim Murat "who covered himself with glory at the battle of Aboukir."[30] The combined naval operations of Britain, Russia, and Turkey had been a supreme flop, thanks to Turkish incompetence. For rather than advancing from their original beachhead, the troops had just dug in and waited, failing even to isolate the city of Alexandria. Among the French casualties,

Napoleon lost a fourth aide-de-camp, Guibert, while Generals Murat, Fugière, and Lannes (yet again) had been wounded, as Napoleon renamed the fort at Alexandria after a fallen general, his Corsican friend Caffarelli.[31]

"The name of Aboukir was detested by every Frenchman before this battle took place; the events of July 25 have now rendered it glorious," Napoleon proclaimed to the army on August 1 before setting out for Cairo. "We have just reconquered the establishments in India and those of our allies. In a single operation we have made it possible for the French government to oblige England, in spite of her previous naval victories, to agree to a glorious peace with the Republic."[32] Napoleona . . .

Even though he now had the badly needed victory with which to return to France, on reaching Cairo on August 11, Napoleon was not in a particularly happy mood. Newspapers he had received from the English fleet reported that Europe was indeed at war again and that a new allied coalition threatened France. War had broken out on March 13—General Jourdan's Army of the Rhine had been beaten at Feldkirch, and General Schérer's Army of Italy had been defeated at Rivoli (of all places). The English navy was successfully blockading both the French and Spanish navies at Toulon and Cartagena. The French, he discovered, had lost Corfu, and Malta itself was effectively sealed off by a British blockade (and would soon fall). As for his Army of the Orient, despite his great victory, Napoleon was still isolated from the outside world, "the prisoner of his own conquest."[33]

Meanwhile the Sublime Porte was marshaling fresh armies, by land and sea, and most of Egypt remained unconquered. Relations between Napoleon and his senior commanders were as bad as ever. Kléber worked with Napoleon only out of his sense of duty to the republic he loved, but Desaix, it seems, had disobeyed earlier orders to abandon the south and to advance to Balbais. On learning of this Napoleon snapped: "I have not been at all happy with your conduct, Citizen General. . . . Regardless of the circumstances one finds oneself in, they must never prevent a soldier from obeying orders."[34] Napoleon also managed to complain about the incompetence of General Destain and, for the first time, one of his favorites, the Pole, Zayoncheck.

On top of everything, he found fresh trouble brewing in the Divan, and even open rebellion and talk of treason in the gilded halls of the Egyptian Institute, despite the presence of Monge. With this to greet the triumphant warrior, the day following his return to Cairo Bonaparte secretly notified Ganteaume to pack and store the recent war trophies, taken in Syria and at Abukir, aboard ship. He would be returning to the coast shortly, he informed him.[35]

﹡   ﹡   ﹡

Although Bonaparte carefully concealed plans for his secret departure from Egypt, nevertheless vague rumors soon began to circulate, mainly in the harbor of Alexandria, where feverish preparations were under way to arm and victual four French ships. Ganteaume's unusual interest and daily quayside visits, and the delicacies included among the victuals, made it clear that these vessels were not being prepared for just another messenger. Indeed, apart from Bourrienne, Ganteaume, and Berthier, Napoleon confided in no one, not even Monge.[36] (Monge was incapable of subterfuge, and Napoleon did not inform him until the day of departure itself.) On August 17 General Dugua complained to Napoleon: "They say that you are leaving for France, that you are taking Monge, Berthollet, Lannes and Murat with you." Although it was only a rumor, he continued, it was "having a very bad effect on army morale. I hope you will refute it at once."[37]

To put everyone off the scent, Napoleon announced that he was preparing for an immediate tour of the north. "I am leaving tomorrow for Menouf, whence I am going to make several different tours of inspection of the Delta to see for myself what injustices are being committed in the countryside and to better get to know the people of this land," he told the Divan on the seventeenth.[38] To Dugua he varied the theme, stating vaguely that he was setting out for the Mediterranean "to study the position of the enemy along the coast."[39] When Monge was cornered by his esteemed colleague Costaz at the institute, he blushed and did indeed dissimulate sheepishly and incoherently. He was sure by now that the rumors were true. When next pressed by the suspicious poet, Parseval-Grandmaison, who for one had no intention of being left behind in this hellhole, Monge muttered, "I don't know a thing. I believe we are going to Lower Egypt."[40]

At 10:00 P.M. on August 17, Napoleon's carriage pulled up before the institute. Monge, Berthollet, and Denon hustled inside with their baggage, as their betrayed colleagues bade them adieu. Embarrassed, they were no doubt greatly relieved as they left among a clatter of hooves, Monge leaving the institute he had founded and was never to see again. Arriving at the Elfi palace, Monge, Berthollet, and Denon joined Bonaparte. Casually kissing Pauline Fourès good-bye as she strolled through the lush gardens of the palace in her favorite hussar's uniform, Napoleon told her he would be back in a few days. In fact he had no intention of ever seeing her again, nor did he.

At midnight several vehicles set out from the palace with the chosen, including four of his aides-de-camp—Eugène de Beauharnais, Duroc, Lavalette, and Merlin—his Armenian servant, Roustan Raza, Jaubert, and five future marshals of France—Lannes, Marmont, Murat, Bessières, and

Berthier. Reaching Bulaq in the early morning they embarked on the vessels that took them down the Nile to Alexandria.[41] To Bonaparte's great annoyance Grandmaison had secretly followed and begged to be permitted to join them; aided by a guilty Monge, he succeeded.

Even before reaching Alexandria, to further put his own senior commanders off the scent, Napoleon dispatched couriers to Menou (ordering him to meet him at the port) and to Kléber (to leave for Rosetta), deceptions they learned of only after Napoleon's departure. It was under these circumstances that Kléber was subsequently informed by letter that he was appointed Napoleon's successor as commander in chief of a bereft army about to be attacked by further Turkish forces.

Because of France's precarious state, Napoleon informed Kléber in this final communication that he felt it incumbent on himself to return to the homeland, to repair their national fortunes. He also left orders for Kléber to send Aide-de-camp Junot and General Desaix back to France that autumn. On reaching France, he assured him, he would have a fresh convoy sent out with weapons, munitions, "and enough reinforcements to repair the losses incurred during the last two campaigns." But if things continued to go badly in Egypt, Napoleon instructed Kléber:

> You are authorized to conclude a peace treaty with the Ottoman Porte, on the principal condition that you be permitted to evacuate Egypt.... Accustomed as I am to see the recompense for the pains and labor of our undertakings in the later opinion of our posterity, needless to say I am thus abandoning Egypt with the greatest regret. The interest of the fatherland, its glory, duty, the extraordinary events occurring there alone have decided me to pass through the midst of enemy squadrons to return to Europe. I shall be here with you in heart and spirit.... The army that I confide to you is composed of my children. Over the period of time ... I have been given the mark of their attachment to me.

He closed with "by the very special friendship that I have for you, and for the true attachment I have for them—BONAPARTE."[42] But as Bourrienne put it, he did not have the courage to face his successor; "he wished to avoid his reproaches and Kléber's brutal frankness." Napoleon had made a colossal hash of his Egyptian campaign, and abandoning a condemned army en masse, he left Kléber to cope with the resultant disaster of all his miscalculations. After an earlier clash with Bonaparte, Kléber had referred to him as "that little bugger." What he said on receiving this astounding betrayal was not recorded.

Just before weighing anchor on the twenty-third, Napoleon sent a warmer message to Dugua, informing him that "an urgent duty" required his return to France and giving Dugua permission to return to France to take up his position in the legislature.[43] In a later note he assured the Executive Directory: "I have left Egypt well organized ... and the Nile more beautiful than it has been in the last fifty years."[44] Pure Napoleona. He had in fact left in his wake burning villages; an empty treasury; an army decimated by battle, climate, and disease, its morale absolutely shattered, surrounded by a resentful, hostile Muslim population just waiting for the first ripe occasion to turn on them. In the army Bonaparte's name was anathema, and every major commander except Desaix and the deceased Caffarelli had officially requested to be relieved of command and sent back to France. An army of more than thirty thousand had been reduced to perhaps twelve thousand. Kléber, whom he now left in command, would be assassinated in the gardens of the Elfi palace the following June by a knife-wielding Arab who claimed that he wished to shake his hand; while Desaix, who would indeed reach Napoleon later that year, would die on the battlefield after helping to win the Battle of Marengo. General Jacques Menou, who succeeded Kléber, converted to Islam, changed his name to Abdullah, married a beautiful teenage Arab girl. He arrested the faithful General Reynier for treason, no less, and ultimately surrendered to the British in 1801. The Egyptian fiasco was complete. Or, as Bourrienne so aptly summed it up, "So ended that disastrous expedition."[45]

For Napoleon the Egyptian campaign had been a turning point in his life and career. His faith shaken in Josephine, whom he had adored, their marriage would never again be the same, later ensured by her inability to have any more children. For the French army, it was a crossroads as well. Many hundreds of officers would finally be repatriated to France by their British captors in 1801, but the vast majority would never forget or forgive their abandonment and betrayal by Bonaparte. Most would achieve higher rank, some even becoming marshals of France, but all knew that in Napoleon Bonaparte they had a commander in chief whose word and loyalty were worthless, a man who abandoned them to save his own skin. Napoleon himself for the first time realized the limits of even his own abilities and conceptions. The Egyptian campaign made no strategic sense at a time when France was barely holding its own in Europe. Further, it had been hastily conceived and most unprofessionally executed, resulting not only in its ultimate failure but also in the destruction of close to two-thirds of the men who had been entrusted to him by the families of the first French Republic.

And yet, ironically, this misadventure made possible the greatest event of his life. On returning to France and landing in Saint-Raphaël Bay on October 9, 1799, much to his utter astonishment, the thirty-year-old Napoleon Bonaparte found himself greeted by a madly exuberant French people who knew little of his phenomenal disasters and instead saw only the man who had captured Malta, the Pyramids, and Egypt, the latter-day republican crusader who had taken Cairo from the heathens, capped by his final resplendent victory over the Turks at the Battle of Abukir. It was in this light that he was permitted to rush to Paris the conquering hero and sweep all before him. "The little bugger" had succeeded in spite of himself, and Kléber for one could never quite understand it.

Prelude to a Coup

The directors believe that they are using him, but one fine morning he is going to gobble them up, without their being able to do anything about it.
— GENERAL PICHEGRU TO FAVRE DE L'AUDE, 1797

n May 3, 1748, during the reign of Louis XV, in the sleepy port of Fréjus, a son was born to the town's postmaster and most obedient royal tax collector. The infant would one day be responsible for the shaking of the very foundations of the House of Bourbon, bringing it down and with it the entire *ancien régime*.

Coming of humble stock, Emmanuel Sieyès was fortunate in having parents who believed in educating their children. He was first sent to a Jesuit school in Fréjus and then on to colleges in Draguignan run by the Doctrinaires. At seventeen he was dispatched to Paris to the prestigious Petit Séminaire de Saint-Sulpice to continue his studies (a young Talleyrand meanwhile attended its sister institution for the aristocracy, the Séminaire de Saint-Sulpice). After five years of rather mediocre results, however, he was abruptly asked to leave: The reasons were never made public, the priests simply indicating that they did not wish to have the pleasure of ordaining him as a product of their institution. And thus it was that only two years later, on July 28, 1772, Sieyès finally left the nearby Lazarist

Séminaire de Saint-Firmin an ordained priest.[1]Although Sieyès's childhood hopes had been for a glorious military career, a weak constitution and chronic poor health and eyesight had destined him instead for a career in the church. Although ordained at the relatively late age of twenty-four, and despite a personal recalcitrance vis-à-vis church authority in general, he succeeded—thanks to his native ability and perseverance, and the good fortune of having a few powerful friends, including the bishop of Fréjus, behind him when it counted.

Graduating fifty-fourth in a class of eighty, he emerged with his *baccalauréat* and *licence* secured.[2] But it was hardly a propitious beginning for an impecunious young man. His childhood heroes—Alexander, Hannibal, and Caesar—had gradually given way to more cerebral giants, who had occupied most of his thoughts and study ever since, including among them such political theoreticians and philosophers as Rousseau, Montesquieu, Descartes, Condillac, Helvétius, Grotius, and Hobbes. In particular he was inspired by the works of the seventeenth-century British physician-philosopher John Locke. As his daily life and reading reflected, the Abbé Sieyès was by no means a devout or religious gentleman, preferring administration to ontology, and he was soon appointed secretary to Jean-Baptiste Joseph de Lubersac, bishop of Tréguier. Not taking his clerical vows overly seriously, the otherwise grim priest enjoyed the favors of an occasional mistress and more frequently the repose of Monseigneur de Lubersac's elegant estate of Bougainval. And yet such earthly pleasures were of no real, intrinsic value or interest to this compulsively serious young man with few friends or acquaintances. But with the bishop's promotion from the wilds of Brittany to the more pastoral surroundings of Chartres—the nation's wealthiest and most prestigious bishopric—came promotion for Sieyès as well, who on accompanying him was soon named *grand vicaire*—in charge of administering the thirty vicars attached to the cathedral.[3] This in turn was to lead unexpectedly to politics, as his new post permitted him to spend most of his time in Paris, where the nation was astir.

Of a reclusive nature, he was not a particularly warm or lovable human being and thereafter rarely corresponded with or saw his family. Nor was he even remotely handsome. Of average height, hollow chested, with a somewhat hooked nose, pale, bald with long stringy hair on the sides reaching down to his shoulders—this dry, humorless, awkward young man seemed devoid of any social graces or charms whatsoever. To make matters worse, he was troubled with a lifelong chronic hernia and often crippling eye problems. Food, clothes, fine furniture, elegant surroundings, beautiful women, and even money were of no lasting interest to the introverted

Sieyès, as the one or two semibarren rooms he rented in Paris throughout his life attested, with their two or three chipped chairs and table buried beneath stacks of books and papers, and a coat hanging from a nail on the wall. Nor during his twenties and thirties, was he a familiar sight in an age of superb salons given by the capital's grandes dames and their imitators. Later Madame de Staël, famous for her own fashionable if unconventional salon, which Sieyès did attend, admired the abbé's intelligence but nevertheless acknowledged that "the human race displeased him and he did not quite know how to deal with it."[4] And although she found his ideas interesting, not so his personality; she declared him to be "a very moody character . . . not the best sort of person for communicating with other men, so easily did he become irritated by their views, when not actually wounding them with his own."[5] No doubt to the astonishment of just about everyone, including himself, by the eve of the Revolution of 1789 the forty-one-year-old grand vicaire had turned into an important personality, if ever the curmudgeon, preoccupied only with political philosophy and theory—how to better the plight of France, its ruling institutions, and even its people.

Unhappy with the absolute monarchy of the Bourbons, as well as the pervasive influence of his fellow churchmen (more than eighty thousand strong) and church institutions, Sieyès now turned his long-simmering rebellion and his philosophical quest into two slender, if most timely, revolutionary pamphlets that shocked Louis XVI and much of the nation— *What Is the Third Estate?* and *Essay on Privileges.* "What is the third estate [that is, the common people, as opposed to the clergy and the nobility, comprising the other two]?" he asked. "Everything," he replied. Yet they had no voice in government, and this, he insisted, must now be changed. "If we do not have the right constitution," he argued, "then we must draw one up" to enable the people to have a say in how their lives were governed. (What is interesting is the fact that Sieyès wrote these pamphlets only after he and his father had exhausted all attempts to prove that they themselves were aristocrats related to the ennobled de Sieyès family.)

Much to his surprise, Emmanuel Sieyès soon found himself out of his black cassock and in a frock coat, acclaimed as one of the founders of the French Revolution and one of the earliest members of what was to become known as the infamous Jacobin Club. Naturally, just as his fame quickly spread, so did his number of acquaintances, a small handful of whom he was to become relatively intimate with, including the rebellious Madame de Staël, daughter of King Louis's onetime finance minister, Jacques Necker, the celebrated mathematician and philosopher, the Marquis de Condorcet, as well as the widow of Claude Adrien Helvétius (the wealthy tax-farmer-general, better known as a philosopher), though admittedly the theme of such friendships remained purely political in scope. Warmth and human companionship however, still remained quite beyond his ken, and in that sense the grim abbé had no real social life at all.

Despite the fire of his occasional speeches and printed rhetoric and of his private conversations, when critical moments actually arose, Sieyès was generally not found among those haranguing crowds or making masterful decisions. Indeed, throughout his life he attempted to recede into the background, a timid, undecided, almost cowardly soul, avoiding political leadership and in particular its responsibilities, which he generally excused on grounds of poor health. On the few occasions he did stand out, he had a firm majority behind him, as in January 1793, when he joined Talleyrand, Barras, Carnot, and most of the other leaders of the Revolution in voting for the execution of Louis XVI. Although he served on the Committee of Public Safety on more than one occasion, it was not in the limelight but in a less abrasive position, for example concerning himself with the nation's educational system.

Subsequently, when on May 28, 1795, the assemblies ordered the arrest of all members of both the Committees of Public Safety and of the Sûreté Générale and their political appointees, culminating in some twelve hundred detentions, the name of the elusive Sieyès was not to be found on the list. In fact, the month before he had safely maneuvered himself into nothing less than the presidency of the Convention, the perfect haven.[6]

With the overthrow of the Convention in the summer of 1795 and its infamous committees, the Constitution of the Year III (as it was to be known hereafter) replaced the old government with a new executive power comprising five directors, supported by a Council of Five Hundred (it had 500 members) and a senior Council of Ancients (of 250 members). Sieyès, though not happy with this constitution (preferring another of his own making), did reluctantly accept it, but, unlike the opportunistic Barras, declined to serve on the first Directory that October.[7] Sieyès did accept membership in the newly created institute, however, when he was named to the section on Moral and Political Sciences,[8] and of course he was elected to the first Council of Five Hundred, from which he launched a series of attacks against the repressive acts of the new Directory in a country already struggling after devastingly bad harvests and a severe winter.

One of the many fascinating aspects of the French Revolution was the bizarre array of human specimens it spewed forth, including two men so antithetical in character, values, outlook, and goals as Abbé Sieyès and Napoleon Bonaparte. The perspicacious Madame de Staël, after laying unsuccessful amorous siege to General Bonaparte, noted that she found "something disdainful about him when he is pleased with himself, and quite vulgar when he is fully relaxed."[9] This same disdain, blended with a pervasive distrust, was shared by both Bonaparte and Sieyès, vis-à-vis not only each other but many of the same political leaders of the day. For his part, Abbé Sieyès's hostility to this conquering hero increased sharply following his victorious return from Italy in December 1797, after Bonaparte's negotiations at Leoben and the temporary occupation of Venice, not to mention drafts in hand of the preliminary treaties of Tolentino (with Pius VI) and of Campo Formio (with the Austrians, resulting in the ceding of Holland and Belgium to France, and northern Italy as well, in the guise of the Cisalpine Republic).[10] Then, rubbing salt in the wound, Sieyès was obliged to attend three of the subsequent celebrations given in the general's behalf, including a dinner given by the politician François de Neufchâteau, for a couple of dozen distinguished personages, including members of the Institute (to which Bonaparte was elected two weeks later), followed by a private dinner given by the lovely Madame de Staël, and finally an enormous banquet given by the combined parliamentary councils in honor of Bonaparte's role in making the new peace treaties (and loot) possible.[11] Never a subtle man, Napoleon in his abrupt manner warned the French people during his speech that night where he stood and what to expect, concluding, "When the happiness of the French people will one day finally be based on the best organic laws, Europe will then be freed."[12] Only one man present apparently listened to his words with special concern: Emmanuel Sieyès.

In 1798, in order to avoid the political dilemma facing the Directory, Abbé Sieyès had—with Talleyrand's full support—suddenly had himself appointed French minister to Berlin, although he had no diplomatic experience whatsoever and could not speak a word of German. To aggravate matters, the dispatching of Sieyés, regicide par excellence, to the very antirepublican Prussian court of King Friedrich Wilhelm III was hardly likely to heal wounds or bring about a rapprochement between the two antagonistic states.[13]

In the meantime all was not going well for France, despite the government's momentary respite after overthrowing the attempted Jacobin electoral landslide. The country's traditional archenemy, England, had formed a working agreement with Russia in December 1797, followed by General Jourdan's defeat at Stokach on March 25, 1798, and Gen. Jean-Victor Moreau's further defeat at the hands of the Russians and Austrians at Cassano on April 27, 1799, while General Bonaparte's badly needed army was far across the sea, stranded in the sands of Egypt, where it was of no use to anyone. As if this were not bad enough, Czar Paul I had declared war on France in September 1798, while Franco-Prussian relations quickly plummeted, thanks in part to Minister Sieyès. But then in his absence, on May 16, 1799, Abbé Sieyès was elected to the Directory. He immediately abandoned Berlin for the French capital.[14]

If Barras, who had been ruling the Directory with an iron hand since its inception, considered Sieyès politically as well as personally detestable, other "republicans," including Madame de Staël's most recent lover, Benjamin Constant, welcomed the abbé's presence as "the last hope . . . of this poor republic which has been struggling so against immorality and stupidity for these past eighteen months."[15] Sieyès had left the country at a time of national crisis and had returned at an even worse time of constitutional jeopardy. While he was still en route to France, on June 5, the Council of Five Hundred, meeting in camera, had sent an ultimatum to the Directory demanding that it justify its actions and policies at home and abroad. No answer had been forthcoming three days later, when Abbé Sieyès was officially sworn in as the newest member of the Directory.[16]

This then was the grave situation facing France—of which Bonaparte was still quite unaware when planning to return home. The constitutional crisis, the great open clash between the Ancients and the Five Hundred, on the one hand, and the Directory on the other, was coming to a head. On June 16, eleven days after issuing this ultimatum, the two councils still had received no response from the Directory; they declared themselves in permanent emergency session. Retaliating, the Directory did likewise and the next day succeeded in ejecting from their board Director Treilhard (on the grounds that his election had been technically invalid), replacing him with the more manageable former justice minister Gohier. The political temperature in the French capital was now at the sizzling point.

On June 18 the angered Five Hundred attacked, the eloquent Jacobin firebrand Bertrand launching into the Directory and accusing them of having "annihilated public spirit, muzzled our liberties, and of having persecuted the republicans,"[17] while others denounced Directors Merlin and La Révellière, who were forced to resign. Sieyès, an old friend of Merlin, sat by silently without protesting or attempting to come to his aid. These two directors were now quickly replaced by ex-Jacobin and member of the Convention Roger-Ducos and General Moulin (a friend of Barras). At the same time the complete cabinet of ministers was swept away, including Foreign Minister Talleyrand, who was replaced by Reinhard, Cambacérès taking over the Justice Ministry, Fouché heading the Police Ministry,

Quinette the Interior Ministry, and the occasionally energetic republican General Bernadotte, the War Ministry.[18] Curiously enough it was Sieyès who now took the initiative in canceling the former decision to dispatch Admiral Bruix to Egypt to rescue General Bonaparte and his army and bring them back to France. But what could not be swept away so easily was the moral corruption of French society at the top, as whores and demi-mondaines replaced wives among public functionaries, reflecting the two new kings of a corrupt Paris, money and power. Meanwhile Director Barras remained "the very model of these [corrupt] new times: going from business to pleasure, from pleasure to politics, and from politics back to business."[19] For the less sybaritic Sieyès the decline in France reached a startling new low when he witnessed the old revolutionary salutation of "Citizen" being replaced again by "Monsieur" and "Madame." "That is simply scandalous!" the shocked abbé muttered.[20]

Meanwhile, at his new post War Minister Bernadotte did not find himself in any more enviable a position, with the French military in full retreat abroad, General Moreau's defeats in Italy resulting in the French evacuation of that country, while in Germany, General Jourdan was likewise defeated, not to mention the parlous state of the French army in Switzerland, following Masséna's defeat by Russian forces now threatening French frontiers.[21] In France itself Jacobins, despite the severe thinning of their leadership, continued to make themselves and their causes felt, by the end of June calling for a fresh revolutionary-style *levée en masse* (mass draft) of army conscripts and the abrogation of the right to buy a substitute for army service, while the "red" General Jourdan demanded that "the rich" provide forthwith a one-hundred-million-franc "loan" to the nation.[22] Perhaps even more frightening to those who had survived the horrors and atrocities of Robespierre's Reign of Terror was the creation by the Councils of Ancients and Five Hundred of the "law of hostages." This permitted the government of every department to arrest and take hostage relatives of émigrés or *chouans* (royalist rebels), who could be deported every time a public official was assassinated. For every such murder victim, four hostages (persons not personally responsible for or guilty of the crime) were to be deported from the country to penal colonies. What is more, this new law provided for the seizure of hostages in the event of acts of rebellion, stealing of crops, arson, pillage, and so on, all of which Abbé Sieyès quietly acknowledged without raising objections, thereby repeating his former role under Robespierre's régime. "We need a great burst of republican action," superpatriot Sieyès warned. "Do not forget, the enemy is at our very gates and simply must be repulsed."[23] But all continued to go badly for France throughout the summer of 1799, accompanied by fresh royalist uprisings around Toulouse and in the West, while Sieyès's good friend General Joubert, on whom he had been secretly counting for his own plans, was killed at the Battle of Novi (in Piedmont) on August 15, followed ten days later by the landing of English troops in Holland, even as uprisings took place in Lyons.[24]

Meanwhile, belatedly, the more conservative Council of Ancients cracked down on the immediate Jacobin threat within, on July 26 expelling their club (now calling itself the Friends of Freedom and Equality) to move out of the Salle de Manège, or riding hall of the Louvre, Sieyès proclaiming that "those calamitous days [under Robespierre] will not take place again. We, like you, detest everything that is contrary to the law and order of the land and the tranquillity of our citizens. . . . Our government exists to provide justice."[25] Nevertheless, on August 5 the Jacobins arrogantly adopted a frightening new program, demanding the abrogation of all existing laws contrary to the constitution and calling for the "redistribution" of property from the wealthy and middle classes to all those without any.

The Directory had to act vigorously if it was not to be overthrown by the incorrigible Jacobins. Thus it was they had called in the tough ex-terrorist and Jacobin Joseph Fouché, "the Executioner of Lyons" and regicide, to head the nation's Police Ministry. On August 13 Sieyès—fully supported by Barras and Roger Ducos (against the opposition of Gohier and Moulin)—demanded the official suppression of all Jacobin clubs, and because of the strong popular support for General Bernadotte (with his open ties to the Jacobins), Sieyès and Barras had to get rid of him as well. This was the same Bernadotte who was responsible for finally reinvigorating the army and bringing in badly needed reinforcements, money, and supplies that would soon result in fresh French victories abroad by Generals Brune and Masséna.[26] But, as war minister, Bernadotte could also turn triumphant French troops against the Directory, therefore Sieyès wanted him out.

Meanwhile tension continued to build, even as Bonaparte was en route from Egypt, and on September 14 government troops narrowly prevented hostile mobs on the Left Bank from breaking into the Bourbon Palace, where the Council of Five Hundred was being addressed by another Jacobin general, Jean-Baptiste Jourdan, who harangued the deputies, warning them of the great danger facing the republic. With this as the perfect excuse, Sieyès demanded Bernadotte's resignation, over that general's vehement protest, and got it the next day.[27] The Directory was now literally living on a hair-raising day-by-day existence, everyone wondering just how long this could continue. It was against this chaotic background on September 23 that the president of the Council of Five Hundred, Antoine Boulay de la Meurthe, during a celebration of the anniversary of the creation of the first French Republic, praised Director Sieyès as "the first founder of the Republic."[28] It was a surrealist nightmare.

With the situation continuing to deteriorate, however, by now even Sieyès, like Barras, was wondering how they were to be saved. He had, he felt, most of the answers: Overthrow the present constitution and with it the Directory and its outrageous councils, to be replaced by a new constitutional republic of his own design, headed by two consuls, including himself, naturally, aided by a powerful general, without whom he could not act. "I am looking for a sword," he had told General Joubert during a frank discussion earlier on, "but the shortest one possible."[29] When Joubert, his first choice, was killed in mid-August, Sieyès was left to resume his desperate, if unsuccessful, search for the one soldier he could count on, reluctantly turning to the ineffectual but manipulable General Moreau. To the abbé's surprise, Moreau not only declined but instead recommended Bonaparte, who, he said, "will carry out your coup d'état far better than I."[30] Moreau wanted no part of this volatile situation.

With the unexpected news reaching the Directory on October 13 of Bonaparte's seemingly miraculous appearance in France, the situation in Paris, still uncontrolled, changed yet again. No man in French politics seemed less likely to be able to bring about a decisive change of government, not to say a coup d'état, than the bald, puny, scruffy-looking Abbé Sieyès, who, Edmund Burke joked, seemed to have a fresh constitution in every cubbyhole of his desk. No man seemed less energetic, less effectual, and so lacking in the unusual leadership qualities required of such a unique moment. Indeed, no man seemed a less likely collaborator and ally of the arrogant, thumping, rude, impatient, egotistical, and demanding Bonaparte. Despite his appearance—later miraculously transformed by David's magical paintbrush into a fairly handsome man with a full head of hair!—Sieyès, with his impeccable republican credentials, did wield an immense amount of influence in the country and he did badly want the whole present regime and constitution swept aside in order to permit him to seize personal control. It was indeed ironic that this now somewhat jaded and tarnished idealist, frequently weak, indecisive, and lacking the moral courage to stand up when outnumbered, nevertheless remained perhaps the one key who could, in tandem with the right, vigorous, decisive "sword," strike the death knell of the very republic he had been so instrumental in launching just a decade earlier.

*   *   *

No fellow revolutionary could have been more antithetical in character, morality, decision, and action to Sieyès than the sybaritic Viscount Paul François de Barras.

The military was hardly a surprising choice for Barras, born in Fox-Amphous, Provence, in 1755, of an ancient, aristocratic family dating back to the army commanders it provided during the Crusades, and descended from a long line of soldiers ever since.[31] His career began quite normally after serving in the cavalry in France for five years, setting sail from Marseilles for the fabled East and the French enclave of Pondicherry in India, and a few years later on to South Africa. But on returning permanently to France in 1783, instead of delivering a report to Marshal de Castries, Louis XVI's irascible war minister, he got into a hot dispute with him, failing to observe the normal conventions incumbent on a very junior officer vis-à-vis a superior. Not only was he cashiered as a result, but an order was subsequently issued for his arrest, which the young man managed to evade. Four years later he was permitted to return to the capital, albeit without a career or future, though in his private life he already boasted a formidable list of ardent beauties to his name.[32] In spite of his well-publicized escapades and affairs, in January 1791 his parents, in exchange for a handsome dowry, somehow got him married off to Pélagie Templier, daughter of a rich Provençal merchant. That the marriage proved unhappy was hardly surprising; though it was never dissolved, the couple rarely saw each other again in the course of their lives.[33] Barras, by now an "incurable epicurean and impenitent seducer,"[34] was not about to change.

Unlike most of his family, with the coming of the Revolution, Barras turned not only to politics but to Jacobin politics, joining the extreme left wing in bringing down and destroying his own class and the French monarchy, and like Sieyès, voting for the death of the very king he had earlier (as an officer) sworn to defend. "I neither pretend to justify, nor pretend that I even have to justify to anyone, the conduct which those times required of me, and further which my conscience then also demanded of me,"[35] he wrote decades later.

After a stint in the newly created National Convention, to which he had been elected in 1792, he was named political commissar with the Army of Italy, in charge of maintaining the army's political loyalty to the Convention and the republic. With the fall of Toulon to the British in August 1793, Barras was given command of the overall military and political situation of that region and in the course of his duties appointed Bonaparte to take charge of the port's siege artillery. There, for the first time, another aspect of Barras's character appeared, as he personally ordered the murder and execution of hundreds of innocent French people in retaliation for their alleged support of the British. After stealing a fortune in booty from French citizens, he returned to Paris, where he somehow managed to survive Robespierre's animosity, while joining in the plot to overthrow him in July 1794.

The year 1795 marked a great rise in Barras's career, amid the nationwide turbulence and insurrection following the downfall of Robespierre and his cohorts. Now hurriedly reintegrated into the army and promoted to the rank of *général de division*, or major general, and commander in chief of the armed forces, Barras attempted to cope with the thousands of armed rebels fighting in the capital. The creation of a new constitution—that of the Year III, attended by the revolt of 13 Vendémiaire (October 5), was expeditiously quelled when General Barras called in Brigadier General Bonaparte (promoted by Barras in December 1793) as his second-in-command.[36] Thus, ironically, Barras once again was responsible for launching Bonaparte in his career and catapulting him to national fame. It was to Barras, more than to any other single individual, that the young officer owed his meteoric rise. Subsequently, as commander in chief of the Army of the Interior, Barras named Brigadier General Bonaparte his second-in-command once again. Then, upon Barras's elevation to the Directory on October 26, he had Bonaparte appointed his successor, raised in rank to divisional general (he had risen from lieutenant in less than three years), and six months later transferred to command the new Army of Italy.[37] And just for good measure, no doubt giving the debauched director much sadistic joy, Barras acted as witness to the wedding of his former mistress, Josephine de Beauharnais, to General Bonaparte. Thanks to Barras's continued support in the Directory and Bonaparte's own successes with his army in Italy, his career continued on its course.[38]

Barras's choice of this soldier had been vindicated. He needed the army behind him to support his own political ambitions and had carefully selected and groomed Bonaparte as his protégé because of his lack of the traditional ties and loyalties found in most other officers: Bonaparte, the Corsican outsider, had not a drop of French blood in his veins and no ties to court or party. Moreover, his military record already indicated more than one black mark against him—being AWOL for months at a time, chiefly in Corsica, even leading attacks against French forces there, not to mention having supported Robespierre's regime and later refusing to take up the command of an army in the West. Without Barras to cover for him, time and again, he probably would have had little chance of a successful military career. Thus Bonaparte literally owed Barras everything, and in return he provided the ideal "sword" to support Barras's political role. Barras's biggest mistake, however, was in underestimating the young general, whom he thought he could manipulate to his own advantage, as he had everyone else.

Barras and the Directory were not without their own trials, however, as they cracked down on the anarchist Gracchus Babeuf—"The Revolution is not over. The rich still have all the money"—and his fellow communist conspirators, who were finally condemned for treason in February 1797. Royalist pressure in the south continued to develop as well, as Director Barras ordered General Hoche's Armée de Sambre et Meuse back to France from Austria. Such emergencies required money, of course, and despite the vast booty sent by Bonaparte, more was needed, as Barras informed him. "At one fell blow you can save the Republic, stop the émigrés and destroy the base of foreign influence here," Barras wrote. "If you need force to accomplish this, then call up the armies."[39]

Although his protégé did not come in person to aid Barras in Paris, he did send General Augereau, but in fact it was General Hoche who provided the first fifty thousand badly needed livres (out of his own pocket) for the director's emergency expenses.[40] Meanwhile the royalist plot to overthrow the French government continued apace, General Pichegru, one of its leaders (and Napoleon's former math teacher), ironically warning the government that it was Bonaparte, not he, who was the real threat to the Republic: "Tell them [the government] not to trust your Buonaparte, this little monsieur. . . . The directors believe that they are using him, but one fine morning he is going to gobble them up, without their being able to do anything about it."[41] Pichegru, it seems, was one of the very few in France who really understood the extent of the Corsican general's ambitions.

The crisis came at the beginning of September 1797. Barras, on behalf of the Directory, ordered General Augereau to bring up his troops and artillery to protect the major bridges and government buildings of the capital, and then, on the fourth (18 Fructidor), the Directory ordered General Pichegru's arrest for treason. In addition dozens of leftist conspirators were also sought by the police, and the election of 157 newly returned Jacobin deputies was quashed as well. A total of 163 "conspirators" were in the end deported to the dry guillotine, as French Guiana was called, and thirty-one opposition newspapers were suppressed.[42]

This smashing of Barras's political opponents, generally referred to as his coup d'état of 18 Fructidor, proved but a temporary reprieve. The immediate threat was over; both royalists and Jacobins were stunned, if not uprooted. And yet, perhaps not surprisingly given his devious character, Barras—with Talleyrand acting as middleman—had also been secretly negotiating with Louis XVIII. The success of 18 Fructidor giving him full independence again, he did not follow up the royal option—all reference to which was carefully hushed up.

Meanwhile Bonaparte had returned to France from Italy as the greatest national hero of his day. This was followed by the general's demand to become a member of the government and Barras's rejection of the idea. Rastadt of course had not worked out, nor had the invasion plans for England, Bonaparte instead being dispatched safely across the Mediterranean to capture Egypt. Barras and the other directors could breathe more easily. With a bit of luck the ambitious general would not be seen again for years, perhaps never.

But, as 1798 gave way to 1799, the disintegration of French politics and society continued unabated. "The invasion of [Jacobin] republicans continues to penetrate all levels and classes," Barras, the former good Jacobin, complained,[43] while whispered tales of his sexual orgies in the Luxembourg and at his nearby estate of Grosbois circulated among the government's growing number of enemies. Decadence and corruption, not politics, were the order of the day. Even Madame de Chastenay, well informed by Police Minister Fouché, lamented Barras's leading role in this decline, including the immense fortune he was making through the illicit sale of army horses and supplies—while fresh police reports informed Paris that "all organization [within the country] is deteriorating at an unabated rate, everything is collapsing."[44] France had been teetering on the edge of internal collapse for several years, and a series of military disasters in the spring of 1799—beginning with the defeat of General Jourdan's army at Stockach, Germany, in March—only made matters worse. As already noted, this was followed by the even more incredible news of the double disaster in Italy that April, when first General Moreau was crushed at Cassano, resulting in the loss of Milan, capped by General Schérer's evacuation of the whole of Lombardy, not to mention the continuing threat of a possible Russian thrust through Switzerland. All that Bonaparte had earlier won in Italy had been lost.

It was under these circumstances that on May 9 Sieyès was recalled from his diplomatic post in Prussia to replace Rewbell in the Directory, much to the dismay of Barras, so fearful of this puritanical theoretician. Barras needed an influential soldier to support him. The once tall, handsome, dashing army officer, was now a tired, jaded politician, prematurely exhausted by his constant political intrigues and dissolute personal life. Thus had he been transformed, pasty unhealthy flesh gathering about his body, so replete with all the excesses Paris had to offer, that he was practically moribund, incapable of acting vigorously in the face of fresh upheavals. Hence his anxiety about the return of the more active and still ambitious Sieyès who, though perhaps a fanatic, could nonetheless become a real determining force if left unchecked.

As seen earlier, the crisis broke on June 15 when the Councils of Ancients and Five Hundred, having received no reply to their demand to the Directory of a fresh assessment of the state of French foreign and military affairs, now defiantly declared themselves in permanent session (and beyond the orders of the Directory). Agitation was increased when Treilhard, the newly appointed leftist director, was quickly disqualified, ostensibly because of a minor technical infraction.[45] Having executed this move, on June 18 Barras carried out his next coup, ousting two more opposing leftist directors, Merlin and La Révellière (subjecting the latter to a crude verbal barrage, involving language rarely heard in public). In fact La Révellière, so outraged by the dissolute viscount, had drawn his sword, and the flash of clashing metal was averted only by the timely arrival of some deputies.[46]

Meanwhile the country's internal disintegration continued unabated as brigands closed public roads everywhere; Jacobins threatened the entire administrative structure of Normandy; and industrial Lyons was shaken by severe unrest; while in the West, royalists supported by English gold and munitions erupted in fighting. France's worst enemies were always the French.

Celebrating his immediate victory resulting from the June 18 coup, Barras returned to his usual spate of luxurious dinner parties and nightly entertainments, while Sieyès quietly returned to France in June to join the Directory and, like Barras, seek "a sword" to support his own coup. "He continues ceaselessly to plot surreptitiously with the Assembly ... he creates factions, eggs them on, one against the other, and then stands aside [innocently] to profit from the outcome. . . . He is more dangerous and guilty so far as our personal liberties are concerned than all those previously brought to justice,"[47] Robespierre (of all people) had complained of Abbé Sieyès years earlier, just prior to his own downfall. These words now perfectly described the situation on October 13, when word reached Paris of Bonaparte's totally unexpected landing near St.-Raphaël.

18–19 Brumaire

There are those who would like to return to the days of the
Convention [and Robespierre], to the revolutionary
committees and the scaffold. . . . Just remember that I am
marching with the gods of victory and war on my side.

On October 8, 1799, Bonaparte's last dispatch from Egypt had reached Paris, announcing his final victory at Abukir Bay, just prior to his abandoning that country. The Directory immediately ordered celebratory artillery salvos fired throughout the city, joined by the peal of bells from the capital's hundreds of desecrated churches. The directoral ecstasy gave way, however, to utter consternation when, five days later, they learned that the great hero—whom they had all thought safely stranded on the other side of the Mediterranean—had in fact just returned to France, AWOL, and was even then en route to Paris! In fact Bonaparte's journey from Fréjus had been greeted by hysterical mobs following his coach for miles, attended by "unanimous applause" and "general euphoria . . . this inconceivable enthusiasm . . . this explosion of feeling and admiration . . . this spontaneous outburst . . . the like of which will never be seen again,"[1] leaving even Bourrienne quite staggered. Unabashed hero worship, singing, dancing in the streets, torchlit parades, and hastily erected flower-covered triumphal arches complete with tricolor bunting were to be seen

from Marseilles to Lyons and all the way to Paris, where a weary, dust-covered General Bonaparte finally reached his small house in the Rue de la Victoire at dawn on October 16, after an exhausting all-night drive from Burgundy. Josephine was still in Lyons, having missed him en route, thus Bonaparte entered an empty house—except for a servant—and went upstairs to his bedroom, collapsing still dressed into a deep sleep.[2]

Nevertheless, after just a few hours, he was up washing and changing his clothes, then setting out across the Seine to report to the Luxembourg Palace. As his carriage pulled into the courtyard, he jumped down and hurried up the long stone staircase to pay his respects to the Directory's current president, Louis Gohier. But he was anxious rather than triumphant, for—in addition to the humiliating tale he bore of his abandoned army of more than twelve thousand, with its horses, artillery, and stores—he was preoccupied with that whore of a wife, Josephine, news of whose flaunted affair with the young, "pretty" Captain Charles had even crossed the Mediterranean, consuming Bonaparte the cuckold with a fury such as he had never known, all because of a woman he had not only married and truly loved but madly adored. And to his great chagrin his brothers had met him en route to Paris and confirmed everything he had heard and more.

Although this initial meeting was to have been simply a brief courtesy call, Napoleon was nonetheless taken aback by the "glacial reception" he received.[3] In fact, a deputation of republican deputies was already requesting his arrest for the desertion of his army and for having violated the forty-day quarantine period* on debarkation. They also demanded the appointment of Bernadotte as military commander of the Seventeenth Military District (in which Paris was situated) in order to prevent a possible coup d'état by the desperate Bonaparte. Despite the ignorance of the masses and their vociferous welcome, no one of importance had any illusions about why Bonaparte had returned. But Barras, fearful of Bernadotte and his Jacobin associates, and of the growing chaos and disintegration of the country described in daily police reports, delayed these delegations and their demands, ultimately refusing to act against the general.[4]

Nevertheless, after leaving the Luxembourg, Bonaparte could not concentrate on politics with Josephine's outrageous deceit obscuring all else. Thus it was later that same evening that he paid an unofficial visit to another part of the Luxembourg Palace, this time to the posh apartments of his earlier protector, Barras, immediately bursting into a long, uncontrolled

*All passengers and crew on ships reaching French Mediterranean shores were automatically quarantined for forty days for health reasons.

denunciation of his wife, threatening to divorce her forthwith.[5] "But I told him that he had to look at the matter from a truly philosophical point of view,"[6] Barras related. Napoleon was seething with resentment and anger, and it was only after a long talk that Barras was able to cool him down enough to make him realize that, if nothing else, divorce would hurt his career. Nevertheless, he continued to harangue Barras, listing the history of her scandalous behavior, first as Alexandre de Beauharnais's wife, then living openly with General Hoche, not to mention subsequent affairs with Hoche's aides-de-camp and even more junior officers.[7] She was worse than a whore or courtesan, she was a nymphomaniac. Naturally Bonaparte did not mention what he and all Paris also knew: her other notorious affairs with numerous influential figures, including even Barras, though before Bonaparte had come into her life.

But now that she was married to General Bonaparte, "a new code" was imposed on her—and him—Barras pointed out, and with it a new discipline: "Everyone must submit to it, for there is in it an obligatory restraint without which society cannot function, which is even more indispensable than even military discipline, for just look at the consequences if it is ignored: the veritable upsetting, annihilation of, all social order."[8]

Although the law of divorce had been introduced by the Revolution, Barras continued, he could not think of a single self-respecting person of quality who had taken advantage of it, for fear of the political and social consequences. "Take my own case, for instance, I am hardly an angel . . . I could never afford to agree to a divorce . . . because of the permanent stain to one's name in the eyes of all the leading people of society."[9] After a couple of badly needed cognacs and much more talk, a sullen if somewhat more resigned Bonaparte left Barras's apartments.

If Barras was on surprisingly friendly terms with Bonaparte, given the unpleasantries of their last meeting before the departure for Egypt, it was because—despite his forebodings—he thought he could still use him. And as he admitted in private, "Immediately upon his return from Egypt, I thought Bonaparte was still with me, sharing the same special confidence that had existed from the earlier days of his military promotion and subsequent marriage."[10] But of course that was not at all the case, and Barras was quickly disabused of this view, though he continued to think that Bonaparte was still very much dependent on his political clout, favors, and protection, if for no other reason than the charge of desertion now hanging over him.

The next morning Bonaparte was back at the Luxembourg—no courtesy call this time—in front of the full board of five directors to deliver his report on the situation in Egypt and to face the menacing accusation of desertion, for which he had indeed jeopardized his entire career—and perhaps his neck. Two and a half hours later, an understanding was reached, however. No charges were to be pressed, and a much more relaxed if heavily perspiring Bonaparte escaped the Luxembourg and its snares, at least for the moment.[11] Once again Barras had intervened to save his career.

Returning home late that night, Josephine (accompanied by Hortense and Eugène) arrived in her traveling coach, only to find her husband locked in their bedroom. Terrible scenes ensued as Joséphine pleaded and pounded on the door, crying, imploring, beseeching, joined by Hortense, Eugène, and even Bourrienne, who pointed out the dangers to his career from such deplorable publicity, reinforcing Barras's earlier argument.[12] "After three days of marital pouting," as Bourrienne put it, and more tears and melodrama, Napoleon's bedroom door was finally unlocked and "their union . . . was not again troubled," though Josephine's other chronic problems, namely her spending sprees and debts, continued to plague her husband.[13] Despite the apparent reconciliation, however, the doting Napoleon she had known before the Egyptian expedition was gone. Josephine discovered a husband more demanding, more insistent on getting his own way, less open to her wiles, and less good humored, adamant for instance that she now break with "the Directory crowd," as he put it, particularly the courtesans attached to it.

The next day General Bonaparte set to work on his political career ordering his faithful aide-de-camp, Regnault de Saint Jean d'Angély, to invite Pierre Louis Roederer over to talk with him. The conversation proved most profitable for Bonaparte, Roederer agreeing to serve in the general's ranks in his attempt to seize power.[14] This was a particularly important coup for Bonaparte himself, as Roederer had a long and solid list of republican credentials and an equally solid reputation in the capital.

His father having served as a counselor to the king, and himself a celebrated jurist from Metz, Roederer had established a reputation as an economist and parliamentarian, first supporting the king and later the republic, when he held office as prefect of the Seine. But like Mirabeau, he strongly favored the moderate English system of constitutional monarchy, ideas that he later espoused in the influential *Journal de Paris,* which he edited for several years. In 1796 he, like Bonaparte a year later, was elected to the institute. It was not until March 1798, however, that he was finally introduced to General Bonaparte (by none other than Talleyrand).[15] They kept in touch thereafter, Roederer supporting Bonaparte and his ambitions because he genuinely wanted to see an end to the corruption and incompetence riddling the government at every level, and a return to law, order, and national stability not to mention to genuine republican democracy, which Bonaparte now assured him was his fervent wish as well. Roederer's open support was not merely a feather in the general's cap but a sign of the times, for as Bourrienne acknowledged, "one so easily believes what one desires," adding, "in all social classes, in every sector of public opinion, an 18 Brumaire was desired and expected"[16]—though of course not necessarily one led by Napoleon.

Meanwhile, Bonaparte was meeting almost daily with his "secret committee," as he called it, including Talleyrand, Roederer, Boulay de la Meurtre, Berthier, Joseph Bonaparte, and another influential politician, Volney, quite apart from a special committee of military experts.

Bonaparte's initial days in Paris were hectic but measured, as he assessed the political situation and decided what ultimate objective to set for himself—a place in the existing Directory, or preferably in an entirely new government. Next he had to decide how best to achieve that goal, as he continued to make those humiliating official visits to the Luxembourg and eat humble pie, while behind the scenes the Bonaparte brothers were hard at work, even Josephine visiting Barras and more frequently her old friends, President and Madame Gohier, trying to show her husband in a more favorable light.

The day after Napoleon's unexpected return to the capital, the cool, calculating Talleyrand (until that summer foreign minister under the Directory), along with Admiral Bruix and Roederer, called on Bonaparte in the Rue de la Victoire.[17] Prior to the general's departure for Egypt, Foreign Minister Talleyrand had promised to smooth the way for his conquest there by going personally to Constantinople to arrange affairs with the Sublime Porte. His failure to do so, however, resulted in the Ottoman sultan's declaration of war on France and his subsequent naval and land attack on Bonaparte's army.

What Bonaparte did not know, of course, was that—like both Barras and Sieyès—Talleyrand too had been planning on working for a change of government with the much more congenial and obliging General Joubert, whose untimely death that August on the battlefield had left them all with but one remaining feasible, if disagreeable, alternate choice. Hence Talleyrand's visit on October 17 to mend relations between them, bringing Bruix and Roederer as human buffers in the event Bonaparte became violent. Yet Bonaparte, still without a specific plan in mind, needed all the help he could muster, including the wily talents of the extraordinary if unscrupulous Talleyrand. It was at this time that Bonaparte revealed that he was interested in holding more than just the military portion of a political partnership.[18] Talleyrand, ever confident of his own superior faculties of managing men—any men—and situations, was not averse to working with the potentially powerful young Corsican general. Over the next couple of days all existing differences between them were cleared away, allowing for closer relations, while at the same time permitting Talleyrand to bring Bonaparte up-to-date on the intricacies and significance of the current political situation. If Gohier, with General Moulin, wanted to maintain the present Directory and follow its current destructive course, not so the irritable Sieyès and more amenable Roger-Ducos. As for Barras, always his own man, he remained strictly aloof, joining no party. To be sure, before Talleyrand's new relationship with Bonaparte, the general, goaded by his wife, had first hoped to exclude the execrable Sieyès from their plans, preferring to win over the more malleable Gohier, and perhaps even General Moulin.

Despite the acute political tension of the capital, in particular at the Luxembourg Palace, President Gohier gave a dinner party to which Bonaparte and Josephine were invited. The four-foot eleven-inch Josephine arrived in a ravishing gown, and the general, shorn of his long revolutionary hair, appeared in a stylish frock coat, his boots actually shining for once. Sieyès, who made no attempt to conceal his disdain for the hero of the Pyramids and conqueror of Egypt, found his feelings fully reciprocated: Napoleon pointedly ignored him, which turned out to be a colossal political miscalculation. Bonaparte soon came to realize that there could be no political success without Sieyès's full support. Meanwhile the abbé, much peeved by the arrogant soldier, snapped that he "should have had that insolent little fellow shot long ago!"[19] It was under these arctic conditions that the reception was held amid the neoclassical splendor of the Luxembourg, combined with the past elegance of Louis XIV and Louis XV. Here Bonaparte was able to converse with a more friendly group, including Talleyrand, Boulay de la Meurthe, Berthollet, Monge, the scientist Laplace, Volney, and, for the first time, General Moreau. More important, by inviting General Bonaparte tonight, the Directory announced to one and all that he had been exonerated and was again persona grata.

The climate changed dramatically over the following two days when a more confident Bonaparte returned to the Luxembourg to see first Gohier privately, and then General Moulin, to sound them out about his replacing one of the current members of that exalted board, probably Sieyès. He encountered utter shock, disbelief, and fear.[20] Thus it was that Bonaparte, at Talleyrand's urging, changed his tack. It was Sieyès who was the key to his success. "You want power," Talleyrand pointed out to Bonaparte with unusual bluntness, "and Sieyès wants a new constitution. Therefore join forces."[21] Though it meant swallowing his pride, it was the only sort of language Bonaparte understood.

"I was given the task of negotiating the political arrangements" with his old friend Sieyès, Roederer later recalled. "I transmitted their respective views on the proposed new constitution, first to one, and then the other,"[22] while Talleyrand with his impeccable credentials handled the day-to-day political tactics, gradually closing the remaining gulf separating Sieyès and Bonaparte. Following a series of stealthy late-night meetings, Roederer at last won over the reluctant abbé, as Sieyès and Bonaparte finally exchanged visits. The seemingly unbridgeable gulf of hostility between them overcome, the way for the eventual coup moved one step closer. Talleyrand's overall strategy was working.

Meanwhile brother Joseph was inviting influential politicians and soldiers to his posh Paris mansion in the Rue des Errancis or as weekend guests to his new 248,000-franc estate of Mortefontaine north of the city,[23] while Lucien worked closely in Parisian political circles, particularly among the Five Hundred, though occasionally seeing Sieyès as well. And then on October 25 Lucien pulled off his own little coup, arranging for his own election as president of the Council of Five Hundred. (He lied about his age—he was only twenty-four instead of the requisite thirty. Had any sort of credentials commitee been in place, Lucien would have been thrown out on his ear, or worse.) As for the Council of Ancients, there Sieyès still maintained sufficient influence, if not control, which Bonaparte badly needed to enlist if he was to succeed in that quarter.

But matters got completely out of hand and nearly came to a disastrous head on October 28, when Bonaparte was called to appear before a formal session of the Directory that had feted him so gloriously less than a fortnight earlier. Now he found himself charged not with desertion but with having enriched himself and his family while commander of the Army of Italy, back in 1797–98. In other words he was accused of having swindled the French government. Bonaparte was furious. Never before had anyone dared to call him a thief to his face—nor would they ever do so again. To be sure, newly acquired Bonaparte wealth was on glittering display for all to see. Lucien had bought an ostentatious mansion in the Grande Rue Verte. Napoleon himself had poured tens of thousands of francs into refurbishing Josephine's house in the Rue de la Victoire, and her several jewel boxes were literally overflowing with looted Italian gems. And then there was the matter of that bauble La Malmaison, which she had purchased in the spring of 1799. Not to mention Joseph's luxurious estate and splendid Paris residence.[24] Nor did Bonaparte deny it. A fortune had been spent by the clan, but, he protested angrily, not a penny had come from army funds. It was in fact all bona fide Italian war loot. Every senior officer, indeed every lieutenant, had availed himself of the circumstances, as was the tradition of the day. If Bonaparte had come back with more, it was quite simply because as commander in chief it was his natural right to do so. But steal from the French government? Never! The stormy meeting ended satisfactorily, exonerating the outraged general. But a fresh wedge had been driven between him and the directors, who now secretly agreed on the necessity of again ridding themselves of the hot-tempered, ambitious Bonaparte, offering him a fresh army command, which he declined.[25]

On the surface this latest attempt by the Directory to discredit him did not appear to bode well. Privately Bonaparte managed to keep open the lines of communication with Barras—whose political influence he could not yet do without—reinforced by Barras's contact with Roederer and Talleyrand. Meanwhile Police Minister Fouché, now openly beginning to favor the Bonaparte-Sieyès coup, was a more frequent visitor to the Rue de la Victoire, where he also came across Berthier, Bruix, Paris Police Commissioner Réal, Volney, and Roederer.

And then on November 1 (10 Brumaire), Lucien gave a special dinner for Sieyès and Napoleon, marking the cementing of relations. Following dinner they retired to the study, and by the time they broke up in the early hours of the morning, they had elaborated their general plan. There would be a coup d'état. The revolutionary Constitution of the Year III (1795) would be replaced by a new one, eliminating the Directory, the Council of Ancients, and the Council of Five Hundred, thereby sweeping away all vestiges of the corruption undermining the integrity and functioning of the first French Republic. Having arrived at Lucien's still somewhat wary of each other, they parted fellow conspirators, Sieyès promising to gain as much parliamentary support as he could, seconded in this effort by Lucien. Bonaparte would continue his efforts to gain the backing of as many of the senior army commanders as possible. As for the details of the day of the coup, they would cope with those later.[26]

As Bonaparte and Sieyès were now under close scrutiny, they could not afford to meet alone again—in private, anyway—and Roederer, under Talleyrand's guidance, was to continue as their middleman while Eugène de Beauharnais kept tabs on Barras (on the pretext of visiting some of his aides-de-camp, whom he had known in the army). Nor was the opposition uninformed of events, Police Minister Fouché, as usual playing both sides at once, working with Bonaparte through Réal, while secretly enlightening

Barras about the developing plot to overthrow him and the Directory. But neither Barras nor Fouché decided to act, apparently feeling that they could not muster enough force to foil Bonaparte and that under the circumstances it behooved them to go along with the planned coup given the general upheaval reported throughout the country, with nothing or no one powerful enough to counter it or the conspirators. Given Gohier's and Moulin's antipathy, however, naturally Barras and Fouché deemed it equally inadvisable to apprise them of Bonaparte's secret plans.[27]

By November 6 (15 Brumaire) the great plot to overthrow the government was well in hand, Fouché declaring himself more firmly on Bonaparte's side. On that date a huge subscription banquet was given in General Bonaparte's honor by the Council of Ancients, held in the former Eglise Saint-Sulpice. It was in fact originally conceived by Lucien as a good means of feting his brother and reconciling most members of the Ancients to Bonaparte, at the same time providing an excellent opportunity for the conspirators to take a reading of public opinion and how their chances stood. It proved a "bizarre feast," as Bourrienne put it, where everyone spoke quietly, with considerable reserve, there being "no freedom, no open comments ... no gaiety ... everyone carefully observing one another and saying little."[28] Though they were colleagues when meeting daily as the Council of Ancients, there was little camaraderie among them now. Indeed, extraordinary caution was evident in the hushed conversations taking place in that unheated seventeenth-century edifice, where about the only thing anyone was thinking about—apart from wondering what Bonaparte had up his sleeve—was how to keep from freezing. Napoleon himself got quickly irritated with the whole affair, and after gulping down his food, with General Berthier at his side, made his rounds, circumnavigating the immense U-shaped chain of tables, rubbing his hands to keep warm as he said a few words to most of the 250 guests. Then, suddenly taking his coat, he darted out into the cold drizzle and ordered his carriage to take him to the Luxembourg Palace for another secret meeting.[29] Despite everything, however, the dinner had achieved its goal, drawing to his side most of those members who had previously shied away from him, thanks in large part to the work of Sieyès. As for Bonaparte's fellow soldiers, only three important ones refused to support him: Generals Jourdan, Augereau, and, of course, Bernadotte.[30]

Though close to Barras, Bernadotte remained wary of both his brother-in-law, Napoleon (his wife, Désirée Clary, was the sister of Joseph Bonaparte's wife, Julie), for his egotistical antirepublican plans, and Abbé Sieyès, for having fired him that summer as war minister. But at least Joseph Bonaparte had succeeded in bringing Napoleon and Bernadotte together again, if hardly on cordial terms. The Bernadottes then gave a splendid dinner party for the entire detestable Bonaparte clan, though interspersing them among other guests, including General and Madame Moreau, Pierre Louis Roederer and his wife, Prince Talleyrand, and the Volneys. But at this chic dinner in a fashionable mansion in the Rue Cisalpine, even the presence of a bevy of beautiful ladies and fine old wines could not close the gap of intrinsic distrust and hostility between Napoleon and his brother-in-law, whom Napoleon described in private as "a very zealous republican"—a point of view that worried him. "He is a curious fellow, this Bernadotte," he confided to Bourrienne. "He is stubborn . . . a man who creates obstacles. . . . He has Moorish blood in his veins: he is enterprising and hardy . . . he does not like me. I am almost certain he will oppose me. . . . He is too idealistic . . . a devilish fellow."[31] And thus it was as enemies they met that evening and as enemies they parted.

In Paris, so it is said, when one entertains lavishly there is no plot afoot. With the coup initially set for November 7 (16 Brumaire), it was under just such culinary cover that Josephine gave a sumptuous dinner on the sixth in the Rue de la Victoire, where friends and foes alike could be found rubbing elbows, including Director Gohier and his wife.[32]

But at the last minute the conspirators had to postpone the critical date to the ninth (18 Brumaire). Two final steps had yet to be taken if success was to be assured: moving the sessions of the two councils—the Ancients and the Five Hundred—from the heart of Paris, where a vociferous Jacobin opposition had many friends and could physically break up and destroy Bonaparte's plans; and replacing Gen. François-Joseph Lefebvre, the commander of the Seventeenth Military District, with Bonaparte himself, to ensure a disciplined control of the ten thousand or so troops garrisoned in and around Paris.

On November 8 the various Bonapartist henchmen—and there was now a sizable number of well-informed conspirators—were busily at work on the final preparations—including such details as what each individual would be doing and which senior officers would be in command of which military units, and where. With the coup set for the next day, yet another dinner had to be hastily arranged, this time at Justice Minister Cambacérès's spacious residence, while still later that night Sieyès and President Louis Lemercier arranged to convene an emergency session of the Council of Ancients at dawn, in order to execute the final two items of business required prior to putting the coup in motion.[33]

Meanwhile the last of those joining the by-now-large conspiracy went over their roles, as the circle widened to include Cambacérès and Napoleon's banker, Collot, who agreed to ensure the financial side of operations. During the night of 17–18 Brumaire, General Lefebvre, who was about to be replaced as the commander of the Paris region, moved up cavalry regiments along the Champs-Elysées and the principal boulevards,[34] while Fouché and Réal ordered the police to take up positions before the main government buildings.

Just before the crack of dawn on 18 Brumaire, Saturday, November 9, 1799, President Lemercier duly issued the orders for an emergency convocation of the Ancients within the hour at the Salle de Manège, the Royal Riding School of the Tuileries Palace. At about the same time Talleyrand, Louis Roederer, and his son met secretly to draft Barras's letter of resignation. With that accomplished, at seven o'clock they set out for the Rue de la Victoire, where they found the narrow street crowded with army brass. Surprisingly, among their numbers they found a new convert, General Moreau, "a soft man lacking enterprise," Bonaparte said of him privately.[35] Although the Gohiers had also been invited to breakfast with Josephine, only Madame Gohier had turned up. Her husband had heard the endless round of rumors circulating throughout the capital and, fearing a trap, had sent his wife to see what was in the wind.

On his arrival Bourrienne seemed equally startled by the "great number of generals and other high officers [including Berthier, Bruix, Leclerc, and Murat] all those devoted to him. I have never seen such a great number in the Rue de la Victoire . . . all in full-dress uniform, overflowing from Bonaparte's little town house into the courtyard and the side paths." As for Napoleon, Bourrienne found him "calm, just the way he always was immediately prior to a battle."[36] Then, with the arrival of Joseph Bonaparte, bringing Bernadotte (in mufti), the assembly was complete, though a heated scene ensued between Bonaparte and the influential and popular Bernadotte, the latter denouncing any "rebellion" against the government and refusing to go along with the intended coup, of whose details he was only now fully informed. "[He called it a] rebellion! Can you imagine that!" Bonaparte afterward related to Bourrienne, unaccustomed to and shocked by the full truth. "A pack of fools!" Nevertheless, the general tried to reassure Bernadotte, informing him that he would be acting legally, not in rebellion, in fact commanding government troops under the direct orders of the Council of Ancients, which he expected to receive at any moment, though acknowledging to Bourrienne that he would not be able to win over Bernadotte, whom he described as "hard as a stick. . . . What a pity."[37]

While all this was taking place in the Rue de la Victoire, not far away at the Tuileries, Deputy Cornet, another Bonaparte stooge and a member of the "commission des inspecteurs" (roughly equivalent to party whips), was addressing the Council of Ancients. In the flamboyant language of the day he denounced another fearful "Jacobin plot," describing the "alarming symptoms" that had been uncovered, those *"poignards"*—literally, knife-wielding assassins—and "vultures," along with "sinister reports" reaching the authorities. Standing before that august assembly at that ungodly hour, in the drafty, unheated Riding School, Cornet harangued them, sounding the familiar clarion "The fatherland is in danger," and warning that "if they did not take immediate measures" to leave the capital, all would be lost.[38] Deputy Régnier, another man in on the plot, invoking Article 102 of the Constitution of the Year III, moved that their proceedings be continued the next morning at the royal residence at St.-Cloud, where their safety from invading mobs could be more easily assured. In a final motion he concluded the proceedings by nominating General Bonaparte, "this illustrious man who has so merited of his country [and] is burning to crown his national achievements," to replace General Lefebvre as the commander of all troops stationed in and around Paris, including the special Guards assigned to protect the Directory and the two parliamentary councils.[39] Lemercier then ordered a vote on both motions, which were carried. They duly agreed to meet, along with the Council of Five Hundred, the next day at St.-Cloud.

Instructed to notify General Bonaparte posthaste of his new military command, Cornet set off for the Rue de la Victoire, where he ordered Bonaparte to take "all necessary measures to ensure the safety of the nation's representatives."[40] Looking on with consternation as Cornet handed Bonaparte his written instructions to repair immediately to the Tuileries to take his new oath of office, Bernadotte finally acquiesced in the inevitable. "I will not march against you," he told Bonaparte, "but if the Directory orders me to act, I will march against any and all troublemakers," which of course would include Bonaparte himself. With that Napoleon leaped into the saddle and, with his full entourage of generals, galloped off to the Royal Palace.

Appearing before the Ancients, Bonaparte was duly called upon to take the loyalty oath (which in fact he had personally drafted for the occasion), ending: "We want a Republic founded on true freedom, on civil liberties, on full national representation. We shall have it, I swear it, in my name and in that of my companions-in-arms."[41] No one bothered to point out that the Ancients' replacing of Lefebvre with Bonaparte was quite illegal, exceeding the authority granted them by the Constitution, not one of the dozens of lawyers present protesting.

The clock for the greatest coup in French history had now begun to tick, as Bonaparte mounted his horse and went into the Tuileries Gardens to address the nearly ten thousand troops assembled there:

> The Republic has been badly governed for two years now. You have hoped that my return would put an end to such ills. . . . Liberty, victory, and peace will once again place the French Republic in the position it formerly occupied in Europe, and which only ineptitude and treason had forced it to relinquish.[42]

While all this was happening, the people of Paris could read Bonaparte's own proclamation to them, put up earlier by Fouché: "Under the present special circumstances, it [the nation] needs the unanimous support and confidence of its patriots. Rally round it, for it is the sole means of seating the republic on the foundation of civil liberty, national happiness, victory, and peace."[43]

Next, in his new capacity as the commander of the Seventeenth Military District, Bonaparte named General Moreau commander of the Guard for the Luxembourg Palace, while ordering the immediate sealing off of the city and the closing of its gates. It was hardly subtle, but with orders in hand from the Ancients, and the Army behind him, there was no body powerful enough to challenge him.

Meanwhile, across the Seine, at eleven o'clock that same morning, Lucien Bonaparte convoked the emergency rump session of the Council of Five Hundred in the National Assembly—the more volatile opposition Jacobin members not having been notified—where he, as its new president, had the earlier decree passed by the Ancients read aloud. They were stupefied, and there was soon much open anger, but Lucien, keeping a lid on events, immediately closed the session to all debate, pending the transfer to St.-Cloud the following day. Napoleon's timetable continued to run on schedule.

Meanwhile Director Sieyès had gone to the Tuileries as planned, where he was soon joined by fellow director and conspirator Roger-Ducos, remaining there for the moment under the protection of Bonaparte's troops ringing that ancient palace, while Gohier, Moulin, and Barras remained as usual at the Luxembourg Palace, still more or less ignorant of these immediate events.

Toward noon Talleyrand stepped briefly into the limelight, arriving at the Luxembourg with Barras's letter of resignation in his pocket, next to a banker's draft for a couple of million francs to soften the blow. Barras, who had never refused a good bribe, was expected to comply.[44] Nevertheless Barras, the Red Viscount, was not altogether uninformed of what had been transpiring in the capital in the past couple of weeks. Thanks to his close friend and confidant Fouché, and numerous other friends and "ears" throughout society, he knew of course that his former protégé, General Bonaparte, was preparing a coup d'état and that it was imminent. Hence his lack of surprise when he saw Talleyrand approach the table where he had been breakfasting late with the financier Gabriel-Julien Ouvrard, who had reported earlier seeing Bonaparte riding past his mansion with a bevy of senior officers at his side. Though he acted astonished, Barras acquiesced without a struggle, not even asking for compensation in exchange for signing the letter of resignation now thrust before him. Talleyrand, only too pleased with the proceedings, thus left the palace with the bribe—fortunately made out "to the bearer"—intact, his task completed, and himself unexpectedly a couple of million francs the richer.[45]

Meanwhile General Moreau arrived at three o'clock to escort the remaining two directors, Gohier and Moulin, to the Tuileries to sign and therefore "legalize" (albeit under duress) the decree drawn up earlier by the Ancients, along with their own resignations. In the meantime ex-Director Barras, also under military escort, vacated his apartments in the Luxembourg, leaving Paris for his estate of Grosbois for the last time as a former public official.[46]

That same Saturday evening, there was a final meeting of the conspirators in the Rue de la Victoire, including Lucien, Joseph, Roederer, Sieyès, Murat, Réal, Cambacérès, and several generals, apparently little realizing that they had already made one nearly fatal error by neglecting the cardinal principle of any coup—speed. By not having concluded the whole thing the first day, they jeopardized everything, giving their powerful Jacobin opposition time in which to rally. Nonetheless Bonaparte was not displeased with the results, as he saw the last of the conspirators to the door that night. "All in all it has not turned out badly today," he said as Bourrienne was taking his leave. "We shall see what happens tomorrow."[47]

The capital remained peaceful during the night, thanks to the presence of troops and police in great numbers. At dawn on a cold, overcast Sunday, November 10 (19 Brumaire), Bonaparte ordered some five thousand troops to set out for the Palace of St.-Cloud, including Milet and Sébastiani (a fellow Corsican), who had been with Bonaparte's army in Italy.[48] Once again, but for the last time, everything was going precisely according to schedule.

Upon arriving at St.-Cloud, Sieyès and Roger-Ducos immediately installed themselves in an unheated dilapidated room on the second floor of the palace. Like the rest of the once-elegant royal residence, this room had been ransacked by mobs during the Revolution, leaving a wantonly vandalized shambles in its place. It was from this small command center, however, that all operations were now directed. Meanwhile, up the road, in a private residence—all arranged by Napoleon's discreet banker, Collot, Talleyrand, Roederer, and a few others met quietly to monitor the day's events. As usual Talleyrand did not choose to be seen *sur place*.[49]

But at the palace itself all was not well. Finding themselves ringed by thousands of troops as they arrived for the sessions of both councils, the deputies gave vent to angry murmurs and comments, which did nothing to improve Bonaparte's already flagging popularity. Immediately on the opening of the session of the Five Hundred in the Orangerie at one o'clock, these deputies, who had been so effectively muzzled by Lucien Bonaparte the day before, now got completely out of control: "No dictators!" "Down with dictators!" "The Constitution is dead!" "Bayonets don't frighten us!" The Jacobins, who not only appeared the noisiest but who were also clearly in the majority, demanded the retaking of their loyalty oath to the Constitution and the Republic.[50]

Fortunately the scene (in the Galérie d'Appollon within the château itself) was not quite so tumultuous when the Council of Ancients reconvened at two o'clock and Lemercier announced the resignation of the Directory. However, the outraged Jacobin minority did demand information about the alleged plot that had forced them to seek refuge at St.-Cloud. And later one deputy suggested adding Bonaparte to the Directory, a move attended by a considerable hubbub as the party whips temporarily suspended the session. As for the man responsible for this national political eruption, Bonaparte was upstairs pacing back and forth, as Roger Ducos and Sieyès looked on, all three impatiently awaiting the outcome of the session in the Galérie d'Apollon and word from the Orangerie. Instead Bonaparte was met by infuriating silence. This was not the way he was accustomed to dealing with a situation. When finally the door did open, it was only to admit Generals Augereau and Leclerc. Napoleon burst out: "The wine has been drawn, now we must drink!" But then he simply withdrew into a stony silence once again and resumed his pacing. The minutes, then the hours, passed slowly, painfully, without word from either assembly, and by five o'clock Bonaparte's nerves snapped. It was obvious that things were not going well, no one coming to call on him as their national savior or to establish a dual or triple consulship with him at its head.

Suddenly he pivoted and stormed out of the room without a word, stopping outside only to gather Berthier and Bourrienne. Then, sweeping down the main staircase of the château, he barged in to the Galérie Apollon just as the Ancients were taking a break. Bonaparte carried out what his secretary described as "neither a noble nor dignified conversation" with Lemercier.[51] "You are sitting on a volcano!" Napoleon exclaimed. "The Council of Five Hundred is divided; everything now depends upon you. It's you who gave me my new powers. You must take action! Speak out! Do something! I am here to execute your decisions. Preserve our liberties!" It was as pathetic as it was nonsensical, but he felt he had to say something—anything—to break the deadlock. "And the Constitution?" one deputy asked. "You already destroyed the Constitution when you violated it. No one respects it anymore."[52] When pressed about the alleged plot threatening them and about its leaders, he replied: "Barras and Moulin— they have made certain proposals to me." And in fact both the Jacobins and the royalists had secretly approached Bonaparte, who had rejected them all. After all, he had his own plot. "There are those who would like to return to the days of the Convention [and Robespierre]," Bonaparte continued, "to the revolutionary committees and the scaffold. . . . Just remember that I am marching with the gods of victory and war on my side," he added threateningly, "and if certain spokesmen here in the pay of foreigners ever attempt to declare me an outlaw . . . just let them take care that they do not instead find themselves outlawed!" Turning to the general officers serving as his aides-de-camp and standing protectively around him, he continued that he would call on "my brave companions-in-arms here." Bourrienne urged: "Leave, General! You no longer know what you are saying." Bonaparte blurted out incoherently: "He who loves me, will follow me!" ("His place was clearly before an artillery battery, and not before this assembly," Bourrienne later lamented.) The general had bungled it, and as Bourrienne and Berthier hustled him out, his secretary commented, "I had the distinct feeling that instead of sleeping in the Luxembourg Palace tomorrow [as Napoleon had predicted], he would be ending his career in the Place de la Révolution"—where Louis XVI had been guillotined.[53]

Stymied and at the breaking point, Bonaparte strode out of the château and across the garden. "We have to play every card we have now," he said as he passed cheering troops. Entering the Orangerie without being announced or requested, his hat in one hand and riding crop in the other, escorted this time by four strapping grenadiers armed with campaign swords, the little general with the big shinning boots, found himself in the middle of a session of the Council of Five Hundred, where Barras's letter of resignation had just been read:

The glory accompanying the return of the illustrious warrior whose splendid career I had the good fortune of opening for him, along with the astonishing marks of confidence the legislators have shown him and the decree of the National Convention, have convinced me that, whatever post he is called on by the nation to fill, the threats to liberty will be overcome and the interests of the army guaranteed.

Thus it is that I joyfully return to the rank of plain citizen.[54]

After the mollifying words of ex-Director Barras, the timing of the "illustrious warrior" could not have been more unfortunate. "What are you doing here?" the infuriated deputies demanded. "General, is it for such unconscionable acts as these that you conquered for us on the field of battle?" Cries of "Down with the dictator! The sanctuary of the nation's laws has been violated. Down with the tyrant! Down with this Cromwell!" "Outlaw him! Long live the Constitution!"[55] pelted him from every direction, as the angered men in their white state robes and blue sashes closed menacingly around him. Bonaparte was only saved at the last minute as the four grenadiers shoved back the threatening hands and bodies—but not before one deputy grabbed him by the collar and shook him.

Leaving utter mayhem in his wake, the trembling Bonaparte stomped back across the gardens to the château, to relate to Sieyès what had just transpired, as he gathered his general staff around him.[56] Beside himself, he rushed back outside. Telling the troops assembled outside of the attack on his person by the Five Hundred, he shouted: "Soldiers! Can I count on you?" By now Generals Murat and Sérurier were at his side, and many other senior officers were equally wrought up. In the Orangerie, Lucien Bonaparte, doing all in his power to prevent his brother from being outlawed, pounded his gavel furiously, his voice unheard in the ensuing pandemonium. Exasperated, he tore off his presidential sash and toga, shouting, "I hereby place on this tribune, as a sign of mourning, the badge and costume of the supreme magistrature." Then, practically unnoticed, he left the hall.[57]

Outside, encountering Napoleon and Sieyès, a shaken Lucien told them: "If you don't stop them within the next ten minutes, all is lost."[58] And, mounting a horse, Lucien shouted at the troops: "The majority of the council is being threatened by the Terror [Jacobins], some even wielding daggers … and threatening to outlaw the general who has been charged with executing the council's decree. You must expel the rebels from the Orangerie. Those brigands are no longer the representatives of the people, but of the dagger." Then withdrawing a sword and pointing it at

Napoleon's heart, he swore before all of them to run his own brother through then and there if he did not respect their liberties, which finally won cheers and smiles from the soldiers.[59] "Lucien," said Bourrienne, "showed an activity, an intelligence, a courage, a hardiness, and a presence of mind rare in any man at any time. From what I have seen, it is incontestably to him and his conduct that the ultimate success of 19 Brumaire was due."[60]

Napoleon, pale but calmer, turned to address the troops: "Soldiers, I have led you to victory in the past. Can I count on you here?"[61] Apart from an occasional hesitant cheer, a curious, tentative silence and sense of bewilderment hung over the thousands of men. Old soldiers who had campaigned with Bonaparte to their great glory in the Army of Italy, and others in Murat's old cavalry unit, were clearly moved and on the brink of going over to their general, but they held back, aware of the gravity of marching against a duly constituted government body of their legally elected representatives. Napoleon could think of nothing else to say or do to convince them. He stood there, riding crop in hand, white, speechless, incredulous that his enthusiasm and his wishes had not ignited them. Finally the tension was unexpectedly broken as General Murat urged his horse ahead of Napoleon and Lucien, waving his long cavalry sword, calling out to the troops to move. That crude gesture seemed to do it: Drums suddenly rolled and all the troops moved en masse, following Generals Murat and Leclerc on their horses into the Orangerie.[62] Shouting "Vive le général!" they rushed into the glass building, where they were greeted by shouts of abuse from the swarming deputies in their white robes, Murat's angry voice thundering above them all, "Dammit, get the whole lot out of here!"[63] Terrified, most of the deputies poured out through the nearest exits, and within ten minutes the Orangerie was swept clean and still. It was 7:30 and dark outside. Napoleon's schedule was a shambles.

Meanwhile, in the Galérie d'Apollon, the Ancients, learning of what had just transpired, hastily reconvened.[64] Here at least the steady guiding hands of Napoleon's fellow conspirators Sieyès and Roger-Ducos had maintained order and direction. Most of the few dozen remaining Ancients drew up the formal draft of a new decree naming a new "temporary executive committee" consisting of Bonaparte, Sieyès, and Roger-Ducos to replace the defunct Directory. "This semblance of legal representation was essential," Bourrienne noted, "for Bonaparte, in spite of the illegalities committed the previous day, wished to present the facade of having acted legally"[65]—window dressing for public consumption, and for history.

After stopping to rest and get something to eat, Lucien managed to convene sixty-one of the remaining deputies of the Council of Five Hundred. Meeting in the cold hall, lit only by a handful of candles, at 1:30 in the morning on 20 Brumaire, Boulay de la Meurthe—another member of Bonaparte's inner circle—addressed them, declaring that there remained in France "neither public liberty nor personal freedom," merely "a phantom government."[66] A new one had to be installed under an entirely new constitution. To ensure no further problems from the Left, they voted to exclude all Jacobin members of the present Five Hundred and Ancients from any future legislative body, and then seconded the earlier motion of the Ancients by authorizing the creation of "an executive consular commission."[67] Bonaparte, Sieyès, and Roger-Ducos were then summoned to take the oath of office. Until a new constitution could be written, the former two assemblies would be replaced by a special twenty-five-man commission to help govern the country and administer the policies and decisions of the executive consuls. With only two members now opposing these measures, the motions were carried and the Constitution of the Year III proclaimed null and void. Bonaparte had successfully pulled off what Alexis de Tocqueville called "one of the most badly conceived and executed coups d'etat imaginable."[68]

The night session had gone "smoothly and quietly," Bourrienne recorded:

> At three in the morning all was finished and the Château of St.-Cloud, . . . once again enveloped in a vast solitude, resumed its customary state of calm. . . . I climbed into the carriage with Bonaparte as we took the road back to Paris. Bonaparte was so exhausted after so many trials and tribulations that—[as] a whole new future unfolded before him—he was entirely lost in thought, and during the journey back did not utter a single word.[69]

CHAPTER 14

The Consulate

We have lived together for so many years, and have been so closely united that our hearts are one, and you know better than anyone how fond I am of you.

—To Joseph

 am greatly disposed to think, that the present [French] Government is much inclined to correct, at least in part, the follies of the past," Secretary of State John Marshall informed President John Adams in the spring of 1800.[1] War with France could be averted if the new French government, the Consulate, as it was called, would make amends, substantial reparations for past attacks on American citizens and property during the violent revolutionary years. For months three upright and wary senior American ministers plenipotentiary—Chief Justice Oliver Ellsworth, William Vans Murray, and William Richardson Davie—had been negotiating with their French counterparts, led by Joseph Bonaparte. For months they had been in deadlock, first because Napoleon had been stalling and as a result of very real differences and then because the latest military campaign against the Austrians took First Consul Napoleon Bonaparte to battlefields far from the Parisian conference table. Nor had relations between the stern, puritanical American diplomats with the easygoing Joseph Bonaparte been smooth. Ellsworth and Murray in particular had more than once been at the point of despair. But finally there had been a breakthrough, for even Puritans are willing to compromise, and on September 30, 1800, they had agreed to the articles and wording of a new treaty between the American and French Republics.

Now, at four o'clock on Friday, October 3, the spacious courtyard of Joseph Bonaparte's sprawling country estate of Mortefontaine was filled with hundreds of the most important government officials of the French Republic. Joseph and Julie Bonaparte, as hosts to the multitude—a queue of more than a thousand carriages stretched back some twenty miles to Paris—waited with smiles and a little anxiety. Trumpets pierced the air, and drums rolled as cavalry units of the Consular Guard suddenly appeared, the ground shaking beneath the thunder of their hooves and those of the six white horses recently given First Consul Bonaparte by Austrian Emperor Franz I, the state carriage coming to a halt in the Court of Honor as other elite troops of the Guard snapped to attention.

This was clearly Joseph Bonaparte's great day, and if the signing of this Franco-American treaty was hardly his most important coup, it was nevertheless a bold step forward in his own career, to be followed in a few months by the even more spectacular treaties of Lunéville (concluding hostilities with Austria) and Amiens (with England). But this was the first important treaty to be concluded at his estate, with the eyes of the nation—nay, of the world—on him. Mr. and Mrs. Murray and William Davie stood near Joseph, and even the crotchety Oliver Ellsworth had left his bed, to which he had been confined because of a severe attack of kidney stones. William Murray, who had found Joseph Bonaparte the diplomat rather a fierce contender for a while, now saw Joseph the chatelain graciously indolent, warm, even charming, full of surprises, including his "flow of literary knowledge" that "comes from him like an insensible perspiration."[2]

The estate of Mortefontaine seemed to shrink as more than three thousand dignitaries and special guests invaded the gracious salons, overflowing into the vast park that was in turn encompassed by a village, mills, and numerous farms, all set on well over a thousand acres in all directions. The English garden, so uncontrolled and informal after the rigid constraints that his brother Napoleon so preferred in the gardens of the Tuileries, Versailles, and Fontainebleau, somehow came as a relief. Lakes with wooded isles, rocky hills, temples, and peacocks, along with magnificent old chestnuts, oaks, elms, and lime trees stood as backdrop, as the ministers of First Consul Bonaparte's government witnessed Foreign Minister Talleyrand's presentation of the Convention of Peace, Commerce, and Navigation to Bonaparte. All the ministers were here, as were consuls, the somewhat reduced diplomatic corps, dozens of senior general officers of the French army and navy, members of the all-important and newly created State Council, the highest judges of the land, and the presidents of the various national institutions, including those of the Tribunate, the Corps Législatif, and the Senate. Farther back were their ladies in all their magnificence, in gowns specially made for the occasion, arms, bosoms, and coiffures glittering with gems, the fruit of Napoleon's campaigns. But it was the rare sight of a man whose appearance Napoleon was shortly to ban, a man whose name rang in the hearts and imaginations of Frenchmen and Americans alike—perhaps even more than that of Bonaparte himself—the forty-three-year-old Gen. Gilbert du Motier, Marquis de Lafayette, and his lovely wife, Adrienne, that attracted as much attention and comment as anyone there.

Signed on October 1, 1800, by Joseph Bonaparte and his three colleagues, and of course by the three American "commissioners," the treaty was pending final ratification by both governments.[3] War between France and the United States, war that Secretary of State John Marshall believed to be inevitable had these negotiations fallen through, had been averted, though just barely. Ending the state of quasi hostilities existing between the two countries, it now established free commerce between them, while outlawing contraband of war (anything from guns, ammunition, and swords to cavalry saddles) that could be seized by either party. France had successfully removed the fledgling American democracy from the ties of London, creating a new crack in the slate of nations England was attempting to assemble for the purpose of further isolating France. This was just the beginning, however, as Napoleon's gaze fell farther afield on a seemingly unbounded horizon.

As the document was handed over, cannonfire shook the great house, announcing to the world this diplomatic coup, as everyone celebrated with vintage champagne and conversation. Then Joseph's butler announced that dinner was served, and some 180 special guests filed into three of the largest reception rooms, all decorated in Franco-American motifs.

The main dining room, now dubbed the "Salle de l'Union," had several American inscriptions on the walls, in the form of shields placed over the crossed flags of France and the United States, including one reading, "Fourth of July 1776, American Independence," another, "Lexington," followed by "Saratoga," "York Town," and other battles and events of the American Revolution. The remaining two halls bore the names "Salle de Washington" and "Salle de Franklin," with appropriate busts of those two gentlemen set off by tasteful floral displays. Various toasts were offered, Napoleon lifting his glass "to the memory of the French and Americans who died on the field of battle for the independence of the world."[4]

Following dinner, the guests stepped out into the garden briefly to watch a colorful fireworks display above the nearest lake, representing the motif of the union of France with its new American friends, over a flotilla of model warships sailing across the water, complete with sails and miniature French and American flags. Yet another hint for the Americans. As everyone stepped inside once again, a concert of French and Italian music was given, followed by two light plays. These were followed in turn by a grand ball that lasted well into the morning, but from which Napoleon and Josephine, and the Americans, retired shortly after midnight.

Early the next morning the indefatigable first consul was off on a hunt, bringing down a doe. Afterward he strolled in the gardens with a curious Murray, the latter's first real tête-à-tête with Napoleon. The American diplomat was much impressed, finding Bonaparte

> grave, rather thoughtful, occasionally severe—not inflated nor egotisti-cal—very exact in all his motions wh[ich] show at once an impatient heart & a methodical head—not the exactness of a special pleader—but of a most skilful self possest fencing master. . . . He speaks with a frank-ness so much above fear that you think he has no reserve—He is a pleasing man with the Soldier drawing into the politician—He could never have been a trifler in his life.[5]

A shrewd assessment.

As Ellsworth and Davie were taking their leave and about to board their carriage for Le Havre, thence to sail for America with their new treaty, Napoleon presented them each with a handful of gold Roman coins recently excavated in the region. Taken aback, they put their heads together momentarily and then handed back the gifts, explaining to a baffled first consul—and a much bemused Talleyrand—that they were not permitted to accept foreign gifts.[6]

Unknown to the three Americans, on that very October 4 the one person obviously absent at Mortefontaine, General Berthier, was at Madrid signing the secret Second Treaty of Ildefonso, ceding the vast region of Louisiana and the Spanish half of the island of Hispaniola to France. It was not a good bargain for Spain; the Spanish received only the Duchy of Tus-cany for the Spanish king's daughter, Maria Luisa, and his son-in-law, Louis de Bourbon, duke of Parma.[7] Although later disturbed by this decep-tion, the pragmatic Americans nevertheless duly ratified their treaty. They were in no position to do otherwise, and in the long run it proved a most fortunate event so far as the United States government was concerned.

Leaning back in his carriage as he returned to Paris that same Saturday afternoon, momentarily free of the unrelenting demands of his counselors, ministers, family, and general events, First Consul Bonaparte could smile, fairly if not fully content with his achievements since 18 Brumaire. His brief sojourn in the Luxembourg Palace had been quickly followed in February by a transfer of establishment to the Tuileries, which gave him and his staff much more space, his two fellow consuls now being required to reside in smaller separate residences of their own. Not only were he and Josephine permitted grander quarters (Josephine's apartments included the entire ground floor of the Tuileries) but also more ostentatious, even royal, trappings, correctly reflecting Napoleon's new position of power. Chamberlains, equerries, valets, and whole platoons of servants of every variety were adorned with the new personal livery and colors of the first consul. The once simple Bonaparte household had overnight taken on princely pretensions and accoutrements, surrounded and protected by a new, rigorous etiquette worthy of Louis XVI himself, which carefully isolated the first consul from everyone whenever he chose, even from his closest military colleagues and the highest government officials.

Napoleon's first few months in power had in fact achieved staggering results, most of them for the better, enough to impress even the stern John Marshall. First he had discarded the corrupt Directory and its government and constitution, replacing them with Sieyès's newly inaugurated—if modified—Constitution of 1799, which created the triconsulships and Napoleon's dominating position—complete with full decree powers—as the nation's first consul. Then Sieyès and Roger-Ducos were edged out and replaced by the new second consul, Cambacérès, and Third Consul Charles-François Lebrun, and of course three new "representative" bodies replacing the former Council of Ancients and Council of Five Hundred: a hand-picked Senate, which introduced new legislative proposals (given by Napoleon); a one-hundred-member Tribunate, empowered solely to discuss these new proposals; and a legislative body that could vote on (but not debate) them. Divide and rule.

Thus First Consul Bonaparte had cleverly emasculated and manipulated the entire legislative process. The only real opposition came from the Tribunate, and Napoleon was finally to eliminate that institution in 1807. This revised structure was capped with the government ministers for the various traditional departments (foreign affairs, interior, war, and so on) responsible to, and named by, Bonaparte. But above the entire institutional hierarchy was found something new, the State Council, which was to revolutionize the governing process.

This highest of all councils, and the only really important one so far as Napoleon was concerned, was divided into five sections—laws, interior (national affairs), finances, army and navy, and legislation. Its tasks included drafting required legislation—on proposals submitted by the first consul— and prior study of these projects and of any other subject assigned by him, and him alone. The first consul personally convened each of the five sections monthly. It was perhaps the first coherent, deliberately established think tank in history. In addition the State Council served as a final court of appeals, not only in legal matters but also acting against administrative abuse by the nation's bureaucrats, something badly needed and greatly welcomed in a country where a challenge to persons in authority had hitherto been an exercise in futility. The council, in its several aspects, was to prove a most effective creation, and it would outlast Napoleon and his subsequent Empire, a Second Empire later in the century, and every subsequent republic that followed, down to the present day.

For the most part the ministers selected by Napoleon were very bright and well prepared for the tasks they were to undertake, with only a few subsequent changes required. Considering how many of the previous years Bonaparte had spent out of the country, and that he had never been directly involved in day-to-day politics and national administration—thus lacking that necessary contact, intimacy, and background—the first consul's choices proved to be remarkably adroit, including those of Cambacérès and Lebrun, who were to remain close to Napoleon later under the Empire, as his arch-chancellor and arch-treasurer, posts they retained to the very end.

Apart from his ministers and state counselors, there was one person on whom Napoleon depended to a considerable degree during the first ten years, despite grave differences of opinion, and that was his brother Joseph.

For Joseph Bonaparte the festivities at Mortefontaine celebrating the new Franco-American treaty of friendship were halcyon days. To be sure, festivities on later occasions were more spectacular, as when two years hence the Treaty of Amiens was concluded there, but in a sense this was the best time, still uncomplicated by the jealousies and growing differences that were to divide Joseph and his younger brother and eventually ravage the entire Bonaparte family.

Of all the Bonaparte children, Joseph was by far the best educated and the most highly cultured, with a real, if amateurish, interest in literature, music, and the arts—and, unlike Napoleon, he could sing in key.

Had the family not been forced to flee their native land and certain arrest, Joseph could have anticipated a fairly easy life in an influential position in national politics or the judiciary, probably as a high court judge. As head of his family he was responsible for brothers Lucien, Louis, and Jérôme, sisters Caroline, Pauline, and Elisa, as well as his mother. Like Lucien, he was a warehouse guard at St.-Maximin, a temporary and humiliating job that scarcely kept a roof over the heads of his family. But thanks to contact with a wealthy merchant family of Marseilles, Joseph soon became engaged to the eldest daughter, Julie Clary. Their nuptials were celebrated on August 1, 1794,[8] at a time when, thanks to the rising military star of Napoleon, the twenty-six-year-old Joseph was earning a substantial income as a quartermaster, providing the French army with supplies—always a lucrative position.

Marriage changed his and the family's circumstances. Julie brought a substantial dowry, fidelity, stability, and devotion to her young husband and future family. She gave Joseph not only the working capital needed to launch the sizable fortune he was soon to build into millions, but the partnership of a woman whom he could respect and count on, in good times and bad. Like the entire dozen Clary siblings, Julie was religious, embarrassingly honest, stubborn, and intelligent, thereby making her highly antithetical to so many of the Bonaparte family values in general. But "Madame Mère," as Letizia was known, admired and respected Julie Clary, and without that blessing for a new wife in the Bonaparte clan, life could be extremely unpleasant, as Josephine in particular was to discover.

A father within a year of marriage, Joseph quickly became a stereotypical paterfamilias, and as the oldest Bonaparte male, the head of the entire Bonaparte family as well, it was a position he assumed naturally, unquestioningly, with pride and pleasure. All the family's finances were placed in his hands for many years to come, even Napoleon handing over his salary and "outside earnings" to Joseph for investment and dispersal. "Whatever circumstances fate reserves for you," Napoleon wrote his brother at this time,

> you certainly know, my friend, you can have no better friend than I, who holds you most dear and who desires most sincerely your happiness. Life is a wisp of thought that disappears before our eyes. . . . If you leave [on a business trip], and feel it will be for a considerable time, send me your portrait. We have lived together for so many years, and have been so closely united, that our hearts are one, and you know better than anyone how fond I am of you. I find in writing these words an emotion I have rarely felt in my life.[9]

It was indeed a most rare moment in Napoleon's young life, with his guard down and heart open, at a time just before his fame swelled across the land

and a warm brotherly heart changed, growing into a hard ambitious one with no room for such sentiments. These feelings lasted barely another year, for in October 1795 the Committee of Public Safety nominated Napoleon the new commander in chief of the Army of the Interior, and the heart that had recently revealed itself just as quickly closed.

Nor was the change in relations one-sided. Despite growing prosperity and even considerable affluence, Joseph the businessman gradually became more and more jealous of Napoleon's national and familial dominance. This was aggravated by the greater success in another arena, for which Napoleon was chiefly responsible, politics. Napoleon introduced Joseph to some of the governing elite of Paris, including Barras, Napoleon's own patron since his rise from obscurity at Toulon. Most reluctantly, at Napoleon's insistence, Joseph left the warmth and comfort of his position in Marseilles for the lure, lights, fortune, and women of the French capital. This, Napoleon assured him, was where real fortunes were made, where real power and influence lay.

It began humbly enough as young General Bonaparte obtained for Joseph letters of marque, authorizing him to launch two armed corsairs (now with the blessing of the government) against enemy merchantmen in and around the waters of Corsica and the ninety miles of sea between that island and the French coast. This was nothing, of course, for Napoleon had in mind far greater enterprises than a mere Joseph could imagine in his wildest dreams. But Napoleon knew Joseph very well indeed, a man with little willpower when confronted with temptation. The lucrative possibilities thus revealed to him would seduce him as not even the most beautiful woman could, although there would be plenty of them, now, as well. Once having been the sun of the family galaxy, Joseph saw his star rising, but, lacking Napoleon's depth of vision and genius, he failed to realize that his star was actually being subtly reduced to the status of a satellite, as the younger brother's own light began to outshine his with a blinding brillance. It was something Joseph was never to excuse—or accept.

Before Joseph had married Julie, Napoleon had had a brief tryst with her sister Désirée. An intimacy and understanding of sorts was established between Napoleon and her, lacking only a formal acknowledgment and commitment by the family. Then the young general was recalled to Paris to resume his duties there.

Though the rift betweeen the Clarys and Napoleon—opened when he fell head-over-heels in love with Josephine and dropped their daughter Désirée—healed slightly, the rift between Josephine and the Bonaparte clan was immediate, bitter, and permanent. She was a woman who had children and a "reputation." Also, unlike the Bonapartes, she was a real member of the old aristocracy.[10]

Joseph, offended by the way Napoleon had dropped Désirée, and indirectly humiliated as the link between the Clarys and the Bonapartes, found his position as head of the family distinctly uncomfortable. A simple man, Joseph always got on well with people and wanted everyone to like him, whereas Napoleon couldn't have cared less. From this moment, therefore, Joseph, pushed by his mother and supported by the rest of the clan, remorselessly attacked Napoleon's marriage, opposing Josephine and her children every step of the way. Nor did they relent over the months and years to come, their virulence and acrimony instead intensifying. It was the first time Joseph had ever challenged Napoleon; it would not be the last.

This ongoing internal familial war, however, in no way seemed to impair their public lives, as Joseph got involved in the shadows of Parisian political life and then was elected to the Council of Five Hundred in 1797. Scarcely had he taken his seat, however, than he was diverted to a diplomatic career, beginning with an appointment by the directors as French consul to Parma. But to Divisional General Bonaparte, such a position for his brother was an insult. Thanks to Barras's intervention Joseph was promoted overnight to minister plenipotentiary to Rome, with the curiously undiplomatic task of "introducing representative democracy" there.[11]

With part of his sixty-thousand-franc salary in his strongbox, he and Julie set out for Italy, reaching Rome at the beginning of September 1797, where his credentials were duly presented to, and accepted by, Pope Pius VII.[12] Little did the pontiff realize that Minister Bonaparte had come with formal orders to overthrow papal secular rule, replacing it in Rome with a new French satellite, under the guise of a new "Roman Republic." He had been given specific, secret orders to execute this by bribery and by undermining the status quo, and then by instigating an "incident" that would provide the French Republic with an excuse for military intervention. (General Berthier's military units in Mantua had already been put on standby alert, to be prepared to move quickly.)

All went well. Bribes were discreetly dispersed, antipapal republicans were won over to the French view, and the "incident" was then arranged by Joseph's military attaché, General Duphot (now Désirée Clary's fiancé), who lured the police of the Papal States to the French Embassy and manufactured a shooting incident. Unfortunately for Duphot the situation literally backfired, and he was killed in the ensuing scuffle. But the "incident" had been created.

Joseph, who had little stomach for the realities of his own egregious actions, bolted with his wife and staff at the crack of dawn the following day, December 29.[13] But Paris was delighted to see the objective reached and executed in a mere four months, and on February 15, 1798, Gen. Alexandre Berthier duly arrived in the heart of the Papal States, proudly proclaiming a new "independent Roman Republic."[14] Joseph's first "diplomatic mission" had been a clear success, although Désirée Clary would have to resume the arduous search for yet another fiancé.

Unlike the other Bonapartes, Joseph, now safely ensconced back in Paris, could concentrate on the acquisition of Mortefontaine, for despite his brief stay in Rome, and his rather precipitous retreat, he had not left with empty coffers. Topped off by a few handsome bribes and gifts, he managed to provide the full cash outlay of 258,000 francs for the estate, not to mention hundreds of thousands of francs more over the next eight years on adjacent acreage, interior decoration, furnishings, and improvements.

Joseph's love of art led him to clutter the vast rooms with hundreds of paintings and pieces of looted sculpture, rare furniture, rugs, and tapestries. He installed his own small chamber orchestra and lined his first real library with splendidly bound volumes, especially of French and Italian literature. Much of this he professed to have devoured when he was not courting the ladies—like most of the Bonaparte men he had a weakness for actresses—giving weekly dinners, attending the opera, playing cards, or simply glowing in the social world, for Joseph was the most socially oriented Bonaparte. Indeed, he somehow even found time to write a novella, *Moina,* a literary weakness of sorts to which both Lucien and Louis later fell victim as well.

During his state reception for the American envoys, Joseph Bonaparte was perhaps as happy as he was ever destined to be, with future diplomatic assignments awaiting him that, if successful, would bring peace to France and the Continent, and a French nation grateful to him, while assuring him a footnote or two in French history. Had he been alone in the world with his wife and children, he no doubt would have remained contented. But he was not alone, and indeed was being demoted to a secondary position even within the Bonaparte family, as brother Napoleon continually pushed himself forward, depriving Joseph of his place of respected seniority. This was aggravated by the growing role of politics in family affairs, an envious Joseph now coveting Napoleon's position as head of state. Should Napoleon decide to retain office permanently, he would need to name a successor. And as Josephine had thus far proved incapable of producing any more male children, this meant that the succession would revert to the Bonaparte family. As the senior member of that clan, Joseph naturally intended to insist on his due. The result was that hereafter Joseph would be eating his heart out over what he had been deprived of politically, and possibly even over his inability to definitely secure a hereditary post as head of state.

"Clearly you do not understand me at all, if you think I lack the initiative to defend my interests where my personal honor is concerned," Joseph later remonstrated with Napoleon over the succession. "I have to remind you of my position and of the decisions I shall be forced to take, that you might not otherwise misjudge my apparent moderation concerning your ultimate decision in the matter. I hardly need say more on this point."[15] Napoleon knew that something appropriate would have to be done, but he could not readily envisage a place that would satisfy such a disgruntled Joseph, at least not under a mere republic.

The "succession" issue was to undermine Napoleon's relations with all his brothers and sisters for years to come, pitting one against another and all against Napoleon himself. The weakest link in all his plans for the future was to prove his own family—as brother Lucien was soon to confirm.

The post of interior minister, like those of foreign minister and minister for war, was of critical importance to the smooth transition of the new government, the Consulate. It was the interior minister who controlled and administered the country's entire internal political machinery, from the naming of mayors and prefects (the governors of every department, or province) to the overseeing of the gendarmerie and the National Guard. He also ordered the implementation of all laws and decrees, not to mention overseeing all public elections, and was even responsible for providing the army with its annual allotment of conscripts.

The person named for this portfolio, therefore, had to be a very senior, experienced, adroit hand, capable of maintaining stability and calm throughout the land when executing sometimes exceedingly unpopular measures. Such an individual had to possess firmness of resolve, wisdom, and a wide knowledge of men and recent political history. Finally he had to command popular political respect. In brief, this had to be a man who could be trusted above all others. That Napoleon should have disregarded all these elementary requirements in favor of his twenty-four-year-old brother Lucien was as mad as it probably was inevitable. Without Lucien's help, of course, the coup of 18–19 Brumaire would have never come off. Napoleon was in his brother's debt, and a true Corsican honored his debts.

Certainly Lucien was affable; everyone said so. He never failed to charm the ladies and to delight the gentlemen as a raconteur. However, that his manners in society were not yet exactly up to snuff was irrelevant compared to his complete lack of formal education. He had no real love of or interest in learning, despite later ostentatious literary affectations for public consumption. Indeed, two years at Brienne with Napoleon and then a brief stay at Uncle Joseph Fesch's seminary at Aix comprised the whole of his "education." Furthermore, displaying no interest in the military, the church, or commerce, of the five Bonaparte brothers he was the only one naturally attracted to the political arena. Growing into manhood in the more ferocious days of Jacobin politics under Robespierre, he felt himself strongly drawn to the left wing of the Revolution and considered himself a "born republican."

He joined political clubs in Marseilles, where, despite his obvious youth, he debated and spoke frequently. Indeed, a little too brash and outspoken, the bumptious Lucien continued his vociferous politics throughout the summer of 1795, even as the counterrevolutionaries were attacking. That Lucien, among hundreds of other left-wingers, then found himself in a crowded cell in Aix that July should have surprised no one. Fortunately his brother General Bonaparte had just enough influence to extricate the feckless youth in September from his latest difficulties.

That same autumn Napoleon won further support and praise from Barras in quelling Parisian riots. Again thanks to his older brother, Lucien obtained the position of *commissaire politique*, or political indoctrination officer, with the French army, a position that also had its lucrative financial perks. From the accused and the condemned, overnight he became the accuser of unorthodox political thought and the judge of who was fit for French society within the ranks of the French army, who was politically suitable, who was toeing the republican line, who was a true and loyal patriot. And then of course he was elected to the post of president of the Council of Five Hundred.

Meanwhile his pleasant young wife, Christine, and their first child moved into his barren, treeless, expensive estate of Plessis-Chamant near Senlis, whose sole apparent advantage was that it made him a neighbor of his brother Joseph, of whom he was very fond.

Rewarding the young man with the portfolio of the Ministry of the Interior—as Napoleon did in October 1799—was a mistake from the beginning. Apart from briefly presiding over the Council of Five Hundred, Lucien had had no administrative experience whatsoever. It did not bode well.

Shortly after his arrival in France, when he was working as a warehouse guard with Joseph, he had met Christine Boyer, the daughter of a local publican. Despite her peasant stock, obvious lack of any but the most rudimentary education, not to mention an equal lack of good looks, everyone liked her, even the difficult General Bonaparte. She was tall, full-figured, but otherwise slender, and as Laure Junot described, she "had in her figure and carriage that native grace and ease which are imparted by the air and sky of the South." Although her face bore traces of smallpox, aggravated by small eyes and a broad nose, "she nevertheless was pleasing because of her kind expression, sweet smile and lovely voice." In brief, "she was as good as an angel" and devoted to her husband, in spite of his ever-roving Bonaparte eye.[16]

Even an angel, however, could not alter Lucien's basic values, actions, and shortcomings. Although quite bright and lacking no degree of self-confidence, he had accepted this staggering ministerial responsibility far too glibly. He now controlled the lives of hundreds of employees, yet to him it was all a game. And what a delight, after the financial inconveniences of the past, to have a major ministry, with its own budget and treasury, available at his fingertips! Not surprisingly funds quickly found their way home, as his pockets jingled with the sound of government gold, and his latest mistress found a golden key to a new mansion. As rather substantial amounts continued to disappear (he was, after all, a Bonaparte), his frustrated underlings and accountants floundered in an attempt to deal with the unexpected hole in their coffers—a fact eventually duly noted by Police Minister Fouché's minions.

Laure Junot, a close family friend, knew Lucien better than most. She described him as "tall, ill-shaped, with long spidery arms and a small head. . . . [He] was very near-sighted, which made him stoop and peer through squinting eyes." His smile, nevertheless, she found "harmonious," and

> although he was rather plain looking, he pleased generally . . . [and] he had a very remarkable success with women who were themselves remarkable in their own right. . . . He was endowed by nature with many talents. His mind was comprehensive, his imagination brilliant and capable of great designs. . . . His heart was kind, and although he was sometimes carried away by his passions, no serious charge can be brought against him [regardless of accusations to the contrary] and his conduct toward his brother [Napoleon] was irreproachable. . . . But I would not with equal confidence acclaim the soundness of his judgment.[17]

Like so many of her assessments of those around her, this one was perspicacious. Lucien's lack of judgment would prove his undoing.

Thus in Lucien, First Consul Bonaparte had nominated a very strange minister of the interior. Nevertheless he had his reasons, beyond mere recompense for services rendered, for in this ministry Lucien could prove most useful indeed, for instance when overseeing various national elections and plebiscites. And he proved his worth when arranging the national plebiscite to legalize the Constitution of the Year VIII, which had discarded the Directorate and replaced it with the Consulate and its entirely new administrative structure. With the deft forger Lucien at the helm, it was hardly surprising that 3,011,007 people allegedly "voted" for Napoleon's new constitution and only 1,562 rejected it (out of an eligible electorate of nine million). In reality more than five million had cast their votes, but only 1.5 million for the new constitution. Lucien had eliminated 3.5 million negative votes.[18] Future interior ministers would follow his example during the referendums for the life consulship and the acceptance of the Empire, thus Napoleon's entire career was built on a policy of voter fraud. The one involved now was not only self-evident but blatantly so, and—openly criticized by Napoleon's many opponents—it resulted in one of the greatest vote-rigging scandals in French history. Nonetheless one is tempted to ask what would have happened if Napoleon had not ordered this fraud to ensure his new consular rule? The alternative was the corruption (of another genre) and instability of the Directory.

Fouché also had a hand in the election and manipulating the outcome—further documenting his private dossier on Lucien. Alas, hundreds of individuals were in on the "secret," so the truth was certain to come out. But it was done, and in any event there was no practical means of appeal available to the shocked or disgruntled, except of course through the newly created State Council, over which Napoleon personally presided. Once again he was in the debt of his perversely talented brother.

Thereafter, however, everything that Interior Minister Bonaparte did seemed to go awry. The administrative problems and confusion arising in Lucien's ministry were the natural and inevitable results of his own disastrous administrative incompetence—he loathed paperwork and detail—and news of this soon reached Napoleon's (and Fouché's) ears, compounded by Lucien's outrageous pilfering of that ministry's coffers. This state of affairs would not perhaps have been totally hopeless in Napoleon's eyes had there not been aggravating factors, including Lucien's personal, nonministerial peccadilloes. After all, every ministry had its permanent secretary-general for just such a purpose as guiding new officials, and as for money—well, books could be doctored and the necessary funds restored by brother Napoleon.

On top of Lucien's disastrous political position, his personal life was an utter shambles—and there he had no secretary-general to guide and protect him. His flaunting of his mistresses at a time when his wife was pregnant again, his penchant for foppishly theatrical public appearances, not to mention his glaring display of new wealth and his exorbitant personal expenditures on his Paris mansion—none of this could be concealed, unlike his handiwork behind the closed doors of the Interior Ministry. For Napoleon, who spent his millions privately—apart from the inevitable display made by Josephine—who always dressed conservatively and spent relatively little on himself, and who, further, avoided crowds and public acclaim like the plague itself, this was all outrageous.[19] The last thing the first consul wished to do was draw public attention to himself and his family, in a country where poverty and hardship had for so long dogged the French people.

Oblivious to all this, Lucien continued on his merry way, continuing to appear frequently in public—he was a popular figure—and spread his largesse in such a brash manner that talk of it became common in the Tuileries, the Tribunate, the Corps Législatif, the Senate, as well as in every street market in the capital. Lucien's worst offense, according to current gossip, was his expenditures on one of his most famous mistresses, the celebrated Mlle. Mézeray of the Théâtre Français. This lovely actress had even more of a flair than did her lover for displaying the unexpected windfall that glittered on her arms and neck, to say nothing of the elegant new mansion Lucien had obligingly just bought for her. And all this as his wife was entering the third—and as it turned out, fatal—trimester of her pregnancy.[20] But Lucien, being not only Lucien but a Bonaparte, could not even let it go at that. Word soon leaked to the thirteen remaining newspapers in Paris (Napoleon having suppressed forty-seven others) of the interior minister's dazzling speculations on the Bourse, and of his illegal concessions of national monopolies to certain well-known figures (in exchange for purses of gold, naturally). Indeed, it was hard to imagine a transgression this flamboyant young Bonaparte had somehow managed not to commit during the months of his public rampage.

For Police Minister Fouché, lurking in the shadows and avidly documenting every item in his special file on Lucien, it was all superb material. It permitted him to put into effect his own plan to remove Lucien from the public scene while undermining the unity of the Bonaparte clan as well as Napoleon's position as political leader of the country. Fouché was well pleased with the new interior minister.

The unrestrained and insatiable Lucien had apparently not yet had enough: He now believed that in the event of a national election, the republican electorate would find his candidacy preferable to that of his rather high-handed brother, who was clearly veering sharply to the right. Indeed, he could already picture himself replacing Napoleon as the leader of France (especially as Napoleon had deemed it impossible for one of his brothers to be named second consul, as Lucien had at first hoped).

For Napoleon, who was busy trying to bolster his position nationally and to ensure the acceptance of his new government, Lucien's irresponsibility was drawing too much attention and rocking the boat; this he could not tolerate. In fact the first consul had already warned his brother on more than one occasion, but to no avail.

By the summer of 1800 Lucien's appointment had become an absolute nightmare. (Napoleon's worst political enemy could hardly have devised a better means of attacking him.) Yet, continuing on his spree, apparently feeling himself immune, Lucien finally committed an indiscretion that topped all the others. He had a highly critical (of Napoleon) pamphlet, *Parallels Between Caesar, Cromwell, Monk and Bonaparte,* published at government expense and then officially distributed on his personal orders to hundreds of influential politicians and departmental prefects throughout the country.

This was all Bonaparte's archenemy from within, Police Minister Fouché, needed to complete his by-now-bulging dossier on the crimes and misdemeanors of Lucien Bonaparte. Lucien had had several scenes with the first consul, sometimes even before Fouché (of all people), regarding Napoleon's discarding of republican principles and policies, the very ones Napoleon himself had professed to support at St.-Cloud on 19 Brumaire. Discussing this ongoing wrangling with Napoleon's aide-de-camp General Junot and his young wife Laure Permon, Lucien affirmed: "Well, I shall always speak that way to him, and threats on his part will not make me deviate from my path. If the men who surround my brother in the Government choose to assist him in measures oppressive to the country, I, for my part, refuse to join them, and on the day that personal freedom disappears from the Republic, I shall go and seek another country."[21] Little did he then realize.

Fouché finally struck, making a special appointment with the first consul on November 1, 1800. Interior Minister Lucien Bonaparte was summoned to Napoleon's small office on the second floor of the Tuileries. On entering, the twenty-five-year-old Lucien found himself facing Napoleon, Bourrienne (required as a witness), and a slyly smiling Fouché, with the infamous file in his hands.

Without any ado Napoleon ordered Fouché to read the summary of his voluminous report. It was an inquisition. Lucien grew more and more agitated as he realized the extent to which his every move and conversation had been spied on and duly documented month after month. He interrupted, screaming, and—flinging down his own portfolio—he stomped out of the room and out of the French government. Eight days later Lucien, now a widower in black, with his four young daughters, piled into a heavy coach laden with trunks and left to take up his new appointment as ambassador to the court of Madrid.[22]

"Because of the present state of affairs in Europe," Napoleon informed the King of Spain, "I have felt it necessary to send as special envoy and new Ambassador, Citizen Lucien Bonaparte, my brother, to represent to Your Majesty just how important the conquest of Portugal is."[23] Lucien's demotion had been surgically swift and clean. He was never to return to the French government. It had been humiliating for Napoleon, too, to have that loathesome outsider Fouché read that scandalous disclosure before him, the first consul, about his own brother, but it had to be done.

The hesitant King Carlos IV was soon won over by Lucien's natural charm and affability. Lucien then began negotiating a peace treaty—the final version ultimately known as the Peace of Badajoz—among France, Spain, and Portugal. Napoleon had instructed Spain to strike at England (its navy and commerce) by invading and seizing Portugal. He was not satisfied with the original signed draft and its unprofessional wording, sent by an eager Lucien. Nor was he happy with the meager war indemnities intended for France. As was the custom (at least in some countries), substantial bribes had been paid to the leading negotiators, King Carlos IV breaking all records by presenting Lucien with five million francs' worth of diamonds and throwing in twenty old-master paintings for good measure.[24] A treaty favorable to Spain was essential, and Carlos IV did not want Bonaparte for an enemy.

Napoleon, however, not only rejected the signed treaty sent by Lucien without his prior approval and consultation but sharply rebuked him in the process. This was too much for Lucien. He would have to return the loot if he could not achieve all he had promised the Spanish king. But once a Bonaparte always a Bonaparte, at least a Lucien Bonaparte, and—stashing his treasure in trunks and strongboxes—he secretly ordered them secured in his carriage. Packing up his children once again, he fled in the middle of the night, not even having the courage to request the return of his passports or to take leave of a very bewildered king. The ex-president of the Council of Five Hundred, ex-minister of the interior, and now ex-ambassador to Madrid reached Paris in a record five days, on November 19, 1801, one year after his departure, much to Napoleon's astonishment. The bounder, liar, forger, and thief had returned. "Lucien's complete lack of judgment, and of any moral sense, pushed ambition to the point of utter frenzy, and the thirst for riches, to sheer robbery,"[25] historian Louis Madelin remarked. As for the second treaty with Spain, it was eventually signed, successfully linking Spain to Napoleon's foreign policy.

Fresh problems arose later in 1803, when Napoleon informed an idle Lucien that he was going to alter the Constitution of the Year VIII to permit him to hold the first consulship "for life," which Lucien needless to say strongly opposed. Napoleon had in fact tried to neutralize him and squeeze him out of public politics by foisting a politically inert senatorship on him. Frustrated over his political impotence, Lucien announced, "I intend to obtain real political freedom and the suppression of all despotism,"[26] but of course he was helpless to act.

The final severing of relations between Lucien and Napoleon came in the spring of 1804, as Napoleon was preparing to exchange his consular blue for imperial purple and in so doing, bypassed Lucien in the legal succession. The excuse for this final break was Lucien's choice of a second wife, Alexandrine Jouberthon, a ravishing beauty and the goddess of the Paris demimonde, the alleged "widow" of one Hippolyte Jouberthon (who had fled to the West Indies earlier to escape criminal prosecution for banking irregularities and was never heard from again). She, meanwhile, had become the talk of the town, first after "posing" for various artists, then for her role as mistress of the young Comte Alexandre de la Borde, while ignoring her baby daughter.

For Napoleon this was too much, especially after Lucien whisked her away to the country and installed her as his official mistress at Plessis-Chamant. Then in May 1803 Lucien's and Alexandrine's bastard, Jules-Laurent-Lucien, was born, followed by a hasty civil wedding ceremony. "Betrayal! It's sheer betrayal!" a disconcerted Napoleon fumed to Josephine on receiving the news.

On April 4, 1804, Monsieur et Madame Lucien Bonaparte left Paris for an Italian exile from which they would never return.[27] For Napoleon it was the first disappointment, the first divergence from the great master plan he was preparing for the roles allotted to his family in the conquest of Western Europe. But then the first consul had three other brothers—and with them three even greater shocks lay in store for him. The burden of genius was not always easy.

CHAPTER 15

The Foreign Minister

He was always in the process of betraying me.
—ON TALLEYRAND

Of all Napoleon's ministers over the years, he considered only one to be of his own stature and value, worthy of the respect of a distinguished peer, and that was Talleyrand. In fact Napoleon spent more time with his foreign minister than with various ministers on internal developments, except when dealing periodically with something important of the moment, such as judicial or educational reform, financial and commercial matters, or religious affairs. War was quite another matter, of course, involving numerous conferences, but of a lower level, regarding technicalities of a particular campaign, not long-term national policy.

There was nothing periodic or temporary about Napoleon's interest in foreign affairs: They were the very core of his existence, attended usually by the subsequent military ramifications. Napoleon was always contemplating moves abroad— diplomatic, commercial, or military actions, whether concerning England, Spain, Russia, the Prussian emperor and his states, or the Austrian emperor. He was constantly considering possible moves into central or eastern Europe, the Middle East, the Far East, the West Indies, or even North Africa. But whatever the country or the campaign, the one man Napoleon constantly consulted was his Foreign Minister.

*   *   *

Born in Paris in 1754, Charles-Maurice de Talleyrand-Périgord had a personal history as unusual as one might hope to find and certainly worthy of revolutionary France.

As scions of one of the nation's oldest and most distinguished families, Talleyrand and his two brothers were entitled to expect a high place in French society. But because of a deformed foot, supported by a heavy metal brace and an array of leather straps, Talleyrand's expectations had been severely narrowed, precluding any active physical career, including the military. Thus his father, Charles-Daniel, comte de Talleyrand-Périgord, and his mother, the comtesse, Victoire-Eléonore, had settled on a clerical career for the boy, in an age when preferment in the church hierarchy was determined largely by birth and an archbishop's or cardinal's miter could be expected even in one's twenties or thirties. With little money or land left, his parents had not much choice, given the boy's physical limitations and temperament.[1]

In his youth and early adulthood Talleyrand had extremely effeminate physical features, an aspect reflected in some of his actions over the ensuing years. This man who spent a full hour every morning before the mirror with his valet, dressing and preparing his coiffure, was always more at ease in the perfumed elegance of the boudoir than in a smoke-filled billiards room. Declining years combined with overindulgence and vice would accelerate an alteration of his once-slender figure and delicate face, finally reflecting in that very mirror stout, sagging features.

Meanwhile, as a product of the élite Seminary of Saint-Sulpice in Paris, he could expect to encounter few difficulties in his clerical career. Having completed his theological thesis at the Sorbonne and taken his minor orders by the age of twenty, in the following year, 1775, as a deputy deacon, he assisted at the coronation ceremony of the new Bourbon king, Louis XVI, at Reims; four years later he was ordained a priest and then named vicar-general of that same prestigious diocese. His numerous sexual exploits, which had begun when he was a teenage seminarian, continued apace. His bastard son, Charles de Flahaut, was born in 1785, when Talleyrand was appointed secretary to the General Assembly of the Clergy.

At the rather late age of thirty-four he was nominated bishop of Autun. Following his installation in 1789, Talleyrand was elected to represent the clergy at the newly convened National Assembly, becoming that body's president a year later. In 1791 he "resigned" his position as bishop (though officiating at the installation of the first "constitutional bishops," who swore their first allegiance not to the pope but to the French Republic).

In 1792, at the age of thirty-eight, he was sent on his first diplomatic mission, to London (where, as an aristocratic revolutionary, he was shunned as a turncoat by the British). During his absence the Convention turned against *all* aristocrats, issuing a decree for the arrest of the head of its own diplomatic mission in the English capital. The next year his name also appeared on the much feared "list of émigrés," followed in January 1794 by an order of His Majesty's Government expelling him from the British Isles. Persona non grata in London and outlawed in France, the nearly penniless refugee embarked for the United States at the age of forty.

His prospects were bleak, his life at its nadir, but Talleyrand was never one to despair, not even remotely. And with his name finally removed from the list of émigrés by the National Convention in December 1795, he returned to Paris the following September. In December 1797 the Directory appointed him foreign minister, and it was in this capacity that he met the young General Bonaparte for the first time.

Talleyrand was much impressed by this unlikely diminutive Corsican, and as foreign minister theoretically supported both the Egyptian campaign and the subsequent coup d'état of 18 Brumaire. Having resigned as foreign minister in July, he was duly reappointed by Bonaparte in November 1799. At the age of forty-five, Talleyrand had found his true calling.

In later years, under the Restoration, Talleyrand was criticized for his earlier support of Bonaparte's coup and government, but although devious he was never a coward, and he parried the accusation with his praise of Bonaparte's "noble task." "I liked Napoleon," he insisted. "I was even quite attached to his person, despite his faults. At the beginning I felt myself attracted to him by that irresistible aura that only a genius can emit. He had produced definite benefits for the country, for which I was deeply grateful. Why should I be afraid to acknowledge this?"[2] It was the only time the arrogant, egotistical, aloof, grand cynic Talleyrand ever praised anyone to such an extent. He may have been a member of the hated Convention, dishonest, destructive, an accomplice to murder (he designed the seizure of Enghien), but he was honest in this rare moment of praise for a kindred spirit who was as pessimistically forthright as he himself in stating his objectives and in taking whatever ruthless measures were required to effect them. Both Talleyrand and Bonaparte were geniuses, both adopted more or less similar moral values and political principles. Both men respected scholarship and were fascinated by classical history. (Talleyrand ultimately built the finest private library in France, second only to that of the Bibliothèque Nationale.) To be sure, Talleyrand had let Napoleon down during the Egyptian campaign (he had probably had no intention of going to Constantinople in the first place), although Napoleon obligingly cast that painful memory aside.

Napoleon also recognized genius and the extraordinary man that Talleyrand was, as well as his equally astonishing practical abilities. During his entire career there were few men who deeply impressed Bonaparte, and only one who truly dazzled him—Talleyrand. He needed this brilliant statesman to help construct his new government. Nevertheless Napoleon made one great error: thinking that he was the cleverer of the two and could thus always manage this Talleyrand as he did everyone else, as he appointed him to head the Foreign Ministry in the splendid new Hôtel de Gallifet in the Rue du Bac. The two men now had very long talks and appeared to understand each other perfectly, both having studied, and adhering to, the precepts of Niccolò Machiavelli.

Talleyrand was a gentleman. In Bonaparte's eyes he represented the old aristocracy at its best and most talented. At the same time, he saw in Talleyrand a man very much like himself, capable and willing to commit any act, however ruthless, brutal, or morally outrageous, in order to achieve the objective of the moment, and not only without a qualm but with unmatched expertise and even elegance and finesse. On the other hand there certainly were vast differences between the two men. Napoleon's personal frame of reference included something important lacking in Talleyrand's case: The Bonapartes were after all of Florentine origin, and Napoleon was strongly influenced by the historical precedents of the great Italian Renaissance warlord-politicians—the Sforzas, the Borgias, and, above all, the Medicis—all successful in carving out personal empires for themselves. Here Napoleon and Talleyrand differed, as did their value systems, including their attitudes toward military despoiling and conquest.

More important, their ultimate objectives differed. In the final analysis, regardless of his own personal aims—restoring his family's wealth and position—Talleyrand also always sought to reestablish the fortunes and place of France as a nation superior to all others (not necessarily through geographical empire, but through national genius and degree of civilization attained). Not so Napoleon, who was seeking to establish for the first time the wealth, power, and greatness of his personal empire, and that of his family. France, his adopted country, the conqueror he had so detested as a schoolboy, was of secondary importance to him in accomplishing this and always would be. The Napoleonic ego came first, although his personal accomplishments were to be reflected, on the surface, in French national conquests, themes, institutions, and glory.

Regardless of their quite separate aims and goals, each man needed the other to attain them. First Consul Bonaparte had to have Talleyrand on his ministerial team now, supporting him. There was no choice in the matter—he never settled for second best—and certainly no statesman in France, or indeed the world, came close to matching the wily foreign minister's extraordinary abilities. As for Talleyrand, he would manipulate Napoleon with all the considerable subtlety at his command to reach his own ends. They were two individual thoroughbreds harnessed in tandem to one coach. At this initial stage there was just one road to follow, but an unseen fork lay ahead, when one of them would be turning left, and the other right. That a harnessed team could not turn and separate in two directions at once meant either disaster or a parting of the ways—or both.

Whether in office or out, in France or abroad, Talleyrand was a formidable and unique force to deal with. But who was this man on whom so much depended and who could enthrall even a Napoleon? What was he really like?

One aspect of Talleyrand remained unaltered throughout his long life, and that was his outward ancien-régime elegance, charm, and wit. But for all that he could be intimidating with his low voice and, as Comte Molé put it, his "dead eyes" set off by his continuous "supercilious expression" that so often upset those about him, including the ladies, especially the rare ladies of chaste reputation in his social circle. Because of his limp and having to drag his lame right leg in a "slithering manner, one could almost see in him one of those fabled monsters, or ogres, half man, half serpent," as one contemporary put it.[3]

Victorine de Chastenay, who was also greatly fascinated by Talleyrand's enemy Fouché, found the foreign minister to be "most witty . . . and remarkably able to an unusual degree."[4] Henriette-Lucy, marquise de La Tour du Pin de Gouvernet, who along with her father had known Talleyrand for decades and who was put off by his notorious reputation, his debauched parties, and the impressive number of affairs attributed to him, nevertheless acknowledged: "kind as he has always been to me, with that delightful conversation so unique to him. . . . One personally regretted having so many reasons for not being able to respect him," she sighed, "but after an hour with him all was forgotten."[5] A less charitable Hortense de Beauharnais, who later had an affair with Talleyrand's illegitimate son, Charles de Flahaut, by whom she in turn had an illegitimate son, commented on his *indulgence pour les vices.*"[6] And Molé shrewdly remarked, "One found in him the *grand seigneur,* a feminine streak, a catlike nature and a bit of the priest, the priest and *grand seigneur* predominating." And thus, "when he wished it, perhaps no one could quite fascinate you as M. de Talleyrand."[7] The Marquise de La Tour du Pin added, "I must confess, I found in him a charm that I never discovered in any other man,"[8] and even the hostile Hortense once admitted, "The day he condescends to speak to you, he is already too kind, you feel, and you are only too ready to adore him if he so much as asks after your health." So gracious and charming could he be, that regardless of everything one knew about him, "he always won you over to him, like the bird hypnotized by the serpent," she noted.[9]

Talleyrand's work habits as foreign minister were also a throwback to the days of the ancien régime. His hours of public appearance ranged from 11:00 A.M. until 11:00 P.M. (when the doors of the salons of his private receptions were opened). As foreign minister he had no sympathy for wars, which he felt to be as puerile as they were destructive, as a means of settling human differences. Although he generally understood Napoleon's character and aims as the great man invaded one country after another, he did not appreciate them. He found it unprofitable for France and Europe to wage foreign policy by the sword—leaving strife, hatred, jealousy, anger, as well as social, political, and economic instability, in their wake. If he despised the English as much as Napoleon did—and he could never forget how he had been ejected from British soil—at the same time he felt there were less energetic and more effective and civilized means by which to cope with them.

He approached his professional work in a seemingly inefficient, even slothful manner, causing considerable delays in any diplomatic proceeding. For his permanent undersecretaries, he described his own diplomatic philosophy: "Circumspection," "discretion," and "a disinterested dedication open to no outside influence," he maintained, were essential. "A certain elevation of feelings that makes the individual feel it is grand and noble to be able to represent one's country," was a necessary element. Nevertheless his own actions appeared to put some of the above ideas in the tongue-in-cheek category, for despite his official policy of *"festina lente"*—making haste slowly—and claims of disinterestedness, his primary interest often appeared to be the quest for money and power, at a time when senior diplomats usually received a tenth of the salary of an equivalent general officer.

Unlike Napoleon, he did not believe that he should have to concern himself with the minor aspects and details of his daily work, when those could easily be delegated to underlings. "I have always made others work to avoid doing it myself," he acknowledged.[10] And yet the results were invariably good and satisfactory, achieving what he had set out to do. What is more, he was generally respected and even admired by his ministerial subordinates, including Jaucourt and Caulaincourt, who later succeeded him.

When actually at the negotiating table he epitomized the centuries-old technique of avoiding giving an official response by his government on a particular issue. "A negotiator or minister . . . can, by giving an immediate, definitive answer without adequate consideration, do, in a thoughtless moment, such harm to his cause and country that often cannot be undone afterward even by several years' good service." Therefore not only was it possible to avoid a premature commitment, but it behooved one to do so. The means were simple enough. When pressed by a diplomatic opponent,

> the lack of instructions and the necessity of consulting one's government are always legitimate excuses, in order to obtain delays in political affairs. . . . never give an immediate reply to any proposition whatsoever made to you, nor to any complaint or unexpected offer. . . . One must always have time to reflect, and it is better to put off to tomorrow what one cannot do readily and well today, than to act precipitously.[11]

If over the years Napoleon was to find hints and even proof of Talleyrand's disloyalty to him, he kept him on time and again. "His own self-interest," Napoleon insisted, "guarantees me his loyalty, much more than does his character."[12] The ineffable Talleyrand, however, put his own negative philosophy on the matter on record: "Political regimes may come and go, but France always remains. Occasionally one may betray all his country's interests by serving one particular regime too fervently, and yet in so doing, at least one is sure of betraying her only intermittently."[13] In other words, one can justify anything.

In later years, after having dismissed Talleyrand (only to beg him to return), Napoleon turned on him, attacking both his character and ability, sometimes lying, and generally distorting the truth and his own real estimation of him when emotionally wrought up at a particular moment. "I do not even think . . . that he is very intelligent, certainly not extraordinarily intelligent," he once complained most unconvincingly, as he pointed to the mismanagement of Talleyrand's personal life and to his disastrous marriage to a woman whom Napoleon himself was largely responsible for forcing him to marry. "Part of his reputation is due to luck more than to his own merit"—something Napoleon's lifelong detractors suggested about Bonaparte's own military career. "He was by birth and class one of the first personages of the nobility and clergy, and yet he did all in his power to bring them down," he pointed out disparagingly, and this was perfectly true. "As we all know, he has stolen more than anyone else in the world, and yet he does not have a *sou* to his name." It was indeed true that Talleyrand, a high-stakes gambler who played cards nearly every night, sometimes lost staggering sums, necessitating that Napoleon come to his rescue. Napoleon reminded everyone, "I am obliged to support him out of my private funds, as well as pay off his latest debts."[14] Despite the enormous sums Talleyrand earned or "received" by dubious means, he was constantly coming back to Bonaparte to bail him out. It was also Napoleon who was responsible for purchasing for the dissolute foreign minister one of the largest estates in the whole of France, the 1.6-million-franc, fifty-thousand-acre Renaissance estate of Valençay, in Berry.[15]

Admittedly, at various times he was a very wealthy man, mainly as a result of the fabulous purses acquired through the bribes he so openly demanded of various diplomatists and foreign princes when they were negotiating with France or otherwise simply needed a favor. But even Talleyrand could not be compared with Europe's greatest thief, the looter par excellence of his age, Napoleon. Bonaparte sent entire mule trains and ships laden with his war booty from Spain, Italy, Holland, Austria, and the German states back to France, in part for the state, in part for his own coffers and for those of his family. They bought dozens of estates and then filled them with millions of francs' worth of jewels, art, gold, and silver. Yet he had the audacity to claim that Talleyrand had surpassed him. But this of course simply followed Napoleon's pattern of denigrating anyone who ultimately abandoned or rejected him.

It was certainly true, however, that as France's foreign minister, Talleyrand did obtain the most outrageous sums as bribes. The list of these perversely colorful achievements was known to the whole of Europe to gape and wonder at, and the subsequent ire and outrage simply made Talleyrand smile all the more mischievously. Great princes can commit great crimes—it is expected of them. But it was not always "enemies" of the French state who bribed him: Frenchmen played the same game. Marshal Murat, for example, paid Talleyrand substantial amounts for helping him secure his Italian claims, including one impressive payment of eight hundred thousand francs in (looted) gold. The margrave of Baden reputedly gave the French foreign minister 1 million francs, and King Ferdinand IV of Naples, 3.7 million, for the right to retain title to lands they wanted. The king of Saxony upped the ante by giving Talleyrand a cool 6 million francs in exchange for a Berlin prison cell.[16] The negotiators at Lunéville later reputedly gave him 7 million.[17] Gold was flowing in almost as regularly as the tide. The hapless Prince van Weilbourg was to present Talleyrand with another five million francs in exchange for the presidency of the Batavian Republic. Although Talleyrand received his coffer of gold, Weilbourg failed to receive his quid pro quo. The French foreign minister never guaranteed results, of course, and never returned a sou. Nor were the German princes and princelings of the various Rhineland states—shortly to be assigned new frontiers and titles in what was to become the Confederation of the Rhine—any less worried about their future condition and largesse. Even more generous in an attempt to assure their claims, they sent convoys of gold under heavy guard directly to Talleyrand's palace in broad daylight. The amount? Ten million francs. One German diplomat who did not appreciate being given this princely squeeze, and who did not fare well in Talleyrand's hands, a certain Baron Gagerneda, complained that the French foreign minister was demanding payment in "hard cash" for his influence and "considered his high diplomatic position a gold mine."[18] He was, and it was. In the case of the realignment of the Rhineland states, after receiving the usual pot of gold from, in this case, Prince von Reuss, the elegant Talleyrand wrote in the margin of the treaty sent him: "The French Republic is delighted to have made the acquaintance of Prince von Reuss."[19] The inimitable Talleyrand had struck again.

Yet there was a mutual respect between Talleyrand and Napoleon. Talleyrand rarely emitted any semblance of personal feeling or emotion, especially in the political world, but when he did so, it was invariably disparaging. Was he being facetious a few years later, in 1805, when taking leave of Napoleon (who was departing for the battlefield), when he said he "felt an emotion that is impossible to describe"?[20] With Talleyrand one never knew. Napoleon, too—despite later negative remarks—admitted he found it "most painful to leave the two persons [Josephine and Talleyrand] I love most."[21] The love-hate relationship between these two geniuses amused many and baffled most.

In the field of diplomacy, Napoleon and Talleyrand agreed on the tactics required to subdue their unfortunate opponent of the moment, and they applied the crudest, harshest measures in achieving this goal. Holland was virtually ravaged—militarily, financially, socially, and politically—by the brutal measures applied by Talleyrand and Bonaparte. But ultimately the foreign affairs objectives of the two men were to diverge dramatically. Both men hated Great Britain, but only Talleyrand was wise enough to wish to compromise and end the decades-long mutually destructive struggle between the two nations. Napoleon remained an uncompromising warlord, while Talleyrand, a despiser of the military profession, sought a full, enduring European peace. Sooner or later the two men were bound to break and go their separate ways.

Naturally, therefore, Talleyrand was to oppose most of Napoleon's continental expansion, particularly in areas well beyond the historical frontiers of France. "My humble brain has much trouble in convincing itself that what we are doing beyond the Rhine will outlive the great man who is creating it,"[22] Talleyrand said to Metternich following Austerlitz and subsequent central European conquests. They were, he insisted, "most foolish steps," all the result of "ambition, pride, anger on his part, and of some imbeciles he listens to, thereby blinding his vision. . . . You will see how he will finally compromise himself one of these days."[23] When later Talleyrand secretly corresponded with the English, and with Czar Alexander I, opposing Napoleon's formidable expansion throughout Europe, the foreign minister justified himself by quoting Corneille's famous lines: "'Treachery is a noble thing when enacted against tyranny.'. . . The only time in my life I ever plotted," Talleyrand quipped, "was when I had most Frenchmen as my accomplices, and when the well-being of the country required it."[24] But that of course was many years later. Still, Talleyrand's sly, secretive ways and rather questionable foreign connections, as well as his own history, led Napoleon to entertain suspicions against him. "When M. de Talleyrand is not plotting," Chateaubriand remarked, "he is selling bribes." And everyone knew it.

Much later on, there were to be some rather disagreeable scenes between Talleyrand and Napoleon—or, one should say, by Napoleon against Talleyrand—accusing him of all sorts of things, especially when, after a series of battles, Napoleon refused to establish a lasting European peace. Talleyrand was gradually to come to the conclusion that the only way for France to achieve peace was "to banish the doctrines of [Bonaparte] usurpation and to revive the principle of legitimacy, which is the sole remedy for all the woes afflicting us."[25] This led to a furious scene, when Talleyrand, summoned peremptorily to the Tuileries, found Napoleon surrounded by Fouché, Cambacérès, Lebrun, and Decrès. Napoleon, who always stage-managed everything, obviously had something special in mind. He lashed out at Talleyrand, calling him

a thief . . . a coward, a faithless wretch. . . . All your life you have failed to fulfill your duties, you have deceived and betrayed everyone. . . . Nothing is sacred to you! You would not think twice about selling out your own father! I could break you like a glass! . . . I really don't know why I haven't had you hanged from the gates of the Carrousel!"[26]

Even the tough Admiral Decrès, himself an old aristocrat, winced. "A pity, don't you think, that such a great man was so badly brought up,"[27] Talleyrand quipped later, as he reached those very gates outside the Tuileries. In reality, however, he was shaken and had never been so humiliated in his life. Yet he knew he was right. France needed peace at last, and Napoleon of course throve only on war.

"It is not that I fail to recognize his talents," Talleyrand remarked, "for he is superior to everyone else, *mais c'est l'or à côté de la merde.*"[28] "My affairs went well all the time that Talleyrand was in charge of them," Napoleon one day acknowledged, "and in the final analysis, he is the one man who best knows and understands France and Europe."[29] But that lay many, many years in the future. In 1800 Napoleon and France were just beginning their adventurous saga.

CHAPTER 16

Fouché's Police

He is the sort of man we need in an affair like this.
—ON FOUCHÉ

n May 21, 1759, Joseph Fouché, one of the most sadistic and versatile political actors and opportunists in French history, was born at Pellerin, on the Loire River just a few miles west of Nantes. The scion of well-to-do sea captains and merchants, young Fouché was too frail to follow in his father's more robust footsteps to sea. Instead he received a good scientific and classical education at the Oratory of Jesus at Nantes, where he found himself in his element and throve. He considered but then abandoned the idea of a career in the church,[1] though he retained his strong attachment to the Oratory and its unique fraternity. Indeed, he decided to remain within the Oratory system but in a lay capacity, teaching science.

Beginning his teaching career at the Oratory College of Niort in 1782, within five years he had been transferred to the élite Oratory College at Juilly, where the aristocracy and the influential sent their favored sons. Among the students and colleagues, some were to be prominent in Fouché's own political career within a few years, including Eugène de Beauharnais, Jérôme Bonaparte, Etienne-Denis Pasquier, Mathieu Molé, and Antoine Arnaud, all of whom were later closely associated with Napoleon's regime, especially Minister Molé and Chancellor Pasquier.[2]

Despite his brief stay there, Fouché made a few lifelong friends and left an indelible impression on many as well, if for no other reason than his celebrated hot-air-balloon ascent with his upper classmen. (Joseph and Etienne Montgolfier had launched their first "mongolfière" in 1783 from the very field just outside Lyons, where, less than a decade later, Fouché was to inaugurate a mass execution of the notables of that same city.) But no sooner had he arrived at Juilly, which he found an academic paradise, than he was transferred yet again in the new year, this time to the Oratory College at Arras.

It was in that grim northern industrial city that Fouché's political education began and where he met Carnot, still a frustrated army engineering officer, and, more important, an equally frustrated local lawyer by the name of Maximilien Robespierre, into whose family Fouché was welcomed. Although Robespierre's sister declined Fouché's offer of marriage, nevertheless a timely loan by the affluent schoolmaster enabled Robespierre to reach Paris in 1789 and to launch his bloody career. In October 1790 Fouché was transferred a final time, back to the Oratory College at Nantes, and soon was promoted to headmaster.[3]

By now, however, his mind tended to be more on revolutionary politics than on education, especially in the watershed year (for him) of 1792, when the government closed his school, along with thousands of others. Running for the seat as deputy for Nantes and elected to the Convention, he proclaimed himself a "constitutional royalist," a position he was quickly to abandon. That same year Fouché's father died, in theory leaving him comfortably off, and before departing for Paris he married the daughter of the most influential politician of revolutionary Nantes, Bonne-Jeanne Coiquaud.[4] It was to prove a fruitful and happy union, of which Fouché himself was proud and protective. At the age of thirty-three, Fouché was beginning a new career and a new life. Entering the assembly as a moderate from the Gironde, promising "to maintain freedom and equality or to die defending them,"[5] he soon passed over not merely to the Left but to the extreme Left, to the Montagne of Jacobin politics. Voting now for the execution of his king, Louis XVI, he denounced both the nobility and the very church that had nurtured him.

But no sooner had he joined Robespierre's faction than he was dispatched as special envoy of the Convention to enforce another execution, this time of the revolutionary principles still defied by some sections of the country. The French people were not yet sufficiently appreciative of what the Revolution had to offer, and his job was to encourage them to change their mind. Religion and the Roman Catholic church had to disappear—

"de-Christianization," they called it—to be replaced by the "Cult of Reason," as did the nation's aristocracy and most of the manufacturers, merchants, magistrature, and the wealthy in general. While some 600,000 French citizens were ultimately killed in France during the Revolution as a result of military and nonmilitary action, another 145,000, mostly aristocrats and the educated classes, managed to flee the country. For those less fortunate, imprisonment, torture, or some form of brutal summary execution remained the usual alternative.

Fouché, the man of his hour, who had hitherto passed himself off as a middle-class "gentilhomme" and teacher, now changed personality, ordering the desecration of the churches and cathedrals of Nevers and Moulins, where he humiliated and literally publicly defrocked Bishop François Laurent and thirty of his priests who, stripped of their vestments, were paraded before the shouting citizens as if they were circus clowns.[6] Burning the priests' vestments and missals while smashing religious statuary—though keeping the more precious objects—Fouché played up to the crowd, denouncing "these impostors who persist in continuing to perform their religious comedy,"[7] as he put it. "It is they who have been enslaving us more and more over the past 1,300 years,"[8] he exclaimed later in Lyons, when he personally ordered the invasion of Bishop Lamourette's residence and had him placed ignominiously on a donkey, his miter strapped to the beast's head, and the bishop's Bible and crucifix tied to its tail, as the wretched clergyman was led through a howling mob that kicked, beat, and spit on him. All religious objects in Lyons were also destroyed, again on Fouché's personal orders. A few weeks later he could proudly report to Paris that Christianity had "been struck down once and for all."[9]

It was here at Lyons, in his role as proconsul for the Convention, that the darkest side of Fouché's bizarre nature fully emerged. He and Collot d'Horbois, his fellow coordinator of Lyons, signed orders for the destruction of sixteen hundred of the city's finest residences and for the execution of 1,905 citizens—all in the name of the newly proclaimed First Republic. "A bayonet piercing a human heart," executioner Fouché remarked, "makes me tremble. However, this bayonet is guiltless, and only a child would wish to break it,"[10] he insisted in one of the most contorted sentences ever created. "Terror," he continued, "salutary terror, is now the order of the day here. . . . We are causing much impure blood to flow," he concluded, "but it is our duty to do so, it is for humanity's sake"[11]—which is precisely what the Spanish Inquisition had declared in the sixteenth century. Clearly he had found the formula for achieving the revolutionary objectives of liberty, equality, and fraternity, and under him the French Republic triumphed and rejoiced.

Alas, Fouché's enthusiasm had proved a little too effective, for when the blood from the mass executions in the center of Lyons gushed from severed heads and bodies into the streets, drenching the gutters of the Rue Lafont, the vile-smelling red flow nauseated the local residents, who irately complained to Fouché and demanded payment for damages. Fouché, sensitive to their outcry, obliged them by ordering the executions moved out of the city to the Brotteaux field, along the Rhône. Beginning late in 1793 and continuing into the early spring of 1794, batch after batch of bankers, scholars, aristocrats, priests, nuns, and wealthy merchants and their wives, mistresses, and children were transferred here from the city's jails, tied to wooden stakes, where firing squads and mobs were permitted to dispatch them. Day after day these murders went on, and ex-headmaster Fouché, whose personal library was filled with hundreds of leather-bound volumes in Greek and Latin, looked on. And every night this same Fouché, the model husband and father, smilingly, modestly returned to his wife and children at home, where a warm hearth and clean bed awaited the Executioner of Lyons, as he was known thereafter, both locally and to history.

Things were not always accomplished as neatly as he had planned or might have hoped, however. On one afternoon the execution of a twenty-six-year-old nun did not go according to schedule, when the good wives of Lyons' working classes slashed at her bloodied head with their meat cleavers several times before succeeding in beheading the young woman, whose only crime had been refusing to stop praying to God when ordered to do so by "the people."[12] Clearly democracy and freedom were on the march. "We must be fierce in order to fear becoming weak and cruel," Fouché commented. ". . . Let us strike like lightning and let the very ashes of our enemies disappear with the approach of freedom."[13] His famous "terror, salutary terror" was now indeed "the order of the day" here in Lyons,[14] Fouché dutifully reported to Paris. In any other country he would either have been committed to an insane asylum or executed as a homicidal maniac, but in revolutionary France he was a hero.

Indeed, Paris appreciated his patriotic acts. "Citizen Fouché has brought about miracles. . . . The infirm have been succored, the poor given fresh respect, [religious] fanaticism has been destroyed . . . suspicious persons have been arrested, great crimes punished . . . such is the summary of the achievements of the representative of the people, Fouché."[15] And as Legendre confirmed in a special report to the Committee of Public Safety, "Public spirit is evident everywhere . . . the vigor of the measures taken [by Fouché] will cause republicanism to triumph in such a manner as to make the enemies of freedom and equality despair."[16] The tenets of the Revolution were the new gospel of the land, and Fouché was their apostle.

Following the change in tide, however, by the summer of 1799 the slippery political chameleon par excellence had put considerable distance between his recent unsavory past and the Jacobin officials and policies he had so warmly espoused and even personified. The Council of Five Hundred with its pro-Jacobin leanings, supported by its president, General Jourdan, and War Minister Bernadotte, was, in the eyes of the Directory, a danger to the Republic and a direct threat to their own existence and national stability. Having dismissed the previous nine unsatisfactory police ministers over the past three years, the Directory desperately sought a strong new minister willing to accept full responsibility for ruthlessly crushing all opponents. The reviled Executioner of Lyons was the only one capable of filling their requirements. Fouché convinced the five-man Directory that he could indeed restore order and firm government control of the country. If it took an ex-Jacobin to quell the Jacobins, so be it. What the Directory did not realize, of course, was that Fouché could not only squelch their opponents but help drive the final nail into their own directorial coffin as well.

Duly appointed the tenth minister of the General Police on July 20, 1799,[17] Fouché acted swiftly. After giving the Jacobins warning that he intended to close them down, he wrote a crude, threatening letter to one of their prominent spokesmen, War Minister Bernadotte: "Imbecile! What are you doing? What do you expect to accomplish? Just remember, as of tomorrow, when I deal with your club, if I find you still there at its head, yours will fall from your shoulders. I give you my solemn word on it, and shall keep it, I warn you."[18] General Bernadotte wisely stepped into the shadows. The police minister personally led the assault, and, with the wideranging powers granted him, his police then made what they euphemistically called "domiciliary visits," or house roundups of Jacobins, aristocrats, and priests alike. With that expedited, the new police minister surrounded the conspiring Council of Five Hundred and temporarily closed it down. Then Fouché "put the keys in his pocket and later calmly handed them over to an astonished Directory."[19] He was as good as his word.

His policies as police minister sometimes seemed contradictory, as he tried to reestablish national order according to his own lights. For instance, while asking for powers to impose sweeping newspaper censorship, he freed some well-known journalists from prison. At about the same time he persuaded the Directory to allow the first aristocratic émigrés to return to France from their long exile. He also succeeded in removing from the government's banned list the names of some nonjuring priests (those who had not sworn allegiance to the revolutionary constitution), the very priests he

had attacked at Lyons. As a result Fouché, the proconsul who had so ter-
rorized and persecuted Lyons' aristocrats and priests, became a regular
guest at a few of their remaining chic salons in the Faubourg Saint-
Germain, including those of the marquise de Custine and the marquise
d'Esparbès, hobnobbing with distinguished names and leading churchmen.[20]
Who could begin to understand the twisted mind of this political opportunist, as he now mingled with the oldest French families while carrying in
his pockets warrants for their arrest?

And while actively attempting to stanch the tide of royalist-extremist
groups hoping to overthrow the Directory, the inveterate conspirator
Fouché was seeking out "a strong soldier" to carry out his own little coup
d'état against those same directors who had just appointed him to office. If
all went well he would soon be appointing himself head of state! For this
coup, however, he needed a flexible soldier without strong personal interests in politics, someone who would not vie with him afterward for control
of the government.

His ultimate choice for this unique position was finally decided on as
Fouché began visiting that individual's beautiful aristocratic wife in the Rue
de la Victoire, none other than Joséphine Bonaparte. Curiously enough the
general's wife found the police minister a delightful if "correct"
companion.[21] Fouché, apparently always faithful to his wife, was paying
only political court to Joséphine. Her lifelong weakness being money, of
which there never seemed to be enough, Fouché had been able to help her
out on several occasions in exchange for information about Bonaparte's
headquarters, personal actions, and intentions. Joséphine became a police
informer against her own husband. Thus it was that Fouché soon realized
that General Bonaparte was already preparing his own little surprise for the
Directory, seeing himself in the role Fouché had reserved for himself.
Fouché was reluctantly obliged to modify his plans, while Joséphine filled
him in on what she knew, handing over documents and even her husband's
personal letters to her. With the tide against him, as usual Fouché decided
to swim with it, now attempting to ingratiate himself with Lucien and
Joseph Bonaparte—whose attentions were not reciprocated, however. His
aim now was to be accepted by the accomplices involved as "one of the
leaders of the conspiracy," as Director Gohier attested.[22]

After Napoleon abandoned his army in Egypt and returned to Paris,
Fouché had requested an interview with the general, who kept the influential minister of police waiting a full hour in his anteroom with everyone else
before receiving him. Fouché was outraged but remained outwardly calm,
though he would not forget this slight—sitting there, hat in hand, like a

fourth-former before his headmaster. He passed muster, however. "He is the sort of man we need in an affair like this," Napoleon afterward confided to a colleague, and admitted Fouché "into the secret,"[23] as he put it.

Talking with Fouché at some length and quizzing him in depth, chiefly on the current political situation in the country, General Bonaparte had realized that the infamous police minister about whom he had heard so much over the years was in fact the only man for the disagreeable job of being *his* police minister. What is more, Fouché proceeded to steal nine hundred thousand francs from police funds for Bonaparte and his preparations for the 18–19 Brumaire, and then helped secure the streets of the French capital for him as well, preventing any possibility of revolt. Unlike Talleyrand, whom he respected in spite of their differences, Napoleon often felt disgusted by Fouché's very presence. Few men had ever affected Bonaparte so strongly. These feelings were reciprocated,[24] but Fouché needed him and there were no better offers in sight. Fouché for his part had a comprehensive understanding of the political situation, its undercurrents and its leaders (all of whom he knew personally), not to mention the national situation, and a useful, detailed knowledge of administrative procedure. He already had hundreds of trusted men in place, while his ideas for reorganizing and reinvogorating the police were without parallel. For better or worse there was only one Fouché.

Now, at the beginning of consular rule, Fouché set out reorganizing the entire Police Ministry. Determined to erase his reputation as the Proconsul of Terror at Nevers, Moulins, and Lyons, Fouché first secretly destroyed most of the documentary evidence concerning his earlier participation, including his official correspondence, speeches, and reports submitted to Paris. Meanwhile, to the public he stressed the moderating aspects of his new police policy, describing it as "gentler and firmer" than that of the past—as usual a contradiction in terms. To publicize his new image he had the names of some proscribed and outlawed citizens of prominence removed from the official government's lists, including those of Maurice Barthélémy and Lazare Carnot. At the same time he attempted to mollify the very groups he had previously attacked with such pathological ferocity—aristocrats, priests, and Jacobins—by arranging for the return of some aristocrats, including Lafayette from a dreary Austrian prison.[25] Fouché was naturally only too pleased to act the great man, the obliging patron, as more aristocrats with ancient titles threw their doors open to him or discreetly sought his help in some matter. This did not, however, prevent the police minister from fully supporting and executing First Consul Bonaparte's vigorous policy of crushing the Chouans, or the monarchist rebellion in the West. Fouché would accept aristocrats as long as they were willing to abide by his rules, which included reporting regularly to the police and being kept under close observation. Power was a wonderful thing.

And yet there are further contradictions, for while Bonaparte favored negotiations to gain international recognition of his fledgling triumvirate and a rapprochement with the exiled Bourbons and Louis XVIII himself, Fouché worked behind the scenes to undo all that. (Later he would do just the opposite, negotiating with the Bourbons for peace *against* Napoleon.) Although maintaining a firm hand on the controls, so far as the more violent Jacobins were concerned, the police minister resumed reasonably friendly relations with their backers, including—of all people—Generals Bernadotte, Jourdan, and Moreau.[26] Ever the political opportunist, he believed in keeping his options open.

He likewise modified his policy regarding the church. In addition to attempting a reconciliation with the more moderate churchmen, he was to favor Napoleon's Concordat and the normalizing of relations with Rome, whose very church he had ridiculed and vandalized.[27] What had been condemned yesterday was today supported by the government, and by none more strongly than Fouché himself. Nonetheless, harsh repressive measures were also being taken by that very government. On Bonaparte's orders, for instance, Fouché began cracking down on the capital's newspapers, eventually reducing them through state censorship and police action from a thriving sixty to thirteen.[28] No one really knew what to expect in "this country . . . so strangely troubled by a thousand different passions," as Louis Madelin so aptly put it.[29]

Fouché's ideas for reorganizing the police fitted in reasonably well with those of First Consul Bonaparte. To enable the surveillance and control of the entire country, he had to have sweeping powers, and for that purpose Fouché asked for the creation of prefects of police for every department— that is, alongside the first consul's new political prefects. Napoleon found this proposition rather alarming, no doubt rightly seeing in such a move the creation of a powerful adversary, should the police minister himself turn against the first consul. What is more, Interior Minister Lucien Bonaparte— traditionally in charge of the nation's police in the provinces through the gendarmerie—protested at the transfer of those powers from his own ministry. But Fouché persisted and through a change of title managed to effect roughly the same thing. In the major ports and cities of the country, Fouché was now permitted to create prefects of police in everything but name, designating them "general commissioners of police," while those at a lower level, for certain ports and regions, were labeled "special commissioners."[30] Thus all the Channel ports, for instance—from Boulogne down to Bordeaux and along the Mediterranean coast as well—were now controlled directly by Fouché's own men, while all major cities and regional capitals, such as Strasbourg, Toulouse, and Lyons, were equally covered, as were non-French territories as they were conquered, including Geneva, Turin, Mainz, Cologne, Ostend, and Antwerp.[31] As part of the compromise made by Fouché, the general commissioners were technically, administratively, under the prefect of each department (or state), but in reality they were detached from Lucien Bonaparte's Interior Ministry and made directly responsible to Fouché. Fouché's police now legally controlled the entire country.

The overall daily administration of the entire Police Ministry was handled by Fouché's friend and close collaborator Secretary-General Lombard Tardeau. After him Fouché relied heavily on three senior officials: Pierre François Réal, a former Paris police commissioner and friend of Danton, who was in charge of nearly half the country's provincial police, including those of the northern and western departments; State Counselor Pelet de La Lozère, who in turned administered the remainder of the country, with the exception of Paris. All general commissioners thus reported directly to these two men alone. And finally there was Charles Desmarests, a vicious defrocked priest, who headed France's Secret Police, his grasping tentacles reaching out in every direction.[32] All these department heads, along with the prefect of police of Paris, usually met in Fouché's office every Wednesday.

Unlike the rest of the country, Paris was allotted its own separate police prefecture, created on February 17, 1800. The prefect was far more powerful and influential than any of the general commissioners in the provinces, and in theory was at the same administrative level as Réal and Pelet de La Lozère. But in reality he gradually became a rival of and challenge to the police minister himself, Paris being the seat of government and the hub of all national political and commercial activity. Fouché soon found that Prefect Louis Dubois, with whom he had at first worked so closely, gradually began to vie openly with him. Indeed, in some cases Dubois clearly outshone Fouché in results, such as when he uncovered the most complex and murderous assassination plot ever concocted against Napoleon—a plot that Fouché had dismissed as unimportant until an explosion proved how terribly wrong he had been.

Every now and then one comes across the names of individuals, prominent or distinguished for some reason, who are known among the upper echelon of government or society but unknown to the public. Little is written about their private lives, then or later. Even high-ranking government officials acquainted in their official capacity with such individuals afterward found in fact that they knew very little indeed about their past or personal existence. When the individual in question also deliberately conceals his tracks and fails to oblige us with memoirs—in an age when nearly everyone wrote them—we are left at a loss. Such is the case of the early years of Napoleon's first prefect of the Paris Police, Louis Nicolas Pierre Joseph Dubois.

Born in Lille in 1758, Dubois lived to be nearly ninety, his life ending in utter obscurity in the closing days of 1847, just before the collapse of Louis-Philippe's July Monarchy. Under the Bourbons the policing of Paris had been left in the hands of the lieutenant-general of police. But with the arrival of the Consulate, Napoleon created the prefecture of police and named Dubois to that post on March 8, 1800, a job he held until the autumn of 1810.[33] Although the new prefect had served as a magistrate during the Revolution, he had apparently had no direct police experience before taking up his new post.

Fortunately for Fouché and Dubois, General Bonaparte believed in a strong police authority and gave it his full support. Indeed, Napoleon was fascinated by its daily activity and always delighted in listening to Dubois—whom he highly esteemed—tell police stories, the more lurid the better.[34] In fact, as Napoleon's associates, friends, and family soon learned, there was little happening in Paris, and in their own lives, that he did not know about.

Dubois was the only police official apart from his superior, Fouché, who had direct access to Napoleon whenever he wished. If Dubois, like just about every other Bonaparte appointee, was vain and hardly scrupulous in financial dealings, nevertheless he was an effective administrator governing the most volatile capital in Europe. What is more, Prefect Dubois was held directly responsible for the safety and well-being of Bonaparte and his entire family, as well as of every other member of the government. It was a tall order, and if anything untoward happened to the first consul, for example, if any attempt was made on his life or to overthrow his government, it was Dubois—not Fouché—who was charged with uncovering such conspiracies—well in advance. The prefect's powers and responsibilities were therefore not merely second to those of Fouché, but inevitably overlapped and duplicated some of them, leading to mutual jealousy and acrimony. Although it was Fouché who had hired Dubois in the first place, it was only natural that Fouché would become wary as the prefect began to steal some of his thunder, eventually resulting in Fouché's plotting to remove Dubois. Ironically, when the prefect did ultimately fall from power many years later, he did so with Fouché at his side.

*   *   *

Fouché, as police minister, bore the overall nationwide responsibility for everything from arresting murderers and administering prisons to guarding public baths and garbage collection. The reports and information arriving daily from the four corners of the "Republic" were submitted to Réal or Pelet de La Lozère, who in turn passed them on to Secretary-General Tardeau, who finally presented them to the police minister. Fouché and his staff next carefully studied, sifted, and edited their contents for a special creation of the Ministry of Police, the most select and secret newspaper in France, the *Bulletin de la Police*. Early each morning only two copies were printed, covering from between fifteen to twenty pages. One copy was kept under lock and key in Fouché's office. The other was tied in a green—Napoleon's favorite color—silk ribbon and dispatched to the secretary of state, Hugues Maret, at the Tuileries, who was responsible for deciding who and what should have access to the first consul. Maret then personally handed the daily *Bulletin* to Napoleon.[35]

The *Bulletin* included every major and minor item of interest occurring in the whole of France during the previous twenty-four to forty-eight hours, and Napoleon spent a great deal of time studying it. When, during one campaign hundreds of miles from Paris, the *Bulletin* was late in reaching him, he raged: "That is incredible negligence!"[36] Indeed, he came to feel that he could not run the country without it, for every Frenchman of importance was spied upon with a thoroughness that would have shocked the world had it been known. Although he specifically forbade the interception of most mail at the outset of his regime, and denounced the Directory for having censored all mail, Napoleon soon permitted Post Office Director Lavalette to expand his efforts. Nor were the police without means of similar procedures. The French, accustomed to this sort of humiliating interference, shrugged their shoulders and accepted it. And as the vast majority of the citizens were illiterate, government intervention of the nation's post affected only a small percentage of the population. In any event, it was better than the chaos, distortions, and rampant brutality of the Revolutionary regimes. There was always a price to pay.

Napoleon frequently met with Fouché at eleven each morning to discuss a variety of subjects, including items in the *Bulletin,* as well as special proposals and subjects brought up by the police minister. In addition the police minister communicated with the Tuileries by letter on a frequent basis, totaling some eleven hundred items over the course of Napoleon's fourteen-year reign.

At the beginning of the Consulate a still-optimistic Bonaparte had made it known that he considered Fouché's role and that of his police to be of critical importance to the success of his new régime. "I wish to be informed about everything [concerning the police] in the greatest detail and to work with you personally at least once, even twice a day when necessary," First Consul Bonaparte had instructed his new police minister.[37]

Nor was Fouché slow to act, issuing his own national proclamation informing the country of his philosophy of the national police and how he interpreted its execution:

> All the repressive measures required have been effectively taken [that is, against the individuals attempting to prevent Bonaparte's initial coup of 18 Brumaire and of undermining his new regime]: the instigators of the troubles, the royalist provocateurs, in short everyone who could serve as a threat to public or individual safety will be seized and prosecuted. All good republicans should therefore remain calm, because all their wishes are being carried out.[38]

It was typical of Fouché and a clear warning to the people of the new Police Minister's concept of his office and what to expect. France had been threatened by émigrés abroad and Jacobins and royalists at home; he, Fouché, would protect the country. That meant taking stern measures.

"The police, such as I perceive it, must be established to anticipate and prevent crimes in order to contain and stop even that which has not yet been foreseen by the present laws,"[39] Fouché warned. This was hardly calming or reassuring, echoing as it did the mentality witnessed in the blackest days of the Revolution. He literally expected to act unhindered extrajudicially and with the blessing of First Consul Bonaparte. He could execute a dictatorial policy of harsh "preventive measures" if he merely suspected certain individuals, for instance, of being guilty of acting against the state (while lacking any solid evidence to that effect). As for humane treatment and general respect for the principles of humanity being flaunted—yet flagrantly defied—by the Revolution, Fouché considered that issue as well. "None of the measures that the public well-being now necessitates requires inhumane treatment" of suspects and prisoners, he assured the citizenry. "Nevertheless, humane action remains a virtue only so long as it does not conflict with the public interest, and this interest is ultimately the sole motive that might justify taking extraordinary precautions in imprisoning certain individuals."[40] No one dared to ask who defined what consituted a "conflict with the public interest."

Several months after taking office, Fouché reported to the first consul:

It is possible, it is even true no doubt, that a few enemies of our liberty and laws are still at large, hiding in France. But they will hardly be in a position to act with impunity in any concerted effort. We have all their movements, words, acts, and most secret plans under the closest scrutiny, preparatory to penetrating their groups and arresting them. Every means of surveillance is available to the police, whose love for our nation renders this surveillance and its enforcement more sweeping, faster, and more infallible.[41]

What powerful words, reflecting equally powerful action, in this proclamation of new police policy. What a transformation from the schoolmaster, what a development from the science enthusiast launching montgolfières to launching spies and filling the nation's prisons with "enemies of the state." What sort of individual created the most ruthlessly efficient police system that Europe had ever known? Who indeed was Joseph Fouché?

CHAPTER 17

Fouché the Man

A heart as hard as a diamond, a stomach of iron and a
tearless eye.

—TALLEYRAND ON FOUCHÉ

ALL, thin, hollow chested, slightly stoop shouldered, with thin reddish-blond hair, a pale—indeed colorless—unhandsome face, as expressionless and dead as his watery gray eyes, his thin-drawn bloodless lips rarely emitting more than an occasional caustic sentence or order, completed by a cold, aloof, forbidding bearing—this was the image the new police minister presented to the world.

And yet there were times when he suddenly began gossiping, relating embarrassing comments or stories about the highest officials of the land, including his own closest colleagues.[1] This deceptively quiet exterior concealed a man of ceaseless energy, who rarely slept more than a few hours or wasted more than a few minutes on anything but the most abbreviated of dinners, even interviewing people in the morning while he was still dressing. When standing at an official reception in his dark, simple dress—in stark contrast with the heavily encrusted gold or silver of the uniforms of his fellow high officials and of the military—he rarely moved, apart from his long, bony hands, only his weasel eyes and alert ears following everyone and every conversation, noting everything, missing nothing. Fouché's name and reputation were as feared as much as they were detested.

Napoleon was still impressed by this bizarre creature that had been vomited forth by the Revolution. There was not another police official in the country who could even begin to replace his seemingly mournful police minister. He had his *mouchards*—spies—in every salon, in every ministry, and, it was said, even in the army. On Napoleon's orders he had just closed forty-seven of the nation's newspapers, the prisons were crowded once again as his gendarmes cracked down on the brigands attacking travelers, coaches, and even government depots and cashiers in forty-six of the country's eighty-seven departments. As for crime in the capital, it was still staggeringly high, daily burglaries, muggings, and murder requiring every male citizen to be armed.

Outwardly devoid of emotion and human feeling of any kind, Fouché seemed to retain that perfect equanimity, the "unflappable calm"[2] for which he was renowned, even when facing General Bonaparte's thunderous tirades. By now, at the age of forty-one, Fouché seemed imbued with a philosophy that protected him from the world of mere human beings, he existing on another plane, far above them all. Men and women would be arrested, interrogated, tortured, imprisoned, or executed on his personal orders, and he continued to eat the same amount, sleep the same hours, day in, day out. He felt nothing; he was simply doing his job. (At least Napoleon was seen to break down in tears at the sight of his maimed and dead warriors on the battlefield.) Unlike Talleyrand at the Foreign Ministry, Fouché was the first to arrive at his Police Ministry in the Quai Voltaire and the last to leave. Again unlike Talleyrand, no detail was too small for him; aided by a superb memory, Fouché mastered everything with in-depth knowledge of events in every department of the land, down to the names of the officers and agents concerned. All was recorded and stored in the swelling secret files—some in his own office—of his ministry—files to which not even Napoleon had access.

But for all his simplicity of manner and dress in daily life, Fouché was not loath to attire himself in one of his several silver-encrusted blue velour state uniforms. Nor did he decline official, ostentatious cavalry escorts on occasion for his carriage, as he was whisked through Paris's teeming streets. He considered himself a statesman, a great man, not a mere policeman, and he secretly longed to exchange his portfolio for that of foreign affairs.

For all that, however, deep down Fouché was a born policeman and throve in this role alone. One aspect of this required him to act "the mole," as biographer Stefan Zweig so aptly referred to him. Victorine de Chastenay noted this characteristic even in the salon, during seemingly innocent chit-chat. He was "a true Breton," she claimed, "invariably meddling in everything that was happening."[3] It went much deeper, of course, and Talleyrand quite agreed: "The minister of police is a man who begins by taking up that which concerns him and then that which does not concern him in the least."[4] It was this constant burrowing and ferreting out of fresh scandal, plots, shameful acts, indiscreet slips of the tongue, or simply discreet confidences that provided him with the pretext for visiting some very varied drawing rooms in Paris, whether Jacobin (he still had some old friends among them), clerical (he always protected his fellow Oratorians), republican, or aristocratic. That he was frequently looked on with unease and caution, regardless of the social or political milieu, was hardly surprising, and Fouché would even jest about it, secretly relishing the very fear he caused: "When you have something bad to say about the emperor and the government, wait for my arrival. The [police] spies will disappear when they see me."[5] But few found anything to laugh about. Napoleon, who naturally spied on his own superspy, would thus receive bewildering, confusing reports of his police minister observed in intense conversation with alleged friend and foe alike.[6] Napoleon was stymied, and a smiling Fouché knew it and delighted in the mystification. To Fouché stealth was sublime, convoluted plottings not only a way of life but as necessary as the air he breathed. Without them, he simply had no raison d'être. François Guizot, the future scholar and statesman, despite his youth at the time, was one of the few to understand this man in gray, at least in part, recognizing his "hardy, ironic, cynical indifference, indeed phlegmatic attitude [to all about him], applied in his unsated quest for embroilment."[7]

This man who had no softness in him when it came to his work was, on the other hand, a doting husband and dedicated paterfamilias. Unlike most of his colleagues, Fouché rarely permitted official life to intrude into his quietly sumptuous homes in the Rue du Bac and later in the Rue Cérutti. Only close and special friends were invited to spend an evening *chez lui,* and again unlike most of the higher officials with social pretensions and obligations, he did not hold an open house once a week. His wife rarely appeared at receptions or in the famous salons. This was not the result of shyness on the part of this hardened woman, who had personally witnessed her husband's blood-curdling massacres without a murmur of dissent, but simply that she completely shared his values, insensitivity, and utterly bleak view of humanity and society.

Unlike almost every other high French official at this time, Fouché was not only a proud father and husband but also contentedly monogamous.

"My only wish is to make life pleasant for my wife and children,"[8] he insisted. "Follow my example," he warmly advised his old friend, Raoul Gaillard, "dictate your letters to your wife. It is so pleasant being able to kiss your secretary."[9]

Indeed, his happiest moments were spent at home with his family, where he actually guffawed at the pranks of his four children (who could do no wrong). In French society at this time, of course, children were never allowed to be seen or heard with guests present, but not so in the Fouché household. There the children were vociferously present, running wild, which quite astonished new arrivals to his salon and left Fouché filled with amusement: "You have probably been told that they are spoiled, but they are delightful and the supreme joy of my life," he confessed.[10]

Victorine de Chastenay was a good example of the aristocratic ladies to be found frequently in chez Fouché. The former head of a religious order, she was not entirely without criticism of the new police minister, which nonetheless did not seem to deter her visits there. She felt instinctively that there was something of "the charlatan" in his pretensions, as he coldly and arrogantly vaunted his "superiority over all men, over all social ranks, over every opinion and passion, giving one the impression that he alone was in full control [of what was transpiring in France]."[11] He always acted with dignified condescension, permitting his friends to feel that they were being given confidential information about some event of the day, only to learn subsequently that Fouché had in fact imparted nothing of importance.

One of the factors that seemed to attract his female admirers—and most of his admirers were, as in the case of Talleyrand, female—was no doubt his fidelity to his wife, especially in an age when sexual permissiveness was considered the norm (even the great national hero Lafayette was known for his conquests). Added to this was his equally obvious love of, and dedication to, his children, whom he idolized and showered with the affection he had never received from his parents. Madame de Chastenay was equally impressed by his wife's devotion to him.[12]

He would not brook the presence of loose women, advising his sister, Alexandrine Broband, to keep a close eye on her daughters, his nieces: "Recommend that they behave themselves properly in public. Let them realize that a woman's empire in society is established by the firmness of her principles, spirit, and moral values."[13] Like Napoleon, he did not at all approve of the permissive society fostered by the Revolution and still continuing. It was hardly surprising, therefore, that Police Minister Fouché, later the duke of Otranto, rarely allowed his wife to appear in public, nor—in his exceptional case—did Napoleon insist.

Despite Josephine's lurid history of sexual exploits, Fouché genuinely liked her and was often able to obtain information from her, including Napoleon's personal letters to her from Egypt (for which he paid her handsomely). Josephine the police informer did not make a pretty picture. But at the same time Fouché admired her honesty in the matter—her grace, warmth, and generosity—even naming one of his daughters after her. If Fouché did not throw open the doors of his home to most high Napoleonic officials—not that they would have cared to join him, least of all the Bonaparte clan—select guests *were* welcomed, even Josephine on occasion. Perhaps the most surprising guest to appear there was the archbishop of Paris, Cardinal du Belloy,[14] who chose to ignore the ignoble past of this priest-killer and despoiler of the church.

Although Madame de Chastenay could find "a certain nobility of character" to admire in Fouché, not so his colleagues, including Talleyrand, who summed him up with unusual pithy precision as a man with "a heart as hard as a diamond, a stomach of iron and a tearless eye."[15] (Others had of course attributed similar qualities to the foreign minister himself.)

If Fouché had no apparent weakness for the temptations of women, food, and drink, nevertheless he was enticed by another siren (apart from the lust for power): money—despite his public declarations to the contrary during the Revolution ("Let us scorn vile gold and silver, and leave those monarchical gods in the filth where they belong"). Although some of his wealth came from a few very discreet "gifts," and larger amounts were annually siphoned off from unaudited gambling "taxes" collected by the police, Napoleon himself was not to prove ungenerous, eventually giving him millions over the years.[16] This money Fouché safely invested with his wealthy financier friends, or he at least acted on their advice. But perhaps even more important than this and his priceless art and gem collections—mostly acquired at little or no cost from the monasteries, churches, and châteaux looted during and following the Reign of Terror, including a few choice items from Lyons—was Fouché's real estate empire.

This impressive gallery of properties included the quietly impressive mansion he was shortly to acquire in the Rue Cérutti (next to the Paris residence of Queen Hortense of Holland) and two superb estates fairly close to Paris, Ferrières (later owned by the Rothschilds) and Pont Carré; two other sizable domains in the South of France; elegant town houses in Aix, Toulon, and Nice; two entire parishes in Champagne—every house, shop, mill, tannery, farm, and field; and tens of thousands of acres and dozens of farms and houses, chiefly between Aix and the Var. Nor should one omit future large income-producing estates in conquered German and Italian provinces, as well as the family sugar and indigo plantations he had inherited in Santo Domingo.[17] Quite exclusive of his private investments was the combined income received from his government posts as minister, senator, and state counselor, bringing another 223,000 francs annually to the family coffers. As a frugal Breton he managed to save a considerable amount of this, despite the great costs of maintaining such properties and the hundreds of domestics and retainers required for them. Unlike the chronic spendthrift and gambler Talleyrand, Fouché ultimately accrued an estimated fortune of about 15 million francs,[18] in an age when a workman with a thousand francs in cash each year would have considered himself very fortunate indeed. Some of this wealth was derived from killings he made on the Bourse as a result of "insider information" of some forthcoming peace agreement or spectacular military victory, a pastime he shared with Joseph Bonaparte. Of Fouché's two great lifelong passions, it is hard to say which took precedence, political intrigue or collecting real estate.

While remaining surprisingly loyal to his Oratorian friends over the years, in politics Fouché betrayed just about everyone, including Robespierre, Sieyès, Barras, Talleyrand, Lafayette, Carnot, and of course Napoleon.[19] Curiously, though, despite his great thirst for power, he was not vindictive when it came to transgressions against himself personally, unless such actions interfered with his own professional plans and objectives. The great skeptic so far as human behavior and values were concerned, he expected and accepted just about anything. "I excuse all human weaknesses," he nobly conceded, and on occasion even helped political enemies who found themselves in a difficult position.[20] Fouché always claimed to aim for moderation and "clémence," which seemed a bit far-fetched given his own bloodstained record of revolutionary excesses. As Louis Madelin so cogently perceived:

> He had . . . studied his neighbors. He had seen at firsthand the shameful capitulations made by men he had hitherto considered to be upright, and the debauchery of those who had previously descried similar actions of the tyrants before them. . . . The Minister of Police had personal experience of every type of ignominious act and had explored the worst humanity had to offer. He had known better than anyone else . . . the lamentable trafficking of the human conscience. [For him] the world was comprised of either . . . hypocritical scoundrels or contented imbeciles.[21]

But of course he who had permitted the fishwives of Lyons to hack a woman to death with carving knives and meat cleavers, and who had filled his stately residences with a museum's ransom in stolen or despoiled objets d'art, was above reproach as he now stood officially as overseer of national morality. If Fouché was the greatest skeptic in a nation of skeptics, it was because he recognized all the traits he now denounced in his own sadistic, even psychotic, acts; in his own treachery, ruthlessness, brutality, and egotism, which he had then seen repeated by those around him. He knew that such a man as he, once in a position of real power, was capable of doing anything. As he frankly confided to his oratorian friend Raoul Gaillard, "I have to be able to be complete master when I govern."²² And that he was at the Police Ministry.

As for policies and objectives, did he in fact have any? He was, like Napoleon himself, a disturber of the public peace. He was a conspirator, a conniver, a man bent on upsetting any government in power. "He sought out storms, he created complications for the sheer pleasure of unraveling and solving them, just as an actor shapes his plays to fit his own particular style. That is why he was contented when dealing with especially formidable adversaries," and "at times he revealed a stupefyingly bold and furious force" when grappling with them.²³ It amused him to say the most outrageous things about his colleagues, and even about Napoleon, knowing full well that such remarks would get back to them within the hour. "Bonaparte does not like me," he confided with the slight trace of a smile, "and he knows that I do not like him."²⁴ These remarks would set tongues wagging once again. Ever since his proconsulship days at Lyons, where he deployed almost sovereign power over the lives of that city's inhabitants, he felt himself to be above everyone and everything. He could do anything, and indeed had done so, down to sacking hundreds of churches and murdering young nuns and old ladies. He was duplicity and immorality personified and had "a strange and constant need to mystify" those around him,²⁵ relishing their ultimate failure to understand him. "One finds a mixture of everything [in him]," Chateaubriand acknowledged, "religion along with impiety, virtue with vice, the royalist with the revolutionary.... I have never found a more bewildering combination in anyone."²⁶

Thus once again we must ask, What in fact were his political objectives, which Chateaubriand among others found so perplexing? Was he a Jacobin, bent on revolution at any price? Was he a moderate republican? Was he a monarchist in disguise? In fact he was nothing and everything, according to the demands of the hour. He believed in nothing but himself, his own power, and the game he was then playing. But one thing was certain, he despised religion, democracy, the masses, and any and all authority (when he was not wielding it). "He felt there could be neither indecency nor impossibility in the game of politics. Moreover, he had but one concern, that of rendering himself always indispensable, the man of the hour, and that was the secret of his good fortune under every régime. He was always, under the government of today, the man preparing for the government of tomorrow," Louis Madelin observed.[27] Or, putting it more simply, as he himself admitted to Chancellor Pasquier, "One must have one's hand in every pie."[28] Perhaps it was Guizot, however, who best summed up the man and his politics:

> No man had more completely shown such hardy, ironic, cynical indifference, such an imperturbable sang-froid, along with an immoderate need of action and in a commitment to do whatever was needed to succeed—not in order to fulfill a predetermined plan—but, rather, simply to take advantage of the chance offered by that particular passing moment.[29]

As far as policy was concerned during Napoleon's First Empire, Fouché's could best be summed up as anti-Napoleon: Napoleon was forever at war, and Fouché always sought peace. Napoleon ruled the land, and Fouché envied him. Fouché made no secret of this, though he did conceal his various plots in the years to come, while attempting to ease relations with the various European powers, England in particular. But there was apparently no one even remotely able enough to replace all aspects of Fouché's police work in France, except perhaps Dubois, and he was needed as prefect. Napoleon acknowledged his own dependency on this strange man. When in 1802 Fouché opposed the general's bid for a life consulship, having further irritated Napoleon by revealing Lucien Bonaparte's corrupt practices, crimes, and indiscretions in his private life and at the Interior Ministry, not to mention hints of lists of indiscretions of each member of the Bonaparte clan, Napoleon finally sacked the police minister—with a 1.2-million-franc golden handshake. Yet Napoleon could not do without him, it seemed. He retained his services by naming him a life senator (with a generous salary) and a state counselor (also with a good salary), calling him occasionally to the Tuileries for advice and to sit on various government commissions. Following Fouché's dismissal and the closing of the entire Police Ministry, however, the crime rate soared, probably aided by Fouché in a few instances, especially in the provinces, where royalist brigands carried out a reign of terror even as fresh conspiracies to overthrow the Corsican general came to light. There was no second-best police official with sufficient expertise, experience, and administrative know-how. It was as simple as that.

It was hardly surprising, then, that on establishing the Empire two years later, Napoleon would revive the defunct Police Ministry and return the former police minister with greater powers than ever and orders to clean up the country and restore order. This did not preclude friction between the two men from resurfacing from time to time. Fouché would never change his ways any more than would Napoleon. It was on such occasions that Fouché, as disdainful and independent as ever, showed his true phlegm and mettle, making Napoleon laugh despite his consuming anger. And frequently Napoleon even baited Fouché, to see what droll response he would arouse, for Napoleon liked a good show as much as Fouché an appreciative audience. For example, Napoleon was not loath to remind Fouché what a good Jacobin and terrorist he had been in the early years of the Revolution, a subject on which Fouché generally remained entirely reticent. "You voted for the death of Louis XVI, Monsieur le Duc d'Otrante?" he asked with a glint in his eye and a lurking smile. "Indeed I did, Sire," Fouché replied in a loud clear voice. "In fact that was the first service I was able to render Your Majesty,"[30] Napoleon burst into laughter. That Fouché! Later, in 1815, when the emperor discovered that the police minister was again negotiating secretly—and without his authorization—with the English and their allies in order to avoid a fresh war, Napoleon called him a traitor. "Duc d'Otrante, I ought to have you hanged." An unruffled Fouché replied, without batting an eye, "I am not of the same opinion, Sire,"[31] and continued to retain his office. On another occasion, after Napoleon returned unscathed from battle, his Corsican humor got the better of him again, leading him to pose a devilish question that would have flummoxed any other minister: "What would you have done if I had just been killed by a cannonball, or in an accident?" With perfect equanimity, not moving a muscle or even altering his expression or tone, Fouché replied: "Sire, I would have seized as much power for myself as I possibly could, so as not to have become the victim of events." Eyeing him intently, the by-now-beaming Napoleon quipped: "Splendid! That's the way to play the game!"[32] Which is precisely what he continued to do.

CHAPTER 18

The Christmas Eve Plot and Others

I don't like having to bring conspirators to trial, for the government invariably loses when the condemned man becomes a public hero.

round 5:45 P.M. on Christmas Eve of the year 1800, a little over thirteen months after Napoleon Bonaparte had carried out his successful coup d'état, three men dressed in long blue workmen's blouses were seen boarding a stout wooden cart at 23 Rue du Paradis in Paris and driving its lone horse in the general direction of the Louvre.[1] Before the hour was out the cart entered the darkened Rue St.-Niçaise, across from the Tuileries, where the three men parked the vehicle, bearing two large barrels surrounded by heavy stones, just before a clothing store, more or less barring the narrow street. Two of the men walked toward the nearby Rue de Rivoli, while the third gave a young girl a coin to hold the horse's bridle and then moved several paces away.

Seconds before eight o'clock, the other workmen signaled the one nearest the cart, who ignited some straw near the barrels and darted away, just as First Consul Bonaparte's state carriage appeared, emerging from the Carrousel. Instead of going up the Rue St.-Niçaise as it invariably did, it turned into the Rue de la Loi,[2] which would take it to the Opéra in the Place Louvois, where General Bonaparte was awaited for the opening performance of Haydn's oratorio *La Création*. No sooner had Napoleon's mounted guard and carriage disappeared around the corner than the two wooden barrels on the cart exploded, killing and maiming several dozen persons, including the proprietess of the Café d'Apollon, whose breasts were severed by a piece of one barrel's metal hoops, and the little girl holding the horse. Bodies were strewn everywhere in the street and apartments above the shops, particularly at the café around the corner, hurling Napoleon's mounted grenadiers from their bloodstained mounts, smashing windows, and bringing down an avalanche of tiles and loose stones from the façades and roofs. Nevertheless Napoleon and his three aides-de-camp Generals Lannes, Bessières, and Lauriston, emerged unscathed from the carriage, as an immense cloud of dust and rubble momentarily obliterated everything in the dim lamplight.[3] Quickly assessing the situation, and looking back for Josephine's carriage (still out of sight behind his own), the first consul returned to his carriage and ordered the mounted guard and coachman to continue up the street to the Opéra. There a quarter of an hour later he received a standing ovation from the audience and performers, in the very building where just a few months earlier assassins had lain in wait, only to be captured minutes before attacking Napoleon. But this time the police had failed to act in time, and he and Josephine were saved only by what he was wont to call "*sa Providence.*" Indeed, it seemed to be a case of double good fortune, for Josephine's carriage, which should immediately have followed the first consul's, had been delayed when she unexpectedly returned to the Tuileries to change part of her costume. Had she followed directly behind her husband's carriage, she would have been exposed to the full blast of the explosion and no doubt killed outright. Nevertheless she was hysterical for hours afterward.[4]

Both Fouché and Dubois had been caught unawares. There had been rumors of the vaguest sort that something was about to happen, and the Opéra itself had been thoroughly searched before the general's arrival, although nothing was found. Warnings were received every day; this had seemed to be just another false alarm.[5]

While Napoleon was listening to *The Creation*, Chazot, police commissioner of the Tuileries, began directing the initial investigation in the Rue St.-Niçaise, evacuating the dozens of grievously wounded and directing the four corpses discovered in the rubble to be taken to the morgue in the Châtelet. Stopping a passing carter, Commissioner Chazot requisitioned him and his cart, as the police went through the debris of human limbs, gathering everything that was left, including the mutilated remains of the unfortunate mare, and one hoof, both shafts of the cart (surprisingly intact), two pieces of one wheel, and heaps of blackened and bloody clothes and shoes, which on Prefect Dubois's orders Chazot then sent over to prefecture headquarters near the Quai Desaix.[6] He also began interviewing witnesses and taking statements. Back at the Tuileries at one o'clock in the morning, Chazot began analyzing everything he had gathered thus far and then drafted his initial report. Many more were to follow.

During the rest of the night and the following days, panic set in and accusations multiplied regarding those behind this diabolical plot. Prefect Dubois had no quick answers, but an angry Napoleon immediately blamed the former Jacobins and their fellow revolutionaries, Septembrists, and fanatics who had so vociferously opposed Napoleon's coup d'état and consular government. And with the panic came the inevitable anonymous denunciations by the good citizens of Paris, as in the days of Robespierre and the Reign of Terror—neighbors denouncing suspicious strangers or even neighbors against whom they had some long-standing grudge. During the first seventy-two hours, well over thirty such denunciations reached Dubois's desk alone, all of which proved not only to be unsubstantiated but some even vicious, permitting thirty innocent names to enter police records. Even Dubois's chief inspector, Limodin, finally got fed up. "We must speak out, for if this awful system of cowardly anonymous denunciations is allowed to continue, who among our honest and law-abiding citizens cannot be tainted in this manner?"[7]

Although Police Minister Fouché felt the plot to be the work of the Chouans (royalists) and their military leader, Georges Cadoudal, Napoleon continued to insist—without proof of any sort—that it was the Jacobins who were behind this, and ordered their mass roundup. Forty-eight police commissioners and their teams dispersed through the capital seeking out the culprits. And thus the accused were rushed in indiscriminately for questioning. Not content with this list of 130 names—to which General Bonaparte himself sent lengthy additions—and on his instructions Fouché ordered still other former Jacobins and revolutionaries, against whom nothing could be found, to be expelled from the city. So the panic continued, despite warnings and considerable hesitation on the part of both Dubois and Fouché.[8] Dubois's team of interrogators, led by Limodin, thus pursued their fruitless questioning of the endless stream summarily accused and brought to their cells.

But if it was not the Jacobins and instead the royalists who were behind this plot, then proof had to be found, as Dubois well realized. On Christmas Day he concentrated his personal investigation on the facts alone, beginning with the grisly remains of the horse. Enough pieces remained for it to be identified, he felt, including the one remaining recently shod hoof, and perhaps the owner or blacksmith could be found. The veterinarian consulted by the police was considered the best in France. By reassembling the animal's remains in the courtyard of the prefecture, he was soon able to provide a full description of the horse, which in turn was given to police agents throughout the city.[9] It did not seem like much, especially in a city filled with tens of thousands of horses, but it was a beginning, however slender.

At the same time the twenty-seven National Guardsmen on duty along Napoleon's route to the Opéra and in the Rue St.-Niçaise that night were intensively interrogated, and one of them revealed that one man standing near the fatal cart had asked him for a light for his pipe. Obtaining a description of him and his accent, Dubois ordered the questioning of all surviving inhabitants of that street as well.

The first real break came on December 26, when an inspector reported that a cart like the one carrying the "infernal machine"—as the French press referred to the explosive device—had been stored for three or four days in the Faubourg Poissonière, by a man with a large scar above his left eye. Focusing on this, the police interviewed a grain merchant by the name of Lambel, from the Porte Saint-Martin, who had come forward of his own volition to inform them that, just a few days earlier, he had sold a cart and horse like the ones described to a man calling himself an itinerant cloth merchant. Excited, the inspector took Lambel into the courtyard where the remains of the horse, harness, and wooden cart were laid out on the cobblestones. The stench was horrendous, and it was a slow procedure, but Lambel took his time and afterward definitely identified the remains of the mare's head, the few bits of the leather harness, and the fragments of wood from the cart. He had sold the horse and cart for two hundred francs—which was paid by another man by the name of "Citizen Brunet"—on December 20 to that itinerant merchant. Brunet even gave him a six francs' tip, and Lambel invited the two clients out for a drink in the Rue du Temple, where he got a good look at them, though the purchaser still refused to give his name. Lambel thus provided the police with the first detailed description of both men.

Luck now continued to favor Dubois, as a blacksmith, also from the Faubourg du Temple, came to the prefecture out of curiosity, where he, too, studied the gruesome remains. The horseshoe was definitely his work, he declared, having shod the poor beast for the past four years. Who was the owner? he was asked. "Lambel."

The focus tightened when Dubois learned that the "itinerant merchant" had rented a coachhouse at 23 Rue du Paradis, up the street from one owned by General Marmont. Dubois himself stepped in to question the owner of that property, Citizen Mesnager, and his concierge, Citizeness Rocher, and their twenty tenants. Interrogating one of the renters, he discovered that she had found the itinerant merchant somewhat curious, considering the type of work he allegedly did, and had spied on him through a hole in the wall, observing him meeting with two other men in his room. Thus the police discovered for the first time that there were possibly at least three men involved. Concierge Rocher, with great zest and in the best Parisian tradition, described the other two men in vivid detail, including their accents and clothes. Regarding the vehicle itself, she said it was laden with two heavy *caisses*, not cloth, and that it had remained at 23 Rue du Paradis until about 5:45 P.M. on December 24.[10] Luck was continuing to hold. Then the prefect discovered that a master cooper had been earlier hired to reinforce two stout barrels with heavy iron bands. He next discovered that this same individual had just bought those barrels at 22 Rue du Paradis. Everyone confirmed the description of the suspect, locally known as "Petit François," and another man with him.

On learning that "Petit François" came from the area between the Portes St.-Denis and St.-Martin, they quickly located his sister, who lived on the seventh floor of an ancient apartment building in the Rue St.-Martin. Although known locally as Madame Valon, her name in fact was Carbon, and they discovered the "itinerant merchant's" real name to be François Carbon, the man with the scar over the eye.

Two weeks into the new year, 1801, came another break. During the search of Madame Valon's squalid rooms the investigating commissioner found a half-empty barrel of fine gunpowder, some cartridges, and a variety of men's clothing. Madame Valon and her two teenage daughters were arrested by Dubois and whisked away to a secret detention center for questioning. Carbon of course was going to be the initial key to unraveling the plot, and bulletins for his arrest were issued throughout the French capital and the eighty-seven departments.

Meanwhile the grueling interrogation of Valon and her daughters was intensified. The daughters admitted that their uncle François had been staying there and was now hiding with two former nuns, the Saint-Michel sisters, in the Rue Nôtre-Dame-des-Champs. The girls said that he had been seeing some friends, but they had no idea what he had been up to. Dubois was surprised to learn that Carbon, a rough Breton sailor who had eventually joined Cadoudal's ranks, was now in fact with a group of aristocratic

ladies. Clearly this was no Jacobin plot, and Fouché for one had been completely right after all. Thus at seven o'clock on the morning of January 16,
the police raided the luxurious residence of the two ex-nuns, where in a
small room in the garret they found Carbon fast asleep.[11]

Dubois personally began grilling the scar-faced Carbon, but he
remained obdurately silent. The interrogation went on throughout the day
without results. After a break, at nine o'clock that evening the prefect
resumed the questioning, which continued hour after hour, until suddenly
at four o'clock the next morning Carbon cracked. Not only did he admit to
being the "itinerant merchant" who had bought the cart and horse, and who
had kept them at 23 Rue de Paradis, but he even revealed the names of his
accomplices: "Pierrot," in reality Pierre Robinault de Saint-Réjant, and
"Beaumont," another important aristocrat by the name of Limoëlan.

Dubois could not believe his good fortune, for Saint-Réjant had been a
former divisional general in the Chouan army and Limoëlan, a major general serving under the infamous Cadoudal![12] This was a royalist plot
through and through, there could be no doubt of it. Other names were also
revealed, and although Saint-Réjant was soon captured, other conspirators
escaped.

As Prefect Rigotard put it later, Fouché could well savor "his own
Austerlitz," while accusing his rival Dubois (and his police) of "weakness"
and "indulgence" for having permitted such a dastardly attack ever to have
taken place.[13] Dubois was furious, both with Fouché and the fact that so
many had escaped his dragnet. Fortunately Napoleon took a different view
and strongly praised the work of the prefect of police, capping it with a
generous "bonus" and a May 1802 appointment to the prestigious State
Council, as a reward "for his conduct and the good order he maintained in
the capital."[14]

This initial royalist plot to murder First Consul Bonaparte marked
what was only the beginning of a long-drawn-out war between the
Chouans and Napoleon Bonaparte, the origins of which were now traced
back to their headquarters across the Channel.

The plot in the Rue de Paradis was in fact finally linked to General
Cadoudal himself, who, under orders from London that summer, had prepared Saint-Réjant's original mission: to kidnap (not kill) General Bonaparte, this directly financed by the British government. "I will provide you
with the means by which to reach the capital, where you will get in touch
with people whose names and addresses you will be given," Cadoudal had
instructed him. "With those funds you will arrange to buy a number of
horses, arms, and clothes that I shall be needing at a later stage."[15] General

Cadoudal—commissioned by Louis XVIII—would then personally take command in Paris.

Saint-Réjant, however, desired more vigorous action than a mere kidnapping. Thus, once in France, he independently contacted his friend M. de Limoëlan, a leading royalist, and with the help of an engineer fabricated the bomb eventually planted in the Rue St.-Niçaise.[16]

The rest of course was history, for Cadoudal, still in England, though now blamed by Fouché for the attempt on the first consul's life, in fact only learned of it afterward and was as surprised as anyone else, thinking it the work of Jacobins. But with the proof presented by Dubois, a sullen Napoleon reluctantly released some 223 persons arrested erroneously after the explosion, including Jacobins or Jacobin sympathizers, but not before executing both Carbon and Saint-Réjant.

Time now passed, and Cadoudal, the tall, heavily built, forty-five-year-old scion of Breton peasants, was a little more subtle and intelligent than the impatient Saint-Réjant, although just as stubborn. Not about to give up his plans to overthrow the usurper Bonaparte in favor of the rightful heir, Louis XVIII, he slowly prepared yet again in 1803 for his return to France.

Until this point Cadoudal had refrained from acting, but with the more cautious General Pichegru's acceptance to support it, Cadoudal thought he could now proceed. What he did not realize, however, was that Pichegru was doing so now only under the mistaken assumption that General Moreau had given his full support as well. A royalist envoy had assured Pichegru of Moreau's support, whereas in reality it had been only Moreau's mother-in-law, Mme. Hulot—violently hostile to Bonaparte—who had encouraged the envoy to proceed to England. "If Moreau and Pichegru agree, I will soon be back in France," the Comte d'Artois (the brother of King Louis XVIII and himself the future Charles X) announced enthusiastically, if prematurely, giving the blessing of the House of Bourbon for a major concerted attack (assassination) by the Chouans.[17]

Cadoudal, a vigorous man despite his obesity, only too glad to get back to France to work actively, set out from London on August 21, 1803, with his coconspirators (including two from the unsuccessful Christmas Eve plot).[18] Financed generously by Prime Minister Henry Addington's government, they sailed to a point near Dieppe, where a Chouan officer by the name of Raoul Gaillard greeted them and arranged for their travel to Paris.[19] (Gaillard, an ex-Oratorian, was an old friend of Minister Fouché.)

Once in the French capital, however, everything depended on the coordination of efforts by Generals Pichegru and Moreau. As for Cadoudal, his hands were tied until these two gentlemen finally met and agreed to the joint course of action. But weeks passed, and for a variety of reasons, mostly contrived, nothing was arranged between Pichegru and Moreau. After further problems they finally met secretly on January 25, 1804. It was only now that Moreau's real feelings were disclosed, however, and he emphasized, as he had in the past, his staunch *republican* values—no matter how he detested Bonaparte—and that he would certainly not support the Bourbons or anyone else to the throne. Cadoudal and Pichegru were stunned. Unless they could pull the proverbial rabbit out of the hat, all plans for a concerted military uprising would have to be abandoned or greatly reduced.

It was also in late January that Police Director Réal informed Napoleon that a royalist in the Abbaye Prison had just revealed that he had participated in Cadoudal's recent landing at Dieppe. The prisoner described the plans for a vast military uprising. focusing around the kidnapping plot to remove General Bonaparte himself.

Fouché and Dubois immediately put out a dragnet for the conspirators, in February capturing Bouvet de Lozier, a Chouan leader, who gave them the background on the "Moreau-Pichegru conspiracy."

Informed of this, Napoleon personally ordered the arrest of the two generals. Moreau was captured on February 15 and taken to the towering medieval dungeon in Paris known as the Temple. Five days later Pichegru, Napoleon's former teacher at Brienne, was apprehended in the house of one M. Leblanc, who had betrayed him for a purse of silver. Under the circumstances Cadoudal decided to find a safe place for himself, selecting the house of a pro-Bourbon perfume manufacturer. Fellow conspirator Louis Léridant, with the aid of his friend Goujon, was to have a cabriolet ready to transport Cadoudal. What no one knew, however, was that the worthy royalist Goujon was in fact in the pay of the police. On March 9 a cabriolet duly arrived in the Place St.-Etienne du Mont, right on schedule, which General Cadoudal and three of his officers promptly boarded.[20] At that same moment, however, four policemen in civilian clothes suddenly sprang forward, attempting to grab him, only to be shoved aside by Cadoudal's friends as he escaped in the carriage. But on reaching the Place de l'Odéon, two more policemen cut him off, Cadoudal shooting one of them dead as he reached for the horses and wounding the second superficially in the hip just as he was about to strike Cadoudal with a club. As Cadoudal leaped from the cab and began to run away, the wounded officer gathered enough strength to reach Cadoudal and strike him over the head, aided by two passing civilians. Within the hour public enemy number one was in Dubois's clutches at the prefecture.

Beyond admitting to Dubois that he had come to Paris to seize Bonaparte and take him prisoner, Cadoudal refused to disclose anything else.

"Where did you stay in Paris?" Dubois asked.

"Nowhere."

"Was Pichegru one of the conspirators?"

"I have no idea."

"Moreau?"

"Don't know him, never met him."

"Where were you lodging when you were arrested?"

"In a cabriolet."

"Are you aware that you killed a family man [the police agent]?"

"Next time send bachelors," the prisoner grimly quipped.

Dubois got nothing more out of him, and after days of interrogation he was dispatched to the Temple to join the others.[21]

At the trials of these royalists, Cadoudal was sentenced to death and Moreau given only a two-year prison term, followed by his expulsion from the country. Two other accomplices, Armand and Jules Polignac, were also sentenced. Jules Polignac (a future statesman under Charles X) received two years, while Armand was condemned to death, later reduced to life imprisonment. As for General Pichegru, he was found dead in his prison cell in the Temple, having died, according to the official police report, of "self-inflicted strangulation," like an inordinate number of Temple prisoners. And with that ended the second serious Chouan attempt against Napoleon, one he would not easily forget.

First Consul Bonaparte had acted quickly, accusing men of crimes before even knowing who was involved in the Christmas Eve plot, because of an earlier attempt on his life at the Opéra by some knife-wielding "republicans," mostly Corsican inspired (as were so many of Bonaparte's enemies). On the night of October 10, 1800, Police Prefect Dubois's men had lain in wait for Arena, Ceracchi, Topino-Lebrun, and Demerville as they assembled to assassinate the first consul, who, although he attended, had been warned of the situation. They were duly captured, tried, and executed, but Napoleon had been shaken by the incident.[22]

Prior to that an ambush had been set for him on the road to Malmaison, from which he had narrowly escaped.

These threats and attempts on his life from the outset of his regime had clearly affected the first consul. Despite his obviously dictatorial means for laying down the organization of his new government under the Consulate, behind it all had been an innate, if diluted, idealism of sorts. He genuinely wanted good things for France, hoping to bring law, order, stability, and prosperity to the country. He wanted all traces of the fear of the Revolution and its terroristic wake to be removed once and for all, forgotten, and dismissed. He had great dreams for France, but with the first concerted attack by so-called republicans, something happened to him, causing him to retrench psychologically, gradually leading him away from some of the ideals he had been so seriously contemplating. The Rue du Paradis conspiracy reinforced that, causing him to clamp down severely on dissident groups and suspected dissidents, whether royalist, republican, or Jacobin. Censorship—written and spoken—had to be tightened. Even the vaguest hints of treason had to be suppressed. Newspapers had to disappear. Even the renowned François Joseph Talma of the Théâtre Français had to submit and read before Napoleon personally every new play he planned to produce in public.

Attendant on this was Bonaparte's great drive to crush the Chouans in the West. He had begun this vigorous campaign immediately after 18 Brumaire in November 1799, and continued his efforts strenuously after Christmas 1800, personally ordering the seizure of Chouan leaders, Cadoudal in particular. "Take that wretched Georges dead or alive. Once you take him, have him shot within twenty-four hours."[23] His Chouan supporters were to be shown no mercy: "Act vigorously against the rebels," he instructed. "Burn their villages if necessary." But what Napoleon could not forgive himself for now was his own gullibility, for back on March 5, 1800, he had actually met with this same Cadoudal in Paris, face to face, hoping to win the Chouan leader to his side.[24]

Bonaparte was never one to lose sleep over missed opportunities or past mistakes, however. Meanwhile, so successful were Fouché's police in their surveillance of royalist activities in the country that only one more serious royalist plot was launched, at least in part. Though it occurred years later, it was the final stage of what Cadoudal and the others had begun back at the beginning of the Consulate. By then Emperor Napoleon would sometimes dismiss alleged threats reported by Fouché or Dubois, on occasion even calling them "chimeras." In any event, that was their problem, what they were paid to deal with. "Very well, then, see to it," he once said, dismissing Fouché, who had just revealed a new plot. "That's your affair. You are the police; take whatever measures are required."[25] He had inured himself by then, through some sort of philosophical assurance: "Having submitted to every type of danger for years," he was to say in 1808, "We have acquired the right to think no man will make an attempt on Our life until Providence so wills it."[26] He had not only survived various assassination attempts, including at least four in the first year of the Consulate alone, but battle after battle, leaving behind him hundreds of thousands of maimed and dead, including several of his closest colleagues, aides-de-camp, staff members, and favorite generals, to find himself years later still unscathed. Unlike the tormented Junot, Napoleon's sleep was not even disturbed.

In addition to conspiracies to kill him, there had been and would be numerous one-man suicide missions, including a student who had come from Germany with a trunkload of pistols, intent on avenging the French occupation of German territory. The police of the Paris prefecture intervened, however, before he could attack. Nevertheless, on Napoleon's personal orders, he was not executed but merely imprisoned. "The young man's age is clearly the reason for his actions," Napoleon argued. "After all, one does not become a hardened criminal so early in life. . . . Give him good books to read, have him write to his family and talk it over with the Archchancellor [Cambacérès], who always has good advice to offer."[27] Released by the Allies in 1814 on Napoleon's reappearance in Paris during the One Hundred Days, the hapless young student likewise rematerialized, this time with a homemade bomb under his arm, which, alas, exploded when he tripped and fell from the steps of a Parisian cab. Again imprisoned by Napoleon, after several weeks in a hospital, he was released by Louis XVIII a second time in 1815, only to end his own life in the murky waters of the Seine. With the disappearance of Napoleon he had lost his own raison d'être.[28]

"It is not so easy to make me part with my hide," Napoleon confided to Marshal Davout after one assassination attempt. "I have no fixed daily habits, no precise schedule. All my activities end at different times, and I come and go at irregular hours."[29] "In the midst of so much danger, and so many ambushes, it never occurred to him to take the slightest precaution, at least nothing obvious to me," complained Secret Police Director Desmarest. "It was even necessary to conceal from him certain steps we took when he appeared at the theater, the opera, or during his hunts and journeys."[30] But then something happened to revive the whole royalist scare of December 1800—something Napoleon could not so easily dismiss.

It began at eleven o'clock in the morning on March 11, 1808, when Napoleon was perusing the *Bulletin de la Police* just handed him by Fouché. It concerned a minor item about another landing of royalist agents along the coast of Brittany. When Napoleon pointed out this particular item, about one Prigent, it was Police Minister Fouché's turn for once simply to shrug his shoulders, dismissing it as a minor matter. But Napoleon, who often at critical moments lived by his instinct, sensed something more. Asking questions and still dissatisfied, he instructed Fouché to keep him informed with daily reports.[31]

Fouché immediately put more men on the case, assigning them to St.-Malo, where the incident had first been reported. Ever since the Revolution there had been landings along this stretch of coast by the British and the Bourbons. In this case Fouché notified Napoleon that late in January 1808, a fishing smack out of Jersey had dropped off four men on a deserted stretch of Breton coast not far from Dinard.[32] A certain Ballet reported to the police about "four peasants" who had stayed with him at St.-Servan for more than a week. Their names: Jean, Nonote, Fauchinot, and Blondel, all false of course. Their leader, the so-called Blondel, was the key to the situation. A robust man of about forty-five, he spoke with a local accent, probably from St.-Malo. When General Commissioner Réal then gave Ballet the description of one François-Noël Prigent, the son of a St.-Malo fruit merchant, he identified him at once as Blondel. It all fell into place after that, for Réal's police had been after this elusive Prigent for many years. He was in fact one of the principal Bourbon agents working for Joseph, Comte de Puisaye, himself thought to be working out of London and financed directly by the British government. With this information now before him, Napoleon reiterated the urgency of finding these men and their papers, and of making them talk.

Time after time report after report had reached Paris of sightings of British vessels signaling to the French shore and unknown agents, or attempting to land men and supplies from Ostend and Boulogne. Such sightings had been made along the Norman and Breton coasts right down to the Charente. In January a boat had been seized and taken to Calais, where a packet of mysterious papers was found and handed over to the police. Four Chouan agents were captured at Nantes, and a suspicious vessel flying the American flag had been seized at Morlaix. At Amsterdam secret correspondence between London and the firm of Henrique was unearthed. Another secret letter sent to London but intercepted by the police came from Fauche-Borel, whose "Comité de Paris" continued "to pursue . . . the overthrow of the [French] imperial throne."[33]

Meanwhile, when on February 21, 1808, a play entitled *Kokoli* was presented at the Théâtre du Pavillon, the police cracked down when the principal character, Kokoli, said to the king: "Recall your army . . . reduce taxes . . . make peace"—obviously aimed at Napoleon. In any event, the local *commissaire générale* duly informed Paris: "Long and warm applause proves that this play could affect and change public opinion [in favor of the royalists]," and he promptly closed it down.[34] Sedition and unrest were to be found every-where, and Fouché's police had to remain ever vigilant if they were to save France.

Another item in the *Bulletin,* on March 10, sparked interest in the search for the aforesaid Prigent. An alarming secret letter, probably from the Comte de Puisaye in London, to a royalist agent in the Charente, was reported to Paris. The critical line read: "I told you about a month ago that Prigent and some Chouan subalterns had left [London] for Jersey."[35] What worried Napoleon about this newly discovered letter was that it was dated three months earlier, which meant that the enemy agents were well on their way with their work and objective, thus tying in with the report from St.-Malo on the sighting of Prigent. "I recommend your following up this case with dispatch!" Napoleon urged the police minister.[36]

Fouché set to work increasing the number of gendarmes and police officials all along the Channel. But it was only five weeks later, on April 27, that the general commissioner of St.-Malo was finally able to report back that he had found Prigent's initial January hiding place at St.-Servan.[37] The royalist agent's trail still remained more than three months old. Over the next month the net continued to widen, and the police discovered that Prigent had been corresponding with the important royalist leader, the Prince de Bouillon, and had had contact with other royalist agents from the Côtes-du-Nord the previous year. What is more, one of Prigent's lieutenants, the so-called Fauchinot, was in reality a man named Deschamps, a known Chouan agent whose mother had been found to be hiding him back in 1803 (for which she had subsequently been imprisoned for three years). They all would be tracked down. It was merely a matter of time, Fouché assured Napoleon. But would they strike first? And at what? At whom? And how—with guns, knives, bombs? Clearly time was of the essence.

Finally, early on the morning of June 7, Police Minister Fouché requested an urgent meeting with Napoleon and informed him that Prigent had been arrested two days ago at Saint-Gilles, near Rennes, along with Deschamps and Leclerc.[38] The police had earlier captured the fourth man in the group, "Jean," whose real name was Bouchard and who had in fact betrayed Prigent, making the arrest possible. Knowing how Napoleon relished the details of such plots, Fouché filled him in:

Disguised as a gendarme, he [Bouchard] guided the brigade [of gendarmes] commanded by Captain Géry. That same evening the three brigands were traced to a room in a granary. [When confronted] they opened fire, wounding one gendarme in the leg. Leclerc was shot twice, probably mortally. Such are the results of the vigilant measures taken over the past seven weeks by the Commissaire général of Police of Saint-Malo.[39]

Fouché went on to praise his work, announcing:

Prigent's arrest may be considered an important operation, given this individual's considerable activity and audacity in the past, and who indeed—one may say without exaggeration—has made more than two hundred [clandestine] trips to the French coast over the past fifteen years. It was he who was responsible for the principal landings of émigrés and Chouan leaders, for the supply of arms and munitions, and for maintaining the constant flow of communications.

What is more, "Prigent has confessed to being Puisaye's agent, Puisaye who in turn has the ear of the British government [under the prime minister, the Duke of Portland], as well as that of the Bourbons, for their affairs in the West." It turned out that other agents had also been sent out back in January, all of them with secret correspondence from London for "royalist committees in several parts of the interior, . . . [which] confirms what our agent in London also tells us."[40]

Prigent had apparently broken quickly under rigorous police interrogation and was now providing them with an enormous amount of material, Fouché said, including important documents, and generally cooperating. All his papers and notes were now in the hands of the prefect of Rennes. Finally he admitted that he had been given letters for agents in Paris and had received replies from them. Although he was unable to provide the real name of the party to whom they were sent, he did have the address, which in turn resulted in the disclosure of that person, a Monsieur Mars, at 118 Rue de Miromesnil. Fouché, by now excited by these revelations, had already given orders to have Prigent transferred to the ministry in Paris for trial. "Appropriate measures have been taken to prevent his escape," he assured the Tuileries.[41]

Pleased with the work done by Fouché's men in the field, and spellbound by the unraveling of these events, Napoleon asked to see everything found in Prigent's wallet and papers. He added, "Have him write out a journal of everything he did day by day, indicating where he had been to dine and sleep. I find it difficult to believe that it is all as simple and clear as you tell me. He must make a completely frank confession, including the names of English agents in Paris and along the coast."[42]

Four days later, on June 11, Fouché returned with the daily *Bulletin* and a long report with further disclosures regarding what he now referred to as "L'Affaire Prigent." Prigent had had both general and special instructions from Puisaye, he informed Napoleon, including a coded list of twenty-six royalist leaders throughout the West—a list he had burned. These detailed instructions concerned the royalist committees to be established in Brittany, in the Imperial Navy, and throughout France.[43]

Napoleon's initial intuitive anxiety about the report on Prigent back in March had been correct after all. If he had listened to Fouché and not pursued the investigation thoroughly, a vast underground royalist network might have been reestablished in the country. Fortunately Fouché's men had nipped the conspiracy in the bud, for Prigent's original efforts at sounding out members of the old royalist "Comité de 1797" had turned out to be not at all encouraging. Several people ignored him, and others dismissed his plan as foolhardy or impossible.[44] Indeed, even the comte de Puisaye's brother, who had been contacted at his estate in the Orne, refused to communicate with him at all. (Fouché had had the brother arrested anyway and interrogated by Desmarest's Haute Police, though he was finally released.) As for the burned list of twenty-six other conspirators, Prigent could remember only a few of the names and addresses—which, admittedly, he did give the police—most of them in and around Rennes.[45]

In any event Prigent was providing them with all sorts of valuable contacts in various capacities throughout the western regions of the country. If Napoleon was generally pleased with these unexpected results, he was not as satisfied as Fouché. The police had the names of at least a hundred people, many of them property owners. Napoleon ordered Fouché to "draw up a list of them and send it to the appropriate prefects and to the office of property registration, and then order the sequestration of those properties as well as those belonging to their wives, while placing their relatives under special police surveillance."[46] Napoleon could be lenient in the case of a crazed student, but not when a full-scale conspiracy and possible revolt to topple his regime were involved. Everyone concerned—men, women, and children—was to be punished.

The result of Fouché's intensive interrogations was finally presented to Napoleon at the Tuileries on June 16. Outlining the general situation, Fouché explained that apparently Puisaye had decided on this new plan to revive the Chouan movement against Napoleon back in October 1807. On January 18, 1808, Prigent was duly landed on French shores from a boat from Jersey, carrying plans and instructions for the establishment of the Royalist Committee of Rennes. Fouché further informed Napoleon that

Prigent was to hand over three thousand gold louis, or sixty thousand francs, as a fund for the émigré committees in Brittany and Normandy, to be used for transporting émigrés back to France for the uprising and operations against Napoleon.[47]

Although the police had apparently scotched the plot, the *Bulletin de la Police* announced on June 22 that it had learned that three more important royalist agents were expected to land at any moment along the Normandy coast, and thus Fouché's police were remaining on the alert.[48] But Prigent, almost enthusiastically aiding the authorities now—in exchange for a promise of immunity from prosecution by Fouché—was drawing up suggestions of the best way to intercept enemy communications with the coast of France. Fouché acknowledged that he had never seen anything like this before. "The great detail he has provided establishes his intelligence, good faith, and strong desire to attain the purpose he had promised." To show further good faith, Prigent disclosed the signal he used to contact the vessel now being sent to collect him and ferry him back to Jersey.[49] The work and information that Prigent contributed to this affair are "quite remarkable," Fouché concluded.[50]

The immediate result of this top-priority police operation by hundreds of Desmarest's Haute Police ultimately involved the arrest of sixty-three individuals, ten of whom were condemned to be executed by a firing squad, while another twenty-nine were eventually acquitted. The first seven were duly executed at 3:00 A.M. on October 3.[51] As for Prigent and the man who had turned him in, Bouchard, Fouché had promised that they would be pardoned by Napoleon in exchange for their extraordinary cooperation. But when word of this got out, there was a great cry of public indignation and Prigent unexpectedly found himself before a firing squad on October 11,[52] a fact omitted by the *Bulletin de la Police*.

Napoleon was not ungrateful for the work carried out by the commanding officers of the police units in the Prigent affair. "These men have rendered me such a great service that I wish to demonstrate my gratitude to them," he said, ordering Fouché to distribute twenty-four thousand francs in rewards (taken from money found on the captured men).[53] So ended the last serious London-directed royalist attempt against Napoleon—while of course not forgetting Malet's unique plot several years later.

CHAPTER 19

"The Revolution Is Over"

I do not wage war as a profession, no one in fact is more peaceful than I.

rom the moment Bonaparte assumed the position of head of state, as the senior of the three ruling consuls, the lives of everyone around him, especially that of his secretary, Bourrienne, became a nightmare. A thousand ideas and objectives concerning the running of a great country like France now filled Napoleon's mind, and they all seemed to spill out at once.

After announcing to the nation on November 12, 1799, that the badly contrived Constitution of the Year III was dead, and with it all the corrupt undemocratic apparatus, he immediately set out to replace every aspect of it. "Everyone talks to me about goodness, abstract justice, and the natural laws of society," he said. "Well, the first law is that of necessity, and the first principle of justice is ensuring the public welfare."[1] What he considered a necessity and the requirements of establishing and maintaining the public welfare, however, were not even remotely similar to those envisioned by such contemporaries as Sieyès, Lafayette, Talleyrand—or Thomas Jefferson. France was in store for a shock that would rock the very historical foundations of the land and from which it would still be reeling two centuries later.

"I listen to advice from all sides, but in the end, my head is my only counsel," he remarked before the newly created State Council, by which he was largely to govern the country thereafter. "The art of governing," he said, "involves nothing more than the application of common sense when dealing with important political matters."[2] The pace he was now setting for himself and the hard-pressed Bourrienne (who began work at seven every morning and continued until eleven or later at night, seven days a week, month in, month out) was grueling. The results poured out daily in an avalanche of papers, decisions, and orders to state counselors, ministers, and institutions. "Weakness in the supreme power is the worst sort of calamity that might befall a people," he later informed the Corps Législatif, and he was determined to avoid that now, as he seized the reins of power with an iron grip that only the combined armies of all the European powers would years later be able to force him to release. "It was in fact not simply the matter of an absolutist form of government that Bonaparte was now attempting to establish in France, but of a military dictatorship," Bourrienne pointed out, and that was "worse yet."[3] The truth of that observation was not long in manifesting itself.

Although the nation lay shattered and exhausted after ten years of revolutionary fratricide, internal mayhem, and willful self-destruction, Napoleon's first thoughts, apart from orders to Finance Minister Gaudin to reorganize completely the state's finances and to create the Banque de France, turned to the army and war. France was still at war with Austria, for instance, which had reconquered from France its former Italian provinces, and Napoleon was determined to get them back.

Before his new administration was seven weeks old, he had put the nation on a war footing, preparing depots, artillery, and troops for the Armies of the Rhine and of Italy. This included stripping the beleaguered Army of the Orient, still in Egypt, of four of its best remaining commanders (Desaix, Davout, Vial, and Lanusse) and recalling them to France, while instructing that same abandoned army to strive to maintain control of France's splendid new province. Addressing the Armies of the Rhine and of Italy, he reminded them that they had already conquered Holland, the Rhine, and Italy and that "Victory will give you bread."[4]

"Everyone is so fearful these days, I swear, they would let the Devil himself rule, if he promised to suppress the revolution for ever," Roederer observed. Indeed, the last thing the people wanted was war, even on foreign soil. Napoleon quickly reassured them that this new government was quite unlike the previous ones. In effect he told a startled but largely delighted French Republic that the Revolution was over.

This had begun back on December 15, 1799, when he proclaimed that "a [new] constitution is being drawn up for you ... founded on the true principles of representative government, based on the sacred rights safeguarding private property, equality and freedom. ... The powers instituted by it will be strong and stable, as they must be in order to guarantee the rights of our citizens and the interests of the State."[5] All the key elements were in that message: private property, which had been sacrificed during the Revolution, would finally be secure, along with individual equality; a government with great authority would ensure the stability of the land and the interests of the state, including a prosperous commerce and agriculture. The only misleading statement was the promise that representative democratic institutions would be introduced. They would appear in name, to be sure, but they were to prove powerless illusions.

Bonaparte was perfectly sincere in stating that the disruptive Revolution was over once and for all. Effective immediately all the revolutionary holidays were to be suppressed (except for July 14, celebrating the fall of the Bastille, and 1 Vendémiaire, the festival commemorating the founding of the First French Republic).[6] What is more, the class with which Napoleon personally associated himself—that of the aristocrats, the émigrés—was no longer to be harassed. They would be permitted to return to France, their confiscated property returned. These measures were kept from the public, however, for it would take time to wean the masses from their revolutionary prejudices.[7] He ordered a proper public burial with full honors for Pope Pius VI, who had died earlier at Valence while a prisoner of the French Republic. Churches were to be reopened throughout the country and priests permitted to carry out traditional services. There must be freedom of worship in the land for Jew and Christian alike, he declared, as he prepared the way for improved relations with the Vatican (not because of personal religious reasons, but because it was necessary to gain the support of the people and to maintain stability in the country). This would soon lead to the concluding of a Concordat on July 15, 1801, normalizing relations between the Roman Catholic church and France for the first time since the beginning of the Revolution. "Religion," Napoleon confided to Bourrienne, "is useful for the governments of every country. We must use it to control the people. In Egypt I was a Muhammadan, in France I am a Catholic."[8]

This great political coup for Bonaparte was a disaster for the Bourbons, who had counted on the support of the Vatican as an important card in their favor. "When the leader of the [Roman Catholic] Church abandons the interests of religion and the cause of kings," a dismayed comte de Vaudreuil wrote his mother, "upon whom can we count?" The young duc d'Enghien was equally disturbed. "It takes only a cheap action to become a great man these days, that is, when that man is Bonaparte. Nothing seems to stop him, not even God," he lamented.[9]

At the same time, as a part of his plan to restore stability in the country, the first consul announced his intention of putting down the royalist uprising in the West. Civil war had to be crushed.[10] But at the same time Napoleon wanted a "reconciliation" with these rebels, who, with Bourbon support in London and elsewhere, had doggedly fought the Revolution. Napoleon ordered the harsh measures taken against them by the Directory to be revoked: No more "loans" were to be extorted from them, no more hostages were to be taken, no more villages destroyed, and all religious restrictions were to be lifted at once. "Rally round our new constitution," he encouraged them. "The ministers of a God of peace will be the first means of achieving national reconciliation and concord. . . . Hereafter only one sentiment must stir us all, the love of the fatherland."[11]

When this peace offering was rejected out of hand by the Chouans, Napoleon issued a brutal "Proclamation to the Army," ordering French troops to crush the tens of thousands of French citizens rebelling in the western provinces. Attack them vigorously, "surprise your enemies . . . and exterminate those wretches," he ordered. "Weakness now is inhumanity. . . . Only with vigorous action can you succeed. Therefore, to arms! To arms!" On January 5, 1800, General Hédouville was ordered to march sixty thousand French troops into the West.[12] No one turned down Napoleon with impunity.

From the beginning the first consul expected blind obedience, whether from Frenchman or foreigner. The Italians were soon to suffer the same fate as the previously conquered Dutch, Swiss, Bretons, and Vendeans. On December 18, 1799, Napoleon had instructed the people of the Ligurian Republic that he expected them to be annexed to France, whether they liked it or not. If they did not sign a treaty of annexation with France, General Masséna would be "authorised to raise a contribution [of millions of francs] from the principal merchant houses [of Genoa]," as he had already done in Switzerland and in Holland.[13]

Napoleon had made his warning to Europe clear from the start. France could and would expand when and where it wished to do so. War would continue. Although the first consul had written to both King George III of England and the Austrian emperor on December 25, 1799, calling for peace, Napoleon not only did not expect a favorable response but did not even allow time for one to be sent. On that same day he had already issued his famous proclamation "To the French Soldiers" instructing them to prepare for a new war that would take them well beyond French frontiers "to invade the enemy states."[14]

With his new government safely installed by New Year's Day, 1800, Napoleon was moving with lightning speed and resolve to secure his regime before opponents could either protest or revolt. To demonstrate to the world, and to the French in particular, that his administration was not to prove another spineless, corrupt Directory but a resolute one-man rule, on February 19, in a symbolic move, he transferred the entire government, including cabinet ministers and State Council, in an enormous procession, escorted by three thousand troops, from the Directory's headquarters in the Luxembourg Palace to the Tuileries. Thereafter his fellow consuls would have to seek shelter under their own roofs.[15] Napoleon was literally replacing the Bourbon kings of France, moving into the very palace where Louis XVI and Marie Antoinette had resided and ruled the nation.

In other spheres as well the diminutive first consul was soon proving himself a giant, not just another revolutionary politician. On Finance Minister Gaudin's recommendation, he created the Banque de France to help bring order, stability, integrity, and sense of planning to the jumbled world of revolutionary finances and currency problems. He ordered the drawing up of new law codes that would ensure the respect, stability, and position of the propertied classes, while establishing and regularizing civil, criminal, and commercial legal codes. The State Council, assigned to draft the Civil Code, for instance, moved with remarkable rapidity, over great protestations by the Tribunate. It was duly published in March 1803 and went into full effect in January 1804. To Napoleon, who had literally discussed and debated every article of the proposed code with the Judicial Commission of the Council, it was of critical importance to the establishment of the new France he now envisaged. This was probably the first consul's greatest single contribution, State Counselor de Fontanes congratulating the country on "the consummation of this great enterprise, which had defied Charlemagne himself." Napoleon commented years later: "The great glory of my reign is not in having won forty battles. . . . That which can never be denied, and that [which] will live on forever, is my Civil Code."[16]

On May 19, 1802, Bonaparte created the Legion of Honor, despite much anger on the part of frustrated Jacobins and much of the republican-dominated Tribunate. They wanted no more kings, no more one-man rule, nor did they want to see men separated and distinguished by rank, achievement, and distinction. All men were equal, they argued; all men had exactly the same talents and abilities. Therefore all achievements were of the same value, and there should be no artificial distinctions. Even Napoleon's hand-picked State Council balked at the idea, only fourteen of the twenty-four counselors voting for it. It was with considerable trouble that Napoleon crushed and overcame opposition from the Tribunate, which finally voted in its favor, and he now counted the days until such time as he could completely suppress this troublesome political institution altogether (which he did on August 16, 1807). "The noisy minority have not understood what I am attempting to do," Napoleon argued.[17]

Nor were the arts or education forgotten in this phenomenal blizzard of national legislation, which included the creation of the lycée system and the refounding of the national university, including special new schools for law, the sciences, art, military science, and three schools for girls. More than ten thousand national scholarships were created (of which the young Victor Hugo was among the recipients) to open the ranks of the nation's best schools to the talented, regardless of their financial condition.[18] (After all, without a similar scholarship, First Consul Bonaparte himself would not then have been ruling France.) But this also involved the introduction of a new and insidious regimentation into all aspects of national life, one that has continued to this day. For the first time education was to be centrally directed by Paris—and Napoleon. All lycée students were to wear uniforms (to eliminate outward differences in individual students' wealth) and march to class in measured step, literally at the drumbeat. The psychological left-right-left mentality of the soldier was instilled from youth. They would be ready to accept orders from Napoleon and the state to hasten to the colors when they were called up under the national conscription, which greatly expanded under Bonaparte. This in turn had to be reinforced by the same values and knowledge: Everyone must accept the same views, which must be held sacrosanct and unquestioned. "Education," Napoleon insisted, "must impart the same knowledge and the same principles to all individuals living in the same society, in order to create a single, uniform body, informed with one and the same understanding, and working for the common good on the basis of uniformity of views and desire." Differing or alternate views were unacceptable, inadmissible in Napoleonic schools; only the state's interpretations of subjects and official views, dictated by the Tuileries, were permitted. Woe unto him or her who questioned them. There was no room for the individual or the independent thinker in Napoleon's new France. There was no room, either, for politically incorrect thought or conduct, and naturally unacceptable works (in the view of Napoleon) were to be banned from every classroom and library of the land, including works by Montesquieu, Rousseau, and Tacitus. "Instead let youth read Caesar's *Commentaries* [and] Corneille," he ordered. Napoleon alone knew what was acceptable.[19]

The national curriculum set for all schools and classes was almost entirely concentrated on the subjects required to make good citizens, future army officers, and heads of bureaucratic departments in the various government ministries. History was rewritten to suppress anything detracting from French and Napoleonic glory; knaves and crooked politicians, scandals, or defeats in the field of battle, were either hushed up or so altered as to defy historical recognition (a policy continued in French schools and universities to this day). Glory was extolled at the expense of truth, French leaders preferring to treat their citizens like children and leave them in ignorance, in a world of dreams. It was a move as pathetic as it was to prove destructive, stifling a need for integrity without which no nation can reach maturity or achieve respect at any level.

This educational censorship was mirrored in everyday life. As already noted, several dozen of the nation's newspapers were suppressed, and one quickly assumed official position as the vehicle for announcing Napoleon's national policies: the *Moniteur Universel*. It was to be supplemented by the *Journal des Débats* and other official administrative publications. Napoleon ordered the publishing of a new history of France, reflecting his views on the nation's developments. Individual works by scholars had to be subjected to his censors (through the Ministry of Police and the prefect of Paris). This extended to the theater, Bonaparte announcing that historical themes and "historical tragedy" were too dangerous to be presented to the public: antigovernment opposition might easily be found or interpreted through such plays. The French needed only lighthearted works, "Give them comedy," he insisted. When a new play was to be considered, the author or its leading dramatic actor was ordered to bring it to the Tuileries, Malmaison, or St.-Cloud for a reading. If an author did not please Napoleon, his career was finished, his works neither published nor produced. Napoleon alone was empowered to dictate censorship policy in the land, deciding what was fit for the public. Occasionally a few plays were actually produced in the provinces without his knowledge, but thanks chiefly to Fouché's ever vigilant police, they were soon brought to Napoleon's attention.

As of 1802 the first consul spent most of his time at the Palace of St.-Cloud, which he had completely renovated and refurbished by Percier and Fontaine at a cost of six million francs.[20] Vandalized and then devastated by earlier revolutionary mobs, the entire interior of this spacious palace was gutted and restored. Malmaison, for its part, was difficult to get to, lacked a sweeping river perspective, and was simply too small, not to mention Napoleon's loathing of Josephine's English gardeners (with whom he was constantly at war) and gardens. St.-Cloud, more than any other palace, represented Napoleon and his tastes. Spacious new formal *French* gardens were laid out, as well as a theater and facilities of every kind, including accommodations and apartments for dozens of people. St.-Cloud also had the advantage of being situated overlooking the Seine in a heavily wooded area far from crowded, noisy Paris. Unlike the siuation at the Tuileries, the public could not stroll by and peer into the windows of the room where Napoleon and Josephine were sitting and talking. Napoleon despised and feared the masses and took appropriate measures to secure himself against them. No howling mob was going to break into the spacious but well-guarded estate of St.-Cloud, as had happened at the Louvre. And in later years Bonaparte would have massive gray-green-and-gold iron grilles and fencing erected around the Tuileries, the Luxembourg Palace, Fontainebleau, St.-Cloud, and dozens of government buildings, all bearing his imperial initial.

Napoleon, much influenced by the spectacular monuments he had seen in Egypt, from the very beginning planned to make major changes in Paris. Beginning with a series of new bridges—the Ponts des Arts, St.-Cloud, Sèvres, and later Austerlitz and Jena—he ultimately had additions made to the Louvre and to the Invalides, then built the Bourse, later the new Foreign Ministry on the Quai Bonaparte (now Quai d'Orsay), barracks, broad new boulevards, including the Rue Impériale, put up war trophies, had obelisks placed near the Tuileries and in the Place de la Révolution, and of course erected the massive Arc de Triomphe, which was to bear the names of his most famous generals and admirals. "The purpose of all these works," he freely admitted to Bourrienne, "is to ensure that my name is indestructibly linked with the name of France." "The destruction of men and the construction of men's monuments seemed perfectly compatible in Bonaparte's mind," his secretary wryly commented, "and his passion for monuments almost equaled his passion for war." Although Paris never witnessed structures as impressive as those that dominated Rome or Egypt, Napoleon did have more utilitarian projects in mind, including the extension of the St.-Quentin Canal, a new road built over the Simplon Pass for his armies— "there are no more Alps"—and a wide new military highway through the forests and swamps to link Metz and Mainz.[21] But the monuments that really concerned Napoleon most were not those made of stone but rather of paper. His glory recorded in history books was in the last analysis the only

Bonapartes,
Relatives, and Friends

Lieutenant Colonel
Bonaparte at Toulon, 1793.
(*Musées Nationaux*)

Letizia Bonaparte,
Napoleon's mother.
Portrait by Gérard,
lithograph by de Villain.
(*Dawson Collection, Morrab
Library of Penzance*)

Joseph Bonaparte, Napoleon['s]
older brother, king of Naple[s],
then usurper king of Spain,
womanizer, war contractor,
speculator. Following the fa[ll]
of the First Empire, as the
count of Survilliers, he mov[ed]
to the United States, where [he]
purchased the estate of Poin[t]
Breeze, near Bordentown, N[.J.]
Portrait by J. Goubaud,
engraving by S. W. Reynold[s.]
(Dawson Collection, Morrab
Library of Penzance)

Lucien Bonaparte, impetuous, unsta[ble]
political schemer, exiled in Italy in 1[8]
Portrait by Fabre. *(Montpellier)*

Louis Bonaparte, king of Holland, forced
to retire from the world because of mental
illness. *(Dawson Collection, Morrab*
Library of Penzance)

Jérôme Bonaparte, Napoleon's youngest and most troublesome brother; admiral, general, king of Westphalia, and bigamously "married" to Princess Catherine of Württemberg. *(Dawson Collection, Morrab Library of Penzance)*

Napoleon's sister Elise Bonaparte Bacchiochi, princess of Lucca and grand duchess of Tuscany. Portrait by Belliazo, lithograph by Delpech. *(Dawson Collection, Morrab Library of Penzance)*

Caroline Bonaparte Murat, queen of Naples.
Portrait by Vigée-Lebrun. *(Musée de Versailles)*

Pauline Bonaparte, princess Borghese.
Portrait by Lefèvre. *(Musées Nationaux)*

Josephine. Portrait
by Prud'hon.
(Musées Nationaux)

Empress Josephine
at the coronation,
December 2, 1804.
Portrait by Gérard.
(Proctor Jones Collec-
tion, San Francisco)

Napoleon's second wife,
Empress Marie-Louise,
who provided her hus-
band with his first "legal"
son, the king of Rome.
Portrait by Desnoyers,
engraving by P. M. Alix.
(Dawson Collection, Morrab
Library of Penzance)

François-Charles-Joseph Bonaparte,
Napoleon's son by Empress Marie-Louise,
known as the king of Rome and Napoleon II,
was held prisoner in Vienna, where he died
under highly suspicious circumstances at the
age of twenty-one. Drawing by N. N. Carter,
engraving by C. Hullmandel. *(Dawson
Collection, Morrab Library of Penzance)*

Julie Clary, queen of Spain
much-betrayed wife of Jos
Bonaparte. Portrait by Lefè
(Musées Nationa

Hortense de Beauharnais,
estranged wife of Louis
Bonaparte. Portrait by
Fleury. *(Bibliothèque
Nationale)*

Napoleon's Uncle Fesch, pirate, war profiteer, cardinal. Print of Meynier's original. *(Musées Nationaux)*

Napoleon's stepson, Prince Eugène de Beauharnais, viceroy of Italy. Though Eugène was promised the crown of Italy, as usual Napoleon reneged on his word. *(Dawson Collection, Morrab Library of Penzance)*

Eléonore Denuelle de la Plaigne, the first of Napoleon's mistresses to provide him with a son. Portrait by Léon. *(Proctor Jones Collection, San Francisco)*

Countess Marie Walewska, Napoleon's favorite mistress, who gave him his second son, Count Alexandre Walewski. *(Dawson Collection, Morrab Library of Penzance)*

A defeated Emperor Napoleon. Print of Delaroche's original. *(Musées Nationaux)*

Ministers, Aides, and Associates

Foreign Minister Talleyrand, who attempted in vain to resist Napoleon's expansion beyond French borders, the invasion of England, and the creation of the Continental System. *(Dawson Collection, Morrab Library of Penzance)*

Napoleon's heinous police minister and mass murderer, Joseph Fouché, the duke of Otranto. Engraving by Couche fils. *(Dawson Collection, Morrab Library of Penzance)*

Gaspard Monge, a founder of the Ecole Polytechnique and Napoleon's early confidant in Italy and Egypt. Portrait by David d'Anger. *(Dawson Collection, Morrab Library of Penzance)*

Gen. Armand de Caulaincourt, duc de Vicence, foreign minister, was with Napoleon throughout the harrowing Russian campaign, which he had strongly advised against. *(Dawson Collection, Morrab Library of Penzance)*

Archchancellor J. J. Cambacérès, who ruled France when Napoleon was on his various military campaigns. *(Dawson Collection, Morrab Library of Penzance)*

Louis de Bourrienne, Napoleon's classmate and later faithful and industrious private secretary. When he decided to resign, Bourrienne was defamed, falsely accused of theft, and became the victim of character assassination by Napoleon. *(Bibliothèque Nationale)*

Claude-François de Méneval, who replaced Bourrienne as Napoleon's private secretary in 1802, serving until the end of the 1812 Russian campaign, when, he lost the use of one leg due to frostbite and transferred to the service of Empress Marie-Louise. *(Collection of Baron C. F. Méneval)*

Dr. Dominique Larrey, head of the army's medical services after Egypt, whose requests for help and improvement were largely ignored by Napoleon. *(Musées Nationaux)*

Charles Tristan de Montholon, aide to Napoleon on St. Helena, who became his poisoner. *(Bibliothèque Nationale)*

Soldiers and Sailors of France

Adm. Denis Decrès, Napoleon's
naval minister, prepared for the
invasion of England, 1803–5.
(Musée de Versailles)

Adm. Eustace de Bruix,
commander in chief of
naval operations for the invasion of England, 1803–5.
(Musée de la Marine)

Adm. Villeneuve, commander
in chief of the Franco-Spanish
combined fleet at Trafalgar,
October 21, 1805, who
was probably murdered on
his return to France.
(Musée de la Marine)

Marshal Soult, ever intriguing and conniving, on the eve of retirement. (*Dawson Collection, Morrab Library of Penzance*)

Marshal Alexandre Berthier, prince of Neuchâtel, Napoleon's irreplaceable permanent chief of staff, who committed suicide in 1815. (*Dawson Collection, Morrab Library of Penzance*)

Marshal Bernadotte, Napoleon's bête noire, who married Napoleon's rejected Désirée Clary. Constantly plotting and jealous of Napoleon, Bernadotte betrayed the French on the battlefield. (*Dawson Collection, Morrab Library of Penzance*)

Marshal Louis Davout, duke of Auerstädt, prince of Eckmühl. Napoleon's finest field commander. Portrait by Maurin, engraving by V. Adams. *(Dawson Collection, Morrab Library of Penzance)*

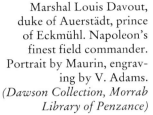

Marshal Joachim Murat, who replaced Joseph Bonaparte as king of Naples. Portrait by Belliard, engraving by Delpech. *(Dawson Collection, Morrab Library of Penzance)*

Gen. Andoche Junot, duke of Abrantès, who was seduced by Caroline Murat. He lost Portugal to the British and ultimately committed suicide. Portrait by Maurin, engraving by V. Adams. *(Dawson Collection, Morrab Library of Penzance)*

Marshal Jean Lannes, duke of Montebello, one of Napoleon's most dependable commanders. Portrait by Belliard, lithograph by Delpech. *(Dawson Collection, Morrab Library of Penzance)*

rshal André Masséna, duke of Rivoli, prince f Essling, who during the early years of the Empire was an effective field commander. Portrait by Maurin, engraving by Delpech. *(Dawson Collection, Morrab Library of Penzance)*

Marshal Michel Ney, duke of Elchingen, prince of the Moskowa, who proved the ultimate national scapegoat for Napoleon's destructive swath through history. Portrait by Maurin, lithograph by Delpech. *(Dawson Collection, Morrab Library of Penzance)*

Marshal Auguste Frédéric Louis Viesse de Marmont, duke of Ragusa. Portrait by Maurin, lithograph by Delpech. *(Dawson Collection, Morrab Library of Penzance)*

Gen. Christophe Duroc, Napoleon's closest confidant in the later years. Portrait by Belliard, engraving by Delpech. *(Dawson Collection, Morrab Library of Penzance)*

Gen. J. B. Kléber, gravely wounded in taking Alexandria, later falsely accused of being overly protective of its inhabitants and of financial mismanagement by Napoleon, and then abandoned in Egypt along with the entire French expeditionary force by Napoleon, where he was assassinated by a Syrian in 1800. *(Proctor Jones Collection, San Francisco)* "monument" that really counted. To ensure that his version of events was remembered, he falsified army reports and bulletins, as he had already done in Egypt, aided by numerous articles he personally inserted in the *Moniteur* throughout his career.[22] He was less concerned with the present than with posterity.

Bonaparte's arrival on the scene was definitely different from that of any previous ruler, politician, or soldier, in France—or elsewhere, for that matter. "His incredible activity had something very catching about it, electrifying all those around him ... even government employees," Bourrienne remarked. "During these early days of the Consulate, it was really quite wonderful to see, the haste every individual seemed to make to help the First Consul in the execution of his projects for the regeneration of France. Everything seemed animated by a new spirit in the land, and everyone made an extra effort to contribute to it." Napoleon insisted: "'Impossible' is not a French word." "Bonaparte," commented Schopenhauer, "is the finest example of a human destiny manipulated by sheer will power." "We need a man of steel," Champagny had said back in 1799,[23] and now France had one.

This invigorating force also resulted in the will to restore stability and confidence in the country, a stability and confidence not seen since before the horrors of the Revolution. Gold coin, long buried or hidden, reemerged, commerce revived, new industries gradually developed, the small Paris stock exchange once again opened its doors, and government securities and investment funds rose dramatically. As Napoleon discouraged the informal "you"—the *tu/toi*—in public speech, and was to do the same for the revolutionary titles of "Citizen" and "Citizeness" that had replaced the traditional "Monsieur" and "Madame," the people began to realize there was indeed to be a real change in the land. "The Revolution is over," Bonaparte informed Chouan leader d'Andigné. "The revolutionary laws will not return to devastate the beautiful soil of France."[24]

Theaters and music halls opened throughout Paris. For the first time in eleven years the French people could sing and dance freely. It was a good start, and the new law codes—civil, criminal, and commercial—would secure the present while ensuring a stable future for their children and grandchildren. But instead of devoting most of the nearly six hundred million francs of the annual national budget in the reconstruction of a devastated land, instead of rebuilding the tens of thousands of buildings damaged or destroyed during the human firestorm known as the Revolution, instead of repairing the old canals and the sadly neglected but once superb national highways, instead of rebuilding the ports and putting money into the much-reduced merchant fleet, instead of building badly needed government facilities, schools, and hospitals throughout the land, First Consul Bonaparte unilaterally dedicated most of these funds for war.

The French had been at war, internally and externally, since the execution of Louis XVI, and Napoleon realized he could not afford to undertake a long military campaign at this time. The people wanted peace, despite his own personal ambitions for expansion throughout Europe and even North Africa. Thus he set out to recapture the Austrian provinces of northern Italy and then conclude a fresh peace, if only a temporary one, with England.

First he would deal with the Austrian emperor. He appointed Moreau as commander in chief of the Army of the Rhine with orders to drive into southern Germany, and with Berthier as commander of the new Reserve Army, he was ready. But the armies as usual lacked everything, and the national treasury held only sixty-seven thousand francs when he seized the government in November 1799. He found the solution, however, as he usually did: extortion. He demanded vast sums from the merchants of Paris, Lyons, Marseilles, and Bordeaux. That not sufficing, he extorted at bayonet point more millions from Dutch merchants, the Swiss, the Italians, and even the Portuguese (from whom he demanded "8–9 million francs" to cover a portion of the costs of invading Italy.)[25] He ordered General Augereau, the new commander of the French Army in Batavia, to demand that "the Hague . . . furnish us with a subsidy to help defray the costs of [France's] forthcoming campaign" in Germany, part of it to go to Masséna in Italy as well.[26] Moreau was ordered to threaten the Swiss. A few months later, on March 8 he extorted another 10 to 12 million francs from citizens and officials of Amsterdam. Still not satisfied, less than three months later he demanded more money from them, plus thousands of Dutch troops for the new war effort against Austria. "Imperiously insist on everything that government owes us!" he ordered Augereau. Neither the Portuguese nor the Dutch owed France one franc, quite the reverse; nor was this their war, but that was irrelevant. And he demanded the same from the Swiss. Explain "the circumstances of the war" to the Swiss government, and "our [France's] wish to protect Helvetic territory," Napoleon instructed Minister Reinhard on 11 May 1800.[27]

Nor were the French spared Napoleon's demands for "loans." "Summon the 12 most powerful merchants [of Paris] to demand the immediate payment of additional millions for the specific purpose of paying and supplying 'the French army,'" he ordered Finance Minister Gaudin. Similar orders were issued to "the 12 most important merchants of Lyons and Marseilles. When these sizable sums still did not suffice, Napoleon had recourse to private individuals, even ordering the arrest of the wealthy financier Ouvrard along with the demand "to return" 62 million francs to the government. (At the same time *Bonaparte* refused to return the 24 million francs he had "borrowed" from another banker, Collot, who had financed the coup of 18 Brumaire, even having him thrown out of his house.)

It was only as a result of his extortion of massive sums from these unwilling victims that he was finally able to launch his two principal armies across the Rhine and over the Great St. Bernard Pass. Setting out from Paris on May 5, 1800, the first consul enjoined Cambacérès and Lebrun to keep Paris calm during his absence, no matter how. "Strike vigorously at the first sign of trouble, at the first person, no matter who it is, who steps out of line."[28]

After the rapacity of his financial extortions to launch these armies—which he had kept secret from the public—the subsequent military campaign itself, usually so admired by soldiers and historians alike, takes on a different perspective altogether. General Moreau's Army of the Rhine, 120,000 strong, was ordered to march in mid-April against the Austrian General Kray's 100,000 men, while General Berthier (who had just stepped down as war minister, replaced by Carnot) led a newly created Reserve Army of almost 60,000 men over the Great St. Bernard Pass on May 20 (though in fact it took weeks to get all the troops, horses, supplies, and artillery through the deep mountain snow). General Masséna's smaller Army of Italy was already operating in the northwest around Genoa, where it faced General Melas's much larger Austrian force of 97,000 men.[29]

The campaign held some nasty surprises for Napoleon, beginning with Moreau's refusal to cross the four bridgeheads over the Rhine as instructed, followed by his overcautious dithering when he finally did obey instructions. His resentment at taking orders from the young Corsican general, whom he despised, clearly aggravated and even jeopardized the situation. Meanwhile General Melas took Napoleon by surprise when he went on the offensive and attacked Masséna, his aim to drive through Genoa and Nice, straight to Toulon, where he expected support from Admiral Lord Keith's fleet and marines. Facing Melas in Italy were General Suchet's 36,000 men and Masséna's force of 15,000 to 18,000 (after leaving garrisons in Genoa, Gavi, and Novi). Masséna quickly found himself isolated in Genoa, cut off from the rest of the French troops.

Napoleon ordered him to hold on as best he could, while privately acknowledging the strong possibility of his surrender, given the odds against him, not to mention the lack of supplies and mutinies he found in the besieged city. But Masséna was holding down a large number of Aus-

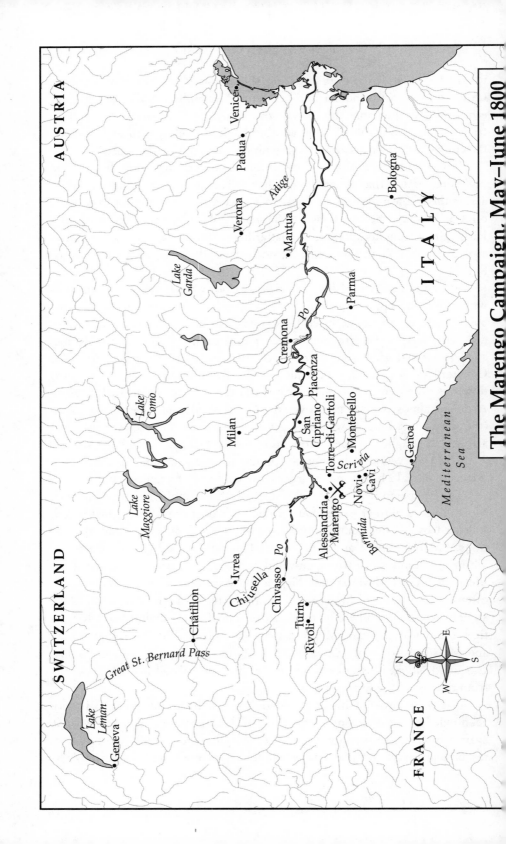

The Marengo Campaign, May–June 1800

trian troops, thereby permitting Bonaparte, with Berthier's Reserve Army, to descend southward from the staging area in Geneva. Masséna was soon forced to surrender Genoa, but permitted to withdraw with his entire army intact, while General Suchet's small force was attempting to defend Nice from the Austrian troops pouring through the Colle de Tenda. A series of minor but often dramatic battles ensued, as Berthier and Bonaparte descended through Châtillon, Ivrée, Chiusella, Verceil, Chivasso, and Piacenza. Murat's victorious troops, along with Napoleon, reached Milan on June 2, where a Te Deum was chanted "to celebrate the fortunate delivery of Italy from the heretics and infidels"—that is, the Roman Catholic Habsburgs—as the first consul announced to the world.[30] But so quick were the victories and advances of the French that Napoleon's commanders sometimes received three or four conflicting sets of orders on the same day. Such was the background leading to Marengo.

Berthier, as "general-in-chief" of the Reserve Army now spearheading operations in Italy (with Napoleon looking over his shoulder), prepared for the confrontation with Melas's main force. Generals Lannes and Victor defeated the Austrian General Ott at Montebello (and years later Lannes would tardily receive the title duke of Montebello for this battle). Napoleon moved in for the kill despite his inferior force. In fact, of Berthier's force of fifty-eight thousand men, only thirty thousand (with a mere forty-one pieces of artillery) formed the actual field force. The Reserve Army crossed the Po at San Cipriano on June 11, the same day as General Desaix arrived after his long journey from Egypt. It next crossed the River Scrivia in search of the Austrians, who Bonaparte mistakenly thought were avoiding a confrontation.

Through a series of bogus and misinformed intelligence reports, Napoleon was hardly expecting the major battle with the Austrians he had so long sought, when, early on Sunday morning, June 14, 1800, he and his entire army were caught completely off guard by a full-scale attack by Melas's thirty-one thousand Austrian troops and their one hundred cannon. Napoleon still completely misjudged the entire situation and remained at Torre-di-Garfoli, thinking this just an Austrian side action.[31] Indeed, he even *detached* some troops from Berthier's command. But finally the penny dropped, although even with the arrival of Lannes's and Murat's troops to support Victor, Berthier still had only fifteen thousand men and very few guns. Napoleon ordered Lapoype's division and General Desaix at the head of Monnier's division to reinforce them in the plain of Marengo, before the River Bormida and the city of Alessandria.

Although he already considered the battle lost by three o'clock, with the arrival of Desaix's fresh division in further support of the hard-pressed Generals Victor and Lannes, later reinforced by the brilliant young Brigadier Kellermann (whose talents Napoleon so resented back in Italy in 1796) at the head of his small but now most effective cavalry unit, a couple of hours later Napoleon launched one final, fateful counterattack. Breaking through the Austrian ranks, the French Army suddenly turned near-defeat into a spectacular victory, after twelve grueling hours of intense fighting in sweltering temperatures.

The price paid was heavy for both sides, including some seven thousand French casualties, among them the unfortunate Desaix, killed early on. The Austrians had suffered a worse fate with fourteen thousand casualties, almost half the men actually engaged in the fighting on the plains of Marengo, not to mention the loss of forty cannon. Within twenty-four hours, an amazed Melas was forced to ask for a temporary armistice, resulting in the Convention of Alessandria, which eventually gave France the whole of northern Italy. (In one of the great ironies of history, both Desaix, killed at Marengo, and Kléber, who was assassinated by an Arab in Cairo, fell on the same day, June 14, 1800.) If there was not the promise of an immediate peace treaty with Vienna, at least negotiations were on course, permitting a triumphant Bonaparte to leave Italy for Paris on June 17. Immediately after his return to the French capital, Bonaparte ordered his brother Lucien at the Interior Ministry to commission "the six best artists" to paint large scenes of the battles of Rivoli, Moekirsch, Mt. Tabor, the Pyramids, Abukir, and of course Marengo (most of which he had not even witnessed).[32] The great Egyptian myth was about to be born.

After the signing of a full armistice on July 5 in Italy, further victories and pressure by Moreau's Army of the Rhine pushing up the Danube resulted in the Battle of Hohenlinden on December 3, 1800, finally forcing the Austrian emperor to admit defeat and sign the Peace of Lunéville on February 9, 1801.

Lunéville was indeed a triumph, confirming the terms of the Treaty of Campo Formio (the cession to the French of most of northern Italy, the left bank of the Rhine, and Belgium). The Austrians recognized the three French satellite states—the Batavian, Cisalpine, and Helvetian Republics. What is more, Archduke Ferdinand ceded Tuscany to the Spanish infanta, married to the Duke of Parma. With the French flag officially replacing that of the Habsburgs on the left bank of the Rhine, Napoleon was effectively beginning what would result in the total collapse of the thousand-year-old Holy Roman Empire, to be confirmed in a few years by the creation of the French-controlled Confederation of the Rhine.

With these great diplomatic and military victories behind him, added to the overwhelming desire for peace at home, Napoleon decided to press for a peace treaty with the one remaining French enemy, England. That, however, could not be concluded until the Egyptian question had been settled.[33]

Following Napoleon's abandonment of the Army of the Orient on August 23, 1799, morale had plummeted in Egypt, resulting in Desaix's surrender to Commodor Sir William Sidney Smith at al-Arish on January 28, 1800. But Smith's rather lenient terms, allowing the French to retain their arms and return to France, were rejected out of hand by the commander in chief of the Mediterranean fleet, Lord Keith. Instead he demanded unconditional surrender, rejected by Desaix this time. The fighting had then resumed, Kléber winning a decisive victory with his reduced force of about 10,000 men against a Turkish army of 75,000 at Heliopolis on March 21.

But Napoleon, who had apparently given up any real hope of retaining Egypt—despite dramatic public words to the contrary—had, as already seen, ordered four of his best generals there, including Desaix, to return to France. This had left Kléber and General "Abdullah" Menou in command. Turkish armies were closing in from al-Arish, and Gen. Sir Ralph Abercromby's sixty-thousand-man force landed at Abukir Bay, defeating the French on March 21, 1801. With the death of Kléber on June 14, Cairo fell to the Turks thirteen days later. Menou officially surrendered with his remaining eleven thousand men (out of the original thirty-four thousand) to the British on September 2. Bonaparte's great Egyptian fiasco was complete.[34]

Desaix of course had brought news of the tragic events in Egypt, and Napoleon realized, even before learning of the subsequent death of Kléber and surrender by Menou, that for his army there—without provisions and reinforcements since the initial landings in 1798, and with its best commanders dead or now in Europe—all was lost.

"And what were the results of that memorable expedition?" Bourrienne asked in retrospect. "The destruction of one of our finest armies, the loss of the best of our generals, the utter destruction of our navy, the loss of Malta, and the complete domination of the Mediterranean by the English. And what remains of all that today? A scientific work."[35]

Earlier, on March 21, 1801, France had signed the Treaty of Aranjuez, confirming the articles of the San Ildefonso Agreement, binding Spain more closely to France, while another secret treaty, that of Madrid, on September 29, 1801, authorized the passage of French troops across Spanish territory to attack Portugal. And in March 1801 the king of Naples had, like the Spaniards, finally buckled under French threats, agreeing to close his ports to the English navy while ceding a minor islet, by the name of Elba, to

France. Still earlier that same year, however, Napoleon had learned of the destruction of the Danish fleet at the Battle of Copenhagen on April 2, 1801, by Admirals Nelson and Hyde Parker to end their "armed neutrality." Malta of course had also fallen to the British, who remained everywhere triumphant. Then came the bad news received in Paris on April 12, 1801, of the death of France's ally, Czar Paul I. Napoleon was at once checked in the Baltic, the Mediterranean, and the Caribbean (with the loss and failure of the Leclerc expedition to Santo Domingo).

While Bonaparte had been in Italy for the Marengo campaign, however, Talleyrand was concluding the Franco-Portuguese Treaty of June 6, 1801, signed initially by brother Lucien Bonaparte and Pinto de Sousa, at Badajoz, then modified, ratified, and exchanged on October 19, giving France not only a large portion of Portuguese Guiana in South America but also a stranglehold over Portuguese naval support of British ships, which so badly depended on that nation's strategically situated neutral ports.[36] The French had further countered British military success with the successful Italian campaign, leading to the victory at Marengo over England's subsidized allies, the Austrians, culminating in the Treaty of Lunéville. Four days earlier, on February 5, William Pitt tendered his resignation as prime minister, to be replaced by the much more malleable Addington. The last English coalition against France had collapsed with Lunéville, and Addington, who had long opposed Pitt's unrelenting war against France, immediately opened negotiations at Amiens with Napoleon's government, leading to the Peace of Amiens, signed on March 25, 1802.

That treaty clearly represented the British government's avid wish for peace, regardless of their own great military victories, and despite the great losses of territory and prestige they were willing to suffer as a result of this new agreement with France.

"My unchangeable opinion is that firmness will, and that firmness alone can, extricate the country [England] from the difficulties which the success of France upon the Continent have brought upon us," Lord Grenville had advised Lord Hawkesbury, his successor at the Foreign Office.[37] But Hawkesbury, like the new prime minister, was bent on peace, no matter the cost. With the Americans, Portuguese, and Austrians at peace with the French, and with Belgium in French hands and Holland under the iron control of Paris as well, and the new czar not committed to Britain at this stage, Lord Hawkesbury felt that England had no choice. Nevertheless, negotiations advanced slowly and painfully until the very end of December, when Napoleon finally gave Joseph Bonaparte authorization to conclude them quickly.

The treaty was signed at the Amiens Hôtel de Ville on March 25, 1802, by France, Holland, Spain, and England. The British were to restore Malta to the Order of St. John of Jerusalem within three months of the treaty's ratification, and Egypt was to be returned to the Ottoman sultan. The various islands the British navy had taken over the years were to be restored to Spain, Holland, and France, except Ceylon (Dutch) and Trinidad (Spanish). (No mention was made of the French seizure of Belgium and Piedmont.) The Cape of Good Hope was to be given back to the Dutch, its ports open to all countries. The Republic of the Seven (Ionian) Isles was recognized. French troops were to evacuate Rome and the Kingdom of Naples, and the British to evacuate Elba and all the other Mediterranean or Adriatic ports and isles occupied by them. Finally the Treaty of Amiens declared that henceforth there should be peace and friendship among the contracting parties.[38]

Although France and England were still wary of each other, after ten years of unremitting warfare there was nevertheless a real sense of relief and joy on both sides of the Channel. An astonished General Lauriston, bringing the signed preliminaries of the treaty to London, found himself surrounded by a large delirious crowd that unhitched the horses from his carriage,[39] pulling it and him the two miles across the English capital to his new apartment. Nor was there less excitement in Paris. "The epoch of the Peace of Amiens must be considered as the most glorious in the history of France," Bourrienne rejoiced.

On May 6, 1803, the peace treaty was duly presented to the Tribunate for ratification. That same day a grateful nation, or to be more precise, the hand-picked Senate, rewarded its head of state with an extension of his national mandate by ten years. This didn't satisfy Napoleon. He wanted the position for life (including his official state salary of five hundred thousand francs a year).

"I have lived but to serve my country," he responded, and then indicated that he could consider such a magnanimous offer only if it were confirmed by a favorable national plebiscite. The Tribunate was upset, but they submitted in silence; not so, however, Lafayette, who, after arguing with Bonaparte, admitted, "I cannot do anything with him. It is frustrating."[40]

On August 2 Interior Minister Lucien Bonaparte, in charge of the national plebiscite, announced the (unsurprising) results: 3,600,000 to 8,374. Two days later Napoleon proclaimed the revised "Constitution of the Year X." In fact Lucien, who had earlier perfected his vote "counting" when Napoleon's new constitution was overwhelmingly approved, had now committed perhaps the greatest voter fraud thus far in French history, dumping millions of negative votes and adding fresh ones to give his brother the winning number he desired. Napoleon had in fact been disastrously defeated at the polls, but only he, Lucien, Fouché, and a few others were privy to this "recount." With this crucial accomplishment behind him, the final steps—to hereditary rule for his family and his elevation as emperor—were child's play. The Bonapartes now knew how to cope with future plebiscites. Confident of his new position, on November 2 Napoleon took the bold—but wise—step of firing the troublesome, prying Fouché, who was in on too many family secrets. At the same time he suppressed the Police Ministry (which he would restore, along with Fouché, in July 1804).

The period from 1799 to early 1804 marked one of prodigious activity. The first consul submitted most of his productive projects at this time. "The Emperor labors relentlessly and yet never manages to sow any seed. Nothing so annihilates the present as that which kills the future," Réal commented to Victorine de Chastenay. And that was in fact Napoleon's great tragedy: He did sow ample seed, but as a result of his other less admirable qualities, he personally destroyed the young plants before they had an opportunity to mature. Above all, his veritable obsession with dominating others—whether French, English, German, Austrian, Italian, Belgian, Dutch, Swiss, Polish, Russian, Spanish, or Portuguese, precipitating one unnecessary war after another—would lead his own armies to trample down the very seed he himself had so tenderly planted. He could never come to terms with his own deep internal anger, rejection by his own parents and humiliating schooldays, and the whole of Europe suffered as a result.

But alas, despite all his protests to the contrary—"I do not wage war as a profession; no one in fact is more peaceful than I"—Napoleon was not in the least interested in peace.[41] It was hardly surprising then that barely a year later, by mid-May 1803, he was arming once again for renewed hostilities. The ostensible cause for it was Britain's refusal to observe the terms of the Peace of Amiens by failing to withdraw from Malta. The British on the other hand blamed fresh French expansion in, and annexation of, Italian territory to be the root of the matter, contravening both the spirit and the letter of the treaties of Lunéville and Amiens. The British were also greatly disturbed by "Ambassador" General Sébastiani's strongly anti-English report published by Napoleon in the *Moniteur* that spring, following that diplomat's return from Constantinople and North Africa, where he had been attempting to convince the Turks to permit Egypt and most of the Maghrib to be handed over to France, if only as protectorates.[42] (The French capitulation to the British in Egypt had of course specifically recognized the return of Egypt to Turkey and the full permanent withdrawal of all French troops from that province.)

Both England and France were right, but Napoleon was looking for any excuse, real or imaginary, to renew the war and set in motion a vast new plan he had been secretly nurturing since the spring of 1802. In fact, the one country that was ever to defy and elude him was now, for the first and only time, to be his single, principal objective. With pathological obsessiveness he privately instructed his war and naval ministers to prepare for nothing less than the conquest of England. Clearly he had forgotten his own "first principle of justice"—that of "ensuring the public welfare." He told Bourrienne, "It is true that in less than two years I have conquered Cairo, Milan, and Paris. . . . Well, if I were to die tomorrow, ten centuries hence, only half a page in a world history would be dedicated to me."[43] Clearly that was an underestimation. After all, no one had forgotten William the Conqueror's great feat of 1066. "[Napoleon] would have had to have changed very much indeed during the past six months since our last meeting," Bourrienne concluded, "if he did not now feel a real thrill at the very idea of a vast new war whose various operations could be nourished by his insatiable genius."[44]

War Once Again

We have six centuries of insults to avenge.
—TO GENERAL AUGEREAU, SUMMER 1803

f Napoleon's disastrous Egyptian expedition had taught him anything, it certainly did not seem apparent in the spring of 1803, as he contemplated an even more hazardous and utterly unnecessary campaign, based on even riskier, more fantastic assumptions and preparations—the invasion of Great Britain.

In the longest, the most elaborate military campaign of his entire career, he now strained every muscle of the French people and of their subjected allies—the Dutch, Belgians, Italians, West Bank Rhinelanders, and, soon, the Spaniards—in order to achieve his latest pipe-dream-become-*idée fixe*. The mass extortion of hundreds of millions of francs, the draining of the French national treasury, and the mobilization of an international corvée would have astonished the Sun King himself. Beginning in 1803—with the country enjoying the first stable political period since the upheavals of the French Revolution, a revived, thriving national prosperity, real hope in the land, and a full treasury—Bonaparte was to jeopardize all, including a hard-earned general European peace, leaving the French treasury once again tottering on the verge of bankruptcy.

The idea for such "a descent upon the British Isles" had been slowly germinating since the early months of 1798, when Bonaparte had been tentatively assigned to take command of the small flotilla and expeditionary force forming along the Channel for a proposed invasion. He had rejected the idea out of hand after studying the situation. Such a land and sea assault as this, he felt, could be achieved only if greatly enlarged in scope and with full national support—but it *could* succeed. Nothing in his eyes was beyond feasibility, and as he was wont to say, "Only achieving the impossible is admired in France."[1] Since Napoleon was a bit of a magician, and never one to dismiss illusions, this project was assured of success if approached correctly, intelligently, and with the full resources of the richest most populous land in Europe, as France was at this time. To cross fewer than twenty-five miles of sea between England and France was nothing. The Normans, in the most primitive of vessels, had achieved this very feat seven centuries earlier. He himself had launched a major expeditionary force from one end of the Mediterranean to the other. Clearly those opposing this invasion were being led by their emotions, politics, or simply limited outlook, but not by their intellect.

Yet the entire operation was certainly far more complex than any land operation he had ever conducted. It had been difficult enough back in 1796–97, when he had led a ragged, poorly armed and supplied French republican army across the Alps to conquer the plains of Lombardy. The preparations for Egypt, however, had provided him with the background for the other element required for a sea expedition. Despite errors, Egypt had proved that the French could launch an entire army across hundreds and hundreds of miles of enemy-infested waters. To be sure, the number of men involved had been relatively small, thirty-eight thousand, and, of course, initially luck had been on Napoleon's side, but then it usually was.

General Bonaparte's close, if brief, study of the Channel coast in January and February 1798 had revealed logistical problems he had not properly understood before, especially for the launching of a large invasion force. The shortest distance between England and France was between the coasts of Calais and Dover, but there were no real ports around Calais and Boulogne now, the closest one being farther south at Le Havre, and Napoleon did not like that position. And if one was considering an invasion right up the Thames to London, it was a matter of a minimum of seventy nautical miles just between Boulogne (where no port yet existed) and the mouth of the Thames, not a mere twenty-some miles between Boulogne and the Kentish coast. Moreover, whatever the distance agreed on, it had to be traversed again, if French troops were later to return home safely.

In 1797–98 the Directory had ordered the hasty construction of a flotilla of some 1,130 small coastal craft, for the sole purpose of *defending* the Channel ports, yet by the spring of 1801 only 167 of those vessels remained afloat.[2] But in that spring of his second year in office, First Consul Bonaparte was still intent only on protecting French ports and commerce from British guns and possible small landings. Accordingly, in a secret decree of March 10, 1801, he ordered the creation of what he referred to as a "light flotilla" of 450 small craft to continue coastal defense and nothing else (similar to England's "sea fencibles"), to protect the coast from Morbihan in France to Flushing in Holland.[3]

Napoleon's first naval minister, Pierre Forfait, no sailor but in fact a naval engineer and architect, was responsible for the new light flotilla. Although he made some important contributions during his stint in office, he was not liked by professional sailors. Not only had he never served at sea, but he had developed a flat-bottomed-boat design for river commerce that he wanted to see extended for coastal use. He thought like a river sailor, not like the men who had to traverse and live on the high seas for months and years at a time. By the spring of 1803 First Consul Bonaparte began looking for a sailor with a larger view of things, real sea experience, and greater talent and intelligence. The individual he settled on was Denis Decrès.

Decrès, a nobleman, was born at Château-Villain in the Haute-Marne in 1761. After receiving a good education, he joined the navy at the rather late age of seventeen, serving first under Admiral de Grasse in the Antilles, and was promoted to the rank of lieutenant in 1786. From his first command (a schooner) he soon advanced to frigates and finally to the largest of warships. But in the antiaristocratic reaction that swept France between 1792 and 1795, most of the French officer corps had been arrested, cashiered from the navy and some executed, as a result of the prevailing Jacobin prejudice against their birth and class, although most of those officers had in fact been loyally serving, to protect their country. The result: The French navy was reduced to a mere forty-two post captains.

Decrès, too, despite an entirely honorable and most praiseworthy career, was duly arrested in 1794, though released and reintegrated again the next year following the fall of the Jacobins when he was assigned to Rear-Admiral Villeneuve's squadron, first in the Mediterranean and then at Brest. Promoted to the rank of rear admiral in 1798, he was transferred to Admiral Brueys's fleet escorting Bonaparte to Egypt. He was one of the few to escape the debacle of Abukir Bay, and with Villeneuve he managed to reach Malta. There, commanding the *Guillaume Tell*, although he managed to break through the British blockade, he was soon surrounded by three

British ships. Despite devastating and sustained fire, Decrès, by now wounded several times, held out until half his men were casualties and all three of his masts were reduced to shredded stumps. A prisoner of war for many months, after his release by the British from Port Mahón in 1800, Decrè was appointed naval prefect of Lorient in March 1801 and presented by Napoleon with a sword of honor, a rare thing for the first consul ever to do for any sailor.

This was precisely the sort of man Napoleon was looking for. Indeed, if he could find a few dozen Decrèses, the French navy would not be in the dolorous plight in which it now found itself. Here was a man who understood every kind of warship afloat, who could command the respect of men, prepare for major expeditions, organize ports, and fight like a madman, literally until he dropped. What is more, he was not only a gentleman born but an educated one. The forty-year-old Decrès was summoned to the Tuileries, where on October 1, 1801, he was handed the portfolio for the Ministry of the Navy and the Colonies. It was to be his for the next thirteen years.

The gruff, unsociable Decrès was surprisingly subservient to Napoleon, but to no one else. He could take orders, any orders, usually without protest. He had a reputation for loyalty (to Napoleon) as well as ironclad firmness. Napoleon liked that. In addition he was an indefatigable worker. Decrès was one of the few men who failed to achieve goal after goal yet avoided swift and final retaliation from the great man.

There were reasons for the admiral's future failures. Decrès usually surrounded himself with yes-men instead of experts. He was petty and jealous. What is more, Rear-Admiral Decrès expected full compliance with his written orders and general ideas. If someone disagreed with him, he was removed and his career diverted. A really talented but contrary individual might find himself cashiered, a promising career ended. Unfortunately it usually happened only to superior, intelligent, well-qualified officers.

On the other hand, if Decrès felt indebted to someone, that person would be protected through thick and thin, regardless of his incompetence and of the disasters it wrought. One example was the hapless Ganteaume. The most egregious example, however, was Rear-Admiral Villeneuve, under whom a younger Decrès had served many years, including at Abukir Bay in 1798, when Villeneuve had declined the honor of exchanging fire with the British or to protect his hard-pressed colleagues and even his commanding officer. Rather than fight, Villeneuve had set all sail and fled the field of battle unscathed, as usual. Earlier, during the attempted invasion of Ireland, he had somehow failed to arrive in time to partake of that disaster. The fleet had left without him.

That in spite of everything Naval Minister Decrès permitted Villeneuve
to continue to fly his drooping pennant was shocking, unprofessional, and
clearly not the action of a competent, self-respecting sailor. And it was to
prove gravely detrimental to the service, ultimately leading to the worst
naval catastrophe ever suffered by the French at the hands of the Royal
Navy. On the other hand, it was largely due to Decrès's superb knowledge
of the working navy and his administrative abilities that the navy's fleets,
organization, and ports were thoroughly reorganized. In addition Decrès
instituted a badly needed crash building program, requiring the launching
of twelve new ships and sixteen frigates, annually—a feat Great Britain
could not even begin to match.

At best Decrès, because of his weaknesses of character and sense of
insecurity, should have been kept at a secondary level under a more mature
and competent naval minister. But Napoleon was somehow blinded by the
man and stood by him.

Perhaps the most obvious general defect in the French Navy at this
time was its form of administration and lack of proper authoritative channels. The British, although having no naval minister per se, did have a First
Lord of the Admiralty, who sat in on cabinet meetings at Downing Street.
The First Lord oversaw the Admiralty Board, which, made up chiefly of
admirals, was alone responsible for the actions of the Royal Navy. Political
direction naturally came from the prime minister, but how those naval
objectives were to be best achieved lay entirely in the hands of the Admiralty Board's sea lords, the commissioners. The Admiralty Board and its
First Lord alone were responsible for issuing all orders to the fleets. The
navy's shipyards, supplies, hospitals, and treasury were in turn administered by an entirely separate institution, the Naval Board. Although the
French did create a Naval Commission in an attempt to imitate the British,
it was given no real power, could not draw up and issue orders to fleets and
commanders, and therefore could not initiate action. It had no real, independent authority.

Instead Decrès held dictatorial powers over the naval commissioners,
who simply gave their views when asked, clicked their heels, and obeyed all
orders and decisions handed down to them by the naval minister. Decrès
could and did bypass those gentlemen whenever the spirit moved him,
sometimes later calling for their signature, ex post facto, to reinforce or
legalize a particular action. All naval appointments, promotions, and dis-
missals of officers, which in London were handled by the Admiralty Board,
in Paris fell to one man alone, Denis Decrès. Too many of the naval minister's appointments and decisions were to prove disastrous. And if this were

not bad enough, Napoleon frequently interfered with naval operations, often bypassing Decrès and communicating directly with captains and fleet commanders, sometimes without even informing the admiral. It was this lamentable "system" that was responsible for what was now about to transpire.

"If, as I speak here at this moment, you were to be informed that the English had carried out a major landing on our shores, who among you would not have been greatly disturbed?" Pierre-Antoine Daru, Napoleon's spokesman, addressed the Tribunate on May 23, 1803. "Imagine then how alarmed they in turn will be in England upon learning of the arrival of a French army there. . . . We are already masters enough to be able to conquer the King of England's [German] states on the Continent, and once we land on his own island, we will have broken all English power once and for all."[4] Thus it was that Napoleon officially announced to France and the world his decision of May 17 (with the official ending of the Peace of Amiens between France and England) to invade Great Britain.

Within forty-eight hours the British fleet off the coast of Brittany had been notified of the resumption of hostilities:

> The Right Honourable Lord Hobart, . . . having signified his Majesty's pleasure that all ships and vessels belonging to the French Republic should be seized or destroyed by any of his Majesty's ships that may fall in with them; you are, in consequence therefore hereby required and directed to seize or destroy all ships and vessels belonging to the French Republic.[5]

Thus were the orders issued by the Hon. Sir William Cornwallis, admiral of the blue and commander of England's largest fleet, the Channel Fleet off the French coast, to his captains. France and England were at war again, after scarcely a year's respite.

Napoleon now resuscitated Forfait's implausible plan to build an entire "national flotilla" comprised of flat-bottomed riverboats for a major sea invasion, an idea that a staggered Decrès denounced as "monstrous." For perhaps the first time, he contradicted Napoleon, explaining that the notion that these small craft could vanquish frigates and ships of the line was ludicrous. The whole thing, he concluded, was based on "conceptions that are as false as they will prove to be disastrous." These craft were "bad sailers, too frail to withstand the elements, while carrying artillery far too heavy for their feeble design."[6] And Adm. Laurent Jean François fully concurred.

Vice Admiral Bruix was even more outraged by the folly of attempting to invade England with "this swarm of pretty little boats." Napoleon, unaccustomed to being so adamantly rebuffed, was losing his patience, as his best admirals rejected out of hand this brilliant concept for invading the world's greatest sea power with modified flat-bottomed riverboats. Even if half of them did somehow manage to reach the Thames Estuary, some seventy miles from Boulogne, all agreed on the inevitable failure of the enterprise. Such fragile, unseaworthy boats, even if armed with one or two pieces of small artillery, would not stand a chance against real warships such as Admiral Lord Keith was keeping permanently on guard off the English coast. It was absurd, all the experts agreed.

A defiant Napoleon nevertheless dismissed his critics. He had been told it was impossible to bring huge cannon over the snow-covered Alps, but he had succeeded in doing just that. He had been told it was impossible to transport an entire French army across the Mediterranean to invade Egypt, but he had again succeeded. A by now frustrated but determined First Consul Bonaparte finally put the question to the one obsequious sailor who never let him down, Honoré Ganteaume: "Do you think it [the flotilla] will land on Albion's shores?" After considerable hesitation the embarrassed rear admiral replied, "I consider the flotilla expedition, if not impossible, then at least extremely chancy.... This attempted crossing would be extremely tough, extremely dangerous, but I do not think sailors would consider it altogether impractical."[7] (It is amusing to recall Bonaparte's own earlier rejection of the 1798 invasion plan as "extremely chancy.")

"Not altogether impractical" was all Napoleon needed to hear. He pressed Ganteaume for details. These boats "might be able to cross," Ganteaume went on, perhaps unnoticed by the enemy during a long winter's night, during a period of "utter calm" following a major storm, if—and this was his only contingency—all two or three thousand of them were launched "on a single tide." "But what I consider to be extraordinarily difficult, is being able to keep a prodigious number of small craft that would be encumbering all our ports, without considerable damage to them during storms fierce enough to drive away the enemy."[8]

Despite all difficulties involved, some of which Napoleon recognized, he was set on continuing. He decided to visit the Channel in midwinter to study the few fishing boats still putting to sea, to investigate for himself the problems of navigation in howling seas. This was precisely the time of year both Forfait and Ganteaume recommended for launching the expedition "under cover of one long winter's night," in the calm following the usual storm. Alas, although the winter solstice did indeed provide very long nights, they were accompanied by an unrelenting series of ferocious storms, leaving even stout fishing smacks too battered to sail. If the Channel did this to sturdy, seaworthy vessels, frail flat-bottomed craft would not stand a chance. What perhaps was even more dismaying as Napoleon, lashed by wind and rain, stood on the cliffs of Boulogne, telescope in hand, was that although the English warships remained farther out to sea to weather the storm, most of them did not abandon their stations, as Napoleon had predicted they would. Drenched and windblown, he got back into his coach and returned to the warmth and calm of the Tuileries, admitting that his invasion flotilla would have to sail in the summer, during the shortest nights of the year. So be it. It could and would have to be done, although his idea that such a cumbersome crossing could be effected in "six hours," or even twelve or eighteen, was utter nonsense.

It quickly became apparent to every sailor in the French navy that Rear Admiral Ganteaume's other requirement for a successful crossing—launching an entire flotilla of more than two thousand boats "on the same tide," even in the most favorable weather—was equally impossible. It would take at least two or three tides to achieve this from even the best and most spacious of harbors. This in turn meant that Napoleon would have to rework his suppositions, for the element of surprise would be lost. In any event one could hardly conceal two to three thousand vessels from the English warships continually hugging French shores, their telescopes scanning all activity. Indeed, even a few dozen very small craft could be easily spotted by telescope all the way from Dover!

There were still more alarming elements of this already incredible plan. With large numbers of English ships ever present and vigilant all along the Channel coast, these flat-bottomed boats needed to be armed with at least a couple of pieces of artillery, Napoleon insisted. Naval architects, on the other hand, protested that such single-deck shallow-draft vessels were not capable of supporting cannon, howitzers, and mortars, and that the recoil from them would sink the boats or shatter their frames. Indeed even without guns, light frames, in swells and choppy seas, would soon take a beating. Nevertheless Napoleon thought that so arming these craft would largely eliminate the necessity of a powerful naval escort, while providing them with sufficient firepower to protect their own landing in England.

Now arose the problem of finding a few thousand additional pieces of artillery. The navy certainly had little enough to spare, as did the army. Then hundreds of pieces of artillery would have to be brought up to protect the coast and harbors as well. Where was it all to come from? Napoleon had neglected this matter. Even more difficult to answer was the question of where Napoleon or Decrès or anyone else was going to find the thousands of junior naval officers required to man and guide this massive flotilla, when the French navy was still grossly undermanned by officers of all levels. Indeed, five ships of the line were at present in mothballs at Brest for want of officers.

The French navy would also have to be involved in the separate role of providing a protective shield, convoying this curious herd of sheep across the open waters. For as Napoleon was to admit, even a thousand armed erratically sailing boats would hardly be capable of protecting themselves from a full-fledged attack by British battleships. Admiral Cornwallis had a fleet of forty-five ships of the line and frigates under his orders. These would first have to be scattered, and preferably destroyed. But how? One or more tactical feints would have to be devised, unfortunately involving large numbers of French warships to accomplish—warships they did not possess.

The problems continued to accrue with maddening severity and regularity as Napoleon, at St.-Cloud, where he now spent much of his time, paced the floor for hours trying to juggle all the balls. And yet he was neither baffled nor unhappy. If there was one thing he loved, it was a challenge, a real challenge that had defied everyone else. Thus Forfait's "impossible" plan was the one he selected. Thousands of those wretched flat-bottomed boats would have to be built. But of greater difficulty was the fact that no ports yet existed along the stretch of coast he had selected from which to assemble and launch his armada. The very ports themselves would have to be planned and constructed if Napoleon was to continue to insist on the shortest possible crossing of the Channel. Cherbourg had never been completed by Louis XVI and would require years of work. Brest was a superb port, but too far south from which to launch small craft, as were the anchorages of Lorient and La Rochelle. The expedition would have to be launched from the northern Channel ports. But the sole harbor there, Le Havre, could accommodate only a few boats and was also judged to be too far south. In addition to all the above, an army had to be created, bivouacked, housed, and supplied. Boatyards would have to be built, supplies ordered, thousands of workers found, orders tendered. Then of course money had to be found—enormous sums of money.

Although Napoleon was later to dismiss this nautical fiasco as a feint, a charade, created to deceive Austria, Russia, and England, in fact it was a very serious affair. This gross miscalculation would weigh heavily on the French people and their subjected allies, who would have to bear the entire burden of a soldier's whim.

*   *   *

The shortage of senior naval officers capable of commanding large-scale operations was critical, and under the circumstances the choice of the forty-four-year-old Vice Admiral Bruix to serve as commander in chief of the national flotilla was wiser than most, despite his rather curious hobbies of practicing alchemy and writing occasional libretti for light opera.[9]

Born ten years before Napoleon, in the French colony of Santo Domingo, Bruix was the descendant of a long line of army officers, but his first love was the sea. Following a good education in France, at the age of sixteen he joined the French Royal Navy. He served in the Atlantic, then in the Caribbean, participating in the capture of Tobago. He was promoted to post captain in 1793, only to find himself arrested on his return to Brest because of his aristocratic birth. Restored to the navy's active list in 1794, he organized the ill-fated Irish expedition of 1796. Named to the prestigious Académie de Marine, he was promoted to flag rank in 1797, as rear admiral. Between 1798 and 1799 he served as naval minister, when he canceled the next futile plan for the invasion of England (following Napoleon's departure for Egypt) and instead allocated those funds for the construction of sixteen badly needed ships of the line and eighteen frigates. His primary objective as naval minister, in the face of Directory opposition and revolutionary incompetence, was to rebuild a French navy once again capable of protecting French shores and interests. In 1799 he was duly promoted to vice admiral.

This cultivated, gracious, and even elegant gentleman of the old school didn't hesitate to speak his mind, however. When asked by Decrès to provide "a donation" for the commissioning of a new statue of Napoleon, and what sort of uniform he thought the great man should be wearing, Bruix snapped, "Keep him completely nude, it will be easier for you to kiss his ass!"[10] Decrès did not ask a second time. But despite some hesitation over aspects of the admiral's independent nature, Napoleon finally agreed to his appointment as commander in chief of the flotilla, for among other factors in his favor, Bruix had supported the coup of 18 Brumaire.[11] Napoleon rarely forgot his political and military obligations.

On July 30, 1803, First Consul Bonaparte officially announced the creation of the "National Flotilla" intended for the specific purpose of invading England. But it was not until two months later that he ordered Bruix and Forfait to draft the first detailed plans for the organization of the proposed invasion scheme, including the number of vessels required. In reality, however, Napoleon had already ordered hundreds of vessels without any blueprint at all, and he was planning on 114,000 troops (excluding all naval personnel) and seven thousand horses (for staff, cavalry, and artillery), although these figures would be increased in the ensuing months. Over the strong objections of both Decrès and Bruix, the nucleus of the proposed flotilla was to comprise four classes of armed vessels to be custom-built to transport these troops:[12] *prames, chaloupes canonnières, bateaux canonniers*, and *péniches*, following Forfait's designs and specifications. All were flat-bottomed, keelless boats. The largest craft, the three-masted *prame,* would have an overall length of 110 feet, capable of transporting 120 soldiers and a few horses, armed with twelve twenty-four-pound guns on her single deck. The smallest vessel, the lug-rigged *péniche*, could in theory transport 71 troops, armed with a couple of howitzers. Most of these overloaded boats were to have little freeboard and to prove completely unseaworthy, but instead of testing models of each class first, an impatient Napoleon ordered the whole lot, an error for which he and the navy were to pay a heavy price.

All the vessels swamped easily, even when riding at anchor, and without a keel had difficulty in holding a given course.[13] The advantages in using them were their very low building cost compared with traditional warships, and the brief time and work required for their construction (obviating as they did the complex, time-consuming work involved in laying down the usual hull design). These boats also had the advantage of being able to land in very shallow water, leaving even light warships behind. In that sense they would have been ideal for the shores of nearby Kent or the muddy banks of the Thames Estuary.

Even before announcing the official plan and initial number of vessels required, an ever impatient Bonaparte put in an order for the construction of the first 1,050 flat-bottomed vessels, with the stipulation that the first 310 were to be delivered in seven months, by December 23. Timber, tar, hemp, and canvas had to be ordered, skilled shipwrights found, and boatyards stocked and prepared. Scarcely had the contracting boatyards received these orders, when, five days later, he informed the naval minister that he wanted the first 310 boats delivered in four months' time. He further instructed a now exasperated Forfait to "try to have twice that number completed by the end of September." Bonaparte was not an easy man to work for. "Just keep in mind that every hour is precious," he reminded Forfait. Anticipating his next question, the first consul assured him: "There will be no shortage of money."[14]

In order to build these boats—and they were just a part of the initial orders—Napoleon ordered new boatyards to be created at once throughout France wherever there were rivers available for the launching of vessels.

These would be in addition to the traditional coastal shipbuilding yards at Cherbourg, Brest, Nantes, Rochefort, Marseilles, and Toulon, not to mention new boatyards to be erected overnight in Paris. The newly conquered territories and countries were ordered to pitch in as well, and vessels were soon being built as far east as Mainz and the Rhine, and throughout Belgium.

Where were the boatwrights to be found to cope with these orders? "Conscript them," Napoleon ordered Admiral Decrès. "Requisition all the laborers in Belgium and along the Rhine," and do the same in France. But it was the theoretically independent miniature Dutch, or Batavian, Republic that was forced to bear a surprisingly large brunt of the burden for the construction of the French armada.[15]

On June 25, 1803, the Dutch government, under severe duress—the country had been occupied by French troops since early in the previous decade—reluctantly signed the Franco-Batavian Convention. The terms, dictated by Napoleon himself, forced a full-time military partnership on the Dutch. Dutch ports had long been major importers and transshippers of British goods. The country was a famous international trader in its own right, thanks to a large merchant fleet. By controlling the Dutch, Napoleon could seriously hurt British trade there and elsewhere on the Continent. Holland always remained a wealthy financial center from which France could demand sizable "loans." Then, of course, Dutch frontiers had access to northwestern Germany, from which French armies could easily launch invasions. Under French military occupation, however, the Dutch could not move without prior French approval. The Netherlands had become a de facto prisoner state.

According to the terms of the Franco-Batavian Convention, the Dutch were forced to cut their own throats. First they were required to provide two military expeditions for the French. One comprised five ships of the line, five frigates, and enough transport vessels to ferry some 25,000 French troops and 2,500 horses. In the other they were required to provide 350 more ships with which to transport another 36,000 men, their artillery and equipment, and some 1,500 horses. Altogether they were held responsible for shipping some 61,000 French troops and their equipment and mounts to British shores. Not only that, but then Napoleon insisted—quite contrary to the terms of the convention—that the Dutch fully rig, arm, and outfit—and in some cases even man—all these vessels at their own expense. For the people of Holland, which had a population of fewer than two million, it was not only humiliating but onerous if not impossible. This, combined with the closure of all Dutch trade with Great Britain, would result in the near bankruptcy of their maritime trade, the country's lifeblood.

Not content with that, the French government then obliged the Dutch to hand over their entire navy—again contrary to the terms of the convention—thereby leaving the Dutch coast virtually unprotected except for one older French warship sent for that purpose. That still not sufficing, Napoleon next demanded—this time contrary to *any* convention ever drawn up in Europe—the handing over of the entire Dutch naval officer corps.[16] Ultimately Holland was expected to provide nearly half of the vessels of the entire "French expedition" to England, quite exclusive of later demands for Dutch troops and vast sums in gold.

Dutch foreign affairs spokesman Rutger Jan Schimmelpenninck, future grand pensionary heading the republic, protested that his minuscule state could not satisfy the instatiable French demands, pointing out the "great hardship" they were under, while protesting the seizure of the remaining 280 Dutch naval officers. Nor did the Dutch—hardly a nation of warriors like the French—possess the hundreds of cannon Napoleon also quite illegally demanded, even if they stripped their own navy. Nevertheless Napoleon ordered them to do just that.

With no apparent alternative, Schimmelpenninck capitulated:

> We shall spare neither hardship nor trouble in order to comply with your orders. . . . [But] my government wishes to be convinced and persuaded that the First Consul does indeed appreciate the efforts sustained by a country exhausted by such long, enormous sacrifices. . . . It expressly enjoins me to represent to him once more that the financial situation of my unfortunate fatherland is truly heartrending.[17]

Foreign Minister Talleyrand, on Napoleon's orders, warned the Dutch of the "unfortunate consequences" should they fail. The result was that by the end of 1803 the entire Dutch navy had disappeared, apart from three small coastal vessels, the largest with a crew of sixty men. Decrès himself was then dispatched to the Dutch ports to see for himself, reporting back to Napoleon that "the Batavians have stripped all points of their coast" and were now "completely defenseless. There is nothing left."[18] He also praised the Dutch rear admiral, Charles-Henri Verhuell.

Bonaparte remained unmoved, Talleyrand complained of his "great disappointment" that the latest boats delivered were "all in the worst possible state . . . and without crews or artillery. . . . You have no idea how upset the First Consul is by all this," he concluded.[19]

*   *   *

While snapping at the heels of the Dutch people, Napoleon continued preparations in France. First he gave Naval Minister Decrès perhaps the largest naval budget in the history of the country, 130 million francs (out of a total national budget of only 589 million), or just under one-quarter of the French income for the entire fiscal year.[20] Next he borrowed 20 million francs from various banks. When this was still not enough to meet the sky-rocketing expenses involved in the invasion preparations, he resorted to what he referred to as "patriotic contributions."

After notifying Eugène de Beauharnais in Italy that he expected the Italians "to offer" to build some flotilla vessels, he was able to report that "the Italian Republic has offered us twelve chaloupes canonnières." Talleyrand then popped off another threatening letter to the unfortunate Schimmelpenninck, informing him that the first consul expected an even better offer from the Dutch. A favorable response was again duly received, the Dutch offering to prepare, at their own cost, an additional thirty completely outfitted *chaloupes.*[21]

These were followed by patriotic offers, extorted for the most part, from the grateful people of every department of France. Nor did individual cities ignore this opportunity, sometimes vying with their neighbors for an honorable place. Military units were invited by their commanding officers to give up a day's pay, and by October some 24 million francs' worth of cash donations or the equivalent in constructed boats had been pledged or received. To this were added most of the proceeds from the sale of the Louisiana Territory to the Americans for 80 million francs (in fact 54 million, after deducting earlier American claims). The first consul thought that amount quite sufficient and ordered a halt to further offers. Money now seemed to be the least of Napoleon's problems, and yet somehow naval contractors were to find it extremely difficult to obtain payment from the government, causing substantial delays in delivery.

Napoleon's audacious invasion plan encountered grave obstacles and unforeseen setbacks from the beginning, from which the national flotilla itself was not excluded. As early as August 22, 1803, for example, the first consul informed Admiral Bruix that the composition of the flotilla could now be "definitively decreed" as to the number and type of craft needed. Theoretically some 2,008 vessels were already reported completed and prepared. But when Bruix made a special tour of inspection of the ports to take a precise tally of the boats actually in the water, he found only 1,026 (including 172 former fishing boats converted to transports, and dozens of Dutch vessels). Napoleon's figures reflected an error of 982 nonexistent boats, a miscalculation of nearly 50 percent.[22]

What was happening? an astonished Napoleon asked Decrès and the newly appointed Inspector General Forfait. Dishonest shipyard owners, was the naval minister's answer. They had accepted payments but had not begun building the boats, he said.[23] Forfait, on the other hand, in permanent contact with all the Channel boatyards, strongly disagreed with the assessment by Decrès. He insisted that, quite the contrary, the shipyards had not yet received a single payment. It was Decrès's Naval Ministry that was responsible.[24]

Caught between two contradictory reports, Napoleon dispatched Monge—the one person he could trust—to look into the situation. Napoleon finally conceded that there might be some truth to Forfait's allegation. He announced that all the contractors who had not completed their orders by January would be given until March. Though it was not much of an extension, it was an admission of government culpability. Indeed, the failure of Napoleon's government to pay every sort of contractor and bank over the next ten years was to continue to undermine the efficacy of many of his national reforms and military campaigns. In some cases the first consul deliberately refused to pay the full sums agreed on through bona fide contracts. In other cases, such as the present boat-building phase, bureaucratic incompetence and widespread corruption among government and military personnel siphoned off many of the millions allocated by the treasury for official payment. The situation was very bad indeed, and by the time Pitt resumed office as British prime minister in May 1804, France had only 1,273 of the 2,008-vessel flotilla ordered thus far—and of those only 149 were fully outfitted, armed, supplied, and properly crewed.[25] Every set of figures seemed to be contradictory. As for the British, they were worrying in vain at this stage, even one year following the resumption of hostilities.

Ironically, of the entire vast shipbuilding effort it was thanks principally to the virtually enslaved Dutch nation that the flotilla was even beginning to take shape; they soon delivered 371 fully outfitted and armed vessels, complete with Dutch crews and officers. Little Holland was contributing the nucleus of the entire flotilla.[26]

The French were obviously in no position to launch an invasion expedition against Britain when war resumed in May 1803. Not only were transport vessels just being ordered, but not even the specific geographical areas for staging and launching the army for this projected conquest had been established.

With the collapse of the Peace of Amiens merely a matter of time, Napoleon had instructed War Minister Berthier to prepare for the inevitable.

As early as April 18, 1803, the general duly presented the first tentative army plans, calling for the creation of five major encampments (one in Holland, one in Germany, and three in France). However, over the next six months the plans for campsites were changed no fewer than five times, Napoleon finally settling on plan number six, calling for three principal training/staging camps at Bruges, where General Davout would command a corps of three divisions; a corps of four divisions at St.-Omer, under Gen. Jean Soult; and another camp at Montreuil (near Boulogne), where Gen. Michel Ney would head his corps of three divisions. In addition there were dozens of smaller support units at other camps, while army units of all sizes and kinds were being transferred to the Channel in a blizzard of moves. It was not until December 12, 1803, that Napoleon officially, "definitively" announced "the organization of the great expedition."

By March 1804, as a result of the usual vigorous action by General Berthier, the three principal staging centers at Bruges, St.-Omer, and Montreuil had some 71,336 troops in place. That figure would soon be doubled.[27]

Napoleon had at long last settled on a massive invasion of Great Britain, one intended to bring the French army to Piccadilly Circus itself. He had yet to decide, however, on the ports of embarkation or the plans for the warships required to escort the flotilla across the Channel, on which in the final analysis all would depend. Officers at Boulogne may already have toasted: "To the first review of French troops in St. James's Park!" but the twenty-odd miles of sea separating Calais and Dover were to prove the longest Napoleon would ever attempt to traverse.

The great expedition occupied him more and more. He spent hours on it daily in an attempt to cope with the seemingly insoluble problems that tested even his prodigious abilities. At the same time the very array and complexity of the difficulties enthralled him, and thus despite them all, he loved every minute of it. It was this soldier's hour of supreme happiness.

That the problems were monumental seemed only appropriate for a Napoleon (a view not fully shared by his hard-pressed general staff). Housing, for instance, was almost nonexistent along the dank, windswept Channel coast, apart from fishing villages. At the camp of St.-Omer, for example, quarters suddenly had to be found overnight for some thirty thousand troops arriving from all parts of the country. Eventually some 2,750 barracks and huts were built, providing semipermanent housing for an army of 167,500 men. This was one problem the first consul left to General Berthier to resolve. Procuring, transporting, storing, and distributing mountains of food, clothing, arms, munitions depots, artillery and transport parks, and thousands of horses (to be stabled, fed, and maintained) soon reached night-marish proportions along that bleak stretch of sparsely inhabited coast, which offered no facilities of any kind. Obtaining forage and grain supplies for the horses became a feat. Great wagon trains of all these supplies were converging on the Channel camps daily from every corner of the land.

The navy had similar problems, being required to stockpile in the uncompleted port facilities not only for thousands of sailors but for all the troops once they actually boarded the transport vessels. The demands on Finance Minister Gaudin and on the French treasury were intimidating. To this complex problem was added Napoleon's constant interference, ever traveling among the camps, demanding to see the books, insisting on has-tening preparations. That a reasonable sense of efficiency and order was finally established was due in large part to War Minister Berthier.

Berthier was fifty years old in 1803, when he began organizing the entire army side of the expedition. After an initial meeting with a young General Bonaparte back in 1796, he had found himself summoned and appointed chief of staff to Bonaparte's Egyptian expedition.[28] It was as Napoleon's chief of staff that he was to spend most of the remainder of his career, and it was in this position that he excelled above all others.

Although mediocre in just about every other way—and forever the butt of jokes by most of his fellow officers, including Bonaparte himself—the slender, tense, neurotic, nailbiting Berthier was an excellent mathematician and a first-rate organizer and administrator. It was thanks to his unique set of abilities that Napoleon went from victory to victory. Bonaparte could win some battles without Berthier preparing the way, but he had a far bet-ter chance of doing so with him at his side.

It was the job of the chief of staff to prepare the orders for troop move-ments, instructing each commander clearly on his precise orders for the forthcoming campaign. It was he who dispatched supplies, arms, and muntions well in advance along the projected route of the army, so that all was in readiness when Napoleon himself required them. It was Berthier who was responsible for having all troops and commanders in their allotted places on time prior to a battle, at Napoleon's beck and call. In the course of these operations Berthier completely reorganized the concept and work of the French general staff.

Despite his many insensitive jokes at poor Berthier's expense, Napoleon ultimately grew to depend upon him as on no other individual in the French army (the only battle at which Berthier was not present was the disastrous Battle of Waterloo). If Berthier was an elusive character, a loner—apart from the one love of his life, Giuseppa Visconti (wife of the Marquis Visconti, president of the Cisalpine Republic) with whom he lived openly in Paris—he was dedicated to Napoleon in an almost symbiotic relationship. If Napoleon and Berthier were never intimate personal friends, such as Napoleon and Monge had become, nevertheless they were close professional colleagues, usually meeting daily regarding the military campaign of the hour.[29] Thus with the expedition's army in Berthier's capable hands, Bonaparte could confidently concentrate his own enormous energies on all the rest.

While Rear Admiral Decrès was also coping with his own major preoccupation, the flotilla, there remained two more aspects to be dealt with before this invasion force would be operational: ports and the navy. The most baffling in its complexity and infinite difficulties, and on which all success initially depended but to which Napoleon had paid the least attention, was the problem of ports from which to launch a couple of thousand vessels. These ports were still largely nonexistent. It is astonishing that Napoleon even contemplated such an expedition with so many basic elements of his plan not in place, but it was no doubt the very challenge of "achieving the impossible" that so attracted him. There was not an admiral or post captain in the entire French navy who thought that an armada could be launched from this part of the coast, simply because of the lack of ports.

From the very beginning, the lack of ports large enough to hold all the needed vessels would be a crippling factor, limiting Bonaparte's options, helping to eliminate a military surprise, on which he initially claimed success depended. And from the outset all estimates as to the time and money needed for these engineering feats and their ultimate completion were so out of kilter with reality as to result in delay after delay, threatening financial ruin. But with the eyes of the whole of Europe now on this venture, Napoleon could not back down, even if he wanted to. As in the case of the Egyptian campaign, he was yet again prisoner of his own bizarre genius and his own vivid imagination that failed to face the realities of human limitations.

Deciding which ports to sail from was of crucial importance. As already mentioned, Napoleon had earlier considered basing the flotilla as far south as Brest, but the very design of the flat-bottomed boats precluded such a long crossing. Le Havre and Dieppe were closer and offered the advantage of being already in existence, but they were neither large nor close enough. Eventually he settled on the one place along the Channel coast that no naval officer in his right mind would have contemplated—

Boulogne, where no port (apart from a primitive jetty) even existed. What is more, there were no natural, existing protecting bays, basins, or harbors anywhere along this entire northern stretch of coast. "It is one of the worst port sites of the Channel," one engineering report concluded succinctly. Only a soldier could have made such a decision.

Naval ministry files revealed previous assessments of developing ports at Boulogne and elsewhere right up to Dunkirk, and Napoleon commissioned others.[30] Then he rejected all negative feasibility reports (including his own) on Boulogne and nine other ports, and on July 21 he ordered tentative plans that they be prepared to handle a total of 2,380 boats, capable of transporting (at this stage at least) some one hundred thousand men and three thousand horses. That these ports did not yet exist was quite immaterial. That similarly negative reports had been submitted by engineers for most of the other proposed sites was equally irrelevant. Incredulous and dismayed, chief engineer of bridges and highways Sganzin and his staff left the Tuileries wringing their hands.

Beginning work on sinking huge pilings and excavating an enormous boat basin at Boulogne, Sganzin set some three thousand men to work in early May 1803, foolishly agreeing to completion of that port by October, the date insisted on by Napoleon. "There will be no shortage of money," Bonaparte assured him, promising the 2,126,846 francs he estimated it would require to finance the entire project. He wanted a temporary port only, he pointed out, the bare minimum needed for the launching of the flotilla. He was not interested in the future of that harbor.

Despite the use of very cheap labor, including the troops seconded from the nearby camp at Montreuil, Boulogne alone was soon costing 393,000 francs a month, and instead of completion by October, the works (including massive artillery batteries) would not be finished even by October of the following year. The cost of the port would double and then treble even the highest estimates. The artillery batteries alone were to cost an additional 3 million francs. A large jetty had to be built, along with quays, docking facilities, and a basin capable of holding many hundreds of flat-bottom boats, not to mention the expensive locks engineers insisted were required to raise and maintain the water level in the port.[31]

Napoleon personally inspected the entire northwestern Channel coast. "I have found an important place for [another] new port," he announced enthusiastically, "in a swamp" near the seaside hamlet of Wissant. But this time Sganzin categorically rejected it, and even Napoleon could not overrule him, so vehement was the exasperated engineer.[32]

The much smaller projected port of Ambleteuse, which Sganzin had optimistically informed the first consul could also be operational by the autumn of 1803, using a mere 600 laborers at a cost of 180,000 francs per month, was still far from completion by January 1804, although some 3,300 men were now working on it round the clock. Millions were again spent. The same occurred subsequently at Wimereux and at Etaples.

Was Bonaparte completely mad? He certainly had no practical grasp of reality—despite his strong mathematical background—concerning engineering feasibility, or time, or the vast sums involved (and where they were to be found). He was translating his daydreams into nightmares, not only for his hard-put engineers but also for the French people and his allies.

And now the challenge of constructing the port sites and installations was being compounded by another most urgent situation. Ships from Admiral Lord Keith's Home Fleet were bombarding Boulogne and the other coastal projects. Some of these bombardments were very heavy from ships less than a mile offshore, killing or scattering unprotected laborers.

In London the Admiralty Board began receiving ominous reports from across the Channel before 1803 was out. "It seems evident an expedition of some extent is being prepared" along the Channel coast, Commander in Chief Lord Keith informed Adm. John Markham. "Boulogne is undoubtedly the place," Lord Keith concluded. A Portsmouth newspaper warned its readers in the autumn of 1803: "It appears that the information communicated to the Government induces it to believe that the French [war] preparations are in such a state for execution that an immediate attack from the French coast may be expected." Emigré general Charles François Dumouriez agreed about the danger in a private memo to King George III: "If the French do carry out this expedition,[33] movements are sure to be abrupt. Eight days," he solemnly predicted, "will decide the fate of the war."[34]

Duly warned, England hurriedly armed its traditionally weak land forces. A series of crash defensive measures were taken, as the country's military forces and the coasts of Kent and Essex were fortified, including the banks of the River Stour and the islands of Mersea, Sheppey, and Grain. Signal, or beacon, hills along hundreds of miles of coast were prepared with large stores of wood, hay, and tar, to be ignited in the event of enemy landings, while some seventy-four squat stone martello towers were hastily erected along the nation's beaches. A triple line of defense was established from the coast to points several miles inland. A dozen sprawling new army camps sprang up in support of them, from which troops could march at the first sighting of the French, while alarums and rumors of impending disaster caused some coastal residents to load their mattresses and valuables on carts and flee to the safety of the interior.[35]

All preparations for the defense of the British Isles were heightened as of May 18, 1804, as William Pitt once again kissed the king's hand and returned to Downing Street as prime minister (the very day that Lord Nelson was taking command of the Royal Navy's Mediterranean fleet off Toulon). Legislation was quickly passed by Parliament and the war budgets increased. Several hundred thousand men rushed to join newly formed "volunteer regiments," though ultimately only 275,000 were accepted (for want of guns and munitions), their number reinforced by 99,411 militiamen and a beefed-up regular army now totaling 116,000 men in England and another 55,000 in Ireland. Troops were garrisoned around London, or in the large coastal army camps at Harwich, Lowestoft, Colchester, Canterbury, Chichester, Winchester, Weymouth, and Launceton, the remainder dispersed among the nation's sixteen military districts. Everyone was joining up, including the royal family. "My dear son," wrote George III to the Prince of Wales, "should the implacable enemy so far succeed as to land, you will have an opportunity of showing your zeal at the head of your regiment."[36]

Nor was the navy slow to act, with its new, vigorous First Lord of the Admiralty, Lord Melville (replacing Lord St. Vincent—"the greatest seaman that ever existed"), spurred on to new patriotic steps. The number of sailors was increased to some one hundred thousand, to whom were added twenty thousand marines. The number of warships of the Royal Navy was increased from 469 to 551 between 1803 and 1805, as the navy's wartime budget rose sharply from £12,350,000 in 1804 to £18,864,000 the following year. The long, irregular shoreline was divided into twenty-eight coastal districts, its shallows and minor ports and estuaries—from Falmouth in the southwest all the way to the Firth of Forth in Scotland—guarded by some seven hundred or so small gunboats and their crews—the so-called sea fencibles. Lord Melville added 119 vessels to the Royal Navy by the beginning of 1805 to give Britain an average of 83 to 88 ships of the line and between 101 and 128 frigates at sea between 1804 and 1805, depending on the month. And yet of all those imposing ships of the line, only eight carried powerful twenty-four-pound cannon, and mostly twelve- and eighteen-pounders, as opposed to the French navy, which was largely armed with the mighty twenty-four-pounders. (What is more, thanks to Admiral Decrès's impressive shipbuilding program, the French fleet was now being strengthened by approximately 20 ships and frigates annually.) Despite superior gun power at sea, on the few occasions when the French actually dared to challenge the

British, the British led in the critical element, professional manpower, with close to 3,700 career officers, including fifty vice and full admirals alone. Indeed, the British had more vice admirals than all the French flag officers combined (rear, vice, and full admirals), while the junior British officers greatly outnumbered those available to the French.[37] In this respect there was clearly no contest.

Not only were the senior British naval officers aggressively alert to the portent of invasion and fully determined to end that threat quickly and rigorosly, but their patriotic determination was fully supported by the British public.

Unlike the heavily stifled and severely censored French press and theater, for instance, the British were completely free to express their feelings, which they did without any artificial prodding by His Majesty's Government. Theaters in London were bursting with ingenuity, drawing full-house crowds most nights of the week. The Theatre Royal in the Haymarket, the Sans Souci Theatre in the Strand, the Theatre Royal in Drury Lane, and the Royal Amphitheatre at Westminister Bridge, to mention but a few, were vying with one another in support of "the boys" at sea and defending the clifftops of Dover. Such offerings as *The Surrender of Calais, The Ship Launch,* and *The Female Hussar* were matched by patriotic songs—"The Country Squire a Volunteer," "Flat-bottom'd Boats," "The Strutting Emperor," and "Albion Will Govern the Sea."

Posters joined in the fun. One demanded the arrest of

> a certain ill-disposed Vagrant and common Disturber, commonly called or known by the name of NAPOLEON BONAPARTE, alias Jaffa Bonaparte, alias Opium Bonaparte . . . [who] hath been guilty of divers Outrages, Rapes, and Murders," ordering that he "be forthwith sent to our Jail for WILD BEASTS . . . with the Ouran Outang, or some other ferocious and voracious animals like himself.[38]

But, as ever in the face of adversity, above all the British were a nation of singers; the most popular war song, "The Invasion," heard in pubs throughout the capital, reminding one and all: "Bright honour now calls each true Briton to arm,/Invasion's the word which hath spread the alarm."

With the resumption of hostilities between France and England in May 1803, the First Lord of the Admiralty, the Earl St. Vincent, had dispatched warships into the Channel, ordering them to hug the French coast and bombard the impressive new port construction as well as the new port batteries. Even as old a sea hand as Lord Keith was visibly staggered by the reports reaching his flagship off the Downs: "The new works ... proceed night and day with the basin and entrance of Ambleteuse," one dispatch read. At Boulogne another 2,400 laborers were estimated to be working. "At Wimereux ... they work incessantly, and have a camp adjoining which has latterly increased much, and an additional 1,900 men were seen to work there as well, hundreds of torches alight at the new works far into the night. The camp on the heights northeast of Boulogne appears also increased in extent. . . ." Keith grimly acknowledged now, "I think the plot begins to thicken on the other side [of the Channel]," and after personally reporting sixty-one very large artillery pieces just installed on the cliffs of Cape Gris Nez alone, the forty-year veteran confessed, "I never saw a shore so covered with artillery in my life. . . . We are all alert here. I have the secret orders: everything is as ready as possible, and myself too. I have ordered all the ships [of the Home Fleet] to their stations as fast as possible."[39]

British ships began a rigorous, unrelenting series of attacks from Flushing to Boulogne that would last for more than the next two years. Napoleon himself witnessed one such bombardment by three English warships on June 29, 1803. He was furious that the enemy could carry out such destructive acts more or less with impunity, because few French batteries were yet in place—and the artillery pieces and mortars that were lacked the power and range to reach the British ships.

Boulogne was in such a weak position that initially even the normally optimistic Inspector-General Forfait was dejected. "How can you promise the port and city that they will be protected from a bombardment?" he asked the first consul. "This work simply cannot be carried out while we are at war."[40] Napoleon ordered the creation of a series of forts at Boulogne, and the improvement of the existing ones. Within a matter of weeks the first of dozens of powerful twenty-four-, thirty-two- and thirty-six-pound cannon and ten- and twelve-inch mortars were in place.

The ultimate result, some two hundred cannons, mortars, and howitzers, covered a two-mile-long line on the cliffs and beaches of Boulogne. Similar batteries were being constructed all the way up to Ostend and Antwerp, to form an impenetrable wall of fire such as had never been seen before by Lord Keith or any other British admiral. But that was still months away.[41]

A group of 150 master masons was set to cut and place stone for each of the big batteries in Boulogne, aided by hundreds of unskilled laborers. The task was enormous and the work slow. "Here the dominant feeling is still that of fear," Decrès informed Napoleon while on an early tour of inspection at Ostend, "fear of bombardment [from the British] . . . disrupting all work." "What is more, [French] short-range mortars along the coast have permitted the British ships to get close to our forts, their artillery reaching them and even beyond, while our batteries could not even begin to reach them in return," the director of fortifications at Boulogne informed Paris. "I intend to have the work continue on the forts," Napoleon angrily riposted. "Regardless of the cost, it must be done. Have fires lit all night long at the end of the jetties and in the batteries and have our naval forces spend every night out of doors, ready to man their stations at a moment's notice."[42] He had done it at Toulon, why couldn't they?

The result was as inevitable as the morning tide. Napoleon was there in person, pacing, inspecting, dictating, and correcting. Whether in his green-and-yellow traveling coach, filled with stacks of engineers' plans, maps, and artillery officers' reports, or in the saddle, he was relentless; he was everywhere, and neither soldier nor sailor could predict where he would appear next. French officers feared his lightning inspection tours almost as much as they did the big British naval guns.

The batteries at Boulogne naturally came in for the greatest scrutiny, and the first consul's initial reaction on arrival was hardly cheering. "It is indeed curious that four months after receiving the king of England's message [regarding the resumption of hostilities], I find the coasts still undefended." After inspecting one new battery on a still-uncompleted jetty at Boulogne, he angrily dispatched a courier to War Minister Berthier: "The engineering officer's report [claiming that unit to be fully operational] is not at all correct. I spent four hours at that battery, which was unable to fire a single round!" The war minister at this stage was still responsible for building and manning the new batteries, and when a nervous Berthier, gnawing on his well-mauled nails, blamed the whole thing on the navy, Napoleon snapped: "It is not the naval engineers who are fault, it is army engineers and the War Minister."[43]

Yet even a Napoleon could not be everywhere along the coast all the time. He had a country and growing satellite empire to administer and had to depend on the daily reports reaching him at the Tuileries, or more frequently, at his favorite palace, St.-Cloud. Both Berthier and Decrès came in for a withering barrage of criticism, sometimes receiving three, four, or five messages a day. No battery was too small for him, no detail too minor.

Napoleon, once made aware of such a glaring problem as the vulnerability of the nation's coasts, pursued the matter with his usual indefatigable, relentless resolve. He ordered Berthier to transfer sixty thousand regular army troops from the interior to man coastal defenses. With the appearance of the first division of newly completed gunboats, he created flying (horse-drawn) artillery batteries of four twelve-pound guns each, attended by a fifty-man cavalry rescort, to shepherd each new group as it proceeded along the shoreline. Special roads were built along the beaches and clifftops for these mobile batteries, extending all the way from Lorient to Ostend. No point along that long coast was to be left unguarded. On occasion, however, the British would slip through and bombard or land and seize some of the new *chaloupes* or even small French warships, despite all the first consul's precautions and adamant orders. Fuming, he would demand reports from the officers in charge and then frequently descend on them as well. He would suddenly appear in the midst of a gale, or during the darkest hours of the night, guided by young aides-de-camp carrying torches to light the way. In fair weather or in the more typical foul Channel variety, Napoleon Bonaparte seemed to pop up out of nowhere.

But his vigilance paid off, and after the first several months of such intensive efforts on the coast, powerful guns were finally in place, trained on the British warships that were now forced to withdraw to a more respectful distance. Napoleon was slowly achieving his end, but at a dreadful financial price to the nation.

As if Napoleon did not have enough to cope with in his preparations for the invasion of England, he was simultaneously involved with several major controversial personal and political changes. In May 1802 Napoleon announced his intention to reintroduce slavery in the French colonies—slavery that had been abolished years earlier by the French revolutionary government. But when that same month Napoleon declared his decision to name himself consul for life, Joseph, Lucien, and Letizia had opposed the idea vigorously, opposition repeated even more vehemently in May 1804, when Napoleon ordered the Senate to proclaim him emperor. And although he spent most of his time now on the English invasion preparations, he stubbornly overruled his entire family regarding his new empire, as he decided to establish an international Bonaparte dynasty linking him with all the crowned heads of Europe. What is more, he would order Pope Pius VII himself to officiate at his coronation ceremony, which he proposed for the end of 1804. War or no war, Napoleon's long-term plans for the domination of the Continent continued apace—plans that were not only to alter his life but to change the map and history of Europe for the next hundred years.

CHAPTER 21

The Coronation

I have been called upon to change the face of the world.

t six o'clock on the evening of December 1, 1804, the salvos of hundreds of cannon, from the Champ de Mars and the Invalides to the quays and the Hôtel de Ville, began firing and continued on the hour until midnight. Even with the much reduced ceremonial charges, however, the thunder was infernal. Ears and heads ached, conversations and chamber music were drowned out, and medieval buildings that had withstood the catastrophes of the ages shook to their deep stone foundations. The Empire that had been announced at the Palace of St.-Cloud by the hand-picked Senate on May 18 and confirmed by a national plebiscite on November 6 had given Emperor Napoléon I the final "legalized" approval he required, rendering his position seemingly impregnable.[1]

The vote announced—3,572,329 for the creation of the Empire, 2,569 against—reflected less than half of the votes actually cast. Even by government figures this meant that in just under half the nation's six thousand or so cities, towns, and villages, only a single negative vote each had been registered in rejection of the Empire, or from another perspective, that in 57 percent of those communes, not a single person had opposed Napoleon. Approximately 99.9993 percent of the French people had approved the Empire, a virtual statistical impossibility.[2] But Napoleon controlled the nation's armed forces, police, press, publishing, and theater. There existed no independent means of contesting or questioning the voting procedure and results. The coronation could now take place, and Napoleon just laughed, for all had been foreordained on his personal orders.

It was cold and damp under ominous gray skies, threatening more rain and snow for the French capital. The original idea of holding the ceremony in the Invalides had been canceled with the belated, if reluctant, agreement of Pope Pius VII to perform the ceremony himself. For this a cathedral was required.

Throughout the night the ladies of the court and of the new imperial society had been up with their seamstresses and hairdressers, some, according to Laure Junot, with their hair stacked so elaborately high they were forced to sit bolt upright all night. Before the crack of dawn on December 2, eighty-four senators in their blue velvet cloaks and culottes, and wearing black felt hats with large white feathers, led by their president, the pliable Neufchâteau, in almost a precise repetition of their performance at St.-Cloud on May 18, set out for the Ile de la Cité and the Palace of Justice to take the new Imperial Oath of Allegiance. By 7:00 A.M. they were walking the remaining few hundred yards, past thousands of troops in dress uniform, to Nôtre-Dame Cathedral.[3] At that same hour deputations of soldiers, sailors, and National Guardsmen, some five thousand of them, were forming in the Place Dauphine. At eight o'clock members of the Legislative Body, the State Council, the Tribunate, and the Court of Appeals set out in streams of carriages or on foot from their respective palaces, each escorted by between eighty and one hundred cavalry and infantry. An hour later, also under strong military escort, the diplomatic corps assembled, including the Turkish ambassador and dozens of German princes (although emissaries from the three most powerful European states, Great Britain, Russia, and Austria, were noticeably absent).

At that same hour Pope Pius VII, led by a full squadron of dragoons, set out from the Carrousel. The cortege of carriages following him bore cardinals, bishops, and lower church personnel totaling some one hundred in all. Monsignor Speroni, mounted on a gray mule, immediately preceded the pope's carriage. "That is the pope's ass," some irreverent Parisian called out. "That's what you have to kiss!" The pope, ignoring the crowd, sat thoughtfully, quietly resplendent in a cape of gold and silver, the rest of his costume white. His silver tiara and three separate slender golden crowns, encrusted with emeralds, rubies, diamonds, and pearls, had been presented to him by Napoleon. For the pope it was a strange moment, as he passed through this city whose population just a few years earlier had so loudly denounced Christianity while rampaging through and desecrating every church and cathedral of the land, humiliating, torturing, and in some instances, executing priests and nuns.

As late as September 15 the pope still had not accepted the invitation to participate in this coronation. A panicked Napoleon first implored and then threatened ("I will reduce him to the status of a mere Bishop of Rome") if he did not obey the summons.⁴ After two postponements and much haggling, chiefly over the new role and power of the church in France, with assurances (most of which he had no intention of honoring) from Napoleon, a still reluctant Pius VII had acquiesced at the very last moment and set out on the arduous journey over the snow-covered Alps for this very country where his predecessor, Pius VI, had recently died a French state prisoner—and to which he would one day return himself a captive.

For Napoleon it was a tremendous coup, this recognition throwing the full support of the Vatican behind him, raising his stature across the civilized world, giving his regime and coronation a prestige and acceptance such as even the greatest military victory could never confer.

At 10:00 A.M. fresh artillery salvos announced the departure of Napoleon himself from the Tuileries, preceded by the Imperial Guard, trumpeters, and kettle-drummers, all giving the appearance more of an imperial Roman procession than of a French coronation. Security was very tight, troops three deep on either side of the street, totaling some eighty thousand men. Marshal Murat, as military governor of Paris, resplendent in his uniform, led the way, followed by his staff and four squadrons of *carabiniers*, another four squadrons of glistening cuirassiers, one regiment of *chasseurs à cheval* of the Imperial Guard and a squadron of Mamelukes in Egyptian costume, then by the heralds-at-arms, on horseback, followed by eleven elaborate state carriages bearing the master of ceremonies, the comte de Ségur, the grand officers of the Empire, the ministers of state (including Talleyrand, Berthier, and Fouché), another carriage bearing the grand dignitaries of state, yet another with imperial princesses Caroline, Pauline, and Elisa, and finally the emperor's.⁵

Napoleon's carriage was paneled in glass and bore a gilt-covered frieze containing medallions representing each of the departments of the Empire, while its doors bore the Emperor's coats of arms, four allegorical figures holding up the heavens encircled by a garland of laurel in gilded bronze, with golden eagles, and four more eagles in the middle, as well as the crown of Charlemagne on a golden altar. Napoleon sat on the back seat of white velvet embroidered in gold, golden lightning bolts traversing the ceiling, on which a double crown of olive and laurel appeared, along with two golden *N*s also crowned with laurel. This coach was driven by Napoleon's favorite coachman, César (who had saved his life during the bomb attack that fateful Christmas Eve back in 1800), drawn by eight isabelle (gray) horses caparisoned in white, their manes braided and adorned with red and gold cocardes set off by bright red Moroccan leather harnesses and bronze-colored reins. Napoleon's aides-de-camp—all general officers—led the horses, with two colonels general of the Imperial Guard riding along each side of the vehicle, which was mounted by equerries standing at the rear, the carriage followed by the inspector general of the Gendarmerie.

Napoleon was wearing a Spanish costume of purple velvet, embroidered in gold and covered with precious stones. To his left sat Josephine in a mantle of white satin embroidered in gold and silver, her only jewels diamonds in a dazzling profusion—a diadem, a necklace, earrings, and even a belt. Facing them, also in Spanish costume, sat the only two Bonaparte brothers who had agreed to partake in the events of the day, Joseph and Louis. Of the four, only Josephine was smiling, at least at times, while Napoleon sat as grimly as his brothers. To be sure, it was the great day he had been planning for such a long time.[6] France was practically being presented to him on a golden platter, but at a price he would be paying until the very end—the enmity and jealousy of the entire Bonaparte clan, personified by Joseph and Louis, who were all but glowering as they turned in the direction of the Pont-Neuf and the Ile de la Cité. The battle over the political inheritance of the newly born Empire had resulted in colossal scenes between Napoleon and his siblings. Who was to be his successor? Josephine had of course been the number one "enemy" in the eyes of the family ever since her marriage with Napoleon, the entire clan setting themselves against her with an unrelieved Corsican determination that had frequently left her in tears. If she had not wanted the Empire itself, once decided upon, she had been determined to secure her own place in it and was even desperate enough to achieve this to sacrifice her daughter's happiness.

The marriage of Louis Bonaparte and Hortense de Beauharnais had been an utter disaster from the very start. Louis's military career, on which Napoleon had set so much store during the Italian campaign of 1796–97, had by the time of the Egyptian fiasco already begun deteriorating. Then Louis, along with the vast majority of the French officers, rebelled, demanding early repatriation to France and leaving Egypt and a much embarrassed Napoleon in the lurch in midcampaign. Once a quiet, charming young man and a cheerful, pleasant member of his regimental mess,

Louis changed noticeably after a long and painful treatment for gonorrhea. The enthusiastic young soldier, although proficient as an officer, began to lose interest in everything military, much to Napoleon's consternation. Preferring literature to military exercises, Louis withdrew from army activities, eschewing society and the company of soldiers in favor of a few artistic and literary companions. He grew melancholy, introspective, suspicious of everyone, reclusive, and violent. On very rare occasions he revealed a sense of integrity and idealism not seen in the rest of the family (with the exception of Joseph, later). Although, thanks to his brother he was ultimately to rise to the rank of general officer, he spent very little time with the army. He became the despair of the Bonaparte family—of Napoleon in particular—he was so unlike the good-natured Joseph, the optimistic, outgoing Lucien, or the hell-raising Jérôme. They simply did not know what to make of the young man. And then, when he showed an interest in Josephine's niece, Emilie de Beauharnais, the clan panicked.[7] They who had been so determinedly against Josephine from the very beginning—indeed, it was one of the few unifying themes in the family—were hardly about to permit her to strengthen her position by allowing another Bonaparte to marry another Beauharnais, and Emilie was expeditiously married off to Napoleon's aide-de-camp Chaman Lavalette.

At the same time Josephine, who had long abandoned any real hope of giving her second husband children, and fearful of being ejected as a result of Napoleon's growing insistence on the need for heirs, and of continuing strong clan pressure in favor of divorce, suggested the one remaining means of saving her marriage—sacrificing her obedient Hortense to the morose Louis. Hortense, on receiving this order, "broke down and sobbed."[8]

At this time Hortense was in fact infatuated with Napoleon's favorite aide-de-camp, Gen. Gérard-Christophe Duroc. And although the latter apparently did find Hortense equally attractive, from a purely political viewpoint he knew that Napoleon preferred to marry his stepdaughter to someone bearing an important title, in order to bolster his own fledgling dynasty. Nevertheless, being very attached to both Hortense and Duroc, Napoleon for once wavered. In 1800 he suggested the possibility of their marriage, offering the otherwise penniless Duroc a five-hundred-thousand-franc nest egg. Never allowing emotions to get in the way when hard practical questions had to be resolved, Duroc coolly declined the offer and returned to the consolation of one of his several actresses. Napoleon arranged a substitute marriage for him in 1802 with a school friend of Hortense, the wealthy young Maria de la Nieves, the daughter of Don José Martinez de Hervas, the marquis d'Almenara.[9] Alas, this marriage, like most of those contrived by Napoleon, proved singularly unhappy for both parties, and Duroc hastened back to his actresses.

Louis and Hortense were married in Josephine's home in the Rue de la Victoire on January 4, 1802.[10] The union proved an unmitigated disaster from the very beginning, and Hortense, who had made no pretense of liking the idea of such a union, had been tearful before and after the ceremonies. To this was added the undisguised hostility of the entire Bonaparte clan, especially Madame Mère, to the marriage of Louis to a daughter of "the whore," as Letizia Bonaparte referred to Josephine. Yet Hortense was a sweet, gentle, lively girl, incapable of harming a soul.

To the regret of all, Napoleon simply closed his eyes to the crippling gravity of his brother's mental illness. The importance of his own position in France, first as life consul, and then as Emperor, only aggravated the situation, as the issue of "succession" to the throne became a major preoccupation over the years as a result of his own childlessness. This preoccupation soon permeated the psyche and being of the entire covetous Bonaparte family, pitting one against another, as each sibling insisted on fresh titles, wealth, and honors, while maneuvering to establish the priority of each individual claim to the throne in the event that Napoleon did not return one day from one of his numerous military campaigns. As the announcement of the creation of the Empire approached, jealousy and bitterness hardened into a fratricidal feeling that was to undermine not only family stability but also that of the new Empire itself.[11]

Napoleon did his best to avoid the insane power plays among his brothers and sisters. "I must therefore isolate myself from everyone. I can count on no one but myself. Very well, then!" But at the same time he was determined to protect himself, his power base, and his monumental plans. If he could not count on his own family, then the Bonapartes be damned. Thus Napoleon dropped the unobliging Lucien from any place in the imperial succession, and the wayward Jérôme as well.[12] That left Louis and Joseph.

Having previously displaced the elder Joseph as head of the family, he now carried this one step farther in the newly devised imperial succession. Joseph, Napoleon decided, was unfit to succeed him. On learning of this decision, Joseph was outraged (assuaging his anger at Mortefontaine by firing his pistol at brother Napoleon's portrait): "If my brother cannot entrust this to me, if he does not do for me what is expected of him [then] ... to sacrifice one's tastes, one's ambitions, for nothing, for the mere possibility of an eventual position of power, to endure all that, and then possibly in vain, one must be either insane or a born intriguer."[13] These sentiments did not prevent Joseph from doing just that—plotting and intriguing to the very end in an attempt to secure his "rightful" place in the Empire.

The quarrels over who was to get what were horrendous, sometimes violent, and forever unending, leaving everyone angry, shaken, and dissatisfied, culminating in a supreme battle on October 12, 1804, when Napoleon summoned brothers Joseph and Louis, as well as the newly promoted archchancellor of the Empire, Cambacérès, and archtreasurer, Lebrun. Napoleon always insisted on having witnesses present during business conversations, even—especially—with his own outrageous brothers. Tempers flared, unguarded voices rose, and coarse language and wild accusations—which even thick solid walls, closed doors, and heavy Savonnerie tapestries could not mute—reverberated throughout the luxuriously refurnished Palace of St.-Cloud. Joseph heatedly protested Napoleon's decision to crown Josephine, not to mention the naming of Louis and Hortense's son as his direct heir, bypassing Joseph's daughters. Joseph reminded Napoleon of the rights due him as the eldest. All to no avail. however. "How dare he speak to me of *his* rights and of *his* interests! To do this before me, his brother, to arouse his jealousy and pretensions, is to wound me at my most sensitive point. I shall not forget that!" On their departure Napoleon fumed: "It is as if he had said to an impassioned lover that he had f—— his mistress. Well . . . my mistress is the power I have created. I have done far too much to achieve this conquest to permit someone else to ravish or even covet her."[14]

When Roederer, who fully supported the creation of the Empire, attempted to intervene on behalf of his good friend Joseph, Napoleon lashed out:

> You forget therefore that my brothers are nothing without me, that they are great now only because I have made them so. . . . There are thousands of men in France who have rendered far greater services to the State. But let's face the hard facts. Joseph is not destined to reign. He is older than I: I will live longer than he, and in addition, I am in good health. Moreover, he was not born in a high enough social position to have warranted such an illusion on his part. . . . He, like myself, was born in a most common position. But I raised myself by my own abilities. He, on the other hand, has remained exactly the same since birth. To rule in France, one must either be born in grandeur . . . or else be capable of distinguishing oneself above all the others. . . . For the succession to the throne to succeed, it must therefore be passed on to our children born in that grandeur.[15]

What is more, Joseph had only daughters, not sons.

Regardless of all Napoleon's explanations, Joseph continued to see matters differently, the acrimony remaining at the breaking point, until Joseph finally threatened not to participate in the coronation ceremony if he did not get his way: "If you refuse to come to the Coronation," a furious Napoleon replied.

> and to fulfill your functions as Grand Elector and Prince . . . from that very moment you may consider yourself my enemy. In such a situation how do you propose to fight me? Where is your army with which to carry out your attack? You lack everything, and I will annihilate you. . . . I have been called upon to change the face of the world. . . . Therefore be satisfied with being the first of my subjects. It is quite a fine role to play, that of being the second most important man in France and perhaps in the whole of Europe. . . . Be content with being a prince, then, and don't fret about the possible consequences of bearing such a title. When you succeed me one day, you may do whatever you wish and follow your own policies. I will no longer be there to prevent you.[16]

The matter was, however, finally smoothed out. Joseph would get a royal crown of his own, elsewhere in Europe. As Louis's emotional problems were now so grievous as to preclude considering him as direct heir, he was bypassed in favor of his eldest son, Napoléon-Charles, as the immediate successor to the throne.

Hortense reluctantly agreed to this, but Louis literally had a fit, furious that his brother wanted to bring up his son, bestowing on Louis only visiting rights.[17] "What have I done to deserve being disinherited!" a bewildered Louis asked, like a wounded animal. "No, I shall never consent to it! Rather than renounce my rights to the throne, rather than agree to bow my head before my own son, I will leave France. . . . Then we will see if you will dare to kidnap a son from his father in broad daylight!"[18] A compromise was finally worked out, but Louis, who now hated his brother as only an insane man can, would never forgive him. On May 13 Napoleon had pushed through the famous *Sénatus Consulte*, creating the Empire and defining precisely the order of succession. Title II, Articles 5 and 6, named "Louis Bonaparte and his descendants" to succeed to "the imperial dignity" through the right of primogeniture, "from male to male," while providing for the option of adoption: "Napoleon Bonaparte may adopt the sons or grandsons of his brothers, providing they have reached the age of eighteen years and that he himself has no male children of his own at the time of adoption. His adopted sons enter into the direct line of descendance."[19] Napoleon had won, but at the price of gaining another implacable foe.

The unforgiving Louis now sat in the imperial coronation carriage, glaring at Napoleon as they proceeded to Nôtre-Dame. That he and Joseph would now become "French princes" with annual state salaries of 1 million francs each was irrelevant to Louis. That he also would be named colonel general of the *carabiniers* (with another 30,000 francs a year), or promoted to grand officer of the Legion of Honor, or named senator and state counselor, and given the ancient, prestigious title of imperial constable (with a salary of an additional 333,333 francs per year)—all this was irrelevant.[20] Louis Bonaparte was seething, in a state verging on madness.

His "Imperial Highness," as Louis was now styled, had found the one victim who could not fight back, however—the gentle Hortense. Jealous of her every action, wishing to isolate her from all her friends, and especially her mother—for clearly "they" were all plotting together against him—he had her spied on twenty-four hours a day, every day of the year, even posting armed male servants in the halls and outside her bedroom door all night long. He also ordered her secretly—she was forbidden to tell a soul—never to spend another night under her mother's roof! For years to come she was a virtual prisoner. Still not content, Louis threatened his pregnant wife in writing:

> If you support your mother's interests at the expense of mine, I
> swear I will make you regret it. I will separate you from your son. I will
> have you locked up behind high walls in some utterly unknown place
> from which no human power can ever extricate you, and you will spend
> the rest of your life paying for your condescending views of me and my
> family. And just you take special care that none of my threats reaches
> my brother's ears! All his power cannot protect you from my wrath.[21]

The gay, lively Hortense grew pale and fearful, and for years lived in a state of virtual terror, her only place of refuge the little house in the Rue de la Victoire she had been given as a wedding gift. It is not clear if Hortense ever revealed this note and the dangers of her situation, but her dramatic physical changes and isolation could not be concealed, nor could her depression and the obvious breakdown of this tragic marriage engineered by the hapless Josephine and a blind Napoleon. For all his faults, Napoleon would never have forced this on Hortense had he fathomed Louis's character and what a dangerous person he had become. But this was the twenty-six-year-old Prince Louis who now sat in the carriage before them in his white coronation costume. It did not bode well for the newly laid foundations of the Empire.

As for the other "Imperial Highness" seated across from Napoleon, Joseph Bonaparte, at least his anger verged only on jealousy, not deranged malevolence. To be sure, Joseph was just as greedy for power as Louis, despite the munificence of wealth and titles heaped on him by Napoleon as sops and distractions. In addition to his state salary of 1 million francs a year, as grand elector of the Empire he received 333,333 francs per year, not to mention a new official state residence in Paris, the Luxembourg Palace. To further soothe him, Napoleon had given him an additional tax-free sum of 350,000 francs just before the coronation. Still Joseph was not happy.[22] Thus the two unsmiling Bonaparte brothers stared straight ahead at the new imperial couple as the glittering coronation carriage clattered across the Pont-Neuf.

Nor were sisters Pauline, Elisa, and Caroline, in the carriages preceding Napoleon, any happier with their brother on this splendid day. Their animosity toward Josephine had, if anything, hardened since the announcement of the creation of the Empire. Indeed, all three Bonaparte sisters were no longer merely outspoken enemies of the gracious Josephine, but jealous and furious now that they had to curtsey whenever she entered the room and even had to carry her train in the ceremony. She was to be *Empress,* while they were but humble princesses—it was unfair! Nor would they ever forgive Napoleon's earlier personal interference in their lives, in particular Pauline and Caroline.

At the age of sixteen the headstrong Pauline had announced her love for the Jacobin regicide politician Stanislas Fréron. Napoleon seemed to be surrounded by hot-blooded women. Memories of Josephine's outrageous participation in orgies, with Thérèsia Tallien and Fortunée Hamelin in their diaphanous neo-classical Greek gowns, and nightlong champagne parties at the Chaumière in the Champs-Elysées, were hard to live down. Excesses of every kind had been carried out into the wee hours of the morning, month after month. It still rankled, not to mention Josephine having been Barras's official mistress at the Luxembourg and at his country estate; and then there was the matter of that elegant little fop Hippolyte Charles. Now Pauline, still a teenager, was throwing herself at every man in sight. "I am determined to do whatever is necessary to prevent this marriage," brother Napoleon declared.[23]

But scarcely had he disposed of Fréron than Pauline was caught in an embarrassing embrace with the handsome young colonel Victor Emmanuel Leclerc. Clearly something had to be done. Napoleon decided to rush through a marriage with Leclerc, whom at least he liked very much. Thus, barely a month after the end of the Fréron fiasco, on June 17, 1799, the civil and religious ceremonies of Pauline and Leclerc took place in Napoleon's palace outside Milan at Montebello.[24] Now she would have to behave herself.

Napoleon was pleased with the choice of Leclerc. Having first met him during the siege of Toulon, he found him honest, courageous, and a good officer with great potential. Unfortunately the marriage was to prove short-lived. Leclerc, heading an invasion force to recapture the island of Santo Domingo, fell victim—like most of his army—to yellow fever, and died in November 1802. Pauline returned to France in 1803, in broken health and aged by many years, despite later flattering portraits by famous artists.

On November 6, 1803, she married the very wealthy, remarkably unintelligent Roman prince Camillo Borghese.[25] The once-beautiful Pauline remained for the rest of her life in "a state of admirable ignorance, lacking any intellectual endowment" but at least secured in a nominal marriage, though not one that prevented her from engaging in a long career of sexual exploits that only her sister Caroline managed to surpass. It was many years before Pauline could forgive her brother's interference in her private life. (The Bonapartes knew how to carry a grudge.)

Maria Nunziata, rechristened by Lucien and thereafter known as Caroline, not only matched the record of the provocative Pauline, but, being a little more intelligent—if equally ignorant—proved a real troublemaker later for Napoleon in political matters. Murat, the tall, powerful, dashing cavalry officer with black curly locks and a wide smile, was Caroline's ultimate choice as mate. From Napoleon's viewpoint it could not have been much worse (which delighted Caroline all the more). Murat, a womanizer of repute (he had even broadcast his earlier conquest of Josephine), came from a much lower social class than the Bonapartes. The son of a reasonably prosperous estate manager and innkeeper near Cahors, he had been surprisingly well educated, remaining in school until 1787, when at the age of twenty he joined the army. Indeed, he was far better educated not only than most of the newly proclaimed marshals of the Empire in 1804 (except, for example, Berthier and Davout), but probably than Napoleon himself. Although Murat had a flair for bizarre costumes and uniforms, the perceptive Bourrienne found Caroline's husband to be "noble, polite, gallant, and, on a battlefield, twenty men commanded by Murat were worth a regiment."[26]

Murat and Caroline seemed to be in the throes of wild infatuation, which worried Napoleon. "I do not at all like these marriages of little love-birds," he reflected. "These impassioned couples consult only their own volcanic feelings. . . . To be sure, she is marrying a brave man, but in my position that simply does not suffice."[27] Nevertheless the civil marriage took place near Paris on January 18, 1800, with brother Napoleon's grudging approval in the face of Caroline's tantrums and emotional pyrotechnics. "Murat pleases my sister, and no one can possibly call me a snob now, seeking only *grandes alliances*. If I had given my sister a nobleman for a spouse, all the Jacobins would have protested against the counter-Revolution."[28] It was acceptance by rationalization of a situation he was helpless to prevent.

All these female problems were simply too much for him, as exhausting as any military campaign. For better or worse the Murat who had cuckolded him had joined the Bonaparte clan and their destinies. Of all Bonaparte's sisters, Caroline was to prove the most independent "anti-Bonaparte," the greatest hindrance to Napoleon and his fledgling Empire, openly conspiring in political opposition, out for herself even at the expense of her husband. By the time of the coronation she was already a budding foe and outspoken opponent of Napoleon.

Finally came sister Maria Anna, or Elisa, as brother Lucien had dubbed her, who because of her complete lack of physical charms was not overwhelmed with handsome young generals. At first she seemed fortunate enough to find Capt. Felix Bacciochi, marrying him precipitously at Marseilles on May 1, 1797, with her mother's full approval but before Napoleon even learned of their engagement. Bacciochi, a member of an old titleless Corsican family that was a traditional political opponent of the Bonapartes, was an incompetent officer who had remained a captain for an embarrassing number of years and was generally described as being neither honest nor intelligent—indeed, as having no redeeming traits or qualifications of any kind. Although Napoleon reluctantly gave it his blessing, ex post facto, this union too soon proved a disaster.[29]

For Napoleon, then, reaching the archbishop's palace just before 11:00 A.M. on this coronation day, the moment was fraught with many conflicting emotions and nagging, unresolved problems. "The Emperor is truly rendered unhappy by his family," Madame Desvaisnes confided to Gen. Antoine Thibaudeau. "They are all acting like a pack of devils deliberately bent on tormenting him."[30]

Moreover the situation had been aggravated in a most embarrassing manner by Letizia Bonaparte's unexpected rebellion and departure from the capital, in order to join and support the "outlawed" Lucien, her favorite son, in his Roman exile, which she preferred to attending this coronation. There was little love lost between Napoleon and his mother, and she had already been given a residence of her own at Pont-sur-Seine, far from the Tuileries. She preferred to spend most of her time with her brother, the mild-mannered Cardinal Fesch, who provided her with a separate set of apartments in his Paris mansion, where he could at least speak her Corsican dialect. In addition she was personally upset with Napoleon for not giving her a title of her own, she instead finally accepting the designation "Madame Mère." Nor did it help matters that Letizia detested the French, and that her vendetta against Josephine and then her children was bitter, ruthless, and relentless, and Napoleon, caught in the middle, in turn could not forgive either his mother's ill will or her interference in this matter.

But Napoleon somehow cast these personal problems aside now:

> I mount the throne to which I have been called by the unanimous voice of the Senate, people, and the army," Napoleon had informed the Senate just the day before, "my heart filled with the feeling of the great destinies of the people whom I first greeted from the midst of our army camps. . . . I must say here that my only pleasures and pains now are those involving the happiness or unhappiness of the people. . . . My descendants will hold this throne for long hereafter. They will remain ever vigilant to prevent any disregard of our laws and the threat to the social order that inevitably result from weak and uncertain princely rule.[31]

He for one would not imitate the weak Bourbons. He had brought order out of the revolutionary chaos and had restored a national stability unknown for more than a decade. The economy had begun to revive, with new markets in newly acquired satellite republics—and their number was growing, although they were now hesitating over the stalemated invasion of England and unpaid government bills to a variety of contractors. Napoleon had also introduced a sweeping new educational system and the first of a series of new law codes, while putting the law courts back on a firm foundation after years of corruption and destructive incompetence. What is more, most of the rebellion in the West and the South was being put down.

But a price had to be paid for this stability—powerful one-man rule—and mass conscription was about to begin in earnest (Napoleon drafting legislation to call up eighty thousand young men in the following year). There was little public freedom of movement, little freedom of self-expression, as newspaper after newspaper was closed or heavily censored. Thirty theaters in the capital would soon be reduced to eight, their productions personally censored by Napoleon, resulting in the growing mediocrity of the French stage. Anyone who criticized Napoleon in public risked immediate imprisonment, often without trial. Private communications weren't safe either. Mail was intercepted by the police, sometimes resulting in the expulsion of Napoleon's critics from the capital, including the controversial and outspoken Madame de Staël (to her mountain retreat of Coppet, in distant Switzerland).

For the time being, however, the public knew little of the heavy censorship or of the forthcoming conscription (which was to be repeated incessantly, annually, in ever increasing numbers). On the other hand, the people could appreciate peace, at least within the nation's frontiers. To be sure, the French treasury had been drained systematically since 1803 in order to build the Grande Armée forming along the coast and the mighty Boulogne flotilla, but Napoleon had a list of seemingly impressive military victories behind him, including Rivoli, Arcola, the Pyramids, Abukir, and Marengo. He had also lost *two entire armies* in foreign invasions, only one-third of the troops returning from Egypt, and then a mere three thousand of the original thirty-four thousand dispatched under Leclerc's ill-fated Santo Domingo campaign (even as Napoleon was ordering the reestablishment of slavery in the colonies). An invasion of England therefore had to succeed now, or else he would have to be saved by his much vaunted "destiny," that guiding star of his existence.

Finally, his kidnapping and summary execution of the duc d'Enghien earlier in 1804 had backfired, and Napoleon still could not understand why the world was in such an uproar. As far as he was concerned, Enghien had been a part of the royalist plot to destroy him, and he had simply retaliated. The Christmas Eve plot to assassinate him and his family had been financed and executed by the Bourbons, and the English, and Cadoudal, and the rest until Cadoudal himself had been captured and executed.[32] Napoleon had had a clear right to strike back at Enghien (though the Russian ambassador, among others, was not present at the coronation precisely because of that). Still, it had had to be done, despite public protests and utter shock: "I had the Duc d'Enghien arrested and judged," Napoleon was to state later at St. Helena, "because that was necessary for the security, the interests, and honor of the French people.... Under similar circumstances today, I would do the same thing all over again. After all, am I simply some miserable dog one can kill in the street with impunity, while my assassins are held sacrosanct? When they attack my person, I return blow for blow."[33] There would be no weakness, no indecision, so long as Napoleon ruled the French Empire.

Toward 11:45 A.M. Napoleon and Josephine emerged in their ceremonial costumes, passing beneath the Gothic wooden arcade that had been specially built between the palace and Nôtre-Dame, Napoleon wearing a crimson velvet mantle, embroidered in gold and silver and lined in white satin, beneath it a jacket of crimson velvet topped by a crown of golden laurel offset by white feathers set in diamonds. Over a lace collar he wore the grand cordon of the Legion of Honor, while at his side he carried a ceremonial sword, its scabbard encrusted in diamonds, with the enormous Regent's diamond in its hilt. His stockings were of white silk and his small ceremonial slippers of white velvet embroidered in gold. In his small, impeccably manicured hands, gloved in white, he carried Charlemagne's scepter and the traditional Bourbon ceremonial symbol, the Hand of Justice.[34] All at a total cost of just over 99,000 francs.

The court ushers, in black and green, led the procession, followed by the heralds-at-arms in violet, followed in turn by the pages in green and gold. Next came the grand master of ceremonies, the comte de Ségur, in silver and violet, followed by his aides and assistants; and members of the empress's household, including three field marshals—Sérrurier, bearing the cushion with the coronation ring; Moncey, carrying the golden basket for the empress's train; and Murat, carrying her crown.

Empress Josephine was the focus of much scrutiny as she was escorted into the freezing cathedral by her first chamberlain and first equerry. She was beaming with joy and had never looked more beautiful, thought Laure Junot. Beneath a long embroidered crimson velvet train lined in Russian ermine, she wore a short-sleeved white satin gown and white silk embroidered stockings, her other undergarments of velvet or tulle richly embroidered and covered with emeralds, while her white gloves were embroidered in gold. Her diadem, earrings, and necklace were of seemingly numberless diamonds. The cost of her costume and jewelry was some 101,000 francs.

If her closest friends and admirers were happy for her, not so four of the five princesses following in her wake, supporting her magnificent crimson train: Julie, Elisa, Caroline, and Pauline. Josephine's only ally was her daughter, Hortense. After a last-minute battle at St.-Cloud, when the family harridans had confronted their brother en masse, Napoleon, who was by now quite fed up with the entire clan, had given the women an ultimatum: They would either hold Josephine's train or be exiled with their husbands and lose their titles and wealth. Thus they sulked grimly now with the eyes of the nation on them.[35]

As the long procession of marshals and imperial officials finally approached the choir, the pope, who had been waiting for nearly two hours, became the center of attention. His tiara—a gift from Napoleon, considered a masterpiece, adorned with 4,209 diamonds, rubies, and emeralds—cost 181,931 francs. Total expenses for the superb costumes, designed principally by Isabey and David along with the architectural modifications to the Archbishop's palace and to Nôtre-Dame Cathedral, totaled another seven hundred thousand francs.

Two side altars and the choir screen had been removed in the cathedral, and enormous tapestries and a painted special-effects backdrop hung behind there now, while the orchestra and choir, over four hundred, provided with 17,738 pages of hand-copied music, under the direction of Jean François Lesueur, played and sang as Luigi Paisiello's *Mass* and *Te Deum* filled the massive Gothic, 427-foot-long twelfth-to-thirteenth-century stone structure, startling pigeons and sparrows, their wings suddenly flapping 115 feet above the audience of thousands, as hawkers sold drinks, sausages, and rolls.

It was after one o'clock by the time the imperial couple reached the altar. Napoleon genuflected and received the triple papal unction, followed by the empress, which of course constituted a deviation from the traditional ceremony historically carried out by the archbishops of Reims (Napoleon declining to take the host). Then, taking the golden crown from the cushion, turning his back on the pope, according to earlier agreement, Napoleon crowned himself, to the astonishment of the audience before him. He next crowned Josephine as she genuflected at his feet, tears in her eyes as she looked up at a smiling Napoleon and then at the throne high on the platform behind him.

Napoleon was handed the imperial ring, consecrated by the pope, who explained it as representing "the sign of the Holy Faith, the proof of the strength and solidity of your empire, by means of which, as a result of its triumphant power, you will conquer your enemies and destroy heresies, on this imperial throne which Jesus the Christ, the King of Kings and Lord of Lords in his eternal kingdom, affirms your reign with him."

The pope then embraced the emperor and turned to the audience, calling out: "*Vivat imperator in aeternum!*" his assistants responding: "*Vivent l'Empereur et l'Emperatrice.*" The presidents of the Senate, Tribunate, and Corps Législatif stepped forward to administer to Napoleon the singular Constitutional Oath, creating an empire based on a republic, which Napoleon now read out:

> I swear to maintain the integrity of the territory of the Republic; to respect, and cause to be respected, the laws of the Concordat, the freedom of worship; to respect, and cause to be respected, the equality of rights, political and civil liberties, and the irrevocability of conveyances

of national property; to levy no taxes or duties except as laid down by law; to maintain the institution of the Legion of Honor; and to govern with a view solely in the interests, happiness, and glory of the French people.

The heralds-at-arms then proclaimed in a united powerful voice: "The most glorious and most august Napoleon, Emperor of the French people, is anointed, crowned, and enthroned!" "*Vive l'Empereur!*" the assistant heralds-at-arms called out. "*Vive l'Empereur!*" the heralds-at-arms in turn echoed, only to be drowned out by the roar of hundreds of cannon up and down both banks of the Seine, the sudden shock waves reverberating through the vast stone basilica. The pope now led the Te Deum, as the parchment with the Imperial Oath was handed to Napoleon for his signature, thereby completing the coronation ceremony. The Empire was officially launched, stamped with the approval of the Vatican itself. Napoleon was satisfied.

The police estimated that some two million persons were present in the French capital, representing every department of the land and a dozen different countries.[36] The peal of hundreds and hundreds of church bells, large and small, rang out in a deafening din acclaiming the great event, which was followed by fireworks, festivities, formal balls, and dancing in the streets for the next fortnight. Hundreds of celebratory cannon thundered throughout the new imperial capital every hour on the hour until midnight, and through every city of the land, from Marseilles to the newly erected batteries overlooking Boulogne, and heard across the Channel as far away as Dover.

At 6:00 A.M. on December 3 the cannon resumed their explosive fortissimo. By 11:00 musicians were again playing in the squares and at street corners everywhere, and at noon, despite the freezing temperature, a formal concert was given in the Carrousel as golden balloons were launched and exploded against a gray sky. Wine flowed, and soon thousands were dancing in the Place de la Concorde, over paving stones still stained red by the blood of their relatives and of their late king and queen, where an obelisk of fire supporting a twenty-five-foot star exploded in a dazzling illumination. Sideshows and hawkers of food and drink tempted the celebrants, while that evening fireworks again lighted up the skies against low-lying clouds, and crowds passed beneath hundreds of Chinese lanterns strung along the streets and gardens leading to Catherine de Medici's monumentally long sixteenth-century palace. Heralds-at-arms, still in their violet uniforms, worked their way through the teeming masses around the Tuileries to distribute nearly ninety thousand bronze coronation medallions, and another twelve thousand golden ones given to the Imperial Guard—all at a cost of 229,642 francs. Another 276,000 francs were distributed by the interior minister as dowries for the poor.

Napoleon personally distributed eagles for the regimental flags to army and National Guard deputations in the Champ de Mars, during a long ceremony carried out before the court, Senate, State Council high court judges, officers, and the entire diplomatic corps, despite a terrible rainstorm mixed with snow. A young student, intent on putting a bloody premature end to the day's events by assassinating Napoleon, managed to shout out: "Freedom or death!" before he was intercepted by the Imperial Guard and whisked away as the five-hour-long ceremony continued. "Soldiers, here are your colors!" Napoleon addressed the thousands of troops before him. "These eagles will always serve as a rallying point. They will be found everywhere your emperor judges them to be necessary for the defense of his throne and people. You will now swear to sacrifice your lives to defend them through your courage, on the road to victory."[37]

The festivities continued in full swing over the next ten days, the Senate offering military music, fireworks, and a feast in the Luxembourg Gardens, the deputy mayors of Paris offering one of their own, followed by an even more sumptuous affair for thousands presented at the Hôtel de Ville by "the City of Paris." Murat did the honors in the newly proclaimed "Salle des Victoires," at the unbelievable cost of 1,745,646 francs. Similar celebrations were given by the newly created marshals in the Opéra, and another later on by the Corps Legislatif, while at the Opéra-Comique, Marie-Joseph Chénier's latest production, *Cyrus*, calling on Napoleon to end all war and bestow justice and love—"The first requisite of the people and support of good kings"—on France."[38] The next day an irate Napoleon ordered the police to close down that theater.

Nor could the many hundreds of thousands of visitors to the city at this time forget, as they passed the Place de Grève for the festivities at the Hôtel de Ville, that Georges Cadoudal, royalist general and "rebel," had been executed on this very spot earlier that year, and that just a few miles to the east, another Frenchman, the duc d'Enghien, lay buried in a shallow grave in the drained moat of the dungeon of Vincennes.

French tributary and satellite states, meanwhile, were—at bayonet point—continuing to send boats, troops, supplies, and gold for the Channel army camps preparing for the invasion of England, as French troops of occupation beefed up garrisons already in place in Holland and Belgium, on the left bank of the Rhine, and in Geneva, Turin, Milan, and Genoa.

Napoleon's imperial purple mantle was beginning to cast a pall across Europe, not to mention his gradual closure of all trade with Great Britain, which resulted in commercial and financial hardship and ill will on both sides of the Channel.

The costs of creating and maintaining the new Empire were to prove staggering, including the expense of creating an entirely new aristocracy and rewarding the nation's top soldiers on a most munificent scale. Even more expensive was the cost of maintaining and training an inactive "peace" army, the 167,500 men at Montreuil, St.-Omer, and Bruges, along with the maintenance costs of the invasion flotilla to keep boats manned, fully supplied daily with fresh food and ammunition, and seaworthy. Unknown to the French general public, Napoleon continued to extort the vast sums needed for this war effort from not only foreign bankers and merchants at Amsterdam, The Hague, Mainz, Brussels, Genoa, Milan, Lisbon, and Madrid, but also from those of Paris, Lyons, Marseilles, and Bordeaux. The large armed convoys of gold had to be kept moving in the direction of Paris, although Napoleon did not always repay major contractors and bankers supplying the French armies, thereby reinforcing a growing nation-wide lack of trust in him and the government. But increasing restlessness in the soldiers encamped along the Channel and the pressing finances required to keep them there persuaded Napoleon that this situation could not endure. To relieve all sources financing the "war effort," the only real answer was another war and more conquests.

The cost of the coronation day's events and ceremonies, of the alterations to Nôtre-Dame, the state dinners, preparations for the pope, public celebrations and costumes, Finance Minister Gaudin ultimately put at 8,527,973 francs, to be paid by the combined crown and state treasuries.[39]

To Napoleon it was all worth the price. The pope, the head of the entire Roman Catholic church, had come *to him*. Papal approval had given his new Empire international acceptance, legitimacy, and respectability. This in turn permitted him to think about new family alliances—*royal* alliances—previously denied him, as well as fresh international agreements. And to be sure that the significance of the coronation ceremony was not forgotten, Napoleon commissioned his new imperial court painter, David, to paint four massive nineteen-by-thirty-foot canvases depicting these events (only two of which ultimately were completed, however: *The Anointing* and *The Distribution of the Eagles*).[40]

And yet as the last bells ceased chiming, and the words "*Vivat imperator in aeternum*" hung silently in the now empty basilica of Nôtre-Dame, and the smoke of the last celebratory cannon dissipated above the capital, there were already disquieting signs of grave problems, as Finance Minister Gaudin, Archchancellor Cambacérès, and Foreign Minister Talleyrand conferred with Napoleon, after which the newly crowned emperor would have to rush back to the Channel camps and boatyards to urge on his preparations for the invasion of England.

"A Humiliating Business"

With God's help, I shall put an end to the destiny and very existence of England.

apoleon may have had all the elements of his great invasion plan in his head, but apparently not all at the same time. It had taken him the better part of six months to decide where he wanted to place his major embarkation camps. Then ports had been selected between April and December of 1803 on a hit-or-miss basis. But it was only gradually, as blueprints were translated into reality and cannon were hoisted into the new batteries at Boulogne, that he came to realize that a flotilla, even an impressive task force of a couple of thousand gunboats and transports, however heavily armed, could not successfully cross the English Channel in the face of powerful British warships—not, that is, without protection.

It was a most reluctant first consul who ultimately acknowledged that, although he might send some fleets to attack Scotland or Ireland or other points as part of a sweeping tactical feint, in the hope of luring Adm. Sir William Cornwallis and his forty-five or so ships and frigates away from Brest and the English Channel, he would nevertheless still have to cope with Lord Keith and the Home Fleet, stationed off the Kent Downs. As Napoleon was just beginning to appreciate between 1803 and 1804, Corn-

wallis, in his three-decked flagship *Ville de Paris,* at Ushant, off the coast of
Brest, was successfully holding captive the entire French Atlantic fleet. The
commanders of the Brest fleet of twenty-one superb ships of the line—Vice
Adm. Laurent-Jean François Truguet and then his successor, Rear Admiral
Ganteaume—seemed unable to break out of that Breton port, while smaller
squadrons were able to slip out of Lorient and La Rochelle only on very,
very rare occasions, and then never with enough ships to be able to confront Cornwallis. And while Admiral Decrès was doing his best at the
Naval Ministry, he—and therefore Napoleon—was not without his problems, on a most intimidating scale.

To begin with, Admiral Bruix, who was in declining health despite
being only in his early forties, was to die in March 1805 before the operation was ever put into motion. Another competent admiral, Louis
Latouche-Tréville, commander of the Mediterranean fleet at Toulon, was
also ailing and died in port in August 1804 before ever putting to sea. The
one other commander of critical importance, Vice Admiral Truguet, with
the French navy's largest and most powerful fleet at Brest, was to be fired
on political grounds in the summer of 1804 because of his attempt to dissuade Napoleon from accepting the imperial purple. Thus, in less than nine
months' time, France was destined to lose its three best senior naval officers, and there was no one even remotely capable of replacing them.

Rear Adm. Jean-Baptiste-Raymond Lacrosse, hardly of the same mettle
as Admiral Bruix, was to succeed to the command at Boulogne in March
1805. Napoleon's favorite sailor, the pultaceous Ganteaume, was to replace
the excellent Truguet at Brest and, not unexpectedly, prove a spineless,
indecisive, and sycophantic disaster, doomed to ride at anchor behind the
protection of that port's guns. The forty-two-year-old Pierre de Villeneuve
was now promoted to Vice Admiral and nominated as Latouche-Tréville's
successor at Toulon. This same Villeneuve who had earlier deserted Admiral Brueys at the Battle of Abukir Bay without firing a shot was shortly to
prove himself to be one of the most incompetent and ignominious commanders, indeed the greatest wimp in the history of the French navy.

In brief, however hard he worked, and despite his commandeering of
the entire French national treasury for two entire years (1803–5)—not to
mention his blatant extortion of untold millions from Dutch, Belgian, German, Italian, and Spanish allies—for the sole purpose of launching his
flotilla "to avenge six centuries of [English] insults," Napoleon had not
even remote assurances of success. No senior naval or army officer supported the plan. "Battles should not be fought," Napoleon himself was to
admit a few years later, "if one cannot calculate at least a 70 percent chance

of success," adding, however, "And yet [at times] one should fight even when there appears to be no chance of winning, since by its very nature, the outcome of a battle is never predictable. But once it has been decided to fight, one should do so to the very end, to conquer or perish."[1] Even if he did successfully land some troops in Kent or along the Thames Estuary, that hardly ensured the seizure of London and the subjection of the obdurate and patriotic Anglo-Saxons. Nor did it in any measure rationalize his diverting all the nation's energies and resources and bankrupting the French treasury just to bring off the colorful publicity coup of repeating William the Conqueror's unique feat.

Napoleon's manner of drafting and dictating naval strategy was hardly reassuring either. He knew that he wanted to invade England. To do that he knew that he needed to create ports, coastal batteries, an entirely new flotilla, and a large expeditionary force, but he wavered on the selection of its commanders and on the means required to achieve his end. The strategy devised for launching the invasion force proved the final flaw. One major plan after another was drafted for the navy's principal fleets—ordering, then canceling or aborting them—each only to be replaced in turn with the next, and in such numbers (nine different plans in all) as to leave the few remaining competent, seasoned commanding officers bewildered, frustrated, and despondent.

Meanwhile the British government mobilized quickly for an anticipated extensive French landing as early as the autumn of 1803. But, ironically, at that time the first units of Napoleon's new flotilla were not even remotely ready, nor were the basic harbors in any position to receive them until well into the following year. Indeed, despite Bonaparte's brave words and pronouncements regarding the creation of the national flotilla, it was not until over one year later, on July 2, 1804, that he and Admiral Decrès secretly revealed to the senior commanding officers concerned the first set of invasion plans.[2]

With the exception of this initial plan, those that followed required a major French naval force sailing from Europe to Ireland, or to the Caribbean to land troops in the French colonies and attack nearby English island possessions. The objective was to draw large numbers of British warships away from the French coast and the Channel. This sweeping movement—assuming that the British fell for it—was to be foiled from the outset by the fact that the principal French fleet was never able to escape from the port of Brest. This was due in large part to the hovering presence of Admiral Cornwallis's powerful fleet (reaching down to El Ferrol–La Coruña and Cadiz). Therefore there was no reason for Admiral Lord Keith ever to quit British waters. His

primary objective remained unchanged: to protect "hearth and home."
Admiral Decrès seemed most remiss in not explaining this to the first consul.
The annual convoys of sugar, spices, and indigo sailing from the Caribbean,
however, were of vast importance to English merchants and London in particular; French attacks in the Caribbean were of grave concern. But in the
final analysis, protecting English shores came first. The small British
squadron in the Antilles would have to cope as best it could. The even more
lucrative—and far larger—annual convoys from India and the Far East, after
clearing the Cape of Good Hope, sailed along the west coast of Africa,
directly up the English Channel to the Thames Estuary, and up the river to
the sprawling East India Docks. If this vital convoy, sometimes involving
hundreds of commercial transports, was intercepted and destroyed by the
French, London would be left nearly bankrupt. The City in the final analysis
dictated Admiralty strategy, and the Channel therefore remained heavily
protected. The powerful British fleets would remain in place. It is hard to
conceive of Napoleon's failure to grasp such basic concepts, but then he
never did understand the English—nor did he even try.

Napoleon's initial plan to invade England was probably the best. Admiral
Latouche-Tréville was to sail from Toulon with ten or eleven ships of the
line, into the Atlantic, around Spain to collect the small squadron at
Rochefort and the large one at Brest, and proceed directly to Boulogne. It
was aborted on August 14, 1804, however, with the death that day of the
long-ailing Admiral Latouche. As Napoleon once stoically commented, "In
every great enterprise one must always allow something to chance."[3]
    After that, everything seemed to go wrong, perhaps because Bonaparte
now ignored his own rule that a perpendicular line is always shorter than an
oblique one[4] and employed instead a complex strategy that allowed too
many opportunities for chance to intervene. To make matters worse, he
continued to juggle too many possibilities, and when he announced his second invasion plan on September 29, it was very different indeed, setting an
unfortunate pattern for the events to follow. The choice of the aloof, pusillanimous, indecisive Villeneuve to replace Latouche could doom even the
best-laid plans.
    In any event Villeneuve was ordered to sail from Toulon by October 12
at the very latest, to lay by at Cadiz to collect Spanish warships to be joined
to his command, and to chart a course straight to South America and Suri-
nam, where he was to land 5,600 troops, and then to continue on to Martinique, where Rear Admiral Missiessy's very small squadron (arriving from
France) would join him. While in the Antilles he was to attack British pos-

sessions and seize the islands of St. Lucia and Dominica, landing 3,500 more men there. Meanwhile another, smaller French squadron was to be sent from Toulon south along the African coast, destroying British trading posts, with the final objective of seizing a certain tropical isle in the South Atlantic by the name of St. Helena.

"The English will find themselves simultaneously attacked in Asia, Africa, and America," Napoleon argued. "These successive shocks at the main points of their [global] commerce will make them realize at long last just how very vulnerable they really are." After these sweeping operations in the Caribbean and Africa, they "will certainly not be expecting anything else. It will be easy to surprise them. . . . The Grande Armée de Boulogne . . . will then enter the county of Kent."[5]

Part of Napoleon's evaluation was based on the assumption that the Brest fleet—now ordered to land 18,000 troops under General Augereau at Lough Swilly Bay in northern Ireland, with orders to "march straight for Dublin"—would also have sailed. "Lord Cornwallis will go to wait for him [Truguet with the Brest fleet] in Ireland," Napoleon insisted. With the Brest fleet gone, the British were to think that the national flotilla would not cross the Channel. Meanwhile Villeneuve with his combined fleet was to return directly to Boulogne, where he would in turn be joined by the Brest fleet on its return voyage (after sweeping around northern Scotland). Thus they would have only Lord Keith's Home Fleet with which to contend. It would be child's play. "One of these two operations must succeed," Napoleon assured his naval minister. "Whether I am in England or Ireland, in either event we will have won the war."[6]

It was certainly a daring plan in its sweeping strategy, involving the landing of some 194,000 men on both sides of the Atlantic. Unfortunately, its boldness had only one purpose, the destruction and subjection of other human beings. Still not knowing how unreliable Villeneuve was, and with the able Truguet still in place at Brest, Napoleon felt confident of success. But the unexpected happened again: On October 8 Napoleon was informed that the British had intercepted a full copy of these complicated orders. The whole operation had to be scrapped once more.

A frustrated Bonaparte was not to be put off that easily, however, and on October 26 he issued his third invasion plan. Missiessy would sail with his small squadron from Rochefort to Martinique, and Villeneuve would sail to South America and then on to Martinique, from where, with his flock in hand (including Missiessy), he would return to Europe. This time, for security reasons, no mention was made of Boulogne, which was to be continued in separate orders.[7]

As the old year gave way to the new, January 1805 found Admiral Villeneuve still snugly in his Toulon berth, hesitating. He was against the whole venture and had informed Decrès explicitly that he did not desire to be in the limelight of such a dangerous command as this. Meanwhile, however, the Spanish had declared war on England on December 12, 1804, following Cornwallis's capture of three royal Spanish treasure ships (sinking one) in October and two months of very considerable pressure from Napoleon. As a result a Franco-Spanish defense pact was signed in Paris on January 4, 1805, by Talleyrand and Adm. Don Federico Gravina, the Spanish emissary to Paris, the latter assuring his new French allies that he would endeavor to support them "with all my zeal and energy." (He was to prove himself a man of his word.) Hereafter the Spanish navy would throw its full resources behind the French and their campaign against England.

After weeks of procrastination and the usual excuses by Villeneuve—lack of supplies, insufficient crews, bad weather, and the presence of the British—on January 16 without warning Napoleon again modified all naval campaign plans. Missiessy was to sail for the Caribbean (and in fact had already done so but following an earlier plan), while Villeneuve's Toulon fleet was to proceed to the Caribbean and land troops to reinforce Admiral Villaret-de-Joyeuses, governor of Martinique, supported by the Brest and Rochefort fleets, as well as French and Spanish vessels from El Ferrol. Their objectives were to "ravage" the British colonies and then return to Europe or the Canaries, depending on the situation, when final orders would be given for Boulogne.[8]

Much to the astonishment of just about everyone, on January 18 Villeneuve's fleet finally hauled out of Toulon harbor with 6,333 troops aboard his ten ships of the line and seven frigates. Admittedly there was much less astonishment on his return, with a few sails sagging, three days later. Caught by a moderate storm and fearing interception by the British, he had put his helm hard about and made for a safe haven. "Had I been seen by the English squadron [headed by Nelson]," he argued feebly to Decrès, "it would have been quite impossible to escape from it."[9] And yet he had not been seen by a soul.

French naval morale at Toulon, which had sunk after Latouche's replacement by Villeneuve, reached a new low. Villeneuve's secret report to Decrès revealed a very troubled mind indeed. "You will be so good as to recall that I have not asked for the command of this squadron," it began. The navy, he insisted, was in a pathetic, useless state:

I should like to point out to you that about all one can expect from a career in the French Navy today is shame and confusion, and anyone

who denies this I declare to be presumptuous, utterly blind, and incapable of straight thinking. . . . [Therefore] it is my ardent wish that the
Emperor decide not to commit any of his squadrons to the hazards of
these events, for if he does, the French flag will be seriously compromised. The fact of the matter is that *it is utterly impossible for us to
defeat the enemy when both sides are equal, indeed, they will beat us
even when they are a third weaker than we are.* . . . under no circumstances do I intend to become the laughing stock of Europe by being
involved in further disasters. . . . I should therefore view it with the
greatest pleasure if the Emperor would replace me in this command.[10]

Decrès made sure that the document's dark contents never reached the
Tuileries. That the hapless Villeneuve was kept in command of a fleet he
held to be doomed to disaster was as irresponsible as it was perplexing.
Admiral Decrès could not conceal Vice Admiral Villeneuve's unscheduled
return to port, however. "I really believe your admiral does not know how
to command," a frustrated Bonaparte confided to his former aide-de-camp
General Lauriston, who was then aboard Villeneuve's flagship, the *Bucen-
taure.* "We would have to renounce ever putting to sea, even during the
finest of weather, if we were always worried about losing a few ships."[11]

Even while the ships were undergoing repairs, however, Napoleon was
mulling over Villeneuve's latest action. Could he entrust the command of
such an important campaign to him? The result was that he rescinded his
fourth invasion plan (of January 16), replacing it on March 2 with yet
another variation on the theme. Villeneuve, although kept in command of
the Toulon fleet, was demoted to overall second-in-command, his junior
colleague Ganteaume succeeding him. While Villeneuve would (in theory)
be sailing to Martinique, Ganteaume would (also in theory) be hauling out
of harbor with the larger Brest fleet heading for the same rendezvous,
although via El Ferrol (where a smaller French squadron and some Spanish
warships would join him). The final objective remained the same, however:
Sometime between June 10 and July 10, Ganteaume would have to appear
before Boulogne, where Napoleon himself would be waiting.[12]

On March 22, eight days before Villeneuve finally successfully cleared
the Toulon roadstead with his entire fleet, the constant juggler of destinies,
Napoleon Bonaparte, rescinded his fifth plan, issued just twenty days earlier. Instead of proceeding to Martinique, Villeneuve was to sail directly to
Ireland and thence back to Boulogne, while Ganteaume would proceed to
Martinique and then return to escort the flotilla from Boulogne. But this
modified plan (the sixth) was rescinded on April 13, when Napoleon

decided that Villeneuve was not only to rendezvous at Martinique after all, with eleven ships and six frigates, but was to resume overall command in the Antilles with the arrival of Missiessy and Ganteaume![13]

With this veritable deluge of orders and counterorders, in an age where naval communications traveled at the speed of the fastest sailer, chaos and grave complications often arose when dispatches did not reach their addressee in time. Frequently during this period even the best admirals in the French navy were left in the lurch after several changes of instruction from the high command in Paris. Such was again the case now. Following the third plan—the only one he had yet received—Missiessy duly sailed from Martinique for La Rochelle on March 28. Two days later Napoleon's fifth plan (ordering Missiessy to remain at Martinique after all to await the rendezvous with the whole fleet) reached Missiessy's empty berth at Fort de France. That same day Villeneuve set sail for the West Indies. "I am leaving, my dear General," Villeneuve wrote on the thirtieth. "May fortune smile upon me, for I badly need it.[14]

This time it was Ganteaume, as commander of the critically important and more powerful Brest fleet, who was to cause problems for Napoleon. Theoretically, with five of Missiessy's ships, eleven from Toulon, twenty-one from Brest, and another six Spanish ships from Cadiz, Villeneuve should ultimately have been sailing with perhaps forty-one ships, after leaving General Lauriston behind in the Antilles with some twelve thousand troops. On returning to Europe, Villeneuve was to destroy the British naval blockade of El Ferrol–La Coruña to release another fifteen French and Spanish ships there to join him, giving him a total of fifty-seven ships of the line and at least a dozen frigates. With these he was to plow up the Channel in one of the mightiest armadas of the nation's most powerful warships ever seen, sweep aside the remainder of Cornwallis's fleet, and convoy the Boulogne-Kent flotilla crossing, scattering Keith's ships as they arrived. In the event that Ganteaume was unable to break through Cornwallis's intimidating blockade, Villeneuve on his return from the Indies was ordered to Brest to rendezvous with Ganteaume's fleet and together enter the Channel and advance to Boulogne.[15]

In fact Admiral Ganteaume failed to break out of Brest, despite a series of personal orders directly from the Tuileries to do so. On the one occasion he did actually reach the harbor's roadsteads at Berteaume, Cornwallis came thundering in under a full press of sail. Ganteaume immediately put about and hurriedly retraced his own wake back into Brest. He was, he claimed, a virtual prisoner there, as a result of contrary winds, gale-force storms, massive desertion of crews, lack of competent officers and men, and the need for repairs—not to mention the presence of the British.

By now a frustrated Napoleon was writing directly to Ganteaume, sometimes once a week, enquiring what the problem was this time. "Be honest with me, how many ships do you have ready to sail. . . . How many can I actually count on?" "Our ships are in a pitiful state," the plump, pink-cheeked Ganteaume replied. "It is frightening to think of the small number of qualified men we have . . . and if we have to sail in bad weather, we would be greatly embarrassed." The men, Ganteaume complained, were all "lacking the will, the force, the courage to succeed," which of course was a damning condemnation of their leader—himself—whose job it was to instill just those qualities. "You cannot ask for the impossible," a momentarily discouraged Bonaparte replied. "I cannot perform miracles." Time and again Napoleon harried the unharriable Ganteaume. "Put to sea as quickly as possible," Napoleon ordered him on March 2. "Attack and capture the 7 or 8 English ships [before Brest] and sail directly to Ferrol." But Ganteaume would not budge.[16]

> "Ballasted vessels, but not his own head,
> Thus leaves Admiral Ganteaume;
> Going from Brest to Berteaume;
> And returning from Berteaume to Brest in its stead."

So his men sang nightly in the taverns of Brest, and Ganteaume no longer showed his face in public.[17]

Meanwhile the seemingly infinite catena of errors, disasters, misunderstandings, and plain bad luck plaguing the French navy was being compounded by another unforeseen factor. It included, quite unknown to Villeneuve, a stubborn English vice admiral by the name of Horatio, Lord Nelson, who was feverishly seeking the elusive Toulon fleet that had escaped him. Unfortunately for Villeneuve, his British counterpart accepted neither excuses nor the limitations of restrictive orders. On discovering that Villeneuve had crossed into the Atlantic, he would soon be on his trail with his entire Mediterranean fleet, determined to track him down "even to the Antipodes," as he put it.

Duly reaching Martinique on May 16, the antipodal Villeneuve remained largely inactive, adamantly refusing even to land Lauriston and his 12,440 men, despite Naval Ministry orders to do precisely that, and the insistence of the bewildered colonial governor, Captain General Villaret. Another glorious tropical dawn broke on May 30, finding the stubborn Villeneuve still nobly riding at anchor in the delicious clear waters of Fort-de-France, when the frigate *Didon* arrived from France with a set (the seventh) of Napoleon's invasion plan orders, dated April 13. Then, on June 4, Rear Admiral Magon arrived with two more ships of the line, which were attached to the fleet (giving Villeneuve—with Gravina's six Spanish battle-ships—the command of twenty ships of the line thus far), while unknown to Villeneuve, that same day, Nelson's Mediterranean fleet reached Carlisle Bay, Barbados. Finally learning of this a week later, on June 11, while off the coast of Guadeloupe, Villeneuve panicked, and to Villarets's amazement, signaled Gravina and the fleet to follow him as he dashed for the vast empty spaces of the mid-Atlantic—on the most direct course for El Ferrol.

If Nelson and Villeneuve were not destined to meet (despite another hot pursuit by Nelson), the French vice admiral did have another disagreeable surprise in store. On July 22, still some ninety miles off El Ferrol, Villeneuve, the master of disaster, encountered a squadron of fifteen British battleships commanded by Vice Adm. Sir Robert Calder. Given the excuse of no wind and much dense fog, eleven of Villeneuve's fourteen battleships once again managed to remain successfully out of the range of fire, Admiral Gravina and his Spanish squadron instead bearing the full brunt of the English guns, losing two of their ships to the enemy. Calder—a man of pulvinated ego, a boastful sailor, and an excellent fleet politician with influential friends and relatives in Parliament—with his remaining fifteen ships declined the honor of closing with the combined Franco-Spanish fleet and permitted them to escape (for which he was later court-martialed and removed from his command).[18]

Even as Villeneuve was sailing from the natural shelter of El Ferrol, where he arrived on August 1 (following a brief respite at Vigo), on July 26 Napoleon had been in the process of issuing his eighth campaign plan, in effect a modification of the seventh: "You are to proceed to Cadiz," Bonaparte personally instructed him.

> I want you to rally the Spanish ships you find there . . . and then sail to Ferrol, where you will then add the fifteen French and Spanish vessels there to your fleet. . . . With all these forces now under your command you will next proceed to Brest [where Gantaume's fleet was to join him] . . . and thence on to Boulogne, where, if you make me master [of the English Channel] for just three days . . . and with God's help, I shall put an end to the destiny and existence of England.[19]

So much for the "six hours'" control of the Channel that Napoleon had originally suggested he needed for that crossing. Villeneuve had failed to attach the warships awaiting him at Cadiz, but apart from that everything was all right. He could add Ganteaume's fleet to his own on the way north.

Meanwhile, with news of the appearance of Nelson and his Mediterranean Fleet reaching even the French capital, Talleyrand suddenly advised Napoleon to drop all invasion plans: "This unforeseen gathering of forces no doubt renders any plans for a descent [on England] quite impracticable for the moment," he argued, even before learning of Villeneuve's clash with Calder. In the jumbled report Napoleon received at Boulogne on August 8, the actions of the combined Franco-Spanish fleet got twisted, Villeneuve making it appear that the Spanish, through their own incompetence, had lost two ships, while thanks to Villeneuve's remarkable skill, he had not only not suffered a scratch (the last was quite true) but had pursued and chased the (inferior) British fleet away— and had in fact won a sea battle in the process!

"The Combined Fleet has been in a battle at El Ferrol," an exalted Napoleon informed Archchancellor Cambacérès. "It chased away the enemy fleet and for four days remained master of the battlefield." Moreover Villeneuve had reported sinking one British ship (untrue) and battering two others (which in fact the Spanish had done). "I feel that we can consider this affair a real success," the emperor concluded. If his fleet had lost two ships, he insisted, it was the fault of "Spanish blunders.... You know how very little one can ever count on them...."[20] Such was the gist of the version written in Villeneuve's hand (which failed even to mention his own astonishing actions at Martinique).

On entering the safety of the spacious double harbor of El Ferrol–La Coruña on August 1, Villeneuve was handed a copy of Napoleon's eighth plan. At least the objective of sailing north to Boulogne had not altered.

Little did Napoleon realize, of course, the tragic, most delicate state of mind Villeneuve was now in, as he took on hundreds of casks of badly needed fresh water and supplies (which he had somehow failed to do during his long stay at Martinique), while attaching the French and Spanish ships he found there to his combined fleet, giving him a total (after discarding some badly damaged vessels) of twenty-seven ships of the line. As thousands of sailors and dozens of senior officers were making ready to sail in all haste for the great day of reckoning with the British, Villeneuve isolated himself in the spacious cabin of his spotless, double-deck, eighty-gun flagship to begin a fateful letter to the naval minister. And even as his combined fleet of twenty-seven of the world's largest ships of the line was weighing anchor on August 10–11, back at Boulogne, Napoleon was finally receiving more accurate independent reports of what had really transpired during the famous sea battle of July 22 and at Martinique.

"Why is it that Admiral Villeneuve never said anything about this in his reports?" a stupefied Bonaparte exclaimed. "That damned Gravina is all genius and action in battle.... If only Villeneuve had those qualities.... How the devil does he have the nerve to complain about the Spanish? Why, they have fought like lions!"[21] It was only then, at his headquarters, in the Pont de Briques on the cliffs of Boulogne, that he discovered not only that the battle of El Ferrol had been very far from a French naval victory (for which in his initial enthusiasm he had ordered the firing of hundreds of cannon along the length of the Channel), but that Villeneuve had—against orders—failed to land and hand over Lauriston's 12,440 troops in the Antilles to Villaret. Instead an angry Napoleon continued, "my islands of Martinique and Guadeloupe were left in jeopardy," and his mighty combined fleet had fled. "All thanks to this incredible Villeneuve" whom he declared to be a man of "double vision," that is, a coward, seeing twice as many enemy forces before him as really existed. "Here is this Navy, which could have done so much harm to the English, but which has returned having accomplished nothing," General Reille complained to Napoleon's brother-in-law, Marshal Joachim Murat, the titular Grand Admiral of the Empire."[22]

And yet the moment was so ripe, Napoleon assured Admiral Decrès, with Nelson out of the way in London and Admiral Collingwood's ships far away to the south at Cadiz, and Cochrane's and the West Indies squadrons also far away at this moment, leaving "only twenty-four" English ships in the Channel and North sea. "Well, truly, what a splendid opportunity . . . what a perfect occasion, if I only had a real man there!"[23]

The moment was not quite as propitious as Napoleon claimed, but it was the last possible time when he could still launch his much-vaunted expeditionary force against the English, with the final hours dwindling fast. Having ordered Villeneuve to return between June 10 and July 10, the emperor could have set his astonishing plan in action if the admiral had arrived even now, a month late. With perhaps close to forty-seven mighty ships of the line escorting the flotilla, even the English navy might have had to concede defeat. But every day now was precious, as top-secret naval inspection reports indicated a rapid deterioration of his hastily built flotilla.

The truth of the doubts of every admiral as to the seaworthiness of flat-bottomed boats, especially if they were caught in high seas during their fabled crossing, had been borne out back on July 20, 1804, when, on reaching Boulogne, Napoleon had ordered Admiral Bruix to launch hundreds of these small vessels, fully manned and laden. He wanted to see for himself a full-scale demonstration of their capabilities and effectiveness.

The barometer had plunged the previous night, and the sky was completely overcast. Bruix informed the newly proclaimed emperor that he could not endanger the lives of his men and the safety of the boats finally assembled there just for the sake of a demonstration that could easily be delayed for a couple of days until the storm had passed. Napoleon who had come all the way from Paris with his full staff just for this naval exercise, remained adamant.

"Do you want me needlessly to risk the lives of so many brave men?" a stymied Bruix asked incredulously.

"Monsieur, I have given you an order. Once again I am going to ask you why you have not executed it. The consequences concern me and me alone. Carry it out!"

"Sire, I cannot," Bruix, standing erect, replied.

"Monsieur, you are insolent!" Napoleon snapped, raising his riding crop as if to lash at the determined admiral.

"Sire, mind what you do!" Bruix responded, his eyes narrowing and jaw set as he stepped back, placing his hand on the hilt of his sword. Napoleon's staff, surrounding him and enjoying the rare public rebuff of the great man, now suddenly froze in their tracks. Napoleon just stood there, pale, startled, and speechless. Finally throwing his riding crop to the ground, he addressed the only other admiral present.

"Rear Admiral Magon, you will carry out this order this very instant!" Turning, he ordered Bruix to leave for Holland before the day was out (an order he later rescinded).

Magon duly gave the orders, and the flat-bottomed vessels left the safety of the Liane basin and new breakwater to enter the raging sea. Soon dozens of boats were capsized and tossed about, many smashed to bits against one another or when they were hurled onto the rocks and beach. Officially the naval chief of staff announced the destruction of thirty boats and the deaths of thirty-one men, but like most official military figures issued by Napoleon, they were falsified. The British, who were offshore watching the whole spectacle and approached closely during the calm the next day, reported a minimum of four hundred sailors and soldiers dead and many, many dozens of boats capsized or smashed.

Napoleon himself gave Josephine quite a different version of this most preventable of tragedies. "The wind freshened during the night, and one of our gunboats dragged its anchor, but we managed to save everything. The spectacle was grand: the alarm guns, the coast a blaze of fire, the sea tossed with fury, and roaring. At 5 A.M. it cleared up. Everyone was saved and I went to bed with all the sensations inspired by a romantic, epic dream."[24]

Clearly Napoleon's view of the universe was different from that of mere mortals.

Despite such momentary setbacks, and the declining number of boats available, preparations continued for the famous Kent landings, although by December 1804 the proposed armada on which France and its allies had by now spent hundreds of millions of francs was already down to 2,054 vessels capable of ferrying only 127,000 men (not the designated 167,500) and 15,764 horses, from the six ports of Ostend, Dunkirk, Ambleteuse, Etaples, Wimereux, and Boulogne. The winters of 1803–4 and of 1804–5, the most horrendous in living memory, had battered these flimsy craft, leaving hundreds of wooden carcasses strewn on the upper banks of each of the coastal rivers and streams of the ports. Funds set aside for maintaining their full daily provisions of food and muntions for the past year and a half—which Napoleon had insisted on, over the protests of Forfait and Decrès—had not allowed either for ship maintenance or replacement. Torn rigging and sails, broken hulls and bottoms, left only one alternative in most cases—abandonment.

The results were obvious but painful. For although the chief of the general staff of the national flotilla reported on August 8, 1805, a total of 2,343 vessels still available, including 1,016 flat-bottomed gunboats, capable of launching 167,500 men and 9,149 horses, a by now most wary Naval Minister Decrès, on further investigation, discovered that only 672 were in seaworthy condition, which, with 1,058 transports (chiefly supplied by the Dutch), gave the flotilla a combined total of only 1,730 vessels. Unknown to Admiral LaCrosse, his chief of staff, Lafond, a bureaucratic officer intent on gaining imperial praise, had deliberately falsified his report, including 613 nonexistent gunboats, boats that had either sunk or been abandoned.

By whatever reckoning, by the summer of 1805 the flotilla simply could not withstand another winter's accrued loss of a few hundred more vessels. If Decrès had estimated the flotilla of being capable of transporting only 127,000 troops back in December 1804, now the most realistic estimate had dwindled to a maximum of perhaps 100,000 men. The flotilla had lost more than one-third of its projected capacity. Nor in fact were there any longer much more than that number of troops still in the camps at Montreuil, St.-Omer, and Bruges, as Marshals Ney and Soult privately informed Napoleon, over Berthier's protests.[25] Napoleon was furious.

Despite the dismaying flotilla reports, as well as revelations as to the true character of Villeneuve's pusillanimous actions both in Martinique and then off Ferrol against Calder, however, in a final personal letter to Decrès, Napoleon reminded him that he and France were still depending on his arrival, "when you must sweep away all that you find before you and come up the Channel where we are awaiting you most anxiously. . . . We should all of us gladly give our lives in order to help bring about an invasion of that power that has been suppressing France for six centuries. Such," he concluded, "are the sentiments that ought to animate my soldiers."[26]

It was hardly surprising that by now many Frenchmen were questioning whether the emperor was serious about the whole operation, army and naval commanders reporting frustration and suspicion among officers and men alike. Had Napoleon changed his mind about invading England, as he had so frequently changed his mind about everything else?

Thus by the late summer of 1805 even the British, who for more than two years had been taking the greatest pains to defend themselves against this impending descent, began to question the French ruler's intentions. To rub salt into the wound, *The Times* now published a long spoof on its front page, poking fun at the emperor himself, entitled "Buonaparte's Soliloquy on the Cliff at Boulogne."

> *T'invade, or not t'invade — that is the question —*
> *Whether 'tis nobler in my soul, to suffer*
> *Those haughty Islands to check my power,*
> *Or to send forth my troops upon their coast,*
> *And by attacking, crush them. — T'invade — to fight —*
> *No more; — and by a fight, to say I end*
> *The glory, and the thousand natural blessings*
> *That England's heir to; — 'tis a consummation*
> *Devoutly to be wish'd. — To invade — to fight —*
> *To fight — perchance to fail: — Aye, there's the rub,*
> *For in that failure, what dire fate may come,*
> *When they have shuffled all from Gallia's shore,*
> *Must give me pause. — There's the respect,*
> *That makes me thus procrastinate the deed:*
> *For would I bear the scoff and scorn of foes,*
> *The oppressive thought of English liberty,*
> *The pangs of despis'd threats, th'attempt's delay,*
> *The insolence of Britain, and the spurns,*
> *That I impatient and unwilling take,*
> *When I myself might head the plund'ring horde,*
> *And grasp at conquest? Would I tamely bear*
> *To groan and sweat under a long suspense,*
> *But that the dream of something after battle,*

That undecided trial, from whose hazard
I never may return,—puzzles my will,
And makes me rather bear unsated vengeance,
Than fly from Boulogne at the risk of all.
Thus the contemplation stays my deep designs,
And thus my native passion of ambition
Is clouded o'er with sad, presaging thought;
And this momentous, tow'ring enterprise,
With this regard, is yearly turn'd aside,
And waits the name of action.[27]

On August 11—four days before Napoleon's thirty-fourth birthday—
Villeneuve was preparing a fateful letter to his friend, Decrès, as he weighed
anchor to clear El Ferrol harbor. "I cannot pull out of this deep depression
into which I have sunk," Villeneuve began. This expedition had been a mistake from the outset, he lamented. "But the 'sailors' in Paris [Napoleon,
Forfait, and so on] . . . who have been interfering in this are indeed blind,
reprehensible, and stupid." Nor could the French depend on the Spanish,
he insisted, who so lacked even the most elementary naval instruction "as to
prevent them from being ready to put to sea." His own officers and sailors,
"who lack wartime experience," were no better:

> It is quite impossible to have been unhappier than I have been since the
> moment of our departure [from Toulon]. . . . I cannot conceal my belief
> that we have no chance of winning. . . . My lord, put an end to this situ-
> ation." As for his very precise orders to sail north to Boulogne, he
> closed—"I am leaving, and depending upon the circumstances, am
> heading for Brest or Cadiz.[28]

Having said that, and made the junction with Gravina's fleet in La
Coruña Bay, Villeneuve and his combined Franco-Spanish Fleet put to sea.
For the next several days no one, not even Napoleon, had the least idea
what had happened to them, where they were, or even what direction they
were sailing in. It was not until August 21 that Villeneuve's powerful task
force was finally sighted by the British as it reached the harbor of Cádiz.[29]

Vice Admiral Villeneuve's report, completed and dispatched from
Cádiz on August 22, reached Paris in record time on September 2. Setting
out immediately from the Naval Ministry, Decrès girded himself against the
inevitable storm about to break when he reached Napoleon's small study
on the second floor of the Tuileries.

"What a Navy! What an admiral! All those sacrifices for naught!" the emperor ranted. "It is sheer betrayal. . . . That Villeneuve is the worst sort of scoundrel. He would sacrifice everything just to save his own hide. . . . Never again mention another thing about *such a humiliating business!* Never again remind me of the existence of that miserable coward!"[30]

Napoleon immediately ordered Decrès to replace Villeneuve. On September 16 he scrapped the entire invasion plan and in his ninth set of orders, instructed the combined fleet to sail from Cádiz to Genoa, the next day naming Admiral Rosily as Villeneuve's successor. On September 20 Decrès wrote to his old friend Villeneuve for the last time, ordering him to strike his flag. He was finished.[31]

But before officially receiving his new orders (which in fact were leaked to Villeneuve by General Beurnonville, the snickering French minister to Madrid), he ordered the combined fleet to sail. "If the only thing the Imperial Navy was lacking was a little character and backbone, I believe I could provide them," the incredible Villeneuve wrote hastily to Decrès, "thereby assuring the crowning of the present mission with a brilliant success." "Upon my word, my dear Minister," a bemused General Beurnonville wrote Decrès after receiving news that the combined fleet had cleared the harbor of Cádiz, "Vice Admiral Villeneuve has flown the coop. The nest is empty!"[32]

The first to spot the emergence of the enemy fleet, Capt. Henry Blackwood of the *Euryalus* signaled the long-awaited news to Lord Nelson on board the *Victory*. On October 21, off the Cape of Trafalgar, Nelson's fleet of twenty-seven ships fell upon the French admiral's augmented combined fleet of thirty-two ships of the battle line. By the end of that day, the Royal Navy had fought and won the greatest victory in naval history, at the price of the death of Lord Nelson but with not a single British ship lost. Combined French and Spanish losses came to some twenty-two ships, while ten others, under the direction of Rear Adm. Dumanoir Le Pelley, had abandoned their own Navy in the face of the enemy, fleeing northward to safety. The English had suffered 1,690 casualties; the French and Spanish, 5,568 dead and wounded.[33] To complete the fiasco, an unscathed Villeneuve had been taken prisoner and sent to England.

The French Imperial Navy would gradually be rebuilt, but with its spirit and morale shattered, it would never again pose a serious threat to Great Britain during Napoleon's reign—or indeed to any country for many decades to come. However, the man responsible for defending British shores throughout the crucial twenty-nine months of crisis, from 1803 to 1805, Admiral Cornwallis, was soon ordered to strike his flag and retire, his name as quickly forgotten by history and an ungrateful British people.

It was not in Paris that Napoleon learned of this great disaster, however, but on the field of battle far away in Austria, for back on August 26 he had finally given up all hope of ever seeing Villeneuve and his mighty fleet. On the twenty-ninth he had ordered Berthier to break camp and march east. Angrily turning his back on a colossal failure that had cost him two years of unrelenting hard work and consumed nearly every moment of his time in the process, Napoleon instead launched the Grande Armée on the first of a series of remarkable military victories that would more than compensate for a dozen Trafalgars—but never for his cherished dream of putting an end "to the destiny and very existence of England."

Intermezzo à la Bonaparte

After all, I have the heart of a human being. I was not begotten by a tigress.

 apoleon had been more than envious of Joseph's magnificent reception in October 1800 for the signing of the Franco-American Commerce and Friendship Treaty, in particular because of the spacious accommodations and extensive open lands of Joseph's estate that he, Napoleon, lacked at Malmaison for hunts and long horseback rides.

To remedy that he attempted to acquire estates contiguous to Malmaison. The first two neighbors he approached, Mlle. Julien and M. de Channorrier, both refused. A frustrated Napoleon settled on his third choice, a parcel of several hundred acres of forest known as Butard Wood. There were few physical objects in the world that impressed the blasé Corsican general—not gold, jewels, fine porcelain, paintings, or even women—but to be a grand seigneur, to have a sprawling estate of thousands of acres—that was something else.

The deed done and contracts exchanged, he proudly bundled Josephine, Laure Junot, and Bourrienne into a calèche, as he mounted a horse and galloped off in the direction of the new wood. It lay between the château and the Seine, requiring the crossing of a brook and some steep ravines. At the brook Josephine, who had a terror of riding in carriages, even on the best of roads, shrieked as the light carriage abruptly descended into a gully. Napoleon—angry, frustrated, and tired of Josephine's constant hysterics over the most trivial matters—ordered the coachman on. Madame Bonaparte, by now in tears, ordered the bewildered postilion to stop immediately before reaching the water. He did, looking first at Bonaparte—who had already crossed the brook ahead of them on horseback and had cleared the steep bank with some difficulty—and then at Josephine, who by now was crying hysterically. A furious First Consul returned angrily and pulled up before the carriage, again ordering the driver to proceed. When he hesitated, in a quandary at receiving two contradictory orders, Napoleon slashed at him with his whip.[1]

But Josephine remained trembling and nothing could soothe her. Napoleon, wanting to show off his broad new acres, the result of months of acrimonious negotiation, was furious with his wife for spoiling his surprise, his great moment. Josephine, however, could not be moved now, and they reached the wood only later in the day. But the unpleasantness was soon forgotten.

Thus the weeks passed. "We led a merry life, and the summer slipped pleasantly away," the seventeen-year-old mother-to-be Laure Junot recalled. They played cards—never for money—at which Napoleon nevertheless always insisted on winning (as he also did with chess, which he played badly). When playing a game called *reversis*, for instance, he would cheat blatantly. And then he would inevitably win and cry out gleefully like a child—"I have all the fish! Who will buy all the fish in the house?"[2] If it was not exactly interesting for the other players, knowing in advance they were fated to lose, at least the First Consul was content.

The summer dragged on too long, however, especially after Josephine's departure for Plombières in the mountains for six weeks to restore her nerves. Malmaison, so gay, so cheerful when the mistress was present, now became unbearable. For the young bride of General Junot (serving as Napoleon's aide-de-camp but stationed at headquarters in Paris), it became unendurable, with only Hortense and herself there, along with the first consul. She wanted to get away, but Napoleon would not hear of it. "We were not exactly prisoners," she lamented, but they were caught in "a gilded cage."[3]

It began before dawn a couple of weeks prior to Josephine's return. "One morning I was in a profound sleep, when suddenly I was awakened by a slight noise near me, and perceived the First Consul beside my bed," Laure Junot recalled. "Thinking myself in a dream, I rubbed my eyes, which produced a laugh from him." "We are going to chat," Napoleon said, sitting down in a nearby armchair. Taking out a handful of mail and newspapers, he put them on her bed and began sorting. His only suggestive remark was about an assignation he was contemplating with a woman unknown to her. An hour later he heard the clock in the hall chime six. He got up, "collected the papers, pinched my foot through the bedclothes, and smiling . . . went away singing in that squealing voice, so strongly contrasted with the fine sonorous accent of his speech—

> *"Non, non z'il est impossiblé*
> *D'avoir un plus aimable enfant.*
> *Un plus aimable? Ah! si, vraiment.'"*

It was seduction à la Napoleon. But what would it lead to? Was it a simple one-time approach? At the crack of dawn? The rest of the day passed uneventfully.

The following morning Laure was again awakened by a knock, and the first consul entered, as before, with letters and newspapers in his hand. After admiring her "teeth of pearl," he sat down and began reading the papers. When he was finished "the First Consul again pinched my foot through the bedclothes and left the room, singing a few false notes." Determined to put an end to this, Laure summoned her maid and "without explanation prohibited her from ever opening the door to anyone who might knock so early in the morning." When the maid asked hesitantly what to do if it was the first consul, she replied, "I will not be awakened so early by the First Consul or anyone else. Do as you are told!"

The next day passed, Napoleon making no reference whatever to his previous two nights of prowling. Laure became anxious and depressed. "I found no pleasure at Malmaison. . . . I spent the night in tears." After an anxious, restless third night, she withdrew the outer key, double-turned the lock, and took the key with her back to bed. Some time later the door burst open and there stood the first consul, glaring, his face red with anger.

"Are you afraid of being assassinated, then?" he asked. She was speechless. "Tomorrow is the hunting party in Butard Wood," he reminded her. "We set out early, and that you may be ready, I shall come myself to wake you, and as you are not among a horde of Tartars, do not barricade yourself again. . . . Adieu!" She afterward discovered that Napoleon had got in with his own master key.

*Hortense's attempt to render Napoleon's Corsican accent.

She told no one about what transpired. To her surprise and great relief, her husband arrived from Paris to talk with Napoleon, who afterward invited him to dinner.

"The First Consul was in high spirits, joked throughout dinner with M. Monge, and made him explain more than ten times over the nature of trade winds. . . ." After dinner they played billiards as usual, and then Laure played another game of chess with Napoleon.

But when Junot was about to leave—aides-de-camp stationed in Paris were required to return to headquarters every night—she called him aside and asked him to take her home. At first he "thought someone had offended me, and his unbounded rage and resentment against the alleged defaulter absolutely terrified me." He gradually calmed down, however, and she convinced him that she simply wanted to go home to see her mother; she was homesick. They talked a long time, but Junot refused. It was an honor to be a house guest of the first consul, he insisted. Finding no other expedient, she instead persuaded him to spend the night with her. After some resistance he agreed.

Early the next morning, the door to her chamber opened noisily, and steps approached her bed. "What! Still asleep, Madame Junot, on hunting day! I told you that—" he stopped in midsentence as he drew the curtain aside and saw Junot. Junot, scarcely awake, propped himself on one elbow and looked at the first consul with an air of astonishment. "Why, General! What are you doing in a lady's chamber at this hour?" Quickly gathering his wits, Napoleon smiled sheepishly. "I came to awaken Madame Junot for the hunt . . . but," and then after a prolonged silence and a glance at Laure Junot, "but I find her provided with a better alarm clock than myself." Various small talk ensued, and Junot himself was invited to join this famous hunt. Napoleon left. "That is an admirable man!" the simplistic Junot replied.

During the hunt Napoleon cornered her in her carriage, bending down from his horse. "You think yourself very clever, do you not? Can you explain the reason why you made your husband stay over?" he snapped angrily. "The explanation is clear and brief, General. I love Junot. We are married, and I thought there was no scandal in a husband remaining with his wife." The conversation grew more acrimonious, and then *she* confronted him. "Yesterday morning you employed a method that might be called unworthy, to enter my apartment."

"Enough!" he interrupted, striking the frame of the carriage as they approached the gathering hunters. "Hold your tongue!" he shouted at her.

As they neared the group, Napoleon insisted that she give him her word of honor that Junot would know nothing of "this foolish affair." "Good heavens,

General! How can you even conceive of such an idea, knowing Junot as you do? He is an Othello in the violence of his passions . . ." clearly indicating that he would challenge Napoleon to a duel and kill him. She extended her arm as he was about to ride away, but "he refused my hand." "On our return from the hunt, General, I have asked Junot to take me home," she said. "You may dispose of my apartment here, I shall not be occupying it again."

Napoleon had had mixed feelings about Junot from the beginning, despite Junot's unabashed devotion to and admiration for him. Relations would remain strained for quite some time. Junot would never become a *Maréchal de France,* whether he deserved it or not, and for years to come Napoleon's personal relations with Madame Junot were polite but cool.[4]

There was a very special atmosphere about Malmaison, totally secluded amid its sprawling park of ancient sombrous trees, where stone walls and iron grillework gates kept the world at bay. Here, more than at any other residence inhabited by Bonaparte, time seemed to stand still and take on more human proportions. As Napoleon's young new secretary, Claude Méneval, remarked, "he found this patriarchal existence attractive. At his retreat of Malmaison Napoleon seemed like any other father in the midst of his family." "The only other place I found Bonaparte as contented as he was on a battlefield, was in the gardens of Malmaison," Bourrienne confirmed.[5] And it was here that Joséphine appeared at her best to her husband, in the gardens that she so loved, collecting flowers, or painting. Here her great spending follies could somehow be forgotten, at least for the moment, including the 1.2-million-franc debt incurred during the Egyptian fiasco (of which Napoleon ultimately paid only 300,000 francs), and the 250,000-franc pearl necklace (formerly owned by Marie-Antoinette) that Berthier had secretly paid for (to avoid Bonaparte's anger) by diverting funds from the army budget intended for military hospitals in Italy.[6]

"He had everything required . . . to be a pleasant man, except the wish to do so," Bourrienne commented. "He was far too domineering to attract people, however." But his secretary and old school friend added, "I can assure you that Bonaparte, when removed from the political world, could be sensitive, good, and capable of showing pity. He liked children very much. . . . He could be genial and even most indulgent so far as human weaknesses were concerned."[7]

Laure Junot also related another incident at Malmaison, this one witnessed by her husband and revealing yet another aspect of the man's complicated character.

One day a young man appeared on foot before the sentries at the estate's main gates, asking to see the first consul. After talking to three of Napoleon's aides-de-camp—de Lacué, Duroc, and Junot—who were summoned to question the suspicious character, his persistent request was finally related to Bonaparte himself.

The young man, who by his bearing, appearance, and educated speech was obviously a gentleman and probably an aristocrat, wanted to enter the newly expanded Ecole Polytechnique but lacked the formal coursework required for admission. The Abbé Bossu, who was responsible for making the final decision on applicants, had categorically rejected this young man, who in fact had never been enrolled in any school but who had instead been educated by his highly cultivated father. This was unacceptable to the good abbé, himself a product of the revolutionary classes. Not completely discouraged, the young man had walked all the way to Malmaison to appeal the case to Napoleon himself. "I am sure that when he has put any questions to me that he may judge proper, he will find that I meet the entrance requirements."

Duroc, still a bit dubious, nevertheless informed Bonaparte. "So the young enthusiast would have me question him?" Rubbing his chin and smiling, he paced back and forth for a while, considering this rather extraordinary request. Then he asked Duroc, "How old is he?" "Perhaps seventeen or eighteen, General." "Let him come in." A few minutes later the young man crossed the miniature drawbridge entrance to the mansion and was escorted to the library.

"Well, young man, so you wish to be examined by me, do you?" The youth was so stirred that he could not even open his mouth, now that his great moment had actually come. Seeing that the boy—amazed no doubt at his own success—was too excited to reply, Napoleon wisely had Duroc lead him to another room to calm down. Half an hour later he was summoned again. This time the young man could speak, giving his name, Eugène de Kervalègne, and explaining that his father, a cultured, retired gentleman and an excellent mathematician, had personally instructed him over the years. Napoleon then started asking him a series of difficult questions. The young man easily answered them all to Bonaparte's satisfaction. The first consul then sat down and wrote a note. He instructed the young man to give it to the Abbé Bossu personally. The dumbfounded lad thanked him profusely and left quickly on his quest. "Do you see that young man?" Bonaparte said to Junot. "If I had a thousand such as he the conquest of the world would be a mere promenade."

Rushing back to Paris, the student returned to the Ecole Polytechnique and entered the office of the Abbé Bossu and silently handed him the note. The arrogant abbé's mouth dropped as he read the following: "M. Bossu will receive M. Eugène de Kervalègne. I have examined him myself, and find him worthy of admission. Bonaparte."

No one could argue with Napoleon. Kervalègne proved an excellent student and later enjoyed a distinguished career as an engineer with the Department of Bridges and Roads.[8]

Whether at the Tuileries, St.-Cloud, or at Malmaison, Bonaparte fluctuated between great activity and almost profound, languishing repose.

"He was indefatigable, not only on horseback and on campaigns, but [in the office, or the garden], he sometimes walked for five or six hours at a time without even noticing it."[9] It was usually just after such long periods of thought that he would summon Bourrienne and begin dictating his most important new projects, decrees, and decisions.

When at work at Malmaison, Bourrienne, who owned a small house in nearby Rueil, would awaken the first consul at seven o'clock, at which time his valet, Louis Constant, would pour his bath. Frequently taking two hours in a steaming tub (with the breakdown of the Peace of Amiens he spent six!), Bourrienne would read translations of the latest English and German newspapers. Afterward Constant would shave him and comb his thin brown hair.

In his study, the long library of Malmaison, he would immediately set to work, reading his correspondence and petitions drawn up by his secretary the previous night. He would then interview the petitioners, though few ever reached him at Malmaison. The restless Napoleon would often sit on Bourrienne's side of the desk, making it difficult for his secretary to write. Occasionally First Consul Bonaparte, the commander of the nation's armies and navy, would plunk himself down on an embarrassed Bourrienne's lap, putting his arm around his neck, even running his hand through his hair. It was bizarre to say the least. Méneval later reported similar incidents. At other times Napoleon, leaving Bourrienne in peace to get on with his work, would hum or sing a line or two from one of his favorite operas (although he didn't enjoy concerts), invariably off key, sometimes in a harsh falsetto, while with his penknife he dug away pieces of wood from the right arm of a chair. Finally, at 10:00 A.M. the butler would arrive, announcing—"*Le général est servi*" and he would repair to the tentlike dining room, where he would often be joined by Monge, Berthollet, and his various aides-de-camp. His favorite dish was *poulet à la provençale*. Dinner, too, was served early, at 5:00 P.M.[10]

As the Bonapartes usually spent the weekends at Malmaison during the early Consulate, Sunday became the day for amusement, although Napoleon as a rule loathed formal gatherings in Josephine's music gallery. Josephine, who unlike her husband could sing in tune, loved the opera; her favorite instrument was the harp, on which however she could play only one or two melodies, which she repeated annoyingly year after year. Fortunately, in the spring of 1802, the Neapolitan composer Giovanni Paisiello was brought to Paris by the first consul, who appointed him director of both the Opéra and of the Conservatory of Music. Although Paisiello played for Napoleon and his guests on weekends at Malmaison and stayed long enough to compose a mediocre opera, *Prosperine,* despite impressive fees and appeals from the first consul, he soon returned to the more placid charms of his native Italy. Another Italian artist brought to Paris, Antonio Canova, was commissioned to do various pieces of sculpture, including large likenesses of Napoleon and Pauline in white marble, but he too left as soon as possible. Napoleonic France did not agree with them.[11]

The greatest pastime and passion of Malmaison was the theater, which involved nearly everyone directly or indirectly. Josephine ordered the construction of a theater seating some two hundred guests, among whom Napoleon was an eager first subscriber. It was one of the very few things that Napoleon and Josephine greatly enjoyed together. He certainly did not permit her even to discuss politics with him. "Let her weave, let her knit," he would say, dismissing the very idea with a wave of the hand.[12]

The theater, however, remained a passion everyone in the family seemed to be involved in to one degree or another. Napoleon soon set himself up as a little god, the final authority capable of censoring the Parisian theater, in particular the Théâtre Français and the Comédie Francaise, and even the Opéra. Thus he had piece after piece suppressed, especially Voltaire's tragedies, including *Zaïre, Mérope, Mort de César,* and *Brutus,* feeling that such serious pieces could incite audiences. Comedies and farces were better suited to keep the French public from dwelling on thought-provoking subjects.[13] His favorite author, however, was Corneille, whom he admired for both his seriousness and perceptiveness, and for "his profound understanding of the human heart, the depth of his political views," as Napoleon put it: "If a man like Corneille were alive today, I would make him my prime minister." Bonaparte loved in particular Corneille's *Cinna,* which was produced time and again at Malmaison.

Theatrical productions at Malmaison were thus taken most seriously, the plays directed either by the greatest tragedian of the day, Talma himself, or by Michot (director of the Théâtre Français). The cast included

Josephine's children, Eugène (his favorite role was that of a valet) and Hortense, Bourrienne (whom Napoleon finally gave a few hours off on Sunday afternoons in order to practice for the latest production), General Lauriston (one of Napoleon's more ambitious aides-de-camp), Vivant Denon (heading the newly organized Louvre), some of the generals' wives, and occasionally one of Napoleon's sisters, including the overbearing Elisa. But Bourrienne, Eugène, and Hortense remained the mainstay of the troupe. They were given an unlimited budget and granted a sumptuous wardrobe, administered by Josephine. The first consul rarely missed a performance when in town.

Méneval, who was to succeed Bourrienne as Napoleon's principal secretary (but not on the stage) in 1802, praised the first consul for "the simplicity of his manner" during his sojourns in the country. "I found him patient, indulgent, easy to live with, not at all demanding, of a gaiety often turning quite raucous."[14] (Young Méneval was probably the only person ever to describe Bonaparte as "easy to live with" and undemanding.)

Although he could be relaxed at Malmaison, wandering about the grounds, inspecting the rare new plants and animals collected by Josephine, including her famous Egyptian gazelle (which he habitually fed his snuff), his absence from Malmaison was noted by practically everyone with evident pleasure, as Napoleon himself was well aware. "Alas, it is not at all pleasant living with a great man," remarked Bourrienne, who knew whereof he wrote, having spent every day with him for the better part of eleven years.[15] Living with an egotistical whirlwind was not easy.

Like just about everyone else, however, Bourrienne did have a real soft spot for the feckless, not very bright, but warm and lovable Josephine, and felt much more at ease in her company. "The good Josephine," he recalled, "who can be reproached only perhaps with having been a bit too feminine. . . . The excellent Josephine carried out the honors of her position with such grace and geniality. Everyone breathed more easily, became more cheerful in the absence of the master. . . . All changed again immediately upon his return."

Napoleon one day asked Fontanes: "What do you think they would say if I suddenly died?" There being no reply from the abashed architect, Napoleon answered his own question: "Well, I shall tell you. They would simply say, 'Ah! we can breathe at last! That's the end of him, and good riddance.'"[16]

It was not only that Napoleon, like both Talleyrand and Fouché, could carry on long, relentless monologues—even a patient Bourrienne admitting that sometimes he talked "a little too much," despite the often riveting quality of his narrative. But on occasion he deliberately went out of his way to upset people, especially women. "He rarely had anything kind to say to them," Bourrienne noted. Napoleon would point out that their arms were red, or that their hairstyles were ugly, or that he didn't like their dresses. He might suddenly ask every woman in the room her age. He frequently humiliated them in public by telling them of their husbands' mistresses. He would never admit to being in the wrong, however, or to having made any sort of error. Sometimes in anger he would clench his fists and threaten to strike someone, as he actually did to Berthier on more than one occasion, or he would horsewhip a coach driver who did not obey his orders. He might later repent and pay the abused person gold, even lots of it (Berthier, for example, became one of the wealthiest men in France), but that did not bring love, friendship, respect, or a sense of loyalty.

Napoleon was extraordinarily jealous of anyone who outshone him or captured the limelight. Thus, when at Marengo, Kellermann helped save the battle, Napoleon scarcely acknowledged his actions, failing even to promote him, unlike less deserving officers there. And yet it was thanks largely to Desaix and Kellermann that Marengo was not a great French disaster. Marshal Davout was not rewarded for winning the Battle of Auerstädt until years later. Augereau and Moreau were both belittled publicly at one time or another, despite their noted martial achievements.[17]

Bourrienne was puzzled by a man he considered the greatest soldier of the day but who felt so insecure that he had to commit blatant injustices against others when they achieved some individual distinction. "One has to be firm," Napoleon would then counter. "One must have a firm heart, otherwise one should not get mixed up in wars and politics," which of course explained nothing.

He would complain to Bourrienne, "I know very well that I don't have any true friends." But he then would add, "'Friendship' is just a meaningless word. I don't love anyone. No, I don't even love my own brothers. Well, perhaps Joseph just a little." Yet there were men who literally would—and did—readily give their lives for him, who were fanatically dedicated to him. Generals Rapp and Marbot at the beginning, Méneval and Lannes for a long time, and foremost of all, Andoche Junot.

Napoleon perplexed just about everyone at one time or another, leading more than one person to wonder about his stability—this man was who was constantly at war—with his friends as well as with neighboring countries, ordering hundreds of thousands of men to their deaths over the years;

this man who could give generals and admirals several contradictory sets of orders for the same campaign; this man who could attempt to strike his own officers; this man who could one day save a family from penury and destitution, and then harass a helpless pregnant woman, such as Jérôme's American wife, or oppress the miniature Dutch state so relentlessly. "The rumor was spread that the Emperor had gone mad, and while not exactly believing it, no one seemed really surprised by the idea," Victorine de Chastenay commented later, after it was whispered that Bonaparte was being treated by the celebrated Viennese alienist, Dr. Philippe Pinel.[18]

If there was one thing Napoleon could not abide it was treachery, especially in the form of abandonment by one of his closest followers (although of course he himself had thought nothing of abandoning an entire army in Egypt). He would react with a sadistic response worthy of a madman. Such was the case with his old classmate and secretary, Bourrienne, who— exhausted after more than ten years of work that did not allow for a single day off—announced that for reasons of health he had to resign.

He first gave notice to Napoleon in the late spring of 1801. Napoleon merely laughed. "Well, now, Bourrienne, [Dr.] Corvisart says that you do not have a year to live!"[19] But nothing changed, the long ceaseless hours, the days of unremitting work, the nonexistence of his family life. Then it happened.

On February 27, 1802, Napoleon dictated a message for Talleyrand and ordered Bourrienne to have it dispatched as usual. There were messengers in the palace for that very service, and Bourrienne arranged to have it sent. But when Talleyrand arrived the next day, it was learned that he had never received the message (he in fact had spent Saturday night away from home). Napoleon summoned Bourrienne before Talleyrand himself, demanding an explanation. Bourrienne explained, but Napoleon, furious with Talleyrand for not having left a message with his servants as to his whereabouts, instead turned all his fury on Bourrienne. "Get out of here! You are a god-damn idiot!" It was Bourrienne's turn to be furious—insulted and humiliated about something he was not responsible for. Then and there he wrote out his resignation again.

Napoleon had Duroc inform him that he accepted it. Bourrienne was pleased, but when Duroc conducted him down to the first consul at 8:00 P.M., Bonaparte screamed at him again: "All right, damn it, that's the way it is then, get out!" Trembling with fury, Bourrienne left, showed Duroc where all the papers and registers were, and found a temporary apartment elsewhere. The following day Napoleon, his old genial self again, summoned Bourrienne to say good-bye, first asking him what post he would like next. When Bourrienne indicated the Tribunate, however, Napoleon turned him down.

That Tuesday, while Bourrienne was in the process of moving out of his small apartment in the Tuileries, he was summoned again at 4:00 P.M. He found Napoleon, Josephine, and Hortense; it was all nicely staged, the women imploring him to continue working. But Bourrienne was adamant. Then, just as he was leaving the palace, Duroc approached him. "*Mon cher*, he wants you to stay. I beg of you, don't resist. Do this for me." Bourrienne reluctantly accepted and returned to Bonaparte. It was to prove the worst mistake of his life. A triumphant Bonaparte invited him to dine with him, something he had not done in a long time.

But the grueling schedule resumed, and Bourrienne "sincerely regretted" having returned, as a result of Napoleon's "affected geniality." He quickly realized that he had been recalled to hold the fort until Napoleon found a replacement for him. No one ever quit Napoleon and got away with it. He finally found Claude-François de Méneval, "a young man of good family, hard-working, mild-mannered, and discreet," as Bourrienne described him. The next thing Bourrienne knew, Napoleon fired him. "He never forgave me for having dared leave him . . . and awaited the moment he could punish me for it." Though assuring him that "I am disposed to place you promptly in a new appropriate post, suitable to the public service, when the moment is right."[20]

But no one got off that lightly when abandoning Bonaparte, who now encouraged a vicious whispering campaign behind Bourrienne's back. The charge was made that Bourrienne had been speculating recklessly on the Stock Exchange (quite true) and had stolen government funds to finance the transaction (quite false).

On April 20, 1803, Bourrienne was summoned without warning to the palace at St.-Cloud, where Duroc was given the disagreeable task of charging Bourrienne with having pilfered government funds, stealing one hundred thousand francs from a naval treasury! Bourrienne was first staggered, and then furious, sending a note to Bonaparte demanding to see him immediately. Duroc left with it and returned some time later.[21]

Bourrienne: "Well!"

Duroc: "Calm down. He asked me to tell you that it was a mistake. Someone has just established that they deceived him about the whole thing. It's over—not to worry about it any further."

Bourrienne of course never had access to any large sums, or to any treasury or government accounts of any kind. Indeed the only funds available to him were "petty cash" in the coffer on the table in the office. As Bonaparte knew perfectly well, Bourrienne was an honest man. The problem was aggravated, however, because he had been speculating on margin at the stock exchange, along with Berthier, Joseph Bonaparte, and many others. He was accused of taking advantage of his position to manipulate the market.[22] In fact Bourrienne was neither interested in nor capable of carrying out complicated transactions of this nature. The worst that could be said of him is that through lack of experience and advice he had invested most unwisely.

Napoleon—who had a very short memory when it suited him—had by now forgotten the many kindnesses Bourrienne had shown an impoverished young army officer just a few years earlier, inviting him to dine frequently over a period of several months when he was otherwise without the means to do so.

And he was not through with the bewildered Bourrienne. Napoleon now sent men over to his former secretary's small house in Rueil (which he had given him and had furnished) to strip it of all its possessions, while a tearful Mme. de Bourrienne looked on in amazement. Nor did Napoleon keep his word about finding employment soon for his former secretary, who, harried by creditors, was forced to flee with his wife, finally settling in Germany. Without Napoleon's support, he could not get work, for everyone feared the great man, and without work he could neither pay his debts or feed and clothe his family. Napoleon continued to turn the screw. The years passed, and finally Bourrienne, weakened by bad health and utter impoverishment, was appointed French minister to the foggy, dank north German city of Hamburg, where the French were loathed. He remained there a broken man.

It was more than ironic that Bonaparte had deliberately assigned him to that particular post, for in 1800 the first consul had extorted four million francs from the Free Imperial City of Hamburg, as damages for having permitted the English to kidnap from there two Irish agents carrying French passports. Hamburg, threatened by French military reprisals, paid up, but the money never reached the French treasury. Napoleon personally pocketed the entire sum, which he used in large part to pay off Josephine's impressive debts and to refurbish Malmaison, including ample extensions. What was left was distributed among the clan. And this was the man who called Bourrienne a thief![23]

Throughout his career Napoleon sadistically pursued several other unfortunate victims and their families. The number included former Naval Minister

Pierre Forfait, whom he kept demoting, and his Corsican political foe and former family house guest, Pozzo di Borgo, whom he hounded from one employ to another, until that gentleman finally secured the post of Russian ambassador (to various countries) for Czar Alexander (one employer who could not be intimidated by Napoleon). His unrelenting destruction of Holland may likewise be considered an example of this deranged streak in Napoleon's character. His vengeful attack years later against his first valet, Constant, when the latter refused to abandon his own family in France to follow Napoleon into exile, is yet another. The emperor publicly called him "a thief" as well, and the amount involved was by coincidence the same as in the case of Bourrienne, and the accusation was a fabrication also, Napoleon having given one hundred thousand francs—before witnesses— to his faithful valet in lieu of a pension, but then changed his mind and demanded its return. The singular case of Elizabeth Patterson, however, surpassed everything thus far.

It all began when Napoleon's nineteen-year-old brother, Jérôme, was enrolled by him in the French navy in February 1802, where he soon gained the reputation of being a hellion. While serving in the West Indies the following year, he abandoned the fleet and sailed to the United States, landing at Norfolk, Virginia. During a visit to Washington, D.C., the French chargé d'affaires, Pichon, advanced Jérôme several thousand dollars and introduced him to society. Soon he was invited to Baltimore, where Jérôme Bonaparte met the leading families of Maryland society, including the lovely and charming nineteen-year-old "Belle of Baltimore," Elizabeth Patterson, the daughter of William Patterson, a wealthy merchant, and his Irish-born wife, Dorcas Spear.[24] Painted by Gilbert Stuart, she proved even lovelier than the portrait itself—possessed of a fine figure, exquisite features, sparkling wit, brown eyes, and jet black hair, not to mention a personality that charmed everyone.

The two got on superbly from the start, and the young man asked her father for her hand in marriage. Patterson accepted, and the initial date of November 3, 1803, was set for the signing of the marriage contract. Pichon pointed out, however, that according to the newly published Napoleonic or Civil Code (which had just appeared on March 27, 1803), the underage Jérôme had to have his mother's consent.[25] Jérôme, a spoiled young man unused to any restraints being imposed on him, grudgingly postponed the date. As a naval lieutenant his pay was negligible at this time, and his big brother was giving him an allowance of sixty thousand francs a year. But the irresponsible Jérôme had gone through eighty thousand in just his first three months in the United States.

Meanwhile Jérôme worked stealthily to prepare his own little coup, and on December 25 Pichon received a note by special courier: "Monsieur, at the request of M. Jérôme Bonaparte, I have the honour to announce to you that his marriage to Mlle. Patterson was celebrated last night. . . ." The note closed with a request for another cash advance of several thousand dollars.

On October 29 Jérôme and Elizabeth (with the consent of her parents) had taken out a special license to be married on December 24. In the presence of a few witnesses, including Elizabeth's father, mother, and brother, Robert, the mayor of Baltimore, James Calhoun (who was also a justice of the peace of the state of Maryland), performed the civil ceremony, attaching the seal of office to the document after signing it himself. The French undercommissioner for commercial relations also signed the document, sealing it with the large red wax emblem of the French Consulate. Copies of the document were made in English and French. Bishop Carroll of Baltimore personally performed the religious ceremony and then appended his own certificate.[26]

Brother Robert, dispatched to Paris to notify personally the Bonaparte clan, was well received by Lucien, who had just entered his second marriage against the wishes of brother Napoleon and who was still feeling the full effect of that storm. In fact Lucien, Joseph, Louis, and Madame Mère all gave their blessings and best wishes to the couple. But not Napoleon. He had wanted to create a great new dynasty by marrying his brothers and sisters to old European aristocracy. Instead he was forced to accept "the innkeeper's son" (as he referred to Murat) as Caroline's husband, Lucien had married "a scarlet woman," and now Jérôme had married not only a commoner but "a Protestant"* at that. "Tell Monsieur Patterson that our mother, myself, and the entire family unanimously and fully approve of the marriage," Lucien wrote. "The Consul does not agree with us for the moment, but he must be considered the sole dissenting voice in the family. . . . We are all highly pleased and proud of this union."[27]

"I hope you approve of my choice [of a bride]," Jérôme wrote home. "You see, my dear mother, that we were carried away by our destiny, and that is something one can neither avoid nor foresee. . . . I look forward to introducing you to a cherished wife, and one who deserves to be just that. I enclose her portrait. . . ."[28]

On April 20 Decrès, quoting the first consul, ordered Naval Lieutenant Jérôme Bonaparte to pack his bags immediately and report aboard one of the two French frigates being dispatched to New York for him. Napoleon

*She was a Roman Catholic.

refused to allow Elizabeth to accompany Jérôme. "If he brings her with him, she will not set foot on French territory. If he comes alone, I will overlook his error."[29]

Jérôme, who was even more hotheaded and stubborn than either Napoleon or Lucien, on June 1, 1804, announced his refusal to board any French boat whatsoever. Talleyrand threw in the weight of the Foreign Ministry, informing him that his marriage would not be recognized in France. Not content with that, Napoleon personally inserted brief articles in the official French newspapers, including the *Moniteur*, declaring that brother Jérôme "may have taken a mistress" but was not married.[30]

Jérôme was sure that once his brother actually met his wife, he would melt and accept her into the family fold, as he had done Lucien's first (working-class) wife. Accordingly, the young couple hired a brig and filled the vessel's cabins with all their wedding gifts, belongings, and several thousand dollars in gold. They set sail for France on October 25, 1804, determined to arrive in time for the imperial coronation. No sooner had they left the harbor, however, than they were beset by a fierce gale that sank the ship, with all their belongings, a drenched Jérôme and Elizabeth barely escaping with their lives. Undaunted, they hired another brig, only to be turned back this time by British warships, as they were sailing to a French (enemy) port. They missed the coronation.

Meanwhile, stepping up his campaign to eradicate this marriage, on March 2 and 11, 1805, Emperor Napoleon issued decrees addressed "to the civil officers of the Empire," forbidding them to either register this "marriage" or to perform a new one, threatening anyone violating this command with six months in prison. It also stated that any "prince" of his family who committed a similar "illegal" marriage attempt would be cut off officially from the family and country (forbidden to hold office or to receive any income).

Back in Baltimore, on March 3, 1805, the battered couple set out for a third time, now aboard a brig purchased by William Patterson for this specific purpose. On reaching Lisbon on April 8, the pregnant Elizabeth was informed by officials that she would not be permitted to set foot on *European* soil—Napoleon had a long reach. She set sail for Amsterdam, while a furious Jérôme landed and set out for Milan (where brother Napoleon was having himself crowned "King of Italy") on March 17. Jérôme assured an anxious Elizabeth that all would be well. "My good wife, have faith in your husband. The worst that could happen now would be for us to have to live quietly in some foreign country. . . . My dearest Elisa, I will do everything that must be done."[31]

In Italy Emperor Napoleon issued the luxury-loving Jérôme a strong ultimatum. If his brother continued to defy him, Napoleon would refuse to pay his by-now-staggering debts, strip him of all titles and rank, and exclude him from the right of succession to the imperial crown. Jérôme would never receive another franc from France or from any member of the family. He would never be permitted to live in France or any French-controlled territory (Holland, Belgium, France, the west bank of the Rhine, Italy, Spain, and Portugal). As far as the emperor was concerned, Jérôme would cease to exist. If he gave up "this liaison," however, he would have titles, untold riches, promotion, and eventually his own royal crown—his very own country.

On May 6 Jérôme Bonaparte agreed to abandon his wife, never to see her again, and to order her to give up the name of Bonaparte. "Mon frère," a delighted big brother replied, "there is no fault you could commit that would not be overlooked by your repentance. . . . Your marriage thus annulled at your own request, I should like to offer you my friendship."[32]

Nevertheless Elizabeth's plight was far from over. Denied authorization to land in French-occupied Amsterdam as well, now late in her pregnancy she crossed the Channel to Dover,where she was finally permitted to touch solid land on May 18, after nearly fourteen weeks at sea. It was thus in England that the son of Elizabeth and Jérôme Bonaparte was born on July 7, 1805. The boy's name: Jérôme-Napoléon Bonaparte. Shortly thereafter mother and infant sailed for America, returning to her father's house.

"Rest assured, your husband will never abandon you," Jérôme had written. "I would give my life for you alone, and for my child." Elizabeth Bonaparte never saw her husband again.[33]

This was still not enough for Napoleon. He wrote Pope Pius VII asking him to have the Roman Catholic church annul the marriage. The pope, who had been humiliated by Napoleon during the coronation in Paris, was hardly amenable. He replied that in the eyes of the church the marriage was, and remained ever after, valid and binding.[34]

Undaunted, Napoleon created a new avenue, and a year later, an iconoclastic priest, doctor of canon law, and former vicar-general of the diocese of Angers, one Pierre Boilève, declared (after substantial remuneration, no doubt) "that no marriage was contracted" and that therefore "the marriage allegedly contracted between the parties is null and clandestine."[35] But of course neither priest nor bishop could overrule a declaration by the pope himself—the papal decision stood. Napoleon never forgave the pope, and years later, when the moment presented itself, he made him, like his predecessor, a French prisoner.[36]

For Jérôme, the "distinguished child," Napoleon proved as good as his word. Quickly promoted to the rank of post captain and then rear admiral (over Admiral Decrès's angry protests), he was proclaimed a French prince and an imperial highness and decorated with the Grand Eagle of the Legion of Honor, all within the next fifteen months. His "salary" was increased first to 150,000 francs a year, and then to 1 million.

Next Napoleon found a second "wife" for him, the Princess Frederika Catherine Sophia Dorothea, daughter of the king of Württemberg. The contract was hastily signed without too many sensitive questions being asked. A month later Jérôme left the navy, joined the army, and was given the command of an entire army corps (comprising three German divisions). A year after that he was named king of Westphalia, and the bigamous civil and religious marriage ceremonies of the unhappy couple took place in the Tuileries. As the union was illegal, all their subsequent children were of course bastards.

The great warlord loved children, as he was wont to point out, even babies. He adored and spoiled his nephews and nieces and thought it perfectly natural to get down on his hands and knees to play with them.

Although Josephine occasionally agreed to serve as godmother to the children of close friends, Napoleon rarely did so. He made an exception, however, in the case of Général Andoche and Laure Junot's fifteen-month-old Joséphine, a beautiful, bright, and already most mischievous child.

The baptismal service was not long, and at its conclusion Napoleon and Josephine stepped closer, to present the child for the sprinkling ceremony. "Give me your child, Madame Junot," Napoleon said, holding out his arms. But the baby gave a piercing cry. "What a little devil!" Bonaparte exclaimed with a twinkle in his eye. "Will you please come now, little Miss Devil!" But the child fixed her eyes on him and answered "No!" Finally she permitted him to hold her for the ceremony, and he rewarded her with kisses on her cheeks. A few minutes later, when Laure Junot attempted to take her back, she would not leave Napoleon's arms. "She is *my godchild*," the childless Bonaparte beamed. "*My child.*"

The following day Josephine Bonaparte sent Laure Junot a valuable pearl necklace, and attached to it without a note of any kind the receipted purchase contract for the residence Junot was having built amid the rural prairies of the Champs-Elysées, marked "paid in full." That baptismal gift alone cost two hundred thousand francs, and a few weeks later it was followed by one hundred thousand in cash, with which to furnish the new mansion.[37] Clearly Napoleon was most relieved and grateful to the discreet Madame Junot. As for Junot, he was promoted to the important post of military governor of Paris.

It All Began with Austerlitz

The battle of Austerlitz is the finest of all I have fought.

 n spite of his official peaceful protests—"Peace is my heartfelt wish"—"the most powerful prince in Europe," as Talleyrand referred to Napoleon, was bent on expansion.[1] For the sake of whitewashing and legalizing the historical record, Napoleon left a neatly edited paper trail of such peaceful overtures. But such documents were at best legal fictions and at worst blatant lies. Meanwhile he continued to make his plans for greater geopolitical expansion. He would push eastward and westward at the same time, and be forced to forgo plans for aggressive expansion in America—in "the Louisiana Territory" ceded to France by Spain in October 1802—only when General Leclerc's army, designated to occupy it, was unexpectedly annihilated in Santo Domingo that same year, before it could continue to North America as ordered.[2]

Although French expansion in America thus came to an unexpected halt, much to the relief of President Jefferson, Napoleon's efforts in Europe were intensified. Not only had he refused to withdraw French occupation troops from the Batavian (Dutch) and Helvetian (Swiss) Republics, but he

had invaded German territory and British Hannover and had even kidnapped a British diplomat, Sir George Rumbold, the minister accredited to
the Hanseatic cities, in Hamburg, taking him hundreds of miles to a Paris
prison. Then, to ensure that he had thoroughly roused the Austrians to
arms (thus permitting France to claim that it was simply defending itself),
he created the Kingdom of Italy, crowning himself its monarch on May 26,
1805, annexing Genoa, Piedmont, and Savoy as he did so. These were
hardly the moves of someone genuinely interested in establishing a lasting
peace in Europe.

The reaction of Napoleon's opponents was swift and dramatic, even
before the Milan coronation. Russia signed a military alliance with England
in April 1805, calling for the restoration of "peace in Europe" and binding
Britain and Russia in a new Third Coalition—William Pitt's "last grand
work"—against this rampaging France. This was joined by Sweden and
Austria that August. (And six months earlier Russia and Austria had framed
a secret defense pact whereby both would make war on Napoleon if he
committed any new aggression in Italy or menaced the Turkish Empire.)
Britain, pushed by Napoleon's seizure of British Hannover and of course
by the threat of a sweeping invasion, had acted vigorously to create this
new allied coalition. Although it could not spare a single man with its own
shores still menaced by the army across the Channel, it did agree to pay
substantial subsidies to cover mobilization costs of the Allied armies, while
deploying the Royal Navy in the Baltic as well. An exasperated Austria had
in fact at last joined the full coalition only after Napoleon's had seized the
ancient Lombard crown in Milan's Duomo that May, followed by the
annexation of the Ligurian, or Genoese, Republic on June 4.

Basically Austria, Russia, Sweden, and Great Britain wanted the immediate evacuation of Hannover, Holland, Belgium, and Italy (the king of Sardinia demanding the return of his northern lands), and then they needed a
means of preventing any further aggression by Napoleon and the French
army. "This man is insatiable," Czar Alexander had exclaimed that summer
on receiving word of the events in Italy. "His ambition knows no bounds;
he is the scourge of the world. He wants war, does he? Very well, he shall
have it, and the sooner the better."[3]

Napoleon now discovered that he had been too effective in fomenting
alarm and precipitating the next campaign. Ironically he now found himself
in a harrowing situation. As late as mid-August 1805 he had still been in
Boulogne awaiting the arrival from America of Villeneuve's sprawling
Franco-Spanish fleet, scheduled to confront Cornwallis's Channel fleet off
Ushant and then escort the invasion force to English shores. Napoleon had

been boasting so long of his invasion and the destruction of "the perfidious English" that he could hardly back down with the arrival of the combined fleet. It had been humiliating enough duirng the past year just waiting for it to appear and for the invasion to take place. If he declined to execute it now, he would become the laughingstock of Europe.

On the other hand, the growing anger of his European neighbors could hardly be ignored. If they were to march westward into France, as intelligence reports and spies now suggested they would, with the arrival of Villeneuve and the launching of the invasion of England with the entire Grande Armée, France would be utterly defenseless, quickly overrun, and Napoleon no doubt deposed. For all his vaunted machinations, somehow he had greatly miscalculated this, perhaps thinking that he could execute his invasion and complete it earlier, within just a few months, but even that seemed far-fetched, given his recent overt annexations.

Thus, when by August 29 there was still no word from, or sign of, Villeneuve, Bonaparte ordered the flotilla into mothballs and his troops to march. In fact it was not until September 2 that Naval Minister Decrès received word that instead of sailing north to Boulogne as ordered, Villeneuve had fled south to Cadiz.[4] It was no doubt with very mixed feelings that Napoleon watched his mighty expeditionary force move east and not west. And yet, with several hundred thousand troops reportedly about to march on France's frontiers, he hardly had time to reflect on the nearly catastrophic predicament he had gotten himself and France into—and for which he alone was responsible.

The crisis could not have come at a worse possible time. Through his channeling of most of the nation's financial resources for the past two years into the creation of the massive invasion force at Boulogne, and his failure to pay in full many of the contractors building boats and supplying his navy and army—not to mention his equal failure to repay some bank loans—Napoleon had caused growing concern and anxiety in business and financial circles. The extent of the large forced loans Napoleon had demanded, in France and in neighboring countries, was well known to the major financiers in Paris. Furthermore, these same financial and commercial circles, which had at first welcomed with outstretched hands Napoleon's coup, for bringing to an end the corruption, instability, and destruction of most French commercial life, culminating in the restoration of European peace, had then been distinctly disturbed by the unnecessary rupture of the Amiens accords and the resumption of war with Britain, whose fleets controlled the seas, thereby greatly curtailing their own Continental and overseas transactions. What is more the French treasury, despite the flow of foreign gold into its coffers, was barely in the black, with only eighteen million francs left by the end of summer. Should war now expand to include campaigns against the Allies—Austria and Russia in particular—commerce and banking would be further restricted, while greater demands would be made on them to meet Napoleon's needs for the supplying of an army at a time when he had not yet repaid his past debts. And then there was the matter of French army pay, many months in arrears, which would have to be brought up to date if Napoleon expected to receive his soldiers' full support in the field.[5]

In brief, by August 1805 Napoleon and his new imperial government had no more credit at home or abroad. No one in his right mind wanted to end up like the bankers who had financed him so heavily thus far, only to find themselves still pleading for repayment and even harassed by the police and threatened with arrest when they did so. Napoleon's verbal attacks were the talk of the Stock Exchange, no banker envying the fate of Collot, Vanderberghe, Desprès, or Ouvrard, for instance, forced to "repay" the government tens of millions, and facing long sentences of imprisonment.[6]

This was a crisis of enormous proportions. Napoleon faced not only a possible British retaliatory landing along the Channel but a looming financial disaster at home at a time when he needed to tap extraordinary new resources for the military. Panic was already setting in, as both Finance Minister Gaudin and Archchancellor Cambacérès warned him.

Napoleon also confronted a self-inflicted ultimatum: Either he was to begin immediate negotiations with England, Austria, and Russia to defuse the explosive international situation and restore a lasting peace in Europe (and thus withdraw all French troops occupying Holland, Belgium, the west bank of the Rhine, Switzerland, and Italy); cancel his fleet instructions for the invasion of England, order his Grande Armée to stand down, and repay the hundreds of millions of francs he owed banks and businesses in several countries; or he had to carry out a lightning attack on the approaching Austrian and Russian armies threatening France, and quickly, decisively defeat them and restore a redefined peace the hard way. In any event, one thing was certainly clear: The French people were insistent on peace, now. If he *was* to wage war, it would have to be brief and brilliant.

On August 26, even *before* learning of Villeneuve's treasonous disobedience of orders, Napoleon reluctantly gave up the idea of invading England. On the twenty-ninth he ordered the three principal army corps at Montreuil, St.-Omer, and Bruges to break camp and march east—to the Rhine. "I must tell you in the strictest confidence," he informed Cambacérès on

September 1, "that there is not a single man left at Boulogne, apart from those few needed for the defense of the port."

Napoleon had again unilaterally rejected the idea of arriving at a peaceful solution; therefore there could only be war. This was one of the watersheds that were to alter his entire career, condemning France and himself to inevitable ruin.

Back at St.-Cloud on September 5, he found the French capital most anxious about the international situation. A few days later, learning that the Austrians had already crossed the Inn, heading for Munich, Napoleon set to work in earnest, drafting his campaign plans. In conference with Chief of Staff Berthier, he issued a complex series of marching orders for seven separate army corps, for the distribution of garrisons and the establishment of supply depots by the general commissary of army stores. The French army, totaling 210,500 men, was mobilized, including 29,500 cavalry and 396 cannon but excluding Masséna's Army of Italy. Top-secret orders went out to the corps commanders by special courier to launch operations and cross the Rhine on October 2–3.[7]

After nearly three intensive weeks of work, all was in readiness. On September 23 Napoleon drove over to the Luxembourg Palace to address the Senate and the nation. "The Emperor," he began, in the third person,

> forced to repulse an unjust aggression against us [by Austria, Russia, England, and Sweden] that he has in vain attempted to prevent, has had to suspend the execution of his original plans [for the invasion of England]. He . . . will be marching at the head of his troops and will put down his arms only after having obtained full and complete satisfaction, and after having achieved complete security for his own states as well as those of our allies.

He closed with an affirmative "I promise you victory and a prompt return to peace.[8]

On the eve of what was obviously to be another major war, Josephine—who had belatedly learned the error of not joining her husband when he was campaigning—insisted on his taking her with him. She had paid an extremely heavy price to secure the new crown on her head—her beloved daughter's welfare and happiness—and was not about to forgo whatever it took to ensure that she remain Madame Bonaparte, though now she probably felt less in love with him and more fearful of his growing tyranny.[9]

Thus it was that when Napoleon set out on September 24 in his famous post chaise and staff to join his army along the Rhine, Josephine was at his side. They reached Strasbourg on the twenty-sixth and remained there till the end of the month. On October 1, dining with Josephine, his first chamberlain, the comte de Rémusat, and Foreign Secretary Talleyrand—and while holding Josephine in his arms, bidding her adieu for the unknown—Napoleon collapsed in a serious epileptic fit. The tension over the past few weeks had been too much for him; his entire empire was at stake. If his decision now was wrong ... Falling to the ground, his body racked by convulsions, he vomited and gagged, fighting for breath, foam covering his lips. Josephine, who had witnessed earlier attacks over the years, was seriously alarmed but not so panicked as were the startled Talleyrand and Rémusat. For perhaps the first time in his life, Talleyrand was truly terrified. He had heard rumors of Napoleon's epilepsy, but this was the first time he had witnessed such an attack. Josephine had hushed up similar past seizures, silencing servants and friends alike with promises and gold. But gold could not prevent Talleyrand's horror now. He realized just how fragile was this new French empire. Quickly limping over to Napoleon, who lay on the floor in convulsions, Talleyrand removed his cravat, pouring out eau de cologne handed him by Josephine, and as Napoleon's breathing gradually returned to normal, his and Rémusat's relief was only too apparent. The attack lasted a quarter of an hour, longer than any of its predecessors. On recovering, with a stiff brandy, Napoleon got to his feet, and after enjoining all present to total secrecy about what had just transpired, ordered his post chaise and set out alone in the night for Karlsruhe and the gathering Grande Armée.[10]

Bonaparte could silence his foreign minister and first chamberlain, but he could do nothing to quell the growing panic in the newly constructed Bourse, or Stock Exchange. As money grew scarce, trading in stocks and shares uncertain, securities and *rentes* dropping precipitously, accompanied by frightening rumors of collapse of the entire French financial structure, the inevitable run on the franc began.

The first serious signs of looming disaster had appeared as early as June 10, 1805, with the collapse of the largest foreign-exchange dealer in Paris, Fould. Rumors of political uncertainty and perhaps of another war naturally had created unease in the French money markets. "There is little activity at the Stock Exchange," Cambacérès informed Napoleon at Boulogne on August 27. "Money is becoming more and more scarce."[11] This was followed by the archchancellor's letters of September 28 and 29, which had reached Napoleon at Strasbourg before dinner on October 1, informing him that the situation in Paris was becoming more worrisome, rumor spreading like wildfire that the regents of the Banque de France were without reserves and withdrawing currency from circulation. Anxious crowds were growing outside the bank, attempting to withdraw their investments in government securities. Rumor also had it that the Banque de France was discounting some of its paper while severely limiting reimbursements to individual investors to the bare minimum of a few hundred francs each. This in turn engendered greater panic. Talk of the numbers required for the year's forthcoming conscription—eighty thousand, more than twice the normal—caused further anxiety, compounded by false whispers to the effect that the bank was annulling notes already held by the public. Echoes of similar situations had reverberated throughout Paris during the Revolution. "Such a measure would be disastrous," an anxious Cambacérès confided. "It would ruin commerce and leave Your Majesty's government without funds." The same day Napoleon had received this information, he had collapsed.[12]

In fact the Banque de France, with just a few million francs left in its coffers (though it was required to keep hundreds of millions), had indeed issued orders to invalidate notes when it was unable to borrow money from other sources, but it was now forced "to modify" measures to do this and withdraw currency on Napoleon's special orders. But when these negative reports were suddenly seasoned by the rumor of forthcoming peace talks early in October, the run on the Banque de France eased. Talk of victory in the field and the taking of Ulm (not in fact accomplished until October 19) momentarily calmed the Bourse. "The triumph of Your Majesty's armies has rendered the emergency meeting of shareholders of the Bank much calmer than it would have been in the event of military reverses," Cambacérès warned him. "Money is beginning to circulate again; yesterday the crowds at the bank were smaller."[13] But when signs neither of peace nor of decisive victories were confirmed that autumn, the unsettling rumors resumed, as persons bearing letters of exchange balked at receiving payment in the bank's freshly printed paper notes. "The crisis will pass," the archchancellor tried to reassure Napoleon.

By the beginning of November, however, the run on the franc resumed at an alarming rate. "Ill will continues to undermine the Bank," Cambacérès complained after news of the greatest French naval defeat in history, at Trafalgar, reached Paris. "The crowds at the Bank continue to grow. They are having trouble maintaining order there.... Cash, which was already scarce, is becoming more so daily, and the value of government paper continues to plunge." Cambacérès wrote on November 7. "The situation in Paris is becoming disquieting." Two days later soldiers were called in to keep angry investors and shareholders in order. "The troops can barely control the bearer of notes demanding payment," he echoed.[14]

When Napoleon ordered his brother Louis to remove those very troops from Paris, "to defend Antwerp" from a possible landing of "Russians and Swedes," the usually easygoing Cambacérès was in a real flap, bewailing that "the Police Minister can no longer answer for the safety of the capital." Napoleon had to produce one of his celebrated military miracles pretty quickly, if all mayhem was not to break out in the French capital. Or, as Cambacérès put it, "If the circumstances become such, and Your Majesty then also strips Paris of the few remaining troops, disorders must almost inevitably ensue."[15]

Despite Napoleon's victory at Ulm, on October 17–20, and the triumphant entry of French troops into Vienna on November 14, uncertainty, rumor, and panic continued in Paris. By November 19 Cambacérès was forced to notify Napoleon of two new banking disasters as momentous as any victory in the field: the failure of the Swiss Deville Bank and, even more important, the collapse of the prestigious Récamier Bank, reportedly with losses of up to thirty million francs, in which many ministers, government officials, and general officers now in the field with Napoleon—and perhaps Joseph Bonaparte himself—had invested their savings. What was worse, when Récamier had asked for an emergency loan of a mere one million francs, the hard-pressed government had been forced to decline. The fall of the House of Récamier led to a chain of subsequent bankruptcies, including four of the most powerful merchants in the capital.[16]

On November 20 an angry imperial highness, Prince Joseph Bonaparte, acting head of the government in Napoleon's absence, called an emergency meeting with Treasury Minister Barbé-Marbois regarding the collapse of most public services. "The Treasury Minister stressed the difficulty in assuring various public services. . . . At the same time, however, the present [military and financial] circumstances require extraordinary government expenses." Napoleon's irresponsible diversion of every franc from the treasury for the invasion of England was now forcing France to pay the full price. "I cannot pretend to disguise from you, sire, that this meeting . . . has been truly painful," the usually optimistic and diplomatic Cambacérès said. "It is feared that the [financial] damage done [to France and the economy] will be long and difficult to heal."[17]

By November, so little cash was available and in circulation that everyone, at every level of society, was affected, with the director of hospices for the poor tendering his resignation after being forced to pay for his department's services out of his own pocket. Perhaps most dramatically for the

French emperor-general and his Grande Armée, Gen. Jean-François Dejean at the War Ministry was no longer able to purchase forage for Murat's cavalry. Then came the unbelievable news that major merchants of Paris, Lyons, and Geneva, now in a panic, were secretly channeling their funds to England (the Switzerland of the nineteenth century)—*the enemy*—for safekeeping. If this news got out, all would be lost.

The absurdity of the situation became even more evident on November 26, when Cambacérès cheerfully reported to Napoleon's headquarters that the full-scale renovation of the Tuileries Palace—on which many millions were being spent—was going ahead right on schedule. Napoleon and Josephine's personal apartments had been completed, as had the large concert hall in the Pavillon de Molière. In addition the staircase leading to the new quarters of the State Council, as well as to the offices around it, were open for use. Workers were expected to begin laying the parquet that week, and the scaffolding for all work would soon be coming down.[18] Meanwhile the cavalry still lacked hay for want of cash.

Napoleon had to produce a victory of truly staggering dimensions if he was to avert the collapse of the Bourse, the Bank of France, and Paris financial markets—indeed of France itself. As late as November 29 Cambacérès reminded him: "The government is financially embarrassed." There were whispers of incompetence and scandals at the highest levels. Treasury Minister Barbé-Marbois's brother "has cut his throat with a razor," Cambacérès despondently reported. "Prince Joseph now merely convokes cabinet meetings in order to complain about these problems, about the difficulties the Bank finds itself in, about the lack of money with which to carry on," the archchancellor added on the very date that was dramatically to reverse the situation and save Napoleon and his Empire, December 2, 1805.[19]

It was only when the results of the Battle of Austerlitz reached Paris by special courier on December 11 that the financial markets in Paris, Switzerland, and Holland began to rebound—slowly, painfully—barely saving Napoleon and his twelve-month-old Empire.[20] But the story of that military campaign had begun nine weeks earlier.

On the morning of September 25, 1805, Marshal Lannes [V Corps] will cross the Rhine at Kehl and establish himself between Rastadt and Ettlingen. Prince Murat [with the reserve cavalry at Strasbourg] is to follow him with Hautpoul's heavy cavalry, four divisions of dragoons and one of foot dragoons ... Marshal Soult [IV Corps] will cross at Speyer. ... Marshal Ney [VI Corps] is to cross the Rhine at Durlach ... Marshal Davout [III Corps] is to occupy Mannheim,

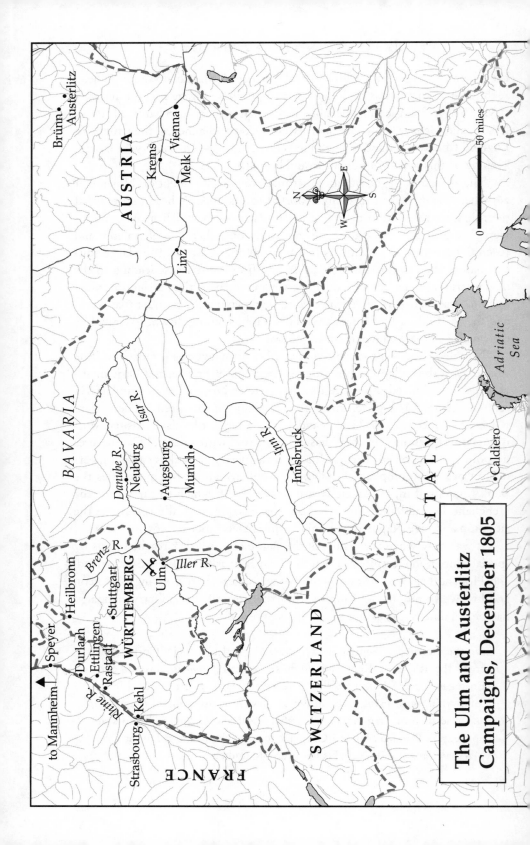

The Ulm and Austerlitz Campaigns, December 1805

Napoleon ordered. Marmont's II Corps was to cross the Rhine at Mainz, while Bernadotte's I Corps now occupying British Hannover was to converge on southern Germany with them. Finally, Augereau's VII Corps was to follow on a twenty-nine-day forced march from Brest. "The marshals are authorized to requisition the food and supplies needed for their troops from the countries they occupy. . . ."[21]

The plan was as magnificent as it was desperate. Napoleon literally stripped France of almost every available soldier, except for Marshal Brune's 30,000 men left to guard the Channel coast. Never before—neither under Louis XVI, Louis XV, nor Louis XIV—had France been left so undefended. Three or four crack British divisions could have marched on Paris with little opposition. But thanks to Napoleon's total government censorship of the press, not a word got out, nor was a single word of criticism published in any newspaper of the land.

Before setting out from Strasbourg, Napoleon had devised the simple, dramatic, and, by military standards, beautiful campaign now being executed against Austrian emperor Franz II's three armies (198,000 men) advancing westward and Czar Alexander I's initial field force (98,000 men). In theory Napoleon had 207,000 men at his disposal now, but in reality fewer than 100,000 under his immediate control. He therefore had to act swiftly to divide and crush the Allies before they could unite and attack him en masse. Napoleon observed operations from his temporary GHQ at Ettlingen, in the Duchy of Baden, during the first week of October, tracing the movement of these corps across his large field map.[22]

In fact Napoleon had decided on this plan of attack only shortly before leaving Paris, as the faithful but hard-pressed Berthier somehow coped with the long stream of complex orders required to set in motion this full-scale campaign. Under the reorganization of the army, Napoleon had carried out many changes, including the replacement of half-brigades with divisions, and the placing of all cavalry under the overall command of one man, Murat, while also centralizing the army's artillery under General Dommartin.[23]

Each corps of the Grande Armée was following a different route to avoid confusion and bottlenecks and in order to ease the inevitable logistical problems involved in keeping artillery, munitions, and food at a pace with the marching units. Napoleon, intent on his invasion of England to the very end, had in fact ignored the glaring logistical problems involved and was to pay a very heavy price from the outset, when it was discovered that the army lacked sufficient numbers of large wagons, and was forced to requisition an additional 3,500 of them, and some 14,000 dray horses to haul them, causing yet another last-minute nightmare foisted on Berthier. Winter clothing would be slow in arriving, and men would have few muskets available to replace their old Charleville 1777 models when they broke or wore out, as they frequently did. Worse, food would often be desperately short, causing thousands and thousands of stragglers and deserters across hundreds of miles, after the first few weeks in the field. To make matters still worse, many units of the army were still long overdue in receiving back pay. Cold, hungry, unshod, unpaid men—it did not bode well at the beginning of a campaign.

This war, like some that preceded it, such as Egypt, and every one to follow to the end of Napoleon's career, was utterly unnecessary, provoked by him alone in what was to prove a long, complicated chain of events, domino-style. Had Napoleon simply removed his occupying forces from Holland, Germany, Switzerland, and Italy, and renounced all claims to those countries, it could all have been avoided. Not a life need have been lost. But Napoleon was set on conquest, which meant war, and this was just the beginning. This war and its ultimate settlement would initiate new grievances, festering wounds, and unsettled accounts that would lead to war after war. "It is said that a man of genius has been seldom ruined but by himself,"[24] one noted historian remarked. In the present instance, Napoleon had deliberately forced Austria (and its ally Russia) to attack him, especially through his latest actions in Italy, while dramatically feigning studied surprise and anger when the Allies were finally forced to retaliate and mobilize as a result.

Nevertheless, despite the crack superbly trained army he had created along the Channel, Napoleon was caught napping, unprepared to meet the avalanche of humanity in military uniform now pouring across Europe to defend various national claims and to put an end to this incessant French aggression. And if Napoleon's logistics were deplorable, his intelligence was little better. Indeed, he had been so hard put in this regard as to send his aide-de-camp General Bertrand and a marshal of the Empire, Prince Murat, on a lightning—if extensive—and most dangerous intelligence mission across the Rhine, probing hundreds of miles into enemy territory. Only Napoleon could have been so brazen and foolhardy as to dispatch one of the nation's nine field marshals on such a risky venture, which could and should have been carried out by someone far junior.

In any event Napoleon had to secure his flanks and rear, for what he planned was an attack on the Austrian emperor's large but widely dispersed armies. Thus on October 1 he forced the duke of Baden to sign a defense pact with him (while promising to spare Heidelberg University from

destruction or rampage, as well as future compensation for the duke himself),²⁵ followed by a similar alliance with the elector of Württemberg four
days later. The elector of Bavaria, however, representing a much larger,
more powerful state centered around Munich, was not so accommodating,
especially when the bargain was complicated by a marriage. Napoleon,
through the good offices of Talleyrand at Strasbourg, ordered the Bavarian
ruler to deliver his daughter as the bride of the viceroy of Italy, Eugène de
Beauharnais, along with a signed defense pact, or pay the consequences.
"The most powerful prince of Europe is a man of the highest character,
magnificent in his affection, while utterly irreconcilable in a reverse position," Talleyrand warned the Bavarian leader. "I hardly need spell out the
consequences."²⁶ The elector, who for all his princely blood was a practical
businessman, held out until October. Then he, too, buckled under to
French military pressure and agreed to provide both a corps of Bavarians
for the Grande Armée and a wife for Eugène de Beauharnais. This gain was
more than set off, however, on November 3 by the signing of the Treaty of
Potsdam, when Czar Alexander persuaded King Friedrich Wilhelm of
Prussia to end his neutral stance and finally join the Third Coalition against
France, following Bernadotte's recent troop violation of Prussian territory
at Ansbach, while en route to join Napoleon.

Casting his corps about in almost parallel, descending routes, like an
enormous fisherman's net, Napoleon set in motion his superb enveloping
movement around the rear of the opposing army, which was to concentrate
at Münster on October 6, cutting off General Kienmaier's 16,000 men at
Neuburg from the rest of Archduke Ferdinand's army straddling the
Danube and the Iller Rivers. So successful was this strategy that in three
days Kienmaier's troops, now isolated, were fleeing hell-for-leather toward
Munich, as Davout's, Soult's, Lannes's, and Murat's troops neatly sealed off
the remainder of Ferdinand's army under the overall command of General
Mack, sending some 40,000 scurrying for the protected battlements of Ulm,
lower on the Danube, as another 11,300 fled south. Meanwhile, Ney's corps
of 24,500 to the north of Ulm prevented escape in that direction. By October 13 Murat, Ney, and Lannes, supported by Bessières and Marmont, had
herded Mack's army neatly between their troops and the walls of Ulm. In a
separate maneuver far to the southeast, Bernadotte's corps sealed off
Munich, although the evasive Kienmaier nevertheless managed to escape
east, avoiding battle. By October 16, thanks to Napoleon's superb envelopment strategy and Mack's obligingly incompetent generalship, Mack's
troops were hopelessly locked up behind their Ulm defenses. Mack, who
had expected Napoleon's army to move into Italy rather than Bavaria, was

unable to cope with the altered situation. Ney's VI and Lannes's V corps cut off Ulm on the west bank of the Danube, while Marmont's II Corp ringed the city on the east bank, as Soult's IV Corps now advanced from the south to close that remaining avenue of escape. Encircled and outnumbered, the hapless Mack signed an eight-day armistice with General de Ségur on October 17.

By October 20, realizing that the first contingent of the Russian Army under General Kutuzov could not arrive in time to save him, General Mack surrendered his entire army at Ulm, apart from 10,000 who had managed to escape earlier. Altogether, some 27,000 Austrian troops officially paraded before a satisfied Napoleon, standing before a huge log fire, stacking arms as they passed, and handing over sixty guns and forty regimental standards. Incurring minimal losses without a major battle, Napoleon had taken an entire army and the river bastion of Ulm with its plentiful supplies of food and munitions.

"The war of the third coalition has begun," a victorious Bonaparte addressed the Grande Armée from imperial headquarters at Augsburg on October 23:

> The Austrian army has crossed the Inn, violated treaties, attacked our ally [Bavaria] and driven him from his capital [Munich]. . . . You in turn have been compelled to hasten . . . to the defence of our frontiers. You have already crossed the Rhine. We shall not again pause until we have assured the independence of the German people, succored our allies, and put to shame the pride of unjust aggressors. We shall not again make peace without firm guarantees. . . . But soldiers, we have difficult marches yet before us, fatigue and hardships of all kinds. Whatever obstacles may confront us, we shall overcome them, and we shall not rest until we have planted our eagles upon the territory of our enemies.[27]

In another order of the day, immediately following the surrender of Mack at Ulm, Napoleon praised Marshals Murat, Ney, Lannes, Soult, and Marmont and the French army. "The result of all these glorious events is that the Austrian army of 100,000 men is destroyed; 50,000 of them are prisoners," he declared, neither of which was true of course, the advancing masses of Archduke Karl's army in particular still posing a very real threat to his southern flank.[28]

Indeed, this was hardly the time to celebrate. The real battles lay ahead of the French, and now that the element of surprise had been lost, victory would be more difficult, given Napoleon's vastly inferior numbers. Half of

Archduke Ferdinand's army had escaped, and, as they attempted to close on the French, the rest of the Austrian army remained as yet untouched by battle, including Archduke John's 22,000 men and Archduke Karl's 80,000. Meanwhile Ney and Marmont continued to attempt to head off Karl's army, aided by Masséna's Army of Italy (35,000 men) to the southwest. Aggravating matters for Napoleon, however, Kutuzov's 38,000 Russian troops were now less than one hundred miles away, followed by the rest of the Russian force—for a total of perhaps 226,000 versus Napoleon's maximum of 152,000 men. And after deducting the garrisons left behind at Ulm and along the road of communications, and the detached divisions with Ney and Marmont, in reality Napoleon found himself with fewer than 100,000 troops available.

It was the Russians who concerned him most at this moment. He ordered Marshals Murat, Soult, Davout, Mortier (and his newly created corps), and Lannes to pursue Kutuzov and the remnants of the immediate Austrian forces, in order to prevent their junction with Czar Alexander's army. At the same time, should the czar join with the Prussians as well, with their separate force of 200,000 men (as a result of the new defense treaty Alexander was negotiating with Friedrich Wilhelm III at Berlin on October 25), all stemming from a situation that Napoleon had himself created, things could prove nasty. As usual Bonaparte was left to juggle his options. Even if the Prussians did achieve their junction with the Russians, they would be slow to mobilize such a large force. That meant that Napoleon might still be able to get at the Russians before either Archduke Karl's army or that of Prussia could reach them. Napoleon was willing to take on the three different allies one at a time, but he simply lacked the numbers and commanders to tackle them as a combined force. Given this background, he decided to close on and dispose of Kutuzov and to secure Vienna.

With Augsburg—safely within Bavarian territory—now the main supply depot for the French army, Napoleon instructed Berthier to make Munich the administrative center of operations. Behind the lines Marshal Augereau's small force was left to garrison newly conquered Ulm, while carrying out harassing operations against the enemy in the Vorarlberg, as Ney and the Bavarian corps were dispatched to Innsbruck in the Tyrol to check Archduke John. It was at this time that Napoleon created a badly needed new corps (VIII) with four divisions taken from other units and placed it under the command of General Mortier. The setting in of an early winter storm, bringing sleet, snow, and plummeting temperatures, did not help matters, however, with the French troops still in the clothes they had worn on quitting the Channel back in August.

Kutuzov's corps, which was the closest Russian force to Archduke Karl and Vienna, much to Napoleon's surprise refused to support his Austrian allies in the defense of their capital. He retreated rapidly (with two Austrian corps in tow as well), escaping across the Danube and up the river valley. Murat, Lannes, and Davout were ordered to pursue Kutusov. As for Archduke Karl, after nearly defeating Masséna at Caldiero on October 29, he resumed his march toward Austria and the strong Austrian force at Venice, reinforced en route by his brother John's smaller army. Together the two archdukes could pose a very serious threat to Napoleon's right flank, especially if the Russians attacked simultaneously from the left. The pressure on Napoleon was growing.

On November 8 Davout severely crippled Meerveldt's corps, though Kutuzov refused to come to the aid of this Austrian ally attached to his own army. And yet Murat, instead of joining Davout's successful strategy in pursuit of Kutuzov, as ordered, unilaterally decided to seize the prize jewel, Vienna. When Napoleon heard at Linz of Murat's grievous error, which in fact was soon to result in a nightmarish position for him as Kutuzov continued his escape up the Danube to reach the principal Russian army in Moravia, the incredulous French emperor went into one of his famous tirades, berating Murat "for acting like a blind fool." The Russians, instead of covering Vienna, had by now retreated over the Danube at Krems, thanks chiefly to Murat.[29] Murat had lost sight of the overall French strategic situation and objective of destroying armies, not occupying undefended cities. By failing to join Davout "to march closely together" per Napoleon's orders,[30] he had altered a very successful and decisive campaign, leaving it in a questionable state, even endangering the entire outcome, should the Allies now be able to coordinate their actions.

In an attempt to make up for this in some small part, Murat and Lannes single-handedly, brazenly walked across the principal bridge of Vienna linking both sides of the broad Danube, and by a courageous if foolhardy ruse (field marshals were not wasted on such missions) successfully seized that bridge from the Austrians before it was destroyed. (This in no way altered the very dangerous situation Murat had helped create, however.) Bernadotte, who was invariably "delayed" somewhere, and now in Melk, certainly also contributed to the tense ambiguities now developing.

Another factor would now be weakening French effectiveness, not only during the remainder of this campaign but in all those to come over the next several years: the jealousy and enmity eroding the coordination required of the French emperor's senior commanders. Real clashes of temper were involved, a bitterness that no doubt alarmed Napoleon and undermined strategic and tactical success.

Back on October 11, Napoleon had ordered Murat, whom he put temporarily in tactical command, along with Ney's and Lannes's corps, more than fifty thousand men all told, to "march as closely together as possible . . . in order to crush the enemy," specifically ordering them to cut off Kutuzov's army before it could reach the Isar River. But in the midst of closing on Ulm—still led by Ney and Lannes under Murat's command—Murat had ordered one of Ney's three division's, General Dupont's, to be separated and left on the other side of the Danube. There Dupont and his four thousand men suddenly found themselves isolated and facing some twenty-five thousand Austrians. He courageously defended himself in a furious all-day battle at Albeck, before he was able to retreat to Brenz.[31] Napoleon had then ordered Murat and Ney to move north to come to Dupont's rescue, and a fierce battle took place on October 14 at Elchingen, on the Danube. Ney in particular distinguished himself, recapturing a damaged bridge, supervising its repair under withering Austrian fire, and then successfully attacking and seizing Elchingen itself (for which he would one day be raised to the peerage as the duke of Elchingen). Thanks to this new bridgehead, that same day Murat had been able to cross the Danube with sufficient troops to a point near Albeck, where the fighting had resumed, arriving just in time to save Dupont's much reduced division from destruction.

Reunited once again, they went on to take Ulm. Ney now furiously attacked Murat, calling him an incompetent commander who had needlessly endangered one-third of his corps. If words could kill, both Ney and Murat would have died many times over in that hot quarrel, until Napoleon personally intervened and separated them. The two men were no longer on speaking terms, or in much of a mood to cooperate in the field again. This was followed by grave, crippling quarrels between Bernadotte and both Chief of Staff Berthier and Marshal Davout.[32]

Perhaps the bitterest of all these disagreements developed later, during the Austerlitz campaign (as a result of Soult's incompetence), between the cold, arrogant, emotionless Soult, with his annoying Catalan accent, and the hotheaded Lannes. At Brünn (now Brno) the good-hearted but emotional Lannes actually challenged Soult to a duel, which was prevented only by Napoleon's intervention once again.[33] And at the conclusion of the campaign, Lannes was in turn bitterly to attack Napoleon for not recognizing his own important contribution to the ultimate success of that battle. Lannes was right; Napoleon had indeed failed to praise him, to give him his due in the *Army Bulletin*, as he frequently failed to do when others were concerned. Napoleon could not abide his commanders sharing the limelight. Later he and Lannes were to have an even more bitter disagreement, which would result in a permanent severing of private relations between the two men.

In other words, during this campaign all five of the principal French field marshals in or around Vienna, who would soon be crossing the Danube to confront the Russian army at the village of Austerlitz on the plains of Moravia, were already or were soon to become, such bitter personal enemies as to undermine their ability to work together on the battlefield against a foreign army. Nor were these enmities forgotten in future campaigns, resulting in near tragedy time and again.

And yet in the final analysis it was Napoleon's long-festering anger with Murat—in which the fact that he had bedded Josephine rankled the most, magnified many times by his permitting Kutuzov to escape, which in turn broke the momentum of the entire campaign—that now came to the fore. Then, days later, as the French army advanced on Czar Alexander's forces, Ney was in hot pursuit of Kutuzov, Prince Bagration holding Oberhollabrünn to protect Kutuzov's retreat, Russian general Winzgerode suggested an armistice to Murat. Murat foolishly agreed, thereby permitting Kutuzov's entire army not only to escape again but now to join forces with Czar Alexander—the very thing Napoleon had so desperately hoped to prevent. "I am at a complete loss for words!" Napoleon shouted at Murat on November 16. As commander of the advance guard Murat had no authority to sign any armistice. "Break the armistice instantly and attack the enemy! March! Destroy the Russian army!"[34] But by then it was too late, and Murat had compounded his original gaffe many times over. He had lost sight of his objective and his personal orders, and as a result Napoleon had in turn lost the initial advantage of this campaign, bringing him to a precarious tactical situation as French armies pushed through Brünn as far as Wischau on the road to Olmütz, where most of the combined Russian army (now including Kutuzov) regrouped, not fleeing from Napoleon but marching toward him.

By November 28, five full weeks after the fall of Ulm, Napoleon still had not confronted the Russian army, and the Grande Armée was far from looking or feeling quite so grand. Napoleon did not know what was wrong with Murat. In the past he had driven to his objective as instructed, often turning the fate of battles as a consequence. Now he seemed almost a hindrance, dragging his feet. But this was his first time in the field as a marshal and the first time since the bitter dispute over the succession to the imperial throne. Since the taking of Ulm he had been demonstrating an independence of action, a willfulness, that was contrary to the spirit and needs of this campaign, clearly demonstrating his unreliability as a corps commander.

Napoleon, too, was not his old self. Everything seemed to be going wrong, compounded by "disorders in the rear of the army" where thousands of troops had deserted and rampaged through conquered villages. "The Emperor is displeased," Berthier had just informed the army. "Scoundrels are doing their utmost to dishonor the army," and Napoleon had been compelled to create five mobile police columns, 150 men each, headed by a commission of four officers and a judge advocate to seize deserters and execute summary courts-martial on the spot, wherever such disorders were occurring. This was relatively minor, but still, things were getting out of hand, and Napoleon had to take strong action to halt mass desertion, including those fleeing hundreds of miles back across the Rhine. He ordered that all deserters were to be arrested,[35] which only increased the large-scale demoralization that set in after Ulm.

The most important objective, however, was still to meet with and destroy the enemy. On the morning of November 28 the Russo-Austrian army under Alexander I approached the French lines, as cavalry and infantry units of Bagration's and General Kienmaier's corps clashed with the French. Napoleon had broken off negotiations with the Austrians, as well as with the Prussian foreign minister, Count von Haugwitz, who had come there on that diplomatic mission, and now all returned empty-handed to Vienna.

At 9:00 P.M. that evening Napoleon and Duroc rode over to Murat's headquarters at the Welspitz posting station on the Brünn-Olmütz Road, some two miles from Austerlitz. It was freezing, the earth as hard as rock, but at least it was not snowing. Napoleon stamped his feet and rubbed his delicate hands. He who found even the Tuileries cold in sweltering July, requiring a fire while others wore the lightest summer clothing, now walked directly over to the large Moravian stove around which he found Murat and Soult comfortably settled, with Lannes sitting nearby at a rough table, hastily completing a letter.

"*Eh bien, messieurs*, all going well here?" he asked, his eyes darting from one to the other as he hovered over the enamel stove. "We don't think so," Lannes said as he approached Napoleon, "and I was just writing to Your Majesty to tell you so." He quickly read Lannes's brief report, looking up with a mock-quizzical expression. Duroc remained discreetly near the door. "What's this, Lannes advises retreat! It is the first time he has ever done such a thing. And you, Marshal Soult?" he said suddenly turning in his direction.

Lannes, who had in fact arrived just a few moments before Napoleon, had found Murat and Soult looking gloomy, both bent on a strategic withdrawal from an untenable position, greatly outnumbered by the combined Austro-Russian force before them. This was aggravated by the threat of Archduke Karl's army (it alone was larger than Napoleon's) still south of Vienna, still uncommitted, threatening to move in their direction. Then there was the growing Prussian threat, as Haugwitz had made only too clear, should they mobilize in time against the French. Napoleon's Grande Armée had gotten itself into a bind of menacing proportions.

Concurring with Murat and Soult, Lannes had thus drawn up this report based on a consensus of the three marshals. Addressing Soult again, Napoleon questioned him further. Soult, usually the most uncommitted, the most reserved, indeed, the shiftiest of Napoleon's first batch of marshals, who had moments earlier fully agreed on the necessity of retreat, now balked. Spinning around to face him, an astonished Lannes lashed out, "Soult is making fools of us!" Tempers flared, the wily, imperturbable Soult remaining emotionless as all three men stared at him, tension in the room rising. "I, too, feel it is necessary to withdraw," Napoleon finally said breaking the painful silence, mollifying slightly a betrayed Lannes and defusing the situation somewhat as the three marshals turned and left the room.[36]

In this room, which was warmer than the large drafty barn he was occupying a few miles away behind the Goldbach, Napoleon started dictating orders to Duroc—not for the withdrawal he had just indicated but for maneuvers of a different nature. In fact, precisely what Napoleon was thinking or planning still remains far from certain. As early as November 21 he had studied the ground between the villages of Austerlitz and Brünn, and at a point some five to six miles west of Austerlitz, on the Brünn-Olmütz Road, he had found a position where he said he wished to lay a trap for the advancing Allied army, the main line of these new positions lying behind the steep banks of the Goldbach.[37]

Although it was later suggested that Napoleon was absolutely set on "luring" the Russians here, the fact is that Napoleon himself had probably been wavering for more than a week as to the choice of actions to take. With only Lannes's, Soult's, and Murat's corps as well as Bessières's Imperial Guard present, Napoleon could not hope to defeat the mighty force being led by the czar himself, which outnumbered and outgunned them. He therefore sent urgent orders to Bernadotte and his remaining 10,500 men, and to Davout, more than eighty miles away with his reduced corps of just 16,300 men, to march from Vienna to join him there as quickly as possible.

Meanwhile Napoleon ordered what remained of his Grande Armée to take up positions in a north-south line along the west side of the Goldbach, with his left flank manned by Lannes's 19,200 men, to dig in straddling the Brünn-Olmütz Road at Santon Hill, where they placed most of their artillery, with a screen of Murat's cavalry before them barring the road. Soult's larger corps of 23,600 men was spread across the center and right flank, with the strongest concentration between Kobeneitz Pond and Lannes's corps. The last of his men stretched out in a very thin line southward, extending Napoleon's right flank to the hamlet of Telnitz and Satschan Pond. Napoleon's entire line remained to the west of the Goldbach and following its course. Behind Lannes stood only 5,500 men of the depleted Imperial Guard.

Despite his later boasting, Napoleon had only about 57,000 men, little artillery (139 guns) and cavalry (fewer than 8,000) to oppose 85,700 men now approaching with 278 cannon and a cavalry that outnumbered their own three to one. If the Allies had struck now, on the twenty-eighth or twenty-ninth, Napoleon probably would have been destroyed or sent falling back quickly in disarray to Vienna. But the Russians were slow and cautious, as usual, and Archduke Karl foolishly failed to close in behind Napoleon and catch the French army between his own superior Austrian force and the czar's, now approaching from the east. Napoleon's famous luck was holding, saving him from almost inevitable destruction. Then Bernadotte's corps finally arrived, bringing the French force up to 67,500, but still leaving them in a greatly inferior position.

As part of his alleged "entrapment" project, Napoleon had made the extremely risky decision to leave the long stretch of the Pratzen Heights, hundreds of feet above and before him across the Goldbach, completely unmanned and undefended, in order to entice the Russians into battle there. This is what Napoleon claimed afterward, but in reality he probably did so because he didn't have sufficient manpower or matériel to hold it properly—which would have required at least an additional 40,000 men with equivalent additional artillery.

Still, the archduke failed to advance from behind and sever Napoleon's link with Vienna, and it was only on December 1 that the Russians arrived at Austerlitz, Napoleon now only awaiting Davout's corps, which was expected to arrive during the night.

The Austro-Russian force was formidable, including Bagration's corps of 13,700 deploying across the Brünn-Olmütz Road facing Lannes, Liechtenstein's, and Buxhöwden's combined force of 59,000 men manning the Pratzen Heights facing Soult, supported behind them to their right by Kollowrat's corps of 16,200 men and Grand Duke Constantine's reserve corps of 10,500 men. Soult's corps alone, 23,600 men, were facing 59,000, including very heavy concentrations around the two weakest points of Soult's line—the center and right flank—where he was hopelessly outnumbered and outgunned.

Napoleon still claimed it was all a trap. He had reinforced his left flank to discourage a major attack there, while leaving Soult's center and right deliberately uncovered to encourage a flanking movement there by the Russians. To make such a move, however, the Allies would have to remove most of their 59,000 men from the Pratzen Heights to complete the swing around and envelopment of Soult, as the rest of their force simultaneously attacked Lannes. Napoleon's apparent plan was then to drive through the emptied center to seize the Pratzen Heights, and swing round Liechtenstein's and Buxhöwden's enveloping force with Soult's and Davout's corps. To what extent this was another case of rationalization after the fact is not clear. Napoleon's real risk remained in the event the Allies did not oblige him by swinging all their troops around his right flank but instead drove right through Soult's thinned center, dividing the entire French army into two separate sections, which could then have been captured or destroyed.

On the eve of battle Napoleon made the rounds of all front-line troops who, in their great enthusiasm, lit hundreds of straw and pine torches, tens of thousands cheering, "*Vive l'Empereur!*" over and over again, their voices carrying across the few hundred yards separating the French and Allied positions. A heavy wintry ground fog set in as Napoleon finally retired in the wee hours of the morning.

At the crack of dawn, the dense fog still concealed French positions as 278 Russian and Austrian big guns suddenly opened fire on them. In theory Allied orders came from Czar Alexander and Emperor Franz at their joint headquarters in the village of Krzenowitz. But it was the Austrian chief of staff, Weirother, who presented the battle plan to the senior commanders at 1:00 A.M. on December 2—a meeting through which Kutuzov allegedly peacefully slept. Weirother it seems was determined to oblige Napoleon and the trap set with Soult's weakened right flank. When Kutuzov, who disagreed with the Austrian strategist, was overruled, he went back to sleep.

By eight o'clock in the morning the Russians and Prussians were hitting Soult's division round Telnitz very hard, forcing the French to withdraw from that hamlet. With Davout's troops from Vienna finally in place, the French would soon order a counterattack, fighting continuing at Telnitz and Sokolnitz throughout the morning.

As the ground fog lifted at about eight o'clock, it revealed the dramatic depletion of Austro-Russian troops along the Pratzen Heights, as they moved in a massive formation against the seemingly weak French right

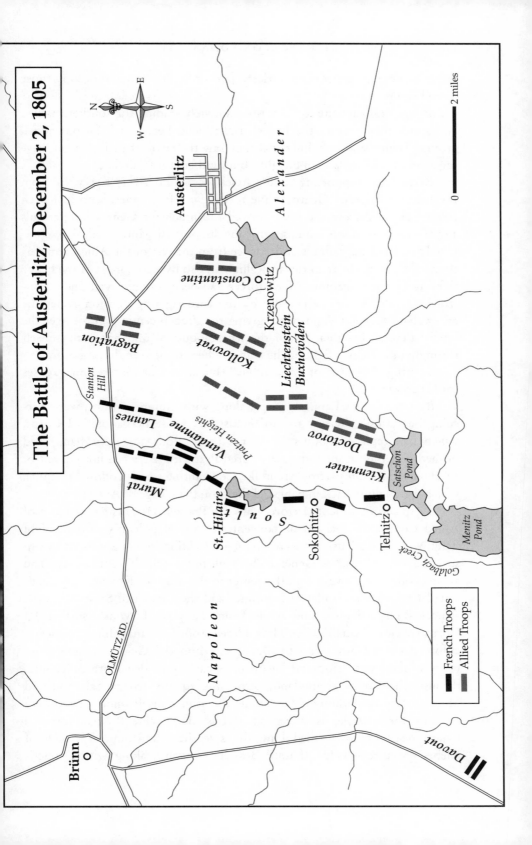

The Battle of Austerlitz, December 2, 1805

Brünn

OLMÜTZ RD.

Napoleon

Stanton Hill

Murat

Lannes

Vandamme

Pratzen Heights

St.-Hilaire

Soult

Bagration

Kollowrat

Austerlitz

Constantine

Krzenowitz

Liechtenstein

Buxhowden

Alexander

Kienmaier

Doctorov

Sokolnitz

Telnitz

Satschon Pond

Goldbach Creek

Menitz Pond

Davout

French Troops
Allied Troops

N E W S

0   2 miles

wing. Napoleon immediately ordered part of Soult's corps to occupy those same heights.

It was only as Kutuzov and Miloradovich, leading the southern Allied corps sweeping around the French right flank, began their all-out attack around Telnitz and Sokolnitz that they saw the error of their ways in having abandoned the Pratzen Heights, but by then it was too late.

Bernadotte, supporting Soult's attack, came under very heavy fire from the Russian Imperial Guard, while to the far left, Lannes, who had been heavily engaged from the start, proved too much for General Bagration's 13,700 men. By noon Lannes, with the support of Murat's cavalry, completely isolated Bagration's entire force from the rest of the Allied army, as they fell back up the road toward Olmütz. Also by noon, most of the heavy fighting by the remaining Allied forces had been brought well under control by Soult's troops, especially by the hard-fighting division under the ever valiant General Vandamme, giving the French center control over the crucial Pratzen Heights. As for the whereabouts of Marshal Soult himself throughout the day's fighting, he was nowhere to be seen, having retired to a safer refuge "because of eye trouble." (He always had interesting excuses for his cowardice.)

By two o'clock Lannes's corps, along with Murat's cavalry, were pursuing Bagration's division toward Haussnitz, while Bernadotte's I Corps, which had replaced Soult's IV Corps (now along the right flank) had pushed past the vacant and now secured Pratzen Heights in hot pursuit of Liechtenstein's and part of Archduke Constantine's and Kollowrat's units, which were falling back in panicked flight on the village of Austerlitz.

By this same time, therefore, with the Pratzen Heights swept clean of Allied troops, the real drama concentrated on Napoleon's extreme right flank, where "the Russians were no longer fighting to win a victory, but to save their very lives," as General Thiébault put it.[38] Soult's entire corps had swung completely away from the center to the south of Kobelnitz, concentrated between the hamlet of Sokolnitz and the Chapel of Saint Anthony, against Buxhöwden's corps, while from the west, Davout's smaller III Corps enveloped Buxhöwden's bewildered troops in a magnificent crescent, enforced on the other end by Bessières's Imperial Guard, forcing Doctorov's infantry division and Kienmaier's cavalry to flee south of Telnitz, through the frozen swampland, across the equally frozen Salschon and Meunitz Ponds. Although Vandamme did find himself under very heavy pressure for a while, as fifteen squadrons of the élite Russian Imperial Guard nearly overwhelmed him, the splendid Vandamme—"a man of Kléber's stature"—held off until Bessière's cavalry, along with Drouet's division, reached him, thereby tightening the closing crescent on the Allies.[39] Napoleon, whose headquarters were in the center of the fighting, foiled an attempted cavalry maneuver by the Russian Imperial Guard by sending in the dependable Rapp with a couple of squadrons of *chasseurs* of the French Imperial Guard, as well as the Mamelukes, crushing the élite Russian cavalry.

By 2:30 P.M. the Austro-Russian force was completely severed into three separate units, all hastily fleeing the battlefield, Bagration up the Olmütz Road in the center; Liechtenstein's, Constantine's, and Kollowrat's corps now at Austerlitz; and Buxhöwden's corps crossing the ponds and marsh along Napoleon's right, southern flank. The fighting had been intense, fierce, and grim everywhere, the French with orders to take no prisoners at all—to leave no man standing, whether he surrendered or not— until the final hour of the battle, when Napoleon finally relented. "Let no one escape!" Davout had echoed.

By three o'clock most of the serious fighting was over as entire Allied divisions threw their arms in the air, while General Doctorov's remaining few thousand men tried to escape over the frozen marshland and lakes. Seeing this, Napoleon directed the fire of twenty-five cannon to smash the thick ice beneath the feet of the fleeing cavalry, infantry, and artillery crews, resulting in as many as two thousand Russians drowning in Satschon Pond in their heavy winter uniforms, packs, and boots, along with thirty-eight guns and at least 130 horses. Rarely had Napoleon shown himself to be so vicious. General Thiébault, himself gravely wounded after a heroic fight, summed up the results of the battle of Austerlitz: fifteen thousand Russian and Prussian dead, thanks to Napoleon's initial inhuman policy of taking none alive; twelve thousand prisoners including 270 lower officers; ten colonels and eight generals; fifty flags and 180 pieces of artillery (which were soon dispatched to Paris to be transformed into a national monument in the Place Vendome).[40]

The victory was complete—indeed no victory could have been more so, as every Russian and Austrian soldier and officer who could flee, did so, including the Austrian and Russian emperors (Czar Alexander, abandoned by his own guard, was nearly captured). Austerlitz—the Battle of the Three Emperors—was over. The Allies, who had not practiced the same brutality on the battlefield battle, had killed only 1,350 French, leaving another 6,940 wounded.

Thus the Battle of Austerlitz, occurring one year to the day after Napoleon's imperial coronation in Nôtre-Dame, and inaugurated under the most anxious of circumstances, finally resulted in the extraordinary victory he so badly needed. Not only did it bring the Allied armies to their knees and the campaign to a brilliant if bloodthirsty end, it resounded throughout the French capital and Empire with such force as to put an end to the financial collapse that had been threatening France's very existence.[41] "I have defeated the Austro-Russian Army commanded by the two emperors," Napoleon proudly informed a most anxious Josephine. "The battle of Austerlitz is the finest of all I have fought."[42] No one could argue with that. But little did Napoleon, or indeed anyone at that time, realize that by having refused to settle accounts peaceably prior to this "successful" military campaign, he had sown the seeds of his own ultimate downfall. The Austerlitz campaign was in fact not to prove his great triumph, ensuring the continuation of his empire. It was rather the first stroke of the death knell of the House of Bonaparte, incurring as it did the irrevocable enmity—ultimately—of the whole of Europe, a Europe that would never rest until Emperor Napoleon I reigned no more. The Austerlitz campaign was to prove one of the greatest mistakes of his career.

CHAPTER 25

The Marches of Empire

Your Holiness [Pope Pius VII] is sovereign of Rome, but I am its emperor.

apoleon's return from Austerlitz had been triumphant. As he traversed the German states, crossing the Rhine, church bells rang as he passed beneath a long series of triumphal arches of flowers in one city after another. The people of Paris cheered even more loudly, giving balls and elegant dinners for this man who, only a few weeks earlier, had been thought to be finished, and with him his tinsel empire. As a part of these celebrations, Imperial Master of the Hunt Marshal Berthier gave hunting parties for Napoleon, including one of his Corsican favorites, a rabbit hunt. Berthier, who personally preferred stag, had gone to considerable trouble to buy approximately one thousand "hares."

On the day of the hunt all was in readiness, the rabbits in massive cages along the wooded sides of an open field, as several carriages finally appeared, Napoleon and his staff soon emerging in full hunting regalia. As Napoleon walked across the field, the signal was given to release the rabbits, and hundreds upon hundreds of black-and-white rabbits leaped forward, enjoying their new freedom. But as the intrepid hunters prepared to go in for the kill, the animals, instead of fleeing in the opposite direction, perversely turned straight for the hunters, coming at them in magnificent bounds.

At first Napoleon could not believe his eyes, nor could anyone else, laughing at the comic absurdity of the whole thing. But laughter soon gave way to perplexity, and perplexity to concern, as the hundreds of animals continued to head directly for Napoleon. Finally a bit anxious himself, he turned and ordered those around him, even the coachmen and postilions, to grab sticks and chase away the insolent animals now poking fun at the emperor's reputation as a distinguished huntsman. But all to no avail. They swarmed around Napoleon, entwining themselves between his legs, even leaping into his arms. He tried beating them off with his riding crop, but more arrived. At last his aides-de-camp and coachmen came to his rescue and got him back safely into his carriage, though it too was quickly besieged.

It had been a narrow escape! A furious Berthier, humiliated by the absurd event, learned only afterward that his men, instead of trapping hares, had purchased a thousand tame rabbits—due to be used for pâté—from farmers. And the mighty victor of Austerlitz, who had soundly defeated a combined force of 85,000 Russian and Austrian troops armed with cannon, muskets, and sabers, had now ignominiously scurried off another battle-field, pursued by a thousand unarmed rabbits, who had mistaken him for the kindly man who was due to give them their daily feed.[1]

"I have few prejudices, and I shall be very glad if the peace treaty dates from the reintroduction of the Gregorian calendar [January 1, 1806], which presages, I hope, as much happiness for my reign as it did for the ancien régime," Napoleon had written Talleyrand from the Schönbrunn Palace in Vienna on December 23, 1805.[2] In fact the suppression of the revolutionary calendar in favor of the old Gregorian one was preceded by the treaty by just a few days. It was signed at Pressburg near Vienna on December 26 by Foreign Minister Talleyrand and Prince John of Liechtenstein and Gyula.

The results were painful indeed for Austria's Emperor Franz, who had to recognize the territories previously lost to France as a result of the treaties of Campo Formio and Lunéville, now adding Venice, Istria, and Dalmatia. Moreover the hapless Habsburg was also forced to recognize Napoleon as king of Italy. Napoleon's new German allies were to be rewarded for their ties with, and support of, France, the electors of Bavaria and Württemberg being raised to monarchs in their own right, their states enhanced by important fresh slices of the former Austrian Empire. The mint-new king of Bavaria thus received Passau, the Tyrol, Brixen, Trent, Augsburg, and the Vorarlberg, while the king of Württemberg's domains were extended to include five small towns on the Danube, the landgraviate of Nellenberg, part of Breisgau, and a few smaller places. Napoleon's other new ally, the elector of Baden, received the remainder of Breisgau and the lovely lakeside city of Constance. The only compensation the Austrian emperor was to receive for his territorial losses would be in the form of Salzburg and Berchtesgaden, which were transferred to him from the lands of his brother, the Archduke Ferdinand (the former grand duke of Tuscany), while Ferdinand received the principality of Würzburg. As for Napoleon, he had secured three delighted new allies, who were to form the nucleus of his new German buffer, along with the previous west bank Rhineland territories, not to mention the forty million gold francs Napoleon was to receive from the defeated Emperor Franz.

"Never had a victor imposed harder conditions on the vanquished," Joseph Bonaparte's good friend Miot commented, little realizing that this was nothing compared to what Napoleon had in store for the vanquished of the future.[3] "Charlemagne was a conqueror and not a founder," Talleyrand had pointed out to the French Senate back on March 18, 1805, when Napoleon first announced the creation of the Kingdom of Italy. "Alexander the Great, incessantly expanding the limits of his conquests, left only death and destruction in his wake. . . . Like these great men . . . we have seen Your Majesty advance rapidly with his arms in Europe and Asia." But, the foreign minister preached, Napoleon was no mere marauding warrior. He was a statesman, a man who would conquer "by the wisdom of your moderation. . . . Your Majesty wanted to remind France of the necessity of order and peace."[4] It was wishful thinking on Talleyrand's part, and Napoleon looked more annoyed than pleased by the remarks. Indeed it was this same Napoleon who at his Italian coronation in May 1805 had placed yet another crown on his head, declaring in Italian: "Heaven gave it to me. Woe unto him who touches it!" That said it all.

At Pressburg he had continued in the same vein, despoiling the Austrian Empire while failing to comprehend how his acts were hastening the disintegration of that empire, with direct effects on Europe as a result. Talleyrand alone seemed to foresee the full extent of the tragedy of Napoleon's ruthless buccaneering and lack of understanding. "I persist in the hope that Your Majesty's latest victory may permit him to assure some repose for Europe, while guaranteeing the security of the civilized world against the invasion of the barbarians." But, the foreign minister then counseled,

> Your Majesty is now in a position to break the Austrian monarchy, or to support and reerect it. Once broken, however, even Your Majesty will not possess power enough to reassemble the ruins of shattered

states and to recompose it as the unit it formerly was. And yet the existence of this single unit is most necessary. Indeed, it is quite indispensable for ensuring the future health of all civilized nations.

For, as he explained, "The Austrian monarchy ... is a poorly composed mass of different states, almost all of them with their own languages, mores, religions, and political and civil systems of administration, and whose only common link is their leader." Put together over the past thousand years, the Holy Roman Empire was in a state of precarious balance, resulting from the quarrels and battles between princes, Protestants, and Catholics, involving more than three hundred principalities, duchies, landgraviates, and free cities, which had been united by the Habsburgs into a relatively peaceful equilibrium. "Today, defeated and humiliated, the Austrian Empire needs a generous, understanding hand from its conqueror. . . . It is that which all the true friends of your glory expect from your political forethought and magnanimity.[5]

The Napoleon who had refused to take alive thousands of defeated Russians and Austrians at Austerlitz was hardly likely to show moderation at Pressburg, nor did he do so. Setting out from Vienna, Napoleon was determined to upset the entire fragile political cohesion of the Holy Roman Empire. There must be a new order in Europe, a Napoleonic order (that would provide him with even larger armies and annual subsidies). There was room for nothing else. Talleyrand was a fool, a dinosaur living in another age.

On his return to Paris on January 26, 1806, Bonaparte wanted to get to work at once. To begin with, the critical financial situation of the government and nation had to be addressed and stabilized. Next the lands taken from Austria and the defunct Holy Roman Empire had to be reorganized to create a vast new northeastern flank for the French Empire, this time on the right bank of the Rhine, as a buffer against central and eastern Europe. And then there was the matter of brothers Joseph, Louis, and later, Jérôme, whom Napoleon had decided to invest with limited monarchical powers of their own, along the marches of his expanding fiefdom.

Within twenty-four hours of his return, Napoleon summoned the finance, treasury, and police ministers to the newly refurbished Tuileries, then ordering that the financiers Desprès, Vanderberghe, and Ouvrard "return" tens of millions (actually of their own money) to government coffers. "I made a dozen rogues cough up," he crudely boasted to Josephine afterward.[6] It had all begun when, at bayonet point, Napoleon had forced Spain to sign a defense pact with Paris, requiring among other things a monthly payment of 6 million francs to the French treasury. (This treaty, signed by the Spanish king under duress, was not legally valid, like most of those drawn up by Napoleon for his allies.) Treasury Minister Barbé-Marbois had just repaid Desprès (representing Ouvrard's interests in the Company of United Merchants) as much as 80 million francs owed his firm. The hard-pressed Spanish government had accepted a large loan from Ouvrard to meet the regular payment due Paris, as well as for grain shipments. In return Ouvrard received tobacco and mining concessions. In addition, on Spain's declaration of war against England, Ouvrard signed enormous contracts by which he was to provision French and Spanish naval vessels in various ports. Spain for its part promised to repay Ouvrard and the French government with government drafts secured by the Mexican treasury. (At the end of 1804 Ouvrard received the first of these Spanish drafts.) It was all as fantastic as it was complicated. By September 1805 the French treasury owed Ouvrard close to one hundred million francs for unpaid war contracts alone. Nor was Spain able to repay the French government for its grain purchases, not to mention the "war subsidies" owed Paris, and the value of the real collapsed, resulting in the freezing of Spanish credits everywhere. By September 1805, as Napoleon was about to set out on his Austerlitz campaign, the Bank of France was all but bankrupt. Meanwhile Vanderberghe, a major war contractor, had to suspend his activities, having no more cash with which to buy materials. Barbé-Marbois finally agreed to repay Vanderberghe's firm some 80 million francs taken directly from the state tax collectors. But by January 1806 Vanderberghe was still owed 147 million francs by the government. Unable to proceed, he terminated his government contract, which infuriated Napoleon. On his return in January, Napoleon extorted more money from the Company of United Merchants, rather than repaying the vast amounts he owed them (and never fully honored).[7]

Napoleon was now blaming others for the financial debacle besetting the government, when in reality the financial crisis was a result of his stripping French coffers to the bone for his invasion of England. Napoleon then fired a quaking Barbé-Marbois—"a fool," he called him to his face—replacing him as treasury minister with Mollien. Next he reorganized the Bank of France, permitting his own hand-picked governor from the Treasury Ministry to administer and control its affairs thereafter, while creating a government disbursement office to regulate the flow of money from the treasury.[8]

The business community was shaken, both by the resounding catastrophe that had caused the failure of some of the most prestigious banks and merchant houses of the nation, and by the harsh threats against their esteemed confrères Desprès, Vanderberghe, and Ouvrard. "I should have had them shot,"[9] Napoleon declared to Josephine.

Nevertheless, as a result of Austerlitz, government "*rentes*," or investment yields, rose within a fortnight from 45 to 66 percent (though still well below their former wartime highs), while interest rates of 24 percent remained forbidding. Austrian gold would literally start pouring in from the vanquished Habsburgs, not to mention the vast new income source he would be tapping from the Germanic states he was intending to reorganize. The treasury would never again be empty. Moreover, commerce and industry were to be encouraged officially by the French government, and there would be an increase in agricultural production as well (the latter one of Napoleon's few temporary successes).[10] In an attempt ostensibly further to increase French revenues (and his own), but actually to harm England, Napoleon was set on creating his Continental System, closing all European markets and ports to British ships, goods, and products. He would bring "haughty England," as he referred to it, to its knees, and any European country violating Napoleon's injunctions concerning this was to be dealt with by his eloquent long sabers. He would brook no disobedience.

Back in November 1805 Elector-Archbishop Dalberg, Baden's minister of state, had submitted a proposal to Napoleon calling for the suppression of the traditional princely houses of the Rhineland then comprising the Holy Roman Empire. Instead they were to be reconstituted as a confederation of such states to serve as a buffer, "to protect it [the French Empire]" from Austria, Prussia, and Russia. Dalberg followed with a plan of his own, and with the conclusion of the Treaty of Pressburg on December 26, 1805, this concept was further developed by Napoleon, Talleyrand, and their advisers.[11] On February 15, 1806, a Franco-Prussian Treaty of Cooperation was signed in Paris by Napoleon's closest confidant, Duroc, and the Prussian minister, Haugwitz, for which the Prussians were promised British Hannover in exchange.

With the preliminaries out of the way, Napoleon now concentrated on the new Rhineland scheme, and the plan for its inception, the Act of Confederation, was duly signed in Paris by Talleyrand on July 12. If the foreign minister himself was not pleased with this destruction of a working political organism and the subsequent seizure of hundreds of sovereign states, he had done his best in the circumstances to reconstitute some sort of balance in their new guise.

First Napoleon had to have strong pro-French leadership within the confederation, and thus had the former archchancellor of the Germanic

Confederation, Dalberg, named its leader with the new title of prince primate. Signatories included the new kings of Bavaria and Württemberg, Elector-Archbishop Dalberg of Baden, the duke of Berg (Murat), the landgrave of Hesse-Darmstadt, various princes, the duke of Aremberg, and Count von Leyen (Dalberg's nephew).

Altogether some 350 principalities, duchies, and other territories would now be reduced to a mere thirty-nine states. Each member of the confederation was to be represented at a Diet to be convened periodically at Frankfurt and divided into a College of Kings and a College of Princes. The theoretical purpose of the Diet was to settle all disputes between member states, presided over by Napoleon's new henchman, Prince Primate Dalberg. Napoleon himself was to be given yet another title, "Protector of the Confederation." Other annexations soon followed, including the two formerly free imperial cities of Nuremberg (annexed by the king of Bavaria) and Frankfurt (which went to Prince Primate Dalberg). Also absorbed into this confederation were "the knightly lands" within their frontiers, that is to say, the property of the Imperial Knights of the Holy Roman Empire, traditionally strongly attached to Austria and the Habsburgs.

The new Confederation of the Rhine was a strictly controlled satellite complex, the main purposes of which were defense and economic union, not to mention the "annual subsidies" each member state was required to pay Napoleon and France. In addition to paying for the complete maintenance of the French military governors and French troops in these states, every state was required to supply troops of its own when attacked. Altogether the Confederation of the Rhine was obliged to provide Bonaparte with 88,400 men in time of war.[12]

The Treaty of Pressburg had left many people bitterly unhappy. The ensuing creation of the Confederation of the Rhine not only angered Austria but gravely upset the balance in Prussia, which hitherto opted for neutrality in times of war with the French. The wheels now began to turn, building in momentum, to convert a weakened, dithering Friedrich Wilhelm III into a ruler finally convinced that he no longer had any choice but to prepare for the worst—war against France. Despite the Franco-Prussian Treaty of February 15, 1806, Prussia maintained secret links with the sympathetic Czar Alexander (due at least in part to Alexander's attraction to Queen Louise of Prussia). The outright seizure of the Rhineland states as French satellites threatened and impinged on the royal Prussian territorial preserves. By giving the Duchies of Cleves and then Berg (ceded by Bavaria) to Joachim and Caroline Murat in March—the two becoming a grand duchy, "the most beautiful gift in the world," Murat called it—

Napoleon aggravated matters considerably. As duke (and then grand duke) of Berg, and a major new Rhineland property owner, Murat immediately began "extending" his territorial boundaries into traditional Prussian possessions. Napoleon's encouragement of this foreign occupation merely acted as a goad to the already anxious Prussians.[13]

In a private letter to Talleyrand, Napoleon had declared his intention of neutralizing Prussia: "Prussia is a great Power, and as a general consideration it would be a serious error to permit her to increase in size. . . . The remedy for this would be to create a brand-new State in Germany that would grow to a size equal to Prussia's," the capital of which would center round Wesel and Düsseldorf (in Murat's duchies). By handing over Cleves and Berg, Napoleon secured this check against Prussia.[14]

A few modifications were made after the initial sixteen princes announced their separation from the Holy Roman Empire in July 1806, including the creation of the three new grand duchies of Baden, Berg, and Hesse-Darmstadt, while Nassau was promoted to a duchy. Several traditional rulers lost all sovereign rights altogether. Naturally Napoleon could not suppress such an important number of pivotal German states and sovereign houses, occupying them with French troops, without arousing lasting, bitter anti-French sentiment. When a patriotic Nuremberg bookseller by the name of Palm published and sold anti-French (that is, anti-Bonaparte) pamphlets, denouncing this latest example of French territorial enterprise, Napoleon had the annoying fellow kidnapped by Berthier's troops and summarily executed, much as he had had Enghien and others disposed of before. So great was Napoleon's megalomania, and so vast his actual power, that he no longer cared what other countries might think about any of his actions.

Then—to worry the Prussians, Austrians, Russians, and English even more—on March 14, 1806, Napoleon announced his intention of naming his brother Louis king of Holland (to avoid overtly annexing that country, which might have caused a bit of an uproar). Before the month was out, Napoleon named brother Joseph to the throne of Naples, territory covering roughly one-third of the country and including (at least in theory) Sicily. Napoleon's Kingdom of Italy included the northern part of the country, apart from the Papal States. (In a decree of December 27, 1805, Napoleon had unilaterally announced: "The Dynasty of Naples has ceased to reign." Queen Maria Carolina for one did not agree, and the French had to fight their way to Naples and then "pacify" the region.) Joseph finally acquiesced to this crown only when Napoleon assured him that he would not be renouncing any of his rights to the French imperial crown.[15]

The seizure of the Neapolitan kingdom was to permit Napoleon to complete his conquest of the whole of Italy. This led to another confrontation with Rome, when Pius VII refused to close his borders and ports to the English. Bonaparte tightened his control over the Italian peninsula by naming Talleyrand prince of Benevento, and Bernadotte prince of Ponte Corvo (lands, incidentally, disputed by Rome and Naples) and then declared these two new princes to be French imperial grand dignitaries. If they were attacked, so was Paris.

On January 15 Eugène de Beauharnais had married Princess Augusta of Bavaria, returning with his bride to Italy, where he was assured by Napoleon that he and Augusta would one day succeed to that country's royal title (a promise shortly to be denied by Napoleon in public). Napoleon further secured the marches of his new empire by marrying off Josephine's niece, Stéphanie de Beauharnais, to the heir of the grand duke of Baden, while forcing a most resentful Berthier to give up his long-standing love and mistress, Madame de Visconti, for a minor Bavarian princess. A year later Jérôme was to add the final link by "marrying" (bigamously—he was still legally married to Elizabeth) into the House of Württemberg. The new Charlemagne had risen, and the allies and Church were duly notified. "Your Holiness is sovereign of Rome," Napoleon proclaimed to Pius VII, "but I am its Emperor."[16]

Throughout this period Napoleon, while moving with decision on Prussia, maintained expansive negotiations with both Russia and England. Initial peace talks between Talleyrand and a recently released British prisoner, the earl of Yarmouth, were followed up by Lord Lauderdale, who arrived in Paris on August 5, 1806. Much to the astonishment of Talleyrand and embarrassment of Napoleon, the British made extraordinary concessions, under the orders of the dying foreign secretary, Charles James Fox. Fox was willing to recognize Joseph as king of the Two Sicilies, Louis as king of Holland, the new kings of Etruria (in central Italy), Bavaria, and Württemberg (in the future), and the grand duke of Baden. England would return the Dutch colonies to Holland (except the Cape of Good Hope) and would even withdraw from Sicily, despite public denials to the contrary. In exchange for these sweeping concessions, Talleyrand promised that England could retain Malta, and that Ferdinand IV (the de jure king of Naples) would be compensated by the Balearic Islands (without the knowledge of Spain), while Hannover was to be returned to its rightful sovereign, the king of England. Napoleon, who had encouraged these talks, now without explanation rejected the draft peace treaty already signed by Talleyrand and

Lauderdale that same August, thereby ending the last and most unexpected opportunity he had of making peace with England.[17] Fox died the following month a disappointed, broken man, having failed to secure the peace he had assured Parliament he could obtain. There would be no other such occasion. Thanks to the French ruler, there would be war to the end.

Simultaneously, negotiations between St. Petersburg and Paris resumed in July, when M. Oubril, the Russian minister plenipotentiary, arrived at the French capital to negotiate a Franco-Russian peace agreement with Talleyrand. The two men signed a draft treaty on July 20, but this time it was a scornful Alexander I who, still furious about the shameful Russian defeat at Austerlitz, refused to ratify it. On receiving the czar's rejection on September 3, Napoleon told Talleyrand, "I cannot have a real alliance with any of the great powers of Europe," and ordered the War Office to call up another fifty thousand army conscripts, while hastening the fortifications of the newly acquired city of Wesel.[18] By September 26 Napoleon was on the move with his army to Germany, making his temporary headquarters on October 2 at Würzburg, where he instructed his eight commanding marshals to hold each of their corps "in readiness, so as to be able to set out within an hour after receiving orders to take the field."[19]

As for Prussia's dilatory King Friedrich Wilhelm III, everything Napoleon did seemed intended to further offend him and the honor of the entire Junker class. Napoleon's seizure of Ansbach, Berg, Wesel, and Hamburg had certainly not helped matters, along with the news that he had been promising Foreign Minister Fox the restoration of Hannover to England (though it was privately promised to Prussia). But naturally it was the French announcement on July 12, 1806, of the creation of the Confederation of the Rhine and its immediate expansion to include Würzburg and Saxony that—even before the ink was dry—shook Frederick the Great's ghost in the Sans Souci Palace at Potsdam. The Prussian monarchy, traditionally fearful and jealous of Saxony (just south of Berlin and including the cities of Leipzig and Dresden), was now doubly incensed by that state's inclusion in Napoleon's new Germanic empire. Napoleon knowingly, deliberately goaded and goaded.

Friedrich Wilhelm's pent-up feelings of outrage could no longer be contained, and on September 26 he sent a voluminous letter—indeed an ultimatum—to Napoleon listing Prussian grievances against France. The language was for once bitter and direct, denouncing the creation of the confederation and Murat's seizure of Wesel. Europe could no longer put up with "this continued fever of fear and suspense." He gave the French until October 8 to reply, little realizing that Napoleon was already on the march

at the head of his armies. On receipt of this document at Bamberg on October 7, the French emperor immediately published the news, describing it as
"a pathetic pamphlet against France."[20]

"Hasten to mobilize your troops. Assemble all available forces . . . and protect your frontiers, while I leap into the center of Prussia and march
directly on Berlin," Napoleon had written his brother, King Louis of Holland, in a top-secret note that September. Marshal Mortier's VIII Corps was
forming at Mainz, where he, along with Louis's army, was expected to
secure the Rhine. Before the Prussian king had even made his final decision
on war against France, Napoleon had begun moving his army forward. "If
the enemy opposes you with a force not exceeding 30,000 men, you should
advance in concert with Marshal Ney and attack it," Napoleon instructed
Marshal Soult on October 5.[21]

The French army was marching forward with a nominal force totaling
little more than 200,000 men, but this included Marmont's 13,500-man corps
in Dalmatia, Masséna's 40,000-strong Army of Italy still in Tuscany, and
Eugène's 40,000 men to the north, as well as Louis's army of 18,000 in
Holland. The Grande Armée actually marching "for Berlin" under
Napoleon's immediate orders in fact comprised six corps: Soult's IV and
Ney's VI along their southern flank; Davout's very tough III Corps and
Augereau's VII Corps to the west; and Lefebvre's V Corps (soon to be commanded by Lannes), and Bernadotte's I Corps, along with Murat's cavalry. In
addition, the new Confederation of the Rhine was assembling an initial force
of 27,000 men to secure its new frontiers. Thus Napoleon could count on just
under 100,000 men, as opposed to 146,300 Prussian troops—that is, if 25,000
men then in eastern Pomerania did not join them, or the two new Russian
armies of 60,000 men each, at Brest-Litovsk.[22]

The three principal Prussian armies facing Napoleon included Prince
Hohenlohe's 42,000 men, the duke of Brunswick's 75,300 troops, and General Rüchel's 29,000. These were maximum figures, of course, for units
would be on detached duty, in garrisons, hospitals, on leave, and so on.
When it came to the actual battles about to be fought, the Prussians had
only 114,500 men available to fight Napoleon's 96,000-man force—much
more reasonable odds.

Finding the Prussians was Napoleon's immediate concern as his wedge-
shaped force advanced to the northeast, in the general direction of Jena,
Naumburg, and Leipzig. The first clashes with the opposing cavalry and
infantry units took place at Schleiz on October 9, one day after the expira-
tion of Friedrich Wilhelm's ultimatum. Brushing aside this initial Prussian

Napoleon's Campaign in Germany, Fall 1806

North Sea

Baltic Sea

Lübeck

Hamburg

MECKLENBURG

Prenzlau

Oder R.

PRUSSIA

Bremen

Elbe R.

HOLLAND

Berlin

Hannover

Potsdam

Brunswick

Magdeburg

Wittenberg

Wesel

SAXONY

BERG

Freiberg Leipzig

Cologne

Dresden

HESSE

Auerstädt Naumburg

Weimar

NASSAU CONFEDERATION

THURINGIA Jena

Koblenz

Frankfurt

Prague

Rhine R.

FRANCE

OF THE

Mainz Würzburg

BOHEMIA

ANSBACH

Metz

Ansbach Nuremberg

AUSTRIA

RHINE

Danube R.

BADEN

Stuttgart

WÜRTTEMBERG

BAVARIA

Munich

N

W E

S

Freiburg

0   100 miles

SWITZERLAND

TYROL

force, Murat and Bernadotte continued their march. On the tenth Lannes's
V Corps attacked Prince Ludwig's force of 8,300 men at Saalfeld, in the
course of which the prince himself was killed, his troops breaking and fleeing northward to rejoin Brunswick's army before Weimar or to seek shelter
among Hohenlohe's force at Jena. The very momentum of the French force
was frightening Prussian commanders.

The French continued to advance, Napoleon expecting a major battle at
Gera. Finding the place empty, Murat's cavalry probed ahead, with Davout
marching toward Naumburg, preceded by Lannes and Augereau. Davout
and Bernadotte were instructed to head off the Prussians should they make
a break for the Elbe and Magdeburg. Meanwhile Friedrich Wilhelm and
Brunswick were still marching to Weimar when they learned that the
French had already seized Naumburg, which lay before them, and Leipzig.

At a war council on the morning of October 13, it was decided not to
fight the French at nearby Jena, but to withdraw, via Auerstädt and
Freiburg. The Prussians, so defiant in August, were now retreating as
quickly as possible, while Napoleon, still ignorant of their whereabouts,
was not expecting to give battle before the sixteenth. In this campaign as in
the last, Napoleon's single greatest weakness was the complete lack of reliable army intelligence as to movements and plans of the opposing force. In
this case it is especially surprising, given his numerous new German-speaking allies with their many direct links with Berlin and the Prussian army
hierarchy.

After receiving a number of reports from Davout, Augereau, and Murat,
at 9:00 A.M. on the thirteenth Bonaparte finally realized that the entire
Prussian army was falling back in the direction of Magdeburg. He issued a
fresh spate of orders to Davout, Lannes, Ney, Soult, and Bernadotte to prepare for a big battle at Jena, or an attack against a retreating Prussian army.
On receipt of a final message from Lannes's courier at 3 o'clock in the afternoon, while himself still en route to Jena, Napoleon made more definite
troop dispositions, to enable him to close in on the Prussians still in place
between Jena and nearby Weimar.

In fact Lannes's V Corps had easily occupied Jena that same morning,
following a hasty Prussian withdrawal, and it was just to the north of that
city that Napoleon joined him later that afternoon. He thought he had the
main body of the Prussian army before him and intended to hold them
there with the 25,000 troops he had in place. Instructions were dispatched
for Soult and Ney to come to Jena on the double, while thousands of
troops, almost every battalion available, were ordered to widen a road to
the top of Landgrafenberg, the highest mountain north of Jena, on which

Napoleon then brought up forty-two pieces of heavy artillery. Still thinking he had the whole of Brunswick's army before him, Bonaparte ordered Davout and Bernadotte (with Murat's cavalry), then just to the west of Naumburg, to rush the long distance from there (near Auerstädt) south-ward to Apolda, to fall on the rear of the Prussian army. After giving orders for Lannes to attack at 6:00 A.M. on October 14, Napoleon returned to his mountaintop headquarters, surrounded by several thousand guardsmen, and retired for what remained of the night.

In fact, however, Brunswick's army of 63,000 men was not before Napoleon at Jena, but just north of Auerstädt facing Davout's 26,000 men, while Napoleon's force instead faced Hohenlohe's 38,000 men and 120 can-non (with Rüchel's 13,000 men, still a total of only 51,000 troops). By noon on the fourteenth, Napoleon would have approximately 96,000 men; and Lannes's V Corps and Augereau's VII Corps, aided by St.-Hilaire's divi-sion, were already causing the Prussians to retreat faster, even before Ney's VI Corps, the rest of Soult's IV Corps, and Bernadotte's I Corps managed to arrive.

At six o'clock on the fourteenth Lannes's guns and troops had duly opened fire on Hohenlohe's right against Generals Tauenzien and Gräwert just to the north of the village of Vierzehnheiligen, as ordered by Napoleon, when their attack was suddenly jeopardized at eleven o'clock by the unex-pected appearance of Ney leading a small number of troops, dashing between Augereau's and Lannes's corps. As usual Ney had acted without orders, and a furious Napoleon managed to save him only by bringing in his last two regiments of reserve cavalry.

This was as good an opportunity as the cautious Prince Hohenlohe had to break through the French line. Instead he foolishly ordered General Gräwert to halt in unprotected country, abruptly ending his successful advance, to await Rüchel's corps to reinforce him. The result was that Gräwert's men were decimated by French fire, suffering very heavy casual-ties for some two hours during a French counterattack.

By 12:30 P.M. Napoleon had 54,000 troops in the front line, with a new powerful reserve of 42,000, including the arrival of Murat's cavalry and the remainder of Soult's and Ney's corps from the south and east. Now the French finally launched a major counterattack, this time across the entire enemy line, with Soult at the far right, Ney and Lannes in the center sup-ported by Murat's cavalry, and Augereau's corps across the French extreme left flank.[23]

Acknowledging the vast superiority of French numbers, Hohenlohe ordered a retreat northward. It was during this flight on the road for Weimar, near Kapellendorf, that Rüchel's badly needed 15,000 men arrived too late and—despite a brief attempt by him to attack—were forced to withdraw. By 3:00 P.M. the French victory at Jena was assured, and an hour later Murat's cavalry were in hot pursuit up the Weimar road. At Weimar the Prussian army split up, some units proceeding north, the rest turning sharply westward on the road to Erfurt. Augereau's reinforced corps followed Murat, while north of Kapellendorf, the remainder of a separated Prussian force, pushed hard by Soult, advanced northward over high country.

As Napoleon ordered an evaluation of the day's battle at Jena, the results slowly came in: 5,000 French wounded and dead, compared to 10,000 Prussians. It was only later that day that he learned that 96,000 of his men had not been fighting the main part of the Prussian army after all, but only 55,000, while to the north at Auerstädt, Marshal Davout with his completely isolated III Corps of 26,000 men had faced the brunt of the duke of Brunswick's army, nearly two-thirds larger than his own.

Davout's corps, like Bernadotte's, had received Napoleon's orders at 4:00 A.M. on October 14 to abandon their northern position between Naumburg and Auerstädt and to march due south to support him at Jena. The dense fog that had been covering Jena throughout much of the day was just as thick here, and it was only at 7:00 A.M., while setting out for Jena, that Davout discovered he had Brunswick's troops before him, when his leading cavalry came upon Prussian cavalry and artillery at Pöppel. As the fog lifted beyond Hassenhaussen, the French, still a little more than two miles east of Auerstädt, found themselves facing Brunswick's army of 63,000 men and 230 guns. Gudin's lead division, with Davout at its head, quickly took up a central position extending to the left, with Friant's division to his right with the cavalry. Facing the French were Kalkreuth's corps, four Prussian divisions, backed up by Blücher's cavalry and infantry and, nearby, the Prussian king and the duke of Brunswick.

Sporadic fighting started immediately, but the real battle began at 9:45 A.M., when Schmettau and Wartensleben advanced with their two powerful divisions, Schmettau's halted by a withering fire, while Wartensleben succeeded against Gudin's overtaxed division on the French left flank. Davout, at the head of his men in the first line of fire, led two regiments of Gudin's line to reoccupy the village of Hassenhaussen, which in turn stopped the Prussians in their tracks—at least momentarily. Having no reserves, Davout was holding out for his third division, under the able General Morand, to reach them. Messengers sent to Bernadotte, marching ahead of them to Jena, were informed that he had no intention of disobeying Napoleon's

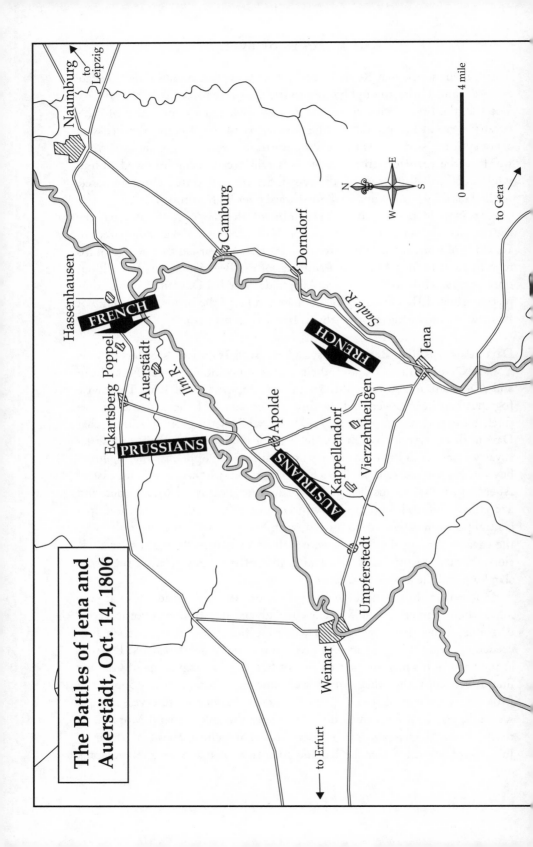

The Battles of Jena and
Auerstädt, Oct. 14, 1806

orders and categorically refused to help Davout, whom he loathed, and his vastly outnumbered men. For the first time in a major campaign, a fellow commanding officer declined to come to the aid of a colleague who was threatened with a real disaster, if not annihilation. In the years to follow it would happen time and again with others, imperiling the Grande Armée—and France.[24]

Continuing to Jena at a lackadaisical pace, Bernadotte and his troops arrived hours later, the only corps of the army successfully to have missed two entire major battles. Napoleon castigated him first for not having come to Davout's rescue and then for arriving deliberately late, taking five hours to cover the last eight miles. Had Bernadotte come earlier, if nothing else he could have prevented most of Hohenlohe's army from escaping, which would thereby have avoided the necessity of the wild pursuit to the north across the whole of Prussia. Napoleon seriously considered bringing Bernadotte before a court-martial for disobedience and cowardice, no doubt recalling the time just a few years earlier when he had discovered that this same Bernadotte, as commander of the Army of the West in Brittany, had been involved in a plot to overthrow Napoleon as first consul. He should have acted then; now the emperor knew it was too late. Since Bernadotte was married to Désirée Clary, the sister of Joseph's wife, the complications would be too great. Thus the marshal escaped punishment yet again.

Meanwhile in the heat of battle at Auerstädt, the very hard-pressed Davout, Friant, and Gudin had two pieces of good luck: the death of the Duke of Brunswick (shot through the head), and the wounding and disabling of General Schmettau. A bewildered Friedrich Wilhelm neither appointed successors to these commanders nor assumed command himself, his inaction leading to growing confusion. A third piece of luck was the arrival of Morand's division at 11:00 A.M., taking over the French left flank and relieving Gudin, who could now consolidate the center.

Once in place, Morand went on the offensive, smashing Wartensleben's units and putting the Prussian right flank out of action. This gave Davout the momentum needed to strike brutally ahead at a stunned Prussian army. The hapless Prussian king then compounded his errors by refusing to release Blücher's strong reserves of fourteen battalions, five squadrons of cavalry, and three batteries of artillery. Forming a crescent, Davout's entire front pushed hard and dislodged Kalkreuth's entire front line, although the powerful Prussian artillery continued to take a lethal toll of the advancing French. As Friant finally turned the Prussian left flank at Pöppel, however, Friedrich Wilhelm panicked, ordering the withdrawal of his entire army.

"By 12:30, the pride of the Prussian army was streaming away to the west and north."[25] By four o'clock, General Kalkreuth's overwhelming numbers were in uncoordinated flight, Napoleon was successfully concluding the battle at Jena. By 4.30, with the Prussians now beyond Auerstädt, even a ruthless Davout knew when his exhausted men could do no more and called a halt.

Davout's victory—which Napoleon himself could not surpass—was one of the most spectacular in French military history, in bravery, steadfastness, professionalism, intelligence, tactics, and destruction of the foe. Indeed, Davout's corps of 26,000 killed outright 10,000 Prussians, wounded thousands more, and took several thousand prisoners not to mention 115 guns. As might be expected, the French suffered extremely heavy losses to achieve this, Davout's tally coming to 7,052 men and officers killed or wounded, some units suffering 40 percent casualties. At Jena Napoleon's casualties had been a negligible 5 percent.

For once even Napoleon was impressed, although it took some time for him to realize that he had been fighting the lesser of the two battles, while Davout with only one-quarter the forces had defeated the larger, principal Prussian force. "Marshal Davout's corps performed wonders," Napoleon briefly admitted. "Not only did he contain, but pushed back and then defeated . . . the bulk of the enemy's troops. . . . This marshal displayed distinguished bravery and firmness of character, the first qualities in a warrior."[26] But in writing home to Josephine, somehow Davout's "distinguished bravery" and extraordinary achievement were omitted, Napoleon as usual emerging without competitors. "*Mon amie*," he wrote the day after Jena, "I executed some fine maneuvers against the Prussians. I carried off a great battle yesterday."

However, Napoleon once again failed to give Lannes and his brave corps their due in official bulletins and press announcements. As in the case of Austerlitz, apparently the great man was jealous. In any event, by now Lannes had grown to despise the Napoleon he had once genuinely admired. At one point, when Napoleon physically threatened Lannes, the latter dropped his hand to the hilt of his long sword and warned the Corsican to mind his manners.[27]

It was only on October 15 that Napoleon finally ordered a full-scale pursuit of Hohenlohe's army, beginning a military odyssey as strange as one might hope to find anywhere, as troops under Württemberg zigzagged hundreds of miles, some to Magdeburg, then joining Hohenlohe's main force past Wittenberg in the direction of the Baltic. Also fleeing from Jena, the duke of Saxe-Weimar's troops joined Blücher, sweeping past the village of Brunswick and far to the west of Magdeburg to the port of Lübeck, where they hoped to escape by sea.

Bernadotte's fresh troops, along with Lannes, Soult, and Murat, followed by Augereau and Davout, carried out the fantastic chase after the defeated Prussian army. By October 24 they had reached the vicinity of Berlin, which Davout's weary but glorious veterans entered the following day. Reaching Berlin himself on the twenty-seventh, Napoleon went immediately to the tomb of Frederick the Great to pay his respects to the one German warrior he most admired.

Meanwhile Lannes went on to seize Stettin on the Oder River, and IX Corps went to Glogau, while Davout was ordered to march to and seize Frankfurt an der Oder, far to the south of Stettin and due east of Berlin. The remnants of the starved and panicked Prussian army were breaking up as they fled northward, Hohenlohe surrendering with 10,000 men to Murat at Prenzlau, followed by the capitulation of the powerful fortress of Stettin with its garrison of a few thousand men to General Lasalle on October 29.

Of the entire Prussian army, only Blücher and the duke of Weimar, with their 22,000 men, remained an effective unit and tried to defend themselves at Lübeck while awaiting ships to ferry them to England, only to find themselves surrounded by Bernadotte's, Soult's, and Murat's troops. On November 5 and 6 an exhausted Blücher and General Scharnhorst duly surrendered.

The last major Prussian stronghold, Magdeburg to the southwest of Berlin, defended by General Kleist, surrendered with 22,000 men and 600 guns to Marshal Ney on November 10. French troops then rampaged through the streets and houses just as they had at Lübeck. As for the Prussian king and his lovely Amazon queen, Louise, they managed to escape with a small force to the Baltic fortress-port of Königsberg.

Within just thirty-three days Napoleon had utterly destroyed the Prussian army, inflicting 35,000 dead and missing while seizing 100,000 prisoners and wounded and some 2,000 cannon. Of the 160,000 or so men comprising the entire Prussian army, only 35,000 had escaped the French, giving Napoleon one of the most complete victories in history—although because of the king's escape, peace negotiations for the official surrender of Prussia were delayed for another eight months.

CHAPTER 26

Point of No Return

Everyone has loved and hated me. Everyone has taken me up, dropped me, and then taken me up again.

he French people were more war-weary than triumphant after the news of Jena (and Davout's magnificent principal victory of Auerstädt was officially accorded a condescending second place of importance). But the French emperor—who had now conquered, or controlled, the whole of western Europe to the Oder River, with the gates of Poland and the east wide open to his victorious legions, had no intention of signing a peace treaty and withdrawing to France—or even to the ample confines of the Confederated States of the Rhine.

Hundreds of miles to the east, on the other side of the Vistula River, the czar was showing his displeasure by maintaining his troops in a state of full alert. Just as he had—quite unknown to the French people—turned down the extraordinarily generous peace treaty offered by Fox less than three months earlier, an insatiable Napoleon was bent on further conquest, set on destroying the Russian army that had escaped him at Austerlitz.[1] The czar was not about to be caught off guard.

The French senatorial delegation watching Napoleon's swaggering victory parade through the Brandenburg Gate was less interested in celebrating his conquest than in pleading for common sense and moderation. It was time to lay down the blood-stained sword and exchange it for a quill of peace. Impatient with this interfering delegation, every member of which ironically he had hand-picked for office, Napoleon hastily ordered them home. Then he issued his Berlin Decrees on November 21, 1806, intended to break England by destroying its commercial lifeblood: "The British Isles are hereby declared to be in a state of blockade. All commerce and correspondence with the British Isles are forbidden." The Continental System was now in effect, and although it initially hurt England, it hardly proved the stranglehold envisaged by Napoleon.

In fact Napoleon's mighty new Empire leaked like Swiss cheese. Napoleon's own family proved to be among the worst offenders, openly permitting their ports, cities, and land routes to be used for the exchange of British commerce: Louis in Holland and, later, Jérôme in Westphalia were openly to defy him, while Joseph's Neapolitan kingdom also refused to close ports to British goods. What is more Marshal Masséna in Italy was making a private fortune by selling trading permits to accommodate British trade, and of course Lisbon was still wide open to the English. Indeed, some of Napoleon's own officials openly flouted the Berlin Decrees. Bourrienne, for example, now minister in Hamburg, was ordered to provide cloth for fifty thousand uniforms. There was no place to get this except England. "Our troops might have perished of the cold had the Continental System, and the absurd group of utterly inexcusable decrees regarding English merchandise, been observed by us," he said.[2] British trade was further sustained as a result of its naval victory at Trafalgar (in October 1805, which gave England undisputed mastery of the seas, especially of the extremely lucrative trade with the West Indies and India, whose annual convoys of more than a thousand merchantmen crammed with spices, tobacco, indigo, sugar, rum, tea, cocoa beans, coffee, silk, and cotton, were the backbone of the City of London.

The outraged British were quick to retaliate, and in a far more practicable manner, by issuing the Orders in Council in January 1807, placing France and all its allies in turn in a state of international blockade. Thereafter neutral countries were hurt as well, forbidden to carry food, cloth, wood, guns, metal, and other useful products for a war machine to any French or French-controlled port. Wealthy Parisians, ministers, and soldiers had to smuggle in cocoa, coffee, sugar, tea, tobacco, and the like if they were to maintain their usual creature comforts. Napoleon's anti-British policies were thus resented more by the French than anyone else, the middle and working classes gradually being denied these products for the next seven years. And if the Tuileries never lacked them, one might ask indiscreetly how they were obtained in such large quantities while the rest of Paris did without.

Never again would Napoleon have the opportunity he had let slip by him with Fox in August 1806, nor did he want it. Peace was incompatible with his particular genius, which could thrive only in a very different environment. "Sooner or later we must encounter and defeat the Russians," he rationalized feebly in Berlin. Russia was in England's pay, therefore Russian armies had to be vanquished.

On November 5 Napoleon dispatched a powerful reconnaissance unit as far as Poznań, as Jérôme Bonaparte (who had given up his unsuccessful naval career for the army), Murat, Davout, Lannes, Augereau, Soult, and Bernadotte were ordered to push through eastern Pomerania and Poland. By November 28 Augereau's III Corps, of 22,700 men and Murat's 18,800 cavalry were coursing the banks of the Vistula, where they found General Lestocq's 15,000 Prussians already in place facing them at Thorn on the far side of that river, supported by Bennigsen's 62,000 men seventy miles or so to the south, near the confluence of the Vistula and Bug. Napoleon "wanted a fight. Very well, he shall have one," Czar Alexander promised.

Eighty thousand French troops now pressed forward, with Davout given the initial objective of seizing Warsaw and sealing it off from the Russians. "I should like to give Poland her independence," Napoleon (unconvincingly) said, "but that will not be easy. Austria, Russia, and Prussia have all had a slice of the Polish cake, and once the new conflagration begins, who knows where it will stop." The partitioning of Poland by those three countries during the past few decades became a dominating, emotional topic in Franco-Polish circles. Napoleon's pronouncements were sometimes evasive, sometimes brutally frank, as when he said of the Poles, "They have allowed themselves to be partitioned. Today they are no longer a nation," the implication being not only that attempting to give them independence was not worth the effort but that it was impossible to do so, given their record in defending themselves.[3]

Repeating his Viennese performance following the fall of Ulm, it was Marshal Murat who first entered an undefended Warsaw on November 28, with Napoleon still back in Prussia. The French emperor was not in such a hurry after the last exhausting, bloody battles, and was intent on bolstering his thinned ranks before again confronting the Russians. In theory he had some 172,000 trained infantry available and 36,000 cavalry. But the 1806 "harvest of recruits"—as his enemies were soon referring to the by-now-unpopular annual event—of 80,000 proved insufficient after the recent casualties, desertions, and the growing number of garrisons left behind to secure the long, precarious logistical route between Poland and France. Thus Napoleon now called up the next crop of 80,000 young men as well, the conscripts of 1807, many months earlier than authorized. In addition Spain, Holland, and Switzerland were forced to provide another 55,000 men to fight French battles of which they wanted no part.[4] Then, to pay the bill for maintaining such an enormous army on a war footing, Napoleon prodded the defeated Prussians and the allied confederated states to come up with more than seven hundred million francs, more than the entire normal French annual peacetime budget. When the more honest of the newly appointed French military governors in the Rhineland Confederation, such as General Thiébault at Fulda, protested against "the numerous, afflicting requisitions and war contributions," in an attempt to protect the people under their authority, they were sharply rebuked by Napoleon.[5] The continued extortion of money and men from the already-much-put-upon Dutch led brother Louis to protest as well, as did King Joseph in Naples, but quite in vain.

Meanwhile Napoleon finally reached Warsaw on December 18, 1806, accompanied by Marshal Bessières and a large escort of the Imperial Guard.[6] At his warm palatial quarters, Napoleon as usual was buried in work. A priority was negotiating a foreign policy with Turkey and Persia, among others, that would force Russia into another war (as he was about to do with Turkey's Sultan Selim III), the aim of course being to require Russia to split its army, committing and deploying large army corps along its southern frontier. He was also working closely with Berthier to secure supply and communications lines with Berlin and Paris, while preparing new campaign plans.

Nevertheless all was not work, for on the very day of his arrival a young, beautiful, mysterious Polish woman had coquettishly greeted him in his carriage, then fled into the crowd without giving her name. Enticed by this "vision," Napoleon gave her description to General Duroc, who finally reported that she had been found. She was Countess Marie Walewska, the eighteen-year-old wife of a distinguished, septuagenarian Polish aristocrat by whom she already had one son. Delighted, even intrigued, Napoleon had her invited to an important ball about to be given in his honor. When she declined, however, he declared that he would not attend if she did not. A great brouhaha ensued, jolting the usual somber corridors of power. Senior members of the ruling aristocracy applied pressure on Count Walewski: They—he—must not offend the man who could free them of both Prussian and Russian oppressors. Countess Walewska duly appeared, if hardly in the best of moods.

Following the ball a series of impassioned "love letters" was dispatched to the countess's elegant palace: "I saw only you, I admired only you, I desired only you," the first began with Napoleon's usual lack of subtlety, and similar ones followed. He was not put off by her resistance. "I want to force you, yes, force you to love me. Marie, I have revived your country's name. I shall do much more for you!"[7] Napoleon let it be known that if the lovely countess did not oblige his sexual desires, the country would suffer. And thus the senior members of her society imposed their will on her and her aging husband again, with Talleyrand brought in to conclude the matter. This was one of his most successful diplomatic missions, and Napoleon and Marie soon became not merely *amants,* but such feverish lovers that Napoleon for once temporarily lost his native lust for war, even promising independence to the Polish aristocracy.

When a Polish delegation had addressed him earlier in Poznań Napoleon had given them a mixed, unexpectedly deflating response. "France," he claimed, "had never recognized the partition of Poland," and "the illustrious Polish nation had rendered the greatest services to all Europe." He went on to explain that "its woes had been the result of internal dissensions." He could not give them permission to reestablish their independence, because they were not ready for it. They had lost their independence by military force, he said, "and that which has been overthrown by force can be reëstablished only by force." But when Poland was united in spirit again and the people eventually reconquered their freedom, "they may always count upon his [Napoleon's] all-powerful protection."[8] It was hardly what they had come there to hear. An angry General Kosciuszko snapped, "He thinks of nothing but himself. He detests every great nation, and even more the spirit of independence. He is a tyrant."

Napoleon said one thing one day, another the next, all the while somehow leading the Poles to believe that he would indeed grant them independence, while more than one ambitious French soldier already had his covetous eye on the new Polish crown for himself, including Murat. In any event, on January 14, 1807, Napoleon created a temporary "directorate" of five distinguished Poles to administer French-occupied Poland, ostensibly under the presidency of Malachowski but in fact carefully masked under the deft supervision of Secretary of State Maret and Talleyrand.

As Napoleon's love affair continued, so did Josephine's imploring letters, insisting that Napoleon send for her. He dismissed them playfully, one after another:

Mon amie, I am touched by all that you tell me, but the season is cold and the roads are very bad and hardly safe. Therefore I cannot allow you to undertake so many trials and dangers. Return [from Mainz] to Paris and pass the winter there. . . . That is my wish. Believe me, it is more painful for me, than for you, to have to postpone by several weeks my happiness in seeing you.[9]

Then he returned to the arms of his Walewska. A few days earlier, he had received a letter from sister Caroline that Eléonore Denuelle, whom the Murats had been keeping secluded for Napoleon in their house outside Paris, had just given birth to his first son.[10]

But the business of conquest was never far off. After seizing Warsaw, the French were involved in several clashes with the Russians, some of them serious enough to leave hundreds of casualties. As already noted, Napoleon had 172,000 infantry and 36,000 cavalry available, scattered over several countries, and of course the first batch of 1806 conscripts were already entering Germany to fill depleted ranks. On January 5, 1807, Napoleon created two new army corps, the IX at Breslau to be commanded by Adm. Jérôme Bonaparte, and the X at Stettin (now Szczecin) under the command of Major General Victor.[11] The Russians had perhaps 115,000 men in this theater, including General Bennigsen's 53,000 infantry and artillery, and 11,000 cavalry, while Marshal Buxhöwden had another 40,000 troops and 7,000 cavalry (excluding the powerful Russian Imperial Guard under the command of Grand Duke Constantine and Lestocq's Prussian Corps of 15,000). In addition the Russians had some 460 guns, compared to Napoleon's 200, a significant difference that could easily decide a battle. But what the Russians, like the Prussians before them, truly lacked were enough good commanders. Even their best—Bagration, Barclay de Tolly, and Platov were hardly in the same league as Augereau, Lannes, Ney, Davout, and Murat. The earlier clashes between the two forces at Pultusk and Golmymin in December had proved inconclusive. The real battles lay before them, but in the spring, when the snow thawed, and on January 7, 1807, Napoleon finally ordered his troops into winter quarters.

The only success Napoleon had in December and January—apart from the conquest of the countess—was seeing the labors of his negotiations with Constantinople come to fruition, the Sublime Porte declaring war on Russia in December and on England late in January. Russia therefore definitely had to commit larger numbers of troops to its southern frontiers, while England saw yet more ports closed to its navy and commerce. If Napoleon could convince the shah of Persia to do the same, he could strike a blow at British India as well. And thus with his men safely in their barracks, Bonaparte expected an interlude of relative calm before spring operations. But he was roused out of his premature reverie at the end of January by the news of unexpected large-scale attacks by Bennigsen against Ney and Bernadotte.

Unknown to Napoleon, back on January 2 at an important war council attended by the czar, the Russians had decided to push the French out of Poland, past the Vistula and then the Oder as well. Napoleon, the master of improvisation, quickly drew up a counterplan on January 28 to entrap and envelop the combined forces of Bennigsen's perhaps 77,000 and Lestocq's 13,000 men. All French corps commanders were ordered to be prepared to launch a big operation on February 1, despite the severe cold and heavy snowfall.

Alas, the copy of operational orders destined for Bernadotte went astray, reaching Bennigsen instead, who had actually been falling into this trap. He quickly extricated himself, and byFebruary 3 Napoleon realized that the Russians knew something and canceled previous instructions. He ordered Ney, Augereau, Soult, and Davout north as quickly as possible after Bennigsen, who continued to withdraw in the direction of friendly Königsberg. This time Bernadotte received his set of orders two days late, which was to have serious consequences for the French. Meanwhile General Lefebvre (who had replaced Victor, captured by the Prussians) held the X Corps at Thorn, and another acting corps commander, Savary, kept the V corps on the Narew River at Ostolenka. Having failed to get at Bennigsen at Ionkovo on February 3–4, the French army was soon in pursuit. A brief clash at Hoff did not prevent the Russians from continuing their march, however, bringing them to Eylau, less than thirty miles from Königsberg.

Soult's and Murat's units reached the vicinity of the Russian army at Eylau in the early afternoon of February 7. They were soon joined by the Imperial Guard and Augereau's corps, for a total of 45,000 men. Ney's 15,000 men, still well to the north trying to intercept Lestocq's Prussians, were ordered back to Eylau by Napoleon. The only other corps within call was Davout's, down to 15,000 men but still well to the south when also summoned north. Facing the French were Bennigsen's 67,000 men already well deployed along the ridge and small hills to the northeast of Eylau, leaving a no-man's land of two-thirds of a mile in low-lying marshy land and small ponds, frozen solid and buried beneath deep snow.

Seizing the hilly ground immediately before and to either side of the town of Preussisch Eylau, Napoleon deployed Soult immediately before and to the left of Eylau, Augereau holding the center just to the right of

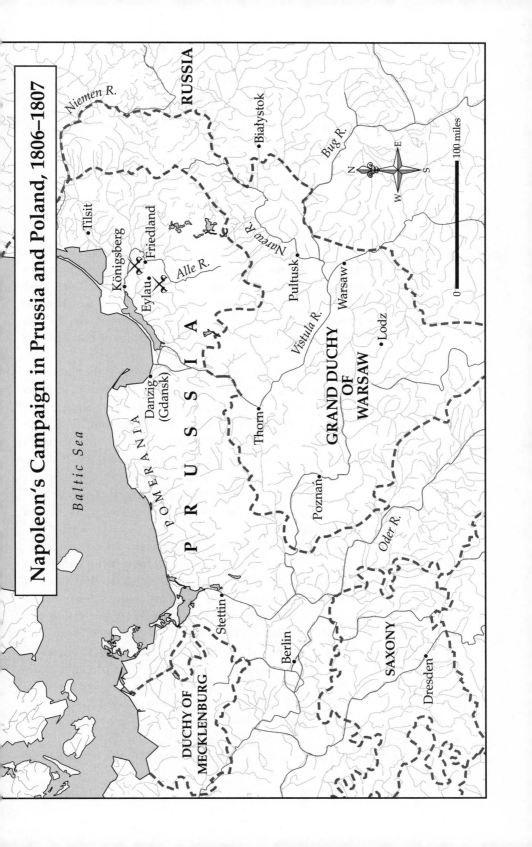

Napoleon's Campaign in Prussia and Poland, 1806–1807

RUSSIA

Niemen R.

•Bialystok

Bug R.

•Tilsit

Königsberg•
•Friedland
Eylau• •
Alle R.

Narew R.

•Pultusk

E
N
W
S

100 miles

0

Danzig•
(Gdansk)

P O M E R A N I A

Vistula R.

•Warsaw

•Lodz

GRAND DUCHY
OF
WARSAW

P R U S S I A

•Thorn

Baltic Sea

•Poznań

Oder R.

Stettin•

•Berlin

DUCHY OF
MECKLENBURG

SAXONY

•Dresden

Eylau and stretching as far to the right as possible, bolstered by one of Soult's divisions and including Murat's four cavalry divisions, with the Imperial Guard and Murat's reserve behind them. There was a very heavy concentration of French artillery before Soult's front line and therefore well before Eylau itself, with seven more batteries on high ground before Augereau's corps, at the center and to the far right.

Bennigsen had not only twenty thousand more men than Napoleon, but also a formidable array of cannon. To Napoleon's 200 artillery pieces, the Prussians had no fewer than 260, and Russian gunners were as renowned as the French. Bennigsen's troops were also well deployed.

The odds were clearly one-sided, even to an optimist like Napoleon, who no doubt prayed that Lestocq's 15,000 men would not arrive in time to bolster the Russian line. On the other hand, he was counting heavily on Davout's 15,000 men, though admittedly the march in subzero weather and unremitting snowfall would greatly delay him. If anyone in the French army could overcome almost any obstacle, it was the stern, hard-driving Davout, who never offered or accepted excuses.

The battle began hours before Napoleon was ready, and then quite by accident, while the French were still arriving. At about two o'clock on February 7 the attendants bringing up Napoleon's personal baggage, field kitchen, and equipment arrived in Eylau and began unpacking. The Russians at a nearby outpost immediately attacked them and the partially unpacked wagons. The attendants and imperial belongings were barely saved. The Russians then sent up reinforcements, and heavy fighting quickly ensued in the streets of Eylau, lasting until ten that night, after which several thousand casualties on both sides were carried away. It was not an auspicious beginning.

Daybreak was scarcely noticeable the next morning due to the continuing heavy snowstorms that hindered both vision and movement, either side barely visible to the other most of the time though only twelve hundred yards apart. Soult's orders were to pin down the Russian divisions opposite him and thereby prevent a major advance on the weaker French positions until Davout could arrive. Rather than just hold his own, however, Napoleon was intent on enveloping the Russians once all his troops had arrived. In any event, full-scale fighting resumed with the little light available at eight o'clock, involving a major artillery duel, but the 130 big Russian guns concentrated between Essen and Sacken easily outdid the French in damage to troops and the stone walls of Eylau, setting fire both to Eylau and the hamlet of Rothenen behind Murat's cavalry.

The massive advance following the bombardment by the Russian right flank against Soult's front lines proceeded through the deep snow and over the ice-covered swamps. Caught off balance, Napoleon threw Augereau's tough VII corps forward beyond French guns, against General Tolstoy's division. Although burning with fever and wobbly on his feet, Augereau carried on. Parallel to him St.-Hilaire's division was also advancing, but blindly through the almost impenetrable snow. Augereau, instead of heading straight ahead for the extreme right end of Tolstoy's division, unwittingly veered to his left, suddenly finding himself within pistol range of Sacken's line and its seventy cannon, which literally obliterated Augereau's entire corps within a matter of minutes. Most of the remainder of his men were then cut down in a savage bayonet attack by Doctorov's reserve infantry driving back the remnants of the French to the edge of Eylau. The result was an enormous hole in Napoleon's center front line. Of Augereau's 14,600 men, only 2,000 or so returned to the safety of their own lines.

At about the same time Napoleon himself was almost captured with his staff near the bell tower in Eylau by several thousand advancing Russian infantry, the emperor saved at the last moment only by Guardsmen literally throwing themselves before him as human shields against the onrushing enemy.

By 11:30 A.M. the situation was so critical, with his center still exposed where Augereau's corps had formerly stood, that Napoleon committed 10,700 of Murat's reserve cavalry to charge through the central gap directly at the massive Russian infantry columns marching in for the kill. The courageous Marshal Murat as usual was leading his cavalry charge through the blinding snow. Murat in turn was followed by Bessières with the Imperial Guard's cavalry and they were followed by four more mounted divisions.

Splitting into two groups, one section of the French cavalry charged magnificently through the Russian cavalry, while the other cleared their infantry, forcing the Russians to withdraw from Eylau. The two cavalry wings then hacked their way through Sacken's formidable center, and, in a marvelously disciplined move, re-formed behind Sacken's line into a single column and retraced their path through the Russians, overrunning and disabling much of the lethal Russian artillery as they went. As Murat's force returned, exhausted and depleted by some fifteen hundred men, Napoleon ordered up the Imperial Guard's cavalry, followed in turn by six squadrons of Mamelukes and *chasseurs*. Murat's superb charge had saved Napoleon from being overrun while permitting Davout's corps, which had finally arrived between the French extreme right and the Russian left, to carry part of the enormous burden. Bennigsen, who had been on the verge of victory, now lost the momentum.

With Davout in place, Napoleon ordered his corps forward along with St.-Hilaire's division, to encircle Tolstoy's left flank, while everywhere else on the line, including Soult's left flank, the French held firmly. For the next two and a half hours Davout's divisions pushed around Tolstoy's division, dislodging them from their ridge positions, forcing them back past the town of Kutschitten on the right and the hamlet of Ankappen in their center. Indeed, the French seemed about to break through the Russian line when Lestocq's Prussian corps, reduced to 7,000 men, appeared. They swung around Bennigsen's rear and struck the French head on, gradually pushing Davout's exhausted men back across the stretch of land they had won over the past couple of hours. At 7:00 P.M. the first of Ney's 14,000 badly needed men reached the French rear lines, resecuring Napoleon's weakened extreme left, both sides now fighting to a bloody standstill.

Later that night Bennigsen decided to call it quits and withdraw. But given the blizzard and the long wintry night, the French knew nothing of this. Indeed, Napoleon had simultaneously given the order to withdraw under cover of darkness from one of the bloodiest battlefields in hundreds of years of European history. It was only an hour or two later that Davout's rear guard noticed the Russian evacuation and Napoleon immediately ordered his troops back into place.[12] The Russians and French had fought a perfectly balanced draw.

The casualties were horrendous. Napoleon claimed in his "Victory" Bulletin—for he had the nerve to call Eylau a glorious French triumph—that they had lost 7,600 dead and wounded, whereas Augereau's corps alone had suffered some 12,000 casualties. The real figure was never published but was probably closer to 25,000 French dead and wounded.[13] Russian casualties probably approached 15,000. As for Marshal Bernadotte, just as during the famous twin battles of Auerstädt-Jena, he failed to appear in time to participate in the combat, although this time he had the perfectly valid excuse of having received his orders two days after everyone else.

For once Napoleon could not come back with captured armies, regimental flags, or even enemy cannon, for there had been no French victory at Eylau this day. Nevertheless this did not prevent him from writing to Josephine: "You must have been anxious. But I defeated the enemy during a memorable day, although it cost me the lives of many brave men." Marshal Ney regarded the bloody battlefield differently. "What a slaughter, and what did we achieve? Nothing!"[14]

Following the battle both General Bennigsen and Napoleon limped away from the corpse-strewn snowfields of Eylau, the French so savagely mauled that they were unable to carry out another campaign now. Back in Warsaw, Napoleon was forced to do something he had never done before in his career, disband an entire army corps, the VII. With the badly wounded Augereau slowly making his way back to France to heal, Bonaparte integrated his remaining two thousand men into other units of the army. He then sent a courier off to the War Office in Paris informing General Dejean to send not only the entire conscript "class" of 1807, but to call up another 80,000 young men designated for 1808, a year and a half in advance. Thus it was that General Lefebvre's unique new X Corps was formed, comprising almost entirely foreign units, a concept to be enlarged upon significantly over the next few years. It included two Polish divisions, two Italian divisions sent by the viceroy of Italy, and a few smaller units from Savoy and Baden, totaling some 27,000 men. Marshal Masséna was next brought from Italy to Poland to help fill the void in commanders.

Napoleon's first important move, even before the recuperating army was out of winter quarters again, was to dispatch Lefebvre's new corps to seize Danzig (now Gdansk). The full investment of that citadel, beginning on March 18, was to prove a formidable task, a stubborn General Kalkreuth not surrendering until May 29.

Meanwhile Czar Alexander fielded his strengthened army of 115,000 troops to resume the struggle against the French invaders, his position enhanced by a new Russo-Prussian defense pact signed secretly at Bartenstein on April 26, 1807. At Finkenstein Castle, in Poland, Napoleon for his part was now intent on accomplishing two things, destroying Bennigsen's elusive army before it reached the Baltic fortress of Königsberg, and then seizing the latter as well. With this in mind he was determined to bring this long, painful campaign to an end as quickly as possible. Thus when Bennigsen's force was reported at Heilsberg, far to the north of Warsaw and not far from Königsberg, Napoleon marched his army there. The fight with the Russians that began on June 10 lasted until 11:00 P.M. that night, French casualties of 10,000 again outnumbering the enemy's 8,000. Once again there was bitter backbiting among the French officers, both Lannes and Savary loudly condemning Murat's "overbearing and insulting conduct" on and off the battlefield. The battle at Heilsburg ended to the Russians' advantage, they afterward withdrawing strategically up the road to Königsberg, past the battlefield of Eylau, heading for Domnau.

By June 13 Napoleon was back at Eylau instructing his commanders on the tactics required of them as they closed in—he hoped for the final time—on the slippery Bennigsen. Lannes was dispatched to the Domnau area, where Napoleon thought the big battle would take place. His orders were to catch up with and hold Bennigsen there until he could arrive with Mortier's, Victor's, and Ney's corps, as well as Bessières's Imperial Guard.

Bennigsen with 60,000 or so troops was determined to cut off and annihilate Lannes's force of 26,000. But in fact Lannes's three infantry divisions with an attached division and Grouchy's two cavalry divisions instead closed in on Bennigsen's two corps at the small town of Friedland on the serpentine Alle River, well to the east of the main road to Königsberg, which lay some thirty miles to the northwest.

At eight o'clock on the morning of June 14 the situation hardly looked encouraging for the vastly outnumbered Lannes. Tough and reliable even in the most difficult of situations, he was a commander Napoleon could always count on. Napoleon for his part was en route for the day of reckoning that had been evading him for more than six months now. With his arrival the French force now totaled 80,000 men, as opposed to Bennigsen's 60,000. If the Russians did not escape yet again, Bonaparte felt confident that he finally had them.

The fighting had begun at 3:00 A.M. The soldiers were beyond exhaustion when, thirteen hours later, at 4:00 P.M. Napoleon launched his offensive, with Mortier on the French left flank, Lannes still in the center but buttressed by Victor, and Ney on the extreme right flank. Facing them were Gorchakov's corps covering the Russian right to the center, divided by the swift-flowing Mühlen River, and Bagration's force covering the left-center all the way to the extreme left Russian flank extending to the Alle, where, on the opposite shore, the Cossack cavalry was moving forward.

Napoleon's aim was to strike hard at Bagration's overextended left flank with Ney's fresh corps, then bring up Victor's reserve corps from behind Lannes's extreme right. It all went just as planned, and so quickly did the Russian line crumble and fall back that French artillerymen literally had to push their guns forward by hand, until within point-blank range of the Russian infantry, which French gunners then ruthlessly destroyed with case shot. Although Gorchakov's infantry along with Uvarov's cavalry attacked the French left in force, Mortier and Grouchy held their own. Bagration then tried to halt Ney's onslaught with a bayonet attack, but that too failed, as Dupont's division continued forward, their own lethal bayonets serving them only too well.

A desperate Bennigsen now unleashed the Russian Imperial Guard, Alexander's much vaunted elite, only to see even them trodden under by the advancing French. By 8:30 that evening Ney's corps had secured Friedland proper, although it was put to the torch by the fleeing Russians. And then, offering the coup de grâce, Napoleon ordered forty squadrons of

Grouchy's cavalry forward, only to see them halted momentarily by Uvarov's enterprising but smaller force of twenty-five squadrons. Grouchy was no Murat, and this was one battle that absent cavalryman would have loved.

Nevertheless the Battle of Friedland was clearly a French victory, as all Russian forces retreated under a hail of fire, the French continuing their pursuit until 11:00 P.M. For once French losses were relatively small—8,000 men, as opposed to nearly 20,000 Russian casualties. There were few Russian prisoners, however, with eighty guns taken, but Bennigsen had finally been decisively defeated. Four days later Czar Alexander reluctantly sued for peace, an armistice going into effect on June 23, 1807. For the first time since leaving Warsaw, Napoleon could smile, having achieved his objective of crushing the czar's forces. "My children have celebrated the anniversary of Marengo in a worthy manner," he wrote Josephine the day after the battle, as Soult took Königsberg and Bennigsen fled up the Baltic coast to a position on the other side of the Niemen (Neman) near a small place called Tilsit.[15]

As the last of the sulfuric smoke lifted over the battlefield of Friedland on June 14, Napoleon successfully brought to a close the long, bloody, destructive, and totally unnecessary military rampage that he had unleashed in the autumn of 1805, which had soon included the major battles of Ulm and Austerlitz, Jena and Auerstädt, Eylau, and now finally Friedland. Some 150,000 men had been killed, wounded, or maimed for life. Following the Battle of Eylau even the patriotic French troops no longer called out the by-now-obligatory "*Vive l'Empereur!*" but instead pleaded for "bread and peace!" The same sentiment was echoed in the streets of Paris. Archbishop de Belloy ordered yet another Te Deum in Nôtre-Dame Cathedral—as he had done after each of the previous victories—but the ancient cathedral bells tolled, not chimed, and mothers and fathers prayed that still another 80,000 French young men would be spared conscription next year. Enough was enough. "This is no longer warfare," an exhausted Bennigsen lamented to Archduke Constantine, "it is a veritable bloodbath." There must be peace at last.[16]

Following an interview with the defeated ruler on June 17, Ambassador Lord Gower reported Czar Alexander I as saying that he "would never stoop to [negotiate with] Bonaparte, he would rather retire to Kazan or even to Tobolsk." But the czar's generals, and Bennigsen in particular, protested the folly of continuing this "bloodbath." Talleyrand, who learned

of Napoleon's latest battle on June 18, while still at Danzig, echoed the
Russian general's sentiments:

> Sire, I have finally heard some details about the battle of Friedland. . . .
> But it is not merely because of the glory of the moment that I now
> rejoice. Rather, I like to think of it as a precursor, or guarantor of peace
> to come, that will ensure the repose Your Majesty and your people so
> richly deserve, after so much toil, hardship, and danger. . . .[17]

Meanwhile Napoleon's agents intimated to the czar that Russia would
be permitted to extend its frontiers westward one hundred miles to the Vistula if peace were now signed. The czar finally relented, signing an armistice
with France on June 22. Negotiations could begin.[18] "The alliance of France
and Russia has always been the object of my desires," a contented
Napoleon wrote the Russian ruler two days later.

Thus it was that Czar Alexander's carriage and strong cavalry escort
arrived at the muddy banks of the Niemen at 11 o'clock on the morning of
June 25, where he was kept waiting half an hour before Napoleon rode up
on the opposite shore. Both men and their staffs boarded large boats that
were rowed out to a raft bearing two tents, anchored at the midway point
of the river. Arriving first, Napoleon in his famous green guard's uniform
and wearing only one decoration—the Grand Cordon of the Legion of
Honor—heartily embraced the amazed Russian leader as he stepped aboard
the platform. There he stood in his dark blue uniform with enormous gold
epaulettes, he so fair and blond, his hair already thinning, towering a full
head above the almost dwarflike Corsican, whose lack of height was minimized only slightly by his beaver hat and high black boots.

They quickly walked over to one of the tents and sat alone for fifty
minutes of initial talks. Afterward, smiling, they introduced their respective staffs, and Alexander helped Napoleon into his boat. At the czar's
request, Napoleon had also agreed to an armistice with shattered Prussia,
and that was signed that same afternoon by Marshal Berthier and General
Kalkreuth for Friedrich Wilhelm III, who had been excluded from this
meeting by Napoleon. Indeed, the Prussian leader, humiliated and fuming, had passed the entire time on his horse on the right bank of the
Niemen, awaiting the czar's return. As for the thirty-two-year-old czar,
who had come to Tilsit with a deep loathing for the French leader, he
came away from this meeting as if hypnotized, admiring him, almost
fawning over him, to the utter astonishment of his aides and staff. "Everyone has loved, and hated me," Napoleon once commented. "Everyone has

taken me up, dropped me, and then taken me up again," as Alexander now proved.[19]

At the second meeting on the raft the following day, the Prussian king accompanied Alexander, Napoleon remaining stiff and arrogant. Rather stilted talks resumed among the three men; Napoleon closed the meeting by turning his back on Friedrich Wilhelm and inviting Alexander alone to dinner that night at his headquarters in Tilsit. The Prussian was affronted, as Napoleon had intended.

Thereafter until the conclusion of the negotiations at Tilsit, the enraptured czar dined with Napoleon every afternoon, and every evening Napoleon took tea, Russian style, with Alexander, whose headquarters had now been moved across the Niemen to Tilsit. The two emperors met daily for several hours in Bonaparte's small village house, usually alone. Indeed, when Foreign Minister Talleyrand arrived on June 29, he was invited neither to participate directly nor even to share Napoleon's confidence until most of the major decisions had already been taken. "If peace is not concluded in a fortnight's time," Savary informed Talleyrand on his arrival, "Napoleon will cross the Niemen." Looking at him in his famous expressionless manner, the foreign minister coolly replied, "And what, pray tell, might he be doing on the other side of the Niemen?"

As Talleyrand no longer had Napoleon's ear—which greatly embarrassed him before the Prussian monarch and the czar, with whom he had hitherto had close relations—he gave advice to General Savary to pass on to his master, especially regarding the role of France in central and eastern Europe:

> You must make him abandon this insane idea of occupying Poland. Nothing can be achieved with these people. The only thing they do is organize disorder. Now is the ideal time to end this and pull out with honor.... If he does not do this, ... he will only be brought back here with greater problems later, all of which can be avoided if he stops his plans [for occupation] today.[20]

Napoleon, however, who was infallible in all matters from drama critique to finance to foreign affairs, had other views on this subject. Indeed, he found Talleyrand's "moderation" rather tedious.

The arrival of the Prussian queen, Louise, on July 6 certainly added a little grace and cheer to these otherwise masculine negotiations dominated by dour Corsican brusqueness. When she attempted to discuss peace terms, however, Napoleon merely smiled condescendingly and complimented her on her dress. "Shall we talk only of chiffons at such a solemn moment as this?" she replied in surprise. Napoleon, who had never permitted Josephine or any other woman to discuss politics with him, had no intention of beginning now. "The Queen of Prussia dined with me yesterday," Napoleon informed his wife the next day. "I had to check myself from not giving in to her and making even more concessions to her husband. But I was most gallant, while holding to my political intentions." Nevertheless, he teased, he did in fact find her *"fort aimable,"* closing, "when you read this letter, peace with Prussia and Russia will have been concluded."[21]

Following mutual troop inspections by both the czar and Napoleon, the two emperors often went out on long rides together and discussed a great variety of subjects beyond the prying eyes and ears of their advisers. Negotiations were finally closed as the two men prepared to break camp following the signing of the draft treaties on July 7, by Foreign Minister Talleyrand and Prince Kurakin. A final treaty was signed with Prussia two days later. Within the space of those couple of weeks together Napoleon had won over the formerly hostile but highly impressionable and mercurial Alexander I—indeed, to an almost embarrassing degree.[22]

The terms of the treaties with Russia and Prussia were not as generous as Alexander had originally been led to believe by Napoleon. They did, however, redesign the map of Europe, leaving France and Russia the undisputed arbiters of the entire continent. The text of the Treaty of Tilsit was in fact made up of three treaties, the "Patent Treaty," the "Separate and Secret Articles," and the "Treaty of Alliance," most of this kept secret and published for the first time only in 1891. "Out of regard for the emperor of all the Russias," Napoleon agreed to restore some of the Prussian territories east of the Elbe, although not including the enclave of Cottbus (which went to Saxony) and the newly created Duchy of Warsaw, which France controlled directly. The Duke of Warsaw was to be Napoleon's straw man, namely the elector—soon to be raised to king—of Saxony. Danzig was to be restored as an independent city. Russia got the Polish district of Bialystok (but not all the land earlier promised by Napoleon). French garrisons were to occupy the Duchies of Saxe-Coburg, Oldenburg, and Mecklenburg-Schwerin. The czar agreed to attempt to mediate a peace treaty between England and France, while Napoleon would do the same for Russia and the Ottoman Empire. Russia lost land, however, including the Turkish provinces of Moldavia and Walachia. The czar also recognized three new Bonaparte kingdoms, Louis's in Holland, Joseph's in Naples, and Jérôme's in the newly created state of Westphalia. In addition Alexander recognized the Confederation of the Rhine. Napoleon and Alexander guaranteed each other's new territories. The Secret Articles also required Russia to hand over to France the Adriatic seaport of Cattaro (now Kotor) and the Ionian Islands. In exchange for giving Hannover to Westphalia, Prussia was to receive an equivalent property on the left bank of the Elbe. The Treaty of Military Alliance required France and Russia to support each other "in every war . . . against any European Power." In the event England refused to make peace with France, Russia could then make "common cause with France." Russia would close its ports to England and would then demand that Copenhagen, Stockholm, and Lisbon do likewise "and to declare war upon England. . . . If Sweden declines to do so, Denmark shall be constrained to declare war upon her in turn." Finally, if the Sublime Porte declined to accept French mediation between the Ottoman Empire and Russia, France agreed to take Russia's side in their quarrel and seize "all the provinces of the Ottoman Empire in Europe, except Constantinople and Rumelia"—in other words, the whole of modern Yugoslavia, Albania, and Greece.

The Treaty of Tilsit was followed two days later, on July 9, by one between France and Prussia, thereby concluding the series of battles following Austerlitz. This ill-advised convention helped further upset the whole political balance of Europe, which had so worried Talleyrand since Pressburg. In fact Prussia lost one-third of her entire territory and nearly one half of her population—4.5 of 10 million—to France and the Confederation of the Rhine. Naturally Prussia would be forbidden to have any further commercial or maritime contact with its former British ally. France agreed to remove all troops of occupation from Prussia within two and a half months, after war "contributions" imposed on the country had been paid. But as that was impossible after having lost nearly half its taxpayers, in reality Prussia would remain an occupied French satellite.

The treaties signed at Tilsit literally turned Europe topsy-turvy. The whole of western Europe was either occupied or controlled by French armies under the orders of one man, Napoleon Bonaparte. The Poles, who had seen their country earlier partitioned and denied independence by Austria, Russia, and Prussia, now came largely under the French yoke for their fourth partitioning. By humiliating and emasculating Prussia, now a nominal French ally, Bonaparte had in reality created a resentful, stubborn, bitter, and ultimately powerful foe set on his destruction. England, which in the summer of 1806 had offered France a most generous peace settlement, was now instead to have the last of its European ports and markets (not to mention the allies of its coalition) cut off, and would be fighting for its very life, because Napoleon alone demanded it. All these events had occurred because of his refusal to withdraw troops from occupied lands in the summer of 1805, when he still had the opportunity to do so. That in turn had led to Austerlitz, when French armies were then unleashed throughout the German states, Prussia, and Poland, terminating on a raft in the Niemen. The result: the undying hatred of the whole of Europe for Napoleon and France. Nor can one forget Talleyrand's wise advice to him back at Tilsit, that the consequences of not withdrawing from eastern Europe and making a moderate peace would inevitably require his return there to cope "with greater problems later."

The extraordinary terms dictated to Russia and Prussia at Tilsit over everyone's objections proved to be the point of no return in Napoleon's career, the final moment irretrievably lost, for which the whole of Europe would now pay the full price over the next seven years. Bonaparte, who had needed a temporary army of 200,000 men to launch this war, would thereafter require a permanent one of 600,000 men to maintain "the peace" in French-occupied Europe.

CHAPTER 2 7

Iberia

To choose the right moment in which to act is the great art of men. What one can do easily in 1807 perhaps cannot be done under any circumstances in 1810.

"hat do you think of all these victories, this armistice, this new peace treaty?" a delighted Regnault de Saint-Angély exclaimed to another Bonapartist officer, General Thibaudeau, on Napoleon's return to Paris on July 27, 1807, after a ten-month absence.[1] "Napoleon is beyond the ken of normal human history," an equally delighted Comte Séguier echoed. "He belongs to the heroic times of yesteryear."[2] The French stock exchange rose dramatically, and Paris rejoiced with genuine enthusiasm, as the first of the victorious French legions marched through the streets of the capital. A grateful nation, which had seen several hundred thousand French boys march off to war, rejoiced as they never had, not even after Austerlitz. But if, following the signing of the Treaty of Pressburg, Bonaparte had returned to face a menacing financial disaster, now he confronted a ministerial crisis of almost equal proportions, requiring his immediate intervention. "I have done enough soldiering. I must now play the prime minister for a bit,"[3] he explained as he convened an urgent cabinet meeting at St.-Cloud.

During Napoleon's long absence, various parties, both at home and abroad, had reported Fouché's intrigues. But Fouché was always playing the mouse during the cat's absence, and the police minister got off with a mere lecture on this occasion. The situation regarding Talleyrand was, however, quite another matter. The foreign minister had been not only the most prestigious member of Bonaparte's team since 18 Brumaire, but the most valuable, the most influential, and in the final analysis, the only one to attempt to guide the emperor directly away from his schemes of European expansion. To show his fury with, and contempt of, the most unobliging Talleyrand, Bonaparte had deliberately excluded him from most of the negotiations at Tilsit. Napoleon had rewarded Talleyrand with untold millions, then purchased for him one of the largest and richest estates in the whole of France, in Berri at Valençay, not to mention raising him to the title of prince of Benevento. He expected complete obedience in return. Instead Talleyrand had had the effrontery to give him sound advice. What is more, Talleyrand had mocked Bonaparte's effort to create a whole new aristocracy out of a pack of working-class oafs who, as a rule, had only one real talent in common, the ability to kill large numbers of opposing troops on the field of battle. Not only that, Napoleon went on to reward Talleyrand "with the only vice he was missing"—as Fouché smirked—raising him to the position of vice-grand elector of the Empire, under brother Joseph, and after that, adding the title of grand chamberlain. Translated into reality this meant another 500,000 francs annually in salary. But why not? Bonaparte had forced the Poles "to fork up" 26,582,000 francs from their confiscated estates. There was no shortage of cash in Napoleon's private coffers.[4] The misguided Polish peasantry considered Napoleon their friend; Finance Minister Gaudin and Treasury Minister Mollien knew otherwise.

Napoleon now had much evidence against Talleyrand, including a stack of private correspondence between him and some of the most influential men in Europe, even with Napoleon's own closest officers and officials.

Talleyrand had returned very slowly to Paris after leaving Tilsit in the first week of July 1807, as he contemplated his own future following Bonaparte's extraordinary contrariness on the Niemen. Having made his decision, Talleyrand handed Napoleon his resignation, the latter nevertheless reluctantly replacing him at the Foreign Ministry with the former interior minister, Nompère de Champagny, hardly of the stature of Talleyrand but at least someone who would not hamper him in his various plans for massive new territorial expansion. "One after another the emperor had defeated Austria, Prussia, and Russia, and now held the destiny of Europe in his hands. What a grand and noble role he could have then played," Talleyrand later reminisced. "But that true glory he simply did not understand." The folly of the Berlin Decrees had been magnified beyond belief at Tilsit when Napoleon had committed France to embroilment in central and eastern Europe to the very end, thereby ensuring the ultimate ruin of France and the total disruption of Europe for decades to come. As if that were not bad enough, on his return to France, Napoleon then dictated a policy that would irrationally involve France in still a further campaign, resulting in an entanglement in Iberia that would of its own right bring Napoleon and France to their knees.[5]

Talleyrand would have none of it: "I was indignant with everything I saw and heard, but I was obliged to conceal my indignation at Tilsit. I do not want to be, or rather, I no longer wish to be, the executioner of Europe. . . . I liked Napoleon; I was even quite attached to him personally, despite his faults," the ex-foreign minister reflected.

> During the period when he was willing to accept the truth, I was loyally frank with him, and indeed, remained so later. . . . I served Bonaparte as emperor with devotion so long as I felt he himself was solely devoted to the interests of France. But from the moment I saw him initiate the revolutionary enterprises [in Austria, Germany, Poland, and Spain], which resulted in losing France, I left the ministry, for which he never forgave me. . . . By 1807 Napoleon had abandoned [the best foreign policy for France], which I clearly recognized, in fact, having done my utmost to adhere to it, but I was not in a position to leave my post until this point [after Tilsit]. In reality it was not as easy as it might at first appear to cease my active functions with him.

Later minimizing the loss to the country in no longer having him as foreign affairs adviser and minister, he jested, "The only difference between [Foreign Minister] Champagny and myself is that, if the emperor ordered him to behead someone, he would execute that order within the hour, whereas, in my case, I should have delayed doing so for a month.[6]

With Talleyrand's departure, Napoleon lost the only serious opponent to whom he would listen regarding his plans for the mass invasion of still other European and North African countries. After Tilsit, however, he was no longer in a mood to listen to anyone: He could do anything, and indeed he had just proved it.

The loss of Talleyrand was to prove a veritable catastrophe for Napoleon and France, and although Napoleon later pleaded on more than one occasion with the former minister to return, it was to no avail. For the superstitious Bonaparte, who knew that Talleyrand, like himself, backed only winners, it was a grave move of which he could never lose sight. Nor could he forgive Talleyrand the great embarrassment of his public abandonment, Napoleon avenging himself by giving out that he had "dismissed" the Prince of Benevento, just as he had earlier "dismissed" Bourrienne.

But the ministerial crisis continued. When Champagny was moved up to the Foreign Ministry in mid-August, Napoleon filled Champagny's former place at the Interior Ministry with another party hack on whom he could always count, Emmanuel Crétet, governor of the Bank of France. This was not the end of this most unexpected cabinet reshuffle. Marshal Berthier, now given his own principality of Neuchâtel, in Switzerland, also had to be replaced as war minister, and Napoleon's choice was again equally bad, Gen. Henri Clarke, the future duc de Feltre, known behind his back as the Desktop General and the Field Marshal of Ink. That said it all, or almost, for not only was Clarke unequal to Berthier in the post, but he was also of wavering loyalty, and in communication with the Bourbons, whom he would more faithfully serve.[7]

Nor was the ministerial turmoil finished with this appointment, for the minister for religious affairs, Count Joseph Portalis, died after a long illness and had to be replaced by someone who supported Bonaparte's policy vis-à-vis the church in France while somehow maintaining diplomatic relations with Rome. Napoleon's choice was State Counselor Bigot de Préameneu. Other appointments were also made, including a seemingly minor change when General Junot was removed as governor of Paris because of his notorious affair with Caroline Bonaparte Murat and ordered to command a newly forming Army of Observation of the Pyrenees, this indirectly reflecting a whole new policy of entanglement, beginning in Portugal and ending in Spain. That Napoleon chose such an erratic commander for such an important post hardly helped matters.

Before donning his military hat once again, rallying his troops, and leaving Paris for fresh fields of glory, Napoleon closed down the most vociferous, critical legislative assembly, the Tribunate, on August 19, 1807. There remained some muted criticism in the few remaining newspapers. Whether such criticism came from the left in the Tribunate, or the right in the press, it was totally unacceptable to Bonaparte. He suppressed one "because it was pro-English," warning two others that if they did not desist from all criticism of his rule and actions they, too, would be shut down.[8] There were other matters to be dealt with as well, regarding the enforcement of his Continental System against England and of his revised policy against Pope

Pius VII, and soon the little matter of Iberia, but the latter he could deal with at the head of his troops in the field.

In a halfhearted attempt to deceive Josephine, Napoleon had resumed his marital role on his return from Poland and the arms of Marie Walewska, although word of his great Polish affair was by now well known to everyone in imperial circles. Josephine—who had closed her eyes to the many dozens of trysts and affairs that had taken place continuously since the beginning of the Consulate, including those with some of her own and Hortense's school friends—on learning of her husband's decision to leave for Italy in November had once again pleaded to accompany him, in vain.

Meanwhile Fouché and Talleyrand manipulated rumors through the French capital concerning the necessity that Bonaparte provide an imperial heir, thereby assuring his succession. In other words a divorce was in order. Fouché's choice for a second bride was the czar's sister, Catherine, and that autumn the police minister went so far as to appeal to Josephine to step down. Bewildered by this unexpected suggestion, she tearfully rushed to Napoleon, who dismissed the idea out of hand. "You know very well that I could not live without you," he assured his wife, though of course they had just been separated for ten entire months without any heartbreak. But the fact is that Napoleon had been acting in a colder, more distant manner toward Josephine since his return from the delights of Finkenstein, and he certainly spent much less time with her, day and night, as the gossipy Austrian minister, Klemens von Metternich, gleefully noted.

Other changes were noticeable following his return from Tilsit. Napoleon now enforced a rigorous court etiquette that kept everyone literally at arm's length, unable to approach him without the approval of Duroc, who among other titles held the post of grand marshal of the palace (or lord high steward).[9] And thus when Napoleon reopened the completely refurbished Fontainebleau Palace for the annual autumn hunt season in 1807, he ordered twelve hundred "guests" to be present, including his ministers, all in formal attire. And when in the evenings, following an equally formal dinner, the inner court gathered in a circle of chairs, scarcely a word was exchanged, the lighthearted nights of cards, billiards, and music at Malmaison during the Consulate already but a fleeting memory. When Napoleon arrived, everyone would stand up, not daring to say a word until the emperor gave permission. The stark change and self-imposed isolation, even amid hundreds of people, was evident to all. Nevertheless Josephine was in tears when Bonaparte left for Italy without her, confessing to her son, Eugène: "My ambitions now are limited to but one, the possession of his heart."

*   *   *

Following a difficult crossing of Mont Cenis, Napoleon reached the Viceroy's Palace in Milan on November 23, 1807, with the specific purpose of expanding and consolidating his power in Italy. Holding only the northern and southern thirds of the country, Bonaparte wanted the middle. His aim was to break the pope's clerical and secular powers, which would among other things permit him to gain control of all the Papal States. Thus Napoleon seized both Ancona and Venice and then the Kingdom of Etruria (which he had earlier given to the Spanish royal house). In fact "Etruria" now disappeared as abruptly as it had first appeared, Napoleon rebaptizing it the Grand Duchy of Tuscany, with its capital at Florence, all of which he handed over to his sister Elisa, with the title of governor, and eventually grand duchess, of Tuscany, keeping it, however, as annexed French territory.

While in Milan, on December 17, Bonaparte extended his Continental System by declaring any ship of any nation submitting to search by a British vessel, or paying any British fees, fines, or taxes, to be a French prize. This he extended on April 1, 1808, by ordering the pope to enter into a military alliance with him, to arrest British diplomatic officials in Rome, and to close it and all ports (for example, Leghorn) to the British. But even before the pope received this command, on April 2 French troops invaded and occupied Rome. With the seizure of the remaining Papal States that same year, followed by the annexation of Istria the year after, Bonaparte effectively closed the entire Italian coastline—apart from Sicily—to the British. When, however, on June 10, 1809, French troops hauled down the papal flag in Rome, the long-suffering Pius VII took action at last, issuing a bull excommunicating Napoleon Bonaparte from the Roman Catholic church. One month later Bonaparte retaliated by invading the Quirinal Palace, kidnapping the pope at bayonet point, whisking him off first to Grenoble, then to Avignon, and finally to Savona.[10] No one, not even the Holy Father, could defy Napoleon and get away with it. Nevertheless the excommunication remained in effect. Napoleon could never again enter a Roman Catholic church, attend cathedral services, or receive Catholic sacraments. He was forever expelled from the Christian community, and even the Grande Armée—all six hundred thousand of them—could not alter that fact.

Bonaparte could close off much of Italy to the British navy and commerce, but British trade still managed to reach the Continent secretly through French-annexed Belgium and Holland, as well as through Denmark and Sweden. As part of the Tilsit agreements, Napoleon had also demanded the closure to the British of all Scandinavian ports, naming Copenhagen in particular. If that major port were closed, along with the narrow Kattegat Sound separating Denmark and Sweden, Napoleon could at one blow deny all British vessels access to the Baltic. Needless to say London was not pleased by such a threat them. To be sure, Britain's astute foreign secretary, George Canning, although receiving general news of the Tilsit meetings, had no precise knowledge of the various clauses, which were kept secret for the next seventy-four years. Nevertheless Canning had before him Napoleon's numerous declarations regarding his intent both to crush England militarily and to apply the Continental System to close all Continental ports and markets to Britain. The actual wording of Article 5 of the secret Treaty of Alliance enjoined the three signatories "to act in concert, and at the same moment summoned the three Courts of Copenhagen, Stockholm and Lisbon, to close their ports to the English, to recall their ambassadors from London and to declare war upon England."[11] Accordingly the duke of Portland's government, following Bonaparte's rejection of Fox's and Talleyrand's sweeping draft peace treaty of August 1806, immediately dispatched a powerful British fleet under Vice Adm. James Gambier to Copenhagen, while instructing Foreign Secretary Canning on August 12 to order the Prince Regent of Denmark to hand over the war fleet of fifteen vessels to the British for the duration of the war and to cease hostilities against England. With French troops at his back, however, that gentleman refused, and a small British force of marines was landed on Zealand as Gambier's powerful fleet began a lethal bombardment of the Danish capital on September 2, resulting in the burning of most of the city by the fifth, when the Danes capitulated.[12] A by-now-sorely-taxed English government was finally reacting with vigor against the enormous French noose tightening around it.

In this case the British successfully seized eight Danish ships of the line and frigates, sailing them to England. Marshal Bernadotte's army of thirty thousand men in Hamburg, already preparing to invade Denmark, had been adroitly if narrowly forestalled. "If the English go on in this manner, it will be necessary to close all the ports of Europe to them!" Napoleon fulminated on receiving news of the fall of Copenhagen. He had anticipated closing the whole of Europe to all English trade in any event, beginning with the creation of the Confederation of the Rhine, enforced by the Continental System and of course by the secret Tilsit accords.[13] Copenhagen had in fact altered none of his prearranged plans for conquest; on the other hand there was no way in the world the French navy could effectively have patrolled Demark's five hundred islands.

And Portugal was quite another matter. That sovereign state, England's oldest Continental ally, dating back to Catherine of Braganza (daughter of the king of Portugal and wife of King Charles II) and the 1703 Treaty of Methuen, had simply ignored Bonaparte's decrees and threats, giving the British navy and merchant marine full access to its ports and facilities. With the intention of sealing off Portugal from England and then using the presence of French troops in Portugal as the first wedge of French military occupation of the whole of the Iberian Peninsula, in the autumn of 1807 Bonaparte ordered General Junot and his newly created Army of Observation to cross Spanish territory to seize Lisbon and the Portuguese royal family, occupying the entire country in the process. The Spanish Bourbons, in a chaotic self-destructive struggle, went nicely along with French plans. Or, as Metternich put it, "The catastrophes that overthrew the Spanish throne are certainly made to measure for the crafty, destructive, and criminal policy of Napoleon." Manuel de Godoy, the "Prince of Peace"—de facto ruler of Spain—"is the rascal who will open the gates of Spain to us,"[14] Fouché predicted, and he proved to be right. The French offered nearly one-third of Portugal in exchange for Godoy's cooperation, promised another third to Spain, and retained the remaining third for Bonaparte, all duly recorded, clause per clause, in the secret Franco-Spanish Treaty of Fontainebleau of October 27, 1807.[15] If Portugal did not close its ports to, and declare war on, England as Napoleon ordered, he promised that "the House of Braganza will not be reigning in Europe two months hence. I will no longer tolerate a single English envoy in Europe. I will declare war on any power that has one [in its capital]."[16]

Lord Strangford, the English ambassador to Portugal, unaware of the extent of French intentions in Iberia, consulted with Prince John, serving as regent for the Portuguese royal family, and informed London on August 13: "The Portuguese Ministers place all their hopes of being able to ward off this terrible blow. . . . But I think that if France could be induced to give up this point [confiscation of British property] and limit her demands to the exclusion of British commerce from Portugal, the Government of this country would accede to them."[17] Working closely together, Britain and Portugal hoped to defuse the situation. Naturally Napoleon was much discommoded by Portugal's surprising compliance with almost every item of his ultimatum, informing Paris that it would declare war on England and close its ports to England's naval and merchant shipping. Because he had hoped that Portuguese rejection of his demands would provide him with an excuse for occupying Portugal, a much-miffed Bonaparte ordered Junot to cross the Spanish frontier that November and invade Portugal anyway. For once the world could legally name Napoleon the aggressor.

The only factor in Portugal's favor now was the choice of Junot to command this invasion force. Junot was of course completely loyal to his chief and usually quite dynamic, but he was erratic and unbalanced, and an incompetent organizer and commander. He was the wrong man for such an assignment, as his army of approximately 25,000 men quickly discovered as they advanced into Portugal under soaring temperatures. Lacking the most elementary logistical support, including food, water, and proper clothing, their numbers dwindled away at a staggering rate, less than two thousand ragged troops finally reaching Lisbon on November 30, 1807.[18] The French arrived too late to kidnap the Portuguese royal family, however, who had sailed for Brazil less than twenty-four hours earlier under a British naval escort commanded by none other than Napoleon's old bugbear and opponent of Acre fame, Sir William Sidney Smith.

More interested in trysts with Portuguese women and in looting Portuguese strongboxes than in making necessary defensive military preparations in the almost inevitable event of British reprisals, Junot took no substantive countermeasures. The result was that Gen. Sir Arthur Wellesley was able to land his initial force of nine thousand men safely at Mondego Bay in August of the following year, finally giving England a tenuous military foothold on the continent. Although Junot's dawdling had helped temporarily delay Bonaparte's campaign in late 1807, Napoleon was relatively satisfied with events.

As noted, Portugal was meant to serve as the wedge of a vast French invasion, Spain to follow, to permit in turn the seizure of Gibraltar and the making of the Mediterranean into Napoleon's very own *mare nostrum*. This would allow him to move his armies into North Africa, in imitation of the Roman legions of yore, while another French army from Naples would invade Sicily and a separate special fleet would take and secure the Cape of Good Hope. This breathtaking plan also required another separate army "of fifty thousand Russians, French, and perhaps Austrians" to march on Constantinople—"the center and seat of universal domination," as Napoleon referred to it[19]—and beyond, Delhi beckoning him on eastward, not to mention the shimmering chimera of the Indies—East and West—and of course South America itself. All these plans of conquest were drawn up in a sweeping master plan he had first conceived in February 1806 and finalized in March 1808—the whole thing intended to destroy all British trade everywhere and place uncontested control of most of the world in his own hands.[20] In breadth, scope, and imagination the scheme was dazzling, involving hundreds of thousands of troops and many dozens of ships of the line that France and Spain in fact no longer possessed. But among other things, Bonaparte had somehow managed to forget about the English navy, which controlled the seven seas, and of course the technical and logistical impossibility of such a worldwide operation. Without Talleyrand there to attempt to keep him in check, Napoleon's surging megalomania was clearly out of hand. Nevertheless Bonaparte—on whose personal orders their very existence depended—was still taken very seriously by most officials and generals.

At this early stage, two more key elements for the enacting of this fresh blueprint for conquest were absolutely necessary: Russian and Spanish cooperation. Napoleon could not commit a major army in Spain without securing his flanks, in particular against an agitating Austria. For this he needed Russian assurances of help and direct military intervention. The second problem involved Spain itself, where Napoleon had foolishly anticipated full cooperation from the Spanish people, thereby permitting his armies to seize the country and then march on to Gibraltar for the next phase of his plan in North Africa. Napoleon did realize, however, that "the aristocracy and the clergy are the masters of Spain. If they fear for their privileges and existence," he explained to Marshal Murat, "they will oppose me and fight on forever. At this time I have partisans there, but if I arrive as a conqueror [at the head of a large army], I will no longer have any."[21] The Spaniards, a most defiant and independent people, had no intention of obliging the French, or any other invader.

With Portugal safely out of the way—and a whopping 100-million-franc war indemnity slapped on it (as compared to Prussia's 140-million-franc reparations)—Napoleon could begin phase two, the invasion of Spain. Fortunately for him, the Spanish royal family was to prove most cooperative, thanks to its general incompetence, compounded by its internecine quarrels and jealousies. Indeed, they literally scampered into the Napoleonic web, although even before Junot's arrival in November, Bonaparte had slipped three small French corps into northern Spain. As for the Spanish army, Napoleon considered it an absurdity that no intelligent commander could take seriously. As for that even greater absurdity, the Spanish Bourbons, they would fit nicely into the plan. King Carlos IV—who had been placed in a secondary position by his ugly wife's lover, the insinuating and ambitious Godoy (a former army private and now virtual dictator of the land)—was as jealous of Godoy and his wife as he was wary of his ever-plotting son, Fernando, prince of Asturias. Promised his very own miniature kingdom of the Algarve, Godoy had proved most cooperative. For Napoleon, who despised the whole lot—Fernando "eats four square meals a day and hasn't an idea in his empty head"—and loathed the corrupt and decadent

Godoy as well, neither the timing nor the situation could have been more opportune. As Napoleon pointed out, "To choose the right moment in which to act is the great art of men. What one can do easily in 1807 perhaps cannot be done under any circumstances in 1810."[22]

And then it happened. Carlos IV ordered the arrest of his son, charging Fernando with treason (for plotting to overthrow him). But as tempers cooled, a reconciliation of sorts took place, and the Spanish king, who had called for French military intervention, relented, informing Napoleon that this would not be necessary after all. Meanwhile French officers in Spain and Portugal were ordered to prepare intelligence reports on logistics, feasible roads, the strength of Spanish garrisons, and so on, accompanied by government-directed attacks in Parisian newspapers against Godoy. Complicating matters was Napoleon's great plan for marrying brother Lucien's eldest daughter, Louise, to Fernando (which in the end, however, came to nought). Nevertheless, by February 16, 1808, Napoleon was finally ready to strike.[23]

On that day French troops seized the Spanish frontier and the cities of Pamplona, Barcelona, San Sebastián, and Figueras. So far, so good.

Meanwhile, if Carlos had had his change of heart about prosecuting Fernando, his son, however, had not yet played all his cards. He in turn now appealed to Napoleon to help him overthrow his father! By this stage even Napoleon was bewildered—first the father, then the son—but in any event he had the excuse he sought for bringing in French troops, 118,000 men to be exact. Godoy advised his masters to flee to South America, following the successful example of the Braganzas, and they rushed for the Atlantic port of Cádiz. News of the attempted royal flight led to national uprisings on March 17, including a revolt in Madrid. Now on the excuse of attempting *to save* the royal family, Napoleon dispatched Marshal Murat at the head of a French army with orders to seize the Spanish capital, which he duly entered on March 24. (Murat had informed his troops that they were marching south to campaign in North Africa.)

As for the royal family, stopped by hostile crowds at Aranjuez, they panicked, the hapless king abdicating on March 19 in favor of his son, to be known as Fernando VII. Within a few days Don Carlos repented as usual. He did not want to abdicate after all, and he appealed to Napoleon, and to the very French army he had been in the midst of fleeing, for help. An incredulous Napoleon, still at Bayonne, could not believe his good fortune. The whole royal family was mad. He could not have devised a better plan himself. Summoning King Carlos, Queen Maria Luisa, Fernando, and Godoy, Napoleon kindly agreed "to mediate" for them and settle the issue once and for all there at Bayonne (on French territory).

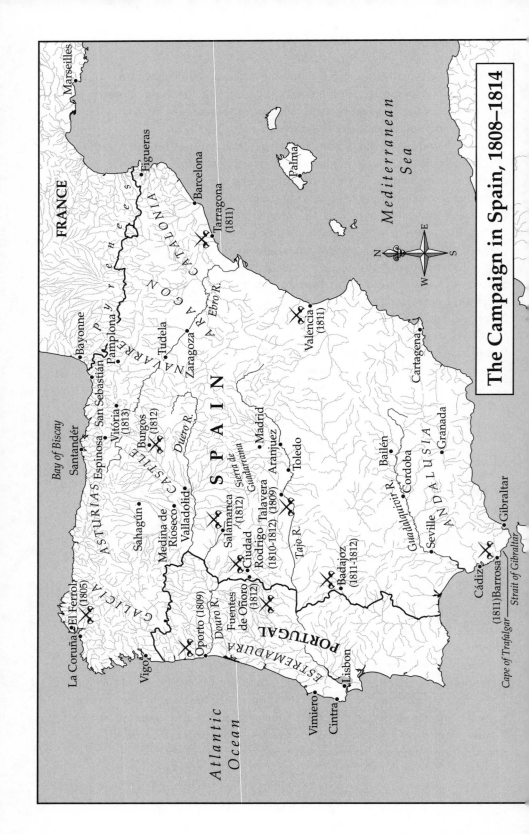

The Campaign in Spain, 1808–1814

The Spaniards, all lured across the French frontier and obligingly into the spider's web, reached Bayonne by April 30, 1808, when Napoleon put his simple but effective plan into action. First he got the dimwitted Carlos secretly to confirm his abdication made earlier at Aranjuez but with one modification: Instead of assigning the throne to his son, he would hand it over to Napoleon, "temporarily," until a solution could be found. Then on May 6 Napoleon in a secret meeting with Fernando convinced him to restore his father to the throne, assigning all his rights to him. Having done this, a beaming Bonaparte produced Carlos's freshly minted modified abdication. Thanks to this sleight of hand, there was no longer either a king or a direct heir to the Spanish throne. *Voilà!* The Spaniards suddenly found themselves exiled from their native land and, under tight military security, escorted to their respective—if luxurious—new prisons, where they would remain under house arrest for the next several years: ex-king Carlos, the ex-queen, and Godoy en route for the Château of Compiègne, and Fernando and his retinue to Talleyrand's sprawling renaissance estate at Valençay. Within a matter of three weeks Bonaparte had polished off the lot of them, the bewildered state prisoners still not quite fathoming what had befallen them.

With Spain now seemingly his for the taking, Napoleon looked for another Bonaparte to succeed to the vacant Bourbon throne. Lucien, his initial choice, still could not be persuaded to discard his second wife, by now the mother of a numerous family. Napoleon denounced his ungrateful, unreasonable brother in a private letter to Joseph on March 11. "Lucien is acting more self-righteous than the Pope!" And he retaliated (as he invariably did when rebuffed) by exiling Lucien from Rome to the provinces. "I thought he was intelligent, but I see now that he is just a fool."[24] Napoleon could never understand any man giving up a kingdom and immense power for a woman.

Napoleon now turned to Louis, who also rejected the Spanish throne but for entirely different reasons. Kings, he lectured brother Napoleon, were not mere government officials to be shunted from post to post. "I am not some simple provincial governor," he reminded him. "The only other promotion possible for me is in heaven. . . . How could I possibly take an oath to faithfully serve another people, when I had not even remained faithful to Holland?"[25] For the hypochondriacal Louis, who spent more time at foreign spas than attending to government business in Holland, it was a surprising remark. Napoleon had no answer for it. Meanwhile Jérôme also declined Spain.

Down to his last choice, Napoleon twice called on King Joseph of Naples. Though his offer was rejected out of hand the first time around,

Joseph accepted the second time on April 18, and then most reluctantly, when among other things Napoleon promised to extend Spanish boundaries to include the Ebro River and the Pyrenees.[26] Joseph agreed to exchange the Bourbon throne of Naples for the Bourbon throne of Spain. He came to regret it almost immediately.

On the very day that Prince Fernando relinquished his claims to the throne, May 6, 1808, Napoleon proclaimed Joseph the new king of "Spain and the Indies," the appointment to become legally effective on August 1, although Joseph was to take up his new post immediately. The news quickly spread through the leading aristocratic circles of the country, the very circles whose support Napoleon himself recognized as being vital to him if he were to execute a quiet, unopposed military occupation of the country. Alas, this ruling élite did not accept Joseph Bonaparte's accession to their throne. "You must be quite aware," Cardinal Desping y Dasseto confided to the archbishop of Granada, "that we cannot recognize as our king someone who is a freemason, a heretic, and a Lutheran, as are all the Bonapartes and indeed all the French people."[27]

Joseph had accepted on the understanding that relinquishing the Neapolitan throne would not result in its falling into unfriendly hands. As he explained to his brother Lucien, with whom he remained on close and friendly terms, "Prince Murat will not be king. The emperor has explained himself on this count by stating ... that only his brothers are to have thrones."[28] Joseph did not learn of Napoleon's latest deception in this matter until he had crossed the Spanish frontier, thereby adding another grudge against a brother whom he by now loathed as heartily as he distrusted, this brother who had so disrupted the calm, comfortable life he had made for himself under the shade of the chestnut trees of Mortefontaine. On May 5 Prince Murat, though himself strongly covetous of the Spanish crown, gratefully accepted the lesser Neapolitan jewel "with tears of gratitude streaming from my eyes," although having in return to sign over to Napoleon the Grand Duchy of Berg as well as Caroline's Elysée Palace.[29]

The imperial French hornets' nest was finally calming down and sorting itself out. Napoleon now had five European crowns "in the family," in addition to that of France: Louis in Holland, Jérôme in Westphalia, sister Caroline and brother-in-law Joachim in Naples, and an obliging Joseph in Madrid (with an increased official income alone of 16 million francs), not to mention his genial young stepson, Eugène de Beauharnais, holding down the fort for him as viceroy of Italy (although Napoleon had gone back on a formal promise actually to hand over that crown to Eugène). Napoleon's master plan for world domination could now proceed.

Joseph made a triumphal entry into Vitoria on June 6, 1808, and was officially recognized as the successor to Carlos IV by the governing aristocratic junta, or council, albeit at French bayonet point. Thereafter the new king was proclaimed as "Don Joseph, by the grace of God, King of Castile, Aragon, of the Two Sicilies, of Jerusalem, of Navarre, Granada, Toledo, Valencia, Galicia, Majorca, Minorca, Seville," and so on, the list of historic titles read filling an entire page, including "Gibraltar, the Canary Islands, and the West and East Indies."[30] The Bonapartes had indeed arrived.

Nonetheless, in spite of a trunkful of ancient, golden, jewel-encrusted crowns, all was not quite as wonderful as Napoleon declared it to be in the pages of the *Moniteur,* for on May 2, even before Fernando had officially signed over all his rights to the crown, tens of thousands of people in Madrid revolted against Marshal Murat and the powerful garrison commanded by General Grouchy, the newly installed governor-general. They were saved only by emergency reinforcements rushed in by Moncey. The results: well over a thousand French and Spanish killed—some put the estimate at close to twenty-five-thousand—and a new rallying symbol of Spanish rebellion against the French invader and usurper resounding through the peninsula: *"Dos de Mayo,"* words that were to haunt the French to the very end. But for the unheedful Napoleon, who was at this moment frolicking in the Atlantic surf with Josephine on a well-guarded beach near Bayonne, it was but a minor incident, or so he declared, as was the further dismaying news reaching France later that month of the Spanish bombardment and capture in Cádiz harbor of the few remaining French vessels that had sheltered there ever since their ignominious defeat at Trafalgar.[31]

Under sunny blue skies Napoleon—having just added two kingdoms to the glorious French Empire—and Josephine duly began their triumphal return journey to Paris, and to the refreshing elegance of St.-Cloud, the heavily censored press kindly omitting the less agreeable details of a few setbacks. But despite official cheers and outward self-congratulation by French imperial officials in the capital, neither Foreign Minister Champagny nor War Minister Clarke could long put off the influx of disconcerting news now reaching them almost daily. Within a single week in May, three French military governors—of Badajoz, Cádiz, and Cartagena—had been assassinated, and three other provinces around Asturias, Seville, and Valencia were already in a state of open rebellion. Indeed, by the end of the first week in June, almost the entire Kingdom of Spain was rising up against the French army of occupation, the Spaniards appealing directly to London for military assistance.

In fact Bonaparte had received news of several major setbacks while en route from Bayonne, in particular by Joseph Bonaparte's new, disliked commander in chief, General Savary (the newly promoted duke of Rovigo), who had caught up with the imperial couple while they were still at Tours.

The assassinations and revolts had taken place chiefly as a result of the *Dos de Mayo* uprising and subsequently after the news of the defeat and surrender of General Dupont's corps of twenty-three thousand men to the Spanish generals Redding and Castaños at Bailén on July 22. Napoleon was particularly concerned about the Dupont catastrophe, which seemed to toll a knell at St.-Cloud and in the War Ministry. It appeared that Dupont's troops, after taking Córdoba, savagely sacked the city and raped thousands of its women and girls, then evacuated with a booty train reminiscent of Napoleon's campaign back in Italy in 1797. Thousands of mules and horses hauled some five hundred wagons crammed with loot, greatly delaying Dupont's escape from the angry Spanish civilians ("rebels," the French called them) and troops that had set out after him, General Redding's garrison at Bailén then preventing his advance north to Madrid.

"If I thought it [the conquest of Spain] were going to cost me 80,000 men, I would not attempt it, but it will not involve more than 12,000 lives," Napoleon had lightly quipped at Bayonne back on April 18, as if twelve thousand lives were a trifle. In fact, however, as he was already beginning to realize, French armies would be able to occupy the whole of Spain only by overcoming vigorous opposition. "I am truly perplexed," he had confided to Marshal Murat. "Do not for a minute lose sight of the fact that you are dealing with a different sort of people there. They have all the courage and enthusiasm one encounters only among men clearly determined to defend their homeland."[32]

It is not that this Spanish resistance surprised Bonaparte so much as the fact that he thought that any good French general, as Dupont had proved himself to be against the Austrians, Prussians, and Russians, at the head of twenty-three thousand or so crack French troops, could easily quell any Spanish force of equal or even larger size. The French were unbeatable, unstoppable. He was dead wrong, as Savary related the defeat at Bailén, accompanied by the incredible news of the flight of *"El Rey Josef"* from Madrid all the way to Burgos. Napoleon was simply stunned.

"We talked for a long time," Savary recalled, "he making me repeat time and again, not being able to comprehend what had taken place in Andalusia. He lamented having committed so many troops there."[33] News of the unexpected disasters—the *Dos de Mayo*, Bailén, Joseph's flight from Madrid—nonplussed a man unaccustomed to such setbacks. "He permitted his communications to be cut," Napoleon said of Dupont's surrender at Bailén, "and his corps to be divided." Furthermore he had attacked incorrectly and then foolishly capitulated in the name of a large portion of his army that had not even been involved in the battle. And then there was the little matter of his five hundred wagons of loot, despite Napoleon's strict orders against all looting. "Could I have expected all that from Dupont of all people, a man whom I greatly liked and was in fact grooming to be my next marshal?... Better, far better they had all died with arms in their hands. Their deaths at least would have been glorious."[34] Napoleon said he would order Dupont to be stripped of his rank and appear before a court-martial.[35] Then, after Savary's verbal report on Joseph's panicked evacuation of his mint-new capital, Napoleon concluded, "Well, General, you certainly bring me some fine news there!... Having fallen back across both rivers [the Ebro and the Duero] is tantamount to evacuating Spain itself."[36] The military genius who had so miscalculated his Egyptian campaign, and then again his attempted amphibious invasion of England, who had lost the naval war at Trafalgar, and who was now holding captive under military occupation Portugal, Holland, Switzerland, Italy, the thirty-nine confederated Rhineland states, Prussia, Austria, and the Grand Duchy of Warsaw, was in the process of making yet another catastrophic error of judgment, and deep down he knew it. Nevertheless he persisted. This would soon tie down the better part of the entire Grande Armée, eventually resulting not in twelve thousand or even eighty thousand unnecessary French deaths, but in a quarter of a million in the Iberian Peninsula alone, not even counting the hundreds of thousands of Spanish and Portuguese dead and wounded and the untold civilian suffering and destruction.

"In this kind of warfare retrograde movements are never any good. Such movements are dangerous enough in a regular campaign, but when dealing with a national uprising, they should never be employed," Bonaparte had advised Marshal Bessières back in mid-June, and now he himself was using just such movements.[37] Indeed, by this time everything in his Iberian calculations appeared to be in retrograde. Having planned on no appreciable Spanish resistance to his occupation, he had instead found himself facing not only national uprisings everywhere but the entire Spanish Royal Army, some one hundred thousand of them, as well. Cardinal Desping y Dasseto and the archbishop of Granada had openly denounced the French, a sentiment that seemed to sum up the feelings of the whole population.

Following the surrender at Bailén on July 22, King Joseph, who had entered Madrid only two days before, had, as General Savary had revealed, fled precipitously northward. Meanwhile Marshal Bessières was frantically attempting to keep open the French logistical lifeline between Madrid and Bayonne. It was a nightmare from the outset—shades of the Egyptian campaign all over again—with outnumbered flying columns trying to cope with flashpoints everywhere on the compass, except now in Spain the local population was larger, better armed, and more determined to oppose the intruder. Instead of just a couple of hostile forces as Napoleon had faced in Egypt, numerous armies now appeared in every direction, generally centered around well-fortified ancient cities and bastions. Instead of laying siege to just one citadel of Acre, he was facing a half dozen. If Kléber and Desaix had somehow managed to achieve some success for a while, not so Moncey and Dupont in Spain, the former failing to take his objective of Valencia and falling back, while Dupont of course surrendered in July. As for Bessières, in the face of tough resistance every step of the way, he had to give up his attempt to drive northward through the damp, cold, heavily forested coastal mountains, even failing to secure the important coastal route as far as the major port of Santandér. Napoleon already had more than 118,000 men in Spain alone, and was everywhere being repulsed. He had not expected any of this. Madrid was becoming another besieged, hostile Cairo. General Verdier, too, had failed, and had been forced to lift his destructive siege of Zaragoza against General Palafox. Junot's entire army of around 26,000 men had then surrendered to Wellesley at Vimiero on August 21, its capitulation signed at Cintra the following day, resulting in the expulsion of the entire French force from Portugal. All this within just three weeks of the initial British landing of 9,000 men at Mondego Bay—the great warrior Junot, his scarred body testimony to his many martial exploits and already a legend in the French army, defeated and expelled from Portugal!

Junot, it now turned out, had failed to prepare defenses against an expected British landing and then had commanded most incompetently at the Battle of Vimiero, followed by his even more bizarre flight in mid-battle in a carriage with a beautiful lady. This all had to be hushed up, as most things were in France. There could be no trials, no public denunciations by Napoleon to attract public scrutiny of the whole French fiasco. But everyone associated with Junot—even General Thiébault who had earlier remonstrated strongly with Junot about his failure to prepare Portugal's defenses—was temporarily sent to Coventry following their return to France as prisoners of war aboard a convoy of forty-five British warships. One humiliation after another. Junot, despite his proven instability of mind and recent incompetence on the battlefield, after being stripped of most of his honorary functions (including his positions as Napoleon's senior aide-de-camp and military governor of Paris), accompanied by an appropriate cut in his nine-hundred-thousand-franc official income, to everyone's amazement was given a fresh field command, that of the III Corps, and later of the VIII, only to abandon his men yet again.[38]

About the only good news from Iberia that summer appeared to be the announcement of Marshal Bessières's victory over Generals Cuesta and Blake at Medina del Río Seco on July 14, 1808. But the French marshal and his twelve thousand men followed this by committing another major war atrocity, putting to the sword thousands of Spanish troops who had honorably surrendered. The ghost of Jaffa continued to haunt them. This news, too, Bonaparte kept out of the French press.

It was not only the unexpected opposition encountered throughout the land that astonished and then dismayed Napoleon. He had not anticipated the intensity and consistency of the opposition or the gravity of the dramatic, unexpected defeats. For the first time since the fall of Egypt, two large French military forces had surrendered. The magic of the emperor's name and legions was tarnished. As Louis Madelin put it, the "virginity of French glory" was now a thing of the past.

Joseph's actions on the arrival of his tattered army at Burgos on August 9 only aggravated matters. Unbelievably, *El Rey Josef* wrote Napoleon that he intended to issue "a decree declaring my intention to renounce reigning over a people who first had to be subdued by arms." Therefore Napoleon had "to stop all plans regarding the Kingdom of Naples" to which Joseph wished to return forthwith. It was not too late, he insisted. The quicker the French pulled out of Iberia, the better. "I am convinced that the new arrangements [that is, the French conquest and his naming as king] will encounter more resistance in this country than Your Majesty might realize and that in the final analysis all this will bring happiness to no one."[39]

It was good, blunt advice, but concepts such as happiness were hardly of any significance to Napoleon. He was neither receptive nor amenable to the idea of Joseph's return to the Neapolitan throne or to the evacuation of his large army from the Iberian Peninsula. Napoleon had already informed the entire diplomatic corps that Spain was his imperial property and that Joseph was its new king. It would be humiliating, he would lose face, should he now suddenly announce that he, his army, and his new puppet king had been thrown out by the Spaniards. Nevertheless Joseph continued to plead in vain to be left on the throne of Naples. In fact Napoleon was so utterly stupefied, even outraged, by Joseph's request and assessment of the situation that he could not respond, apart from a purely formal acknowledgment of receipt of said missive.

Nevertheless the official response from Paris was not long in coming, as a fiery Foreign Minister Champagny harangued the Senate in its Luxembourg chambers. Under no circumstances would France let England claim Spain as one of its provinces. "I am resolved to push ahead most actively with this Spanish business," Napoleon at last informed Joseph. "The future security of my peoples, the prosperity of commerce, and the maritime peace are all dependent upon these important operations."[40] Napoleon would therefore stay, French troops would stay, *Don Josef* would stay. Spain would be "pacified" and Portugal reconquered. It was as simple as that. One of Bonaparte's greatest shortcomings was his arrogant, psychopathic inability to admit an error, especially one dramatically publicized before the world. His Spanish error was to cost him, and France, dearly.

For Napoleon, now back in the French capital, these events could not have occurred at a worse possible time, as he was preparing for an important summit conference with Czar Alexander in Germany, where reports of his latest Iberian setbacks would inevitably undermine his negotiating position. Meanwhile reinforcements would have to be sent to Spain immediately to stabilize the situation and replace the tens of thousands of troops now being returned to France as corpses. Before setting out, in a panic Napoleon authorized troops from France, the Rhineland, and the whole of Europe "to be dispatched to Bayonne without delay."[41]

By mid-July Napoleon well realized that his hope for a quick conquest was proving to be a pipe dream. A hard new reality was setting in. Masses of troops were being hastily assembled and ordered to march from the Rhine, the Vistula, and the Po, and with them crack veteran commanders, tough men capable of coping with such emergencies, including Ney.

> The Emperor, *Monsieur le Maréchal,* wishes you to come to Bayonne in order to join the King [Joseph, in Burgos]. . . . General Dupont in Andalusia has permitted himself to get entangled in inaccessible mountains . . . and has capitulated. . . . This truly incredible event appears to have led the King [Joseph] to recall all his troops to the Duero and perhaps [even as far north as] Burgos. . . . You will therefore appreciate the importance the Emperor attaches to your presence there at this time. . . .[42]

Ney was but the first of a series of marshals now being rushed in to salvage the situation in Iberia.

Another Grave Error

*I want Emperor Alexander to be awed by the spectacle of
my might.*

espite the unexpected setbacks resulting from his brothers'
(including the stubborn Lucien, Louis, and even Jérôme)
refusal to comply with his imperial wishes regarding the
Spanish throne, and the unexpected developments in
Iberia, Napoleon was determined to implement his plan
calling not only for the completion of his conquest of
Europe but of much of the rest of the world as well. For this he needed the
cooperation of Czar Alexander, who would keep the vanquished Austrians
from attempting to mobilize and attack his flanks while he was preoccupied
in Iberia. Thus Talleyrand, who had just tendered his resignation as foreign
secretary on August 9 because of his strong opposition to Napoleon's
unceasing warfare and conquests, suddenly found himself summoned to St.-
Cloud to accompany the emperor on a new, very special diplomatic journey. "We are going to Erfurt," he was informed. "I want to be able to be
free to return to deal with Spain once and for all. Therefore prepare a convention to this effect for me, one that will be mutually acceptable to Czar
Alexander as well."[1]

Never had anything quite like it been seen in the city of Erfurt, as a few
dozen newly crowned heads of the states of the Confederation of the

Rhine, including Bavaria, Saxony, Württemberg, and Westphalia—with their glittering ministers, generals, privy councilors, and equerries—greeted the emperors. Napoleon and Alexander met outside the walls of Erfurt, where Napoleon awarded the czar the Grand Cordon of the Legion of Honor, and Alexander in turn presented Napoleon with the Order of Saint André. Then proceeding together, they arrived on horseback at the head of the enormous procession, as the French cavalry escort, including the eight-hundred-man Imperial Guard, made its grand entry into the medieval city square on September 27, 1808, to the background of martial music and a deafening twenty-one-gun salute for each of the emperors. Napoleon, wishing to impress the czar, had had Alexander escorted from Bromberg to Erfurt by elite French troops, dozens of generals, and two French marshals, the dukes of Dalmatia (Soult) and Montebello (Lannes). But when the overzealous officer in charge of the Erfurt battery was about to repeat the imperial salute for the king of Württemberg, who trailed behind the imperial party, a senior officer angrily snapped: "Stop that, you fool! He's only a king!"[2] With his usual condescending smile and imperious demeanor, Bonaparte dismounted, greeted by the loud acclamation of a fawning crowd of those vanquished earlier by French arms and now on the French payroll. Their imperial majesties then toured their spacious and comfortable accommodations, Napoleon and his vast retinue taking over the government palace in Erfurt, while Alexander and his suite were escorted to "the city's most beautiful mansion," and Grand Duke Constantine found his agreeable quarters in the stately residence of a local senator.

Napoleon's stay in Erfurt proved unexpectedly delightful, he and Alexander seeming to get on well, as if there had been no lapse of time since Tilsit. Napoleon paid assiduous court to the czar, which Alexander insisted on returning, indeed even attending Napoleon's levée in his chamber in the morning. The two emperors also exchanged gifts, the czar outdoing Napoleon by presenting three sable pelisses. Balls were given, as well as splendid state dinners in neighboring castles; there were long rides together and reviews of each other's troops and observations of their field maneuvers. Napoleon's first valet, Constant, however, found the imperial hunts lacking in both sportsmanship and interest, one such event involving the shooting of sixty stags in one afternoon, the deer trapped by beaters using cloth partitions to close off any avenue of escape. The czar, who was very vain and thus refused to wear spectacles in public, could distinguish no living thing beyond a range of twenty feet. This presented a special problem for the organizers of the hunt, who finally walked a large stag (at a distance of twenty feet) before the Russian emperor, who fired at the big blur and brought it down with the first shot. It was a great moment. Bonaparte the sportsman was also delighted with the day's bag.

Germany's great man of letters could hardly be forgotten by the French emperor, who so prided himself on cultural attainments. The aging Johann Wolfgang von Goethe gallantly received from Napoleon's own hand the cross (not the grand eagle) of the Legion of Honor, followed by the French emperor's disquisition on the shortcomings of Voltaire. Later Goethe managed respectfully to decline Napoleon's invitation to Paris.

Most evenings at Erfurt were spent at the theater, Alexander and Napoleon watching, among others, Voltaire's *Oedipus,* performed by the Comédie Française, which Napoleon had brought with him (a full troupe of thirty-two comédiens, including Talma himself and the luscious Antoinette Bourgoin, "the goddess of joy and pleasure," as she was intimately known, whose many charms immediately caught the Russian imperial eye). During one performance, on hearing the line "The friendship of a great man is a blessing of the gods," the czar leaped to his feet and pulled up a dozing Bonaparte and embraced him, much to the delight of the audience below. Understandably Napoleon was to misinterpret this act, as he did Alexander's seemingly warm attitude throughout most of the Erfurt conference, as a sign of his own control and influence over the Russian emperor. This was not the case, the czar having undergone a great change of heart since Tilsit.[3]

Indeed, thinking Alexander was still his man, a sort of Russian Junot completely under his spell, to do with as he pleased, at times Bonaparte got too cocky, overstepping the bounds of the acceptable, acting not only smug but even impudent, deeply offending the sensitive czar, just as Napoleon frequently did those in his own retinue. This proved to be a grave error, with lasting consequences. The mercurial Alexander, who had been so genuinely drawn to Napoleon at Tilsit, had been having serious second thoughts following his cold reception by the Russian aristocracy following the defeats of Friedland and Tilsit. Poland, for example, was, in the czar's eyes, Russian territory, and Napoleon's seizure of the "Grand Duchy of Warsaw" therefore a glaring international slap in the face. "Poland is the sole question about which I shall never change," he had warned the new French envoy, Gen. Armand de Caulaincourt. "In the event of war breaking out, I shall surely have to declare myself king of Poland," Alexander privately acknowledged. "The world is clearly not big enough for us [France and Russia] to come to an understanding over that country."[4] Caulaincourt had duly reported the incident, Napoleon facetiously rejecting the idea with a dismissive smile.

Nor could Alexander forget the equally great humiliation suffered by the king and queen of Prussia (still taking refuge at Königsberg) when Napoleon had seized nearly half their country and people. The czar, loyally and emotionally bound to the Prussian royal family, had a long memory. What is more, the czarina, as a German, continued to hammer away at her son's support of the man whom she referred to in public as "that Corsican parvenu!" and in private as "that bloody tyrant," an exasperated Alexander finally riposting: "We are not hurrying to declare ourselves against him, for we risk losing everything if we do. Rather, let us affirm our alliance by letting him take us for granted. Let us gain some time in order to prepare ourselves for the day of reckoning. When the day comes, we will all vigorously assist in the fall of Napoleon Bonaparte."[5] Thus while openly proclaiming his support of Napoleon to Savary and Marshal Lannes—"I like Emperor Napoleon very much"—the festering resentments of the past were accruing. "Bonaparte considers me a fool," the czar now wrote his sister Catherine from Erfurt. "But he who laughs last, laughs best."[6]

Little did Bonaparte—who as usual thought that he was being most amusing—suspect how that facile unguarded tongue of his, which so amused the French, was creating angry, dangerous foes for him—this at a moment when he thought he was as infallible as he was invincible. "At the very outset, I want Emperor Alexander to be awed by the spectacle of my might," Napoleon had confided to Talleyrand just before his arrival at Erfurt. "That never fails to render subsequent negotiations much easier."[7] But word of the grave setbacks in Iberia had already tarnished Napoleon's image, and in any event the Russian emperor had sharply altered his personal views regarding Napoleon and his French allies. Times had indeed changed, Talleyrand actually warning Alexander in audacious language, "Sire, what are you doing? It's up to you alone to save Europe, and you will succeed only by standing up to Napoleon now. The French people," he added, "are civilized, but their sovereign is not; the sovereign of Russia is civilized, but his people are not. Therefore it behooves the sovereign of Russia to be allied with the French people." As for the present geopolitical situation, "The Rhine, the Alps and the Pyrenees have been conquered by France; all the rest has been conquered by Napoleon, conquests that France in fact does not support."[8] It was not in the best national interests of France to retain Germany beyond the Rhine, Italy, Poland, Holland, Belgium, Spain, and Portugal, he pointed out. Talleyrand clearly was one Frenchman the czar could listen to with interest.

Napoleon had set two principal objectives vis-à-vis Alexander at Erfurt: he wanted a written agreement committing action by Russia against Austria in the event of war, and he wanted the czar's armies to invade the Ottoman Empire, to seize Constantinople (for France!) and advance eastward to challenge British India and British international commerce. In return Napoleon would promise the czar the Ottoman provinces of Moldavia and Walachia and a free hand in seizing Finland and Sweden. Much to Bonaparte's surprise, for once Alexander stood firm, declining the privilege of capturing Constantinople for Napoleon (he of course badly wanted it for Russia, as a Mediterranean port for his otherwise icebound fleet). And despite fair warning by Foreign Minister Champagny—"It is impossible for a dispute over Constantinople not to lead to war between France and Russia"—Napoleon persisted. As for Austria, Alexander agreed only to a vague sort of defense pact with France (while privately informing Vienna that he would in reality remain neutral in the event of hostilities between Austria and France).

Blinded as always by his own egotism, Napoleon misunderstood the significance of the Erfurt talks. "All is going well here," he wrote Josephine. "I am content with Alexander, and he must be with me! If he were a woman, I do believe I could make him my mistress." And yet, just before leaving Erfurt, Napoleon had awakened his valet, Constant, and bodyguard, Rustan, with his screams from a terrifying nightmare. Bursting into his bedroom, Constant called to him twice, without Napoleon replying, his valet shaking him, as he awoke and sat up. "Oh, *mon ami*, what an awful dream I had . . . that a bear was tearing open my chest and about to eat my heart!" "The memory of this dream bothered him for a long time thereafter," Constant recalled. "He spoke about it very often, and each time sought to interpret its meaning."[9] Apparently Napoleon saw no connection between his dreams and the czar.

On October 12, 1808, Foreign Ministers Champagny and Romanzov duly signed the Erfurt Convention, and two days later the Russian and French emperors departed for their respective capitals, never to meet again. Napoleon was confident that he had Alexander in his pocket, while the czar—a most reluctant member of the Continental System—was more convinced than ever that Napoleon had to be stopped.

With, as he thought, his Austrian flank now covered, throughout the autumn Napoleon made final plans for settling the Spanish score. When they had chased his brother from Madrid, they had humiliated Napoleon himself as he had never been humiliated before, and now they would pay dearly, despite his earlier wise words to Murat regarding the foolishness of such a campaign when the country was in full revolt.

On September 4 Napoleon had issued a long letter of instructions for

War Minister Clarke to draft the largest single number of young men ever called up at one time thus far during his rule of France since November 1799: 140,000 men. Of these 80,000 were to be called up prematurely from the 1809 "allotment," and 60,000 from the 1810 conscription "class."[10] There was no legislative body in France powerful enough to question Bonaparte on this extraordinary demand. Prefects throughout the realm distributed the call-up orders, to growing moans and anguish from every department of the country. It was as desperate a move as it was dramatic and unwise. Napoleon had brought peace with England through Amiens and had then abrogated that agreement. He had signed the Pressburg treaty to bring peace with the Austrians. He had fought more battles, concluding with the Treaties of Tilsit to forge a peace with Prussia and Russia, hence bringing peace to the whole continent of Europe. And now he was deliberately, knowingly, developing another full-scale war, in Portugal and Spain, theoretically to break Great Britain but in fact to expand his personal empire. It was hardly the act of a mature, balanced humanitarian. Napoleon was using everything and everyone in (and out of) sight to achieve world conquest. Individuals simply did not count, not even his highest commanders, who were but pawns in this hair-raising game, as his most dedicated aides, commanders, and marshals were now openly admitting. "I have always been the victim of my own attachment to him," Lannes openly acknowledged. "He only loves you by fits and starts, that is only when he needs to use you."[11] To be sure, enormous portraits of each of Napoleon's twenty marshals thus far created hung magnificently in the vast Salle des Maréchaux in the Tuileries,[12] but that was just a petty sop for petty egos, as were the awards of grand eagles and cordons of the Legion of Honor. Nevertheless, even the professional soldiers were now tiring of this incessant lust for warfare. They had wives, children, and mistresses; they had estates and homes of their own; they had their fortunes to tend to and to invest. Enough was enough.

Back on September 10, 1808, while still at St.-Cloud, Napoleon had officially issued the decree announcing his intention to commit France to a full-scale campaign in the Iberian Peninsula, fully reorganizing and expanding the French Army of Spain, bringing it up to a strength of eight full army corps, two of them now being transferred from central Europe and a new IV Corps created by Marshal Lefebvre, comprising chiefly Poles and Germans. With the arrival of the new recruits, Napoleon would leave behind 205,000 troops in central and eastern Europe,[13] with another 100,000 men throughout Italy and Dalmatia.

Orders now streamed out of St.-Cloud like a hail of bullets: Germans,

Poles, and Frenchmen were to march to Spain, while closer to home units were summoned hastily to Bayonne from Vincennes, Boulogne, Ile de Ré, St.-Omer (even the Channel coastal defenses were being stripped to skeletal garrisons), Lyons, Thionville, Venlo, Maastricht, Longwy, Mainz, and Worms.[14]

"You make war like a postal inspector, not a general!" Napoleon had castigated brother Joseph following his precipitous flight from Madrid on July 31, 1808. "Clearly they [King Joseph and company] have lost their heads since the capitulation at Bailén," Napoleon confided to Gen. Mathieu Dumas. "I see that I must go there [to Spain] myself if we are going to get the job done."[15]

Seemingly satisfied with the renewal of relations with Czar Alexander and the resulting agreements, Napoleon had set out from Erfurt with his retinue under heavy escort of Imperial Guardsmen on October 14, reaching St.-Cloud four days later. Isolating himself there for the next ten days, he worked around the clock with his usual unrelenting energy, receiving a series of police and ministerial reports on the state of the French capital and of the Empire, putting all government affairs in anticipation of a long absence from the capital. Most of his time, however, was concentrated on a flow of new orders, directives, and "decisions" to War Minister Clarke, the duc de Feltre, and to Marshal Berthier, the prince de Neuchâtel. (Apart from Berthier's title, which dated back to 1806, since March 1 Napoleon had created the first enormous batch of French Imperial nobility, which would soon include 7 princes, 21 dukes, 452 counts, 1,500 barons, and 1,474 knights.[16]

When Clarke and Berthier completed their work an entirely new army would be preparing itself at Bayonne. Then, after finishing his nearly non-stop whirlwind of dictation, Bonaparte embraced Josephine for a final time as he entered his carriage and set out for Spain at midnight on October 29.

On reaching Marrac Castle at Bayonne on November 3, he was not at all pleased with what he found. He lashed out at the War Minister's chief deputy, General Dejean, for leaving his new army "naked," as he put it.

Monsieur Dejean, you will find herewith a quartermaster's report. You will see by it how inefficiently I am being served! I still have only 1,500 coats in the depots, and 7,000 cloaks, instead of the 50,000 ordered, only 15,000 pairs of shoes, instead of the 229,000 reported [incorrectly] to have been received! Everything is lacking.... My army, about to take the field, is naked and has nothing. There are not even enough uniforms for the conscripts. The reports you sent me are mere fiction, worthless pieces of paper! ... You must work on the assumption that all war contracts are mere excuses for theft [by civilian businessmen supplying the army].[17]

After just two days of further harrying work, inspections, and last-minute dictations, Bonaparte's carriage, crammed with the usual files, reports, and maps and accompanied by a powerful military escort, not to mention an entirely new army, crossed the Spanish frontier, reaching Vitoria by November 7, when he personally opened his second Spanish campaign, which included attacks by Lefebvre's and Victor's corps against General Blake's 24,000 men in Burgos and the armies of Generals Castaños and Palafox to the east.

With the new force of approximately 90,000 men to join the rest of the army already in Spain, Napoleon had two overall aims: to reconquer Portugal and oust the British there; and to shatter the opposing Spanish armies in a direct drive through the peninsula to recapture Madrid. According to the figures given him by Clarke on October 10, his Army of Spain would comprise a total of eight full army corps, totaling 314,612 men, of whom 244,125 were combat troops.[18] Mortier's V and Junot's VIII Corps, serving as reserves, would arrive shortly to complete the picture. Thus tens of thousands of French troops poured across France, converging first at Bayonne, before being assigned their new sectors of operation. Many thousands of wagons and carts followed slowly with the clothes, arms, munitions, and supplies needed to sustain these hundreds of battalions defiling through the cities of the French Empire. With news only of Napoleon's far-reaching European peace agreements at Erfurt, and little talk of Spain in the well-controlled French press, hundreds of thousands of French families now offering their young men to the nation no doubt wondered where the war was.

Facing the French in the peninsula were first of all the forty-seven-year-old Sir John Moore, freshly arrived from England to take command of the British expeditionary force in Portugal, with a maximum of only 50,000 men (half of them Portuguese and Spanish) at his disposal. Alert, intelligent, an able commander in every sense of the word, Moore had campaigned throughout the world, including Den Helder, the Baltic, and Egypt. His troops were noted for always being better trained and equipped than those of most other commanding officers. Once in place that October, Moore was to maneuver with General Baird's 12,000 troops from England about to land at La Coruña. His greatest problems were total ignorance of the geography of the future campaign, compounded by ancient, woefully inaccurate maps, and a growing inability to maintain communications with, and lack of cooperation from, allied Spanish commanders.

Moore's Spanish allies included General La Romana, whose corps, at present with Napoleon's army in Germany, were shortly to desert the French in Denmark, when the British navy in a spectacular rescue operation whisked most of them away right under the noses of the astonished French and back to Spain. La Romana, on the other hand, was a mediocre general, unlike the most capable Spanish field commander, General Castaños. General Blake, a talented young officer of Irish extraction, had only recently received a jump promotion from colonel to captain general of Galicia. The twenty-eight-year-old Joseph Palafox, captain general of Aragon, was "more the courtier than the nobleman," but he did prove to be most courageous when the time required it. General Redding, of the Catalan army, was also considered quite capable, as Dupont had already discovered. The aged captain general of Palma, General Vives, was little more than "an Anglophobic booby." All told the Spaniards commanded only 125,000 troops available for the first line, although with reserves and garrisons they could muster another 75,000 or so, for a total of 200,000 men, few of whom had had military training or real experience in the field. If they could coordinate their communications, tactics, and troop deployments with the British, however, there was hope of foiling Bonaparte's latest invasion plans.

Spain was to prove a problem such as Napoleon had never experienced. Although the extreme heat and aridity were nothing new for the few remaining veterans of Egypt, on the other hand in Egypt the French had not had to cope with half a dozen well dispersed major hot spots of organized resistance at the same time, as was already the case in Spain. What is worse, these battles more often than not involved full-scale sieges of ancient walled cities, such as Vitoria, Salamanca, Burgos, Valencia, Madrid, Seville, Córdoba, and Granada, most of them so far apart as to require the use of totally isolated corps, which meant that Napoleon frequently could not combine two or more corps for a single attack. All this was aggravated by growing guerrilla warfare, which was to prove deadly in the long run.[19] Even on the few occasions when a joint, coordinated effort between corps was required, personal animosity between the commanding officers more than once resulted in their failure to cooperate, as for instance later occurred between Ney and Soult (following Soult's defeat at Oporto by the British), not to mention the continuing hostility between Ney and Lannes, and the general dislike of most commanders of Marshal Berthier. The result was that Napoleon was unable to conclude the occupation of the country and continue on to Gibraltar as planned for the next stage of his conquest, in North Africa. He had instead to fight with the main part of the Grande Armée and most of its famous marshals just in order to recoup his losses in

Portugal and in Spain as far as Madrid, to reestablish his brother on the throne he had held for only a matter of days. To complicate matters further, King Joseph announced that he had already had quite enough and begged to return to the relative calm of his Neapolitan kingdom, or, failing that, to the sane, civilized existence of life at Mortefontaine.

Nor did his problems end in Iberia. The heated words of the German nationalist-philosopher Johann Gottlieb Fichte and Baron von Stein, the Prussian state minister, had ignited the frustrated north Germans, and reports arrived of fresh activity in Austrian military circles concerning a possible new mobilization to avenge their nation and retaliate against the French armies of occupation everywhere surrounding them.

Not even France was free of growing discontent, prefects and military governors reported in growing numbers from every department of the land. Renewed conscription of the nation's youth, not to mention the decline of French commerce and agricultural production (despite and because of Napoleon's ingenious Continental System), aggravated by Britain's unrivaled control of the oceans and overseas markets, all helped to agitate the people. What is more, Napoleon was spending 95 percent of his time on purely military matters—despite great publicity and glaring pronouncements to the contrary—and hence ignoring France and the needs of its civilian population, which, among other things, craved peace.

Within the army, some of Napoleon's commanders were getting more and more out of control, failing to obey orders or to follow elementary common sense. Marshal Bessières, for one, and Generals Junot, Dupont, and Lefebvre were particularly at fault at various times. Indeed, Marshal Lefebvre's latest refusal to obey clear written orders to attack General Blake at Pancorbo actually permitted Blake and his army to escape intact to the west. Napoleon would therefore have to repeat his maneuvers.

To what extent Bonaparte was aware of the pattern of events and of the overall worsening situation everywhere is not entirely clear, although he certainly saw some blunders. "His Majesty is severely displeased," Berthier chastised the unrepentant Lefebvre, the hero of Danzig.[20] It was only on November 11 that "*Beau Soleil*" Victor had finally pulled himself together and shattered Blake's force at Espinosa. The recalcitrant Bessières, a longtime favorite of Napoleon since Egypt, and commander of his Imperial Guard for years, was fired out of hand as commander of the II Corps, as a result of his repeated failure to obey orders. Alas, he was replaced by Marshal Soult, a man of questionable character, loathed almost universally by officers and men alike, and known generally as "Old Nick," who was to cause even more headaches for Bonaparte than did Bessières. As for Marshal Ney, *"le brave des braves,"* with whom Napoleon was growing more and more disenchanted, his corps was drastically reduced in strength.

Advancing on Burgos with 67,000 men on November 10, it was Soult, however, who finally destroyed the army defending the city of Estremadura, thereby permitting the French to occupy that key city of Castile situated on the main logistical route between Bayonne and Madrid. There Napoleon appointed Junot's crack former chief of staff, Divisional General Thiébault, as its new military governor,[21] while Ney's troops continued southward clearing the route to the Spanish capital. Although General Blake had escaped, fleeing northward, Marshall Lannes's 34,000 men then defeated the combined forces of Castaños and Palafox at Tudela on November 23. But if the reconquest of the Iberian Peninsula was on schedule, it was not without grave inherent problems.

For instance, by the end of November 1808, Napoleon had stripped General Dupont of his rank and ordered him to be brought before a general court-martial. Junot had earlier been defeated and taken prisoner with his entire army in Portugal. Bessières had been removed as commander, as had the ineffectual Moncey, while Lefebvre had been strongly reprimanded for incompetence, not to mention Napoleon's anger (unjust, as it turned out) with Ney. Napoleon's magnificent, much-vaunted generals and marshals were proving themselves failures before the whole world. Morale in the French army, and especially in the officer corps, was again plummeting. This was proving to be another Egypt, and yet the econd Spanish campaign had barely begun.

Deciding not to attack Moore's small force approaching Salamanca, on November 28 Napoleon issued orders for the next phase to begin, to retrieve Madrid, this involving some 130,000 troops, with Lefebvre's corps protecting the right flank, Ney taking the left, and Napoleon proceeding with the center. Facing them was a determined Spanish defense force of 21,000 men in the mountains straddling Napoleon's route just north of Madrid. Bonaparte attacked them at Somo Sierra Pass and through the western Guadarramas defiles. The Spanish force, greatly outnumbered, did not stand a chance. But Napoleon, ever impatient to proceed, needlessly ordered a Polish squadron of light horse to charge up a steep mountain to silence a major battery of sixteen pieces of artillery, an unequal task resulting in the decimation of the small Polish unit, only twenty-seven men returning out of the eighty-seven sent up the mountain. One hour later the battery was dislodged by more traditional means. By the end of November the Spaniards had been crushed,[22] and by December 2 Napoleon's army was surrounding the walls of Madrid, which fell to the French on the fourth. As far as Napoleon was concerned, Spain was conquered, Joseph was back on his throne, and once Moore was defeated, Portugal would yet again provide some fine war booty for the Bonapartes.

During his final sojourn in Madrid now, Napoleon established his headquarters in the luxurious Champs Martín Castle, the property of the duke of Infantado's mother, located less than a mile outside the capital itself, while the French army camped in the surrounding fields. Here the rigors of the journey and fighting could be briefly forgotten, as courtiers gathered and the lovely ladies of Joseph's new court lightened the scene, including "a beautiful [fifteen-year-old Spanish] actress ... so pretty, so seductive," whom Napoleon ordered to have brought to his bedchamber.[23] But apart from an occasional outing to the theater after Joseph was reinstalled, Madrid offered few attractions for the French emperor.

Napoleon now had to reassess the constantly changing Spanish scene. His losses were already well above the 12,000 he had once lightly mentioned, and they promised to remain high. This was not a country where one could, by a mere glance at a map, plan a campaign and expect to see it executed according to a prearranged timetable. Now with a reluctant Joseph back in the capital, protected by a permanent force of 40,000 French troops under the command of General Savary, the next stage of their operations had to be contemplated. This included Soult's corps securing the northwest against the small Spanish contingent and equally small British "army" of 25,000 under General Moore, still marching from the Atlantic coast to Salamanca. Napoleon's V Corps was therefore ordered to the northeast to reinforce the French siege of Zaragoza on the Ebro River in the heart of Aragon, while still farther to the east, on the Mediterranean, Gen. Gouvion St.-Cyr was ordered to conquer the whole of Catalonia with his VII Corps.

But on December 19, while in the midst of reviewing troops in Madrid, Napoleon was interrupted by a special courier informing him of Moore's unexpected success in taking Salamanca. Moore, it seemed, was determined to cut off and destroy Marshal Soult's corps, reported to be in the region of Sahagún. The English were always doing the unexpected. Taking no more chances, Bonaparte immediately ordered two powerful corps under Ney and Victor, for a total force of 80,000 men (exclusive of Soult's corps), on a forced march northward.

Alas, Bonaparte's ignorance of the Iberian Peninsula again intervened, throwing off his calculations. His troops were soon slowed by the snow-covered Sierra de Gredos and the Sierra de Guadarrama, separating Madrid from the plains beyond, leaving his dissillusioned, hungry, poorly clad men frustrated to the point of rebellion and large-scale desertions. Openly hostile remarks were even made within earshot of Napoleon himself. "The soldiers . . . [of Victor's I Corps] showed the most sinister disposition against the Emperor's person all the way up [the ice-covered mountain]," Colonel de Gonneville later related, "even calling out loudly to one another to shoot him [Napoleon] and have done with it."[24] But despite the grumbling and growing dissatisfaction with Bonaparte, even within the ranks of the Imperial Guard (which demanded to leave the country), the columns continued to plod ahead to meet Moore's force.

Sir John's objective, on the other hand, was to slow the French final conquest of the southern half of Spain, while preventing Portugal from falling under their control. Having captured a copy of Napoleon's general plan, revealing the strength and location of every French Army corps in the country, Moore, a brave and independent man, realized now what a dangerous spot he and his 25,000 men were in. Nevertheless he persevered until he learned of Napoleon's approach from the rear, when he finally ordered a strategic retreat to the coast. He had little choice. To be slightly outnumbered in a battle meant little to him, but to be isolated and caught between nearly 100,000 French troops now approaching him simply was not reasonable.

With the odds suddenly overwhelmingly in his favor, Soult took up the pursuit to the Atlantic coast, but as usual proceeded far too cautiously. Moore managed to embark 35,000 men (including the garrisons he had left along the coast) at Vigo on the few English ships there, and then proceeded to the northwestern Spanish port of La Coruña, where he had to wait until January 14, 1809, when the Royal Navy finally appeared and began the slow, laborious, and precarious task of embarking the entire remaining force of 16,500 men under the heavy fire of Soult's 20,000 troops. Although Moore succeeded in repulsing the French with heavy losses, the English general himself was killed by a cannonball just prior to the fleet's sailing on January 17.

Twice Marshal Soult had been worsted by the British, but at least he now temporarily held the northwest corner of Spain, including the northern section of Portugal. There was of course no other large organized army left to oppose him.

Napoleon was once again reassessing the situation. Madrid had been secured, albeit at bayonet point amid an openly hostile population, surrounded by an equally hostile people in every province of the land. Some 314,000 French troops had been brought to Iberia, including Junot's repatriated Portuguese corps. But then Junot, more and more deranged, announced he was leaving his new corps and the governorship of one eastern region of the land, and therewith promptly set off for Paris AWOL!

The reports of increasing mass desertion in just about every regiment and battalion of the army were equally disturbing. Bonaparte acknowledged to War Minister Clarke that of every five hundred men sent him from France, only four hundred ever reached Spain. But even this shocking figure proved to be a generous underestimate. In perhaps the most painful case of all, of 295 young recruits recently dispatched from the Loire, only 45 had reached Spain.[25] Napoleon was not only facing a hostile Spanish population, but a distrustful, hostile France as well, to whom he was no longer the great hero and savior of the nation but a veritable warmonger.

All this marked just the beginning of the bad news with which Napoleon had to cope at this time. In addition to everything else, the late Sir John Moore had in fact achieved his principal objective of greatly upsetting Napoleon's timetable for the overall conquest of the peninsula by a good year. What is more, it is estimated that Bonaparte had lost perhaps 75,000 men even before the first year of fighting was out, by January 1809.[26] (As usual, he kept the extent of his Iberian casualty figures out of the newspapers.) His losses here already totaled more than all the French dead and wounded in every battle he had fought since seizing power in 1799—combined.

General Thiébault made a sweeping assessment of the situation of Napoleon's European conquest at this time, concluding:

> Our shameful disasters in Andalusia, and our evacuation of Portugal had altered our military and political position [in Iberia], and the prestige of our former invincibility was now effectively destroyed once and for all. From Messina to St. Petersburg, from Vienna to Texel [Holland], from the Baltic to the Mediterranean, the hatred we now faced— this terrible product resulting from the numerous defeats we had inflicted upon our enemies—now awakened the great desire by the whole of Europe to seek revenge against us.[27]

After placing brother Joseph back on his throne in Madrid, Napoleon returned to Valladolid, where he spent ten days, from January 8 to 18, 1809, studying two more pieces of most disquieting news. During his absence from Paris, Talleyrand and Fouché, seeing clearly what Napoleon apparently could not—the madness of this continuous and expanding state policy of conquest and warfare—had formed an unholy (given their mutual dislike) alliance. Bent on achieving peace and overthrowing the French emperor, even Napoleon's brother-in-law Murat apparently supported the scheme. Then a growing number of intelligence reports brought confirmation of Austrian war preparations, with the apparent objective of avenging all their past defeats and losses on the French. When Josephine now wrote anxiously about such rumors of war with Austria, and perhaps Russia as well, he pooh-poohed the very idea. "Austria will not make war against me," he assured her on January 9. "If she does, however, I have one hundred fifty thousand men in Austria, and as many again on the Rhine, and an additional four hundred thousand German troops with which to deal with them. Everything is going well."[28] In fact at this very moment Bonaparte was in the process of hastily preparing to set out for the French capital, to abandon the direct leadership in this Spanish quagmire for the time being, precisely because of the accuracy of all these rumors. Everything was going very wrong.

Given the secret reports he was receiving from prefects in France and French military governors throughout French-occupied Europe, especially in Holland, the Confederated States of the Rhine, occupied Prussia, and of course mobilizing Austria, Napoleon was finally going to have to begin to face the whirlwind that he himself had set in motion, commencing with the Austerlitz campaign. General Thiébault's assessment had indeed been correct. As a result, while influential high officials in Paris were undermining his position at his very seat of power, Bonaparte would have to face two separate major wars, in two different parts of Europe at the same time. After just four years in existence, his great French Empire would never be the same again.

CHAPTER 29

Another Danube Campaign

Your standing orders are to go wherever there are enemies
to be attacked and destroyed.
—To Marshal Davout, April 21, 1809

n December 31, 1808, Napoleon—while traveling between Benevento and Astorga—had received an urgent dispatch apprising him of the new pending Austrian threat. Canceling his plans, he returned to Paris.

Reaching the Tuileries at 8:00 A.M. on January 23, 1809, he immediately arranged to move his offices and personal quarters into the more secluded and leafy grounds of the Elysée Palace, which he had acquired earlier from Murat when the latter was promoted to the Neapolitan throne. The growing tension and the anger swelling round the imperial court since the outset of the disagreeable Spanish venture had forced Napoleon to rely more than ever on himself, as he withdrew more and more. Those few public functions that now resumed were limited to frightfully formal public receptions, uncomfortable for all. Apart from daily contact with his secretary, Méneval, Napoleon's only really close daily friend and confidant, the only person to be treated almost as an equal and the only one still permitted to *tutoyer* him was Christophe Duroc, on whom he had become heavily dependent psychologically, and who was responsible for a variety of delicate tasks, including diplomatic negotiations. Even some of his closest soldier-friends of yesterday, such as the ever dependable Marshal Lannes, were no longer permitted to address him with the familiar *tu*. This self-imposed isolation was apparent to everyone, especially to Joséphine, who was left behind at the Tuileries.

Bonaparte's official business schedule was as frenetic as ever. He received delegations from the assemblies and the diplomatic corps, consulted daily with Cambacérès and one or two ministers, especially Finance Minister Gaudin and War Minister Clarke, and visited the transformations being carried out by Vivant Denon in the Louvre, as well as the major street and building construction in the Rue de Rivoli, just outside the gates of the Tuileries. And although no great music lover—he could never sing or hum in tune—he managed to get to the Opéra at least once, as public relations necessitated his being seen alive and well in the French capital after yet another long absence.

His daily chats with his older generals—now marshals, princes, dukes, and counts—were a thing of the past, tension, jealousies, and feuds in military circles becoming worse than ever. Scarcely any two or three marshals or senior generals were even on speaking terms. It was to prove a crippling situation, and Napoleon simply did not know how to cope with it.

One of the worst of these military squabbles involved Soult's outright refusal to come to Masséna's aid when facing Wellington before "the lines of Torres Vedras" (Wellington's fifty-kilometer stretch of mountain forts protecting Lisbon). Instead of obeying Napoleon's order to advance briskly to the Portuguese frontier, Soult proceeded to lay siege to Olivenza for nine entire days. And when at last he resumed his march, it was only as far as Badajoz, where he halted his entire army, quite against orders, and began to lay siege to that large city—for fifty-four days! By his "criminal delays" Soult procrastinated just long enough to force Masséna to withdraw from his attack on Portugal. This in turn forced Napoleon to abandon yet another attempted reconquest of that country.[1] Military cooperation at the highest command level was disintegrating everywhere, not helped by the fact that orders to all senior commanders came from the desk of the ruthless, insolent, perverse, frustrated, fingernail-gnawing, permanent chief of staff of the Imperial Army, the universally loathed Major General Berthier.

Thus, although Bonaparte now commanded the largest army in European history, some six hundrd thousand troops, fewer than ever of their commanders were to be found around him in the Elysée Palace, which now offered him the safe isolation and refuge he seemed so badly to need. There "he could walk about in the vast gardens . . . without being importuned, as well as leave without being noticed," his secretary recalled. "There he finally found himself freed of the pompous imprisonment to which he was subjected at the Tuileries."² Indeed, during the remaining days of his stay in Paris, he went to the Tuileries only for meetings of the State Council and for Sunday mass (even after his excommunication by the pope), and of course for the weekly court receptions.

Little seemed to be going right, apart from having restored Joseph to his Spanish throne. That some of his most famous commanders—Junot, Soult, and soon Masséna—had been routed by Generals Wellesley and Moore was more than annoying, little Portugal evading him time and again, and it defended by an English "army" at best one-eighth the size of his own. Napoleon would have to come back and personally give the English a military lesson and a public drubbing, he assured Méneval and Duroc.

There was also the little matter of settling accounts with the conspirators in his own government. Accordingly, on January 28 the day of reckoning came, as Talleyrand and Fouché were peremptorily summoned (Murat, the other party alleged to be in on the plot, was in Italy at the time).

On their arrival they found Archchancellor Cambacérès, Archtreasurer Lebrun, and Naval Minister Decrès awaiting them, along with Napoleon, accompanied by Duroc and Méneval. "Those who have been made grand dignitaries or ministers of the Empire cease to be free individuals in their thoughts and expression upon being named to office," Napoleon began formally, obviously tense, his voice pinched. "After that they can be nothing more than official organs of the state. For them treason has been committed the moment they permit themselves even to doubt [state policy], which is completed when they openly dissent," he said, now looking straight at Talleyrand. "Finally the dike burst," as Méneval put it. "Napoleon, whose indignation and anger grew as he spoke, reached such a pitch that it was inevitable that his scarcely contained fury would burst in a moment."³ Having just reread the conspiratorial correspondence (including a letter from Talleyrand to Murat) intercepted by Postal Director Lavalette and Eugène de Beauharnais, and reports received from Napoleon's own mother, Treasury Minister Mollien, and others—all concerning the extraordinary conspiracy of two hitherto archenemies, Talleyrand and Fouché—Napoleon was livid.

It had been the elegant comte d'Hauteville (a former police official and friend of Talleyrand) who had first secretly brought Talleyrand and Fouché together at his country estate near Bagneux back in October of the previous year, arranging the preliminary reconciliation between the two men. They met again chez the princesse de Vaudémont (an intimate friend of Talleyrand) at Suresnes. Thus far it was all completely confidential.

But then, at the beginning of December, Fouché, who had never before been invited to Talleyrand's present Paris mansion, the Hôtel de Monaco in the Rue de Varenne, not only suddenly appeared there during a reception for several dozen influential personages, but was greeted by a smiling Talleyrand as the two conspirators then walked off slowly, arm in arm.[4] The question on everyone's lips was: Why this blatant display of their intentions?

All Paris was soon talking about this extraordinary collusion. "Formerly so opposed in their views and interests, they have been brought together by ulterior circumstances," Metternich, himself no stranger to ulterior circumstances, reported from Paris to Vienna on December 4:

> I strongly suspect that at this moment they are working closely together to achieve a common goal. They now offer a real chance of success because they conform with the aspirations of an exhausted nation, after the excesses demanded of them for so long, a nation fearful of further demands requiring the destruction of their lives and fortunes, all for but one purpose: satisfying the personal ambitions of their master.

A month later the Austrian ambassador confirmed that "Talleyrand and his friend Fouché are always together, most determined to seize the opportunity, should it arise, but apparently lacking the necessary courage to create it themselves.[5]

The astute Metternich had got it right. They were literally parading their conspiratorial wares, their availability for an attempt to overthrow Napoleon, waiting for an offer of help from the right party to set events in motion. They had attempted to contact Murat, but at least one crucial secret missive had been intercepted. Had they actually been in the throes of a definite plot, however, they certainly would have acted quickly, stealthily, removing Bonaparte while he was still out of the country. Instead they had just flaunted themselves provokingly in public. All this Napoleon had just reread in the reports and letters gathered by his minions. He had worked himself up into a fury.

"You are a thief, a coward, and disloyal," Emperor Napoleon almost screamed at Talleyrand:

> You don't believe in God. All your life you have failed to fulfill your responsibilities. You have deceived and betrayed everyone. Nothing is sacred to you. You would sell out your own father if you found it profitable. I have heaped benefits, veritable fortunes on you, and yet there is

nothing you are incapable of carrying out against me. For the past ten months you have been betraying me, because, for whatever reason of your own, in the final analysis you feel that my affairs in Spain are not going well, thereby entitling you to tell whomever you please that you have always been against my seizure of that kingdom. . . . Well, what are your alternative plans? What would you do instead? Let's hear it!

His temper clearly out of control, clenching his little fists, his darting eyes for once concentrating on the unflinching foreign minister, Napoleon went on before Talleyrand could reply: "Why, I could break you like a glass! I have the power to do so. But I scorn you too much for that. Why didn't I have you hanged in public on the gates of the Carrousel! But there is still time for that. You are just common shit in silk stockings." Trying to arouse a still unruffled, imperturbable Talleyrand, he shouted, "You did not tell me that the Duke de San Carlos [his prisoner at Valençay] was your wife's lover?" Napoleon had finally hit a raw nerve. At last aroused, his mask falling momentarily, Talleyrand nonetheless responded calmly: "Quite, Sire. I did not think that such matters as that could possibly enhance either the glory of Your Majesty or of myself." Taken unaware by this quip, Napoleon flushed, nonplussed. "This violent scene," as the usually discreet Méneval referred to it, continued. But Talleyrand remained calm. "The very immobility of the unflappable gentleman, the utter lack of any sign of emotion, had incensed Napoleon all the more, to the point of forgetting his imperial dignity, by approaching Talleyrand and threatening to strike him." After next briefly lashing out at Fouché, "the paroxysm of his wrath having reached a crescendo," as Méneval put it, "then collapsed by the effort of its own excesses, and Napoleon, finding it futile to continue, left off with the warning: 'Just you remember that in the event of a fresh attempted coup against me, regardless of the role you do or do not play in it, you will be among the first to be destroyed.'"[6] Ten minutes later, as his carriage passed before the very Carrousel where Napoleon had threatened to have him hanged, Talleyrand at last commented, "What a pity that such a great man was so badly brought up!"[7]

Just to twist the knife a little more, the following day, during the usual weekend reception in the Throne Room, as Napoleon was greeting his ministers and state counselors, whom did he find before him as if nothing had transpired but Charles-Maurice de Talleyrand-Périgord! Furious at the rebuked minister's temerity, Napoleon greeted those to either side but deliberately avoided looking at him. When Talleyrand audaciously repeated the same thing one week later, Napoleon dismissed him as his grand chamberlain (replacing him with Count Anatole de Montesquiou) and ordered him not to appear at court again. Fouché, curiously enough, remained in the government for the time being, despite a report that he had burned a good many papers in his office during the preceding week. His days too, however, were clearly numbered. Napoleon had fired the shifty police minister once; he could do so again. As for Murat, hardly a longtime favorite of his brother-in-law, there was no documentary evidence of his complicity, at least not in his own hand, and of course he was "family."

By February 1809 Napoleon was hermetically sealed off from the rest of society by his self-imposed isolation at the Elysée and by the fact that he had no real friends with whom he could discuss matters apart from Duroc. Official matters could still be dealt with in the sessions of the State Council, but even chats with poor Monge were rare occasions now as Monge's mind wandered more and more, he aging quickly ever since his illness and near death at Acre. To be sure, Cambacérès was always there, always faithful, always amusing, and ever dependable to run the government in his absence, but he was not one of Napoleon's confidants. As for Josephine, he rarely spent five minutes with her, deliberately cutting her off as he prepared to make the official decision to divorce her and remarry. She withdrew to the realm of her ladies-in-waiting at the Tuileries, and at her beloved Malmaison, finally inured to the idea of severing marital ties with Napoleon and losing her official role in imperial society.

Even after putting that dreadful scene with Talleyrand and Fouché behind him, for Napoleon back at the Elysée Palace the tension was growing over the dangerous military situation developing in central Europe. Despite the alarums to the contrary back in December, it was only on February 8, 1809, that the Auric Council in Vienna under Count Stadion, in concert with Austrian emperor Franz I, reached the decision to authorize a full-scale campaign against France, to avenge the humiliating wholesale theft of Austrian territory, peoples, and wealth in the previous wars, culminating with Austerlitz and the Peace of Pressburg, back in 1805–6. "The freedom of Europe has sought refuge beneath your banners," Commander in chief Archduke Karl now addressed the Austrian army. "Soldiers, your victories will break her chains. Your German brothers who are now in the ranks of the enemy await their deliverance." On April 9 Austrian forces under the emperor's brother, Archduke Karl, thus once again crossed the River Inn into the territory of King Max Josef of Bavaria, and hence of the Confederation of the Rhine, this time without a declaration of war.

On April 12 Napoleon learned by military "telegraph," shutter-flag tower signals sent from Strasbourg, that Archduke Karl had entered Bavaria. The next day Napoleon and his powerful cavalry escort left the Elysée. Passing Strasbourg, Munich, Ludwigsburg, and Dillingen, they reached the temporary GHQ set up by Berthier at Donauwörth on April 18. The only recent good news Bonaparte had received from the peninsula prior to his departure was of Marshal Lannes's success in taking the devastated city of Zaragoza on February 21, after one of the bloodiest and most destructive sieges in modern history.[8] Thus Lannes was now free to join him.

On paper at least the French military situation in northern and central Europe looked good. In September 1808, on Napoleon's orders, the war and interior ministers initiated the mobilization process for 80,000 more new conscripts (of the classes of 1806, 1807, 1808, and 1809). In December he had demanded another 80,000 recruits from the class of 1810. In January Napoleon issued call-up orders for yet an additional 110,000 conscripts. First eighteen-year-olds, then seventeen-year-olds, now sixteen-year-olds— an entire generation was being swept away. Meanwhile casualties in the peninsula would average 45–50,000 per year, year in, year out thereafter, and unceasing columns of younger and younger replacements were required to maintain the French army in Spain alone. Clearly Napoleon had badly calculated there, or as General Marbot summed it up in later years, "Napoleon too far scorned the nations of the peninsula and believed that he need merely show some *French* troops in order to obtain what he wanted. This was a great mistake," for which the youth of France were now paying in full measure.[9]

The new events in central Europe, particularly the growing Habsburg discontent with the onerous previous peace treaties and the stripping of Austrian territory and citizens, added to the hard fact that French armies of occupation surrounded the Austrians on three sides, and that the Empire had been forced to pay an enormous war indemnities claim by Napoleon, had humiliated and embittered the Austrians beyond the point of reconciliation. On February 23, 1809, Napoleon created the Army Corps of Observation of the Rhine. The situation was tense as Napoleon ordered Ambassador (General) Andréossy to leave Vienna. War, it seemed, was inevitable. French troops remained in northern and northeastern Europe, of course. Davout's III Corps included some 80,000 men, while the Confederation of the Rhine member states provided more than 88,000 troops, and Viceroy Eugène de Beauharnais theoretically had nearly 150,000 men available in all categories, although front-line troops comprised a small percentage of that figure. But no sooner had Napoleon marched tens of thousands of troops all the way from central Europe down to Spain in 1808, than by 1809 he was marching more than 100,000 of these same troops all the way back up to central Europe again. Among their number were some of the principal commanders in that theater, notably Marshals Lannes, Masséna, and Bessières (again at the head of the Imperial Guard). In addition Napoleon was enlarging he prestigious Imperial Guard by adding a new, less select unit, the Young Guard, taken from the raw conscripts (not from volunteers, as of yore). He was also preparing a new Reserve Corps of seventeen regiments.

Napoleon thus reckoned that by May 29, 1809, he would be in a position to announce the creation of what he now called the Grand Army of Germany, expected to have an approximate effective strength of 174,000–177,000 men with which to confront the Austrians. To this number he could add 134,000 new recruits, Poles, Saxons, and some of Eugène's troops. If several of the old commanders were still in place (some for the last time), most of the infantry units were composed of green recruits, many of them scrawny sixteen-year-olds. Clearly this was not to be the Grand Army of Austerlitz and Friedland. Even the artillery was much reduced, with only 311 guns available, dispersed among all units.[10]

The outlook of the French people, too, had altered, Rumblings were growing in all directions, as parents bemoaned the disappearance of 270,000 young men in less than a year's time, this in a population of around 27 million. The conquered nations of Europe—which is to say the whole of Europe except Russia—suffering French armies of occupation were becoming more vehement in their protests, even diplomats openly expressing their discontent. "It is no longer the French people who are waging war," Metternich wrote in December 1808, "it is Napoleon alone who is set on it. . . . Even his army no longer wants this conflict."[11]

Napoleon, who had hoped ultimately to count on a force of up to 177,000 men (including noncombatants, engineers, and the like), united four basic corps to fight a fresh Danube campaign that would probably concentrate in the vicinity of Ratisbon (Regensburg), hoping to catch the Austrians off guard as they gathered large forces to the south, expecting Napoleon to cross the mountains and alps into Italy. His aim was to destroy the major part of the Austrian army in one big battle before the rest of the Austrian forces could be brought up from Italy. The Auric Council, dictating Austrian war plans, had, however, decided (at Karl's urging) to concentrate their forces along the Danube instead, and drive westward into Bavaria, to crush the Army of the Confederation of the Rhine before Napoleon himself could arrive from France to take command.

In addition to his immediate army in Austria of perhaps 161,400, to the north Karl had Bellegarde's smaller force of 48,000 men. Well to the south of Bavaria, in the vast area beginning with Lake Constance in the Vorarlberg and extending through the mountainous Tyrol all the way south to the Adige River and the northeast above Rovereto, anti-French revolt was prevalent in an area held by a mere 10,000 French troops. The French were very vulnerable. The one other large remaining Austrian force was commanded by the less competent archducal brother, Johann, with 76,200 men divided between Italy, at the northern end of the Adriatic between Venice and Trieste, and Dalmatia. Facing the latter was Viceroy Eugène de Beauharnais's immediate force of anywhere from 50,000 to 68,000 men, and Marshal Marmont's isolated corps in Dalmatia.

Ideally Napoleon's intention was to strike hard and fast at Archduke Karl's army before he could be reinforced by General Bellegarde and Archduke Johann. If all went well, after one major victory Bonaparte would drive along the Danube to take a defenseless Vienna once again, as in 1805. But this time around he was to have one or two surprises in store for him.[12]

In fact Napoleon's mighty, monolithic Grand Army of Germany was neither as mighty nor as monolithic as the resplendent name indicated, nor was the situation secure even within the confines of Napoleon's Empire. To the northeast the rumbling in Prussia had intensified since Napoleon had ordered the arrest of Friedrich Wilhelm's state minister, Baron von Stein, for speaking out against him. His patriotic correspondence and speeches calling for the removal of the French had led to Bonaparte's unilateral order to have the man seized and thrown into irons. Apprised of this plan, Stein fled safely across the frontier into Austria before the French could arrest him. He had no intention of becoming another Enghien, another Rumbold, another Palm. At the same time this attack against one of their own ministers irritated the Prussians all the more, hardening their resolve.

In Hamburg, Kassel, and throughout "King Jérôme's" newly created state of Westphalia, there were many grave problems, even well-developed plans for open uprisings. Napoleon had as usual demanded tens of millions in war contributions and separate sums for the maintenance of the army there. Jérôme himself already owed the French treasury more than 20 million francs for state expenses, not to mention millions to friends, local financiers, moneylenders, and businessmen to pay for his own tinsel court, with its outlandish new uniforms, new medals, and even a new currency, the gold "Jérôme" (which infuriated brother Napoléon, with his own coin of the realm in use everywhere else in the Empire). Jérôme's continual, staggering expenses for his endless balls, parties, extravagances, jewelry, clothing, and castles were so far out of control as to bewilder even Napoleon. Then he fired the supervisors and state officers Napoleon had assigned to him and the administration of his court, and even declared a little war of his own against Napoleon's customs officials, whom he defied by openly importing and trading in the prohibited English manufactured goods.

This was the unsettling situation in Westphalia when, in April 1809, Napoleon appointed Jérôme commander of the new X Corps, ordering him "to keep an eye on everything happening in Dresden, Hannover, and Hamburg." Though in theory a field command, this was one corps Napoleon wanted to keep far from the battlefield. The twenty-five-year-old Westphalian Jérôme naturally saw things differently, addressing his men: "*Soldats*! I shall always be there to lead you!"[13] which no doubt was enough to frighten any Frenchman—or Westphalian. In any event one Colonel Dörnberg, commanding the *chasseurs* of Jérôme's Royal Guard, had by now had quite enough of the French occupation of his country and of this spoiled and marauding Jérôme Bonaparte, and planned a coup d'état that included invading Jérôme's palace and sweeping the strutting young man from the stage. This was to be followed immediately by a major uprising of the region. (General Thiébault had had to put down an even earlier uprising when military governor of Kassel.) Other insurrections were planned throughout the rest of Westphalia. Learning of the plot just in time, Jérôme brought in French battalions to put it down, even as his stouthearted "wife" fled across the Rhine all the way to Strasbourg. The virus was everywhere in the air. One determined Major Schill, for instance, quickly raised several hundred regular soldiers to aid in his attack on the Confederation of the Rhine. By the end of May, Schill, despite setbacks, had taken Rostock and Wismar with six thousand men and was stopped only when he was killed at Stralsund. Those two uprisings, and as well as another by Colonel Katt, had stirred the flames. The duke of Brunswick for one was still openly calling for the overthrow of the French. Napoleon repeated the same orders he had given in Hesse and Westphalia in 1807: "My intention is that the main village where the insurrection began shall be burnt, and that thirty of the ringleaders be shot. An impressive example is needed to contain the hatred of the peasantry for our soldiers." He then increased the figure of hostages to be shot to sixty and finally to two hundred.[14] He did the same, far more extensively, in the Kingdom of Naples, and in Spain and Portugal.

In the case of Westphalia, Napoleon naturally blamed the whole thing on Jérôme. "Your kingdom has no police, no finances, and no organization.

One does not found monarchies by living in the lap of luxury, by not lifting a finger. I quite expected that revolt to happen to you, and I hope it will teach you a lesson." It did not, however. Instead it instilled in Jérôme a bitterness toward Napoleon that the emperor would one day have to pay for, at a moment when he badly needed his brother's help.[15]

Nor was the situation more reassuring under King Louis Bonaparte in Holland, where Napoleon also found his orders rebuffed and rejected with a maddening regularity, not to mention his attempt to keep his own "advisers" in control there. In fact Louis's recalcitrance marked a double setback for Napoleon, for unlike Jérôme, Louis, a competent, well-qualified officer, could have substantially aided Napoleon.

King Louis's mental problems had, if anything, increased over the years, however, one such manifestation being his inability to decide where to establish his residence. In the past two years alone, from December 1807 to December 1809, he had moved from Utrecht to the castle of St.-Leu, then to the south, then to Aix-la-Chapelle, then to Loo, and next to Amsterdam. Each move involved the availability of a large palace for his personal advisers, staff, and servants, with adequate quarters for his ministries and the diplomatic community. Louis's peripatetic existence left the state bureaucracies and numerous embassies in a state of perpetual upheaval, to the point that on April 9 the diplomatic community took the unprecedented step of petitioning the king to stop moving. But no sooner had he heeded their request and settled in Amsterdam than one month later he moved back to Utrecht. Finally he found an estate in Haarlem that pleased him. Alas, it belonged to Holland's most prestigious banker, Hope. But Louis insisted, and Hope had to leave his ancestral home. After a few weeks there, Louis moved out, never to return.[16]

What is more, Louis the hypochondriac was constantly out of the country taking the waters at one spa after another. Next he proclaimed himself to be neither Corsican nor French but Dutch, and demanded that the clothing, furniture, and language round him be Dutch. Louis even insisted on speaking Dutch—however badly. He became so Dutch that he even sent away most of the French advisers with whom he had arrived, or whom Napoleon had assigned to him. He even forced all Frenchmen remaining in Holland to renounce their French citizenship. Indeed, only one French national defied him—his wife, Queen Hortense. She remained adamant for once, resulting in colossal quarrels and painful scenes for months to come.

Then, when on April 24, 1808, their son, Charles-Louis-Napoléon, was born in Paris (where Hortense was seeking refuge from her demented husband), more serious battles arose over custody of the baby. Louis demanded that his son be sent to him immediately in Holland. Hortense, strengthened by her citizenship victory, and by the knowledge that Louis could not touch her in Napoleon's capital, refused even to answer the letter, although Louis asked her only "to consent to separate yourself from him for several months." (She knew what "several months" meant.) Nevertheless, this did not prevent good King Louis from announcing in all the Dutch newspapers the forthcoming arrival of his son. Angered, Louis addressed her again and again, but no replies were forthcoming from Hortense. Finally Louis sent a formal demand, which she formally refused. Beside himself, Louis next asked Napoleon to intercede directly and send him the boy. This time it was Napoleon who declined to reply. He was surrounded by enemies, Louis proclaimed, and this was yet another instance of this pervasive plot!

In theory Louis obliged Napoleon regarding the halting of all commerce with England, shipping dropping dramatically from 1,450 seagoing vessels reaching Amsterdam in 1807 to just 361 in 1808, although somehow British goods nonetheless seemed to be plentiful in Holland. Louis even sent (albeit reluctantly) three thousand Dutch soldiers to join Bonaparte in Spain. But when on August 8, 1808, Napoleon suddenly informed Louis that he intended to annex two Dutch provinces, Brant and Zeeland, Louis categorically refused. Napoleon then threatened to cut off all colonial commodities imported via Holland, which would have hurt Dutch commerce severely. The Franco-Dutch war of 1808 continued apace.

Yet despite these continuous fraternal quarrels and misunderstandings, and Napoleon's obvious intent of chipping away at brother Louis's miniature kingdom, Louis deeply loved Napoleon, though such moments of conflicting sentiment could shift on the spur of the moment, gyrating from love to hate, the old battle resuming like something out of a Greek tragedy. When, for instance, Napoleon returned to Spain, Louis, receiving all sorts of disquieting news about French setbacks and enormous casualties in the peninsula, wrote to his former army friend Lavalette: "I am most anxious about this wretched Spanish business. Do send me news by my courier as quickly as possible. . . . It is not the progress of the war that concerns me, but my brother's welfare! Tell me, or let me know, I beg of you, all you can to reassure me about my brother's health."[17]

Nevertheless acrimonious relations began again on Napoleon's return to France in January 1809. First Napoleon informed Louis that he was supporting Hortense's request not to send their son (now a year old) to Holland for a "visit." (He had obviously seen some of Louis's threatening letters to Hortense.) This Napoleon compounded on March 3 by suddenly decreeing that he was adopting Hortense's son, bestowing on the infant the

title grand duke of Berg and Cleves (Murat's former title and state).
Charles-Louis-Napoléon would thus remain with his uncle, to be educated
by him, the emperor further making him heir to the French imperial throne.
Perhaps even more curiously, Louis just as suddenly acquiesced without
further ado. With the queen of Holland now permanently out of her kingdom, the king's son publicly removed from his custody, and reverberations
of the new war brewing in central Europe already reaching every country
of the Continent, conditions for even greater conflict between the two
brothers Bonaparte seemed ripe.

Despite such minor distractions as Spain, Holland, and the disruptions
in Westphalia, not to mention acts of rebellion elsewhere in Germany, in
April 1809 Napoleon had to concentrate on the more immediate Austrian
military threat and the launching of his second Danube campaign.

On April 19, two days after reaching Chief of Staff Berthier at Donauwörth,
Napoleon unleashed his forces in a series of five battles over four days, at
Thann, Abensberg, Landshut, Eckmühl, and Ratisbon. "We are fighting to
give her [Bavaria] independence and to return to Germany her national
honor," he informed his troops. "Within a month we will be in Vienna."

It was not quite that simple, however. Napoleon was confident of
crushing the Austrians, while the Austrian commander in chief, Archduke
Karl, was equally assured of destroying the French war machine once and
for all. Both sides were to be disappointed now, especially the Austrians
defending their very homes. Archduke Karl had hoped the Bavarians, seeing the deployment of such an impressive force of men and guns in the
newly reorganized Austrian army, would join them in the struggle to overthrow the French overlords. King Max Josef, however, had remained loyal
to Napoleon. Marshal Berthier, who had been in command prior to
Napoleon's arrival at Donauwörth, had not followed his orders, and troops
were not properly deployed when hostilities began. Some of Bonaparte's
far-flung army corps had rushed considerable distances to reach the
approaches of Ratisbon, including Davout's III corps, which had come
from the Erfurt area, Oudinot's II Corps from Augsburg, and Masséna's
newly formed IV Corps from Strasbourg. Other units had had to remain
behind to keep an eye on their French allies, just in case.

During the initial clashes Napoleon could muster only 79,000 men
(including part or all of the corps of Davout, Lannes, and Lefebvre) with
whom to cross swords with Archduke Karl's imposing 110,000 men, well
armed and in place, to be completed shortly by the arrival of Kollowrat's
and Bellegarde's corps, adding 48,000 men to the Austrian total.

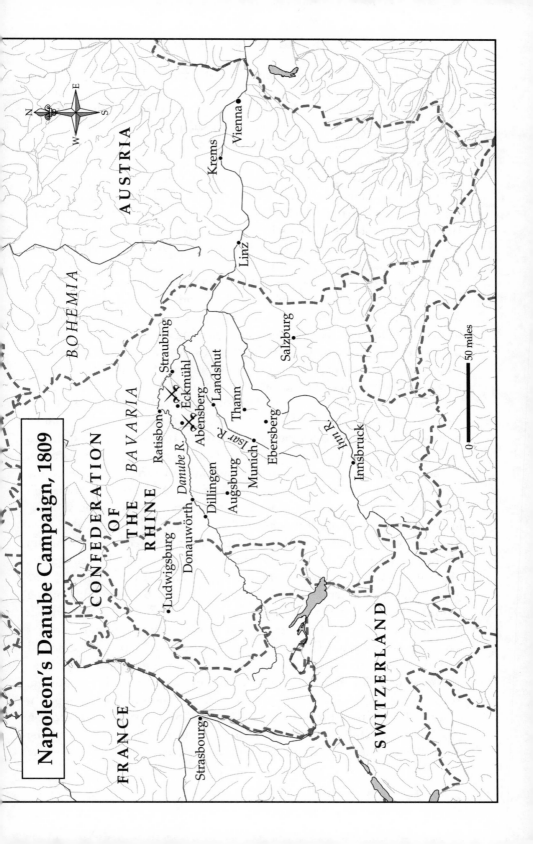

Napoleon's Danube Campaign, 1809

N

FRANCE

CONFEDERATION

OF

THE

RHINE

BAVARIA

BOHEMIA

AUSTRIA

SWITZERLAND

Strasbourg

Ludwigsburg

Donauwörth

Dillingen

Augsburg

Ratisbon

Straubing

Eckmühl

Abensberg

Landshut

Thann

Munich

Ebersberg

Salzburg

Innsbruck

Linz

Krems

Vienna

Danube R.

Isar R.

Inn R.

0   50 miles

Despite the inferiority of forces, the French moved up along the south-ern bank of the Danube toward Thann, Abensberg, and Eckmühl, Napoleon confident that he had the enemy where he wanted them. He was pleased with the results of the initial clashes, as he informed Marshal Davout from Bachl on 21 April. "Much has occurred in just a few days. All the Austrian forces in your area are routed. . . . On all sides, cannon, colors, and prisoners have been taken. It is a second Jena."[18] Even the next day Napoleon had jauntily informed Davout, "I have decided to exterminate Prince Charles's [Archduke Karl's] army today, or tomorrow at the very latest." Then, suddenly, things had begun to go very wrong indeed. Karl had in midbattle suddenly retreated successfully to nearby Ratisbon, and due to the exhaustion of French troops after a long day's fight, there had been no significant French force with which to pursue them.[19]

Having earlier been ordered to seize the critically situated fortified city of Ratisbon, Davout now discovered that on the twentieth the very force he had left behind there had been defeated, yielding the city's stout walls and the strategic bridgehead to Archduke Karl's army. This had altered the whole situation, as the Austrians began to escape to the north side of the Danube, ultimately making for the mountains of Bohemia.

Early on April 23, when Napoleon finally started his pursuit, he found himself stopped in his tracks by a mere six thousand troops manning Ratisbon's stalwart fortifications, the very walls one of Davout's detached regiments had earlier held but lost. Napoleon immediately ordered Lannes's corps to take the city, that marshal literally carrying and mounting the first ladder against the city walls. "It was just before this, while still talking with Marshal Lannes about his attempt to retake Ratisbon and giv-ing him his final orders, that a spent bullet from a carbine, probably fired from a considerable distance, struck Napoleon in the right ankle," Captain Marbot, a witness, related. "The pain was so great that he fell against Marshal Lannes, who caught him and placed him on the ground."[20] The head of the medical service, Dr. Larrey, was sent for, but he found nothing serious, apart from an extremely painful bruised Achilles' tendon. Napoleon as usual had been very lucky; another few inches and he might have been crippled for life. However, the rumor quickly spread that he had been wounded, and officers and soldiers rushed to him from all directions. Marbot continued, "In a moment thousands of men surrounded Napoleon, in spite of enemy cannon fire which concentrated on this huge group." In order to dispel any distorted tales as to his condition, a bandaged Napoleon was hoisted carefully onto his little horse "and made the rounds of the entire French line, amid the acclamation of these brave warriors whom he had so often led to victory!"²¹ But on returning to his field headquarters, Napoleon fainted.

Ratisbon and the bridge were finally taken, ending this first phase of fighting, resulting in some thirty thousand Austrian casualties (including prisoners). Archduke Karl did, however, manage to extricate most of his army, retreating to the northeast on the other side of the Danube, while the rest of his force, under the command of General Hiller, remained on the southern bank, pursued by Masséna, but with orders to slow the French advance. This series of battles did succeed in discouraging wavering states of the Rhineland Confederation—Bavaria, Württemberg, and Saxony—from abandoning Napoleon. Despite the escape of the Austrian army, Lannes, Davout, Mouton, and St.-Hilaire had all performed well thus far, Napoleon even promising St.-Hilaire a marshal's baton at the end of the campaign (which, alas, he was not to survive).

Meanwhile, still on the south bank with Napoleon's main force, the valiant General Hiller did his best to hinder the French, clashing with them seriously at Wels on May 2 and then in a more serious battle the following day at Ebersberg. There his forty thousand troops held the town, protecting their own gradual withdrawal safely across the Danube near Krems, despite a vigorous if costly frontal attack by Masséna's corps. The skillful Hiller made good his escape to rejoin the main Austrian army to the north.

After also dispatching Davout's corps after Hiller, Napoleon ordered the main French force still with him to advance on Vienna. As for Archduke Karl, he was in fact doing just what Napoleon (who still wanted a final, all-out, decisive confrontation) had hoped he would, dropping back closer to the Danube to try to prevent the French from entering the Austrian capital. But as usual the Austrians moved too slowly to achieve this objective, and three days after Napoleon entered Vienna, General Hiller's corps rejoined Karl.

Reaching the outskirts of Vienna on May 10, less than a month after leaving Paris, Napoleon found not Karl but another Habsburg brother, Archduke Maximilian, defending the capital and refusing to budge. When Napoleon sent a delegation of key officers to negotiate the city's surrender, they were cut down, all of them severely slashed without warning by a Hungarian cavalry unit. A furious Napoleon immediately ordered a heavy bombardment of Vienna for the next twenty-four hours, his troops finally seizing the city only on the thirteenth.

Not even the already practically deaf Beethoven could work under the continuous thunder of French guns: "What a destructive, disorderly life I see and hear all around me: nothing but drums, cannon and human misery in every form. . . . We are finally enjoying a little peace after the violent destruction after having suffered every hardship imaginable."[22] Beethoven's initial enthusiasm and support for Napoleon had between 1802 and 1805 given way to disillusion, and his Third Symphony, initially titled "Bonaparte," was renamed "Eroica." "What do you say to this *dead peace?*" he asked his publishers. "I no longer expect to see any stability again in this age of ours."[23]

Within easy cannon-shot of Beethoven's apartment, Napoleon now moved back into his old quarters in the sprawling yellow Schönbrunn Palace on the other side of the city walls. That evening, enjoying a nearly full moon, Napoleon ordered one of his equerries to bring up a horse from the royal stables, and then went riding with Marshal Lannes at his side, followed at a discreet distance by his staff and a large cavalry escort. Scarcely had they set out when the unexpected happened, as told by Lannes's aide-de-camp, Captain Marbot: "The emperor's mount suddenly bolted, flinging him heavily to the ground, he lying there stretched out, motionless, not giving the slightest sign of life! We thought he was dead! He was only unconscious, however, and we gradually revived him. Although Marshal Lannes wanted him to return, Napoleon insisted upon continuing the evening's ride." A milder mount was brought up to replace the recalcitrant steed:

> Afterward, having completed the promenade and once back in the vast courtyard of the palace, the emperor ordered his numerous military staff and the squadron of imperial cavalry—everyone who had witnessed his fall—to gather about him in a large circle, where he forbade them from ever mentioning what they had seen, including members of the other ranks. So religiously did they guard that secret that neither the army nor Europe ever learned that Napoleon had nearly broken his neck and killed himself that night.[24]

Why the state secret about something so commonplace as a fall from a horse, albeit a serious one? Apparently Napoleon felt that an emperor must always appear perfect to his men, never capable of mistakes or weakness— or of disappearing permanently without warning, in a mere blink of an eye. Or was it simply that he did not want to be the butt of their jokes, the great man who was conquering the world but could not even ride a horse?

*　　　　*　　　　*

On Napoleon's inspection of Vienna, his consternation at finding the bridges to the other side of the Danube destroyed was great (intact in 1805, they had permitted the rapid crossing of the entire French army, resulting in the battle of Austerlitz). This time, with the bridges burned or blown up by the Austrians, Napoleon and Lannes went out daily to study possible crossing points. One of these was located just upriver of Vienna, across from Schwartze-Laken Island. Although the Danube was already churning rapidly many feet above the normal water level, and filled with all sorts of floating vegetation and even entire trees swept downstream by the muddy current, Marshal Lannes ordered General St.-Hilaire to select five hundred troops to row over to that island, which was already manned by some Austrian outposts, with easy access to the northern side of the river by a small bridge.

The five hundred Frenchmen, using every spare boat available, crossed the few hundred yards of raging water to reach Schwartze-Laken Island, where they encountered much heavier resistance than expected, quickly reniforced from the far shore. In no time at all half the French unit sent to establish a beachhead there had been killed and the remainder wounded. It was a fiasco. Seeing the plight of the men, Lannes and Napoleon ordered a rescue, but there weren't any boats left. Beside himself with anxiety, watching his men being cut down helplessly before his eyes, Lannes tripped over a half-submerged cable and fell headlong into the swirling waters. Napoleon, the only person close to him, quickly jumped into the water up to his waist, just in time to catch Lannes before he was swept out of reach. Other officers quickly ran over to help Napoleon and succeeded in dragging both men back. A grateful Lannes embraced his old colleague in arms.[25] It had been a close call, but nothing could be done for the troops isolated on the island.

Given the altered circumstances he found in Vienna, Napoleon was forced to rethink his situation. Archduke Karl had escaped with his large army intact, and his younger brother, Archduke Johann, had just defeated Eugène de Beauharnais at Sacile and was apparently now advancing toward Vienna. Napoleon, who had hoped to destroy the Austrians at Eckmühl or Ratisbon, thus had to recast his plans completely.

Across the Danube just north of Vienna, Archduke Karl commanded a total of 115,000 men even after the large losses from the previous series of battles and the usual large-scale desertions. Napoleon had only Lannes's and Masséna's corps at present, with the reserve cavalry and guard, for a total of 82,000—a full army corps less than the Austrians—while the rest of the French army remained scattered to the west, keeping an eye on various opposing units. This was a bit misleading, however, for when taking into account the other remaining corps between Staubing and Vienna, Napoleon could call in within a couple of weeks another 95,000 men for a theoretical total of 177,000, although some units would have to be detached to remain behind permanently to guard the long French logistical line with Donauwörth and Strasbourg.[26] With Lannes and Masséna, Napoleon did of course have immediately at hand two veteran commanders on whom he could depend in just about any situation.

Although Napoleon was determined to attack and destroy Archduke Karl before he could join forces with his brother Johann's smaller army of thirty thousand, the destruction of the Viennese bridges had forestalled an immediate French pursuit and attack. The strategic situation—everything—now depended on their ability to cross the Danube.

Bonaparte therefore summoned Gen. Henri Bertrand, the head of the crack French Engineering Corps, to the Schönbrunn and outlined the problem. After studying all the reports submitted by his engineers, a plan of action was decided on, but it was neither easy to put into effect nor particularly secure, given Napoleon's insistence on speed. Bertrand was to build a series of pontoon sections for an enormous bridge near the village of Kaiser Ebersdorf, a few miles south of Vienna on the south bank, at the point where the Schwechat River flowed into the Danube opposite the immense, flat, marshy island of Lobau.

The Danube was flooding and rising daily as a result of melting spring snows and very heavy rains. Bertrand was now required to build a pontoon bridge some eight hundred yards long just to reach Lobau Island, and then another bridge one hundred yards long to link the island with the northern bank of the Danube, which Napoleon needed if he was to attack Archduke Karl. This left Napoleon very vulnerable. Napoleon was also entirely dependent on those two unprotected wooden bridges over which to transfer all his supplies, his artillery, his entire cavalry, and more than eighty thousand men, not to mention the rest of the army later. Such bridges were, to be sure, prime targets for Austrian artillery and fireboats. Should the Austrians disable those bridges, in particular the long one, Napoleon's force would be cut in two and entirely isolated, thereby cutting them off from all supplies and help from Vienna. It would also result in the severing of his sole means of retreat, in the event Karl's forces were successful in counterattacking.

Bonaparte was clearly intending to act rapidly, thrusting his entire two corps quickly across the river, in a wild gamble of somehow destroying a complete field force that easily outnumbered him and had more than twice as many guns. Great efficiency and speed were required, but also proper protection for his long, completely exposed bridge. But in the hope of advancing quickly and catching Karl off guard, Napoleon, fatefully as it turned out, vetoed a long period of preparation of defenses—pilings in the river, gun emplacements, a flotilla of gunboats to protect that lifeline. He would strike before the Austrians knew what had hit them. This, added to the fact that he would begin his attack with insufficient cannon power to compensate for the lack of troops, and with the other corps of his army still far away, looked, at best, like the longest of his shots. But if he brought it off, he would be considered a miracle worker.

The order was given to begin building the first pontoon bridge, with a second one at Nussdorf a couple of miles north of Vienna as a feint. Although Austrian troops were situated right up to and including Lobau and even a small outpost at Lob Grund opposite the massive bridge-building operation, and hence totally aware of French preparations to launch a new offensive, Karl and his army were taken unawares. At least they did nothing to prevent Napoleon from acting on May 20, when sections of the eight-hundred-yard-long pontoon bridge were swung into place by Bertrand's engineers, as Marshal Masséna's IV Corps secured Lobau, crossed over to the northern bank of the Danube, and seized the surprisingly undefended, unoccupied twin villages of Aspern and Essling.

The size of the force now facing Napoleon now proved a real shock, for his intelligence reports as usual were slapdash, in this instance having informed him that there was still no major Austrian presence there.

In reality, by the afternoon of May 20, six entire Austrian corps, along with Kienmaier's reserve grenadiers, had moved into the area from Bohemia and the Upper Danube between the villages of Langzenersdorf and Baumersdorf on the other side of Wagram.

At 10:00 A.M. on the twenty-first, four of these Austrian corps, totaling 89,000 men, advanced in a line extending from the banks of the northern shore all the way inland for six miles. By one o'clock that afternoon, the first units reached the village of Aspern, dislodging Masséna's surprised units, and by five o'clock, with his army fully in place, Archduke Karl launched a massive attack all across the line. In the midst of the fierce fighting that ensued, Aspern changed hands several times in vicious man-to-man combat, while the French managed more successfully to hold on to the village of Essling to the right. Bessières's cavalry did surprisingly well given the odds against them but, like Masséna's troops, suffered heavy casualties, including the loss of the most able General d'Espagne.

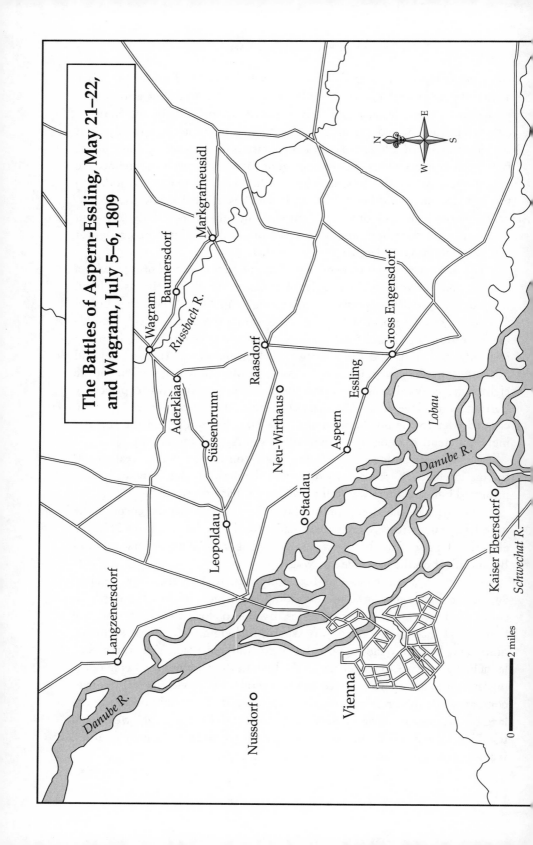

The Battles of Aspern-Essling, May 21–22, and Wagram, July 5–6, 1809

By nightfall a dazed Napoleon still had only 31,400 troops on his side of the Danube, as he desperately sent out couriers with orders for all units, in particular Davout's III Corps occupying Vienna, to come to his aid and to bring artillery and supplies. During the night a barrage of fireboats, floating bombs, logs, and other obstacles was launched into the muddy, churning Danube, causing several breaches, though repairs were completed before dawn broke on the twenty-second, permitting Lannes's II Corps to cross over and reinforce Masséna's IV Corps, giving Napoleon a total of 62,000 infantry and cavalry, with 144 guns, versus the Austrian army's nearly 96,000 men (including 15,000 cavalry) and 264 guns. The French, still greatly outnumbered and outgunned, were practically fighting with their backs to the Danube. Attacks and counterattacks followed by both armies around Aspern and Essling in particular, Napoleon desperately attempting to hold on until Davout could come to the rescue.

At 7:00 A.M. Napoleon foolishly launched Lannes's fresh corps through the center of the Austrian line between Aspern and Essling, although Davout had not yet arrived to support him in the event the attack proved successful. Lannes did indeed succeed, "advancing bravely over the plain," as Captain Marbot recalled. "Nothing could stand in his way. . . . The Austrians fell back . . . and their center . . . finished by breaking!"

Victory seemed in sight when, to everyone's astonishment, Napoleon ordered Lannes to halt. There was a very good reason: Napoleon was isolated again, for the pontoon bridge had been smashed again by a continuing series of floating fires, bombs, and barges hurled against it by the raging current. Napoleon, low on ammunition and food, and with no medical supplies, could not be resupplied, nor could Davout's corps now waiting impatiently on the south bank of the Danube cross over to him.

Archduke Karl naturally took immediate advantage of the situation and launched a fresh attack, concentrating on the French force in the smoldering ruins of Aspern, where the heaviest fighting of the day now continued. Veteran Generals Mouton (at the head of the Young Guard) and Rapp found it impossible to hold and secure the flaming village in the face of such overwhelming forces. In Rapp's words, the situation had become "most dangerous." Although Rapp managed to retake the village, Napoleon came under such an intense hail of musketry and cannonballs that his own élite guard insisted on his retiring to a safer area. Unlike Soult, who generally fled when the fighting got intense, Napoleon was not only in the thick of it throughout the day, but appeared even to be attracted to it like a moth to a candle. And it was now that he received further bad news—irreparable this time.

When Lannes had halted his attack and fallen back to a more tenable position between Essling and Aspern, the archduke had counterattacked, Napoleon sending in St.-Hilaire's cavalry to stop them. They did, but at a great price: The troops were decimated by the withering musketry, and St.-Hilaire himself a casualty, his leg shattered. He died shortly thereafter in a field hospital.

At the same time Lannes's principal aide-de-camp, Captain Marbot, received a painful wound in the thigh, though he could still stand. "The situation was most critical," Marbot recalled. "The Emperor, now on the defensive, formed his army in an arch round the Danube. Our right reached down to the river just behind Essling. Our [contracting] left was secured behind Aspern. We would have to hold that line throughout the day [22 May], or risk being thrown into the river."[27] A little later Marshal Lannes saw one of his favorite commanders, General Pouzet, killed before him. Visibly upset at the sight of his friend's body being placed on a stretcher, Lannes cried out in anguish as he looked at the corpses around him, "Oh, I shall never be able to forget this terrible spectacle!" Marbot reported that he sat down near the edge of a ditch and crossed his legs, his right hand covering his eyes. "He was seated there lost in somber reflection when a small, three-pound cannonball fired from Enzersdorf ricocheted, striking the marshal just where his legs crossed!"[28] Both legs were shattered, and Lannes fell to the ground in agony, though he remained conscious.

The stretcher bearing General Pouzet's body was now emptied hastily for Lannes, who was rushed past a stack of amputated arms and legs into Larrey's blood-splattered, fly-infested tent. No anesthesia being available, a scarcely conscious Lannes was given a glass of wine before Larrey had his stretcher placed on the table, where he swiftly severed one of the legs at the knee. "Awake throughout the ordeal, he acted with great courage," Marbot continued. "It was scarcely over when the Emperor arrived. It was the most touching interview. The emperor, kneeling on the ground next to the stretcher, burst into tears and threw himself over the marshal, whose blood soaked Napoleon's white cashmere waistcoat a bright damp crimson." Napoleon insisted: "You will live, my friend, you will live!" tears streaming down his face.[29]

Meanwhile the battle raged that May 22, with only Masséna left to command the entire force. Napoleon had no choice finally but to fall back to the safety of Lobau Island. The slow evacuation lasted far into the night, and at 3:30 in the morning the bridge's cables were severed by the French, and it swung back to the banks of the island.

The Battle of Aspern-Essling, an appalling French disaster, was over, a defeated Napoleon in retreat from the field. In the morning Napoleon had a boat brought over to Lobau in which to transfer Lannes to the right bank. Not only was there no anesthetia or even soap, but no clean drinking water, and Marbot was forced to filter the muddy Danube water through a fine cloth shirt. Despite daily visits by Napoleon and Marbot's steadfast attention (in total disregard of his own wound), Lannes died a few days later. Napoleon could not be consoled for the loss of this remarkable soldier, who had begun his career so humbly as a dyer's apprentice in the Gers, and who—like Napoleon—had celebrated his fortieth birthday that year. "The Emperor's grief was so great that for the next two days, wherever he was, whenever he thought of Marshal Lannes, he burst into tears, despite his great effort to conceal this," Constant, his valet remembered.[30]

French losses were extremely high, probably as many as 16,000 dead and perhaps double that wounded, some medical reports giving even higher figures, although Napoleon publicly announced to the world only 4,100 dead and wounded. The Austrians officially suffered 23,000 casualties,[31] and were the clear winners of the unequal two-day battle.

Napoleon remained stunned. Never before had the Austrians fought so valiantly. And thanks to his own impatience, he had launched an attack against the enemy's main force when he not only lacked half his army but had failed even to secure the vital logistical communications, his very lifeline, across the Danube. Had a mere brigadier general committed such an error, Napoleon would have broken him. It was fortunate for him, however, that over the next few days, and then weeks, the victorious Archduke Karl for some inexplicable reason remained in his usual moribund Austrian state and failed to follow up on his triumph. He could easily have smashed a now helpless Napoleon and his badly mauled troops on Lobau, "misery island" as the French now called it, where he had them and their wounded cornered. With the bridge repaired again, the thousands of wounded were gradually transported back to Vienna, a steady stream of ambulances and wagons, some five miles long, making the journey over the next week, although the majority didn't survive.

The scandal of the numerous tiffs and tilts among Napoleon's senior generals and marshals was by now widely known. Every other marshal's dislike of Berthier marked but the introduction to this pathetic page of Napoleona, leading to outrageous acts even on the field of battle. The case of Soult and Masséna in the Iberian Peninsula has already been noted. Before that was Bernadotte's blatant refusal to come to the aid of the outnumbered Davout at Auerstädt, while at the same time managing to avoid all fighting that same day at Jena as well. Bernadotte had refused to fire a single shot in behalf of the 123,000 French troops who had been involved in heavy, sometimes desperate, fighting all day long. Longer-standing still was the animosity between Lannes and Murat, which resulted in a bitter side feud between Lannes and Bessières. This came to a head during Aspern-Essling, adding to the tragedy of the day.

It had all begun long ago under the Directory, when first Lannes, and then Murat, had been serving as Napoleon's senior aide-de-camp, while both of them had been vying for the hand of Caroline Bonaparte. Both men were handsome and brave, as well as favorites of Napoleon, but Murat had an extra supporter in Bessières. The latter, close to Napoleon at this time and soon to head his personal guard, took Murat's side in this marital question, ending in success for the strapping Murat. Lannes never forgave Bessières for his interference in his private affairs. Then on May 21, 1809, the long-pent-up bitterness erupted in the middle of the Battle of Aspern-Essling, when Marshal Lannes ordered the less-than-adventurous Marshal Bessières (placed directly under Lannes's orders by Napoleon) to "*chargèr à fond*," to lead the cavalry of the Imperial Guard right through the Austrian battle line and then swing around. It was Lannes's aide-de-camp, Captain Marbot, who was given the task of delivering the humiliating verbal instructions to Bessières before his entire staff. (A general officer or marshal never had to be "ordered" to drive right through the enemy line, that being taken for granted, and Bessières was indignant upon receiving them. Moreover, a marshal never "ordered" another marshal to do anything but instead invited him to do so.) This unpleasant task done, Marbot quickly returned to Lannes.

That night after the battle, Bessières, while talking to Masséna, saw young Marbot limping toward them. "They could see me at once in the bright moonlight, intensified by the glow of the fires still consuming the villages of Essling and Aspern," the captain recalled. Bessières, still smarting from that day's order by Lannes, lashed out verbally at Marbot, not seeing Lannes following behind him. Lannes stepped forward quickly to protect his aide, as an astonished Bessières stopped in midsentence. "It is simply outrageous that you chew out my aide-de-camp!" a hot-tempered Lannes intervened, then praised Marbot's many merits, including his several recent wounds. "What do you reproach this officer for?" he demanded. "Monsieur, your aide-de-camp earlier 'ordered' me to charge straight through the enemy line!" "That is correct, Monsieur, and it is *I* who dictated that order to him!" The words got hotter as tempers rose, Bessières informing Lannes that he would gladly have "acceded" to a polite "request." Lannes snapped,

"Just you listen, Monsieur, one does not 'accede' to an 'order,' one simply 'obeys'! If in the present circumstances the Emperor had placed me under *your* command, I can assure you I would have resigned on the spot!" Masséna, in whose camp they were standing, surrounded by dozens of officers and soldiers, saw the hands of the two marshals drop to the hilts of their swords. He quickly attempted to quell a dangerous situation. "I am your senior [in age], gentlemen. You are in my camp. I have no intention of permitting you the opportunity of giving my troops the scandalous spectacle of seeing two imperial marshals fighting one another, and that on the battlefield still before the enemy. Leave immediately!" Then, Marbot recorded in his memoirs, "he took Marshal Lannes by the arm and walked off to his quarters, "as a brooding Bessières betook himself off to his own camp."

Learning of this incident as he was sitting down to dinner, Napoleon summoned the two men. He walked over in great strides, turned to Marshal Bessières, and strongly reproached him. "The commander of his Imperial Guard seemed truly bewildered by these strong words, a feeling intensified all the more when the Emperor then turned his back on him and returned to his table to eat, inviting Lannes to join him."[32]

Lannes had used outrageous language. But Bessières, who had already failed to follow orders in Spain and had been removed from a corps command as a consequence, was now clearly in Napoleon's bad books. Relations between Napoleon and Bessières never fully recovered. Quarrels in the general officer corps grew more and more divisive until the very end.

Despite the humiliating defeat at Aspern-Essling, the grievous dissensions among his marshals and generals, and the considerable tactical limitations presented by the Danube barrier, Napoleon's stubbornness and genius rose to the fore. He gradually formulated a new plan of attack, for he had no intention of abandoning Vienna and Austria now. Astonishingly enough Archduke Karl continued to oblige, failing to launch an all-out attack against the French army still penned down in their island fortress. Indeed the Austrians moved neither forward nor backward, remaining on the battlefield for the next several weeks; Napoleon, for one, had never seen anything quite like it and once again his old self, determined to succeed despite the initial defeat. After all, he still held Lobau Island, however tenuously, while retaining the Austrian capital as well. Although he spent most days supervising large new fortifications and other works at Lobau, each night an exhausted Bonaparte would cross the Danube to return to his luxurious "camp of Schönbrunn Palace," as he referred to it, to complete the details of

the next stage of this campaign or to be soothed by the available local feminine charms, until the arrival of Countess Walewska later that summer.

More determined than ever to prove to the world that he, Napoleon
Bonaparte, and his invincible army of yore were not done for, that there
would be no more humiliating Bailéns, Vimieiros, and Aspern-Esslings, he
patiently, methodically prepared to build bridges linking Lobgrund and
Lobau. But instead of an enormous single-span bridge, he decided first to
build a bridge halfway across the main channel of the Danube to the small
island of Schneidergrund, and then two more bridges linking the rest of the
channel to Lobgrund and Lobau. The bridges would be shorter, stouter,
and less vulnerable in size and structure. If one were temporarily out of
action, the other would be standing, while the remaining set of bridges linking that midchannel islet with Lobgrund and Lobau would be even better
protected. To further ensure the security of the link with the south bank of
the Danube, an enormous series of pilings was driven into the riverbed
across the channel, which protruded well above the water level to act like a
massive wooden sieve to catch any fire, bomb boats, or other obstacles
launched upstream by the Austrians, preventing them from reaching the
bridges. It was a major engineering feat, but without it there could be no
crossing of troops. To complete this project Napoleon ordered the creation
of a flotilla of gunboats, manned by units of his Imperial Guard, to patrol
the river and protect the works. Meanwhile hundreds of wagons could be
seen traveling daily between Vienna and the bridgehead of Kaiser Ebersdorf
on the south bank, and from outlying areas south of that village, bringing
enormous supplies of timber, metal, and coal, not to mention vast quantities
of ammunition, powder, and more than 350 additional cannon taken from
the walls and arsenals of Vienna.

Clearly Napoleon was planning something big, and yet day after day,
Archduke Karl just watched these preparations and did not lift a finger to
hinder or attack the French or to destroy the mountains of supplies
clearly visible on low-lying Lobau. Napoleon did attempt some feints to
put the Austrians off the scent, however. For instance, he started preparations for building another bridge across the Danube well above Vienna at
Nussdorf, and he dispatched large numbers of cavalry to the south and
away from Vienna, but to any intelligent man, the real work, the basic
concentration, obviously was at and around Lobau Island. One could
hardly conceal tens of thousands of men and many thousands of horses at
work there.

Troops too now began concentrating. First Eugène's army of 23,200
men and one hundred cannon under the command of General MacDonald

reached the region, defeating Archduke Johann's army at Raab in early June, sending the Austrian commander fleeing into Hungary. General Vandamme arrived at Vienna with his troops, Bernadotte with his force at Engerdorf, Marmont with his 10,000 men, all of whom joined Davout's corps and Eugène's army at Lobau. By the beginning of July Napoleon had almost 160,000 men with him, and another 29,000 or so in outlying districts along the Danube between Ratisbon and Vienna.

As for Archduke Karl, despite reinforcements, after heavy casualties suffered since Eckmühl, he was down to about 136,000, to which he hoped could be added Archduke Johann's remaining 12,500, although the Archduke Palatine's army of another 19,000 Hungarians seemed too far away to be of any help.

Meanwhile Napoleon sent messenger after messenger to Czar Alexander asking him to attack the Austrians through Poland, as required by the Treaty of Erfurt. The czar, however, had no intention of obliging Napoleon in the dismantling of the Habsburg Empire. He warned him that "the destruction of the Austrian Monarchy would be a calamity for the whole of Europe," echoing the advice Talleyrand had given earlier. Alexander also warned Napoleon that he could not permit any further partitioning of Poland to go to Napoleon or his allies, "for anything added to the Duchy of Warsaw would be a step to re-establishing Poland, and therefore contrary to the first interests of Russia."[33] Never before had the czar spoken so bluntly. When Napoleon reminded Alexander of his Erfurt obligations to aid the French in a war against Austria, Russia finally sent a symbolic force into Austrian Galicia (in Poland). Alexander was determined to hedge his bets against the omnivorous French. There would be no further effective Russian military collaboration. To be sure, as late as May 13, 1809, the czar had told Caulaincourt that "the Emperor will find in me a supportive ally. I shall take no half measures." In fact, the czar was all the while secretly informing the Austrians that they had nothing to fear from him. Alexander "assures me that everything humanly possible will be done to avoid attacking us," General Schwarzenberg informed Vienna.

Prince Poniatowski for one openly warned Napoleon from Warsaw of what he referred to as Russian "perfidy." Napoleon duly took heed. Indeed, during a visit earlier in the year, Alexander had warned Prince von Schwarzenberg *not* to attack the French, for Austria could not possibly win. If Austria did attack, "you will set Europe ablaze and you will be the first victim."[34]

Austrian Emperor Franz I had ignored this advice and was now preparing for the third and final round with Napoleon in the latest Danube campaign.

By the end of June Napoleon was nearly ready to launch this third offensive. Lobau Island had been transformed into a massive garrison, complete with enormous supply depots linked by a network of new roads in and around the buildings and fortifications, the whole of which ringed by 129 pieces of large artillery. If Archduke Karl finally decided to attack the French here, it was now too late. He did, however fortify his positions between Aspern and Essling, now defended by Generals Hiller and Klenau, supported by several thousand fresh troops and two hundred more cannon. Archduke Karl was apparently still awaiting the arrival of Archduke Johann and his small army, while worrying about a possible descent from Galicia by the Russians. Clearly there would be another French attack, but Karl was still dithering.

In Vienna, life was hardly cheerful, with thousands of French wounded crowded into grossly understaffed Viennese hospitals, and sequestered princely palaces were converted into temporary hospitals. Captain Marbot, after tending to Marshal Lannes day and night until the very end, was himself finally forced to seek treatment in the officers' quarters of Prince Albert's castle in the Old City, where the continuous ninety-degree heat further discomfited the wounded.

Many weeks earlier Napoleon had personally promoted Marbot to the rank of major, but then battles had ensued and the written confirmation of this brevet had never arrived through channels. Following the battles of this campaign and the ultimate victory at Wagram, all the officers involved were duly promoted, and some made officers of the Legion of Honor as well. Marbot, however, still recovering in his hospital ward, heard nothing. Had Lannes lived, no such oversight would have been permitted.

Claude-Philippe Mounier, one of Napoleon's secretaries and later a peer of France, often came to visit another wounded officer and close friend of Marbot. Having heard of Marbot's various wounds and exploits, and now seeing him recuperating from yet another wound, asked what reward he had received. "Nothing," Marbot told him. "Surely it has been an oversight," Mounier responded. "I am certain I have seen your name among a stack of brevets in the Emperor's portfolio." The next day Mounier brought the matter to Napoleon's attention. Napoleon immediately announced that as a special reward for Marbot's exceptional services, he would be made a major in the Imperial Guard cavalry. As any rank held in the guard was equivalent to one rank above its nominal rank, Marbot had received an immediate jump promotion to lieutenant colonel. His devotion and fidelity to Lannes had not been forgotten.

On receiving the good news, the twenty-seven-year-old Marbot was speechless. "It was simply magnificent!" he recalled in old age, still deeply moved by the memory, leaving the new lieutenant colonel more devoted than ever to Napoleon.[35] The war would go on with his full support.

CHAPTER 30

Wagram

*Once my great empire has been launched, no one must be
allowed to get in its path; woe unto him who gets crushed
under its wheels.*

iven all the activity it is difficult to imagine how Napoleon
thought he could possibly hoodwink the Austrians about
his intentions on Lobau. With the arrival of Oudinot's II
Corps, the massing French force now totaled 188,500
troops (including engineers and other noncombatants) and
488 guns. Arriving secretly at "misery island" from Schönbrunn on the night of July 4–5, Napoleon was at last ready to launch five
full army corps, exclusive of Bessières's small reserve of Guards—Masséna's
IV Corps of 29,000, Bernadotte's IX Corps of 18,400, Eugène's (MacDonald's) Italian Corps of 20,300, Oudinot's II Corps of 28,200, and last,
Davout's III Corps of 37,900, exclusive of a few detached units—giving him
142,600 men ready for the initial attack.[1]

Facing the French, Archduke Karl had seven corps under Reuss,
Kollowrat, Klenau, Liechtenstein, Bellegarde, Hohenzollern, and Rosenberg,
for an immediate field force of 121,700.[2] With only 136,000 men, including
noncombatants, and 446 guns, the Austrians were at a numerical disadvantage.
The weeks of wavering and indecision, resulting in their failure to crush
Napoleon after his defeat at Aspern-Essling, had actually left them weaker.

Napoleon was ready to avenge himself for the humiliating defeat in May. Marmont's XII Corps was now marching to Lobau to join the others. In northern Germany "General" Jérôme Bonaparte was still showing the flag, if not in quite the right place, with 11,500 men to intimidate further German rebellion for the moment, while the by-now-untrustworthy General Junot was brought up with a small reserve force stationed on the right bank of the Rhine, near Mainz. For all his numerical superiority, Napoleon sorely missed the tough Marshal Lannes. And the valuable Marshal Suchet was absent as well, his presence badly needed in Spain to offset the deleterious effect of the sly, perpetually excuse-finding, and politically plotting Soult.

In addition the Austrian defenses were more imposing than ever, extending all the way from the Danube (just west of Aspern), solidly linking Aspern with Essling, then over to Gross Enzersdorf and several hundred yards beyond. This bristling line of armament was situated directly opposite the northern branch of the Danube, separating Lobau Island from the north, in part in reaction to Napoleon's very convincing feint of having his engineers build ultimately six new bridgeheads from Lobau to the north shore. These were visible to the Austrians and could be swung out from the shore whenever needed. What the Austrians did not see, however, were four more pontoon bridges concealed well to the south of the last part of the Gross Enzersdorf fortification line, intended to link the swampy southern end of "misery island" with the Austrian-held shore of the Danube. Napoleon had not been idle these past six weeks. Never before had he made such elaborate plans for a river crossing, which would permit *three entire army corps* to cross and debouch simultaneously from Lobau Island. Once across, the French plan was to swing right around Archduke Karl's massive static defenses and avoid them altogether. Simply bypassing this line would not prove enough, however, for the archduke had placed his principal force on a curving line well away from the river, to the north of the Russbach, stretching from Gerasdorf on the left to the village of Wagram, and from there all the way over to Markgrafneusiedl on the right. That line was strong in numbers, but there were neither major immediate fortifications to support it nor depth of reserves behind it.*

Napoleon initiated the new offensive by sending small units across the river at Mühlau and Stadlau, north of Vienna, to throw the Austrians off balance. The real attack began at 9:00 P.M. on July 4, 1809, under cover of yet

---

See map on page 508 for the locations involved in this battle.

another heavy thunderstorm. Napoleon launched Oudinot's troops by boat and bridge from the southernmost tip of Lobau over to the northern bank round the Hansel Grund, silencing the lone Austrian outpost there. At the same time a massive coordinated artillery barrage was unleashed against the principal Austrian village fortifications, leveling Aspern-Essling and Gross Enzersdorf, taking the Austrians entirely by surprise. Under cover of this lethal barrage by a few hundred French cannon, one of the large concealed pontoon bridges, nearly 180 yards across, was swiftly swung into place, connecting the island with the north shore and permitting Masséna's IV Corps to pass over quickly and in good order. Meanwhile the rest of Oudinot's II Corps completed its crossing, and by 2:00 A.M. Davout was leading his men across a third bridge, between Masséna and Oudinot. Thanks to Napoleon's plan and Bertrand's superb engineers, the French had achieved complete tactical surprise. They pushed rapidly ahead, meeting little initial resistance, swinging around and bypassing Gross Enzersdorf and the elaborately fortified line of villages, just as anticipated. Napoleon had lost none of his cunning. By dawn on July 5 French troops, cavalry, and artillery had safely crossed over to the north shore and reformed, while Archduke Karl desperately began to dig in behind the low banks of the Russbach, reinforcing the center position before Wagram. Napoleon's attack was one of the most remarkable achievements of its kind in modern French military history.

By 7:00 A.M. the French were thus deployed right on schedule, Masséna pushing to the left, toward Leopoldau and Süssenbrunn, facing Liechtenstein's corps, while Eugène's "army," which had followed Davout across the bridge during the night, advanced toward the central Austrian line at Wagram, facing Bellegarde's corps, with Oudinot to his right, along with Davout's corps, to face the rest of the Austrian line, held by Hohenzollern's and Rosenberg's two corps. Everything was still going like clockwork.

Just after seven the full thrust of the main French attack was unleashed, as more than four hundred French cannon bombarded the Austrian line. Napoleon's aim was to throw Davout's and Oudinot's corps against the Austrian left while launching Bernadotte's and Eugène's combined force against the still relatively weak center before Wagram. If all went well, the French army could separate the two wings, then envelop them separately.

The Austrian left wing, however, proved far stronger and more determined than Napoleon had anticipated, resulting in unexpectedly heavy French casualties. When Archduke Karl himself then appeared at the head of strong reserves, the French were stopped in their tracks. Marshal MacDonald, directing Eugène's Italian army, had to cope with not only a reinforced enemy but also with thousands of his own unenthusiastic Italian troops as they panicked and broke ranks, abandoning their line and their comrades on either side. They were stopped at the rear only by the bayonets of the French Imperial Guard.[3] This unexpected setback was compounded by Bernadotte's failure to storm Wagram as ordered, his men too falling back for the night. As usual the cowardly Bernadotte could not be relied on.

Napoleon's great lightning offensive was stopped dead. Bernadotte, not content with his own failure even to hold his key place in the line, that evening loudly blamed the day's setback on Napoleon's poor battle plan. Things would have been different if he, Marshal Bernadotte, had been in command, he boasted. His criticism soon got back to GHQ and Napoleon himself, who immediately summoned Bernadotte for a well-deserved dressing down.

During the night Bonaparte reorganized his plan of attack and before dawn moved Masséna down to take Essling and Aspern, held by Klenau's corps, while dropping MacDonald's force in a massive square to face Kollowrat's and Liechtenstein's corps. Eugène and Oudinot were ordered to attack Bellegarde and Hohenzollern at Wagram, with Marmont's corps directly behind them. As for Davout, to the French far right, he had orders to turn and envelop Rosenberg's opposing Austrian corps. Unknown to Napoleon, however, the Austrians were planning to concentrate opposite the French left, in an attempt to dislodge and turn Masséna. Up with his staff and commanders most of the night, Bonaparte dispatched the day's final instructions, all units ordered to open fire at four o'clock the following morning, July 6. This would not be another Jena or Austerlitz.

Nevertheless, this time it was Napoleon who was taken by surprise. Just before four in the morning, General Rosenberg unleashed a murderous artillery barrage and frontal attack against Davout's III Corps on the extreme French right, preparatory to the main Austrian thrust along the French extreme left. Davout, bolstered by fresh reserves and a powerful additional battery, fought for his life for the next two hours before being able to halt the surprisingly fierce Austrian drive. Despite their exhaustion, it was only then that Napoleon, who had been with Davout's corps much of the time, ordered that marshal to prepare for a sharp counterattack. If any man in the French army could be counted on in any situation, especially the most critical, it was Louis Davout, clearly one of Napoleon's most talented and reliable commanders.

Meanwhile fighting had developed all along the line, and as Bonaparte left Davout he discovered that brother-in-law Bernadotte, having abandoned the key village of Aderklaa without orders and instead having moved between Masséna on his left and Eugène on the right, now found his IX Corps again retreating in wild disorder. The Austrians of course had immediately moved in and seized Aderklaa. In one fell blow Bernadotte had undone all the day's plans, and Napoleon, beside himself with anger at Bernadotte's utter incompetence, now ordered that marshal, along with the more reliable Masséna, to retake that village—regardless of the human cost—although Archduke Karl was finally to retake it yet again.

While trying to rally his men, now falling back once more, Bernadotte found himself face to face with none other than this very Napoleon whom he had so royally criticized before his staff the night before. Napoleon, equally caught off guard, and so outraged by Bernadotte's having compromised the entire battle plan, not to mention by the stories reported to him, shouted at him over the deafening thunder of guns as that bewildered marshal came to a halt before him: "You are relieved of your command, which you have so bungled. Leave my presence and the Grande Armée immediately."[4] It was electrifying. Bernadotte and his aides-de-camp and staff sat there on their mounts, stunned, as Austrian cannonballs fell thickly all about them. Finally Bernadotte turned to leave the field of battle. Never in the history of the Consulate or the Empire had anything quite like it been seen, and despite the fury of the fighting, word soon reached every corner of the smoke-covered battleground.

As if this were not confusing enough for Bonaparte, Archduke Karl had finally unleashed his primary thrust against the French left at about eight o'clock that morning, after four hours of very hard fighting. As most of Masséna's corps had been moved up to fill the gap left by Bernadotte to counter Liechtenstein and Bellegarde around Aderklaa, that marshal was now no longer in a position to prevent the large-scale breakthrough on the left by Kollowrat's and Klenau's combined corps, which then threatened the approaches behind Napoleon's lines to the bridgeheads leading back to Lobau Island. Archduke Karl, for all his faults the best of the Austrian army commanders, still managed to summon a few lethal surprises for Napoleon.

"The Emperor remained perfectly calm [throughout this latest crisis]" Marshal Marmont later recalled, as Eugène spontaneously ordered Marshal MacDonald to fall back on the left and form an immense square, supported by General Nansouty's cavalry, in order to push back Kollowrat and Liechtenstein as well. But there were not enough French troops to fill all the gaps, and stopping the unopposed Klenau was quite another matter. Making a risky snap decision, Napoleon completely disengaged three of

Masséna's hard-pressed divisions from the front line and ordered them to march southward nearly five miles to take up a new emergency position before the Austrian-held village of Essling, with Bessières's reserves brought up to fill the breach in the main line as they changed sectors in the heat of battle. It was a complicated, delicate procedure, which the veteran Masséna carried out with great skill.

There remained several hundred yards of still insufficiently protected ground around Neu-Wirthaus, just south of MacDonald's new position on the left, however, and Napoleon, ever the brilliant improvisor, ordered forty artillery pieces from Eugène's army and another seventy-two cannon from the Imperial Guard to be brought up to form an enormous new battery under the able command of the tough General Lauriston. Long ago Napoleon's aide-de-camp and being preened for a position as marshal, Count Lauriston had blotted his copybook with his arrogant boasting and his incessant demands for promotion, wealth, and honors, forever to be denied that supreme nomination thereafter. For all that he was an ideal man in this desperate situation, as he issued the complex orders required to bring up enormous supplies of powder, ball, and canister, not to mention the large artillery crews and all the horses for 112 big guns, all under very heavy fire. An extraordinary, hazardous move, nearly one thousand horses and fifteen hundred gunners weaving through French lines. But Lauriston did it.[5]

Even as the guns belched forth the first of hundreds of lethal missiles against the surging Austrians along the French left, on the far right Davout was ordered again to launch his hard-pressed and already battle-worn troops against Rosenberg's powerful corps. They must hammer at the Austrians, Napoleon ordered unrelentingly as exhausted troops on their feet under intensive fire for many hours were pushed seemingly beyond human endurance in the stifling heat. Lauriston's roundshot and case now hurled in continuous fiery sheets, stunning and then finally stopping the intrepid Austrians, but only after their guns had decimated large numbers of the exposed French battery at Neu-Wirthaus. The casualties on both sides were simply appalling.

As for Klenau's maverick corps closing on Essling, it was stopped only by the remaining large guns on Lobau, permitting Masséna to quick-march his exhausted troops to seize the fortifications of Essling, thereby barring Klenau's route. The Austrians would advance no farther; nevertheless Napoleon's great plan had gone very, very wrong.

If Napoleon could depend on any two men in the entire French army, they had always been Lannes and Davout. Once again Davout fearlessly led his assault against murderous opposition, General Gudin at his side brought down by four simultaneous wounds, and Davout's own horse killed under him, hurling him to the ground. An aide-de-camp quickly brought up a spare mount, and Davout was back in the saddle again. Although Rosenberg's crack IX Corps did for a while penetrate and threaten Davout's haggard line, nevertheless he did regain control, pushing Rosenberg's entire front and second lines back well past Markgrafneusiedl.

Sweeping the whole scene again with his telescope, Napoleon dispatched his aides-de-camp with a rash of fresh orders as he launched the final drive to break the brave Austrian army before him. While Davout was to continue to roll back Rosenberg's corps, Oudinot was to charge the heights protected by Hohenzollern's corps, and MacDonald, supported by Lauriston's new battery, was to break through the Austrian line to the left, at the hinge linking Kollowrat's and Liechtenstein's corps in the direction of the hamlet of Süssenbrunn behind them.

Despite the sweltering heat of the day, again in the nineties, MacDonald marched his twenty-one battalions in a bristling square formation forward to the beat of drums, protected by Imperial Guard Cavalry to the right and confident heavily armored cuirassiers to his left. But even the finest infantry square could not defy concentrated musketry and the flashing Austrian batteries. Kollowrat and Liechtenstein reduced MacDonald's force of 8,000 men by 5,500 casualties in a matter of minutes. With barely 2,500 men left, a much shaken MacDonald pleaded for help, and Napoleon sent in Wrede's Germans to the rescue.

By two o'clock the diminutive Masséna was gaining full control of the ruins of Essling, preventing any further advance there by Klenau, while at the center the remainder of Eugène's Italian army, now supported strongly by Marshals Oudinot and Marmont, were finally sealing the fate of the Austrian forces at Wagram. The splendid Davout remained in full control on the far right as he continued to rout Rosenberg's corps, which was falling back quickly now.

With the slaughter and his own casualties reaching phenomenal proportions, outnumbered from the start and apparently unconfident in his own plan while continuing to face this staggering French ferocity, Archduke Karl conceded defeat and began an orderly withdrawal of his troops from this immense battlefield. Far to the west, across the broad reaches of the Danube, the people of Vienna manned the walls of the ancient Habsburg capital, some with telescopes, and watched the tragic spectacle, or at least what could be seen of it through the long pall of sulfuric smoke thickened by the raging fires in the various villages and the burning fields of wheat around Wagram. The two mighty French batteries now had to silence their many dozens of big guns for fear of hitting their own men, who were advancing through the blazing fields, past smoldering villages and the charred remains of Austrian troops and horses frozen in place for eternity. The archduke's army was departing for the hills of Bohemia once again. By four o'clock the fate of the enemy was sealed, and Napoleon at last realized that he had won the Battle of Wagram—one of the most extraordinary events in the annals of military history.

The Austrians escaped in a long methodical retreat that the exhausted French were unable to pursue, although Marbot for one claims that Napoleon could have mustered a large enough force to smash them once and for all had he been more aggressive. But Napoleon, too, was weary, physically and mentally, after directing his troops for more than a dozen hours without a respite of any sort. His troops were in worse shape, many of them literally falling asleep where they stood or collapsing from wounds. Had the Austrians had a more confident commander, things might have turned out very differently indeed, for the archduke's basic battle plan was a superb one. But he lacked character and confidence.

Nevertheless, by the close of that afternoon, the Austrians had lost the battle, paying a very heavy price in 37,146 casualties (including killed, wounded, and prisoners) of whom 747 were officers (four of them generals) but only twenty guns. Precise French casualties were never established, but it appears they included at least 32,500 dead or wounded and another 7,000 men prisoners of the Austrians. In reality the French wounded figure was probably much higher. Unlike the Austrians the French had lost among their dead and wounded some 1,866 officers (including more than three dozen generals), not to mention the loss of twelve regimental colors and twenty-one guns.[6] Not since Eylau and Auerstädt had the French suffered so grievously.

Never before had the French lost so many big guns and regimental colors. Never before had Napoleon lost so many senior officers. Never before had he dismissed a marshal of the Empire—and on the field of battle before the enemy! For the first time in his career he had actually been outfoxed by excellent opposing battlefield tactics, as he would have been earlier at Aspern-Essling had Archduke Karl's excellent plans been matched by an equal self-confidence and willpower to pursue the French. Here at Wagram the archduke's superb feint along the extreme French right, while launching his massive turning attack on the extreme French left, had taken Napoleon utterly by surprise, for which he paid very heavily in troop losses. But if he had shamed and lost one marshal in Bernadotte, he had created and gained another in MacDonald. Really all French corps commanders performed superbly today, apart from Bernadotte. On the other hand, for the first time many thousands of green conscripts, French, Italian, and German, had broken and run under fire, forced back to their positions only at bayonet-point. Wagram was a very different sort of battle in most respects, and although a technical victory, hardly a sweeping, crushing one. And then, too, Napoleon had lost among his dead and gravely wounded many senior officers he could not easily replace, including d'Espagne, St.-Hilaire, LaSalle, and of course the irreplaceable Lannes, who had been with him since the early days of the Italy campaign under the Directorate.

On July 8 Masséna, Marmont, Oudinot, and Davout were ordered to search for the retreating Austrians, resulting in some sharp rear-guard actions adding further to the calamitous casualty list. Spreading a wide net in this search, it was André Masséna who finally found the main body of the still well-organized Austrian army north of Znaim on the Thaya River reaching into southern Moravia, where a new battle was fought on the 10th. This proved too much for Archduke Karl and his exhausted and thoroughly demoralized army, which finally began breaking ranks and fleeing in all directions. The archduke duly sent a messenger asking for an armistice on the eleventh. That brief document was drawn up and signed by Masséna and Karl in the wee hours of the following morning.

An angry Austrian Emperor Franz I, smarting over yet another defeat at the hands of that wretched Bonaparte and this humiliating armistice, one week later fired his brother, Archduke Karl, though there was no one to replace him.

The war was over. After spending much time with the wounded, first on "misery island" and then in Vienna, Bonaparte returned to the "Camp of Schönbrunn Palace" with his bevy of aides-de-ccamp and staff, to analyze the entire campaign and to draft the final terms of the peace treaty with Austria.

There was another side to Wagram, all the Wagrams, Friedlands, Eylaus, Jenas, Auerstädts, and Austerlitzes—the medical side as seen by the surgeons and the wounded.

"The general who consumes 6,000 men a day!" is how General Kléber had summed up Bonaparte during the Egyptian campaign. "The Empire turned its back on humanity," two medical historians fully concurred more than a century later. "This is not the nicest part of war. It is sad and moving to see so many victims," Napoleon himself had confessed to Josephine on leaving one of his famous battlefields "covered with the dead and wounded."[7] And yet after that terrible slaughter at Eylau, which he alone was responsible for, he continued to wage war rather than make an all-out effort to seek a lasting peace. There was something very sadomasochistic, something very perverted, about Napoleon's wish to continue with slaughter after slaughter, followed by ritualistically contrite, tearful visits to the body-strewn fields of battle after the silencing of all guns. He was truly tormented by the sight of these hundreds of thousands of maimed and dead, and yet apparently it was a sight that he could not live without, even when it meant endangering those very close to him, not to mention his own existence. "I have 300,000 men to spend!" he revealingly boasted to Czar Alexander just before another great battle.[8] "Once my great empire has been launched, no one must be allowed to get in its path; woe unto him who gets crushed under its wheels." He was a human steamroller, crushing all those in his path—after having deliberately placed them in his way.

With the same cold, calculating ruthlessness, Napoleon ignored the dead and wounded, and despite the pleas of the army's chief surgeon, Dr. Dominique Larrey, year after year refused to create a permanent army medical corps. "There is no Medical Service whatsoever!" even the tough Marshal Davout had complained during the first Danube campaign. "On the eve of Austerlitz . . . Monsieur Larrey did not have a single bandage at his disposition," Dr. d'Héralde, the sole surgeon attached to Soult's corps, recalled. "He asked me to give him some. I had some cloth, and cannon swabs, but only enough for four or five hundred wounded, and a double amputation kit," this before a major battle in which 9,000 or so French casualties were thus all but abandoned by Bonaparte.[9] When Dr. Larrey's fellow army surgeon, Pierre François Percy, presented a sweeping plan of reorganization for the medical service, it was neither approved nor appreciated. "I hope that Your Majesty will allow me to tell him how grievously the entire Army Medical Service has been affected by his rejection of the plan prepared by M. Percy, regarding the establishment of a regular field service on a permanent basis," Dr. Jean-Baptiste Turiot complained to Napoleon following the debacle of Eylau and just nine days before the great Battle of Friedland.[10] The lamentations of physicians in his military medical service mounted, and even greater numbers of surgeons refused to consider service under such appalling conditions—one group of sixty such doctors, upon reaching a battlefield, were so shocked by what they saw that they immediately fled and returned to France.

On April 13, 1809, Napoleon finally authorized the first permanent field service, including ten companies of army nurses (all male), comprising a total of 1,250 men for the entire army, and a few ambulances.[11] And although Napoleon could mobilize and march an entire army (literally on foot) from Boulogne to the Rhine in one month, by the time of Wagram, three months after announcing the creation of this medical service, it still existed only on paper. When Napoleon commanded that something be done, it was. In this case there had been no such command.

Almost as pathetic, the few surgical ambulance teams organized and dispatched from Madrid back at the beginning of March 1809 reached Vienna only on June 27, too late to help the French victims at Aspern-Essling in May, which Larrey put at 16,000 dead, and where he had operated literally almost single-handed. (As for the troops in Spain, they would simply have to do without.) It was following this butchery and the unattended dying that Napoleon's troops renamed Lobau *"l'île de misère."*

In a sense the tragedy of Wagram brought the full impact of all these unnecessary battles into focus, through a series of unsolicited letters to Napoleon Bonaparte by Turiot, the deputy chief surgeon of the Grand Army's medical service. Writing angrily to Bonaparte on July 17, 1809, eleven days after the Battle of Wagram, Turiot barely remained civil as he explained the results of the lack of all basic services in those field hospitals. On his arrival at Lobau from Spain, he said that despite "an enormous armed place, complete with streets, workshops, depots and encampments . . . from the medical viewpoint everything was missing, except the devotion of the surgeons."[12] And what surgeons, in reality few of them qualified in medical schools/hospitals, and the majority of those so incompetent as to be unable to earn a living as a physician in French civilian life!

At Essling, Surgeon Herteloup had found nothing available, even for rudimentary field operations, and after having operated as best he could, he attempted to protect the survivors against the sun, rain, and the night cold by building lean-tos of river reed covered by the coats taken from the dead. "All those wretches suffered from thirst and hunger," and such food as could be found, butchered cavalry horses, was cooked in the armor of dead soldiers hammered into the shape of pots, for not even cooking utensils were made available by Napoleon for those hospitalized. For water, there was only the Danube. "But even the zeal and surgical virtuosity of Dr. Larrey could not prevent many from dying of tetanus, because most of those surviving operations were bandaged in dirty cannon swabs." But, he added sarcastically, at least "you and your officers in full dress uniform visited the wounded on April 27, followed by four servants in your livery bearing baskets of gold pieces."[13]

Turiot added that he had personally seen "the field of carnage" at Wagram, the wheat "aflame, and all the villages about us destroyed by artillery. . . . But in the afternoon, after twelve hours of fighting, the victory, albeit hesitant, finally gave way before your implacable will. To be sure, so many laurels have not been acquired without immense sacrifice. Never was there such bloody fighting!" But there were few surgeons on the battlefield, no medicine of any kind, no anesthesia, not even bandages or beds. The newly operated on—and frequently 60 to 70 percent of those never left the "hospital" alive[14]—were permitted to keep the blood-covered stretchers they were brought in on, though most usually were placed on the ground, and if straw was available, on it. More frequently the men were placed on muddy, blood-splattered dirt floors, or simply shoved aside.

"For all the enormous size of your Grand Army, and the complexity of its organization," Turiot continued:

> it was incapable of providing not only a reasonable sort of field medical service, but even the most rudimentary aspects of one. I am also going to take the extreme liberty of again telling Your Majesty how much bloodshed could have been spared, how many human beings could have been saved here, if M. Percy's plan [for reorganizing the medical service] had been put into effect.

At Wagram, "Certainly, we have all done our best," Turiot insisted. "However, even the special medical service reserved for your Imperial Guard was quickly swamped, incapable of coping, as a result of the extent of the battle. . . . The number of wounded increased in terrifying proportions to the increased severity of the bombardment," and their field hospital "has been rapidly filled" by the wounded, leaving it "in total disorder. I even saw one colonel whose arm had just been amputated laid on a pile of manure and straw. I hate to mention the fate of just ordinary soldiers!"

The soldiers who could not be brought in were left unattended in the burned stubble of the wheatfield where they had fallen. The fierce July sun left them parched, many dying of thirst and hunger, Turiot continued, covered "by that sort of enormous flies that are attracted to slaughterhouses." Several days after death thousands were still left in the fields, "their wounds filled with maggots. Next to one burned-out ambulance, I saw the pieces of an arm and leg, the stench of the putrefaction filling the air," the battle-hardened surgeon noted. It was worse for the wounded, forgotten for days, lying helplessly watching the maggot-infested corpses of their companions being eaten away, inch by inch, before their very eyes, driving many of them insane. Other bodies lay half buried by explosions. "Many of those unfortunate men were found only five or six days later. Those who were still strong enough called out or else waved a cloth on their rifle above the wheat . . . others, although half charred, somehow were still alive, which

seems quite incredible," having survived "by drinking their own urine. . . .
Most of the wounded collected after Wagram had almost bled to death,
their tongues thickened and swollen out of their mouths, and they died
shortly after reaching a hospital." Blood transfusions were of course still
unknown.

There, medical orderlies—with an average of three weeks' total training—were forced to carry out many hundreds of amputations themselves,
the only supervision a passing surgeon quickly "marking the place for the
incision with a piece of chalk." When such "operations" were carried out in
the field, there were practically no survivors, the victims dying in the greatest agony—there was no anesthesia for soldier or officer—their amputated
limbs tossed on one of the stacks of arms, legs, feet, and organs typical of all
such French battlefields. To compound matters, the wounded were not separated from the large numbers with infectious diseases. What is more,
Turiot lamented, among the wounded, many were "adolescent conscripts
whose bodies were not yet fully developed and capable of coping with these
hardships."

But still no French Military Health Service organization in existence,
Turiot concluded. "It is essential that the means put at the disposal of the
Health Service be increased to cope with the efficacy of the new more murderous arms and tactics." Fortunately, Turiot closed, "military virtue has
not weakened in the greatest of war leaders, those civil virtues, and the sight
of the blood, tears, suffering, and cries of agony that Your Majesty always
reacts to so profoundly will not have suppressed in him that which makes
him the greatest of sovereigns."[15]

The initial peace negotiations that followed at Altenburg, beginning on
August 18 between Champagny and Metternich, were to prove fruitless in
the face of Austrian instransigence. By September 9 an impatient Bonaparte
had had enough of "this Altenburg farce," as he called it. When Franz I sent
his personal envoy, General Bubna, to talk with him, Napoleon gave him a
message that left the Austrian emperor trembling: "You can tell Monsieur
von Metternich that if the emperor wants to abdicate in favor of the Grand
Duke of Würzburg, I shall leave your country as it is, with its present independence, and shall then form an alliance with you that will allow you to
govern yourself."[16] If the emperor proved contrary, Bonaparte continued,
then he would strip further large sections of Austrian territory from the
Habsburg Empire. (He had of course already taken much of its land.) If he
could suppress the thousand-year-old Holy Roman Empire, he could obviously do the same to the remainder of the truncated Austrian Empire.

Franz I was Napoleon's most stubborn continental opponent at this stage, and Bonaparte wanted him out of the way.

Although Franz I then dispatched Prince von Liechtenstein to reason with the emperor, Napoleon remained unshakable. Nor was Franz I any more willing to compromise, even after consulting with senior members of the Austrian royal family. He refused even to consider abdication. Meanwhile the Austrian ruler had been negotiating secretly with the czar, his special envoy returning from St. Petersburg empty-handed, however. The French emperor's victory had frightened everyone. Both the Prussians and Russians insisted that they wanted to support the Austrian emperor, but they felt they were too weak to do so at this time.

There had been nothing secret about growing Prussian frustration with the French forces occupying their land and dictating their state policy, and their fervent wish to oust the French once and for all. Not surprisingly, the Prussian envoy to Paris had been intriguing against France, as Fouché informed Napoleon. "Then expel that animal!" the French emperor instructed his police minister-cum-acting interior minister with the usual Bonaparte panache.[17]

In Prussia State Minister Goltz warned Queen Louise that "if the King hesitates much longer to take the resolve to stand up against France now as demanded by public opinion, an immediate revolution will be inevitable."[18]

Of course there had already been very real recent attempts at military rebellion, any one of which might have ignited not only Prussia and the Germanic world but also the whole of a seething Europe, almost all of which was occupied by hundreds of thousands of French bayonets. Thanks to King Jérôme's feckless administration of his newly minted kingdom of Westphalia, that entire region was now a veritable hotbed of intrigue and unrest, especially after the endless new tax assessments inflicted on the people by their new master(s), not to mention the extension of military conscription insisted upon by Napoleon. The result was the famous Dörnberg affair of April 22, 1809. To be sure, the Dörnberg plot had been nipped in the bud, narrowly, followed by Major Schill's uprising, which was put down bloodily at Stralsund on May 30, 1809. In consequence Napoleon had been required to keep several thousand troops around Westphalia, troops that otherwise could have been sent to Austria, and had finally created the X Observation Corps of twenty thousand men, initially under Junot's command and then under Kellermann's, though still under the titular command of King Jérôme.[19]

With those embryonic rebellions snuffed out for the moment, and the new campaign opening against the Austrians, Napoleon had ordered brother Jérôme's corps to proceed to Dresden at once. In the post-Wagram battle that ensued there, Junot was defeated and Jérôme fled. When Napoleon learned that Dresden had been abandoned, as Jérôme returned hastily with his entire "royal entourage" to Kassel and the comforts of his castle, Napoleon attacked him without restraint:

> I have just seen an order issued by you that makes you the laughing-stock of Germany, Austria, and France! Have you no friends there who can advise you and tell you a few home truths? You are king, and brother of the emperor, qualities that are quite ridiculous in wartime. One must be a soldier first, and then a soldier again, and finally, still a soldier. There must be no ministers, no diplomatic corps accompanying you, no pomp. You must campaign with the advance guard of the army, be in the saddle day and night, and march with the forward units in order to be up-to-the minute as to what is happening. But you make war like a satrap! God, almighty, you haven't learned such things from me! I, with an army of 200,000 men now, am always to be found at the head of my troops. . . . Stop making an utter fool of yourself: send the diplomatic corps back to Kassel, take no baggage train with you, and bring just enough provisions for yourself alone. Make war like the young soldier that you are, a soldier in search of glory and fame, and try to merit the rank you have been given, to be worthy of the estime of France and Europe, who are watching your every move. And by God! be sensible enough to write and speak in a civil manner![20]

As if Napoleon did not have enough on his plate already, the worries multiplied: anxious reports from Spain with the English on the move again; insurrections or threats of rebellion throughout the German-speaking world; reports by his own spies of anti-French communications flowing from Berlin, Russia, and Austria; and now warnings from Fouché of English plans for the landing of an enormous expeditionary force at Walcheren Island in the North Sea, apparently with the aim of seizing Flushing and Antwerp. Then, too, there were the ramifications of his seizure and arrest of the pope. Life was indeed complicated: All was in jeopardy.

With the defeat of the Austrians at Wagram, followed by the submission of Archduke Karl in July, despite postponements by Emperor Franz I and delays to avoid concluding a final peace treaty, Napoleon continued to put pressure on the Austrians following the stalemated talks at Altenburg in mid-September. Prince von Liechtenstein warned, "He [Napoleon] spoke of one thing only—partitioning the Austrian monarchy and establishing instead several independent states out of the ruins, unless Emperor Franz abdicates." That threat was dismissed out of hand by the Habsburg ruler. "The destruction of the Austrian monarchy would be a calamity for the whole of Europe," the czar pleaded directly with Napoleon.[21]

Metternich, who had recently replaced the unsuccessful Stadion as the Austrian chancellor, now in turn pleaded with French Foreign Minister Champagny: "Let us join your [Continental] System and then you will be able to be really sure of us," but keep Franz I as the Austrian ruler and do not partition the great Habsburg Empire. "That is the basis—honorable for us, practical for you—upon which we hope to establish peace."

As for the position of the French and their allies, the Russians and the Poles, neither Champagny nor Napoleon was content. "The Russians did not fire a shot against the Austrians. In fact the only blood they spilt was Polish,"[22] the French foreign minister complained to Napoleon even as Metternich was confiding to Franz I that Russia "has privately assured us of her support for our side." Metternich had to convince the Austrian emperor of the necessity of signing a peace treaty now and biding his time until he was in a better position to act, his advice resembling very much Czar Alexander's on that subject to his mother earlier. "Our principles remain unalterable," Metternich insisted to Franz, "but we also face certain elementary realities. We have no choice but to conserve our strength for better times to come, while gradually preparing for that moment."[23] Peace had to be made with the French, but only as a means to the final end of one day overthrowing the French invaders.

As for Napoleon's stalwart allies, the Poles, who had volunteered tens of thousands of troops to the Grand Army in hopes of an ultimate national settlement in their favor, Napoleon privately informed Champagny that he had other plans, as Champagny in turn revealed to Caulaincourt:

> The Emperor not only does not want to see the revival of the idea of a rebirth of Poland—an idea very far from his views—but he is even disposed to work with Emperor Alexander in doing everything possible to eliminate the very memory of such a thing from the heart of those people. His Majesty approves the idea of ensuring that the words 'Poland' and 'Polish' disappear not only from all our negotiations but from European history itself.[24]

This was reflected in all of Napoleon's subsequent actions.

Even before the negotiations had been concluded, Prussia's Friedrich Wilhelm III was also secretly seeking to rally allies, in particular the Russians, against the French. "How different the situation would be, Sire," he wrote Czar Alexander "if you were to judge it in the best interests of your empire to renounce your current foreign policy by declaring yourself against France."[25] If officially the by-now-much-more-cautious Alexander avoided open commitments of any kind, the situation was nevertheless patently clear: Although in no position to oppose the French on the battlefield, Prussia, Russia, and Austria were preparing for the future, and under the circumstances Franz I had no alternative but to agree to a "temporary" peace treaty ending the Second Danube Campaign.

After many weeks of negotiating and unpleasant haggling, the Treaty of Schönbrunn (or of Vienna, as it was variously known thereafter) was signed and exchanged during the night of October 13–14, 1809. In its eighteen patent—and six secret—articles, Austria paid a staggering price for its independence, including the loss of some 42,000 square miles of territory, and 3,500,000 Austrian subjects. The real estate lost came from Austria's provinces in Poland (including Krakow), which were first handed over to the king of Saxony and thereafter annexed to Napoleon's Duchy of Warsaw, a small section of western Austria—handed over to Napoleon and annexed to Bavaria—and finally a large section of Austria's "Yugoslav" provinces to the south. All this became part of the ever-growing Confederation of the Rhine. What is more, Austria was required to reduce the size of its standing army and pay a war indemnity to Napoleon Bonaparte of 85 million francs.[26]

For all the French threats, a shaken Franz I did remain on his throne (albeit much reduced), angrier than ever, despite Metternich's official soothing words and rationale. Alexander felt betrayed and cheated because of the small Polish tidbits of Galicia eventually thrown his way from the French feasting table, while Prussia's Friedrich Wilhelm felt more determined than ever to destroy France and Napoleon Bonaparte. Napoleon's "victorious" second Danube campaign, concluded on the plains of Wagram, had ensured his own eventual downfall.

One of the reasons Napoleon had put immense pressure on Austria during the negotiations—which explained at the same time why Austria had so dithered—was the knowledge that the government of England's George III, under Lord Portland, was preparing an unprecedented troop landing somewhere along the Belgian or Dutch coast. A successful British operation might spark a European conflagration that even a Bonaparte could not stanch. He therefore had to break the spirit of Britain's allies in advance. British troops might land, but they would receive no help from Berlin or Vienna.

For all that, this pending English invasion was to rock Napoleon's fragile empire to its very foundations, frightening him as no Austrian army ever had, and dividing the French government in Paris as never before.

It had all begun in the late winter of the previous year (1808), when Police Minister Fouché reported to the government the first signs of what appeared to be unusual military preparations in England, reports that had been dismissed out of hand both by Admiral Decrès at the Naval Ministry and by War Minister Clarke. Archchancellor Cambacérès, ever unswervingly loyal to Napoleon, yet a weak, cautious man afraid of making decisions and commitments, was fully supported by the ministers of every portfolio—Champagny (Foreign Office), Mollien (Treasury), Gaudin (Finance), and Bigot de Préaumeneu (Religious Affairs)—in rejecting Fouché's harum-scarum warnings. Time and again the police minister had produced incorrect prognostications. Or could this be yet another pretext for yet another plot by Fouché himself? In Paris no one trusted either his neighbor or his colleague.

Over the months, however, more reports reached the ministers confirming Fouché's claims, and Clarke agreed to hold a couple of battalions along the Scheldt River, Decrès contributing a few warships along the coast, but nothing beyond that.

Aggravating the international uncertainty was Napoleon's ill-advised and worse-timed decision of May 16, 1809, to annex the Papal States (occupied by France since January 1808), followed by the further gaffe on July 6 of arresting and kidnapping Pope Pius VII himself, who had just excommunicated Napoleon. Europe was already roused against the French, and this act against the Roman Catholic Church deepened the resolve of his foes everywhere—of course he no longer had friends anywhere. Populations, including those of Belgium and Holland, which would be needed to reinforce the French against a British invasion, were still further estranged, indeed outraged, against the French forces occupying their lands.

With the opening of the second Danube campaign in April 1809, King Louis Bonaparte had written to Napoleon pleading for troops with which to defend his kingdom, a request his brother had ignored. Hard pressed by having to wage war on two fronts, and already calling up young students and older retired soldiers, Napoleon had stripped French garrisons to the minimum everywhere, and in the instance of Holland leaving a bare nine thousand men (and those unfit for front-line service) for the entire country.

And then Fouché's warnings were fully confirmed. News reached the French capital by special courier late on July 29, 1809, that an English armada had indeed arrived off the Dutch coast and was preparing for a landing. An *armada*, not just a few ships with a few hundred men. (Sir Arthur Wellesley, of course, had landed earlier that same year in Portugal with another thirty thousand men, which had since resulted in two French defeats in the peninsula, at Oporto in May, when he had defeated Soult and reconquered that country, and at Talavera in July.) Unlike the previous British naval attacks along the French coast over the years, however, now 264 warships and troop transports were landing some forty thousand troops on Walcheren Island.

Thanks to Fouché's urging, the first of a series of emergency cabinet meetings was convened that same day at the Tuileries by Cambacérès. After much hemming and hawing, Fouché, in his capacity as interim interior minister, got approval to mobilize the National Guardsmen of the fifteen districts between Antwerp—the primary objective of the English—and Flushing and Walcheren. Some thirty thousand citizen-soldiers would be under arms within a few days. Even now, however, Cambacérès was aghast at Fouché's audacity,[27] including his insistence on naming the recently fired Marshal Bernadotte, now back in disgrace from Wagram, as the man to command them. The reason? There simply was no one else with corps command experience available, Fouché explained.

When on August 12 Napoleon finally received word in Vienna of what had transpired in Paris during the crisis, he was incredulous that all his ministers had pooh-poohed Fouché's earlier warning of such a landing and then had even tried to prevent the organizing of enough troops with which to repel any invaders. "I am most upset that during the ministerial meeting you did not take it upon yourself to call up the National Guards," Napoleon lashed out at an amazed Cambacérès, hitherto immune from imperial ire: "That really was most irresponsible." And then Cambacérès had authorized the calling up of a mere thirty thousand men! "You must have 80,000 men armed and ready, and impress the nation so as to discourage the English from any further such expeditions, by seeing that the French people are ready to take up arms against them. Walcheren Island must be retaken.... Convene the council of ministers regularly," he ordered Cambacérès. "Don't let the English catch you napping!" he snapped at War Minister Clarke. As for Fouché, "He simply did what you yourself ought to have done."[28]

French troops and National Guardsmen were soon marching, the British, under the baleful command of Lord Chatham, failing to take their objective of Antwerp. Falling back to Walcheren, where some 4,000 died of disease and illnesses in the marshy land, and another 106 in the actual fighting, most of the British force was whisked away to safety in a complex if spectacular Royal Navy operation on September 30 by Admiral Lord Strachan, and the final contingent was rescued on December 22. If—unlike their skillful operations in Portugal—the English expedition in the Low Countries proved a lamentable fiasco, it was thanks alone to its extraordinarily inept commander, not because of the equally incompetent French who had done nothing to prevent their initial landing.

The English had left "15,000 dead" behind, Napoleon boasted to the world (as opposed to the actual figure of 4,107), adding that they would soon "find their graves" in Spain and Portugal as well.[29]

The descent on Walcheren and South Beveland had the unanticipated effect of a complete break between Louis and Napoleon. Louis had been scolded by Napoleon for immediately assuming command of the few French troops in Holland against the British landing force. Louis, a former general officer in the French army, was rebuked for daring to interfere in "French military affairs." "Can I not consider myself deeply humiliated," Louis responded. "You are simply hurting yourself and your dynasty, and it will hurt Your Majesty more than you realize." "This poor Dutch nation of yours certainly has a right to complain about you," Napoleon parried in response. "What she is suffering from today results from the instability of your own character and from the lack of judgment in the measures you have taken."[30]

The gloves were off, as a desperate Napoleon sought to stabilize a Europe he himself had destabilized through his unrelenting conquests and subsequent territorial divisions. He had hastily razed to the ground centuries-old, time-tested geopolitical structures, replacing them with new ones of his own fabrication, all poorly constructed and fatally flawed in design. And now he informed Louis that he intended to dethrone him and annex Holland along with the rest of Europe. Louis declined to abdicate at first, although he did withdraw from public affairs to devote himself to writing an epic poem, *La Mort de Marie*. When he did finally agree to step down, it was on one condition: "There is only one way I will agree to this, if Your Majesty absolutely wants it, and that is by replacing me with my son." Napoleon rejected this out of hand; he wanted Holland for himself. "If the king abdicates, in no case do I intend to replace him by the prince royal [the eldest surviving son]. . . . His throne has been destroyed as a result of the English expedition, when the king demonstrated his total inability to defend himself, and therefore Holland can no longer exist," Napoleon announced.[31] One year later, on July 19, 1810, he officially annexed that country. The English invasion and Louis's mental instability proved the ideal excuses for sequestering yet another state. Brother

Napoleon, who had defied Louis by separating him from his wife and giving her refuge, and had then condoned forbidding Louis even to see his own son, capping that by stealing him—adopting the baby as his own—had now stolen his crown as well!

Meanwhile, although the English threat was over for the moment, Napoleon's absence from Paris at this time had created another menace. Revolt was near the surface in France. If Bonaparte did not defeat the Austrians, the prefect of the Ourthe had warned Fouché on July 6 before news of Wagram had reached Paris, "there will be an immediate insurrection against Napoleon."[32] The French Foreign Ministry, the Interior Ministry, the General Police, and the War Ministry were all receiving similar reports.

Even with the victory of Wagram, because of the immediate failure of Napoleon to wring a peace treaty—or even an admission of defeat—from the Austrians, all sorts of rumors of revolt reached the French capital. Cambacérès's mobilization of National Guardsmen throughout much of France, some thirty thousand in Paris alone, put Napoleon in a state of panic. All those armed citizen-soldiers could now turn against *him*. War Minister Clarke echoed these fears: "It's another levée of [17]93 all over again," he warned. This fear appeared to be centered round Bernadotte, who had earlier joined in a plot in Brittany to overthrow Napoleon and who now, legally in charge of the troops and guardsmen in the Low Countries, might serve as a rallying point to French National Guardsmen as well. Bernadotte "is preparing to play a great role . . . of grave consequences," General Clarke warned. What is more, immediately on reaching Antwerp Bernadotte had acted like a dictator, not an army commander, assuming all civil and military authority in the region. Napoleon assured Clarke that he was fully aware of Bernadotte's complicity.[33] "There is a sort of national vertigo in France now turning everyone's heads," Bonaparte explained to Fouché. "All the reports reaching me inform me that the National Guardsmen have been issued arms, even those in Piedmont, in Languedoc, in Provence, and in the Dauphiné! Why the devil was this authorized? Under such circumstances as these the least incident could spark off a crisis! It could ignite the whole of France."[34] In fact only Acting Interior Minister Fouché had the authority to call them up. In any event the guardsmen were gradually disarmed over the next several weeks, and Bernadotte—who was allegedly named in a plot to have replaced his brother-in-law, Napoleon, and now caught corresponding with Napoleon's enemies—was immediately removed from his command in Holland. (Despite the proof in hand, Napoleon once again failed to take punitive action. Instead he offered Bernadotte distant posts at Ponte Corvo in Italy, and in Spain, all of which were declined. Although Bernadotte finally accepted the post of governor-general of Rome, he never actually took it up. Much to Napoleon's astonishment, he was eventually offered the crown of Sweden. On September 4, 1810, Bernadotte received the official document naming him heir to the Swedish throne.[35]

By mid-October the crisis was over, but Napoleon was more aware than ever how very insecure was his imperial throne. It was not just insurrection in the Low Countries, or in the Confederation of the Rhine, or in Prussia, or the open rebellion in Austria, not to mention disquieting signs in Russia, or even the news of fresh disasters in Iberia. It was in Paris itself; it was in France. Bonaparte could no longer afford to leave the French capital for any length of time, it seemed. He who had at Vienna announced his personal return to Spain in order to drive Sir Arthur Wellesley and the English into the sea would not only never see Spain again but was no longer sure of his own capital. As for his splendid plan to take Gibraltar and North Africa . . .

CHAPTER 31

The Last Rose of Summer

A prince who is considered . . . a kind man is a king who is doomed.

harles the Bald had built the first castle there in the ninth century, the future Charles the Wise had convoked the Estates-General there back in 1358, and Jeanne d'Arc had been held prisoner there by the Burgundians in 1430. Louis XV, or Louis the Beloved, who ruled France for all but five years of his life, from 1715 to 1774, had rebuilt the small, dank medieval fortified castle into a sprawling, elegant country palace with a light-colored limestone facade and immense cobbled *cour d'honneur*. Surrounded by some thirty thousand acres of forest and field, Compiègne was a favorite of the Bourbons, to which this same King Louis had brought two of his celebrated mistresses, Mesdames de Pompadour and du Barry.

Like Napoleon that king had taken an unusually strong interest in Polish affairs, but unlike him Louis had tried to prevent its partitioning. Like Napoleon, he is remembered for a series of wars, including the Seven Years' War, which ended so disastrously for France with the loss of vast territories in India and Canada. It was during his reign, however, that both Lorraine and Corsica had been added to the French monarchy, and thus thanks to him that Napoleon Bonaparte had been born a French citizen. Also like Napoleon, he had been interested in closer ties with Austria, if not with the same intention.

Now, at the end of March 1810, after a week of incessant preparations, a small figure in a gray coat, protected from the heavy spring rain by umbrellas held by equerries and footmen, and joined by another gentleman, tall, broad-shouldered, and towering over him, entered a calèche. Despite the downpour he called for his secretary, ordering the drenched young man to see to some dispatches, and then snapped the window shut as he ordered the coachman to make all haste along the road to Soissons, some twenty-one miles distant. The little man was of course Emperor Napoleon, a fact that his last-minute, incognito change of clothes could hardly have disguised, had it not been for the rain. It was cold, and he was cold. He was always cold, even in July when he had a fire going. Next to him in an extraordinary uniform of his own concoction, concealed by a bulging overcoat, sat his brother-in-law, King Joachim of Naples.

The whip cracked as the horses hurled the light coach forward across cobbles and mud toward Soissons. All the carefully planned arrangements had been cast aside on a whim. A courier had arrived twenty minutes earlier, informing Napoleon that his bride and new empress, the eighteen-year-old Austrian archduchess Marie-Louise, was near Soissons. Elaborate marquees had been set up on the near side of Compiègne, and on the other side by Soissons, from which both parties were to have alighted and made final preparations prior to meeting at an even larger tent set up at a midway point. But, as impatient as ever, Napoleon was advancing at a dangerous speed, given the state of the roads. How many times had he and his closest officers been thrown from overturned carriages in just such weather? But no matter; fate was on his side. If he could escape a dozen major battles without a scratch, apart from that bruised heel back at Aspern-Essling, he need hardly worry about a little rain.

Reaching the hamlet of Courcelles, he encountered the last courier sent by his bride just moments earlier. She would soon be passing. He ordered the coachman to stop here, and he and Murat descended at the doorway of the medieval church to take shelter from the rain. In a few minutes the cavalcade of nearly three dozen carriages, preceded and followed by hundreds of cavalry, hove into sight as the curious little figure stepped into the rain and flagged them down. The empress's equerry hesitantly intervened, until at last, when only an arm's length away, he finally recognized the drenched emperor. Throwing the carriage door open despite the deluge, Napoleon—ignoring his sister, Queen Caroline (Murat), whom he had earlier dispatched to greet the archduchess at Strasbourg, threw his arms around the astonished young lady. Slamming the door again, Napoleon ordered them to proceed directly to Compiègne. That there might be dozens of servants and officials still standing under those marquees awaiting their arrival was irrelevant.

At 10:00 P.M. the courtyard of Compiègne was crisscrossed with flickering shadows from torches in the continuing rain. Carriage after carriage arrived, equerries and chamberlains barking out orders, as Napoleon and Marie-Louise were swept into the reception rooms of the palace, where for once Napoleon failed to rush over to the nearest fire.

Méneval, who now met her for the first time, recalled the impression she made:

> Marie-Louise's figure—she then in the full blush of youth—was perfect. The cut of her dress was longer than that worn [in France] at this time, which only added to her natural dignity and contrasted happily with the disgraceful shortening of the hem of our ladies. Her color was animated by the movement of the journey and by her timidity; her fine, abundant, and light chestnut-colored hair framed a full and fresh face, to which her eyes, filled with sweetness, gave a charming expression. Her lips, a bit thick, recalled those of the reigning family of Austria, just as the slight convexity of her nose distinguished those of the princes of the House of Bourbon. She gave off an aura of candor and innocence, and a plumpness that she was to lose after childbearing announced the state of her good health.[1]

A warm dinner had been awaiting them in the marquee along the road, and another here, but after making preliminary introductions, Napoleon whisked the startled empress to her bedroom where, he informed her, he would be joining her shortly. Although no French civil or religious ceremony had been carried out, the couple had been married by proxy in Austria, Napoleon represented by Marshal Berthier, prince of Neuchâtel (and more recently, of Wagram), and by the bride's uncle, none other than the same Archduke Karl he had fought at Wagram. Uncle (Cardinal) Fesch, now hastily summoned by Napoleon, assured his impatient nephew that legally they were married.

According to the long, elaborate schedule of events, Napoleon was to have slept at the Chancellery. "But he did nothing of the sort," his valet, Constant, recalled. An impatient Napoleon bade the dozens of courtiers and family members, including his latest mistress, the lovely Madame de Mathis, who had shared his bed the night before, a hasty goodnight and disappeared. Never in the long, varied, and sometimes unsavory past of the Bourbons had anyone so flouted the conventions, customs, and decorum of the court and country as this parvenu Bonaparte. The officials laughed, the ladies tittered, and Napoleon betook himself back to the apartments. "After a long conversation with the empress," Constant continued, "he returned to his chamber, undressed, perfumed himself with eau de cologne, and then, wearing only a dressing gown, he returned secretly to the empress."

Emerging late the next morning, beaming an unusually broad smile, Napoleon said to Méneval as he pulled his ear, "Mon cher, marry a German. They are the best women in the world: sweet, good, naive, and as fresh as roses."[2] His remarks were soon making the rounds, Murat and Caroline in particular laughing at this uninhibited Napoleon.

After creating three new marshals—Oudinot, Marmont, and MacDonald—and three new principalities (Wagram for Berthier, Essling for Masséna, and Eckmühl for Davout, not to mention six new duchies for Gaudin, Champagny, Fouché, Régnier, Maret, and Clarke), Napoleon also announced the creation of a new honorary order of the Trois Toisons (Three Fleeces). This new honor would be granted only to officers who had received at least six wounds, irrespective of rank, Lieutenant Colonel Marbot being personally named by Napoleon as its first member. It was probably meant to supersede the overly powerful and independent Legion of Honor, which had assumed too much influence as a new form of "landed aristocracy" to suit Napoleon.[3]

Following the Austrian emperor's ratification of the Treaty of Schönbrunn on October 14, 1809, Napoleon and his staff had returned to France via Munich, reaching Fontainebleau on the morning of October 26.

There he remained for the next few weeks. Determined to break the bonds of marriage with Josephine, he summoned her to the eighteen-hundred-room castle. But, as Méneval put it, "he could not bring himself to do it at first, and then one evening after one of the saddest and most silent of meals, he finally broke the ice," officially informing her of the necessity of a divorce. "One can readily understand the pain and despair Empress Josephine felt at this moment, when at long last the final glimmer of hope had been dashed forever." "I need a womb," as Napoleon summed it up with his characteristic Bonaparte bluntness. Josephine of course had known of this intention for years and had pretended to turn a deaf ear to it. But now, confronting the reality of the situation, she burst into tears:

> Napoleon, for his part, having relieved himself of this unbearable burden, remained profoundly moved by the anguish he was causing her, and from this moment hence he did not cease to surround her with the

most tender attentions and to heap consolation upon her in this hour of despair—care, attention, and consolation that Josephine at first heard with utter indifference.[4]

It had been as heartrending a decision regarding another human being as Napoleon had ever had to make, and it left him shaken. Josephine was the only woman he had ever been truly devoted to—after his own fashion of course. Moreover, and this was the real test, she was the only woman he felt completely responsible for—more than his mother, more than his sisters, more than any of his numerous mistresses, however much he might have found certain of them, especially Marie Walewska, warm, sincere, and attractive. Josephine had come first, and she would always remain first in his thoughts.

Everyone had commented on Josephine and, remarkably enough, everyone had agreed almost precisely on the traits and qualities they had found so appealing in her, which the young Baron de Méneval best summed up:

> Joséphine had an irresistible attraction; she was not outstandingly beautiful, but rather, "her grace surpassed any beauty," as our good La Fontaine [the celebrated French fabulist] put it. She had that light abandon, that supple and elegant movement, that casual grace of the creole. She was always even-tempered. She was good and sweet, affable and indulgent with everyone without exception. She was neither extremely intelligent nor well educated, her exquisite politeness, her great pleasantness in society and at court, and her innocent artifices were always at her command, allowing her to know precisely what to say and do at a given moment. The emperor had loved her very much and always remained fond of her, [feelings] fortified by habit and by her attractive qualities. One might have said she had been born for the role that the elevation of rank had imposed upon, and which rose with, her. . . . She had married his [Napoleon's] glory as well as his person.[5]

Napoleon, who had been so enraptured with Josephine in the early days of his marriage, carried away emotionally as he would never again be by any woman, had had all his hopes and faith in her or any other woman dashed forever on learning of her public affair with Captain Charles. Napoleon had ended that humiliation, while also forcing Josephine to break off all relations with the other feckless souls, the other light ladies of her acquaintance of her wild Chaumière days. Thereafter a much chastened and quickly aging Josephine dedicated herself to her husband and family but could produce no more children, which for Napoleon was an unbearable disappointment. His dozens of sexual flings over the ensuing years (usually arranged by Christophe Duroc, obliging courtiers, or occasionally the Murats, who wanted to destroy Josephine) had resulted in scene after scene of tears and hysterics, and indeed Josephine remained highly nervous and easily upset emotionally. But Napoleon loved her, and he always would, while laughing at her antics and even scorning her. After she insulted him before his entire army in Italy, and then in Egypt, Commander in Chief Bonaparte had lost all respect for marital fidelity. Thereafter anything would go, and did, beginning with his much flaunted affair with Pauline Fourès in Cairo. And now, nearly a dozen years later, they had come to the end. Once betrayed by someone, Napoleon never again trusted him or her. At the same time, had Josephine produced progeny for the mighty Bonaparte dynasty, he probably would not have divorced her, although even that is not certain, given the great plans he had in store for his career.

The decision made to dissolve his marriage, Napoleon summoned Josephine's son, Eugène, and his wife, Princess Augusta, from Milan to Fontainebleau, informing them of his intention to remarry and at the same time to remove him as Viceroy of Italy. He was going to reserve the Italian crown for his own offspring. His eldest son—Napoleon was absolutely confident he would have a son—was to be known as the king of Rome, before succeeding him as emperor. Nevertheless Napoleon remained genuinely fond of Eugène, and now instead offered him the crown of Sweden or that of some newly and specially created miniature kingdom somewhere north of Italy. Eugène proudly declined all offers, retaining only his title as Prince of Venice, although finally accepting the Grand Duchy of Frankfurt and a separate annual income from France of some 2 million francs. As for the unfortunate Hortense, she would be forced to serve in the court of her mother's replacement, in her capacity as the *"Princesse Protectrice des Maisons des Filles de la Légion d'Honneur."* It was painful and humiliating for her, but an insensitive Napoleon as usual chose to ignore it. "Come along now, *ma fille,* a little courage!" he said with a smile. "Oh! Sire, I have courage," she barely uttered before falling into his arms sobbing, her entire world shattered by these Bonapartes.[6]

Meanwhile a divorce was necessary. Napoleon arranged for an official annulment of the civil bands, and a special episcopal council selected by him agreed to an annulment of the religious vows, based on what Fesch pointed out as the technical illegalities of the ceremony he himself had performed at the Tuileries on December 1, 1804. In particular these included the absence of the local Paris priest and the required witnesses. More important, that ceremony had been carried out under duress, he now insisted. Without it the pope had threatened not to officiate on the morrow at the coronation ceremonies. Thus Cambacérès now informed Pius VII that both the civil and religious marriage had been dissolved because of irregularities. That Napoleon had been expelled from the Roman Catholic Church, excommunicated by this same Pius VII, somehow seemed irrelevant to French officialdom, which, in any event, took its orders from its paymaster, Napoleon Bonaparte. Due process had to be followed.

At 10:00 A.M. on Friday, December 15, 1809, the entire Bonaparte clan gathered in Napoleon's office, including Louis, Jérôme and Catherine, Pauline, Joachim and Caroline Murat, and of course Madame Mère—all openly gloating in their ultimate triumph in witnessing the downfall of "that Beauharnais woman." There they found Napoleon and Josephine, Hortense and Eugène, Duroc and Méneval. Napoleon read from a piece of paper in a loud, confident voice, but when he came to "She has graced my life for fifteen years," he was obviously upset. Josephine then read a text prepared for her: "We are each of us glorious in the sacrifice we are now making on behalf of the country—" Tears prevented her from continuing. The document of annulment was duly signed by the two parties, and properly witnessed. Napoleon embraced Josephine and led her to her apartments. His brothers and sisters barely concealed their delight as the couple left. Later Napoleon came to take Hortense to Josephine. "I found her completely overwhelmed . . . crushed,"[7] Hortense reported.

Napoleon returned to his office and "slumped down on the sofa, completely dejected," Méneval relates. "He remained there for some time, leaning forward, resting his head in his hands, and when he finally got up again, his face was cloaked in anguish." He then had Méneval follow him down the small private staircase to Josephine's apartments.

> Upon hearing us enter, she threw herself into his arms and burst into tears, he holding her protectively close to him, kissing her several times. But then, overwhelmed, she fainted. . . . The emperor still holding her, put her in my arms once she began to come to, instructing me not to leave her, as he hastily left via the main salons of the ground floor to the entrance, where his carriage was waiting.

Earlier, in another twist of the knife, he had ordered her son, Prince Eugène, to appear before the Senate to announce officially the dissolution of the imperial marriage. Despite the humiliation he felt, Eugène obeyed, as he always did. And now Napoleon settled back into the carriage that was taking him to Versailles and the Trianon Palace.[8] "The next morning," Hortense continued, "I helped my mother into her carriage. . . . Our journey to la Malmaison was sad and silent." Josephine never returned to Fontainebleau.

After issuing a new decree on January 10, 1810, effectively removing all his brothers and sisters from the line of succession to his expanding imperial domains in favor of the son he expected to have, on January 28 Napoleon had convoked what proved to be a boisterous privy council meeting, including his ministers and high state dignitaries, as well as some male members of the family, including King Louis, Murat, and Uncle Fesch (now archbishop of Paris, following the demise of Cardinal Belloy). Their task, in Fouché's words, was "to discuss, decide, and declare" the name of Josephine's successor. Emotional personal interests were to have nothing to do with it. Napoleon had had quite enough of that sort of thing. It must be a hard-boiled, well-calculated decision. The three bridal candidates—the daughter of the king of Saxony, the younger sister of Czar Alexander, and the daughter of Austria's Emperor Franz—were discussed in considerable detail by these gentlemen, seated before him in their state uniforms of blue velour, encrusted in silver and gold according to their rank. To Napoleon's surprise Louis opted strongly for the princess of the House of Saxony, while Murat, in the guise of a scion of the Revolution, protested his outrage at the very idea of marital ties with Austria: "always so odious to the nation."[9] Their differences resolved by February 2, 1810, their final decision was announced in favor of the eighteen-year-old Austrian archduchess and princess royal of Hungary and Bohemia, Marie-Louise.

For Josephine, shortly to become France's first ex-empress, a new life had to be planned, and Napoleon was not ungenerous. In addition to Malmaison, he gave her the historic, rambling Château de Navarre in Normandy—a good distance from the court—then created it a duchy. A steady stream of correspondence flowed between Napoleon and Josephine, which gradually dwindled over the next few weeks, Napoleon all the while protesting his deep fondness for her and his concern for her well-being, partially ensuring this with the promise of an annual income of five million francs. It helped soften the blow.

Just as Napoleon had ordered Prince Eugène to announce the divorce to the Senate, he was now given the further painful task of making what Fouché described as "the diplomatic overture to Prince von Schwarzenberg," requesting the hand of Marie-Louise, which was accepted forthwith.[10] One of the first persons to be notified of this decision was Czar

Alexander, who had kept Napoleon dangling for two and a half months without a final reply to Napoleon's earlier proposal of marriage to the czar's sister. It was now too late; Alexander and Russia were out of the picture. Thereafter Russia would play only a secondary role at best, Austria now taking precedence, with all that that implied. The Archduchess Marie-Louise had a wide network of aristocratic relations through both her father, Franz (or to be more precise, Franz II, emperor of Austria until 1805, thereafter reduced by Napoleon to the lesser status of Franz I); and her mother, the former Princess Maria-Theresa, daughter of Ferdinand IV, king of the Two Sicilies.

Marie-Louise had been raised in utter isolation from popular, and even from court, life, yet educated to speak many languages, including French, Italian, Spanish, English—even Latin—in order to render her more marriageable. In the words of Méneval: "She regarded herself almost as a victim to be devoured by the Minotaur [Napoleon]," a man who for the past dozen years she had been taught to hate as the devil incarnate. But "raised in the family custom of passive obedience, Marie-Louise had to resign herself to whatever fate awaited her."[11]

A personal exchange of correspondence passed between the conquering Minotaur and his defeated future father-in-law, Franz I of Austria. The mere writing of the critical letter, however, proved most embarrassing for Napoleon, almost more of a trial than all his previous battles with the Austrians. After writing and rewriting this document several times, even the devoted Méneval was forced to admit that it was "just barely legible," and then only after "he had me correct some of the letters, without making this appear too noticeable. . . . I did my best as his school prefect, and then had that letter, along with marriage documents, dispatched by courier to 'Sa Majesté monsieur mon frère l'empéreur d'Autriche.'"[12]

Count de Montesquiou was dispatched to Vienna bearing a portrait of the French emperor, and Berthier followed as ambassador extraordinary to the Schönbrunn, escorted by Prince Paul Esterhazy, passing the ancient walls of the city that were being razed to the ground on Napoleon's imperious orders. On March 8, Emperor Franz's brother and Napoleon's stalwart foe at Wagram, Archduke Karl, under duress, signed the necessary papers on behalf of his niece, and the next day she solemnly renounced all claims to the succession of the imperial throne and swore her new allegiance to France. That same evening the official marriage contract was signed at the Schönbrunn Palace, and Berthier was handed a strongbox containing the bride's dowry—the equivalent of five hundred thousand francs in stacks of gold ducats. Content with the proceedings, the sycophantic Berthier reported back to Napoleon that "all is truly worthy of the spouse of the greatest man in the world."[13] Two days later the religious ceremony was performed in the Church of the Augustins, followed by a gala state banquet, despite noisy public demonstrations in the streets of the Old City against this heinous marriage to the ravager of their country, the excommunicated Napoleon. For, as Méneval acknowledged, "the Peace of Vienna and even the marriage were far from having established good relations between Paris and Vienna. Austria was humiliated but not beaten. She bowed her head for the moment, bitterly biding her time until she could avenge herself."

Unlike the unchallenged one-man rule in France, some three hundred ancient aristocratic families had considerable influence in the affairs of the Austrian Empire. "Politics made this marriage," a prophetic Schwarzenberg warned, and "politics can unmake it later," although he himself had been given the unenviable task of replacing Metternich as ambassador to Paris, to keep an avuncular eye on the Austrian war bride.[14] Napoleon dismissed these unsettling reports, just as he had lightly dismissed the assassination attempt against him by a knife-wielding Thuringian university student with the unfortunate name of Stabb just prior to his departure from Vienna. Time would heal all wounds, Napoleon insisted optimistically, and even if it did not, what could the Austrians possibly do now?

And thus it was that despite vociferous public protests against the French in Vienna and the festering anger of the three hundred ruling families, the archduchess, followed by nearly three dozen carriages, under strong military escort, made her way to Strasbourg, where she was greeted by Queen Caroline of Naples. Instead of putting the young lady at her ease, however, Caroline—whom Talleyrand pithily described as having "the head of a Machiavelli and the body of a pretty woman"—immediately demanded that the bride's entire retinue, including ladies-in-waiting and even her closest confidante, be sent back across the Rhine to Vienna. Then, for good measure, the sadistic Caroline, with the usual Bonaparte twist of the knife, demanded that Marie-Louise send back her little dog as well. (As Napoleon himself acknowledged, "Of my entire family, it's Caroline who most resembles me.")[15] Clearly Marie-Louise was now on foreign territory, in the hands of that ruthless Corsican ogre. This disheartening impression was only partially offset by a series of letters and bouquets of flowers she received from Napoleon en route between Strasbourg and Soissons. Her father's instructions had been most explicit: to obey her husband's every wish. Literally entirely on her own now, she was another pawn in the great game of survival.

*   *   *

Everyone agreed that Bonaparte's actions over the ensuing weeks were bewildering. Acting more like a very young bridegroom just beginning life than a forty-year-old rogue with at least two bastards tucked away well out of sight, Bonaparte threw himself into feverish activity in preparation for this marriage, which would cement the Bonapartes of Ajaccio with the Habsburgs of Vienna. With Josephine now out of the way, he gave orders for any trace of her to be removed, her state quarters converted into "virginal white apartments," as the caustic Victorine de Chastenay called them, while a special new suite of apartments was also prepared for the son he was positive he would have by this daughter of the remarkably fertile Habsburgs. Special outfits and uniforms, including miniature—but real—pistols, swords, and cannon, were ordered: No boy should be without them. Napoleon was humming again, for the first time in years, as usual out of tune. He was rushing about, harrying everyone: Everything had to be perfect. Having had his bride-to-be's measurements sent him, along with a portrait of the rosy-cheeked, slightly plump girl, he ordered an entirely new wardrobe for her, much of it in white silk, including dresses, formal gowns, undergarments, hosiery, shoes, hats—Josephine's personal dressmaker receiving the brunt of the order. And then came the jewelry, seemingly without limit or budget. Napoleon personally inspected every item, one by one, as it arrived. There must be no imperfection, no blemish. Méneval and Duroc were quite bewildered by this intense, frenzied concentration, to the exclusion of everything else. When all seemed in readiness in the Tuileries, he rushed off with dozens of domestics and staff to Compiègne, again feverishly inspecting all preparations, not to mention his own wardrobe.

Meanwhile foreign affairs, state finances, France's internal problems—including vast agricultural shortfalls and a declining economy—even the military and the Spanish situation, received at most but cursory attention. Never before had Bonaparte ignored the military, especially when in "midcampaign," as France still was in the Iberian Peninsula, with well over two hundred thousand men fighting there and the position steadily deteriorating. Napoleon lost all interest it.

If he was agitated, irritable, never satisfied with the smallest detail, despite the occasional smile and badly hummed tune, it was because this was a period of great crisis in his life. His second Danube campaign had deeply shaken him—all those military checks and setbacks, ending with the fiasco at Ratisbon and then the disaster at Aspern-Essling. Of course there was ultimately the victory of Wagram, but how narrowly won, and at what a price! Never before had he had to concentrate, tax every fiber of his ability and energy to cope with one close shave after another on the battlefield, and after making unheard-of military preparations with a superior field force. At forty Napoleon found himself getting too old for active campaigning, now a twenty-four-year veteran with so many battles behind him that he could not count or even remember them all. Was he finished? Emotionally he could not afford another Wagram campaign. He was, like everyone else now, patently war-weary, but was he also slipping, losing that Bonaparte touch, his special genius on the field of battle? Nevertheless, superstitious, he believed in his star. All had to be swept away in his path. He was untouchable. He could walk across dozens of major deadly battlefields, with hundreds of thousands falling on every side, and go untouched—or could he?

Something had clearly happened during this last military campaign. He found himself without real allies; even Czar Alexander had distanced himself from him. The invincible Lannes, whom he loved after his own fashion, perhaps more than any of his own brothers, was gone, with no one to replace him. All those years together, all those dangers shared. Masséna had held, thank God, and along with the stout-hearted Davout, Oudinot, and MacDonald, helped save the day that July before Wagram. And there was the accident at Ratisbon, when he, Napoleon himself, had nearly had his foot shot away. This had never happened before. There were portents in the air. And now not only the faithful Lannes, whom he had treated so shabbily years before by refusing to give him the money he had promised to cover the costs of his new Paris mansion, was gone, but so was his beloved Josephine, the only woman in the world he truly loved, if in his own brutal, callous manner. She who had brought him his good fortune, who had helped start him on his way with those important introductions, who had shared in his great triumphs as a general in the field, as life consul, and then as emperor of the French, was offstage, never again to participate in his life or career. And then he had dismissed his faithful stepson, Eugène, from his position as viceroy of Italy. This same Eugène who had just marched at the head of his army to stand by him on the bloody fields of battle round Wagram, summarily dismissed! Despite his usual outward arrogance, Napoleon was feeling old, tired, jaded, uncertain of himself and his future. He who had promised to return to Spain within a month was instead counting his new wife's underwear and shoes, directing painters, harrying his officials to have all in order for the young bride who was to replace the discarded Josephine, while his troops were dying by the thousands.

Behind it all loomed the problem of Spain. This full-scale war continued to tax heavily the French national budget and economy, despite the enforced annual "war contributions" of hundreds of millions of francs extorted from Napoleon's dozens of "allies," allies whom he barely kept in check with his armies of occupation. Remove one major army and one commander, the vigilant, tough, and demanding Marshal Davout, and Napoleon knew in his heart that the whole of Europe would come tumbling down over his head as easily as any house of cards. As for Spain, could it be conquered? If so, could he admit to the world that Bonaparte had made a horrendous miscalculation, forcing him to withdraw all his forces? Those few associates courageous enough to point out the Spanish ulcer, and the necessity to evacuate the peninsula, were quickly put in their place. Napoleon, who had never liked gratuitous advice, was even less open to it now and continued to brook no contrary view. After the wedding ceremonies he was ordering a most reluctant Masséna—that wily old Niçois looter who had salted away literally tens of millions and who now strongly hinted that he wished to retire to enjoy his last few active years—back to Spain. Another war-weary veteran tired of this state of perpetual warfare would soon be returning to the Iberian war zone.

Iberia was in fact the true test for Napoleon, the true indicator that something was gravely wrong in his life, in his seemingly resplendent career. With more unchallenged power at his personal command than either the king of England or the Austrian emperor, Napoleon was going downhill rapidly. For the first time in his career, he refused to rejoin a major, deadly military campaign, for in his heart of hearts he probably realized he could not win, at least not for many years, in a land where half a dozen major battles might be fought in half a dozen distant places, seconded by Spaniards and Portuguese who were determined to fight to the last man and in the process carry out such barbarous atrocities as to frighten even him. The captured General Foy had been paraded stark naked through city streets. There were reports of captured French officers having their eyes and tongues cut out, or being castrated and left just barely alive, for all to see, insult, jab, and jeer at, while others had fingers, hands, arms, and legs chopped off. Soldiers and female collaborators were tortured and disemboweled. The women, reported eyewitness Capt. Charles François, were eviscerated from the navel to the vagina and their breasts hacked off. But it was the large numbers of men who suffered most frequently over the years, the Spaniards even placing live officers between two boards and sawing them in two. Others were buried alive up to their shoulders and left to die, some were hung upside down over fires, their heads roasted over the flames, and in one case at least Thiébault tells of a general officer captured by the Spaniards and boiled alive in a huge caldron of water, like a human lobster. It was a nightmare. What had Napoleon done? What had he gotten himself into?[16]

So Bonaparte escaped into the unreal world of wedding preparations, not stopping for a moment, faster and faster, until all could be forgotten. He was a genius, everyone said so. If he worked harder than ever, took a new wife, begot many sons, he could save his mighty empire, as mighty as any seen since the fall of Rome, even surpassing that of Charlemagne. To be sure Louis, Jérôme, and Joseph were letting him down. But he needed no man's help. He could do the work of all of them. What is more he could even expand his frontiers. This marriage with Marie-Louise marked the rebirth of Napoleon, the rejuvenation of a prematurely aging man, while serving as a colorful illusion of present and future stability.

They had come for three days from Compiègne to St.-Cloud, with all thirty-two cardinals attending (including the large delegation from Rome), where on April 1 the French civil ceremony was carried out, despite the continuing heavy rain. The following day "the solemn entry into Paris made by the emperor and empress was magnificent." A procession of some three dozen elegant carriages passed beneath the temporary canvas facade of the Arc de Triomphe, which although begun four years earlier had scarcely advanced. Clouds had finally given way to radiant sunshine, bathing the long procession of polished carriages and their large, handsome military escort as they made their way up the still largely uninhabited Champs-Elysées, across the spacious former Place de Louis XV and through the tree-covered gardens to the Tuileries. "It could not have been more touching or magnificent," commented the scathing Fouché, adding, "What a beautiful day. What light-heartedness so prodigiously affirmed!"[17] Hundreds of minor prisoners were released throughout the land, and some six thousand soldiers would receive special pensions and dowries for their daughters. Thousands of small gold and silver medallions bearing the likeness of Napoleon and Marie-Louise were to be distributed among the populace, as a government-organized food lottery was preparing to distribute thousands of chickens, geese, and legs of lamb, all to be washed down by large vats of wine imported into the center of the city. Throughout the capital on his wedding day every bell and church belfry would ring out, and cannon at the Invalides would thunder. Napoleon would show them all; he would prevail and continue to recast the whole of French and European life in his own image.

Following a brief respite, the unrelenting schedule resumed, as a pro-

cession on foot slowly formed in the Galérie de Diane of the Louvre and
proceeded to the large Salon d'Apollon, where a temporary chapel had
been installed for the occasion, the bride's long train borne by Queen
Julie Bonaparte of Spain, Queen Hortense of Holland, Queen Catherine
of Westphalia, and Princesses Elisa and Pauline—Queen Caroline Murat
had adamantly refused to participate—and surrounded by some four hundred select guests. Although Napoleon's uncle Cardinal Fesch naturally
performed this religious ceremony, as he had that of Napoleon and
Josephine six years earlier, only eleven of the thirty-two cardinals summoned agreed to appear, the other places reserved for them remaining
conspicuously empty, although these same gentlemen had been seen
parading through the Tuileries earlier in their bright red costumes. (As
Napoleon looked at the two empty rows he became infuriated. Following
the marriage ceremony he ordered the imprisonment of most of them and
had their estates seized. When they were later released, Napoleon was to
forbid them from wearing red; hence thereafter they became popularly
known as the Black Cardinals.[18])

Napoleon was soon distracted by the religious ceremony and subsequent celebrations. He and his bride then appeared on the balcony of the
Pavillion de l'Horloge, as the Imperial Guard, thousands strong, marched
by in the courtyard in all their shining splendor.

Inside, the reception rooms were filled with royalty, though for the
most part self-made Bonaparte royalty. All of them partook of the imperial
banquet in the theater of the Tuileries, at 6:00 P.M., followed by a concert in
the towering Salle des Maréchaux as well as a fireworks display and the illumination of the principal buildings of the capital, reflected in the waters of
the Seine.

Although Napoleon had hoped that his two wives, past and present,
would meet, Marie-Louise proved jealous and defiant, demanding the ban-
ishment of Josephine and the confiscation of Malmaison. Despite assurances
that Malmaison would remain hers, Josephine wrote back in panic: "Bonaparte! You promised that you would never abandon me! I need your
advice. You are the only friend I have left. . . . I have been banished completely from Your Majesty's memory." He stoically replied:

> You will need courage to maintain yourself and to find happiness, and
> in particular to maintain your good health, which is so precious to me.
> If you are attached to my well-being and love me, you must get a good
> grip on yourself. You can never doubt my friendship for you, and
> indeed, must know very little about my real feelings toward you if you

ever thought I could possibly be happy knowing you are not. Adieu, mon amie, good night.[19]

Although he did come to see her a few times before the marriage, afterward his jealous young new wife kept a firm grip on the mighty Bonaparte, forbidding any contact. After temporary moves to both Malmaison and the Château de Navarre, Josephine decided that a year's travel away from Paris was the best answer for getting over this difficult period, and set out for Aix, Savoy, and Switzerland. Hereafter Josephine would never again appear at Court.

A few days after the marriage ceremonies, they had returned to the Palace of Compiègne, where one evening in one of the long series of reception rooms, the Salon de Jeu, Empress Marie-Louise was seated at a table playing whist while all about her a veritable bevy of royalty mingled with German and Russian princes, French marshals, and high military brass of Europe, and the principal diplomats of the day. Everyone wanted to be seen talking with the great man himself, of course, and he insisted on walking slowly from table to table, exchanging a few bland words or nodding in acknowledgment, and addressing a few gallant, and for once startlingly polite, words to the ladies. His bride was already having a civilizing influence on him. How far he had come from those days in the early 1790s when, as a nearly starving junior officer, he had importuned his former classmate Bourrienne and his wife for a hot meal.

"Having reached the end of the game room, and finding himself before the large open connecting doors, he entered the next room, and immediately almost everyone got up ... and formed a long procession behind him," General Thiébault recorded. "Strolling slowly he reached the middle of the salon, then stopped, crossed his arms across his chest, stared at the floor six feet before him, and did not budge." The kings, queens, princes and princesses, dukes and duchesses, and the other eminent personnages following him also stopped suddenly. Those closest to Napoleon drew back and hesitantly formed an immense circle about the emperor, leaving him immobile in the center, the vast room with its hundreds of candles and sparkling crystal chandeliers. "At first, embarrassed, everyone even avoided looking at one another," Thiébault continued.

Then, curious, little by little they raised their eyes and looked about them. Several moments later, however, their expressions changed to puzzlement, seeming to ask what sort of game Napoleon was now up to. But no one spoke a word as the moments continued to tick away, the French in particular quite ill at ease before so many distinguished foreigners. In fact this abrupt, unexplained act by Napoleon, which seemed as bizarre as it was out of place, made me at first think that he had suddenly remembered something of importance and had stopped to think about it. And yet all the while he did not even bat an eye, and after five, six, seven, eight minutes had passed, no one could make any sense whatsoever of his action. But he remained the master, apparently pleased with this singular spectacle he was presenting, and under the circumstances it seemed best to do nothing at all.

After a quarter of an hour of this, the fifty-two-year-old Marshal Masséna, now known as the duke of Rivoli, had had enough and stepped out of the circle, walking slowly over to Napoleon. "No one else dared move, or even consider[ed] doing so, as they watched spellbound." Not a breath could be heard in the vast salon lined with liveried footmen in powdered wigs, as Masséna addressed a few words very quietly to him. "Without lifting his eyes, or making any movement whatsoever, the Emperor suddenly bellowed at him in a thunderous challenge. 'Why are you pestering me!' . . . he little caring how he was mortifying this great military leader by this cruel game of his." His face turning scarlet, the dapper Masséna in his magnificent uniform bedecked with prestigious decorations returned to his former place in the circle as if nothing had transpired. "I had never been so ashamed," Thiébault acknowledged. "Never before had Napoleon appeared so arrogant and impudent by so harshly addressing one of our oldest and most illustrious warriors. His action was as gratuitous as it was cruel, and at once insulting to France itself before all those foreign dignitaries."

Napoleon remained standing there for another minute or two in "his statuary scene," and then finally, ever so slowly, raised his head "as if coming out of a dream," uncrossed his arms, looked about the circle of dozens of perplexed courtiers surrounding him, and without a word or change of expression turned back in the direction of the Salon de Jeu. As he reentered the room, on a sign from him, Empress Marie-Louise, obviously confused, put down her cards and rose. Passing before her, Napoleon said "in a dry voice, 'Let us go, Madame,'" and continued to walk on, Marie-Louise following three paces behind him, the double doors at the end of the long room suddenly closing behind them as they disappeared from sight.

"It was not yet nine-thirty in the evening, but Napoleon had been coughing a great deal and seemed tired. Such is the scene I cannot yet get out of my head." Thiébault added, "I am still trying to find some sort of explanation for it."[20] The next day Thiébault, against his will, was ordered back to Burgos and the terrible war in Spain, a war to which, after nearly two years of grim fighting, no end appeared in sight.

Though no one had understood what Thiébault called "the bizarre scene" that April day at Compiègne, they all instinctively suppressed it from their memoirs. It was perhaps the only time during his career that Napoleon lapsed into an epileptic state in public, in this case a rare epileptic trance of which he later remembered nothing. His long history of epileptic seizures generally followed a pattern, usually occurring in the evening or late at night, after weeks of hard and tense work. Ever since his return from Vienna the previous autumn, the long, detailed marriage negotiations and subsequent preparations, combined with a series of other problems, including his family, had preoccupied him to the exclusion of all else and induced the inevitable result.

One of the deeper, compounding causes triggering this extraordinary epileptic trance no doubt stemmed from a letter of congratulations on his marriage from brother Lucien, still confined on his estate of Canino in Italy. Lucien had closed, however, by affirming that he would never abandon his devoted second wife, Alexandrine.

First Louis, then Jérôme, then all that bother with Joseph's growing problems in Madrid. This was simply too much, and Napoleon now had a message dispatched to yet another recalcitrant Bonaparte. Things had in fact changed very much since Lucien's self-imposed exile from France back in the spring of 1804. Then the entire clan had taken Lucien's side when he refused to rid himself of his second wife, the former Madame Jouberthon. Madame Mère had even preferred to remain in Italy with Lucien rather than attend Napoleon's imperial coronation. By the spring of 1810, however, with the Bonapartes now linked in marriage with the Habsburgs, opinion had veered 180 degrees, with even his mother and brother Joseph, resigned to the inevitable, advising Lucien to give in and be done with it. Napoleon—who had initially demanded the annulment of Lucien's marriage and had insisted on declaring all his offspring by Alexandrine as bastards—had generously agreed to demand only that Lucien divorce his wife, not that his children be treated as bastards. "Your position, that of your family, mine, that of us all, depends upon you," Letizia Buonaparte pleaded with Lucien in the stilted language of a letter clearly dictated by Napoleon: "It is no longer simply a question of logic, my dear son. Nothing you can tell me will make me change my mind now. . . . This is the last time I shall ask you. There is only one thing that would render my happiness complete, and that is seeing your differences with the Emperor resolved."[21]

Lucien was staggered by this betrayal by his own mother, demanding that he abandon his wife and take their children from her. The pressure Napoleon had put on him since 1804 was enormous. Despite Lucien's by-now-vast independent wealth, and his new title as a Roman prince, his lot was not enviable, with France's complete occupation of the Papal States now placing all of his numerous estates in French territory. He was a virtual prisoner on his own land, not permitted to leave it even to visit the nearest city or another one of his properties without permission from the French military governor of that region.

Thus it was at the beginning of April that Lucien had written brother Napoleon one last time. Even Alexandrine, desperately threatened, pleaded with her brother-in-law. "Sire, I throw myself at your feet. It is as impossible for me to separate myself from Lucien, if only secretly, as it is for him to leave me publicly. We belong to each other till death do us part. . . . Sire, we ask only that you permit us to live peacefully together in some quiet corner of your Empire."[22] But Napoleon was unrelenting in his determination to rid Lucien of his wife. "I don't want any part of her," he said, quickly explaining, "I base this decision solely on political reasons." He then dispatched an official to Lucien to argue with him one final time, but Lucien remained intransigent. "I cannot, without dishonoring myself, divorce a woman who has given me four children. . . . I shall instead go to America, if forced to do so." But, he added, he would prefer to remain in Europe with Napoleon. "In the Imperial administration I could perhaps usefully serve my brother. Why can I not be allowed to prove my devotion to him by holding a nonhereditary post, where the position of my wife and children would not matter?" Finally repeating, "In the event it proves utterly impossible to work with the Emperor under these circumstances, then leaving for America would be the least painful alternative after all."[23]

"I know France," Napoleon reflected. "I know better than anyone else what she wants. All men of common sense would be indignant to see my throne associated with the wife of a bankrupt," he said, referring to Alexandrine's first husband, who had fled the country because of debts. (He apparently forgot that the entire Bonaparte clan had been forced to leave Corsica, bankrupt, years earlier.)

> So be it! Let him live and die as he pleases. I know what I must do, what politics dictates. Lucien implores my clemency. That clemency would include my recognition of his children, provided that he rids himself of that wife of a bankrupt. . . . What he has proposed, however, is quite absurd. Lucien can assume a proper role in my empire only by assum-

ing the role of a dynastic prince, nothing less, and his children can serve me properly only as princes of my house. Lucien cannot accept that. All right! It is all over! I charge you with instructing my family never again to speak to me about this matter.[24]

When in June Lucien received this final refusal to recognize his wife and marriage, he made secret arrangements to start selling his estates, crating hundreds of pictures and pieces of statuary, not to mention a fortune in jewels, dispatching them in the night to the port of Civitavecchia, near Rome, where he hired a small American ship out of Salem, Massachusetts. He was indeed resolved to go to the United States, but to leave Italy he needed "passports" from the French, the king of Sardinia, and the British, who controlled Italian waters, Sicily, Malta, and Gibraltar. On August 7 Lucien and Alexandrine were given French passports, and at 4:00 P.M. the couple and their six children set sail, still hoping for British authorization when they reached Cagliari in Sardinia. By August 22, still without a decision by the British, and with the family living in tight quarters aboard the small American vessel, they sailed without authorization, only to be seized immediately by the Royal Navy and taken to Malta, prisoners of the British and of the governor, Gen. Sir Henry Oakes. Through the intervention of the British Ambassador accredited to Constantinople, who happened to be in Italian waters at this time, Lucien applied directly to the British Foreign Secretary, the Marquis of Wellesley (General Sir Arthur Wellesley's brother) for permission to sail.

At long last a letter from Richard, Lord Wellesley, dated October 15, reached Malta. "His Majesty has commanded me to express to you that in the circumstances in which you find yourselves placed, he cannot permit you to go to America or to remain on the island of Malta. His Majesty is disposed, however, to permit you and your family to install yourselves in England." Transferring to a British frigate, Lucien and his family set sail from Valletta on November 20, 1810, reaching Plymouth on December 12.

Much to Lucien's astonishment, given his brother's fulminating anti-British propaganda, they were kindly received by "the perfidious English." Not only was he not seized and murdered by the crowds, but instead was received by "applause and cheers," as he and his family made their way to Ludlow.[25] Several months later he acquired the rambling estate of Thorngrove and its rolling acres, where his famous house parties, not to mention his fabulous art collection (mostly looted), became the talk of Worcestershire. And as another surprise, although he was kept under "house arrest" and not permitted to leave the estate without government permission, none of his hundreds of crates and trunks had been seized, not a single Spanish diamond or Austrian gold ducat impounded by the British. After years of harassment by Napoleon and the French military authorities, Lucien, Alexandrine, and their family at last found peace.

"Betrayal! Betrayal! It's sheer betrayal!" Napoleon had thundered at Josephine on learning of Lucien's flight from France back in 1804. Now the curses were multiplied, resulting in Napoleon striking Lucien's name from the rosters of the French Senate and the Legion of Honor (and ending the handsome lifetime salaries attached to both). As far as Napoleon was concerned, brother Lucien had betrayed him by seeking freedom and shelter from his own continuous persecution, with his greatest foes, the dastardly English, thereby rendering Napoleon Bonaparte the laughingstock of the whole of Europe . . . and there was absolutely nothing he could do about it. "My family," Napoleon was to write years later, "did much more harm to me than the good I did for them."[26] But as he had once commented: "A prince who is considered . . . a kind man is a king who is doomed!" Napoleon would never have to worry about that particular accusation. Nor was this year, 1810, to spare him further ill tidings. Napoleon's great Empire, even on attaining its zenith with the Habsburg marriage, was already well on the wane.

CHAPTER 32

Chimes and Alarm Bells

Now begins the finest period of my reign.

N apoleon was determined to break England. If he could not do so on the battlefield, for England never fielded large armies on the Continent, relying instead on a strong navy, then he would follow up the trade war begun during the Revolution.

In 1798 the Directory had ordered the seizure of all neutral vessels that had called on British ports. The British retaliated by taking French colonies and trade through them. Great Britain, as a traditional exporter, depended heavily on colonial products, textiles, and iron products destined for the Continent, while also reliant on corn and timber imports. By 1800 English exports had more than doubled, while imports had risen by 64 percent. In 1803 Napoleon had forbidden trade in British products. After the French navy and merchant marine were irreparably crippled by the decisive naval defeat at Trafalgar in October 1805, Napoleon decided to strike another blow, and in November 1806 issued his Berlin Decree, placing Great Britain under a French blockade. This unique blockade, however, would be enforced by land, not by sea: No ship thereafter was allowed to come directly from British ports or colonies to France or French-controlled ports. England had countered French restrictions by shipping more of its goods under neutral flags, and by 1807, 44 percent of British commerce was thus conveyed. Trade was carefully controlled in London by the selling of export-import licenses. Napoleon tightened the noose on British commerce in November 1807 with his Milan Decree, which required the automatic confiscation of all shipping and goods that had touched English ports. The United States, as a neutral, trading with both France and England, was caught in the middle, attempting to solve the conundrum in 1807 by placing an embargo on trade with both countries.

Despite evasive action by Britain, Napoleon's measures were daily taking a stronger bite. The surest way was through conquest, seizing or controlling one continental power after another and hence those additional ports and markets. He tightened his control of France, the Low Countries, Italy, and central Europe. By 1808 British exports, which two years earlier had reached £40.8 million, dropped to £35.1 million. Violent industrial strikes and shortages of products hurt England, and thus for instance the raw cotton imports reaching Liverpool dropped from 143,000 sacks in 1807 to a mere 23,000 in 1818. Corn imports fell, as did timber, and although British exports to South America rose sharply between 1805 and 1808, from £8 million to £20 million, this often involved onetime sales and irregular payment. On the other hand, British exports to the Mediterranean increased fourfold between 1805 and 1811, particularly in Turkey and Persia. But 1808 had been a very bad year, things only gradually recuperating thereafter. Meanwhile the United Kingdom continued to use neutral shipping when possible, thereby providing sugar, coffee, cotton, and soda for Holland, Frankfurt, and Leipzig. A struggling France tried to compensate for its own loss by introducing grape sugar and linen in place of real sugar and cotton, and by the mandatory planting of one hundred thousand hectares of sugar beets, but Paris failed to close Frankfurt and Leipzig to English products and goods.

Nonetheless 1808 had indeed frightened the British and the French both, as major commercial and banking houses lapsed into bankruptcy. The trade war was double-edged, almost equally destructive to both nations. If Russia was a major partner of Napoleon's Continental System, it also served as an important sieve in Napoleon's system, as Riga and other Baltic ports continued to accept British goods. For all that, France's great commercial war continued greatly to harm the Russian economy.

The year 1811 marked another new low for the British, their exports to the Continent dropping by 80 percent from the previous year, exports to the United States and South America falling by a similar figure. British exports, which had finally risen to £60 million in 1810, had plummeted yet again. Great was the anxiety of the City, and unchecked inflation and poor harvests in 1809 and 1810, aggravated by the flow of English gold to pay its continental allies, only compounded the matter. The coalition against France depended on just such flows of English gold. Bankruptcies swept England again in 1810 and in 1811, resulting in large-scale unemployment or at best reduced three-day workweeks. Many desperate firms and traders blamed not Napoleon but the British government, and on May 11, 1812, a bankrupt businessman by the name of Bellingham walked into the lobby of the House of Commons and shot Prime Minister Spencer Percival. Napoleon rejoiced when he heard the news.

Meanwhile a bull-headed Bonaparte, the genius behind this massive economic chaos afflicting Europe, continued to tighten the screws whenever and wherever possible, even when it meant alienating his own allies. In 1810 he officially annexed Holland; the Valais Republic of Switzerland; the Hanseatic cities of Hamburg, Lübeck, Bremen; and by January 1811 the Duchy of Oldenburg. That this gravely aggravated Napoleon's relations with the various Germanic states, including those within the Confederation of the Rhine, and Russia in particular, seemed to him quite irrelevant: Napoleon never learned from past mistakes. If his "allies" misbehaved, he could send in Davout's troops to bully and even occupy them, as indeed he had already done in the case of Hamburg. No one envied that city's fate and the subsequent "war contributions." But that Napoleon chose to do this at a time when events—although stabilizing briefly in 1810—grew more alarming than ever, proved as illogical as it did counterproductive.

England's trade by 1812 was finally improving again, reaching an export figure of £50 million pounds, while France's much-vaunted Continental System could not even begin to equal that. The French economy was sinking desperately, irretrievably. But Napoleon remained intent on destroying the impudent British, regardless of the cost, regardless of the harm to the French and continental economies, and regardless of the destructive cost to his tenuous relations with his political allies and even to his own position.[1]

From the moment that he seized power at gunpoint in November 1799, apart from one year, 1802–3, Napoleon had been in a state of perpetual war, and at one time or other with just about every country and principality in western and central Europe. Waging war being an expensive proposition, it required money and lots of it. Austro-Italian war booty helped bridge the financial gap during the Consulate, but on February 25, 1804, a desperate Napoleon, then in the throes of his invasion preparations for England, introduced what he called "the combined duties." These began with a tax on drinks, then another on salt (which had been abolished during the Revolution), and an increase on tobacco (which finally became a government monopoly). Local taxes also increased now, to help pay for the prefects, and local administration and maintenance, as well as the growing network of local canals, exclusive of normal annual contributions to the national budget. In addition local toll roads, abolished during the Revolution, were reintroduced, and in some cases even pressed-labor gangs (also abolished during the Revolution). Napoleon showed very little interest either in the small taxpayer or the plight of the provinces, and as of 1807 only 37 million francs were set aside by the national treasury for the totality of French public works and the maintainenance or building of churches, schools, and roads. Where did the money go? War. More than half of French annual revenue went to the vast war machine, despite Napoleon's huge "war contributions" from conquered "allied states." Everyone paid, or else.

If the French people had revolted in 1789 in large part because of heavy taxes, King Louis XVI's last budget of a mere 298 million francs looked positively pale in comparison with Napoleon's, which by 1804 had leaped to 588,066,203 francs and finally to 876,266,180 francs by 1812. Napoleon had trebled the French national budget and taxes.[2]

He could argue that perhaps a quarter of the French national budget was paid by such foreign "contributions," but that still left three-quarters of the budget, and it was the small French taxpayer who carried this growing deficit.

Part of the burden paid by the countries of occupied Europe went into the Army Fund, set up on October 28, 1805, milching 743 million francs just from Austria and Prussia between 1805 and 1810.[3] Spain was in theory to contribute another 350 million francs, but in reality it was many times that, as will shortly be seen. But the gap grew. France continued to maintain various state monopolies, including all armaments, the manufacture of gunpowder, the minting of currency, and of course the sales of salt and tobacco, and the control of the nation's mines and forests. Napoleon did a little to encourage commerce and industry, offering national competitions to increase production, for example the development of a small steam engine and a flax-spinning loom, while creating new schools for mining and dyeing, but all with one aim, increasing taxable income. He encouraged silk production, cotton spinning, metallurgy, tools, cutlery, sheet iron, tin, brass, pins and needles—all to replace products cut off by the blockade of British products. But generally, if France could not produce it, then the country went without.

That was just one ramification of Napoleon's creation, the Continental

System. Because the English retaliated by permitting only ships friendly to London to sail the high seas, all French ports were soon effectively closed and moribund, apart from local fishing vessels. The once bustling harbor of Marseilles, with thousands of merchantmen in 1789, was reduced to nine by 1811, while Bordeaux's population fell from 120,000 to 70,000. Other cities and industries suffered similarly. French manufacturers worth 50 million francs in 1789 fell to 12 million by 1811 (while that same year England's exports rose to 1,250,000,000 francs). This resulted in massive unemployment, hundreds of thousands of peasants being forced to eke out an existence on wild herbs and chestnuts, tens of thousands dying annually of malnutrition. Inflation soared even when harvests were relatively good, placing everyday staples well beyond the reach of the masses. The wealthy, too, were affected and could only purchase colonial products at outrageous black-market prices, although Napoleon himself always had a plentiful supply of tobacco and sugar on hand at the Tuileries (largely stolen for him by his customs agents). The bankruptcy of hundreds of major and minor firms occurred throughout continental Europe, and no worse than in Paris, Lyons, and the once prosperous Nantes, Bordeaux, and Marseilles. Two famous companies, Richard-Lenoir and Gros-Davilliers, were only narrowly saved at the last moment by government loans. Nor were the larger, more powerful and prestigious banks of the day spared, as one after another folded, including Laffittes, Foulds, Tourton's and Rodde's,[4] not to mention the collapse of France's wealthiest financier and entrepreneur, Ouvrard, along with his various associates, including Desprès and Vanderberghe.[5]

In an attempt to protect the French people, and to prevent riots, Napoleon did try to maintain state granaries and to peg prices on certain products, including cheap bread, though inflation and high demand made prices increase drastically. It was not surprising that commercial life and the stock exchange and the treasury reflected the worsening situation, as Napoleon desperately ordered Treasury Minister Mollien to come up with millions in "extraordinary revenue" by selling, or privatizing, state and communal properties, including state forests. Then the most desperate of all measures was introduced, the "*centimes de guerre*," special war taxes bringing in another 60 million francs.

But the fact is that when Junot, Masséna, Fouchet, Talleyrand, Berthier, and others were each paid more than nine hundred thousand francs a year, 60 million from "*centimes de guerre*" did not go very far. The French peasant, when fortunate enough to escape or survive conscription, was in a more miserable plight than ever he was under Louis XVI.

As for the large commercial and manufacturing houses that supplied the government, Napoleon arranged for their gradual payment, or repayment, through reserved national sinking funds. But in most cases these businessmen were rarely repaid in full. Thus when Napoleon sought larger government loans, reaching out in all directions, few would oblige him, for a promise by Bonaparte was worthless, and sometimes even dangerous, several prominent businessmen being thrown into prison "for noncompliance" when Napoleon later failed to repay them.[6]

Even with massive extorted funds from occupied territories, the French could not meet the financial and commercial crisis resulting from a permanent wartime economy foisted upon them and the rest of Europe by the unrelenting soldier, Bonaparte. But after his marriage to Marie-Louise, Napoleon's warlike attitude altered significantly. For the moment at least, no doubt with the guns of Wagram still reverberating in his memory, for the first time in his career Napoleon sidestepped open campaigning. On three occasions in 1810 alone he stated his intention of going to Spain to save the situation there, and each time found excuses for not doing so. Had Napoleon finally matured a little and grown tired of warfare and of taking those enormous personal risks? Everyone around him was struck by the changes in him. Clearly Marie-Louise had achieved something.

Following his return to St.-Cloud from his honeymoon in the Netherlands, Napoleon sharply changed his tactics, concentrating most of his efforts on a dramatic new economic attack on England, as he signed four harebrained decrees in July, August, and October 1810, tightening his crackdown on all commerce. No ship from any European nation was permitted to sail without an export-import license personally signed by Napoleon. Heavy new import duties were placed on all colonial produce, including sugar, tobacco, tea, cocoa, and coffee. All colonial products discovered in any country in Europe were to be destroyed. The results: on four days in early November alone, French customs officers seized whole shiploads of such illicit products, burning them dramatically before public rallies.[7] "As a result of not having made peace sooner, England has lost her markets in Naples, Spain, Portugal, and Trieste. If she delays much longer, she will lose those of Holland, the Hanse towns, and Sicily," Napoleon boasted to Foreign Minister Champagny in 1810, still refusing to acknowledge the full extent of his suicidal Continental System, and the reality of the declining French exports compared with those of England.[8] Thus Napoleon's campaign was waged more and more on the economic front, even in the face of the economic catastrophes it was wreaking on France and her allies.

But until such time as England was finally destroyed, France had to find new indirect taxes from dwindling sources to pay for the continuing war. "Our taxes must be varied," Napoleon insisted, "that they might appear less onerous to the public. . . . France must pay greater taxes," he insisted before the State Council in 1810, "and even higher ones today since we have become the premiere nation of Europe. We must maintain ourselves at the level of importance we have achieved. And when I have clobbered England, I will be able to cut our taxes by 200,000,000 francs per year."[9]

"You are still complaining [about the Continental System], aren't you?" Napoleon addressed the governing body of the Council of Commerce and Manufacturers in the spring of 1810:

> When I issued my Berlin and Milan Decrees, England laughed. And you, too, gentlemen, you laughed as well. I was, however, doing something very effective. I had given much serious thought to England. . . . And you can now see for yourselves that the situation of England is today a result of my policy. . . . In ten years' time I will have crushed England. . . . And in any event *I have no pressing wish for peace with England at the present time*. Moreover [thanks to my conquests], I have brought more than one billion francs in war reparations into France since 1807. I am the only one in Europe with money today. Austria is bankrupt, Russia will be shortly, as will be England.[10]

The self-damning speech contained not only blatant lies but also the admission that his Continental System, foisted on his allies, had destroyed their economies. The pall of despair was felt in every quarter, police official Blanc de Hauterive confiding to Talleyrand, "Commerce is finished here. Another two months like this and there will be more business to be found in a provincial American town than in Paris."[11] But when the leaders of the French business community beseeched Napoleon to lift his Continental System, he snapped, "For a mere cup of coffee, badly sweetened at that, they would stop the hand that wants to liberate mankind!"[12]

By 1813, 5 percent Consols, or bonds—so popular among the wealthy as safe investments—dropped from 80 to 50 on the Bourse, while the shares of Bonaparte's prestigious Banque de France plunged from 1,480 to 690 francs a share, but Napoleon blindly refused to recognize the disaster he had brought on France and its allies.

As noted, it was the occupied territories that had to keep paying France, year after year. Once-flourishing Holland was a good example of the realities of the situation.

For example, by 1809 Holland's reduced budget of 70 million florins (or 32,258,000 francs) was not covered by its annual revenue of only 52 million florins (or 23,963,133 francs), and with another 55,128,332 florins (or 25,404,761 francs) in interest, the Dutch national debt had risen to 1,475,807,742 florins. It became much worse each successive year. What is more, Dutch troops were forced to fight for the hated French in lands with which they were not at war, such as Spain and Germany, their entire navy seized by the French and the entire Dutch naval officer corps forced at gunpoint to serve on French warships under the French tricolor! The French troops, officers, and officials who had governed that unfortunate land before the rise of King Louis Bonaparte were once again to take control when Napoleon forced Louis to abdicate in 1810, while the Continental System and war with the English completed the destruction of Holland by virtually annihilating its trade and leaving the port of Amsterdam as empty as those of Marseilles and Bordeaux.[13] To this deliberate financial destruction must be added Napoleon's irrational hatred of the Dutch, evident from the moment in 1803 when he began preparing his impressive invasion plans for England. Napoleon the Latin, the Corsican, had a downright loathing and scorn of northern Europeans and of any group that prized hard work and commercial enterprise above the martial attainment achieved on the field of battle. Napoleon would never understand or even attempt to sympathize with the people of Holland.

Nor was Jérôme Bonaparte's growing kingdom spared his brother's financial exactions. Westphalia stretched from the Lahn and Werra Rivers in the south to the North and Baltic Seas, bordering on the Confederation of the Rhine on the west, a stone's throw from Holland, and on Prussia on the East.

It should have been a wealthy, contented kingdom, but it was not. The Duchy of Brunswick and the Electorate of Hesse-Kassel formed the heart of this new kingdom carved out of formerly independent German states. Napoleon had reshaped it employing French military governors, enforced by French law. In theory initial French rule should have been beneficent, with the abolition of serfdom and feudal rights and privileges, and a fairer system of taxation. It was even given a miniature parliament. But Jérôme Bonaparte, named that institution's president, could prorogue or dismiss it at will, and after 1810 he simply ignored it altogether. Above this stood Jérôme's powerful and influential Council of State. Jérôme enjoyed almost supreme control over the land, down to the naming of the country's magistrates. And although the Napoleonic Code was introduced, so too was universal conscription. An unwanted French army of occupation initially

12,500 strong ultimately increased to more than 30,000, was entirely supported by the kingdom's annual revenues and budget.

Jérôme and his lovely if somewhat hysterical young queen, Catherine, officially began their reign at Kassel on December 7, 1807. Jérôme—like Louis in Holland—swept away most of Napoleon's administrative officials and replaced them with his own men, including his minister of police. His well-meaning officials protested Jérôme's own growing financial irresponsibility and personal and state indebtedness. At the same time Jérôme resisted brother Napoleon's decrees to enforce the Continental System, openly defying him by permitting the sale and transshipment of British industrial and colonial goods. Then there were his wild "flings"—the state of near perpetual festivity, lavish balls, theatricals, and entertainments accompanied by uncontrolled expenditure on gifts, clothing, jewelry, new court uniforms, and state decorations. (He even offered Beethoven the post of *Kappelmeister*, which the celebrated composer wisely declined.[14]) To all this had to be added Jérôme's generous expenditures on his long line of mistresses.

But in the long run, it was Napoleon who called the tune. Westphalian troops were employed by him largely outside Westphalia, in Germany, Austria, Spain, the Baltic fortresses, and finally Russia, while French troops continued to subdue Westphalia itself. Of all the states allied to France, Jérôme's kingdom had the most professional, best-paid, best-equipped army, with the only officer corps in Europe comprising Catholics, Calvinists, Jews, and Lutherans. (This was in stark contrast to the situation in the Grand Duchy of Warsaw, where, at the insistence of the Poles, to which Napoleon acceded, Jews were not allowed to serve as officers and were divested of all political and voting rights as well.) And like Louis, who in the Netherlands stressed the Dutch character of his people, Jérôme emphasized that of the Germans. With little formal education himself, he maintained education at a high—if aberrant—level (although sometimes threatening to destroy it). Jérôme was full of surprises. But he had suffered from uprisings during Napoleon's second Danube campaign leading to Wagram, including armed attempts against the state by Katte, Dörnberg, Martin, Schill, Colonel Emmerich, and the duke of Brunswick-Öls with his Black Legion of Vengeance, ten thousand strong.[15]

The real undoing of the Westphalian hodgepodge was, however, finances. Jérôme certainly added a generous strain of indebtedness, but it was Napoleon who clearly and decisively broke the proverbial camel's back. On naming Jérôme as his latest puppet king, Napoleon immediately heaped enormous indebtedness on the population of 2 million, with a French debt of 34 million francs, while claiming another 26 million resulting from the indebtedness of the former ruling family. As usual in all the countries he conquered, Bonaparte put his own hand into the till, allocating for himself annually another 7 million francs from Jérôme's personal royal domains. A hand here, a hand there. French troops of occupation added a further 20 million francs to the annual Westphalian budget, exclusive of the even higher annual costs for Jérôme's own private Westphalian army. The invisible costs to quarter and maintain the French army over the next few years rose to 200 million francs, which Jérôme of course had to pay. To these had to be added the official outstanding domestic debt of 47 million francs—all this from a state with total annual revenues of just 34 million francs! To this was added the crippling effects of Napoleon's Continental System, forcing Jérôme to sell many prime national properties and all of the kingdom's royal domains—but still the state's indebtedness grew. No one could begin to appease a bloodsucker like Napoleon. Jérôme and Napoleon then extorted "loans" from businessmen and financiers. Taxation, which had begun modestly, was forced sharply upward, taxes on family income (called "hearth taxes"), food, salt, stamps, licenses for various businesses, and indirect taxation reaching unbearable levels. To these burdens were added a "personal" tax on most males above the age of sixteen, while a separate land tax rose to 20 percent by the end of Jérôme's régime. Although Napoleon handed over Hannover to Westphalia in January 1810, he soon burdened this acquisition with debt and military occupation as well, enforced by none other than the ruthless Marshal Davout, prince of Eckmühl, who was brought in to administer the region, facilitate tax collection, and sequester all supplies needed to support his Army of the North.

By October 30, 1810, twenty-six-year-old Jérôme was practically broken by the incessant ravages of Napoleon's demands. Jérôme pleaded that "if he [Napoleon] leaves me here [as king in Westphalia] . . . then he cannot deny me the means by which to maintain myself with honor." Napoleon's reply echoed the unrelenting acquisitiveness and harshness earlier issued to both Joseph and Louis. "It seems unnecessary to repeat that you have made agreements with me, and they must be kept, but you have not done so." The Godfather had spoken. When by the end of the year a weary Jérôme still could not begin to meet the arrears in pay to the French troops of occupation, Napoleon annexed half of Hannover, Osnabrück, and most of Minden, leaving Jérôme with the same debts but fewer means than ever of paying them.

Thus the once prosperous fairy-tale kingdom of Westphalia, like Holland before it, was brought to a state of ruin. As for the domestic debt, which Jerome had found at 47 million francs on his accession to the throne in December 1807, that had risen to a staggering 220 million.[16] Napoleon's Continental System had been at work.

Nor was Spain spared Napoleon's economic scythe. Napoleon found brother Joseph—like Louis and Jérôme—difficult, independent, and contrary. Like Louis and Jérôme, Joseph for his part found brother Napoleon avaricious, arrogant, thieving, outrageous, and meddlesome, with no interest whatsoever in the welfare of the people he had chosen to govern.

There were two principal causes for the collapse and shattering of the Spanish economy during the years of French military occupation: the enforcement of the Continental System, involving the closing of Spanish ports along the Atlantic and the Mediterranean to Anglo-Spanish commerce, and the costs of war and of the occupation itself. In no other single country did Napoleon insist on maintaining such an enormous full-time military force, ranging in size from 250,000 to 300,000 men.

The initial force, which had cost 142 million francs to maintain in the first year ending 1809–10, had by the following year already doubled to 284 million francs. The cost for maintaining and paying the French army, along with the expenses for administering the country that first year alone—800 million francs—was almost equal to the entire French annual budget. In addition, as usual Napoleon had to lend the local Bonaparte king, brother Joseph in this case, some 228 million francs during the initial two years, for which the Spanish government was held responsible.

Meanwhile the new Spanish domestic debt increased from 9,600,000 francs in 1808 to 87,200,000 francs by 1813. National revenue on the other hand did not rise, remaining at about 32 million francs. Then of course there was the little matter of Spanish indebtedness to France, which, beginning at 28,533,333 francs in 1808 ultimately reached 165 million francs by 1813. As for the French army of occupation, that cost soared from 141,866,666 francs to 864,533,000 francs by 1813.[17]

To meet these staggering sums, "rebel" property was seized and sold by the French (when buyers could be found), including royal domains, sprawling church properties, and large private estates, and of course taxes were increased, in a country where little enough specie was to be found even among the oldest aristocratic families, poverty rising along with inflation. Spanish government monopolies involving the sale of liquors and liqueurs, sealing wax, tobacco, and playing cards were ended, and royal manufactories (including china, crystal, and cloth) were privatized, as were the Bourbon gaming houses. The result was a disastrous loss of official income for the new French government under El Rey José, despite the enormous amount of private booty seized and the raising of taxes and internal tariffs.

Nevertheless taxes and sweeping confiscation of properties did not suffice, as war intensified in every corner of the land and commerce was squeezed to a trickle, thanks again to the Continental System. For Napoleon, of course, this was the ideal rationale for intervening, for taking direct control of parts of Spain, just as he had done in Holland and Westphalia. Even before his magnificent wedding ceremony with Marie-Louise in the spring of 1810, Napoleon had seized Aragon, Catalonia, Navarre, Biscay, Burgos, and Valladolid—in other words almost the entire northern part of the country.[18] Joseph himself really directly administered only New Castile (and the southern part of Old Castile), Segovia, and Avila in the center, under the protection of French armies battling to pacify the peninsula.

But even with French military governors and commanders collecting revenue directly from the Spaniards, the military indebtedness of the French army ballooned beyond control, costing Paris between 24 and 34 million francs a *month* in direct subsidies to Spain and its armies. With the exception of the Egyptian campaign, never before had Napoleon determined to persist in a state of permanent active warfare with one particular country, month after month, year after year. In the Netherlands; in the various German states; in Prussia, Austria, and Italy there had been wars, but they were defined and limited to a few months and battles. In Iberia between 250,000 and 300,000 French troops (including units added by his allies) were in a state of permanent war. The casualties continued to mount, as did the price in gold. "The enormous costs of the war in Spain are too much for me," Napoleon had warned Joseph by 1810. But instead of admitting defeat, reducing the growing debt and loss of manpower, Napoleon *increased and extended* his armies and his costs. "Your Majesty is imposing a burden on this country that it simply cannot bear," Joseph riposted in vain.[19]

The pressures on a baffled Joseph continued, and it seemed that—as with Louis in the Netherlands and Jérôme in Westphalia—Napoleon was deliberately attempting to squeeze his brother out by rendering his life impossible and humiliating, while the opportunist Soult was openly hinting at his desire to receive an independent Portuguese crown for himself. Meanwhile, the principal French commanders, including Ney, Masséna, and Marmont, ignored Joseph's orders for the most part, only Marshal Jourdan supporting him. In addition guerrilla warfare everywhere undermined Joseph and the French military, resulting in attacks even on well-armed troop columns, seizing supply convoys and grain.

Throughout this period the position of King Joseph had never been satisfactory from either Napoleon's viewpoint or his own. Spanish hatred of the French would disappear, Joseph had predicted at the beginning, once they saw that France was bringing "wiser, more liberal laws, better adapted to the times we live in than those of the Inquisition."[20] Joseph's opinion had changed, however, as soon as he reached Madrid, where he experienced firsthand the hatred of the people so brutally put down by Marshal Murat's sabers following their famous Dos de Mayo uprising. And as Joseph also quickly discovered, there was no room for liberal ideas in wartime, and Spain was by now literally one enormous battlefield. Not a region of the country went unscathed, and despite Joseph's sincere wish to alleviate the woes then afflicting the Spaniards, he could not do so as long as the country was at war with France. Joseph pleaded time and again with Napoleon to end the war and instead win over the people by love and trust. Napoleon grew so irritated with Joseph's pathetic "naïveté" that he gradually reduced his brother's effective power, even removing Joseph's personal commander in chief, Marshal Jourdan, replacing him with his own men, including Soult and Masséna, who remained directly under his orders and openly refused to obey Joseph's. Soon there was scarcely a French general or marshal in Iberia who would take orders from Joseph.

Joseph in return dissociated himself more and more from the French officers and officials at his court, replacing them with Spaniards, again following the example of Louis in Holland and Jérôme in Westphalia. The court of "the puppet El Rey José" soon became an opposing camp for Paris. "The emperor was the personal butt of the hatred and sarcasms of most of the King's court," General Sébastiani reported to Napoleon.[21] A frustrated Joseph made little attempt to conceal his anger as he protested his rights as the legal head of state as well as of the family. "Joseph still believes himself to be my elder, he still has pretensions to head the family. Is there anything more absurd!"[22] Napoleon exclaimed behind his back. The almost continuous check met by Napoleon's forces in Iberia merely embittered both Bonaparte brothers all the more, each feeling himself the victim. "[Spanish] public opinion is entirely turned against us today," Joseph confided to Queen Julie, who remained in Paris and refused to join him. Napoleon had to start following his advice. "Tell this to the emperor and remind him that he has more at stake, his greater glory and responsibility, so far as posterity is concerned, than do I."[23] "The profession I practice here is, under the circumstances, quite impossible today," Joseph confided in another letter to his wife:

If his ... purpose is to make me feel disgusted with Spain, he has achieved his ends. ... The vexing position in which he wishes to leave me as ruler of a great country is quite unacceptable. I want to know what precisely he wants of me, and if that position includes humiliating me, then I wish to retire from here. I do not want to be under the tutelage of those beneath me [French officers and officials]. I do not want to see my provinces administered by men I do not trust. I do not want to be merely a crowned child-king, because I do not need a crown to prove myself a man, and I feel myself quite great enough on my own merits without having to put up with such charades.[24]

"He [Napoleon] repeated to me that you had only two possibilities open to you," Julie replied on January 13, 1811. "To remain in Spain and quietly accept his wishes, or to return to France as a French prince, and, he added, 'if he has any sense, he will remain in Spain and follow my orders, unless of course he rejects both possibilities and decides to follow Lucien's example, by going over to the English.'" While making up his mind, Joseph took the precaution of sending over several hundred thousand francs in gold for investment in English banks.[25]

One of Joseph's closest friends and advisers, predating even the creation of the Consulate, was Count Miot de Mélito, who thought Joseph himself was not really sure of what he wanted: "The truth of the matter is that he cannot positively make up his mind. The lust for greatness does not disappear easily from the souls of those who feel themselves made for just such power."[26] This was only partially true, for the fact was that Napoleon had not only displaced Joseph as head of the family but forced him to move, first from Marseilles, and then from the quietly influential life of Mortefontaine, first as king of Naples, then as king of Madrid, against his will and instincts. He was a wealthy man in his own right and did not need it. But he was resentful and jealous of Napoleon and could not allow his younger brother to supersede him.

"If I have lost your friendship, then simply permit me to retire in complete obscurity," Joseph pleaded with Napoleon. "If not, I shall find a glorious death through the risks with the name that I bear, at the head of the troops I command, troops that hitherto have brought only victory. Regardless of what happens, however, never forget that you never had a friend more worthy of you, or a brother with more tender thoughts for you, than I, and above all, do not recall this when it is too late to act."[27] When the chips were down, he was in fact the one brother, the one person, on whom Napoleon could count, as he was to prove one summer's day at the Ile d'Aix a few years hence.

By March 1811 Joseph had had quite enough, having found himself, as he informed Julie, "reduced to the abject state of a mere criminal or of the most humble of men. . . . Therefore announce to the Emperor that I shall be leaving [for Paris]. . . . I feel the agony of political death in this country; however, I shall not cede . . . and I shall not of my own free will declare myself dead and assist at my own political funeral."[28]

Napoleon of course was already annexing Spanish territory, and in February of that same year he had published in the *Moniteur Universel* his intention of annexing all of Spain to the French Empire.

Setting out for Paris on April 23, 1811, Joseph stayed till June 16, but only meeting Napoleon a few times. He pleaded for more political and military independence for himself and more financial help for the country. Joseph's French and Spanish troops had been unpaid for more than half a year, and his ministers and high officials remained unpaid for more than a year, so indeed impoverished that they had to plead for army rations for themselves and their families. Joseph reluctantly left the French capital in mid-June after Napoleon had promised to restore to him complete civil and military command, bolstered by substantial loans.[29] But on June 22, scarcely four days after his brother's departure, Napoleon issued an even more humiliating decree regarding his sibling kings, establishing that all members of the Bonaparte clan then serving as ruling monarchs within his empire were thereby reduced from kings to mere French princes.[30] Joseph's journey to Paris had been a failure; war would continue. "Joseph," the Cortes of Cádiz announced, "is more than ever a marionette in the power of the French, a man without authority . . . [and] can be considered only an object of profound contempt by all Spaniards who love the independence and honor of their country."[31]

Despite all that, Joseph remained at his post in Madrid. "If we have war with Russia," he had perceptively written Julie even before setting out for Paris, "the emperor must send me money and show much confidence in me, and I shall second him perhaps more than he expects."[32] The following year, although Napoleon had not improved Joseph's position, his brother still stood by him as he prepared for the Russian campaign, while lamenting that he had "to hopelessly watch the devastation of this land that I have so hoped to render happy."[33]

By then Wellington was meeting with increasing success throughout the Iberian Peninsula against the French. Napoleon, however, saw it differently, announcing that England was "compromising [Spanish] independence and integrity."[34] France of course had not even begun to conquer Spain, whose independence and integrity Napoleon had been determined to overthrow, forcing Spain to invite England to come to its rescue. But Napoleon always had a perverse way of looking at events. When he now failed against the English, he blamed the Spanish debacle on El Rey José, just as he had blamed the Egyptian debacle on Kléber. There was always someone to blame. "He [Joseph] was the most incompetent man I could have chosen there," he later told Las Cases. "All the follies in Spain are due to the mistaken consideration I have shown the King [Joseph]," he complained to War Minister Clarke, "who not only does not know how to command, but who is incapable of recognising his own limitations." Of course the example did not apply to Napoleon himself. "It is hard to imagine anything so inconceivable as what is now going on in Spain," Bonaparte lamented to General Savary later, with the fall of Vittoria. "With 100,000 good men, the King could have defeated the whole of England."[35] And yet when Napoleon had earlier led 300,000 French troops in Spain he had failed as well, as had every commanding general and marshal under his command thereafter, including Junot, Ney, Soult, Masséna, and Marmont. As for El Rey José, he would keep his word and hold on, until 1813, when Napoleon himself was defeated on the field of battle.

Back in the autumn of 1811, Count Miot had already considered Spain a lost cause, though for very different reasons:

> Scarcely five months had elapsed since our return [Joseph's return from Paris] and we have already sunk ... into the same position that had forced us to leave Madrid in the first place. The same financial difficulties, the same scarcity of food, the same political situation, generals as independent as ever before the King's authority, and no master plan on which to work. Moreover, we had lost all hope of improvement there and even the delusions that had formerly sustained us were gone.[36]

In the end, with the Spanish economy shattered and the Spanish government foundering in debt, Napoleon read a balance sheet prepared for him by Finance Minister Gaudin. It made the growing imperial debt elsewhere in Europe appear almost reasonable in comparison: Iberian indebtedness to France approached 1 billion francs. But still Napoleon blamed Joseph, blamed Wellington, or anyone else he could think of at the moment.

What in fact had Napoleon achieved since his coup d'état of November 1799? Every country under his control was staggering under the weight of debt. An entire generation of French manhood had been annihilated by the annual military harvest, and France itself suffered and staggered like the most heavily occupied land. Instead of withdrawing all his troops from eastern and central Europe—from the Netherlands, the Balkans, Italy, and the Iberian Peninsula—and realistically consolidating his position and admitting the self-evident failure of his economic, military, and geopolitical plan, Napoleon persisted, even in the face of the gradual Russian withdrawal from his sphere.

Following Napoleon's epileptic episode at Compiègne near the end of April 1810, Napoleon and Marie-Louise had set out on their honeymoon, a long tour of northern France, "Belgium," and Holland. He stopped to inspect France's major naval shipyards and personally to launch the mighty eighty-gun ship of the line, the *Friedland,* the pride of the new fleet he was rebuilding to replace the one Nelson had destroyed at Trafalgar back in 1805.[37] His pleasure was marred, however, when on April 27 he received an explosive confidential report informing him that brother Louis, Police Minister Fouché, and even Talleyrand were in the midst of separate, secret, top-level negotiations with London.

It had all begun back in November 1809, Napoleon now learned, when Fouché had secretly dispatched an Irish army officer by the name of Fagan with a note for the marquis of Wellesley, Wellington's elder brother, then serving as foreign secretary in the Percival government. Meanwhile, unknown to Fouché, Louis Bonaparte had made separate contact with the British Foreign Office through the good offices of the Dutch banker, Labouchère. Napoleon would deal with Louis later. It was Fouché who roused Napoleon's ire as no one else could, this same Fouché whom he had just rewarded with a peerage as duke of Otranto. Fouché had also been employing Ouvrard in the transfer of these communications to Amsterdam and London. A cultivated man of the world, Ouvrard was Napoleon's long-standing bugbear; indeed there was no businessman and bourgeois in the whole of France he loathed more. What were they up to, this traitorous Louis Bonaparte and the ex-schoolmaster–mass murderer, Joseph Fouché? Carrying out secret peace negotiations with perfidious Albion! All this behind Napoleon's back even as he was waging a tough commercial war to destroy England.

The day after his return to St.-Cloud on June 1, via Lille, Le Havre, and Rouen, Bonaparte summoned an extraordinary meeting of his council of ministers, including Decrès, Clarke, Champagny, Gaudin, Mollien, Regnier, Biget, and Fouché. "You are in charge of making war and peace now?" he scathingly harangued Fouché. "Do you know what the penalty is for such a betrayal? I should march you right up to the guillotine!" But the main event occurred following mass on June 3, when the meeting resumed (without Fouché). This time, in addition to the ministers, various officials and "grand dignitaries" of the realm were summoned, including Talleyrand (of course no longer a minister), Archchancellor Cambacérès, Pasquier, and Maret. "What do you think of a minister who abuses his position by insulting his sovereign and communicating secretly with a foreign power, and opening diplomatic negotiations without authorization and in contradiction to the foreign policy of his own government?"[38]

Napoleon, his temper rising, roundly denounced Fouché's treachery in detail. How dare he open peace negotiations! Napoleon did not want peace. Peace—that was utter treason!

Following the meeting, his temper having cooled, he dictated a long letter to Fouché, in surprisingly civilized language given his public tirade. Despite his detestation of this "traitor," so persistent in acting as the kingpin in the peace negotiations, the fact is that Fouché was simply too powerful to dismiss out of hand. Since the 1790s he had stealthily been gathering detailed, embarrassing files on every member of the Bonaparte clan, their illegal financial dealings, their accumulated profits, the sexual exploits of Joseph, Jérôme, Pauline, and Caroline, not to mention a numerous litter of bastard progeny. Napoleon had to tread very warily indeed.

"I am aware of all the services you have rendered me over the years, and I believe in your attachment to my person," Napoleon's letter began:

> Nevertheless, it is impossible for me to leave you with your portfolio without harming my own position. The post as minister of the Police requires a full, absolute confidence, and that confidence simply no longer exists ... because you have compromised my tranquillity and that of the state, which even the legitimate motives you claim for your actions cannot excuse in my eyes. ... The singular manner in which you have interpreted the powers of your ministry of police in no measure squares with the well-being of the state. ... As a result I am forced to keep a close, continuous watch on you and your activities, which I find quite taxing, and in any event, totally unacceptable. [Through] your overtures with England ... their minister [Foreign Secretary Wellesley] inevitably thought that you were acting on my behalf."

This in turn could result in "a total upheaval in all my political affairs, and were I to countenance it, it would reflect badly on my character as well. ... You clearly have no idea of all the harm you might have caused me." The situation quickly became public knowledge. "The downfall of the Duc d'Otrante,"

Austrian Minister to Paris Prince Karl von Schwarzenberg informed Vienna, "has produced the greatest consternation here."[39]

On the evening of March 19, 1811, carriage after carriage clattered into the Carrousel, pulling up before the main entrance of the Tuileries. Dozens of court dignitaries, ministers, and senior army commanders and their wives, in formal attire, gathered to attend a special evening in the "Petits Aparte-ments" of Empress Marie-Louise. Tonight, however, was different from hundreds of previous such entertainments given here, for the mighty and influential had come to await the birth of Napoleon's child.

Drs. Dubois (the imperial obstetrician), Corvisart, Yvan, Bourdier, Bourdois, and Auvity—the senior members of the Faculty of Medicine—had arrived at 7:00 P.M., when the first telltale labor pains had begun.

Then suddenly the widow of Marshal Lannes, the lovely if distrait-looking duchess of Montebello, appeared, still only half dressed for the evening's event, to consult hastily with Napoleon, then just as quickly dis-appeared. The voices grew loud and more excited, the ladies gesticulating, the gentlemen wagering one thousand ducats to one hundred that the nine-teen-year-old empress would be delivered of a boy, as Napoleon had been boasting for months. The hours passed, and at midnight Napoleon ordered a cold collation of wine, punch, meats, chocolate, and fruit to be served. More hours passed, and the voices and partylike atmosphere grew subdued.

At six o'clock the next morning, Napoleon had a brief medical bulletin read to those still present, tersely announcing that "Her Majesty is in the best of health," awaiting the happy outcome. A tense and tired Napoleon withdrew to his private apartments to bathe and breakfast, only to be inter-rupted in his bath at seven o'clock by a pale, anxious Dr. Dubois, the obste-trician. "Eh bien! What is it! She hasn't died!" was Napoleon's first reac-tion. Her water had broken, he was informed, and it would be a breech birth. Clearly Dubois was most distraught. As for Napoleon, everyone knew how anxious he was, having divorced Josephine for the sole purpose of being presented with an heir. Now seeing the effect of the mounting pressure on Dubois, Napoleon tried to calm him. "Relax, pretend she is just another shopgirl from the Rue St.-Denis. Forget that she is the empress." "But, Sire, I shall now have to use forceps." "Ah! Mon Dieu!" Napoleon exclaimed in horror. "Will it be dangerous?" "Sire, it may be a case of hav-ing to make a choice, of saving the mother or the child." "Come along now, Dubois! Don't panic. Save the mother, I am behind you," and Dubois hur-ried down the stairs again.[40] If it was a question of life and death, the empress had to be saved. She could always have another child. Dried hastily by Constant, and wearing only a bathrobe, Napoleon followed Dubois down his small private staircase, past the crowd of astonished onlookers.

"He went up to her bed, pretending to be cheerful. Kissing her tenderly, he spoke soothingly and reassuringly to her," Méneval recalled.[41] Dubois, who was by now in a real state, insisted that Corvisart, Napoleon's personal physician, stay at his side. The cries were agonizing, and grew worse as Dubois Corvisart, Bourdier and Yvan struggled to deliver the baby.

When it was over, Napoleon "glanced at the infant on the blanket, thinking the lifeless creature dead, turning immediately to his wife, saying nothing about the silent, still baby." Madame de Montesquiou, to whose care the child would be entrusted hereafter, lifted and cleaned it, and put a few drops of eau-de-vie in its mouth, then covered the silent red baby with warm towels. Seven entire minutes passed before at last the baby gave its first cry, its first sign of life. Only now did they notice that it was a boy, twenty inches long, weighing nine pounds. "In the fever of his joy, Napoleon leaned over the infant and suddenly took it in his arms and walked toward the outer salon where by now all the great personnages of the empire were again congregating, as he proudly held up the child proclaiming: "Voilà! The King of Rome!"[42]

The signal was given to the celebratory batteries waiting to announce the news to Paris: twenty-one cannon to fire in the event of the birth of a girl, one hundred for a boy. The Imperial Guard's artillery began their thunderous announcement, echoed far to the east by the batteries of Vincennes. One after another they discharged as tens of thousands of people gathered in the courtyard, in the Tuileries Gardens, in the Place de la Concorde, in the Rue de Rivoli, in the Cité, in the Latin Quarter, everyone counting attentively eighteen, nineteen, twenty, twenty-one . . . and then twenty-two, twenty-three, twenty-four, twenty-five . . . as cheers and applause filled the French capital, and a veritable flow of carriages converged on the Tuileries.

Meanwhile Prince Eugène and the grand duke of Würzburg, after serving as official witnesses to the birth, returned to the salon where Archchancellor Cambacérès ordered the drawing up of the birth certificate for Napoléon-François-Joseph-Charles. François for the father of Marie-Louise, Emperor Franz I of Austria; Joseph for brother Joseph and for one of the godfathers, the grand duke of Würzburg; and Charles of course after Napoleon's father. After fifteen painful years of waiting and uncertainty, a legal child was at last born.

This long-awaited son was to be royally pampered. Madame de Montesquiou was to be permanently in charge, attended by deputy governesses, guards, equerries, chamberlains, and servants. The baby would never be alone, never unguarded. Meanwhile whole platoons of imperial couriers were dispatched with the news of the imperial birth and that Empress Marie-Louise herself was all right. Off they went, to the Senate in the Luxembourg Palace, to the Hôtel de Ville, to the embassies, to Josephine at the Château de Navarre—"He has my chest, my mouth and my eyes," Napoleon informed her. "I trust that he will fulfill his destiny."[43] Off they went to Berlin, Vienna, and St. Petersburg, to every prefect of every department, and to every military governor of Napoleon's vast empire, to every mayor and garrison of the country, aided by the Chappe system of military telegraph towers informing Brest, Boulogne, Metz, Strasbourg, Brussels, Lyons, and Milan. A Te Deum was chanted in the chapel of the Tuileries, a literal fountain of wine flowed in the Châtelet, fireworks dazzled the eye before the Hôtel de Ville (which had presented the baby with a priceless solid gold-and-silver cradle), every bell in every church, convent, school, and *mairie* (local town hall) in the French capital—thousands of them— ringing out. It was deafening, hour after hour. The infant in the arms of Madame de Montesquiou, preceded by four pages, army officers, one of Napoleon's aides-de-camp, four chamberlains, two equerries, and his own master of ceremonies arrived in the baby's apartments, where he was presented with the cordon of the Legion of Honor and Charlemagne's famous Iron Crown. Three more batteries then repeated the one hundred salvos. Napoleon in his ecstasy rewarded everyone. First a string of pearls worth 500,000 francs to his beloved wife, tens of thousands of francs to the successful Dubois and the other doctors. In the name of the empress 250,000 francs were distributed among the poor of the city.

But in other respects the celebration differed from that of his coronation five and a half years earlier. Large numbers of prisoners were not freed from the prisons this time—Ouvrard and his partners, Séguin and Desprès, still behind bars and stone walls of debtors' prison, Ste.-Pélagie, falsely accused by Napoleon of owing the state twelve million francs. Nor after the initial announcement on the twentieth were there large crowds or much deeply felt cheering by the public. Their numbers had been diminished over the years by the permanent state of warfare, hundreds of thousands buried but not forgotten in foreign lands from the Baltic to the Mediterranean. Napoleon could well rejoice over the birth of a son, while hundreds of thousands were mourning the deaths of theirs. Nor were the popular medals with the effigies of the emperor and empress distributed among the public this time, not even lead or tin replicas; the few medallions of gold, silver, or bronze struck by the mint were limited solely for the princes,

princesses, and members of the court. Nor did anything like the vast number of congratulations seen in December 1804 flood the Tuileries this time.
Official documents were received, of course, from the capitals of occupied
Europe and from some Masonic lodges, but nothing from the French people. There were few cheerful songs in the streets, or even the theater. To be
sure, the official delegations made their appearances, the ambassadors
extraordinary were dispatched—Prince von Hatzfeld from Berlin, Chernichev from St. Petersburg, Prince Karl from Vienna, from the kings of
Bavaria, Saxony, Württemberg, from El Rey José, delegations from the Senate, the Corps Législatif, and the nation's university and magistracy. But
strangely enough—and no doubt it struck everyone at the time—representative delegations from Napoleon's ultimate base of power, his army, were
deliberately excluded from the ceremonies, apart from the Paris military
governor's staff officers. Even the delegation dispatched by the Imperial
Guard was not admitted. And then of course there was that slight problem
with his family, for when Napoleon named sister Caroline Murat as one of
his son's godmothers, requiring her presence at the child's baptism at
Nôtre-Dame, the pouting Caroline declined to participate.[44] She had been
brooding ever since the interloper, Marie-Louise, had arrived in France and
was devastated when she learned of the new empress's pregnancy. The birth
of their son sent Caroline into temper tantrums, for Joachim would never
be named as Napoleon's successor now. Nevertheless Napoleon repeatedly
extended the invitation to come to the Paris ceremony, finally losing his
patience and removing her name altogether as godmother. No one ever
crossed Napoleon Bonaparte and got away with it.

What was happening in France? What was happening to Napoleon?
Everyone had noted the changes in him since his exhausted return from the
Wagram campaign at the end of 1809. He had gained weight; he had withdrawn from society; and most strangely he had repeatedly procrastinated
leaving for the battlefields of Spain, where his 280,000 men were awaiting
him. Was Napoleon tired of war? But even as Napoleon was deliriously celebrating the birth of his first legitimate heir, proclaiming loudly, "Now
begins the finest period of my reign," the growing rumble of marching
boots and the rat-a-tat-tat of distant drums were already faintly heard far to
the east, beyond the Oder, the Vistula, and the Niemen, in a new theater of
war at once so vast and limitless as to reduce the voracious Iberian battlefield to insignificance in comparison.

CHAPTER 33

Russia

As a Roman emperor once said: the body of a dead enemy always smells good.

ith his invasion and annexation of Hamburg, Bremen, Lübeck and the Duchy of Oldenburg, in December 1810 and February 1812, Napoleon had at once ensured a war to the death with Russia, and eventually with the rest of occupied Europe. With the French closing of the very last commercial outlets with England, indeed with the outside world, Czar Alexander realized he had no choice. Although in full sympathy with Alexander, Bavaria, Prussia, and Austria declined to join Russia openly in opposing French armies of occupation in 1812, if only through fear of further rapacious French reprisals.

Czar Alexander had finally retaliated against the French with his famous decree of December 31, 1810, placing high import duties on all French goods, chiefly luxury items, while reopening Russian ports to British trade. "Is that what Russia calls an alliance and a state of peaceful relations?" Napoleon asked Champagny.[1] When Napoleon then ordered Marshal Davout, on one of his rare visits to Paris, suddenly back to Germany, the Russian ambassador advised St. Petersburg immediately: "Marshal Davout's abrupt departure has produced quite a sensation here. It is considered the automatic harbinger of war. Two hundred cannon have already been shipped across the Rhine to Wesel."[2]

Although Alexander dissimulated to Ambassador Caulaincourt, protesting his devotion to Napoleon, all the while he was preparing for the inevitable break. Napoleon for his part did not mince words. "Your Majesty's last ukase [of December 31] both in essence and form was specifically directed against France," Napoleon wrote St. Petersburg on February 28, 1811, ". . . and therefore in the view of Europe and England, our alliance no longer exists." As for Poland, it was French territory, Napoleon warned, and "I therefore have the right to insist that no one interefere in what I do beyond the Elbe," even as he received reports of fresh Russian fortifications being raised along the River Dvina.

> I am amazed by this new evidence and by the realization that Your Majesty is quite disposed—once circumstances permit—to come to an arrangement with England. As far as I am concerned, that is equivalent to igniting a state of war between our two empires. Your Majesty's abandoning of our alliance and burning of the Tilsit Conventions would inevitably lead to war within the next few months.[3]

Although Alexander continued to dissimulate his protestations of friendship to French Ambassador Caulaincourt, it was simply to buy time. Secretly the czar was confiding to the other occupied European powers straining under the harsh French yoke, "I am sick and tired of Napoleon's continued meddling in our affairs. I have 200,000 good troops ready, and another 300,000 men in my militia, with which to challenge him, and we shall then see."[4]

"Order that this operation [for increased arms manufacture] be executed with the greatest secrecy," Bonaparte informed War Minister Clarke on February 18, 1811, instructing him to prepare for war with Russia, and to have guns ready by May. "They must be able to be shipped within twenty-four hours' notice" to the army munitions depots at Mainz.[5] "There is no doubt about it now," commented Comte Charles de Damas on March 22, 1811, "that Napoleon wants to wage war on Russia."[6] "I am not so stupid as to think that it is Oldenburg [the property of the husband of the czar's favorite sister, Catherine] that troubles you," Napoleon warned Russian Minister Prince Kurakin on August 15, 1811. "I see that Poland is the real question. You believe I have designs on Poland. However I begin to think that you wish to seize it for yourselves. No! *If your army were encamped on the very heights of Montmartre itself, I would not cede an inch of the Warsaw territory, not a village, not a windmill.*[7] . . . Am I to be forced into abandoning the [Continental] System I have set up [because of you?]. . . .

I will not yield an inch of Poland. Nothing that has been annexed to France shall be taken from her.[8] The following day, August 16, Napoleon was convening a ministerial conference in which he outlined his intended campaign against Russia.

"We are in a state of highest alert," Czar Alexander wrote his sister Catherine on November 10, 1811. "The situation is so delicate, so tense, that hostilities might break out at any moment now." A month later he concluded, "It seems that blood must flow yet again." "You know that I have eight hundred thousand men, and that every year another two hundred-fifty thousand conscripts more are placed at my disposal," Napoleon bullied Prince Kurakin in Paris. As far as Alexander was concerned, "The moment a French army passes the River Oder, for I can no longer hold the Elbe, I believe I have the right to consider war to have been declared against me, and Divine Providence alone will decide the outcome."[9]

Alexander was attending a ball at the estate of Gen. Baron Levin Bennigsen on June 24, 1812, when a special courier arrived with a dispatch informing the czar that the French army had just crossed the Niemen, the Russian frontier. Despite the blatant invasion of sovereign Russian territory, Alexander decided to make one last effort to save the peace. He wrote to Napoleon:

> *Monsieur mon frère*, I learned yesterday that, in spite of the loyalty I have demonstrated in maintaining my engagements with Your Majesty, his troops have crossed the Russian frontier. If Your Majesty has no wish to spill the blood of his people over a misunderstanding of this nature, and if he agrees to withdraw his troops from Russian territory, I shall choose to overlook the matter, thereby allowing an accommodation to remain in effect between us. . . . It lies within Your Majesty's hands alone to spare mankind the calamities of another war.[10]

"I have undertaken great preparations, and my forces are three times greater than yours," an uncompromising Napoleon wrote back from his new GHQ at Vilna, Lithuania. "At this time, with the whole of Europe behind me, how do you expect to be able to stop me?"[11]

The orders had already gone out to Napoleon's family and the imperial command to prepare for war. Jérôme was named commander of the VIII Westphalian Corps. But Louis, living in his Austrian exile writing poetry, would not take part, while brother Joseph assured Julie and Napoleon of his intention of holding the fort in Spain. Brother Lucien of course was happily ensconced in his comfortable English estate, protected by English guns. Prince Eugène de Beauharnais, still in temporary administrative control of the Kingdom of Italy, received his marching orders from Major General Berthier on April 30, 1812, to join the Army of Italy, as the new IV Corps of the Grande Armée in Poland. "It is sad for me to see you go to war again, but I hope that God will protect the good son of a good and tender mother," Josephine now wrote. Her sentiments were shared by hundreds of thousands of mothers all across Europe.[12]

The situation regarding the final member of the Bonaparte clan, brother-in-law Joachim Murat, king of Naples, however, was far more delicate. Joachim and Caroline Bonaparte, who had separated after numerous acrimonious quarrels, especially concerning her latest open liaison, this time with Prince von Metternich, now agreed to a reconciliation, for public consumption at any rate, as Murat desperately needed Caroline to intercede with Napoleon. Napoleon was openly threatening to annex Naples, just as he was threatening Joseph in Spain and had already done in the case of Holland. The situation had been aggravated on June 14, 1811, when Murat, who had been firing high French officials personally placed in Naples by Napoleon, decreed that all French generals and officials serving in his new kingdom had to drop their French citizenship and instead become naturalized Neapolitan citizens under his own rule. That was the last straw. Napoleon immediately reinstated most of the key officials peremptorily removed by Murat, topped by an embarrassing slap in the face: a superseding decree from Paris. The Kingdom of Naples, Napoleon reminded King Joachim,

> comprises the Kingdom of the Two Sicilies [Naples] an integral part of Our Empire, thereby considering any prince ruling that state automatically to be a French citizen ... and that that particular prince [Murat] has only been placed, and maintained upon, that throne thanks to efforts of our people [Napoleon's French Army], and thus we have decreed and do hereby decree: ARTICLE I. All French citizens are [automatically] citizens of the Two Sicilies. ARTICLE II. *The Decree of 14 June* [1811] by the king of this country [Murat] is not applicable.[13]

Rumors spread like wildfire throughout Paris and Naples that the arrogant Murat had finally gone too far and would shortly be removed, as Napoleon announced the official dissolution of the Army of Naples, replacing it with a French-run Armée d'Observation.

A panic-stricken Murat made up with Caroline, who reluctantly left

Metternich's bed to trudge over to the Tuileries to intercede with Napoleon on Joachim's behalf. She had no intention of losing *her* kingdom in the process. Napoleon reluctantly gave in, on the condition that Murat apologize and formally declare himself a vassal of Napoleon, and hence his willingness to join him in the forthcoming war with Russia. Murat capitulated, whining and as innocent and subservient as Soult had been in Spain when that marshal had declared his interest in seizing a kingdom for himself in Portugal. "And what, Sire, have 'they' done to so alarm you about my feelings to you?" Murat cheekily replied.

> How could I not tremble at the very thought, when in fact all my thoughts and efforts have had but one sole purpose, that of never acting contrary to your vast projects, indeed, quite the reverse, to second you entirely? . . . Your Majesty dishonors his brother-in-law, his lieutenant, by removing him as commander of his own troops, by accusing him before the whole of France as being anti-French. . . . To my dying breath I shall be, and have always been, your faithful friend. There is nothing more I can add. I am so distressed by all this.[14]

Murat would now behave himself, and Napoleon could employ his badly needed sword in Russia, and on May 12, 1812, King Joachim duly set out as commander of the four cavalry corps of the Grande Armée, and Caroline could return to the comfort of Metternich's perfumed featherbed.

In May 1811 Napoleon had recalled Ambassador and Grand Equerry Armand de Caulaincourt from St. Petersburg. Caulaincourt was a fool, he said, hoodwinked by Alexander, whom he fawned over. He believed all the czar's professions of peaceful intentions toward France. That Napoleon had in turn misled both the czar and Caulaincourt through his belligerent annexations of the Grand Duchy of Oldenburg and the Hanseatic states was quite another matter, of course. Not so for an embarrassed Caulaincourt, however, who requested to be replaced as French ambassador to St. Petersburg.[15] Technically basing his request on grounds of failing health due to the harsh Russian climate, he in fact had been caught between the czar's anger over the recent French annexations, and by Napoleon's own displeasure with the czar's breaking with the Continental System and reopening of the Baltic to English trade. Napoleon, who never permitted anyone to resign from his personal service, ignored Caulaincourt's request and instead immediately "recalled" him.

Then, on his return to Paris on June 5, Caulaincourt had been sum-

moned to St.-Cloud to receive an imperial dressing-down over his failure to
have properly represented France's vested interests there, vis-à-vis the deteriorating relations between the two great empires.[16] Caulaincourt, a most
reasonable man, tried in vain to reason with Napoleon. "Given these circumstances, my duty is to plead with Your Majesty [to understand the situ-
ation]," he began. "I am neither approving nor criticizing. I am merely
recounting all the events that have transpired. Your Majesty will then judge
for himself if all his criticisms of my actions were well founded after all."[17]
But instead Napoleon harangued him, Caulaincourt commenting, "As
regards the unjust harshness of a sovereign who can never admit he is in the
wrong, I refused to accept any personal complaint against me," something
Bonaparte was quite unaccustomed to since the days of Talleyrand. "The
Emperor was angrier than ever at me."[18] For all his ranting and raving, however, he did not dismiss Caulaincourt, though his presence was not always
tolerated at court. Napoleon secretly respected a man who stood his ground
and was not intimidated by him, and a courageous Caulaincourt held firm
to the very end.

By the summer of 1811, Napoleon's actions had again altered dramatically.
He shed his recent lethargy and left behind the easygoing interlude that had
begun following his marriage to Marie-Louise the previous year and lasted
until the birth of his son in March, as a locust leaves behind its old shell on
the bark of an elm. Suddenly there was new action, new tension, acrimonious political discussions with his ministers and the State Council, and
above all a fresh flow of orders to War Minister Clarke. The sleeping giant
was awake again.

Napoleon was restless, some thought even unhinged or at least unnatu-
rally frantic. The languid days of domestic bliss and early fatherhood were
over. He was constantly on the move now. The empress could not keep up
with this stranger, nor could his ministers, or his enormous staff, or the
commander of the Imperial Guard responsible for providing the military
escorts for his frequently unplanned movements. On July 10 Napoleon
moved from St.-Cloud to the Trianon Palace, then back to St.-Cloud. On
August 6 he suddenly announced his departure for Rambouillet, and on the
fourteenth he rushed back to the Tuileries, then to St.-Cloud, then back to
the Trianon. Just as abruptly he set out for the Palace of Compiègne, followed in September by a sudden journey to Boulogne. Massive stores of
provisions and elaborate palace personnel had to be ready at all these establishments, for Napoleon flew into a rage when on a whim he left one palace
for another only to find nothing in readiness for him and his suite.

After inspecting the massive batteries and fortifications at Boulogne, Bonaparte suddenly ordered a tour of the north, arriving at Ostend at three o'clock in the morning, where he transferred to a ship and sailed up the coast to Flushing, then off to Middelburg, then to Terneuzen, next up the Scheldt to the primary French naval shipyards and fortifications at Antwerp where he was joined by a bewildered Marie-Louise at one o'clock in the morning of September 30. (Life in the Schönbrunn had never been like this.) In rapid succession over the next few days he visited Willemstad, Hellevoetsluis, Hogplat, Dordrecht, Gorkum, and Utrecht. On the seventh and eighth he carried out a full military review at La Bruyère. From there to Amersfoort, Amsterdam, the Helder, then touring the new series of forts at Texel before continuing to Alkmaar, Haarlem, Muiden, Naarden, and on to Katwijk, Leiden, Scheveningen, and The Hague,[19] concluding his lightning tour with Bonn, Liège, and Compiègne and reaching St.-Cloud again on November 11. Not since Napoleon had suddenly announced his intention of building a couple of thousand boats and hundreds of fortresses preparatory to invading England had anyone seen him in such a frenzy. Clearly it was to be war again, as never before.

The hectic pace of Napoleon's new war preparations could not conceal the deep malaise within the French imperial establishment itself. Fouché, in his quest for peace, had been exiled beyond French frontiers, and Talleyrand was persona non grata at the Tuileries for the same reason. And of course the presence of ex-Ambassador Armand de Caulaincourt scarcely lessened tensions.

Upon his return to Paris in 1811, Caulaincourt, although remaining grand equerry of the imperial court, found himself snubbed and excluded from major public functions. Indeed, he was summoned again to the Tuileries only twice in the spring of 1812, to discuss the disagreeable subject of the forthcoming war with Russia, which Caulaincourt continued to oppose. He bluntly pointed out that if by crushing Russia, Napoleon would strike a real blow against England, nevertheless it would also be a calamity to the rest of the world. "I have to tell you quite frankly that everyone—in Europe and in France—sees in the war against Poland and Russia for which you are preparing, only an excuse, a pretext for further expansion." To which Napoleon angrily snapped, "I have not asked for your opinion!"[20] "Do you want me to tell you the truth about the situation, about our future?" one minister had confided to Marshal Marmont about Spain back in 1809. "The Emperor is crazy, stark staring mad, and we are all going to pay for it, all will end up a colossal catastrophe for us."[21] This applied doubly to the Russian campaign of 1812.

Curiously Napoleon summoned Caulaincourt one more time that spring of 1812, just before setting out for Poland.

> I spoke to him of the reproaches he would continue to suffer for running so many risks, for putting up for lottery such fine and great destinies, when instead he could exercise such a great, such a powerful influence through his government in the cause of peace. I spoke to him about the effect of his risking the lives of the youth of France would have on the people.... I represented to him the reproaches already made against him about this loss of life in the war in Spain, and added how dangerous it would be by now starting yet another distant campaign [in Russia] before the Spanish campaign was brought to a successful conclusion.... I also reminded him of the great privations and discomfort his troops had suffered during the last campaign in Poland [at Eylau and Friedland].... It was therefore also a matter of conscience and moral conviction. "Your Majesty is being led astray by false councils. He is closing his ears to the truth and instead believing illusions. He believes he is marching toward a great political objective, and I believe he is wrong."

Unaccustomed to such plain speaking, Napoleon lashed back, claiming, in Caulaincourt's words, that "I had become Russified and that these matters were really quite beyond my humble understanding, closing in a heated manner telling me that it was in fact the Emperor of Russia who wanted to make war now, not he...."[22] Napoleon capped this with the final irony of all by ordering Caulaincourt to accompany him on this very Russian campaign against which he had so valiantly argued against.

Napoleon's departure from Paris on May 9, 1812, for the new theater of war, astounded everyone who knew him. For the first and final time in his career he left in broad daylight, in a magnificent regal procession of carriages, with Empress Marie-Louise at his side and a major retinue of imperial officials, as well as his special confidant General Duroc, Secretary Méneval, and the unfortunate Caulaincourt. The imperial carriages were preceded and followed by hundreds of mounted élite Imperial Guardsmen in all their splendor. Here was a very confident man indeed: Napoleon Bonaparte would show the world. He had summoned all the princes, kings, and emperors within his imperial fold to meet him at Dresden, where he would hold a prestigious confab on the most ambitious campaign of his career. Napoleon had already secured his diplomatic flanks by concluding a

series of defense pacts and commitments to provide troops, including one
with King Friedrich Wilhelm III of Prussia on February 24, 1812, and
another with his own father-in-law, Emperor Franz I of Austria, on March
14, 1812. Unfortunately, he had let a similar engagement with Sweden slip
through his fingers, throwing Stockholm into the arms of St. Petersburg.

The regal procession reached the Saxon capital of Dresden on May 16,
welcomed by a torchlit parade and blaring trumpets (an event to be imitated
there nearly 150 years later by another conqueror). The kings and princes
were there in all their splendor, Napoleon and Marie-Louise the center of
this carefully prepared rally, as the king and queen of Saxony personally led
them to their quarters in the castle. Friedrich Wilhelm, who so loathed this
Bonaparte, was there with a forced smile, joined by the kings and queens of
Bavaria, Württemberg, and Westphalia. Amid the clutter of minor new royalty, the emperor and empress of Austria, Marie-Louise's parents, arrived
two days late. Balls were given night after night, and long, unpleasant talks
were held behind closed doors during the day, as military commanders
received their marching orders and attempted to coordinate their efforts. As
for Alexander I of Russia, he refused to have anything to do with this,
merely passing on a message informing Napoleon that he, Alexander,
would "not draw the first sword. I have no intention of being held responsible in the eyes of Europe for the blood this war will cause to be shed. You
have been threatening me for eighteen months now. French troops . . . line
my frontiers. But I remain in my capital, arming and fortifying us."[23]

Bidding adieu to Empress Marie-Louise, whom he would not see again
for seven months, Napoleon set out from Dresden on May 29, the magnificent state carriages replaced by caissons and cannon, and tens of thousands
of troops, traveling via Glogau and Posen, reaching Thorn on June 2, where
he spent four days before going on to Danzig where he arrived on 7 June to
inspect the largest French military depot in that region.

Danzig proved to be more than a mere stopover. Here it was that he
finally confronted his brother-in-law, King Joachim of Naples. Still embittered over the tiff he had over Murat's attempt at independence, Napoleon
had forbidden that monarch from joining the major convocation of rulers
and commanders just held at Dresden. Instead a smarting Murat had been
ordered to the isolated Baltic fastness of Danzig.

Relations between the emperor and the king of Naples were "more
than merely chilly," eyewitness Caulaincourt reported. Bonaparte complained that Murat no longer considered himself a Frenchman and had forgotten to whom he owed everything he had. "'When he sees me, he belongs
to me,' Napoleon commented, 'but as soon as I am out of sight, he acts like

all other people without real character. Out of sight, out of mind.' . . . In public the emperor received the king well enough, but alone he began to harangue him fiercely."

Meanwhile Murat was complaining to anyone who would listen that in reality Napoleon had made him only a viceroy, not a real king, a mere pawn through whom Napoleon could enforce his will. "He wants to be king of the whole of Italy," Napoleon snapped on learning of Murat's words. "It's that dream alone that prevents him from asking for the crown of Poland!" He then continued to vent his spleen by attacking his brothers. "Jérôme is only interested in a lot of glitter, women, pomp, and feasts. None of my brothers supports me. I have to govern for them all. Without me, they would ruin their poor subjects. . . . My brothers think of no one but themselves. But I at least provide a good example for them."[24]

After raising Murat's hackles and inspecting the fortress and impressive supply depot there, Napoleon set out from Danzig on June 10, with Murat heading his cavalry, continuing via Marienburg, to Königsberg where he spent four days preparing that stronghold, and "on the 23rd [of June] we camped along the Niemen."[25]

The man wearing a Polish soldier's hat and overcoat rode along the banks of the Niemen that morning, studying the slopes and river level, then scanning the opposite shore, the Russian frontier, with his telescope. He could see little movement, nary a sign of the enemy army. The man in the costume of a Polish light cavalryman was of course Napoleon, and the man at his side was General Haxo, chief of his engineers. Their aim was to find the best point at which to throw across the pontoon bridges. Time was of the essence. Surprising everyone, Napoleon had reached Marshal Davout's I Corps at the village of Alexota only a few hours earlier. He had to hurry. But while returning across a wheatfield, Napoleon, "who invariably rode badly," was thrown heavily to the ground by his mount. Badly dazed, he complained to Caulaincourt later that everything still seemed very dark. The word quickly spread through the ranks of the superstitious guard and troops. The last time Napoleon had been thrown from his horse, at the Schönbrunn Palace during the Wagram campaign, it had been followed immediately by an attempt on his life by a German student. "It would be best not to cross the Niemen," an equally superstitious Berthier insisted. "This fall is a bad sign," he argued, and a large number of previously hesitant senior commanders agreed. What is more, "The Prince of Eckmühl [Davout] and the general staff all complained about the total lack of solid intelligence reports" regarding the Russian army.[26]

Napoleon ignored all such objections, and the Niemen was successfully bridged the next day, Napoleon himself among the first to cross with General Morand's leading division, as he continued to remain with the advance guard, "pressing the pace of the entire army" and outstripping his already lagging supply trains, in spite of the warnings of the wary Berthier.

Advancing via Kovno, Napoleon entered the freshly evacuated major Russian citadel of Vilna, Lithuania, on the twenty-eighth. He felt angry and cheated. The Russians had refused to fight. Despite the speed of his advance, they had evaded him, if by just a few hours. What was happening? Caulaincourt explained that the czar had plenty of territory and was deliberately withdrawing to weaken further Napoleon's fragile supply and communication lines, to isolate the French in hostile country. The truth of his grand equerry's assessment was not lost on Napoleon, only four days after crossing the Russian frontier. "This rapid movement without supply depots exhausted and destroyed all the resources of the local inhabitants unfortunate enough to find themselves along Napoleon's invasion route." Nor was the Grande Armée spared by Napoleon's precipitous advance and poor planning. "The advance guard of the French army lived well enough off the land, consuming everything in sight," Caulaincourt recalled, "while the remainder of the army as it advanced in its wake found itself without even elementary food supplies for the troops or horses, both literally dying of hunger. . . . Exhaustion, added to the very cold rainy nights, resulted in the loss of 10,000 horses, and even of many men of the Young Imperial Guard just during the first few days." And yet this was only the beginning; the enemy had not even been sighted. It did not bode well, but Napoleon persisted, as he always did.

As for Vilna, "It was quite mournful." Napoleon complained about the hostility of the local population, "all the Lithuanians praising Emperor Alexander," instead of their French "liberators." After just four days in Vilna, without enough supplies even for Napoleon's headquarters staff, they had to move on.[27]

Then a courier arrived with a special letter from the czar. Napoleon smiled knowingly. Alexander was already asking for terms; he was capitulating. Napoleon had won. "My brother Alexander . . . already wants to surrender. He is afraid. My armies have sent his flying. Before the month is out, the Russians will be on their knees before me." After crossing the Niemen, he had exclaimed: "*Alors*, now Poland is mine!" and this had come true without firing a single shot.[28]

Alas, the note from the czar immediately dispelled all Napoleon's premature bombast. Alexander had the audacity "to demand the reasons for the invasion of his country, and in a time of peace, without even a declaration of war." He ordered Napoleon to withdraw immediately behind the Niemen, after which he would be willing to open negotiations with the French. "Alexander is poking fun at me!" an astounded Bonaparte exclaimed. "Does he really believe I have come all this way just to negotiate some minor commercial treaty with him? I have to finish once and for all with the colossus of the barbarians of the North. I have drawn my sword!"[29]

The fact is that the czar's unexpected evacuation of his frontier, including the major stronghold of Vilna, had deprived Napoleon of the great, initial sweeping victorious battle he had predicted, which could end the campaign quickly and decisively—another Austerlitz. He was more than upset, he was bewildered.

Napoleon's mighty force was phenomenal in size and strength as it continued its advance. They were marching by the thousands, the tens of thousands, the hundreds of thousands. It was incredible, it was fascinating, it was awe-inspiring but above all, it was terrifying. All Europe was trembling at the very thought of this massive Gallic-led horde, the likes of which had not been seen since the eighth-century invasion of Europe by the Arabs and Berbers, and before that by Attila the Hun. Bavarians, Württembergers, troops from Berg, Hesse-Darmstadt, Frankfurt, Nassau-Aremberg, Isenburg, Hohenzollern-Sigmaringen, Würzburg, Saxony, Anhalt-Berburg, Schwarzburg-Sondershausen, Waldeck, Schaumburg-Lippe, Westphalia, Mecklenburg-Strelitz, Oldenburg, occupied Denmark, occupied Prussia, occupied Spain and Portugal, occupied Holland, occupied Switzerland, northern Italy, the occupied Papal States, Danzig and Illyria, tiny San Marino and the miniature principality of Liechtenstein, to Marseilles, Lyons, and Paris—they marched hundreds of miles, some ultimately two thousand miles, because once more Napoleon Bonaparte had refused peace, because—obsessed beyond any definition of rational thought—he demanded war and further conquest. He clenched his little fists and denounced the British, the Russians, his ministers and generals, all the subdued people of Europe immediately under his yoke, and the whole of Europe, with psycopathic persistence and perversity. Seven engineer battalions, twenty-two army train battalions, military police, hundreds of bakers' ovens, thousands of horse handlers and smiths, and even so Napoleon had had to leave behind 275,000 troops in France and Italy in 1812 to quell his own angry people.[30]

And thus they continued to converge on eastern Poland, 265 French infantry battalions, 291 foreign battalions, 219 French cavalry squadrons, 261 foreign squadrons, all told, 513,500 infantry and foot artillery, and 98,400 cavalry and horse artillery, for a grand total of 611,900 men, exclusive of well over 25,000 civilians, officials, servants, and whores and camp followers. Nor was Napoleon neglecting the backbone of his army, including 130 heavy siege guns and 1,242 field artillery pieces of every caliber. More than six thousand wagons were required just to carry the daily food provisions, and altogether 32,700 official army wagons, carts, and caissons streamed across every major road leading to Warsaw and the Baltic, hauled by 183,911 army horses. But even these wagons did not suffice, and more had been sequestered once French troops had crossed the Rhine and entered the German states, where, among other things, an additional 150,000 draft horses were stripped from every farm and village they passed ... 333,911 horses all told! The average division of 10,000 heavily laden men could trudge at best fifteen miles per day, and each division occupied a solid stream three to four miles long. The French army, along with the allied contingents forced to join them, formed the largest traffic jam in European history, which backed up hundreds of miles over the next several weeks. Nothing quite like it had ever been seen before.[31]

The largest army ever assembled by any one force in European history was an unwieldy multilingual organization divided among three levels of command. The first line of 450,000 men, directed by Napoleon himself, was divided into three armies. The first of these, approximately 250,000 strong, commanded by Bonaparte in person, included Murat's two cavalry corps, the Imperial Guard, and Davout's three infantry corps (he was Napoleon's finest field commander), while Oudinot's II Corps and Ney's III Corps were accordingly smaller. Oudinot and Ney were hardly of the caliber of Lannes, who was now so badly missed, nor were they equal to Masséna or Suchet, whom Napoleon was forced to keep in Spain in this multifront conflagration. The Imperial Guard was now beefed up to include the Young Guard, under Mortier; the Old Guard, under Lefebvre, while the Guards Cavalry as usual remained under Bessières.

In addition Napoleon created two auxiliary armies to support the "first line," one comprising 70,000 Westphalians, Saxons, Hessians, and Poles, under King Jérôme (for the moment), and to be known as VIII Corps, and the other, IV Corps, under the titular command of Prince Eugène de Beauharnais, including 80,000 Italians and Bavarians. There were two more semiautonomous corps: Macdonald's reliable X Corps guarding Napoleon's extreme left flank along the Baltic, and Prince von Schwarzenberg's Austrian corps protecting the Grande Armée's extreme right, or southern flank. (Additional changes of command would include Poniatowski's Polish V Corps, St.-Cyr's Bavarian VI Corps, and Reynier's Saxon VII Corps.)

Napoleon's second line was in effect really a massive reserve force of 165,000 men intended to provide replacements for the three principal armies of the first line, including Marshal Victor's multinational IX Corps (33,000). The third portion of the Grande Armée included the final, fallback reserve of 60,000 men, the XI Corps commanded by Marshal Augereau, comprising garrisons left at Danzig and along the Vistula. Napoleon's principal army and second line included some 302,000 "Frenchmen"; the Swiss, German states, Austrians, and Prussians provided another 190,000; the Poles and Lithuanians some 90,000; and the Spaniards, Portuguese, and Illyrians another 32,000 or so.[32]

Russia was not without its own substantial resources, reinforced after the signing of the Peace of Bucharest with Turkey in May 1812, releasing tens of thousands of troops for the northern campaign, and a treaty of alliance between Russia and Great Britain that was being drafted even as Napoleon crossed the Niemen and would be signed and made operative as of July. And of course the Swedes had also joined Russia in the diplomatic and military campaign. Since the humiliating defeat at Austerlitz, Czar Alexander had more or less reorganized and enlarged his army, including thirty-six new training centers across the country for recruits. The Russian cavalry was considered to be the best in Europe, supported handsomely by the Cossacks (literally, "freebooters"). The czar put much more emphasis on heavy artillery now, including forty-four batteries of eighteen-pound howitzers and twelve-pound cannon alone. Still, the Russian army totaled only some 409,000, 211,000 of them available first-line troops supported by a small reserve force of 45,000. Another 153,000 troops were scattered in garrisons separated by immense distances. Napoleon had numerical superiority, easily doubling the Russian front-line force. A major Russian weakness lay in its incoherent, untrained, amateurish administrative general staff, further weakened and divided by the inevitable petty loyalties among various senior commanders and gentlemen of influence. Baron Barclay de Tolly, the fifty-one-year-old Livonian general, was commander in chief of the First Army until he was superseded in August by the one-eyed, sixty-seven-year-old Russian prince Mikhail Kutuzov. The arrogant Hanoverian general, Baron Levin Bennigsen, who had faced Napoleon at Eylau and Friedland, though currently out of favor in St. Petersburg, would soon be called on again. The Prussian General Phull was largely responsible for preparing the Russian strategic plan—if such it may be called—of 1812, while the ablest Gen. Matvi Ivanovich Platov commanded the formidable

Don Cossacks. Other generals in the field included Bagration, Wittgenstein, Miloradovich, as well as Ostermann.

"The aim of all my moves will be to concentrate an army of 400,000 men at a single point," Napoleon instructed Davout.[33] As for the choice of invasion routes, he did not have much latitude, given the dense forests, numerous river crossings, large marshes and swamps—including the Pripet Marshes to the east of Warsaw, some two hundred miles long and one hundred miles wide—and the lack of roads, good or bad. The three principal routes included the northernmost one at Kovno on the Niemen; Grodno, also on the Niemen but nearly one hundred miles farther south; and finally at Brest-Litovsk, just east of Warsaw.

The Kovno Road led to Vilna, where the czar purportedly was assembling a major force; then to Vitebsk, Smolensk, and Borodino and on to Moscow. The Grodno route to the south passed through Minsk before rejoining the Vitebsk route. From Brest-Litovsk, Napoleon could travel well to the south of the Pripet Marshes to Kiev in the Ukraine, an enormous swing to the south before regaining the route to Moscow. The czar's general headquarters' best estimation was that, given the inordinate distances he would have to travel just to reach Russian territory, Bonaparte would take the shortest, most direct route, via Kovno and Vilna, so that is where the main Russian army of 27,000 men under Barclay lay in wait. The rest of the Russian army was dispersed over some 250 miles, from Rossitent in the north to Grodno in the south. This army included five regular army corps, Archduke Constantine's Imperial Guard, and three cavalry corps. To the south and east of Warsaw stood General Bagration's Second Army of 48,000 men. Since Bagration was a difficult man who could not tolerate Barclay, this separation was perhaps not such a bad idea. The only other immediate Russian force was General Tormassov's Third Army of 43,000 to the south of the Pripet Marshes near Lutsk.

After crossing the Niemen on June 24, Napoleon had been followed to the north by Macdonald's X Corps. To the south Davout's I Corps, Oudinot's II, and Ney's III drove past Kovno with St.-Cyr's VI Corps and Prince Eugène's IV Corps to their south, as Jérôme's VIII Corps theoretically pushed up from Warsaw. As usual, Murat's cavalry was leading the drive, now east of Kovno, and had been the first to reach Vilna on the twenty-eighth.

If Napoleon had originally hoped to draw Bagration's Second Army to the Vistula in pursuit of Jérôme's and Eugène's armies as they drove north, so

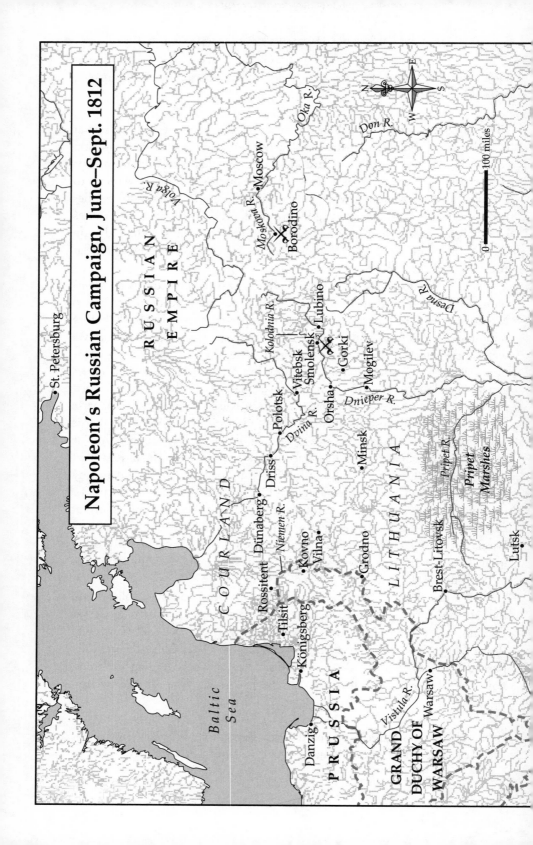

Napoleon's Russian Campaign, June–Sept. 1812

as to permit him meanwhile to attack and envelop the principal Russian force under Barclay before those forces could join under one command, he was to be disappointed. Not only were the czar's commanders proving contrary by withdrawing before the oncoming French, but two of Russia's three great natural factors were already playing major roles, disrupting Napoleon's overall strategy: time and distance.

It took time to march men into position, weary men who had already marched many hundreds of miles, and to coordinate schedules. Both Eugène and Jérôme in particular were well behind schedule and not in their designated positions when ordered. The problem was aggravated by the yawning distances that seemed uncharted on even the best of maps, which Napoleon in any case never bothered with. It was utter folly to launch such a massive campaign in a vast region where it was well known that food, supplies, and fodder would be at a minimum, and roads of any sort few and far between. It was Egypt all over again, and Napoleon had learned nothing then or since. For a campaign of such overwhelming numbers, Napoleon needed good roads, and many of them—at least one per corps—not to mention efficient logistical support for supplies of food, water, and fodder for each corps. This simply did not exist. Instead Napoleon was forcing his eleven army corps, exclusive of the guard and large cavalry and their enormous supply and baggage trains and hundreds of pieces of artillery, to keep to just a couple of principal routes. He had been here before and should have known better. Consequently, few corps commanders could adhere to Bonaparte's orders, which, moreover, sometimes went astray or at best were delayed by the vast distances and the general confusion.

The third great natural force in Russia, weather, added the final ingredient to the by-now all-encompassing chaos: First there were spells of wilting, almost subtropical heat, as columns of hundreds of thousands of men under heavy kit, and three hundred thousand horses, kicked up miles-long dust clouds, literally choking man and beast alike, followed by sudden torrential, monsoonlike rains that persisted for days on end, turning hard, deeply rutted roads into axle-deep quagmires. Sunny days would then follow, baking solid the ruts, hindering the advance of 32,000 horse- and ox-drawn vehicles, impeding the arrival of all munitions and supplies. But whether deep dry ruts or vats of sucking mud hundreds of miles long, all resulted in broken legs of men and horses, not to mention cracked and broken axles and wheels. From the moment the French crossed the Niemen, there were ceaseless bottlenecks of enormous proportions on every route. Repair crews, thousands of men, called up from the sappers and even front-line troops, worked all day, all night, only to see the situation deteriorate daily. The hard-slogging infantry, with their heavy field packs, abject, practically on the verge of starvation, far from home, and demoralized even before the first shot was fired, began throwing away their heavy flour supply and even cartridges. Napoleon simply did not understand the limits of human beings—nor for that matter did he understand the demands of elementary logistics.

Worst of all were the difficulties involved in moving and giving top priority to Napoleon's "daughters," as he referred to his beloved artillery. Even the smaller six-pounders weighed 2,010 pounds, each with cannon and limbers, while the formidable twelve-pounders, Napoleon's favorites, each weighed 3,440 pounds. Furthermore it took eight horses to haul each six-pounder—when not bogged down in mud—and a dozen horses to pull the twelve-pounders. Once the artillery pieces were bogged down in knee-deep mud, hundreds of troops and additional animals had to be brought in to help extricate them. The loss of horses alone was calamitous from the very start; most of the 150,000 or so farm horses stolen from German and later Polish farms were the first to go. They could work hard for a few days or even a few weeks, but never having traveled more than two or three miles from their farms, they were quickly broken by the insufficient food, lack of rest, and especially the unrelenting distances. Then there was the endemic problem of colic, as ravenous beasts were given damp thatch from cottage roofs, or green corn or grain, to eat. Their bellies and intestines distended, literally bursting open, tens of thousands of the bewildered beasts dying in agony along the army's path, adding to the logistical nightmare that Napoleon in his haste and blind determination had failed to consider. The stench was stifling in the overwhelming heat, and the sight demoralizing to the troops as they passed by the maggot-infested beasts. If these were the conditions in midsummer, what would winter bring?

Thus when Napoleon ordered Jérôme's corps here, or Eugène's there, or Victor's or Macdonald's or Ney's anywhere, it was not simply a case of moving men from point A to point B on a neat map in general headquarters. Morale collapsed even among the high-spirited Young Guard, and the usual 20 percent desertion rate soon left entire divisions so weakened as to be of little use, until they could be artificially reinforced by the fragments of other units. The food supply trains in theory accompanied them, but frequently were late. Men foraged and killed and ransacked every farm and village they passed, the situation aggravated by the lack of clean water. Dysentery and typhus were epidemic. Chief of Staff Berthier, a brutal, angry man when thwarted, was beside himself by the time Napoleon reached Vilna on the twenty-eighth. Every commander in the French army, Berthier among them, had argued vehemently against this campaign and thought crossing the Niemen madness if not suicide. Napoleon overruled them all in the superiority of his intellect and greater personal vision. Forward! he ordered. And anxiously, wearily they trudged on, although the first battle had yet to take place.

One of the first grave psychological setbacks for Napoleon came not from the Russians but from his younger brother, King Jérôme of Westphalia. "Tell him that it would be impossible to maneuver in a more incompetent manner than he has just done," Napoleon instructed Berthier. Jérôme had failed to follow orders as usual, neglected to deploy his men properly, and in general was not adhering to the established campaign "plan" and schedule. Jérôme in fact was still only at Grodno as late as July 3, when he should have been harassing General Bagration's army far to the south, pinning them down. Tell him, Napoleon continued, that "he has caused my initial maneuvers to fail, thereby permitting the best opportunity of the war to escape me, all as a result of his singular inability to understand the first thing about how to wage war!"[34] And yet Napoleon should have known this from previous experience. Jérôme was furious, but instead of taking it out on his big brother, he did the next best thing. He got into a furious quarrel with the very tough Marshal Davout, who quickly, roughly squelched that young upstart, Bonaparte or no. If Louis Davout would not suffer that sort of insult from Napoleon, he certainly wouldn't take it from the pampered Jérôme. A week later, on July 14, a sulking Jérôme abandoned his entire Westphaliam army and decamped for the west and the comforts of Kassel, leaving Davout temporarily in command of that additional corps until it could be handed over to the by-now hardly reliable General Junot. As for the Russians, despite Davout's very hard push, Bagration's army had escaped, thanks to Jérôme's incompetence.

Even as Davout continued to pursue Bagration's Second Army toward Orsha, Napoleon was concentrating on pursuing Barclay de Tolly's First Army as it effectively retired to the powerful defenses of Driss and Dünaburg on the Dvina. Leaving Murat's cavalry along with Ney and Oudinot's infantry before these fortresses, Napoleon moved the main part of the French army to the north to isolate Barclay from the rest of the Russian army and its own life of communications, in other words, an end-run attempt to outflank and attack him from the rear, the *"manoeuvre sur les derrières,"* as he called it. This second attempt to bring to battle and to defeat the principal Russian force had to work, Napoleon felt. Meanwhile, far to the south, St.-Cyr's VI Corps, Eugène's IV Corps, the VIII Corps, and Davout's large I Corps were driving in a sweeping line, Davout still intent on cutting off Bagration. From the west Jérôme's former corps was pressing Bagration from the west, and by July 24 they and Davout were closing in on Bagration before the Dnieper. Meanwhile, to the north that same day, Murat's cavalry, Ney, Eugène, and the Imperial Guard were forcing Barclay farther up to Vitebsk.

Davout had finally caught up with part of Bagration's army at Mohilev on July 23 and did inflict a few thousand casualties, yet most of that Russian force managed to escape intact, shortly to join with the main force after all. Although Napoleon had anticipated taking Barclay's army at Polotsk, it was in fact on the Dvina before Vitebsk on July 27 that the French army finally trapped the elusive Barclay. But when on the twenty-eighth Napoleon had finally entered Vitebsk, great was his disappointment in finding another deserted city: Barclay's troops having withdrawn eastward during the night. "The Emperor was completely lost in thought, often in a foul mood, to the point of not addressing anyone round him in a civil manner, a rare enough event in itself," Caulaincourt recalled:

> He was dismayed by the departure of the inhabitants of the city and by the flight of the troops into the countryside. This system of retreat perhaps finally opened his eyes to the eventual consequences that such a war as this could have on us, a strategy that was daily drawing us farther and farther from France. But then with the slightest hope in our favor again he cast aside such practical considerations and their consequences, his hope once again unrealistically rekindled [for a fast victory].[35]
>
> "Time and again the Emperor repeated that the Russians whom everyone had claimed to be so numerous, in fact had no more than 150,000 men. . . . [He] added that he was sure that we [Caulaincourt and the other French generals opposing Napoleon's campaign] had deceived him personally about everything, down to the problems of the Russian climate, insisting that winter here was like that in France, except that it just lasted longer. These accusations against us were repeated on every occasion. I reiterated to the Emperor, quite in vain as it turned out, that I had not been exaggerating in the least, and that as his most faithful servant I had revealed the full truth about everything. But I failed to make him change his mind,"

an exasperated Caulaincourt lamented.[36]

Nor was Chief of Staff Berthier spared the results of Napoleon's frustrations. He was "heaped with wild abuse for his frank advice, as a reward for his constant hard work and devotion" to his chief. Bonaparte complained that much of the work of Berthier's general staff—several hundred of them—was badly done, "no one planned ahead." Yet Napoleon refused to trust anyone, not even Berthier, to make the smallest decision or give the simplest order without his own stamp of approval. As Caulaincourt painfully witnessed: "The Emperor's irritation with him [Berthier] reached such a point that he now often told him that he was good for nothing and ought to leave the army and return to [his estate of] Grosbois and the arms of his Visconti." Many of the army administrative services were indeed run badly, but given the extraordinary situation, they could justifiably blame Napoleon, who had led them into a country where they were unable to obtain even basic supplies. "Everyone was miserable and eventually it took all the Emperor's will and insistence to maintain some sort of control over the situation."[37] Even before the first major battle took place at Smolensk, French morale was disastrous at every level, everyone angry, openly opposing the system, the campaign, and their own colleagues. It boded very badly indeed for the future.

Napoleon, invariably in a foul mood now, continued to attack everyone around him. When General Junot, the new commander of Jérôme's corps, advanced apathetically with his troops, Napoleon immediately turned on him. It was Junot's fault that the Russians had escaped. He would be responsible for Napoleon losing this campaign. Then he blamed the Poles for being unreliable. And why didn't Andréossy prevent the treaty between Russia and the Turks? It was all his fault that tens of thousands of fresh Russian troops were now freed for service against the French. Nor did Napoleon spare his brother-in-law Bernadotte, whom he accused of joining forces with the Russians. On and on he criticized everyone, clearly on the verge of a mental breakdown, but never did he himself admit to a single mistake.

And all this was compounded by the czar's continued silence over peace proposals Napoleon had finally submitted to dispatch to him. "Alexander can see perfectly well how incompetent his generals are, and that as a result he is losing his country!" What was the matter with the man? Napoleon angrily demanded. Was he blind?[38] Caulaincourt wondered just how long things could continue like this, with Napoleon in control, before all collapsed around their heads.

The reason for this prolonged, bitter outburst was the fact that the Russians had fled a second confrontation as a result of their successful evacuation of Vitebsk. The next opportunity for a big decisive battle was at Smolensk, eighty miles away. Schwarzenberg's Austrian Corps and Reynier's VII did manage to contain General Tormassov's Third Army of the West near Brest-Litovsk, however, ending that immediate threat to the French flank, while Oudinot's II Corps, aided by St.-Cyr's VI (Bavarian) Corps had managed to inflict a minor if temporary victory over Wittgenstein at Polotsk back on July 18. Unfortunately Napoleon paid a heavy price, as Oudinot was wounded and put temporarily out of action, though St.-Cyr was rewarded with a marshal's baton for his contribution.

Now, on July 28 at Vitebsk, Bonaparte had to reshape his campaign plans as a result of Barclay's escape, matched by Bagration's escape from Davout at Mohilev back on the twenty-third. What he had dreaded most was taking place: Barclay's and Bagration's armies had by now joined forces many miles to the east, at Smolensk. Napoleon's line of communications with the rear all the way back to Dresden was at the breaking point, with tens of thousands of dead horses marking the milestones between Danzig and Russia, and a straggling line of supplies stretching literally back to the Rhine. Worst of all was the loss of perhaps 100,000 troops through massive desertion, illness, poor and irregular rations, and unrelenting fatigue. By August 4 Napoleon's immediate force was reduced to no more than 185,000 men, while Barclay and Bagration had some 125,000 effective troops at their command. Napoleon's huge numerical superiority was quickly dwindling in the Russian vastness.[39]

At a war council on August 6, the Russian high command finally decided it was time to stop withdrawing. Not only would they stand and fight, they would also launch a powerful counteroffensive, as Barclay, with 650 guns, marched 118,000 men west of Smolensk along the Dnieper. Once again the Russian plan failed, however, due to jealousy of command, Bagration refusing to close and coordinate his efforts with his rival Barclay. In fact Bagration advanced only hesitatingly, finally refusing any effective cooperation whatsoever. As a result the Russians ordered a temporary halt, which permitted Napoleon to advance in two columns along a fifteen-mile front heading toward the Dnieper, while sending another force to secure the Smolensk-Moscow Road, with the intention of cutting off the Russian line of retreat.

During the night of August 13–14, French engineers threw four substantial pontoon bridges across the Dnieper, and by dawn most of Napoleon's army was already across. The Russians under Barclay began wavering, and after a few days withdrew to the east, back to Smolensk, leaving one crack division of 9,500 men under General Neveroski to guard the Dnieper and bar the main road to that city.

Barclay ordered General Rayevski's 20,000 troops and seventy-two guns to occupy Smolensk and hold off the French until Barclay's and Bagration's armies could fully reinforce them and the city walls. Bagration, still holding himself aloof well to the east of the city, and completely separated from Barclay's force, refused to cooperate, however, leaving Barclay with only the vague consolation of knowing that two more large Russian armies would soon be on the move to aid them, including those of Finland (Russia was now at peace with Sweden) and Moldavia (thanks to the Treaty of Bucharest). But Russian armies were notoriously slow and cumbersome, and the distances to be covered vast. Barclay de Tolly understood this only too well.

Once over the Dnieper, Napoleon launched Murat's still-powerful cavalry, Ney's corps, the Imperial Guard, and Prince Eugène's army toward Smolensk, while to the south Davout formed a second column comprising I, V, and III Corps, as Latour-Maubourg's reserve cavalry executed a diversionary attack down the Dnieper. But barring the Orsha-Rosasna Road stood General Neveroski's crack division, formed in a powerful square. Murat, who had apparently forgotten the lesson the French squares had given the Mameluke cavalry at the Battle of the Pyramids, charged the square, time after time, to no avail. Contrary to orders. Ney was forced to intervene and stop the useless carnage of Murat's irreplaceable cavalry. Murat and Ney had not been on speaking terms for years, however, and Murat adamantly refused to clear the road for Ney's infantry, regardless of orders and pleas from GHQ to do so. Murat would show them. He could do it all alone. The result was that Murat's cavalry took a severe mauling and was forced back with grievous losses. And as the French did not have artillery with them at this point, they could not bombard the otherwise vulnerable Russian square. General Neveroski therefore succeeded in attaining his objective of delaying the French advance, as Barclay strengthened his position in and to the north of Smolensk.

By dawn on August 16 the French began arriving around the massive walls of ancient Smolensk, and by the next day the battle was on, Murat's greatly weakened cavalry and Poniatowski's corps attacking the city from the southwest; next to them Davout's I and Ney's III Corps to the north of Davout sealing off everything to the banks of the Dnieper itself, while Barclay's main force remained one mile away on the northern side of the Dnieper, protected by several powerful artillery batteries. Bagration, who made no real attempt to protect Smolensk—or Barclay—crossed the Kolodnia River and fled eastward toward Lubno and Moscow, while General Doctorov, now in charge of Smolensk's city defenses, was slowly being encircled and crushed by the overwhelming French numbers. Throughout the following day Doctorov held on grimly, still denying the French access to the city. If that Russian commander suffered up to fourteen thousand casualties, yet he held off Napoleon, who, surprisingly, showed very little vigor in his attack. It was bewildering. Napoleon did not even bother to send a strong force to occupy the empty miles separating Bagration from Barclay. As for Doctorov, he successfully withdrew from the burning city and finally rejoined Barclay's main position to the north. Murat's two cavalry corps gave pursuit on August 19, as Barclay's force, still well north of the Dnieper, hastily withdrew eastward. The French pursuit was maintained by Ney in the direction of Gorbunovo, crossing the Kolodnia also in the direction of Lubno; Davout and Ney followed in a more direct line along the Smolensk-Lubno Road. "In a month," Napoleon had earlier pronounced, "we will be in Moscow. In six weeks a peace treaty will be signed." But as Caulaincourt admitted, "This prophetic tone of his did not convince a soul," nor was it fulfilled.[40]

By August 24, with more negative reports just received from Spain, including that of Wellington's decisive defeat of Marshal Marmont at Salamanca a few weeks earlier, Napoleon nevertheless gave the order for yet another final drive against the gathering Russian army now at Borodino, the last large city between them and Moscow. Marshal Kutuzov, obese and infirm, was a Russian born and bred, and a determined fighter. If, as Clausewitz claimed, he "no longer possessed either the activity of mind or body of yore . . . nevertheless he knew the Russians, and how to handle them."[41] Czar Alexander had just appointed Kutuzov to supersede the disappointing Barclay, despite Kutuzov's irascible reputation, but because he remained the one Russian general capable of commanding the respect of his officers and troops alike, and because of his unflagging determination to fight. Napoleon, only too familiar with Kutuzov and aware of the significance of the demotion of Barclay, thought the long-awaited confrontation with the czar's army now definitely lay ahead at Borodino. "His genius was slow, vindictive, and crafty," de Ségur informed Napoleon, but he was the first real Russian opponent they had met, and thus the French resumed their seemingly endless march eastward, along the road to Borodino, nearing their objective by September 5.

The French camp, which still totaled some 166,000 men and cavalry and 587 guns before setting out on this trek, had by the time they reached Borodino been reduced to 131,000 men and cavalry. Morale and divisions within the French command and in the ranks were already at a dangerous level. The physical and mental condition of Napoleon's men of all ranks could be described at best as fast fading as malnutrition, illness, and a despairing homesickness made rapid inroads.

The lack of cooperation between some of Napoleon's senior commanders continued to be appalling. This was aggravated by the open mutual distrust and dislike between Napoleon and Murat, and then Murat's outrageous refusal to allow Ney's corps to advance to meet the enemy. Next a veritable shouting match between the brash Murat and the unmovable Davout at Smolensk over a difference in tactical use of Murat's cavalry. Davout, a difficult man, was nonetheless by far the most brilliant military commander, second only to Napoleon, whereas Murat was hardly on an intellectual par with Davout. Indeed Murat had made blunders with his mismanagement of the army's precious but fast-disappearing cavalry, now reduced effectively to perhaps 28,000 as they approached Borodino. As for Berthier, neither Ney, Murat, nor Davout could stomach the man, feelings that Berthier, as chief of staff, was in a powerful position to reciprocate with a malign vengeance.

Finally there was Napoleon himself. Time and again he had been advised, even by the sometimes surprisingly timid Berthier, that this entire campaign had been an unconscionable error, that they should never have crossed the Niemen, that the French general staff could no longer cope, that their lines of supply and communications were dangerously overstretched, that less than one-third of the original Grande Armée were French-born, the rest "allies" supporting them in a war that not a single one among them had wanted and from which they had everything to lose and nothing to gain. In brief, if it came to a down-and-out battle, Berthier assured Napoleon that the French could count on no one but themselves, and already tens of thousands of deserters, malingerers, and genuinely ill troops were daily depleting the effective fighting force while undermining the mental attitude of even the more robust of commanders. This was now compounded by Napoleon's own growing anxiety over this campaign, which he had initially hoped to complete within the first thirty days, and had then reluctantly revised to "two months"—and that was back in May. It was now September, with temperatures still mild but beginning to fall during the night, adding to the daily death toll and reduced muster roll every morning. Not only was Napoleon rightly anxious, with the terrible news from Iberia—a military theater he now realized he personally had to rush back to if he was to save it at all—but he was tired, suffering from hemorrhoids, a lingering cold, a painful urinary infection, and the burning pain of his gastric ulcer piercing his side, forcing him more and more to hold his right hand in that famous "pose," inside his jacket over the left side. Every time his horse slipped in the heavily rutted roads and he was thrown, he was reminded that he was now forty-three and had spent the better part of the last twenty-seven years as a soldier. For the first time in his career he was beginning to feel old, and tired of his own profession. Indeed, all the signs appeared to be against him. Thus it had to be Borodino, now or never, the battle to decide the fate of the latest war he himself had chosen to inflict on Russia, France, and Europe, in the face of all opposition.

The Russians' numbers were now temporarily reduced as well, they having left a long train of dead and wounded in the burning ruins of Smolensk and by desertion. Kutuzov could marshal effectively perhaps 106,000 men (including 24,000 crack cavalry still in superb condition, unlike their weakened and dispirited French counterparts), but only 82,000 infantry, perhaps 90,000 at most, including untrained militia just brought up. The Russian high command was weak, disunited, and communicating very badly, each army more or less on its own, with almost independent commanders. But Kutuzov not only outgunned Napoleon, he had the advantage of doing at Borodino what Napoleon had done at Austerlitz, and doing it better: getting there first and choosing his own battlefield.

The small town of Borodino was situated on the west bank of the snaking Kalatsha River, which, continuing a few miles north of the town, then joined with Moskva River. In addition there were several smaller rivers and streams dissecting the region, particularly along the bluffs and steep banks of the Latsha River Valley, with its numerous hills and dispersed woods. With Moscow only seventy-two miles to the east, the czar's command still ringing in his ears, Kutuzov had to act with vigor, and this he did. He built redoubts and batteries all along the commanding hills and crests, with Platov's and Uvarov's cavalry securing the northernmost point of his right flank on the east side of the Kalatsha. From his headquarters at nearby Gorki, Kutuzov ordered his generals to surround the city. The southern flank numerically was the weakest link in the Russian line, as the commanding hilltops and river bluffs and dispersed wood cover gave way to open plains. As for the Russian Imperial Guard, or V Corps, under the Archduke Constantine, it remained behind the lines in reserve. Kutuzov had found a far superior defensive position than Napoleon had at Austerlitz. Here French cavalry, cannon, and mass troop movements were automatically thwarted by the terrain.

Finally in place on September 5 and 6, Napoleon deployed his troops before the Russians. While his engineers built five pontoon bridges over the

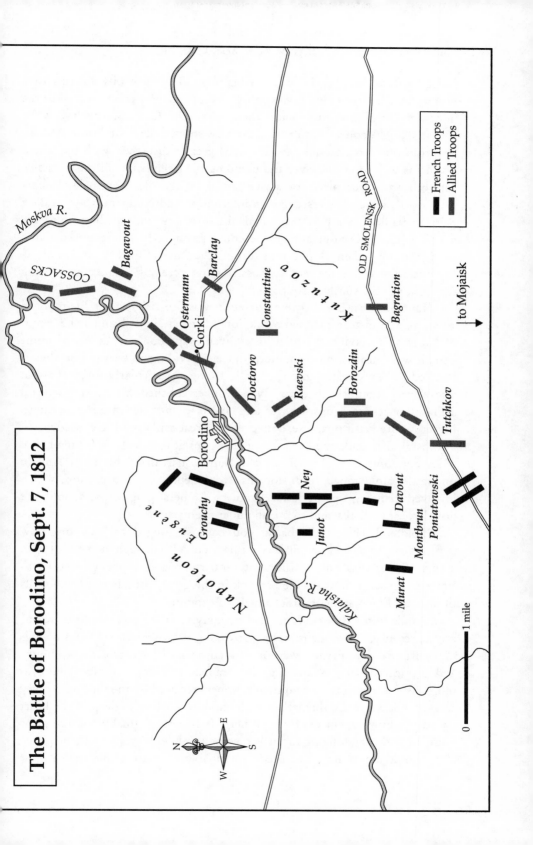

The Battle of Borodino, Sept. 7, 1812

Moskva R.

COSSACKS

Bagavout

Ostermann

Barclay

Gorki

Constantine

Doctorov

Raevski

Borozdin

K u t u z o v

Bagration

OLD SMOLENSK ROAD

to Mojaisk

Tutchkov

Borodino

Ney

Junot

Davout

Montbrun

Poniatowski

Murat

Grouchy

Eugène

N a p o l e o n

Kalatsha R.

French Troops

Allied Troops

N
W   E
S

0   1 mile

Kalatsha River, Bonaparte finalized his plans. The most obvious offensive was to launch a sweeping cavalry thrust, supported by infantry well to the north of Borodino. But facing them were the Cossack cavalry, while Murat's much reduced cavalry was by now in mediocre condition. Attacking from the north would have involved greater distances, with the added problems of fording the river and climbing the steep banks of the Kalatsha. The other obvious place for attack lay along the old Smolensk-Moscow Post Road, which traversed the southernmost and comparatively weakest Russian flank. Once past the initial hills bristling with artillery, into the opening plains, Davout argued, he could strongly hit the exposed flank, swing around and envelop it, thus turning the Russian line. What was more, Davout pointed out, the mighty Russian guns were dug in and aimed facing the west, not the south or southeast.

Napoleon insisted that this operation was too risky, given his reduced strength, and instead planned a headlong drive straight through the center of Kutuzov's heavily defended line. Given Napoleon's weakness of numbers, it was hardly a wise counterproposal. Dividing an enemy line always resulted in heavy losses, and they were facing a particularly tough Russian line. Compounding his error, Napoleon established his most powerful artillery pieces, 120 guns in three large batteries, just out of effective range. Never before had Bonaparte, above all the great artillery officer, made such a colossal miscalculation. As the opening guns at 6:00 A.M. on September 7, 1812, announced the French attack, Napoleon realized his error, and in midbattle, amid much confusion, had to redeploy all 120 cannon, which involved bringing up the horse handlers, limbers, gun crews, supplies of powder, cannonballs, and so on, all under enemy fire.

"Soldiers! This is the battle you have so longed for! Victory now depends on you, and we do need this victory! Through it we will gain plenty of supplies and warm winter quarters, and a prompt return to France. . . . Let it be said, 'He partook in the great battle beneath the walls of Moscow!'"[42] Napoleon proclaimed at Borodino.

Morale in the Russian army had strongly revived now, thanks to Kutuzov's presence, not to mention the proximity of Moscow, the religious capital of Russia. The French were hardly enthusiastic, most of them hungry and all more or less anxious and demoralized as every day saw them ever more distant from France and their numbers reduced by the thousand every week, while knowing themselves to be hundreds of miles deep in the heart of eastern Europe, cut off from all help. If Napoleon finally had the great battle he had been longing for, it had come too late. It was a battle he probably should never have accepted, but unable even to admit an error or defeat, he felt he had no choice but to order the opening salvos, shattering the morning stillness.

Eugène's corps easily overran Borodino's nominal Russian garrison. But Davout, who had been placed to the left-center of the Russian line—the very position he had so adamantly argued against attacking—found himself battering against a solid Russian wall of grit, guns, and bayonets, just as he had predicted.

Less than an hour after the initial French attack, Kutuzov launched a massive counteroffensive, throwing back Davout, Eugène, and the French line, wounding Davout and General Rapp in the process, inflictng four more wounds on the courageous Ney (making him eligible for the Order of the Three Fleeces), not to mention killing several French generals, including the valiant cavalry commander Montbrun and his successor as well, Gen. Auguste de Caulaincourt, Armand's brother. So severe was the monumental blast from all along the Russian line that by 8:30 A.M. Napoleon had been forced to commit Junot's reserve corps. It was almost another Eylau, Bonaparte fighting for his very existence despite the inferior Russian numbers. The French had been repulsed from left to right. Davout's plan would have avoided this. But there was always a great intellectual-military rivalry between Bonaparte and Davout, and Bonaparte would never admit that someone might have a plan superior to his own. Indeed, he attempted a similar headlong thrust through the very center of the enemy later at Waterloo. . . .

After recoiling in confusion, just before 10:00 A.M. Napoleon's right flank launched another attack, only to be thrown back by the highly motivated patriots of Bagration's troops and their three hundred big guns. Napoleon had never seen anything like it. "The huge Russian redoubt belched out a veritable hell against our center," Caulaincourt reported.[43] Napoleon was further hampered by the superb defensive position taken by Kutuzov, which everywhere divided the French forces into tightly packed narrow columns, leaving no large open space for the intimidating full-line attack Bonaparte so favored, and when the narrow French columns did advance, they were mowed down by superb Russian sharpshooters and a devastating artillery. Nor could French cavalry advance easily in most areas, given river barriers, streams, woods, hills, and narrow valleys, although the Russians, too, paid a very heavy price for their valor in defending their country, including the loss of Marshal Bagration himself, as the Russian army was finally forced back to consolidate its position. The French pushed hard along the southern and northern Russian flanks, but soon the equality of the two armies simply ended in stalemate.

Throughout the battle Napoleon refused to commit his Old Guard, despite the appeals for their help by all the French commanders. Finally, slowly pulling himself together, he gathered four hundred French guns to concentrate on the principal Russian redoubt, blasting away the seemingly impregnable Russian position.

Armand de Caulaincourt watched with fascination this awesome tug-of-war between the French and Russians:

> They threw out a hellish fire against our center in return. Marshal Ney and the viceroy [Eugène] launched a combined attack to take their position but were repulsed. Nor were they any more successful after another attempt and in fact Ney even lost some ground. . . . But our artillery finally checked the enemy offensive, they then being caught in a murderous cannonading by us.

As the action continued:

> His Majesty rushed up at a gallop ahead of our own cavalry, joining the king of Naples, to assure the success of his next attack, while Marshal Ney and the viceroy supported General de Caulainourt's decisive attack. But the enemy's attempt to retake their lost terrain now proved futile. To better see personally what their [Russian] position was at this time, the emperor advanced to our front line. The [musket] balls whistled so intensely round him that he ordered his personal escort back for safety, and me as well. . . . I thanked him but remained at his side. It was certainly a dangerous moment for the emperor, the fusillade becoming so furious that the king of Naples, along with several other generals, again pressed the emperor to retire. He not only remained there, but personally led the reserve columns into the battle,

for by now "almost every division and several of the regiments had lost their commanding officers, killed or wounded."[44]

At about two o'clock in the afternoon, French cavalry followed up this bombardment by sweeping through the remains of that Russian redoubt, supported by Eugène's infantry, every man of the enemy position exterminated. But still Napoleon would not commit the Old Guard, his only remaining unscathed reserve. When Doctorov and Duke Constantine attempted a counterthrust, they were smashed by a fresh battery of eighty French guns, although the Russians still held fast everywhere else. By now both sides were so utterly exhausted after nearly twelve hours of intensive combat that all firing gradually ceased. "Night alone finally put an end to the fighting," Caulaincourt summed up. Napoleon had no stomach to continue, nor had Kutuzov. Both armies held in disciplined formations.

That night Napoleon placed his headquarters right in the middle of the battlefield before the great redoubt, amid the cries of the dying. "Never had a battle cost us so many generals and officers," Caulaincourt commented, without mention of his own brother among their number. "Never had a position been attacked with more vigor and intelligence and so stubbornly defended." As Napoleon himself attested, "These Russians let themselves be killed as if they were not men, but mere machines, refusing to surrender, and therefore we are taking no prisoners now, and that is not advancing our position one whit."

Crossing the battlefield that same evening, Caulaincourt summed up the appalling sight, "so cluttered with so many dead. In the village [of Borodino] around which the fighting had centered, the Russian dead were stacked one on top of another. In the plateau behind it, the field was heaped with the dead." During the night, Caulaincourt continued, "the Russians made such an orderly retreat, such as no enemy has ever made, not leaving a single cart."

When the French passed through the ruins of the village of Mojaisk at noon the next day,

> Napoleon was much too preoccupied to talk. His thoughts were as much on the developments in Spain as they were in Russia, and in spite of having won a battle, he was no less anxious than he was before. The condition of our men was appalling, and he was deeply distressed. And all units were badly reduced.... To be sure the prospect of entering Moscow now was cheering, but with the Russian Army still out there before us, nothing was finished. Everyone noticed the emperor's obvious concern, regardless of the meaningless phrases he repeated before them, that the seizure of Moscow meant peace at last, even as Kutuzov was regrouping around that city.[45]

For all his feverish personal intervention on the field, Napoleon had steadfastly refused to commit his reserves, including most of his guard, even most of Eugène's reserves and Junot's (Jérôme's Westphalians, which could possibly have given him a decisive rather than just a nominal victory over the Russians). Even so, the Russian force was left with barely 52,000 effective troops. Napoleon, however, had been so utterly shaken by the fierce wall of fire and human flesh he had encountered that he only left Borodino on September 10 to continue his slow march on Moscow, even then harassed severely by the undaunted Cossacks.

Borodino was technically a French victory. Nevertheless the Russians had withdrawn in remarkably good order and, despite the bloodletting, had strong fresh reserves coming up. Kutuzov was in the heart of his own country, supported by Russians who had seen village after village, city after city, burned and destroyed and looted by the French, these French who were now nearly two thousand miles from their own capital, while Kutuzov was only sixty miles from his own. The French were completely isolated.

As for the casualties, they were catastrophic, the French suffering more than forty thousand dead and wounded, the Russians probably close to fifty thousand.[46] No one kept accurate figures, for the French and Russian "medical corps" were inundated with the vast stream of butchered troops. The French alone lost forty-eight wounded or dead major or lieutenant generals, and with brigadiers that figure probably came closer to seventy, not to mention an additional eighty-six aides-de-camp and thirty-two staff officers. Never had there been such a bloodbath.

It was this slaughter with which Dr. Turiot—writing another of his blunt, gratuitous medical reports from the Galitzine Hospital in Moscow twenty days after the human disaster at Borodino—was so preoccupied. He summed up the entire tragic venture from the time the French had first crossed the Niemen. "The [French] victory at Smolensk merely added to our predicament," the medical corps lacking everything as they watched the city burn around them. Napoleon had equipped them with neither bandages, medication, clean water, nor even sufficient personnel. The French surgeons as usual lacked a proper field hospital.

> The city's archives building was therefore transformed into a hospital, the documents found were rolled up to serve as splints, cannon plugs and gun cotton replacing bandages and linen, while government files were used as bedding for those operations. . . . Under such conditions it was not without some merit to have carried out all the emergency operations within the first twenty-four hours. Nevertheless almost all the amputees died,

due to unsanitary conditions, gangrene and infection setting in on a wide scale. "And as usual for want of a professional and adequate ambulance service the rest of the wounded remained for a long time on the battlefield where they had fallen ... complicated by the incessant rainfall, the air infected by the rotting corpses admidst the wounded, and the plunging night temperatures." The mortality rate was staggering.

Smolensk proved a victory for us because the logistical services brought up five hundred cannon and two thousand five hundred caissons and munitions wagons, [but] as a result of the negligence and incompetence of those same logistical services, they had abandoned far behind our advance route the immense quantities of linen, bandages, and medications we had earlier prepared.

Thus the thousands suffered and died, "that number increased because no lamps were provided for us, limbs amputated and wounds stitched by torchlight, whenever that was available ... with the deplorable results as one can readily imagine." What is more, only forty-five surgeons were available to cope with the casualties, while "the entire corps of nurses deserted us en masse." Forced to use "untrained surgeons"—that is, men with no medical training or experience—the medical corps "did more harm to our army than all the enemy's batteries combined." The French needed at least one hundred more qualified surgeons, "and our losses would then have been less terrible, especially if aided by a properly run medical service." But corrupt and incompetent army contractors and administrators were largely responsible for many of these woes.

The same situation then recurred many times following Borodino:

My Belgian colleague, Kerckhoven, who had to operate in the church of Borodino, tells me that the wounded lay on the raw ground, for want even of straw bedding ... without any sort of medication being available to help their wounds or reduce their pain. Everywhere, therefore, we saw only fright and despair. Several of the wounded trapped in the fire [that swept Borodino] perished in the flames,

while others who somehow survived this "soon died of hunger or as a result of putrefaction." One soldier badly wounded and abandoned in the field was found two weeks later "half his body buried in the belly of a dead horse, eating its raw flesh like a wild dog." Those who could be saved were taken to temporary medical quarters in Moscow, at the Galitzine Hospital, the Orphanage, the Paul Hospital, and at the Empress's Hospital, but still that did not begin to suffice for the tens of thousands without beds. Much of the suffering, Dr. Turiot repeated to Napoleon, was due to French maladministration and to soldiers through their "pillage and waste, and the deliberate pilfering of the immense provisions that would have amply allowed us to bring much physical comfort to the troops. In a word, the army administrators responsible for this débâcle thought only of themselves and of lining their own pockets." But now the few survivors could not be moved. They had to be be left in Russian cities, in Moscow, for they would never survive the return journey. "To leave Moscow would be to leave the wounded and the healing at the mercy of the army administrators and war contractors, or to their fate in the hands of ruthless wagon drivers, even the bakers," who were interested only in loading loot, not human beings. "The taste for loot and blatant venality have transformed those whose job it is to devote themselves entirely to the wounded and the troops into veritable parasites."[47] Surgeon Turiot prayed for no more great French victories.

Opponents

Louis XVIII, who plotted
from England to overthrow
Napoleon. Portrait by Gérard.
(Kunsthalle, Hamburg)

His Most Gracious Majesty
George III. Portrait by William
Beechy. *(Hulton, Deutsch)*

Pope Pius VII, arrested and imprisoned by Napoleon. Portrait by David. (*Proctor Jones Collection, San Francisco*)

Prime Minister William Pitt the Younger, who vigorously armed Great Britain against the threat of French invasion, 1804–5. Portrait by Gainsborough, engraving by I. K. Sherwin. (*Dawson Collection, Morrab Library of Penzance*)

Lord Liverpool, Robert Banks Jenkinson, who first as secretary for war, 1809–12, and then as prime minister, from 1812 onward, fully supported Wellington in Iberia, and the Allied Coalition, with the objective of defeating Napoleon and removing him from the French throne. (*Hulton, Deutsch*)

Robert Stewart, viscount Castlereagh, who as foreign secretary from 1809, pursued a vigorous course against Napoleon, in which he was strongly supported by Lord Liverpool. *(Hulton, Deutsch)*

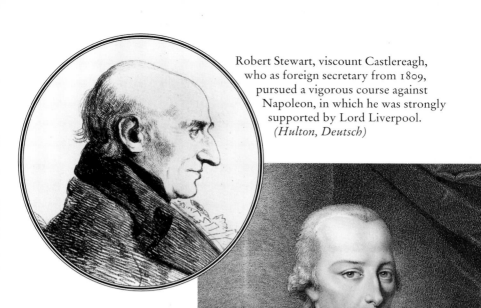

Emperor Franz I of Austria, whose thousand-year-old Holy Roman Empire was seized, dismantled, and replaced by Napoleon's Confederation of the Rhine. Portrait by Dumont, engraving by Bourgeois de la Richardière. *(Dawson Collection, Morrab Library of Penzance)*

Frederick William III, king of Prussia, who lost half of his kingdom to Napoleon and his allies. *(Proctor Jones Collection, San Francisco)*

Czar Alexander, friend and foe of Napoleon.
A rare portrait by Gerhard Kuchelchen,
engraving by Alexander Tardieu. *(Dawson
Collection, Morrab Library of Penzance)*

Field Marshal Gebhard Leberecht von Blücher, prince
of Wahlstadt, who with Wellington defeated Napoleon
at Waterloo. Portrait by F. Rahberg, engraving by
J. Swaine. *(Dawson Collection, Morrab Library of Penzance)*

The Spanish royal family,
kidnapped and imprisoned by Napoleon.
Group portrait by Goya.
(Museo Nacional del Prado)

Prince Mikhail Golenishchev Kutuzov, who, as commander in chief of the Russian army, succeeded in forcing Napoleon to withdraw his army from Moscow in 1812 with catastrophic losses. *(Dawson Collection, Morrab Library of Penzance)*

Arthur Wellesley, the duke of Wellington, who successfully defeated every French general and marshal in Iberia, and then with Blücher defeated Napoleon at Waterloo. Portrait by John Simpson, engraving by H. Phillips. *(Dawson Collection, Morrab Library of Penzance)*

Battles and Other Events

Siege of the Tuileries Palace, August 1792, as witnessed by Napoleon and Bourrienne.
Engraving by Berthault. *(Dawson Collection, Morrab Library of Penzance)*

The French Channel Fleet, locked in the harbor of Brest by Adm. Sir William Cornwalli
preventing its participation in the invasion of England, 1803–5. *(Musée de Versailles)*

Napoleon builds a navy and flotilla for the invasion of England, 1803–5. *(Musée de la Marine)*

Napoleon's Coronation at Notre Dame Cathedral, December 2, 1804, officially launching his new empire. Engraving by Dupreel. *(Dawson Collection, Morrab Library of Penzance)*

Napoleon and his staff inspect invasion preparations at Boulogne, 1805. *(Musée de la Marine)*

British defeat of combined Franco-Spanish fleet, Trafalgar, October 21, 1805.
Painting by Harold Wyllie. *(Royal Naval Museum, Portsmouth)*

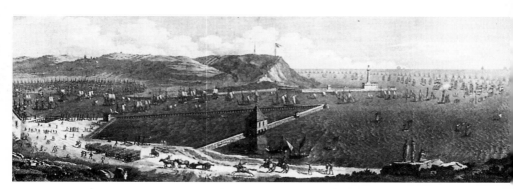

Boulogne, 1805, preparations for the invasion of England. *(Musée de la Marine)*

The Grande Armée on parade in the Champs-Elysées.
(Dawson Collection, Morrab Library of Penzance)

Napoleon and his marshals at the Battle of Friedland, 1806. Print of Vernet's original. *(Musées Nationaux)*

A victorious Napoleon and Grande Armée enter Berlin's Brandenburg Gate and seize Prussia. Print of Meynier's original. *(Bibliothèque Nationale)*

Emperors Napoleon and Alexander I meeting on a raft in the Niemen River, resulting in the peace treaties of Tilsit, July 7–9, 1807, between France, Russia, and Prussia.

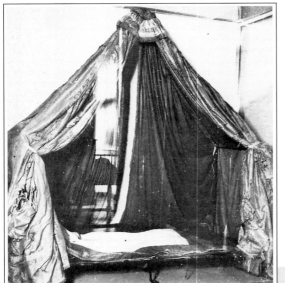

Napoleon's iron campaign bed. *(Archives de l'Armée)*

Bonaparte inspects cannon during a battle. Lithograph by F.C. Vogel. *(Dawson Collection, Morrab Library of Penzance)*

Napoleon at Wagram, 1809.
Print of Vernet's original.
(*Bibliothèque Nationale*)

French retreat from Russia, 1812. (*Dawson Collection, Morrab Library of Penzance*)

The French army gathers at Leipzig, where it was to be defeated by the Allies, October 16–19, 18
(*Dawson Collection, Morrab Library of Penzance*)

A gloomy Napoleon and French army defending France against Allied invasion, 1814.
Print of Meissonier's original. (*Bibliothèque Nationale*)

Victorious Allies enter Paris, March 31, 1814.
(*Dawson Collection, Morrab Library of Penzance*)

March 1, 1815: Napoleon, having escaped Elba, lands in the Golfe Juan near Cannes.
(Dawson Collection, Morrab Library of Penzance)

Napoleon on the day of his defeat
at Waterloo, June 18, 1815.
(Dawson Collection, Morrab Library of Penzance)

Places

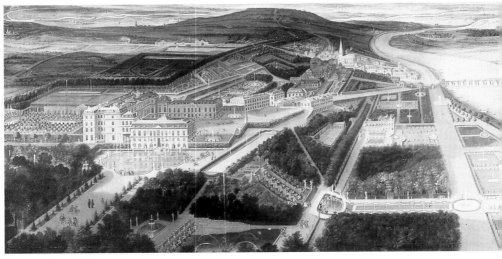

Napoleon's favorite residence, the Palace of St.-Cloud, burned down by the Germans in 1871. *(Bibliothèque Nationale)*

One corner of Fontaine's Hall of the Marshals, in the Tuileries. Drawing by Fontaine. *(Bibliothèque Nationale)*

Place Vendôme, bronze column made from 1,200 enemy cannon, upon which a statue of Emperor Napoleon was briefly placed. *(Dawson Collection, Morrab Library of Penzance)*

Versailles during the 1790s. Drawing by
Rigaud, finished by Tinney. *(Dawson
Collection, Morrab Library of Penzance)*

Port St.-Denis, the major northern entrance
into Paris. Drawing by Captain Batty,
engraving by Charles Heath. *(Dawson
Collection, Morrab Library of Penzance)*

The Palace of the Legion of Honor.
Engraving by Hensball. *(Dawson Collection, Morrab Library of Penzance)*

Malmaison,
facing the park.
(*Bibliothèque
Nationale*)

Paris's
Hôtel de Ville
as it looked in
Napoleon's time.
Engraving by
Charles. (*Dawson
Collection, Morra
Library of Penzar*

Longwood—the residence, stables, and grounds of the British lieutenant governor
of St. Helena—made available to Napoleon and his staff for his final home.
Watercolor by Marchand. (*British Library*)

CHAPTER 3 4

Malet's Malaise

I need to make an example of someone in order to prevent this from recurring.

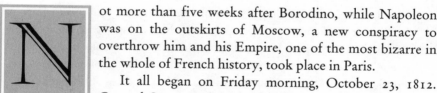

ot more than five weeks after Borodino, while Napoleon was on the outskirts of Moscow, a new conspiracy to overthrow him and his Empire, one of the most bizarre in the whole of French history, took place in Paris.

It all began on Friday morning, October 23, 1812. General Savary, minister of police since the dismissal of Joseph Fouché two years earlier, had just completed the long daily report for the special courier about to leave for Moscow, where a triumphant Emperor Napoleon was believed to be quartering his troops for the winter. It was tedious, and Savary, despite his mere thirty-eight years, was exhausted by this unending paperwork. Although Fouché's *Police Bulletin* had not been continued, the amount of work remained the same if not greater.

After two years in office Savary still was not used to being called a policeman. A soldier by profession, he had passed his entire career in the army, campaigning or at Napoleon's side as an aide-de-camp, and had even served a short stint as imperial ambassador to St. Petersburg. The only work he had ever done that had anything to do with the police was as commander of the nation's special troops, known as the *élite gendarmerie,* which in fact were soldiers called in by the police when needed for maintaining law and order. Louis Dubois was no longer at the prefecture of police, having been replaced in 1810 by the former imperial chancellor, the mild—some thought hopelessly weak—Etienne-Denis, duc de Pasquier. As many saw it, with the removal of both Fouché and Dubois, the police had fallen into a state of lassitude, a feeling that the day's events were only to reinforce.

As dedicated as Fouché had been to his work, Savary in addition was equally dedicated to Napoleon, and took every task assigned him seriously. It was no doubt because of this unquestioning loyalty that the emperor had entrusted him with this sensitive if irksome portfolio—for which in fact he was not as well suited as his predecessor.

Finishing the night's work at five o'clock in the morning, the minister signed the report and left it on his desk for his assistant to dispatch. Unlike Fouché, Savary—a bachelor—resided at his ministry and thus simply retired to his bedroom next door. Bolting the door and snuffing the candle, he fell into a deep sleep. Two hours later there was a terrible ruckus in the adjoining apartments, loud enough eventually to awaken the police minister:

> I was very tired, and, when I heard the wooden panels of the door to
> my office crack, splinter, and fall to the floor, at first I tried to ignore it.
> Then I thought the building was on fire and that they were making all
> that noise to wake me up. I got up with a jolt, walking across my darkened bedroom, groping for the door to the study. As I unlocked it and
> entered the office, I saw armed soldiers trying to force the other door,
> and there were others in the courtyard outside as well. . . . Still standing
> in my nightshirt, I opened the door and asked who had brought them
> here.

Instead of answering, the soldiers shouted, "Call the general!" Savary was astonished to see enter his study General Lahorie, his comrade in arms of Revolutionary days and former chief of staff of General Moreau's Army of the Rhine, but who had since been involved in antigovernment activities resulting in his imprisonment. Not surprisingly there was no smile on Lahorie's lips, no greeting whatsoever to this former friend.

"You are under arrest," he said brusquely to the bewildered Police Minister. "Just be grateful that you are in my hands, at least no harm will come to you." Then he explained: "The Emperor is dead, killed beneath the walls of Moscow on June 8," adding that in consequence there was a change of government and that he had been ordered by the military governor of

Paris to arrest the minister. "You are talking a lot of nonsense." Savary suddenly smiled. "I have a letter from him here of that same date. I can show it to you." "But that cannot be, is that possible?" General Lahorie said, genuinely taken aback. "That is not possible," he said, looking more resolute. Leaving a couple of men behind, he left the room.[2]

Savary grew anxious. He had recently ordered the arrest of General Lahorie for treason and had thrown him into the much-dreaded La Force Prison. Clearly he had broken out: How, When? During Lahorie's absence, Savary tried to get a few answers: "Who are you?" he asked the officer in command. "I am a captain and adjutant major of the 10th Regiment of the National Guard." "Very well," the police minister continued. "These soldiers belong to your troop?" "Yes, sir." "Then you are not revolting against the government?" he asked. The soldiers looked astonished, protesting, "No, no, we were ordered here by our officers. We were brought here by a general." "Very well, then, do you know this general?" "No," they admitted. "In that case, what I see does not surprise me," Savary continued. "As for me, I know him, and I am therefore going to let you know precisely the dilemma you are in. He is a former aide-de-camp of General Moreau [convicted of treason] . . . who should have been in prison where I put him. He is a conspirator! And do you know who I am?" Clearly they did not. "Do you know what building you are standing in?" Again they shook their heads. But then one young officer stepped forward, indicating that he knew that Savary was the minister of police. "In that case," the latter said, "I order you and if needs be, demand, that you arrest General Lahorie immediately."[3]

Meanwhile the captain and a lieutenant were securely holding both of Savary's arms, while he tried to extricate himself from this situation, noting that the soldiers' muskets were not even armed with flints or ammunition and were thus useless. "My dear sir," Savary said, turning again to the captain, "you are playing at a most deadly game which you dare not lose, and thus prepare to be shot in a quarter of an hour, if I myself am not first. For it will take only that long for the Imperial Guard to get mounted and be on its way, and then you are lost." In fact the barracks of Napoleon's guard were located just a few hundred yards away, on the other side of the Seine. Seeing the captain waver, clearly in doubt, Savary pursued his ploy. "If you are a man of honor, do not get involved in this crime, and don't prevent me from saving all of you. I only ask that you release me." Savary then reached out and tried to grab the hilt of the captain's sword, but he was not fast enough. "No, you will march when we tell you to," said the officer, suddenly reasserting himself.[4]

Through the tall windows Savary saw General Lahorie returning "with a man with a hideous face," the "sergeant" he had been looking for. "They returned to our room looking quite furious," Savary later recalled, Lahorie dropping back behind the troops. The "sergeant" then approached, but so drunk he slammed into a heavy table. Stunned for a moment, he stopped to massage his leg; then, cursing, he approached Savary, pointing the tip of his sword at his chest, asking if he recognized him. "I am General Guidal whom you had arrested at Marseilles and brought here to Paris," he declared defiantly. And then in a flash it all came back to the police minister. This Guidal—whom he had never seen—had been arrested on his orders after having been caught communicating with the British fleet off the coast of Toulon. "Have you come to dishonor yourself by a cowardly murder?" Savary asked boldly. "No, I will not kill you, but you are going to come with me before the Senate."[5]

Guidal ordered the police minister to get dressed, which he did as slowly as possible, and when one of his secretaries—a former army officer—finally arrived, Savary signaled to him to go back, calling out, "Go tell my neighbor not to worry, no harm has befallen me."[6] The secretary quickly made his way out before anyone could stop him. Savary's "neighbor" was in fact one of the senior police directors, the much feared Pierre François Réal, who lived just around the corner from the Police Ministry in the Rue des Saints Pères.

Guidal and Lahorie escorted Savary briskly out of the building past the police guards stationed there, who did not even attempt to halt or question the intruders grasping their minister by his arms as they led him to a waiting cabriolet. Although Savary managed to escape as they proceeded along the Quai des Lunettes, he was quickly recaptured by the troops and eventually taken to La Force Prison (not the Senate).[7] What next transpired constitutes one of the most curious tales of conspiracy ever heard.

It all began, as it ended, with Gen. Claude-François de Malet, "one of those men produced by revolutions," as Réal put it, "but who, lacking the qualities necessary to succeed, finds himself stymied and then succeeded by those more talented than he."[8]

Malet, born a gentleman and native of the Franche-Comté in 1754, began his career as an army officer, serving in the revolutionary Armies of Italy and the Rhine, and promoted to the rank of brigadier general by 1799. But with the elevation of Bonaparte first to the Consulate and then to the imperial purple—to which Malet vociferously objected—the general's career was brought to an abrupt halt. He was dismissed from his post in

Rome after disagreeing sharply with the French military governor there, General Miolis.[9]

Angered by the injustice of the army authorities, along with the arrogance of Bonaparte, who had the effrontery to crush his beloved First Republic, this genuinely dedicated republican lived in Paris with his wife on half pay. General Malet gradually began meeting other prematurely retired and equally disgruntled army officers—including Generals Lemoyne, Demaillot, Guillaume, Marescot, and Dupont—who made no secret of their own loathing of Bonaparte. It was under such circumstances that one group, meeting daily in a café, first began plotting the overthrow of the Bonaparte regime. This conspiracy differed from most others hatched by the Jacobins and royalists by focusing on one of Napoleon's many absences from France, preferably on a distant battlefield. The basic formula also differed from others in that it lacked solid organization, funding, and planning. And because for the most part Malet rarely confided in more than one or two senior military officers, he also lacked effective army support in the critically placed garrisons. Nor did he have nationally recognized leaders to take over and administer the new government once the coup had been executed. But none of this seemed to bother the cold, haughty, dreamy Malet, or divert him from his idée fixe.

His standard plan—from which he did not deviate much—was to print and sign a series of forged government documents—proclamations, senatorial decrees, and orders—announcing the (fictional) death of Napoleon on some far-off battlefield and the (equally fictitious) resolution by the Senate to create a new government, ousting and arresting members of Napoleon's cabinet and high command. He then drew up a list of important officials, mostly senators, whom he would like to appoint to replace the old government, but without consulting or informing them that they had been chosen.

General Malet's suspicious activities first came to the attention of the police in 1807, and then in June 1808 Fouché reported that Generals Malet, Guillaume, and Demaillot were plotting to overthrow the government and replace it with a dictatorship. Confronted by the police, General Guillaume confirmed that Malet and Demaillot had indeed discussed just such a plan, including the creation of a directory of five members. One police agent reported that Malet had offered a man five hundred thousand francs to assassinate Napoleon. "Malet had told him to be ready to act upon receipt of the orders he would be given two hours before the coup was to take place." Thus Fouché and Dubois finally acted, ordering Malet's arrest. Somehow warned, Malet had fled, though the police found three carbine rifles and two pairs of pistols at his apartment. "Malet's is an overly stimulated mind," Fouché reflected, "belabored by Jacobinism and discontent." The plot, he insisted, despite the testimony of witnesses and the cache of guns, "never existed, or rather, existed only in the heads of two people, that of Malet and M. Dubois, State Councillor and Prefect of Police." Dubois, who had uncovered the plot, was "making far too much of this whole affair,"[10] though upon capture Malet was imprisoned in La Force.

Nevertheless, one year later reports reached the Police Ministry that Malet, still in La Force, was at it again, now conspiring with three fellow prisoners to overthrow Emperor Napoleon. This was confirmed by an Italian inmate in whom Malet had confided.

Malet's new plan was to go into effect before Nôtre-Dame Cathedral on Sunday, May 28, 1809, when a Te Deum—to be attended by the highest officials of the land—was scheduled to celebrate Napoleon's recent victories over the Austrians at Eckmühl and Aspern/Essling.[11] Once again broadsheets and documents had been secretly printed and forged—"Bonaparte no longer exists. Down with the Corsicans and the Police! Long live freedom!"—and uniforms and arms stashed nearby. And although Fouché took the elementary precaution of moving three of the alleged conspirators to other prisons on May 26, he continued to dismiss the plot out of hand in a report to Napoleon, ridiculing Dubois again, whom he claimed had been taken in,[12] summing up the whole thing as merely a harmless "plot of hypotheses."[13]

By 1812, however, both Fouché and Dubois had been dismissed from office, replaced by two lesser individuals, Savary of course at the Police Ministry, and Pasquier at the Police Prefecture. It was their decision in 1812 to release this Malet, now deemed quite harmless, from La Force and transfer him to a small mental institution, "une maison de santé." And there once again he was forgotten.

But General Malet, a man obsessed with his own curious brand of destiny, was hard at work carefully forming a new coven in the old mold, drafting the usual documents, proclamations, and decrees, including again a senatorial document organizing the new government, naming its directors (quite unknown to them), which as usual he himself would soon "sign" on behalf of the absent senators. Among the new documents created this time was one appointing Malet as the new military governor of Paris, thereby giving him command of all the troops and National Guards in the First Military Division, which included Paris and the immediate region.[14]

At the maison de santé Malet had met a Spanish priest by the name of Cajamano, who had since been released and agreed to abet the hapless general in his latest conspiracy. Another priest, one Abbé Lafond, also an inmate of this hospital, joined them, and recommended two young protégés, a Corporal Rateau, serving in a Paris garrison, and a Vendéen law student by the name of Boutreux. As unlikely as it seems, given his extreme youth, Boutreux was to be appointed "Prefect of the Seine," while Corporal Rateau was to become an officer, indeed, Malet's aide-de-camp. Malet then duly forged the appropriate documents confirming these nominations. At the same time he prepared brevet promotions for a couple of army officers to be used later, as shall be seen, complete with one-hundred-thousand-franc drafts drawn on the treasury to be given these men as a special "bonus." For Malet all was possible.

In order to carry out his own coup this time, Malet decided he needed force, that is to say, troops, and fortune could not have been more accommodating, placing as it did the Popincourt Army Barracks in the street directly behind the mental institution. Naturally he would need help to maneuver the various military detachments envisioned by his plans. This included nothing less than arresting the minister of police, the prefect of police, the war minister, and members of the government, while securing the directory of post and telegraph (all communications with the city), the treasury, and certain government buildings, and sealing the city's gates. For this delicate task he selected two real but at present "embarrassed" generals—Guidal and Lahorie—currently detained at his majesty's pleasure in La Force Prison.

Barring any unforeseen complications, with Malet's uncanny verve and audacity, taking over the nearby army barracks and deploying those troops should present no problem at all. For this he would also need his old uniform and another for his new "aide-de-camp," and he sent word to his wife, instructing her to pack them and some light arms and ammunition in a trunk and deliver them to the Spanish priest. With everything ready, the fateful countdown began late on Thursday, October 22, 1812. The stage was now set, and with Napoleon well out of the way—in fact in the process of evacuating Moscow at this very moment—Malet was free to act.

After the main gates and massive doors of the *maison de santé* were locked at ten o'clock, Malet and Lafond put their operation into effect. Climbing out of Malet's ground-floor window—there were no bars—they swiftly traversed the long enclosed garden and clambered over a small wall. Free at last, they set off for the Spanish priest's flat, where they found everyone waiting. There Malet and Corporal Rateau donned their uniforms, and the new prefect of the Seine, Boutreux, a tricolored sash of office.[15] Then, displaying his large leather portfolio of forged documents, Malet explained each one and what it was to be used for, and made duplicate packages for the conspirators to distribute later.

At one o'clock on the morning of Friday, October 23, Malet, Prefect Boutreux, and Aide-de-Camp Rateau set out for the Popincourt Barracks, where Malet easily talked his way past the sleepy guard on duty, demanding to see the commanding officer, Colonel Soulier.

Soulier was ill in bed, and Malet, with a candle in his hand, pushed his way into the bedroom and introduced himself as "General Lamotte." "I can well see that you have not been apprised of the situation," Malet blurted out. "We have had the misfortune of losing our emperor." Soulier, still half asleep and trying to take in what was happening here in his bedroom, broke down sobbing. "There has been a change of government. Here are the orders General Malet gave me for you just a little while ago," he added as he handed him his instructions to prepare his men and follow "Lamotte's" orders to the letter, which he in turn had received from the Senate. At the same time he informed Soulier that he had just been promoted to the rank of brigadier general, handing him the nomination along with a one-hundred-thousand-franc draft. "Lamotte" ordered Soulier to assemble his troops in the large stone courtyard below.[16]

A quarter of an hour later "Lamotte" was addressing the twelve hundred men of the Tenth National Guard Regiment, reading a proclamation informing them of the death of Napoleon and change of government, and that they would now be following his orders. He instructed Soulier to take one company to the Hôtel de Ville to prepare for the convening of high officials forming the new temporary governing junta, and to await his own arrival there. "Lamotte" himself commanded the remainder of the garrison to follow him, but, acting in great haste he forgot to issue flints or ammunition for their muskets.

As Friday was the traditional day for the weekly dress parade in the Place Vendôme, the movement of so many troops in the street during the night apparently did not arouse anyone's suspicion. Malet led the remainder of his troops right up the Rue St.-Antoine to La Force Prison, where he ordered the concierge to open the gates for him and release Generals Guidal and Lahorie in his custody. The latter, as bewildered as the concierge—not having been apprised by Malet of his big "putsch"—gradually began to understand and then embraced him.

"There is no time to lose," he told them once they were alone. "Here are your instructions; take these troops and carry them out. I need only a half-company with me to seize the government, and when that is done I'll await your news."[17] For Lahorie, an old hand at conspiracies—he had been in on Napoleon's coup d'état of 18 Brumaire—and now facing a long prison term as a result of the Moreau affair, there was nothing to lose as he and Guidal accepted the packets of instructions.

General Lahorie immediately set out with his troops for the Prefecture of

Police on the Ile de la Cité. Arriving there at six o'clock in the morning, he found Pasquier already at work. Forcing his way into the Prefect's office, Lahorie arrested him on the spot, Pasquier not even protesting. Lahorie marched him over to La Force where he had him locked up, along with Police Minister Savary. At this very moment other troops were on their way to arrest War Minister Clarke and Archchancellor Cambacérès, while Malet was assembling two more National Guard regiments with which to close all gates and exits to the city of Paris, and to occupy the Banque de France, the treasury, and main administrative offices.[18] All was going according to schedule.

The most amazing aspect of this whole fantastic affair up to this point was that no one had considered the news of Napoleon's death startling or, apart from Savary, had even challenged its validity or the orders and actions of the conspirators.

With growing confidence Malet thus set out to arrest the military governor of Paris, General Hulin, at his official residence in the Place Vendôme, next door to his headquarters, which he had surrounded with a detachment of twenty-five men. Pushing his way into the luxurious apartment, Malet informed the incredulous Hulin of Napoleon's death and the order for his own arrest. Hulin, amazed and still sleepy, insisted on reading the orders himself. But as he turned around to read the orders, Malet whipped out a pistol and shot the general in the face, his wife screaming in the background. Calmly putting the pistol away, Malet, attended by an infantry captain who had witnessed this entire assassination without even a protest, then returned to the Place Vendôme and entered the adjacent general headquarters with his own nomination as Hulin's successor.

Having been preceded by his officers, Malet found the second in command, Adjudant Général Doucet, still going through the documents he had been handed, obviously perplexed by it all. Malet went over these instructions, explaining that Doucet was now promoted to the rank of brigadier general and ordering him to arrest his commanding officer, General Laborde. But Doucet still could not take in any of this. Stalling for time, he sent for Laborde. When he was informed of events, Laborde left the office before anyone could stop him, taking the batch of documents to study, he said. On the ground floor, he saw an inspector general from the Ministry of Police attempting to enter his office but being prevented from doing so by a detail of sixty troops from the Tenth Regiment. Laborde ordered them to let him pass, which they did. Taking him aside, General Laborde quickly explained the situation, the inspector general then insisting on returning upstairs immediately, as he not only knew Malet but had personally escorted him from prison to the *maison de santé* a few months earlier.

Suddenly bursting into Doucet's office, the two men confronted Malet. "Monsieur Malet," the inspector general said sharply, "you have not been authorized to leave your *maison* without my permission." Then he turned away to Colonel Doucet. "There is something phony about all this. Arrest him. I am going over to the [Police] Ministry to find out what is happening." Malet, leaning against the mantelpiece on the other side of the room, reached into his jacket for his pistol, an action reflected in the opposite mirror, and all three of them—Laborde, Doucet, and the inspector general—seized and disarmed him. At that moment an orderly came running in with the news that Malet had shot the military governor, who was dying.[19]

With Malet's arrest, it was all over, and all the culprits, including the army and National Guard officers who had played a role in the affair, were dispatched to La Force, pending military trial. Of eighty-four persons arrested in the subsequent investigation and officially accused, fourteen were found guilty of treason and sentenced to death for attempting to overthrow Napoleon. And although most of the senior officers involved had no knowledge that the written orders handed them by Malet were forgeries and had thus acted in good faith, nonetheless they were executed by firing squad in the Grenelle Plain immediately after the trial—for there was no process of appeal—among them, Generals Malet, Guidal, and Lahorie and Colonel Soulier, as well as lesser individuals, including Boutreux. Only one colonel and the Spanish priest were ultimately pardoned.[20]

But on reflection what struck the senior officials involved was that one isolated madman had nearly succeeded in overthrowing Napoleon, a man who had successfully defeated the combined forces—hundreds of thousands of them—of Britain, Prussia, Austria, and Russia. And as Police Minister Savary later acknowledged, "General Malet could indeed have been in complete control of much of the government in very little time."[21]

Savary continued:

> [Given] the sad situation of our military in Russia, [Malet] could have even seized the emperor himself upon his return from that campaign, without the least interference. . . . The threat facing the nation was certainly great, and we realized too late how unprotected and unprepared we were from just this sort of attempt against the state. . . . We were especially struck by how easy it was to persuade our troops that all was lost and the emperor dead, without any of their officers even questioning the authority of such claims, and certainly without a thought to Napoleon's son and successor.[22]

Of course Malet's charade would have been quickly revealed, certainly within a matter of hours, and he had no junta with which to replace Napoleon's government. But "the contagion would have spread," as Savary put it, and shaken the public to the quick, perhaps providing the opportunity for some other enemies of the emperor to step in and take advantage of the situation, or at least to cause a nationwide revolt and chaos. If Fouché was right, in the sense that Malet certainly did not have a mature, fully developed plan for running the government once he had carried out his coup, on the other hand he was proved wrong about the earlier steps (in Malet's ability to arrest key officials and to seize control of critical government offices and agencies). That Napoleon's reappearance in Paris within a few weeks might have restored order in the long run was by no means assured, or even relevant. Nor can the fact be minimized that in the final analysis this entire plot was the result of just one man, in a French lunatic asylum, who had rocked the most powerful empire in the world. But as Police Minister Savary summed up: "We were none the wiser for what transpired. They were scared and truly shaken in Paris, finding themselves on a volcano, when for so long they had felt themselves to be so secure, on such solid ground."[23]

Death March

I could hardly be better situated than where I am now, at Moscow, to sit out the winter.

apoleon—as usual—had survived completely unscathed the Battle of Borodino, suffering from nothing more serious than a case of laryngitis.

Having spent the night of September 14–15 at a tavern outside Moscow, Méneval reported Napoleon's entry into Moscow as "without any of the usual tumult accompanying the victories associated with the taking of a large city. The streets were perfectly still, apart from the rumbling of the wheels of the gun limbers and the caissons of munitions. . . . The streets we crossed were lined with beautiful houses for the most part, but the doors and windows were locked." They passed "colonnaded palaces, churches, and beautiful public buildings . . . all reflecting the life of ease and luxury of a great city enriched by commerce and inhabited by a large, opulent aristocracy." There was no life to be seen, however, not a face in a window, not a child in a garden, not a horse, carriage, or wagon in the streets or courtyards. Instead, "Moscow appeared to be lost in deep sleep, like those enchanted cities described in the *Arabian Nights.*" But unlike those cities this one was dead, most of its three hundred thousand inhabitants having fled.[1]

We hoped to find rest at last, especially bountiful supplies of food and provisions. It was truly a curious and imposing sight, the sudden appearance of this vast city, more asiatic than European in appearance, this city suddenly appearing out of a naked, deserted plain, with its twelve hundred steeples, towers, clocks, and sky blue cupolas strewn with golden stars and linked by golden chains. We had paid dearly for this conquest, but Napoleon found reassurance in the hope that its seizure would result in the dictation of a solid peace. The King of Naples, who was the first to enter the city, remarked anxiously to Napoleon, however, that the city appeared uninhabited and that no military or civil delegation, no nobleman or even a priest had come forth.[2]

He was bewildered. The vanquished did not act like this.

At the head of the long column of cavalry, Napoleon made straight for the immense walls of the Kremlin, looming dramatically before him: "Within its ramparts stand the Imperial Palace, the arsenal, the Senate Palace, the National Archives, the principal public buildings, a great number of churches and temples filled with historical curiosities . . . including some of the trophies and regimental colors recently taken from the Turks," not to mention the celebrated basilica containing the tombs of the czars in its "semi-barbarous magnificence, . . . its walls covered with heavy gold and silver plaques."[3]

On entering the Kremlin at noon on September 15, Napoleon discovered that "nothing had been disturbed, all the clocks still striking every quarter of an hour, chiming as if their Russian masters were still there." It was quite uncanny, as Napoleon moved into the czar's private apartments, while Marshal Mortier, as commander of the Young Guard, was made responsible for maintaining order in the city, which the former governor, Fyodor Rostopchin, had left barely an hour before.

The lack of anyone to greet him in the name of the city, along with "all the strange reports he was receiving, left the Emperor more anxious than before," Caulaincourt noted. "The most mournful silence reigned. . . . We had not encountered a soul during our entry."[4] The army took up positions around the Kremlin, and other units were quartered in the imperial barracks.

At 8 P.M. on the fifteenth, fires were reported in the . . . Chinese quarter, an immense bazaar of long galleries enclosing a vast series of warehouses and cellars . . . filled with precious merchandise of every description, from fur stoles, to the delicate cloths and silks from India and

China. All efforts to extinguish the fire in the bazaar proved fruitless, as
it spread, now threatening the whole city.... whole streets of houses
igniting simultaneously. The city became an immense furnace.[5]

Initially French officials did not take the fire seriously; it was attributed
to some drunken soldiers and looters. "The Emperor had retired early . . .
but at 10:30 P.M," Caulaincourt related, "my valet de chambre . . . woke me
up to tell me that the city had been on fire for three quarters of an hour. I
could hardly doubt it, as it flooded my room, leaving it so light that I could
have read by the flames. I leapt out of bed and had the Grand Marshal of
the Palace [Gen. Christophe Duroc] awakened...." The Imperial Guard
was called out, although it was decided "to let the Emperor rest for a while
yet." Caulaincourt continued: "I quickly got on my horse to see for myself
what was happening, and to organize what help I could . . . [But] a strong
wind was blowing from the north, the direction from which the initial two
fires could be seen, their flames pushed towards the center of the city, giving them an extraordinary violence."

By 12:30 A.M. another fire had started, and then another, and yet
another. The danger was now so imminent that it was decided to awaken
Napoleon, who had slept through all the commotion. All the pumps and
hoses, it was discovered, had been sabotaged by Rostopchin before leaving,
but Caulaincourt managed to get two pumps working in the Kremlin, while
servants and soldiers alike carried out buckets of water and brooms to
extinguish the ring of fiery ash around the walls, the heat becoming so
extreme that windows shattered, though the magazines of the arsenals were
protected by hundreds of men. "At first Napoleon thought that the fires
had been set by our own disorderly troops," Caulaincourt continued. "He
simply could not believe that . . . the Russians themselves were deliberately
destroying their own city to prevent us from occupying it." But arsonists
captured by the French soon established that Count Rostopchin had left
specific orders to burn the city, himself torching his own resplendent mansion. "I next went over to the imperial stables where some of the European
horses were kept along with the official state carriages of the czar,"
Caulaincourt reported. "It took all the zeal, and I must say, all the courage
of everyone there to save them. We were literally breathing the fire, and our
lungs were inhaling pure smoke." The bridge to the south of the Kremlin
was saved only thanks to the intervention of the Imperial Guard. The heat
was so intense everywhere "that one could not remain for more than a
minute in any one place, the fur on the shakos singed on the heads of the
grenadiers."[6]

At 4:30 that afternoon Napoleon finally gave the order to depart and to leave nothing behind. Their destination was the Petrovskoye Palace, only a few miles outside Moscow on the road to St. Petersburg. But even so Napoleon had a hard time escaping the city. Winds were fanning the fire, and the western part of the city was already destroyed. Napoleon finally reached the safety of the suburbs at nightfall.

At Petrovskoye Palace, Napoleon was silent and distant. Originally he had planned on remaining in Moscow to negotiate a peace settlement with the czar. But it now finally dawned on him that the Russians would not have sacrificed Moscow if they were desperate to conclude a treaty. Napoleon decided to cut short his stay here, and everything was put in order for a final retreat. But this atmosphere was countered brilliantly by a fresh series of reports from Murat, who informed Napoleon that, after having interrogated many Russian officials and prisoners, he was convinced that the Russian army was in total disarray, in poor morale, and that the czar would soon be forced to capitulate. This persuaded Napoleon to prolong his stay after all.

On September 18 Napoleon returned to the Kremlin. In only two days the city had been sacked. Even the houses that had been saved from the fire had been pillaged, while the Sloboda Palace—the sprawling mansion Napoleon had reserved for himself outside the Kremlin walls—had been burned to the ground, along with three-quarters of the entire city, including some eight hundred churches. French troops had to turn their bayonets on their own rioting comrades, and many a summary execution took place.

Napoleon was convinced that the Russians would capitulate and sent messages to St. Petersburg to open negotiations. "The Emperor repeated that the war he was waging was purely political . . . not one of personal animosity, and that achieving a rapid peace was his main objective, . . . and that indeed he had been forced to come to Moscow in spite of himself."[7]

Meanwhile, in St. Petersburg events were seen in a very different light. Kutuzov had announced a great victory over Bonaparte at Borodino, and the czar had ordered the chanting of the Te Deum in the capital's cathedral. Gradually, however, as more detailed reports followed, Alexander came to realize that although Kutuzov had indeed inflicted heavy losses on the French, he had been unable to prevent them from occupying Moscow and forcing Kutuzov's army to flee. The jubilation on the Nevsky gave way to clamors for peace, beginning with Chancellor Rumanzov, Grand Duke Constantine, and even by the dowager empress.

The czar would have none of this, however. No one had ever seen Alexander so angry, so determined, silencing all treasonous talk of surrender. Bonaparte and the pillaging French invaders had to be stopped and exterminated, whatever the cost. "It is Napoleon or I, I or he!" the czar proclaimed, despite the numerical superiority of the French, with roughly 248,000 troops including French garrisons from as far away as Königsberg, Danzig, and Warsaw, and another 59,000 or so recruits en route to eastern Europe. Nevertheless the French were thousands of miles from home and lacked the troops and horses required to keep their extensive line of communications and supplies, literally their lifeline, open. And winter was not yet upon them. Bonaparte's immense cavalry under Murat had been so reduced in numbers, including mounts and superior officers, that they had literally had to walk their few remaining horses most of the way from Borodino to Moscow. The czar might have only 193,000 troops immediately at hand, but his large cavalry was well mounted and fed, accustomed to the rigors of this climate and land, and the men were more determined, defending their own country.[8] Czar Alexander was in no mood to negotiate.

As Caulaincourt reflected:

> Our return to Moscow was at least as depressing as had been our departure. I cannot begin to find the words with which to express everything I felt since the death of my brother. The spectacle of the most recent events left me simply stunned, overwhelmed. The horror of everything now surrounding us just added to my loss. . . . I was at the end of my tether! Fortunate indeed are those who did not witness this awful desolation, this scene of awesome destruction everywhere around us!

Several days after their return to the Kremlin, Napoleon announced his decision to make his winter quarters in Moscow after all. Troops were ordered to bring in food, grain, provisions, furs, clothing. Fortifications had to be strengthened, and fresh levees of conscripts from France and Poland ordered up. The long network of posting stations linking Paris with Erfurt and then with Danzig, Warsaw, and Moscow also had to be reinforced. Comte Lavalette was held responsible for maintaining full messenger service, twenty-four hours a day, the posting stations to be situated between fifteen and twenty-one miles apart, with a minimum of four fresh mounts available at each one. This involved hundreds of such stations and the assigning of thousands of fresh troops to guard this vital line of communications. Despite warnings by everyone that he had no idea what a Russian winter was like, Napoleon was determined. He would show Alexander yet and defy the Cassandras. What is more, once the czar saw how determined he was to stay in Moscow, he would give in, just as Napoleon had predicted from the very start.

If the unusually warm autumn had misled Napoleon into believing that everyone had been hoodwinking him, the great distances separating him from Vilna, Warsaw, Dresden, and Erfurt, however, were no illusions. When his couriers were murdered—one was expected to deliver mail to Napoleon *daily* from Paris and vice versa—and his personal dispatches from his own ministers seized, along with all the mail for the army, even Napoleon grew uneasy about the decision to stay. And Caulaincourt, who spent hours with him daily, noted that despite the burning of Moscow, Napoleon remained "always prepared to believe in his guiding star, and that the Russians, tired of this war, would seize any occasion to put an end to this struggle."

As for the weather, Caulaincourt continued:

the mild temperatures that lasted much longer than usual this year all contributed in lulling him. . . . Even in private so strongly did the emperor express his conviction of remaining in Moscow now that those held in his closest confidence continued to believe him for quite some time. Such then was our situation ten to twelve days after our return to Moscow.[9]

Napoleon kept busy as never before, reviewing military parades in the courtyard of the Kremlin, ordering the construction of large new baking ovens for the troops, mills for the preparation of flour, extending his defenses, sending out strong detachments of troops "to collect the cattle that were becoming very rare now" for the long winter ahead. Napoleon's activity went beyond the phenomenal to the frenetic or, as Caulaincourt put it, "the nights doubled the length of his days." Behind all this intense activity, however, his growing private anxieties he kept largely to himself, except for Duroc, his closest friend and confidant, and to Caulaincourt:

Paris and France remained his ultimate concern, as his daily decrees and decisions dispatched from Moscow attested. The Spanish War [and its setbacks] too aroused his concerns more and more [Wellington marched into Madrid on August 12, and Marshal Soult raised his siege of Cádiz on the twenty-fifth]. . . . Accustomed to dictating peace upon arriving in the palaces of his newly conquered capitals, he was astonished by the unique silence that now greeted him. . . .

But if he left Moscow now, after all his boasting, he would be forced to eat his own words. Instead of admitting his error, Napoleon insisted "that his position in Moscow was most disturbing and even threatening for Russia." Nevertheless, after dispatching more personal messages to the czar in St. Petersburg, he gradually, finally began to realize "that by the silence of his enemy over the very real dangers of his position, he had no choice but to quit the country."[10]

From the military point of view his position was also worsening daily, as the Russian troops reached Podolsk on September 18 and General Miloradovich seized Desna—only fifteen miles south of Moscow—by the twenty-first. With fresh campaign plans, morale in the Russian lines was raised. In October the czar ordered Wittgenstein's and Chitchagov's armies to the Berezina. Meanwhile due to his poor intelligence service, Napoleon had no idea of the extent of the Russian threat that was slowly closing in him, intent on exterminating him and the entire French army. What is more, many of the reports Napoleon did receive were contradictory or misleading, and in any event the exhausted and demoralized French army had neither the strength nor the will to fight, with Cossack units now striking successfully even at the suburbs of Moscow itself. Frightened French troops sometimes panicked, rampaging through empty shops and mansions, despite harsh penalties for looting announced by Napoleon. By October 6 the Russian army had moved into some effective positions, its army established at Tarutino and Vinkovo. With the main Russian army now successfully regrouped, its leaders promised the czar to wreak full vengeance on the French capital itself.

"I waged war on Your Majesty without personal animosity," Napoleon had written Alexander on September 20. "The fine, beautiful city of Moscow no longer exists, because Rostopchin had it burned. . . . A letter of capitulation from you before or after the battle [at Borodino] could have stopped my march. . . . If Your Majesty still holds some of his former attachments toward me, he will take this letter to heart."[11] The czar of course did not condescend to reply. "The emperor, my master, has a sincere desire to end the differences between our two great and generous nations, and to end them forever," General Lauriston told Kutuzov. "I have received no instructions on that subject," Kutuzov curtly replied, for "the Russian people consider the French as destructive as they did the Tartars of Genghis Khan himself!"[12] Lauriston was sent back to Moscow.

Meanwhile Napoleon's activities throughout this period varied from ceaseless activity to utter apathy, reflecting his own inner conflicts; between September 19 and 29, for instance, he had left the Kremlin only once. Had he had more epileptic seizures? Had he been paralyzed by his own errors at long last? Indeed, was he going quite insane, as rumor had it in both the officers' mess and in the barracks? "The Emperor is mad, completely mad," one French minister had confided to Marshal Marmont well before the conception of the Russian invasion.

Even within the walls of the Kremlin, Napoleon further isolated himself. A French theatrical group, brought all the way from Paris, did present an occasional play for Bonaparte and his inner circle, and Napoleon actually tolerated two half-hour concerts offered by an Italian tenor. Otherwise he now saw little of Caulaincourt or the others; he was tired of their advice to leave Moscow. Even Duroc was often not admitted into the quarters of the great man. If he even ate alone, he did invite Berthier, Duroc, and Eugène occasionally to join him for a coffee afterward. The faithful Berthier in particular was singularly excluded from such intimacy.

On two separate occasions Napoleon had asked Caulaincourt, as former ambassador, to travel to St. Petersburg to open negotiations with the czar, and twice he had refused to do so, pointing out that clearly Alexander had no intention of surrendering to the French. Lauriston had thus been sent instead, only to receive the blatant rebuff Caulaincourt had predicted. Napoleon complained constantly that he could get no information about what was happening in St. Petersburg.[13]

Murat, the only senior officer in regular contact with Kutuzov's GHQ, continued to send absurdly optimistic reports about the softening of the Russian position, whereas in fact the Russian army was closing in. By September 22 even Napoleon had had enough of Murat's foolishness and ordered Berthier to instruct him formally that Napoleon "had decreed the death penalty for any French officer who opened unauthorized negotiations with the enemy,"[14] which the cocky Murat merely dismissed with a scornful laugh. He continued seeing the Russians. Alas Napoleon could not shoot his own brother-in-law, however great the temptation.

The continued despondency, centered around Berthier's GHQ, which initially numbered more than four hundred officers, got more and more on Napoleon's nerves. "You just want to go back to Grosbois to be with your Visconti," Napoleon repeated, leaving Berthier frustrated, trembling, gnawing his nails, and cursing everyone in sight. But following Lauriston's final failure with the czar at the end of the second week of October, Napoleon summoned Caulaincourt once more. "Emperor Alexander is stubborn," he insisted. "He will regret it. He will never have had a better opportunity for a more favorable peace than what I am now offering." But Caulaincourt, although tired of repeating ad nauseam the same sound advice, reminded Napoleon yet again that the czar was well aware that the French were in no bargaining position. "What do you mean by 'our weaknesses here'?

Napoleon snarled. 'But winter, Sire,' [Caulaincourt] responded." He continued:

> We are already in great jeopardy, our shortage of supplies, of transport
> animals for our artillery, our great number of ill and wounded, the lack
> of proper winter clothing for our troops. Everyone needs a sheepskin
> coat, fur-lined gloves, heavy hats, stockings, and thick winter boots
> against the ice and snow. We lack everything. Our smiths don't even
> have the proper heavy horseshoes used here [in winter]. How can teams
> of horses be expected to haul our artillery across ice? And then there is
> the question of our lines of communications. It is still unseasonably
> warm now, but what will it be in two weeks' time when winter sets in?

Napoleon listened with obvious growing impatience. "Then you think I
intend to leave Moscow after all that I have said?" "Yes, sire," Caulaincourt, now resigned to the inevitable sharp reply, continued. "I have
decided nothing yet." "I could hardly be better situated than where I am
now, at Moscow, to sit out the winter."[15]

In fact by October 3 Napoleon was already secretly preparing to leave.
On that date, even before Lauriston's next return from St. Petersburg, he
ordered his men to be able to move out of the city by the fifteenth or sixteenth. The news, which still continued to arrive from Paris almost daily,
was bad, and worse from Spain, where Wellington was undoing everything
Napoleon had achieved. But Napoleon's courier service had broken down
twice again, and his messengers had been seized or killed. Then followed
the czar's final rejection.

With the few reinforcements that got through, counting troops in the
outlying areas, Napoleon had entered Russia with nearly 450,000 men.
Now he had a total immediate effective force in Moscow of 102,260, including 14,760 cavalry, while his 41,500-man Imperial Guard was reduced to
21,500 at most. He also had 533 pieces of artillery of the original 1,372, but
lacked horses to haul even that number and their caissons. There were also
some ten to fifteen thousand French wounded and ill in hospitals, as the
wretched Dr. Turiot kept reminding him. How was he to move them?[16]

But nonetheless the decision was made. Horses, wagons, carts, and anything else with wheels were loaded with the wounded and staggering mountains of loot, including gigantic statues and paintings, huge pieces of furniture, and even enormous Persian carpets. And then the orders that
Napoleon had so long refused to give came from his lips. At noon on October 19, thirty-five days after their triumphant arrival, Bonaparte, his

coaches, and the Imperial Guard at the head of an enormous column slowly, cumbersomely marched through the gates of the Kremlin and Moscow for the last time, leaving behind Marshal Mortier with some 7,000 or so troops with orders to protect their rear and blow up the entire Kremlin on October 23. The order was never executed.

The plan was to take the southern route via the by-now-well-provisioned French army warehouses in the ruins of Smolensk, Napoleon hoping to defeat Kutuzov in one final battle at Kaluga and thus clear the way for the rest of this ignominious withdrawal. While the Cossacks continued to harry the French lines, already dozens of miles long, snapping at their heels like enormous packs of jackals, Murat was caught napping by the Russians. General Sébastiani's corps was defeated at Vinkovo, as Kutuzov attempted in vain to capture Murat's entire cavalry. But feeding more than one hundred thousand men and tens of thousands of horses was difficult at the best of times. With the first heavy frosts setting in with a vengeance, and with some forty thousand carts, wagons, carriages, caissons and limbers, it was a mad scheme at best. But off they went down the old Kaluga Road, via Desna in the direction of Maloyaroslavets. Junot's corps was on the Borodino Road at Mozajsk, where they were to meet. But Junot, who had ultimately replaced Jérôme Bonaparte, was by now clearly mentally unbalanced, failing to follow orders or to appear on schedule and arguing violently with every other senior commanding officer and marshal. Having been stripped first of his prestigious post as Napoleon's senior aide-de-camp, next of his title military governor of Paris, then of his appointment as commander in chief of the French invasion of Portugal (where he had been defeated by Wellington, losing Portugal in the process), Junot had ever since been going downhill precipitously. Yet with the loss of well over sixty generals at Borodino alone, Napoleon had no choice but to keep a man of Junot's field experience.

The first two days of the march from Moscow alternated from chilly downpours to warm weather, followed by frigid nights, Méneval—himself shortly to suffer from severe frostbite and the loss of the use of one leg—recorded in his *Memoirs*. On October 22 Doctorov's corps set off from Tarutino, hoping to block the head of Napoleon's army, then led by Prince Eugène, at Maloyaroslavets, while Kutuzov headed north of Kaluga. On the twenty-fourth a fierce battle began at Maloyaroslavets between Doctorov's troops and one of Eugène's divisions, Eugène remaining in control, as Napoleon's army moved up along the north bank. Although Doctorov retreated, the French had lost seven more generals. On October 25, during

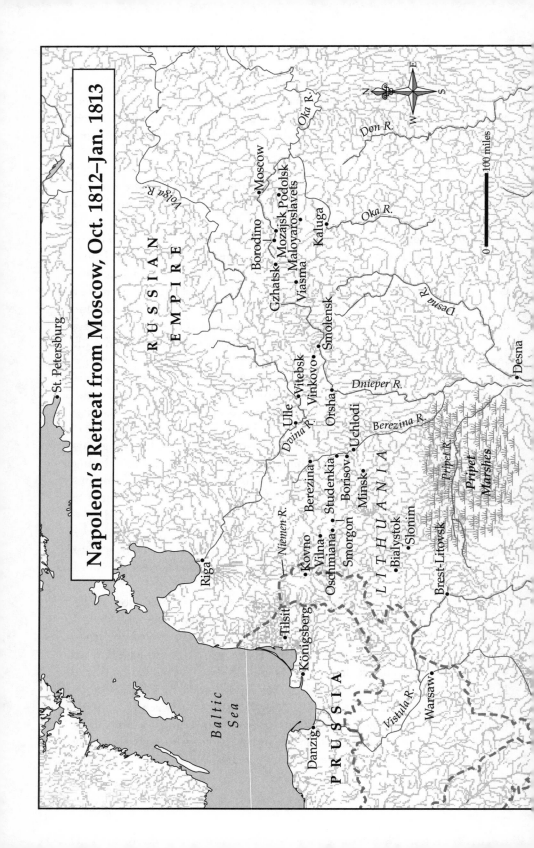

Napoleon's Retreat from Moscow, Oct. 1812–Jan. 1813

one of his usual reconnaissance tours, Napoleon, with just a handful of the Imperial Guard as an escort, was nearly captured. He just barely escaped, his staff officers drawing sabers to defend him, he then declining to discontinue his march on Kaluga, returning instead via Oshigovo to Mozajsk. The unwieldy army now straggled in a column some fifty miles long, accompanied by fresh skirmishes and casualties.

French horses were dropping by the thousands, as wounded troops, baggage, cannon, and loot were abandoned along the route. Colonel Marbot now referred to the vast land of Russia that was swallowing them up as "this enormous tomb," they leaving behind some "30,000 corpses half eaten by wolves."[17] They reached Gzhatsk and then Viasma, in the direction of Smolensk, even as Prince von Schwarzenberg abandoned the French army for Warsaw. To the north, a Russian Army now under General Tschashniki, was keeping the combined II and IX French Corps off balance, endangering Napoleon's approach to the critical Berezina River crossing, while Admiral Chitchagov was barring the route between Brest-Litovsk and Slonim.

Napoleon literally had only the garrison of Smolensk upon which to depend, as Kutuzov's advance guard under Miloradovich pressed on. "The [French] regiments began to dissolve and collapse," one French officer recorded, with tens of thousands of horses littering the wayside, their wagons and munitions burned. And all along the road, Russian civilians who had suffered so brutally at French hands during the initial invasion of the country were now carrying out atrocities against these same French troops and stragglers as they retraced their steps. While Napoleon was at Slavkoyvo, Miloradovich's army finally reached and attacked Napoleon's rear guard. Davout found himself surrounded, saved at the last minute only by the valiant intervention of Prince Eugène. Ney's III Corps was ordered to take over the rear guard from Davout, though by now Ney himself was fighting off pretty savage attacks by the Russians. The French cavalry was down to just a few thousand men from the nearly fifteen thousand that had set out from Moscow. They could not be protected and were incapable of protecting themselves. In the first week of November, as the entire French army disintegrated, large packs of wolves moved in, and Cossacks and regular cavalry units ravaged the haggard French line, the snow began to fall, burying the dead in some cases for the next 154 years. "I must inform Your Highness that the past three days of suffering have so dispirited my men that as of this moment I believe they are no longer capable even of defending themselves," Prince Eugène de Beauharnais reluctantly reported on November 8.[18] Similar reports were reaching Berthier and Napoleon from every unit of the French army.

That same week Napoleon received news of further setbacks in Spain, and more immediately, of Savary's crushing of General Malet's attempted coup d'état which, though thwarted, had unsettled Paris and even the staunchest of Napoleonic governmental institutions. Meanwhile, ahead of him, Wittgenstein's and Chitchagov's armies, totaling seventy thousand Russian troops, were closing in on Minsk and the Berezina River crossing.

Napoleon finally reached Smolensk on November 9, even his Imperial Guard refusing to obey orders, going amok, killing, destroying, raping, and looting warehouses and homes, as the temperature continued to drop. Then came news of General Baraguey d'Hillier's surrender to the Russians not far from Smolensk. There were to be no new reinforcements for Napoleon.

As the Grande Armée gradually straggled into Smolensk over the next four days, Napoleon was already setting out for the next depots at Vitebsk and Minsk. The French army had lost some sixty thousand men just since leaving Moscow a little less than a month before. The guard still maintained fourteen thousand men, but they were out of control and, what was worse, the most powerful corps of the entire army, under Davout, had dwindled to ten thousand, while Ney was down to three thousand and the VI and VIII Corps combined totaled only fifteen hundred. Napoleon's only hope, and it was not much of one, lay in the twenty-five thousand men awaiting him at Orsha, that is the IX and II Corps under Marshals Victor and Oudinot.

But instead of heading northwest toward Vitebsk, on November 12 the head of the French column set off southwest for Krasnoe, Borisov, on the Berezina, and Minsk, with Kutuzov's army and cavalry harrying them every step of the way, and Platov's ever vigorous cavalry and Miloradovich's main force pressing respectively from the north and south. Moreover, Wittgenstein's army of perhaps twenty-five to thirty thousand troops, in control of Vitebsk and Polotsk, already further to the north were moving westward as well, while General Chitchagov's army of thirty-four thousand were coming straight at Napoleon's "army," head on from the direction of Minsk, where the French had been hoping to find a refuge. Bonaparte still appeared to have no idea just how completely he was surrounded, with Macdonald's force of twenty thousand isolated at Riga, on the Baltic, well out of the picture, while the Bavarian Count von Wrede, commanding Napoleon's VI Corps west of Polotsk, was abandoning his army. Only Oudinot's eight thousand men, now to the northwest of Minsk, seemed to offer any real hope, along with Victor's reported eleven thousand.

Reaching Krasnoye on November 15, Napoleon waited for two entire days for his army to catch up with him, while the Imperial Guard smashed through Kutuzov's forces barring the road to Minsk, sending 35,000 Russians fleeing (an encounter sometimes referred to as the battle of Krasnoye).

But the situation was still desperate. With Russian forces literally surrounding him on all sides, Napoleon could wait no longer. Taking advantage of this minor victory, he ordered the French army to push on brutally, abandoning Ney's rear guard in the process, for he had just learned that Chitchagov had seized Minsk from the French garrison that had been under Schwarzenberg, at one fell blow cutting off his last major supply center and escape route. As for Schwarzenberg, he was falling back to Warsaw.

Napoleon drove hard, passing Orsha toward the Berezina before Chitchagov and Kutuzov could block that exodus as well. With Minsk fallen, and the road cut to Warsaw, where there was heavy fighting, Napoleon was left with only one immediate option, to move to the northwest, past the Dnieper and Dvina and Ulle, in the direction of Smorgon and Kovno, retracing his steps over the Niemen, to the French-held bastions of Königsberg and Danzig (still held by Rapp's 30,000 men).

Much to his surprise, Napoleon's abandoned rear guard, Ney's III corps given up as lost, now appeared through the driving snow from Smolensk, where Napoleon had in fact forgotten to give Ney the order to retreat. (Ney, who had 10,000 men at the beginning of September, was now down to 1,000.) Meanwhile the snow, which had begun on November 3, continued, perhaps aiding Ney in his escape, which took place also thanks to Prince Eugène's courage in sending a detachment to help them through.

Now with the news that General Dombrowski's much reduced French cavalry had lost the bridgehead it was holding for Napoleon over the Berezina defeated by Chitchagov's much larger force of thirty-four thousand men, came the dreaded confirmation that Wittgenstein's thirty-thousand-man army—larger than Junot's, Poniatowski's, Murat's, Ney's, Eugène's, and Davout's combined—was nearing Borisov, on the Berezina. That escape route, too, would now be cut. The French could never reach Kovno or Königsberg, it seemed—until once again Napoleon's fabled good fortune saved the situation: Brigadier General Corbineau had managed to find a suitable ford upriver of Borisov.

Laying an elaborate trap, Napoleon sent in Oudinot's reinforced II Corps to carry out a feinted fording of the Berezina, even threatening to take Borisov, to draw off the Russians opposite Corbineau's ford at Studenkia. Oudinot's men set to their task noisily enough at a river crossing near Uchlodi, and the Russians immediately withdrew all his forces from Studenkia, to oppose Oudinot's effective diversion. A delighted Bonaparte threw up two makeshift bridges over the Berezina at Studenkia.

Despite the snowfall, the land was not yet frozen, nor was the river, which made the going hard, but Napoleon's artillery and engineers managed to achieve their task, permitting what remained of the French army to cross to the west bank on November 26–29. Napoleon had escaped an elaborate trap, though Marbot admitted that the size of the Berezina at this point was in reality "no wider than the Rue Royale" in Paris.

Scarcely had most of Napoleon's forces crossed the river, trudging through marshland while Victor IX's Corps held the tenuous bridgehead, than they were finally attacked in force, Oudinot and Ney holding the enemy off. Nevertheless, with Platov's Cossacks descending from the north, and Wittgenstein's army corps closing in on the eastern shore, not quite all the French escaped, and by December some four thousand men of Marshal Victor's valiant rear-guard divisions were captured before they could make their escape from the Russian pincer movement. They never returned to France.

Napoleon had most of his remaining effective troops on the west bank now (less some 36,000 French stragglers who had reached the burning bridges too late and also fallen prisoner to the Russians). There weren't many left: nearly 40,000 men, a large percentage of them officers and senior noncoms, though only 14,000 infantry, 2,000 cavalry, and perhaps 200 cannon. The once fabulous French Imperial Guard was reduced to 6,000 men, while the combined corps of Napoleon's, Davout's, and Eugène's forces totaled no more than 3,600.

The escape across the Berezina may have been a partial success, but the winter Caulaincourt had been so anxious about now set in with a vengeance, temperatures dropping from minus four degrees Fahrenheit to minus twenty-nine. In the first half of December the French lost another 36,000 prisoners to the Russians as well as 311 pieces of heavy artillery. Indeed, three days after Napoleon's crossing of the Berezina, the famed Grande Armée had dwindled to 8,823 men.

After reaching Molodesczo, on December 5, a very depressed Napoleon drafted the famous 29th *Army Bulletin* and issued decrees for the raising of another 300,000 men. That same day at Smorgoni he gathered together his senior commanders for the last time, placing an unhappy Joachim Murat in command of the remnant of his army, another grave error, for Murat too would shortly be abandoning them.

At 10 P.M. precisely, we climbed into our carriages, the Emperor and myself [Caulaincourt] in his enormous sleeping coach, with the brave Wonsowicz riding alongside on his horse, along with Roustam and a couple of others. The Duc de Frioul [Duroc] and the Comte de Lobau followed us in the next calèche, and behind them the Baron Fain and Louis Constant in the other. All measures were so carefully prepared, and the secret so well guarded, that no one had the least idea what we were about.[19]

Setting out from Smorgoni accompanied by a two-hundred-man guard, they reached Oschmiana at midnight. After Napoleon ordered everyone to change into heavy sheepskin coats and boots, and even equipped with bearskin rugs, they set out for Vilna and Kovno, crossing the frozen Niemen into the frozen wastes of Poland. Progress through the snow soon became impossible, forcing them to change into sleighs over the next several hours until they reached Warsaw. Thence on to Dresden, where the formerly gaily lit, chandeliered state reception rooms of the Saxon palace were dark and cold. Napoleon dictated to Méneval's replacement, Baron Fain, orders calling forth another 40,000 Austrian and Prussian troops to come to his aid. The balls, the glittering uniforms of the bevy of kings, and the ravishing gowns of their queens, duchesses, and princesses, which had so filled these vast rooms just a few months earlier, now haunted them, as Napoleon, disguised as Caulaincourt's secretary, scuttled back into his sleigh and headed for Erfurt, Fulda, Mainz, Metz, and Meaux, where his last relay of exhausted horses gave out. He had to ask the head of that posting house for his personal chaise and a fresh team of horses for the last leg of the journey. The postilion was sent on ahead in the December darkness, "passing at a full gallop beneath the half-finished Arc de Triomphe" to announce their arrival. By now Napoleon's large escort had been reduced to a few cavaliers as they finally pulled into the cobbled courtyard of the Tuileries.

> [Napoleon] descended safe and sound . . . just as the clock was striking the last quarter before midnight. The concierges took us for some officers bearing dispatches and let us pass as we reached the entrance to the gallery opening into the garden. The Swiss Guard, who had been asleep, came to the door in his nightshirt, a lantern in his hand, to see who was knocking. He was bewildered by our appearance [Napoleon still in disguise] and called his wife. I had to give my name several times before they agreed to open the door for us. He had to rub his eyes before he finally recognized us.[20]

Meanwhile, back in eastern and central Europe, nature and the Russian forces had taken their toll of the remainder of the Grande Armée. Divisional General Loison left Vilna with his remaining garrison of 14,000 men, which now was down to some 4,000. Murat, Macdonald and Schwarzenberg had also withdrawn, abandoning 141 more guns and tens of thousands of men unable to continue to Tilsit and Bialystok. In vain the valiant Ney held Kovno until December 14. Pursued by Russians across nearly six hundred miles of desolate frozen land, the last remnants of the French army, approximately 43,000, recrossed the Niemen. The famed Napoleonic Imperial Guard was down to fewer than 1,000 men.[21] The final tally was stark: Of 612,000 French and allied soldiers, 400,000 had died and 100,000 were left behind as Russian POWS. According to official records, the Russians burned or buried 243,612 men of the Grande Armée. On New Year's Day, 1813, the Russian army, still in pursuit, crossed the frozen Niemen, heading for the Rhine, while in Prussia Baron Karl von Stein was reminding his people of the necessity of "restoring the independence of Germany."[22]

Caulaincourt may have regretted being one of the survivors during the two-week ride from Smorgoni to Paris. He was a captive audience for endless diatribes and denunciations by a defeated Bonaparte who blamed all his woes on Murat, Eugène, Berthier, Lefebvre, Bessières, Mortier, Ney, Davout, Poniatowski and his faithless Poles, the Russians, the weather, and of course the English, for in the final analysis, it had all been the fault of the English. As for the French, how they had betrayed him! But he would show them.

The Saxon Campaign

I will sacrifice a million men yet if necessary. Honor before all.

ll the women and wives were truly to be pitied," ex-Queen Hortense of Holland commented on the French invasion of Russia. "The whole of France seemed to be in Russia. Our wishes, fears, and hopes, all were on that campaign. Never before had the nation found itself so cut off from its defenders, and the great distance from the theatre of war itself merely made it all the more frightening for us." And then came Napoleon's twenty-ninth *Grand Army Bulletin*, describing his defeat. "What a reversal from our mighty position in the world. What a blow to our national pride! This great northern Empire [Russia], which had earlier retreated before us, now instead sent back to France the debris of its wreckage, its amputees, wounded, and shell-shocked, but although fugitives, they remained conquerors in our eyes."[1]

A shocked and dismayed Hortense added, "Only our deep pain equaled the greatness of our disasters. Everyone was in mourning. For so long confident in, and used to, obeying one man alone, France found itself as depressed as it was astonished by the news of its defeat, but nevertheless gradually pulled itself together, ready again to face the future."

As Napoleon had hoped, his presence in Paris checked the full effect of that fateful bulletin. "His sudden return, his firm, confident attitude stopped our despair. One heard no more whispers [of his fall]. We felt too humiliated to complain, and national pride would not permit us to dwell on the sacrifices we had made." As for Napoleon, "He seemed tired, lost in thought, but not beaten.... Never was he more master of himself than in difficult or unhappy times." And it was true. His superior intelligence always seemed to overcome an immediate setback, however grave, putting physical distance between himself and the event in order to better view the catastrophe, in this case, the loss of more than half a million men and the collapse of his empire.

"So worried by what I had read, I asked him if the Army's disaster had indeed been as cruel as the Army Bulletin had announced. He replied, obviously deeply pained, 'I told the complete truth.'"[2] But it was far from the whole truth, far from the ultimate truth, for in fact this war, too, had been quite unnecessary. The world, even the French people, had wanted peace, desperately so, but instead he alone had demanded more bloodshed. Nor had the bulletin stated that from a purely technical, logistical viewpoint, that entire campaign had been ill conceived and pathetically executed, beyond even his capabilities.

And yet just a few weeks earlier, Hortense recalled, "Never had the annual winter carnival of 1812 been so brilliant," everyone having such utter faith in Napoleon's invincibility. "The balls and parties following one another in rapid succession seemed by their very din and activity to drown out the reality that we had just launched the greatest military expedition ever seen. France was happy, our friends dancing, all our ambitions having been reached, our every wish fulfilled." But then came the weeks of waiting and finally the news of the great setbacks.[3] "Gradually the brilliant, gay carnival turned more somber, everyone more worried as time passed." The balls went on, because they always did, but the numbers of those present declined noticeably, the almost wanton, frenetic gaiety extinguished.

Napoleon retired to Versailles and the Trianon for a fortnight to sort out his affairs in peace and solitude. But no sooner had he arrived than he was again thrown by his horse, a repetition of the accidents at Vienna and before crossing the Niemen to Moscow. It augured ill for the superstitious, and this time he was forced to spend several days in bed. It was a good place for reflection, however, and Hortense, who visited him, thought it would prove fruitful. "Our misfortunes in Russia had been so grievous that I now had no doubt that, under the circumstances, the Emperor would renounce any further grand projects.... I had not the slightest doubt that he would now make the greatest personal sacrifices in order to bring peace, a peace demanded by France and indeed the whole of Europe," she noted.

"Madame, you who know the character of the emperor so well, tell me honestly, do you think we can hope for a European peace from him at last?" Prince Karl von Schwarzenberg, the new Austrian ambassador, asked her. Yes, she told him, even if he needed just one more nominal victory in the field to save face.[4] But Hortense was utterly wrong. It seemed that in spite of his Russian debacle, his portentous third fall from a horse, so symbolic of present events, in fact, disregarding one and all, he had no interest in peace, for that would mean concessions, losses, and admission of poor judgment.

Napoleon had not given up, although he had made some drastic decisions. If he had learned one thing from the Russian campaign, it was that he could not carry out two wars in two different theaters simultaneously. Thus on January 4, 1813, he ordered War Minister Clarke to instruct El Rey José Bonaparte to withdraw from his capital of Madrid and from Castile, and to move his temporary new GHQ far to the north, on the main road to France, at Valladolid. At the same time Napoleon consented to allow him to be his own master at last, his own commander in chief, permitting him to rid himself of the arrogant Marshal Soult—"this wretch" as Joseph called him—who was being recalled to France. Now Joseph was to concentrate on quelling the north, consolidating everything from Valladolid to the Pyrenees. What Napoleon did not tell his elder brother, however, was that this was the end of his rule, the end of the French in Spain.[5] Nor did he inform him that he would shortly be writing to Fernando VII, still Napoleon's state prisoner at Talleyrand's luxurious castle at Valençay, that "the present state of affairs within my empire has made it necessary for me to bring my Spanish affairs to a close." A new treaty recognizing him in place of Joseph as king of Spain would be drawn up as soon as the English quit the country.[6] Napoleon, who rarely trusted anyone, least of all one of his own brothers, was hardly about to apprise Joseph of his fate:

> I have sacrificed thousands, hundreds of thousands of men, in order that he [Joseph] should be able to reign in Spain. It was a mistake on my part to have thought my brothers necessary in order to assure my dynastic rule. My dynasty is now assured without them. It will be guaranteed in the future come what may, simply by force of circumstance. The existence of the empress alone now assures its continuation. . . . It therefore no longer makes the slightest difference to me that Ferdinand will be replacing Joseph,

Napoleon confided to Roederer.[7] As usual he blamed his failures on his family. "All the setbacks in Spain," he told Clarke, "are the result of my misplaced trust in the king [Joseph]," failing to point out that not only had Joseph been against the invasion in the first place but had strongly objected to being removed from Naples to come to this country, to assume a crown he did not want,[8] and moreover, that for the past four years the French field commanders in Spain had been following Napoleon's orders, not Joseph's.

The fact of the matter was that the entire Iberian campaign had been as ill conceived as the Russian one (not to mention that little Egyptian miscalculation), and it had started from the very beginning: Junot defeated by Sir Arthur Wellesley at Vimiero on August 30, 1808; then Soult chased from Portugal in May 1809; followed by Marshal Victor's defeat by the same Wellesley at Talavera on July 27–28, 1809. Viscount Wellington, as he was known thereafter, next defeated Masséna at Bussaco on September 27, 1810, chasing him from Portugal the next year, followed by his conquest of Fuentes de Oñoro on May 4, 1811. Nor had 1812 improved the French situation, beginning with Wellington's capture of Ciudad Rodrigo on January 19, and then of Badajoz, even temporarily seizing Joseph's capital as a result of his victory over Marmont at Salamanca on July 22, while Marshal Soult was forced by the Spanish to lift his siege of Cádiz. Indeed the only French general to triumph in arms now was Marshal Louis-Gabriel Suchet, who captured Valencia from the Spanish.

And, finally, in 1813, Napoleon at last realized that he could no longer fight the whole of Europe at once, not even an English army of forty thousand soldiers in Spain, at least while the one general he always underestimated was in command, Arthur Lord Wellington, who had stoutly defeated every general and marshal sent against him.

The unfortunate Rey José left Madrid for the last time on March 17, 1813, and within three months' time on June 21 would suffer ultimate defeat at Vitoria, putting an end to the French occupation of the Peninsula—but only after losing between 250,000 and 300,000 French lives, all for nought.

The Spanish decision had been long in the making, in part because Napoleon did not know what to do with Joseph, who if deprived of his Spanish crown had to be provided with another, or at least with something equivalent. But suddenly Europe, French-occupied Europe, was shrinking daily before Napoleon's very eyes. The only alternative would have been to make Joseph regent, but that was out of the question now, with Marie-Louise and his son and heir, the king of Rome, having altered that situation.

That in turn brought other complications. The excommunicated Napoleon wanted Pope Pius VII, confined at Fontainebleau since June 1812, to sign a revised Concordat with France *and* perform the coronation ceremony, first for Empress Marie Louise, and then for the king of Rome. Regardless of the absurd situation, everything had to look legitimate in the eyes of the world. Although the pope did initially give in under duress and sign the Concordat on January 25, 1813, he immediately regretted it, on learning of Napoleon's premature announcement of the event before even clearing it with him. The pope resisted many sticky issues outstanding between the Vatican and Paris, including the procedure for the nomination of bishops and supervision of higher church personnel, and the pope adamantly refused to move the Vatican to Paris as Napoleon now demanded. But so confident was Bonaparte that he had already arranged to buy the Château de Crachamp at Avignon for the pope.

On March 24 the pope suddenly declared his opposition to the new Concordat. The document had, he announced, "torn his spirit" and in consequence, "with the help of God we desire that it be completely broken." Nor did he have any intention of anointing and performing the coronation ceremony of Marie-Louise and of Napoleon's beloved son. Thunderstruck, a furious Napoleon ordered his carriage in the Cour du Cheval Blanc, never to see the pope again, whom he eventually released from his French prison on January 21, 1814.[9]

Napoleon decided that he could manage quite nicely without his brothers or even the pope and ordered a *senatus consultum** officially recognizing Marie-Louise as regent, celebrated at a ceremony at the Elysée on March 30, 1813. She would rule in his absence, advised by a special Regency Council.[10] Although Article VIII of the Imperial Constitution in fact denied the regency to a woman, Napoleon simply overruled it. As for Joseph, by the summer of 1813 he was back in France, Napoleon ordering him to isolate himself at Mortefontaine with his wife. Like Louis, Lucien, and Jérôme, brother Joseph was a failure and an embarrassment.

For the first time in his imperial career, on returning from a major military campaign, Napoleon had not received hearty congratulations on yet another splendid victory. Instead eyes were awkwardly averted in the great man's presence. His own courtiers and officials did not know what to say, what to do. Thus no one was more taken aback than Napoleon himself when early in January he received a most extraordinary letter from brother Louis Bonaparte, who had apparently been temporarily awakened from his literary hibernation at Graz:

*A decree enacted by Napoleon that theoretically was taken after consultation with the Senate (whose members he personally nominated). It was in fact a legal fiction.

Deeply grieved by [what I have just heard of] the suffering and losses inflicted on the Grand Army after the long series of successes that have carried your arms to the North Pole itself, and knowing how terribly pressed you are at present, and how urgent it is to assemble all the defenses possible, and as furious preparations are apace for the terrible struggle that will shortly continue, and therefore convinced that there has never been a more critical moment for France, for your reign, for you personally, I come, sire, to offer the country of my birth [*sic*] and to you, despite my poor health, whatever assistance I possibly can, provided that I am permitted to do so with honor.[11]

Napoleon was staggered. This letter was almost as much of a shock as the loss of Russia itself! Even more amazing, he replied positively to Louis. "*Mon frère*, I have received your letter of January 1 and greatly appreciate your kind sentiments. . . . Return here as quickly as possible and I shall receive you, not as a brother whom you offended [when King of Holland], but as the brother who brought you up."[12] By Napoleon's standards it was the warmest letter he had written anyone in years.

Bonaparte immediately informed his equally amazed mother of Louis's extraordinarily change of heart, and she more than seconded Napoleon's invitation that Louis should return to "hearth and home." "I, as your mother, order you to do so, as it is necessary [for Napoleon]."

That did it. Louis's mood, which changed as abruptly as the weather over the Hebrides, replied sullenly: "Why, my dear mother, always repeat the same old things to me? I can only return to Holland [as King], not France." This was how he interpreted offering "assistance." He then closed: "Not another word on the subject."[13]

That was too much for Napoleon. The imperial invitation to Paris was withdrawn, and Louis returned to his poetry. Months later, as a good patriot during the Saxon campaign, Louis could no longer bear to reside in Graz and moved to Basel, where he penned fresh poems: "Absence," "Regrets," "Hopes," and "Doubts." Only on receiving on November 3, 1813, the news of Napoleon's later defeat did Louis finally return to France, staying at his mother's residence at Pont-sur-Seine. "If he is coming as King of Holland, and persists in this fantasy of his, I cannot receive him in Paris. . . . Let him remain with her 'incognito,'" Napoleon instructed Archchancellor Cambacérès. "I should rather see Holland handed over to the House of Orange than to my brother." "I have renounced the country of my birth, absolutely everything," Louis wrote to Napoleon, and now "I find myself without a country, without friends, and without even a roof over my head."[14]

*   *   *

All the countries the French had invaded and occupied under Napoleonic rule had been thoroughly stripped of their assets. No two countries had been hit harder than Holland and brother Jérôme Bonaparte's once-thriving Kingdom of Westphalia.

Napoleon had not only extracted the usual "war reparations," gold, artworks, jewels, and stashes of fine wines in ancient princely cellars, but had destroyed much of the economy through the implementation of the Continental System, completed by the constant flow of new financial demands that by January 1813 had left Westphalia with an empty treasury and its national debt beyond any means of control. In addition Napoleon had milked the kingdom for his own private treasury and family needs, to the point that Jérôme had been forced to sell all national and royal properties. What is more, Napoleon had insisted that Jérôme produce an army corps of twenty-five thousand for the Russian invasion, of whom only 5 percent returned.

As a result there had been several attempts at revolt, all of which Napoleon had naturally blamed on Jérôme's incompetence and frivolity. Knowing only too well how irresponsible and shallow a young man Jérôme was, Napoleon had nevertheless wedded him (bigamously) to Catherine of Württemberg. Catherine was as lightheaded and as insouciant as her prodigiously unfaithful husband, living for the same glitter, pomp, and constant schedule of plays, masked balls, and dazzling bejeweled presents. In addition Queen Catherine, like Josephine, easily became hysterical. In January 1813, therefore, when the full impact of the destruction of Napoleon's Grande Armée was felt in Westphalian commercial and royal circles, Catherine panicked, fearing the vengeance of advancing armies from the east, be they Russian or Prussian.

Westphalia of course bordered on the much reduced western Prussian frontier at the Elbe River, less than two hundred miles from Berlin. Minuscule Prussia, literally halved by Napoleon, in turn now acted as a buffer state between the Kingdom of Westphalia and Napoleon's Grand Duchy of Warsaw farther to the east. Westphalia's southeastern frontier was opposed (or supported, depending on one's viewpoint) by the Kingdom of Saxony, with its capital of Dresden less than one hundred miles from Westphalian territory. Due north of Westphalia lay the state of Mecklenburg and the much smaller enclave of Swedish Pomerania, both bordering the Baltic. A little farther to the northwest stood the Hanseatic cities of Hamburg, Bremen, and Lübeck, while only about a hundred miles directly north of Jérôme's capital of Kassel on the River Fulda was King George III's private

state of Hannover (now in French hands, of course). Napoleon had originally carved out the Grand Duchy of Berg, which was in turn absorbed into
the Kingdom of Westphalia.

Westphalia therefore stood as the linchpin of Napoleon's north German defenses, both controlling the Confederation of the Rhine and protecting French possessions from any hostile incursions from the east, from the
other side of the Elbe. That Napoleon should have placed the shallowest,
least intelligent, and least reliable of his brothers on that throne was the
folly of follies. In the early days of 1813 Napoleon depended more than
ever on the stability and dependability of any state in his realm. Yet Westphalia, as a result of his own imaginative financial extortions and Jérôme's
total administrative incompetence, was in a highly unstable state.

By January 1813 relations between Paris and Kassel could not have
been worse. Napoleon still could not forgive the humiliation of Jérôme's
abandonment of his army at the beginning of the Russian campaign the previous year. Jérôme, who had been attempting to correspond with Napoleon
ever since, had met a wall of total silence. The coronation of the infant king
of Rome, scheduled in Paris, in March 1813 should have been an ideal time
for the mending of relations, except that Napoleon denied the Westphalian
royal family an invitation.

On January 11 Jérôme's chamberlain, who was in Paris on official business, took the opportunity to bring up a new matter that took Napoleon by
surprise. Queen Catherine wanted to come to Paris urgently. Rumor was
rife of "enemy forces" driving westward toward Berlin. Catherine was terrified—she had already fled earlier during the Dörnberg plot—and wanted
to leave immediately. The queen not only desired to come to Paris but in
great state, which would mean being received officially and at the frequent
state functions held at the Tuileries. Napoleon wanted none of this. As for
the alleged danger of approaching enemy forces, that, he insisted, was nonsense, and he would not issue an invitation to his sister-in-law.

By February 21 Jérôme was becoming desperate and informed Paris
that if Catherine were not invited to France he would send her to Stuttgart
with its large French garrison.[15] The ostensible urgency concerned the
impending war and invasion, hence the need for the queen's flight from
Kassel. Napoleon was always suspicious of any request or action by any
member of his family. Nevertheless finally, if reluctantly, he did give tentative approval, but on one condition only: "Immediately following the entry
of Emperor Alexander and General Kutuzov into either Berlin or Dresden,
you will arrange for the departure of the queen via Wesel, thence on to
Paris, *but not before that!*"[16] He was adamant. Jérôme, who saw none of the

implied nuances, was delighted, as was silly Catherine. She could hardly wait to leave. She would be staying at Uncle Fesch's enormous mansion in Paris. Jérôme, a little too precipitously, then announced in the *Westphalian Monitor* that "the Queen was leaving for Paris at the invitation of His Imperial Majesty." The very next day, March 9, Jérôme informed Napoleon that the enemy had entered Berlin "in force" and thus he was seeing off his good lady. Bidding adieu to his wife on the tenth, Jérôme ordered the coachman and accompanying military escort to avoid the more direct Frankfurt-am-Main route, now "encumbered by an army of one hundred thousand men," sending her instead via Bonn, Aachen, and Brussels.[17]

Upon receiving this news by special royal courier, Napoleon was incredulous. The Russian army already in Berlin, about to invade Westphalia! Impossible!

In reality the king of Westphalia simply wanted his wife not only out of his bed, but out of his castle, out of his kingdom, and out of his life, for he had found a lovely if ruthless replacement. The stunning Countess von Löwenstein-Wertheim was immediately installed as mistress in residence at the royal palace in Kassel. Everyone knew about it but Napoleon. When Jérôme had abandoned the battlefield in Poland in 1812, it had been to rush back to the charms and wiles of this lovely countess now "in her early thirties," who had arrived here from Württemberg in 1808, along with an impoverished and redundant husband, not to mention three unwanted children.

By the autumn of 1812, the determined countess had already secured her position at the court of Westphalia. Determined as any Lady Macbeth to prepare a solid power base for herself, she had already "persuaded" the feckless Jérôme to remove several of his closest officers in favor of soldier-friends of *her* own choice, not to mention establishing an intricate network of spies riddling the royal palace. Jérôme was apparently happily unaware that his every word and action, even his private correspondence, was being reported back to the scheming Löwenstein. Needless to say Queen Catherine's mail, even to her father, was not spared the countess's rigorous scrutiny, and when the queen discovered this and complained, the matter was dismissed out of hand.

Catherine had grown more and more fearful of this intruder's power, especially when she realized in the autumn of 1812 that her husband wanted to marry the hussy.

There were two more things Jérôme's mistress desired before striking the final blow. First she wanted to be made a princess, which she did by inveigling Jérôme to persuade the king of Bavaria to raise the title of her

father-in-law from "Count" to "Prince" von Löwenstein, which the obliging Max Joseph officially did, thereby automatically elevating the countess
to princess. (That she had long ago abandoned her estranged husband, the
good von Löwenstein, appeared immaterial, even to the king of Bavaria.)
The next step was to get rid of Catherine, which she succeeded in doing
with the scare of "the Russians are coming." Deadlier than any enemy
troops, the enemy had in fact already arrived.

Now it was simply a case of buying off the church with another annulment. Napoleon had it in his power to do anything, and after all the unfortunate pope was still a state prisoner at Fontainebleau. Given a few more
months, perhaps a year, and she would be able to elevate her title once
again, this time to queen.

Alas, here our Lady Macbeth made two slight miscalculations. Under
no circumstances would the pope have obliged Jérôme with a divorce or
annulment (Pius VII still considered him married to Elizabeth, his
American wife), and in any case the pope was no longer on speaking terms
with Napoleon or any other Bonaparte. The scheming Löwenstein's second
error was greater, for she did not know that in fact not only were the
Russians indeed coming but so were the Prussians. Furthermore, the
resplendent castle she so coveted in Kassel would soon be reduced to a heap
of ashes and rubble (not by the marauding Cossacks but by overzealous
royal servants feeding an overheated oven). Jérôme's tinsel Kingdom of
Westphalia would be swept off the map before the year was out. As for the
ousted Catherine, she soon found herself first at Compiègne and then in
Paris, an annoyed brother-in-law Napoleon footing all her bills thereafter.[18]

"Sire, your army no longer exists," Chief-of-Staff Berthier had informed
Napoleon on his return to Paris in December 1812. And as Méneval
acknowledged, "He [Napoleon] had to conquer continuously, absolutely,
and in every direction, and his first real defeat on the battlefield would
overnight transform his 'allies,' hitherto bound to him at gunpoint, into
relentless enemies."[19]

On January 22, 1813, Karl August von Hardenberg, the Prussian chancellor who had been dismissed years before on Napoleon's personal orders
but since reinstated, gave a glittering dinner party in his Berlin mansion for
the entire diplomatic corps and the senior French generals in the city,
announcing casually that King Friedrich Wilhelm was about to leave Potsdam to assemble the new Prussian force required by the French. He was
indeed raising a new army, but one with which to fight the French occupying force in his kingdom.[20]

Deep-seated hatred of the French now appeared overtly in every direction. The hitherto dry, stuffy Professor Steffens, entering the amphitheater for his usual boring lecture at the University of Breslau, instead set aside his lecture notes and indignantly harangued his astonished audience on their patriotic duty to overthrow the French despots. He marched out of the entrance of the university with some two hundred students to volunteer for militia service at the local garrison. Similar scenes were repeated in Berlin and elsewhere.

On January 13 Alexander gave full authorization for his newly prepared war plans, while naming the outlawed (by Napoleon) Baron Stein to administer the districts of Prussia proper as they were recaptured by Russian troops. Beginning with Königsberg, he was to summon the Provincial Assemblies of East and West Prussia and with their approval prepare to arm and launch a new *Landwehr*, or militia.[21] Full-throated voices, long choked off by the French, resounded loudly their determination, echoing from the banks of the Pregel to those of the Rhine itself.

Meanwhile the Prussian king had not only been successfully calling up new army units, but also conferring secretly at Breslau with Chancellor von Hardenberg and Gen. Gerhard von Scharnhorst, drafting an emergency defence pact that would be presented to Czar Alexander on February 28 at nearby Kalisch. Scharnhorst, who had directed the Royal Prussian Military Academy, also had his own personal account to settle with Napoleon Bonaparte. A veteran of both Auerstädt and Eylau, he had then been taken prisoner by the French at Lübeck. Since 1807 he had reorganized the Prussian army, boosting the morale of its officer corps to such a point that military leaders were now champing at the bit to attack the French.

The Treaty of Kalisch was fully approved by the czar and formed the basis of the new grand alliance, the coalition of powers that were gathering everywhere. The instrument called for "the total destruction of the enemy forces," proclaiming "the great epoch of independence for all the States which shall be ready to seize it and free themselves from the yoke which France has imposed upon them for so many years."[22] The Kalisch Accords further called for full and immediate cooperation between Russian and Prussian armies, swearing both countries not to sign any separate peace treaties with the French. They had to work together if they were to succeed this time. Russia agreed to restore Prussia "to the same degree of power," population, and land that that kingdom had held before the war of 1806, though the two countries differed on which portions of Poland would go to whom. On March 15 Alexander, Friedrich Wilhelm, Hardenberg, and Scharnhorst duly met again at Breslau to launch their new campaign, although in reality the troops of both armies were already on the march and had recaptured Berlin itself. Their goal was to bring in Austria as well, but—wary of Napoleon's power—Vienna balked at the idea (while secretly in agreement with both the feelings and objectives of the new Allied Coalition).

On March 17 a wider Russo-Prussian Convention was signed at Breslau with very precise objectives, including the liberation of Germany from France, the destruction of the Confederation of the Rhine (as a French organization), and the summoning of all German princes to join them (or else suffer the loss of their territory). Friedrich Wilhelm closed this pivotal congress by creating the order of merit to be known as the Iron Cross, to be awarded to German patriots in the new campaign. The aging poet-philosopher Goethe cast the only shadow with his famous dictum: "Shake your chains as you will, the man [Napoleon] is too strong for you."[23] Neither Goethe nor his skepticism was present at Breslau that momentous day, however, as orders were issued to the general staffs to prepare full-scale attacks against the French.

Austria's hands were still officially tied at this time, through its earlier military pact with Napoleon. Nevertheless it was slowly coming around to the realization that it would soon have to change sides and, indeed, had already taken one initial step that had very much upset Napoleon—concluding a separate armistice with the Russians back in January 1813. As a result Emperor Franz I now offered to act as mediator of a peace accord between France and its opponents. Napoleon immediately countered this by dispatching Ambassador Narbonne to Vienna to hamstring those negotiations, an act not appreciated by the Austrians, even as Alexander and Friedrich Wilhelm were advancing with their troops and reaching Dresden. The Austrians would eventually join the Allies, but only when they were sure that this time they could not lose. One of the key factors soon to render this possible was Great Britain's joining the Russo-Prussian Kalisch Accords officially signed at Reichenbach, Silesia, on June 14–15. The British were to pay £666,666 per month as a special subsidy to Prussia, another £1 million total to Russia, while guaranteeing a separate £5 million war chest with both Russia and Prussia. Independently of this, on March 3, the British government had signed another defense pact at Stockholm with Crown Prince Bernadotte, ensuring a Swedish declaration of war against Napoleon and the landing of up to thirty thousand men in Swedish Pomerania, in exchange for another British subsidy. A new coalition was formed.

Napoleon of course had made it perfectly clear to Ambassador Narbonne that he was not interested in peace or concessions. It was to be continued war. Hortense's estimation, given earlier to Schwarzenberg in perfectly good faith, assuring him of Napoleon's peaceful intentions, had proved 100 percent incorrect. Apparently having forgotten the five hundred thousand men of the Grande Armée left behind in Russia less than a year before, he was now bent on a war of annihilation.

Bonaparte did not seem to grasp the reality of the rapid disintegration of his imperial holdings throughout Europe. Warsaw had fallen to the Russians back in February, Rapp was isolated at Danzig with up to thirty thousand men, and on March 4 Prince Eugène and the French army were forced to evacuate Berlin. Hamburg was the next to fall, Gen. Carra St.-Cyr forced to retreat on March 12, as the Freikorps moved in. The next day Prussia declared war on France, catching Napoleon completely off guard. He who was so accustomed to deciding when a campaign would begin was not ready. Hold the Oder, he instructed his commanders, if at all possible, while Davout was ordered to head for Hamburg to undo the damage done there. But the bad news continued. General Reynier's southern army had been forced to evacuate the Saxon capital of Dresden, which was occupied by Field Marshal Blücher and the Prussian army on March 27. Napoleon, who had planned on driving to the Vistula, was instead fighting just to hold the Elbe.

That Bonaparte remained in Paris as long as he did, given the grave situation, is puzzling. The usually decisive—indeed impetuous—commander did not set out from the French capital until April 15, after Warsaw, Berlin, Hamburg, and Dresden all were lost. This Saxon campaign, as it was to be known, was to prove one of the longest and most costly ever fought. Time, along with all the other factors, was favoring the new Allied Coalition against him. Although determined to hold the Elbe, he could no longer count on his once mighty Confederation of the Rhine, already in the throes of rebellion. His revised plan was to let the Allies "penetrate toward Bayreuth" while Napoleon at the head of his main army headed for Dresden, now in Prussian hands.[24]

Lacking anything like accurate intelligence on Allied numbers and positions, Napoleon spent a week at Mainz gleaning what he could, further revising his plan of operations and issuing final orders.

On April 25 Napoleon moved on to Erfurt, preparatory to gathering his armies near Merseburg and Naumburg along the Saale River, just west of Leipzig. Combined, Napoleon's Army of the Elbe and the Army of the Main totaled about 179,000 men, but with a very small cavalry and thus far only 372 guns (he had lost his entire cavalry in Russia, not to mention more than one thousand artillery pieces). The French still held two bridgeheads over the Elbe at Magdeburg and Wittenberg, however, and they had to be held at all costs.

Bonaparte had placed his northern army of 58,000 men under the command of Prince Eugène, with Latour-Maubourg's cavalry and part of the new Guard, with orders to deploy along the Elbe as far north as Magdeburg. Meanwhile Davout's independent command of 20,000 men and Sébastiani's cavalry of 14,000 men were to secure the far northwest to the Baltic. At this time Napoleon had actually with him only about 121,000 men (including Oudinot's, Bertrand's, Marmont's, and Ney's corps, and most of the Guard, perhaps 15,000 or so, commanded by Bessières, Mortier, and Soult).

The Allies were not as well coordinated and surprisingly still fielded only about 106,000 men, even as late as April. The Russian army was temporarily the largest, while the dying Kutuzov was replaced as commander in chief by Wittgenstein (who had defeated the French time and again the year before). Their four corps were deployed along the Elbe opposite Magdeburg down as far as Halle. To the south of them stood Blücher's Prussian army, near Leipzig.

By May 1, 1813, Napoleon's main force reached a point just south of Lützen, opposite Wittgenstein's Russians (whose numbers had increased), giving them five corps, though their precise whereabouts still remained unknown at French GHQ. Marching on the road to Leipzig on May 1, Napoleon was startled to hear heavy guns and intensive small-arms fire from between Lützen and—when he checked his map—the sleepy village of Kaja.

It had all been such a surrealistic nightmare ever since the flight from Moscow, their narrow escape over the Berezina, the humiliation of having to flee in disguise as Caulaincourt's secretary, with packs of wolves literally snarling around them as their terrified horses pulled them mile after mile across the frozen wastes of Poland, to the Elbe, the Rhine, and the Seine, Napoleon's body so shrunken beneath those strange clothes that neither his concierge nor his own wife had recognized him at first. His thoughts were only to avenge himself with another army, one as large as the one he had just obliterated from the face of the earth. And what a nightmare it had been assembling this totally new army.

In September 1812, through another special *senatus consultum*, Napoleon had called for 137,000 conscripts from the class of 1813, and another 78,000 National Guards were assigned to active military duty with the army. On January 11, 1813, he had called for an additional 100,000 men from the class of 1812, who, through various loopholes, had earlier evaded service. In

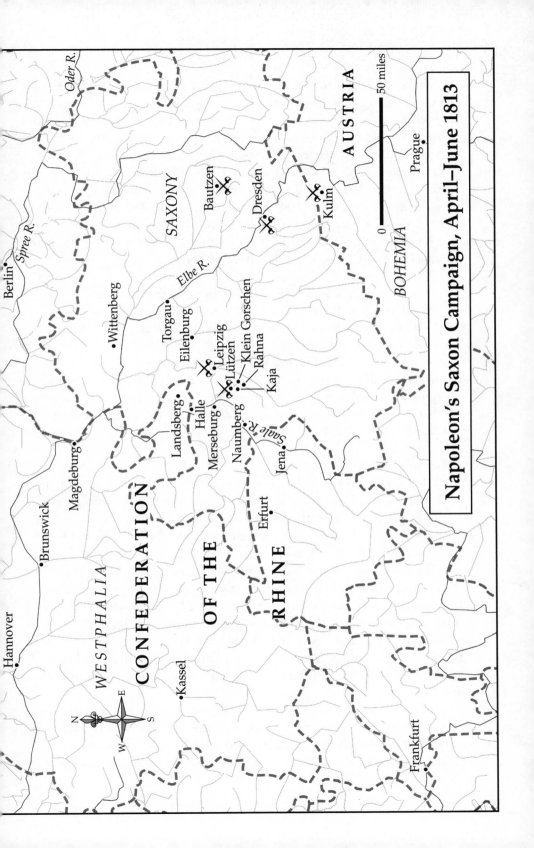

Napoleon's Saxon Campaign, April–June 1813

50 miles

0

AUSTRIA

BOHEMIA

Prague

Kulm

Dresden

Bautzen

SAXONY

Berlin

Spree R.

Oder R.

Wittenberg

Elbe R.

Torgau

Eilenburg

Leipzig

Klein Gorschen

Rahna

Lützen

Kaja

Halle

Landsberg

Merseburg

Naumberg

Saale R.

Jena

Erfurt

Magdeburg

Brunswick

Hannover

WESTPHALIA

CONFEDERATION

OF THE

RHINE

Kassel

Frankfurt

N
E
S
W

February, Napoleon ordered the conscription of 150,000 young men from the Class of 1814. He transferred 16,000 naval gunners to the army, then stripped most of the ships of the line of their crews and added them to the army as well. Still not satisfied, on April 3 Napoleon drafted a further 80,000 men from the classes of 1807–12, plus 90,000 more from the class of 1814. A special 10,000-man *Gardes d'Honneur* was drafted from the wealthy and well-connected young men who had escaped military service by influence or the purchase of a substitute or two.[25] Napoleon was desperate: He would take anyone, even old rejects—except brother Jérôme.

When the king of Westphalia had volunteered his services for the forthcoming campaign, Napoleon had instructed Berthier:

> Inform the king that he will never be given another command in the French Army if: (1) he will not first acknowledge his disgraceful conduct last year by leaving the army without permission . . . and (2) if in being reintegrated he does not agree to take orders from every marshal of my army . . . and if he will not further agree to holding the rank of général de division and no higher. . . . For he must realize that war is a profession, which one must learn and prepare for, and that as the king has never even been in a major battle, he therefore is not fit to command.[26]

Jérôme did not reply.

After calling up every conscript he could think of, even some old, crippled soldiers who had already served their long years, and putting the navy in mothballs (because of the lack of crews, also conscripted), he was left with trying to find cavalry and especially mounts, finally reduced to drafting the nation's mounted gendarmerie.

Then there was the problem of actually rounding up French conscripts themselves, so violently had public reaction turned against Napoleon's continuous, fatal wars. By 1813 there were at least forty thousand deserters or men who had escaped the recruiters' bayonets, roaming the French countryside in gangs, terrorizing one and all, as they desperately attempted to flee the glorious call to arms, to avoid the fate of the hundreds of thousands of corpses frozen beneath those immaculate white fields of snow in Poland and Russia.

But the vast majority of the French recruits did fall in behind the recruiting sergeant. Onward they came, these unfortunate men and boys, only to find themselves scorned by their own French people as they were marched from village to village, to the high roads, as if they themselves were the enemy, pariahs. And each night en route they found themselves quartered in the local prison, or a barn, if they were fortunate enough, or else simply herded to the nearest field, even having to pay for their daily food ration. The rate of desertion rose the closer they got to the Rhine and then the Saale.

More reinforcements of "allies" were formed. Three more battalions of Westphalians had just been conscripted by force (they would later desert in mid-battle), not to mention one Badenese squadron, to whom were added the Poles, Bavarians, Lithuanians, Saxons, and so on. War Minister Clarke promised another 27,000 men by mid-February, Poles and Germans from the Warta, the Oder, Posen, Warsaw, Zamość, and Czestochowa, some from places even Napoleon had never heard of. Another 24,488 reinforcements would also be marching toward the Elbe by February, including Franco-Italian troops, eight battalions of sailors, and a few hundred more Badenese.[27] Altogether Clarke promised a theoretical force of 200,000 men. These angry men of all age groups openly cursed Napoleon as they passed the burned rubble of villages and once-proud towns, destroyed during previous campaigns.

Napoleon was mystified by the guns he heard south of Lützen on May 1. He did not even know who was fighting, apart from the fact that Ney's III Corps had been "resting" there while en route. In fact a few hours earlier Ney's troops had been assigned to occupy the sleepy, picturesque villages of Kaja, Rahna, Gross, and Klein Görschen to the south of Lützen and the main road, to cover Lauriston's and Macdonald's march on Leipzig, while waiting for Marmont's lagging and dispirited VI Corps to catch up with them.

Incomplete intelligence reports finally reached GHQ. It was the Russians. It appeared that Wittgenstein had been advancing from the southeast with some 73,000 men, when, much to their surprise, they had come upon a mere 2,000 of Ney's troops out in the open cooking breakfast. An angry Ney, who had argued against this new campaign, had not even posted pickets. It was practically a picnic and apparently easy pickings for the Russians. But great was the surprise of Blücher (who was serving under the Russians here) at 11:45 that May morning as his cavalry swept down on Ney's unsuspecting conscripts, to find his Prussian cavalry before not just 2,000 men but an entire French army corps. Blücher immediately stopped his charge and returned to his lines as his artillery was brought up against the French, supported by four full army corps. General Souham held them off as best he could as Napoleon ordered Marmont's corps, the Old Guard, and Macdonald's XI Corps to come to their aid, while Bertrand's IV Corps was advancing from the southwest.

Napoleon did not reach the battlefield with reinforcements until 2:30 that afternoon, where he found Ney's corps single-handedly still holding off the entire Russo-Prussian army. With the smell of gunpowder and apparent near disaster close at hand, the Napoleon of yore suddenly came to life, true to legend, personally leading up fresh, hesitant regiments of green recruits. The old Bonaparte magic worked again as morale suddenly soared, jubilant cries of *"Vive l'Empereur!"* clashing with the roar of cannon. As Marmont later reported, Napoleon as usual soon was in the center of the most deadly fighting. It was Borodino all over again. The casualties were great on both sides, Blücher himself wounded and out of action, replaced by Yorck. Napoleon's aim was to outflank Wittgenstein, and at 6:00 P.M., with a newly massed seventy-gun battery, he unleashed his main attack, which continued right until nightfall, forcing the Allied line to fall back in confusion. It would be a French victory, but not a complete one, as the crack reorganized Prussian cavalry launched an unexpected and most impressive counterattack at 9:00 P.M., immediately stopping all French preparations for pursuit, thereby permitting the Allies to withdraw in good order.

The price for the unplanned Battle of Lützen was high, Ney losing most of his corps, the French suffering a minimum of twenty thousand casualties, and Wittgenstein's Allies an equal number. As all parties evacuated the latest field of battle, they left behind at least four burning, destroyed villages, the innocent civilians as usual the real losers.

Despite his late arrival Napoleon had had the real advantage at Lützen in finally greatly outnumbering his opponents. After some days of rest, but once again with insufficient intelligence data, he decided on a two-pronged follow-up attack. He would threaten Berlin, Wittenberg, and Torgau with the remnants of Ney's corps supported by Victor, Reynier, and Sébastiani's cavalry. His aim was to divide the Allies, forcing the Prussians to abandon the Russians in order to protect their capital. Meanwhile Napoleon, leading the principal part of his army, would drive toward Dresden to destroy Wittgenstein and the Russians. Alas for the French, apart from Blücher's corps of 30,000 men, the Allied army remained together, including the other Prussian corps, all in and around Dresden. In fact, Wittgenstein had already passed Dresden, reaching the banks of the Spree River, where he found a good defensive position and dug in well prepared for the French onslaught he expected. Napoleon advanced with Bertrand commanding his left wing, Marmont and Macdonald the center, and Oudinot directing the right flank. Much to their surprise they entered an undefended Dresden on the evening of May 8. Napoleon moved into the palace that Czar Alexander and King Friedrich Wilhelm had hastily evacuated. As for the amiable but weak-willed king of Saxony, he assured the French emperor that he would not abandon him again.[28] For the moment both sides were better matched, Wittgenstein with 96,000 men, Napoleon with some 115,000, despite an infusion of reinforcements for both of them.

Napoleon decided to wait until he had more substantial reinforcements, however, including Ney's additional four corps, some 84,000. He would soon outnumber Wittgenstein two to one, the sort of odds Napoleon liked. French troops continued to pour into the region around Bautzen, a two-day march to the northeast of Dresden.

Finally satisfied, Bonaparte gave the signal for the opening heavy bombardment at noon on May 20, followed three hours later by the first major attack, with Ney's army group approaching the Spree at Klux, along Napoleon's western flank, Soult and Bertrand commanding the left center, and Marmont's VI Corps along the right center; while to Marmont's right were Macdonald's XI Corps before the town of Bautzen itself, and to the extreme French right, Oudinot's XII Corps. Facing them were the veteran Allied commanders Barclay, Blücher, Kleist, Yorck, Berg, Gorchakov, and Miloradovich.

Intensive fighting lasted all day, with nothing concluded by nightfall. It was only after resuming the fighting the next morning that Ney finally joined them after a long hard march, adding his 84,000 men to the French side. It proved a tough, head-on battle, Napoleon ordering Ney's group to swing around Wittgenstein's right flank cutting him off along the Görlitz Road. Soult would follow up with his 20,000 men near the left center.

As so often happened, orders were fouled up in the heat of battle, Ney not understanding his instructions and consequently launching a series of very heavy assaults against the Allied line instead of outflanking them and cutting off the enemy's escape. Despite outrageously unequal numbers, the Russians and Prussians held grimly fast until five o'clock on the afternoon of the twenty-first, when seeing himself hopelessly outnumbered, Czar Alexander, who had interfered with Wittgenstein's command all day, now initiated the beginning of another orderly tactical retreat. Soult, who was hardly a wonder even at the best of times, simply kept battering at the Allied center, which staunchly withstood his superior numbers. Napoleon was finally forced to call up the Imperial Guard against Blücher's flank but was unable to prevent a successful Allied withdrawal in the direction of Görlitz to the southeast, the route that Ney had failed to sever. Both Ney and Lauriston were in Napoleon's bad books that evening, as they watched an army half the size of theirs escape. Soult as usual had not done much better. Thus the Allied army withdrew, though suffering casualties of some 25 percent of their force. Again the French had suffered an equal number of casualties.

The French pursuit continued the following day, May 22. It had started off well enough, Napoleon desperately urging on his men after the Russian rear guard, when he was stopped by a volley of cannonballs striking around him. He complained to Duroc, "That lot are not leaving anything behind, not even a single prisoner for us. Ah, luck is not on our side today!" He was particularly upset at taking no prisoners, large numbers indicating a real defeat and a demoralized foe. Just then an aide-de-camp rode up to inform him of the death of General Bruyères, who had been with Napoleon since his Italian campaign. Several minutes later, with Caulaincourt, Mortier, General of Engineers Kirgener, and Duroc, Napoleon left the road to get a better view from a nearby hilltop. Just as he was passing an isolated tree, it was cut in half by a Russian cannonball, Napoleon continuing on to the crest of the hill. Turning round, he could not see Duroc, who was invariably at his side. The cannonball that had just split the tree, narrowly missing Napoleon, had ricocheted, cutting General Kirgener in two, and almost completely disemboweling Duroc. Still alive but suffering horribly, Duroc was taken down the hill to a nearby house, accompanied by Napoleon, Berthier, Caulaincourt, and Dr. Yvan. Christophe Duroc was clearly close to death. "It was a terrible sight," recalled Constant. "The Emperor, in a state of despair, leaned over and embraced his faithful friend several times, trying to utter a few words of hope, but the Duke [Duroc], who knew perfectly well how serious the situation was, did not answer . . . and then finally only to ask for opium. At these words, no longer able to bear it, Napoleon left. The Duke of Friuli died the next morning."

Napoleon returned to his camp. "He sat down on a stool outside his tent, his head hung low, his hands tightly gripped together, and there he remained for about an hour, without saying a word. . . . Sobs were heard from his tent all night long." Afterward he ordered Duroc's body to be taken back to Paris for burial in the Invalides. He also bought the house in which his friend had died, ordering a plaque to be placed in it: "Here General Duroc, duc de Frioul, grand marshal of the palace of the Emperor Napoléon, was hit by a cannonball and died in the arms of the emperor, his friend."[29] He also arranged to have prayers read regularly there.

Duroc was indeed his only close friend, the only person in the entire army who still used the informal *tu* with him. Napoleon was silent and remote for days thereafter, just as he had been following the death of

Lannes at Wagram. The effect of the loss of Duroc is difficult to calculate, but it was certainly great and permanent, leaving Napoleon a different man, more distant than ever before. He was now all alone in the world, a vast chasm separating him from the rest of the living.

On May 22, because of Duroc, Napoleon suddenly broke off the pursuit of the Russians despite his favorable position. It all seemed so irrelevant now. The last fall from his horse at the Trianon had indeed been an omen. Duroc had advised Napoleon against both the Russian campaign and the present one, and now he was reaping the whirlwind. He had killed his best friend.

As for the Allies, they were at loggerheads, a furious Wittgenstein resigning from the Russian army as a result of Alexander's having effectively superseded him and his orders throughout the battle at Bautzen. Barclay de Tolly took over command once again as both the Prussians and Russians withdrew strategically to Schweidnitz, in Silesia. Napoleon, at last getting a grip on himself, ordered his main force in the direction of Katzbach, which he took on June 1, along with the important city of Breslau, even as good news arrived from the north: Davout had retaken Hamburg, lost earlier by St-Cyr.

But by now both sides were overextended and licking their wounds after having suffered enormous casualties, complicated by poor supply lines and unsatisfactory field commanders for the most part.

On June 2 both Alexander and Napoleon agreed to a temporary ceasefire, followed on the fourth by a conference at Pleiswitz, where they signed a truce until July 20, during which time they would negotiate a peace settlement. As Napoleon informed War Minister Clarke, he had agreed to this interruption "in the course of my victories" because of the desperate shortage of cavalry—which could not stand up to the superior Cossacks and Prussians—and because of his anxiety over what he referred to as "Austria's hostile attitude."[30]

Yet Napoleon, now offered the ideal occasion for making peace after two bloody but victorious engagements, had no intention of losing face by making a compromising peace, involving the return of land he had taken. For him it was all or nothing. No longer living in the world of reality, he was intent on destroying both the Prussian and Russian armies that had somehow escaped him, and to march to Königsberg. Napoleon thought Metternich was quite mad, coming as a mediator to Dresden on May 27 and counseling Napoleon to be both generous and reasonable in this hour of victory. He asked for the dissolution of the Duchy of Warsaw, Napoleon's renunciation of the territory recently "annexed" at gunpoint in the north of Germany, including Hannover and Hamburg, and the return of Illyria to

Austria. Napoleon dismissed him with a contemptuous wave of the hand. "I have not asked for your mediation. . . . *I will sacrifice a million men yet if necessary*. . . . You wish to tear Italy and Germany from me. You wish to dishonor me, *monsieur*. Honor before all!" he all but screamed at him.[31]

It was under this prevailingly negative mood that the Armistice of Pleiswitz began on June 4 and extended ultimately until August 10. It was another great lack of judgment on Napoleon's part, for not only were more Prussian and Russian troops advancing westward to meet him, but England was in the process of joining the coalition along with Austria.

When Napoleon finally learned about the secret Treaty of Trachtenberg, signed on July 9, 1813, in which England agreed to subsidize Austrian and Swedish participation against France, is not clear, although the final agreement formally bringing Austria into the new Allied Coalition, with Prussia and Russia, was not signed until September 19.[32] Suddenly in mid-July Napoleon summoned Marie-Louise and most of his ministers to an urgent meeting at Mainz.

Arriving on the twenty-fifth he was warmly greeted by his wife and members of his cabinet. Long hours were spent behind closed doors as Napoleon reviewed the situation in Paris—he wanted no more General Malets attempting to overthrow his government again during his absence—and had to make further preparations for the war effort. No doubt one of the main reasons for this unscheduled last-minute meeting was to address the princes and heads of the principal states of the Confederation of the Rhine, and many appeared as commanded, but many other of his devoted "allies" were absent. Metternich's demands for the dismemberment of his great empire had clearly frightened Bonaparte, and he had no doubt already received Prince von Schwarzenberg's hardly subtle double-entendre threat that "Politics have made this marriage, and politics can just as easily unmake it."

Napoleon had been corresponding constantly with his regent-empress, his letters always awkwardly addressed to "Madame, chère amie," every one of them businesslike, lacking warmth, love, and any indication that they were even vaguely related (in contrast to his letters to Josephine, which often had been affectionate and loving). Perhaps Napoleon felt that she had already betrayed him and was working behind his back to overthrow his regime. And although as a sign of love she had brought the portrait artist Isabey in tow, to prepare some quick miniatures of him, Napoleon was wary of her, never trusting anyone—except of course Duroc, and Duroc was no more. He also managed to spend a surprising number of hours alone, as the now crippled Méneval, serving as Marie-Louise's new secretary, reported. And then on August 1 Napoleon was gone as suddenly as he had appeared, and by the 4th back at his GHQ in Dresden.[33]

Meanwhile at the Congress of Prague, convened to resolve this conflict, the negotiators met almost too casually, too lacking in their resolve to arrive at a mutually acceptable European peace, Narbonne and Caulaincourt representing France. Although the armistice had been extended until August 10, they convened in the Bohemian capital for the last time on August 7, when Metternich confidently raised the ante, as additional troops continued to swell the forces of the Coalition. Not only did the Austrian chancellor now insist on the dissolution of the French Grand Duchy of Warsaw (already in Russian hands) and the reestablishment of Hamburg, Bremen, Lübeck, and Hannover, but also on the dismemberment of the Confederation of the Rhine, the return of an independent Holland, the restitution of the old Prussia, the Illyrian provinces to Vienna, and the evacuation of Iberia. In brief France was to withdraw to its former frontiers.

Napoleon remained defiant. "Do you wish to rob me? . . . I will not give up one inch of ground." How dare they demand the return of their rightful property?! And at midnight on August 10, 1813, the Congress of Prague silently dissolved into history. The war was to continue, for Napoleon demanded it.[34]

CHAPTER 37

Leipzig

The Grand Empire no longer exists. It is France itself we
must now defend.
— TO THE FRENCH SENATE, NOVEMBER 14, 1813

s the armistice—and with it the fruitless negotiations at Prague—drew to an end in the second week of August 1813, Napoleon knew despite his poor intelligence service that the immediate post-Bautzen situation had deteriorated so far as the French and their dwindling allies were concerned. At Bautzen on May 21 he had outnumbered the Russo-Prussian army. By the end of August, although still in control of all the strong points along the Elbe, including Magdeburg, Wittenberg, Orgau, and Dresden, and isolated Leipzig, Napoleon's main force was concentrated along the Saxon-Bohemian frontier up to Dresden, reaching eastward as far as Zittau in the Isser Mountains, with perhaps a total force of 220,000 men. Thus, despite his recent victories at Lützen and Bautzen, he controlled only the Elbe and the main cities of Dresden and Leipzig.

Berthier spread out a large map on the table in the castle of Dresden, serving as the French general headquarters, and pointed out to Napoleon four major Allied armies closing in on him. Their numbers and pincerlike movement were very worrying indeed, for this was one reality the French emperor could understand. It could have all been avoided had he signed after his last victory. Then the Austrians had switched sides, none other than Prince von Schwarzenberg—whose sparkling dinners Napoleon had personally attended just a few months earlier—now gathering his 230,000-man Army of Bohemia along the southern Elbe. Far to the east, a second force, the 60,000-man Army of Poland, commanded by Bennigsen, was rapidly moving westward. To the south of Breslau, Blücher commanded the Prussian Army of Silesia, some 95,000 men. Far to the north, Berlin, occupied by the Allied Coalition since March, was being handed over to its new commander, Napoleon's brother-in-law Bernadotte, whose 40,000 Swedes joined the Prussians and would soon be in a position to push southward toward Dresden. All told Russia-Prussia-Austria-Sweden had at least 511,000 men with 1,380 pieces of field artillery and reserves of another 350,000.[1] It was hardly encouraging as Berthier read out the statistics.

In theory Napoleon boasted 400,000 men, 40,000 cavalry, and 1,284 guns, *if* he counted every soldier in every outpost in every country in northern Europe, including all his remaining French allies within the Confederation of the Rhine. In theory Prince Eugène's new Italian army and Wrede's Bavarians could add another 200,000 men, but that was to prove illusory; the Bavarians were already considered questionable if not downright unreliable. When it came to the actual fighting, then, Napoleon could count on only the immediate availability of 220,000 men, and as for his cavalry, it was new, largely untrained and unblooded. What is more this force was scattered along the Elbe and to the south.

Since Duroc's death and the loss of his Austrian allies, Napoleon had a difficult time establishing his objectives: whom to hit first, what areas to secure. Suddenly the very goals of his life had become blurred, shadowy, meaningless. First he moved from Dresden to Bautzen on August 17, only to reverse his orders and march south to Zittau on the Saxon-Bohemian frontier to stop the approaching Russians, only to change his mind yet again, moving to the northeast to head off the larger Silesian army of 95,000 men under Blücher, approaching menacingly from the Oder. Orders were issued and countered, then reissued with variations. His couriers delivered first one set of plans, then another. His commanders were confused. Napoleon had thought the Allies were advancing on Leipzig to the north, and instead they were coming straight for him and Dresden. On August 22 he suddenly rushed back to Dresden to reinforce Marshal St.-Cyr, with news of the sighting of Schwarzenberg's Austrian army.

Napoleon's revised plan to deflect the march of the Allies to the north had failed, however, while Oudinot's XI Corps, aided by Davout, also failed to frighten Bernadotte's now superior force of 110,000 men in Berlin.

That capital could not be retaken, and Oudinot's small corps had been sent fleeing to the safety of Wittenberg. Blücher's Prussian-Silesian Army had by now passed Breslau and the Oder. Even as Schwarzenberg's large Army of Bohemia was moving up to the west and south of Dresden, Blücher, after passing Breslau to the east, was checked by Macdonald's army, while Poniatowski's corps remained as a protective buffer between Macdonald to the east and the now seriously threatened Dresden.

Napoleon wanted another battle, and he would have one. His immediate force came to only 70,000 men for the time being, including Murat, St.-Cyr, Mortier, and Guard units, while awaiting Latour-Maubourg's cavalry, Victor's II Corps, and Marmont's VI Corps, ordered there from Bautzen.

In fact it was only late on August 25 that Napoleon had learned how grave the situation at Dresden had become, when he had issued orders for Marmont and Victor to march on the double to save the city. When he finally entered Dresden at nine o'clock the next morning, Bonaparte found to his dismay the place already ringed by Schwarzenberg's army, some 158,000 of them, solidly cutting off the city's southern banks of the Elbe from the north at Schustenhauser, all around the walls past their southeasternmost boundaries, reaching right up to the Elbe. (At this time Austrian reinforcements under Wittgenstein and Barclay were far to the east of Dresden.) There was not a break in the long, gripping Austrian line.

Fortunately Napoleon's troops still held the entire length of Dresden's walls, as well as the three bridgeheads crossing the river to the north bank, which would permit Latour-Maubourg, Victor, and Marmont's corps to reach them, increasing French forces from 70,000 to 120,000 within a matter of hours.

Although often capable of preparing excellent operational plans—at Wagram, for instance—Schwarzenberg was overcautious by nature, added to a lack of confidence in his own ideas and men. Now, on seeing Napoleon enter the city, the Austrian commander suddenly delayed his own offensive. When it did begin, it was sluggish, and Murat and Ney pushed out powerfully against the attacking Austrians, aided by French batteries from the other side of the Elbe, severely pounding Schwarzenberg's positions. By nightfall Schwarzenberg had lost ground everywhere.

As the battle resumed on the morning of the twenty-seventh, Napoleon was in a stronger position, with 50,000 additional troops thanks to the arrival of Victor and Marmont. Meanwhile well to the southeast of the city Vandamme's 40,000 men had checked Wittgenstein's reinforcements. Mortier, joined by Ney and St.-Cyr, now pushed back Wittgenstein's right flank. Marmont, Victor, Murat, and Latour-Maubourg were equally successful against the Austrians, now reduced to perhaps 170,000. And to com-

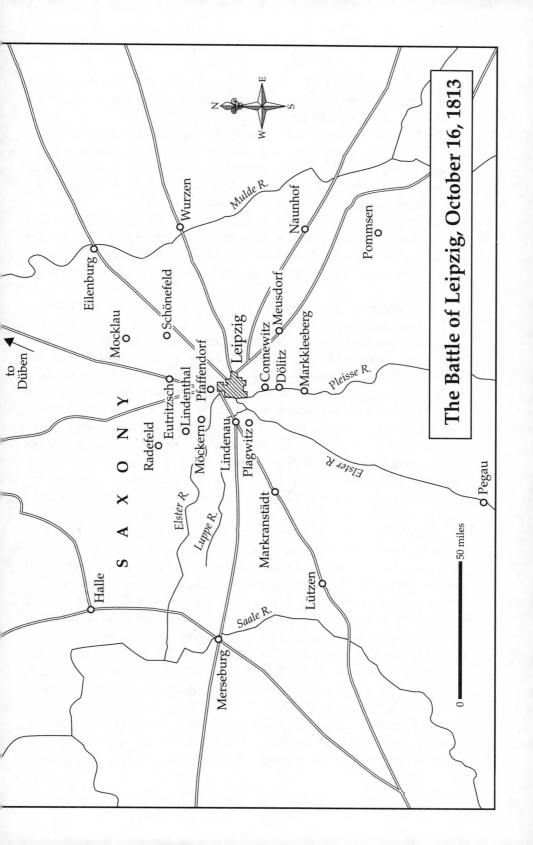

The Battle of Leipzig, October 16, 1813

plete a dreary picture for the Austrians, a heavy rain had fallen the previous night, leaving them—as well as the French—soaked, sleepless, and exhausted by the time the fighting resumed.

Nonetheless the French offensive opened against Schwarzenberg's right at six o'clock that morning and did not stop. Despite some weakness in the French center, success had followed their army. The czar himself, well within range of the lethal artillery, watched in dismay as Allied casualties mounted and the troops gave way: They had had enough.

During the night of August 27–28, the large Russo-Prussian army that two days earlier had appeared to have an ironfast stranglehold on Dresden retreated in defeat toward the mountains of the Bohemian frontier, having suffered some 38,000 casualties, compared to a relatively light 10,000 for the French.

On the twenty-eighth the French pursuit got off to a good start but then suddenly slackened as bad news reached Napoleon's headquarters, where he reportedly was ill. Oudinot had been defeated by Bernadotte near Berlin. Meanwhile Macdonald had in his enthusiasm separated himself from the main French force by pursuing Blücher. Seeing this French marshal now isolated, the Allies turned back and attacked, defeating Macdonald's army decisively on the twenty-sixth at Katzbach. What is more the Prussians had taken 15,000 French prisoners and one hundred field pieces. Then on the twenty-ninth came still more bad news. Vandamme and his I Corps, instead of pursuing the Allies, likewise found themelves defeated decisively by Ostermann at Kulm. What is more, Vandamme and another 13,000 French troops were taken prisoner. Green troops, recalcitrant conscripts, and generally low morale were taking their effect everywhere in French ranks.

Napoleon, though outwardly unmoved, was staggered by two such immense losses after his masterful victory at Dresden: 28,000 French prisoners taken within hours. As for the Allied Coalition, these new French defeats altered the situation completely, restoring their confidence and determination to smash the French once and for all. Clearly the Grande Armée of yore had been buried in the tundra of the north, even as further news of Lord Wellington's triumphant drive through northern Spain reached Napoleon now. The British general had defeated Marshal Jourdan and Joseph Bonaparte at the decisive battle at Vitoria on June 21, forcing the harried Joseph, along with the remnants of the French army, to scurry back over the frontier into France.

In Germany the fleeing Allied armies were halting and regrouping, while the defeated French were retreating to Dresden and the Elbe. The tide of battle and the fate of nations again had been changed all across the continent of Europe. Meeting at Töplitz on September 9, the newly determined Allies signed a fresh Austro-Russo-Prussian Alliance to eradicate Napoleon and his *fameuse armée* from the face of Europe.

The situation was changing rapidly, fresh Allied armies appearing out of nowhere, often covering great distances, forming and reforming, drawing ever closer, like leucocytes isolating a bacterium—the French who were devouring Europe. But for all their rapidity, the new Coalition was still very wary of the Napoleon Bonaparte who had defeated them in the last two battles in May. Even with a mere 100,000 men he was dangerous, and they did not underestimate him now as they concentrated even more troops. Their plan was to begin with attacks on the most vulnerable French positions, the isolated Elbe strongholds.

On the other hand, Bonaparte had not only fought many of the opposing generals on several occasions in the past, defeating them almost every time, but knew some of them and their characters personally. For one of the first times in his career he was in a position to outthink and anticipate his opponents' tactics and actions, but this was complicated by the new factors added to the equation—namely that of old, separate opponents. Recent Allied victories, along with the news of Napoleon's defeat in Spain, along with the French disaster in Russia the previous year, multiplied and aggravated by years of anger and humiliation under the French yoke, culminated in their furious determination to be done with this man once and for all.

Napoleon finally pulled himself together and concentrated on the essentials: the Elbe fortresses, Leipzig, and Dresden. By mid-October the general strategic situation had altered dramatically. The slow-moving army under Bernadotte descending from Berlin, although deflected by Ney, had nevertheless bypassed Magdeburg and Wittenberg, crossing the Elbe, while Blücher's Silesian Prussians, despite running skirmishes with Macdonald, had also crossed the Elbe on October 30, defeating General Bertrand. Indeed, they reached the Saale, not far from Bernadotte, while the Bohemian army, still by far the largest of the Coalition forces, was moving east across the Saale, and north, its apparent objective Leipzig. Napoleon reacted by marching rapidly to the south to be near Leipzig, heading an army comprising five infantry corps (Bertrand's IV, Marmont's VI, Souham's III, Reynier's VII, and Macdonald's XI) supported by Sébastiani's and Latour-Maubourg's cavalry. At Leipzig the French general Arrighi was literally holding the fort, with Murat's wall of cavalry protecting Leipzig's southern approaches, bolstered by Victor's II, Lauriston's V, Poniatowski's VIII, and Augereau's IX Corps.

Napoleon was therefore still in a highly maneuverable position, but at the price of having left Dresden unprotected, held by only St.-Cyr and Lobau, ringed by Ostermann's troops. Allied numerical superiority was finally paying off. As for Davout and his 35,000 men, they, too, found themselves isolated far to the north around Hamburg and thus well out of the picture. Then came more bad news that former French allies—including the jolly Max Joseph of Bavaria, Eugène de Beauharnais's father-in-law—were abandoning Napoleon. That left Westphalia and what remained of the Confederation of the Rhine all the more exposed. Saxony alone still backed the French, and that would last only as long as Napoleon held their capital of Dresden. In fact, since the middle of August the French had lost 150,000 men of their original force, mainly through desertion, to join the new Allied Coalition. Furthermore, French low morale was aggravated by the lack of supplies and rations.

Having lost nearly half of his guns—Napoleon was down to 784—and his total initial force of just over 400,000 now reduced to around 260,000, with manpower and supplies fading quickly,[2] the French leader realized that he had to act immediately and decisively if he was to retrieve the situation, and he had no intention whatsoever of asking for peace terms. First he would have to withdraw forces, shortening French lines of communication and tightening defenses. Leipzig was to be the new center of operations for his army, hence the decision to leave only St.-Cyr and Lobau at the otherwise unprotected capital of Dresden in face of a growing enemy force gathering around them.[3] Given his weakened numbers, maintaining Dresden and not consolidating those forces with him now was an error. But as even the faithful Méneval pointed out, it was his greed, his need to hold everything, everywhere, that was to prove his undoing, distorting his military judgment.

Having originally moved north from Dresden on October 7, 1813, with 150,000 troops, Napoleon had hoped to catch Blücher's Prussian army of 60,000 men unawares. He marched northwest toward Düben, catching up to them on the ninth. But Blücher's smaller, better-fed, and more alert army had reacted quickly, avoiding that confrontation by moving over to the Saale. Napoleon had still been debating his next move when he received urgent word from Murat at Leipzig that he was under attack by Schwarzenberg's army. Napoleon immediately marched south with his entire force to Eilenburg, just a few miles north of Leipzig, gathering more intelligence reports from the tenth to the fourteenth of the month. Although Blücher was just one day's march away at Halle, on the other hand Ney had earlier inflicted heavy casualties on Bernadotte, reducing his army to 80,000 men, though it was still approaching. Murat was withdrawing slowly before the

Allied armies of Schwarzenberg and Bennigsen, now totaling 240,000 men, but unable to prevent their steady advance. Blücher too was on the move, intent on a junction of his 60,000 men and Schwarzenberg's near Leipzig. Bernadotte as usual dithered, avoiding battles and commitments.

By October 13 Napoleon had finally made his decision. He would march south to Leipzig and intercept Blücher's and Schwarzenberg's armies separately before they could join forces. That meant his entire army must reach Leipzig by the next morning. With 200,000 men under his single command, Napoleon felt he could do it. "There can be no doubt," he wrote Marshal Macdonald on the fourteenth, "that sometime tomorrow—the fifteenth—we shall be attacked by the armies of Bohemia [Austria] and Silesia [Prussia]. Come as quickly as possible and when you hear the cannonade. Simply follow the sound of the guns."⁴

Colonel Marbot, serving under Napoleon, described Leipzig at this time as "one of the greatest German centers of German commerce and wealth, situated in the middle of the vast plain extending from the Elbe to the Harz Mountains of Thuringia and Bohemia," at the confluence of four small rivers—the Elster, the Pleisse, the Partha, and the Luppe—creating a veritable maze of waterways and marsh. "The city . . . had four main gates and three smaller ones. The [western] road, from Lützen via Lindenau and Markranstädt, was the only one left by which the French army could still freely maintain communications and supply lines [back to France]."⁵

It was through the main northern gate that Napoleon entered Leipzig on October 14, although the last of his forces, Reynier's VII Corps, was still many miles to the north. Bonaparte was not at all pleased with what he found. His men were stretched in a line two to four miles to the south of the city, a thin defensive line of troops to the west of the city, and separated by a wide, marshy, wooded area from Leipzig on a single causeway and bridge connecting it. What is more this marsh extended from north of the city for a few miles to the south, presenting a great barrier to the maneuverability of friend and foe alike. For the moment his troops to the west of Leipzig held their tenuous French lifeline from Lindenau, Markranstädt, back to Lützen and Erfurt. Although no enemy was yet actually laying siege to the city, it would be difficult to keep that vital logistical route open across relatively flat prairie with very few hills or defensive positions. To the southeast, on the other hand, where the initial French troops had already dug in, there were some hillocks, open plain, and some wood, but no marsh—ideal country for the larger infantry and cavalry tactics Napoleon so favored.

He immediately started planning a major offensive against the principal Austro-Russian force by now in some strength to the southwest, with the intention of enveloping it with his cavalry around the Allied right flank. He did not know the extent of the Allied force (203,000, which outnumbered his own 177,500 men and seven hundred guns). Nor was he yet aware that Blücher's Prussian army, down to 54,000 men, was also quickly approaching Leipzig from the northwest near the Halle-Leipzig Road.

On October 15 both sides deployed their troops, the Austro-Russian army already in full control of the road extending southward from Leipzig to Pegau and several miles to the east as far as the Leipzig-Naunhof Road. Their principal force was followed by Russian and Austrian reserves up the Pegau Road, while already deployed stood Kleist's corps; Prince Eugene's, Pahlen's, and Gorchakov's cavalry; as well as Klenau's corps of 33,000 holding the extreme right wing.

Facing them was Poniatowski's VIII Corps, anchored on the Pegau Road as far as the hamlet of Markkleeberg, where Victor's II Corps took over, extending to the French extreme left, held by Lauriston's small V Corps controlling the Leipzig-Pommsen Road. General Arrighi held the critical French line opposite the marsh to the west of Leipzig, while Marmont's VI Corps formed from the Halle-Leipzig Road north to the village of Radefeld. Reynier's VII Corps was still many miles to the north on the Düben Road, however, and could not be counted on. But immediately north of Leipzig, Souham's III and Bertrand's IV Corps were moving into place even as Macdonald's XI Corps and Sébastiani's small cavalry were arriving from the northwest. South of Leipzig, Napoleon's main cavalry, including Latour-Maubourg's and Pajol's, were placed behind Victor's and Lauriston's line, with the Imperial Guard, 47,000 strong, behind them. Just to the east of them stood Augereau's IX Corps. Such was the position by the beginning of October 16.

Schwarzenberg was in command of Austrian operations, and the czar as usual the smaller Russian force, nominally under Barclay but delegated to Wittgenstein, directing 177,500 Allies.

When the fighting broke out on the morning of the sixteenth, the heaviest was on the northern and western lines, catching Napoleon off guard, for while Gyulai's corps now moved across barring the Lindenau-Lützen Road, engaging General Arrighi, Blücher's 54,000 Prussians suddenly appeared in force, dropping on Marmont's unsuspecting corps, quickly forcing them to fall back on a much more contracted defensive position around the village of Möckern. Bertrand's IV Corps moved through the northern suburbs of Leipzig to reinforce Arrighi on the westernmost

French flank, even as the main French line to the south was also being reinforced. Poniatowski deployed his men along the western French flank anchored on the Pleisse, supported by Augereau behind him, next Victor still in place, bolstered in turn behind him by Oudinot's Guard (Bessières had been killed in May), and Lauriston to the east of Victor, supported by Mortier.

By 11:00 A.M. Austro-Russian forces were already starting to spread farther east and north. All Napoleon's plans were going completely awry. Heavy fighting took place most of the day to the north, west, and the long principal southern line. The unexpected heavy Prussian attack that morning had spoiled everything. Ney's III Corps, originally in the center to help launch the enveloping movement, was awkwardly divided. As for the misty weather, it nicely concealed the Austrians' dense columns as they moved up. There were too many surprises for Napoleon, as General Meerveldt's units plowed through marshy land to attack the French unexpectedly around the villages of Dölitz and Connewitz.

For all that the Allied attack was not well coordinated, some units arriving as late as 9:30 A.M. The heavy fighting around the hamlet of Waschau between Victor and Prince Eugene of Württemberg was as hot as it was uncertain, even as Kleist took the village of Markkleeberg. By eleven o'clock Schwarzenberg's principal southern attack had in fact petered out. More Russian and Prussian reserves and Guards were moved up, while the Allies waited impatiently for another surprise they had up their sleeve, a fresh force of 70,000 men under Bennigsen and Colloredo, still marching up from Dresden, and Blücher was due to launch his offensive at 2:00 P.M.

Due to all these uncertainties, during the morning, Napoleon had delayed the French offensive until noon, when he finally ordered their main attack, concentrating the fire of 150 pieces of heavy artillery against Kleist, Prince Eugene, and Gorchakov, with the aim of throwing his reserves through them while Murat at the head of 10,000 cavalry cleared the Allied center. Struck hard, the Austrians reeled back. Meanwhile, to the north of Leipzig, Blücher duly unleashed his own attack on schedule at two o'clock, thus holding down Marmont and Souham, who were to have taken part in Napoleon's swing around the Allied right flank. By now the fighting was very intense all along the line, as 2,500 *cuirassiers*, Napoleon's heavy cavalry, led by General Doumerc, charged forward against Prince Eugene's flank. So successful were they that they cleared a path straight through the Allied front lines almost back to the command post of a surprised Czar Alexander, only to find themselves unsupported by French units that were to have followed. Exhausted and bloodied, the *cuirassiers* were in turn hurled back to their own lines. Their entire action took only a half hour, between 2:30 and 3:00 P.M., ending Napoleon's much-hoped-for and badly needed success, as the Austrians gradually regained land and advanced, even threatening the French right.

As a result of the successful attack by Blücher, Napoleon had to abandon his post and move up to Möckern to direct operations. Although Marmont's corps at Möckern were as good as any in the present army, holding off the equally fierce Prussians, they still required two of Ney's divisions as well. As a result of the defection of some of his officers, however, Marmont found himself unable to break through the Prussians, checking his own hoped-for offensive. And there was nothing even Napoleon could do about that. The Prussians, under the command of Yorck, continued bull-headedly in the face of withering fire and heavy casualties to launch one attack after another. Never had Napoleon seen such Prussian leadership and tenacity. In the end Yorck unleashed his entire cavalry, finally overrunning Marmont's courageous VI Corps and their artillery, the Prussians then seizing Möckern. But darkness now intervened, preventing the Prussians from following up this important northern sector success.

So ended the first day of the Battle of Leipzig, or Battle of Nations, during which the Allies had already lost 30,000 casualties and the French at least 25,000. The only reinforcements the French could expect were Reynier's 14,000 men, while the Allies still were awaiting Bennigsen's 70,000 men and Bernadotte's Army of the North of 85,000. Napoleon had no idea of the forces working against his chances of success.

So battered were both sides that little fighting took place on the seventeenth, an unusual event in any Napoleonic battle. Every day they waited, the Allied position strengthened. When Reynier's corps finally did arrive, this gave Napoleon just under 200,000 men. But with the arrival of Bennigsen from the east and Bernadotte from the north, the Allies had more than 300,000 men, 155,000 of them perfectly fresh. In addition the Allies had 1,500 guns to 650 French artillery pieces.

With their now overwhelming numerical superiority by the dawn of the eighteenth, the Allied supreme command decided to enclose the entire French force in their coils, gradually contracting, squeezing the French toward Leipzig proper, despite the heavy downpour that night, which rendered all movement slow and exhausting.

With all the additional firepower, the fighting consisted of confusion and constant movement. Gyulai's corps sealed off most of the western flank as Blücher's three corps, aided by Bernadotte and Winzingerode, pushed heavily, forcing back Dombrowski, Marmont, and Reynier. The encirclement coincided from west to east as well, as Wesse-Homburg's 50,000 men, supported by Barclay's 65,000 Russians, hit the extreme French left flank under Poniatowski and Victor, very hard. At the same time, further pressing the French back sharply from the east, Bennigsen's and Colloredo's 70,000 fresh troops hit Macdonald and Sébastiani along a line from Hayda to the village of Möklau. The French were hopelessly outnumbered. As if things were not bad enough, more of Napoleon's "allies" defected in mid-battle, including two brigades of Saxons, along with their badly needed artillery—which did not help the morale of those remaining behind. To cinch the Coalition's victory, which was now obvious to all, Bernadotte from the northwest and Bennigsen from the east launched another massive attack, forcing the French closer to the walls of Leipzig, followed by Barclay's tough onslaught from the southwest.

Almost completely encircled; low on ammunition, food, and supplies; and with very high casualties, as darkness approached a stunned Napoleon knew he was lost. Riding back to Leipzig he prepared to retreat. Keeping open the bridges and the route through Lindenau, Bonaparte ordered the remnants of his battered army to withdraw from Leipzig, taking the road to Lützen, in the direction of Auerstädt and Erfurt.

Gradually during the night of October 18–19, haggard though they were, the French withdrew in good order, leaving 30,000 men behind to protect their rear.

It was only after seven o'clock the next morning that the Allies began to realize that for the first time they had completely routed the mighty Napoleon, whose troops were now fleeing toward Erfurt, abandoning 35,000 French garrison troops now isolated behind them along the Elbe. Requesting a truce, Napoleon gained a little more time, as the last French units continued to pour through Leipzig's ancient narrow streets, along the battle-torn passages, and across the Lindenau causeway, Bonaparte himself leaving the city just after 11:00 A.M. on the nineteenth.

"Nothing was more difficult than getting out of Leipzig, this city surrounded on all sides by the enemy," Constant recalled. "The emperor headed for the [western] Ranstadt Gate, but it was so completely blocked by men and debris that it was impossible to work our way through. He then had to retrace his steps, crossing the city again. Successfully getting through the northern gate, he then circled back to the western road to Erfurt."[6]

It was a textbook withdrawal, as orderly as could be expected under the circumstances, that is until once again the unexpected occurred. An incompetent Colonel Montfort, disobeying orders to remain behind to supervise the destruction of the Lindenau bridge after the last of the rear guard had cleared Leipzig, had followed the all-too-prevalent *sauve qui peut* (every man for himself) tradition of the French army and abandoned his post, leaving just one corporal in charge of that critical task.

Although the bridge was still crowded with thousands of French troops, seeing his own commanding officer running away, this corporal panicked and at one o'clock on the nineteenth blew up the bridge, killing hundreds of French troops while entrapping most of the French rear guard under Marshal Oudinot's command. Although Oudinot was able to swim to the safety of the other side, the valiant but badly wounded General Poniatowski was not, drowning in midstream. With all escape impossible, the last of the French rear guard, directed by Generals Lauriston and Reynier, put up a stiff but futile fight that afternoon, until they were forced to surrender to prevent the complete slaughter of their troops.

The losses for all sides were horrifying, the Allies suffering 54,000 casualties, the French losing close to 75,000 men, including 30,000 POWs and a few thousand defectors. In addition forty-eight French general officers were lost, thirty-six as prisoners and another dozen killed or wounded.

And then there were the usual innocent civilian bystanders, caught helplessly by forces beyond their control or comprehension, whose casualties were never counted. Dresden had been heavily bombarded and Leipzig, like Smolensk and Borodino, left in flames and ruin, not to mention the dozens of villages surrounding those battle sites. Thousands of civilians were killed or wounded and thousands more left homeless.

The French continued to make their way to Frankfurt and Mainz as the Allies pursued, taking the less seriously wounded with them, abandoning the rest along the wayside, along with their dead. In addition, they left behind their dead horses, hundreds of vehicles, and another 325 cannon. Some "70,000 combatants and 40,000 stragglers finally reached the Rhine in safety, but almost 400,000 troops had been lost."[7]

The Saxon campaign had not completely bypassed brother Jérôme. Although he formally denied his brother a command at the beginning of the war, on August 12 Napoleon, already beginning to realize how desperate the situation was, authorized General Clarke to write to Jérôme to prepare to defend Kassel.[8] On August 22 and 23 at Zittau the First and Second Westphalian Hussars, recruited earlier by Jérôme, had defected to Coalition forces.

By mid-September Thielmann's and Platov's cavalry were approaching Kassel and temporarily seized Merseburg, Bernadotte himself directing the attacks against the Kingdom of Westphalia. A Russian column under General Chernichev, including 4,000 Cossacks and dragoons and ten cannon, was approaching from the east. When just four miles from Kassel at Munden, they were challenged by 552 Westphalians under General von Zandt, and at Heiligenstadt by another 1,100 men under General Bastineller. At Kassel itself Jérôme had perhaps another 1,050 men, including his grenadiers, hussars, and local citizens.

On September 25 Jérôme sent a desperate appeal to General Kellermann asking him for reinforcements. Meanwhile, bypassing General Bastineller's force, Chernichev continued his march, via Sondershausen and Mulhausen, detaching 800 Cossacks and four cannon toward Kassel. At 4:00 A.M. on the twenty-eighth, Jérôme was awakened by a gendarme saying the Cossacks were at Helsa, about five miles away. Assembling his thousand-man force under the command of General Allix, Jérôme prepared for the defense of his capital, closing the Leipzig Gate, protected by two cannon. But the Cossacks continued to advance to the city walls.

After a hearty breakfast, a uniformed King Jérôme appeared on his horse at the Vieux Châteaux and announced his intention of clearing the enemy. One convoy of carriages filled with courtiers and French employees had already left precipitously for Holland. Jérôme now bade good-bye to his fairy-tale kingdom, as they passed through the southern gate, accompanied by his generals and ministers, abandoning Allix and his men. Jérôme led the remaining few hundred men, including his personal guard, two squadrons of hussars, and a battalion of grenadiers, and attacked the Cossacks at the river, who then fled.

Jérôme waited, hoping for reinforcements. When none had arrived by three o'clock, Jérôme fled for his life, not even stopping at Marburg. On the thirtieth General Chernichev bombarded Kassel with field guns. At 7:00 P.M. Allix, heavily outnumbered by army veterans and abandoned by his own king, surrendered. That evening the Russians took possession of the Kingdom of Westphalia, pronouncing the dissolution of the kingdom and the dethronement of Jérôme Bonaparte. That same day, riding so fast that he left far behind his own valet de chambre, French chef, and all his possessions, with literally only the shirt on his back, ex-King Jérôme reached the Rhine. As for the abandoned, angry Princess von Löwenstein, she had earlier left for greener pastures, all her plans in shambles.

Traveling incognito, Jérôme's movements were as uncertain as they were erratic. He first set out for Koblenz, then for Cologne. There on November 3 Jérôme received a castigating letter from brother Napoleon informing him to take up residence along the Rhine and to send for his wife, Caroline, immediately. On Napoleon's orders the duc de Bassano formally forbade Jérôme from returning to Paris or France, or even Mainz. "The King continuously having failed to heed the Emperor's advice, while likewise failing to do any of the things upon which his interests, and those of his kingdom, depended, His Majesty therefore would find any meeting [between the two brothers] as painful as it would be pointless." As far as the emperor of the French was concerned, brother Jérôme no longer existed.[9]

In the meantime Napoleon, reaching the Rhine on November 2, spent a few days at Mainz, setting out from that city for the last time on November 7 and reaching St.-Cloud two days later. On November 11 Marshal St.-Cyr surrendered Dresden to the Austrians. On the fourteenth, addressing the French Senate, Emperor Napoleon solemnly announced: "The Grand Empire no longer exists, it is France itself we must now defend." And then, as if matters could not be worse, he received a final letter from brother Louis, who had since taken refuge at Madame Mère's estate of Pont-sur-Seine, near Paris. Louis still wanted to be King of Holland! "The Empire has been invaded and I have the whole of an armed Europe against me. . . . If you persist in your idea of returning to Holland as its king, then the sooner you leave Paris the better and do not come within forty leagues [120 miles] of it ever again!"[10] First Leipzig, then Jérôme and his crazy wife, now Louis—while his entire world was collapsing all around him.

CHAPTER 38

"The Cossacks Are Coming!"

Make no preparations for the abandonment of Paris. If worse comes to worse we will bury ourselves under its ruins.

ou have seen the emperor? How is he? What is he doing? What does he say about his defeat?" the Marquise de LaTour du Pin asked Talleyrand immediately on his arrival at her soirée. "Oh! Don't bother me about your precious emperor. That man is finished," Talleyrand replied, his expression as cold and as emotionless as ever.[1] "It's too painful to describe that horrible day when the news of Leipzig reached Paris," Victorine de Chastenay recorded in her *Memoirs*. "It appears that the emperor made a complete shambles of it there." The French capital, she continued, reacted quickly. "The idea of returning to the ancien régime and the Bourbons began to spread, almost becoming popular. I was simply staggered at the idea and at how many people were turning to it overnight. . . . The young ladies wore rings freshly engraved with: '*Domine, salvum fac regem*'"[2]—"Lord, protect the king," Louis XVIII, who had been in exile since 1791.

"The happiness on seeing his wife and son again acted as a real balm for Napoleon's wounds," Méneval remarked, but it served only as a momentary diversion from all the anxieties besieging him. Every one of these called his attention to the urgent necessity of coping with the defense of French territory. Emergency administrative councils presided over by the Emperor were held all day long. Extraordinary measures had to be taken to recruit a new army, remount the cavalry, manufacture arms, etc. His private treasury amassed in the cellars of the Tuileries over the past ten years was now used to cover the costs of these urgent military expenses,

as the official French treasury had been emptied to launch the last campaign in Saxony.[3]

Then on December 15, 1813, Saint-Aignan, the French minister to Weimar, arrived unexpectedly from Frankfurt-am-Main, where the Allies had assembled. Russian Foreign Minister Nesselrode, Chancellor Metternich, and Lord Aberdeen offered Napoleon a peace treaty, requiring France to evacuate the rest of Europe and return to its "natural frontiers." With the country still in a state of shock, and the French Army reduced to fewer than 70,000 men actually available in and near France, the situation obviously required peace. But instead of responding promptly to the Frankfurt proposals, an angry Napoleon fired Foreign Minister Maret and replaced him with Caulaincourt.

It was only on January 1 that Napoleon finally authorized a favorable reply to Frankfurt. Meanwhile, not having received word from Paris by the fourth, the impatient Allies unanimously signed and issued a new declaration, that French frontiers would have to be cut back farther, to those of 1792, which meant losing a slice of Switzerland, the left bank of the Rhine (including Aachen), and Belgium right up to Antwerp.[4] For Napoleon that was the final insult—but one he could cope with. He had been rearming from the time of his return for one final campaign.

Again the call went out for conscripts. Napoleon demanded a new army of another 300,000 men immediately, and added a levée en masse, ultimately calling up a total of 936,000 men and boys. The nation was at hazard and had to be protected. But as Méneval admitted, the country remained "inert," well over 100,000 men actually openly fleeing the French conscripting authorities. In the end Napoleon would assemble a total of perhaps 120,000 men, adamantly rejecting the services of the former leaders of the Revolution, the Jacobins.

The Legislative Body, newly reconvened by Napoleon in the third week of December, ordered a special committee to study the situation, and on December 28 it gave its report.

Instead of calling the nation to unite firmly under its leader, the Commission ... presented a list of complaints and grievances against the oppression of the French people, demanding guarantees against further arbitrary authority and insisting on the execution of laws in favor of freedom in general, including the free exercise of political rights,

an outraged Méneval, ever loyal to Napoleon complained. What is more the "Legislative Body then adopted the committee's report by a sweeping majority of votes." Both the Senate and the Corps Législatif demanded peace.

The leader of the rebellion, Joachim Laîné, a lawyer and royalist from Bordeaux, was personally castigated by Napoleon as he harangued the Corps Législatif for its outrageous independence. "You have done more harm to us than had we lost ten battles to the enemy. One does not wash the family's dirty linen in public!" "What is a throne? Four pieces of wood covered by green velvet," the unperturbed Laîné riposted, greeted by the strong applause of the delegates assembled there for the last time. It was a threat, and Napoleon did not like threats. Infuriated, he retaliated by proroguing that assembly altogether two days later. Political freedom, indeed!

There would be no more interference from that quarter. Word soon went out that Napoleon had ordered Fouché's replacement at the Police Ministry, General Savary, to arrest the "traitors," and most fled the city. Issuing a statement for Allied consumption, Laîné proclaimed, seeking his excuses for the past fourteen years of Franco-Napoleonic conquest: "The virtues of this country belong to it alone. All the wrongs done belong to the master [Napoleon] who still wishes to enslave her." Laîné failed to mention, of course, that it was the French people who had been supporting Napoleon all those years, and conquering Europe.

Méneval confessed that Napoleon had been deeply hurt by this unexpected open rebellion. "I found him quite worried now ... in public, however, he remained calm and reassuring.... For the first time he was no longer happy. I could not help but notice this with sad interest, and seeing Napoleon so wretched only increased my admiration of him."⁵

"The Cossacks are coming!" the Parisians soon cried out in the streets. In fact the Austrians, the Prussians, the Italians, the Spaniards, the Dutch, the Swedes, and the English would indeed soon be advancing on the French capital. "The fate of Paris was not at all certain," Victorine de Chastenay recalled. "The burning of Moscow let us fear the worst.... 'Moscow burnt down, Paris burnt down; Moscow burnt down, Paris *kaputt*!'" Even the usually buoyant Colonel Marbot confessed, "It is impossible to describe the great anxiety and agitation one found in that capital."[6] Back on December 2, the annual celebration for the victory at Austerlitz was poorly attended, and though it was customary on that day to throw open all the theaters of the capital free to the public, attendance was sparse.

The throbbing excitement and growing frustration of all of Europe to get rid of Bonaparte and the French was, however, already being drowned out by the sound of hundreds of thousands of feet all marching in one direction—toward France. If quarrels and differences of opinion existed amid the ranks of the Coalition—Austria, for one, was not overly anxious for another clash of arms with Bonaparte—nevertheless they had finally concluded there was no other way: The Houses of Habsburg, Romanov, and Hohenzollern were agreed. Anticipating Napoleon's by-now-standard arrogant defiance, by December 1813 three major armies were on the march again. The Army of the North, comprising a joint British-Prussian force, was to be launched from liberated Holland, with a separate northern force under Bernadotte, Winzingerode, and Bennigsen concentrating around Magdeburg and Hamburg (where a stubborn Davout still refused to capitulate). The second army, Prussia's Army of Silesia, under the command of Field Marshal Blücher, had begun crossing the Rhine near Mannheim on December 29. The third force, the Austrian army, directed by Prince von Schwarzenberg, was already descending on Colmar from Basel by January 1, 1814. By February some 400,000 Allied troops could be expected on French soil.[7]

In fact Blücher alone was soon approaching the Meuse River with 107,500 troops, and Schwarzenberg with another 209,000 was heading for Champagne. Then there was the Anglo-Spanish Army, under the successful Lord Wellington, pouring over the Pyrenees, closing in on Soult and Suchet at Toulouse. In Italy another Austrian army under Bellegarde, 74,000 strong, was approaching Prince Eugène's 50,000 north Italians. To make matters worse, on January 11, King Joachim Murat of Naples (with Caroline Bonaparte's prodding and blessing) went over to the Allies, imitated by King Frederick VI of Denmark three days later. Murat's declaration of war against France was too much for Napoleon, calling his brother's-in-law action "infamous, and as for that of the queen . . . there is no name for it! I hope I live long enough to wreak full vengeance on them for this outrage!"[8] In brief France would shortly be invaded from just about every direction except from the sea, and there the mighty Channel Fleet of the Royal Navy lay in wait, several dozen of its men of war with thousands of marines prepared to land at a moment's notice.

With fewer than 70,000 men, what could Napoleon do? Augereau was attempting to form another "army" at Lyons, but one does not begin forming an army from scratch when already under attack. There were also Marshal Mortier's Old Guard of 9,000 men and perhaps 30,000 National Guardsmen. That was about it.

Still the enemy kept coming, unhindered, Blücher crossing the Meuse and already well into France by January 22. As for Paris, almost nothing had been done for its defense, so fearful was Napoleon of adding to the panic already too visible on the faces of the people. The city's old fortifications were patchy at best, left over from the days of earlier Bourbon triumphs. "Make no preparations for the abandonment of Paris," Napoleon warned. "If worst comes to worst we will bury ourselves under its ruins."[9]

"I attended mass at the Tuileries," ex-Queen Hortense recalled.

> The Duchess of Montebello [Marshal Lannes's widow], looking most anxious, came up to me and whispered, "Madame, have you heard the news? The Allies have crossed the Rhine. Paris is in a panic. What on earth is the Emperor doing?" . . . Returning for dinner with the family that evening I found the Emperor alone with the Empress. He was holding her in his arms, making fun of her. "Well then, Hortense!" he said with a teasing smile as I approached. "Everyone in Paris is afraid, are they? They have already seen the Cossacks there. Well, they are not yet there, I can assure you, and we still have not forgotten our profession. Stay calm," he admonished his wife, "we are going to go to Vienna to beat Papa François [Franz I] yet."

Then during dinner his son was brought in for the dessert. "Napoleon repeated several times to the boy: 'Let's go beat Papa François,' and the child repeated this phrase so often and so well that the Emperor burst into laughter." For Marie-Louise, caught between her husband, child, and new country on the one hand, and her father and Austrian family and friends on the other, the scene was no doubt extremely painful.

After dinner they retired to a small salon, and Napoleon had Berthier summoned. "Sit down over there," he commanded, pointing to the green card table. "We are going to have to prepare another Italian campaign." An unsmiling Berthier, still looking haggard after a severe illness the previous year, took a seat as Napoleon

dictated to him before us for the next hour, outlining the entire organization and plan of attack for the army. . . . He then had four generals of
his Guard come in, questioning them on the number of men available,
or ill, going into great detail about each of their corps. That lasted quite
a while, then, after dismissing them, he turned to us again and said:
'Well now, Mesdames, do you feel better about the situation? Do you
still think we are going to let them take us so easily?'[10]

This "Note on the Actual Situation of France" prepared on January 12,
1814, predicted that the Allies would have a difficulty in breaking through
French defenses along the frontiers, resulting in a considerable delay before
they could possibly be in a position to threaten the French capital, by
which time Napoleon anticipated having a minimal force of 120,000 men
ready, along with a city garrison of another 30,000. By that time
Schwarzenberg and Blücher combined would be reduced to a total of only
80,000, the analysis optimistically reported.[11]

As for Napoleon's campaign plan, in its final phase it was to drive hard
and fast to Lorraine and Alsace, to attack and separate the Prussians and
Austrians before they could join forces, and at the same cut them off from
their supply lines on the other side of the Rhine. In doing this he hoped to
draw them away from Paris itself. It sounded so simple when he explained
it, but then it always did.

The night before his departure from the Tuileries, Napoleon summoned the officers of the newly formed National Guard to the impressive
Salle des Maréchaux, presenting the empress and his son to them, closing
with, "I am leaving to fight the enemy now. I confide for your safe keeping
what I prize most in this world, the Empress, my wife, and the King of
Rome, my son."[12] On January 25, under the usual Imperial Guard escort,
Napoleon set out for Châlons-sur-Marne on his first campaign on French
soil, fighting for his nation's very existence. In his absence the queen and
the Regency Council, presided over by the faithful Cambacérès, would rule
in his stead.

Napoleon was drawing in all available units, Marmont from Metz, to join
Ney and Victor behind the Meuse, and Macdonald from south of Strasbourg. Meanwhile the Allies had plans of their own, permitting them to
close on their ultimate objective from at least four different routes. Bülow's
combined corps, added to the 10,000-man English division, was advancing
south from Holland to the French frontier near Mézières, while Blücher's
Prussians were thrusting from Metz and Nancy, heading for Châlons-sur-

Marne, the principal route from the east to Paris along the Marne via Château-Thierry and la Ferté, which Napoleon now hoped to stop. To the south Schwarzenberg's large army was concentrating along the main road from Langres to Bar-sur-Aube, another important route to Paris via Troyes, Nogent-sur-Seine, the Marne, and the capital. Finally the southern-most of the main easterly roads leading to Paris extended from Châtillon to Auxerre, up the Yonne toward Fontainebleau.

Once again Napoleon was taken by surprise, not so much by the num-bers—the Allied forces swollen by all of Napoleon's former allies—but by the unusual rapidity of both the Prussian and Austrian armies. Even as Napoleon was finally setting out from the Tuileries on the twenty-fifth, Schwarzenberg's 150,000 men were nearing Bar-sur-Aube, and Blücher with 50,000 men was near Napoleon's old school at Brienne, defended by the remnants of Victor's and Macdonald's men. Napoleon had between 34,000 and 42,000 men under his immediate command, Mortier with another 20,000 at Troyes, and Macdonald with 10,000 closing in. On Jan-uary 29 Bonaparte made his bid to prevent the linkup of the major Allied forces by attacking Blücher, who fell back on Bar-sur-Aube. But on Febru-ary 1 it was Blücher's turn to send Napoleon reeling with bloody losses from La Rothière to Troyes.

At a war council that followed, the Allies argued among themselves, the czar insistent on crushing France, leaving it permanently a second-rate power, while both Castlereagh and Metternich argued for a moderately strong France, to help maintain the balance of power in Europe, which in turn would result in a more lasting peace. They did not want to see Europe again left with one or two menacing superpowers. Thinking Napoleon fin-ished after his flight from La Rothière, Schwarzenberg at the head of his 150,000 troops began his march on Paris via Sens. Blücher, whose command included Russian corps, now resumed his advance in three columns.

Despite the inferior number of his troops, Napoleon, to the consterna-tion of the Allies, struck hard, with all his old skill, even as Marmont and Ney destroyed the enemy at Champaubert on February 10, while Bona-parte himself with only 20,000 men defeated Sacken's Corps at Montmirail the next day. Reinforced by Marmont, Napoleon succeeded in pushing back Blücher's third column toward Bergères. Within a matter of days, with fewer than 30,000 troops, he had not only sent Blücher's 50,000 men falling back but had inflicted 15,000 casualties on them. It was only now, however, that Napoleon learned of Schwarzenberg's advance via Fontainebleau and Bray-sur-Seine, seriously threatening Paris for the first time.

* * *

Amid much distrust among themselves, on February 5, 1814, the Allies opened the Congress of Châtillon-sur-Seine. Present were the czar and his dour, aloof foreign minister, Nesselrode, the foppish, elegant Metternich, a determined Hardenberg attending Friedrich Wilhelm, and the calm, phlegmatic British foreign secretary, Lord Castelreagh. Here they prepared their list of demands, handing them to Caulaincourt two days later: France was to withdraw everywhere and French boundaries were thus to return to those of 1792. (Earlier the Spanish Regency and the Cortes had rejected Napoleon's proposal for the return of Fernando VII.) Czar Alexander, invariably a poor judge of men, however, wanted to see Bernadotte as the new French monarch, an idea dismissed out of hand by his amazed fellow Allies.

Meanwhile Joseph, while supporting Napoleon, nevertheless realized what his brother failed to acknowledge, the impossibility of their situation. He wrote to him on February 9, explaining that the position of Paris alone was untenable. There were only six thousand muskets available, apart from the arms of the regular troops and

> thus it is impossible to create a new reserve force of 30 to 40 thousand men in Paris. Some things are quite beyond the power of man, Sire, and when that becomes self-evident, as it now does, it seems to me that the only true glory left to us is to make the best possible peace terms, to keep as much as we realistically can. To endanger even one human life against an overwhelming threat is not a glorious or praiseworthy act, because it will bring no advantage to the great masses of men who cherish their own existence as well as yours. . . . One must face reality with courage, which will either permit you to bring happiness to the people, or else by forcing you to commit yourself, no longer leaving you with the choice between death and dishonor.

Yet at the same time he continued to counsel Napoleon to retain his throne, for if he abandoned it "that would bring misfortune upon a people protected by, and dependent upon, your government." But for all that the only real solution was peace. He must end the fighting. "If you can possibly make peace [at Châtillon], do so at whatever the price. If that is not possible, you must be prepared to perish."[13] Never before had Joseph spoken out so strongly, so directly, so honestly.

Replying from Nangis, Napoleon seemed to concur—in part. "I hope to reach a peace settlement promptly, based on the Frankfurt proposals [that is, natural frontiers], which is the minimum I can accept with honor."

In other words he still demanded to retain western Switzerland, the left bank of the Rhine (including Aachen), and Belgium right up to the Dutch frontier. If this could not be, Napoleon went on, "I have decided to win or perish . . . with one more battle to stop the Allied threat to my capital. . . ." After that "I owe it to the best interests of the Empire and to my own glory to enter into negotiations for an enduring peace." But, he stressed, if the Allies forced him to evacuate Belgium and the left bank of the Rhine, he would sign nothing. "If I had accepted the reduced old frontier [of 1792], I would have been forced to resort to arms again in a couple of years to regain that land. I therefore hope to be able to conclude a favorable peace accord, one that any reasonable man might be expected to desire."[14]

Joseph continued to go along with him. "Peace is absolutely indispensable now!" he wrote from Paris on March 4:

> Therefore make a temporary truce, since the injustice of our enemies will not allow you to make a lasting just peace, and since our present situation in France and public opinion will not support the great effort needed [to raise a large enough army]. . . . By so doing you will be able to remain in France . . . and you who saved the country once [in 1799] will be in a position to save it a second time, by signing a peace treaty today. Once done you will be recognized by England, when you will be free to liberate France of the Cossacks and Prussians."

After rebuilding his army, in a couple of years he could reconquer those natural frontiers. "But whether or not you have won a battle today, *you must agree to a peace settlement.* That is the conclusion I have drawn, that is what everyone I have discussed this with thinks and wants here."[15] Peace above all, they must have peace.

When Blücher also resumed his advance toward the capital, however, Napoleon resumed his attack against the Prussians, now at Craonne, on March 7, sending them falling back to Laon, where Blücher got his revenge by defeating Marmont's corps, which now fled for safety toward Paris. Although he was then on the Else River, when he learned of a renewed threat to Paris by the Austrians, Napoleon diverted his 23,000 men to Arcis-sur-Aube, where he was defeated by 60,000 Austrians.

Too greatly outnumbered to prevent the Austrians and Prussians from joining, Napoleon decided to put into effect his earlier plan for driving far to the northeast, to Lorraine, to cut off Schwarzenberg's line of communications. "I am expecting great results by this movement, which should cause chaos and confusion among the enemy's rear guard and general staff,"[16] he boasted to Joseph from Epernay on March 17.

This letter, with details of his plans, was intercepted by the Allies, however, and the czar was able to persuade Schwarzenberg, who had actually begun to withdraw from his attack on Paris, to turn around and work in a concerted push with Blücher and his own troops, concentrating on Paris. With Napoleon well out of harm's way to the northeast, they had their best shot at capturing the French capital. Napoleon's ruse had backfired. As for Bernadotte and Sweden, Napoleon's last-minute attempt to woo him away from the Allies failed, and the Châtillon Peace Congress ended on March 19, after dismissing Foreign Minister Caulaincourt's plea for an armistice. With a new twenty-year mutual defense pact signed by England, Austria, Prussia, and Russia, and guaranteed by another £5 million subsidy and hence a hardening of their resolve to continue, it was now a complete French surrender they demanded, and no more of Bonaparte's ruses.[17]

By now Napoleon was so tired of hearing of fresh defeats and defections by French leaders that he would no longer even tolerate the mention of the word "peace" in his presence. "The first person who petitions me to agree to 'peace' I will have tried for mutiny!"[18] But it was real panic that was now gripping the nation, as Méneval witnessed for himself:

> The presence of enemy troops at the gates of Paris had caused the inhabitants in the countryside to flood the capital, with their furniture, their sacks of grain and vegetables, their cattle, sheep, and chickens, all completely snarling the traffic at the gates leading into the city. Rich families were fleeing from the Loire. In Paris itself, thousands of members of the working classes roamed the streets aimlessly, hopelessly in a daze. . . . Everyone of all classes was fleeing the theater of war,

fanning rumors of atrocities committed by the barbaric invaders, seemingly confirmed by a couple of dozen French villages and towns already heavily bombarded or burned to the ground, thousands of French men, women, and children homeless, refugees streaming aimlessly, mile after mile. Troyes, Arcis-sur-Aube, Montmirail, Vauxchamps, Clacy, Craonne, Laon, and on and on read the list, the French now suffering as the Germans, Austrians, Italians, Poles, and Russians had earlier suffered at French hands. Panic spread, and "thus the absence of the Emperor at this critical moment" paralyzed the French capital all the more.[19]

※　　　※　　　※

As late as March 13 there had still been no plan authorized for the defense of Paris, Napoleon rejecting the complicated one Joseph had sent him. "Keep it as simple as possible," he insisted. By now even Napoleon was alarmed about the morale in Paris. "I receive complaints from all sides about the mayors and the middle classes who are preventing the defense of the capital from being carried out," he confided to Joseph. Even Méneval was anxious about the number of Napoleon's courtiers and administrators, who were openly going over to the Allies, Talleyrand and the duc de Dalberg leading the list. They in turn were "aided by the perfidy of foreign diplomatic actions, [and] by our own domestic treason silently eating away at the imperial structure." Nor could he forget "the discouraging actions by French army commanders who were no longer obeying orders, fearing they would not be supported, or if supported, only in a half-hearted manner." Nevertheless it was imperative that Joseph complete the city's defenses, for the Allies were advancing in greater numbers in spite of all Napoleon's efforts to stop or divert them.[20] By the last week of March, the situation in Paris looked truly bleak, Marie-Louise expecting the worst, as she confessed to Méneval, "It appears that things are going so badly for us that we must certainly expect a visit [by the advancing Allies] in a matter of days. What a frightening prospect!"[21]

The empress was correct. The coordinated Allied offensive on Paris was launched on March 25, Schwarzenberg setting out from Vitry and Blücher from Châlons-sur-Marne, with Yorck and Kleist to the west approaching Lizy, and another Prussian corps encircling the French at Soissons and Compiègne. On that same day both Marmont and Mortier were defeated and sent flying from La Fère-Champenoise, their shattered corps precipitating toward Paris.

When they reached the capital, Joseph placed the remnants of their troops at the foot of Montmartre, where the final defense of the capital would take place. Joseph took up his command post high atop that hill with brother Jérôme at his side, a sight to discourage even the most optimistic of commanders.

For all his bright, confident words, in mid-March Napoleon had dispatched a special courier to Joseph enjoining him "under no circumstances to permit the Empress and the King of Rome to fall into the hands of the enemy.... If the enemy should advance on Paris with such superior forces as to render all resistance impossible, then send the Regent, my son, the highest officials, dignitaries, and the ministers, and Baron Bouillerie with the treasure, to the Loire. Do not leave my son's side," he concluded with apocalyptic menace, "and just remember that I should prefer to see him at

the bottom of the Seine than in the hands of the enemies of France. The fate
of Astyanax, suffered as a Greek prisoner, always struck me as the most
wretched of all in history." Then for the first time in many years, he signed
his letter, "Your affectionate brother, Napoleon."[22]

By March 28 the sense of inevitable disaster pervaded every quarter of
Paris, although Napoleon had announced his intention of turning around
and coming directly back to save the capital. That evening an emergency
council was convened at the Tuileries, including the highest officials of the
empire, the ministers, and the president of the Senate. There was only one
question on the agenda: whether the Empress should leave Paris with her
son, or remain here. Although the majority at first insisted on her remaining, when Joseph revealed Napoleon's own handwritten orders for her to
depart, they acquiesced, as they always did. Marie-Louise herself made the
ultimate decision to leave the next morning.

The lights burned all night as orders were given to prepare a couple of
dozen carriages and the necessary teams of horses for the morrow, while
maids and ladies-in-waiting worked until dawn packing. Under Méneval's
supervision, the emperor's head archivist spent the same night burning
important documents and sensitive correspondence in the fireplace, while
deep in the cellars of the Tuileries the most valuable jewels and a sizable
quantity of gold were being packed and brought up.

By daybreak the carriages were drawn up in the courtyard, Marie-
Louise ready by seven. At first everyone talked quickly, nervously, followed by "a painful silence," embarrassed perhaps by their own relief at
being able to escape. Joseph had gone out with Jérôme and Louis once again
to study the military situation around the capital and still had not returned
when War Minister Clarke sent an officer to the Empress urging her immediate departure. The advance guard of the Prussian army had already been
spotted outside the city walls. Still they did not leave, the empress postpon-
ing the decision hour after hour. Then her three-year-old-son put up a ter-
rific row, screaming, "I don't want to leave my house!" kicking all the way
into the courtyard.

Just before noon everyone was finally aboard the coaches, and as
Joseph still had not returned, Marie-Louise gave one of the most difficult
orders of her life, to abandon the capital and proceed to Tours. Ten heavy
green berlins, the imperial arms on the doors, followed by dozens of carriages carrying grand dignitaries of the realm, ministers, palace personnel,
army officers, servants, and baggage, pulled out of the Carrousel through
the Pont-Royal Gate, turning in the direction of the Place de la Concorde
and the Champs-Elysées, as some eighty or so bystanders watched "this

cortège in mournful silence, as one might a passing funeral procession."
And indeed, Méneval commented, "they were in fact watching the funeral
of the Empire."

The night was passed at Rambouillet. They continued on to Chartres
the following day, where one of Napoleon's few remaining aides-de-camp,
General Dejean, announced that the emperor was heading a column of
troops to defend Paris. But in fact Marshal Marmont, while arguing vehemently with Marshal Mortier, was then in the midst of following Joseph's
order to surrender the French capital to the Austrians on the thirtieth. Marmont and his eleven thousand men were allowed to keep their arms and
leave the capital for Essonnes, to the southwest. A few thousand men holding off a couple of hundred thousand troops—it would have meant a bloodbath and the destruction of the city. Everyone accused Marmont, but he
made the only intelligent choice possible. Meanwhile Hortense had left
with her children to join Josephine at her castle of Navarre in Normandy.

On March 31, on reaching Vendôme, Marie-Louise received another
special courier from Napoleon. With only a light cavalry escort he had
passed through Juvisy near the village of La Cour de France at 10:30 A.M.
on the thirtieth, when he had come upon General Belliard at the head of a
column of French soldiers coming from Paris. It was Belliard who informed
him of Joseph's order to capitulate and of the subsequent surrender of Marmont. Paris lost! He was too late after all. This changed everything. After
roundly cursing both Joseph and the war minister, Napoleon gathered his
wits about him and ordered Foreign Minister Caulaincourt to continue on
to the capital "to present himself to the Allied sovereigns [and] . . . to negotiate a truce or peace treaty," while sending a messenger to Marie-Louise to
change direction and head for Blois. Then turning his carriage, Napoleon
set out for Fontainebleau at 3:00 A.M., where he arrived at the crack of
dawn.

Marie-Louise and the king of Rome arrived at Blois on April 2, followed shortly thereafter by Joseph, Jérôme, and Louis. Prefect Baron
Christiani made spacious quarters available for the empress within the security of the ancient prefecture buildings.[23]

Placards had appeared throughout Paris announcing the empress's departure. Meanwhile Prince Talleyrand, who for months had been corresponding with the comte de Lille (later Louis XVIII), the eldest brother of the late
Louis XVI and hence heir to the throne, preparing the way for the Bourbon
Restoration, was now convening a special session of the Senate to authorize
a provisional committee (including Talleyrand, General Beurnonville, the

duc de Dalberg, Senator Jaucourt, and Abbé Montesquiou) to replace the defunct imperial régime. (It was this same Abbé Montesquiou who soon became famous for his exclamation, "Won't someone get rid of this little man for us!") Back at his mansion Talleyrand also persuaded the czar, now his house guest, and the Prussian King Friedrich Wilhelm to refuse to negotiate with Napoleon "or with any member of his family." The Corps Législatif, still stung by their rough treatment last December, quickly supported Talleyrand and the Senate's actions.

Not far away, at his office in the Foreign Ministry, Armand de Caulaincourt learned of the arrival that March 31 of the victorious Allied armies through the Pantin Gate at eleven that morning, preceded by the Russian Imperial Guard, wending their way to the Rue Royale and the Champs-Elysées. There Czar Alexander and Friedrich Wilhelm, followed by the colorful and surprisingly orderly Cossacks, rode past in a solemn procession taking many hours as the tens of thousands of foreign troops filled the boulevards. "The most mournful silence reigned," Caulaincourt remarked, "anxiety and fear were seen on every face." But instead of the rapine, looting, and slaughter expected by the Parisians, "there were only orderly columns of well-disciplined troops. The Allies were most exemplary," he added, every soldier wearing a white armband to distinguish the Allies (in their variety of uniforms and colors) from the French. "Vivent les souverains!" some shouted, "Vivent les Alliés! Vivent nos libérateurs!" mingled with a few "Vive le roi! [Louis XVIII]" and "Vive Napoléon!" "Intrigues and treason" had already made fast inroads among the conquered French, who were ready for anything.[24] Although thousands had already fled the city to the south and west, the roads filled with panic-stricken refugees, the vast majority who remained were gradually filled with a sense of relief.

It was not simply that the troops were restrained, thanks to the presence of their sovereigns, but something far deeper, more fundamental. After nearly fifteen years of Napoleonic warfare, after the massive conscription that had literally obliterated an entire generation, leaving not one family untouched, the fighting had ended. There was to be no more war. And this Caulaincourt openly acknowledged. "I must admit, that there was general unhappiness everywhere [among the French] that Napoleon had pushed events to the point that foreign armies were now marching down the boulevards of Paris," but at the same time they were relieved, as the full significance of this dramatic change in their lives sank in.

In the negotiations that ensued, "the greatest opposition that I encountered with the monarchs was their adamancy against Napoleon himself and any wish to accord him and his dynasty any rights whatsoever," Caulaincourt noted, and his task would indeed prove fruitless, so engrained was the bitterness of the whole of Europe against Bonaparte. But even as the Cossacks pitched their tents along the Champs-Elysées, extending back into the Bois de Boulogne, Foreign Minister Caulaincourt stuck to his painful task, negotiating with little leverage with the czar, Foreign Minister Nesselrode, Prince von Schwarzenberg, and the Prussians.

Although the Allies were at first tempted to continue their pursuit of Napoleon and his forces, Caulaincourt, employing all his skill and powers of persuasion, delayed and then stopped them. "Are you going to let one hundred thousand Austrians get killed in order to put the Bourbons on the throne of your emperor's daughter and grandson?" he argued with Schwarzenberg. Lyons had already fallen, Augereau retreating to Valence, while the Fleur de Lys had been flying over royalist Bordeaux since March 12. Reims had fallen on the thirteenth. Soult, already besieged in Toulouse, would shortly see its surrender to Viscount Wellington on April 10. Daily all public officials were turning against Napoleon, like jackals, denouncing the man who had placed them in office and, in many instances, brought them riches. The tide was turning overnight. There would be no further need of fighting, Caulaincourt assured the Allies.

Meanwhile the French vented their anger on the man who had brought all this evil upon them:

> Inhabitants of Paris, your officials would be betraying you and the country if, through vile personal considerations, they compromised their voices and conscience, which cry out to them that you owe all the woes which have befallen you to one man and one man alone. It is he who, year after year, has decimated your families by his continuous conscription. . . . who has closed the very seas to us, who has destroyed our national industry, who has seized the cultivators of our fields, our workers from their factories.

This proclamation on April 2 by the General Council of the Seine did not have to mention the name of Napoleon Bonaparte. The people, the legislators, and the leaders of society all stared in the direction of Fontainebleau.

The man now directing the opposition—preparing both Friedrich Wilhelm and Czar Alexander, and finally the reluctant, easygoing Austrian emperor, Franz I, along with the French Senate itself, not merely to overthrow Napoleon Bonaparte and his once mighty First Empire but to demand unconditional surrender—was none other than Talleyrand. Caulaincourt's brave diplomatic battle to save Napoleon had failed.

Dismayed, Napoleon instructed Caulaincourt that if he could not save his own crown, then at least he should save the regency for Empress Marie-Louise on behalf of their son. But the Allies would never allow that. A boy with his father's blood in his veins would be at their throats on reaching manhood. There would be more warfare, more conquests, more conscription, the destruction of hundreds of additional towns, villages, and cities across the face of Europe. The apocalypse would inevitably repeat itself.

On April 2 the Senate, under Talleyrand's leadership, officially voted the overthrow of Napoleon "and of his entire family." As Prince von Schwarzenberg plainly told Caulaincourt: "It's all over now. There is nothing he can do about it.... He brought it all upon himself. We warned him.... I complained to France, I complained to you. As for the Emperor he desired this wretched state of affairs. He has only himself to blame for it."[25]

In fact on April 1 the czar had written to Napoleon, informing him there was nothing to negotiate about. Napoleon retaliated by threatening to march on Paris. Marshals Berthier, Ney, Oudinot, Lefebvre, and Macdonald argued with him, but Napoleon refused to see reality. Then Caulaincourt and Maret attempted to persuade him. "The army will obey me," Napoleon insisted. "No!" snapped an impatient Ney. "From now on it will obey only its commanders, us." "Our horses can go no farther," Macdonald pointed out. "We don't have enough ammunition for even one more skirmish," and if Napoleon were to attack the Allies, who had proved remarkably lenient thus far, they would take it out on France, on the French people. "The whole of France will be destroyed," Macdonald persisted, the others in full agreement. Finally after hours of heated argument, Napoleon gave in. They would lay down their arms.[26]

"Born a soldier, I won't need a throne. I can revert to being just a plain citizen again. My happiness does not depend on grandeur. I wanted to see a great, powerful France; I want that above all else." Then he added ominously, "I would rather leave the throne, abandon it, than sign a shameful peace treaty." He veered in one direction, then another; he had been doing so for days now. In spite of Austria's betrayal, Marie-Louise's father "does not wish to dethrone his beloved daughter and grandson.... But men are blind, so blind! It is their hatred that is guiding their actions today, and nothing else. In the present frenzy, reason and political requirements are no longer listened to."[27]

Then he would revert to war as the only solution, keeping Caulaincourt up night after night, till dawn itself, arguing, trying to convince him. "He seemed to think that he could alter the situation and change the outcome yet by marching against the enemy and attacking them before Paris....

And I saw for myself that there were still many young officers who wanted to fight one more big battle, to save face and the army's honor. He wanted to fight the last battle to avenge himself, he told me, against the shameful conduct of the Parisians." By now Caulaincourt had had enough. "I did not hide from the Emperor the fact that whatever he did, he had to act quickly, there was no time to lose. The Army was exhausted, but if he were to fight it would have to be today, or else fall back on the Loire, surrender and abdicate."

"We shall be fighting for the honor of France," Napoleon went off on another tangent, "to prove that the French are not a people to accept the dictates of mere Cossacks." Then he tore into his ministers and officials, Fouché, Talleyrand, Dalberg, and especially Clarke for his "incompetent defense of the capital." He was so unstable that Caulaincourt grew very anxious, not knowing what to expect. Then the next day Napoleon ordered his troops into the Cour du Cheval Blanc and addressed them: "Soldiers! The enemy got to Paris three days ahead of us, making them masters of the city. We must chase them away. Swear before me now to conquer or to die, to make the tricolor cocarde respected, that cocarde with which we have lined the roads of Europe with honor and glory for these past twenty years!"[28]

But on learning of the Senate's vote and determination to dethrone him, supported by the Corps Législatif, he finally agreed to order the army to stand down. He would abdicate after all, after summoning his marshals and generals again to sound them out. "The marshals and many of the generals have lost their heads," Napoleon later complained. "They said nothing, but I could see that they wanted my abdication. . . . The imbeciles simply cannot see that the health and safety of France depends on me alone. . . . Born a soldier I could get on very well without an empire, but France cannot get on without me." In spite of everything, he still was not convinced, nor was he rational.

He ordered Caulaincourt back to Paris, with Marshals Macdonald and Lefebvre this time, for one last attempt to sway the Allies. En route they stopped at Essonnes and tried to win over Marmont. But no sooner had they arrived in Paris on April 4, with Marmont at their side, than they learned that General Souham, in Marmont's absence, had taken over the entire corps of eleven thousand men to the Austrians. The game was up. That corps had been Napoleon's trump card. "If I win," he had told Caulaincourt before setting out for Paris, "we will have an honorable peace settlement. If I lose, it is our poor France that will have to suffer the consequences."[29]

The next day, Caulaincourt received a summons to the rue Saint-Florentin where the czar was waiting for him. His worst fears were immediately borne out. "Bad news . . . we are lost," he recorded. "He knows all about it." News of the defection of Marmont's corps had arrived earlier. "At this unhappy conference we were ordered to return promptly with an unconditional abdication."[30]

Reaching Fontainebleau at two o'clock in the morning of April 6 with Marshals Lefebvre and Macdonald, Caulaincourt found Napoleon with Marshal Oudinot waiting for him. On receiving the news, Napoleon attacked everyone viciously, from the Senate to Marshal Marmont, accusing him "of deserting to the enemy with his corps. . . . And when? . . . At the very moment when an almost certain victory would have crowned our last great effort, making Europe truly repent for having occupied my capital."[31]

Napoleon had reached the breaking point, his hysteria, his illusions, his utterances embarrassing to them all. "That's the lot of sovereigns for you!" Napoleon went on irrationally. "They merely create a lot of ungrateful people." After hours of tirade, an exhausted Napoleon conceded defeat. "They want me to abdicate, all right then, I'll abdicate!"[32]

Caulaincourt rushed back to Paris again, this time to conclude the negotiations, drawing up and signing the necessary documents. The Senate having already proclaimed Louis Stanislas Xavier, the comte de Lille, Louis XVIII, king of France, the stage was set. Between the seventh and eighth, Marshals Lefebvre, Oudinot, and Jourdan surrendered to the Allies while Talleyrand insisted to Caulaincourt that Napoleon, Marie-Louise, and their son must all disappear from France and French history forever. On April 11 Napoleon drafted and signed his abdication at the Palace of Fontainebleau:

> The allied powers having proclaimed the Emperor Napoleon to be the sole remaining obstacle to the re-establishment of peace in Europe, Emperor Napoleon, faithful to his oath, declares his renunciation of the thrones of France and Italy, for himself and his heirs, and that there is no personal sacrifice, even that of life itself, that he is not prepared to make in the interests of France.
>
> NAPOLEON

He had already been informed that his wife and son would not be allowed to join him, and that the island of Elba had been assigned as his place of exile, over which he would be granted complete sovereignty—against the strong objections of Talleyrand and Fouché, who demanded that he and his entire clan be sent far from European shores. Napoleon, fearful of assassination attempts by the Bourbons and his many other enemies, had ironically first hinted at exile in England, with Marie-Louise and their son. But of course Lord Castlereagh, who had just reached Paris with Metternich, was adamantly against that. What Napoleon really desired was protection, and therefore next *insisted* that the British government place an English army officer at his side on Elba to protect him. This "Perfidious Albion" that he had so vehemently denounced throughout his entire career was in the end the only country he could literally trust with his life. At first taken aback, Castlereagh and the British government agreed to this extraordinary request.[33]

Meanwhile all was chaos in Napoleon's mind and world. Marie-Louise and his son, whom he had ordered from Blois to Orléans, soon found their "treasury" of jewels and cash taken from them by the Allies and she and her son ordered back to Rambouillet. Napoleon would never see his wife or son again.

The Allies signed all the final documents pertaining to Napoleon's dethronement at 1:00 A.M. on April 12.[34] Only Napoleon's signature was missing.

An exhausted Caulaincourt and Macdonald reached Fontainebleau with their precious portfolios that same afternoon. But instead of finding the thousands of troops and hundreds of staff officers, court officials, and servants, there remained only the loyal Polish lancers under General Krasinski and a few units of the Old Guard. When Napoleon asked Berthier and Caulaincourt to follow him into exile, they both declined, as did Constant. Napoleon retaliated against his valet alone, calling him a thief, which was as untrue as the accusation against Bourrienne years earlier when he, too, had tried to leave his service. "Ah, Caulaincourt, I have lived too long," Napoleon sighed, "Poor France . . . I don't want to see her dishonored!" clearly referring to himself and his own humiliating position now. "A little more effort by everyone, a few more months of suffering and she would have triumphed over all her enemies."[35] He continued to ramble on for hours, lost in a world very far from reality, his mind wandering in and out of the past and present, then suddenly reverting back to his great triumphs of yesteryear.

At three o'clock in the morning on April 13, Napoleon sent for Caulaincourt. He was in bed, the usual night lamp giving off a feeble light. "Come close, sit down," he said in a weak voice. He made Caulaincourt promise to hand-deliver a letter he had just written to Marie-Louise.

My good Louise, I have received your letter. I approve of your
going to Rambouillet where your father will come to rejoin you. That is
the only consolation that you can expect to receive under the present
circumstances. I have been waiting for this moment for an entire week.
Your father has separated us and has been bad for us, but nevertheless
he will be a kind father to you, and your son. Caulaincourt has returned
here. Yesterday I sent you a copy of the arrangements he has agreed to
and signed on your behalf and that of your son. Goodbye, my good
Louise. I love you more than anyone else in the world. My misfortunes
hurt me only because of the pain they cause you. Love your most tender husband always. Give a kiss to my son. Adieu, chère Louise. All the
very best.

Napoleon

He had in fact just taken the vial of poison he always carried around his
neck, prepared a couple of years earlier by his doctor, in the event of capture by the enemy. He now soon became incoherent and then cried out in
agony as the poison took effect, perspiring and vomiting all over his bed.
Caulaincourt realized what he had done and sent for Dr. Yvan:

The Emperor suffered atrociously. . . . I cannot begin to express the
great pain this scene caused me. "How difficult it is to die," Napoleon
cried out. ". . . Tell Josephine that I have been thinking about her. . . .
Give me your hand. Kiss me!" and he pulled me to his heart, breathing
heavily. I choked and could not hide my tears, which flowed in spite of
me, falling on to his cheeks and hands.

For hours Dr. Yvan and Caulaincourt remained by his bedside, helpless, as
the poison ate into his system. But finally by morning the crisis was over.
The poison was too old, having lost its potency, and Napoleon slowly
recovered over the next couple of days.[36]

By April 16 he was strong enough to write a final letter to Josephine:

Today I congratulate myself, for an enormous burden has been
removed. My fall has been great, but at least it is useful, or so they say.

When I go into my retreat, I am going to replace my sword with a
pen. The history of my reign should prove to be most curious, for I
have been seen only in profile, but I shall reveal the whole. . . . I have
heaped benefits upon thousands of wretches. But what have they done
for me in return, at the end?

They have betrayed me, yes, all of them, except the good Eugène, so worthy of you and me. . . .

Good-bye, my dear Joséphine, resign yourself, as I have had to do, and never forget him who has never forgotten you and never will.

Napoleon

Brother Jérôme's reaction to the news of Napoleon's abdication and failed suicide attempt was typical: "The Emperor, after having caused all our troubles, has survived!"[37]

Louis XVIII would be reaching France and Compiègne on April 29, preparing for his grand entrance into the French capital, even as his new naval minister ordered two frigates to transfer Napoleon to the island of Elba. Only Generals Drouot and Bertrand of his entourage would be accompanying Napoleon immediately, along with six Allied officers as far as the French coast. They insisted on disguising their prisoner in an Austrian general's uniform later for his own protection, against hostile French crowds. The carriages and escort finally prepared to depart on the twentieth as Napoleon bade farewell to the Old Guard assembled before him, most of whom would be left behind. The procession then pulled out of the Cour du Cheval Blanc through the Forest of Fontainebleau for the Mediterranean coast. Reaching St.-Raphaël on April 27, Napoleon boarded the English frigate HMS *Undaunted* the following morning, the two French vessels not yet having arrived—or did Napoleon simply feel safer aboard a British warship? Unknown to him, on the very day of his sailing, Josephine had died of pneumonia at her beloved Malmaison. Aboard the *Undaunted* Napoleon was, according to Caulaincourt, "received with all due consideration and distinction possible and treated with all the privileges of his rank."

On May 30 the various Treaties of Paris concluding the peace settlement were signed and exchanged, reducing French frontiers to what they had been in 1792, while England generously returned the French colonies taken during the long wars, except for Mauritius, Tobago, and St. Lucia. No reparations of any kind were to be demanded by the aggrieved parties, for a war that had cost England alone £6 hundred million. Lord Castlereagh, never an orator, tried to pacify his outraged fellow countrymen about the unusual leniency of the peace terms. He explained: "It is better for France to be commercial and pacific, than a warlike and conquering State." Peace was worth the price, he felt. Never had a more lenient treaty been adopted, given the tormented and ravaged Europe that France and Napoleon had left in their wake over the past fifteen years: the hundreds of burned towns and villages; the hundreds of thousands of rapes; the looted cities; the occupied lands; the tortured and murdered citizens; the three million dead European soldiers alone (one million of them French); the destruction of an entire continent's economy, industry, and trade; and the sowing of international hatred and distrust that in some instances have lasted to this very day.[38]

In Napoleon's eyes all his marshals and generals had abandoned him in the end, although he finally excused a few of them. Berthier, whose health had been shattered permanently as a result of the Russian campaign, was a changed man, now over sixty and looking much older. All he wanted was to spend his last days with his German wife and children, away from soldiers, fighting, and Napoleon's almost daily abuse. Macdonald had stayed to the very end, failing to follow the course of the other "traitors." As for Caulaincourt, no man had served with greater dedication and loyalty under the most unpleasant of circumstances, until the very last moment. Napoleon could never thank him enough for what he had done, including all through the night and early morning hours of that dreadful April 13.

As HMS *Undaunted* left him behind and hove out of the harbor of Portoferraio on May 4, 1814, Napoleon instructed the island's French governor that he had specially selected Elba "because of its climate and for the gentle ways of its people." He of course had had no say in the matter of his exile, but that was Napoleon, and in any event, it sounded good. Most of minuscule Elba's population of 13,700 had come out to greet their new sovereign, the outlawed war criminal, with *"Evviva l'Imperatore!"* It had a nice ring to it.

Accompanying him were Gen. Henri Bertrand, who had replaced Christophe Duroc as grand marshal of the palace (although there was no building on this island even remotely resembling a palace, the island itself appearing as a mere dot on the map). Guillaume-Joseph, baron Peyrusse, served as his new treasurer and finance minister, and Gen. Antoine Drouot as war minister, while at the same time replacing the departing French governor. The hapless General Cambronne commanded the nearly thousand-man force the Allies had foolishly allowed Napoleon as protection. Dr. Labi headed the Directory of Domains [state lands and property], and André Pons de l'Hérault managed the island's iron mines (the main source of state revenue; the Allies, although sworn to provide Napoleon with 2 million francs a year, were never to pay a single centime). The English government had been as good as its word, however, sending the good-natured Col. Sir Neil Campbell to remain with him, to help avert any would-be assassination attempt, and to report back to the Allies on Napoleon's activities. The Allies would do their best to intercept all mail to and from Napoleon and Europe, including with his own family. His mother and Pauline, his favorite sister, whom some claimed also to be his lover,[39] would soon come to join him permanently.

Marie-Louise and the king of Rome were whisked off to Vienna and kept virtual prisoners in the Schönbrunn, on Metternich's particular insistence. As for the rest of the clan, that was a complex issue as they flitted about Europe. No country really wanted anyone bearing the name "Bonaparte" on its territory; they were all to move several times over the next few years. Louis had been allowed to settle temporarily in Lausanne, under heavy police surveillance; and Joseph, thereafter known as the comte de Survilliers, nearby at the castle of Prangins, overlooking Lake Geneva, though ultimately he ended up a resident of the state of New Jersey, much to the surprise of the American people. Jérôme (with Catherine) was chased out of Württemberg by his irate father-in-law, moving to Graz, Austria, for a while. Elisa was even more peripatetic, moving several times before finally settling in Trieste temporarily. Caroline and Joachim Murat were allowed to remain in the royal palace at Naples for the time being, until the following spring, when Murat suddenly declared war on Austria while trying to capture the whole of Italy, only to be defeated. Fleeing to France during Napoleon's One Hundred Days, he was offered refuge in the wilderness mountains between Grenoble and Sisterone, but he preferred the balmy breezes and palms of Cannes. (Following Napoleon's second fall in June 1815, the mad Murat attempted to invade Corsica, only to be ejected. Landing in Calabria and proclaiming himself king again, he was ordered by King Ferdinand to be summarily executed by a firing squad, on October 13.) As for Lucien and his wife, Alexandrine, whom he had refused to give up even for a kingdom, they were permitted by the British government to exchange their Shropshire manor house for a sprawling Italian villa, he apparently considered the only "neutral" Bonaparte. Hortense, who had remained temporarily in France and now was known as the Duchess of Saint-Leu, was eventually forced to move to northern Switzerland. Her brother, Prince Eugène, and the lovely Augusta were given permanent refuge by the king of Bavaria, her father.

On the island there were no women, at least until the arrival later of Pauline. Hortense, whom he dearly missed, was still in mourning at Malmaison. Countess Marie Waleska had come to Fontainebleau at Napoleon's behest, only to be kept waiting hour after hour, Napoleon then changing his mind and refusing to see her. She had left in tears, without Napoleon either bothering to say good-bye or even to inquire about their son. Had he not risen to such power, it is unlikely that any woman would have been attracted to this emperor whose favorite pastime remained insulting the fair sex in public and in private.

His new kingdom was not much, a mountainous spot in the sea. He selected as his "palace" the former garrison-cum-court-cum-windmill, appropriately called I Mulini (the mills), situated some thousand feet above his port-capital of Portoferraio, overlooking the Tyrrhenian Sea. The palace was small, and even with the addition of apartments upstairs, where Pauline would later reside, it came to less than a dozen rooms. Madame Mère, with whom he barely got on, would be shunted to a smaller house of her own in a nearby village. Napoleon also acquired a small seaside house at Portolongone, "the grange" at San Martino (a gift of Pauline), and he later built a small bungalow atop Mt. Capanna. The island had just a few miles of road, which Napoleon immediately began extending, while improving the facilities of his capital. His other major building project was military in nature—fortifications—for he was still obsessed with the idea that assassins would be landed here, and in fact plots were already being hatched.

Without money, however, on Elba—"a great refuge for an old fox," as one soldier dubbed it—Napoleon's hands were tied. Louis XVIII stated quite openly that he had no intention of sending the annual sum of 2 million francs stipulated by the Allies in the Fontainebleau treaty (signed by everyone, in fact, but the Bourbons). The island's mines provided him with a total of 607,309 francs annually, and that was it. Apart from the money he brought with him, and the generosity of Pauline, Napoleon had nothing. Sir Neil Campbell wrote angry letters to the Allies, reminding them of their unfulfilled obligations. It was vital, he insisted. "I persist in my opinion that if Napoleon receives the sums stipulated by the treaties, he will remain perfectly contented [at Elba], barring any unforeseen event in Italy or France," he informed Castlereagh.[40]

For a man of Napoleon's energy—admittedly greatly reduced since his suicide attempt (he had been wheezing and coughing ever since) and imagination—Elba was a boring backwater. As for the famous "history" he had told Caulaincourt he intended to write, not a word. For entertainment he went out on his horse for long daily rides, and every Sunday the traditional "imperial levée" took place at I Mulini, followed by mass, just as it had been done at the Tuileries. Although his handful of courtiers and their wives turned out in their uniforms and gowns for an occasional "state dinner," they usually passed the evening playing cards, or preparing a new amateur theatrical production, enhanced by officers' wives. Even with the arrival of the lively Pauline that winter, life at the palace was lackluster, if not deadly. Everyone was bored and frustrated. Nerves snapped and tempers flared. Nor could Napoleon pay his troops or his personal entourage. The good Bertrand and his wife, Fanny, who had by now joined him, did their best to enliven things. But with his daily circle limited to Bertrand, Drouot, the dreary Cambronne, Major Malet (no relation to the mad general) and Colonel Jerzmanowski (now commanding the Polish Red Lancers), life was pretty tedious, and this dreariness was reflected on Napoleon's face, worrying Colonel Campbell more and more.

A few foreign visitors were permitted to land briefly. Two of Napoleon's former mistresses even managed to escape Allied naval vessels for brief sojourns, including the ever faithful Countess Walewska and Emilie de Pellapra, both of whom had borne his sons. But then they were gone, and the masked balls launched by Pauline, artificially light-hearted, left a ringing emptiness, a painful reminder of the better days of yore. Nor did Marie-Louise—now in the arms and bed of Gen. Albrecht Adam von Neipperg, the Austrian hussar assigned to protect her—any longer wish to return to him.

By the end of December 1814, an anxious Colonel Campbell reported to London that Napoleon was withdrawing more and more, avoiding him and just about everyone else.

Meanwhile Talleyrand, who had insisted on the unconditional abdication of Napoleon in his own name and that of all heirs, and who had earlier hired an assassin in Paris to kill Napoleon, was now planning another attempt to kidnap and perhaps kill him, just as he had drawn up the initial master plan for the kidnapping and murder of the duke of Enghien back in 1804. "Napoleon frequently goes over to Pianosa [an islet next to Elba]," French Consul General Mariotti reported from Livorno to Talleyrand. "I have been assured that having no lodgings on that island, he always sleeps aboard one of his ships. It will be easy . . . to kidnap him." Colonel Campbell warned Lord Castlereagh of various plots against the sovereign of the island of Elba, including one by Gen. Louis Brulast, the new Bourbon commanding officer of Corsica, which included hiring Arabs from Algiers to sail over in the night and seize him. Others included open murder attempts. "Let them kill me," a dejected Bonaparte told Campbell, "but I do not want to be deported." He did not want to end his days in a French dungeon, buried alive forever from any contact with another human being.[41]

By the spring of 1815, as the Congress of Vienna (opened on November 1, 1814) was convening to provide a long-lasting overall European peace settlement to unscramble the political mayhem Napoleon had left for them, the man himself—bored, broke, depressed, anxious, and frustrated—came to the conclusion that he could no longer abide the enforced limitations of his new existence. "Friends" got messages to him. The French people wanted him back, they said; he must liberate them from the Bourbons. With the arrival of former Deputy Prefect Fleury de Chaboulon on February 12, 1815, Napoleon finalized plans to escape his island prison. When Colonel Campbell then obligingly left Portoferraio on February 16 for one of his periodic rendezvous with his mistress on the Italian mainland, the plans went into action.

A seven-vessel flotilla was assembled and rapidly armed, victualed, and prepared for the embarkation of an expeditionary force of 1,026 officers and men, including the Polish lancers, the 551 grenadiers of the Old Guard, and every available Elban willing to join this venture.

After attending mass at 10:00 A.M. on Sunday, February 26, Napoleon once again donned his famous green uniform as colonel of grenadiers. He appeared at the harbor with his new general staff—Generals Bertrand, Cambronne, and Drouot, and General Commissioner Pons—and proclaimed to his men: "Grenadiers, it has been decided. We are going to France, we are going back to Paris!" "Vive la France!" roared hundreds of jubilant homesick voices, "Vive l'Empereur!"

After bidding adieu to Madame Mère and Pauline for the last time, at 9:00 P.M. that evening, with his new white Elban flag with its diagonal red stripe and three bees flying over his flagship, Napoleon boarded the brig the *Inconstant*, ordering Captain Cautard to hoist the signal to sail, and they weighed anchor and put to sea. Meanwhile off the Tuscan coast, the jolly Colonel Campbell, having been apprised of the events on the island, was aboard a small warship rushing back from Livorno. They passed each other unseen in the night. Despite the sighting of a couple of distant French and British warships, Napoleon's luck held, his Elban odyssey on course and on schedule, proceeding across calm seas under a clear sky.

And thus it was that at 10:00 A.M. on March 1 they first glimpsed the distant mountains behind Cap d'Antibes, as the captain lowered the Elban flag and replaced it with the tricolor. Rounding the cape, and concealed from the fort at Antibes, with the Ile Ste.-Marguerite to their west, the flotilla entered the protected shallow waters of the secluded Golfe Juan and began landing their few cannon and "army," as they set out to march along the beach to the narrow peninsula of La Croisette, and Cannes. "I am the sovereign of the Island of Elba," he proclaimed as he entered that sleepy city, "and have come with six hundred men to attack the King of France and his six hundred thousand soldiers. I shall conquer this kingdom."[42]

CHAPTER 39

"Projects of Troubles and Upsettings"

I want to return to my throne without having spilled a single drop of blood.

ad the sixty-seven-year-old mayor of Cannes, Notary François Poulle, been expecting trouble on the afternoon of Wednesday, March 1, 1815, no doubt he would have posted guards on the parapet of the seventy-foot, eleventh-century stone Tour du Suquet on the heights of the Old Quarter and near the Eglise Nôtre-Dame d'Espérance, overlooking the town's ancient fishing port and twelve thousand peaceful inhabitants. The Phoenicians had passed there, the Romans had given the city its name (after the reeds growing in the lagoon), the Arabs based at nearby La Garde–Freinet had ravaged the area from the eighth through the tenth century, leaving behind only mountainous slopes covered with cork, oak, olive, and chestnut trees to recall their presence.

Such then was the scene when at 3:00 P.M. the good mayor was suddenly summoned most urgently to the Hôtel de Ville, where a domineering man—in fact, General Cambronne—had arrived out of the blue, first demanding "passports" for himself and his friends required to continue on to Marseilles, next returning with a further demand for dozens of horses and a couple of dozen carriages and wagons, and then finally adamantly ordering the bewildered mayor to deliver three thousand rations of beef and bread to their bivouac amid the sand dunes ringing the Bay of the Angels, for as the mayor of Cannes was now informed, Emperor Napoleon had returned to save the realm. With much of the city unwalled and undefended, the mayor had no choice. He summoned all the butchers and bakers, who slaughtered three head of cattle and produced hundreds of loaves of bread.

The town's three principal roads, leading to Fréjus to the west, Antibes and Nice to the east, and Grasse to the north, were barricaded by uniformed troops, but not securely enough to prevent Mayor Poulle from getting off a desperate message to Count de Bouthillier Chavigny, the royal prefect of the Var, at Draguinan, informing him that "sixty soldiers" and an Elban general had seized the city. This was before Cambronne had returned a final time demanding three thousand rations and informing him of the arrival of Napoleon Bonaparte, while leaving him with the latter's "Proclamation to the Army": "Napoleon, by the grace of God, Emperor of the French," had returned to save them, it announced:

> I heard you calling me in my exile and crossed every obstacle and peril to be here.... Take up those colors that the nation has proscribed, those colors round which we have rallied for twenty-five years, in fending off the enemies of France. Put on the same tricolor cocarde that you wore during our finest days ... [and] take up again the eagles that preceded you at Ulm, Austerlitz, Jena, Eylau, and Friedland.... Soldiers! Come rally around the banners of your leader![1]

Given the very limited military resources at his disposal, Napoleon had skillfully prepared his invasion plan. Without cavalry, without heavy artillery, and without large numbers of troops, he was in no position even to attack Vauban's Square Fortress at Antibes, where he had been held prisoner briefly following the downfall of Robespierre. He certainly could not attack the major garrisons farther up the coast at Toulon and Marseilles, where Marshal Masséna now commanded the Eighth Military District in the name of the Bourbon royal house. To be sure, Napoleon had already dispatched one vessel to inform Masséna of his arrival and intentions, and another to Joachim Murat at Naples, asking them both for their support.

Bonaparte knew, however, that he had to march quickly on Paris, for if he got bogged down in conflict here in this traditionally strong pro-Bourbon region, he would be lost. Thus he had landed in one of the very few undefended places that at the same time gave him the most direct access to the route he intended to follow: via Grasse, then climbing into the mountainous back country through Castellane, Digne, Gap, Laffrey, Grenoble, Lyons, and Châlons. This permitted him to put much distance, and tough terrain, between him and any pursuers. Furthermore, he knew the region well, and what little it had to offer large numbers of troops, with its muddy roads weaving up narrow valleys, sometimes heavily forested and always rocky. But it would be hard going for his own men too. High morale was as important as food for his 1,026-man expeditionary force. If all went well, Napoleon's first real challenge would come as he descended the high mountains overlooking Grenoble, where there was a large garrison of at least 7,000 men, with heavy artillery, munitions, and supplies—all of which he had prepared for his earlier campaigns into Italy and Switzerland while still emperor. He therefore had to win over that garrison. He was not relying entirely on luck, however, having dispatched a messenger to Col. Charles de La Bédoyère, who commanded the Seventh Infantry Regiment at Grenoble, and with whom he had been in secret correspondence since his arrival at Elba. Napoleon was counting on winning over more troops and preventing a clash. "I want to return to my throne without having spilled a single drop of blood," he lectured his troops sternly before breaking camp at a little after 4:00 A.M. the next day, March 2, knowing that otherwise the French would turn against him.

Reaching Grasse later that same morning, they encountered the outraged royalist mayor of that city, the marquis de Gourdon, who summoned the local National Guard, only thirty men answering the call. Instead Napoleon now gave the orders, demanding more food for his men, wagons, horses, and mules. No sooner had they finished eating than they resumed their march, this time up the steep route into the mountains, to St.-Valliers, Escragnolle, and Seranon, abandoning animals, cannon, and carriages by the time they reached the snow level and severe cold. Making their way along the narrow road used by local mules and peasant carts through the pine forest, at well over three thousand feet, they finally reached Castellane. There they rested as Napoleon requisitioned five thousand rations for the troops—needed through the mountains before them—forty carts, and two hundred mules, only to set out once again, deeper into the desolate mountains, where scarcely a house or shepherd could be found, reaching Barême on March 3 and Digne by the fourth.

Napoleon's recognition of the potential dangers back in the Var in fact proved to be too true. Prefect Count Bouthillier had ordered an initial force of fewer than one hundred men to march to the coast via Le Muy on the second. On learning that it was Bonaparte himself, with a much larger force than initially reported by Poulle, he rushed off a messenger to Masséna to inform him "that troops HEADED by Bonaparte would be at Digne today," and that he, Masséna must act quickly. By 7:00 P.M. Bouthillier had prepared another dispatch, this one for his immediate superior in Paris, Interior Minister Montesquiou, apprising him of the emergency. Nevertheless, "it is quite impossible for those troops [of Bonaparte] to advance very far in a country entirely devoted to H. M. [Louis XVIII] before receiving their just deserts for such a rash act." He closed by assuring the minister that he was taking "all precautions necessary . . . to ensure that this aggressor would be repulsed. . . . Vive le Roi!" On March 4 he ordered a fresh detachment into the hills as far as St.-Vallier.[2]

The prudent Masséna, safe and snug in a secure berth at long last, had no intention of wrangling with Napoleon or getting involved in any of this. He would remain neutral. He had received Bonaparte's initial message sent the first day, but claimed utter surprise on receipt of Poulle's later message on March 3, stating "that fifty men from the Guard of the ex-Emperor Napoleon . . . landed in the Golfe Juan yesterday." To buy time he sent out two or three agents in various directions to gather more precise information, which was always good for a day or two, and after that ordered a regiment into the mountains to Sisteron to pursue the sovereign of Elba. "You can count on my zeal and devotion," Marshal Masséna informed Louis XVIII's new war minister, none other than the wily Marshal Soult. "I swore my fidelity to the legitimate King. I shall never deviate from the path of honor," Masséna, one of the greatest looters in the army, reported.[3] And thus it was that Napoleon safely got away.

But by March 7 he was facing the first real test at Laffrey, where he found himself confronting a battalion of nearly eight hundred men. Gen. Jean-Gabriel Marchand, the commanding officer of Grenoble (awarded the Grand Eagle of the Legion of Honor by Napoleon himself) had no intention of seriously preventing this man who had given him his fortune from marching on Paris. Nor did the local battalion commander sound very convincing: "If you do not withdraw, I shall arrest you."[4] That is not how determined troops stop dangerous invaders. "Soldiers of the 5th Infantry Regiment, I am your Emperor," Napoleon shouted, ignoring the impudent officer. "If there is any one among you who wishes to kill his emperor, here I am," he said defiantly holding his coat open for them to fire at his heart. Although one captain did order the men to fire, nothing happened, and suddenly there was a thundering spontaneous outburst—"*Vive l'Empereur!*"—as hundreds of men threw down their weapons and broke ranks. They rushed over to Napoleon, knelt before him, and kissed the hem of his winter coat, even his sword.

Shortly thereafter Colonel La Bédoyère arrived at the head of the Seventh Infantry and joined forces with Napoleon's men. They marched by torchlight through the heavy snow, down the mountain, passing through the open Bonne Gate of the city, which General Marchand and the prefect had just abandoned. Grenoble was his, giving Bonaparte some eight thousand troops and more than enough artillery and munitions to arm a powerful column to Lyons. His gamble had worked thus far, and his route of march was right on schedule. The hurdle of Lyons could prove much more difficult, however.

At 4:00 P.M. on March 9, Napoleon's newly requisitioned coach, preceded by his Polish lancers in their red-and-gold uniforms, set out with his greatly increased force for the plains of Burgundy and the confluence of the Rhône and Saône Rivers.

On that same day in the Place Bellecour of Lyons, the king's brother, the comte d'Artois, attended by General Damas and Marshal Macdonald, was addressing General Brayer's large garrison, reminding them of Bonaparte's past and of the necessity of preventing him from "again imposing his yoke on a great nation. . . . Put an end to these criminal projects. We are all going to advance together on the enemy! Long live the King!"[5] But instead of a loud "*Vive le roi!*" there was a resounding silence. A much rattled Artois, after hastily dismissing the troops and consulting with Macdonald and the two generals, fled the city with the marshal early the next morning, leaving behind only General Brayer, who had decided to throw in his lot with his former commander, Napoleon.

At 10:00 P.M. that same day, March 10, Napoleon and his troops drove unopposed through the gates of the city of Lyons and into the same Place Bellecourt. He was greeted by thousands of vociferous soldiers and civilians—"*Vive l'Empereur!* Down with the priests! Down with the nobles! Death to the Bourbons! *Vive la liberté!*"[6]

After spending a comfortable night in the archbishop's palace (the former residence of Uncle Fesch, the onetime pirate, war commissar, priest, and, latterly, cardinal), "the emperor," in excellent spirits, emerged with General Brayer at his side to address the troops and townspeople, with a surprise for them all: "I am coming back to protect and defend the interests that our Revolution has given us. I want to give you an inviolable constitution, one prepared by the people and me together." He concluded with the announcement that he was abolishing the Bourbon aristocracy and replacing the white flag with the revolutionary tricolor.[7] The roar of the massive

crowd was deafening. In effect he was proclaiming a constitutional monarchy and a return to some of the revolutionary principles, this same
Napoleon who had done everything he could as emperor to eradicate every
trace of that very Revolution. Politics were politics.

After emptying the till of the Banque de France of six hundred thousand
francs, Napoleon, at the head now of some fourteen thousand troops, set off
on the road for Paris, determined to arrive on the twentieth, just in time to
celebrate his son's fourth birthday. But he was not in a great hurry as the
troops marched north along the Saône, past Mâcon to Châlons, reaching
Autun on the fifteenth. He was closing the distance to his objective.

"I believe I can assure Your Excellency that we have nothing to worry
about," Prefect Gamot had informed the interior minister from the provincial capital of the Yonne at Auxerre. But when, on March 15, Gamot
"appealed to every man of goodwill" to step forward and form reserve battalions, he, too, met with silence, even as rumors from Paris announced the
mass desertion of more officers and troops from the Bourbon Royal Army,
culminating in the incredible news of the fall of both Grenoble and Lyons
to Napoleon and his army's approach to Auxerre itself. The result: On the
sixteenth, Gamot—who had just assured the interior minister of the loyalty
of the people of his department—now addressed these very people: "Inhabitants of the Yonne.... Let us unite around this hero whom glory has
recalled to us."[8]

The king, with strong assurances from his war minister, "Old Nick"
Soult, and Marshal Ney, who was gathering a small reserve force at Lons-
le-Saunier, may have felt anxious but not desperate. On March 14 Marshal
Ney described Napoleon Bonaparte to the prefect as a "mad dog upon
whom one must fling oneself in order to avoid his savage bite. If I have the
good fortune to arrest him, I intend to bring him back to Paris alive in an
iron cage!"[9] Aglaé-Louise Ney reassured her husband: "What utter madness
could have seized the emperor? But he will soon be its first victim. Who
will support him? Not a soul!"

Nevertheless, all was not quite what it seemed, for privately a confused
Ney was even angrier with the king, who had provided him with only six
thousand against Napoleon's approaching fourteen thousand. Ney had seen
for himself what sort of miracles the little Corsican could pull off even
when outnumbered. That same day Ney, who could at times become hotheaded and make violent changes of judgment, did it again. He suddenly
declared that he had decided to support that "mad dog" Bonaparte. "But
don't worry about a thing. Napoleon is returning with the finest intentions
in the world. He wants to forget the past and reconcile all parts of society

and save France."[10] (It should be mentioned in passing that Ney was the brother-in-law of Prefect Gamot at Auxerre, whose lead he was following.)

At 8:00 A.M. on March 16, Marshal Ney arrived just as his brother-in-law and Napoleon were about to sit down for breakfast. The "mad dog" gave Ney a big hug and exuberant thanks, as the marshal's forces now swelled Napoleon's to at least twenty thousand, the equivalent of two divisions.[11]

Although the country did not know any of the current members of the Bourbon dynasty, they did know that Louis XVIII represented a great change from Bonaparte. France was accepted by the international European community, and, more important, the nation was finally at peace. Louis XVIII's predecessor, Louis XVI, had had many faults, but he had not been a warmonger, and furthermore taxes under the Bourbons had been considerably lower. Though the French might poke fun at a monarch obsessed by his clock collection, they could think of far more fatal passions. "Peace is the country's only desire. . . . By one final effort worthy of you, obtain that peace for yourself and the French people," the Senate had implored Bonaparte back in December 1813, in vain.[12] But the Corps Législatif had supported the Senate. "Commerce has been annihilated . . . industry is on its last legs. . . . What has been the cause of these unutterable woes?" Deputy Laîné had demanded angrily:

An overbearing government, overtaxation, the deplorable means applied in the collection of taxes, and even more cruel, the excesses of the system used for army recruitment. . . . Conscription has become an odious plague for the entire country. . . . For the past two years the men of this nation have been harvested three times a year. A barbarous and pointless war has been periodically fed by our youth, torn from their education, from agriculture, commerce, and the arts.

Laîné's motion to initiate peace talks had then won a sweeping majority vote of approval, 223 for, 51 against. "We want only one thing, peace," Senator Lapparent agreed. "It is the general cry of everyone, from every corner of the land."[13] "Do you really want me to tell you the unvarnished truth?" an exasperated Naval Minister Decrès had confided to Napoleon's protégé and former aide-de-camp Marshal Marmont. "The Emperor is crazy, completely insane, and is going to throw us over, landing us in an incredible catastrophe."[14] Of course the admiral's prediction had been borne out by the events of 1814.

Thus if Louis XVIII had not been cheered wildly by the majority of Frenchmen, at least no one had jeered. Moreover, he brought with him a "Constitutional Charter," or to be more accurate, seventy-four articles forced upon him by the victorious Allies bent on removing the traditional Bourbon dictatorial control over the country that had so incited the people leading to the Revolution in 1789, which in turn had unleashed its violent armies across Europe, ultimately resulting in Napoleon's appearance on the scene.

On June 4, 1814, Louis XVIII had signed the document theoretically creating a constitutional monarchy, with a permanent bicameral legislature, including a Chamber of Peers, or Senate, and a Chamber of Deputies. Slavery, which Napoleon had reintroduced, was again abolished. However, the former electorate of approximately five million of the Empire was now reduced to just ninety thousand, while only ten thousand persons were actually qualified to hold office because of the clause limiting eligibility to those paying high enough taxes. What is more, Roman Catholicism again became the official state religion.

When it came to the army, however, King Louis was in a bind, for he could find only a few dozen professional officers of aristocratic birth to assume command, thus forcing him to reemploy most of Napoleon's officer corps. General Dupont, of Bailén memory, was named the first war minister, later to be replaced by Marshal Soult and finally by Napoleon's own General Clarke. What is more, two of Napoleon's marshals had been named to command the king's personal six-thousand-man "Household Guard," none other than Marmont and Berthier.[15]

On March 5, learning of Napoleon's landing near Cannes, King Louis, in coordination with War Minister Soult, decided to launch three armies against the intruders.[16] Two of them would be commanded by King Louis's nephews. The duc d'Angoulême would form one around Nîmes with ten thousand men with which to pursue Napoleon, and the duc de Berry in the Franche-Comté would form another small one, while Marshal Soult was dispatched to Lyons to form a third corps of thirty thousand. None of these armies was fully established, due in part to mass desertions from the Royal Army, and in part as a result of the utter incompetence of the royal nephews, but in particular because of the even more disastrous inability of Soult, a professional soldier, to follow orders at Lyons, where thirty thousand men could easily have stopped and destroyed Napoleon's embryonic force. Indeed the only good news reaching Paris now was that two premature pro-Bonaparte military uprisings, by Generals Drouet d'Erlon and Lefebvre-Desnouëttes, were quickly put down in the north.

On learning of the fall of Grenoble and Lyons, the king ordered most of the Paris garrison to Villejuif and Melun, where the duc de Berry was reassigned as commander, with Macdonald serving as his deputy. As for Soult, he was denounced by the king's closest adviser and companion, the comte de Blacas d'Aulps, charging him with conspiring with Napoleon to overthrow the monarchy. Pouting, Soult resigned and stalked off in a huff. But in fact even Berry's new army was not taking shape, as desertions accelerated. A by-now-much-more-anxious King Louis had then also sent Marshal Ney to Lons-le-Saulnier to assemble the army Berry had failed to, the results of which Napoleon saw for himself at Auxerre by the seventeenth.

But on the stormy afternoon of the sixteenth, the king, still in blissful ignorance of Ney's betrayal, and despite a downpour, set off in a grand procession to the National Assembly to convene personally for the first (and last) time the new combined chambers. They proceeded in somewhat dampened magnificence attended by the comte d'Artois, the duc de Berry, the duc d'Orléans (the future Louis-Philippe), as well as the principal state and palace officials, in a stream of state carriages, preceded by cavalry units of the Paris National Guard and the king's famous musketeers in their glorious red-and-black uniforms.

At 4:00 P.M. the king's arrival was announced to the mighty of the land—"*Le Roi, Messieurs, le Roi*"—attended by trumpeters' fanfares as the king in all his grotesque enormity was helped to his throne. He then addressed the assemblage. "Gentlemen, in this moment of crisis . . . I come in your midst to draw close those ties uniting you to me. . . . I have seen my fatherland again, and I have reconciled it with all the foreign powers. . . . I have labored for the happiness of my people. . . . And now at the age of sixty, how could I better end my career than by dying in defense of my country." They must avert civil war and Napoleon's "iron yoke," he reminded them, for "he comes to destroy this constitutional Charter." The people had to act. "Then let us rally, gentlemen, let us rally around it [the charter]; let it be our sacred standard."[17] When the king waddled back to his coach, it was still pouring. Politics were still politics.

The moment he reached the Tuileries, and after receiving everyone's congratulations, his majesty was informed by a special messenger of Ney's defection. Summoning Gen. Nicolas Joseph Maison, the governor of the First Military District around Paris, along with General Dessolles, he informed them of the situation and ordered them to replace Soult and Ney at the head of new armies. Could he count on them? the king asked these two former Napoleonic officers warily? Of course, the shocked gentlemen reassured him, but, because they would be risking their necks in the event

Napoleon succeeded, they would first need a little insurance, say two hundred thousand francs each, in gold, in advance. At this stage nothing surprised the king anymore, and he consented. Maison left to rally the regular troops in the garrisons around Paris, while Dessolles called out the National Guard, even as War Minister Clarke assured his commanders that all was now well in hand and that all the damage done by Soult had been repaired. The *Journal des Débats,* however, surpassed even Clarke, informing the French populace that armies under General Marchand and Marshal Masséna had joined forces and had retaken Lyons. (Masséna of course had not even left Marseilles, while Marchand had returned to the Napoleonic fold.) In that same newspaper the pro-Bourbon liberal, Benjamin Constant, described Bonaparte as "this Attila, this Genghis Khan . . . this man stained with our blood."[18]

But with the quadruple failures of Berry, Angloulême, Soult, and Ney, no one took newspaper reports seriously any longer. As the upper bourgeoisie and the aristocracy hastened to the Hôtel des Postes to apply for their passports, a flow of carriages with encrusted crests on the door panels left the city for the northwest.

Back at the Tuileries, Treasury Minister Louis was arranging to transfer 25 million francs in silver from the capital, matched by an almost equal sum withdrawn by individuals from their banks. Then just to cap it all, on Saturday March 18, an irate Marshal Macdonald arrived most unexpectedly at the Tuileries, denouncing the interference and follies of the so-called commander at Villejuif and Melun, the Duc de Berry. Even for the phlegmatic king this was too much. He fired Berry on the spot and replaced him with Macdonald. As even the king's close adviser, the baron de Vitrolles, confessed, "the knell of our agony was ringing across the land." The king, now in a real panic, remained unable to make the decisions necessary—"a sort of paralysis set in," the baron admitted.[19]

By the following day there was pandemonium in the Tuileries, and although no one yet knew it, for he had refused to share this information with even the highest aristocrats of the land, the king had determined to flee the country, covering his tracks by scheduling a review of the Royal Household Guard at the Champ de Mars at noon. Ironically the only two people he did confide in were two Napoleonic officers, Marshals Berthier and Macdonald, not even his own war minister, however.[20]

The king set off for the review—it was raining again—but because of hostile crowds, he turned around and returned to the Tuileries, not even informing a rain-soaked Marmont, who was left waiting for him with thousands of troops. Later that evening the king's ministers were finally informed of his planned flight, agreeing to follow him—after each had received one hundred thousand francs in cash. Bidding adieu to his staff and capital, the King set out from the Tuileries just after midnight.²¹ It was March 20, the king of Rome's fourth birthday.

Fortunately the Allies, meeting at the Congress of Vienna since September 1814, had been a little more efficacious and organized than the Bourbon brothers, though not without some initial division. Convening as a result of the Treaty of Paris (May 30, 1814), the Congress had set out to settle the fate of Europe and its new frontiers, in an attempt to undo the confusion and damage done by Napoleon's conquests, various dethronements of rulers, and the redrawing of international frontiers, and to name new rulers and governments to replace some of the old. Indeed, one of their first decisions had been to recognize the return of the Bourbons to France and the dissolution of the former Napoleonic Empire. They also had to cope with the conflict between Prussia and Russia over the spoils, Saxony and Poland. Then of course there was the question of a newly independent combined state of Belgium and Holland.

The key individuals making these fateful decisions at Vienna were Lord Castlereagh, the British foreign secretary; Prince Klemens von Metternich representing Franz I of Austria; Karl August von Hardenberg, Prussia's King Friedrich Wilhelm III; and Count Nesselrode, Czar Alexander. France, although specifically excluded from participation in this Congress by the Treaty of Paris, was nevertheless represented by King Louis's new foreign minister, the ubiquitous Talleyrand. As another main purpose of this congress was to arrange French and European affairs in such a way as to preclude any future warlike activity on the part of the turbulent French, the Allies very nearly undid much, including their own coalition, by allowing Talleyrand's presence.

Talleyrand, who seemed to personify the most perverse traits of the traditionally perverse French when it came to international affairs, through his great intelligence, finesse, and skill was able to insinuate himself into a place at the negotiating table and then to set ally against ally. An unusually lax Castlereagh was equally responsible, by supporting Talleyrand, who succeeded in manipulating a nearly decisive division among France's foes by the drafting on January 3, 1815, of a secret Treaty of Alliance among Britain, France, and Austria. In theory a simple mutual defense pact, it was in fact aimed deliberately at the suspiciously vigorous expansionist policies of Czar Alexander, who had already swallowed up both Bessarabia and Finland. Britain protested against Prussia's desire to annex Saxony. "I confess little kindness for the King of Saxony," the prime minister confided to Lord Castlereagh, "but I do not wish to see the system of totally annihilating ancient States extended beyond what is necessary."[22] But at least the decision regarding the Low Countries was made in February 1815, transforming Prince William into King William of the Low Countries, thereby combining Holland, Belgium, and Luxembourg. France must never again be permitted to possess those countries, Castlereagh insisted.

Meanwhile Talleyrand played on Allied fears of a possible return of Napoleon. Bonaparte's "principles," he claimed, "must be expelled from Europe once and for all. . . . Yes, we have removed him from the battlefields, *mais il est au bout de notre lorgnette* [but he is still right under our noses]," he warned Prince von Schwarzenberg. "If they had listened to us," Castlereagh added, "he would have been deported 16,000 leagues from here." Or, as Talleyrand himself had earlier put it back in February 1814, "The evil never change their ways."[23]

The immediate result of Talleyrand's sinuous manipulations and subtle perversities alienated all the rest of the allies from Russia, without the czar even realizing it. "The Coalition is dissolved, and dissolved forever," Talleyrand assured Louis XVIII in January 1815.[24] But even the wily Talleyrand could make grievously wrong assessments of situations, and everything was suddenly and irretrievably altered on March 11 as Lord Clancarty, assisting Lord Wellington at Vienna, explained in an urgent message to Castlereagh:

> We were at Court the night of the arrival of Burghersh's dispatch, containing the news of Buonaparte's flight; and though there was every attempt to conceal apprehension under the masque of unconcern, it was not difficult to perceive that fear was predominant in all—[including] the Imperial and Royal personages there assembled. The overwhelming circumstances . . . [left nothing but] black and bloody prospects for the whole of Europe and any lasting peace.[25]

The congress acted swiftly. On March 13 all seven powers (including Russia, Spain, Portugal, and Sweden) signed a declaration outlawing Napoleon:

> In breaking the Convention which established him in the Isle of Elba, Bonaparte is destroying the sole legal title to which his existence is attached. In reappearing in France with projects of troubles and upsettings, he has deprived himself of the protection of the laws, and has

manifested in the face of the universe that it cannot have peace or truce with him. In consequence The Powers declare, that Napoleon Bonaparte is placed outside civil and social relations, and that as an enemy and disturber of the peace of the world, he has delivered himself over to public prosecution.[26]

The Allies, for all their disagreements with Russia, were quick to re-form their coalition—the seventh—and Talleyrand's scheme for its dissolution was foiled. Before closing the Congress of Vienna, "the Big Four"—Britain, Austria, Prussia, and Russia—signed the Treaty of Vienna on March 25, 1815, agreeing to quickly rally their armies until Bonaparte "be put absolutely beyond the possibility of exciting troubles."[27]

"If we are to undertake the job, we must leave nothing to chance," Castlereagh wrote Lord Wellington in Vienna. "It must be done upon the largest scale . . . you must inundate France with force in all directions. If Bonaparte could turn the tide, there is no calculating upon his plan." As for England, the foreign secretary continued on April 3, "there is no hesitation on the part of the Prince Regent's Government . . . in prosecuting the war against Napoleon . . . and will embark heartily in the contest . . . for the salvation of Europe." The Russians fully endorsed this determination, or as Nesselrode put it in an awkward phrase, half English, half French—"*C'est pour nous tous, le cas du* last shilling, [the] last drop of blood." They would spend every penny they had and fight to the last man.

"I have the honour to acquaint you," Lord Clancarty informed London, "that his Grace the Duke of Wellington set out this morning from Vienna, to take command of the army in the Low Countries."[28]

Meanwhile Napoleon, still living in his fantasy world and remaining blissfully ignorant of the hornets' nest he had stirred up (or, for that matter, what Marie-Louise had been doing in his absence), wrote to his wife on March 19 before setting out for Paris from Auxerre: "My good Louise, The people are running to me in droves. Entire regiments are quitting and joining me. . . . I shall be in Paris by the time you receive this letter. . . . Come and rejoin me with my son. I hope to embrace you before the month is out."[29]

"I wish to be less the sovereign of France and more the first of her citizens," Napoleon had declared at Lyons. "I am a product of the Revolution . . . [and] have come to free the French people from the enslavement in which the priests and nobles wanted to entrap them. . . . I shall hang the lot of them!" If this blatant rabble-rousing politicking did hoodwink tens of thousands of troops, not so the civilians. "If we are not careful, we shall see the same bloody scenes of 92 all over again," one prefect warned. "I am fearful of the upheaval threatening us, ready as it is to vomit forth terror and proscription over France yet again," an uneasy comte de Molé confided frankly to Napoleon. "It was sheer folly," Madame de Staël was to comment within a few weeks. "The moment we accepted Bonaparte, a return to dictatorship was inevitable."[30]

Such were some of the sentiments expressed as Napoleon's glorious cavalcade passed unchallenged through the suburbs, reaching Paris in the cold of night and crossing the Seine on the Pont Louis XV, the bridge's lamps casting a dull glow over the damp tricolor flags just erected there. Reaching the Tuileries, they passed under the arches of the Pavillon de Flore, clattering into the courtyard where units of National Guardsmen snapped to attention and a large crowd of officers, civilians, and dignitaries rushed over to the coach. "Seeing that he could advance no farther, the Emperor descended in the midst of the immense crowd, which quickly engulfed him," eyewitness Saint-Denis reported. But once inside and looking about these welcoming courtiers, what no doubt he noticed most were those of the faithful who were absent, including Berthier, Clarke, Jaucourt, and Talleyrand, all now attached to Louis XVIII's court at Ghent, but in particular, his marshals—Brune, St.-Cyr, Jourdan, Macdonald, Marmont, Soult, Augereau, Moncey, Mortier, Oudinot, and Suchet—the others too weak and ailing to be of use. And then there were the phantoms of another age who would never return: Duroc, Bessières, Poniatowski, Junot, and of course Lannes.

Nevertheless there were many familiar faces, not all of them of the first order, to be sure, including former Secretary of State Maret; Admiral Decrès, despite his sense of doom; Gaudin, the former finance minister; Treasury Minister Mollien; and the inimitable but much aged Cambacérès, who would agree to accept the one very sensitive portfolio in his new government that no one else would touch, that of justice. There was also Marshal Davout, the best commander he had ever had, but who would only grudgingly accept the War Ministry now, and of course, Caulaincourt, Lavalette, and a few others. But the vast majority were either over the border or on their estates in silent protest, demanding only to be left alone by Napoleon Bonaparte.

With Bertrand at his side, still serving as his grand marshal, after accepting the congratulations of the assemblage, Napoleon withdrew to begin organizing his new government. In addition to Maret, Decrès, Gaudin, Mollien, Cambacérès, and an extremely unhappy Davout, he gave Lavalette his old portfolio as postal minister and again named Caulaincourt to head the Foreign Office, despite the latter's request for an army command. Nor did anyone want the other sensitive portfolio, as interior minister. With his profession of a return to the principles of the Revolution, Napoleon needed someone with a sense of command and decision, a man who knew the workings of the government and whose name would silence any criticism from the left. The next day he was to summon a most wary Lazare Carnot, the very man who had denounced Napoleon's position as life consul and emperor, preferring the seclusion of his country house to that of participation in a dictatorship. Leaving the Tuileries afterward, the tough Carnot simply sighed, "At a time like this, one could refuse him nothing." If Carnot's nomination took everyone utterly by surprise, that of Napoleon's final appointment left them staggered: none other than the infamous Joseph Fouché, returning to the Police Ministry after years in the wilderness. "Thus the government was completed," ex-Chancellor Pasquier, no longer a participant and soon to be harried by Napoleon's police, concluded, "but not without very considerable difficulty."[31]

"I am a product of the Revolution," Napoleon repeated, and that was to be his theme as he promptly ordered all royalists to leave the French capital, Fouché issuing warrants for the arrest of Talleyrand, Montesquiou, La Rochefoucauld, Lynch, Bellard, Beurnonville, Jaucourt, and of course Marmont and the highly dangerous Bourrienne, ordering the seizure of their estates and wealth—although Bourrienne had never had anything to seize. Next Napoleon reintroduced slavery, while theoretically abolishing the press censorship he himself had earlier established. But when the royalists immediately unleashed a torrent of abusive anti-Bonapartist articles and propaganda, Napoleon grew uneasy, and the faithful General Hugo, whom Napoleon had so faithlessly fired years earlier over the Egyptian fiasco, protested, *malgré tout*: "Is it possible to so horribly outrage the great man!" And yet even within his own ranks, indeed even among his ministers, there was not only a singular lack of enthusiasm for the new enterprise but open doubt. "He is going to be up against the whole of Europe," Foreign Minister Caulaincourt confided to the former chancellor, Pasquier. "The Emperor is not in an enviable position," Michel St.-Jean d'Angély echoed.[32]

Despite the doubt and criticism he encountered, Napoleon was determined to play his last card, his claim of wishing to introduce the new "Liberal Empire." The onetime dictator had changed his proverbial spots: There would now be representative government and peace. "I should rather perish than fall into his hands," Benjamin Constant declared to his mistress, Juliette Récamier, after having openly attacked Napoleon in the columns of the *Journal de Paris*. "I shall not change and become a wretched turncoat, going about with hat in hand, from one régime to another. . . . Along with Marmont, Chateaubriand, and Laîné, I am now certainly one of the most compromised men in France." But when Bonaparte now summoned this selfsame gentleman to the Tuileries, he came away beaming. "What an amazing man he is!" he exclaimed to Recamier. "I am to bring him an outline for a new constitution!"[33] She and Chateaubriand were both aghast.

On April 19 Constant duly returned to the Tuileries with the draft of the new "Additional Act" to the Imperial Constitution. It called for the abolition of all press censorship, as well as any state religious affiliation. All conscription thereafter would have to be authorized by the chambers. Government ministers were to be given wider powers. The document did make a surprising number of concessions to Bonaparte, who would be allowed the right to continue to appoint all members of the hereditary Chamber of Peers, and the nation's judges, while also retaining the right unilaterally to prorogue and dissolve the chambers and to propose new legislation.

After completing his reading of the entire text of sixty-seven articles, an anxious Constant looked up to see Napoleon's reaction. Much to his surprise Bonaparte accepted the entire thing, Constant's "Benjamine," as it was soon dubbed by the royalists. Napoleon would now submit it to a new Constitution Committee for study. With a vigorous new step, Constant rushed off to Madame Récamier's boudoir to relate the good news.[34]

But immediately following Constant's departure, a furious Napoleon exploded to his secretary, Baron Fain: "They are pushing me in a direction I do not like. They are weakening me, tying my hands." The French people, he said, were asking what had become of "the Emperor's famous firm hand, which France needs now in order to master Europe again. They can talk to me all they want about their concepts of 'goodness,' 'abstract justice,' and 'the natural laws,' but the first real law is 'necessity,' while the most essential form of 'justice' is 'national safety.'"

"That man has learned nothing," Fouché commented, "and has returned as much of a despot, as keen on conquest, as insane as ever."[35]

Napoleon knew he needed a device by which to regain the support of the masses, and his new "republicanism" was just the thing. Naturally he confided nothing of this to the fundamentalist republican Carnot at the Interior Ministry, while publicly calling for a new national plebiscite to approve Constant's Additional Act. The results would be announced at an enormous rally, the "Champ de Mai" ceremony in Paris on May 26 (a date later changed to June 1). Postal Minister Lavalette, an intimate of the Bonaparte inner circle who knew Napoleon very well indeed, for one was not taken in by this little charade. "Do not rely on this liberal constitution, which he appears willing enough to give us today. Once at the head of a victorious army again, he will have soon forgotten it." A. N. de Salvandy fully agreed: "He has learned nothing, he has forgotten nothing."[36]

Next Napoleon went to work on the window dressing, calling for the convening of the electoral colleges to elect the new deputies to the Chamber of Representatives, while he ordered brother Joseph—who, like Lucien and Jérôme (but unlike Prince Eugène de Beauharnais), had most reluctantly returned to Paris—to draw up a list of 120 candidates for the proposed new Chamber of Peers, from whom Napoleon would select 80.[37] Between April 26 and 30, Bonaparte personally launched the national plebiscite, as his prefects went to every town and village of the realm to "count" the votes.

If Napoleon had somehow convinced himself that all would fall nicely into place again, with the country fully behind him, Caulaincourt, who had lectured him on the way back from Moscow to Paris in 1812, asked: "What direction is he heading in now? He does not even know himself.... He is entirely out of his depth. And why is he so blind to the fact that the only real feeling he inspires in the people is fear itself?"[38] Indeed there was much fear in the land, resulting in political instability, revolt, repression, and growing turmoil. Even Interior Minister Carnot was taken aback by the treasonous reports he was receiving from the nation's prefects, who governed with full powers in the country's provinces, Carnot finally forced to dismiss sixty-one of a total of eighty-seven of their number. Then, with ever-growing reports of revolt and discontent, he fired every mayor in the country, replacing them with his own men.

"The government's action here is entirely null and void," read the report of one southern prefect. "Everything is collapsing and falling into a state of anarchy."[39] At Aix-en-Provence, Marseilles, Bayonne, Versailles, and Amiens, official government decrees and proclamations were torn down, often replaced by royalist counterpropaganda. At Boulogne the white Bourbon flag was hoisted defiantly. "Down with the eagles! String up Napoleon! Up the royalists! Death to the Bonapartistes!" were heard and duly reported by prefects throughout the land. Even the headmasters of the few schools in the country, lycées that Napoleon had earlier created, reported open defiance of anything celebrating Napoleon, students adamantly refusing to cry out *"Vive l'Empereur!"* at school assemblies, knowing of course that they would soon be called up for national service once war resumed. Nor was it surprising that the numerous newly returned clergy, humiliated by Bonaparte for nearly fifteen years, now preached against him in just about every church of the land, and there was nothing the prefects could do about that. TWO MILLION FRANCS REWARD FOR ANYONE FINDING THE PEACE LOST ON 20 MARCH, read one poster boldly plastered on the very walls of the Tuileries Palace. Not only were the prefects, mayors, and schoolboys defying Paris, but in the capital itself the newly elected president of the Chamber of Representatives, the undaunted Laîné, openly called for his constituents not to heed Napoleon's new decrees or pay their imperial taxes.

But perhaps the greatest change to be found since Napoleon's return, and for him the most dramatic, was public attacks on the army, the very base of his power. Following Laîné's speech, two hundred rioting young army conscripts in Bordeaux were put down only at bayonet point. There and elsewhere officers were insulted in the streets and began to appear publicly more often in civilian disguise. In one case some citizens called up for temporary National Guard service opened fire on some regular army officers. Marshal Brune, the military governor in Provence, received death threats in the mail (he would later be murdered). At Lisieux one regimental colonel who refused to discard his uniform was seized by civilians and publicly horsewhipped. Some of his prefects, Carnot admitted, lacked "energy and firmness." But it was these very prefects and mayors who were ultimately responsible for issuing the call-up orders to the recruits for the new army Napoleon was forming. "All the reports received express the same apathy and ill-will on the part of the mayors," the war minister confirmed.[40]

Despite the early April reports by some prefects—"Fears of civil war in the West have now completely disappeared"; "Everywhere the people are happy"—massive unrest was in fact building. At the heart of the royalist rebellion about to break out were Louis, the marquis de La Rochejacquelein, and his brother, Auguste, with their headquarters at the family château at St.-Aubin de Baugîné. There their lieutenants—some of whom Napoleon had known as a student at the Ecole Militaire—came for their instructions, including d'Autichamp, Sapinaud, St.-Hubert, de Suzannet, Robert, the Charettes, La Salmonière, d'Andigné, and others. The entire region from Brittany to the Vendée was a virtual hotbed of rebellion, and this time well armed, with the support of the majority of the civil population behind them.

General Caffarelli was one of the first to report the gravity of the situation, sending a dispatch rider to War Minister Davout on April 16: "The revolt here will explode out of control if the remaining troops are withdrawn. Then instead we will need an entire army in Brittany." In fact, due to Napoleon's conviction that he remained the people's overwhelming choice, he had ordered almost all troops to be withdrawn from the provinces to form a part of his new army. He continued to turn a cold shoulder to such hysteria. Rebel attacks until this point—led by La Rochejacquelein, d'Autichamp, and Suzannet, for instance—had been small and scattered, the leaders deliberately holding off major operations throughout the western provinces until they could coordinate it with the expected Allied invasion in June. Meanwhile the British continued to land along the coast of Brittany almost with impunity, due to Napoleon's having put most ships in mothballs back in 1814.

Some of the royalist commanders would not wait for the big day, however, and began to launch serious attacks. "It's civil war just like '93 all over again!" a distraught General Charpentier reported. "The entire Department of Morbihan is in rebellion. "Rennes is being threatened. I am surrounded by ten thousand insurgents!" General Bigarré, no hysteric, warned from Brittany. "The country is in danger, discontent is general and continuing to spread in the provinces, as it is in Paris," Carnot himself personally alerted Napoleon. "Civil war is about to break out in several parts of the country."

It was not until the end of May, however, that Napoleon finally conceded that he had misjudged the situation in the West. He then ordered General Lamarque to form a special new army, including regiments of the "Young Guard," twenty-five battalions of infantry, eight squadrons of cavalry, and three artillery batteries—more than twenty thousand additional men—to march quickly to the aid of the various besieged garrisons, even as rebellion was spreading to Bordeaux and Provence. Ultimately Napoleon would be forced to leave 105,151 troops behind, occupying France.[41] By the end of May he not only had all of Europe against him but most of France as well.

Napoleon's almost-full-time preoccupation now was neither political reform nor the expanding civil war but the creation of his new army with which to confront the Allies. That he was successful in mobilizing and arming such a force so quickly, literally within less than three months, was thanks to the astonishing efforts of two men supremely suited to do just that: the forty-five-year-old Marshal Louis Davout, the duke of Auerstädt and prince of Eckmühl, and the sixty-two-year-old mathematician and republican turned imperial count, Lazare Carnot.

Born in 1772, the scion of minor Burgundian aristocracy, Louis Nicolas Davout entered the Ecole Militaire just as Napoleon was receiving his commission. Second Lieutenant Davout began his military career in 1788. He proved as brilliant a soldier as he had a scholar and rose quickly in the new revolutionary army. He was already a brigadier general in March 1798, when Gen. Louis Desaix introduced him to Major General Bonaparte, whose Egyptian expedition he then joined. In Egypt he proved to be the most effective field commander, inflicting the heaviest overall casualties on the Mamelukes.

Participating in most of Napoleon's subsequent campaigns, he continued to distinguish himself time and again, the one senior commander who always executed his orders, and was on the initial list to receive a marshal's baton in 1804. He singlehandedly defeated the Prussians at Auerstädt and performed superbly again at the Battle of Eckmühl (though a jealous Napoleon withheld the peerages due for those victories for several years).

A grim and sometimes brutal commander, the brilliant Davout was one of the very few general officers who proved impeccably honest. In addition he was a superb administrator, resulting in Napoleon's naming him military governor of the Grand Duchy of Warsaw. Following the Russian debacle, he continued in that capacity at Hamburg over the Hanseatic cities, and ultimately was the last French commander to hold out against the Allies.

In consequence Davout's nomination as war minister in 1815 had caused many a raised eyebrow and was criticized in military circles then and ever after. Napoleon badly needed Davout at the head of one of his wings in June 1815 and was to suffer grievously for having made yet another wrong decision. On the other hand, because of General Clarke's and Marshal Berthier's defections to the royalist cause, Napoleon appeared to have no other senior general as capable and as reliable as Davout, nor one with his detailed knowledge of the workings of the French army. Carnot no doubt would have done an equally good job if he had not been out of the army and office since the Consulate. It would have taken too long to bring him up to date, and Napoleon had not a day to spare.

As for Carnot himself: The son of a prosperous Burgundian notary, born at Nolay in 1753, he was educated first at the Collège d'Autun and next at the seminary in that same city. After two years' study of artillery and engineering in Paris, Carnot completed his preparation at the famous Mézières engineering school, from which he graduated in January 1773 with the rank of lieutenant. But because he could not establish noble birth, he was not permitted to rise above the rank of captain, which helped turn him against the Bourbons. As a member of the National Convention he voted for the execution of Louis XVI and Marie Antoinette. In fact he became a fanatical supporter of the Revolution and served as one of the members of the hated Committee of Public Safety in 1793, where he was responsible principally for reorganizing the army, thereby making possible significant victories in the field, for which he was ever after known to the nation as "the Organizer of Victory."

Trained as an engineering officer, Carnot became a specialist in the designing of fortifications, over which he often clashed with General Bonaparte, who thought his own views superior. Carnot also was a brilliant mathematician and an active member of the Institute's Academy of Science.

Forced to flee arrest and deportation in 1797, Carnot returned to France only following Napoleon's coup d'état in November 1799, the first consul appointing him inspector general of military reviews and then war minister, in which post he quickly established a reputation as a most effective (and honest) administrator. But for Bonaparte, Carnot remained a problem, and his jealousy of the independent, mule-headed Carnot's views and mathematical abilities, added to his fundamentalist revolutionary principles, led to a parting of the ways, especially after Carnot rebuked him for his dictatorial and hereditary leadership. "I shall vote against the reestablishment of monarchy in any form," he had told the first consul to his face. Carnot retired to the provinces, and although he was a member of the Tribunate from 1802 until it was dissolved in 1807, he never again served Bonaparte directly in any capacity. Unlike just about every other high official, Carnot was devoted to his wife, and they spent their last years together, she dying, however, before Napoleon's return to France. "Monsieur Carnot, I really got to know you far too late," Bonaparte later admitted at Saint Helena.[42]

If Lazare Carnot was thus very much out of touch with the army and its administration by the spring of 1815, he could organize the nation's material resources and draft the men needed for the army. Thus Carnot, Davout, and Napoleon formed a bizarre, if powerfully effective, triumvirate in mobilizing the country for war.

Bonaparte made an attempt through Foreign Minister Caulaincourt to contact the various capitals of Europe, hoping somehow to delay the Allied armies from marching against France, but it was quite in vain. Nevertheless it had almost worked, when on taking over foreign affairs Caulaincourt discovered the secret treaty signed by Britain, France, and Prussia back in January. Taking advantage of this explosive document, he immediately revealed it to the Russians, who—though greatly upset about this anti-Russian plot—nonetheless remained even more furious with this Napoleon, who had destroyed their cities, burned their land, and slaughtered their people. The czar thus agreed to continue to support the Seventh Coalition in its determination to attack and destroy Bonaparte and the French army.

Money was always a problem, and now Napoleon found only 50 million francs in the treasury. His budget back in 1812, for instance, had reached

876,000,000 francs, but 226,389,000 francs of that had come from forced
annual war contributions extorted from the occupied states all over Europe.
That money had stopped, of course, in 1813.[43]

Napoleon took ruthless action. He had already put the entire French
fleet into mothballs, leaving only five ships of the line (out of nearly one
hundred), transferring their officers and men to the army and the navy's
budget to the army's budget. As he informed an incredulous Admiral
Decrès, "So long as this crisis lasts, it really does not matter whether or not
we have a navy."

Where was he to get the many hundreds of millions he needed to raise
overnight? Amazingly, the much abused Ouvrard offered a loan of 40 million, and Finance Minister Gaudin promised another 150 million franc loan
for the government. Gaudin thought another 240 million could be raised
through revenue gradually due the government over the next several
months. Treasury Minister Mollien next offered to produce 440 million in
"extraordinary revenue" by selling the remainder of state and communal
property, state forests, and cut timber, and through the reintroduction of
his special war tax, the "*centimes de guerre*." But when that minister
attempted to obtain "patriotic offers," as Napoleon had most successfully
done for the creation of the invasion flotilla back in 1803–5, it proved a
colossal flop. So desperate was Bonaparte that the lycée students of Grenoble were *ordered* to send Paris 400 francs; those of Nancy, 500; the Collège
de France another 1,500; and Monge's Ecole Polytechnique yet another
4,000. One aging war veteran offered his year's pension of 1,081 francs, and
the police prefect of Paris came up with 20,000 (its source undisclosed).[44]
And thus the process worked, Napoleon forced to steal schoolboys'
allowances in order to buy bayonets.

Carnot and Davout also got the arsenals working overtime, to provide
three hundred thousand muskets "in the shortest time possible." The muskets were finally produced, and some army recruits did arrive, but they
could not be outfitted. "I have 100,000 men at the induction centers whom I
cannot even use because of the lack of funds with which to clothe and equip
them," Bonaparte complained to Mollien, ordering him "to work day and
night" to get the job done.[45]

Mobilizing the necessary troops proved an even bigger task. On March
26 Napoleon had ordered the creation of eight new army corps, and by
June he envisaged a regular standing army of 300,000 men. An additional
112,000 men could be found by drafting "former soldiers" (mostly deserters
from 1814). But the 120,000 recruits—chiefly teenagers—from the 1815
conscription lists fizzled, and the figure revised downward to 85,000 men.

He needed 40,000 men for the newly promoted Marshal Grouchy's cavalry—Grouchy a second-rate replacement for Murat, whom Napoleon understandably refused even to see. Carnot promised a *levée en masse* that would raise 2.5 million men, including 234,000 National Guardsmen initially. But by June only 90,000 had materialized, and only 52,500 former soldiers could actually be rounded up. Of the 445,800 men promised by Napoleon's minister, only 142,500 ultimately appeared by June. With these added to men already serving, Napoleon had a grand total of 284,000 men under arms, but with 105,000 of these needed to put down French national uprisings, he was in fact left with a mere 179,000 with which to face several hundred thousand Allied troops, and of course some would have to be left to defend the frontiers.

With news of more and more Allied army units assembling under Wellington, and of the approaching Austrian forces to the south and east, and of course the Prussians, followed by the Russians, Caulaincourt's anxieties seemed to sum up the situation: "What will be the outcome of this terrible war into which he is leading us?" he asked his old friend Pasquier. "The most valiant generals are themselves afraid, and upon seeing the approach of hostilities the nation will take fright and turn against him [Napoleon]."[46]

But Napoleon would show them yet. He could do it, and the "Champ de Mai" ceremony now about to take place on June 1 was intended to stir every male citizen to his patriotic duty. Moreover, the Bonaparte family was back at his side, at least part of it, including Joseph and Julie, Madame Mère, Hortense, a pouting Jérôme, a wary Lucien after an absence of eleven years, and Uncle Fesch, who had been brought to France by a French warship on May 26. Murat and Caroline, however, were not allowed by Napoleon to come to Paris, following King Joachim's little stunt back in Italy. (At Rimini on March 30, 1815, Murat had suddenly proclaimed Italian independence, reserving the entire peninsula for himself. After being routed from Occhiobello by the Austrians that April, ending in his final defeat at Tolentino in May, the Murats had fled the country. Once in France, they were informed they had to stay out of harm's way, Napoleon indicating the region between Lyons and the Alps as their abode. Disregarding his instructions, they chose the Riviera.)[47] The most glaring absence, causing considerable comment, however, was that of Empress Marie-Louise and the king of Rome.

Police Minister Fouché estimated the crowd assembled on the vast acres of the Champ de Mars before the Ecole Militaire at a couple of hundred thousand, while hundreds more filled boats and barges in the Seine, across from the sharply rising right bank, where Napoleon had earlier planned to build a palace for his son. The ministers, five hundred electoral college delegates, peers, representatives, members of the Institute, distinguished professors, mayors, and commanding officers were all gathered together once again in their splendid array of uniforms and colors. At 11:00 A.M. sharp a thundering explosion stopped all talk as one hundred cannon along the Seine near the Tuileries and another five hundred at the Ecole Militaire, the Invalides, atop Montmartre, and at distant Vincennes left eardrums numb and the very land beneath their feet rolling. For a few moments all those civilians present were given their first inkling of what it might possibly be like on a battlefield, but now only to announce the departure of the emperor from the Tuileries, preceded by his Polish Red Lancers and the Imperial Guard.

The overcast skies soon gave way to a sunny, in fact broiling, day, as the procession of state coaches, including Napoleon's refurbished 1804 coronation carriage, reached the special Scandinavian-style stands built by the imperial architect, Pierre Fontaine. The purpose of this extraordinary gathering was in theory to announce the results of the constitutional plebiscite, but in reality to show the world that Napoleon was back at the helm and that nothing had changed. But of course everything had changed very much, for these very Parisians had also witnessed the vast armies of the triumphant Coalition recently parading in this very field and then had briefly glimpsed the results of peace, freedom, and the end of mass conscription. What is more, although Joseph, Lucien, and Jérôme were now back at Napoleon's side, they looked tense and peeved, as did the five marshals who had agreed to serve on the forthcoming campaign—Davout, Grouchy, Mortier, Ney, and Soult. Seven additional marshals had reluctantly consented to make a brief appearance for old time's sake before retreating quickly to their estates and seclusion—Jourdan, Kellermann, Lefebvre, Masséna, Moncey, Oudinot, and Sérurier—and they now deliberately separated from the rest. As for the absent sixty-one-year-old Marshal Berthier, that very afternoon he was climbing the tower of his castle in Bamberg, Germany, about to leap to his death.

Perhaps the greatest symbol of the change, however, was Napoleon himself, who looked ten years older since his attempted suicide just over a year ago, his pronounced paunch nearly bursting the resewn buttons on his coronation costume, first worn more than a decade earlier. He was wheezing, and saliva occasionally was seen on his lips, and the face of this forty-five-year-old retread emperor was rounder than last remembered, as he sweated under the heavy robes.

At last the ceremony began, late as usual, with only an occasional *"Vive l'Empereur!"* despite the patriotic music filling the air. Welcoming Napoleon, the spokesman for the electoral delegates announced that "a new contract has been formed between the nation and Your Majesty," a new "tablet of laws." Then he criticized the impending invasion threatened by the Allies—"But what do all these Allied kings want with us ... drawn up for a war that so astounds Europe and afflicts humanity?"—and continued with his speech, which had been carefully vetted and rewritten by Cambacérès and Jean-Antoine Chaptal, leading to the purpose of this discourse—"If they force us to fight, then let one great cry resound in every heart. Let us march on the enemy!" There it was, the ultimate reason for the assembly: a pep rally for the war. "Every Frenchman is a soldier," he concluded. "Victory will follow our eagles!"[48]

The results of the great national plebiscite on the Additional Act to the Imperial Constitution were announced: 1,532,357 votes for, only 4,802 votes against, out of more than 5 million electors. 99.993 percent of the votes cast, for Napoleon.[49] The usual remarkable results ...

Napoleon then addressed those present: "As Emperor, Consul, Soldier, I owe everything to the people. In prosperity, adversity, on the battlefield, before the council, on the throne, in exile, France has been the sole and constant object of my thoughts and actions." He had "sacrificed" himself, he said, in exchange for "a long era of peace." But the unjust Allies would not permit the French to live in peace, the foreign kings saying that they wanted only Napoleon out of the way, when in fact "it is this country they really want, and not just me, otherwise I would gladly give myself up to them." But so long as "the French people continue to manifest the many examples of their love for me, the rage of the enemies will be rendered harmless."[50]

There was fairly loud applause, mainly from the thousands of troops, with cries of *"Vive l'Empereur!"* but clearly the crowd remained anxious and withdrawn. The speech had lacked the old stirring spark. He then took the oath, before the archbishop of Bourges, "to observe the constitutions of the Empire," all the new state officials following suit. The Te Deum was chanted and the imperial eagles of the National Guard, navy, and army units passed in review, thousands strong.

Following that, Napoleon then crossed the field to a large platform in the middle of the troop formation and addressed the men: "I hereby confide the eagle to the national colors. Do you swear to perish if need be in the defense of the nation? Do you swear to die rather than allow them [foreign troops] to come and dictate their laws to us?" *"Nous le jurons!"* "We swear it!" came the response like a deafening thunderclap, followed by salvos of *"Vive l'Empereur! Vive l'Empereur!"* It was electrifying. Napoleon had finally roused them. "It is impossible to describe its magnitude," English eyewitness John Cam Hobhouse, remarked, duly impressed by the spectacle.[51]

Throughout the remaining few days Napoleon was preoccupied with war preparations, and having reinstated Marshal Soult in May, appointed him Berthier's replacement as chief of staff. On Sunday, June 11, Napoleon's last full day in Paris, he received a delegation from the combined chambers at the Tuileries, these chambers that Gen. Gilbert de Lafayette had dubbed "the Napoleon Club." "I shall be leaving tonight to join and lead my armies," he informed them in the magnificent Hall of the Marshals. "In all my undertakings my step will be firm and straight. Help me now save the country."[52]

After ordering Marshal Ney to meet him at his field headquarters at Avesnes on the fourteenth, Napoleon convened his final Council of Ministers in the throne room to instruct them that they, in the presence of *"notre frère le prince Joseph,"* and seconded by "Prince Lucien," would be responsible for governing in his absence.

Back in his apartments that evening brother Joseph handed Napoleon eight hundred thousand francs' worth of diamonds, just in case (Pauline had earlier given him one of her necklaces worth three hundred thousand francs). Then after sending final notes—along with a large cache of arms— to two of his former mistresses who had borne him sons, Mesdames Pellapra and Walewska, preceded by his Red Lancers and a four-hundred-man Imperial Guard escort, Napoleon's famous green-and-yellow berlin clattered out of the courtyard of the Tuileries, taking the road north for Soissons—and his last campaign.[53]

"To Conquer or Perish"

*Once it has been decided to fight, one should do so to the
very end, to conquer or perish.*

s Napoleon was moving north to assume command of his
army, the Allies were very slowly putting their own plans
into effect for a second invasion of France. Wellington with
a theoretical force of 92,300 men was to drive south via
Mons as Blücher's 130,200 Prussians simultaneously
attacked from the east through Charleroi and Maubeuge,
while 168,000 Russian troops crossed the frontier east of the Moselle and
Metz, marching for Nancy; and finally 225,000 Austrians under Schwarzenberg would be attacking between the Russians and the Rhine, with the
remainder of their force invading France from Switzerland (37,000 men)
and Italy (60,000 men).

By mid-June, however, the Prussians were just leaving the regions
around Koblenz and Liège, while Schwarzenberg's principal force was still
extended on the eastern banks of the Rhine from Mannheim down to the
Swiss frontier facing General Rapp's meager 23,000 men on the opposite
shore around Strasbourg. Opposing the Swiss force, Napoleon had only
Lecourbe's 8,400 troops, while farther to the south the Austrian army
under Frimont was advancing against Suchet's and Brune's combined force
of just under 30,000 men. Counting every man from Toulon to the frontier,

Napoleon had 179,000 men facing a total of about 719,000 allies, a force 74 percent greater than his own, a disparity he was probably not aware of.

Back on June 7 Napoleon had told the French army that they "must be prepared to die rather than survive and see France degraded and dishonoured,"[1] and he at least was prepared to do just that, although lacking the numbers he had counted on. In fact his own immediate army theoretically totaling 128,000 was reduced slightly to 122,652 men, comprised by four infantry corps: General Drouet d'Erlon's I Corps, Reille's II, Vandamme's III Corps, Gérard's IV, Lobau's VI, and finally Marshal Mortier's newly reconstituted Imperial Guard.

Bonaparte left Paris June 12, traveling northward via Soissons, Laon, and Avesnes, reaching Beaumont just on the French side of the frontier on the fourteenth. Although Ney failed to appear, Napoleon summoned his obsequious but crafty new chief of staff, Marshal Soult, and dictated his marching orders for what he anticipated to be a lightning drive toward Brussels, with the intention of separating and attacking individually Wellington's Anglo-Dutch Army and Blücher's Prussians. As for the Austrians, he hoped they would wait their turn. Napoleon's army included 21,600 cavalry and 101,000 infantry, with 358 pieces of ordnance.[2]

Between 2:30 A.M. and 8:00 A.M. on June 15 the offensive was set to begin: General Vandamme's III corps was to lead a central column northward followed by Lobau's men, the Imperial Guard's "Young Guard," and the remainder of Grouchy's reserve cavalry. At the same time a left column would set out for Charleroi along the west bank of the Sambre River, including General Reille's corps, with orders to secure Marchienne as Drouet d'Erlon's corps marched on Thuin on the east bank. At the same time Gérard was to head a right column advancing on Charleroi from Philippeville.

But no sooner had Napoleon given the orders than Marshal Adolphe Mortier, commanding the Imperial Guard, was immobilized by sciatica at Beaumont, to be replaced by his second-in-command, Comte Antoine Drouot (not to be confused with General Drouet, Comte d'Erlon, commanding I Corps). Soult, who had bungled campaigns before, and most recently in Spain, made the blunder—and one can only presume it was deliberate—of sending only one set of orders to each of the corps commanders. Napoleon invariably sent at least two different messengers to each one in the event of some mishap, especially when traveling through unknown fields in the dark of night in potentially hostile territory. Thus the messenger dispatched ordering Vandamme to lead the attack did not reach his headquarters until 5:00 A.M., only to find Vandamme not there. The aide-de-camp sent after him was then crushed by his horse when it fell in the dark, leaving him unconscious. And thus Vandamme was still ignorant of events when he returned, only to learn of the marching orders when he found Lobau's VI Corps marching up the road behind his encampment. Napoleon's entire invasion plan was thrown into chaos and hours behind schedule. Lobau had to stop in his tracks with the road before him blocked, while a cursing Vandamme set his men out on the double, causing an immense traffic jam for the sixty thousand men of the central column, backing up many miles, not to mention all the caissons, artillery limbers, and thousands of horses congesting the road as far as Charleroi. So great was the confusion that it spilled over to the right column under Gérard also marching on Charleroi, but now forced to seek an alternative bridgehead over the Sambre at Châtelet, to the east. Only the left column under Reille and d'Erlon reached its objective, though delayed by most unexpected Prussian resistance.

Charleroi was not even secure when Bonaparte reached it at noon on the fifteenth, Vandamme ultimately arriving five hours late, three hours after Napoleon. The Army of the North was off to a bad start, thereby signaling the Prussians in that sector of this surprise attack. And then just to ensure that result, General Bourmont, attached to Napoleon's army, went over to the enemy with his entire campaign plans. He did not "want to help establish a bloody despotism in France," Bourmont said in a note he left behind. Fortunately for Napoleon, when Bourmont's information was passed on to the Prussian I Corps commander near Charleroi, General Ziethen, he cast such aspersions on any turncoat that he did not bother to transmit this valuable piece of intelligence to Marshal Blücher's headquarters until 1:30 that afternoon, when it was already too late.[3]

The one good thing to happen at Charleroi that afternoon was the belated arrival of a sultry Marshal Ney at 3:30. "Hello, Ney," a relieved but cool Bonaparte greeted him, ordering him to take command of Drouet d'Erlon's and Reille's corps, as well as the Guard's light cavalry. Tomorrow he would be joined by Kellermann's cuirassiers. For now he was to push the enemy up the road toward Brussels and take up a position at Quatre-Bras. These instructions, mentioned in just a few moments, were to affect the outcome of the entire campaign. Ney, whom Napoleon privately derided as "brave and nothing more ... good at leading 10,000 men into battle, but other than that ... a real blockhead," had just been handed command of half Napoleon's entire army. Ney for his part, usually so energetic and decisive, had been unable to make up his mind about joining Bonaparte. In the end, however, he had decided to throw in his lot with the Army of the North, giving Napoleon his second marshal in the field, three counting Soult, out of the surviving twenty-three marshals he had created.

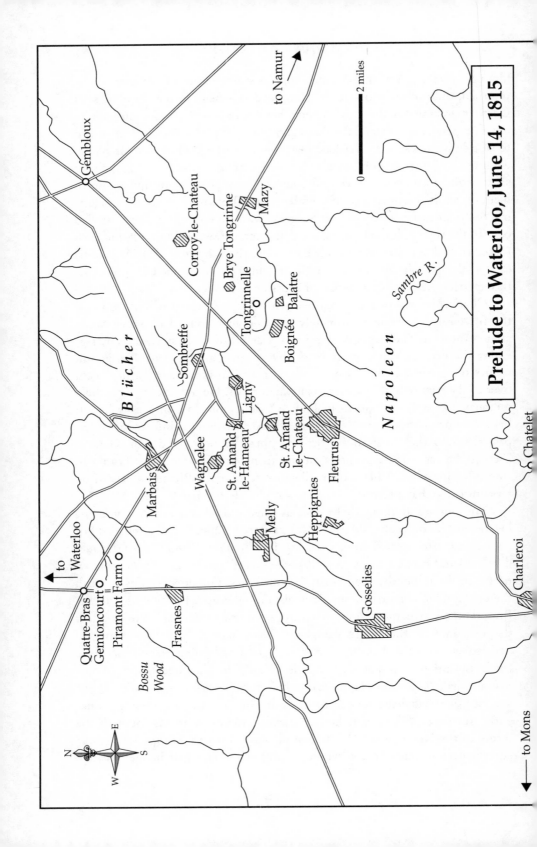

Prelude to Waterloo, June 14, 1815

(This for instance compared with the ten he had during the Russian Campaign.) For the simple Ney, it was a decision he would soon regret most bitterly, his hesitancy over the next few days reflecting his own real qualms. As Ney went to take command of Drouet d'Erlon's and Reille's corps, Napoleon made another decision that he was soon to regret, giving Grouchy a marshal's baton and the command of the right column or wing of his army, over the vociferous protests of its two corps commanders, Vandamme and Gérard, who detested Soult just as much.

Field Marshal Prince Gebhard Leberecht Blücher von Walstadt—"Old Marshal Forward March," as his troops called him—a native of Rostock, who was again commanding the Prussian force—was surprisingly active for a soldier of seventy-three who had experienced many a bloody battle, including several nasty defeats at the hands of this same Napoleon. His army, the result of the major reorganization and new training program introduced years earlier, following Prussia's initial defeat by the French, now comprised four corps: Lieutenant General Ziethen's I Corps, Major General Pirch's II, Lieutenant General Thielmann's III Corps, and Graf Bülow von Dennewitz's IV Corps.[4] Blücher's quartermaster-general and chief of staff, Lieutenant General Graf von Gneisenau, was a very capable man, though not always on the best of terms with some of the corps commanders, while serving on the staff of Thielmann's III Corps was an unknown but highly observant colonel by the name of Carl von Clausewitz.

The smaller Anglo-Dutch Army, in reality left its commander in chief, Field Marshal Arthur Wellesley, Duke of Wellington, with only 69,000 infantry and 14,500 cavalry, only a third of them British. It was hardly a brilliant army, including an inexperienced young Prince of Orange (a political necessity), commanding I Corps. The able lieutenant general, the earl of Uxbridge, headed the small, predominantly British cavalry corps, and Lieutenant General Lord Hill commanded Wellington's own Reserve Corps. Altogether the British government had provided Wellington with only 27,985 men, or one-third of his new army.[5]

The forty-six-year-old Wellington had a superb reputation after vanquishing Marshals Jourdan, Kellermann, Marmont, Mortier, Ney, Soult, and Victor during the Peninsular campaign, even the defeated General Foy comparing him to "our great Turenne." For all that, however, Wellington had encountered one obstacle after another from London as a result of the political tug-of-war between Tories and Whigs.

After his arrival at Brussels from the Congress of Vienna on April 11, he had requested a *minimal* British force of 55,000 men (including infantry and cavalry) and moreover had specifically asked that he be sent as many of his 47,000 Peninsular Army veterans as possible. Although the Tory prime minister, Lord Liverpool—Robert Bank Jenkinson—apparently did his best against formidable opponents, including the Royal Family, others in authority balked. The incompetent commander in chief of the entire British army, Frederick, duke of York, resented this Wellington who had achieved in the field what he had singularly failed to do. And it was York who decided what forces were to be sent his subordinate. When Wellington again asked him to send and promote a list of his veteran officers from Iberia, York snarled at him, "The power of appointment to commission is not invested in you." "I am overloaded with people [officers] I have never seen before," Wellington complained to the secretary of war, Lord Bathurst, "and it appears to be purposely intended to keep those out of my way whom I wish to have."

The result was hardly encouraging. "I have got an infamous army. . . . In my opinion they are doing nothing in England," Wellington summed up his new Anglo-Belgian-Dutch army in a private letter to Lord Stewart. Ending up with about half the small force of British soldiers he had requested, he would be largely dependent on foreign troops, the newly created army of the new King William of the Netherlands, which was riddled with officers and troops strongly sympathetic to memories of the former Grande Armée and to its leader. What is more, King William's choice of war minister could not have been worse: General Janssens, who had fought *against* the British in South Africa and Java, and made no secret of his open hostility to Wellington. In a real crisis, in the heat of battle, all would ultimately depend on fewer than 28,000 British troops, most of whom had never been under fire before, whereas the majority of Napoleon's army was comprised of veterans of several campaigns. The Allies might boast to the world of having theoretically fielded 715,000 men or so, but they were not present in Belgium now.

Napoleon simply dismissed his opponent, this Wellington born in the same year as himself, with a mocking smirk and dismissive wave of the hand as "a mere Sepoy general."* A good commander studies his opposition; Napoleon could not be bothered. The English and Wellington were not worth the trouble. For all those defeats at this same soldier's hands in Iberia, Napoleon had learned nothing.

All was quiet in Wellington's headquarters in Brussels on June 15, when around three o'clock in the afternoon three dispatch riders pulled up

---

*A sepoy was an Indian soldier.

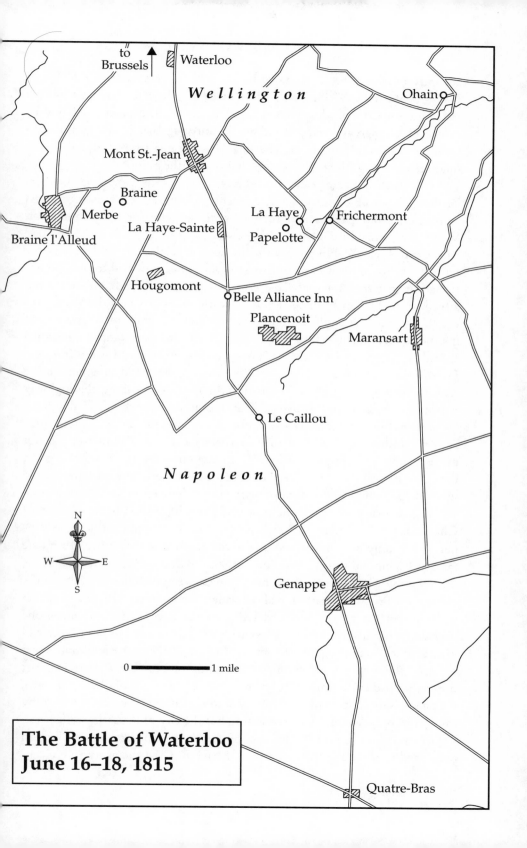

to
Brussels

Waterloo

Wellington

Ohain

Mont St.-Jean

Braine

Merbe

La Haye

Papelotte

Frichermont

Braine l'Alleud

La Haye-Sainte

Hougomont

Belle Alliance Inn

Plancenoit

Maransart

Le Caillou

Napoleon

N
W E
S

Genappe

0 ▬▬▬▬ 1 mile

Quatre-Bras

The Battle of Waterloo
June 16–18, 1815

abruptly outside. The first one rushed in with a message from Blücher at Namur, informing Wellington of the attack at Charleroi and that he was moving his general headquarters to Sombreffe. The next one came from the prince of Orange at Braine-le-Comte, confirming that heavy gunfire had been heard around Charleroi. The final report came from Ziethen's head-quarters repeating Blücher's—*eleven hours* after the event.[6]

The British were caught completely unawares, because General Ziethen, responsible for the southern sector, had been lax in posting pickets and sending out patrols and then in notifying the foreign commander, Wellington, when he did have vital news.

In any event Wellington, who had been expecting an attack along the most direct route from Paris to Brussels, via Mons, now had to obtain con-firmation that the attack at Charleroi was not just a feint. He could not afford to move men from such widely scattered points until he knew pre-cisely, and thus he could do little over the next several hours, apart from instruct all commanders to move their troops to prearranged divisional assembly points, to be ready to move quickly when word came through. He ordered Orange's I Corps to Nivelles, Enghien, and Soignies, rather than to secure Quatre-Bras, the main crossroads controlling the highway between Charleroi and Brussels. This meant that much of Wellington's force would be too far away to support any action taking place at Quatre-Bras the following day. And then, curiously enough, Wellington did not prevent most of his senior officers from attending a supper and ball given that very night by his good friend and aide-de-camp, General Lennox, the duke of Richmond, and indeed prepared to go there himself.

The reports confirming the powerful French position in the vicinity of Charleroi finally reached Wellington later that evening at the duchess's sup-per. It was only now he learned that in the absence of the Prince of Orange (also at Richmond's now), his Chief of Staff, Baron de Constant Rebecque, uneasy about the immense unmanned gap between Nivelles and Sombreffe, the nearest Prussian position, had overruled Wellington's orders and at two o'clock that afternoon had ordered General Perponcher to move one brigade to occupy the critical crossroads at Quatre-Bras.[7] Even as the ele-gant couples were preparing to set out for the duchess of Richmond's that evening, these men were clashing with some of Ney's initial troops, just down the road at the hamlet of Frasnes. While the prince of Orange danced, Constant Rebecque reinforced the position with another brigade, thereby saving not only Wellington's reputation but the city of Brussels itself.

"Napoleon has humbugged me, by God!" an embarrassed Wellington exclaimed to the duke of Richmond. "I have ordered the army to concentrate at Quatre-Bras."[8] And by 7:00 A.M. the next morning, June 16, Wellington and his staff officers were heading south under lowery skies, reaching Quatre-Bras at 10:00 A.M. After studying the situation and the latest reports, the Duke turned east to confer with *"Alter Vorwärts"* Blücher at the hamlet of Byre, near Sombreffe.

"There are systems one applies on the battlefield," Napoleon explained at Charleroi, "just as when laying siege to a fortress, and in this case it means concentrating all one's firepower on a single point," the road from Charleroi north, where the two allied armies joined—"attacking the central position," he called it.[9] It sounded good, but half of "the system" would not apply now because instead of having a concentrated army to destroy, Napoleon was to discover Wellington's army scattered irregularly in more than twenty separate places, from Brussels westward across to Ghent, from Nivelles to Oudenaarde, from Mons to Tournai. The English were not very logical.

That was not the only setback now. Both Ney and Grouchy had ignored their orders, and instead of advancing on the double—Ney due north from Charleroi toward Quatre-Bras and Grouchy coming up the road to the large village of Fleurus to face the Prussians round Sombreffe—by nightfall on the fifteenth both wings of the French Army of the North were far from their objectives.

Ney was surprised to encounter Wellington's forces at 5:30 P.M., when he repulsed the Nassau battalions near Frasnes, south of Quatre-Bras. But although Ney's two corps had some 44,500 men, and had only two enemy battalions opposing him, nevertheless he stopped dead in his tracks and would not budge. Thus Orange was permitted to reinforce his hold on the critical Quatre-Bras crossroads with a mere 8,050 men. Ney even dropped back, his left wing camping for the night between Marchienne and Gosselies. The usually vigorous Ney was suddenly cautious, hesitant, indecisive, already regretting having volunteered to join Napoleon on this campaign. In any event the previously clear open road to Brussels was now blocked, with more troops pouring in.

Reassessing the situation early on the morning of the sixteenth, Napoleon issued new instructions. "I am moving Marshal Grouchy's 3rd and 4th Infantry Corps up against Sombreffe," he informed Ney, and "I am taking my [Imperial] Guard to Fleurus where I shall arrive before noon . . . and then clear the road [of the Prussians] as far as Gembloux." Unfortunately, having heard nothing to the contrary, Napoleon thought Ney was in possession of Quatre-Bras, and ordered his left wing, theoretically in place there to "start marching for Brussels this evening [to arrive] there at seven o'clock tomorrow morning. I shall support you with the Guard ... and hope to arrive there myself tomorrow just after you." Thanks to Ney's silence, Napoleon, knowing nothing of the Allied seizure of Quatre-Bras, continued, issuing instructions to Grouchy: "If the enemy is at Sombreffe, I want to attack him. Indeed, I want to attack him even if he is beyond at Gembloux, securing that position as well.... Therefore, *do not lose a moment*... [and] keep the road open [to Fleurus] for me. The Prussians certainly cannot muster more than 40,000 men," he closed. As usual, Napoleon's almost nonexistent intelligence of either the enemy's strength or positions was to recoil on him with a shock. It had happened throughout his career, during the two Italian campaigns, at Wagram, at Eylau, during the campaign of 1812. The final instructions simply stated that the Imperial Guard would be held in the rear, to be able to reinforce either wing, as events required.[10]

On reaching Saint-Amand at 11:00 A.M. Napoleon quickly realized that there were indeed more than 40,000 Prussian troops there—in fact there were 84,000 arriving from Namur—and that he would not be simply skirmishing but unexpectedly facing a full-fledged battle. What is more, his own troops, Grouchy's right wing, were not even in place. Facing the French were Pirch's II Corps on the Quatre-Bras road west of Sombreffe, Ziethen's I Corps before Brye and St. Amand-La-Haie, extending over to the village of Ligny, with Blücher's III Corps, Thielmann's, straddling the Charleroi-Gembloux Road and securing the east side of Sombreffe.

Napoleon found a seven-and-a-half-mile-long front covered with prepared Prussian positions. But despite their 224 guns, their troops were too thinly deployed to hold such a long line (Blücher's IV Corps, of another 31,000 men, had not yet arrived). Napoleon's own troops were still moving up, however—Vandamme's corps anchoring his left flank before St.-Amand-le-Hameau and Wagnelée and St.-Amand-le-Château, with Gérard's corps holding roughly the center before Ligny, and Excelleman's and Pajol's cavalry securing a mobile right flank.

Even as Napoleon's ultimate force of 76,800 men were taking up their positions, a little after one o'clock Wellington was conferring with Blücher at Bussy Windmill in Brye. The duke saw immediately the weakness of the overly extended Prussian line and told Blücher in his usual forthright manner that the French "had it in their power to cannonade them and shatter them to pieces," but that because of an extensive marshy area separating the two forces, the Prussians could not easily advance and attack the French. "I said that if I were in Blücher's place ... I should withdraw all the columns I saw scattered about the front, and get more of the troops under shelter of the rising ground. However, they seemed to think they knew best, so I came away shortly." Before leaving, Blücher asked him to reinforce him, and Wellington agreed, "provided I am not attacked myself."

Meanwhile, ascertaining the full gravity of the situation before him, Napoleon dispatched a courier to Ney to advance on the double from Quatre-Bras "so as to bring about the envelopment of those enemy troops."[11] If all went well, with the arrival of Ney's troops by 6:00 P.M., reinforced by the Imperial Guard along the central position, he could entrap Blücher's entire force. The whole battle would be over by sunset. It would be so easy.

The full French offensive began between 2:30 and 3:00 P.M. on June 16. Some 140 French guns poured a barrage against the exposed Prussian front lines, returned even more intensely by the Prussians, while Vandamme's Corps hit the Prussians' strongest point, at the center and right-center at St.-Amand-la-Haie. "Do not lose a minute," Napoleon wrote in another hurried dispatch to Ney. "This [Prussian] Army is lost if you act quickly. The fate of France is in your hands." The French continued to pound the Prussians as Wellington had predicted, but the Prussians continued to throw them back.

Independent of Napoleon's orders directly to Ney, one of the Emperor's staff officers also ordered Ney's I Corps, commanded by Drouet d'Erlon, to come immediately to Sombreffe. But then another messenger arrived with other instructions, and d'Erlon, understandably confused, changed direction and started instead to march toward Saint-Amand. When d'Erlon's corps finally did appear at 5:30 P.M., from the wrong direction behind General Vandamme and Napoleon, they at first thought it was the enemy. Bonaparte was about to launch his principal attack of the day, but he postponed it, waiting impatiently for an entire hour before establishing the identity of d'Erlon's force approaching from the rear. D'Erlon then received yet another courier, this time from Ney, ordering him back to support that marshal's left wing. Thus Drouet d'Erlon, though a little more than a mile from Napoleon's troops, turned about and started counter-marching back to Ney, leaving only one division with Bonaparte, d'Erlon ultimately keeping his troops out of all effective fighting that day.

Meanwhile Marshal Blücher remained supremely confident of his own superiority, secure in the knowledge that Count Bülow's thirty-seven squadrons of cavalry and eighty-eight pieces of ordnance would soon be supporting him. In fact the contrary Bülow was not en route at all, refusing to advance from Liège, despite the fresh orders he had received from Blücher at 11:00 A.M. on the fifteenth.

Two intensive areas of fighting continued unabated that afternoon of the sixteenth, at Ligny and St.-Amand. No sooner would Vandamme repulse Ziethen from St.-Amand at four o'clock, than it was followed by a powerful counterattack. The gallant Blücher, mistaking a movement by the French Imperial Guard for a full retreat, personally led a superb cavalry charge of forty seven squadrons against St.-Amand-le-Hameau and St.-Amand-la-Haie,[12] the Prussians succeeding in retaking St.-Amand and holding it for the next few hours. But this last extraordinary charge by the bulk of the Prussian cavalry left them with dwindling reserves, and seeing this Bonaparte prepared to launch his main attack.

At the village of Ligny, the Prussians were fighting in an intensive house-to-house drama, with sixty cannon firing sometimes at point blank range. By four o'clock Blücher met Gérard's ferocious attempt by ordering in a brigade of reserve cavalry and another infantry brigade, giving him 14,000 men by eight o'clock, versus Gérard's 16,000. By now Blücher was clearly worried, and neither Bülow nor Wellington had come to his aid.

Meanwhile, in the French camp at 7:30 P.M., giving up all hope of d'Erlon's reappearance, Napoleon finally gave the signal for the delayed major attack against Ligny, after five hours of fierce resistance by the Prussians. In the midst of severe hand-to-hand fighting in the narrow village streets, Blücher led another counterattack at the head of thirty-two squadrons. Just as the Prussians were stopped in their tracks by a fierce barrage of artillery and musketry, the Prussian field marshal's horse was shot from beneath him while at a full gallop, throwing the septuagenarian Blücher heavily to the ground, where he lay unconscious and trampled in the churned-up mud as French *cuirassiers* passed over him.

Nevertheless the Prussians held on to Ligny until about nine o'clock, the slaughter great on both sides. Then, with their commander down, they began a complete retreat once Blücher had been found, battered but alive, by one of his aides. The Prussians made good their escape, but at the cost of 18,772 casualties, and twenty-two guns, leaving the honors of the day to Napoleon once again, with his 13,721 casualties. The bulk of the Prussian army made an orderly withdrawal, however, leaving few prisoners, and would soon be joined by Bülow's still entirely fresh corps of 31,000 men. Napoleon Bonaparte therefore was far from happy with the results, for the Prussians could now regroup and join Wellington after all. All that fighting, all those deaths for nought.[13]

*   *   *

That day, June 16, proved to be a bizarre one for Marshal Ney, when Soult's order, repeating Napoleon's initial instructions, reached him at 6:30 A.M. Ney literally had not moved an inch in the past thirteen hours, and even now, instead of advancing as ordered, he sat down to a hearty breakfast, then set out to inspect his outposts at Frasnes. Ney, Soult, and Grouchy, although personal enemies, nevertheless all acted in the same manner, with the same unpardonable laxity. Napoleon's secretary, Fleury de Chaboulon, explained that "these men were simply sick and tired of war," and no doubt he was right.

In any event, after next receiving a third set of orders brought personally to Ney at 11:00 A.M. by Napoleon's aide-de-camp, General Flahaut (Talleyrand's bastard, and the father of Hortense's bastard, the future duc de Morny), Ney finally broke camp at noon and set out for Quatre-Bras. "It is my express desire that you be ready to march [from Quatre-Bras] on Brussels," the last dispatch had read.[14] But when Reille's 24,336 men reached Frasnes and found Wellington's 7,806 men there, Reille refused to obey Ney's orders and instead called for reinforcements before resuming the march. French morale was at rock bottom.

At 2:00 P.M. an angry Ney finally led the new attack himself, in three columns comprising three divisions marching north to seize the crossroads of Quatre-Bras itself. The third column, under the command of Lt. Gen. Jérôme Bonaparte, was ordered to secure Pierrepont Farm and Bossut Wood, while Reille's fifty guns and howitzers provided a protective barrage of steel, shot, and canister.[15]

At Quatre-Bras itself, just before 3:00 P.M., Wellington returned from his meeting with Blücher and instructed the first units of his Reserve Army from Mont St.-Jean to take up positions, while General Reille's corps rebuffed the Prince of Orange's initial cavalry charge a half hour later. Although Ney's 24,000 men at first well outnumbered Wellington's, reinforcements kept arriving, soon giving the Allies 23,000 men. This was the situation at four o'clock that afternoon when yet another courier reached Ney with Napoleon's two-o'clock orders to come immediately to Wagnelée and Sombreffe to execute the enveloping operations. As if that were not enough, d'Erlon's chief of staff, General Delcambre, now also arrived, informing Ney to support the right wing at Sombreffe. Turning purple with rage, Ney finally said, "Tell the Emperor what you have seen here!" He pointed with a sweep of his arm at the thousands of Allied troops just up the road reinforcing Wellington. "I will hold on where I am, but nothing more." At the same time he ordered General Delcambre to disregard Napoleon's orders and to proceed instead at once to Quatre-Bras.[16]

With his adrenaline and ire up, Ney threw himself into battle with all
the energy of yesteryear, leading his lancers in a mighty, frenzied charge
against the eccentric Gen. Sir Thomas Picton's newly arrived division at
Quatre-Bras, now deployed in squares bristling with long bayonets and
successfully repulsing the French. Undaunted by high losses, Ney next
ordered Marshal Kellermann's son, Gen. F. E. Kellermann, and his cavalry
to attack again. Young Kellermann, considered the finest cavalry commander in the army, balked at the order to commit suicide, but when Ney
repeated the order, personally taking the lead of four thousand *cuirassiers*,
Kellermann gave in. *"Pour charger!"* Ney commanded. *"Au galop! En
avant! Marche!"* His voice cracked like a whip as the thundering mass of
heavy cavalry pitched themselves headlong against Picton's division,
deployed in a line of infantry squares again. Wellington himself personally
directed the first volley, when the *cuirassiers* in their shining heavy chest
armor and steel helmets were only thirty yards away, killing and wounding
hundreds of the cavalry and their mounts, supported by five batteries of
cannon fired at point-blank range and by the rolling half-company volleys
of musketry all along the Allied front. The duke, with little cavalry and less
artillery at his disposal, nevertheless succeeded in halting a bewildered Ney
and Kellermann, who were not used to such resistance. "The finest fellow I
ever saw," Col. Sir Augustus Frazer recalled in admiration, as the French
cavalry beat a bloody retreat, Kellermann himself grounded when his
mount was shot under him, barely escaping by grabbing hold of two passing horses.[17] But with Wellington's troops extremely low in ammunition,
the situation seemed pretty grim for the Allies.

Returning from the charge after having lost his second horse of the day,
Ney now found *another* courier waiting with an even more urgent order
from the emperor: "Regardless of the situation Marshal Ney now finds
himself in, it is absolutely imperative that Comte d'Erlon's orders [to join
him] be executed. It is of little consequence what happens over there [at
Quatre-Bras]." A furious, mud-splattered Ney, covered with his horse's
blood, and cursing a blue streak at this impudent officer before him,
ordered a third mount to be brought up. Swinging into the saddle, he
ordered all the remaining cuirassiers, lancers, and hussars forward as he
launched another blind charge against the Allied squares.[18]

At long last a much relieved Wellington saw fresh reinforcements arriving from Mont St.-Jean and Nivelles. The wounded Picton formed one of
these two fresh brigades into four regimental squares barring the Brussels
Road, extending over to Bossut Wood, only to have his order counter-
manded by the foolish young prince of Orange, redeploying Halkett's fresh

British brigade in a thin line at the moment Ney's cavalry reached them, savagely slashing through four fully exposed regiments before turning against Picton again. It was only thanks to Wellington's intervention, countermanding Orange's orders, re-forming the remnants of those much reduced regiments into squares, that he was able to repulse Ney's nearly successful charge.

From this point on, time was on Wellington's side. By 6:30 P.M. he had 36,000 men and seventy guns, with fresh caissons of ammunition rolling in. Ready at last, he launched his first major attack of the day, hurling Reille's corps back from Bossut Wood, Gémioncourt Farm, and Piraumont Farm, and by nine o'clock that evening the Allies had regained all the ground they had lost, bringing the Battle of Quatre-Bras to a successful conclusion. The price paid was 5,200 Allied casualties, compared to Ney's 4,100. Meanwhile Drouet d'Erlon's corps was still marching, having not fired a single round all day.

"I attacked the English position at Quatre-Bras with all I had," Ney informed Napoleon, "but an error on the part of the Comte d'Erlon deprived me of a fine victory." Napoleon wrote back by return courier: "If Marshal Ney had attacked the English with all his troops, he would have crushed them, and at the same time given the Prussians their coup de grâce. And if after having committed that first error he had not made his second blunder, by preventing the Comte d'Erlon from joining me Blücher's entire army would have been captured or destroyed."[19] In fact Ney had lost the Battle of Quatre-Bras the day before, when he had refused to obey his marching orders.

It was not until 7:30 in the morning of the seventeenth that Wellington received the report of the Prussian defeat and retreat north. "Old Blücher has had a damned good licking and gone back to Wavre," he sighed aloud to Captain Bowles of the Coldstream Guards. With Blücher gone, Wellington was exposed, for Napoleon would soon be marching up the very road he had traveled from Byre yesterday. Thus at noon the duke gave the orders to withdraw from Quatre-Bras to the village of Mont St.-Jean, about three miles south of Waterloo, which would place the Prussian army at Wavre, a little more than ten miles due east of them. With a bit of luck the two allied forces could finally join. Little did Field Marshal Wellington realize how fortunate he was even to have the Prussians moving to Wavre. While Blücher was still unconscious, his second-in-command and chief of staff, the strongly anti-British General Gneisenau, had blamed their defeat on Wellington's failure to come to their rescue, and had initially ordered the retreat not north to Wavre but east to Liège and the German frontier. Fortunately, when the loyal old Blücher did revive, he proved fit enough to ride and resume command, chastising Gneisenau, rescinding his earlier orders, and now directing his army to Wavre after all. Although several thousand wounded and deserters did continue up the road to Liège and Namur, the main Prussian force remained intact with the field marshal.[20]

The French had sent the Prussians flying and remained the technical victors. Yet confusion reigned in their camp the evening of June 16. An exhausted Napoleon retired for the night still thinking that Ney had defeated the Allies, who would now be falling back in disarray toward Brussels. It would be just like the old Danube campaign, marching practically unopposed to Vienna. Unfortunately an overconfident Napoleon had not bothered to send out patrols either to nearby Quatre-Bras or after the Prussians. Indeed, he ordered no real pursuit of the Prussians that night, thinking that the stream of Prussians reported on the road to Liège constituted their whole army. It was very sloppy, and very cocky, but typical of Bonaparte, who had done this time and again in previous campaigns. Even as late as eleven o'clock the following morning, Napoleon was receiving reports that the entire Prussian army was still retreating to Namur and Maastricht. Fortunately he now took the trouble to demand confirmation of the enemy's flight back to Germany, "to learn what precisely Blücher and Wellington intend to do, in the event they do plan on joining forces after all . . . and fight."[21] Had Napoleon been more energetic and decisive, he could have dispatched fresh troops—such as Lobau's ten thousand men, whom he had *forgotten* to deploy during the Battle of Ligny—to participate in a vigorous pursuit and stop the battered and momentarily shaken Prussians from getting anywhere near Wavre. By the time he finally learned that Blücher was heading north in two columns, via Walhain and Mont St.-Guibert, and not to the east, it was too late. And it was only on the morning of the seventeenth that he also discovered that d'Erlon had not joined Ney before Quatre-Bras and that his marshal had instead been defeated there. "It was with great dissatisfaction that the Emperor saw that you did not succeed yesterday," Soult admonished Ney, preventing Napoleon from taking "perhaps some 30,000 Prussian prisoners." That did not help sagging French morale in Ney's defeated left wing.[22]

When Napoleon finally reached Quatre-Bras at two o'clock in the afternoon of the seventeenth, he did not find a single French soldier anywhere in sight. Instead he discovered Ney and his men several miles to the south sitting leisurely around campfires enjoying their lunch. This time, out of control, Napoleon shouted at a mortified Ney before his aides-de-camp, staff, and troops, ordering him to pursue the withdrawing Allied force on the double. As usual Bonaparte's presence had an electrifying effect, d'Erlon's corps unstacking their arms, forming up, and moving out in the direction of Quatre-Bras and Genappe, followed by Reille's and Lobau's corps, with Napoleon at a full gallop at the head of the column with the Imperial Guard and d'Erlon's cavalry.[23]

Just as the first units of French cavalry approached the British rearguard cavalry, a thunderstorm broke over the entire area, soon turning the highway to Brussels into a long, narrow strip of mud, slowing the French troops and causing hundreds of cannon, including 3,400 12-pounders and limbers, to sink axle deep in the road, effectively reducing the French pursuit to a crawl.[24] By 6:30 P.M. Wellington was already in position around Mont Saint-Jean when the initial French troops began to reach the Belle Alliance Inn.

After catching a couple of hours' sleep at the Gros Caillou Farm, Napoleon was awakened at three o'clock in the morning of the eighteenth to receive a dispatch from Marshal Grouchy then at Gembloux, dated 10:00 P.M. the seventeenth, finally confirming that Blücher was indeed marching toward Wavre and that he was in pursuit. But Napoleon failed to send any reply or instructions whatsoever. Unknown to Napoleon, the dithering Grouchy set out, after an eleven-hour siesta, from Gembloux at 8:00 A.M. on the eighteenth, while everywhere the rain continued to fall.

Bonaparte now had 74,500 men and 254 pieces of ordnance (including many 12-pounders) with him—the Imperial Guard, the I, II, and VI Corps and two Reserve cavalry corps for a total of 104 battalions of infantry and 113½ squadrons (15,830 troopers). Grouchy, slowly making his way north many miles to the east, had under his command III and IV Corps, for a total of nearly 30,000 men.[25]

Wellington had finally beefed up his army to give him 74,300 men including Orange's I Corps, Hill's II, the Army Reserve and Uxbridge's cavalry, divided into 84½ battalions of infantry, 93 squadrons of cavalry (14,457 and only 157 guns, nine-pounders being his largest). Well to the west at Hal, Prince Frederick had another 17,000 men in reserve. Napoleon in fact had a superiority in cavalry with thousands of *cuirassiers*, of which Wellington had none, and 97 more pieces of ordnance. In addition Napoleon had a cohesive, entirely French force, largely veterans of other campaigns, compared to Wellington's mostly new recruits. Nor did Wellington have a large number of veteran commanders to spare— Uxbridge, Clinton, Hill, Cook, Colville, and Alten against at least sixteen

French generals.[26] On the other hand Wellington had the advantage of selecting the battlefield best suited to his needs and style of fighting, while Blücher's remaining effective field force, reduced to 89,000 men, was within marching distance of Mont Saint-Jean.[27]

To take advantage of his immediate superiority, Bonaparte had to act promptly and destroy Wellington's force before Blücher could arrive. But the mud just got deeper and mobility slower.

As a gray dawn broke on June 18, 1815, the deployment of the two enemy forces could at last be seen, at least in part. General Chassé's Third Belgian-Dutch Division was anchoring Wellington's extreme right flank around the village of Braine l'Alleud, joined by Clinton's division behind the Braine l'Alleud Road, along with Cooke's and finally Alten's division, extending to the junction with the Brussels Road. Wellington's own reserve corps there held the center of the Anglo-Allied front, continuing up the Ohain Road, straddling the Brussels-Charleroi Road intersection, opposite La Haie Sainte Farm. Picton's division continued up the Ohain Road as far as Papelotte and La Haie (not to be confused with La Haie Sainte), and where Saxe-Weimar secured the left flank, supported to the rear by Uxbridge's cavalry. The men were literally packed one against another.

Napoleon deployed his men more than seventeen hundred yards to the south, before the Belle Alliance Inn, in roughly a parallel line, his left flank anchored at the Mont Saint-Jean-Nivelles Road, extending eastward across the Brussels Road, and anchoring on the extreme right opposite the hamlet of La Haie. Beginning at the extreme left, Napoleon placed Piré's cavalry and Reille's corps, the cavalry of Kellermann and Guyot behind. Right, or east of the Brussels Road, the first French line was held by d'Erlon's I Corps, with Jacquinot's cavalry on the extreme right flank, supported to the rear by Milhaud and Lefebvre-Desnouëttes. Napoleon placed his principal battery of eighty-four guns to the right of the Belle Alliance Inn. Given the deep mud, it was difficult to transport them far from any road. Lobau's VI Corps and the Imperial Guard formed the main reserves.

Bonaparte's plan could not have been simpler: to batter his way through Wellington's central position along the Brussels Road, while attempting to turn his extreme flanks, then drive to Mont Saint-Jean Farm and cut off the Brussels Road and the entire right flank of the English army. If Blücher somehow managed to attack, d'Erlon was assigned to halt him, supported by the Imperial Guard and "a detachment of troops from Marshal Grouchy."[28]

Because of the heavy rain throughout the night, and the inevitable mist and soggy ground, instead of launching a dawn attack, Bonaparte was still taking breakfast at the Caillou farmhouse with his senior commanders and brother Jérôme. But the main reason for this extraordinary delay was the enormous difficulty of moving up men, artillery, and supply wagons through the wheat- and cornfields that soon became vast quagmires of heavy mud. Thus the original attack, postponed to eleven o'clock, was delayed again until one o'clock on the afternoon of June 18.

Jérôme Bonaparte, as a divisional commander in Reille's corps, was to begin a diversionary attack at 11:50 A.M. from the extreme French left flank against the large walled Château de Goumont, or Hougoumont Farm, as it was locally known, in order to draw as much of Wellington's attention and firepower as possible to that sector, while Napoleon prepared for his big central drive. The farm itself was already controlled by Wellington's Nassauers, Hanoverians, and British troops dug in behind the walls.

After 11:50 the firing became general along the line. Time and again Jérôme threw all four brigades against Hougoumont, only to be repulsed every time. Clearly needing more men, Jérôme "sequestered" half of Foy's division, over the latter's outraged protests. But the British in turn were reinforced by the Coldstream Guards and the Scots Guards, for Wellington was determined not to have that flank turned. Nevertheless it was surprising that Napoleon did not interfere, permitting this useless slaughter of troops as Reille and Jérôme attacked first with troops rather than bombarding Hougoumont Farm with howitzers and cannon.[29] But Bonaparte's whole attitude today was very different from the past: He merely observed from a distance with his telescope, far from the actual fighting.

Just before one o'clock, while Jérôme was continuing his attack and Napoleon was preparing to order his superbattery of eighty-four guns before La Belle Alliance to open fire, an unknown column was spotted some eight miles distant in the direction of Wavre. Were they French or Prussian? Napoleon suspended operations until the approaching army could be identified. Half an hour later Colonel Marbot rode up in a spray of mud to give Napoleon the bad news: It was General Bülow von Dennewitz's IV corps, no doubt ahead of the rest of Blücher's army.

Before the main attack even began, a greatly outnumbered Napoleon had the choice of continuing with a swift full-scale attack or withdrawing to the south. "Even now we have a sixty percent chance of winning," he optimistically summed up, and then remembering Grouchy's still unanswered letter of the night before, he hurriedly dictated instructions ordering him "not to lose a moment in closing in in this direction to join us in crushing Bülow, whom you will certainly take by complete surprise." Incorrectly estimating that a fast courier could reach Grouchy, near Walhain, within an hour, he was determined to launch his attack and hold on until that marshal arrived. In fact, however, the messenger took the long route and didn't deliver the instructions for four hours. "A more careful man would have broken off the engagement and retreated," Colonel Clausewitz concluded.[30] But of course Bonaparte had rarely been careful in his life.

Reassessing the situation, Napoleon ordered Comte Lobau's Reserve Corps of 20,330 men and thirty-two guns to cross the Brussels Road to secure d'Erlon's rear and right flank by forming a perpendicular line across the fields extending from Frichermont almost to Aywiers, where it appeared that the first Prussian units would debouch from the forest in their attempt to envelop Napoleon.

With these orders issued at 1:30, Bonaparte finally unleashed a ferocious artillery barrage from Belle Alliance, the powerful 12-pounders landing well within English lines though not doing as much harm as Napoleon had predicted. Many of the Allied troops were concealed over the lip of the hill, denying the gunners a precise target, and many of the cannonballs just sank in the deep mud instead of ricocheting and plowing through British troops.

At two o'clock d'Erlon launched three of his divisions in the direction of La Haie Sainte Farm, but instead of deploying in smaller units by battalion, two of the divisions proceeded in two massive columns two hundred men abreast—a superb target for the British, who simply mowed them down. It was a slaughter. They "appeared to wave like high-standing corn blown by sudden gusts of wind ... their caps and muskets flying in the air,"[31] one eyewitness described the advance. Although they did rout a Dutch-Belgian brigade under van Bijlandt, and destroyed one of Ompteda's battalions, the rest of the Allied line held, as Wellington in the heart of the heaviest fighting popped around giving instructions and encouragement.

Unfortunately d'Erlon's divisions had chosen to attack part of Wellington's finest troops, commanded by General Picton. Although seriously wounded back at Quatre-Bras, Picton courageously led his men against d'Erlon, repelling them from Ohain Road and Papelotte Farm, though being killed himself as he did so. These English, even Anglophobe Fleury de Chaboulon admitted, were "recklessly bold in withstanding the charges of our infantry and cavalry with such great firmness." For Bonaparte, who had never personally come up against Wellington before, it proved a disagreeable surprise, the resistance stunning. The British were at their most heroic; not only was Picton killed now, but thirteen of his fifteen brigade and regimental commanders were either killed or wounded by nightfall.

Still they did not give way, as Uxbridge's cavalry charged forward sweeping the French back, though paying a high price in 40 percent overall casualties, including Uxbridge and seven of his nine commanding officers. By three o'clock Wellington was still holding his line, if barely, and this was just the first serious French attack.[32]

With the exception of Reille's II Corps, still attempting to take Hougoumont Farm, there was a lull across the rest of the muddy fields of corn and grain as both sides licked their wounds. Kempt replacing Picton, while Prince Bernhard von Saxe-Weimar's Second Nassau Brigade reoccupied the hamlet of Papelotte.[33]

If Napoleon was to win, it had to be very quickly now, but time was not on his side. He now received another message from Grouchy, sent from Walhain at 11:30 A.M., announcing that he was still intent on marching toward Wavre, some nine miles away, though he could hear the big guns round Mont Saint-Jean even from that distance and despite the vociferous protests of both Generals Gérard and Vandamme. Meanwhile the Prussians had set out from Wavre for Mont Saint-Jean. It was a sad comedy of errors and betrayal.

At 3:30 Napoleon pressed Marshal Ney to try to take the stoutly walled and enclosed farm of La Haie Sainte, just below the important crossroads of the Brussels Road and the Wavre–Braine l'Alleud Road. Ney personally led a cavalry attack against the farm, while overhead Napoleon's "belles filles," as he called his 12-pounders, belched forth death, announcing a second French attack. But Ney was repulsed by the King's German Legion, holding La Haie Sainte Farm.

The hotheaded—or desperate—Ney now took actions leading to a whole chain of disastrous consequences for the French. Mistaking a long stream of wounded men and vehicles behind the British line for a major retreat, Ney ordered the crack IV Cavalry Corps to make an extraordinarily bold if uncoordinated charge, some five thousand men plowing right up the slope of the Allies' central position on the west side of the Brussels Road, at the very point where Napoleon was still concentrating his principal artillery barrage. An incredulous Bonaparte stopped the barrage just in time. Somehow slipping and sliding up the muddy slopes, Ney found himself before tightly packed squares of bright red uniforms. "Prepare to receive cavalry!" the British commander shouted above the din of screaming cavalrymen and pounding horses, as thousands of Brown Bess muskets and Baker rifles, along with double-shotted British artillery tore through Ney's brave but badly led men. Still the British fired, reloaded, and fired again and again, the muzzles of some of the guns "bent down by the excess

heat [and] many touch-holes melted away." Watching through his telescope, Napoleon was beside himself about this "fatal charge" and Ney's
blockheadedness. "Never did cavalry behave so nobly or was received by
infantry so firmly," Colonel Frazer attested.[34] "What indescribable confusion," another officer more accurately put it.

> The horses of the first rank of cuirassiers, in spite of all the efforts of
> their riders came to a standstill, shaking and covered with foam, at
> about twenty yards' distance from our squares. Unable to renew the
> charge, but unwilling to retreat, they brandished their swords with loud
> cries of 'Vive l'Empereur!' and allowed themselves to be mowed down
> by the hundreds rather than yield.

The British too paid a high price. In one regimental square "it was impossible to move a yard without treading on a wounded comrade, or upon the
bodies of the dead." After one final lethal volley, assisted by more double-
shot, even a confused Ney had to recognize the failure of his charge, falling
back down "the corpse-strewn acres," urged on by Uxbridge's cavalry.[35]

Ney, by now no longer knowing what he was doing, regrouped some
of the survivors at the bottom of the slope, and despite their exhausted,
blown, and frequently wounded mounts launched another attack up the
crest, this time at a walk through the thick mud, however further slowed by
the hundreds of dead and dying men and horses. Once again the British
squares, "suffocated by the smoke and smell of burnt cartridges," poured
out more death. Ney again turned back, only to rush over to a furious
Napoleon and ask for reinforcements to try again. "Where the devil do you
expect me to find them!" the emperor snapped at this man who seemed
bent on committing suicide.[36]

Sensing just how critical their position was, by five o'clock Gen. F. E.
Kellermann and his III Cavalry Corps of 3,858 men, along with Guyot's
2,068 cuirassiers, joined Ney as Napoleon looked on in hopeless silence
through his telescope. It was insane. Some 9,000 French cavalry under
Ney's lead were emerging from between Hougoumont and La Haie Sainte,
galloping pell-mell along a five-hundred-yard-wide front straight at the
British. The whole appeared "one moving mass," recalled Captain Siborne,
"and as it approached the Anglo-Allied position, undulating with the con-
formation of the ground, it resembled a sea in agitation. . . . Like waves following in quick succession . . . and the devoted [British] squares seemed lost
in the tumultuous onset." "Never, no never did the French strike their
adversaries with such murderous force," Fleury de Chaboulon exclaimed

from the French lines. "Hard pounding this," a more phlegmatic Wellington admitted. "Let us see who will pound the longest." And the
redoubtable British squares repulsed this "tempestuous and hazardous"
attack with thousands of musket balls and the defending British cavalry.
"Thundering murderous work," one soldier called it.[37]

Re-forming yet again, the stunned French cavalry somehow forced
themselves up that same slope against the bloodied British squares, Generals Friand and Michel falling mortally wounded, and Ney himself, though
miraculously untouched, having his fourth and last horse shot from beneath
him, hurling him headfirst into the mud. After six o'clock and "the most
horrible carnage I have ever witnessed," as Ney himself later described it,
he found his way back to the French lines on foot, not a single French officer or trooper willing to offer him a place behind his saddle.[38] Ney had foolishly advanced without even ordering Reille's and d'Erlon's infantry to follow, nor did he have adequate artillery. It was perhaps one of the most
incompetent moves of any French marshal in history. Not even the Imperial Guard could stand up against the British infantry, Wellington had once
boasted, and he had now proved it.

Napoleon, still isolated, continued to watch in dull amazement. Everything that could possibly go wrong had, from the very beginning. Ney had
lost the battle on the fifteenth and sixteenth, when he had disobeyed orders
to advance. Soult was an incompetent, even mischievous, chief of staff.
Grouchy . . . one could not find the words with which to describe the cowardly commander of the phantom right wing.

It simply could not end this way, and Napoleon ordered another attack
against La Haie Sainte Farm, Ney finally succeeding in seizing it, now that
the cut-off German legion was out of ammunition. Coming to life again,
Napoleon quickly ordered his artillery to concentrate fire on Wellington's
already badly battered center, annihilating brigades of both Ompteda's and
Kielmansegge's forces, in the process killing Ompteda himself.[39] Wellington's original core of 28,000 men, now reduced to just a few thousand and
greatly shaken, was barely holding on.

When Ney now pleaded again for reserves from the Imperial Guard,
Napoleon refused outright, though they were probably in a position to
drive through the British center at last. The news had just reached GHQ
that the Young Guard, badly mauled, had withdrawn from nearby Plancenoit. Napoleon had only fourteen battalions in reserve and would not
risk his fate by giving one more to Ney.

Nor had the Prussians been inactive this June 18. Blücher had finally
joined Bülow's corps at Chapelle-St.-Lambert at one o'clock, bringing with

him two more corps, leaving only Thielmann's much reduced corps to cope
with the likes of Grouchy. Blücher was still not very steady on his legs after
the severe ordeal he had been through at Ligny, and he reacted slowly to
the fast-moving events before him at Mont St.-Jean. It was not until 4:00
P.M. that Bülow's first few brigades began debouching from near the Bois
de Paris, between Frichermont and Aywiers.[40] On came Bülow toward
Plancenoit, just two miles away, scattering General Domon's Third Cavalry
Division by five o'clock as he advanced, and although Lobau's 7,000 men
tried to stop Bülow's 31,000 troops, it was quite in vain. At 6:00 P.M. they
abandoned Plancenoit, from which a road linked directly with the Brussels
Road behind the Belle Alliance and Napoleon's own position. GHQ was
now exposed.

Having to seek shelter from Bülow's bombardment, a desperate
Napoleon, literally fighting for his life, called up some 4,000 Young Guards,
along with twenty-four pieces of field artillery, briefly retaking Plancenoit
before falling back, while Durutte attacked Papelotte, just before the
French line. Bülow hurled fresh forces against the Guard, killing their commander and recapturing Plancenoit. Once again that Prussian corps commander was in a position to cut off Napoleon's retreat. Reacting to this new
check, Napoleon deployed eleven of his reserve Guard battalions in squares
along the Charleroi-Bruxelles Road, between La Belle Alliance south to
Rossommée Farm. Still not giving up, he ordered another attack on Plancenoit with two battalions of the Old Guard's *chasseurs*, actually retaking
Plancenoit by seven o'clock as news arrived of the French recapture of
Papelotte and La Haie by Durutte's redoutable Fourth Infantry Division.

At about the same time, Jérôme Bonaparte was still vainly laying siege
to Hougoumont, as he had been doing without success since before noon,
the sun finally breaking through for the first time all day. Napoleon's situation, despite the temporary successes, was by now hopeless, as thousands of
fresh Prussian troops supported the exhausted Anglo-Dutch army. If he
withdrew now he could perhaps regroup around Philippeville in order to
defend the northern French frontier from invasion, and unless Grouchy
appeared (and predictably he did not), that was about the only option. It
really was the end, but instead of retreating, Napoleon decided on another
attack against Wellington's center before La Haie Sainte, for as he had often
put it, "by its very nature the outcome of a battle is never predictable."[41]
Given the increasing military revolts throughout France, he could not return
to Paris defeated and hope to retain his throne or perhaps even his head.

As the ever loyal Fleury put it, "the brave presence of the Guard and a
dramatic talk by Napoleon now inflamed the troops again." Colonel

Clausewitz, observing the entire tragic fiasco, saw things differently. "Never had Bonaparte committed a greater error. There has always been an immense difference between leading an invincible army in an orderly withdrawal from a battlefield in the face of an overwhelmingly superior force, and returning like a veritable fugitive, guilty of having lost and abandoned an entire army."[42] Unlike his position after having abandoned his army in Egypt, however, here there would be no second chance.

Nevertheless, despite the vastly overwhelming odds, Bonaparte now deployed two Guard battalions between Hougoumont and La Haie Sainte, ordering Ney to spearhead another drive with an additional seven Guard battalions across the Ohain Road, even as he ordered a final heavy artillery barrage against what remained of Wellington's center. At seven o'clock that evening, just as Napoleon was about to give the signal for the final counteroffensive, he heard a loud artillery barrage to the northeast. It was Blücher's fourth and last remaining corps arriving from Wavre.

Despite knowing that it was futile to go on, Bonaparte lied to Ney, informing him that it was Grouchy. They were saved. With cheers of "*Vive l'Empereur!*" echoed thousands of times by his troops, Ney gave the order to charge.[43] Advancing smartly forward, seventy-five men abreast, the seven Guard battalions in a "dark waving forest of bear-skin caps" advanced, but then accidentally divided, while across much of the line French troops advanced in support. Ney's force continued forward, coming under heavy fire of the musketry of the brave Dutch-Belgian infantry, while Wellington's troops lay concealed on the other side of the Ohain road. Suddenly confusion erupted, as the extreme French left flank came under unexpected fire from the British emerging through a cornfield. Wellington, in his blue coat, white buckskin breeches, and gold Spanish sash from his peninsular days, stood up and waved his hat, signaling the Allies to counterattack all across the line. The moment had come.

When Ney's troops were fewer than sixty yards away, some forty thousand Allied troops suddenly appeared from nowhere. Sending a stream of lethal volleys into the ranks of the stunned Imperial Guard. The Allied soldiers charged with bayonets, and the Guard's drummers suddenly broke off the "*pas de charge*," as the French Imperial Guard broke and fled.[44] Forming three Guard battalions into squares, Napoleon hoped to check the flight of the other Guard units, but shouts of "*Sauve qui peut!*" drowned out his orders.

By eight o'clock that evening, even Napoleon had to admit that he had lost. He "entirely disappeared," as Ney summed it up, without even notifying Ney or any other commander of his intentions. It was shades of Egypt all over again. "A complete panic at once spread throughout the whole field of battle," one official French battle report read, as the greatest army in the world fled in pandemonium. "In an instant the whole army was nothing but a mass of confusion," Ney later recalled, "and it was utterly impossible to rally a single unit. . . . Even the cavalry squadrons accompanying the Emperor were overthrown and disorganized," deserting Napoleon. "I owe my life to a corporal who supported me on the road and did not abandon me during the retreat," Ney acknowledged.[45]

Bonaparte was forced to abandon his coach at Genappe, along with all its contents—the gold, banknotes, diamonds, sister Pauline's necklace, and his personal papers. He grabbed a horse and galloped south, followed only by Drouot, Bertrand, and his staff, Grouchy executing a similarly swift retreat before Wavre.

Meanwhile, behind them, units of Gneisenau's cavalry were beginning a pursuit, as the victorious Duke of Wellington and Prince Blücher finally met at 9:30 P.M. at the Belle Alliance Inn, the Prussian army band striking up "God Save the King." It was only now that Wellington realized what a beating Blücher had taken back at Ligny and what remarkable endurance he must have had to continue. After many toasts the two men discussed their immediate plans for a coordinated advance on Paris, though it took all Wellington's efforts finally to dissuade Blücher from executing his pet project of vengeance by blowing up the Pont d'Iéna and other war memorials and buildings in Paris, not to mention executing Napoleon himself. "Blücher wants to kill him," Wellington afterward related, "but I advised him to have nothing to do with so foul a transaction."[46]

Napoleon, after turning over the command of his troops to Marshal Soult, beat a hasty retreat to Laon on June 20, reaching the Elysée Palace at 5:30 A.M. on the twenty-first, after having told Bertrand back at Philippeville: "If I return to Paris and have to get my hands bloody, then I'll shove them in right up to the elbow!"[47] The French people and the Allies had different ideas on the subject, however.

France left 25,000 dead and wounded and 220 cannon on the now silent battlefield of Waterloo and a total of 64,602 men during the entire Belgian campaign. The Allies suffered 62,818 casualties.[48] Dazed, bruised, and disillusioned, Napoleon now sat in the library of Hortense's home at Malmaison, lost in another world, far from thoughts of future battles, for that he had given up. Instead he was again reading Alexander von Humboldt's study of America, his *Voyages et Contrés Equinoxiales du Nouveau Continent,* which he had earlier discussed with poor old Gaspard Monge, at sixty-nine now a mere shadow of his former self. So much had changed, but Monge and brothers Joseph, Lucien, and Jérôme, had promised to come with him to seek refuge in America. Napoleon planned elaborate fantasies—explorations "from Canada to the tip of the Horn. Henceforth, without any army and empire, only the sciences remain strong enough to attract me." "I want to start a new career, leaving behind some works truly worthy of me," he had told Monge.

A devoted Hortense had welcomed him to Malmaison on June 25, breaking the news of Josephine's death. He now wandered around the eight-hundred-acre estate, seeking Josephine's ghost. "That poor Josephine," he murmured. "I cannot get used to living here without her. I always expect to see her emerging from a path gathering one of the flowers she so loved. She was the most graceful woman I have ever known." he confided to Hortense in a rare lapse into sentimentality.[49]

"I am sorry to see you in Paris," Caulaincourt had greeted him on his arrival at the Elysée on Wednesday, June 21. The army, he insisted, was the only source of Napoleon's power and safety. Now it was all over, too late, there would be no more fresh armies, no more mass call-ups of nonexistent recruits. Instead he reread old leatherbound volumes of Humboldt. "Tell me frankly," he said, cornering the faithful Regnault, "it's my abdication they want, isn't it?" "Given the current situation," he replied, "I believe it preferable if Your Majesty were not to oppose it and instead to offer it of your own accord before the Chambers demand it." Lucien had protested: Napoleon must "assume dictatorial powers, put France under martial law, and call upon all patriots and good Frenchmen to come to its defense." Napoleon looked at this younger brother who had never carried a rifle in his life, forever living in a world of dreams. He had been gone too long and simply no longer knew the country. It was no longer 1804.

Then Napoleon received an urgent message from the Chamber of Representatives, declaring itself in permanent session and warning him that any attempt by him to dissolve it would be considered "a crime of high treason." "Peace with the Powers is not possible unless you hand over Bonaparte," Lord Castlereagh's half-brother, Sir Charles Stewart, frankly told General Lafayette.[50] "I hope it [Napoleon's reign] comes to an end quickly," Lafayette told Joseph Bonaparte, for this was no time for mincing words. "The truth has been revealed at last," Henri Lacoste declared before the Chamber of Representatives, "You know as well as we do that it is against Napoleon alone that Europe has declared war." Whether Napoleon agreed or not, he was now mentally defeated. With the whole of France rising against him, he had no choice.[51]

The following day, Thursday, June 22, a small delegation from the chambers presented Napoleon with their ultimatum to abdicate. A beaten Napoleon acquiesced, signing his "Declaration to the French People" that same day:

> At the beginning of the war to maintain our national independence, I was counting on the union of all our efforts. But since then the circumstances appear to me to have changed, and I hereby offer to sacrifice myself to the hatred of the enemies of France. My political life is over, and I proclaim my son, under the title of Napoleon II, *Empereur des Français.*[52]

Then he had moved to Rueil and Malmaison, even as 66,000 Prussians and another 52,000 men under Wellington were driving through France heading directly for Paris. Napoleon now found himself a virtual prisoner at Malmaison, on War Minister Davout's orders, although Generals Bertrand, Gourgaud, Montholon, and the two Allemand brothers were also staying with him. "We were continuously on the alert," Hortense recalled, Napoleon appearing to be the only person quite indifferent to all that was taking place about him, literally living in another world. "You will guard all avenues and all sides leading to Malmaison," Marshal Davout had instructed General Beker. "The interests of the country require that the evil-doers be prevented from rescuing him and using his name to cause uprisings in the country."[53] Hortense was horrified by these measures.

"What will you do there?" a bewildered Fleury asked Napoleon about his decision to seek final asylum in the United States. "They will give me some land, or I shall buy some, and we will cultivate it. I shall live on the products of my fields and flocks." But if that was not possible? Fleury persisted. In that case "I will go to Mexico, to Buenos Aires, or to California, or if worst comes to worst, I will travel from sea to sea until I find a sanctuary against man's evil and persecution." Clearly he expected to find no justice in the world.[54]

Meanwhile, in Paris, Naval Minister Decrès took Napoleon seriously, ordering two frigates near Rochefort, *La Saale* and *La Méduse,* to prepare to receive Napoleon, his family, and staff for the journey to the New World, although they could not move without British safe-conduct passes. To be sure, the British had other ideas on the matter, an exhausted Prime Minister Lord Liverpool confiding to Lord Castlereagh, "We wish that the King of France would hang or shoot Bonaparte, as the best termination of the business."[55] Although Lucien told Napoleon he would go personally to

London to plead with the British, he instead simply bolted, à la Bonaparte, returning to Italy again, even as Jérôme fled to Germany. *Sauve qui peut.*

In Paris, immediately following the news of the French defeat, Napoleon's government had been swept aside and replaced by a five-man Executive Committee headed by none other than the resilient Joseph Fouché. On June 23 it sent its plenipotentiaries—including La Fayette, Benjamin Constant, and General Sébastiani—to negotiate an immediate armistice in order "to save the country." The abdication forced upon, and accepted by, Napoleon on June 22 "automatically returns the nation to a position of peace with the other Powers," Fouché's official letter to the Allies read, "since their only aim had been to remove him." But, he continued, the Allies now must "renounce without reservation any plans to again place the French government under the Bourbon family," creating instead a regency in the name of Napoleon's son. The Executive Committee also demanded that the Allies "stipulate the safety and inviolability of the Emperor Napoleon once he has left his territory," with Napoleon choosing his own place of exile.[56] Needless to say these proposed terms, arrogant and unrealistic, were dismissed out of hand by the Prussians, and the new acting French foreign minister, Bignon, had to submit new proposals, while Fouché personally favored establishing the duc d'Orléans on the throne.

With 110,000 Allied troops already ringing the French capital and hundreds of thousands more on the way, Davout, the acting war minister, acknowledged the inability of the French to gain anything by further resistance. At a war council convened at Villette on Saturday, July 1, it was agreed to surrender, to avoid "dismemberment of France, [and] the pillage and devastation of the capital."[57] Early the next day Fouché called an emergency meeting of the ruling committee, preparing the eighteen articles of the armistice to be called the Convention of Paris, which were completed and signed on Monday, the third. Davout then personally brought the document to the Allies, at the Neuilly bridge at six o'clock in the morning of the fourth. All parties duly signed then and there. It was over at last—or almost, for in much of the country, the "white terror" was unleashed, long-suppressed royalists attacking and murdering Bonapartist supporters, perhaps in the thousands, and among them, Marshal Brune.

"Who would have ever thought that I would see the emperor of the French held prisoner at Malmaison!" Hortense exclaimed in a rare moment of anger, as Napoleon was ordered to pack his things in two carriages and leave for La Rochelle. Of the entire Bonaparte clan, only Joseph remained faithful to the end, willing to accept exile with Napoleon in America. One last-minute appeal to General Beker to persuade the committee at least to permit Napoleon to head an army in defense of France—"I offer my services as a general only, still considering myself the first soldier of the land"—had been rejected with outraged laughter.[58]

And then the day came to leave, as Hortense quietly handed Napoleon a present he had long ago given her, a two-hundred-thousand-franc diamond necklace, as he stood in the Cour d'Honneur for the last time, looking back. "How beautiful Malmaison is, isn't it, Hortense. It would be wonderful to be able to stay here." Then he turned, his shoulders stooped, and climbed into the unmarked calèche with brother Joseph and General Beker, with Generals Gourgaud and Montholon, along with Las Cases in a second carriage and his staff and younger officers in a third. And thus on June 29, 1815, General Beker now gave the orders for them to set out for the coast.

Reaching the port of Rochefort on July 3, General Savary exchanged one hundred thousand francs in banknotes for gold, which Marchand then sewed into a dozen leather money belts. On July 7 Prussian troops duly made their victorious entry into the French capital. At 10:00 P.M. the next day Napoleon and his party were rowed from Fouras (opposite the Ile d'Aix) to the frigate *La Saale*, where the ex-emperor was received by a cool but correct Captain Philibert. "Once [he is aboard] the frigates must put to sea within twenty-four hours," read Decrès's sealed orders to Philibert, and they were then to sail "as quickly as possible . . . landing Napoleon and his suite either at Philadelphia or at Boston, or at such other port of the United States as would be promptly and easily reached." *La Saale* did not even raise its anchors, however, for blocking the channel was the seventy-four-gun British ship of the line, the mighty *Bellerophon*, a famous veteran of Trafalgar. When Savary, Las Cases, and General Lallemand met with Frederick Maitland, the captain of *Bellerophon*, to obtain the passes required to permit them to sail, they of course were denied. Maitland had been authorized, however, to receive Napoleon and his entire party and to convey them to England.[59]

Although Joseph proposed going aboard *Bellerophon* posing as his brother, thereby permitting Napoleon to escape, the latter would have no part of it. He was too tired for any more delays and ruses. As he confided to General Bertrand on July 14, "it is not without some danger, in putting myself in the enemy's hands, but it is better to risk confiding oneself to their honor than to be handed over to them as *de jure* prisoners." No English gentleman would do what he had done to the duc d'Enghien and to so many others. "I have concluded my political career," Napoleon now wrote the Prince Regent of England. "I come to take my place before the hearth of the British people. I place myself under the protection of their laws . . . as that of the most powerful, most consistent, and most generous of my enemies."[60]

A little after six o'clock the morning of Saturday, July 15, 1815, Napoleon was piped aboard *Bellerophon*, receiving full honors, and escorted to the captain's own cabins, which he had vacated for his special guest.[61] As the sails were unfurled and they put to sea, Napoleon watched the shores of his empire slowly fade from sight, Joseph sailing in another ship for the United States.

Meanwhile, after Bonaparte's one-hundred-day fiasco, France found its frontiers reduced again, this time to those of 1789, and the country was ordered to pay a war indemnity totaling seven hundred million francs, while foreign troops occupied the land. On July 24 the restored Louis XVIII took his revenge, the reprisals beginning with a list of fifty-seven officials and soldiers—including nineteen marshals and generals—who were accused of high treason. Orders for their arrest were issued.

Davout protested directly to the Tuileries, for the list was very selective indeed, omitting Fouché, Decrès, Caulaincourt, and Davout himself. These "officers have merely obeyed the orders I gave them in my capacity as war minister," he argued. "Therefore you must replace all their names with mine alone." When the king ignored this request, Davout wrote secretly to those named "to think about their safety," warning them that they had not "a moment to lose."[62] The celebrated cavalry hero, General Lefebvre-Desnoëttes, was last seen vanishing in the guise of a traveling salesman—but minus his enormous mustache, while General Lavalette escaped from a stone cell in the Conciergerie disguised in his wife's dress. Ultimately only five had the misfortune to be captured—including the twenty-nine-year-old newly promoted Brigadier General La Bédoyère, as he was bidding adieu to his wife—and executed. Another fourteen generals and politicians were condemned to death in absentia, while others were dismissed from office or banished, including Bassano, Boulay de La Meurthe, Cambacérès, Carnot, Defermont, Fouché, Masséna, Regnault de Saint-Jean d'Angély, Merlin de Douay, Quinette, Thibaudeau, and of course the wily, ingratiating Soult, while Grouchy managed to have himself declared "incompetent to stand trial."[63]

There was to be one more execution later. At 9:20 A.M. on Thursday, December 7, Marshal Michel Ney found himself standing before a firing squad in a Paris street. Having refused to kneel and be blindfolded—"a man such as I does not get down on his knees"—he stood there defiantly. And then as the commanding officer shouted, "*Apprêtez armes!*" Ney said, "I protest against my judgment. . . . Soldiers, straight at my heart!" "*Joue! Feu!*" As the drums rolled, twelve musket balls riddled his body, three of them shattering his face. The only marshal to have been captured—after betrayal by a fellow French officer—Ney had been tried before a court of 150 peers in the Luxembourg Palace and found guilty the day before his execution. Of the court, 5 peers had appealed for clemency and 17 had called for deportation, while 122 had demanded the death penalty, among them Ney's four fellow marshals Pérignon, Kellermann, Sérurier, and Victor, not to mention the pink-cheeked Admiral Ganteaume and numerous generals, including Beurnonville, Compans, Dessolles, La Tour-Maubourg, Lauriston, Maison, Monnieur, and Soulès.

"Failing to recognize the king's authority, cowardly putting his life under the orders of the foreigner [Napoleon], are acts so unworthy of a Frenchman," the *Journal des Débats* editorial concluded, "that they silence any commiseration that we might have otherwise felt for him. . . . Now we have accomplished a great act of justice."[64]

Meanwhile, at Plymouth, ex-emperor Napoleon, having been transferred from *Bellerophon* to *Northumberland* on August 7, 1815, accompanied by General and Mrs. Bertrand, the Montholons, General Gourgaud, and Las Cases and his son, ten weeks later stepped ashore on an isolated island owned by the East India Company, called St. Helena, the same island a twenty-year-old Lieutenant Bonaparte had recorded in one of his notebooks—the only item he had not had time to complete. Now he would do so.

CHAPTER 41

Final Casualties

French historians will have to deal with the Empire . . . and will have to give me my rightful due.

oney! Boney!" the two English schoolgirls cried out in the garden of the house not far from Jamestown, the port and only town of the forty-seven-square-mile-island of St. Helena. The girls giggled as they tied the blindfold over the eyes of the smiling, portly ex-emperor, much to the dismay of their parents, the William Balcombes, while a seething comte de Montholon looked on helplessly. "Boney," indeed!

That had been during the good days, the first days at the house known as the Briars, shortly after the ten-vessel British naval squadron—including troop transports and the seventy-four-gun *Northumberland,* commanded by Adm. Sir George Cockburn—had finally sighted "this black wart rising out of the ocean," as naval surgeon Henry described this volcanic outcrop jutting some 2,500 feet out of the South Atlantic, following an exhausting seventy-one-day voyage from England, dropping anchor at Jamestown on the evening of Saturday, October 17. Mr. Balcombe in particular had been kindness itself, something Napoleon had not expected of an Englishman, an employee of the East India Company, to which this island belonged but now placed at the disposal of His Majesty's Government for a unique assignment.

Then came the move up the sharply rising heights to the more arid but refreshingly cooler slopes to Longwood House, a couple of miles away from the Briars and four miles from Jamestown, while to the east, less than two miles distant, precipitous cliffs dropped abruptly to a raging surf below. It had been raining on December 9 as they made their way up the winding mountain road to the house of Lieutenant Governor Skelton, situated at an altitude of 1,730 feet, where the Skeltons gave Napoleon and his large entourage a warm welcome before a much needed glowing fire in the sitting room, Mrs. Skelton then giving her house guests a tour of their eleven-room country house. They were quite charming about relinquishing their home, as Napoleon later remarked.

It was hardly surprising that London had insisted on tight security for the most hated war criminal in Europe, and Longwood was the best choice, situated high up the windward side of the island buttressed by forbidding cliffs. Furthermore, there was room for an army camp just a few miles away, to foil the anticipated schemes to rescue the dethroned emperor. The British were not about to take any chances. Indeed, it was not long before London learned from the Spanish ambassador accredited to Washington, D.C., that Joseph Bonaparte was plotting to launch a flotilla of a half dozen vessels carrying some three hundred mercenaries to rescue brother Napoleon in June 1816.[1] This led to London reinforcing both the St. Helena garrison and the South Atlantic squadron by several thousand men. They had peace at last, and an exhausted Europe was not about to jeopardize it by taking half-measures at St. Helena.

Despite the spaciousness of Longwood and its pleasant gardens, it could hardly accommodate Napoleon's entire entourage, including their wives and children, not to mention twenty servants. The Bertrands and their children, for instance, were housed at the cottage known as Hutt's Gate, a mile away, and most of the servants were much farther than that. But His Majesty's Government had foreseen this problem and had already ordered a large amount of lumber and stone to be hauled up the mountain with which to build a spacious additional wing, waiting only for Napoleon's personal specifications and wishes—which, as it turned out, he declined to offer.

From the very beginning, following the departure of the Skeltons from their home, a formal decision was made by the French to appeal to European public opinion about the cruel and unusual conditions inflicted on the great man by the brutal, insensitive English, not to mention the evil "vexatious interference" of the British governor to render life intolerable for them in this tiny, windswept "cabin" where they were being starved and ill-treated.[2] Letters were immediately written and some safely smuggled out to Europe. Who was to know that in fact the prisoner was provided with a stable of horses for himself and his staff and was allowed to ride in any direction within a circumference of twelve, later reduced to eight, miles of Longwood, his to use whenever he chose? Far from being chained to walls of a stone cell in the Temple in Paris, as he had done to his English captives, he had instead comfortable furniture, staff, and servants, even his own French cook, all of his own choosing, waiting on him hand and foot. Indeed, far from starving, he was provided with seventy pounds of beef and mutton, along with seven chickens, *daily,* not to mention his own wine cellar, while he and his friends dined off rare porcelain and fine silver plate. And yet Napoleon complained to the governor: "What is the use of silver plate when you have no food to put on it?"[3] Well, it sounded good in the grim letters Napoleon, Montholon, Bertrand, and Gourgaud were carefully concocting for the gullible back in the old country.

Napoleon, certainly the most successful public relations man of his day, had elaborated this plan of attack at a long meeting convened on November 30, as eyewitness Las Cases remarked:

> We were possessed of moral arms only, and in order to make the most advantageous use of them, it was necessary to reduce to *a system,* our demeanour, our words, our sentiments, *even our privations,* with the intention of exciting a lively interest in Europe, and to rouse the political opposition in England to attack their own government regarding their violent conduct towards us.[4]

Soon the complaints of the "inhumane" living conditions the French were forced to endure at Longwood reached Rear Adm. Sir George Cockburn, and the governor, and were repeated in secret corresondence. As Napoleon himself put it to Las Cases: "All eyes are focused on us and this island. We remain the martyrs of an immortal cause. Millions of men are weeping for us, the fatherland sighs, and national glory is in mourning. We struggle here against the oppression of the gods."[5]

The Napoleon who had drafted the highly imaginative *Army Bulletin* about his alleged destruction of the fortress of Acre had lost none of his editorial skill. When he ordered Gen. Henri Bertrand personally to carry one complaint after another to the governor, the honorable man flinched and protested but in the end obeyed, as he always did.

Prisoner of war Napoleon Bonaparte found it outrageous that the British did not trust him and required a small escort of one or two soldiers to accompany him when he left the grounds of the house, and that all letters sent to, or received from, the outside world had first to be submitted to the governor's office for careful perusal. "Any protest from me would be beneath my dignity," he told his inner circle. Therefore it was up to them to "make your protests . . . and make Europe learn how badly we are being treated here, so that they may become indignant. . . . The Government has declared that he is a prisoner of war. The Emperor is not a prisoner of war." Such were the ploys and fantasies spread by Napoleon and the inmates of Longwood House. When years later Montholon was asked about these attacks against the British and the blatant defamation of Sir Hudson Lowe's character, he merely shrugged his shoulders and replied, "C'était notre politique, que voulez-vous?"[6]

In reality the governor of the island not only meticulously followed his instructions from London but when ordered by them later to cut back on Napoleon's rather luxurious level of living and to reduce the Longwood budget to £8,000 per annum, the new governor, Sir Hudson Lowe, not only vigorously protested to the secretary of state but unilaterally rejected it, adding on his own authority £4,000 which Napoleon of course never mentioned. And then when Bonaparte sent down some of his silver plate to Sir Hudson, asking him to sell it for him, Lowe instead sealed it and saved it in storage for the emperor, while giving him its value, £250, out of his own pocket, without telling Napoleon its source.

Gen. Sir Hudson Lowe arrived at Jamestown on April 14, 1816, to assume command of the troops and the island. The forty-seven-year-old Lowe knew Bonaparte's homeland well, and in addition to French and German, spoke the Corsican dialect of Italian he had learned while serving on that island and later commanding a corps of Corsican exiles in various campaigns, including Egypt. In 1813 he was transferred to Russia and assigned as liaison officer with Blücher's staff, giving him the opportunity to witness several Prussian battles with Napoleon, including the final battles in France in 1814, leaving him in great admiration of Bonaparte's astonishing military abilities. It was Lowe who brought the first news of Napoleon's abdication to London in the spring of 1814, and he was subsequently knighted for his many years of active service by the Prince Regent, and decorated by both Friedrich Wilhelm of Prussia and the czar. In 1814–15 he served as quartermaster general of the British forces in the Netherlands, old Blücher himself praising him, even the Anglophobe General Gneisenau complimenting him on "your rare military talents, your sound judgment on the great operations of war, and your imperturbable sang froid on the day of battle." Finally,

Lowe had been present at Waterloo when Napoleon fled the battlefield, and that was one humiliation Bonaparte could never forgive him. In fact, the British government could not have selected a more qualified man for the disagreeable job.

Lowe was a dedicated public servant who found himself saddled with the unenviable task of having to enforce the strict, detailed orders given him by London. The rigidly upright Lowe was precisely the sort of gentleman Napoleon could never begin to understand, nor did he make any attempt to do so.

On Sir Hudson's initial visit to Longwood at nine one morning in April 1816, Montholon rudely informed the English general that the emperor was "indisposed" and could not see him until four o'clock the following day. Lowe arrived punctually the next afternoon, with Admiral Cockburn at his side. General Bertrand, aided by a muscular valet, stood before the British officer, physically barring the way. A determined Lowe sidestepped them and went into the room, introducing himself to Bonaparte, and they were soon talking in the Corsican dialect. Apparently it had never occurred to Bonaparte, Montholon, or Bertrand that Lowe could summarily have summoned him to Plantation House instead. From the beginning Sir Hudson made every attempt to be conciliatory.

Later, when Lowe learned of the French complaints to the Prince Regent, relations between the governor and Longwood grew strained. But still Lowe attempted to improve the situation, and when for instance Las Cases, serving as Napoleon's secretary, came to Plantation House in the spring of 1816, Lowe put his entire library at Napoleon's disposal. This, however, drew Napoleon's ire, as did occasions when the new governor invited Napoleon and his suite—General Gourgaud, the comte and comtesse de Montholon, General and Mme. Bertrand—to dinners and soirées. For the ladies in particular these occasions were a great relief from the constraints of an ever glowering Napoleon. But when *la Grande Maréchale*, Bertrand's wife—*née* Fanny Dillon and a native English speaker—dared leave Napoleon's table at one such supper and ball to join her new English friends, Napoleon afterward sharply rebuked her and Madame Montholon publicly. Bonaparte insisted on severing all social relations with Plantation House, forcing the minuscule French community to withdraw into its own world, which in turn led to severe repercussions, including insipid quarrels between those couples.

This was further complicated when the members of Napoleon's immediate male entourage vied for the privilege of becoming his favorite. Gourgaud quarreled with Bertrand and Montholon, Montholon despised them both, and Napoleon thought the whole thing amusing. The wives rarely spoke to one another, and Madame Montholon was jealous of Madame Bertrand having a separate house away from Longwood, while she and her husband and children shared three rooms under Napoleon's roof. Then, just to complete this petty state of affairs, on the visit of the wife of the governor general of India who was stopping off at St. Helena before continuing her long voyage, Governor Lowe considerately sent a dinner invitation to Napoleon, but addressed him as "General Bonaparte" instead of "Emperor Napoleon." A furious Napoleon interpreted this as the insult of insults, in his reply calling Lowe his "executioner," while managing to slip in a complaint that he was allowed to travel only within a limited area around Longwood, and that Lowe had added to this humiliation by posting soldiers on the island. (Britain of course had never recognized the "Empire" or the title "emperor," and Lowe was therefore required by London to use the title "general.")

The last two interviews between Lowe and Bonaparte took place on August 17 and 18, when Napoleon again taunted the governor in outrageous language about the disgraceful habitation he had foisted upon him, the lack of food, and so on. "You make me smile, sir," the phlegmatic five-foot-seven, blond, blue-eyed Lowe said, looking down at the plump little man. "How is that, *monsieur*?" "You force me to smile, because your misconception of my character and the rudeness of your manners excite my pity. I wish you good day." He turned about, leaving a dumbfounded Napoleon Bonaparte turning red with anger. No one had ever done such a thing to the mighty conqueror.[7]

Thus Napoleon increased his campaign of the grossest character assassination of Lowe, and when the governor next dismissed the British ship's surgeon, Barry Edward O'Meara, who had been permitted to act as Napoleon's physician, O'Meara added to the defamation in his book, *A Voice from St. Helena*. In fact Lowe had no choice but to dismiss O'Meara when it was learned that he had been sending mendacious reports from Longwood to Plantation House, and was in fact in the pay of Napoleon, even managing to aid the French in sending letters abroad.[8]

No true view of the events taking place at Longwood over the next five years or so can be understood properly without a brief description of the entourage with which Napoleon decided to surround himself—in particular the four men with whom he spent most of his time: Gourgaud, Bertrand, Las Cases, and Montholon.

Gaspard Gourgaud was born in 1783, the son of a classical violinist employed by Louis XVI, while his mother worked as a domestic in the same palace. Gourgaud, though he had numerous relatives in the theater, instead chose to attend first the Ecole Polytechnique and then the Ecole de Châlons, emerging with a commission as an artillery officer. He participated in various campaigns, including Austerlitz, where he was wounded; then fought with distinction at Pultusk. Like many with the Grande Armée, he was ordered to Iberia, where he took part in the siege of Zaragoza, followed by rapid promotions. By 1811 he was serving as imperial ordnance officer with Napoleon on the long, bitter Russian campaign, resulting in another wound at the battle of Smolensk. Raised to the peerage as a baron for his zeal, intelligence, reliability, and loyalty, Gourgaud was at Napoleon's side for part of the retreat from Moscow, himself only escaping at Berezina by swimming that icy river.[9] He was promoted on his return, named Napoleon's first ordnance officer, and followed him into battle before Dresden in August 1813 when he was awarded the prestigious Grand Eagle of the Legion. On January 29, 1814, he reached the pinnacle of his military career at the Battle of Brienne by shooting a Cossack who was about to stab Napoleon, which the latter later denied, while Gourgaud staunchly held his ground. Wounded again, at Montmirail, he was made a commander of the Legion of Honor. On taking leave of Napoleon at Fontainebleau on April 24, he was one of the few strongly praised by the emperor. He next served in the newly reconstituted Bourbon army of Louis XVIII, promoted to the rank of general, and awarded the Cross of Saint-Louis. But with the return of Napoleon, he abandoned the king.

A vexed Napoleon at first refused to see Gourgaud. The highly emotional general screamed, cried, and swore he would blow out his brains. Two weeks later Napoleon relented, "pardoning" him with a simultaneous promotion as *maréchal de camp*.[10] Gourgaud was to prove an unstable character, emotionally and fitfully jealous of his other three companions in exile.

Of all those associated with Napoleon now, Gen. Comte Henri Bertrand proved throughout the years to be the most faithful and reliable. The son of a wealthy upper-middle-class family from Berry, he emerged with his commission from the Ecole du Génie Militaire (Military Engineering School) and the Ecole Centrale des Travaux Publics (Central Civil Engineering School). He later served with the Army of Italy, and again with Napoleon in Egypt, returning from Egypt a brigadier general at the age of twenty-three.

Thereafter he served constantly with Napoleon, next in charge of the engineers at the St.-Omer invasion camp (1803–1805), and then named aide-de-camp to Napoleon himself. In 1807, at the age of thirty-four, he was promoted to the rank of major general and married Fanny, daughter of the late Gen. Arthur Dillon. As wedding gifts Napoleon heaped riches on the couple, including a small country house, entirely furnished, and hundreds of thousands of francs in one form or other.

For services rendered during the second Danube campaign in 1809, Bertrand was awarded the Grand Eagle of the Legion, and in April 1811 found himself named the governor general of the unruly Illyrian Provinces. With the death of Duroc in 1813, Bertrand was called on to replace him as grand marshal. Reliable, honest, hardworking, and intelligent, on his arrival at St. Helena with Fanny and their two children, initially he was the closest person to Napoleon.[11] He was forty-two years old.

Emmanuel de Las Cases was quite another kettle of fish, totally unlike General Bertrand. Las Cases was born in the Château de Las Cases, in Languedoc, in 1766, the eldest son of the marquis. Raised in refined surroundings, he was well educated at the Collège de Vendôme, and then at the Ecole Militaire in Paris. Like Napoleon and Gourgaud, Las Cases was abnormally small, which apparently was the reason for his choosing a career in the French Royal Navy over the army. He was wounded fighting the British during the siege of Gibraltar in November 1782, and was eventually promoted to naval lieutenant and presented at court in July 1790. He was one of the many thousands of fellow aristocrats emigrating, keeping alive by tutoring the children of friends.

He finally returned to France in 1803 and swore his allegiance to Napoleon. Although he was refused the Cross of the Legion of Honor in 1809, Napoleon did make him a baron of the Empire as a result of his book, *Atlas Historique et Généalogique*. In 1810 he was appointed to the position of master of petitions for the naval section of the Council of State, next presiding over the Debt Liquidation Commission for the Illyrian Provinces, resulting in a boost up the peerage as count. Although he was capable of hard work, he intrigued far more strenuously at obtaining honors and was considered quite an egotist by his colleagues. With the approach of the Allied armies in 1814, he was named temporary commander in the Paris National Guard and simultaneously was promoted to naval captain and state councillor, after which he fled the country for England.

He was accepted back by Napoleon during the Hundred Days, serving as president of the Commission of Petitions, and with Montholon served as one of Napoleon's chamberlains. At Malmaison in June 1815 he agreed to go into exile with Napoleon, who asked, "Do you know where we are going?" "I haven't the slightest idea," Las Cases replied, "but my supreme wish is only to be granted this favor of accompanying you." At the age of forty-nine he would leave his wife and all his children behind, with the exception of his fifteen-year-old son, whom he withdrew from his lycée.

Unlike Bertrand, however, the insecure Las Cases was not truly loyal or devoted to Napoleon, though he certainly admired him. Nor had he agreed to follow him in hope of financial gain. Perhaps as he approached his fiftieth year, at a crossroads in an unhappy marriage, without having really achieved anything of permanence, flitting from one post to another, he simply wanted a change. But what a change! It hardly boded well for Napoleon that thus far he had selected two men who for various reasons seemed particularly unreliable in the long term, especially under conditions of considerable stress—the curious Las Cases, and the emotionally unstable Gourgaud with his enormous inferiority complex.[12]

What was to prove the most disastrous personnel decision of Napoleon's entire life, however, was the selection of the obsequious Charles Tristan de Montholon to join him in exile. Born in 1783, Tristan de Montholon was given the title of comte de Lee at birth. His father died when the boy was five, and his mother remarried Huguet de Montaran de Sémonville, a man who was to have much influence in Paris and in future promotions for Tristan as a result of his own spectacular rise, first as a parliamentary counselor and then as future ambassador under Napoleon. One of Montholon's sisters, Félicité, was to marry first General Joubert and later Marshal Macdonald, who was also to give Montholon a leg up the ladder. At the age of sixteen Tristan de Montholon was sent off to the Army of Italy, receiving his commission the following spring and promoted to captain when attached to General Augereau's command in 1801.

But thereafter most of the long military career he subsequently claimed at St. Helena was one of the most extraordinary web of lies and fabrications ever recorded in the annals of the French army. He said, for instance, that he had fought and distinguished himself during the Hohenlinden campaign, for which he received a sword of honor, whereas Montholon was not only not present at Hohenlinden in December 1800, but was in fact in the process of being cashiered from the army for incompetence. Thanks to influential friends, no doubt brother-in-law Macdonald among them, Montholon was reintegrated into the army, soon as aide-de-camp to General Macdonald himself. For such a brave and enterprising warrior, clearly promotion was long overdue, and thus influential stepfather Sémonville had a word with his good friend War Minister Berthier, and in November 1804 the twenty-one-year-old Montholon, who had never commanded even a platoon, was breveted lieutenant colonel. However, Sémonville, not satisfied with such a mediocre reward for a stepson who had spent almost two and a half years in the army, had another one of his famous chats with Marshal Berthier, and then with Secretary of State Maret, both of whom then personally recommended young Tristan to Bonaparte. On looking at his service record, Napoleon rejected the request, stating what was obvious to anyone who could add and subtract, that "this officer has not served the requisite time." Thus Montholon merely got himself transferred to a soft general-staff posting with Macdonald again.

In 1809, thanks to effective politicking on his part and more string-pulling on the part of his stepfather and brother-in-law, the persistent Montholon was promoted to full colonel, created a peer of the realm (as comte de Sémonville), awarded a state pension of four thousand francs a year, based on property stolen in Hannover. Naturally, achieving all that in less than twelve months was fatiguing. Pleading that "the breakdown of my health resulting from my exhausting war service no longer permits me to serve as an active officer," the twenty-six-year-old colonel sought instead a position at the Tuileries as chamberlain to Napoleon. The record he now submitted to Napoleon was once again a superb list of colorful lies: wounded at Jena—not true, according to an affidavit from his commanding officer later; singlehandedly saved several battalions of Savary's division from destruction at Heilsberg—alas, a little too imaginative, there having *been* no Savary division at Heilsberg at that time. Not satisfied with these yarns, the boundless Montholon, emboldened, now embroidered further, waxing truly eloquent over a famous cavalry charge he had led at Eckmühl, followed by another in Madrid at the head of the marines in recapturing the main arsenal, while not forgetting his distinguished leadership at Wagram—total fabrications, the lot, but a jolly good read for all that. Moreover Montholon, though legally a colonel, neglected to mention that he had never earned any of his promotions on the battlefield, a unique record even in those corrupt times.

As a civilian Montholon—thus saved from the arduous duties of high field command, not to mention the rigors of life as a court chamberlain—in 1811 got himself named minister plenipotentiary to the grand duke of Würzburg at a salary of forty thousand francs a year. But by the age of twenty-eight, finding all those state balls a little too fatiguing and the ducal receptions a little too boring, in May 1812 our hero abandoned that post too (without permission) and returned to Paris to marry one Madame

Roger. Alas, he had failed to request Napoleon's blessings on these nuptials, and the slighted emperor was most put out. Moreover, Napoleon did not approve of young men of *bonne famille* marrying divorcées: It set a bad example. As a result the dumbfounded Montholon at the age twenty-nine found himself dismissed as both court chamberlain and minister plenipotentiary, and with that went the loss of a considerable income and the usual bribes, which really hurt—Tristan being an inveterate gambler and spendthrift, and of course a bounder par excellence. The official communiqué from the foreign minister informed him that he had "judged the marriage you have just contracted to be incompatible with the honorable functions that have been conferred upon you." That was in October 1812, in the midst of the Russian campaign. Then the second blow followed, for shortly after their marriage his wife gave birth to their first child, clearly conceived out of wedlock. That proved the final straw for both Napoleon—with two bastards of his own—and the foreign minister, as the ex-soldier, ex-diplomat was ordered to retreat to his estate near Nogent-sur-Vernisson at Changry and not to show his handsome face in Paris again.

After the disastrous Russian campaign, however, Napoleon literally needed every man who could still walk—or at least limp—and thus Montholon was called to the colors again in April 1813 by a desperate war minister, who was truly scraping the bottom of the barrel. Montholon's assignment was to serve as chief of staff of the Second Light Cavalry Division. But the idea of all that exertion, not to mention the real danger this time, was too much for the thirty-year-old, who replied: "It is with the greatest regret that as a result of my wounds . . . I am unable even to mount a horse without causing awful hemorrhaging," and tossed those egregious orders into the fire. When in December of that year the war minister wrote again with a fresh assignment not involving horses—in damp, foggy Holland, clearly a most disagreeable place to pass the winter and to fight a war—the elusive Montholon added yet another notch to his flummery, replying, "I would have set out immediately had I not been kept in bed with a raging fever," as he threw the second set of orders into the fire. But by now General Hulin (who had ordered the murder of Enghien at Vincennes) had had quite enough and peremptorily ordered the evasive Montholon to appear forthwith—which Tristan as usual declined to countenance. Surely if he were patient enough, the war minister could come up with something a little more amenable. And lo! patience duly had its reward in the form of a direct order straight from the Tuileries, this time to take command of the troops of the Department of the Loire, for the final defense of France. It was getting better and better.

This time "General Montholon"—another hard-earned promotion—actually went to Montbrison on March 12, 1814, to form an army with which to defend the region. Ordered to lead his four-thousand-or-so-man army to aid General Augereau at St.-Bonnet-le-Château in the mountains, Montholon set out, only to abandon his troops in mid-March to rejoin his wife and children, informing the war minister that the Austrians had advanced quickly and seized St.-Etienne, and that he was making a "strategic retreat" to beef up his "weak corps." Finally rejoining his troops but abandoning his entire department to the approaching Allies, he fell back to Clermont-Ferrand, well out of gunshot, just long enough to seize the 5,970 francs' pay due some of his troops, and on April 16 abandoned his entire army, now totaling some eight thousand men, absconding with the funds, fleeing not the enemy but the gambling debts he owed his own junior officers.

Montholon later wrote Napoleon that he had been betrayed at Lyons by Augereau and had thus withdrawn, but he was now offering to bring an entire brigade to the Emperor's aid. "Entirely devoted to Your Majesty," he informed Napoleon, "I have sacrificed everything for Him." Meanwhile, that same day, Montholon wrote another letter, this time to Louis XVIII's staff, explaining that "after having suffered eighteen months of disgrace at the hands of [Napoleon's] government," he would like to serve the Bourbons. "My Lord, permit me to request of your goodness the rank of brigadier general. I shall serve the king as faithfully as my forefathers served Henri II and François I." He now signed himself "the Marquis de Montholon." In a follow-up letter he added, "I have served my country in thirteen campaigns and ten great battles in the course of which I was wounded three times and had several horses shot out from beneath me." All lies including his new title of "marquis."

Needless to say, the king could hardly pass up an officer of such sterling qualities, and on August 24, 1814, duly accorded him a commission as brigadier general in the Bourbon army. But scarcely had the ink dried on the parchment when Montholon's past finally caught up with him—not in the form of all those fictitious campaigns he had never witnessed and wounds he had never received but ironically a little heist from an army safe in Clermont-Ferrand. An arrest warrant was ordered for the "brigadier." The outraged Montholon immediately reminded the king of his "long and good services to the crown"—he had held his commission for seven days—and explained that the only reason he had not handed over the pay to his men was because of the approach of the enemy, and in the past four months he had not had an opportunity to pay them.

This time it simply did not wash, and General Augereau—whom Montholon had denounced at Lyons—ordered a court-martial, Montholon saved at the eleventh hour by the timely intervention of Louis XVIII's brother, the comte d'Artois (the future Charles X), who quashed the proceedings but ordered Montholon to return to his estate and not to appear in public again.

Thus when Napoleon had made his appearance at the Tuileries in March 1815, it proved a godsend for the ill-used Montholon. Cautiously waiting to see if Bonaparte would stay the course, it was only at the beginning of June that Montholon finally wrote officially to War Minister Davout demanding a command, followed by a personal letter to Napoleon on June 5 in which among other things he pleaded: "Sire, by the devotion I have shown you [listing two full pages of previous exploits], I retain the hope of being called to serve Your Majesty in a military capacity ... and that you accord me an active and honorable post." No response from either the War Office or the Tuileries, but that did not prevent Montholon from concocting the story in his *Mémoires* that Napoleon had named him an aide-de-camp and promoted him to the rank of major general during the Hundred Days, whereas of course Napoleon had declined the honor of calling on Montholon's redoubtable military talents in any capacity.[13]

That Montholon was able to inveigle himself in Napoleon's good graces after Waterloo, while awaiting deportation at Malmaison, remains perhaps his greatest coup of all—and Napoleon fell for it.

Now at Longwood, 4,400 miles from Malmaison in the absolute middle of nowhere, Tristan de Montholon had finally succeeded in edging out the faithful Bertrand himself, becoming to all intents and purposes Napoleon's chief of staff and closest intimate, causing severe rifts and jealousies among a bewildered Bertrand, hysterical Gourgaud, and a pouting Las Cases. The latter, after filling his notebooks with all the confidences and remembrances, real and imagined, that Napoleon had purportedly shared with him since his arrival in 1815, left in a huff in November 1816, after quarreling with Napoleon over the insults he had received from both Gourgaud and Montholon. Gourgaud, himself terribly insecure, had attacked Las Cases for coming to St. Helena solely "in order to be talked about" on his return to France "and to write anecdotes, which he intends to exploit financially."[14] (Las Cases would in fact publish his long talks with Napoleon in eight volumes entitled *Memorial of St. Helena* shortly after Napoleon's death, not to mention his own personal *Mémoires*.) As for Montholon, he was delighted to have succeeded in chasing away the nervous Las Cases, leaving now only two men between him and Napoleon.

In fact Sir Hudson Lowe had first ordered Las Cases to leave Long-wood when he learned that, on Napoleon's orders, he had bribed a servant to send two letters to Europe. But later, when the governor offered to permit Las Cases to return to Napoleon, he instead begged to be allowed to take the first boat back to France. Having been insulted by Montholon and Gourgaud—both goaded by Napoleon—Las Cases never wanted to see the great man again.

The growing acrimony at Longwood was not helped by the weather, with frequently long periods of rain, wind, and low-hanging cloud over nearby Diana Peak. Napoleon always reacted sharply to chilly, gloomy weather. To this was added the isolation, not just from Jamestown but also from civilization even on the island, since Napoleon had ordered them all to keep their distance from the English, the pressure stemming from their self-imposed intimacy playing havoc with everyone's nerves.

The women were the first to react, and although Sir Hudson provided a billiards table when requested, and then a piano, and hundreds of books, nevertheless petty disputes and disagreements, along with daily friction, increased. Harmless games of whist during the long, repetitive evenings frequently ended in tiffs, and Fanny Bertrand could not abide the presence of "that woman," the notorious comtesse de Montholon. Even when they did manage an evening of cards or chess, Napoleon's outrageous cheating—tolerated at Malmaison—set their hackles up at Longwood. It was perhaps even worse for Gourgaud, however, for unlike Bertrand and Montholon, he had neither wife nor children there.

Napoleon himself was in the same position, of course, for the first time in his life finding himself without a woman, or even wanting one, as his depression increased, along with a decline in health. "I don't like women very much," he said at Longwood, "or games of any kind, or anything else. I am I suppose a purely political creature." Nor was he very sympathetic to the plight of those caught in the political upheaval he had left behind in France. On learning of the arrest and execution of two of the men who had so helped him during the Hundred Days—young La Bédoyère and Michel Ney, instead of commiserating on their fate and praising their contributions, he merely snarled to Gourgaud: "One ought never to break one's word.... I despise traitors."[15] (They had sworn allegiance to Louis XVIII before returning to him.) Gourgaud, scarcely believing his ears, sat there speechless. Was this really his great hero, around whom he had centered his life and career? If he said that about two men who had volunteered their lives for him, what would he say about Gourgaud himself in his absence? As for Las Cases, both Montholon and Gourgaud had rejoiced at his departure: "the little Jesuit," Gourgaud spitefully called him. Napoleon seemed disappointed in only one respect—he would be unable to continue his English lessons, which Las Cases had been attempting to inculcate, without much success, however, as Napoleon's last letter in English reflected.

Count Lascases,

Since sixt week y learn the English and I do not any progress. Sixt week do fourty and two day. If might have learn fivty word, for day, i could know it two thousands and two hundreds. It is in the dictionary more of fourty thousand: even he could most twenty; bot much tems. For know it or hundred and twenty weeks, which do more two years. After this you shall agree that the study one tongue is a great labour who it must do into the young aged.[16]

With Las Cases gone, Gourgaud came under greater attack by both Bertrand and Montholon, who now taunted "Gogo," Napoleon chuckling in the background. Gourgaud, who felt he should have precedence over the fake soldier and upstart, saw his enemy superseding him in Napoleon's esteem. Montholon now even went so far as to tease Gourgaud about having saved Napoleon at Brienne, which Napoleon even fully denied had ever happened. That did it. Gourgaud snapped, challenging Montholon to a duel. But like all bullies, Montholon was a coward and backed off, and Napoleon intervened, forbidding the action and criticizing Gourgaud for his part in it, but not Montholon for his.

That was the final insult, and General Gourgaud asked Napoleon's permission to leave the island, which was quickly granted. Bonaparte was also unhappy with Gourgaud for having written positive letters to his mother about their living conditions, assuring her that they had been treated well and even generously by Sir Hudson Lowe. Some of these letters reached official circles in Paris, countering the black tales of horror Napoleon's clique had been manufacturing and circulating.

On February 13, 1818, Gourgaud left Longwood, spending his remaining weeks at a cottage near Plantation House awaiting the next ship. Napoleon refused to advance him any money, money legally due him, leaving the penniless Gourgaud in a predicament until Governor Lowe advanced him one hundred pounds out of his own pocket. Perfidious Albion . . .

On reaching England on May 1, Gourgaud spoke with the Under Secretary of State, warning him that Napoleon had been plotting, sending apocryphal accounts of their living conditions and of Sir Hudson's adminis-

tration to Europe. He also pointed out how easily he could escape. Gourgaud did admit that, "However unhappy he [Napoleon] is there, he secretly
enjoys the importance attached to his custody, the interest that the Powers
take in it, and the care taken to collect his least words." Las Cases confirmed this independently, quoting Napoleon just before leaving the island:
"Our situation here may even have its positive points. Everyone in Europe
is looking at us. We remain the martyrs of an immoral cause."[17]

Intrigue, the intense intimacy enforced on the inmates of Longwood
House, and their conflicting personalities were taking their toll. Las Cases,
Gourgaud and O'Meara were gone, and now both Mesdames Bertrand and
Montholon insisted on departing with their children. To be sure, there were
a few pleasant days, when even Napoleon would appear in his wide-
brimmed hat, his body gaining more and more flesh, his hair growing thinner and thinner. At night they would read aloud, or play chess or billiards,
to which Napoleon added a new twist, using his hand instead of a cue.

Three Corsicans arrived at St. Helena, sent by Uncle Fesch, including
two priests and Dr. Francesco Antommarchi. But it hardly improved the
almost lethal atmosphere of Longwood. A depressed Albine de Montholon
was permitted to sail with her children, including her newborn daughter,
Napoléonne, in the first week of July 1819. Alas the lovely, tall, blond
Fanny Bertrand, who so disliked Napoleon after his months of insults that
she refused to visit Longwood anymore, was forced to remain. Life was
reduced to a dreary bachelor existence, becoming quite unbearable. The
only reason Tristan Montholon did not leave was because Napoleon had
bribed him, too, offering to pay large sums to his wife and children once
they reached France, with hints of a spectacular legacy in his will if Montholon stayed.

Meanwhile Madame Bertrand too was becoming more and more desperate to escape the island altogether, especially after having learned of her
mother's death back in 1817. When in 1820 she was finally about to leave
with her son, Arthur, and daughter, Hortense, however, Bertrand
announced that he would join her that same year. Napoleon forbade it. A
simmering Fanny unpacked her trunks but refused any further communication with Bonaparte until just hours before his death.

However, there had earlier been three successful, if involuntary, departures
from Longwood, beginning on February 24, 1818, with Napoleon's Corsican butler, Cipriani, who in fact was his intelligence officer (their two families had been old friends back in Ajaccio). A very strong man who never

suffered from even a cold, on February 24, 1818, he suddenly collapsed with severe chills, sharp burning abdominal pains, nausea, and vomiting. Forty-eight hours later he was dead. The doctors consulted were puzzled, but there it was, and the poor man was buried nearby. But when an inquiry was launched from a suspicious Longwood, and an autopsy ordered, it was discovered that the body had disappeared. Within a matter of weeks a young maid also died, with similar symptoms, and then the child of a servant—all residents of, or people working at, Longwood House.

Napoleon was not without his own growing number of health problems, even collapsing on at least one occasion. It is not clear when the first signs of serious illness were noted, but certainly by early 1818 they were well in evidence. Napoleon complained of violent stomachaches, "burning" he called them, chills, vomiting, accompanied by loss of appetite. Finally, by the end of 1820, he was reduced to a diet of fluids and cold drinks—no more bread, meat, or vegetables—yet he continued to gain weight. He knew he was ill, very ill, and William Balcombe, who still occasionally visited Napoleon, had suggested poisoning as the cause as early as 1818, after the suspicious deaths of Cipriani and the others.

From 1820 onward all life at Longwood seemed to come to a standstill. The large stacks of timber and stone intended for the new wing of the house gathered mildew, because Napoleon still refused to authorize the new construction. After all, what would world public opinion say about the poor man's sufferings at the hands of the cruel British if it were learned that he was living in a twenty-room country house? With those additional rooms Napoleon could hardly have continued to dispatch the by-now-most-embarrassed General Bertrand to complain about the "appalling living conditions" there.

Bertrand continued to make his appearance at Longwood, but it was for shorter and shorter periods, as he found himself supplanted by the controlling Montholon, who still wanted to rejoin his wife and children but also wanted the substantial sum Napoleon was dangling before him. Napoleon's valet, Marchand, was still there, but he spoke with Napoleon only in the morning when dressing and shaving him, and in the evening. Lunch and supper became painful affairs, with all those empty chairs, leaving only Montholon and Napoleon, the latter on a liquid diet, finding even the sight of food repulsive.

To prevent Napoleon from vomiting what little food he was now taking, calomel was administered, with strict instructions from Dr. Antommarchi that not more than one-quarter of one grain be given at a time, due to its toxicity (it contains mercury chloride). But in fact the cause of Napoleon's steady, dramatic decline was arsenic poisoning.

Prior to Cipriani's death in February 1818, it would have been difficult for anyone to do this, for the Corsican "butler" was responsible for ordering Napoleon's food supplies from abroad, including his favorite Capetown claret, and for carefully inspecting the kitchen and the food served Napoleon. Now that the devoted but more suspicious Cipriani was out of the way, and seven servants had been fired in a belt-tightening exercise, not to mention the departure of the ever-present Las Cases and Gourgaud, there was far less supervision of supplies received and food served. In addition, there was one item that was reserved solely for Napoleon, his special wine, which no one else touched. Arsenic, largely odorless and tasteless, could be readily introduced into wine without being detected, and apparently that was how it was done. But after the sudden deaths of three perfectly healthy individuals, the killer had to conceal his or her tracks. If Napoleon suddenly died, especially from the same cause as the butler, the maid, and the child—and he had the same symptoms—the British would demand an autopsy, and many questions would be asked. Therefore the would-be murderer had to switch tactics, adding a different poison.

In March 1821 Dr. Antommarchi allowed Napoleon to be given a new lemonade drink with a tartar emetic. The drink would quench the patient's insatiable thirst while countering the severe problem of constipation. But the base of this emetic was antimony potassium tartrate, a highly toxic substance. Napoleon was now taking two potentially lethal substances, arsenic and the emetic. Then on April 22 a new fruit drink, orgeat, was introduced, to which the murderer added an oil of bitter almonds. (A case of bitter almonds had been delivered to Longwood in April; before that an oil of ground peach stones, which contain hydrocyanic, or Prussic, acid, had been used.)[18] This of course was done without the doctor's knowledge. Napoleon was now ingesting four toxic substances including the calomel, for the arsenic continued to be administered secretly (if irregularly) in his wine, thereby increasing Napoleon's thirst, causing him to drink more of the poisoned orgeat, resulting in the toxic chemicals combining to form mercury cyanide. And, as the vomiting was now largely stopped by the calomel, the mercury cyanide remained in Napoleon's body.

"The Emperor had a sudden relapse," Dr. Antommarchi recorded on February 21, 1821. "He is worse than yesterday," he noted the following day, Napoleon feeling nauseous, complaining of a burning sensation in his abdomen, a "burning thirst," and coughing. Clearly another large dose of arsenic had been administered. Now, in the waning days of winter and the dawning of spring, Napoleon was confined to his bed. "Today he is a corpse animated by a mere breath of life," Montholon described to his wife on March 5. Part of the poisoning was purely accidental, of course. The physician-prescribed tartar emetic, beginning on March 22, aggravated the situation, which grew critical a month later, when Napoleon began drinking large quantities of the orgeat. Napoleon declined rapidly and remained in constant pain now.

By April death appeared not only inevitable but imminent, which did not prevent Napoleon from continuing with his accusations, haranguing the latest British physician, Dr. Arnott, as late as April 20: "I came to sit at the hearth of the British nation, asking only for honest hospitality ... [and instead] was put in chains.... How have I been treated since my arrival here? There is not a single indignity that has not been heaped upon me by my captors.... And now perishing on this loathsome rock, I bequeath the name of my death to the Ruling House of England."

After April 22 Napoleon no longer had the energy for tirades against anyone. With a patient suffering from so many conflicting symptoms, his personal physician was stymied, and feeling that the end was near summoned Dr. Arnott from Plantation House. After a long consultation they agreed to increase the dose of calomel. "This is one last desperate attempt," Bertrand recorded, "for the emperor is lost. We must not leave ourselves in a position afterward where we could reproach ourselves for not having taken every possible measure to save him."[19]

Before receiving the massive dose at 5:30 P.M. on May 3, Napoleon could still occasionally mumble a few words, most of them unintelligible except for "Josephine" and "my son." The calomel was administered in sugared water, after he had earlier swallowed large amounts of the poisoned orgeat. Bertrand's coded diaries, only recently deciphered, describe the results: "Shortly thereafter he became unconscious and completely paralyzed."[20] The mercury cyanide was eating into his system.

At 7:00 A.M. on Saturday, May 5, Fanny Bertrand reappeared at Longwood House to pay her last respects, taking a chair at the foot of Napoleon's bed, and then all the French staff working around or in Longwood were brought into the bedroom as well. Napoleon Bonaparte died at 5:49 P.M., the paralysis so complete that he could no longer swallow or breathe. Moments later a signal cannon was fired to notify the governor and the island. The most destructive man in European history since Attila the Hun was no more.

The faithful Henri Bertrand approached and, kneeling at the bedside, kissed his master's hand. Dr. Arnott brought in an ordnance officer to witness the death, as two more doctors were dispatched from Plantation House by Sir Hudson Lowe.

Following their instructions, the testamentary executors retired to the billiards room to read the last will and testament and its thirty-seven articles, dividing perhaps six million francs left with Napoleon's banker, Laffitte. After bequeathing a few hundred thousand francs to both Bertrand and his valet, Marchand, nothing to Marie Louise or any of his brothers, and only his properties in Ajaccio to his son, to the astonishment of everyone he left the major portion, 2 million francs, to Tristan de Montholon.

An official autopsy attended by seven physicians discovered that his stomach was seriously ulcerated, leading to the unanimous decision that Napoleon had died of cancer, like his father before him, despite the fact that the corpse before them was fatter than before his arrival back in 1815. After removing the rather small heart and stomach—the latter to be sent to England for further medical study—the body was cleaned and placed in Napoleon's favorite uniform as a *chasseur* of the Guards, with its white cashmere underjacket and breeches, and a green jacket. A hat with a tricolor cocarde was placed on his head, while the orders of the Legion of Honor and the Iron Crown were pinned on his chest and the Grand Cordon of the Legion attached as well.

After being left in a *chapelle ardente*, the body was finally placed in four caskets, one inside another, two of metal, two of mahogany, all of them sealed with lead. After Abbé Vignali celebrated the mass and twelve British grenadiers in dress uniform carried the heavy casket into the garden of Longwood and placed it on the hearse, Bertrand covered it with the blue cape Napoleon had worn at Marengo, and his sword. Two thousand British troops in immaculate scarlet uniforms stood at ramrod attention, presenting arms as the British military band played the funeral dirge. Sir Hudson Lowe, in dress uniform, attended by his wife and daughter, a rear admiral, and a representative of the French government, stood over the newly finished stone crypt, eleven feet deep and six feet wide. Fifteen grenadiers fired three salvos as the heavy mahogany coffin was lowered. Because the French had insisted on a tombstone bearing the words "Emperor Napoleon" and the British, refusing a title their government had never officially recognized, suggested instead "Napoleon Bonaparte," the French declined any marker whatsoever. Napoleon Bonaparte, or Emperor Napoleon, was finally laid to rest, and Europe could sigh with relief.

The autopsy conclusions notwithstanding, there is no doubt that Napoleon was murdered. Recent scientific analyses of Napoleon's hair have found arsenic levels from 35 to 640 times that found in the hair of a healthy human being. Facts are facts.

Needless to say, if the killer had given Napoleon one enormous, lethal dose, it would have been too evident. Therefore the doses remained just strong enough gradually to break down his constitution, while adding the powerful hydrocyanic acid. Thus, though he was administered arsenic in his wine for many months, Napoleon ultimately died of cyanide poisoning.

Only a few people were consistently in Napoleon's intimate proximity the last few months and thus in a position to murder him: General Bertrand, Marchand, Napoleon's bodyguard Ali Saint-Denis, and Montholon. Marchand and Ali had respectable pasts and personalities inconsistent with that of a stealthy poisoner. The same applied to the loyal, steadfast Bertrand, who in any case lived well over a mile away from Longwood. The killer had only a few hours in the middle of the night when the kitchen was empty in which to prepare the poison and add it to the food or drink. With Cipriani out of the way, the poisoner was free to act.

Montholon was not only present throughout this period but also had the devious personality required to execute such a diabolical plot. He was a consistent deceiver, as his military record clearly shows, not to mention a little larceny in the process. Moreover, he had a double motive: to leave the island and gain a fortune. Persona non grata with King Louis XVIII and deeply in debt and harried by French creditors, he wormed his way into Napoleon's good graces through his ancien régime manners, courtesies, and unusual charm. This boundless bounder escaped debtors' prison by serving Napoleon on faraway St. Helena. When Montholon discovered that Napoleon preferred his company to that of Las Cases, Gourgaud, and even Bertrand, Montholon took advantage of it, gradually forcing both Las Cases and Gourgaud to flee, and nearly doing the same in the case of the Bertrands.

Napoleon's promise to provide a substantial income for Montholon's wife and children in France and also to leave a major portion of his fortune to him proved to be the former emperor's undoing. The sooner Montholon killed him, the sooner he could escape from St. Helena and return to France in style. The scheme would have worked—if the Bonaparte clan, in a rare moment of family solidarity, had not blocked his access to the loot, thanks to the cooperation of his banker, Lafitte. Montholon died penniless in Belgium.

One final irony: The French emperor, who had successfully escaped death time and again from Prussian, Russian, British, Austrian, German, Italian, and Spanish artillery, muskets, swords, and bayonets, had been killed by his closest chosen companion—a Frenchman.

EPILOGUE

or all the attempts to restrict, suppress and muffle me, it will be difficult to make me disappear from the public memory completely. French historians will have to deal with the Empire . . . and will have to give me my rightful due." Clearly Napoleon had forgotten the hundreds of smoking villages he had bombarded or burned to the ground, from Moscow to Warsaw to Prussia, throughout northern and southern Italy, and sweeping across the plains and mountains of Iberia. He had forgotten the thousands of genuine POWs he had subsequently executed in cold blood. He had forgotten the hundreds of thousands of civilian refugees rendered homeless by his wars, the thousands upon thousands of old women and young girls raped by his Grande Armée, of the hundreds of towns and cities he had ruthlessly looted, the three million or so dead soldiers of all nations left rotting across the face of Europe, and the millions of wounded and permanently handicapped, the destroyed political institutions of a few hundred states and principalities— the shattered economies, the fear and dread he had left behind everywhere, France included. The memory of Genghis Khan paled in comparison. "What utter madness to believe that one can prevent the truth of history from eventually being written," a much tried but undaunted Emile Zola reflected at the end of the nineteenth century, in the midst of the Dreyfus affair. I have attempted to give Napoleon Bonaparte his rightful due.

Finally, in perhaps one of the most ironic twists of fate, a direct result of Napoleon's having destroyed the hundreds of Germanic states belonging to the Holy Roman Empire, and reunifying them along with Prussia, Bavaria, Saxony, and the rest, was the facilitation and stimulation of German nationalism and unification under Bismarck's guiding hand later in the century, leading to Prussia's successful invasion and occupation of France.

APPENDIX A

Napoleon's Marshals

1. Pierre-François-Charles Augereau, 1757–1816, duke of Castiglione
2. Jean-Baptiste-Jules Bernadotte, 1763–1844, prince of Pontecorvo
3. Louis-Alexandre Berthier, 1753–1815 (suicide, Bamberg, Bavaria), prince of Neuchâtel, prince of Wagram
4. Jean-Baptiste Bessières, 1768–1813 (Lützen), duke of Istria
5. Guillaume-Marie-Anne Brune, 1763–1815 (murdered by French mob)
6. Louis-Nicolas Davout, 1770–1823, duke of Auerstädt, prince of Eckmühl
7. Laurent Gouvion St.-Cyr, 1764–1830, count
8. Emmanuel de Grouchy, 1766–1847, count
9. Jean-Baptiste Jourdan, 1762–1833
10. François-Etienne-Christophe Kellermann, 1735–1820, duke of Valmy
11. Jean Lannes, 1769–1809 (Aspern), prince of Sievers, duke of Montebello
12. François-Joseph Lefebvre, 1755–1820, duke of Danzig
13. Etienne-Jacques-Joseph-Alexandre Macdonald, 1765–1840, duke of Taranto
14. Auguste-Frédéric-Louis Viesse de Marmont, 1774–1852, duke of Ragusa
15. André Masséna, 1758–1817, duke of Rivoli, prince of Essling
16. Bon-Adrien Jannot de Moncey, 1754–1842, duke of Conigliano
17. Adolphe-Edouard-Casimir-Joseph Mortier, 1768–1835, duke of Treviso
18. Joachim Murat, 1768–1815 (executed, Italy), grand duke of Berg and of Cleves, king of Naples
19. Michel Ney, 1769–1815 (executed, Paris), duke of Elchingen, prince of La Moskowa
20. Nicolas-Charles Oudinot, 1767–1847, count, duke of Reggio
21. Cathérine-Dominique de Perignon, 1754–1818, count
22. Joseph-Antoine Poniatowski, 1763–1813 (Leipzig), prince of the Holy Roman Empire

23. Jean-Mathieu-Philibert Serurier, 1742–1819, count
24. Jean de Dieu Soult, 1769–1851, duke of Dalmatia
25. Louis-Gabriel Suchet, 1770–1826, count, duke of Albufera
26. Claude-Victor Perrin, called Victor, 1764–1841, duke of Bellune

APPENDIX B

Medical Notes

Three phases of Napoleon's medical history appear to predominate:

1. The arsenic poisoning by Montholon has been clearly established by Ben Weider and his Swedish scientist colleague, the late Dr. Sten Forshufvud, through an exhaustive series of modern tests executed by (among others) the Harwell Nuclear Research Laboratory, London; and the FBI on August 28, 1995 (in a graphite furnace atomic absorption spectroscopy procedure). Their findings appear in *The Assassination at St. Helena Revisited* (New York: John Wiley, 1995).

2. Napoleon's epileptic attacks continued throughout his adult life, but were for the most part successfully hushed up by Josephine and Duroc. I have recorded a few such instances to indicate their gravity.

3. From a psychiatric viewpoint, all my medical friends confirm that Bonaparte—like so many dictatorial rulers—would according to the U.K. Mental Health Act of 1983 be described as a psychopath, a term that includes in its definition:

    a. Failure to make loving relationships

    b. A propensity toward highly impulsive, irrational actions

    c. Lack of sense of guilt or sensitivity for own actions

    d. Failure to learn from adverse experiences

The combination of all four traits is reflected by the various kidnappings, murders, lies, and wars he perpetrated to the very end.

Napoleon was also very paranoid long before coming to power, even as a child. Indeed, in addition to having servants first taste all food and drink presented, when General Thiébault, his loyal new military governor of a recently confiscated Rhineland state, sent him several thousand bottles of choice wines he had just seized, Napoleon wrote back angrily adominishing him for wanting to poison him and ordered every bottle broken.

Bonaparte was of course also sadomasochistic, as is evident time and again throughout this book, for example resulting in his unrelenting "vengeance" against those who "betrayed" him, whether Elizabeth Patterson (whom he vigorously persecuted in her private life, through his agents, till the end of his reign); his outrageous attempt to destroy the Bourriennes; or his attacks on Constant, Pozzo di Borgo, and numerous others down to a humble German bookseller/printer, and even his own brother Lucien.

NOTES

1 "A DANGEROUS ISLANDER"

1. Frédéric Masson, *Napoléon et sa famille* (Paris: Ollendorff, 1920), vol. 1, *1769–1802*, chap. 1; Frédéric Masson, *Napoléon dans sa jeunesse, 1769–1793* (Paris: Ollendorff, 1905); Arthur Chuquet, *La Jeunesse de Napoléon* (Paris: Colin, 1898); vols. 1–3; Louis Madelin, *La Jeunesse de Bonaparte* (Paris: Hachette, 1927), chap. 1.

2. Joseph Bonaparte, *Mémoires et correspondance politique et militaire du roi Joseph* (Paris: Perrotin, 1853), vol. 1, pp. 26–27; Gabriel Girod de l'Ain, *Joseph Bonaparte, le roi malgré lui* (Paris: Perrin, 1970).

3. Frédéric Masson and Guido Biagi, *Napoléon inconnu* (Paris: Albin Michel, 1895); Masson, *Napoléon dans sa jeunesse;* François Gilbert Coston's *Premières années de Napoléon* (Paris: Plon-Nourrit, 1840).

4. Girod de l'Ain, *Joseph Bonaparte*, p. 22.

5. Masson, *Napoléon et sa famille*, vol. 1, p. 28; Madelin, *Jeunesse de Bonaparte*, p. 43.

6. Madelin, *Jeunesse de Bonaparte*, p. 47; A. Fournier, *Napoléon I, Eine Biographie* (Vienna: Verlag Bauer, 1891), vol. 1, pp. 12–13.

7. Laure Junot, Duchesse d'Abrantès, *Memoirs of the Emperor Napoleon, from Ajaccio to Waterloo* (Akron, Ohio: St. Dunstan Society, 1901), vol. 1, p. 85.

8. Masson, *Napoléon et sa famille*, vol. 1, p. 156.

9. Madelin, *Jeunesse de Bonaparte*, vol. 1, 55.

10. Ibid., p. 53.

11. Napoléon Bonaparte, *Manuscripts inédits, 1786–1791* (Paris: Albin Michel, 1927), doc. 2, dated May 3, 1786, pp. 5–6.

12. See the complete manuscripts on all these subjects, ibid.

13. Ibid., doc. 29, pp. 523–28; doc. 13, p. 87.

14. Sieur Surirey de Saint-Rémy, *Mémoires d'artilleries où et traité des mortiers, pétards, arquebuses à croc, mousquets et fusils,* n.p., n.d.

15. Napoléon, *Manuscrits inédits,* doc. 41, cahier 19, pp. 504 ff.

16. Ibid., passim.

17. Ibid., doc. 51, p. 536; doc. 43, p. 521; doc. 51, pp. 536, 390, 396.

18. Ibid., doc. 37, 443, p. 396.

19. Madelin, *Jeunesse de Bonaparte*, p. 61.

20. Ibid., p. 71.

21. Napoléon, *Manuscrits inédits*, doc. 38, p. 446 ff; John Holland Rose, *The Life of Napoleon I* (London: Bell, 1924), book 1, p. 31.

22. Ibid., doc. 52, pp. 538 ff.

23. In April 1791 a papal bull condemned the oath to the new Civil Constitution, required by the French clergy. Madelin, *Jeunesse de Bonaparte*, p. 168.

24. Ibid., p. 209.

25. See ibid.; Masson, *Napoléon dans sa Jeunesse*; and Chuquet, *Jeunesse de Napoléon*.

2 "To Destiny"

1. Girod de l'Ain, *Joseph Bonaparte*, pp. 41–42.

2. Joseph du Teil, *Les Généraux du Teil* (Paris: Nourrit-Plon, n.d.), pp. 150–55.

3. David G. Chandler, *The Campaigns of Napoleon* (New York: Macmillan, 1967), p. 27.

4. Rose, *Napoleon*, book 1, pp. 44 ff; Madelin, *Jeunesse de Bonaparte*, pp. 234 ff; Masson, *Napoleon dans sa jeunesse*.

5. Madelin, *Jeunesse de Bonaparte*, pp. 260, 254.

6. Salicetti to the Comité du Salut Public, 19 Thermidor an II, François Alphonse Aulard, *Recueil des Actes du Comité du Salut Public* (Paris: Imprimerie Nationale, 1889–1923), vol. 15, p. 778; Masson, *Napoléon et sa famille*, vol. 1, p. 92.

7. Coston, *Premières années de Napoleon*, vol. 1, pp. 232–41, 304–6; Jean-Antoine Chaptal, *Mes Souvenirs sur Napoléon* (Paris: Plon, 1893), p. 197.

8. Madelin, *Jeunesse de Bonaparte*, pp. 265 ff.

9. Ibid., p. 304–6; Aulard, *Actes*, vol. 15, 778, 780.

10. Napoleon to Junot, "du fort Carré, à Antibes, *Correspondance de Napoléon I* (Paris: Imprimérie Impériale, 1858), no. 35 (there are thirty-two volumes in this series, quoted hereafter as *Corr de Nap*, followed by the document number); Napoléon to Tilly, 19 Thermidor an II, regarding views on Robespierre, Coston, *Premières années*, vol. 2, p. 286.

11. Ibid., vol. 1, pp. 340–48, 357; Masson, *Napoléon et sa famille*, vol. 1, p. 105; Masson, *Napoléon dans sa jeunesse*, p. 285.

12. Masson, *Napoléon et sa famille*, vol. 1, pp. 120–24; Madelin, *Jeunesse de Bonaparte*, p. 313. *Correspondance de Napoléon*, nos. 56, 65.

13. Madelin, *Jeunesse de Bonaparte*, p. 315.

14. Masson, *Napoléon et sa famille*, vol. 1, p. 126.

15. Napoleon, *Correspondance*, vol. 1; Barras, *Mémoires*; Madelin, *Jeunesse de Bonaparte*; Masson, *Napoleon dans sa Jeunesse*; Masson, *Napoléon et sa famille*, vol. 1; Abrantès, *Memoirs*.

16. Abrantès, *Memoirs*, vol. 1, pp. 115–29.

17. Evangeline Bruce, *Napoleon & Josephine: An Improbable Marriage* (New York: Scribner's, 1995). Frédéric Masson dedicated several works to her life: *Joséphine de*

Beauharnais, 1763–1796 (Paris: A. Michel, 1925); *Madame Bonaparte, 1796–1804* (Paris: A. Michel, n.d.); *Joséphine Impératrice et Reine, 1804–1809* (Paris: A. Michel, 1919); and *Joséphine répudiée, 1809–1813* (Paris: A. Michel, n.d.).

18. J. Bourgeat, *Napoléon: Lettres à Josephine* (Paris: Guy le Prat, 1941), p. 34; Charles Tennant, *A Tour through Parts of the Netherlands, Holland, Germany, Switzerland, Savoy and France in the year 1821–2* (London: Murray, 1823), appendixes.

3 "A NEW ALEXANDER THE GREAT"

1. Dieudonné-Paul-Charles-Henri Thiébault, *Mémoires du général baron Thiébault* (Paris: Plon, 1984), vol. 2, p. 29.
2. Jérome Zieseniss, *Berthier, Frère d'Armes de Napoléon* (Paris: Belfond, 1985).
3. Auguste Frédéric Louis Viesse de Marmont, *Mémoires de 1792 à 1841* (Paris: Perrotin, 1856), vol. 1.
4. Jean Tulard, *Murat, ou l'éveil des nations* (Paris: Hachette, 1983).
5. Jean-Claude Damamme, *Lannes, Maréchal d'Empire* (Paris: Payot, 1987); Louis Chardigny, *Les Maréchaux de Napoléon* (Paris: Tallandier, 1977); Jacques Jourquin, *Dictionnaire des maréchaux du premier empire* (Paris: Tallandier, 1986).
6. See Chandler, *Campaigns of Napoleon*, pp. 63 ff; Emmanuel de Las Cases, *Le Mémorial de Sainte-Hélène* (Paris: Flammarion, 1951), vol. 1, pp. 823–95.
7. Napoléon, *Correspondance de Napoléon Ier*, no. 91. See also Hubert Camon's series of military studies, *La Guerre Napoléonienne: Batailles* (Paris: Chapelot, 1910); *La Guerre Napoléonienne les systèmes d'opérations* (Paris: Chapelot, 1907); *La Guerre Napoléonienne: Précis des campagnes* (Paris: Chapelot, 1925). For historical and political events, Louis Madelin, *L'Ascension de Bonaparte* (Paris: Hachette, 1937), pp. 33 ff.
8. Tennant, *A Tour through Parts of the Netherlands*, appendixes.
9. "Campagne d'Italie," p. 828, *Mémorial de Ste-Hélène*.
10. Chandler, *Campaigns*, p. 77.
11. *Corr de Nap*, no. 234.
12. Felix Markham, *Napoleon* (London: Weidenfeld, 1963), p. 28; and *Mémorial de Ste-Hélène*, vol. 1, p. 119.
13. *Corr de Nap*, no. 421.
14. R. W. Phipps, *The Armies of the First French Republic* (Oxford, England: Oxford University Press, 1939), vol. 4, p. 39.
15. Madelin, *L'Ascension*, p. 79.
16. Ibid.
17. Markham, *Napoleon*, p. 28; *Mémorial de Ste-Hélène*, vol. 1, p. 119; quote by Ida de Saint-Elme, *Mémoires d'une contemporaine* (Paris: J. Savant, 1827), vol. 2, p. 42.
18. Saint-Elme, *Mémoires*, vol. 2, p. 47.
19. Antoine Vincent Arnault, *Souvenirs d'un sexagénaire* (Paris: Garnier, 1908), vol. 1, p. 348.
20. Bruce, *Napoleon & Josephine*, p. 184.
21. Ibid., p. 173. Napoleon to Josephine, Marmirole, July 171796, *Archives Nationales*, 400 AP 6, vol. 1, no. 3; Louis Hastier, *Le Grand Amour de Joséphine* (Paris: Corea Buchet/Chastel, n.d.).
22. "Campagne d'Italie," *Mémorial de Ste.-Hélène*, I, pp. 839–40.

23. *Corr de Nap,* no. 806.

24. "Campagne d'Italie," vol. 1, pp. 841–42.

25. Thiébault, *Mémoires,* vol. 2, p. 47; Chandler, *Campaigns,* p. 95.

26. "Campagne d'Italie," vol. 1, pp. 844–47.

27. Ibid., pp. 846–47.

28. Ibid., p. 848.

29. 29. Ibid., pp. 849–52.

30. Thiébault, *Mémoires,* vol. 2, pp. 37–38.

31. "Campagne d'Italie, pp. 851–852; Ida de Saint-Elme, *Mémoires,* II, 53.

32. "Campagne d'Italie," pp. 853 *et seq.*

33. Ibid., pp. 858–61; Damamme, *Lannes,* p. 39.

34. Madelin, *L'Ascension,* p. 127.

35. Ibid., p. 112; *Corr de Nap,* no. 2025.

36. Madelin, *L'Ascension,* p. 118; *Corr de Nap,* no. 1748.

37. Madelin, *L'Ascension,* p. 130; *Corr de Nap,* no. 1748.

38. André Soubiran, *Napoléon et un million de Morts* (Paris: Kent-Segep, 1969), pp. 34–44. Emphasis in original.

4 CROSSROADS

1. André-François, Count Miot de Melito, *Memoirs of Count Miot de Melito* (New York: Scribner's Sons, 1881), pp. 91–92.

2. Ibid., pp. 93–95. Emphasis in original.

3. Ibid., p. 105.

4. Ibid., p. 113.

5. Ibid., pp. 106–7.

6. Ibid., pp. 110–11.

7. Antoine Chamans Lavalette, *Mémoires et souvenirs du Comte de Lavalette* (Paris: Mercure de France, 1994), pp. 167–73.

8. Louis de Launay, *Monge, un Grand Français, Fondateur de l'Ecole Polytechnique* (Paris: P. Roger, n.d.), p. 167.

9. C. de la Jonquière, *L'Expédition d'Egypte, 1798–1801* (Paris: Charl Lavauzelle, 1899), vol. 1, p. 324.

10. Miot, *Memoirs,* p. 113.

11. Louis Fauvelet de Bourrienne, *Mémoires de M de Bourrienne, Ministre d'Etat, sur Napoléon, le Directoire, le Consulat, l'Empire et la Restauration* (Paris: Ladvocat, 1829), vol. 2, p. 3.

12. Ibid., pp. 26–27.

13. Ibid., pp. 31, 32.

14. Ibid., p. 32.

15. Ibid., pp. 32–33; De Launay, *Monge,* p. 180.

16. Bourrienne, *Mémoires,* vol. 2, pp. 37–38.

17. Ibid., p. 38; de la Jonquière, *L'Expédition d'Egypte,* vol. 1, p. 170. (This work, my primary source for all aspects of the Maltese and Egyptian campaigns, is cited hereafter as *LJ.*

18. Bonaparte, "Rapport au Directoire Exécutif, le 5 ventôse an VI [Feb. 23, 1798]," *LJ,* vol. 1, pp. 172–76. Emphasis added.

19. Bourrienne, *Mémoires*, vol. 2, pp. 34, 38–39.
20. Ibid., pp. 38, 44.
21. *LJ*, vol. 1, p. 17.
22. Ibid., p. 181.
23. Ibid.
24. Ibid., p. 186.
25. Ibid., p. 151.
26. Talleyrand's project "Sur la conquête de l'Egypte, Rapport au Directoire Exécutif, 25 pluviôse an VI [Feb. 14, 1798]," in ibid., pp. 154–68.
27. Ibid.
28. Ibid. Emphasis in original.
29. Ibid., p. 186.

5 THE DECISION

1. *LJ*, vol. 1, pp. 149–50.
2. Miot, *Memoirs*, p. 3.
3. *LJ*, vol. 1, pp. 25–26.
4. Ibid., p. 29.
5. Ibid., pp. 197–200.
6. Ibid., pp. 201–4.
7. Ibid., pp. 204–6.
8. This "Instruction pour la Commission Chargée de l'Inspection des Côtes de la Mediterranée" was issued by Bonaparte himself, and not by the Directory, who had given him more or less carte blanche regarding all aspects of its preparation. Ibid, pp. 207–8.
9. Ibid., p. 218.
10. Ibid., p. 225.
11. Ibid., p. 235.
12. Ibid., pp. 229, 230–31; 49–251.
13. Ibid., p. 225.
14. Ibid., p. 221.
15. Ibid., pp. 249–51.
16. Bourrienne, *Mémoires*, vol. 2, p. 48.
17. *Moniteur*, 12 germinal an VI (April 1, 1798).
18. Ibid., April 4, 1798. See also *LJ*, vol. 1, pp. 254–55.
19. *LJ*, vol. 1, p. 247.
20. Ibid., 265.
21. Ibid., pp. 265–66.
22. Ibid., p. 242.
23. Ibid., p. 270.
24. Ibid.
25. Ibid.
26. Ibid., pp. 245–46.
27. Ibid., p. 255.
28. Ibid., pp. 274–81.
29. Ibid., p. 324.

30. Ibid., pp. 338–39.
31. Ibid., pp. 280, 281–83.
32. Ibid., pp. 341–42.
33. Ibid., pp. 343–44.
34. Ibid., pp. 345–46.
35. Ibid., pp. 350–53.
36. Ibid.
37. Ibid., pp. 355–56.
38. Ibid., p. 283.
39. Bernard Chevallier and Christophe Pincemaille, *L'impératrice Joséphine* (Paris: Presses de la Renaissance, 1988), pp. 166 ff. See also Ernest John Knapton, *Empress Josephine* (Cambridge, Mass: Harvard University Press, 1963), pp. 151–53, 160–66.
40. Chevallier and Pincemaille, *Joséphine*, p. 167.
41. Ibid., pp. 133, 137, 154, 163–68, 180, 198.
42. *LJ*, vol. 1, p. 372. The Armaments Commission comprised Rear Adm. Blanquet du Chayla, Army Ordonnateur Sucy, Naval Ordonnateur LeRoy, and General Dommartin.
43. Ibid., pp. 363–64.
44. Ibid., p. 359.
45. Ibid., p. 371.
46. Ibid.
47. Directoral Arrêté, April 24, 1798, *Archives Nationales*, AFIII, 518; see also *LJ*, vol. 1, pp. 284–87.
48. *LJ*, vol. 1, p. 390.
49. Ibid., p. 391.
50. Ibid., pp. 378–88.
51. Ibid., pp. 388, 389.
52. Ibid., p. 389.
53. Paul Barras, *Mémoires de Barras* (Paris: Hachette, 1896), vol. 3, pp. 215 ff.
54. Ibid.; Bourrienne, *Mémoires*, vol. 2, p. 54.
55. *LJ*, vol. 1, pp. 396, 395.
56. Bourrienne, *Mémoires*, vol. 2, pp. 54, 56.

6 THE ARMADA

1. *LJ*, vol. 1, pp. 459–61.
2. Ibid., pp. 407–8.
3. Ibid., p. 409.
4. Ibid., p. 478.
5. Ibid., p. 419.
6. Ibid., pp. 419–20.
7. Ibid., p. 459.
8. Ibid., p. 473.
9. Ibid., p. 469.
10. Ibid., pp. 406, 411.
11. *Moniteur*, le 19 floréal an VI (May 8, 1798).

12. *LJ*, vol. 1, p. 461.
13. Ibid., p. 477.
14. Ibid., p. 478.
15. Ibid., p. 481.
16. Ibid., pp. 483, 487.
17. Ibid., p. 491.
18. Ibid., p. 488.
19. Bourrienne, *Mémoires*, vol. 2, p. 49.
20. *LJ*, vol. 1, pp. 495–96.
21. William James, *A Naval History of Great Britain* (London: Macmillan, 1902), vol. 2, pp. 166–71.
22. *LJ*, vol. 1, pp. 496–97.
23. Ibid., p. 501.
24. Ibid., p. 502.
25. Ibid., p. 531.
26. Ibid., p. 537.
27. Ibid., p. 538.
28. Ibid., pp. 519, 526. See also Naval Ministry Chart, ibid., p. 283.
29. Ibid., p. 359.
30. Ibid.
31. Ibid., pp. 513–15.
32. Ibid., pp. 514–15.
33. Ibid., pp. 663–64.
34. Ibid., pp. 512, 513, 517.
35. Ibid., p. 542.
36. Ibid., p. 553.
37. See "Journal de Laugier" in ibid., p. 546.
38. De Launay, *Monge*, pp. 14–15.
39. Ibid., pp. 23–25.
40. Ibid., p. 38.
41. Ibid., pp. 65–66.
42. Ibid., p. 98.
43. Ibid., pp. 84–85.
44. Ibid., p. 88.
45. Ibid., p. 99.
46. Ibid., pp. 104–6.
47. Ibid., p. 109. See also René Taton, *L'Oeuvre scientifique de Monge* (Paris: Presses Universitaires de France, 1951), pp. 36–37.
48. De Launay, *Monge*, p. 112
49. Ibid., p. 127; Prof. Roger Hahn, holding the chair of the History of Science at the University of California, Berkeley, has kindly provided me with background on Monge and his work at and for the Ecole Polytechnique.
50. Ibid., pp. 140–42.
51. Ibid., p. 146.
52. Ibid., pp. 145, 148, 154–55, 164–65.
53. Ibid., p. 180.

54. Bourrienne, *Mémoires,* vol. 2, p. 45.

55. Ibid., p. 73.

56. Ibid., p. 70–71.

57. Ibid., pp. 72–73.

58. See James, *Naval History,* vol. 2, pp. 166–71.

59. A. T. Mahan, *The Life of Nelson, The Embodiment of the Sea Power of Great Britain* (London: Low, Marston & Company, 1897), vol. 1, p. 325.

60. "Journal de Damas," *LJ,* vol. 1, pp. 552–53, 555.

61. Ibid., p. 560.

62. J. Christopher Herold, *Bonaparte in Egypt* (New York: Harper & Row, 1962), pp. 40–42.

63. See the official chart in *LJ,* vol. 1, pp. 533–38.

64. "Journal du Contre Amiral Blanquet," in ibid., p. 562.

65. "Journal du Général Belliard," in ibid., pp. 575–77.

66. See ibid., pp. 577–79. An already ailing Baraguey d'Hilliers was to be repatriated after landing at Malta, and replaced by General Bon.

67. *Corr de Nap,* no. 2629.

68. *LJ,* vol. 1, p. 586.

69. Ibid., pp. 587–94.

70. Ibid., pp. 596–97.

71. Ibid., pp. 613–616.

72. Ibid., p. 643.

73. Ibid., p. 617.

74. Ibid., p. 622.

75. Ibid., pp. 643–45.

76. Herold, *Bonaparte in Egypt,* p. 47.

77. *LJ,* vol. 1, pp. 643–45.

78. Ibid., p. 646.

79. Ibid., pp. 634–37.

80. Ibid., p. 639.

81. Ibid., pp. 629–30.

82. Ibid., p. 648.

83. Ibid., pp. 533–34.

7 LAND OF THE PHARAOHS

1. A. T. Mahan, *The Life of Nelson, the Embodiment of the Sea Power of Great Britain* (London: Sampson, Low, Marston, 1897), vol. 1, p. 322.

2. Ibid., p. 323.

3. James, *Naval History,* vol. 2, p. 166.

4. Carola Oman, *Nelson* (London: Hodder & Stoughton, 1947), p. 245.

5. James, *Naval History,* vol. 2, pp. 171–72.

6. Oman, *Nelson,* p. 246.

7. *LJ,* vol. 1, p. 533, naval chart; Mahan, *Life of Nelson,* vol. 1, p. 328.

8. *LJ,* vol. 1, p. 534.

9. Oman, *Nelson,* p. 280; James, *Naval History,* vol. 2, p. 176. See also Ludovic Kennedy, *Nelson's Band of Brothers* (London: Odhams Press, 1952), pp. 118 ff.

10. *LJ*, vol. 2, pp. 32–33.

11. Ibid., p. 33.

12. Ibid., pp. 37–38.

13. Ibid.

14. Ibid., pp. 42–49.

15. Ibid., p. 45.

16. Ibid., pp. 47–48.

17. Ibid.

18. Ibid., p. 62.

19. Ibid., pp. 23–26, 62–64, 67.

20. Ibid., p. 64.

21. Ibid., p. 65.

22. Ibid.

23. Ibid, p. 69.

24. Ibid., pp. 68–69.

25. Ibid., p. 74.

26. Ibid., p. 68.

27. Ibid., pp. 75, 100.

28. Ibid., p. 100.

29. Ibid.

30. Ibid., p. 98.

31. Ibid., pp. 107–8, 113–14.

32. Ibid., pp. 117–22, 132.

33. Ibid., p. 123.

34. Ibid., pp. 124–25.

35. Ibid., p. 136, n. 2.

36. Bourrienne, *Mémoires*, vol. 2, pp. 102–3.

37. *LJ*, vol. 2, p. 139.

38. Ibid., pp. 141–42.

39. Ibid., pp. 143–44.

40. Ibid., pp. 148–50

41. Ibid., p. 150.

42. Ibid., pp. 152, 154–55.

43. Ibid., pp. 158–60.

44. Ibid., pp. 154, 156.

45. Ibid., p. 162.

46. Ibid., pp. 162–64.

47. Ibid., p. 164.

48. Ibid., p. 165

49. Ibid., p. 166; A. J. M. R. Savary, *Mémoires du duc de Rovigo pour servir à l'histoire de l'Empereur Napoléon* (Paris: Bossange, 1828), vol. 1, p. 56.

50. *LJ*, vol. 2, p. 166.

51. Savary, *Mémoires*, vol. 1, p. 57; *LJ*, vol. 2, p. 167.

52. See Chandler, *Campaigns of Napoleon*, p. 222.

53. *LJ*, vol. 2, p. 169.

54. Ibid., pp. 171–72.

55. Ibid.
56. Ibid., pp. 173–74.
57. Ibid., p. 178.
58. Ibid., pp. 179–80.
59. Kaoula el Turk, *Histoire de l'Expédition des Français en Egypte* (Paris: Imprimerie royale, 1939), pp. 29 ff; *LJ*, vol. 2, pp. 175–78.
60. *LJ*, vol. 2, pp. 181–83.
61. Ibid.
62. Ibid., p. 183.
63. Ibid., pp. 183–85.
64. Ibid., pp. 188–189, 193.
65. Ibid., pp. 189, 191.
66. Ibid., pp. 194.
67. Ibid., pp. 158, 197.

8 DEEP WATER

1. *LJ*, vol. 2, pp. 390–94. Emphasis added.
2. Ibid.
3. *Corr de Nap*, no. 2727.
4. Ibid., no. 2728.
5. James, *Naval History*, vol. 2, p. 208.
6. *LJ*, vol. 2, pp. 84–85. Emphasis added.
7. Ibid., p. 87.
8. Ibid.
9. Ibid., pp. 93–94; *Corr de Nap*, vol. 4, no. 2765.
10. *LJ*, vol. 2, pp. 250–51.
11. Ibid., p. 251.
12. Ibid., pp. 251, 252.
13. Ibid., pp. 252–54.
14. Ibid., pp. 254–56.
15. Ibid., p. 257.
16. Ibid., pp. 314–16.
17. Gaspard Gourgaud, *Sainte-Hélène, Journal* (Paris, n.d.) vol. 2, pp. 435–36.
18. James, *Naval History*, vol. 2, p. 208.
19. Oman, *Nelson*, p. 252.
20. James, *Naval History*, vol. 2, p. 183.
21. *LJ*, vol. 2, pp. 420–21, 399–400, 401–7.
22. Ibid., p. 421.
23. James, *Naval History*, vol.2, pp. 184–94, 206–7; Ludovic Kennedy, *Nelson's Band of Brothers* (London: Odhams Press, 1951), pp. 124 ff.
24. James, *Naval History*, vol. 2, pp. 194–96.
25. See Louis Dureste, "L'Ecroulement du rêve égyptien," *Samothrace* 1, no. 1: 41–47, 45.
26. *LJ*, vol. 2, pp. 398–99.
27. *Corr de Nap*, no. 3045; *LJ*, vol. 2, pp. 426–30.
28. *LJ*, vol. 2, 415; James, *Naval History*, vol. 2, p. 208.

29. *Corr de Nap*, no. 3045; and *LJ*, vol. 2, p. 422.
30. Bourrienne, *Mémoires*, vol. 2, pp. 147–54.
31. *Corr de Nap*, vol. 4, no. 3226.

9 IN THE SHADOW OF DEFEAT

1. *LJ*, vol. 2, p. 449.
2. Ibid., p. 451.
3. Ibid., pp. 452, 454.
4. *Corr de Nap*, no. 3034.
5. Ibid., no. 2837.
6. Ibid., no. 2858.
7. See Bonaparte's orders and decrees of July 24–August 3, 1798, ibid., no. 2829; see also nos. 2869, 2870, 2923, and *LJ*, vol. 2, pp. 285–87.
8. *LJ*, vol. 2, pp. 288–91.
9. *Corr de Nap*, nos. 2883, 2895, 2896, 2897, 2898, 2899; see also *LJ*, vol. 2, p. 689.
10. *Corr de Nap*, vol. 4, no. 2835.
11. *LJ*, vol. 2, pp. 294–96.
12. Ibid., p. 300.
13. The Rosetta Stone was discovered in August 1799, handed over to the British by Menou in 1801, and later deciphered by Jean-François Champollion. See *Corr de Nap*, nos. 3083, 3084; *LJ*, vol. 3, p. 554, no. 1.
14. *Corr de Nap*, no. 3083, art. 2.
15. Paul V. Aubry, *Monge Le Savant Ami de Napoléon Bonaparte, 1746–1818* (Paris: Gauthier-Villars, 1954), p. 251.
16. *LJ*, vol. 3, pp. 556–57; Aubry, *Monge*, p. 252.
17. Ernest John Knapton, *Empress Josephine* (Cambridge, Mass: Harvard University Press, 1963), pp. 150–53, 160–66; Chevallier and Pinceaille, *L'impératrice Joséphine*, pp. 133, 137, 140, 142, 149, 154, 162, 163, 165–68, 180, 198.
18. Napoleon Bonaparte, *The Confidential Correspondence of Napoleon Bonaparte with His Brother Joseph* (New York: Appleton, 1856), p. 48.
19. Bourrienne, *Mémoires*, vol. 2, p. 135.
20. *LJ*, vol. 2, pp. 624–25.
21. Bourrienne, *Mémoires*, vol. 2, p. 137.
22. Ibid., p. 130.
23. *LJ*, vol. 2, pp 479–82.
24. *Corr de Nap*, vol. 4, no. 3040.
25. Ibid., no. 3056.
26. Ibid., no. 3059.
27. *LJ*, vol. 2, pp. 508–10.
28. Ibid., p. 510.
29. Ibid., p. 512.
30. Ibid., p. 519.
31. Ibid., pp. 519–20.
32. Ibid., vol. 3, p. 77.
33. Ibid., pp. 80–81.
34. *Corr de Nap*, no. 3210.

35. *LJ*, vol. 3, pp. 90–91.
36. Ibid., p. 93. Emphasis added.
37. Ibid. pp. 93–94.
38. *Corr de Nap*, no. 3418.
39. Bourrienne, *Mémoires*, vol. 2, p. 161.

10 TIVOLI AND BEYOND

1. *LJ*, vol. 3, p. 271.
2. *Corr de Nap*, no. 3486; *LJ*, vol. 3, pp. 273, 276.
3. *LJ*, vol. 3, pp. 289, 290–91.
4. Ibid., p. 277.
5. Ibid., p. 279.
6. Ibid., p. 283.
7. Ibid., pp. 282–83, 284.
8. Ibid., p. 286; Bourrienne, *Mémoires*, vol. 2, pp. 186 ff.
9. Bourrienne, *Mémoires*, vol. 2, p. 185.
10. *Corr de Nap*, no. 3527.
11. Ibid., no. 3539.
12. *LJ*, vol. 3, pp. 290–91.
13. Ibid. pp. 281–82.
14. Bourrienne, *Mémoires*, vol. 2, pp. 185.
15. *Courrier de l'Egypte*, October 31–December 1, 1798.
16. *LJ*, vol. 3, pp. 383–85.
17. Ibid., p. 385, n. 1.
18. Bourrienne, *Mémoires*, vol. 2, pp. 174–75.
19. Ibid., p. 177.
20. Ibid., pp. 422, 387.
21. Comte de las Cases, *Le Mémorial de Sainte-Hélène* (Paris: Flammarion, 1951), vol. 1, pp. 131–32; H. Christopher Herold, *Bonaparte in Egypt* (New York: Harper & Row, 1962), p. 82.
22. Bourrienne, *Mémoires*, vol. 2, p. 137.
23. *LJ*, vol. 3, pp. 387–90, 391.
24. Ibid., p. 389.
25. Ibid., p. 387.
26. René-Nicolas Desgenettes, *Souvenirs d'un médecin de l'expédition d'Egypte* (Paris: Calmann-Lévy, 1893), vol. 3, p. 198.
27. *LJ*, vol. 3, p. 88; *Corr de Nap*, vol. 5, nos. 3503, 3439.
28. *LJ*, vol. 3, pp. 393, 394–99.
29. See *LJ*, ibid., pp. 534–39.
30. Ibid., pp. 66–68.
31. *LJ*, vol. 3, pp. 406–7.
32. Ibid., pp. 406–9, 260.
33. Ibid., pp. 334–35, 257.
34. Ibid., pp. 252–56.
35. Ibid., p. 260.
36. Ibid., pp. 261–68.

37. Ibid., p. 268.
38. *Corr de Nap*, no. 3234.
39. *LJ*, vol. 3, p. 208.
40. Ibid., pp. 503–39; 698; 617 ff., 626 ff., 642 ff., 675 ff.
41. Ibid., pp. 312–17, 422.
42. *Corr de Nap*, no. 3357.
43. Ibid., no. 3375.
44. Ibid., no. 3269.
45. Ibid., no. 3387.
46. Ibid. vol. 5, no. 3374; see also vol. 4, nos. 3357, 3252.
47. *LJ*, vol. 3, pp. 444–45.
48. *Corr de Nap*, nos. 3736, 3737, 3740, 3734, 3738: *LJ*, vol. 3, pp. 466–69.
49. *LJ*, vol. 3, pp. 480–81.
50. Bourrienne, *Mémoires*, vol. 2, p. 197; *LJ*, vol. 3, pp. 481, 491–93; *Corr de Nap*, no. 3804.

11 ROAD TO DAMASCUS

1. Bourrienne, *Mémoires*, vol. 2, p. 205.
2. *Corr de Nap*, no. 4011.
3. Quoted in Désiré Lacroix, *Bonaparte en Egypte (1798–1799)* (Paris: Garnier Frères, 1899), pp. 275–76.
4. Ibid.; Bourrienne, *Mémoires*, vol. 2, pp. 223, 221–27.
5. Ibid., pp. 226–27.
6. Tom Pocock, *Thirst for Glory: The Life of Admiral Sir William Sidney Smith* (London: Aurum Press, 1966) fills in the preparations.
7. De Launay, *Monge*, pp. 218–19; Aubry, *Monge*, pp. 268–70.
8. *Corr de Nap*, no. 4138; Bourrienne, *Mémoires*, vol. 2, p. 248.
9. Ibid., pp. 250–52.
10. *Corr de Nap*, no. 4188; Bourrienne, *Mémoires*, vol. 2, p. 249.
11. Ibid., p. 266.
12. *Corr de Nap*, no. 2197.
13. De Launay, *Monge*, p. 220; *Victoires, Conquêtes, Disastres, Revers et Guerres Civiles des Français de 1792 à 1815* (Paris: 1819), vol. 10, p. 313; Desgenettes, *Souvenirs*, p. 213.
14. *Corr de Nap*, no. 4225.
15. Ibid.
16. Ibid., nos. 4281, 4282.
17. Ibid., nos. 4283, 4288, 4285, 4289, 4290.
18. Bourrienne, *Mémoires*, vol. 2, pp. 302 ff.
19. *Corr de Nap*, no. 4290.
20. Ibid., nos. 4302, 4303.
21. Ibid., no. 4294.
22. Ibid., no. 4300.
23. Ibid., no. 4301.
24. Ibid., no. 4303.
25. Ibid., nos. 4304, 4305, 4307.

26. Ibid., no. 4310.
27. Ibid., no. 4317.
28. Tulard, *Murat*, p. 43; *Corr de Nap*, no. 4323.
29. *Corr de Nap*, no. 4316.
30. Ibid., no. 4322.
31. Ibid., no. 4325.
32. Ibid., no. 4329.
33. Tulard, *Murat*, p. 36.
34. *Corr de Nap*, nos. 4337, 4338.
35. Ibid., no. 4343.
36. Bourrienne, *Mémoires*, vol. 2, p. 306.
37. Ibid.
38. *Corr de Nap*, no. 4367.
39. Ibid., no. 4370.
40. Herold, *Bonaparte in Egypt*, p. 325; Aubry, *Monge*, pp. 273–74.
41. Aubry, *Monge*, p. 275.
42. *Corr de Nap*, no. 4374.
43. Ibid., no. 4376.
44. Ibid., no. 4382.
45. Aubry, *Monge*, p. 277; Bourrienne, *Mémoires*, vol. 2, p. 249.

12 PRELUDE TO A COUP

1. Jean-Denis Bredin, *Sieyès, La clé de la Révolution* (Paris: Fallois 1988), pp. 21, 23, pp. 24–30.
2. Ibid., pp. 30–31.
3. Ibid., p. 56.
4. Germaine de Staël-Holstein, *Considérations sur les Principaux Evénements de la Révolution Française* (Paris: Delaunay, 1818), vol. 2, p. 248.
5. Ibid., vol. 1, p. 304.
6. Bredin, *Sieyès*, pp. 343–46.
7. Ibid., pp. 372, 377.
8. Ibid., p. 378.
9. Quoted in ibid., p. 401.
10. Ibid., p. 400.
11. Ibid. pp. 401 ff.
12. Bourrienne, *Mémoires*, vol. 2, pp. 26–27.
13. Bredin, *Sieyès*, pp. 403, 409.
14. Ibid., p. 416.
15. Ibid., p. 419.
16. Ibid., p. 420.
17. Ibid.
18. Ibid., pp. 420–21.
19. Ibid., p. 426.
20. Ibid., p. 424.
21. Dunbar Plunket Barton, *Bernadotte* (Paris: Payot, 1983), pp. 108 ff.
22. Bredin, *Sieyès*, p. 425.

23. Ibid., p. 435.
24. Ibid., p. 435.
25. Ibid., p. 437.
26. Ibid., p. 459.
27. Ibid., pp. 437–38.
28. Ibid., p. 438.
29. Ibid., p. 446.
30. Ibid.
31. Eric Le Nabour, *Barras, Le Vicomte Rouge* (Paris: Lattès, 1982), pp. 15–16.
32. Ibid., p. 27.
33. Ibid., p. 37.
34. Ibid., p. 32.
35. Ibid., p. 41.
36. Ibid., pp. 108 ff; Jean Tulard, *Napoleon, The Myth of the Saviour* (London: Methuen, 1984), p. 53.
37. Le Nabour, *Barras*, pp. 111 ff.
38. Ibid., pp. 159–71.
39. Bourrienne, *Mémoires*, vol. 1, pp. 236 ff.
40. Le Nabour, *Barras*, pp. 186–87.
41. Ibid., p. 181.
42. Ibid., p. 191.
43. Ibid., p. 244.
44. Ibid., pp. 244, 245; Victorine de Chastenay, *Mémoires, 1771–1815* (Paris: Perrin, 1987).
45. Le Nabour, *Barras*, p. 248.
46. Ibid.
47. Ibid., p. 246.

13 18–19 BRUMAIRE

1. Bourrienne, *Mémoires*, vol. 3, p. 33.
2. Ibid., p. 36.
3. Ibid., p. 38.
4. Barton, *Bernadotte*, p. 120.
5. Le Nabour, *Barras*, p. 265; Paul-François de Barras, *Mémoires de Barras, Membre du Directoire* (Paris: Hachette, 1896), vol. 4, *Consulat, Empire, Restauration*, pp. 31 ff.
6. Barras, *Mémoires*, vol. 4, p. 31.
7. Ibid., p. 32.
8. Ibid.
9. Ibid.
10. Ibid., p. 31.
11. Georges-Albert Morlot and Jeanne Happert, *Talleyrand, une mystification historique* (Paris: Veyrier, 1992), p. 323.
12. Bourrienne, *Mémoires*, vol. 3, p. 38.
13. Morlot, *Talleyrand*, p. 323; Madame de Rémusat, *Mémoires* (Paris: Calmann Lévy, 1880), vol. 1, *1802–1808*, pp. 148–49; Bourrienne, *Mémoires*, vol. 3, p. 38.

14. Pierre Louis Roederer, *Autour de Bonaparte, Journal du Comte Roederer* (Paris: Daragon, 1909), pp. 213 ff.

15. Ibid., pp. vi–viii.

16. Bourrienne, *Mémoires*, vol. 3, p. 34.

17. Louis Madelin, *Talleyrand* (Paris: Flammarion, 1944), p. 95.

18. Morlot, *Talleyrand*, pp. 324–25.

19. Bourrienne, *Mémoires*, vol. 3, p. 61.

20. Morlot, *Talleyrand*, p. 325.

21. G. Lacour-Gayet, *Talleyrand 1754–1838* (Paris: Payot, 1933), vol. 1, p. 354.

22. Roederer, *Autour de Bonaparte*, p. 213.

23. Gabriel Girod de l'Ain, *Joseph Bonaparte* (Paris: Perrin, 1970), pp. 278, 281.

24. Masson, *Napoléon et sa famille*, vol. 1, *1769–1802*, pp. 209, 250, 251. See also Girod de l'Ain, *Joseph Bonaparte*, pp. 81–86.

25. Morlot, *Talleyrand*, p. 326.

26. Ibid., p. 328.

27. Ibid., p. 331.

28. Bourrienne, *Mémoires*, vol. 3, pp. 57–58.

29. Morlot, *Talleyrand*, p. 331.

30. Masson, *Napoléon et sa famille*, vol. 1, p. 286.

31. Bourrienne, *Mémoires*, vol. 3, pp. 58–59.

32. Lacour-Gayet, *Talleyrand*, vol. 1, p. 356.

33. Morlot, *Talleyrand*, p. 331.

34. Bredin, *Sieyès*, p. 452.

35. Bourrienne, *Mémoires*, vol. 3, p. 44.

36. Ibid., p. 68.

37. Ibid., p. 81.

38. Bredin, *Sieyès*, pp. 452–53.

39. Morlot, *Talleyrand*, p. 331; Bredin, *Sieyès*, pp. 453 ff.

40. Morlot, *Talleyrand*, p. 331; Bredin, *Sieyès*, pp. 453 ff.

41. Bourrienne, *Mémoires*, vol. 3, p. 81.

42. Ibid., pp. 73–74.

43. Ibid., pp. 77–78.

44. Morlot, *Talleyrand*, pp. 333–36.

45. Lacour-Gayet, *Talleyrand*, vol. 1, 358.

46. Bredin, *Sieyès*, p. 454.

47. Bourrienne, *Mémoires*, vol. 3, p. 82.

48. Masson, *Napoléon et sa famille*, vol. 1, pp. 284–85.

49. Bredin, *Sieyès*, p. 454; Otto Wolff, *Ouvrard, Speculator of Genius* (New York: McKay, 1962), p. 232.

50. Bourrienne, *Mémoires*, vol. 3, pp. 81 ff.

51. Ibid., p. 83; *Corr de Nap*, no. 4388.

52. Bourrienne, *Mémoires*, vol. 3, pp. 81 ff; *Moniteur*, 20, 21 Brumaire; Bredin, *Sieyès*, pp. 456–57; *Corr de Nap*, no. 4388.

53. Ibid., no. 4388; Bourrienne, *Mémoires*, vol. 3, pp. 86–87.

54. Bourrienne, *Mémoires*, vol. 3, p. 88.

55. Ibid., pp. 92 ff.

56. Bredin, *Sieyès*, p. 458.

57. Ibid., pp. 458–59.

58. Ibid., p. 458; Morlot, *Talleyrand*, p. 340.

59. Bourrienne, *Mémoires*, vol. 3, pp. 95–97.

60. Ibid., p. 57.

61. Bredin, *Sieyès*, p. 458.

62. Morlot, *Talleyrand*, p. 340.

63. Bredin, *Sieyès*, p. 458.

64. Ibid., p. 459.

65. Bourrienne, *Mémoires*, vol. 3, pp. 101–2.

66. Ibid., pp. 102 ff.

67. Ibid., p. 105.

68. Alexis de Tocqueville, *L'Ancien Régime et la Révolution*, in *Oeuvres complètes* (Paris: Plon, 1898), vol. 2, p. 309.

69. Bourrienne, *Mémoires*, vol. 3, pp. 103–5.

14 THE CONSULATE

1. Andrew J. Montague, ed., *The American Secretaries of State and Their Diplomacy* (New York: Knopf, 1927), vol. 2, p. 254.

2. Peter P. Hill, *William Vans Murray* (New York: Macmillan, 1975), p. 195.

3. See Ruhl J. Barlette, *The Record of American Diplomacy* (New York: Knopf, 1964), pp. 100–102. See also *Moniteur*, 14 vendémiaire an IX, pp. 1, 2; 11 vendémiaire an 9, p. 2.

4. Ibid., 14 vendémiaire an IX, and *The Times* (London), Thursday, October 16, 1800, p. 2. See also William Garrott Brown, *The Life of Oliver Ellsworth* (New York: Macmillan, 1905), pp. 305–8.

5. Hill, *William Vans Murray*, pp. 195–96.

6. Brown, *Oliver Ellsworth*, p. 308; and *Moniteur*, 14 vendémiaire an IX (October 4, 1800), pp. 1, 2.

7. R. B. Mowat, *The Diplomacy of Napoleon* (London: Edward Arnold, 1924) pp. 135–37.

8. Masson, *Napoléon et sa famille*, vol. 1, pp. 94, 95.

9. Ibid., p. 118.

10. Ibid., p. 132: Girod de l'Ain, *Joseph Bonaparte*, pp. 64 ff.

11. Masson, *Napoléon et sa famille*, vol. 1, pp. 192–93.

12. Ibid., pp. 212, 214.

13. Girod de l'Ain, *Joseph Bonaparte*, pp. 72–75.

14. Masson, *Napoléon et sa famille*, vol. 1, pp. 212–18.

15. Ibid., pp. 405 ff.

16. Abrantès, *Memoirs of the Emperor Napoleon*, vol. 1, pp. 165, 168.

17. Ibid., pp. 148–65.

18. Jean Tulard, *Napoleon, the Myth of the Saviour* (London: Methuen, 1984), pp. 85–86. Antonello Pietromarchi, *Lucien Bonaparte, Prince Romain* (Paris: Perrin, 1980), pp. 30–31, 75–76. See also Louis Madelin, *De Brumaire à Marengo* (Paris: Hachette, 1949); Alfred Cobban, *A History of Modern France* (Harmondsworth, England: Penguin, 1971), vol. 2, p. 13. Lucien's biographer Pietromarchi claims

that five million votes were cast, of which only one and a half million were for Napoleon's new constitution (*Lucien Bonaparte*, pp. 75–76).

19. Pietromarchi, *Lucien Bonaparte*, p. 79.
20. Abrantès, *Memoirs*, vol. 1, p. 148.
21. Ibid., p. 309.
22. Louis Madelin, *Le Consulat* (Paris: Hachette, 1939), p. 48.
23. *Corr de Nap*, no. 5165.
24. Pietromarchi, *Lucien Bonaparte*, pp. 127–19; Masson, *Napoléon et sa famille*, vol. 2, pp. 15–17, 21.
25. Madelin, *Le Consulat*, p. 241.
26. Pietromarchi, *Lucien Bonaparte*, p. 153; see also Miot, *Mémoires*, vol. 2, 114–15.
27. Pietromarchi, *Lucien Bonaparte*, p. 161.

15 THE FOREIGN MINISTER

1. See G. Lacour-Gayet, *Talleyrand, 1754–1838* (Paris: Payot, 1930), vol. 2.
2. Ibid., p. 9.
3. Louis Mathieu Molé, *Le Comte Molé, sa vie et ses mémoires* (Paris: Champion, 1922), vol. 1, p. 272.
4. Chastenay, *Mémoires*, p. 559.
5. Henriette-Lucy Dillon, marquise de la Tour du Pin, *Mémoires de la Marquise de la Tour du Pin, Journal d'une femme de cinquante 1778–1815* (Paris: Mercure de France, 1989), p. 340.
6. Hortense de Beauharnais, *Mémoires de la Reine Hortense* (Paris: Plon, 1930), vol. 1, p. 160.
7. Molé, *Mémoires*, vol. 1, p. 272.
8. La Tour du Pin, *Mémoires*, p. 340.
9. Hortense, *Mémoires*, vol. 1, p. 253.
10. Lacour-Gayet, *Talleyrand*, vol. 2, p. 44.
11. Ibid., pp. 43, 44, 46–47.
12. Ibid., p. 47.
13. Ibid., pp. 48, 322.
14. Molé, *Mémoires*, vol. 1, p. 193.
15. Jean Orieux, *Talleyrand* (Paris: Flammarion, 1970), p. 451.
16. Ibid., p. 605; Lacour-Gayet, *Talleyrand*, vol. 2, p. 439.
17. Orieux, *Talleyrand*, pp. 393–96.
18. Ibid., p. 448.
19. Ibid., p. 397.
20. Ibid., p. 433.
21. Ibid.
22. Ibid., p. 471.
23. Alan Schom, *One Hundred Days* (New York: Oxford University Press, 1992), p. 97.
24. Orieux, *Talleyrand*, p. 570; Madelin, *Talleyrand*.
25. Orieux, *Talleyrand*, p. 574.
26. Lacour-Gayet, *Talleyrand*, vol. 2, p. 272.
27. Ibid., p. 273.

28. "... but he's a blend of gold and shit." Armand de Caulaincourt, *Mémoires: La Campagne de Russie, L'Agonie de Fontainebleau* (Paris: Perrin, 1986), p. 200.

29. Orieux, *Talleyrand*, p. 575.

16 FOUCHÉ'S POLICE

1. Louis Madelin, *Fouché, 1759–1820* (Paris: Plon et Nourrit, 1945), vol. 1, p. 7.
2. Ibid., p. 11.
3. Ibid., p. 21.
4. Ibid.
5. Ibid., p. 41.
6. Ibid., p. 104.
7. François Alphonse Aulard, *Histoire politique de la révolution française, 1789–1804* (Paris: Nourrit, 1901); François Alphonse Aulard, *Recueil des Séances du Comité du Salut public* (Paris: Nourrit, 1895), vol. 7, p. 149.
8. Joseph Fouché, *Mémoire sur les troubles de Lyon* (Lyons: Guillon de Mostléon, 1797), vol. 2, pp. 357–75.
9. Ibid.
10. Peter de Polnay, *Napoleon's Police* (London: W. H. Allen, 1970), p. 43.
11. Aulard, *Histoire politique*, vol. 9, p. 713; Aulard, *Recueil des Séances*, vol. 9, p. 363.
12. Madelin, *Fouché*, vol. 1, p. 138.
13. Aulard, *Recueil des Séances*, vol. 9, p. 555.
14. Ibid.
15. *Moniteur*, September 9, 1793.
16. Aulard, *Recueil des Séances*, vol. 7, p. 290.
17. Ernest d'Hauterive, *Napoléon et sa Police* (Paris: Flammarion, 1943), p. 11.
18. Madelin, *Fouché*, vol. 1, p. 251; de Ségur, *Mémoires*, vol. 3, p. 407.
19. Ibid., p. 253.
20. Ibid., pp. 256–57.
21. Ibid., p. 261.
22. Louis-Gérôme Gohier, *Mémoires* (Paris: Bosange, 1824), I, 51.
23. Madelin, *Fouché*, vol. 1, p. 264.
24. Ibid., vol. 1, pp. 264 ff.; Chastenay, *Mémoires*, p. 611.
25. Madelin, Fouché, vol. 1, pp. 278, 298–300, 303.
26. Ibid., p. 278.
27. Ibid., pp. 280–81.
28. Ibid., p. 295.
29. Ibid., p. 282.
30. *Moniteur*, 8 brumaire an IX.
31. Madelin, *Fouché*, vol. 1, p. 290.
32. Polnay, *Napoleon's Police*, p. 49.
33. Jean Rigotard, *La Police parisienne de Napoléon: la Préfecture de Police* (Paris: Tallandier, 1990), pp. 9–10, 19–22, 48, 55; Polnay, *Napoleon's Police*, p. 10; Madelin, *Fouché*, vol. 1, 288.
34. Rigotard, *Police parisienne*, p. 31.
35. Hauterive, *Napoléon et sa Police*, pp. 27, 28.

36. Ibid., p. 29.

37. Ibid., p. 20.

38. *Moniteur*, 20 brumaire an VIII (November 13, 1794).

39. Madelin, *Fouché*, vol. 1, p. 285.

40. *Moniteur*, 11 frimaire an VIII.

41. Madelin, *Fouché*, vol. 1, p. 293.

17 FOUCHÉ THE MAN

1. Madelin, *Fouché*, vol. 1, pp. 395–96.

2. Ibid., p. 399.

3. Chastenay, *Mémoires*, p. 368.

4. Hauterive, *Napoléon et sa police*, p. 11.

5. Pierre-François Réal, *Indiscrétions (1798–1830): Souvenirs anecdotiques et politiques tirés du portefeuille d'un fonctionnaire de l'Empereur* (Paris: 1835), vol. 1, p. 411.

6. Madelin, *Fouché*, vol. 1, p. 441.

7. François Guizot, *Mémoires pour servir à l'histoire de mon temps* (Paris: Michel Lévy, 1858), vol. 1, p. 73.

8. Madelin, *Fouché*, vol. 1, p. 388.

9. Ibid., p. 387.

10. Ibid., pp. 387–88.

11. Chastenay, *Mémoires*, 329, 363, 364, 366, 368.

12. Ibid., p. 364.

13. Madelin, *Fouché*, vol. 1, p. 386.

14. Chastenay, *Mémoires*, p. 371; Madelin, *Fouché*, vol. 2, p. 438; Joseph Fouché, *Les mémoires de Fouché* (Paris: Flammarion 1945), pp. 143–44.

15. Polnay, *Napoleon's Police*, p. 45.

16. Madelin, *Fouché*, vol. 1, p. 384.

17. Ibid., pp. 382–83.

18. Ibid.

19. Ibid., p. 390.

20. Ibid., p. 393.

21. Ibid., p. 394.

22. Ibid.

23. Madelin, *Fouché*, vol. 1, p. 399.

24. Chastenay, *Mémoires*, p. 611.

25. Madelin, *Fouché*, vol. 1, p. 400.

26. François-René de Chateaubriand, *La Monarchie suivant la Charte* (Paris: Plon, 1891), p. 111.

27. Madelin, *Fouché*, vol. 1, 402.

28. Etienne-Denis Pasquier, *Histoire de mon temps: Mémoires du chancelier Pasquier* (Paris: Plon, 1893), vol. 3, p. 172.

29. Guizot, *Mémoires*, vol. 1, p. 72.

30. Joseph Fouché, *Mémoires de Joseph Fouché, Duc d'Otrante, Ministre de la Police générale* (Paris: Le Rouge, 1824), vol. 1, p. 385.

31. Joseph-Abraham-Bernard Fleury, *Mémoires de Fleury, de la Comédie Française* (Bruxelles, 1835), vol. 2, p. 21.

32. Pierre-Marie Desmarest, *Témoignages historiques, ou Quinze ans de haute police sous le Consulat et l'Empire* (Paris: Levasseur, 1833), p. 219.

18 THE CHRISTMAS EVE PLOT AND OTHERS

1. Rigotard, *Police parisienne*, p. 88.
2. Ibid., p. 73; Masson, *Napoléon et sa famille*, vol. 1, pp. 378 ff.
3. Rigotard, *Police parisienne*, p. 74.
4. Abrantès, *Memoirs*, vol. 2, p. 48.
5. Fouché, *Mémoires*, p. 253.
6. Rigotard, *Police parisienne*, p. 85; see also various newspaper reports of this incident, for example, *Moniteur*, 4, 5, 6, 7, 8, 9, 10 Nivôse an IX (December 26, 27, 28, 28, 29, 1800).
7. Rigotard, *Police parisienne*, p. 82.
8. Ibid., pp. 75–79.
9. Ibid., p. 85.
10. Ibid., pp. 87–89.
11. Ibid., pp. 89–90.
12. Ibid., p. 90.
13. Ibid., p. 91; see also *Corr de Nap*, no. 5246.
14. Rigotard, *Police parisienne*, pp. 95–96.
15. Polnay, *Napoleon's Police*, p. 71.
16. Ibid.
17. Ibid., p. 81. Pichegru had worked as the mathematics instructor at Brienne while Napoleon was there.
18. Ibid.
19. Ibid., p. 82.
20. Ibid., pp. 85–87.
21. Ibid., pp. 87–88.
22. See Napoleon's speech to Tribunate, October 16, 1800, *Corr de Nap*, no. 5129.
23. Ibid., nos. 4877, 5001, 5205.
24. Ibid., no. 4639.
25. Pierre-Marie Desmarest, *Témoignages historiques, ou 15 ans de Haute Police sous Napoléon* (Geneva: Slatkine-Megariotis, 1977), pp. 276 ff.
26. Ernest d'Hauterive, *Napoléon et sa police* (Paris: Flammarion, 1943), p. 49.
27. Ibid., pp. 51 ff.; n. 2.
28. Ibid.
29. Ibid., p. 48.
30. Ibid.
31. Ibid., p. 81; Ernest d'Hauterive, *La Police secrète du Premier Empire: Bulletins quotidiens adressés par Fouché à l'Empereur* (Paris: Clavreuil, 1963), nouvelle série, 1808–1809, vol. 4, p. 157; *Bulletin de la Police*, 11 mars, 22 avril 1808.
32. Ibid.
33. *Bulletin de la Police*, vol. 4, vendredi, 8 janvier 1808, item 17; dimanche, 10 et lundi, 11 janvier 1808, items 24, 25, 26; mercredi, 13 janvier 1808, item 33; dimanche 24 et lundi 25 janvier 1808, item 62.
34. Ibid., jeudi, 3 mars 1808, item 180.

35. Ibid., *Bulletin de la Police,* jeudi, 10 mars 1808, item 198.
36. Hauterive, *Napoléon et sa police,* p. 81.
37. *Bulletin e la Police,* mercredi, 27 avril 1808, item 330.
38. Ibid., mardi, 7 juin 1808, item 446.
39. Ibid., mardi, 7 juin 1808, item 446.
40. Ibid.
41. Ibid.
42. Hauterive, *Napoléon et sa police,* pp. 81, 82.
43. *Bulletin de la Police,* samedi, 11 juin 1808, item 463.
44. Ibid.
45. Ibid.
46. Hauterive, *Napoléon et sa police,* p. 82.
47. *Bulletin de la Police,* jeudi, 16 juin 1808, item 477.
48. Ibid., mercredi, 22 juin 1808, item 503.
49. Ibid., dimanche, 26 juin 1808, item 516, 517.
50. Ibid., vendredi, 8 juillet 1808, item 555.
51. Ibid., samedi, 5 novembre 1808, item 858.
52. Ibid., vendredi, 7 octobre 1808, item 795; jeudi, 13 octobre 1808, item 808; samedi, 5 novembre 1808, item 858; Hauterive, *Napoleon et sa police,* p. 83.
53. Hauterive, *Napoléon et sa police,* p. 82.

19 "The Revolution Is Over"

1. Guizot, *Mémoires,* vol. 1, p. 68.
2. Quoted in Madelin, *De Brumaire à Marengo,* p. 91.
3. Bourrienne, *Mémoires,* vol. 5, pp. 62–63.
4. *Corr de Nap,* nos. 4423, 4450; see also nos. 4407, 4409, 4412, 4413, 4418, 4416, 4423, 4432, 4449, 4450.
5. Pierre Louis Roederer, *Oeuvres du comte P L Roederer* (Paris: Firmin-Didot, 1854), vol. 3, p. 331; *Corr de Nap,* nos. 4422, 4447.
6. *Corr de Nap,* no. 4442; Bourrienne, *Mémoires,* vol. 4, p. 281.
7. *Corr de Nap,* no. 4457, no. 4439; Bourrienne, *Mémoires,* vol. 4, pp. 331–36.
8. *Corr de Nap,* nos. 4471, 4477, 4485.
9. Comte de Vaudreuil, *Correspondance du Comte de Vaudreuil et du Comte d'Artois* (Paris: 1870), vol. 2, p. 307; Boulay de la Meurthe, *Documents sur le duc d'Enghien* (Paris: 1850), vol. 1, p. 116.
10. *Corr de Nap,* no. 4403.
11. Ibid., no. 4473.
12. Ibid., nos. 4498, 4499.
13. Ibid., no. 4425.
14. Ibid., no. 4449.
15. Bourrienne, *Mémoires,* vol. 3, pp. 318 ff.
16. Madelin, *Le Consulat,* p. 204; Las Cases, *Mémorial de Sainte-Hélène* (Paris, n.p., 1823), vol. 2, p. 395.
17. Bourrienne, *Mémoires,* vol. 4, p. 357.
18. Claude-François de Méneval, *Mémoires pour servir à l'histoire de Napoléon Ier depuis 1802 jusqu'à 1815* (Paris: Dentu, 1893–94), vol. 1, p. 169–71.

19. Pieter Geyl, *Napoleon For and Against* (New Haven, Conn: Yale University Press, 1949), pp. 141–42.

20. Bourrienne, *Mémoires,* vol. 4, pp. 43–46.

21. Ibid., pp. 51, 39.

22. Ibid., pp. 349–50, 355.

23. Ibid., pp. 41, 66; quoted in Léonce Pingaud, *Le Comte d'Antraigues* (Paris: Nourit, 1890), vol. 9, p. 206.

24. *Corr de Nap,* no. 4488.

25. Ibid., no. 4521.

26. Ibid., nos. 4540, 4565.

27. Ibid., nos. 4600, 4871, 4872, 4652, 4734, 4778.

28. Ibid., nos 4569, 4570, 4555; Bourrienne, *Mémoires,* vol. 4, pp. 347–48; *Corr de Nap,* no. 4764.

29. See Chandler, *Campaigns of Napoleon,* pp. 264–98; the campaign may be followed step by step in *Corr de Nap,* beginning on March 22, 1800. *Corr de Nap,* no. 4694 ff.

30. *Corr de Nap,* no. 4882.

31. Bourrienne, *Mémoires,* vol. 4, pp. 120 ff.

32. *Corr de Nap,* no. 4993; Chandler, *Campaigns of Napoleon,* pp. 286–98.

33. Bourrienne, *Mémoires,* vol. 4, p. 242.

34. C. de La Jonquière, *L'Expédition d'Égypte, 1798–1801* (Paris: Charles-Lavauzelle, 1899), vol. 5, for complete coverage; Madelin, *Le Consulat,* p. 157.

35. Bourrienne, *Mémoires,* vol. 4, p. 297.

36. Mowat, *Diplomacy of Napoleon,* pp. 87 ff.

37. Ibid., p. 87.

38. Ibid., p. 101.

39. Bourrienne, *Mémoires,* vol. 4, p. 55.

40. Ibid., pp. 366–70.

41. Quoted in Léon Lecestre, in *Lettres inédits de Napoléon Ier* (Paris: Plon-Nourrit, 1897), vol. 2, p. 241, no. 1020.

42. Bourrienne, *Mémoires,* vol. 4, pp. 336–38.

43. Ibid., p. 171.

44. Ibid., vol. 5, p. 221.

20 WAR ONCE AGAIN

1. Alan Schom, *Trafalgar, Countdown to Battle, 1803–1805* (London: Michael Joseph, 1990), p. 62.

2. Auguste Thomazi, *Les Marins de Napoléon* (Paris: Tallandier, 1978), pp. 112, 131.

3. Ibid., p. 112.

4. *Moniteur,* May 24, 1803.

5. John Leyland, ed., *Dispatches and Letters Relating to the Blockade of Brest, 1803–1805* (London: Navy Records Society, 1899), vol. 1, p. 16.

6. Napoléon Bonaparte, *Correspondance de Napoléon avec le Ministre de la Marine, depuis 1804 jusqu'en avril 1815* (Paris: Delloye & Lecou, 1837), vol. 1, pp. 25–31.

7. Thomazi, *Marins de Napoléon,* p. 133; *Corr de Nap,* no. 7501.

8. Thomazi, *Marins de Napoléon,* p. 135.

9. Schom, *Trafalgar*, pp. 81 ff.

10. Thomazi, *Marins de Napoléon*, p. 143.

11. Schom, *Trafalgar*, p. 81; Thomazi, *Marins de Napoléon*, pp. 70–71.

12. Schom, *Trafalgar*, pp. 74–81 ff; Edouard Desbrière, *Projets et Tentatives de Débarquement aux Iles Britanniques* (Paris: Chapelot, 1902), hereafter cited as *Projets*.

13. Schom, *Trafalgar*, pp. 75, 76.

14. *Archives Nationales*, BB^{iv}, p. 167; Schom, *Trafalgar*, p. 396, n. 3.

15. *Archives Nationales*, BB^{iv}, p. 167.

16. Schom, *Trafalgar*, p. 92.

17. *Archives des affaires étrangères*, 607, Hollande, 1803, ans XI et XII.

18. Ibid.; *Corr de Nap*, no. 7453; *Archives Nationales*, AF^{iv}, 1202.

19. Talleyrand to Schimmelpenninck, *Archives des affaires étrangères*, 608, Hollande, 1804, ans XII et XII.

20. Thomazi, *Marins de Napoléon*, p. 120; Schom, *Trafalgar*, pp. 82–83.

21. *Corr de Nap*, no. 7055.

22. Schom, *Trafalgar*, p. 396, n. 3; *Archives Nationales*, AF^{iv}, 1203.

23. *Archives Nationales*, AF^{iv}, 1191; BB^{ii}, 91.

24. Ibid., BB^{iv}, p. 199.

25. Ibid., BB^{i}, p. 29; Schom, *Trafalgar*, p. 90.

26. Schom, *Trafalgar*, p. 96.

27. Ibid., pp. 122 ff.

28. Ibid., p. 120.

29. Jérome Zieseniss, *Berthier, Frère d'armes de Napoléon* (Paris: Belfond, 1985).

30. *Projets*, vol. 3, p. 141.

31. Schom, *Trafalgar*, pp. 101–3.

32. *Corr de Nap*, no. 6870; *Projets*, vol. 3, p. 162.

33. John Markham, *Selections from the Correspondence of Admiral John Markham, 1801–4, 1806–7*, ed. Clements Markham (London: Navy Records Society, 1904), p. 153.

34. *The Times* (London), Wednesday, May 16, 1804; J. Holland Rose and A. M. Broadley, *Dumouriez and the Defence of England against Napoleon* (London: John Lane, 1904), pp. 239–55, 258–62, 278–86.

35. Schom, *Trafalgar*, pp. 47, 54.

36. Ibid., pp. 41, 46–48, 58; see George III to Prince of Wales, August 7, 1803, in H. F. B. Wheeler and A. M. Broadley, *Napoleon and the Invasion of England: The Story of the Great Fear* (London: John Lane, 1908), vol. 2, p. 133.

37. Schom, *Trafalgar*, pp. 142–43.

38. Ibid., pp. 59–62; on theatrical events, see *The Times* and the London *Morning Post* throughout the period; Wheeler and Broadley, *Napoleon and the Invasion of England*, vol. 2, pp. 270–89; George Cruikshank, *A Pop-gun Fired off by George Cruikshank in Defence of the British Volunteers of 1803* (London, n.p., n.d.), p. 11; John Wardropper, *Kings, Lords and Wicked Libellers, Satire and Protest, 1760–1837* (London: John Murray, 1973).

39. Markham, *Correspondence*, pp. 113–14, 129–30, 152–53.

40. Schom, *Trafalgar*, p. 103; *Archives Nationales*, BB^{iv}, p. 73.

41. Schom, *Trafalgar,* pp. 111–16.
42. *Archives Nationales,* AF^iv, p. 1190.
43. *Projets,* vol. 3, pp. 110 ff.

21 THE CORONATION

1. Frédéric Masson, *Le Sacre et le Couronnement de Napoléon* (Paris: Ollendorff, 1908), p. 122; Louis Madelin, *L'Avènement de l'Empire* (Paris: Hachette, 1939), vol. 5, pp. 201–2; The national plebiscite results of 10–14 thermidor were accepted by Senatus-Consulte of November 6, 1804, and published in the *Moniteur,* on November 27, 1804. Tulard, *Napoleon, the Myth of the* Saviour, p. 129.

2. *Moniteur,* 27 novembre 1805; Masson, *Le Sacre et le Couronnement,* pp. 121, 122; Jean Tulard, *Napoléon* (Fayard, 1987), p. 172.

3. Masson, *Le Sacre et le Couronnement,* pp. 192 ff. and the *Moniteur* and *The Times* (London).

4. Masson, *Le Sacre et le Couronnement,* p. 112; E. E. Y. Hales, *Napoleon and the Pope* (London: Collins, 1962), p. 94.

5. Masson, *Le Sacre et le Couronnement,* pp. 202–3.

6. First Consul Bonaparte first officially discussed the creation of a hereditary succession to the proposed new imperial throne at a privy council meeting on April 23, 1804, when the principle was "officially" accepted and adopted, fully supported by Talleyrand. G. Lacour-Gayet, *Talleyrand (1754–1838)* (Paris: Payot, 1930), vol. 2, p. 145.

7. Masson, *Napoléon et sa famille,* vol. 1, p. 225.

8. Bourrienne, *Mémoires,* vol. 4, p. 318.

9. "Duroc, Confident intime de Napoléon," by Gen. Georges Spillmann, in *Souvenir Napoléonien* 296 (Nov. 1977), pp. 3 ff; Bourrienne, *Mémoires,* vol. 4, pp. 319–23.

10. Masson, *Napoléon et sa famille,* vol. 1, pp. 419–20.

11. Madelin, *L'Avènement de l'Empire,* vol. 5, p. 193.

12. Masson, *Napoléon et sa famille,* vol. 2, p. 375.

13. Ibid., pp. 379–80.

14. Ibid., pp. 448–49.

15. Ibid., pp. 451–52.

16. Ibid., p. 457.

17. Madelin, *L'Avènement de l'Empire,* p. 194; Masson, *Napoléon et sa famille,* vol. 2, p. 382.

18. Masson, *Napoléon et sa famille,* vol. 2, p. 373.

19. Ibid., pp. 370, 381. On April 7, 1804, Napoleon first informed Louis and Hortense of his wish to adopt Napoléon-Charles.

20. Ibid., p. 431.

21. Ibid., pp. 431–32.

22. Ibid., p. 382.

23.

24. Ibid., vol. 1, pp. 183, 189.

25. Ibid., vol. 2, p. 263.

26. Bourrienne, *Mémoires,* vol. 3, p. 284.

27. Ibid., vol. 1, pp. 305–20; Tulard, *Murat,* pp. 50–51.

28. Bourrienne, *Mémoires,* vol. 3, p. 292.

29. Masson, *Napoléon et sa famille,* vol. 1, pp. 180–84.

30. Antoine-Clair Thibaudeau, *Mémoires de A. C. Thibaudeau (1799–1815),* (Paris: Plon, 1913), p. 162.

31. *Corr de Nap,* no. 7021.

32. David Hamilton-Williams, *The Fall of Napoleon: The Final Betrayal* (New York: Wiley, 1994), p. 306.

33. Masson, *Le Sacre et le Couronnement,* pp. 329–31. Napoléon had paid a total of 300,667 francs to all those involved in engineering the Enghien affair—State Counselor Réal, Governor (of Paris) Murat, and General Hutlin.

34. Masson, *Napoléon et sa famille,* vol. 2, pp. 293 ff.

35. Masson, *Le Sacre et le Couronnement,* pp. 207 ff.

36. Madelin, *L'avènement de l'Empire,* pp. 206–9.

37. Masson, *Le Sacre et le Couronnement,* pp. 218–23; the *Moniteur* and *The Times* (London) in the issues preceding and following the coronation and the subsequent festivities.

38. Ibid.

39. Masson, *Le Sacre et le Couronnement,* p. 257.

40. Ibid., pp. 274–82. David's new atelier, the Eglise de Cluny, was provided him by the emperor. He was commissioned originally to paint four canvases, thirty by nineteen feet; *Le Sacre, L'intronisation,* the *Distribution des Aigles,* and *L'Arrivée de l'Empereur à l'Hôtel de Ville,* for which he was to be paid a total of 160,000 francs. But when David took much longer than expected, and then charged 100,000 francs for the first picture (*Le Sacre*) alone, Napoleon canceled the order for *L'Intronisation* and the *Hôtel de Ville.* The principal painting, *Le Sacre,* or *The Anointing,* was completed in December 1807. But it was not true to life, David altering Napoleon's sisters (they no longer hold Josephine's train), and adding Madame Mère, who was not even in France at the time. Similar liberty was taken with *The Distribution of the Eagles,* in which Napoleon had Joséphine removed altogether.

22 "A HUMILIATING BUSINESS"

1. Schom, *One Hundred Days,* p. 273.

2. Schom, *Trafalgar,* pp. 168–69.

3. Ibid., p. 173; Madelin, *L'Ascension,* p. 335.

4. Madelin, *De Brumaire à Marengo,* p. 89.

5. *Corr de Nap,* nos. 8060, 8061.

6. Ibid., nos. 8048, 8063.

7. Schom, *Trafalgar,* p. 174.

8. Ibid., pp. 190, 192, 193; *Archives Nationales,* BB[iv], 233, fol. 24.

9. Ibid., BB[iv], p. 230.

10. Ibid.; Schom, *Trafalgar,* p. 198. Emphasis added.

11. *Corr de Nap,* no. 8309.

12. Schom, *Trafalgar,* pp. 195, 196.

13. Ibid., p. 205.

14. *Archives Nationales*, Bb^{iv} 230.

15. Bonaparte, *Correspondance de Napoléon avec le Ministre de la Marine*, vol. 1, pp. 39–45. Additional troops brought by other vessels gave Lauriston 12,440 men.

16. *Corr de Nap*, no. 7996; *Archives Nationales*, AF^{iv}, 1195, fol. 8; Leyland, *Blockade of Brest*, vol. 1, pp. 354–55.

17. Bourrienne, *Mémoires*, vol. 2, p. 238; Thomazi, *Les Marins de Napoléon*, p. 92.

18. Schom, *Trafalgar*, pp. 224–35. Gravina lost the *San Rafaël* and the *Pirme*, and later abandoned two more ships at Vigo.

19. *Corr de Nap*, no. 9022.

20. Bourrienne, *Mémoires*, vol., p. 28, Thomazi, *Lez Marins de Napoléon*, p. 92.

21. Desbrière, *Projets*, vol. 4, p. 739; *Corr de Nap*, no. 9057, 9059.

22. Schom, *Trafalgar*, p. 240; *Corr de Nap*, nos. 9072.

23. Ibid.; *Archives Nationales*, BB^{iv}, p. 233.

24. *Corr de Nap.*, no. 9076.

25. Schom, *Trafalgar*, pp. 97–99; Thomazi, *Marins de Napoléon*, pp. 139 ff.; Constant, *Mémoires*, vol. 1, p. 273. Napoleon to Fouche, 16 July 1809; Lecestre, *Lettres inédites de Napoléon*, vol. 1, p. 325.

26. Schom, *Trafalgar*, pp. 266–67; *Archives Nationales*, BB^{i}, 31; ibid., BB^{iv}; Desbrières, *Projets*, vol. 4, pp. 225–26, 464–65; *Archives Nationale*, BB^{ii}, 10; Desbrière, *Projets*, vol. 4, pp. 464–65; *Corr de Nap*, nos. 8835, 8551.

27. *Corr de Nap*, no. 9076, 9073.

28. "Buonaparte's Soliloquy on the Cliff at Boulogne," *The Times*, September 11, 1805.

29. *Archives Nationales*, BB^{iv}, fols. 230, 263, 252.

30. Schom, *Trafalgar*, p. 276.

31. Ibid., pp. 238–42, 295; *Corr de Nap*, nos. 9179, 9190; *Archives Nationales*, BB^{iv}, p. 230; ibid., AF^{4}, p. 1196.

32. *Archives Nationales*, BB^{iv}, p. 230.

33. Edouard Desbrière, *Trafalgar la Campagne Maritime de 1805* (Paris: Chapelot, 1907), pp. 125–27; *Archives Nationales*, BB^{iv}, p. 234.

23 INTERMEZZO À LA BONAPARTE

1. Abrantès, *Memoirs*, vol. 2, pp. 2–5.

2. Ibid., p. 6.

3. Ibid., pp. 7–20.

4. Ibid., pp. 5–21.

5. Méneval, *Mémoires*, vol. 1, p. 139; Bourrienne, *Mémoires*, vol. 3, p. 223.

6. Bourrienne, *Mémoires*, vol. 3, p. 292.

7. Ibid., p. 224; vol 1, p. 234.

8. Abrantès, *Memoirs*, vol. 2, pp. 101–1.

9. Bourrienne, *Mémoires*, vol. 3, pp. 207–9.

10. Méneval, *Mémoires*, vol. 1, pp. 424–25.

11. Ibid., pp. 201–3.

12. Bourrienne, *Mémoires*, vol. 4, p. 359.

13. Ibid., pp. 257–60; ibid., vol. 5, p. 241; Méneval, *Mémoires*, vol. 1, pp. 424–25; Abrantès, *Memoirs*, vol. 2, 228–29.

14. Méneval, *Mémoires*, vol. 2, p. 142.
15. Bourrienne, *Mémoires*, vol. 4, pp. 36, 61.
16. Ibid., vol. 3, p. 228; ibid., vol. 2, p. 225. Chastenay, *Mémoires*, p. 469.
17. Bourrienne, *Mémoires*, vol. 3, pp. 225–26, 228–30.
18. Ibid., pp. 218–19: Chastenay, *Mémoires*, p. 403.
19. Bourrienne, *Mémoires*, vol. 5, pp. 69–77, 158–88.
20. Ibid., p. 182.
21. Ibid., pp. 185–89, 168.
22. Ibid., pp. 168 ff.
23. *Corr de Nap*, nos. 4482, 4520.
24. Masson, *Napoléon et sa famille*, vol. 2, pp. 304–52; this entire section is based on this source, apart from some documents I uncovered in the *Archives Nationales*, 400 AP 153–54 series.
25. Masson, *Napoléon et sa famille*, vol. 2, pp. 311–12.
26. Ibid.; *Archives Nationales*, 400 AP 153–54.
27. Masson, *Napoléon et sa* famille, vol. 2, pp. 351–52.
28. Ibid., vol. 3, pp. 85–86.
29. Ibid., pp. 87–89.
30. Ibid., p. 90.
31. Ibid., pp. 92–97.
32. Ibid., p. 98.
33. Ibid., p. 100.
34. Ibid., pp. 155–57.
35. Ibid., p. 377.
36. Ibid., pp. 102–3, 371, 377, 395, 409–11, 445. Forty-seven years later, an aging Jérôme Bonaparte was still fighting that battle, and on learning that his nephew, Napoleon III, was about to receive—and recognize the legitimacy of—his son by Elizabeth, Jérôme warned Napoleon III that if he did so, "it would cast doubt on the legitimacy of my children [by Catherine]."
37. Abrantès, *Memoirs*, vol. 2, pp. 179–81.

24 IT ALL BEGAN WITH AUSTERLITZ

1. Quoted in G. Lacour-Gayet, *Talleyrand, 1754–1838* (Paris: Payot, 1930), vol. 2, p. 156.
2. Napoleon had officially promised Spain in writing at the time of the transfer of Louisiana to France (Treaty of San Ildefonso, October 1, 1800, article 3) that he would not in turn transfer this vast territory to yet a third party (note of General Saint-Cyr, French ambassador to Madrid, to the Spanish minister of state, July 22, 1802). R. B. Mowat, *The Diplomacy of Napoleon* (London: E. Arnold, 1924), p. 141. Pres. Thomas Jefferson had been so alarmed by the reacquisition of Louisiana by France that he dispatched James Monroe to Paris to negotiate with Napoleon—resulting in the agreement to sell the entire territory to the United States (Treaty of Cession, April 30, 1803, signed by Treasury Minister Barbé-Marbois, and Ministers Plen. Monroe, and Livingston; the price: 60 million francs, or $11,250,000. Spain finally acquiesced, recognizing the sale to the United States and handing over Louisiana to France on Novem-

ber 30, 1803. On December 20 the American flag was first hoisted over New Orleans.

3. Rose, *Napoleon*, vol. 2, p. 11. Piedmont was of course still legally the property of the king of Sardinia.

4. As late as August 8, 1805, Napoleon was still issuing detailed embarkation orders for his troops and their crews at Boulogne. See Order [no. 149], Camp de Boulogne, 8 Aug. 1805, in Ernest Picard and Louis Tuetey, *Unpublished Correspondence of Napoleon I* (New York: Duffield, 1913), vol. 1 (1804–7). p. 87; Schom, *Trafalgar*. pp. 295 ff.

5. Jacques Wolff, *Le financier Ouvrard. 1770–1846, L'argent et la politique* (Paris: Tallandier, 1992), p. 120.

6. Ibid., pp. 118–26.

7. Quoted in Picard and Tuetey, *Unpublished Correspondence of Napoleon*, vol. 1, pp. 108–10, 122.

8. Quoted in Lacour-Gayet, *Talleyrand*, vol. 2, p. 158; *Corr de Nap*, no. 9216.

9. Bruce, *Napoleon & Josephine*, p. 376.

10. The discreet Méneval managed to suppress reports of most of Napoleon's epileptic attacks, but Talleyrand left a record of this one: Lacour-Gayet, Talleyrand, vol. 2, p. 160.

11. Jean-Jacques Cambacérès, *Cambacérès: Lettres inédites à Napoléon, 1802–1814* (Paris: Klincksieck, 1973), vol. 1, letters 265, 330, and 331, June 10, September 28 and 29, 1805, pp. 244–46, 290–91.

12. Ibid., pp. 290–91; *Corr de Nap*, no. 9124; Marion, *Histoire financière*, vol. 4, 276 ff.

13. Cambacérès, *Lettres*, p. 296.

14. Ibid., pp. 296, 307.

15. Ibid., pp. 309, 308.

16. Ibid., pp. 313, 311, 312, see also 329–30; Hauterive, *La Police secrète du premier Empire*, vol. 2, pp. 200–201.

17. Cambacérès, *Lettres*, vol. 1, p. 314.

18. Ibid., pp. 316, 317; see also Wolff, *Ouvrard*, p. 255.

19. Cambacérès, *Lettres*, vol. 1, pp. 319, 320–22.

20. Ibid., pp. 326–27.

21. Picard and Tuetey, *Unpublished Correspondence*, vol. 1, pp. 115, 118, 120, 122, 124; orders to Marshals Soult and Davout quoted in Alombert and Collin, *La Campagne de 1805* (Paris: Nourrit, n.d.), vol. 2, pp. 523–24, 600.

22. Gen. Vincent J. Esposito and Col. John Robert Elting, *A Military History and Atlas of the Napoleonic Wars* (New York: Praeger, 1964), map 46.

23. For a useful gunnery chart, Chandler, *Campaigns of Napoleon*, pp. 358–59.

24. Catherine Drinker Bowen, *Francis Bacon: The Temper of a Man* (Boston: Little, Brown, 1963), p. 4.

25. Picard and Tuetey, *Unpublished Correspondence*, vol. 1, p. 129.

26. In Lacour-Gayet, *Talleyrand*, vol. 2, p. 161.

27. Ibid., p. 137; Baden signed a defensive alliance with France on September 9, 1805; Württemberg signed a similar defense pact with France on October 5; and on October 12 Maximilian Joseph of Bavaria signed a military pact with France—all agreeing to provide a specific number of troops. See Mowat, *Diplo-*

macy of Napoleon, pp. 154–55; Lefebvre's *Histoire des Cabinets de l'Europe pendant le Consulat et L'Empire* (Paris, 1866), vol. 2, pp. 125–26.

28. Picard and Tuetey, *Unpublished Correspondence*, vol. 1, p. 134.

29. *Corr de Nap*, no. 9470.

30. Ibid., no. 9364.

31. Chandler, *Campaigns of Napoleon*, pp. 397–99; Tulard, *Murat*, p. 78; I also compare and take figures and statistics from Esposito and Elting, *Military History and Atlas of the Napoleonic Wars*, pp. 46–56.

32. Barton, *Bernadotte*, pp. 78, 186.

33. Sir Peter Hayman, *Soult, Napoleon's Maligned Marshal* (London: Arms & Armour, 1990), pp. 62, 66–67; Thiébault, *Mémoires*, vol. 2, p. 63.

34. *Corr de Nap*, no. 9497.

35. Picard and Tuetey, *Unpublished Correspondence*, vol. 1, pp. 147, 149.

36. Thiébault, *Mémoires*, vol. 3, pp. 446–49; Jean-Claude Damamme, *Lannes, Maréchal d'Empire* (Paris: Payot, 1987), pp. 161–63.

37. Chandler, *Campaigns of Napoléon*, pp. 412 ff.; and Philippe Paul Ségur, *Histoire et mémoires* (Paris: Firmin-Didot, 1873), vol. 3, p. 279.

38. Thiébault, *Mémoires*, vol. 3, p. 458.

39. Ibid., p. 462.

40. Chandler, *Campaigns of Napoleon*, p. 432; Jean-Baptiste-Antoine-Marcellin, *Mémoires du Général Baron de Marbot* (Paris: Mercure de France, 1983), vol. 1, pp. 216–19; Thiébault, *Mémoires*, vol. 3, p. 465.

41. Wolff, *Ouvrard*, pp. 124 ff.

42. Claude Manceron, *Austerlitz* (Paris: Laffont, 1962), p. 305; Jean Tulard, *Lettres d'Amour à Joséphine* (Paris: Fayard, 1981), item 87, p. 198.

25 THE MARCHES OF EMPIRE

1. Thiébault, *Mémoires*, vol. 3, pp. 545–46.

2. *Corr de Nap*, no. 9613.

3. Mowat, *Diplomacy of Napoleon*, pp. 148 ff.; Miot, *Memoirs*, vol. 2, p. 150.

4. Lacour-Gayet, *Talleyrand*, vol. 2, pp. 153–54.

5. Ibid., p. 170; Pierre Bertrand, *Les Lettres inédites de Talleyrand à Napoléon* (Paris: Perrin, n.d.) pp. 209–12, 224.

6. *Corr de Nap*, no. 9773.

7. Georges Lefebvre, *Napoleon* (London: Routledge & Kegan Paul, 1969), vol. 1, *From 18 Brumaire to Tilsit, 1799–1807*, pp. 232–37; see also Wolff, *Le Financier Ouvrard*, pp. 118–27.

8. Louis Madelin, *Vers L'Empire d'Occident, 1806–1807* (Paris: Hachette, 1940), pp. 1–15, 83 ff.

9. *Corr de Nap*, no. 9773.

10. Lefebvre, *Napoleon*, vol. 1, p. 243. On April 22, 1806, Napoleon passed a law putting the Bank of France directly under state control: On 14 July 1806 he created the Caisse de Service for the treasury.

11. Mowat, *Diplomacy of Napoleon*, pp. 155 ff.

12. Ibid., pp. 152 ff.; Madelin, *Vers l'Empire d'Occident*, pp. 143 ff.; Lefebvre, *Napoleon*, vol. 1, pp. 243 ff.

13. Masson, *Napoléon et sa famille*, vol. 3, pp. 271 ff. Napoleon encouraged Murat to violate his neighbors' frontiers to expand the confederation, especially at the expense of Prussia. The prince-archbishop of Würzburg entered the confederation on September 25, 1806; the elector of Saxony, only in 1807.

14. *Corr de Nap*, no. 9716; Tulard, *Murat*, pp. 92–95; Mowat, *Diplomacy of Napoleon*, p. 159.

15. Lefebvre, *Napoleon*, vol. 1, p. 246.

16. *Corr de Nap*, no. 1011.

17. Mowat, *Diplomacy of Napoleon*, pp. 168–69; see also *Hansard Parliamentary Debates*, 1st series (1803–20), vol. 8, pp. 140, 130.

18. Lecestre, *Lettres inédites de Napoléon*, vol. 1, p. 74; Picard and Tuetey, *Unpublished Correspondence of Napoleon*, vol. 1, pp. 329–31, 326, 347.

19. Picard and Tuetey, *Unpublished Correspondence of Napoleon*, vol. 1, pp. 348, 353, 359–60, 368, 375.

20. Mowat, *Diplomacy of Napoleon*, pp. 170–71; *Corr de Nap*, no. 10967.

21. *Corr de Nap*, nos. 10815, 10977.

22. Chandler, *The Campaigns of Napoleon*, pp. 476–79; Esposito and Elting, *Military History and Atlas of the Napoleonic Wars*, nos. 57–67.

23. Tulard, *Murat,*. pp. 98–99.

24. Dunbar Plunket Barton's whitewashing of Bernadotte's cowardly actions, in his biography *Bernadotte*, pp. 192–99; Jean-Claude Damamme's lamentable biography of *Lannes* (Paris: Payot, 1987), p. 158, 159; Hayman, *Soult, Napoleon's Maligned Marshal*, pp. 70–71, has nothing good to say about Bernadotte.

25. Chandler, *Campaigns of Napoleon*, p. 495.

26. *Corr de Nap*, no. 11009.

27. Damamme, *Lannes*, p. 159.

26 POINT OF NO RETURN

1. Maynard Solomon, *Beethoven* (New York: Schirmer, 1977), p. 138; Louis Madelin, *Le Consulat et l'Empire* (Paris: Hachette, 1932), vol. 1, p. 307.

2. Bourrienne, *Mémoires*, vol. 2, p. 14.

3. Ibid., p. 3.

4. Chandler, *Campaigns of Napoleon*, pp. 516–17.

5. Thiébault, *Mémoires*, vol. 4, p. 49.

6. *Archives Nationales*, 400 AP 6, vol. 2, no. 79.

7. Bruce, *Napoleon and Josephine*, pp. 403 ff.

8. Picard and Tuetey, *Unpublished Correspondence of Napoleon*, vol. 1, p. 427; Lacour-Gayet, *Talleyrand*, vol. 2, p. 205.

9. *Archives Nationales*, 400 AP6, vol. 2, no. 83.

10. Bruce, Napoleon and Josephine, pp. 385, 400, 403.

11. Chandler, *Campaigns of Napoleon*, pp. 516–20; Picard and Tuetey, *Unpublished Correspondence of Napoleon*, vol. 1, p. 448, no. 856; ibid., pp. 450–54, no. 861.

12. Thiébault, *Mémoires*, vol. 1, pp. 88–89.

13. Chandler, *Campaigns of Napoleon*, p. 548; see also Jean-Baptiste-Antoine-Marcellin, *Mémoires du général baron de Marbot* (Paris: Plon, 1891), vol. 1, pp. 265–69.

14. *Archives Nationales*, 400 AP6, vol. 2, no. 96; Eric Perrin, *Le Maréchal Ney* (Paris: Perrin, 1993), p. 106.

15. Chandler, *Campaigns of Napoleon*, and *Corr de Nap*, nos. 12741-875. See also Esposito and Elting, *A Military History and Atlas*, pp. 76-83; Albert Vandal, *Napoléon et Alexandre I* (Paris, 1914), vol. 1, p. 48.

16. Rose, *Napoleon*, book 2, p. 126; Vandal, *Napoléon et Alexandre I*, vol. 1, p. 48.

17. Lacour-Gayet, *Talleyrand*, vol. 2, p. 211.

18. Mowat, *Diplomacy of Napoleon*, pp. 175 ff.

19. Herold, *Mind of Napoleon*, p. 273.

20. Mowat, *Diplomacy of Napoleon*, p. 178; Lacour-Gayet, *Talleyrand*, vol. 1, pp. 211-12; Savary, *Mémoires du Duc de Rovigo*, vol. 6, p. 35.

21. *Archives Nationales*, 400 AP 6, vol. 2, no. 139.

22. Henri Troyat, *Alexandre Ier, le Sphinx du Nord* (Paris: Flammarion, 1980), pp. 133 ff.

27 IBERIA

1. Thibaudeau, *Mémoires*, p. 219.

2. Lanzac de Laborie, *Paris sous Napoléon* (Paris: Plon-Nourrit, 1903), pp. 129-30.

3. Thibaudeau, *Mémoires*, p. 219.

4. Rose, *Napoleon*, book 2, p. 149. Rose gives the figure of 26,582,000 francs.

5. Louis Madelin, *L'Affaire d'Espagne, 1807-1809* (Paris: Hachette, 1943), vol. 7, pp. 29-32; Rose, *Napoleon*, book 1, pp. 145-49; Lacour-Gayet, *Talleyrand*, vol. 2, pp. 218 ff. Regarding the invasion of Spain, Talleyrand had agreed to the temporary feasibility of invading the northeastern Mediterranean coast of Catalonia and then only until London agreed to peace. Talleyrand refused to acquiesce and abet Napoleon in the full conquest and annexation of Spain.

6. Lacour-Gayet, *Talleyrand*, vol. 2, pp. 214, 217-20; Charles-Maurice de Talleyrand-Périgord, *Mémoires du prince de Talleyrand* (Paris: Calmann-Lévy, 1891), vol. 1, p. 318, vol. 2, pp. 132-33.

7. Madelin, *L'Affaire d'Espagne*, p. 33; Picard and Tuetey, *Unpublished Correspondence of Napoleon*, vol. 1, no. 1248.

8. Madelin, *L'Affaire d'Espagne*, p. 39; *Corr de Nap*, nos. 13677, 14807.

9. Charles Otto Zieseniss, *Napoléon et la Cour Impériale* (Paris: Tallandier, 1957), pp. 158-61.

10. Mowat, *Diplomacy of Napoleon*, pp. 195-98.

11. Ibid., p. 184.

12. Ibid., pp. 186-87; J. Stephen Watson, *The Reign of George III, 1760-1815* (Oxford: Oxford University Press, 1985), pp. 455-56.

13. *Corr de Nap*, no. 13079.

14. Quoted in Clément-Wenceslas-Lothaire de Metternich, *Mémoires, documents et écrits divers laissés par le prince de Metternich, chancelier de la court et d'Etat* (Paris: Plon, 1886), vol. 2, p. 167; Fouché, *Mémoires*, vol.1, p. 13. Napoleon created the Army of Observation of the Gironde on August 2, 1807.

15. The Fontainebleau treaty was signed by General Duroc and Sr. Izquierdo. See Mowat, *Diplomacy of Napoleon*, p. 209, and also the France-Spanish Convention of January 4, 1805, signed by Admirals Decrès and Gravina, regarding mutual war contributions vis-à-vis England.

16. D. A. Bingham, *A Selection from the Letters and Despatches of Napoleon* (London: 1884), vol. 2, p. 324. See also *Corr de Nap*, no. 12928.

17. Rose, *Napoleon*, book 2, p. 148.

18. Picard and Tuetey, *Unpublished Correspondence of Napoleon*, vol. 2, p. 8.

19. Chandler, *Campaigns of Napoleon*, p. 600; Las Cases, *Memoirs of Emperor Napoleon* (London, 1836), vol. 4, part 1, p. 83.

20. Chandler, *Campaigns of Napoleon*, p. 600.

21. Méneval, *Mémoires*, vol. 2, p. 158.

22. Fouché, *Mémoires*, vol. 1, p. 13; *Corr de Nap*, nos. 13778, 11911.

23. Picard and Tuetey, *Unpublished Correspondence of Napoleon*, vols. 1 and 2.

24. Masson, *Napoléon et sa famille*, vol. 4, p. 221.

25. Ibid., p. 220.

26. Ibid., p. 224.

27. Lefebvre, *Napoleon*, vol. 2, p. 19.

28. Masson, *Napoléon et sa famille*, vol. 4, p. 228.

29. Ibid., pp. 238–39. On June 2, 1808, Murat signed over the Duchy of Berg. He was to assume the Neapolitan throne on August 1. Ibid., p. 251.

30. Ibid., p. 245.

31. Ibid., p. 263.

32. Chandler, *Campaigns of Napoleon*, pp. 612 ff; Madelin, *L'Affaire d'Espagne*, pp. 82 ff, 89 ff, 106 ff, 120 ff, 138 ff.; Tulard, *Murat*, pp. 115 ff.; Rose, *Napoleon*, book 2, pp. 159–73; Jacques Bainville, *Napoléon* (Paris: Fayard, 1931), pp. 243–68; Masson, *Napoléon et sa famille*, vol. 4, pp. 197–284; Lefebvre, *Napoleon*, vol. 2, pp. 13–24, 29–32; Watson, *The Reign of George III*, pp. 458–62, 479–2, 485–88, 493–495; Méneval, *Mémoires*, vol. 2, p. 158.

33. Savary, *Mémoires*, vol. 3, p. 455; Thierry Lentz, *Savary, Le séide de Napoléon (1774–1833)* (Metz: Editions Serpenoise, 1993), pp. 129–30.

34. Rose, *Napoleon*, book 2, p. 170.

35. Picard and Tuetey, *Unpublished Correspondence of Napoleon*, vol. 2, pp. 387–88.

36. Mathieu Dumas, *Souvenirs du lieutenant général comte Mathieu Dumas, de 1770 à 1836* (Paris: Gosselin, 1839), vol. 2, p. 317.

37. Chandler, *Campaigns of Napoleon*, p. 603.

38. For good background material on Junot's actions during the French occupation of Portugal, see Thiébault, *Mémoires*, vol. 4, pp. 184–274.

39. Masson, *Napoléon et sa famille*, vol. 4, p. 264.

40. Ibid., p. 267.

41. Picard and Tuetey, *Unpublished Correspondence of Napoleon*, vol. 2, pp. 310–11, 317, 333, 316, 336, 359–62, nos. 2073, 2084, 2107, 2114, 2152.

42. Ibid., p. 363, no. 2155.

28 ANOTHER GRAVE ERROR

1. *Corr de Nap*, no. 1421.

2. Rose, *Napoleon*, book 2, p. 179.

3. Constant, *Mémoires*, p. 331; Rose, *Life of Napoleon*, book 2, p. 179.

4. Troyat, *Alexandre Ier*, p. 167.

5. Ibid., p. 168.

6. Ibid., p. 170.

7. Lacour-Gayet, *Talleyrand*, vol. 2, p. 245.

8. Ibid., p. 246.

9. *Archives Nationales*, 400 AP 6, vol. 3, nos. 150, 149; see also Constant, *Mémoires*, p. 332.

10. Picard and Tuetey, *Unpublished Correspondence of Napoleon*, vol. 2, pp. 423-27, no. 2255.

11. Rose, *Napoleon*, book 2, p. 193.

12. Marshal Jourdan's portrait by Vien fils was shortly to be removed from the Hall of the Marshals. For a complete list of the marshals created by Napoleon, see Appendix A of this book.

13. In occupied central and eastern Europe: 155,000 line infantry, 37,000 cavalry, 13,000 engineers and gunners. Picard and Tuetey, *Unpublished Correspondence of Napoleon*, vol. 2, p. 426. no. 2255.

14. Ibid., pp. 425 ff.

15. Mathieu Dumas, *Souvenirs du lieutenant général comte Mathieu Dumas, de 1770 à 1836* (Paris: Gosselin, 1839), vol. 1, pp. 321-22.

16. For a good example of the long list of intricate orders dispatched by Napoleon from Erfurt, St.-Cloud, and Bayonne, see Picard and Tuetey, *Unpublished Correspondence of Napoleon*, vol. 2, pp. 433-514; document nos. 2326-2429; Madelin, *L'Affaire d'Espagne*, vol. 7, p. 47.

17. Picard and Tuetey, *Unpublished Correspondence of Napoleon*, vol. 2, p. 514, nos. 2429, 2431; See also Constant, *Mémoires*, p. 338.

18. For a detailed breakdown of the *Armée d'Espagne* at this time, see Chandler, *Campaigns of Napoleon*, pp. 1104-6; see also Sir Charles Oman, *History of the Peninsular War* (Oxford: Oxford University Press, 1902), vol. 1, pp. 640-45.

19. On guerrilla warfare, see Col. Jean-Louis Reynaud, *Contre-Guerilla en Espagne (1808-1814), Suchet pacifie l'Aragon* (Paris: Economica, 1992).

20. Picard and Tuetey, *Unpublished Correspondence of Napoleon*, vol. 2, pp. 548-92, nos. 2504-600.

21. Ibid., p. 519, no. 2440; Constant, *Mémoires Intimes*, p. 337.

22. Rose, *Napoleon*, book 2, p. 171; Chandler, *Campaigns of Napoleon*, pp. 641-42. As Lannes and ultimately just about everyone else commented, sooner or later Napoleon used his troops as if they were not human beings, but literally tools to be manipulated to achieve his military goals.

23. Constant, *Mémoires*, pp. 339-44, for events in Madrid. It did not appear to incommode Bonaparte one whit that he had recently ordered the arrest of the owner's son [of Champs Martín], and the sequestration of all his property, and that under the circumstances it might have been awkward demanding shelter in this particular residence where he had to see the young duke's mother daily.

24. Aymar-Olivier Le Hariver de Gonneville, *Souvenirs militaires* (Paris: Didier, 1895), vol. 1, p. 61.

25. Bernard Bergerot, *Le Maréchal Suchet* (Paris: Tallandier, 1986), p. 113.

26. Chandler, *Campaigns of Napoleon*, p. 659.

27. Thiébault, *Mémoires*, vol. 4, p. 244. Thiébault's memoirs for the Iberian campaign provide invaluable background material to understanding the events and thinking of the day.
28. *Archives Nationales*, 400 AP 6, vol. 3, no. 164.

29 ANOTHER DANUBE CAMPAIGN

1. Thiébault, *Mémoires*, vol. 4, pp. 466–67. Napoleon's plan for the reconquest of Portugal was based on the original plan first submitted by Gen. Thiébault.
2. Méneval, *Mémoires*, vol. 2, pp. 233–34.
3. Ibid., p. 227.
4. Ibid., pp. 233–34.
5. Metternich, *Mémoires*, vol. 2, pp 243, 262.
6. Méneval, *Mémoires*, vol. 2, p. 228; Madelin, *Fouché*, vol. 2, pp. 84–85; François-Nicolas Mollier, *Mémoires d'un ancien ministre du Trésor, 1800–1814* (Paris: Fournier, 1837), vol. 3, p. 7.
7. Lacour-Gayet, *Talleyrand*, vol. 2, pp. 272–73.
8. Méneval, *Mémoires*, vol. 3, pp. 236, 239; Rose, *Napoleon*, book 2, p. 190. According to Masson, the Austrians crossed the Inn, entering Bavaria on April 9, 1809; *Napoleon et sa famille*, vol. 4, p. 309.
9. Chandler, *Campaigns of Napoléon*, pp. 630, 668, 669; Marbot, *Mémoires*, vol. 1, p. 301.
10. Chandler, *Campaigns of Napoléon*, p. 670, gives the figure of 311 guns.
11. Metternich, *Mémoires*, vol. 2, pp. 240 ff. Mowat, *Diplomacy of Napoleon*, p. 224.
12. For army strength, see Chandler, *Campaigns of Napoleon*, pp. 669–77; and Esposito and Elting, *Military History and Atlas*, pp. 100–106.
13. Masson, *Napoléon et sa famille*, vol. 2, pp. 286–309, 311.
14. Geyl, *Napoleon For and Against*, p. 172.
15. Masson, *Napoléon et sa famille*, vol. 4, pp. 312–13, 314.
16. Ibid., p. 328.
17. Ibid., pp. 328 ff.
18. Picard and Tuetey, *Unpublished Correspondence of Napoleon*, vol. 3, p. 29, no 3118.
19. Chandler, *Campaigns of Napoleon*, p. 691.
20. Marbot, *Mémoires*, vol. 1, p. 391.
21. Ibid.
22. Maynard Solomon, *Beethoven* (New York: Schirmer, 1977), p. 150.
23. Ibid., pp. 132–37, 150.
24. Marbot, *Mémoires*, vol. 1, p. 419.
25. Ibid., p. 423.
26. On unit strengths, guns, and so on, cf. Chandler, *Campaigns of Napoleon*, pp. 668–69 and Esposito and Elting, *A Military History and Atlas*, pp. 100–106.
27. Marbot, vol. 1, p. 437.
28. Ibid., pp. 440–44; Damamme, *Lannes*, pp. 282 ff.
29. Marbot, *Mémoires*, vol. 1, pp. 440–44.
30. Ibid.; Constant, *Mémoires*, pp. 243–44.
31. Chandler, *Campaigns of Napoleon*, p. 706.
32. Marbot, *Mémoires*, vol. 1, pp 429–34.

33. Mowat, *Diplomacy of Napoléon*, p. 232.

34. N. Schilder, *L'Empéreur Alexandre Ier, sa vie, son regne* (St. Petersburg, n.d.), vol. 2, pp. 301, 355.

35. Marbot, *Mémoires*, vol. 1.

30 WAGRAM

1. Esposito and Elting, *Military History and Atlas*, pp. 237 ff.

2. General Hiller had resigned from the Austrian army after the Battle of Aspern-Essling.

3. Chandler, *Campaigns of Napoleon*, p. 719. For a sketch of the personal role of Eugène de Beauharnais and his Italian Army at Wagram, see Carola Oman, *Napoleon's Viceroy, Eugène de Beauharnais* (London: Hodder & Stoughton, 1966), which gives the material before but not at the battle; and René Blémus's scarcely better *Eugène de Beauharnais, 1781–1824: L'Honneur à tout vent* (Paris: Editions France-Empire, 1993).

4. Marbot, *Mémoires*, vol. 2, p. 273; Barton, *Bernadotte*, pp. 225–29.

5. See Dr. Chandler's useful charts, pp. 358–59, in *Campaigns of Napoleon*. For example, a twelve-pounder had a crew of fifteen men, an eight-pounder a crew of thirteen.

6. Ibid., p. 729.

7. Jean Morvan, *Le Soldat impérial* (Paris: Plon, 1904), vol. 1, p. 58; Brice and Bottet, *Le Corps de Santé Militaire en France* (Paris Berger-Levrault, 1907), p. 213; *Archives Nationales*, 400 AP6, vol. 2, no. 198.

8. Quoted in Maximilien Vox, *Napoléon* (Paris: Seuil, 1959), p. 199; Soubiran, *Napoléon et un million de morts*, p. 15.

9. Dominique d'Héralde papers, Archives du Service de Santé Militaire, Musée du Val-de-Grâce, Paris; Soubiran, *Napoléon*, pp. 14, 98.

10. From "Dantsik," quoted in Soubiran, *Napoléon*, p. 151.

11. Ibid., p. 197.

12. Ibid., p. 200.

13. Ibid.

14. At one point Soubiran states that of seventeen hundred men operated on, thirteen hundred did not survive for lack of proper operative and postoperative treatment—that is, a mortality rate of over 76 percent. Ibid.

15. Ibid., pp. 203–206.

16. Louis Madelin, *L'Apogée de l'Empire*, 1809–1810 (Paris: Hachette, 1944), vol. 3, pp. 124–25.

17. Ibid., p. 125.

18. Ibid., pp. 35–36.

19. Masson, *Napoléon et sa famille*, vol. 4, pp. 311–14.

20. Ibid., p. 319.

21. Madelin, *Apogée*, pp. 91–92; Masson, *Napoléon et sa famille*, vol. 4, p. 345; Troyat, *Alexandre Ier*, p. 176.

22. Vandal, *L'avènement de Napoléon* (Paris: 1905), vol. 1, p. 132.

23. Metternich, *Mémoires*, vol. 2, p. 305.

24. Vandal, *L'avènement*, vol. 2, p. 162; Madelin, *Apogée*, p. 128.

25. Madelin, *Apogée*, p. 94.

26. Mowat, *Diplomacy of Napoleon*, pp. 230–31; Madelin, *Apogée*, pp. 126–27. Trieste, the Carniola, part of Carinthia, Croatia, Istria, and Fiume would soon be added to Dalmatia (taken from Austria by France in 1805), incorporated by Napoleon into the French Empire under the rubric "Gouvernement généeral d'Illyrie."

27. Madelin, *Apogée*, pp. 110–11.

28. *Corr de Nap*, nos. 15629, 15633, 15636.

29. Madelin, *Apogée*, pp. 98 ff., 109; Lefebvre, *Napoleon*, vol. 2, p. 66.

30. Masson, *Napoléon et sa famille*, vol. 4, pp. 329–57.

31. Ibid.

32. Madelin, *Apogée*, p. 102.

33. Ibid., pp. 116–17.

34. *Corr de Nap*, nos. 15670, 15811, 15855, 15866.

35. Barton, *Bernadotte*, pp. 235–36, 250.

31 THE LAST ROSE OF SUMMER

1. Louis Constant Wairy, *Mémoires de Constant* (Paris: Garnier, 1894), vol. 3, pp. 407 ff.; Méneval, *Mémoires*, vol. 2, pp. 333–35.

2. Constant, *Mémoires*, vol. 3, p. 408.

3. Méneval, *Mémoires*, vol. 2, pp. 271 ff.

4. Ibid., p. 288.

5. Ibid., vol. 1, pp. 289–90.

6. Ibid., vol. 2, pp. 290–91; Beauharnais, *Mémoires de la Reine Hortense*, vol. 2, pp. 56–58.

7. Beauharnais, *Mémoires de la Reine Hortense*, vol. 2, pp. 54–55.

8. Méneval, *Mémoires*, vol. 2, pp. 292–93.

9. Masson, *Napoléon et sa famille*, vol. 5, p. 9.

10. Fouché, *Mémoires*, p. 263.

11. Méneval, *Mémoires*, vol. 2, pp. 312–13.

12. Ibid.

13. Zieseniss, *Berthier*, p. 203.

14. Méneval, *Mémoires*, vol. 2, pp. 321, 323.

15. Ibid., p. 398.

16. Thiébault and Marbot discuss these mutilations in several places, as does Capt. Charles François, *Journal du capitaine François (1792–1830)* (Paris: Carrington, 1903), vol. 2.

17. Madelin, *Apogée*, vol. 8, p. 266.

18. Treaty ceding Holland to France, signed March 16, 1810; Méneval, *Mémoires*, vol. 2, p. 350.

19. *Archives Nationales*, 400 AP 6, vol. 3, no. 190.

20. Thiébault, *Mémoires*, vol. 4, pp. 390–93.

21. Masson, *Napoléon et sa famille*, vol. 5, p. 91.

22. Ibid., pp. 72, 73.

23. Ibid., pp. 68–70.

24. Ibid., pp. 88–89.

25. Ibid., pp. 101–21; Antonello Pietro-Marchi, *Lucien Bonaparte* (Paris: Perrin, 1980), pp. 213–19.

26. Las Cases, *Le Mémorial de Sainte-Hélène*, vol. 2, p. 306.

32 CHIMES AND ALARM BELLS

1. J. Stephen Watson, *The Reign of George III, 1760–1815* (Oxford: Clarendon Press, 1985), pp. 462–71; Jean Tulard's phrase, "cette fureur annexiste," in *Napoléon, ou le mythe du sauveur* (Paris: Fayard, 1987), pp. 374–78, 391.
2. Schom, *One Hundred Days*, p. 178.
3. Lefebvre, *Napoleon*, vol. 2, p. 174.
4. Wolff, *Le financier Ouvrard*, pp. 132–46.
5. Ibid.
6. Rose, *Napoleon*, book 2, pp. 103 ff, 216 ff.
7. Ibid., p. 213, pp. 103 ff, pp. 216 ff.
8. Marquis de Noailles, *Le comte Molé, 1781–1855: Sa vie, ses mémoires* (Paris: Champion, 1922), vol. 1, pp. 58–59; Louis Madelin, *La nation sous l'Empereur* (Hachette: Paris, 1948), vol. 11, pp. 355 ff.
9. Lanzac de Laborie, *La domination française en Belgique*, vol. 6, pp. 78–80; Madelin, *La nation sous l'Empereur*, vol. 11, pp. 356–63. Emphasis added.
10. Madelin, *La nation sous l'Empereur*, vol. 11, pp. 170, 356–63.
11. Schom, *One Hundred Days*, pp. 35–36.
12. Schom, *Trafalgar*, for example, pp. 91–96, 396–97; Owen Connelly, *Napoleon's Satellite Kingdoms* (New York: Free Press, 1954), pp. 137–46. On July 1, 1810, French troops seized Amsterdam, and on the ninth Louis fled to Teplitz, Bohemia, and Napoleon annexed Holland.
13. Solomon, *Beethoven*, p. 148.
14. Connelly, *Napoleon's Satellite Kingdoms*, pp. 200 ff.
15. Ibid., p. 208.
16. Ibid., pp. 241 ff.
17. Madelin, *L'Empire et Napoléon*, vol. 10, p. 321.
18. Masson, *Napoléon et sa famille*, vol. 6, p. 122.
19. Quoted in Caulaincourt, *Mémoires*, vol. 2, pp. 234–35.
20. Quoted in Driault, *Le Grand Empire*, p. 137.
21. Roederer, *Oeuvres*, vol. 2, p. 582.
22. Girod de l'Ain, *Joseph Bonaparte*, p. 318.
23. Masson, *Napoléon et sa famille*, vol. 6, pp. 76–77.
24. Girod de l'Ain, *Joseph Bonaparte*, pp. 259, 272.
25. Joseph invested £62,000 with Barings, and another £27,000 with Rougement and Verhend Bank, also in London, not to mention large amounts with Hope and Co., of Amsterdam. Ibid., p. 272.
26. Ibid., p. 263.
27. Masson, *Napoléon et sa famille*, vol. 7, p. 78.
28. Ibid. vol. 6, pp. 172–73.
29. Girod de l'Ain, *Joseph Bonaparte*, p. 260.
30. Madelin, *L'Empire et Napoleon*, vol. 10, p. 27.
31. Miot, *Memoirs*, p. 579.
32. Girod de l'Ain, *Joseph Bonaparte*, p. 260.
33. Masson, *Napoléon et sa famille*, vol. 6, p. 142.

34. Ibid., pp. 171–72.
35. One comment made at St. Helena, the other to Gen. Clarke on July 1, 1813, and then to Savary on the thirteenth, quoted in Rose, *Napoleon.* book 2, p. 313.
36. Miot, *Memoirs*, p. 585.
37. Méneval, *Mémoires*, vol. 2, pp. 358–59.
38. Madelin, *Fouché*, vol. 2, pp. 190 ff.
39. Ibid., vol. 2, pp. 175–90, 196; *Corr de Nap*, no. 16529. This is reminiscent of J. Edgar Hoover's notorious files, held over the heads of several U.S. presidents, including Harry Truman and John Kennedy in particular, not to mention dozens of other high national officials, thanks to which no one had the courage to dismiss Hoover as director of the FBI.
40. Méneval, *Mémoires*, vol. 2, pp. 431 ff.; Constant, *Mémoires*, vol. 3, pp. 424–29.
41. Méneval, *Mémoires*.
42. Ibid.; Constant, *Mémoires*.
43. Rose, *Napoleon*, book 2, p. 227.
44. See Frédéric Masson, *Napoléon et son fils* (Paris: Ollendorff, 1899), pp. 123–43; Frédéric Masson, *L'Impératrice Marie-Louise, 1809–1815* (Ollendorff, Paris, 1900); Comtesse de Montesquiou, "Marie-Louise et le Roi de Rome," in *Revue de Paris* (May 1949), pp. 59–80; and, more important, Claude-François de Méneval's *Napoléon et Marie-Louise: Souvenir Historiques* (Paris: Amyot, 1844–45).

33 RUSSIA

1. *Corr de Nap*, no. 17316.
2. Metternich, *Mémoires*, vol. 1, p. 203.
3. *Corr de Nap*, no. 17395.
4. Troyat, *Alexandre*, p. 179.
5. *Corr de Nap*, no. 17371.
6. Louis Madelin, *Crise de l'Empire* (Paris: Hachette, 1944), vol. 9, p. 317.
7. Rose, *Napoleon*, book 2, pp. 236, 237. Emphasis in original.
8. Miot, *Memoirs*, p. 583. Emphasis in original.
9. Troyat, *Alexandre*, pp. 191, 192.
10. Ibid., p. 199.
11. *Corr de Nap*, no. 15669.
12. Blémus, *Eugène de Beauharnais*, pp. 221–24.
13. *Corr de Nap*, no. 17844.
14. *Arch. Nat.* AP 6, Murat to Napoleon, 20 July 1811; see also Tulard's excellent discussion of this problem in *Murat*, pp. 167–73.
15. Caulaincourt, *Mémoires*, vol. 1, p. 277.
16. Ibid., pp. 281 ff.
17. Ibid., p. 287.
18. Ibid., pp. 305, 306.
19. Ibid., pp. 303–5.
20. Ibid., pp. 311, 318.
21. Tulard, *Napoléon* (Paris: Fayard, 1977), p. 287.
22. Caulaincourt, *Mémoires*, vol. 1, pp. 319–20.

23. Ibid., p. 330.

24. Ibid., pp. 341–42.

25. Ibid., pp. 325–37; Méneval, *Mémoires*, vol. 3.

26. Méneval, *Mémoires*, vol. 3, pp. 29 ff.; Caulaincourt, *Mémoires*, vol. 1, pp. 342–44.

27. Caulaincourt, *Mémoires*, vol. 1, pp. 348–52.

28. Ibid., pp. 346–54.

29. Ibid., pp. 351–54.

30. Richard K. Riehn, *1812: Napoleon's Russian Campaign* (New York: John Wiley, 1991), p. 425.

31. Riehn gives excellent statistics; ibid., p. 441.

32. See Chandler's excellent coverage of these preparations, *Campaigns of Napoleon,* pp. 754–56; for contrasting figures on French troop strengths see Riehn, *1812*; George Nafziger, *Napoleon's Invasion of Russia* (Novato, Calif: Presidio, 1988).

33. *Corr de Nap*, no. 18725.

34. Ibid., no. 18905.

35. Caulaincourt, *Mémoires*, vol. 1, pp. 379–80.

36. Ibid., pp. 381–82.

37. Ibid., pp. 383, 397–98, 406–7.

38. Ibid., pp. 397–98, 406–7.

39. Chandler, *Campaigns of Napoleon*, p. 782.

40. Caulaincourt, *Mémoires*, vol. 1, p. 396.

41. Gen. C. von Clausewitz, *The Campaign of 1812* (London: Bell, 1843), pp. 139, 142.

42. *Corr de Nap*, no. 19182.

43. Caulaincourt, *Mémoires*, vol. 2, p. 423.

44. Ibid., pp. 424–40.

45. Ibid., pp. 424–41.

46. Riehn, *1812*, gives lower estimates, p. 255; Chandler, *Campaigns of Napoleon*, suggests higher losses.

47. For all the following and preceding medical citations, see Surgeon Turiot's letter, quoted in Soubiran, *Napoléon et un million de morts*, pp. 258–64.

34 MALET'S MALAISE

1. Savary, *Mémoires*, vol. 6, p. 2.

2. Ibid., pp. 2 ff.

3. Ibid., pp. 4–5.

4. Ibid., pp. 6–7.

5. Ibid., pp. 7–8.

6. Ibid., p. 8.

7. Ibid., pp. 8 ff.

8. Réal, *Indiscrétions*, vol. 1, p. 211.

9. Pierre-Marie Desmarest, *Témoignages historiques ou Quinze ans de haute police sous le Consulat et l'Empire* (Paris: Levasseur, 1833), pp. 293 ff. Desmarest was officially involved in the Malet case over a period of several years.

10. *Bulletin de la Police*, item no. 255; Réal, *Indiscretions*, p. 224.
11. *Bulletin de la Police*, item no. 144.
12. Ibid.
13. Rigotard, *Police parisienne*, p. 130.
14. Savary, *Mémoires*, vol. 6, pp. 20 ff.
15. Ibid., pp. 23–24; Desmarest, *Témoignages*, pp. 297 ff.
16. Savary, *Mémoires*, vol. 6, pp. 25–26.
17. Ibid., pp. 27–28.
18. Ibid., pp. 29–30.
19. Ibid., pp. 30–36. Savary personally interrogated all persons involved in this attempted coup.
20. Rigotard, *Police parisienne*, pp. 270–71.
21. Savary, *Mémoires*, vol. 6, pp. 39–40.
22. Ibid.
23. Ibid., p. 42.

35 DEATH MARCH

1. Méneval, *Mémoires*, vol. 3, pp. 63–64.
2. Ibid., pp. 62–63.
3. Ibid., pp. 64–66.
4. Caulaincourt, *Mémoires*, vol. 2, pp. 4–6.
5. Méneval, *Mémoires*, vol. 3, pp. 64–66.
6. Caulaincourt, *Mémoires*, vol. 2, pp. 11–14.
7. Ibid., pp. 15–21.
8. Riehn, *1812*, p. 287.
9. Caulaincourt, *Mémoires*, vol. 2, pp. 22–26.
10. Ibid., pp. 26–29.
11. *Corr de Nap*, no. 19213; Méneval, *Mémoires*, vol. 3, p. 118.
12. Quoted in Schilder, *L'Empéreur Alexandre Ie*, pp. 3, 34 ff.
13. Caulaincourt, *Mémoires*, vol. 2, pp. 34 ff.
14. Ibid., p. 36.
15. Ibid., pp. 40, 41, 46, 47–52.
16. Ibid., pp. 5–83.
17. Marbot, *Mémoires*, vol. 2, p. 150.
18. M. Anderson, *The Retreat of the French* (London: 1813), p. 15.
19. Caulaincourt, *Mémoires*, vol. 3, pp. 205–6.
20. Ibid., 340 ff.
21. Riehn, *1812*, pp. 287–399, 417, 441; Caulaincourt, *Mémoires*, vol. 2, pp. 205–347.
22. Quoted in Mowat, *The Diplomacy of Napoleon*, p. 269.

36 THE SAXON CAMPAIGN

1. Hortense, *Mémoires*, vol. 2, p. 151.
2. Ibid., pp. 151–52.
3. Ibid., vol. 3, p. 146.
4. Ibid., vol. 2, pp. 161–62.

5. Masson, *Napoleon et sa famille*, vol. 8, p. 91.

6. Ibid., p. 249. On November 12, 1813, Napoleon finally authorized the duc de Bassano to take this letter to King Fernando.

7. Ibid., p. 248.

8. *Corr de Nap*, no. 20237.

9. Mowat, *Diplomacy of Napoleon*, pp. 263–65: Lefebvre, *Napoleon*, vol. 2, p. 328; Tulard, *Napoléon*, p. 368.

10. Hortense, *Mémoires*, vol. 2, p. 164.

11. Masson, *Napoléon et sa famille*, vol. 8, pp. 261–62.

12. Ibid., *Napoléon et sa famille*, vol. 8, p. 264.

13. Ibid., pp. 266–67.

14. Ibid., pp. 273, 274.

15. Ibid., pp. 30–32.

16. Ibid., p. 32.

17. Ibid., p. 33.

18. Ibid., pp. 34 ff.

19. Méneval, *Mémoires*, vol. 2, p. 522.

20. Mowat, *Diplomacy of Napoléon*, p. 273; Rose, *Napoléon*, book 2, pp. 270 ff.

21. Ibid., pp. 274 ff.

22. Mowat, *Diplomacy of Napoleon*, p. 273.

23. Rose, *Napoleon*, book 2, pp. 277–278.

24. Chandler, *Campaigns of Napoleon*, p. 878.

25. Nafziger, *Napoleon's Invasion of Russia*, pp. 334–39.

26. Masson, *Napoléon et sa famille*, vol. 8, p. 165.

27. Riehn's statistics in his excellent study, *1812*, pp. 503–6.

28. Constant, *Mémoires*, vol. 6, p. 523.

29. Ibid., pp. 527–29.

30. Marmont, *Mémoires*, vol. 5, p. 140.

31. Mowat, *Diplomacy of Napoleon*, pp. 277–78. Emphasis added.

32. On 19 September the Treaty of Töplitz was signed, adding Austria as a full partner with Russia and Prussia.

33. Méneval, *Mémoires*, vol. 3, pp. 129, 137–42.

34. Mowat, *Diplomacy of Napoleon*, pp. 278–80.

37 LEIPZIG

1. Chandler, *Campaigns of Napoleon*, pp. 900 ff.

2. Ibid., p. 916.

3. *Cambridge Modern History* (Cambridge: Cambridge University Press, 1910), vol. 9, p. 533.

4. Agathon-Jean-François Fain, *Mémoires du baron Fain, premier secrétaire du cabinet de l'Empereur* (Paris: Plon, 1908), vol. 2, p. 404.

5. Marbot, *Mémoires*, vol. 2, p. 364.

6. Constant, *Mémoires*, vol. 4, p. 15.

7. Chandler, *Campaigns of Napolon*, p. 938.

8. Masson, *Napoléon et sa famille*, vol. 8, p. 167.

9. Ibid., vol. 8, pp. 166–96.
10. Ibid., p. 196.

38 "THE COSSACKS ARE COMING!"

1. Henriette-Lucie Dillon, Marquise de LaTour du Pin, *Journal d'une femme de cinquante ans, 1778–1815* (Paris: Chapelot, 1913), vol. 2, p. 341.
2. Chastenay, *Mémoires*, vol. 2, pp. 482, 483.
3. Méneval, *Mémoires*, vol. 3, pp. 170–71.
4. Madelin, *Consulat et l'Empire*, vol. 2, *1809–1915*, p. 247.
5. Chastenay, *Mémoires*, vol. 2, 486; Méneval, *Mémoires*, vol. 3, pp 182–84.
6. Chastenay, *Mémoires*, vol. 2, p. 487; Jean Baptiste Antoine Marcellin Marbot, *Mémoires du général baron de Marbot* (Paris: Plon, 1891), vol. 2, p. 424.
7. Chandler, *Campaigns of Napoleon*, pp. 948–49.
8. Gilbert Martineau, *Caroline Bonaparte* (Paris: France-Empire, 1991), p. 222.
9. Chandler, *Campaigns of Napoleon*, p. 952.
10. Hortense, *Mémoires*, vol. 2, pp. 174–75.
11. *Corr de Nap*, no. 21089.
12. Méneval, *Mémoires*, vol. 3, pp. 186–87.
13. Ibid., pp. 193–94.
14. Ibid., pp. 196–98.
15. Ibid., pp. 204–6. Emphasis in original.
16. Ibid., p. 209.
17. The new defense pact was signed at Chaumont by England, Austria, Russia, and Prussia on March 9, 1814, but backdated to March 1.
18. Ibid., p. 223.
19. Ibid., pp. 224–25.
20. Ibid., p. 208, and also Méneval's own comments in ibid., pp. 212, 220.
21. Ibid., p. 218.
22. Ibid., p. 234.
23. Ibid., pp. 228–43. (He was of course an eyewitness, attending the empress.)
24. Caulaincourt, *Mémoires*, vol. 3, pp. 83–89.
25. Ibid., pp. 94–98, 158–60.
26. Rose, *Napoleon*, book 2, p. 427.
27. Caulaincourt, *Mémoires*, vol. 3, pp. 161–63.
28. Ibid., pp. 166–78.
29. Ibid., pp. 179–84, 190.
30. Ibid., pp. 213–30.
31. Ibid., pp. 232.
32. Ibid., pp. 231–43.
33. Ibid., pp. 315, 326, 341.
34. Ibid., pp. 328–33; *Corr de Nap*, no. 21558.
35. Caulaincourt, *Mémoires*, vol. 3, pp. 342–56.
36. Ibid., pp. 359–365; Constant, *Mémoires*, vol. 4, pp. 632 ff.
37. J. Bourgeat, *Napoléon: Lettres à Joséphine* (Paris: Plon, 1941), pp. 216–17; Masson, *Napoléon et sa famille*, vol. 9, p. 439.

38. Caulaincourt, *Mémoires*, vol. 3, pp. 408–19; Bruce, *Napoleon & Josephine*, p. 478; André Soubiran attributes 1 million dead to the French army, and 2 million dead to the other European armies, excluding civilians—Soubiran, *Napoléon et un million de morts*, pp. 12–15; Rose, *Napoleon*, book 2, chap. 32.

39. Masson, *Napoléon et sa famille*, vol. 10, pp. 419–37.

40. For all the above on life on Elba, see Schom, *One Hundred Days*, chaps. 1 and 2, which also provide a complete bibliography.

41. Neil Campbell, *Chroniques des événements du 1814 et 1815* (Paris: Pichot, 1873), p. 78.

42. Charles Alleaume, "Les Cent Jours dans le Var," *Mémoires* (Draguignan: Société d'Etudes Scientifiques et Archéologiques/Oliver Joulian, 1938) vol. 49, p. 15. For greater detail of events on Elba and the return to France, see Schom, *One Hundred Days*, chaps. 1 and 2.

39 "PROJECTS OF TROUBLES AND UPSETTINGS"

1. For a detailed account of these events, see Schom, *One Hundred Days*, pp. 15 ff.; Henry Houssaye, *1815*, vol. 1, *La Première Restauration—Le Retour de l'Ile d'Elbe, Les Cent Jours* (Paris: Perrin, 1896), pp. 181 ff.; Charles Alleaume, "Les Cents Jours dans le Var," *Mémoires* (Draguignan: Société d'Etudes Scientifiques et Archéologiques/Oliver Joulian, 1938) vol. 49, p. 15; Fleury de Chaboulon, *Mémoires pour servir l'histoire* (Paris: Rauveure Cornet, 1901), vol. 1, p. 93; Napoléon, *L'île d'Elbe et les Cents Jours. Correspondance* 31, 24; Jean Orieux, *Talleyrand, ou le Sphinx Incompris* (Paris: Flammarion, 1970), pp. 617 ff.; Charles Florange, *Le vol de l'aigle (1815): Napoléon, La marche sur Paris* (Paris: Clavreuil, 1932), pp. 11–13; Henri Gracien Bertrand, *Lettres à Fanny, 1800–1815* (Paris: Albin Michel, 1979), p. 403; Comtesse de Boigne, *Mémoires de la Comtesse de Poigne* (Paris: Mercure de France, 1986), vol. 1, 307; Hubert Dhumez, "Cannes et les Cents-Jours," *Mélange inédits relatifs au passé du pays cannois. Collection: Documents, textes, inconnus pour servir à l'Histoir du pays de Cannes et de sa région* (Cannes: Aegitna, 1961), vol. 6, p. 117–27; *Archives Nationales*, fte III. Var 12 (liasse 1813); "La nuit de Malijay," published in *Illustration*, 21 Sept 1931; Paul Canestrier, "Rapport d'un envoyé secret de Napoléon, p. l. Report dated 2 June 1815, Antibes, by Officier d'ordonnan Rey, "Sur les bords du Var, pendant les Cents Jours."

2. Préfet Bouthillier to Interior Minister, le 3 mars 1815, *Archives Nationales*, Fte. vol. 3, Var. 12 (liasse 1813).

3. Masséna, *Mémoires*, pp. 4, 6.

4. *Moniteur*, March 9, 1815; Alleaume, *Cent Jours*, pp. 31–35; Houssaye, *1815: Cent Jours*, p. 242.

5. G. Bertier de Sauvigny, *La Restauration* (Paris: Flammarion, 1955) pp. 97–98; Florange, *Vol de l'Aigle*, pp. 90–91; Houssaye, *1815;* pp. 246–61.

6. Houssaye, *1815: Cent Jours*, p. 264.

7. Florange, *Vol de l'Aigle*, pp. 82–83.

8. Claude Manceron, *Napoléon Reprend Paris, 20 mars 1815* (Paris: Laffont, 1965), pp. 22, 103, 119, 120, 144–45.

9. Manceron, *Napoléon reprend Paris*, p. 25.

10. Ibid., p. 53; Bertier, *Restauration*, p. 9.

11. Manceron, *Napoléon reprend Paris*, pp. 147-48, 25, 53; Bertier, *Restauration*, p. 99.

12. Bertier, *Restauration*, p. 13.

13. Ibid., p. 13-15.

14. Ibid., p. 12.

15. Schom, *One Hundred Days*, pp. 40-41.

16. Ibid., pp. 41 ff.

17. Baron de Vitrolles, *Mémoires* (Paris: Gallimard 1884), vol. 2, *1810-1814*, pp. 232, 349 ff.; Houssaye, *1815: Cent Jours*, pp. 321-22; *Journal des Débats* 15 and 18 mars 1815.

18. Houssaye, *1815; Cent Jours*, pp. 138, 321-22, 340-43; the treasury paid out the full sum of four hundred thousand francs at 4:00 P.M. that same day; Vitrolles, *Mémoires*, vol. 2, pp. 291, 321-323; Auguste Frédéric Louis Viesse de Marmont, *Mémoires du duc de Raguse* (Paris: Perrotin, 1857), 9 vols.

19. Fleury de Chaboulon, *Mémoires*, vol. 1, pp. 210, 248; Manceron, *Napoléon reprend Paris*, p. 49; Houssaye, *1815: Cent Jours*, pp. 344, 326, 354 ff., 360 ff.; 413-33; Vitrolles, *Mémoires*, vol. 2, pp. 321 ff.; *Journal des Débats*, 18 and 19 mars 1815; Bertier, *Restauration*, 102-3; Beauharnais, *Mémoires de la Reine Hortense*, vol. 2, pp. 329-33.

20. Vitrolles, *Mémoires*, vol. 2, 354; Houssaye, *1815: Cent Jours*, p. 35.

21. Mowat, *Diplomacy of Napoleon*, p. 299; Talleyrand, *Mémoires*, vol. 2, pp. 561-65; Viscount Castlereagh, *Correspondence, Despatches, and Other Papers of Viscount Castlereagh* (London: Murray, 1853), vol. 10, pp. 239-40, 243; Watson, *The Reign of George III*, p. 565; Lacour-Gayet, *Talleyrand*, vol. 2, pp. 333, 432.

22. Lacour-Gayet, *Talleyrand*, vol. 2, pp. 333, 432; Orieux, *Talleyrand*, p. 618.

23. Mowat, *Diplomacy of Napoleon*, p. 299; Talleyrand, *Mémoires*, vol. 2, pp. 56-65.

24. Castlereagh, *Correspondence*, vol. 10, pp. 263-69, 276.

25. Mowat, *Diplomacy of Napoleon*, p. 3 and in Talleyrand's *Mémoires*, vol. 3, 111, 113.

26. Ibid.

27. Castlereagh, *Correspondence*, vol. 10, pp. 285-286, 297; 288.

28. Fleury de Chaboulon, *Mémoires*, vol. 1, p. 248.

29. Houssaye, *1815: Cent Jours*, pp. 440-42, 486 ff., 494.

30. Schom, *One Hundred Days*, pp. 55-56.

31. Ibid., p. 109; Lazare Nicolas Carnot, *Exposé de ma conduite politique*, p. 22. Napoleon had also offered the Foreign Ministry to Lavalette. Etienne-Denis Pasquier, *Histoire de mon temps: Mémoires du Chancelier Pasquier, duc d'Audiffret-Pasquier* (Paris: Plon, 1894), vol. 3, pp. 165-66, 177.

32. Houssaye, *1815: Cent Jours*, pp. 440-42, 483, 498-45; Constant, *Mémoires*, vol. 2, pp. 47 ff.; "Mémoires de Molé," *Revue de la Révolution* 11, p. 39; Benjamin Constant de Rebecque, *Journal Intime* (Paris: Ollendorff, 1895), p. 100; Las Cases, *Mémoriale de Sainte-Hélène*, vol. 2, 93-95; *Bulletin de Lois*, 24 mars 1815; Pasquier, *Mémoires*, vol. 3, p. 174.

33. Houssaye, *1815: Cent Jours*, p. 540; Constant, *Mémoires*, vol. 2, 122; Françoise Wagener, *Madame Récamier, 1777-1849* (Paris: Lattès, 1986), p. 270.

34. Houssaye, *1815: Cent Jours*, pp. 542-43, 547.

35. Ibid., p. 545; Schom, *One Hundred Days*, pp. 132–33; Pasquier, *Mémoires*, vol. 3, p. 170.

36. Houssaye, *1815: Cent Jours*, pp. 550, 545; Pasquier, *Mémoires*, vol. 3, p. 218; A. N. de Salvandy, *Observation critique sur le champs de mai*.

37. Schom, *One Hundred Days*, p. 134; Houssaye, *1815: Cent Jours*, p. 554.

38. Pasquier, *Mémoires*, vol. 3, pp. 177–79.

39. Houssaye, *1815: Cent Jours*, 496, pp. 500–512; Constant, *Mémoires*, vol. 2, p. 90 (all mayors of communes, towns with populations of more than five thousand).

40. Schom, *One Hundred Days*, pp. 145–49.

41. For details on the civil war, see ibid., pp. 149–54, 201. Of 284,090 men, only 178,929 were available for the Army of the North and northern frontier garrison duty.

42. Davout, *La Correspondance du Maréchal Davout, Prince d'Eckmühl: Ses commandements, son Ministère, 1801–1815* (Paris: Plon, 1885), vol. 4, pp. 352 ff.; Comte Vigier, *Davout, maréchal d'Empire, Duc d'Auerstaedt, Prince d'Eckmühl, 1770–1823* (Paris: Ollendorff, 1898), vol. 1, p. 7; For the long, complex correspondence between Davout and Bonaparte at the time of mobilization, see Schom, *One Hundred Days*, pp. 137 ff., 161 ff., 361–68; Louis Chardigny, *Les maréchaux de Napoléon* (Paris: Tallandier, 1977), p. 193; Marcel Reinhard, *Le Grand Carnot* (Paris: Hachette, 1952), vol. 2, pp. 132, 269–71, and Lazare Carnot's *Révolution et Mathématiques* (Paris: L'Herne, 1984).

43. On budgets and fund-raising, see Schom, *One Hundred Days*, pp. 178–80.

44. *Corr de Nap*, nos. 21803, 21836; Schom, *Trafalgar*, p. 83; Houssaye, *1815: Cent Jours*, pp. 630–31.

45. Davout, *Correspondance*, vol. 4, p. 441; *Corr de Nap*, nos. 21885, 21874, 21886.

46. On mobilization efforts, Schom, *One Hundred Days*, pp. 192 et seq.; Henry Houssaye, *1815: Waterloo* (Paris: Bartillat, 1987), pp. 12, 36–37; entire correspondence of Napoleon with Davout throughout April–June, *Corr de Nap*, nos. 21779, 21819–22042; Madelin, *Fouché*, vol. 2, p. 277; Pasquier, *Histoire de mon temps, Mémoires*, vol. 3, p. 110; Soult was ordered to prepare the marching plans for the Armée du Nord on June 3, 1815. *Corr de Nap*, no. 22005. See also Davout, *Correspondance*, vol. 4, pp. 441–43.

47. Louis Marchand, *Mémoires de Marchand* (Paris: Plon, 1952), vol. 1, pp. 149–50. Napoleon moved into the Elysée Palace on May 21, 1815.

48. Ibid., p. 145; Zieseniss, *Berthier*, p. 212; Houssaye, *1815: Cent Jours*, pp. 595, 598, 599; Fleury de Chaboulon, *Mémoires*, vol. 2, pp. 66–81; *Corr de Nap*, no. 21997; Fleury de Chaboulon, *Mémoires*, vol. 2, pp. 66–81. A note on voting: In villages frequently the entire population queued up before a large leather register, and made their mark before soldiers, officials, and so on. There was no secrecy, and much intimidation. Napoleon gave the mayors powers that they have abused till this day. See John Cam Hobhouse's reflections, *Lettres écrites de Paris pendant le dernier règne de l'Empereur Napoleon* (Gand: Houdin, 1817), vol. 2, pp. 389–92; *Corr de Nap*, nos. 22038, 22044, 22045.

49. On voting see Schom, *One Hundred Days*, pp. 208–9.

50. *Corr de Nap*, no. 21997.

51. *Moniteur*, 2 juin 1815; John Cam Hobhouse, *Lettres*, vol. 2, pp. 329–92.

52. *Corr de Nap*, no. 22039.

53. Schom, *One Hundred Days*, p. 220.

40 "TO CONQUER OR PERISH"

1. Schom, *One Hundred Days*, p. 236.

2. Scott Bowden, *Armies at Waterloo* (Arlington, Tex.: Empire Games Press, 1983), gives a figure of 112,652 men and 358 guns (p. 42); Houssaye, *Waterloo*; lists approximately 124,000 men and 370 guns (pp. 101–4); while Chandler, *Campaigns of Napoleon*, gives a figure of 122,721 troops, including 89,000 infantry, 22,100 cavalry, and 366 guns (pp. 1, 117). According to Gen. Bruno Chaix, the Ecole Royale Belge (military academy) gives Napoleon 126,088 men and 344 cannon; Wellington, 93,643 men and 186 cannon; the Prussians, 117,697 men and 312 cannon. Letter to author, June 2, 1991. For a detailed breakdown of French, English, and Prussian armies later at Waterloo, see Schom, *One Hundred Days*, appendix 3.

3. Von Ziethen's report prepared at Gilly at 1:30 P.M., Houssaye, *1815: Waterloo*, pp. 111–12.

4. Jacques Jourquin, "Dictionnaire analytique, statistique et comparé des vingt-six maréchaux du premier empire," *Revue de l'Institution Napoléon* 146 (Paris: Tallandier, 1986), p. 161; Jourquin has here produced a most valuable little book for the historian. See also *Corr de Nap*, no. 22056; Houssaye, *1815: Waterloo*, p. 120.

5. Schom, *One Hundred Days*, p. 247 and appendix 1; Jac Weller, *Wellington at Waterloo* (London: Longmans, 1967), pp. 31, 242–43, 237 ff.

6. Charles Oman, *A History of the Peninsular War* (Oxford: Oxford University Press, 1902–30), vol. 5, p. 473; Elizabeth Longford, *Wellington*, vol. 1, *The Years of the Sword* (London: Weidenfeld & Nicolson, 1969), pp. 282, 330; *The Supplementary Despatches, Correspondence, and Memoranda of Field Marshal Arthur, Duke of Wellington*, KG (London: John Murray, 1858–64), vol. 10, p. 216; *The Dispatches of Field Marshal the Duke of Wellington, during his various Campaigns* (London: John Murray, 1834–38), 12 vols.

7. Schom, *One Hundred Days*, p. 254.

8. Chandler, *Campaigns of Napoleon*, pp. 1031–32.

9. Ibid., pp. 1032, 1033; Baron von Müffling, *Passages from My Life* (London: John Murray, 1853), p. 230; Wellington, *Dispatches*, vol. 12, pp. 472 ff.

10. General H. Camon, *La Guerre Napoléonienne, Les Batailles* (Paris: Chapelot, 1910), pp. 17 ff.; Chandler, *Campaigns of Napoleon*, pp. 162 ff.

11. *Corr de Nap*, nos. 22058, 22059.

12. Sir Herbert Maxwell, *The Life of Wellington* (London: S. Low Marston & Co, 1899), vol. 2, pp., 19–20; Chandler, *Campaigns of Napoleon*, p. 1040; for a different version, Carl von Clausewitz, *Campagne de 1815 en France* (Paris: Chapel, 1900), pp. 71, 75–79; Clausewitz quotes the four orders issued by Soult/Napoleon to Ney on 16 June 1815, pp. 77–79; Camon, *Batailles*, p. 454.

13. 13. Clausewitz, *Campagne*, pp. 49–50, 91; Camon, *Batailles*, p. 459.

14. Schom, *One Hundred Days*, pp. 252–66.

15. Fleury de Chaboulon, *Mémoires de Fleury de Chaboulon* (Paris: Rouveyre, 1901), vol. 2, p. 120; *Corr de Nap*, no. 22058.

16. Bowden, *Armies at Waterloo*, pp. 106, 124.

17. Ibid., p. 258; Clausewitz, *Campagne*, p. 57; Camon, *Batailles*, pp. 472, 475; d'Erlon first received Ney's order to advance to Quatre-Bras at 12:15 P.M., June 16. Houssaye, *1815: Waterloo*, pp. 200–201.

18. Augustus Frazer, *Letters of Colonel Sir Augustus Frazer* (London: John Murray, 1859), p. 98; Weller, *Wellington at Waterloo*, pp. 61–64.

19. Camon, *Batailles*, p. 474; Weller, *Wellington at Waterloo*, pp. 61–64.

20. Chandler, *Campaigns of Napoleon*, p. 1053; Camon, *Batailles*, p. 474 and n. 2; Fleury de Chaboulon, *Mémoires*, vol. 2, p. 134. Fleury and Baron Fain served as Napoleon's personal secretaries at this time. Fleury was at Napoleon's side throughout the campaign.

21. Chandler, *Campaigns of Napoleon*, pp. 1057–58; Camon, *Batailles*, p. 484.

22. Camon, *Batailles*, p. 477; Emmanuel de Grouchy, *Mémoires du Maréchal de Grouchy* (Paris: Dentu, 1874), vol. 5, pp. 35 ff.

23. Camon, *Batailles*, p. 483.

24. Peter Hayman, *Soult, Napoleon's Maligned Marshal* (London: Arms and Armour, 1990); Nicole Gotteri, *Soult, Maréchal d'Empire et homme d'Etat* (Besançon: La manufacture, 1991), pp. 476–77; Camon, *Batailles*, pp. 484, 486; Chandler, *Campaigns of Napoleon*, p. 1061.

25. French artillery: the 12-pounder gun, model 1802–3, weighed 1,950 pounds and its limber 1,490 pounds. The French 6-pounder weighed 880 pounds, its limber 1,130, while the 6.54-inch howitzer (Gribeauval) weighed 700 pounds, its limber 1,565. The British nine-pounder weighed 1,510 pounds and its limber 1,760 pounds; the British 6-pounder weighed 576 pounds, its limber 1,065 pounds, and the British 5.5-inch howitzer, 448 pounds, its limber, 1,125 pounds. It took twelve horses to pull a French 12-pounder, ten to pull the 6.54-inch howitzer and the 8-pounder, and eight horses to haul the six- and four-pounders. The British on the other hand, used only six horses per team for their largest artillery piece there, the 9-pounder. Weller, *Wellington at Waterloo*, p. 177.

26. Bowden, *Armies at Waterloo*, p. 131; after deducting 18,421 casualties from 122,652, giving Grouchy 29,731. Napoleon gives a figure of 34,000 men. *Corr de Nap*, vol. 31, p. 179; Camon, *Batailles*, p. 203.

27. Schom, *One Hundred Days*, p. 278.

28. Bowden, *Armies at Waterloo*, p. 271; Bowden gives adjusted figure of 74,326. Chandler, *Campaigns of Napoleon*, gives Wellington a force of only 67,661, including a cavalry of 12,408 and 156 guns. (Napoleon incorrectly claimed that Wellington had 90,000 men and 255 guns. *Corr de Nap*, vol. 31, p. 156. Weller, *Wellington at Waterloo*, p. 177; Bowden, *Armies at Waterloo*, pp. 199, 201, 261–68, 327. The Prussian force (including officers), originally 130,246, 15,857 cavalry, 7,125 artillery, 103,345 infantry. Bowden, *Armies at Waterloo*, pp. 199, 201. On June 18, reduced to 99,374 (ibid., p. 327).

29. *Corr de Nap*, no. 1832; Chandler, *Campaigns of Napoleon*, p. 593; Camon, *Batailles*, p. 492.

30. Camon, *Batailles*, pp. 494, 497; Chandler, *Campaigns*, pp. 1072–73.

31. Chandler, *Campaigns*, p. 1076; Clausewitz, *Campagne*, pp. 149–151, 157, 166; Camon, *Batailles*, p. 500. In fact the 1:30 letter did not reach Grouchy until 7:00 P.M., according to Clausewitz.

32. Edward Cotton, *A Voice from Waterloo: A History of the Battle Fought on the 18th of June, 1815* (Brussels: Hôtel du Musée, 1913), p. 126.

33. Bowden, *Armies at Waterloo*, p. 252, 268–71; Fleury de Chaboulon, *Mémoires*, vol. 2, pp. 140–41; for all statistics on Lord Uxbridge's Cavalry Corps, see Bowden, *Armies at Waterloo*, pp. 268–71. Chandler, *Campaigns of Napoleon*, pp. 1078–79; Camon, *Batailles*, pp. 218. (Lieutenant General, the Earl of Uxbridge, Maj. Gen. Lord Edward Somerset (1776–1842) had commanded the Fourth Light Dragoons during the Peninsular War. Maj. Gen. Sir William Pensonby, killed at Waterloo.)

34. Chandler, *Campaigns of Napoleon*, pp. 1070–81; Cotton, *Voice from Waterloo*, p. 116.

35. Rees Howell Gronow, *Captain Gronow, His Reminiscences of Regency and Victorian Life, 1810–60* (London: Kyle Cathie, 1991), p. 137.

36. Houssaye, *Waterloo*, pp. 389 ff.

37. Bowden, *Armies at Waterloo* pp. 83, 124; Chandler, *Campaigns of Napoleon*, p. 1084; Camon, *Batailles*, pp. 501–10; Fleury de Chaboulon, *Mémoires*, vol. 2, 145, 148; Cotton, *Voice from Waterloo*, pp. 117, 311.

38. Ney to Fouché, June 26, 1815.

39. Chandler, *Campaigns*, p. 1086.

40. The Prussians used the term *brigade* instead of the rough British or French equivalent, "division." The average Prussian brigade was almost six thousand men. Bowden, *Armies at Waterloo*, p. 197.

41. Napoleon to Jourdan, 28 July 1809.

42. Fleury de Chaboulon, *Mémoires*, vol. 2, 141; Clausewitz, *Campagne*, p. 167.

43. Camon, *Batailles*, pp. 513–14.

44. Chandler, *Campaigns of Napoleon*, pp. 1087, 1088.

45. Ney to Fouché, 26 June 1815: Fleury de Chaboulon, *Mémoires*, vol. 2, 150; "Official French Report," "Bataille de Mont Saint-Jean."

46. Wellington, *Dispatches*, vol. 12, p. 242.

47. Houssaye, *Waterloo*, pp. 428–31, 432–40; Wellington, *Dispatches*, vol. 2, p. 510; Clausewitz, *Campagne*, pp. 189, 191, 193; Wellington, *Dispatches*, vol. 12, p. 242; vol. 20, p. 529; vol. 12, pp. 510, 499–500; Fleury de Chaboulon, *Mémoires*, vol. 2, pp. 155, 156; Girod de l'Ain, *Joseph Bonaparte*, pp. 317 ff.; Clausewitz, pp. 202, 215, gives Blücher 60,000 men and Wellington 50,000; see Chandler, *Campaigns of Napoleon*, p. 1094.

48. Bowden, *Armies at Waterloo*, pp. 324–27. Total Coalition dead, wounded, deserters, prisoners at Waterloo, 24,143: 6,998 Prussians, and 17,145 Allies (Dutch, Belgian, British, Germans). Separate British losses at Waterloo were 8,458. France lost 64,602 men as casualties, including 43,656 at Waterloo and during the retreat (including POWs, and so on). The Allies suffered total casualties of 62,818, including Prussian figures of 40,237, and the other Allies, 22,581. Of the British losses of 8,458, some 460 included officers, thereby giving the British the highest percentage of battle casualties among the Allies—approximately 30 percent. The French of course had about 51 percent casualties, *Armies at Waterloo*, pp. 324–27. Thus, according to him, the entire campaign in Belgium resulted in 127,420 casualties.

49. Houssaye, *1815*, vol. 3, *La Seconde Abdication—La Terreur Blanche* (Paris: Perrin, 1914), p. 215: Hortense, *Mémoires*, vol. 3, p. 27.

50. Duc de Castries, *La Fayette* (Paris: Tallandier, 1981), p. 366.

51. Fleury de Chaboulon, *Mémoires*, vol. 2, pp. 174–75, 178; Castries, *La Fayette*, p. 361.

52. *Journal des Débats*, 23 juin 1815; Fleury de Chaboulon, *Mémoires*, vol. 2, p. 182.

53. Louis Marchand, *Mémoires de Marchand, Premier Valet de Chambre et Testamentair de l'Empereur*, vol. 1, *L'Ile d'Elbe — Les Cent Jours* (Paris: Plon, 1952), pp. 182–83.

54. Fleury de Chaboulon, *Mémoires*, vol. 1, pp. 222–23.

55. Wellington, *Supplementary Despatches*, vol. 2, p. 47.

56. Fleury de Chaboulon, *Mémoires*, vol. 2, pp. 238–48.

57. Ibid., vol. 2, pp. 253–57, 261, 270–72, 275–76, 287–88, 289, Houssaye, *1815: La Seconde Abdication*, pp. 168 pp.; Fleury de Chaboulon, *Mémoires*, vol. 2, pp. 261, 270–72, 275–76, 287–88, 289; Fouché, *Mémoires*, vol. 2, p. 503; Clausewitz, *Campagne*, pp. 201–2, 215, 220.

58. Fleury de Chaboulon, *Mémoires*, vol. 2, pp. 214–16; Hortense, *Mémoires*, vol. 3, p. 31.

59. Marchand, *Mémoires*, vol. 1, p. 203; Fleury de Chaboulon, *Mémoires*, vol. 2, pp. 231–34.

60. Marchand, *Mémoires*, vol. 1, pp. 203–4, 205.

61. Schom, *One Hundred Days*, p. 310; Schom, *Trafalgar*, p. 346; Marchand, *Mémoires*, vol. 1, pp. 205–6.

62. Houssaye, *1815: La Second Abdication*, pp. 426 ff.

63. Fleury de Chaboulon, *Mémoires*, vol. 2, pp. 327–29; Houssaye, *1815: La Second Abdication*, pp. 427–33.

64. *Journal des Débats*, jeudi, le 7 décembre 1815, pp. 1–4; for the trial. The entire proceedings were immediately published in two cahiers; Record of his execution taken from *Journal des Débats*, 8 décembre 1815, Houssaye, *1815: La Seconde Abdication*, pp. 583–585.

41 FINAL CASUALTIES

1. Rose, *Napoleon*, book 2, p. 556.

2. Tulard, *Napoléon*, p. 446.

3. Rose, *Napoleon*, book 2, p. 555.

4. This passage was carefully suppressed by Las Cases when he eventually published his *Mémorial de Sainte-Hélène*, vol. 2, p. 533.

5. Ibid., p. 566.

6. Ibid., p. 552.

7. Ibid., p. 550.

8. Rose, *Napoleon*, book 2, p. 551; Barry Edward O'Meara, *Napoleon in Exile: A Voice from St. Helena*, 2 vols. (London: Simpkin and Marshall, 1822).

9. Gaspard Gourgaud, *Napoléon et la Grande Armée en Russie* (Paris, 1825), p. 201.

10. Frédéric Masson, *Napoléon à Sainte-Hélène, 1815–1821* (Paris: Albin Michel, 1929), pp. 128–38.

11. Ibid., pp. 88 ff.

12. Ibid., pp. 141 ff.

13. Ibid., pp. 102 ff.

14. Gaspard Gourgaud, *Sainte-Hélène, Journal inédit de 1815 à 1818* (Paris: Flammarion, 1899), vol. 1, pp. 262–70, 316.

15. Rose, *Napoleon*, book 2, p. 558; Gourgaud, *Journal*, vol. 1, pp. 77, 94, 136, 491.

16. Rose, *Napoleon*, book 2, pp. 559–60.

17. Las Cases, *Mémorial de Sainte-Hélène*, vol. 1, p. 806; Rose, *Napoleon*, book 2, p. 565.

18. Henri Bertrand, *Cahiers de Sainte-Hélène* (Paris: Sulliver-Albin Michel, 1959), III, 165.

19. Masson, *Napoléon à Sainte-Hélène*, p. 480.

20. Bertrand, *Cahiers de Sainte-Hélène*, vol. 3, p. 19. For full details on the poisoning of Napoleon, including the scientific documentation, see Ben Weider and Sten Forshufvud, *Assassination at St. Helena Revisited* (New York: John Wiley, 1995), pp. 475 ff.

BIBLIOGRAPHY

BOOKS

Abd al-Rahman al-Jabarti. *Journal d'Abdurrhahman Gabarti, Pendant l'occupation française en Egypte.* Paris, 1838.

Abrantès, Laure Junot, Duchesse d'. *Memoirs of the Emperor Napoleon from Ajaccio to Waterloo.* Akron, Ohio: St. Dunstan Society, 1901.

Agoult, Marie de Flavigny d'. *Mes souvenirs, 1806–1833.* Paris: Calmann-Lévy, 1877.

Alfieri, Vittorio. *Vie de Victor Alfieri.* 2 vols. Paris: Nicolle, 1809.

Alleaume, Charles. "Les Cents Jours dans le Var." In *Mémoires.* Vol. 49. Draguignan: Société d'Etudes Scientifiques et Archéologiques de Draguignan/Oliver Joulian, 1938.

Ampère, André-Marie. *Journal et correspondance d'André-Marie Ampère de 1805 à 1864.* 2 vols. Paris: Hetzel, 1875.

Anchel, Robert. *Les Juifs de France.* Paris: Janin, 1946.

———. *Napoléon et les Juifs.* Paris: Alcan, 1928.

Antommarchi, François. *Mémoires ou des derniers moments de Napoléon.* 2 vols. Paris: Barrois, 1825.

Aretz, K. *Betsy Balcombe, Napoleons Letzte Freundin.* Munich, 1919.

Arnault, Antoine Vincent. *Souvenirs d'un sexagénaire.* 4 vols. Paris: Dufey, 1833.

———. *Une Vie Politique et militaire de Napoléon.* Paris: Dufey, 1822.

Arnold, Erick Anderson. *Fouché, Napoleon, and the General Police.* Washington, D.C.: University Press of America, 1979.

Aubert, Jacques d'. *Mémoires sur les Evénements qui se rapportent à la réoccupation de Hambourg par les Français à l'époque du 30 mai 1813.* Paris: Marchands de Nouveautés, 1825.

Aubry, Joseph. *Souvenirs du 12e chasseurs, 1799–1815.* Paris: Quantin, 1889.

Aubry, Octave. *Le Roi de Rome.* Paris: Fayard, 1932,

Aubry, Paul V. *Monge Le Savant Ami de Napoléon Bonaparte. 1746–1818.* Paris: Gauthier-Villars, 1954.

Audiffret-Pasquier, Etienne Denis, Duc d'. *L'Histoire de mon temps: Mémoires du Chancelier Pasquier, duc d'Audiffret-Pasquier.* Vols. 1–3. Paris: Plon, 1894.

Aulard, François Alphonse. *Histoire politique de la révolution Française, 1789–1804.* Paris: Colin, 1903.

————. *Etudes et leçons de la Révolution françaises*. 9 vols. Paris: Felix Alcan, 1893–94.

————. *L'Etablissement du Consulat à vie*. Paris, 1895.

————. *Paris sous le Consulat*. Paris: Cerf, 1903–09.

————. *Paris pendant la réaction thermidorienne et sous le Directoire*. Paris: Cerf, 1898–1902.

————. *Recueil des Séances du Comité du Salut public, avec la correspondance officielle des représentants en mission* .... Paris: Imprimerie Nationale, 1899–1951.

Autichamp, Charles d'. *Mémoires pour servir à l'histoire de la campagne de 1815 dans la Vendée*. Paris: Egron, 1817.

Avrillion, Marie-Jeanne. *Mémoires sur la vie privée de Joséphine, sa famille, sa cour*. 2 vols. Paris: Ladvocat, 1833.

Ayling, Stanley. *George the Third*. London: Collins, 1972.

Azanza, Miguel-Joseph de. *Mémoires de M Miguel-Joseph de Azanza et D. Gonzalo O. Farrill et exposé des faits quit justifient leur conduite politique depuis mars 1808 jusqu'en avril 1814*. Paris, 1815.

Bac, Ferdinand. *Le Secret de Talleyrand*. Paris: Hachette, 1933.

Bainville, Jacques. *Napoléon*. Paris: Fayard, 1931.

Barère de Vieuzac, Bertrand. *Mémoires de Bertrand Barère*. 4 vols. Paris: Labitte, 1842–1844.

Barral, Georges. *L'épopée de Waterloo*. Paris: Flammarion, n.d.

Barras, Paul Jean François Nicolas de. *Mémoires de Barras, membre du Directoire*. 4 vols. Paris: Hachette, 1895–1896.

Barrès, Jean Baptiste. *Souvenirs d'un officier de la Grande Armée*. Paris: Plon, 1923.

Bartel, Paul. *Napoléon à l'île d'Elbe*. Paris: Parrin, 1950.

Barthélemy, Hyacinthe-Claude-Félix de. *Souvenirs d'un ancien préfet 1787–1848*. Paris: Dentu, 1885.

Bartlett, C. J. *Castlereagh*. London: Goldsmith College, 1967.

Barlette, Ruhl J. *The Record of American Diplomacy*. New York: Knopf, 1964.

Barton, Dunbar Plunket. *Bernadotte*. Paris: Payot, 1983.

Bassanville, Anaïs Lebrun. *Les salons d'autrefois. Souvenirs intimes par Madame la Comtesse de Bassanville*. 4 vols. Paris: Brunet, 1868.

Beatty, Dr. William. *The Authentic Narrative of the Death of Lord Nelson*. London: T. Cadell, 1807.

Beauchamp, Alphonse de. *Collection de mémoires relatifs aux révolutions d'Espagne*. 2 vols. Paris: Michaud, 1824.

Beauharnais, Eugène de. *Mémoires et Correspondance politique et militaire du prince Eugène, 1781–1814*. 10 vols. Paris: Lévy, 1858–60.

Beauharnais, Hortense de. *Mémoires de la Reine Hortense*. 3 vols. Paris: Plon, 1927.

Beker-Martha. *Le Général Beker*. Paris: Didier, 1876

Belliard, Augustin-Daniel. *Mémoires du comte Belliard*. 3 vols. Paris: Berquet et Petion, 1842.

Bellot de Kergorre, Alexandre. *Un commissaire des guerres pendant le premier Empire: Journal de Bellot de Kergorre*. Paris: Emile-Paul, 1899.

Belliard, Augustin Daniel. *Histoire scientifique et militaire de l'expédition française en Egypte*. 10 vols. Paris, 1830–36.

Bergerot, Bernard. *Le Maréchal Suchet*. Paris: Tallandier, 1986.

Bernoyer, M. *Avec Bonaparte en Egypte et en Syrie, 19 lettres inédites*. Paris: Payot, 1976.

Berthaut, Jules. *Manuel du Chef: Maximes Napoléoniennes*. Paris: Payot, 1919.

Berthezène, Pierre. *Souvenirs militaires de la République et de l'empire*. 2 vols. Paris: Dumaine, 1855.

Bertrand, Henri Gratien. *Cahiers de Sainte-Hélène*. Paris: Sulliver-Albin Michel, 1959.

———. *Lettres à Fanny, 1800–1815*. 3 vols. Paris: Albin Michel, 1979.

Beugnot, Jacques. *Mémoires du comte Beugnot, ancien ministre, 1783–1815*. 2 vols. Paris: Dentu, 1866.

Bignon, Louis. *Souvenirs d'un diplomate, la Pologne, 1811–1813*. Paris: Dentu, 1864.

Bigarré, Auguste. *Mémoires du Général Bigarré, aide de camp du roi Joseph*. Paris: Kolb, 1893.

Bigot, Robert. *Les banques françaises au cours du XIXe siècle*. Paris: Sirey, 1947.

———. *La Caisse d'escompte et les débuts de la Banque de France*. Paris: Presses Universitaires de France, 1927.

Bingham, D. A. *A Selection from the Letters and Despatches of Napoleon*. London, 1884.

Biver, Marie Louise. *Le Paris de Napoleon*. Paris: Plon, 1963.

Blémus, René. *Eugène de Beauharnais, 1781–1824: L'Honneur à tout vent*. Paris: Editions France-Empire, 1949.

Bloqueville, Marquise de. *Le maréchal Davout, prince d'Eckmühl*. 4 vols. Paris: Didier, 1879, 1880.

Blumenkranz, Bernhard, and Albert Soboul. *Le Grand Sanhedrin de Napoléon*. Toulouse: Privat, 1879.

Boigne, Eléonore-Adèle d'Osmond, de. *Récits d'une tante. Mémoires de la comtesse de Boigne*. 4 vols. Paris: Plon, 1907–8.

Bois, Maurice, *Napoléon Bonaparte, lieutenant d'artillerie à Auxonne*. Paris: Flammarion, 1898.

Bonaparte, Jérôme, *Mémoires et correspondance du roi Jérôme et de la reine Catherine*. 7 vols. Paris: Dentu, 1861–1866.

Bonaparte, Joseph. *Mémoires et correspondance politique et militaire du roi Joseph*. 10 vols. Paris: Perrotin, 1853–5.

Bonaparte, Louis. *Documents historiques et réflexions sur le gouvernement de la Hollande*. 3 vols. Paris: Aillaud, 1820.

Bonaparte, Lucien. *Mémoires secrètes sur la vie privée, publique et littéraire*. 2 vols. Paris: Delaunay, 1816.

Bonaparte, Napoléon. *The Confidential Correspondence of Napoleon Bonaparte with His Brother Joseph*. New York: Appleton, 1856.

———. *Correspondence de Napoléon Ier*. 32 vols. Paris: Plon/Imprimerie Impériale, 1858–70.

———. *Correspondance de Napoléon avec le Ministre de la Marine, depuis 1804 jusqu'en avril 1815*. 2 vols. Paris: Delloye & Lecou, 1837.

———. *Manuscrits inédits*. Edited by Frédéric Masson and Guido Biagi. Paris: Albin Michel, 1907.

———. *Mémoires pour servir à l'histoire de Napoléon, Campagnes d'Egypte et de Syrie, 1798–1799*. Edited by Gen. Henri Bertrand. 2 vols. Paris: Comon, 1847.

———. *Mémoires pour servir à l'histoire de France en 1815*. Paris: Barrois, 1820.

———. *Mémoires pour servir a l'histoire de Napoléon*. 8 vols. (dictated to Gen. Gourgaud). Paris, 1823–25.

Boucher de Perthes, Jacques. *Sous dix rois, Souvenirs de 1791 à 1860*. 8 vols. Paris: Jung-Trentel, 1863–68.

Boudard, Rene. *Gênes et la France, 1748–1797*. Paris: Mouton, 1962.

———. *La "Nation Corse" et sa lutte pour la liberte, 1744–1769*. Marseilles: Laffitte, 1979.

Boulay de la Meurthe, Alfred. *Histoire de la négociation du Concordat de 1801*. Tours: Mame et fils, 1926.

———. *Le Directoire et l'expédition d'Egypte*. Paris: Hachette, 1885.

Boulay de la Meurthe, Antoine Jacques Claude. *Boulay de la Meurthe*. Paris: Champion, 1868.

Bourgeat, J. *Napoléon: Lettres à Joséphine*. Paris: Guy le Prat, 1941.

Bourgin, G., and J. Godechot. *L'Italie et Napoléon, 1796–1814*. Paris: Sirey, 1935.

Bourrienne, Louis Antoine Fauvelet de. *Mémoires de M de Bourrianne sur Napoleon*. 5 vols. Paris: Garnier, 1899–1900.

Bowden, Scott. *Armies at Waterloo. A Detailed Analysis of the Armies that Fought History's Greatest Battle*. Arlington, Tex.: Empire Games Press, 1983.

Bredin, Jean Denis. *Sieyès, La clé de la Révolution*. Paris: Fallois, 1988.

Brett-James, Antony. *Wellington at War, 1794–1815. A Selection of*.

———. *The Hundred Days: Napoleon's Last Campaign from Eye-Witness Accounts*. London: Macmillan, 1964.

Brice and Bottet, Médecin-capitaines. *Le Corps de Santé Militaire en France*. Paris: Berger-Levrault, 1907.

Bro, Louis. *Mémoires du général Bro, 1796–1844*. Paris, 1914.

Broglie, Achille Charles Léonce, de. *Souvenirs du duc de Broglie: 1785–1870*. 4 vols. Paris: Calmann-Levy, 1886.

Brotonne, Léonce de. *Les Bonapartes et leurs alliances*. Paris: Charavay, 1893.

———. *Les sénateurs du consulat et de l'empire*. Genève: Slatkine-Megariotis, 1974.

Brown, William Garrott. *The Life of Oliver Ellsworth*. New York: Macmillan, 1905.

Bruce, Evangeline. *Napoleon & Josephine: An Improbable Marriage*. New York: Scribner, 1995.

Bruce, H. A. *Life of General Sir William Napier*. London: Murray, 1864.

Cambacérès, Jean-Jacques. *Cambacérès, Lettres inédites à Napoléon, 1802–1814*. Edited by Jean Tulard. Paris: Klincksieck, 1973.

Cambridge Modern History. Vol. 9. London: Cambridge University Press, 1910.

Camon, Hubert. *La Guerre Napoléonienne: Batailles*. Paris: Chapelot, 1910.

———. *La Guerre Napoléonienne: Les systèmes d'opérations*. Paris: Chapelot, 1907.

———. *La Guerre Napoléonienne—Précis des campagnes*. Paris: Chapelot, 1925.

Campbell, Neil. *Napoleon at Fontainebleau and Elba*. London: Murray, 1869.

Canuel, Simon. *Mémoires sur la guerre de Vendée en 1815*. Paris: Dentu, 1817.

Carnot, Lazare. *Mémoires historiques et militaires*. Paris: Baudouin, 1824.

———. *Mémoires sur Carnot, par son Fils*. 2 vols. Paris: Charavay, 1893.

Castelot, André. *Napoleon.* New York: Harper & Row, 1971.

Castlereagh, Robert Stewart, Viscount. *Correspondence, Despatches, and other Papers of Viscount Castlereagh.* London: Murray,.

Castries, René de la Croix, duc de. *La Fayette.* Paris: Tallandier, 1981

Catherine de Westphalie. *Correspondance inédite de la reine Catherine avec sa famille et celle du roi Jérôme.* Paris: Bouillon, 1893.

Caulaincourt, Armand Louis Augustin de. *Mémoires du général de Caulincourt, duc de Vicence, grand ecuyer de l'Empereur.* 3 vols. Paris: Plon, 1933.

Cavallero, Manuel. *Défense de Saragosse, 1808 et 1809.* Paris: Magimel, 1815.

Cerfberr, G. *Souvenirs de la Révolution et de l'Empire.* Paris: Jouvet, n.d.

Chandler, David G., ed. *The Oxford Illustrated History of the British Army.* Oxford: Oxford University Press, 1994.

———. *The Campaigns of Napoleon.* New York: Macmillan, 1966.

———. *On the Napoleonic Wars.* London: Greenhill Books, 1994.

Chaptal, Jean-Antoine Claude. *De l'Industrie française.* Paris: Renouard, 1819.

———. *Mes souvenirs sur Napoleon.* Paris: Plon, 1893.

Chardigny, Louis. *Les Maréchaux de Napoléon.* Paris: Tallandier, 1977

Charles-Roux, François. *Bonaparte, Gouverneur d'Egypte.* Paris: Plon, 1946.

Chassin, Charles. *Les pacifications de l'ouest, 1794–1801.* Paris: Dupont, 1896–99.

Chastenay, Louise Marie Victorine de. *Mémoires de Madame Chastenay, 1771–1815.* 2 vols. Paris: Plon, 1896.

Chateaubriand, Francois August René. 12 vols. *Memoires d'outre-tombe.* Paris: Penau, 1849–50.

Chevallier, Bernard, and Christophe Pincemaille. *L'impératrice Joséphine.* Paris: Presses de la Renaissance, 1988.

Chuquet, Arthur. *L'Année 1814, la campagne de France.* Paris: Fontemoing, 1914.

Chuquet, Arthur. *La Jeunesse de Napoleon.* 3 vols. Paris: Colin, 1897–99.

———. *Quatre généraux de la révolution—Hoche, Desaix, Kléber, Marceau: lettres et notes inedites.* Paris: Fontemoing, 1911–20.

Clarke, J. S., and J. McArthur. *The Life of Admiral Lord Nelson, KB.* London, 1809.

Clausewitz, Carl von. *Campagne de 1815 en France.* Paris: Chapelot, 1900.

Clermont-Tonnerre, Gaspard de. *L'expédition d'Espagne, 1808–1810.* Paris: Perrin, 1983.

Clerq, Charles de. *Receuil des traités de France.* Paris: Plon-Nourrit, 1864.

Cobban, Alfred. *A History of Modern France.* 2 vols. Harmondsworth, England: Penguin, 1971.

Coignet, Jean Roch. *Les cahiers du capitaine Coignet.* 2 vols. Auxerre: Perriquet, 1851–53.

Colin, Jean. *L'Education militaire de Napoleon.* Paris: Chapelot, 1901.

Colomb, Colonel von. *La guerre des partisans contre Napoléon: Carnet de campagne d'un officier prussien.* Paris: Berger-Levrault, 1914.

Colonna de Cesari Rocca, Pierre Paul Raoul. *Histoire de Corse.* Paris: Boivin, 1916.

Colling, Alfred. *La prodigieuse histoire de la Bourse.* Paris: Société d'Editions economiques et financiers, 1949.

Collot, Jean-Pierre. *Un ami du général Bonaparte: Les souvenirs du receveur general Collot.* Lyon: Vitte, 1897.

Comeau, Sébastien Joseph de. *Souvenirs des guerres d'Allemagne pendant La Révolution et l'Empire.* Paris: Plon, 1900

Connelly, Owen. *The Gentle Bonaparte: A Biography of Joseph*. New York: Macmillan, 1968.

————. *Napoleon's Satellite Kingdoms*. New York: Free Press, 1965.

Consalvi, Hercule. *Mémoires du cardinal Consalvi*. 2 vols. Paris, 1864–66.

Constant de Rebecque, Benjamin. *Journal intime*. Paris: Ollendorff, 1895.

————. *Mémoires sur les Cent-Jours*. Paris: Pichon et Didier, 1829.

Constant, Louis. *Mémoires de Constant*. Paris: Garnier, 1894.

Cornwallis-West, George. *The Life and Letters of Admiral Cornwallis*. London: Holden, 1927.

Coston, François Gilbert. *Histoire de Napoléon Bonaparte depuis sa naissance jusqu'à l'époque de son commandement en chef de l'Armée d'Italie*. Paris: Pommeret et Moreau, 1848.

————. *Premières années de Napoléon*. Paris: Plon-Nourrit, 1840.

Cotton, Edward. *A Voice from Waterloo: A History of the Battle Fought on the 18th June 1815*. Brussels: Hôtel du Musée, 1913.

Crestwell, John. *British Admirals of the Eighteenth Century: Tactics in Battle*. London: George Allen & Unwin, 1972.

Crouzel, François. *Britain Ascendant: Comparative Studies in Franco-British Economic History*. Cambridge: Cambridge University Press, 1990.

Cuneo d'Ornano, F. *Napoléon au Golfe Juan*. Paris: Firmin-Didot, 1830.

Curely, Jean Nicolas. *Le Général Curely: Itinéraire d'un cavalier Léger*. Paris: Berger-Levrault, 1887.

Dainville, France de, and Jean Tulard. *Atlas administratif de l'Empire Français*. Paris: Minard, 1973.

Damamme, Jean Claude. *Lannes, Marechal a Empire*. Paris: Payot, 1907.

Darnay, Antoine. *Notices historiques sur S A R le prince Eugène, vice-roi d'Italie, duc Le Leuchtenberg, prince d'Eichstadt*. Paris: Didier, 1830.

David, Louis. *Le peintre Louis David, 1748–1825. Souvenirs et Documents inédits*. 2 vols. Paris: Havard, 1880–82.

Davout, Louis Nicolas, duc d'Auerstaedt. *La Correspondance du Maréchal Davout, Prince d'Eckmühl: Ses commandements, son ministère, 1801–1815*. 4 vols. Paris: Plon, 1885.

Delagrave, André. *Mémoires du colonel Delagrave, Campagne du Portugal, 1810–1811*. Paris: Delagrave, 1902.

Delecluze, Etienne-Jean. *Louis David, son école et son temps: Souvenirs par E-J Delecluze*. Paris: Didier, 1860.

Denon, Vivant. *Voyage dans la basse et la haute-Egypte pendant les campagnes de Bonaparte*. London: Bagster, 1807.

Desbrière, Edouard. *Projects et tentatives de débarquement aux Iles Britanniques*. 4 vols. Paris: Librairie militaire R Chapelot, 1902.

————. *Trafalgar, la campagne maritime de 1805*. Paris: Chapelot, 1907.

Desgenettes, René. *Souvenirs d'un médecin de l'expédition d'Egypte*. Paris: Calmann-Lévy, 1893.

Desmarest, Pierre-Marie. *Témoignages historiques, ou Quinze ans de haute police sous le Consulat et l'Empire*. Paris: Levasseur, 1833.

Des Mazis, Alexandre Jean. *Cahiers*. In *La Jeunnesse inédite de Napoléon*. Edited by Paul Bartel. Paris: Amyot, 1954.

———. *Souvenirs de la fin du XVIIIe siècle et du commencement du XIXe, ou mémoires de R. D. G.* 2 vols. Paris: Firmin-Didot, 1835–36.

Desvernois, Nicholas Philibert. *Souvenirs militaires du Baron Desvernois*. Paris: Tamena, 1858.

Destrème, Jean. *Les déportations du consulat et de l'empire*. Paris: Jeanmarie, 1885.

Dhumez, Hubert. "Cannes et les Cent-Jours," *Mélange inédits relatifs au passé du pays cannois. Collections: Documents, textes inconnus pour servir à l'Histoire du pays de Cannes et de sa région*. Vol. 6. Cannes: Aegitna, 1961.

Dino, Dorothée de Courlande de. *Souvenirs de la duchesse de Dino*. Paris: Calmann-Lévy, 1901.

Dogereau, Jean Pierre. *Journal de l'expédition d'Egypte*. Paris: Perrin, 1904.

Doris, Charles. *Mémoires secrètes sur Napoléon Bonaparte écrites par un homme qui ne l'a pas quité depuis quinze ans*. 2 vols. Paris: Germain Mathiot, 1817.

———. *Le Grand Empire*. Paris: Alcan, 1910.

Driault, Edouard. *Napoléon en Italie, 1800–1812*. Paris: Alcan, 1906.

Drouet d'Erlon, Jean Baptiste. *Vie militaire écrite par lui-même*. Paris: Barba, 1844.

Drujon de Beaulieu. *Souvenirs d'un militaire pendant quelques années du règne de Napoléon Bonaparte*. Belley: Verpillon, 1831.

Dubreuil, Léon. *L'Histoire des insurrections de L'Ouest*. 2 vols. Paris: Rieder. 1829–30.

Dumas, Alexandre. *Mes Mémoires*. 5 vols. Paris: Gallimard, 1954.

Dumas, Mathieu. *Souvenirs du lieutenant-général comte Mathieu Dumas*. 3 vols. Paris: Gosselin, 1839.

Dumoulin, Evariste. *Histoire complète du maréchal Ney*. 2 vols. Paris: Delaunay, 1815.

Duplan, Victor. *Mémoires et campagnes*. Moutiers: Ducloz, 1901.

Dupré de Saint-Maur, Jenny. *Pauline Borghèse jugée par une femme, Mémoires de Madame de Saint-Maur*. 2 vols. Nancy: Georges Thomas, 1948.

Durand, Charles. *Le fonctionnement du Conseil d'Etat Napoléonic*. Gap: Louis-Jean, 1954.

Dutheillet de la Mothe, Aubin. *Mémoires du lieutenant-colonel Aubin Dutheillet de la Mothe*. Bruxelles: Lamertin, 1899.

Dwyer, Philippe. "Duroc, Diplomate, un militaire au service de la diplomatie, ambassadeur de Napoléon." *Souvenir Napoléonien* 399 (Jan.-Feb. 1995), pp. 21–38.

Eckstein, Fernand d'. *De ma carrière politique et littéraire en France et dans les Pays-Bas*. Paris, ca. 1820.

Effendi, Mouhib. *Relation de voyage et de mission de Mouhib Effendi Ambassadeur extraordinaire du Sultan Selim III, 1806–1811*. Paris: Bossard, 1920.

Eiffes, Michel. *Mémoires du sous-lieutenant Michel Eiffes qui command da le peleton d'exécution d'Andreas Hofer*. In *Napoleon et le Luxembourg*, edited by Jacques Dollar, pp. 271–86. Luxembourg: Saint-Paul, 1989.

Escoiquiz, Juan de. *Mémoires*. Paris: Michaud, 1823.

Esposito, Vincent J., and John Robert Elting, *A Military History and Atlas of the Napoleonic Wars*. New York: Praeger, 1964.

Fain, Agathon-Jean-François. *Mémoires du baron Fain, premier secrétaire du cabinet de l'Empereur*. Paris: Plon, 1908.

Fantin des Odoards, Louis-Florimond. *Journal du général Fantin des Odoards*. Paris: Plon, 1895.

Fauche-Borel, Louis. *Mémoires*. Paris: Montardier, 1829, 4 vols.

Ferrero, Guglielmo. *Aventure: Bonaparte en Italie, 1796–1797*. Paris: Plon, 1936.

Fievée, Joseph. *Correspondance et relations de J. Fievée avec Bonaparte pendant onze années, 1802–1813*. Paris: Desrez et .

Fleury, Joseph Abraham Benard. *Mémoires de Fleury de la Comédie Française*. Paris: Gosselin, 1844.

Fleury de Chaboulon, P. A. Edouard, *Les Cent-Jours, Mémoires pour servir à l'histoire de la vie privée, du retour et du règne de Napoléon en 1815*. 3 vols. Paris: Rouveyre, 1901.

Florange, Charles. *Le vol de l'aigle, 1815: Napoléon, la marche sur Paris*. Paris: Clavreuil, 1932.

Fontaine, Pierre François Léonard. *Journal, 1799–1853*. 2 vols. Paris: Ec. N. des Beaux-Arts, 1987.

Fouché, Joseph. *Mémoires de Joseph Fouché, Duc d'Otrante*. 2 vols. Paris: Le Rouge, 1824.

Fournier, A. *Napoléon I, Eine Biographie*. 2 vols. Vienna: Verlag Bauer, 1891.

Franceschetti, Dominique César. *Mémoires sur les événements qui ont précédé la mort de Joachim Ier roi des Deux-Siciles*. Paris: Beaudouin, 1826.

François, Charles. *Journal du capitaine François, 1792–1830*. 2 vols. Paris: Carrington, 1903.

Frazer, Augustus, *Letters of Colonel Sir Augustus Frazer*. London: Murray, 1859.

Frénilly, François Auguste Fauveau de. *Souvenirs du baron de Frénilly*. Paris: Plon, 1909.

Friedrich, J-C. *Mémoires d'un mort, 1805–1828*. 3 vols. Paris: Librairie Universelle, 1913.

Fuller, J. F. C. *The Decisive Battles of the Western World, 1792–1944*. London: Eyre & Spottiswoode, 1954.

Gabory, Emile. *Napoléon et la Vendée*. Paris: Perrin, 1914.

Gaffarel, Paul. *Bonaparte et les républiques italiennes. 1796–99*. Paris: Alcan, 1895.

Gaillard, Maurice André. *Un ami de Fouché d'après les mémoires de Gaillard*. Paris: Plon, 1911.

Galitzin, Nicolas Dimitri Boris. *Souvenirs et impressions d'un officier russe pendant les campagnes de 1812–1814*. St. Petersburg: Kray, 1844.

Gallagher, John G. *The Iron Marshal: A Biography of Louis N. Davout*. Carbondale: Southern Illinois University Press, 1976.

Garnier, Athanase. *La cour de Hollande sous le règne de Louis Bonaparte*. Paris: Persan, 1823.

Garros, Louis. *Itinéraire de Napoléon Bonaparte, 1769–1821*. Paris: Editions de l'Encyclopédie française, 1947.

Gaubert, Henri. *Les Conspirateurs au Temps de Napoléon Ier*. Paris: Flammarion, 1962.

Gaudin, Michel Martin Charles, *Mémoires, souvenirs, opinions et écrits du Duc de Gaëte*. Paris: Colin, 1926, vol. 1

Gazan, Colonel. *Le 1er mars 1815: Débarquement de Napoléon au golfe Jouan.* Grasse: Crosnier, 1898.

George, Marguerite Joséphine Wemmer. *Mémoires inédits de Mlle George.* Paris: Plon, 1912.

Geyl, Pieter. *Napoleon, For and Against.* New Haven, Conn: Yale University Press, 1949.

Gillé, Bertrand. *Les sources statisques de l'histoire de France.* Genève: Droz, 1964.

Gillon, Edouard, *Les complots militaires sous le consulat et l'empire.* Paris: Plon-Nourrit, 1894

———. *Les Guerres d'Espagne sous Napoléon.* Paris: Plon-Nourrit, 1902

———. *Napoléon et la Suisse, 1803–1815.* Paris: Plon, 1910

Girod de l'Ain, Gabriel. *Bernadotte de guerre et Chef d'Etat.* Paris: Perrin:, 1968.

———. *Desirée Clary, d'après sa correspondance inédite au Bonaparte, Bernadotte, et sa famille.* Paris: Hachette, 1959.

———. *Joseph Bonaparte, roi malgré lui.* Paris: Perrin, 1970.

Gobineau, Louis de. *Mémoires du comte Louis de Gobineau.* Bruxelles: Erasme, 1955.

Godart, Roch. *Mémoires du général baron Roch Godart, 1792–1815.* Paris: Flammarion, 1895.

Godechot, Jacques. *Les commissaires aux armées sous le directoire.* Paris: Fustier, 1937.

———. *Les constitutions de la France depuis 1789.* Paris: Garnier-Flammarion, 1970

———. *La Contre-révolution, doctrine et action, 1796–1799.* Paris/Alcan, 1895

Godoy, Manuel. *Mémoires du prince de la Paix.* 4 vols. Paris: Ladvocat, 1836.

Gohier, Louis Jérôme. *Mémoires.* Paris: Bossange, 1824.

Goodwin, Peter. *The Construction and Fitting of English Ships of War, 1600–1815.* London: Conway Maritime Press, 1987.

Gotteri, Nicole. *Soult, Maréchal d'Empire, et homme d'Etat.* Besançon: Editions La Manufacture, 1991.

Gourgaud, Gaspard. *Mémoires pour servir à l'histoire de France sous Napoléon.* Paris: Didot, 1823, 2 vols.

———. *Sainte-Hélène: Journal inédit de 1815 à 1818.* 2 vols. Paris: Flammarion, 1899.

Gouvion Saint-Cyr, Laurent de. *Mémoires pour servir à l'histoire militaire sous le Directoire, le Consulat et l'empire.* 4 vols. Paris: Anselin, 1831.

Grégoire, Baptiste-Henri. *Mémoires de Grégoire, ancien évêque de Blois.* 2 vols. Paris: Dupont, 1837.

Gronow, Rees Howell. *Captain Gronow: His Reminiscences of Regency and Victorian Life, 1810–60.* Edited by Christopher Hibbert. London: Kyle Cathie, 1991.

Grouchy, Emmanuel de. *Mémoires du maréchal de Grouchy.* 5 vols. Paris: Dentu, 1873–74.

Grüber, Karl Johann. *Souvenirs du chevalier Grüber.* Paris: Perrin, 1909.

Guillemin, Henri. *Madame de Staël et Napoléon.* Paris: Seuil, 1987.

Guizot, François. *Mémoires pour servir à l'histoire de mon temps.* Vol. 1. Paris: Michel Lévy, 1858.

Haberkant, Johann, M.D. *Napoleon Bonaparte also affektepileptischen psychopath und seine tentamine suicidi.* Prague, 1914.

Hamilton-Williams, David. *The Fall of Napoleon: The Final Betrayal.* London: John Wiley, 1994.

Harcourt, Levenson Vernon, ed. *The Diaries and Correspondence of the Right Hon. George Rose*. London: Bentley, 1860.

Haswell, Jock. *The First Respectable Spy: The Life and Times of Colquhoun Grant*. London: Hamilton, 1969.

Hastier, L. *Le grand amour de Joséphine*. Paris: Corea Buchet/Chastel, n.d.

Hauptmann, Karl. *Napoleon Bonaparte*. 2 vols. Munich: Callwey, 1911.

Hauterive, Ernest d'. *La police secrète du Premier Empire: Bulletins quotidiens adressés par Fouché à l'Empereur, 1804–1810*. 5 vols. Paris: Perrin, 1908–64.

————. *Napoléon et sa police*. Paris: Flammarion, 1943.

Hauteville, Ernest d'. *L'Enlèvement du sénateur Clément de Ris*. Paris: Perrin, 1926.

Hayman, Peter. *Soult, Napoleon's Maligned Marshal*. London: Arms & Armour, 1990.

Haythornthwaite, Philip. *The Armies of Wellington*. London: *Arms & Armour*, 1994.

Heckscher, Eli. *The Continental System: An Economic Interpretation*. Oxford: Clarendon Press, 1922.

Hennequin, Philippe Auguste. *Mémoires de Philippe Auguste Hennequin*. Paris: Calmann-Lévy, 1933.

Herold, Christopher. *Bonaparte in Egypt*. New York: Harper & Row, 1962.

————. *The Age of Napoleon*. London: Weidenfeld & Nicolson, 1963.

Hill, Peter P. *William Vans Murray, Federalist Diplomat*. Syracuse, N.Y.: Syracuse University Press, 1971.

Hobhouse, John Cam. *Lettres écrites de Paris pendant le dernier règne de l'Empereur Napoléon*. 2 vols. Ghent: Houdin, 1817.

Holland, Henry Richard. *Souvenirs diplomatiques de Lord Holland*. Paris: Rouvier, Le Doyen, 1851.

Holwein, Hans. *Napoleon Bonaparte Kaiser der Franzosen*. Stuttgart: Franck, 1964.

Houssaye, Henri. *1814*. Paris: Bartillat, 1986,

————. *1815*. Vol. 1, *La Première Restauration—Le Retour de l'Ile d'Elbe—Les Cent Jours*. Paris: Perrin, 1896.

————. *1815*. Vol. 2, *Waterloo*. Paris: Bartillat, 1978.

————. *1815*. Vol. 3, *La Seconde Abdication—La Terreur Blanche*. Paris: Perrin, 1914.

Hugo, Joseph Léopold. *Mémoires du général Hugo*. 3 vols. Paris: Ladvocat, 1823.

Hyde de Neuville, Jean Guillaume. *Mémoires et souvenirs du baron Hyde de Neuveille*. 3 vols. Paris: Plon, 1888.

Iung, Théodore. *Bonaparte et son temps, 1769–1799*. 3 vols. Paris: Charpentier, 1885–92.

————. *Lucien Bonaparte et ses mémoires, 1775–1840*. 3 vols. Paris: Charpentier, 1882–83.

Jackson, Basil. *Notes and Reminiscences of a Staff Officer, Chiefly Relating to the Waterloo Campaign, and to St Helena*. London: Harrison, 1877.

James, Lawrence. *The Iron Duke: A Military Biography*. London: Weidenfeld & Nicholson, 1992.

James, William. *The Naval History of Great Britain, from the Declaration of War by France in 1793, to the Accession of George IV*. Vols. 1–4. London: Bentley, 1837.

Jauffrey, Joseph. *Mémoires historiques sur les affaires ecclésiastiques de France pendant les premières années du dix-neuvième siècle*. 3 vols. Paris: Leclère, 1819–24.

Jollois, Jean Baptiste Prosper. *Journal d'un ingénieur attaché à l'expédition d'Egypte, 1798–1802.* Paris: Leroux, 1904.

Jomard, Edmé François. *Souvenirs sur Gaspard Monge et ses rapports avec Napoléon.* Paris: Thunot, 1853.

Jomini, Henri de. *Journal d'Espagne, Extrait des souvenirs inédits du général Jomini.* Paris: Baudouin, 1892.

———. *Précis politique et militaire des campagnes de 1812 à 1814.* Paris: Benda, 1886, 2 vols.

Jomini, Antoine Henri. *Vie politique et militaire de Napoléon.* Paris: Anselin, 1827.

Journal d'un dragon d'Egypte: 14e dragons. Paris: Dubois, 1899.

Jourquin, Jacques. *Dictionnaire des maréchaux du premier empire.* Paris: Tallandier, 1986.

Jouvenal, Bertrand de. *Napoléon et l'économie dirigée, le blocus continental.* Bruxelles: Editions de la Toison d'Or, 1942.

Keegan, John. *The Price of Admiralty, War at Sea, from Man of War to Submarine.* London: Hutchinson, 1988.

Kennedy, Ludovic. *Nelson's Band of Brothers.* London: Odhams Press, 1952.

Knapton, John. *Empress Josephine.* Cambridge, Mass: Harvard University Press, 1963.

Krebs, Léonce, and Henry Moris. *Campagnes dans les Alpes pendant la Révolution.* Paris: Plon-Nourrit, 1895.

Labaume, Eugène. *Relation circonstanciée de la campagne de Russie.* Paris: Penckoucke, 1814.

Lacour-Gayet, Georges. *Napoléon, sa vie, son oeuvre, son temps.* Paris: Hachette, 1921.

———. *Talleyrand, 1754–1838.* 4 vols. Paris: Payot, 1933–34.

———. *Histoire de commerce.* Paris: SPID, 1950–53.

Lachouque, Henry. *Napoléon à Austerlitz.* Paris: Victor, 1961.

———. *Napoleon's Battles: A History of His Campaigns.* New York: Dutton, 1966.

Lacroix, Clément de. *Souvenirs du Comte de Montgaillard, agent de la diplomatie secrète pendant la Révolution, l'Empire et de la Restauration.* Paris: Credté, 1895.

Lacroix, Désiré. *Bonaparte en Egypte, 1798–1799.* Paris: Garnier Frères, 1899.

La Fayette, Marie Joseph Gilbert du Motier de. *Mémoires, correspondance et manuscrits du général La Fayette.* 6 vols. Paris: Fournier, 1837–18.

Laffon de Labedat, André Daniel. *Laffon-Labedat, président du conseil des anciens: Journal de ma déportation à la Guyane Française.* Paris: Ollendorff, 1912.

Lafolie, Charles Jean, *Mémoires sur la cour du prince Eugène.* Paris: Audin, 1824.

Lagarde-Chambonas, A. de. *Fêtes et souvenirs du Congrès de Vienne.* 2 vols. Paris: Appert, 1843.

Lagneau, Louis Vivant, *Journal d'un chirurgien de la Grande Armée.* Paris: Emile-Paul, 1913.

Lainé, Joseph Lous Joachim. *Dans les archives du vicomte Lainé.* Paris: Champion, 1929.

Langeron, Andrault. *Mémoires de Langeron, Général d'infanterie dans l'armée russe: campagnes de 1812, 1813, 1814.* Paris: Picard, 1902.

La Jonquière, C. de. *L'Expédition d'Egypte, 1798–1801.* 4 vols. Paris: Charles Lavauzelle, 1899.

Lamarque, Jean Maximilien. *Mémoires et souvenirs du général Maximilien Lamarque*. 3 vols. Paris: Fournier jeune, 1835–36.

Lanzac de Laborie, Léon. *La Domination française en Belgique, 1795–1814*. Paris: Plon, 1895.

———. *Paris sous Napoléon*. 8 vols. Paris: Plon-Nourrit, 1903.

La Rochefoucauld-Doudeauville, Louis François Sosthène de. *Mémoires de M, de La Rochefoucauld, duc de Doudeauville*. 15 vols. Paris: Michel Lévy, 1861–64.

La Rochejacquelein, Marie Louise Victorine de. *Mémoires de Madame la marquise de La Rochejacquelein*. Paris: Plon, 1857.

Larrey, Dominique Jean, *Mémoires de chirurgie militaires et campagnes*. 4 vols. Paris: Smith, 1812–17. (A fifth volume on Waterloo was published by Baillière in Paris in 1841.)

Las Cases, Marie Joseph Emmanuel Dieudonné. *Mémoires d'Emmanuel Dieudonné comte de Las Casas*. Bruxelles: Walhlen, 1818.

Las Cases, Marie Joseph Emmanuel Dieudonné. *Mémorial de Saint-Hélène*. 8 vols. Paris: Author, 1823.

La Tour du Pin, Henriette-Lucy Dillon. *Mémoires de la Marquise de la Tour du Pin: Journal d'une femme de cinquante ans, 1778–1815*. Paris: Mercure de France 1989.

Launay, Louis de. *Monge, un Grand Français: Fondateur de l'Ecole Polytechnique*. Paris: P. Roger, n.d.

LaValette, Antoine Marie Chamans de. *Mémoires et souvenirs du comte de Lavalette*. 2 vols. Paris: Fournier, 1931.

Lavery, B. *The Ship of the Line*. London: Conway Maritime Press, 1983–84, 2 vols.

Lecestre, Léon. *Lettres inédites de Napoléon Ier*. Paris: Plon-Nourrit, 1897.

Lefebvre, Georges. *Napoleon*. 2 vols. London: Routledge & Kegan Paul, 1969.

Lehmann, Joseph. *Napoléon et les juifs*. Paris: Avalon/Mercure, 1989.

Le Nabour, Eric. *Barras, Le Victome Rouge*. Paris: Lattès, 1982.

Lentz, Thierry Savary. *Le séide de Napoléon, 1774–1844*. Paris: Editions Serpenoise, 1993.

Leyland, John. *Dispatches and Letters Relating to the Blockade of Brest, 1803–1805*. 2 vols. London: Navy Records Society, 1899.

Ligne, Charles Joseph, prince de. *Fragments de l'histoire de ma vie*. 2 vols. Paris: Plon, 1928.

Longford, Elizabeth. *Wellington*. 2 vols. London: Weidenfeld & Nicolson, 1969.

Lombard de Langres, Vincent. *Le Royaume de Westphalie, Jérôme Bonaparte, sa cour, ses favouris, ses mémoires*. Paris: Gide, 1820.

Louis Philippe d'Orleans. *Mon journal, Evénements de 1815*. 2 vols. Paris: Michel Lévy, 1849.

Lowe, Hudson. *Histoire de la captivité de Napoléon à Sainte-Hélène d'après les documents officiels inédits et les manuscripts de Sir Hudson Lowe publiée par W. Forsyth*. 4 vols. Paris: Amyot, 1853.

Ludwig I of Bavaria. *Kronprinz Ludwig von Bayern und Napoleon I*. Munich: Verlage der Bayerischen Akademie, 1942.

M.C. (author). *Napoléon, sa naissance, son éducation, sa carrière son gouvernement, sa chute, son exile et sa sort*. Paris: Vauquelin, 1821.

Macdonald, Jacques Etienne Joseph Alexandre. *Souvenirs du Maréchal Macdonald, duc de Tarente*. Paris: Plon, 1892.

Madelin, Louis. *Fouché, 1759–1820*. 2 vols. Paris: Plon, 1903.

———. *Histoire du Consulat et de l'Empire*. 16 Vols. Hachette, Paris, 1937–43. (Noted under the individual titles of each volume in my notes; for example, *La Jeunesse de Bonaparte, De Brumaire à Marengo, L'Affaire d'Espagne* and so on.)

———. *Talleyrand*. Paris: Flammarion, 1944.

Mahan, Alfred T. *The Life of Nelson, the Embodiment of the Sea Power of Great Britain*. London: Sampson, Low, Marston, 1897.

Mahul, Alphonse. *Souvenirs d'un collégien du temps de l'Empire 1810–1814*. Montpellier: Imprimerie du Midi, 1895.

Mailly, Adrien Augustin Amalric. *Mon journal pendant la Campagne de Russie*. Paris: Gros, 1841

Maine de Biran, Pierre François Marie. *Journal intime de Maine de Biran de l'année 1792 à l'année 1812*. 2 vols. Paris, 1927.

Maistre, Joseph de. *Carnets*. Paris: Vitte 1923.

Maitland, Frederick Lewis. *Relation du capitaine Maitland, concernant l'embarquement et le séjour de l'Empereur à bord de ce vaisseau*. Paris: Bauduoin, 1826.

Malmesbury, Earl of. *Diaries and Correspondence of James Harris, First Earl of Malmesbury*. London: Bentley, 1844.

Manceron, Claude. *Napoléon reprend Paris, 20 mars 1815*. Paris: Laffont, 1965.

Marbot, Jean Baptiste Antoine Marcellin, de. *Mémoires du général baron*. Paris: Plon, 1891 3 vols.

Marcel, Nicolas. *Campagne du capitaine Marcel en Espagne et en Portugal. 1808–1814*. Paris: Plon, 1913.

Marchand, Louis. *Mémoires de Marchand, premier valet de chambre et exécuteur testamentaire de l'Empereur*. 2 vols. Paris: Plon, 1952–55.

Maret, Hugues Bernard, Duc de Bassano. *Souvenirs intimes de la Révolution et de l'empire*. 2 vols. Bruxelles: Potter, 1843.

Marigny, Marie Anne Françoise de Chateaubriand, *Paris en 1814: Journal inédit de Mme de Marigny*. Paris: Emile-Paul, 1907.

Markham, Felix, *Napoleon*. London: Weidenfeld, 1963.

Markham, Clements, ed. *Selections from the Correspondence of Admiral John Markham, 1801–4, 1806–7*. London: Navy Records Society, 1904.

Marmont, Auguste Frédéric Louis Viesse de, duc de Raguse. *Mémoires de 1792 à 1841*. 9 vols. Paris: Perrotin, 1856–57.

Marshall-Cornwall, James. *Marshal Masséna*. Oxford: Oxford University Press, 1965.

Martineau, Gilbert. *Caroline Bonaparte*. Paris: France-Empire, 1991.

Masséna, André. *Mémoires de M. le Maréchal Masséna, Duc de Rivoli, Prince d'Essling, sur les événements qui ont eu lieu en Provence, pendant les mois de mars et d'avril 1815*. Paris: Delaunay, 1816.

Masson, Frédéric. *L'Affaire Maubreuil*. Paris: Ollendorff, 1903

———. *Joséphine de Beauharnais, 1763–1796,*. Paris: Albin Michel, 1925.

———. *Joséphine Impératrice et Reine, 1804–1809*. Paris: Albin Michel, 1919.

———. *Joséphine répudiée, 1809–1814*. Paris: Albin Michel, 1926

———. *L'Impératrice Marie-Louise, 1809–1815*. Paris: Albin Michel, 1927.

———. *Napoléon à Sainte-Hélène*. Paris: Albin Michel, 1930.

———. *Madame Bonaparte, 1796–1804*. Paris: Albin Michel, 1925.

———. *Napoléon dans sa jeunesse, 1769–1793*. Paris: Albin Michel, 1925.

———. *Napoléon et sa famille*. 13 vols. Paris: Ollendorff, 1919.

———. *Napoléon et son fils*. Paris: Ollendorff, 1908.

———. *Le Sacre et le Couronnement de Napoléon*. Paris: Albin Michel, 1925.

———. *Napoléon et les femmes*. Paris: Albin Michel, 1928.

Masson, André, and Guido Biagi, *Napoléon inconnu*. Paris: Albin Michel, 1895.

Matheson, Cyril. *The Life of Henry Dundas, First Viscount Melville, 1742–1811*. London: Constable, 1933.

Maxwell, Herbert. *The Life of Wellington*. 2 vols. London: Macmillan, 1900.

Méneval, Claude François de. *Mémoires pour servir à l'histoire de Napoléon Ier depuis 1802 jusqu'à 1815*. Paris: Dentu: 1893–94.

———. *Napoléon et Marie-Louise, Souvenirs historiques de M le baron de Méneval*. 2 vols. Paris: Amyot, 1844–45.

Merode-Westerloo, Henri Marie Ghislain de. *Souvenirs de Comte de Merode-Westerloo*. Bruxelles: Grusse 1845–1846, 2 vols.

Mesnard, Louis Charles. *Souvenirs intimes de M le comte de Mesnard*. 3 vols. Paris: Potter, 1844.

Mesnile, Ange Benjamin Marie du. *Mémoires sur le prince Lebrun, duc de Plaisance*. Paris: Rapilly, 1828.

Metternich, Clément Wenceslas Lothaire, prince de. *Mémoires, documents et écrits divers laissés par le prince de Metternich, chancellier de la cour et d'Etat*. 8 vols. Paris: Plon, 1880–84.

Meynier, Albert. *Une erreur historique, les morts de la grande armée et des armées ennemies*. Paris: Presses Universitaires de France, 1935.

Michelet, Jules. *Histoire du XIXe siècle*. Paris: Frères, 1875.

Millet, Pierre Jean Baptiste. *Le chasseur Pierre Millet, Souvenirs de la campagne d'Egypte, 1798–1801*. Paris: Emile-Paul, 1903.

Minto, Nora. *Life and Letters of Sir Gilbert Elliot, First Earl of Minto, from 1751–1806*. 3 vols. London: Longmans, 1874.

Miot de Melito, André-François. *Mémoires du comte Miot Melito, ancien ministre, ambassadeur, conseiller d'Etat et membre de l'Institut, 1788–1815*. 3 vols. Paris: Michel Lévy, 1858.

———. *Memoirs of Count Miot de Melito*. New York: Scribner's Sons, 1881.

Moiret, Joseph Marie. *Mémoires sur l'expédition d'Egypte*. Paris: Belfond, 1984.

Molé, Louis Mathieu. *Le Comte Molé, sa vie et ses mémoires*. Paris: Champion, 1922.

———. *Marquis de Noailles, le comte Molé, 1781–1855, Sa vie, ses mémoires*. 6 vols. Paris: Champion, 1922.

Mollien, François Nicolas. *Mémoires d'un ancien ministre du Trésor de 1800 à 1814*. 4 vols. Paris: Fournier, 1937.

Montague, Andrew J., ed. *The American Secretaries of State and their Diplomacy*. New York: Knopf, 1927.

Montchenu, marquis de. *La captivité de Sainte-Hélène d'après les rapports inédits du marquis de Montchenu*. Paris: Firmin-Didot, 1894.

Montesquiou, Raymond Emery Philippe Joseph de, duc de Féranzac. *Souvenirs militaires de 1804 à 1804*. Paris: Dumaine, 1863.

Montholon, Albine-Hélène de Vassal. *Souvenirs de Sainte-Hélène par la competesse de Montholon*. Paris: Emile-Paul, 1901.

Montholon, Charles François Tristan de. *Récits de la captivité de l'Empereur Napoléon à Sainte-Hélène*. 2 vols. Paris: Paulin, 1847.

Morlot, Georges Albert, and Jeanne Happert. *Talleyrand, Une Mystification historique*. Paris: Veyrier, 1992.

Morvan, Jean. *Le Soldat impérial*. Paris: Plon, 1904.

Mowat, R. B., *The Diplomacy of Napoleon*. London: Edward Arnold, 1924

Muller, Paul. *L'espionnage militaire sous Napoléon Ier*. Paris: Berger-Levrault, 1896.

Nabonne, B., *La Diplomatie du Directoire et de Bonaparte*. Paris: Presses Universitaires de France, 1951.

Napier, William F. P. *A History of the War in the Peninsula and the South of France, 1807–1814*. London: Murray, 1886, 6 vols.

Nel, Commandant. *Bonaparte au siege de Toulon*. Toulon: Moutin & Combe, 1921.

Nesselrode, Charles Robert de. *Lettres et papiers du chancelier comte de Nesselrode, 1760–1850*. 11 vols. Paris: Lahure, 1904–12.

Ney, Michel. *Mémoires du maréchal Ney, duc d'Elchingen, prince de la Moskowa*. 2 vols. Paris: Fournier, 1833.

Nicolas-El-Turk, Mou'Allem. "Expédition française en Egypte, par Mou' Allem Nicolas el Turki, secrétaire du prince des Druzes." *Revue Rétrospective* 6–7 (1838), pp. 154–83, 235–77.

Nodier, Charles. *Souvenirs de la Révolution et de l'Empire*. 2 vols. Paris: Charpentier, 1850.

Norvins, Jacques Marquet de Montbreton de. *Souvenirs d'un historien de Napoléon*. 3 vols. Paris: Plon, 1896–97.

Odeleben, Otto von. *Campagne des Français en Saxe en 1813*. 2 vols. Paris, 1817.

Oman, Carola. *Napoleon's Viceroy, Eugène de Beauharnais*. London: Hodder & Stoughton, 1966.

———. *Nelson*. London: Hodder & Stoughton, 1947

Oman, Charles, *A History of the Peninsular War*. Oxford: Oxford University Press, 1902–30.

O'Meara, Barry Edward. *A Voice from St Helena*. London: Simpkin & Marshall, 1922.

Orieux, Jean. *Talleyrand*. Paris: Flammarion, 1970.

Ouvrard, Gabriel Julie. *Mémoires de G-J Ouvrard sur sa vie et ses diverses opérations financières*. 3 vols. Paris: Moutardier, 1826.

Paget, Henry William, marquess of Anglesey. *One-Leg, The Life and Letters of Henry William Paget, 1st Marquess of Anglesey*. London: Jonathan Cape, 1961.

Parkinson, Roger. *The Hussar General: The Life of Blücher*. London: Murray, 1975.

Pasquier, Etienne Denis. *Histoire de mon temps, Mémoires du Chancelier Pasquier*. Paris: Plon, 1893–94, 6 vols.

Pelet, Jean Jacques Germain. *Mémoires sur la guerre de 1809 en Allemagne, sur les opérations particulière des corps d'Italie, de Pologne, de Saxe, de Naples et de Walcheren*. Paris: Roret, 1824–26.

Pellapra, Emilie. *Une fille de Napoléon: Mémoires d'Emilie de Pellapra*. Paris: La Sirène, 1921.

Percy, Pierre François. *Journal des campagnes du baron Percy, chirugien en chef de la Grande Armée*. Paris: Plon, 1904.

Peretti, Lydie. *La mère de l'Empereur, Letizia Bonaparte*. Paris: Plon, 1932.

Perrin du Lack, François. "Journal d'un sous-préfet de Baugé en 1815." *Revue de l'Anjou* (Nov.-Dec. 1913), pp. 183–206, 365–81.

Petre, F. L. *Napoleon's Last Campaign in Germany, 1813*. London: Arnold, 1912.

Picard, Ernest, and Louis Tuetey. *Unpublished Correspondence of Napoleon I, 1804–1812*. 3 vols. New York: Duffield, 1913.

Picton, Thomas. *Memoirs of Sir Thomas Picton*. London: Murray, 1836.

Pietromarchi, Antonello. *Lucien Bonaparte, Prince Romain*. Paris: Perrin, 1980.

Pingaud, Léonce. *Correspondence du Comte de Vaudreuil et du Comte d'Artois pendant l'émigration*. 2 vols. Paris: Plon-Nourrit, 1889.

———. *Une agent secret sous la révolution et l'empire Le Comte d'Antraigues*. Vol. 9. Paris: Plon-Nourrit, 1893.

Polnay, Peter de *Napoleon's Police*. London: W. H. Allen, 1970.

Pons de L'Hérault, André. *Souvenirs et anecdotes de l'île d'Elbe*. Paris: Plon, 1897.

Pontécoulant, Louis-Gustave Doulcet de. *Souvenirs historiques et parlementaires du comte de Pontécoulant*. 4 vols. Paris: Michel Lévy, 1861–65.

Poulle, François-Auguste. "Mémoires du maire de Cannes sur le débarquement de Napoléon ler, 1815." *Revue Rétrospective* 6 (Jan.-June 1887), pp. 216–21.

Pozzo di Borgo, Charles-André. *Correspondance diplomatique du comte Pozzo di Borgo, Ambassadeur de Russie en France, et du comte Nesselrode, 1814–1818*. Vol. 1. Paris: Calmann-Lévy, 1890.

Pradt, Dominique Georges Frédéric de Fourt de. *Histoire de l'ambassade dans le Grand Duché de Varsovie en 1813*. Paris: Pillet, 1815.

Puisaye, Joseph Geneviève de. *Mémoires*. 6 vols. London, 1803–9.

Quesné, Jacques. *Confessions*. 3 vols. Paris: Pellet, 1828.

Radziwill, Louise de Prusse, Princesse Antoine. *Quarante-cinq années de ma vie, 1770–1815, par Louise de Prusse*. Paris: Plon, 1911.

Rambauteau, Calude Philibert Barthelot de. *Mémoires du comte de Rambuteau*. Paris: Calmann-Lévy, 1906.

Rapp, Jean. *Mémoires du général Rapp, aide de camp de Napoléon*. Paris: Garnier, 1895.

Réal, Pierre François. *Indiscretion, 1798–1830, Souvenirs anecdotiques et politiques*. 2 vols. Paris, 1835.

Récamier, Juliette Bernard. *Souvenirs et correspondance*. 2 vols. Paris: Calmann-Lévy, 1869.

Reinhard, Marcel. *Le Grand Carnot*. Paris: Hachette, 1952.

Reilly, Robin. *William Pitt the Younger*. New York: Putnam, 1979.

Rémusat, Charles de. *Mémoires de ma vie*. Vol. 1. *1797–1820*. Paris: Plon, 1941.

Rémusat, Claire Elisabeth Jean Gravier de Vergennes. *Mémoires, 1802–08*. 3 vols. Paris: Calmann-Lévy, 1879–80.

Reynaud, Jean-Louis. *Contre-Guerilla en Espagne, 1808–1814: Suchet pacifie l'Aragon*. Paris: Economica, 1992.

Riehn, Richard K. *Napoleon's Russian Campaign*. New York: John Wiley, 1991.

Rigotard, Jean. *La Police parisienne de Napoléon, La Préfecture de police*. Paris: Tallandier, 1990.

Rochechouart, Louis Victor Léon de. *Souvenir sur la Révolution, l'Empire et la Restauration par le général comte de Rochehouart*. Paris: Plon, 1889.

Roederer, Pierre-Louis. *Autour de Bonaparte: Journal du Comte Roederer*. Paris: Daragon, 1909.

Roederer, Pierre-Louis. *Oeuvres du comte P L Roederer*. 8 vols. Paris: Firmin-Didot, 1853–59.

Rose, John Holland. *The Life of Napoleon I*. London: G. Bell, 1924.

————. *William Pitt and the Great War*. London: G. Bell, 1911.

Rose, John Holland, and A. M. Broadley. *Dumouriez and the Defence of England against Napoleon*. London: John Lane, 1904.

Rostopchine, Fédor. *La vérité sur l'incendie de Moscou par le comte Rostopchine*. Paris: Ponthieu, 1823.

Roustam Raza. *Souvenirs de Roustam, Mameluck de Napoléon*. Paris: Ollendorff, 1911.

Saint-Chamans, Alfred Armand Robert de. *Mémoires du général comte de Saint-Chamans, ancien aide de camp du maréchal Soult, 1802–1823*. Paris: Plon, 1896.

Saint-Denis, Louis-Etienne "Ali." *Souvenirs du mameluck Ali sur l'empereur Napoléon*. Paris: Payot, 1926.

Saint-Elme, Ida. *Mémoires d'une contemporaine ou souvenirs d'une femme sur les principaux personnages de la République, du Consulat et de l'Empire*. 8 vols. Paris: Ladvocat, 1827.

Saintoyant, Jules. *La colonisation française pendant la période napoléonienne, 1799–1815*. Paris: Renaissance du livre, 1931.

St. Vincent, John Jervis, Earl of. *Letters of Admiral of the Fleet The Earl of St Vincent whilst First Lord of the Admiralty, 1801–1804*. London: Navy Records Society, 1927.

————. *Memoirs of the Administration of the Board of Admiralty under the President of the Earl of St Vincent*. London, 1805.

Salvandy, A. N. de. *Observation critique sur le champ de mai*. Paris, 1815.

Sarrazin, Jean. *Mémoires écrits par lui-même depuis 1770 jusqu'en 1848*. Bruxelles: Vancaulaert, 1848

Savant, Jean. *Les espions de Napoléon*. Paris: Hachette, 1957.

————. *Les préfets de Napoleon*. Paris: Hachette, 1958.

Savary, Anne Jean Marie René, duc de Rovigo. *Mémoires du duc de Rovigo pour servir à l'histoire de l'empereur Napoéon*.8 vols. Paris: Bossange, 1828.

Savatier, René. *Bonaparte et le Code civil*. Paris: Librairie générale de droit et de jurisprudence, 1927.

Schilder, Nikola. *L'Empereur Alexandre Ier, sa vie, son regne*. St. Petersburg: Izd-Nie A.S., Suvorina, 1904.

Schom, Alan. *One Hundred Days, Napoleon's Road to Waterloo:* New York: Oxford University Press, 1993.

————. *Trafalgar: Countdown to Battle, 1803–1805*. New York: Oxford University Press, 1991.

Schouvaloff, Paul. "De Fontainebleau à Fréjus—Avril 1814." *Revue de Paris* (1897), pp. 809–23.

Schwarzfuchs, Simon. *Napoleon, the Jews and the Sandhedrin*. London: Routledge & Kegan Paul, 1979.

Sébastiani, Horace François Bastien. *Fragment de mémoires inédites en 1817.* Mortagne: Dampelay, 1864.

Sera, Jean André de. *Souvenirs d'un pré de la monarchie: Mémoires, 1786–1862.*

Ségur, Philippe Paul de. *Histoire et mémoires.* 8 vols. Paris: Firmin-Didot, 1873.

Senfft von Pilsach. *Mémoires du comte de Senfft.* Leipzig, 1863.

Sirtema van Grovestin, Carol Frederick. *Mémoires et souvenirs.* 5 vols. St.-Germain-en-Laye: Toinon, 1866–69.

Solomon, Maynard. *Beethoven.* New York: Schirmer, 1973.

Soubiran, André. *Napoléon et un million de morts.* Paris: Kent-Segep, 1969.

Soult, Jean de Dieu. *Mémoires du maréchal général Soult.* 3 vols. Paris: Amyot, 1854.

Spillman, Georges. "Duroc, Confident et agent secret de l'Empereur." *Le Souvenir Napoléonien* 296 (Nov. 1, 1977), pp. 3–26.

———. *Napoléon et l'Islam.* Paris: Perrin, 1969.

Sprünglin, Emmanuel Frederick. "Souvenirs." *Revue Hispanique* (1904), pp. 299–537.

Staël-Holstein, Anne Louise Germaine Necker de. *Considérations sur les Principaux Evénements de la Révolution Française.* Paris: Delaunay, 1818.

———. *Mémoires, Dix ans d'Exil.* Paris: Treuttel, 1821.

Stendhal (Henri Beyle). *Journal de Stendhal, 1801–1814.* Paris: Garnier, 1888.

Stiegler, Gaston. *Le maréchal Oudinot d'après les souvenirs inédits de la marcéchale.* Paris: Plon, 1894.

Stürmer, Bartholomée. *Napoléon à Sainte Hélène, Rapports officiels, Commissaire du gouvernment autrichien.* Paris: Librairie Illustrée, 1887.

Suchet, Louis-Gabriel. *Mémoires du maréchal Suchet, duc d'Albufera sur ses campagnes en Espagne depuis 1808 jusqu'en 1814.* 2 vols. Paris: Bossange, 1828.

Talleyrand-Périgord, Charles Maurice de. *Correspondance inédite avec le Roi Louis XVIII pendant le congrès de Vienne.* Paris: Calmann-Lévy, 1881.

———. *Les Lettres inédites de Talleyrand à Napoléon.* Paris: Calmann-Lévy, n.d.

———. *Mémoires du prince de Talleyrand.* 5 vols. Paris: Calmann-Lévy, 1891–92.

Tennant, Charles. *A Tour through Parts of the Netherlands, Holland, Germany, Switzerland, Savoy and France in the year 1821–2.* London: Murray, 1824.

Teil, Joseph du. *Napoléon Bonaparte et les généraux du Teil, 1788–1794: L'école d'artillerie d'Auxonne et le siège de Toulon.* Paris: Picard, 1897.

Thibaudeau, Antoine Clair. *Le Consulat et l'Empire, ou l'histoire de la France et de Napoléon Bonaparte.* Paris: Renouard, 1834–35.

———. *Mémoires de A. C. Thibaudeau, 1799–1815.* Paris: Plon, 1913.

Thiébault, Dieudonné-Paul-Charles-Henri. *Mémoires du général baron Thiébault.* 5 vols. Paris: Plon, 1893–95.

Thiers, Adolphe. *Histoire du Consulat et de l'empire.* Bruxelles: Muquardt, 1845–52.

Thiry, Jean. *Jean-Jacques Régis de Cambacérès, archichancelier de l'empire.* 28 vols. Paris: Berger-Levrault, 1935.

———. *La Guerre d'Espagne.* Paris: Berger-Levrault, 1965.

———. *Les Cent-Jours.* Paris: Berger-Levrault, 1943.

———. *Napoléon Bonaparte.* Paris: Berger-Levrault, 1938–75.

Thomazi, Auguste. *Les marins de Napoléon.* Paris: Tallandier, 1978.

Thuillier, Guy. *La Bureaucratie en France aux XIXe et XXe siècles*. Paris: Economica, 1987.

Tranié, Jean, et al. "L'expédition d'Egypte, 1798–1801." In *Samothrace. La Revue d'Histoire Militaire*, no. 1, pp. 5–47, and continued under same title in *Samothrace*, no. 2, pp. 4–44.

Thurman, Louis. *Bonaparte en Egypte: Souvenirs du capitaine Thurman*. Paris: Emile-Paul, 1902.

Trembicka, Françoise. *Mémoires d'une Polonaise pour servir à l'Histoire de la Pologne, de 1764 à 1830*. Paris: Lachèze, 1841.

Troyat, Henri. *Alexandre Ier, le Sphinx du Nord*. Paris: Flammarion, 1980.

Tulard, Jean. *Dictionnaire Napoléon*. Paris: Fayard, 1987.

———. *Le Grand Empire, 1804–1815*. Paris: Albin Michel, 1982.

———. ed., *Lettres d'Amour à Joséphine*. Paris: Fayard, 1981.

———. *Napoléon, ou le Mythe du Sauveur*. Paris: Fayard, 1977.

———. *Murat, ou l'éveil des nations*. Paris: Hachette, 1983.

———. *Nouvelle Bibliographie critique des Mémoires sur l'épopée napoléonienne*. Genève: Droz, 1991.

———. *Paris et son administration, 1800–1830*. Paris: Commission des Travaux historiques, 1976.

El-Turk, Kaoula. *Histoire de l'Expédition des Français en Egypte*. Paris: Imprimerie Royale, 1839.

Valynseele, Joseph. *La descendance naturelle de Napoléon Ier, le Comte Léon, le comte Walewski*. Paris, 1964

Van Hogendorp, Dirk. *Mémoires du général Dirk van Hogendorp, comte de l'Empire*. Paris: Pedone/The Hague: Hijhoff, 1887.

Vandal, Albert. *L'Avènement de Bonaparte*. Paris: Nelson, 1912.

———. *Napoléon et Alexandre I*. Paris: Plon-Nourrit, 1914

Victor, Claude Perrin, Duc de Bellune. *Mémoires*. Paris: Dumaine, 1847.

Vidalenc, Jean. *Les émigrés français, 1789–1825*. Caen: Université de Caen, 1963.

Vidocqu, Eugène François. *Mémoires de Vidocq, chef de la police de sûreté jusqu'en 1827*. 4 vols. Paris: Tenon, 1828.

Vigée-Lebrun, Marie-Anne-Elisabeth. *Souvenirs*. 3 vols. Paris, 1835.

Vigier, Comte. *Davout, Maréchal d'Empire, duc d'Auerstaedt, prince d'Eckmühl, 1770–1823*. Paris: Ollendorff, 1898.

Villiaume, Claude. *Mes détentions comme prisonnier d'Etat sous le gouvernement de Buonaparte, ou mémoires de Claude Villiaume*. Paris, 1814.

Villiers du Terrage, René Edouard. *Journal et souvenirs sur l'expédition d'Egypte, 1798–1801*. Paris: Plon, 1899.

Vitrolles, Eugène d'Arnauld de. *Mémoires et relations politiques du baron de Vitrolles*. 3 vols. Paris: Charpentier, 1884.

Vivent, Jacques. *Barras. le de la république, 1755–1829*. Paris: Hachette, 1938.

Vox, Maximilien. *Napoléon*. Paris: Seuil, 1959.

Wagener, Françoise. *Madame Récamier, 1777–1849*. Paris: Lattès, 1986.

Waldburg-Truchsess, Ludwig Frederik von. *Nouvelle relation de l'itinéraire de Napoléon de Fontainebleau à l'île d'Elbe*. Paris: Panckoucke, 1815.

Warden, William. *Lettres de Sainte-Hélène*. Bruxelles: Parkin, 1817.

Watson, J. Steven. *The Reign of George III, 1760–1815*. Oxford: Clarendon Press, 1963.

Webster, Charles. *Congress of Vienna, 1814–1815*. London: Bell, 1850.

Weller, Jac. *Wellington at Waterloo*. London: Longmans, 1967.

———. Wellington in the Peninsula, 1808–1815. London: Longmans, 1969.

Wellington, Arthur, duke of. *The Dispatches of Field Marshal the Duke of Wellington, during his various Campaigns*. Vol. 12. London: John Murray, 1834–38.

———. *Supplementary Despatches, Correspondence, and Memoranda of Field Marshal Arthur, Duke of Wellington, K.G.* Vols. 9, 10, 11. London: John Murray, 1858–64.

Wheeler, H. F. B., and Broadley, R. M. *Napoleon and the Invasion of England*. London: John Lane, 1908.

Wolff, Jacques. *Le financier Ouvrard, 1770–1846, L'argent et la politique*. Paris: Tallandier, 1992.

Wolff, Otto. *Ouvrard, Speculator of Genius*. New York: McKay, 1962.

Woodward, Llewellyn. *The Age of Reform, 1815–1870*. Oxford: Oxford University Press, 1962.

Zakharovich, Manfred Albert. *Napoléon Bonaparte*. Moscou: Edition du Progrès, 1980.

Zieseniss, Charles Otto. *Napoléon et la Cour Impériale*. Paris: Tallandier, 1957.

Zieseniss, Jérome. *Berthier, Frère d'Armes de Napoléon*. Paris: Belfond, 1985.

Zivy, Henry. *Le Treize vendémiaire an IV*. Paris: Alcan, 1898.

PRINCIPAL PERIODICALS

Observer (London)
Le Courrier de L'Egypte
La Gazette Nationale, ou le Moniteur Universel
The Times (London)
Le Journal des Débats
The Annual Register, or a View of the History, Politics, and Literature for the Years 1804–1815
Morning Post (London)
London Gazette
Morning Chronicle
La Gazette de France
La Gazette Officielle
Le Journal de l'Empire
Le Journal de Paris
La Quotidienne
Naval Chronicle

I N D E X

Europe in 1789, Before Napoleon; and in 1814, Before His Defeat at Waterloo

North Sea

DENMARK Copenh
Lüb
Haml

UNITED KINGDOM
London
Portsmouth Dover
The Hague Amsterdam
HOLLAND Hannove
Bremen
WESTPHA
Ghent Antwerp **CONFEDERATI**
Calais Brussels **OF THE** Le
Waterloo
Cherbourg Amiens **BELGIUM** **RHINE**
Boulogne Reims Frankfurt
Brest Seine Paris Verdun
Strasbourg Rhine **BADEN**
Ulm N
Atlantic Ocean
Loire
Dijon Zürich **BAV**
FRANCE **SWITZ.**
Lausanne Bern
Lyons Geneva **KINGI**
SAVOY **OF IT**
Grenoble Turin Milan
Bordeaux
PIEDMONT Bol
Bayonne Genoa
Nice
Marseilles Toulon Flo
La Coruña **TUS**
Saragossa **CORSICA** Elba
Salamanca Ajaccio
PORTUGAL Madrid Barcelona
Lisbon Tagus **SPAIN**
SARDINIA
Cartagena
Seville
Cádiz
Gibraltar

Rhône

N
W E
S

A F R I C A

Conquered "vassal" states
Conquered "allied" states
Conquered "rebellious" states
European "sovereign" states